COMPANY
PROFILES
for Students

COMPANY PROFILES
for Students

Volume 1: A–L

Donna Craft, Editor

GALE

DETROIT • LONDON

Company Profiles for Students

Staff

Editorial: Donna Craft, *Editor*. Rebecca Marlow-Ferguson, *Associate Editor*. Anja Barnard, Matthew W. Brisbois, Jennifer L. Carman, Susan J. Cindric, Eva M. Davis, Andrea L. deJong, Sheila Dow, Sonya D. Hill, Ken Karges, Christine A. Kesler, Jane A. Malonis, Jenai A. Mynatt, Terry Peck, William A. Petrick, Michael Weaver, *Contributing Editors*. Diane Maniaci, *Managing Editor*. Synapse, the Knowledge Link Corporation, *Indexer*.

Graphic Services: Barbara J. Yarrow, *Graphic Services Manager*. Randy Bassett, *Image Database Supervisor*. Pamela A. Reed, *Image Coordinator*. Robert Duncan, *Senior Imaging Specialist*. Mike Logusz, *Imaging Specialist*. Nick Sternberg, Frontline Design, Ltd., *Graph Designer*.

Permissions: Susan Trosky, *Permissions Manager*. Kimberly F. Smilay, *Permissions Specialist*. Steve Cusack, Kelly Quin, *Permissions Associates*. Sandy Gore, *Permissions Assistant*.

Product Design: Cynthia Baldwin, *Product Design Manager*. Pamela A.E. Galbreath, *Senior Art Director*.

Production: Mary Beth Trimper, *Production Director*. Evi Seoud, *Assistant Production Manager*.

Research: Victoria B. Cariappa, *Research Manager*. Michele P. LaMeau, *Research Specialist*.

Technical Support Services: Theresa Rocklin, *Manager*. Kryzsztof Musial, *Senior Consultant*. Jim Edwards, Mark F. Mikula, *Technical Training Specialists*. Chris Ward, *Programmer/ Analyst*.

Copyright Notice

Table of Contents

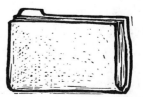

Advisors and Contributors

Advisory Board

A five-member board consisting of teachers and librarians on young adult economics, business, and history needs was consulted to help determine the contents of *Company Profiles for Students.*

The members of the board for this volume include:

Maria Cummins: Cataloger for Yahoo.com; Librarian, Santa Clara County Library/Cupertino Public Library, San Jose, California.

Katherine Bailey: Librarian, Seabreeze High School, Ormond Beach, Florida.

Chris Erdman: Teacher, Skyview High School, Vancouver, Washington.

Bob Kirsch: Librarian, Lake Forest High School, Lake Forest, Illinois.

Alan Nichter: Librarian, Lutz Branch Library, Lutz, Florida.

Contributors

Many writers contributed to the text of *Company Profiles for Students* including:

Daniel J. Alberts

Donald F. Amerman Jr.

Geraldine Azzata

Beth Babini

Maura Basile

David P. Bianco

Darlene Bremer

Larry Budd

Anne B. Burke

Sherri Chasin Calvo

Paula Hartman Cohen

Diane Dickinson

Geoffrey E. Duin

Tim Eigo

Dave Fagan

Jacqueline Gikow

Shirley Gray

Linda Gundersen

Karl Heil

Scott F. Heil

Christopher Hunt

Marinell Jochnowitz

David R. Johnstone

Allison A. Jones

Paula M. Kalamaras

Lisa Musolf Karl

Christine Kelley

Paul Kraly

Brenda Kubiac

Wendy H. Mason

Jennifer Mast

Doris A. Maxfield

Merry McInerney

Cameron McLaughlin

Joan Noechel

Robert Schneider

Fran Shonfeld Sherman

Jane E. Spear

Angela Thor

Denise Worhach

Introduction

Company Profiles for Students (CPFS) has been designed specifically to meet the curricular needs of high school and undergraduate college students taking courses in economics, business, and history. Part of Gale's successful line of business products for students, *CPFS* provides information on both the current operations and performance of 280 contemporary public and private U.S.-based and significant foreign-owned companies, in addition to the historical events, people, and strategies that shaped them. *CPFS* satisfies research assignments regarding a particular company's stock performance, new product lines, or comparisons of the management styles of companies in different industries. By focusing on the many different aspects of a company, which are typically studied in high schools and frequently omitted from standard business publications, *CPFS* meets the strong curricular need for business information written at the high school level. See Gale's *Business Leader Profiles for Students* for in-depth information on nearly 250 prominent individuals who have made significant contributions to business and industry.

An advisory panel of high school teachers and librarians reviewed a list of potential companies and, based on their knowledge and experience, helped select the companies to be covered. Based on this list we then chose 35 industries to profile that best represented the companies covered in this edition. Each company and industry essay was then researched and compiled by a professional writer.

How Each Entry Is Organized

Company Profiles for Students provides users with a single, comprehensive resource. Data was pulled together from annual reports, press releases, numerous print resources, and online databases to give users a one-stop reference source containing a wide variety of information. Each entry in *CPFS* focuses on one company. Each entry heading lists the name of the company, a variant name of the company if one applies, and the year the company was founded. In addition, each entry lists contact information, including address and phone number, as well as fax and toll free number, email, and URL when available. Essays cover some or all of the following topics:

- **Overview:** Provides a brief synthesis outlining the importance of the company, along with its market(s), broad strategies, competitors, etc.

- **Company Finances:** Gives textual information and, in many cases, graphical information illustrating revenues and stock prices over a period of time.

- **Analysts' Opinions:** Discusses various analyses of the company's market share, strategies, stock market position, etc.

- **History:** Gives historical information on the company's genesis and provides a description of inventions or trends that spurred the establishment of the company and of key events throughout the company's existence.

- **Strategy:** Provides an overview of past and current strategies.

- **Influences:** Covers successes or failures that impacted how the company has done business or has positioned itself.

- **Current Trends:** Explains the current influences on company strategy and how the company intends to proceed.

- **Products:** Provides a description of the company's current products and/or information about new products the company plans to introduce in the future.

- **Corporate Citizenship:** Outlines the company's policies and record in regard to the environment, human rights, affirmative action/diversity, etc.

- **Global Presence:** Explains which foreign markets the company has entered and any challenges it faces there. Includes information on the company's global market share, operations, etc.

- **Employment:** Provides information on corporate culture.

- **Sources of Information:** First, a **Bibliography** is provided that includes annotated citations for publicly accessible books, periodicals, and online sources used to compile the entry. Second, a section titled **For an annual report** provides the Internet address, telephone, or address to locate the company's annual report. Third, a section titled **For additional industry research** contains primary Standard Industrial Codes (SICs) and descriptions that apply to the company.

Other Features

Company Profiles for Students includes more than 400 logos and photos, as well as graphs illustrating revenue and stock prices. Most entries also include a chronology of key events in the company's history and, when appropriate, sidebars on prominent individuals and/or products associated with the companies. In addition, each entry includes a "Fast Facts" sidebar that includes all or some of the following elements:

- **Ownership:** Explains whether the company is a public or privately owned company and who it is owned by.

- **Ticker Symbol:** Provides the company's or the company owner's ticker symbol when applicable.

- **Officers:** Contains a list of up to four company officers, their titles, and their ages and salaries (if available).

- **Employees:** Gives the number of employees at the company.

- **Principal Subsidiary Companies:** Supplies a summary of significant corporate relationships.

- **Chief Competitors:** Provides a summary of the company's primary competitors.

An appendix of 35 industry profiles is also included, which give information regarding the industry as a whole. These entries contain all or some of the following topics:

- **Overview:** Provides an overview of the industry, including such aspects as key regulatory bodies affecting the industry.

- **History of the Industry:** Gives historical information on the industry's genesis and development, in-

cluding major technological advances, historic events, scandals, major products, key legislation, and other factors that have shaped the industry.

- **Significant Events Affecting the Industry:** Explains important events that have affected and are currently affecting the industry, such as major advances and the impact of these on the industry.

- **New Trends Influencing the Industry:** Provides information on major advances and their impacts on the industry, including environmental issues if pertinent.

- **Key Competitors:** Covers background information, historical highlights, and current status of specific industry leaders.

- **Employment:** When available, contains information on the employment practices of the industry including data on salaries and benefits, type of worker/education preferred, positions available, and any other information about the industry's employment needs.

- **Global Presence:** Includes information on the leading countries in the world that have key companies in this industry or where this industry provides significant income to the country's economy.

- **Industry Projections:** Explains where the industry is heading in the future.

- **Bibliography:** Provides users with suggested further reading on the industry. These sources, also used to compile the essays, are publicly accessible materials such as magazines, general and academic periodicals, books, annual reports, government sources, and online databases.

Other features include a general business chronology of events specifically pertaining to companies; a glossary of economic and business terms found within the text; a directory of business web sites; and a general index that includes primary people, company names, and brand names.

Comments and Suggestions

Questions, comments, and suggestions regarding *Company Profiles for Students* are welcomed. Please contact:

The Editor *Company Profiles for Students*
Gale Research
27500 Drake Rd.
Farmington Hills, MI 48331-3535
Telephone: (248)677-4253
Toll-Free: (800)877-GALE
Fax: (248)699-8070
Email: Donna.Craft@gale.com

Chronology of Key Business Events

1865: The Civil war brings the value of Confederate paper money down and the value of Union Gold rises. The Confederate money remains worthless for another 13 years.

1866: The National Labor Congress convenes in Baltimore and forms the National Labor Union; Western Union Telegraph absorbs two small telegraph companies becoming the first great U.S. monopoly.

1867: Steel rail production begins in the United States, which had been using iron rails or imported steel; Milwaukee printer Christopher Sholes invents the typewriter; inventor Benjamin Tilghman devises a process for producing wood pulp for paper production.

1868: U.S. businesses resist government intervention by quoting the fourteenth amendment; Congress enacts a law restricting work days to 8 hours for government workers, but in the private sector, most laborers work 10 to 12 hour days.

1869: Wall Street crashes for the first time, ruining small speculators, as a small group of financiers try to corner the market on gold, and close half the banks and businesses in New York in the process; the Noble Order of the Knights of Labor, a secret society, is founded following the death of the president of the National Labor Union; the Union Pacific and Central Pacific railroads meet in Promontory Point, Utah, completing the first transcontinental railroad.

1872: Congress enacts the first consumer protection law, making it illegal to use the mail for fraudulent purposes.

1873: A farmers' convention attacks monopolies, calling them "detrimental to the public prosperity," and urges an end to government subsidies to corporations and an end to tariff protection for industry; The Fourth Coinage Act is passed by Congress making gold the sole U.S. monetary standard and inadvertently making trade dollars legal tender in amounts up to $5.

1877: The Supreme Court sustains the state law of 1871 of state supervised grain elevators and lays the ground work for all regulation of U.S. businesses by government.

1878: Congress votes to reduce circulation of paper money, which has regained its value for the first time since 1865; shares in gas companies plummet as Thomas Edison works out methods for cheap production and transmission of electrical current, making it adaptable for household use.

1883: U.S. railroads adopt standard time with four time zones: Eastern, Central, Rocky Mountain, and Pacific; Thomas Edison pioneers the radio tube.

1886: Labor struggles for an eight-hour work day and better working conditions leads 610,000 workers to strike, the most ever in nineteenth-century America; a new American Federation of Labor (AF of L) is founded; the Supreme Court rules that only the federal government can regulate interstate railway rates.

1887: The Interstate Commerce Act is passed by Congress and orders railroads to keep their rates fair and reasonable.

1890: The Sherman Antitrust Act is passed by Congress to curb the power of U.S. monopolies; the McKinley Tariff Act is passed by Congress and increases the average U.S. import duty to its highest level ever; the United Mine Workers of America is founded as an affiliate of the AF of L.

1891: The first full-service advertising agency opens in New York, providing copy, art, production, and placement.

1893: Wall Street prices plummet and the market collapses, 600 banks close their doors, and more than 15,000 businesses fail as an economic depression hits the United States.

1894: The Wilson-Gorman Tariff Act reduces tariffs by 20 percent and includes an income tax on incomes over $4,000 a year.

1895: The Supreme Court fails to uphold the Sherman Antitrust Act by ruling that controlling the manufacturing process affects interstate commerce only indirectly and incidentally; The Supreme Court rules that the income tax provision of the Wilson-Gorman Tariff Act is unconstitutional; a gold rush to Canada's Klondike begins.

1897: The Dingley Tariff Act raises costs of living by increasing duties to an average of 57 percent; The influx of gold from the Klondike gold rush helps end the economic depression; after a 12-week strike, bituminous coal workers win an eight-hour day, semimonthly pay, abolition of company stores that charge premium prices, and biennial conferences; The Supreme Court rules that railroads are subject to the Sherman Antitrust Act.

1899: Congress passes the Refuse Act giving the Army Corps of Engineers the power to prosecute polluters, providing fines of up to $2,500 for oil spills and other similar pollution, but the act is not enforced.

1901: Wall Street panics as brokerage houses sell off stock so they can raise funds to take over the Northern Pacific Railroad; the stock prices in the railroad fluctuate from a high of $1,000 per share to a low of $150 per share and the Northers Securities holding company ends up owning most of the country's railroads.

1902: United Mine Workers lead a strike of 147,000 anthracite coal workers that cripples the United States; President T. Roosevelt begins instituting antitrust proceedings against many U.S. corporations; Congress passes the National Reclamation Act, which gives the federal government the rights to build irrigation dams throughout the West and limits the size of individual land holdings receiving federal water to 160 acres.

1904: The Supreme Court rules that the Northern Securities trust formed in 1901 violates the Sherman Antitrust Act.

1905: The Industrial Workers of the World (IWW) joins U.S. workers and attacks the AF of L for supporting the capitalist system; a New York law limiting hours of work in the baking industry is considered unconstitutional by the Supreme Court; Upton Sinclair exposes the horrific working conditions in the meat-packing industry in his novel *The Jungle*.

1906: The Hepburn Act is passed, which extends jurisdiction of the Interstate Commerce Commission (ICC) and gives the ICC the power to fix railroad rates; Congress appoints $2.5 million and New York bankers loan hundreds of millions of dollars to San Francisco to rebuild the city after an earthquake and fire devastates the city; a Pure Food and Drug bill is passed by Congress to regulate producers and sellers of food.

1907: New York Stock Exchange prices drop sharply because of financial drains from rebuilding San Francisco, several railroad expansion programs, and the Russo-Japanese War of 1905, sparking an economic depression.

1908: The Supreme Court rules that discrimination against union labor in interstate commerce violates the fifth amendment.

1910: The Manns-Elkins Act amends the Interstate Commerce Act and regulates telephone, telegraph, and cable companies under ICC regulations.

1911: Yale political economic professor Irving Fisher proposes the theory that prices rise in proportion to the supply of money and the speed at which money circulates, and pioneers indexing the economy with price indexes, cost-of-living indexes, etc.; the first SAE handbook on automotive standardization is published by the Society of Automotive Engineers.

1912: The Shirley amendment to the Pure Food and Drug Law prohibits far-fetched claims of therapeutic effects; the Associated Advertising Clubs of America adopts a Truth in Advertising code.

1913: The U.S. Bureau of Labor Statistics computes its first monthly consumer price index to determine the fairness of wages; the Underwood-Simmons Tariff Act lowers import duties by an average of 30 percent, which hurts many U.S. manufacturers who fight for restoration of tariff protection; the Glass-Owen Currency Act establishes 12 Federal Reserve banks in 12 major cities and requires member banks to maintain cash reserves proportionate to their deposits with the Federal Reserve system; the Federal Reserve's board of governors determine the amount of cash in circulation, provide elasticity to the supply of currency, and can act to control inflation.

1914: The New York Stock Exchange closes as Montreal, Toronto, Madrid, London, and many other European exchanges close due to the escalation of war in Europe; the Clayton Antitrust Act strengthens the federal government's power against restraint of trade as outlawed by the Sherman Antitrust Act; A Federal Trade Commission is established to prevent unfair competition in U.S. industry.

1915: Delaware begins revising and liberalizing its corporation laws to attract corporations and soon becomes the national leader in chartering the largest corporations; IWW leader Joe Hill is executed.

1916: The Owen-Keating Act forbids shipment in interstate commerce of goods on which children under 14 have labored or on which children 14 to 16 worked more than eight hours a day; the Adamson Bill provides an eight hour work day on interstate railroads with time and a half pay for overtime; the U.S. railroad industry reaches its peak of 254,000 miles of track.

1917: President Wilson issues an embargo proclamation and places government control over exports of U.S. food, fuel, iron, steel, and war material.

1918: The Supreme Court rules that the Owen-Keating Act is unconstitutional and encroaches on a state's rights.

1919: Four million workers either strike or are locked out in one of the biggest years for labor unrest in U.S. history; World War I costs the United States nearly $22 billion and an additional $9 billion in loans to allied powers.

1921: Nearly 20,000 businesses fail and 3.5 million Americans are out of work; Boll weevils cut cotton production in Georgia and South Carolina in half.

1922: The Fordney-McCumber Tariff Act returns tariffs to higher levels and gives the president the power to raise or lower duties by 50 percent to equalize production costs; a six-month strike by coal miners to protest wage cuts cripples U.S. industries reliant on coal and leads to a period of chronic depression in the coal mining industry, whose operators resort to cutthroat competition to remain in business; the first paid radio commercial airs, setting the pattern for private control of radio airwaves.

1926: Scheduled airline service begins for the first time.

1929: The Dow Jones Industrial Average reaches 381.17 up from 88 in 1924, but it crashes on October 29; a record 16.4 million shares are traded, the Dow plummets 30.57 points, speculators that bought on margin are forced to sell, and almost $30 billion disappears, sending the United States into the worst economic depression in history.

1930: Stock prices regain some of their losses, but investors fearing a business depression continually lower prices; the Smoot-Hawley Tariff Bill raises tariffs to their highest level in history, and other countries raise their tariffs in response; a general world economic depression begins, U.S. unemployment reaches 4.5 million, and more than 1,300 banks close.

1931: The U.S. wheat crop breaks all records, driving down prices and leading to many farmers being forced off their farms as banks foreclose on their property.

1932: The average weekly wage falls from $28 to $17 in 1929; 21,000 businesses go bankrupt, 1,616 banks close, and industrial production drops to one-third the 1929 level; the Dow Jones Industrial Average reaches its low point of 41.22; Congress enacts a Reconstruction Finance Corp. with the power to lend $1.8 billion to the states to finance industry and agriculture; Congress passes a Home Loan Act that will lend money to mortgage loan institutions to rescue banks being forced to close; unemployment reaches 17 million.

1933: The Emergency Banking Act gives the president control over banking transactions and foreign exchange and forbids exporting of gold; President F. Roosevelt declares a bank holiday and only authorizes banks to reopen after an examiner has determined them solvent; all private gold holdings are required to be turned over to federal reserves in exchange for coin or currency; the United States abandons the gold standard; the Glass-Steagall Act forbids banks to deal in stocks and bonds and insures bank deposits; a National Industrial Recovery Act provides for codes of fair competition in industry and collective bargaining with labor; the unemployment rate peaks at 24.9 percent.

1934: The Reciprocal Trade Agreement Act passed by Congress gives the president power to negotiate trade pacts without consent of the Senate; the new act replaces the high tariffs of the Smoot-Hawley Act, believed to have contributed to the worldwide depression; the nation's first general strike starts in San Francisco to show sympathy for a strike of 12,000 International Longshoremen's Association workers; the Securities and Exchange Commission (SEC) is created by Congress to limit bank credit for speculators and to police the securities industry.

1935: An Emergency Relief Appropriations Act is passed by Congress to provide work and employment by "providing useful projects"; the Federal Reserve System is reorganized and establishes an open market committee to buy and sell government securities held by the Federal Reserve and thus control the money supply; a Federal Deposit Insurance Corp. (FDIC) is developed with assistance from the banks; the Committee for Industrial Organization (CIO) is founded.

1936: The Robinson-Patman Act supplements the Clayton Antitrust Act by forbidding manufacturers to practice price discrimination.

1938: The Fair Labor Standards Act limits working hours in the first national attempt to set maximum hours and minimum wages; the Dow Jones average falls to 98.95 but regains to 158.41; the Civil Aeronautics Authority (CAA) is created to regulate the growing aviation industry; the Federal Trade Commission, through the Wheller-Lea Act, is given the power to regulate advertising of food, drugs, cosmetics, and therapeutic devices.

1940: The Export Control Act gives the president power to halt or slow export of materials vital to U.S. defense; exports of aviation gas outside the Western hemisphere, and export of scrap iron and steel to Japan is embargoed.

1942: President Roosevelt calls for production of 60,000 planes, 45,000 tanks, 20,000 anti-aircraft guns, and 6 million tons of merchant shipping; the federal budget of $59 billion has $52 billion marked for the war effort; an Emergency Price Control Act gives the Office of Price Administration the power to control prices; an order by the newly created Office of Economic Stabilization limits salaries to $25,000 per year.

1944: A United Nations Monetary and Financial Conference establishes the International Bank for Reconstruction, which formulates a system, used until 1973, whereby every participating nation keeps its currency within a few percentage points of an agreed dollar value; the first automatic, general-purpose computer, which takes 4 seconds to perform simple multiplication and 11 seconds to perform simple division, is completed at Harvard University.

1946: The worst work stoppage since 1919 idles 4.6 million workers with a loss of 116 million man-days; the Office of Economic Stabilization, shutdown after the World War II, is reinstated by President Truman to control inflation; ENIAC (electronic numerical integrator and computer) is the world's first electronic digital computer and is the first to use vacuum tubes instead of mechanical relays—its 18,000 vacuum tubes perform 4,500 additions per second.

1947: The Taft-Hartley Act restricts a labor union's power to strike, outlaws businesses that can only hire union workers, introduces an 80-day waiting period before a lockout or a strike can begin, and empowers the government to obtain injunctions if the strike is detriment to national safety; the General Agreement on Tariffs and Trade (GATT) lowers tariff barriers significantly and helps revitalize world trade; coal mines return to private ownership after being run by federal government for the last year.

1948: The cost-of-living index reaches a record high as does U.S. production, employment, and national income; President Truman orders the Army to operate the railroad to prevent a nationwide strike.

1950: The Celler-Kefauver Amendment to the Clayton Antitrust Act curbs mergers of U.S. business firms and stops companies from buying up stock in other companies; the Revenue Act increases income and corporation taxes; the Defense Production Act establishes a system of priorities for materials, provides for wage and price stabilization, and curbs installment buying.

1951: The Federal Reserve Board raises stock-purchase margin requirements to discourage credit expansion; the Wage Stabilization Board freezes salaries and wages.

1952: President Truman orders federal seizure of steel mills to avoid a nationwide strike, but the Supreme Court rules the seizure illegal and 600,000 CIO steel workers go on strike; the railroads once again return to private ownership after nearly two years of being run by the federal troops.

1954: The Dow Jones average finally passes its 1929 high of 381 and closes the year above 404.

1955: The AF of L and CIO merge into the AFL-CIO.

1957: Senator Kefauver investigates the effect on consumers of increasing mergers by auto and steel makers, bread bakers, and pharmaceutical firms.

1959: The Landrum-Griffin Act requires labor unions to file financial reports with the secretary of labor and includes a labor Bill of Rights; the federal government gains an injunction against striking steel workers, a decision upheld by the Supreme Court; supermarkets account for 11 percent of food stores, but 69 percent of all food store sales.

1960: In an effort to curb a rising deficit in the U.S. balance of payments, President Eisenhower orders a reduction of government spending abroad; Eisenhower warns against the military-industrial complex that maintains high levels of spending for defense.

1963: U.S. factory workers average more than $100 per week for the first time in history.

1966: There are a record 2,377 corporate mergers in the United States, up from 844 in 1960; Congress passes the Fair Packaging and Labeling Act, which calls for clear labeling of the net weight of every package and imposes controls over the confusing proliferation of package sizes, but food continues to be sold in packages that make it difficult for consumers to determine the price per pound they are paying; many airline companies suffer financial losses because of inability to fill seats on the new Boeing 747 jumbo jets.

1967: The United Auto Workers quits the AFL-CIO, charging a lack of leadership and organizing effort; the record numbers of corporate mergers in the United States continue to rise with 2,975 mergers taking place; a U.S. Federal Meat Inspection Act takes effect as the Pure Food and Drug act of 1906 is strengthened.

1968: Corporate mergers continue to rise as 4,462 take place; Congress passes a Consumer Credit Protection Law requiring banks and other lending institutions to disclose clearly the true annual rate of interest and other financing costs on loans.

1969: Unemployment hits its lowest point in 15 years, and the Dow Jones average rises above 1000 for the first time in history, but does not hold.

1970: The Dow Jones average bottoms out at 631 then jumps 32.04 points, the largest one day jump ever recorded; the Rail Passenger Service Act creates the National Rail Passenger Corp. (Amtrak) to improve U.S. rail travel.

1971: President Nixon imposes a freeze on wages and prices, temporarily suspends conversion of dollars into gold, and asks Congress to impose a 10-percent surcharge to strengthen the dollar as the Vietnam War pushes inflation up; in response to Nixon's news, the Dow Jones average makes a record one-day jump of 32.93 points; the AFL-CIO announces it has no faith in Nixon's plan and refuses to cooperate with the wage freeze; U.S. imports top exports for the first time since 1888.

1972: The Dow Jones average closes at 1003.16, the first time it has ever closed above the 1000 mark; Soviet grain buyers begin buying U.S. soy and wheat and end up buying one quarter of the entire U.S. wheat crop.

1973: Speculative selling of U.S. dollars on foreign exchanges devalues the dollar, and Secretary of the Treasury George Schultz announces that the dollar will be devalued by up to 10 percent against major world currencies in an effort to make U.S. goods more competitive in foreign trade; President Nixon announces an embargo on exports of soybeans and cottonseeds, which lasts only five days; buyers bid up the prices of wheat as foreign buyers redouble their purchase of U.S. grain in case further embargoes are issued; Arab nations begin cutting back oil exports for political reasons.

1974: Economic recession hits the world following a hike in oil prices by major petroleum producers in the Middle East and a rising inflation rate; The Consumer Price Index rises a record 12.2 percent; the Dow Jones average bottoms out at 570.01.

1975: Investors fail to take advantage of the first opportunity since 1933 to buy gold, driving the price down by over $30 per ounce; Wall Street's fixed commission rate ends by order of the Securities and Exchange Commission, leading to lower rates, sometimes by as much as 90 percent, and forcing many brokers and dealers out of business.

1976: Federal Trade Commission figures show that the 450 largest companies control 70 percent of U.S. manufacturing assets and make 72 percent of the profits; the Energy Policy and Conservation Act sets gasoline mileage standards for cars, establishes petroleum reserves, and authorizes the president to develop contingency plans for future energy crises.

1977: Kohlberg Kravis Roberts pioneers the leveraged buy-out, using high-yield junk bonds to finance them; the Foreign Corrupt Practices Act provides for severe penalties, including up five years in jail and up to $1 million in fines, for any U.S. corporation

that offers a bribe to a foreign government, political party official, or political candidate; the Semiconductor Industry Association is formed to lobby against government-subsidized Japanese efforts to dominate the semiconductor industry.

1978: President Carter announces a program of voluntary wage-price guidelines to curb the rising inflation; the Dow Jones Industrial Average sets another one day record by jumping up 35.4 points; the mandatory retirement age for workers is raised to 70.

1979: The Supreme Court rules that the valuation of warehouse items may not be reduced for tax purposes unless it is disposed of or sold at reduced prices; inflation continues to rise uncontrollably and balloons 13.3 percent for the year, the largest jump in 33 years; the Federal Reserve Board announces a 1-percent increase in the discount interest rate to curb inflation; Wall Street reacts drastically to the news, driving down the Dow Jones average by 26.48 points on the day of the announcement, starting a small recession; Gold prices top $400 per ounce for the first time in history as world markets react to worries about inflation.

1980: Banks raise the prime loan rate, which fluctuates between a low of 12.0 percent to a peak of 21.5 percent; President Carter places a partial embargo on the export of grain to the Soviet Union in response to the Soviet Invasion of Afghanistan.

1982: Heavy tariffs are imposed on some steel imports that are foreign government subsidized to help struggling U.S. steel mills; unemployment reaches 10.8 percent, the highest since 1940, and the number of Americans living below the poverty line is the highest it's been in 17 years; fax machines gain popularity as the time per page goes from 6 minutes to 20 seconds, bringing phone bills down for faxing.

1984: Economic growth rises at 6.8 percent, the biggest in over 30 years, and the inflation rate drops to 3.7 percent, the lowest in 17 years, but budget and trade deficits continue to rise to record levels.

1985: Corporate mergers and acquisitions continue to increase and 24 involve more than $1 billion each, with junk bonds used to finance most takeovers; world oil prices collapse, putting pressure on, and in some cases closing, many banks and savings institutions in energy sector states.

1986: Congress restructures the federal tax system raising taxes on businesses, which in turn raise prices; the Dow Jones average rises past 1900; the national debt rises above $2 trillion for the first time in history; Wall Street continues to suffer from insider trading scandals as Dennis B. Levine and Ivan F. Boesky are both found guilty of trading on non-public information.

1987: The Dow Jones average peaks at 2722.42, sets a one-day record rising 75.23 points, then plummets

508 points, or 22 percent, in one day—a bigger one-day drop than the October 1929 crash; the AFL-CIO allows the Brotherhood of Teamsters into the union.

1989: The Financial Institutions Rescue, Recovery and Enforcement Act attempts to bail out the failed savings and loan institutions using tax dollars, but inadvertently jeopardizes commercial banks, and in the end fails in its purpose; the Dow Jones average drops 190.58 points in one day as junk bond financing of mergers and acquisitions shakes investors' confidence, but prices rebound the following week and Dow Jones closes the year at 2753.

1990: The record eight-year economic boom ends and the country goes into a recession; the Dow Jones peaks at 2999.75, then drops to a low of 2365.10; the Federal Reserve Board gives J.P. Morgan & Co. the power to underwrite stocks, the first time a bank has had that power since 1933.

1991: The Dow Jones Industrial Average closes above 3000 for the first time in history, but drops back down amid reports that the recession is not over.

1992: The national debt tops $4 trillion, rising $2 trillion in just six years.

1993: The North American Free Trade Agreement (NAFTA) phases out tariffs and other trade barriers between Canada, Mexico, and the United States, and the agreement is passed despite severe opposition from labor unions who claim it will take jobs into other countries; the Revenue Reconciliation Act seeks to reduce the national deficit by nearly $500 billion through budget cuts and modest tax increases.

1994: The General Agreement on Tariffs and Trade (GATT) is updated to extend patent protection and strengthen anti-dumping laws and sanctions, as well as new coverage for agriculture, textiles, services, and intellectual property rights.

1996: The Telecommunications Act of 1996 deregulates the telecommunications industry and allows any communications company to compete in any market against any other company.

1997: The Dow Jones begins unprecedented growth, growing nearly 1,500 points over five months to top 8000; the unemployment rate drops to 4.8 percent, the lowest figure since before the Great Depression.

1998: The Asian economic crisis begins to spread throughout the world with Japan, China, Russia, and eastern Europe suffering from severe depressions, which threaten to spread to outlying regions in Asia, western Europe, and North America; to keep the economy strong in the United States, the Federal Reserve drops the federal funds rate to 5.25 from 5.50 percent; Wall Street begins to see results of the crisis and, as of October, the Dow Jones average drops from a high of 9337 to a low of 7539, including a response to the federal funds cut with two one-day drops in a row of 237.9 points and 208.8 points; crude oil prices drop from $17.78 per barrel in 1997 to a low of $11.36, leading many oil companies to begin mass layoffs.

3M

ALSO KNOWN AS: Minnesota Mining & Manufacturing Co.
FOUNDED: 1902

OVERVIEW

Minnesota Mining and Manufacturing Company, or 3M as the company prefers to be known, manufactures over 50,000 products in a variety of different markets. From Scotch Tape, which recently celebrated its sixty-fifth anniversary as a home and office staple, to Post-it Notes, the 1980's product rumored to be the result of an engineering mistake, 3M products have significantly impacted how people work in the office and in the home.

Currently organized into three main sectors, 3M's corporate structure reflects the diversity of their product line. The Industrial and Consumer Sector, which includes 3M's profitable office products line, oversees the production and sale of products to the transportation, construction, and electronics industries. The Health Care Sector focuses on health care products including bandages, surgical supplies, and computer software for health care organizations. The Transportation, Safety, and Chemicals Sector develops products for the automotive industry, performance chemicals, and sign materials. The strategy for all three sectors is largely the same; the focus is on creating new products that allow 3M to compete quickly and significantly in new markets. 3M's primary goal is to decrease the amount of time it takes a product to move from the research and development phase to being available for purchase. High growth industries, such as computers and health care services, are being particularly targeted as 3M seeks to improve productivity while expanding its international presence. With operations in 63 countries and product sales in more than 200 countries, 3M is a highly diversified Fortune 500 company with a strong global presence. 3M's continued focus on new product development has been suc-

Contact Information:

HEADQUARTERS: 3M Center
    St. Paul, MN 55144-1000
PHONE: (612)736-1110
FAX: (612)736-2133
TOLL FREE: (800)3M-HELPS
EMAIL: innovation@mmm.com
URL: http://www.mmm.com

FINANCES:

3M Net Sales, 1994-1997 (billion dollars)

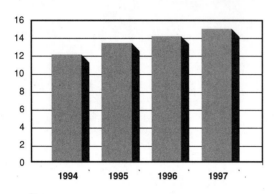

3M 1997 Stock Prices (dollars)

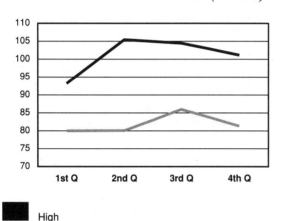

3M's 50,000 products are sold to a well diversified customer base. Sales to industrial customers total 45 percent, while sales to service related industry consumers make up an additional 45 percent of 3M's sales. Ten percent of 3M's products are sold to consumers. In 1997 international sales accounted for 52 percent of the company's revenue total.

ANALYSTS' OPINIONS

As one of the 30 companies of the Dow Jones Industrial Average, 3M will tell any potential investor that because of their long record of innovation, the company has established itself as the market leader in many diverse product lines and has maintained consistent profit and dividend growth since 1916. Many analysts agree with 3M's assessment and consider it a safe and stable stock. For example, *Value Line Investment Survey* reported that 3M, as a diversified company with multiple product lines, will grow slowly and steadily, paralleling the U.S. economy. As a stock purchase, 3M appeals to conservative investors, ones who expect long-term steady growth in their portfolio rather than an immediate high return. Consistently ranked by *Fortune* magazine as one of the country's most admired corporations, 3M will continue to encourage heavy research and development into new technologies in order to insure the company's future success.

HISTORY

3M's reputation as a company that balances innovation and risk-taking with solid financial success was largely the result of its ability to overcome early obstacles. The five businessmen who founded 3M in Two Harbors, Minnesota, in 1902 set out to mine corundum, a very hard mineral that could be used as an abrasive for grinding-wheels. This mining venture was not a success because their mineral holdings were not corundum, but instead anorthosite, which had no commercial value. Abandoning this venture, co-founder John Dwan turned to early investors and solicited funds in exchange for stock. Edgar Ober and Lucius Ordway accepted Dwan's offer and took over the company in 1905. After moving its headquarters to Duluth, they began researching and producing sandpaper products. William McKnight, soon to be a key executive in the firm, joined the company in 1907, and A.G. Bush, McKnight's eventual co-leader, joined in 1909. After years of struggle—not only with production methods, but also with getting the raw supplies necessary for producing their product—3M finally became financially stable in 1916. 3M president Edgar Ober, who had gone without a salary for most of the company's tumultuous early years, announced to company investors: "Gentlemen this is the day we've been wait-

cessful with 30 percent of sales in the 1990s coming from products created since 1994.

COMPANY FINANCES

From 1995 to 1997, 3M has shown steady increases in revenue. In 1995, the company had revenues of $13.5 billion, and this increased to $14.2 billion in 1996. Revenue for 1997 was $15.1 billion. Stock prices rose as well during this time period. For fiscal year 1995, the high was 69.88; for fiscal year 1996, the high was 85.88, and fiscal year 1997's high was 105.50.

ing for, the day some of us wondered would ever come. We're out of debt, and the future looks good. Business has more than doubled in the past two years, and for the first time, we'll have enough left after expenses to pay a dividend."

Early successes for 3M included Three-M-ite sandpaper, Wetordry sandpaper, and Scotch Brand Tape. The development plans of these early products had common elements that contributed to their eventual success. All three products were innovative, fulfilled a customer need, and were either better quality than similar products on the market or were completely new product concepts that filled needs customers had but were unable to describe. Three-M-ite sandpaper was a more effective sandpaper than others that were on the market. The Wetordry sandpaper was a revolutionary product as it was the first waterproof sandpaper that made sanding dust far less dangerous to the health of factory workers. Scotch masking tape filled a customer need by allowing auto workers to temporarily tape and protect car bodies while painting.

Timing was also essential to the success of many 3M products. Three-M-ite sandpaper was introduced shortly before the United States entry into World War I when automotive and machine tool factories were responsible for supplying equipment to the armed forces. Vast quantities of sandpaper were required to complete the job. In 1930, when 3M developers found a way to graft cellophane, a DuPont invention, to adhesive, the company succeeded in producing a product (Transparent Scotch Tape) that allowed workers to repair items rather than replace them, which was of growing importance during the Depression. This helped the company to grow at a time when most businesses struggled to break even. When a 3M salesman invented the portable tape dispenser, Transparent Scotch Tape became 3M's first large-scale consumer product. By 1932 the product was doing so well that 3M's main client base shifted from factories to office supply stores.

Succeeding decades found 3M constantly striving to diversify and expand their product line. During the 1940s, 3M expanded industrial uses of their adhesives to include vinyl electrical tape and Sound Recording Tape, a product innovation that spurred growth in the music recording industry. The 1950s saw the creation of 3M's subsidiary companies in Australia, Canada, France, Germany, Mexico, and the United Kingdom. Health care products were developed for the first time, and the household cleaning product Scotch-Brite Scouring Pads were derived from abrasives traditionally sold into the industrial market. During the 1970s, 3M's technology base continued to expand. As their web site history points out, "the innovative new products they produced held automotive parts in place; fastened diapers; provided backup security for computers; gave dentists new filling materials; helped keep buildings clean; helped prevent theft of library books; and made insulated clothing less bulky and more comfortable." The 1980s brought the creation of Post-it Notes and the establishment of 3M's first research

FAST FACTS:
About 3M

Ownership: 3M is a publicly owned company traded on the New York, Pacific, Chicago, Tokyo, Paris, Amsterdam, Swiss, and German Stock Exchanges.

Ticker symbol: MMM

Officers: Livio D. DeSimone, Chmn. & CEO, 61, $1,598,870; Ronald A. Mitsch, Vchmn. & Exec. VP, 63, $752,411; J. Marc Adam, VP Marketing, 59

Employees: 75,639

Principal Subsidiary Companies: 3M has subsidiary companies and facilities in over 60 countries.

Chief Competitors: Because of its diverse product line, 3M competes with multinational companies in a variety of industries including manufacturers, wholesalers, and retailers of pharmaceuticals, electronics, and industrial supplies. Some primary competitors are: BASF; Johnson & Johnson; DuPont; Exxon; and General Electric.

and administrative complex outside of the company's home state of Minnesota; the Austin Center was established to better enable networking with other high tech electronics and telecommunications firms headquartered in Texas. Noteworthy new products of the 1990s have again demonstrated 3M's ability to make new and successful products out of their most familiar materials and technologies. 3M introduced the O-Cel-O StayFresh sponge, the first sponge to use anti-microbial technology to eliminate odor-causing germs on contact. 3M also introduced large-format graphics with its Scotchprint Electronic Graphic System, which allows advertisers to transfer self-sticking images and text onto unlikely surfaces such as buses, trains, floors, and buildings. The future direction of the company is the same as the direction of the company founded in 1902. 3M continues to expand product lines with new and innovative uses of the technologies they know best.

STRATEGY

In 1948, 3M's corporate strategy was developed by one of the company's key executives, William L. McKnight, and it has remained largely the same

CHRONOLOGY:

Key Dates for 3M

1902: Minnesota Mining and Manufacturing (3M) is founded in Two Harbors, Minnesota

1916: 3M makes a profit and pays its first dividend

1930: Scotch Transparent Tape is introduced

1947: Scotch Magnetic Tape is introduced

1948: Scotch-Brite scouring pads are developed

1950: 3M manufactures its first health care product

1963: Carlton Society is created to reward 3M innovators

1975: 3M creates its 3P Program to encourage pollution prevention

1980: Post-It Notes are introduced

1994: 3M introduces its O-Cel-O StayFresh Sponge, the first sponge to use anti-microbial technology to kill germs

1995: 3M makes its Precise Mousing Surface, a mouse pad that makes use of microreplication technology

throughout the company's history. The updated version, still present in many 3M offices, reflects the company's emphasis on allowing employees to do their work in their own way. "As our business grows, it becomes increasingly necessary to delegate responsibility and to encourage men and women to exercise their initiative. . . . Mistakes will be made. But if a person is essentially right, the mistakes he or she makes are not as serious in the long run as the mistakes management will make if it undertakes to tell those in authority exactly how they must do their jobs. Management that is destructively critical when mistakes are made kills initiative. And it's essential that we have many people with initiative if we are to continue to grow." Corporate goals are clearly aligned to 3M's entrepreneurial environment, including its emphasis on developing and selling distinctive products and services of great quality and dependability.

Financial goals are also tied to their entrepreneurial strategy as the company seeks to provide investors a return on their investment (company dividends paid against purchased stock), that grows at a rate of 10 percent per year. As this type of growth typically requires a steady

stream of successful new products, 3M has established the corporate goal of obtaining 30 percent of worldwide sales from products released since 1994. Customers are an integral part of the new product design process. For example, the development of electronic Post-it Notes started with a survey of the product's users and finished with preliminary copies of the software going to 1,000 potential users who tested and provided feedback on the product. Additional incentives are offered to accomplish the company's other corporate goals that stress earning customer loyalty, encouraging international growth, and continually improving productivity and global competitiveness. In order to achieve these goals, 3M focuses on measurable results; each of the company's business units must report on sales, earnings, market share, inventory and, most important for 3M, percentage of new product growth.

INFLUENCES

3M's emphasis on continual new product development created an environment where risk-taking is rewarded. Some of 3M's most successful inventions came from creating new products based on technologies that failed their original purpose. One such invention was Post-It Notes, the notepad that made use of an adhesive that would not stick. 3M engineers also developed micro replication technology, which is a process of covering surfaces with millions of perfectly made miniature shapes such as cubes or pyramids. This process, used in highly reflective highway signs, lap-top computer screens, and certain abrasives, changes the physical properties of the materials and improves their functionality. As this new technology satisfies 3M's goal of focusing on products that create new markets and has the potential to generate several billion dollars of new sales by the end of this decade, its importance to 3M lies in its future, not current, profitability and success. This ability to transform a failed technology into a successful product encourages 3M employees to continually focus on innovation.

Innovation, however, has not been able to salvage every technology. When faced with a pricing war in the late 1970s, during which TDK and Maxell slashed the prices of their consumer audio cassette tapes, 3M stopped manufacturing cassettes and instead began purchasing the magnetic media from an overseas supplier and placing the 3M label on the imported tapes. While the loss of sales and increased production costs did not seriously impact 3M's profitability, it did reinforce their tradition of abandoning markets where it could not set its own prices. This practice caused difficulties for 3M during the 1970s and 1980s when competition in their traditional markets became more fierce. Faced with an eroding customer base in what 3M considered to be their core technology of abrasives, 3M began increasing the amount of money spent in research and development. For the past 20 years, even when business slowed, 3M has continually increased re-

The 3M headquarters in St. Paul, Minnesota. *(Courtesy of 3M.)*

search dollars in order to stimulate development and meet the company's aggressive new product goals.

3M's method of creative madness carries over into 3M's organizational blueprint. 3M's divisions, groups, and sectors all function in odd combinations. For example, the same division that makes tape for disposable diapers was at one time grouped with the division that makes reflective substances for traffic signs. To some business analysts, these odd combinations of product lines seem chaotic and disorganized, and they have generally applauded 3M's recent reorganizations that grouped 3M subsidiary companies and divisions around common markets, industries, and distribution channels. To supporters, 3M's chaos is a form of creative genius that reflect a very unsystematic approach to successful management.

CURRENT TRENDS

While 3M is still seeking to produce innovative products that fill customer needs, the company is currently focused on consolidating marketing efforts around common product lines. In 1995, the company reorganized into market-centered groups that would focus on different branches of the company's diverse customer base. One such group was the Electronic Market Center, which handles product marketing for 18 electronic product divisions. The goal of these market centers is to leverage 3M's marketing efforts by eliminating multiple calls to customers. The Electronic Market Center, which took over a year to establish, has account managers for key electronic product accounts and will focus on key industry segments such as storage systems, semiconductors, electronic displays, and electronic components.

Other trends affecting 3M management include their continued efforts to reduce pollution during the manufacturing process, lower production costs through streamlining, and increase the speed and efficiency of new product development.

PRODUCTS

A listing of 3M's products would be quite extensive since they have more than 50,000. Some of the company's well-known products include sandpaper, Scotch tape, Scotchguard fabric protector, Post-it Notes, O-Cel-O sponges, asthma inhalers, medical and dental adhesives, and plastic sheeting.

3M's focus on limiting pollution during product manufacturing resulted in new technologies such as its aircraft painting and re-coating technique. Using sticky film, wheat, and dry ice to paint and re-coat aircraft, the company has succeeded in patenting a technique that eliminates hazardous wastes and lessens pollution in the entire aircraft painting and re-coating process. Other new product ventures include electronic Post-it Software

THE POST-IT NOTES STORY

Art Fry, the inventor of Post-It Notes, used 3M's famed 15–percent rule to develop a bookmark he could use for his choir book. Needing a placeholder that would stick temporarily without ripping the pages, he heard of a 3M adhesive developed by Dr. Spence Silver that did not stick to a surface permanently. Working with developers in engineering and production, they developed a unique coating process that would apply the nonsticky adhesive to the back of small pieces of paper. Once the prototype was in place, Fry used company employees to test his bookmark. Initial feedback was not reassuring as critics thought they were too frivolous and expensive. It was only after receiving a letter with his "bookmark" used to add scribbled comments, that Fry realized he hadn't invented a bookmark but rather a new way to communicate or organize information. He was also unprepared for the almost instant demand by employees for additional supplies of "stickies." Today Post-It Notes are one of the five top-selling office products in the United States.

Notes, a software program that allows users to post notes within electronic documents, and 3M Nexcare Waterproof Bandages with Tattoo Designs, which stick to the skin during long periods of underwater wear and looks like a tattoo. 3M also plans to expand its Thinsulate material product line, which is currently used for boots, gloves, and other clothing items; Thinsulate Acoustical Material is an insulating material used in automobiles with potential applications in home theaters, household appliances, and offices. Additionally, 3M Light Fiber is a breakthrough product that provides lighting underwater and to heat sensitive materials.

CORPORATE CITIZENSHIP

In 1975, 3M adopted an Environmental Policy that stated it would solve its own environmental problems, prevent pollution at the source, and develop products that have a minimum impact on the environment. Viewed as a means of reducing production and manufacturing costs, 3M created its Pollution Prevention Pays (3P) Program. This program rewards employees for preventing pollution rather than cleaning it up after it occurs. Since this program was instituted in 1975, 4,651

employee 3P Programs have been organized, saving the company an estimated $810 million dollars. The company received national recognition for the program in 1996 when it was given the Presidential Award for Sustainable Development.

3M continuously seeks to improve the environmental performance of its products by considering the impact at all stages of the product's life cycle, from manufacturing and shipping through use and disposal. By installing air pollution control equipment at 3M locations where it was not required by law, they have since cut air emissions by more than 70 percent. They have also cut waste—what is left after counting raw materials and subtracting product and used byproduct—by one-third. Their goals for the year 2000 include cutting process releases to the environment 90 percent from a 1990 base; they have achieved a 50 percent reduction from air emissions and plan to achieve the remaining 40 percent from pollution prevention.

In addition to a strong environmental policy, 3M also funds educational initiatives through the 3M Foundation and the Corporate Contributions Program. In 1996, they donated approximately $47 million in cash, products, and services to educational and charitable institutions. One such initiative was MATHCOUNTS, a national math program for middle school students. 3M also funds continuing education programs in science and economics, and it sponsors science programs on PBS. Employees are also encouraged to take part in community development programs such as Meals-On-Wheels and Habitat for Humanity. 3M's participation in environmental and community development initiatives have become an integral part of the company's strategy.

GLOBAL PRESENCE

With 52 percent of the company's total 1997 sales of $15.1 billion coming from product sales in more than 200 countries, 3M has a well established international market. It is a major player in the global economy with operations in more than 60 countries accounting for more than half of its business. Its international operations are grouped into three areas including Asia and the Pacific; Latin America, Africa, and Canada; and Europe and the Middle East. Forty-four international companies have manufacturing operations; 29 international companies have laboratories. The company employs more than 36,000 people outside the United States, less than 200 of them being U.S. citizens. 3M's current strategy includes expanding their international presence even further by increasing their global marketing programs. The strongest international growth has been in Eastern Europe and the Middle East. In order to sustain and build growth in these regions, 3M has added more than 600 people to their International Division during the past seven years and established additional sales offices in the emerging economies of eastern Europe and the former Soviet Union. 3M also plans to expand production facilities and distribution centers in Singapore, Korea, and the Philippines in order to build on the 12 percent growth in sales to countries in Asia and the Pacific.

EMPLOYMENT

There are more than 75,000 3M employees worldwide. Boasting a low turnover rate of less than 3 percent annually, 3M encourages career employees and maintains that its formula for success produces workers satisfied enough to spend their work-life at 3M. The company's unique management style demands that employees be creative and take risks. New employees are required to take a class in risk taking, where numerous stories are told of great inventions coming from employees not afraid to contradict their supervisors. Researchers are required to stick to what the company calls the "15 percent rule," meaning the researchers are encouraged to spend that amount of their time working on their own projects. The company is so focused on hiring innovators that it researched and developed a personality profile of successful inventors; successful 3M innovators are creative and resourceful, have broad interests, and are self-motivated problem solvers with a strong work ethic. Creating what the company calls "a culture of cooperation," 3M encourages employees to freely share knowledge and rewards innovations that come from such exchanges.

SOURCES OF INFORMATION

Bibliography

3M Home Page, 5 June 1998. Available at http://www.mmm.com.

Collins, James, and Jerry Porras. *Built To Last.* New York: Henry Holt and Company, 1994.

Loeb, Marshall. "Ten Commandments for Managing Creative People." *Fortune,* 16 January 1995.

"Minnesota Mining and Manufacturing Company." *Hoover's Online,* September 1998. Available at http://www.hoovers.com.

Our Story So Far: Notes from the First 75 Years of 3M Company. St. Paul, MN: 3M Public Relations Department, 1977.

Pederson, Jay P. "Minnesota Mining & Manufacturing Company (3M)." *International Directory of Company Histories.* Detroit, MI: St. James Press, 1995.

Stewart, Thomas A. "3M Fights Back." *Fortune,* 5 February 1996.

For an annual report:

on the Internet at: http://www.mmm.com/profile/report2/index.html **or** write: General Office, 3M Center, St. Paul, MN 55144-1000

For additional industry research:

Investigate companies by their Standard Industrial Classification Codes, also known as SICs. 3M's primary SICs are:

2678 Stationery, Tablets, and Related Products

2891 Adhesives and Sealants

3291 Abrasive Products

3695 Magnetic and Optical Recording Media

ABC Inc.

ALSO KNOWN AS: American Broadcasting Companies Inc.
FOUNDED: 1943

Contact Information:

HEADQUARTERS: 77 West 66th St.
    New York, NY 10023-6298
PHONE: (212)456-7777
FAX: (212)456-6850
URL: http://www.abc.com

OVERVIEW

A multimedia giant, the American Broadcasting Companies (ABC), directly or through its subsidiaries, operates the ABC television network (with 224 affiliates), 10 television stations, ABC Radio Networks, and 26 radio stations. The company's Multimedia Group directs its digital television, interactive television, pay-per-view, video-on-demand, and online operations. The company also has an interest in a number of cable television networks, including ESPN, A&E, and Lifetime. Through joint ventures, ABC is engaged in international broadcast-cable services and television production and distribution. The company also publishes a number of daily and weekly newspapers, shopping guides, and several specialized and business periodicals and books. Additionally, the company provides research services and distributes information from databases.

Throughout its years as one of the leading U.S. television networks, ABC has reported news in the making as well as making a little history of its own. In 1995 the company was purchased by the Walt Disney Company for $19 billion, in what was at that time the second-largest corporate merger in U.S. history.

COMPANY FINANCES

As a subsidiary of Walt Disney Company, ABC does not report independently on its financial operations. However, for fiscal 1997, Disney's Broadcasting Division, which includes most of ABC's radio and television operations, reported operating income of $1.29 billion on revenue of $6.50 billion, compared with operating income for fiscal year 1996 of $1.08 billion on revenue of $6.01 billion. For the entire company, Disney reported net income of $1.77 billion in fiscal 1997, compared with $1.27 billion in fiscal 1996.

ANALYSTS' OPINIONS

"Disney's merger with ABC unites entertainment production and distribution operations that complement each other like oil and vinegar," wrote Stratford Sherman in a 1995 *Fortune* magazine article. The Federal Communications Commission split studios and television networks apart in the 1970s with regulations known as the financial interest/syndication (fin/syn) rules. Such regulations have lapsed in the 1990s, however, leading to Disney's acquisition of ABC. "So long as fin/syn governed their behavior, entertainment companies had to choose between content and distribution," Sherman continued. "In theory, the much-discussed convergence of computing, telecommunications, information, and entertainment creates a hierarchy of value, in which content, the scarcest commodity, bobs to the top. But reality is more complicated than that. . . . After building up great libraries of copyrighted movies and shows, production companies usually make up for lean years by selling out to a new owner for a fabulous price: Every major studio but Disney has done that more than once. But the leading content companies are getting almost too big to buy, making expansion into distribution a more attractive alternative."

He went on to say, "Both Disney and ABC are in the business of introducing new brands to audiences and then exploiting those brands for all they're worth. With ABC in its grasp, Disney can gain more value from its own TV productions by giving them favorable scheduling and promotion. Similarly, stores in Disney theme parks can sell sports merchandise with the logo of ESPN, ABC's sports channel. The opportunities are endless."

Writing in a 1995 *Commonweal* article, John Garvey commented, "The fact that ABC News is now in the hands of the Disney corporation has led to a lot of talk about this concentration of power over news and entertainment in a comparatively few number of hands." The objectivity and independence of news organizations such as ABC are now questioned more thoroughly. Garvey claims that recent mergers and mega-mergers resulting in the creation of monopolies like ABC and Disney creates a climate in where profit—and only profit—is the force that drives our economy. Such situations, Garvey feels, create economies in which "the soul goes out of a society."

HISTORY

Of the three major networks in the United States, ABC is the youngest. The first U.S. broadcasting com-

FAST FACTS:
About ABC Inc.

Ownership: ABC Inc. is a subsidiary of Walt Disney Co., which is a publicly owned company traded on the New York and Pacific Stock Exchanges.

Ticker symbol: DIS

Officers: Robert A. Iger, Pres., 46; Preston Padden, Pres., ABC Television Network; Allan N. Braverman, Sr. VP & Gen. Counsel

Employees: 20,000

Principal Subsidiary Companies: ABC is a widely diversified broadcaster and publisher. Among its subsidiaries are ABC Cable and International Broadcast Inc., ABC Entertainment, ABC News Inc., ABC Publishing Agricultural Group, ABC Radio Networks Inc., ABC Sports Inc., ABC/Kane Productions International Inc., Belleville News-Democrat, Capital Cities Media Inc., Capital Cities/ABC Video Publishing Inc., and Chilton Co. Other subsidiaries include ESPN Inc., Fairchild Publications, Farm Progress Companies Inc., Fort Worth Star-Telegram Inc., Great Lakes Media Inc., Hitchcock Publishing Co., Institutional Investor Inc., Kansas City Star Co., Legal Communications Corp., Miller Publishing Company Inc., National Price Service, Satellite Music Network Inc., Shore Line Newspapers Inc., Star-Telegram Newspaper Inc., and Sutton Industries Inc.

Chief Competitors: ABC Inc. faces keen competition in all of the media arenas in which it operates. These include radio, broadcast and cable television, and publishing. Some of its major competitors include: Advance Publications; Bertelsmann; Cablevision Systems; Capstar Broadcasting; CBS; Cox Enterprises; Discovery Communications; Dow Jones; Scripps; Gannett; Hearst; Knight Ridder; Liberty Media; NBC; News Corp.; TCI; Time Warner; Times Mirror; Tribune; Univision Communications; Viacom; Washington Post; and Westwood One.

pany was the National Broadcasting Company (NBC). By 1928 NBC had grown so large that its parent company, RCA, divided the company into two networks, the red and the blue, and it is in the blue network that ABC's origins lie. In 1943 NBC sold the less-profitable blue network to Edward J. Noble, who had made his fortune as

CHRONOLOGY:

Key Dates for ABC Inc.

1928: The National Broadcasting Company (NBC) had grown so large that its owner RCA divided the company into two networks

1941: The FCC rules no single company could own more than one network and orders NBC to divest itself of one of its networks

1943: NBC sells its less profitable network to Edward J. Noble who dubs his network American Broadcasting Company (ABC)

1953: ABC merges with United Paramount Theatres and becomes American Broadcasting-Paramount Theatres (AB-PT)

1954: AB-PT gives Walt Disney $4.5 million to finish Disneyland and Disney agrees to provide television shows for ABC

1957: Am-Par records, the music division of AB-PT, brings Philadelphia DJ Dick Clark to the station where he developed "American Bandstand"

1961: ABC Sports is founded

1965: AB-PT becomes American Broadcast Companies

1975: Fred Silverman joins ABC and the network soon becomes number one in prime-time ratings

1979: "Nightline" is introduced

1985: Capital Cities Communications purchases ABC; changes company name to Capital Cities/ABC Inc.

1995: Disney purchases ABC and changes name to ABC Inc.

---

the head of Life Savers Inc. Noble dubbed his network the American Broadcasting Company (ABC).

At first ABC was only a radio broadcaster. NBC and CBS had been involved in experimental television production and transmission for more than a decade by the time ABC was created, and the new network found the transition to television difficult, a reputation that dogged ABC for years. It was not until 1953, when ABC merged with United Paramount Theatres, that ABC had emerged as a third network of full stature. The following year ABC began a programming relationship with Disney that was perhaps a hint of things to come. As ABC had little ac-

cess to programs, supplied mostly by advertisers, the president of the newly formed company, Leonard Goldenson, built stronger ties with Hollywood. According to an article in *Newsweek,* Goldenson gave Walt Disney a $20 million loan to build Disneyland in exchange for programming. The next year ABC premiered *The Mickey Mouse Club,* another Disney-created show that would reach number one in the daytime television programming ratings. Roy and Walt Disney took their programming to NBC in 1961.

It was not until 1969 that ABC had its first number one series with *Marcus Welby, M.D.* Other milestones in ABC programming include the network's first television broadcast of *NFL Monday Night Football* in 1970; the 1975 premiere of *Good Morning America;* and the addition of Barbara Walters to the *ABC Evening News* team and her promotion to news anchor in 1976. The following year, propelled by the eight-day telecast of Alex Haley's *Roots,* ABC topped the network ratings. The *Roots* mini-series became the most-watched programming in television history.

It was not until 1980 that ABC finally won the respect accorded to its older TV rivals, CBS and NBC. During the 1980s and the 1990s, ABC broke new ground and stirred up controversy with some of its program offerings, notably *Thirtysomething, Roseanne, My So-Called Life,* and *Ellen.* These shows came under fire from some for their portrayal of homosexuality and other previously taboo subjects.

ABC reported $6.38 billion in operating revenue at the end of the 1995 fiscal year. With the various mergers and consolidations through the late 1980s and 1990s, particularly its 1985 acquisition by Capital Cities Communications, the holding company for ABC changed its name several times before Disney purchased the company in 1995 and redubbed it simply ABC Inc. The 1995 merger of Disney and ABC brought together two very complementary companies.

STRATEGY

As the 1997-98 television season approached in the fall of 1997, ABC's ratings were at their lowest level in some time, having plunged 9 percent during the course of the 1996-97 season. The company began to focus on restructuring the network's prime-time lineup. ABC President Robert Iger put together a new team of senior executives to handle some routine responsibilities so that he could concentrate on reworking the network's schedule to focus on family-oriented programming.

INFLUENCES

According to *U.S. News & World Report,* "Access to ABC's prime-time audience opens an enormous door for Disney's television production business. The Magic Kingdom's TV studios currently produce the top-rated show, ABC's *Home Improvement,* and eight other series airing this fall on various networks." Dennis Hightower, chief of television for Disney, said that he had been hoping to produce a dozen shows over the next couple of years, but with Disney helping to shape ABC's schedule, he will set his sights higher.

CURRENT TRENDS

The trend away from investigative journalism of the type ABC had become known for on its *20/20* news magazine, seemed to accelerate in the wake of suits such as that brought by Food Lion. ABC's *PrimeTime Live* television show aired a story claiming that Food Lion stores had knowingly sold spoiled meat, fish, and poultry to its customers. Sales in the nationwide chain plunged 9.5 percent that month. Food Lion subsequently sued ABC for fraud and racketeering, claiming that ABC had concocted the story. As a result, Food Lion was awarded significant damage compensation. "It's bad enough that news organizations have to worry about defamation charges that, even if overturned, are nonetheless costly and distracting," wrote Dan Trigoboff in *Broadcasting & Cable.* As a result of such settlements, news organizations have been more carefully considering whether it is worth their time and expense to conduct investigative reporting, even if they believe it may benefit the general public.

Since its merger with Disney, ABC has been in the process of restructuring. The network appears to be doing something right because its viewing audience is increasing, as well as its profits. However, CEO Robert Iger is the person to credit with the profitability of the company in 1997 and into 1998. In fact, *Television Digest* reported that ABC and ESPN had increased Disney's operating profit in 1997, and this trend has continued into 1998.

A major challenge and opportunity for growth has been the cable industry. Even if the television broadcasters do everything right, basic cable viewing is on the rise. This trend will continue as new cable networks emerge. Fortunately for the broadcasters, they have expanded their own cable holdings in the 1990s. ABC is a little ahead of its competitors with ESPN, Disney, and interests in Lifetime and A&E, all of which bring in subscriber fees as well as advertising revenues. In fact, the profits from ABC's cable businesses exceeded the profits of ABC's television network in the late 1990s. Nearly 80 percent of children's viewing goes to cable, mostly to Nickelodeon and the Cartoon Network. ABC and the other networks are paying more for programming in an attempt to stop the decline of their viewing audiences. The network attributed its 1997 gain in revenue to "improved performance of sports, news and late-night programming."

PRODUCTS

ABC is a broadcaster and publisher with subsidiaries that include ABC Cable and International Broadcast Inc., ABC Entertainment, ABC News Inc., ABC Publishing Agricultural Group, ABC Radio Networks Inc., ABC Sports Inc., ABC/Kane Productions International Inc., Belleville News-Democrat, Capital Cities Media Inc., ABC Video Publishing Inc., Chilton Co., ESPN Inc., Fairchild Publications, Farm Progress Companies Inc., Fort Worth Star-Telegram Inc., Great Lakes Media Inc., Hitchcock Publishing Co., Institutional Investor Inc., Kansas City Star Co., Legal Communications Corp., Miller Publishing Company Inc., NILS Publishing Co., National Price Service, Satellite Music Network Inc., Shore Line Newspapers Inc., Star-Telegram Newspaper Inc., and Sutton Industries Inc.

CORPORATE CITIZENSHIP

ABC operates the ABC Foundation, which is managed on a day-to-day basis by a board, as well as an executive director, and contributes specifically to the arts, such as museums and the ballet. The company operates a VIP program, which places interested employees into various charitable organizations. There are about 1,000 employees involved in ABC's VIP program.

GLOBAL PRESENCE

ABC is a widely diversified broadcaster and publisher. It operates the ABC Television Network Group, which distributes programming to 224 affiliated stations; 10 television stations, with 6 of them in the nation's top 10 markets; ABC Radio Networks, which reaches more than 3,400 radio stations; and 21 AM and FM radio outlets, all in major cities. As of 1998, there were 6 international Disney Channels in Taiwan, the United Kingdom, Australia, Malaysia, France, and the Middle East.

The ABC Cable and International Broadcast Group is the majority owner of ESPN and ESPN2 in the United States and overseas. ABC Cable is also a partner in the A&E and Lifetime cable networks in the United States. As of early 1998, ESPN, which is seen in 130 countries in 11 different languages, reached 72 million households in the United States and 152 million internationally. The sports network reached 72 million households in the United States. An additional 50 million households subscribed to ESPN2 and ESPNews. Overseas, ABC holds minority interests in the German production and distribution companies TelMunchen and RTL-2, Hamster Productions and TV Sport of France, Tesauro of Spain, the Scandinavian Broadcasting System, Eurosport of London, and the Japan Sports Channel. In addition, it has launched two children's television program services in China.

The ABC Publishing Group owns and operates seven daily newspapers, including the nationally respected *Kansas City Star* and *Fort Worth Star-Telegram.* It also publishes weekly newspapers and shopping guides in several states. Overall, the company's diversified Publishing Group produced more than 100 periodicals in the 1990s.

SOURCES OF INFORMATION

Bibliography
"ABC Will Lay Off About 50 Staffers." *Broadcasting & Cable,* 6 April 1998.

Boroughs, Don L., et. al. "Disney's All Smiles: Michael Eisner Puts the Powerful Magic Kingdom on Top of the Entertainment World with His Blockbuster Purchase of ABC." *U.S. News & World Report,* 14 August 1995.

Garvey, John. "Whistle While You Work." *Commonweal,* 8 September 1995.

Loomis, Carol J. "Buffett to Disney: All Thumbs Up." *Fortune,* 1 April 1996.

McClellan, Steve. "Nets Are Big 4's Weakest Links." *Broadcasting & Cable,* 2 March 1998.

Morgan, Richard. "Mad Ave. Bums Out Boomers." *Variety,* 23 March 1998.

"NABET-CWA Officials Say They Broke Off Talks with Disney/ABC Representatives Wednesday." *Broadcasting & Cable,* 13 October 1997.

Nix, Jennifer. "TV Battles Point Up Labor Pains." *Variety,* 23 March 1998.

Rice, Lynette. "ABC Is ABC Again." *Broadcasting & Cable,* 7 October 1996.

Schlosser, Joe. "ABC Renews Hits." *Broadcasting & Cable,* 16 March 1998.

Sherman, Stratford. "Why Disney Had to Buy ABC." *Fortune,* 4 September 1995.

Trigoboff, Dan. "ABC Thrown to the Lion." *Broadcasting & Cable,* 3 February 1997.

The Walt Disney Company Annual Report. Burbank, CA: The Walt Disney Company, 1997.

"The Walt Disney Company." *Fact Book.* Burbank, 1997.

"Washington Report-Is Mickey Mouse a Good Citizen." *New from the UAW,* 28 May 1998. Available at http://www.uaw.org.

For an annual report:
write: The Walt Disney Co., 500 S. Buena Vista St., Burbank, CA 91521-9722

For additional industry research:
Investigate companies by their Standard Industrial Classification Codes, also known as SICs. ABC's primary SICs are:

2711 Newspaper Publishing & Printing

2721 Periodicals & Printing

4832 Radio Broadcasting

4833 Television Broadcasting

Abercrombie & Fitch Co.

OVERVIEW

Abercrombie & Fitch is a retailer of high-quality sport and casual clothes, with spring and fall lines. The back-to-school and December holiday seasons are its busiest. Merchandise comes from 58 different manufacturing contractors throughout the world. The company operates over 150 stores, primarily in regional shopping malls. Principal customers are college students and the Generation X age group, though older generations can be seen wearing its clothes, too. Chairman and CEO Michael S. Jeffries calls the company a "lifestyle retailer."

COMPANY FINANCES

In the company's 1997 annual report, CEO Jeffries wrote, "[We] surpassed all our financial goals, outpacing even the most generous forecasts. Our growth is managed and healthy. . . ." Sales in 1997 were $521.3 million, with comparable store sales up 21 percent. Net income was $48.3 million, up 96 percent from 1996. Earnings per share were $.94, up 74 percent from 1996.

In its first day of trading on the New York Stock Exchange in 1996, the stock grew 45 percent, from $16.00 to $23.13. Since then, earnings have been spectacular, with significant increases and several quarters beating Wall Street's projections. In 1997 alone, the stock nearly doubled in price. By the end of 1997, Abercrombie & Fitch had seen 22 straight quarters of improved profits. The company's first monthly sales report in April of 1998 triggered a stock price rise of 9.7 percent.

FOUNDED: 1892

Contact Information:

HEADQUARTERS: 4 Limited Pky. E
    Reynoldsburg, OH 43218
PHONE: (614)577-6500
FAX: (614)577-6565
EMAIL: opportunities@abercrombie.com
URL: http://www.abercrombie.com

FINANCES:

Abercrombie & Fitch Net Sales, 1994-1997 (million dollars)

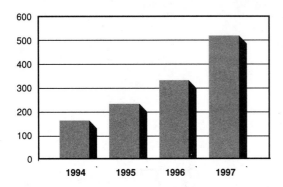

Abercrombie & Fitch 1997 Stock Prices (dollars)

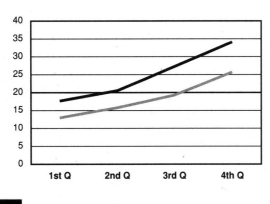

High

Low

HISTORY

Abercrombie & Fitch began as an outfitter of campers, hunters, and fishermen in 1892 in Manhattan with the partnership of David Abercrombie, a former miner and trapper who owned a camping-equipment factory and shop, and Ezra Fitch, one of his customers who was an outdoorsman and an attorney. The two had conflicting visions of the company's mission, and Abercrombie ultimately decamped in 1907. Fitch continued on with new partners, though in 1909 the company al-

most folded due to the expense it incurred in mass-mailing a 456-page catalogue of its inventory. The efforts eventually paid off, however, and the business built up a sizeable customer base.

In 1917 the company opened its first store in midtown Manhattan, which housed its own casting pool and a log cabin that founder Fitch had built. It became a purveyor of hip flasks during the country's Prohibition years. Other non-sporting equipment included cameras and indoor games like mah-jongg. It boasted many prominent patrons such as Teddy Roosevelt, whose African safari's required many of their wares; Charles Lindbergh; Amelia Earhart; Admiral Richard Byrd; and Ernest Hemingway. Fitch retired in 1928 selling his stake to his brother-in-law, James Cobb, and an employee named Otis Guernsy, who would become president and vice-president, respectively. Shortly thereafter, the company acquired Von Lengerke & Detmold, a New York carrier of guns and fishing equipment, as well as the gunsmith Griffin & Howe. In its heyday from the 1920s through the 1960s, the company's stores featured 15,000 kinds of fishing lures and 700 kinds of shotguns. Eventually it diversified to cater to tennis and polo players, ice skaters, and golfers. In the 1920s it gained a presence outside of New York with a yachting-related store in Hyannis, on Cape Cod in Massachusetts. By the time of the stock market crash of 1929, annual sales stood at well over $6 million, but at the high point of the Depression, they sank to a low point of $2.6 million.

The enterprise that had come to tout itself as The Greatest Sporting Goods Store in the World added stores in various other cities, though its store in Manhattan remained its epicenter. It featured taxidermed fish and big-game heads such as, elk, moose, caribou, and buffalo as wall decor. Winter-only stores opened under the Abercrombie & Fitch name in Palm Beach and Sarasota, Florida. Summer-only stores appeared in Southampton, New York; and Bayhead, New Jersey. In 1968 the company held a one-day warehouse sale, where it sold off all manner of archaic and unusual items at terrific bargains, attracting 90,000 patrons. A loss of $500,000 the following year inspired a similar sale in 1970. By that point, Abercrombie & Fitch seemed to have passed its prime as a retailer of products meant to help people experience and enjoy the great outdoors.

The company fell upon hard times in the 1970s, and by 1977 it filed for Chapter 11 bankruptcy protection and shut its doors, possibly forever. In 1978, a sporting retailer called Oshman's bought the company and proceeded to expand the erstwhile number of stores and the range of products it had sold. In 1988 Oshman's sold Abercrombie & Fitch to The Limited, a popular garment marketer, which limited the fallen empire's focus to clothes. In 1992, when it was having further financial difficulties, Michael Jeffries took the helm of Abercrombie & Fitch and shifted the target consumer base toward college-age youth. In 1996, then-owner The Limited spun off about 16 percent of it in an initial public offering, and in 1998 it distributed the rest to its shareholders.

STRATEGY

According to the 1997 annual report, the company will be keeping its annual store growth at no more than 20 percent per year, as it seeks to prevent "dilution of the brand." Brand-name recognition is central to Abercrombie & Fitch's appeal, especially to youth. Many of its garments sport the company's name or initials, often with "1892," the year of its birth. The company envisions itself and its products as being "in." The aesthetic it fosters and conveys in its stores' environments—from the overhead music to the attitude of the personnel—are similarly calculated to instill a sense of leisure. In the 1997 annual report, Jeffries wrote that the customers "come to be part of the lifestyle," and that they "want to be part of the experience," which involves "being seen in our stores."

Company representatives travel the country to visit colleges and youth "hot spots," in order to gain a sense of what its target age group is wearing, or would want to wear, as well as how they live in general. According to Jeffries, "[We] know what they wear, listen to, read, how they spend their time, what's hot, and what's not."

In a rare company/customer relationship, Abercrombie & Fitch individually answers each of the 2,000-plus monthly e-mails it receives from its public. A note on the comments section of the company's web site reads, "Every e-mail we receive is read and considered by a real live person." As further evidence of the company's positive relations with its customers, there is a liberal return policy: "No Sale Is Ever Final."

INFLUENCES

A significant goal is to expand the company's geographic reach. Plans for 1998 included adding 32 more stores. The chain grew rapidly within the United States in the late 1990s. It discontinued selling men's neckties and dress shirts in 1996; but it has diversified by adding additional women's fragrances and personal products. In 1997, the company stopped allocating additional space to women's apparel. A children's garment line is under consideration.

CURRENT TRENDS

Abercrombie & Fitch has created a unique venue as a menu for its next seasons' garments—a quarterly release appropriately named *A & F Quarterly,* which seems

FAST FACTS:
About Abercrombie & Fitch Co.

Ownership: The company was once a wholly owned subsidiary of the clothing retailer The Limited, but it is now fully independent and traded on the New York Stock Exchange.

Ticker symbol: ANF

Officers: Michael S. Jeffries, Chmn. & CEO, $1,796,154; Seth R. Johnson, VP & CFO, $526,923

Employees: 6,700 (5,500 part-time). The company also hires temporary help at peak selling times, such as the December holiday season.

Chief Competitors: Abercrombie & Fitch competes with a number of other retailers of casual clothes, including: The Gap; J. Crew; Spiegel; and American Eagle Outfitters.

to function as a magazine, too. (How many clothing catalogs sell for $5.00 on the newsstands or include editorials and lifestyle articles, such as musical and culinary comment?) It welcomes submissions of stories, essays, and photos. With a circulation of over 100,000, *A & F Quarterly,* has grown more quickly than expected, and in 1998 the magazine began accepting advertisements. Jeffries calls it "a powerful brand reinforcement," and "an innovative sourcebook of what's cool and new." A year's subscription can be had for $10.00 by calling (800)432-0888. The company's web site, a similar medium where the company promotes its wares and culture, with 2.5 million hits per month, also takes subscription order information for the publication.

PRODUCTS

Abercrombie & Fitch sells men's and women's casual clothes, such as sweaters, sweatshirts, shorts, boxer shorts, baseball-type caps, T-shirts, and jackets.

EMPLOYMENT

The company seeks college-age employees for its stores. Its web site includes current employment open-

CHRONOLOGY:

Key Dates for Abercrombie & Fitch Co.

1892: Founded as an outfitter for campers and hunters

1907: David Abercrombie leaves the company

1909: The company almost goes bankrupt because of the expense of a mass mailing of a 456-page catalog of its products

1917: Abercrombie & Fitch opens its first store in midtown Manhattan

1928: Ezra Fitch retires, selling his share to James Cobb

1933: During the Depression, the company's sales dropped from $6.3 million to $2.6 million

1939: Abercrombie & Fitch boasts the most valuable collection of firearms and the widest assortment of fishing flies available

1947: The company records its all-time record for net profits of $682,894

1958: Their first store in San Francisco opens

1968: The company holds a one-day warehouse sale in Manhattan attracting 90,000 customers

1977: Files for Chapter 11 bankruptcy

1978: Oshman's, a sporting retailer, purchases the company

1988: Oshman's sells the company to The Limited, refocusing the company on clothing

1992: The company shifts its target market toward college-age youth

1996: The Limited spins off about 16 percent of Abercrombie & Fitch in an initial public offering

1998: The rest of the company stock is distributed to its shareholders

---

ings, both for local stores and the corporate headquarters. A formal, 90-day management-training program ("MIT") offers recent college graduates an opportunity to become in-store Assistant Managers. Within a year, graduates of the program are eligible for promotion to store manager, and eventual promotion to district and regional managerial positions is possible.

SOURCES OF INFORMATION

Bibliography

"A&F Sizzles on 1st Day on NYSE." *WWD,* 27 September 1996.

"Abercrombie & Fitch, Co." *Form 10-K, for the Fiscal Year Ended 31 January 1998,* June 1998. Available at http://www.sec.gov/cgi-bin/srch-edgar.

"Abercrombie & Fitch, Co." *Hoover's Online,* 25 August 1998. Available at http://www.hoovers.com.

"Abercrombie & Fitch Co." *International Directory of Company Histories.* Detroit, MI: St. James Press, 1995.

Abercrombie & Fitch Co. 1997 Annual Report. Reynoldsburg, OH: Abercrombie & Fitch Co, 1998.

"Abercrombie & Fitch Co. Quarterly Financial Information." 18 May 1998.

Abercrombie & Fitch Home Page, June 1998. Available at http://www.abercrombie.com.

"Abercrombie & Fitch Profits Skyrocket in Third Quarter; First Report Since Public Filing." *Daily News Record,* 20 November 1996.

"Abercrombie & Fitch to Become a Fully Independent Public Company." Abercrombie & Fitch Press Release, 17 February 1998.

Edelson, Sharon. "Net Sales Increase 51 Percent in Abercrombie & Fitch Quarter." *WWD,* 1 August 1997.

"The Limited, Inc. Commences Tax-Free Exchange Offer to Create Fully Independent Abercrombie & Fitch." *PR Newswire,* 15 April 1998.

"The Limited Spinning Off Abercrombie & Fitch." *Daily News Record,* 18 February 1998.

Moin, David. "A&F Finds New Life by Aiming Its Weapons at a Younger Shopper." *WWD,* 2 February 1997.

Sandler, Linda, and Leslie Scism. "Limited's Planned Sale of Abercrombie Isn't Giving the Stock the Lift Many Expected." *Wall Street Journal,* 13 April 1998.

Sheban, Jeffrey. "A&F to Keep Its Sights Mainly on Men's Wear." *Daily News Record,* 21 May 1997.

———. "Abercrombie: Women's to Get New Products, No More Space." *WWD,* 21 May 1997.

Williams, Stan. "Catalog & Cool." *Daily News Record,* 13 March 1998.

For an annual report:
telephone: (614)577-6500

For additional industry research:
Investigate companies by their Standard Industrial Classification Codes, also known as SICs. Abercrombie & Fitch's primary SIC is:

5699 Miscellaneous Apparel and Accessory Stores

Acclaim Entertainment, Inc.

OVERVIEW

Acclaim Entertainment is an independent publisher, developer, and seller of high-excitement, interactive entertainment software. It makes sports-simulation and fantasy/role-playing games for use with Nintendo, SEGA, and Sony game systems, including *Space Jam* and *NFL Quarterback Club '98,* as well as personal computer (PC) games. In fiscal 1997, it released 26 new 32-bit games, 14 multimedia PC games, and 1 64-bit game. Teenage boys comprise most of the company's customers, and Acclaim designs its marketing campaigns according to each product's target audience. The company's Acclaim Comics unit is a publisher of comic books, which markets a superhero series (of characters it either creates itself or licensees from other content providers) under the VALIANT imprint name. Some major retail carriers of Acclaim's products are Best Buy, Toys 'R' Us, and Walmart. Sales are seasonal, with the heaviest period being in December. In 1997 about half of the company's sales were outside the United States.

FOUNDED: 1987

Contact Information:
HEADQUARTERS: 1 Acclaim Plz.
   Glen Cove, NY 11542
PHONE: (516)656-5000
FAX: (516)656-2040
TOLL FREE: (800)759-7800
URL: http://www.acclaimnation.com
   http://www.acclaim.net
   http://www.forsaken.com

COMPANY FINANCES

Acclaim has had financial difficulties in the 1990s—net revenues fell from $566.7 million in fiscal 1995 to $161.9 million in fiscal 1996, but 1997 was a year of encouraging improvement. For the fiscal year ending August 31, 1997, net revenues were $165.4 million and gross profit was $75.6 million. 1998 also represented a remarkable turnaround, as the company posted a first-quarter net profit of $8.0 million, as compared to a loss of $19.2 million a year prior. The change is attributable,

FINANCES:

Acclaim Entertainment Net Revenues, 1994-1997 (million dollars)

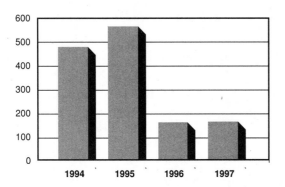

Acclaim Entertainment 1997 Stock Prices (dollars)

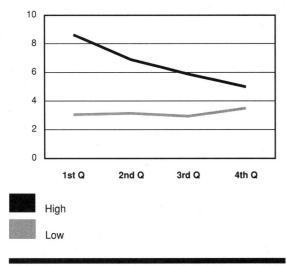

■ High

■ Low

Quoted in an Acclaim press release, Stephen Fleming of BancAmerica Robertson Stevens praised the company's progress: "Acclaim's strategy of making fewer, better games appears to be yielding tangible results, and we were surprised by the strength of Acclaim's E3 lineup." "E3" refers to a high-profile industry trade show called The Electronic Entertainment Expo, which convened in Atlanta in May 1998. Special guest appearances by Acclaim endorsers such as NFL MVP quarterback Brett Favre, NBA rookie star Keith Van Horn, and motocross winner Jeremy McGrath helped to draw record crowds to the company's product display booth.

HISTORY

Co-Chairmen Gregory Fischbach and James Scoroposki founded Acclaim Entertainment in 1987, largely to market home video games for the Nintendo Entertainment System, for which the company was the first independent American publisher of software. The company went public in 1988 and, in 1994, acquired Voyager Communications and renamed it Acclaim Comics. In the same year, the company provided special effects for the movie *Batman Forever*.

STRATEGY

Acclaim prides itself on the details within the graphics of its games. Paul Eibeler, the company's vice president and general manager, explains, "Acclaim Sports has become a premier sports brand because we go the extra mile—sweat the details—with every product we create. Whether it's accurately re-creating an NBA player's face in *NBA Jam* or matching the brownish color and unique design of the dirt of Fenway Park in our *All Star Baseball '99* game, Acclaim Sports will always create the ultimate in sports gaming realism."

The company has fostered relationships with the television network Fox, the Major League Baseball Players Association, the National Basketball Association (NBA), the National Football League (NFL), Warner Brothers, and The World Wrestling Federation (WWF), all with an eye toward continuing product development. In addition to institutional alliances, Acclaim cultivates endorsement deals with major sports figures. Motocross legend Jeremy McGrath was chosen to help design the game *Supercross '98 Featuring Jeremy McGrath* for the Sony PlayStation system, and home-run champ Larry Walker of the Colorado Rockies was chosen to endorse *All Star Baseball '99* for the Gameboy and Nintendo systems. Keith Van Horn of the New Jersey Nets endorses *NBA Jam '99*. Other promotional moves include

in part, to healthy sales of new products. "Hit" titles are always crucial to the company's overall success—during the six months ending on February 28, 1998, Acclaim's top four releases comprised 69 percent of its gross sales. In April 1998 the investment firm BT Alex Brown bestowed a "Buy" rating on Acclaim's stock, citing optimism about near-term growth, an ample balance sheet, positive cash flow, careful control of expenses, and better-than-expected second-quarter earnings. Merrill Lynch gave it a "long-term neutral" rating. Acclaim Entertainment, Inc. has never paid cash dividends on its common stock, and it foresees no plans to do so.

stepping up the company's advertising budget to $15 million for national television advertising, as well as backing the *NFL Quarterback Club '99* release with a sweepstakes in conjunction with Fleer/Skybox football cards. *Supercross '98 Featuring Jeremy McGrath* benefits dually from its advertising in motocross and video-game publications alike, in addition to receiving heavy radio advertising.

INFLUENCES

A key factor in Acclaim's product development is the current hardware available to support its software. Acclaim had made 16-bit cartridge systems—an arena it ultimately exited in April of 1996—but it suffered financially after it was slow to adapt to the newer markets for the more sophisticated 32- and 64-bit systems. In 1997 Acclaim sold the assets of its Acclaim Redemption Games (formerly known as Lazer-Tron). In the same year, it cut its PC games catalog from 60 to 40 in order to pare down those that were not performing well in the market. Acclaim's titles can remain competitive for a three-month time frame or over a year depending upon initial popularity, with the densest sales usually occurring by the fourth month. At any given time the marketed titles tend to be the company's 10 to 15 most recent issues.

Following 1995's purchase of three "software studios": Iguana Entertainment, Inc., Sculpted Software, Inc., and Probe Entertainment, Acclaim began to develop the majority of its software in-house. The balance of the releases are developed at and licensed from independent firms, as were all Acclaim titles before 1995. In order to develop animation technology, Acclaim has invested in a "motion capture studio." This state-of-the-art technology involves electronically mapping the movements of real objects, or people, for incorporation into graphic programs. The results are highly realistic when applied to video animation. An Acclaim software product's development phase falls between eight months and two years, usually at a cost of between $1 and $2 million.

CURRENT TRENDS

Acclaim began to produce children's books in 1997, bringing out its Acclaim Young Readers line of "visual storybooks" in an effort to expand its markets. In planning the 64-page products, the company signed licensing agreements to use characters from Disney, Saban Entertainment, and Fox Kids Network. The Disney-inspired books will be distributed by Penguin under two "sub brands": Disney's Enchanting Stories, which includes *101 Dalmatians* and *Beauty and the Beast,* and Disney's Action Club, which includes *Life with Louie* (featuring the

FAST FACTS:
About Acclaim Entertainment, Inc.

Ownership: Acclaim Entertainment, Inc. is a publicly owned company traded on the New York Stock Exchange.

Ticker symbol: AKLM

Officers: Gregory E. Fischbach, Co-Chmn., Pres., & CEO, 55, $775,000; James Scoroposki, Co-Chmn., Sr. Exec. VP, Secretary, & Treasurer, $500,000; Anthony Williams, Exec. VP, 39, $225,000

Employees: 680 (1997)

Chief Competitors: Acclaim competes with various other video game makers and publishers of comic books, including: Electronic Arts; Nintendo; SEGA; and Marvel Entertainment Group. Inc.

popular comedian Louie Anderson) and *The Tick.* Most of the first year's 35 works are published in paperback.

In March 1998 Acclaim announced that it would close its coin-operated video game unit Acclaim Coin-Operated Entertainment, Inc., in order to concentrate resources on its Acclaim Studios division. Acclaim had been in the arcade machine market since 1995. Said CEO Gregory Fischbach of the strategic decision, "Expanding our studios' head count without impacting our cost structure allows us to create additional development teams, which we expect will increase our output of product."

In 1998 the company announced plans to release PC and video games that are based on the Comedy Central animated series *South Park.* In a press release, Steve Lux, the company's vice president for marketing, commented, "The addictive quality of the show's characters and stories is great fodder for creating mature-rated video games."

PRODUCTS

Acclaim's games are nothing if not action-packed. *Forsaken,* a futuristic war game, has enjoyed rave reviews: *CNET Gamecenter* called it "high-flying, 3D, nausea-inducing excitement." Recent releases in the Acclaim Sports brand lineup include *WWF War Zone, NFL Quarterback Club '99,* and *NBA Jam '99.* One of the most

CHRONOLOGY:

Key Dates for Acclaim Entertainment, Inc.

1987: Gregory Fischback and James Scoropski founded Acclaim Entertainment to market home video games for the Nintendo systems

1988: Acclaim goes public

1994: Acclaim acquires Voyager Communications and renames it Acclaim Comics

1997: Begins producing children's books; lays off 115 employees from its headquarters in a $40 million cost-cutting measure

1998: Closes its coin-operated game division

brisk sellers has been the new *All Star Baseball '99* (licensed by Major League Baseball Properties and the Major League Baseball Players Association), which has startling graphics representing real U.S. baseball stadiums, as well as players' faces. It allows up to four simultaneous players on a screen and uses authentic play-by-play announcements from Yankee colormen Michael Kay and John Sterling. *NFL Quarterback Club '98* has reigned as the widest-selling Nintendo 64 format sports game, and its 1999 follow-up version, designed with input from the New York Jets' offensive coordinator Charlie Weis, improves upon many of its technical features. *Supercross '98 Featuring Jeremy McGrath* lets players choose weather and track conditions and accommodates two racers on a split screen. A "create-a-track" feature allows players to custom design their own driving environments and to store up to thirty environments for future use. The game became an immediate hit upon release.

GLOBAL PRESENCE

Acclaim Entertainment, Inc. is based on Long Island, New York, but it also has marketing and distribution operations in Great Britain, France, Germany, Japan, and Spain. The London-based Acclaim Europe unit oversees the company's European sales.

EMPLOYMENT

Recent years have seen employment cuts at Acclaim. In 1996, 65 employees were dismissed, and in 1997's $40-million cost-cutting measures, the company laid off 115 administrative, customer service, financial, and public-relations staffers at its headquarters. In 1998 the company closed its coin-operated game division, though some personnel were reassigned. Acclaim does not have a pension plan for employees.

SOURCES OF INFORMATION

Bibliography

"Acclaim Applauded at Electronic Expo." Acclaim Entertainment, Inc. Press Release, 3 June 1998.

"Acclaim Closes a Game Division." *Wall Street Journal,* 9 March 1998.

"Acclaim Closes Coin-Operated Division Shifting Development Resources to Acclaim Studios." *Business Wire,* 6 March 1998.

"Acclaim Entertainment, Inc." *Form 10-K, for the Fiscal Year Ended 31 August 1997.* U.S. Securities and Exchange Commission, 1998.

"Acclaim Entertainment, Inc." *Form 10-Q, for the Quarterly Period Ended February 28 1998.* U.S. Securities and Exchange Commission, 1998.

Acclaim Entertainment, Inc. Home Page, June 1998. Available at http://www.acclaimnation.com.

"Acclaim Entertainment, Inc." *Hoover's Online,* 25 August 1998. Available at http://www.hoovers.com.

"Acclaim Entertainment's *Forsaken* Goes Gold; Only 10 Days Till the Beginning of the End." Acclaim Entertainment, Inc. Press Release, 20 April 1998.

"Acclaim Lays Off 115." *Television Digest,* 26 May 1997.

"Acclaim Sports Announces Its Second Half 1998 Release Schedule." Acclaim Entertainment, Inc. Press Release, 2 June 1998.

"Acclaim Sports Starts the Summer with Back to Back Home Runs." *Entertainment Wire,* 12 June 1998.

First Call Research Network. *Morning Meeting Notes,* 7 April 1998.

———. *Morning Meeting Notes,* 8 April 1998.

"From South Park to Ball Park, the Hottest Games at the Electronic Entertainment Expo Are at Acclaim!" Acclaim Entertainment, Inc. Press Release, 21 May 1998.

"Larry Walker Steps up to the Plate for Acclaim Sports' All Star Baseball '99." Acclaim Entertainment, Inc. Press Release, 28 April 1998.

"Marv Albert Will Remain." *Television Digest,* 29 September 1997.

Marvel Entertainment Group, Inc. Home Page, June 1998. Available at http://www.marvel.com.

Milliot, Jim. "Acclaim Books Launches Young Readers Line." *Publishers Weekly,* 14 April 1997.

Motion Capture Research Home Page, June 1998. Available at http://www.visgraf.impa.br/Projects/mcapture/mcapture.html.

"NFL Quarterback Club '98 Breaks the 900,000 Unite Mark." Acclaim Entertainment, Inc. Press Release, 22 May 1998.

"NFL Quarterback Club '99 Ready for August Kickoff." Acclaim Entertainment, Inc. Press Release, 28 May 1998.

"PC Software Selection Changing." *Television Digest,* 7 July 1997.

"Supercross '98 Featuring Jeremy McGrath Revs Up for PlayStation Release in May." Acclaim Entertainment, Inc. Press Release, 14 April 1998.

For an annual report:

telephone: (800)759-7800

For additional industry research:

Investigate companies by their Standard Industrial Classification Codes, also known as SICs. Acclaim Entertainment Inc.'s primary SICs are:

2731 Book Publishing

3944 Games, Toys, & Children's Vehicles

7372 Prepackaged Software

Ace Hardware Corporation

FOUNDED: 1924

Contact Information:

HEADQUARTERS: 2200 Kensington Ct.
  Oak Brook, IL 60521
PHONE: (630)990-6600
FAX: (630)573-4894
URL: http://www.acehardware.com

OVERVIEW

Ace Hardware Corporation is a dealer-owned cooperative that serves more than 5,000 retail outlets across the United States and more than 400 stores in 62 other countries around the world. The company serves as a middleman between its dealers and the manufacturers of hardware supplies. Ace buys merchandise in vast quantities and distributes it through a network of regional warehouses. It also manufactures its own line of paint products. The company is owned completely by its dealers, which receive dividends from Ace's profits.

Ace and other chains of small- to medium-sized hardware stores faced a new competitive challenge in the closing years of the twentieth century with the rise of warehouse-type stores. Ace strategists mapped out a plan to resist the inroads of these retail giants by promoting unparalleled customer service at its own stores. This was an area in which the company felt it had a reasonable chance to outdo its warehouse-sized competitors.

Ace was founded in the 1920s when four Chicago-area businessmen, all of whom had operated their own hardware businesses individually, decided that there was strength in numbers and so banded together to boost their buying power. The concept was a smashing success. Not even the Great Depression could stop the expansion of the hardware chain. In 1973 the last surviving Ace founder sold off the company to its retailers, creating a dealer-owned cooperative.

The company takes great pride in being a good citizen of the communities in which it operates. Through its sponsorship of the Children's Miracle Network and its own Ace Hardware Foundation, Ace endeavors to give something back to these communities and their residents.

COMPANY FINANCES

Ace Hardware posted net earnings of $76 million on revenue of $2.90 billion in 1997, compared with net income of $72 million on revenue of $2.74 billion in 1996. The company posted net earnings of $64 million on revenue of $2.44 billion in 1995, compared with net income of $65 million on revenue of $2.33 billion in 1994. In 1997 sales of paint, cleaning supplies, and related supplies accounted for 21 percent of revenue, while sales of plumbing and heating supplies made up 15 percent of revenue. These were followed by sales of hand and power tools with 14 percent of revenue; farm and garden equipment, 13 percent; electrical supplies, 12 percent; general hardware supplies, 12 percent; sundries, 7 percent; and housewares and appliances, 6 percent.

ANALYSTS' OPINIONS

Industry analysts have sounded a note of caution regarding the growing competition facing Ace and other chains of small- to medium-sized hardware stores from warehouse-type outlets like Home Depot. They feel that the spread of the giants, including the steady expansion of Sears Hardware stores, poses a threat to Ace and its similarly positioned rival, TruServ. Sears Hardware, with 165 stores in 20 states, is seen as the more potent threat because of the moderate size of its stores, which average about 20,000 square feet.

On the plus side, the stores that are linked together in Ace's cooperative are able to keep their prices low through the pooling of their buying power and advertising dollars. "It's not a chain, but it gives a local store the image of being a chain," Ellen Hackney, communications director for the National Retail Hardware Association, told the *Atlanta Journal and Constitution.*

HISTORY

In the early 1920s four men from Chicago—Richard Hesse, E. Gunnard Lundquist, Frank Burke, and Oscar Fisher—all of whom had operated their own hardware businesses, banded together to increase their buying power, increase collective profits, and share common costs. Ace Stores Inc. was born, so named to honor the valor displayed by World War I's victorious "ace" pilots.

Unlike most retail operations, hardware stores managed to thrive during the Great Depression of the 1930s. By 1933 Ace had built a network of 38 retailers and staged its first dealer convention in Chicago so that dealers could evaluate new merchandise and decide whether or not to buy it.

The U.S. economy was sluggish in the early 1940s and rationing was mandated as part of the war effort dur-

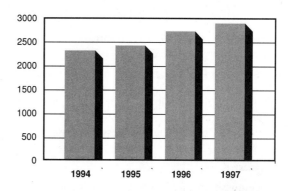

FINANCES:

Ace Hardware Net Sales, 1994-1997 (million dollars)

ing World War II. Ace was forced to become creative in order to survive these difficult years. One of its marketing ploys involved the sale of baby chicks in connection with the country's "Food for Freedom" campaign. Despite the economic obstacles, Ace continued to grow. By the end of the decade the company had amassed more than 130 dealers in 7 states.

The post-war economic boom of the 1950s brought rapid growth to most in America's retail sector, including the hardware business. Ace's sales shot through the roof. By January 1951 the company's sales had reached $9 million. The 1960s were a decade marked by revolutionary change, not the least of which was the arrival of the Computer Age. In 1961 Ace purchased its first mainframe computer. In 1963 the company began expanding into the South and the West Coast.

Ace experienced rapid growth in the 1970s. In 1973 Richard Hesse, the last surviving founder, sold the company to Ace retailers, thus creating a dealer-owned cooperative. In the waning days of the decade, Ace's sales reached nearly $600 million and the cooperative had retailers in nearly every state in the country. The economic recession of the late 1970s and early 1980s did not restrain Ace's continued expansion. By the end of 1980 more than 4,000 Ace stores were operating in all 50 states. In order to better supply its vast network of retailers, Ace doubled the number of its regional retail support centers from 7 to 14. The company also began producing its own line of paint at a state-of-the-art production facility in Matteson, Illinois.

A whole new breed of competition emerged in the 1990s with the rise of warehouse-style chains like Home Depot. Ace, however, resolved to fight back aggres-

FAST FACTS:

About Ace Hardware Corporation

Ownership: Ace Hardware, a cooperative owned by its dealers, is privately held.

Officers: Richard E. Laskowski, Chmn., 54; David F. Hodnik, Pres. & CEO, 48, base salary $450,000; William Loftus, Sr. VP, Retail Operations, 57, base salary $315,000; Paul Ingevaldson, VP, Corporate Strategy & International Business, 50, base salary $280,000

Employees: 4,700

Chief Competitors: Ace Hardware's major competitors include: 84 Lumber; Benjamin Moore; Eagle Hardware & Garden; Hechinger; Home Depot; HomeBase; Kmart; Lowe's; Payless Cashways; Sears; Sherwin-Williams; TruServ; Wal-Mart; and Wickes.

sively, launching its "New Age of Ace" strategy to provide its customers with the best service and hardware products available anywhere. Then, in 1997, Ace's chief rival, True Value, merged with ServiStar to create TruServ, a chain of more than 10,000 hardware stores across the country.

STRATEGY

In response to the arrival of home improvement mega-stores in communities across the country, Ace and its dealers are concentrating on giving their customers a level of service that can't be duplicated by these giant competitors. That there is strength in numbers is apparent from the comments of Ace Hardware dealers, who admit they'd rather not have to compete with giants like Home Depot, but feel confident that, with the backing of Ace corporate headquarters, they can weather the storm.

Connie Hansen, who has run an Ace Hardware outlet in Plano, Texas, for 20 years, told the *Dallas Morning News* that she was not particularly cowed by the opening of a Lowe's warehouse-type store in Plano. Two Home Depot stores are also within a five-mile radius of her store. Ms. Hansen contends the area is large enough to support all the stores. She expressed some concern, however, that the competition might lead to price wars.

Khandoo Nagar, operator of a Dallas Ace Hardware outlet, recalled the threat he faced when Home Depot moved into his neighborhood. "When Home Depot opened, our profits were hurt but not our sales," he said. "We consulted with Ace [corporate headquarters] and worked very hard to increase sales. We expanded and we changed our prices. Customers were mesmerized with the new Home Depot at first, but they soon realized that they can get many of the same prices here and be in and out in five minutes instead of spending more than an hour in Home Depot."

INFLUENCES

One of the factors that is helping Ace shape its strategy for the new millennium and weather the storm of competition is the growing American demand for higher levels of customer service. This gives Ace a leg up on its larger competitors, whose very size makes it difficult to supply that level of service. As the company points out in its literature, Ace truly is the place "with the helpful hardware man." In an open letter to customers on the company's web site, chairman Richard E. Laskowski and CEO David F. Hodnik express pride " . . . in the helpful quality service the folks in the red vests provide to our customers day after day, year after year." Most notably, the company offers its customers a "No Hassle Return Policy" and a "Satisfaction Guarantee".

CURRENT TRENDS

In a world that has become increasingly wired, the hardware industry is no exception. To do business in the most efficient manner possible, companies have had to create high-speed electronic links between themselves and their suppliers. In the spring of 1998 Ace announced it had formed a strategic alliance with EC Company, a leader in the development and sale of electronic commerce software and services, which will allow Ace to offer electronic data interchange (EDI) capabilities to its small- and medium-sized suppliers.

EC Exchange, the trademarked EC terminal system, offers " . . . a quick and easy way for our suppliers to start trading electronically," according to Lynda Moriarty, Ace's quick response manager. "Most importantly, our partners can be up and trading electronically with Ace Hardware in days, not months."

PRODUCTS

Among the products carried in Ace Hardware retail outlets, the biggest sellers are paint and cleaning supplies. The company manufactures its own line of paint.

Other products carried by Ace dealers include plumbing and heating supplies; hand and power tools; lawn, garden, and farm supplies; electrical equipment; general hardware such as screws, nails, nuts, and bolts; and housewares and appliances.

CORPORATE CITIZENSHIP

Ace's dealers are actively involved in the communities in which they operate. The company promotes awareness of the importance of assisting customers in the community as well as in the store. Ace is a national sponsor of the Children's Miracle Network, which helps children's hospitals in every corner of the United States. To promote greater sensitivity to environmental concerns, Ace has developed a corporate Conservation Initiative.

Another way in which the company helps communities is through the Ace Hardware Foundation, which was founded in 1991. The Foundation encourages donations from both Ace Hardware Corporation and its individual stores for disaster relief and the Children's Miracle Network. By 1997 the Foundation's contributions to victims of natural disasters totaled more than $113,000.

GLOBAL PRESENCE

In addition to its vast network of hardware stores across the United States, Ace Hardware supplies more than 400 retail units in 62 other countries. Says CEO David F. Hodnik of the company's international presence, "Based on the success many of our international operators are achieving, we're convinced the Ace retail concept is transportable to most countries, especially where there is an emerging middle class seeking to improve their homes and lifestyle. We see Asia and eastern Europe as having considerable long-term growth potential in that regard."

The company's first Asian store, a 15,000-square-foot outlet outside Indonesia's capital of Jakarta, was opened in 1995. Since then, Kunkuro Wibowo, an Indonesian hardware distributor, has opened three additional stores and hopes to eventually open 50 to 100 more by sub-franchising the Ace concept.

EMPLOYMENT

Ace Hardware offers entry-level positions in a number of departments ranging from MIS to Distributing to Merchandising. The company promotes itself as a company where the recent college graduate "can use your

CHRONOLOGY:
Key Dates for Ace Hardware Corporation

1924: Four Chicago-area businessmen join together to increase buying power and share costs, calling themselves Ace Stores, Inc.

1933: Stages its first dealer convention to view and purchase merchandise

1941: In conjunction with the "Food for Freedom" campaign, Ace sells baby chicks out of its stores

1950: Ace has grown to 130 dealers in seven states

1961: The company purchases its first mainframe computer

1963: Ace begins expanding into the South and the West Coast

1973: The last surviving founder sells the company to retailers, creating a dealer-owned cooperative

1990: Ace has grown to 4,000 dealers in all 50 states

1997: True Value, Ace's chief competitor, merges with Servistar to create a chain of more than 10,000 hardware stores

newly learned skills, while broadening your experiences and positioning yourself for future growth. It's also important to find an organization where you feel like you fit in, that you're part of a team, and that your contributions are valued. At Ace Hardware, you'll find all that and much more."

The company's 4,700 employees are spread among its Oak Brook, Illinois, corporate headquarters, its 17 regional distribution facilities across the United States and Canada, 3 divisional offices, and 2 paint production facilities in suburban Chicago. Ace employees provide services and products to the company's 5,000-plus hardware stores, each of which is independently owned and operated.

SOURCES OF INFORMATION

Bibliography

"Ace Hardware Corporation." *Hoover's Online,* 12 June 1998. Available at http://www.hoovers.com.

"Ace Hardware Delivers EC Exchange Innovative EDI Technology to Supplier Community." *Business Wire,* 29 March 1998.

Ace Hardware Home Page, 12 June 1998. Available at http://www.acehardware.com/ahci0601/ahci100u.htm.

Halkias, Maria. "Nailing Down a Niche: Small Hardware Retailers Brace for Onslaught of Superstores." *Dallas Morning News,* 4 February 1997.

Simmons, Kelly. "Battling Tooth and Nail: Faced With 'Big Box' Competitors Like Home Depot, Hardware Stores Emphasize Personalized Service and Join Buying Cooperatives." *Atlanta Journal and Constitution,* 2 February 1998.

For additional industry research:

Investigate companies by their Standard Industrial Classification Codes, also known as SICs. Ace Hardware's primary SICs are:

2851 Paint and Allied Products

3423 Hand and Edge Tools, NEC

3425 Saw Blades and Handsaws

3429 Hardware, NEC

3452 Bolts, Nuts, Rivets, and Washers

5251 Hardware Stores

adidas-Salomon AG

OVERVIEW

FOUNDED: 1948

adidas' main markets are in athletic footwear and apparel, but the company is developing plans to assimilate its newly acquired sports equipment lines. It is the world leader in soccer accessories and has a strong base in tennis shoes as well. A focus on sports, rather than on fashion, has kept adidas from being subject to shifts in popular styles and tastes. CEO Wynne credits adidas's longevity, rather than trends, for the company's success. Teens make up a substantial portion of the company's customers, and women purchase a significant portion of the men's apparel. One of adidas's goals is to make its products for children "multi-functional" so that they can be used in a variety of sports.

Contact Information:
HEADQUARTERS: 9605 SW Nimbus Ave.
   Beaverton, OR 97008
PHONE: (503)972-2300
FAX: (503)797-4935
TOLL FREE: (800)677-6638
URL: http://www.adidas.com

COMPANY FINANCES

Recent years have seen a dramatic turnaround for adidas's financial picture. By the early 1990s adidas's market share had been eclipsed by fierce competition, and the company was losing about $100 million per year. Partly as a result of new, energetic management, adidas has redeemed itself financially and stands ready to overtake Reebok, which has been experiencing difficulties in recent years. adidas has been reclaiming the market share it had lost to such competitors as L.A. Gear and Fila. A substantial increase in sales of apparel has contributed to the company's good fortune. adidas America exceeded $1 billion in North American sales in 1997, of which about 95 percent came from the United States.

FAST FACTS:

About adidas-Salomon AG

Ownership: Following a 1995 initial public offering, shares of the parent company are traded on the Paris and Frankfurt stock exchanges. Plans for a listing on a major U.S. exchange have been postponed.

Ticker symbol: ADDDY

Officers: Peter Moore, Worldwide Creative Director; Steve Wynne, Pres. & CEO

Employees: 400

Principal Subsidiary Companies: adidas America is a subsidiary of the German-based adidas-Salomon AG—now the world's number-two sporting goods manufacturer. It handles the company's marketing, distribution, merchandising, and sales in North America.

Chief Competitors: Primary competitors include: Nike; Reebok; and Fila.

ANALYSTS' OPINIONS

The parent company's 1995 initial public offering raised almost $2 billion. The share price has risen steadily ever since, from an opening price of $42.50. In 1997 its increase was 77 percent. For market capitalization and trading volume, adidas rates among the 30 largest publicly traded companies in Germany. The share price now reflects the merger with Salomon.

HISTORY

adidas-Salomon AG traces its beginnings to the workshop of a German cobbler named Adolph ("Adi") Dassler (hence the company's name, a blend of his first and last names). Dassler's rise to become a global business player came from humble origins. He began with an entrepreneurial spirit in a depressed economy, cutting his teeth on the business of crafting homemade slippers made from surplus World War I military bags. In 1920 he branched out to make training shoes, and eventually he diversified his work to include footwear for tennis, running, and soccer. In order to maximize safety and dura-

bility, Dassler's designs derived from his own experience as an athlete and also from the advice of contemporary sports professionals. adidas continues to engineer its products in consultation with the very athletes who will be wearing them. To the present day, adidas regards itself as centrally a footwear company.

Persistence and a scientific approach helped Dassler promote his products as offering an unprecedented level of excellence. In his constant research to improve his wares, Dassler eventually began to work with national-team soccer players and Olympic contenders. In fact, the American Jesse Owens boxed in Dassler-made shoes in the 1936 Olympic Games in Berlin and ultimately defeated Dassler's own countryman, Max Schmelling. Says adidas America's director of sports marketing, Robert Erb, of the innovative founder and namesake in *Brandweek,* "He wasn't a business guru or a marketing genius. He was a guy, a craftsman, who was in love with sports and made decent product." Dassler's first decades in the sporting world involved such products as soccer balls, tennis shoes, handball boots, and running spikes.

In 1948 Dassler formed adidas, while his brother started the rival company Puma. In the same year, Dassler's enterprise introduced the world's first indoor track shoe. The following year saw the inception of the company's familiar three-stripe logo, which grew out of a functional role in adding additional support to the sides of shoes. (The ubiquitous "trefoil" trademark did not appear until 1972.) Come the 1952 Olympic Games in Helsinki, adidas shoes appeared on more competitors' feet than any other German brand, and by 1958 a majority of World Cup soccer players sported them as well. Constant product development yielded new ergonomic features, such as padding to protect the Achilles tendon, and the eventual Torsion™ system, which promotes flexibility with natural movement. In addition to footwear, adidas began to produce sports apparel and accessories, and can be credited with designing both the first track suit and the sports bag. Clothing continues to be a substantial source of the company's revenues. Dassler was named to the American Sporting Goods Hall of Fame in 1978, the year of his death.

adidas America is the result of a 1993 merger of adidas USA with a U.S. sports-marketing firm called Sports, Inc., which had been founded by two former executives from Nike. In an effort to strengthen the ties between operations in the United States and Europe, adidas AG, the parent company, acquired Sports, Inc. after a collaboration on the development of the adidas Equipment product line. The project involved athlete input and focused on the functional aspects of use. The result breathed new life into the adidas name and jump-started a return to the company's past prosperity. One of the founders of Sports, Inc. was Peter Moore, who subsequently became adidas America's Worldwide Creative Director.

STRATEGY

Today, adidas truly is a sporting-goods company in a broad sense. In 1997 the company acquired the French sporting-equipment concern Salomon (and accordingly, a name change for the parent company), thus creating the world's second-largest company of its kind. Prior to 1997 adidas had enjoyed relatively little of the high-tech equipment market, but since then it has entered three new businesses: golf clubs, winter sports equipment, and bicycle parts. The two firms had had almost no overlap in their product scopes, enabling them to spread their total risk over more fields of production. An expanded capital base will allow for expanded research and development. The new, larger adidas-Salomon AG expects a seasonal balance among overall sales as well as an increase in market penetration. It has its sights on doubling its 1997 U.S. market share to 12 percent by the year 2000.

In order to realize its stated mission of being "the best sports brand in the world," adidas is focusing heavily on visibility and brand-name recognition. By capitalizing on its stated brand strategy, "to be associated with any activity that is physical and competitive," the company aims to be identified with champions in a range of athletics. Current tactics include the forging of endorsement alliances at both the individual and team levels in order to promote an image of authenticity. adidas wants to be allied with teams and athletes who are respected for their superiority, rather than merely for their style or flair. For example, in 1997 adidas entered a $90-million sponsorship agreement with the New York Yankees. CEO Wynne explained in *Sporting Goods Business,* "In the case of the Yankees, we looked at a team that had some of the same characteristics that we do as a brand." The company is confident in the potential of these partnerships to increase exposure, and does not rely on advertising saturation. adidas has made similar deals with the Women's National Basketball Association and with various colleges such as Northwestern University, whose 380 male and female athletes it outfits with uniforms and practice apparel. It is also a sponsor and licensee of World Cup France '98.

INFLUENCES

adidas has several internal factors working in its favor. It has enjoyed improvements in efficiency thanks to its distribution center in Spartanburg, South Carolina. The company uses its own Portland, Oregon, store to try out merchandising initiatives and to study the results. Company representatives monitor feedback from the public. adidas has asked retailers to compile consumer profiles of their female shoppers for market research. The retailers comply by using sales records, exit polls, and questionnaires.

CHRONOLOGY:
Key Dates for adidas-Salomon AG

1948: Founded by Adolph (Adi) Dassler

1953: Introduces first track shoe with interchangeable spikes

1954: German National team wins Soccer's World Cup in adidas shoes

1963: Adidas begins producing balls

1967: Produces their first track suit

1972: Trefoil trademark is introduced

1978: Adi Dassler dies at age 78 and is inducted into the Sporting Goods Industry Hall of Fame

1984: Adi's wife Kathe dies and his son Horst takes over the company

1993: Merges with Sports, Inc.

1997: Acquires the French company Salomon and changes the corporate name to adidas-Salomon AG

CURRENT TRENDS

From the start, adidas has always involved in-depth research in the design of new footwear. The company continues its methods with cutting-edge technology. Most research takes place at the company's Global Technology Center in Scheinfeld, Germany, which it calls "the ultimate sports manufacturing think tank." A new "Feet You Wear"™ technology was developed at the company's design center in Portland. This shoe concept provides the foot with better support by carefully following its natural shape, thus mimicking the freedom and flexibility of being barefoot. The company is optimistic about applying the concept to the soccer market, which it has long dominated. adidas also has created a high-density foam it calls adiprene™, which absorbs shock at the foot's points of impact, to preserve both the shoe and the foot in it. A "Point of Deflection System"™ uses hollow chambers in the sole to cushion impact. Each of these technologies is calculated to improve athletic performance, and thus, adidas hopes, contribute to the company's business growth.

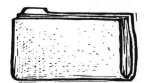

FORM FOLLOWS FUNCTION

The "three f's" have always been Adidas' motto when it came to creating a product. The following is an outline of how an athletic shoe is born:

- Athletes' needs are evaluated by the marketing department, where a basic concept shoe is developed to fulfill those needs

- Marketing presents their concept to the design department, which, in turn draws sketches of possible prototypes

- Marketing and design consider the sketches together, eventually narrowing the selection down to the one they predict will be most successful in meeting the athlete's needs

- Design involves product development. Together they work on creating a prototype product

- Design and marketing meet once again to make final changes to the prototype

- The product is wear-tested to make sure it will stand up to the demands of the sport for which it was designed

- Consumer focus groups and key accounts receive preview samples

- Preview samples are distributed to sales representatives to present to retailers

- The final product is delivered to the retailers that have purchased it

PRODUCTS

adidas's primary products include shoes and apparel for soccer, running, tennis, basketball, and with the recent merger with Salomon, golf, cycling, and winter-sports equipment. adidas makes shoes for a wide range of sports, but the core of its production lies in the tennis, running, and basketball shoes featuring the Feet You Wear™ technology, designed to work with the foot's natural movement. In 1994 adidas resumed its presence in the women's apparel market, which had been a lagging area for the company in the 1980s. In 1998 adidas will roll out its first performance basketball footwear for women, and it has plans for additional women's softball, volleyball, and soccer products. The breakdown of product types in the United States is approximately 55 percent footwear and 45 percent apparel, but internationally the two are just about equal.

CORPORATE CITIZENSHIP

adidas's corporate mission statement professes a commitment to "social and environmental responsibility for the world in which we live, for the rights of all individuals and for the laws and customs of the countries in which we operate." The company sponsors an annual basketball camp, which allows promising high-school players to demonstrate their skills to college coaches. But the company is careful not to exude a political agenda. "We believe in celebrating sports. We don't try to relay social issues or lifestyle issues," explained Wynne in *WWD*. "We have our roots [in sports], and we plan to stay there. We know what we are, consumers know what we are, and we don't try to be anything else."

GLOBAL PRESENCE

adidas-Salomon, the parent company, has a major global presence. Its world market share for sporting goods has risen to 6 percent, as 1997s net sales (aside from Salomon) were up a whopping 42 percent. European sales grew by about 31 percent to contribute most heavily to the year's success. The Pacific Rim also represents several strong markets for adidas products, despite the recent currency crisis. International sports alliances include an agreement to provide footwear and practicewear to the eight teams of the Canadian Football League (CFL), and similar support for the NFL's Europe League. Other international involvement, though on American soil, will include sponsorship of the 1999 Women's World Cup Soccer tournament and the 1999 Women's Global Challenge sports invitational.

EMPLOYMENT

adidas America had approximately 400 employees in 1998, up from 120 in recent years. At the end of 1997, adidas-Salomon AG employed approximately 8,000. The work atmosphere at the Oregon headquarters is described as open, cooperative, and a departure from the more traditional corporate setting. The management style encourages communication among people of all levels.

SOURCES OF INFORMATION

Bibliography
"adidas." *Hoover's Online,* April 1998. Available at http://www. hoover's.com.

"adidas America, an Overview." *adidas America.* Beaverton, OR: n.d.

adidas Annual Report 1997. Herzogenaurach, Germany: adidas AG, 1997.

"Adidas Details International Plans with the NFL; First Sponsor to Support NFL/CFL Alliance." *BW SportsWire,* 16 April 1998.

adidas Home Page. April 1998. Available at http://www.adidas.com.

"adidas 1997." *Business Wire,* 6 March 1998.

"Adidas Turns Purple." *WWD,* 8 May 1997.

Bhonslay, Marianne. "Stars & Stripes." *Sporting Goods Business,* 23 January 1998.

Brand Mission/Vision. Herzogenaurach, Germany: adidas AG, n.d.

Feitelberg, Rosemary. "Adidas Trains for the Long Run." *WWD,* 22 January 1998.

Lefton, Terry. "Robert Erb: Director of Sports Marketing, Adidas America (The Next Generation)." *Brandweek,* 3 November 1997.

Levine, Joshua. "Adidas Flies Again." *Forbes,* 25 March 1996.

Lowry, Tom, "Sports Shoemaker Goes for Rebound." *USA Today,* 21 October 1996.

Lustigman, Alyssa. "Interview with Adidas America CEO Rob Strasser (The SGB Interview)." *Sporting Goods Business,* September 1993.

Million Dollar Directory, Series 1998. Bethlehem, PA: Dun & Bradstreet, 1998.

Pesky, Greg. "Earning Its Stripes." *Sporting Goods Business,* September 1995.

Tedeschi, Mark. "The SGB Interview." *Sporting Goods Business,* 2 June 1997.

Wallace, Charles P. "Adidas: Back in the Game, the Venerable German Shoemaker Has Pulled Its Financial Socks Up. Now It's Scoring Some Points in the U.S. Market." *Fortune,* 18 August 1997.

For an annual report:

telephone: (800)677-6638

For additional industry research:

Investigate companies by their Standard Industrial Classification Codes, also known as SICs. adidas' primary SICs are:

3021 Rubber and Plastics Footwear

3949 Sporting and Athletic Goods, NEC

5136 Men's/Boy's Clothing

5137 Women/Children's Clothing

5139 Footwear

Adobe Systems Inc.

FOUNDED: 1982

Contact Information:
HEADQUARTERS: 1585 Charleston Rd.
   Mountain View, CA 94039
PHONE: (415)961-4400
FAX: (415)961-4480
URL: http://www.adobe.com

OVERVIEW

Adobe Systems Inc. has a franchise position in graphics, printing and publishing technology, and applications. The company built its franchise on the PostScript printing language and utilizes that success to dominate market shares for illustration, image editing, and document publishing applications. In 1994 Adobe purchased Aldus Corporation, acquiring PageMaker, a page layout and document publishing tool, for approximately $440 million. In addition, they purchased rival Frame Technology Corporation in 1995 for $460 million and obtained ownership of FrameMaker, a high-end publishing application. Succeeded by Microsoft and Novell, Adobe continues to market a wide variety of computer software.

Adobe's selected products include: Acrobat (electronic document management software), Adobe Acrobat (document formatting software), Adobe ArtExplorer (painting and drawing software for children), Adobe Fetch (cataloging software), Adobe Gallery Effects (special-effects software), Adobe Illustrator (graphics software), Adobe PageMill (Web-page creation software), Adobe Persuasion (presentation software), Adobe PhotoDeluxe (personalized photo software), Adobe Photoshop (photographic image software), Adobe Premiere (film and video editing software), Adobe SiteMill (Internet link repair software), FrameMaker (document authoring software), PageMaker (page layout software), and PostScript (page description language interpreter). Adobe maintains a 40-percent market share in desktop publishing, which translates into about a 1.7 million user base.

COMPANY FINANCES

Adobe Systems Inc. reported first quarter earnings for 1998 (the 90-day period ending February 27, 1998) of $197.8 million, compared to $226.5 million in the first quarter of 1997. Of those revenues, applications product revenues accounted for $156 million, down from $175 million in the first quarter of 1997. Revenues derived from Windows applications did show an increase, up 18 percent from 1997, while Macintosh revenues declined 36 percent. Windows' share of total application revenues increased from 44 percent in first quarter 1997 to 59 percent in first quarter 1998. Licensing accounted for the remaining $41 million in first quarter revenues (compared to $51 million from licensing in first quarter 1997).

Net income for the first quarter of 1998 was $26.7 million, or $.38 per share, compared to $46.4 million in 1997. Adobe attributes the decrease in first quarter revenues for 1998 to 1997's exceptionally strong opening—Adobe Photoshop 4.0 and PageMaker 6.5 were both released in the first quarter of 1997. In comparison, no new releases or product upgrades took place in the first quarter of 1998.

Annual sales in 1997 reached $912 million, revenue growth of 16 percent over 1996 revenues of $786.6 million. Of the $912 million earned in 1997, revenue from applications products was a record $716 million, compared to $590 million in 1996. Revenues earned from licensing remained at the same level of $196 million each year. 1997 was also the first year that revenues from the Windows platform exceeded that of Macintosh—Windows products accounted for 51 percent of applications products revenue, leaving Macintosh with 49 percent. Net income for 1997 reached $187 million.

Adobe's stock price over a 52-week period ranged from a high of $53.12 to a low of $33.50 per share. As of May 1998, the price per share was consistently hovering near $50.00.

ANALYSTS' OPINIONS

Adobe Systems Inc. reported earnings of $.33 per share in the first quarter of 1998, performing below projected estimates of $.44 per share. The company again cited the lack of new product releases during the quarter as cause for the company's performance, as well as a weak Asian market. Adobe hopes new product releases through the remainder of 1998 will help to raise revenues. However, the shaky up/down performance of Adobe over the past couple of years, as well as its continued association with Apple, has caused analysts to regard Adobe as a fairly high risk for investors.

The general consensus by stock market analysts at Zacks Investment Research, Inc. was to grant Adobe Systems a "hold" rating, meaning investors should hold on

FINANCES:

Adobe Systems Inc.
Revenues, 1994-1997
(million dollars)

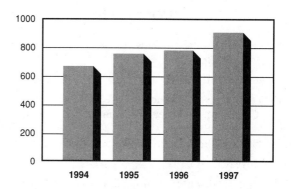

Adobe Systems Inc.
1997 Stock Prices
(dollars)

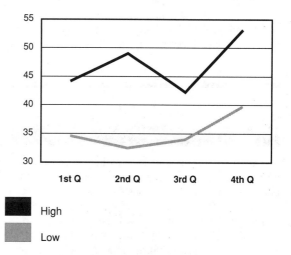

to stock they currently own. Several were willing to place a "moderate buy" rating on the company. Those recommendations were based on such items as the company's growth rate—estimated at 15.0 percent over the past five years, in comparison to a 22.2-percent growth rate in the industry overall. Analysts forecast a negative growth rate of 1.3 percent for Adobe in 1998, but expect the company to see renewed growth of 23.8 percent in 1999. However, those figures are still below projected growth for the overall industry average (29.2 percent in 1998 and 34.4 percent in 1999).

FAST FACTS:

About Adobe Systems Inc.

Ownership: Adobe Systems Inc. is a publicly owned company traded on NASDAQ.

Ticker symbol: ADBE

Officers: John E. Warnock, Co-Chmn. & CEO, 57; Charles M. Geschke, Co-Chmn. & Pres., 58; Jackson Bell, Exec. VP, CFO, & Chief Admin. Officer, 56; Ross Bott, Exec. VP Product Divisions, 46

Employees: 2,702

Principal Subsidiary Companies: Adobe's selected subsidiaries are Aldus Corp. and Ceneca Communications Inc.

Chief Competitors: As a leading software firm, Adobe's primary competitors include: Allegro New Media; America Online; Apple Computer; Autodesk; Avid Technology; Corel; Electronica for Imaging; IBM; Interleaf; Lintotype-Hell; Macromedia; Micrografx; Microsoft; Novell; Quark; and Softkey.

HISTORY

In 1978 John Warnock and Charles Geschke, former Xerox executives, teamed up and developed a revolutionary innovation of a standard computer language and scalable-font called PostScript. When Xerox refused to market the product, the two left the company and founded Adobe Systems in 1982—they began marketing PostScript in 1985. PostScript is a high-level computer language that communicates precise descriptions of computer generated graphics, photos, and text to any output device with a PostScript interpreter.

In 1986, the company went public and in 1987 branched out into the European market with its Adobe Systems Europe subsidiary. In order to market its products in the Pacific Rim, the company started another subsidiary in 1989. By acquiring other software companies, Adobe continued growing during the early 1990s. In 1993, they began licensing Adobe software to printer manufacturers. That same year, they also began marketing Acrobat software. Adobe merged with Aldus in 1994, bringing sales to a new high.

1995 saw the integration of Acrobat's viewing technology into Netscape's Internet software. With Acrobat

the company was moving to establish itself in the online publishing world. Also in 1995, Adobe acquired Frame Technology.

STRATEGY

Adobe has a comprehensive Internet/Intranet strategy that focuses on web site development tools, information distribution and printing, and graphics. With products like PageMill and SiteMill, and its Acrobat electronic document technology, Adobe is well positioned for growth in that market. By simultaneously releasing Windows and Mac versions of its software, the company is making important progress. Adobe also focuses on marketing new and upgraded products to meet new technological demands (e.g., the release of Adobe PostScript 3 to meet the needs of Internet-based printing environments).

In reference to PostScript, "People don't realize it," John Warnock explained, "but the technology that we developed in the early 80's and the desktop publishing revolution have really taken over printing and publishing. So every newspaper today, every magazine uses a piece of our technology, and uses our type library, and uses the graphic arts interface. Every cereal box on the shelf, the titling on a lot of television channels—they all use it."

Adobe began distributing its products to Europe and the Pacific Rim in 1987. A weaker European market (due primarily to weak FrameMaker and PageMaker sales) was offset by stronger sales growth in Japan, from which Adobe derives 20 percent or more of its revenue. By mid-1997 a new Japanese version of FrameMaker was released.

INFLUENCES

Adobe has seen incredible success with several of its most solid performers, such as PostScript. Another of its best performing products is PhotoDeluxe, which was recently ranked by Dataquest as the best selling consumer photo-editing software in the world. And in April of 1998, Adobe Illustrator 7.0 received the Software Publishers Association's Codie Award for Best Text or Graphics Business Program. Adobe attributes the success of these programs, and others, to its consistent attempts to address customer interests, according to group product manager Michael Hopwood.

The company has seen its share of disappointments, however. In the second half of fiscal year 1997, Hewlett-Packard discontinued using Adobe's PostScript technology in some of its laser printers. The estimated Hewlett-Packard-related PostScript revenues were about $41 million in 1996. However, Adobe established a new relationship to incorporate PostScript into IBM printers and released new technologies for the color ink jet printer and production printer markets. When Adobe purchased Frame Technology Corporation in 1995 to acquire FrameMaker, they expected to have about $100 million in sales in 1996. Adobe's hopes for a quick payoff from the Frame deal did not materialize. The company stumbled badly with the acquisition and, in the words of John Warnock, Adobe's CEO, we were "overconfident and complacent" about the deal. Revenue for the fourth quarter of 1995 and the first quarter of 1996 slumped, and earnings were hit hard. Adobe underestimated the importance of a direct sales effort for selling complex software like FrameMaker and discontinued Frame's telephone sales force in the United States. In short, Adobe was forced to absorb operating expenses without an increase in revenues.

CURRENT TRENDS

Adobe restructured and reorganized its businesses into five independent operating units, which allowed management to better focus on its printing and publishing products and also to concentrate on opportunities in the rapidly growing graphics and Internet markets. The company felt restructuring would help Adobe management meet revenue targets and keep future costs down. Also, the company rebuilt the international direct sales team and took a look at possible cost reductions.

Adobe also added key executives to its management team. Jack Bell, formerly of Connor Peripherals and American Airlines, joined Adobe as executive vice president, chief financial officer, and chief administrative officer. In 1996 Bob Roblin, formerly of IBM, joined as senior vice president of marketing. Adobe also announced that Ross Bott, formerly of Silicon Graphics, joined as senior vice president and general manager of the graphics division. One of the explicit aims that Roblin discussed involved solidifying the image of Adobe as the principle provider of graphics tools and software for the corporate and creative professional market.

PRODUCTS

In terms of product development 1997 was a good year for Adobe. The company launched Adobe PostScript 3, designed specifically for Internet-based environments. In a joint venture with IBM, the company offered the IBM InfoPrint 4000, a digital printing system that exceeded 1,000 pages per minute. In addition, Adobe's PrintGear, software architecture designed to improve low-cost printer performance, continued to perform well. Efforts in 1998 included its submission of a proposal to work with IBM, Netscape, and Sun Microsystems to create vector graphics software for Web content. This initiative was termed the Precision Graphics Markup Language (PGML), and is a two-dimensional graphics language that

CHRONOLOGY:
Key Dates for Adobe Systems Inc.

1982: Founded

1985: Begins marketing PostScript

1986: Goes public

1987: Creates Adobe Systems Europe subsidiary

1993: Begins licensing Adobe software to printer manufacturers and marketing Adobe Acrobat

1994: Merged with Aldus Corp.

1995: Acrobat viewing is integrated into Netscape's Internet software

1998: Initiates work on new PGML Web language with IBM, Sun, and Netscape

"provides precise control of layout, fonts, color and printing, which will result in Web pages with compelling text, images and graphics, as well as dynamic events and animation," according to an Adobe press release.

Late in 1996 Adobe shipped upgrades of five of its applications: Photoshop 4.0, PageMaker 6.5, Acrobat 3.0, PageMill 2.0, and Persuasian 4.0. The upgrades included a wide range of new key features and capabilities. In particular, PageMaker 6.5 was the initial professional page layout application to offer document-wide layers and automatic layout adjustment for creating print and web documents. PageMaker became the only application for designing documents with a fixed structure, such as magazines, catalogs, and newspapers. According to *The Wall Street Journal,* Adobe Systems, Apple Computer, and Netscape Communications announced that they would work to define font extensions for Hypertext Markup Language (HTML) to enable Type 1 and True-Type fonts on the Internet. In addition, IBM and Adobe demonstrated its first PostScript production printing based on Adobe's SUPRA architecture. This system offered commercial printing customers and corporate in-plant printers unlimited capabilities and business opportunities.

CORPORATE CITIZENSHIP

In 1997, at the request of the Federal Bureau of Investigation (FBI), Adobe assisted in the "national take-down" of eight bulletin board systems across the country by the FBI in an operation code-named "Cyber Strike." The bulletin board systems were involved in an organized scheme of trafficking illegal copies of software from Adobe and other vendors. The software industry has lost revenue every year to piracy. The revenue lost has a direct effect on job opportunity and research and development for a sector that is critical to our nation's economy.

Adobe is a philanthropic institution committed to supporting programs that improve the quality of life for everyone. Adobe specifically supported non-profit health and human service organizations that: service disadvantaged youth, the homeless, minorities, and victims of abuse; provide disaster relief, medical and hospice care, and meal services; and organizations that support human rights. They also support the arts, environmental organizations, educational programs, and animal rights.

GLOBAL PRESENCE

Adobe's European and international headquarters are located in the United Kingdom, Japan, and Australia. Japan is the leader in sales growth, contributing 20 percent or more of Adobe's revenue. In 1996 Adobe announced its support of the proposed final Information Technology Agreement reached at the World Trade Organization Ministerial in Singapore. The Information Technology Agreement provides for the elimination of tariffs on hardware, software, and other information technology in participating countries. This benefits all participating member countries by making information technology products more widely available at a lower cost to consumers.

EMPLOYMENT

Adobe Systems Inc. is an equal opportunity/affirmative action employer offering a wide range of employment opportunities. Positions include: legal, administration, human resources, engineering, finance, information services, marketing, operations, sales and support, software quality assurance, and technical support/customer service.

SOURCES OF INFORMATION

Bibliography

"Adobe Illustrator Honored with Software Publishers Association's Codie Award." Adobe Systems Inc. Press Release, 6 April 1998. Available at http://www.adobe.com/aboutadobe/publicrelations/HTML/9804/980406.codie.html.

"Adobe Is World Leader in Consumer Photo-Editing Software." Adobe Systems Inc. Press Release, 8 April 1998. Available at http://www.adobe.com/aboutadobe/publicrelations/HTML/9804/980408.leader.html.

"Adobe Products and Application Index," 20 February 1997. Available at http://www.adobe.com/prodindex/main.html.

"Adobe Products for Internet Publishing Overview," 23 February 1997. Available at http://www.adobe.com/internet/overview.html.

"Adobe Submits Proposal to Improve Quality of Web Graphics with IBM, Netscape, and Sun." Adobe Systems Inc. Press Release, 13 April 1998. Available at http://www.adobe.com/aboutadobe/publicrelations/HTML/9804/980413.pgml.html.

"Adobe Systems Announces Adobe PageMaker 6.5," 6 March 1997. Available at http://www.mv.us.adobe.com/aboutadobe/publicrelations/HTML/9609/960909.pm65ann.html.

"Adobe Systems Earnings Miss Their Mark." *The Online Investor,* 27 March 1998. Available at http://www.investhelp.com.

"Adobe Systems Inc." *Hoover's Online,* May 1998. Available at http://www.hoovers.com.

"Adobe Systems Inc." *Microsoft Investor,* May 1998. Available at http://investor.msn.com.

"Adobe Systems Reports First Quarter 1998 Results," 26 March 1998. Available at http://www.adobe.com/aboutadobe/invrelations/PDFS/9803/980326.adbeq1.pdf.

"Adobe Systems Reports Fourth Quarter Results," 23 February 1997. Available at http://www.adobe.com/aboutadobe/publicrelations/HTML/9701/970107.adbeq4.html.

"Adobe's Offices and Phones," 20 February 1997. Available at http://www.adobe.com/aboutadobe/phones.html.

"Employment Opportunities at Adobe Systems," May 1998. Available at http://www.adobe.com/aboutadobe/employmentopp/main.html.

Gable, Gene. "Inside Report." *Publish,* September 1995.

"Letter to Stakeholders," May 1998. Available at http://www.adobe.com/aboutadobe/invrelations/PDFS/stkletter.pdf.

"Software Maker's Net Beats Most Analysts' Forecasts." *The Wall Street Journal,* 8 January 1997.

"Three Firms Team Up to Develop New Fonts for Use on the Internet." *The Wall Street Journal,* 27 February 1996.

For an annual report:

on the Internet at: http://www.adobe.com/aboutadobe/invrelations/main.html **or** telephone: (800)536-4700

For additional industry research:

Investigate companies by their Standard Industrial Classification Codes, also known as SICs. Adobe's primary SICs are:

3651 Household Audio & Video Equipment

3861 Photographic Equipment & Supplies

7372 Prepackaged Software

7379 Computer Related Services, NEC

Allied Waste Industries, Inc.

OVERVIEW

Allied Waste Industries, Inc. is a leading domestic non-hazardous solid waste management company based in Scottsdale, Arizona. Although Allied has a national presence, the company maintains a strong local presence through its decentralized management philosophy. Its objective is to operate collection, transfer, recycling, and disposal businesses in each of its major markets. Allied is a focused company, adhering to a simple operating strategy of vertical integration. The company aims to build efficient, vertically integrated operations that unite the strengths of the collection and disposal operations it has acquired and developed over time. It also seeks to move waste from its collection routes in major population centers to Allied's cost-efficient suburban and rural landfills. By owning the waste disposal facilities that service its collections and improving operating efficiencies, Allied has been able to maximize its operating margins and thus its overall profitability. Allied currently conducts operations in 18 states, with 81 collection companies, 21 recycling facilities, 43 transfer stations, and 56 landfills.

COMPANY FINANCES

Allied is the fifth-largest solid waste management company in the United States as measured by revenues. The company's revenues have grown from approximately $9 million in 1991 to $875 million in 1997, placing Allied in the top ranks of solid waste companies in the United States. Consequently, Allied Waste Industries, Inc. ranks among the top 10 Arizona-based companies. As of 1997 Allied's revenue mix consisted of 59 percent

FOUNDED: 1987

Contact Information:

HEADQUARTERS: 15880 N. Greenway-Hayden Loop
  Scottsdale, AZ 85260
PHONE: (602)423-2946
FAX: (602)423-9424
EMAIL: info@awin.com
URL: http://www.alliedwaste.com/

FINANCES:

Allied Waste
Revenues, 1994-1997
(million dollars)

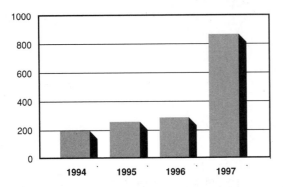

Allied Waste
1997 Stock Prices
(dollars)

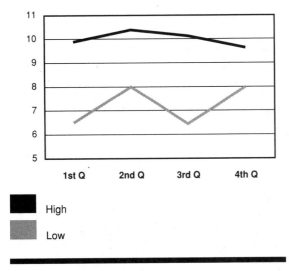

■ High

■ Low

collection, 25 percent landfill business, 7 percent transfer, 3 percent recycling, and 6 percent other.

ANALYSTS' OPINIONS

In October of 1996, *Fortune* magazine listed Allied Waste as twenty-fifth among the 100 fastest growing companies, based on $33 million added to sales with the acquisition of 3 landfills, 15 garbage-collection compa-

nies, 2 recycling facilities, and 3 transfer stations. In the late 1990s the company was receiving widespread attention from Wall Street. Many are particularly impressed by the quality of its management. According to some analysts, Allied is large enough to gain access to capital markets for more consistent, acquisition-driven growth, and the company's presence in 18 states provides geographic diversification, reducing the impact of regional economic downturns. Still, others believe a lack of access to new equity could hinder the company's growth plans and note that the company is highly leveraged. Nonetheless, Allied Waste is expected to be one of the most aggressive acquirers in the industry.

HISTORY

Allied Waste is the product of a merger between several small regional solid waste companies. Thomas H. Van Weelden, Allied's president and CEO, is a second-generation executive in the solid waste industry, having begun his career in a family owned waste company serving Chicago. In 1975 Van Weelden formed an integrated waste management company in southern Illinois. Meanwhile, Roger A. Ramsey, now chairman of Allied's Board of Directors, had co-founded the waste management company Browning-Ferris Industries, Inc. Upon leaving Browning-Ferris, Roger Ramsey formed a private investment company and some years later returned to the solid waste industry with a small company named Allied Waste. Ramsey and Van Weelden merged their companies to form the core of the current business.

STRATEGY

Vertical integration of collection and disposal assets in each market is the single most important element of the company's business strategy. It implements this strategy by acquiring waste disposal assets and by swapping assets with other companies to achieve greater integration in particular regions. Building initially on a base of landfills, Allied then adds collection and, if necessary, transfer capabilities to lower the cost of hauling over longer distances. This integration of waste operations, or waste internalization, is critical to the company's success because it provides guaranteed waste flow into the company's landfills and minimizes the dependence of its collection business on competitors' landfills.

Allied's strategy also focuses on the inevitable results of stiffer regulation and the increased population density of urban areas. As time passes and existing disposal sites in urban areas approach capacity, waste must be transported farther from urban cores to larger regional landfills. Allied's basic strategy is to identify regions where these changes are occurring or are about to occur and to acquire facilities to take advantage of them.

INFLUENCES

The non-hazardous waste collection and disposal industry is highly competitive and requires substantial capital and human resources. National waste management companies and several regional waste management companies have significantly greater resources, but Allied has the advantage of well-regarded, experienced management: 60 percent of the company's managers have more than 20 years of experience in the industry.

Allied exits markets if it believes that achieving vertical integration in accordance with its business model will not be cost-effective. Each of the company's acquisitions and divestitures are consistent with its plan to increase its waste internalization rate and focus on markets where there are good opportunities for future growth. For example, the 1996 acquisition of Laidlaw's waste management assets opened up 17 new markets, including 6 Canadian provinces. However, the Canadian operations, while solid in themselves, were not in markets that Allied could fit into its business strategy. They were sold off, and the resources were freed up to integrate more promising assets. Allied also sold its collection operations in Gaithersburg, Maryland, where 100 percent of the collected waste was disposed of at third-party landfills. The company's Chiquita Canyon landfill in Los Angeles, California, was sold because Allied does not have collection operations in the market. Meanwhile, an addition of a landfill to the company's Carolina operations completed the market entry initiated in 1996 with the acquisition of Container Corporation of Carolina. Allied prefers to own every aspect of the waste management operation in a particular area, from pickup to landfill.

CURRENT TRENDS

The U.S. solid waste market has been consolidating since the late 1970s, driven by increased regulation that fundamentally altered the economics of waste collection and hauling operations in favor of larger regional facilities. The company expects the trend toward consolidation to continue because many independent landfill operators lack the capital resources, management skills, and technical expertise needed to comply with the complex regulations.

Another factor affecting the waste disposal industry is the trend toward outsourcing government services to commercial vendors. In 1997, Allied outbid 26 competitors to purchase all the waste disposal assets of San Diego County for $184 million, the largest privatization of gov-

FAST FACTS:
About Allied Waste Industries, Inc.

Ownership: Allied Waste Industries, Inc. is a publicly owned company traded on NASDAQ.

Ticker symbol: AWIN

Officers: Roger A. Ramsey, Chmn., $1,140,000; Thomas H. Van Weelden, Pres. & CEO, 43, $1,023,000; Henry L. Hirvela, VP & CFO, 46, $530,000; Larry D. Henk, VP & COO, 38, $525,000

Employees: 5,400 (1997)

Principal Subsidiary Companies: Allied Waste's selected subsidiaries include: National Waste Service, Super Services Waste Management Inc., Environmental Control Inc., CRX Inc., and Sanco Inc.

Chief Competitors: Allied competes with other non-hazardous solid waste management companies, including: United Waste Systems; U.S.A. Waste Systems; Waste Management Inc.; Sanifill Inc.; Mid-American Waste Systems; American Waste Services; Browning-Ferris Industries; Republic Industries, Inc.; and WMX Technologies, Inc.

ernment solid waste disposal services to date, which included four landfills, a transfer station, a recycling facility, and several rural collection points.

EMPLOYMENT

Many of Allied's employees come from local companies it acquires. By maintaining continuity in each community it serves and allowing the local districts autonomy in operations management, the company encourages employee and customer loyalty.

SOURCES OF INFORMATION

Bibliography

Allied Waste Industries, Inc. Home Page, 3 August 1998. Available at http://www.alliedwaste.com.

"Allied Waste Industries, Inc." 5 May 1998. Available at http://www.marketguide.com.

"Allied Waste Industries, Inc." *Hoover's Online,* 26 July 1998. Available at http://www.hoovers.com.

Allied Waste Industries, Inc. 1997 Annual Report. Scottsdale, AR: Allied Waste Industries, Inc., 1997.

"Allied Waste Industries Recommended by San Diego County Chief Administrative Officer for Landmark Privatization of Solid Waste System." *Envirobiz,* 30 July 1997.

"America's Fastest-Growing Companies." *Fortune,* 14 October 1996.

The Corporate Directory By Walker's 1997. San Mateo, CA: E. Tollenaere Walsh, 1997.

Gilbertson, Dawn. "Small Arizona-Based Waste-Management Company Plans $1.5 Billion Acquisition."*Knight-Rider/Tribune Business News,* 19 September 1996.

Reagor, Catherine. "New Partner to Help Allied Waste." *The Business Journal,* 10 February 1995.

For an annual report:

telephone: (602)423-2946

For additional industry research:

Investigate companies by their Standard Industrial Classification Codes, also known as SICs. Allied's primary SICs are:

4952 Sewage Systems

4953 Refuse Systems

4959 Sanitary Services

America Online, Inc.

OVERVIEW

America Online (AOL) was originally started as a service provided by a company called Quantum in 1989. Quantum changed its name in 1991 to America Online, offering PC users Internet access, e-mail, and an array of information and services. America Online, Inc. ranks as the world's top online service provider.

American Online, Inc. has three major divisions. First is its AOL Networks unit. This segment is accountable for consumer access to the Internet. AOL Studios, a second division, creates new online features. A third division, ANS Communications, arranges high-speed networking for its customers. The company's reorganization into these three divisions was part of its strategy to build online advertising and commerce revenues.

COMPANY FINANCES

In 1997, America Online's total revenues were $1.68 billion, $1.43 billion (85 percent) of which was derived from its online service revenues. This represented a substantial increase from total 1996 revenues of $1.09 billion and online revenues of $991 million. Though data for the full year of fiscal 1998 (ending 6/98) was not available, America Online had already increased revenues over 1997 in its first three quarters, earning $1.80 billion as of 3/31/98.

In May of 1998, AOL stock was trading between $85 and $90 per share. The company's 52-week high was $92.25 and its 52-week low was $24.12. AOL earnings per share were $.32.

ALSO KNOWN AS: AOL
FOUNDED: 1989

Contact Information:

HEADQUARTERS: 22000 AOL Way
   Dulles, VA 20166
PHONE: (703)448-8700
FAX: (703)265-2039
URL: http://www.aol.com

FINANCES:

America Online Inc.
Net Sales, 1994-1997
(million dollars)

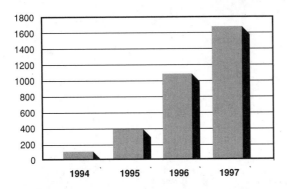

America Online Inc.
1997 Stock Prices
(dollars)

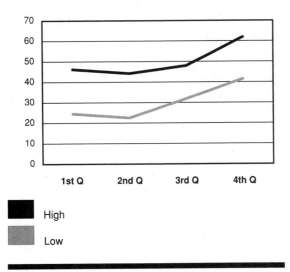

■ High

■ Low

ANALYSTS' OPINIONS

Many analysts see online services as a market with tremendous growth possibilities. Given the Internet's growth in recent years, America Online and other companies providing online service face new market concerns. Briefly, there was controversy stemming from America Online's financial position. Using questionable accounting practices, the company postponed marketing costs, showing higher profits as a result. In September of 1996, the company absorbed a $385 million write off to account for these postponed expenses. That left some analysts to question the company's actual financial status. Even with cost cutting efforts (AOL's flat rate offer), America Online just began to see green again in early 1997. Still, many analysts saw this as a positive sign for the company since much smaller online companies couldn't possibly compete with such low prices. Other critics say America Online will run out of money before it can accommodate all of its customers. The only way for the company to turn a profit, they say, is to charge for prime services and generate advertising profit with company sponsors.

America Online Inc. also faced scandal with flooded lines as a result of drastic price reductions. This led some analysts to see a positive indication of the company's advantage in a profitable market. Most users did wade through the flood of the masses trying to get online during the price war. Users like America Online's user-friendly format, and critics say it's the easiest to use on the market. While America Online's software is not updated as rapidly as downloading from the Internet, it has been praised for giving its customers more than their money's worth.

AOL surpassed analyst estimates for the first three quarters of the 1998 fiscal year, however, and its stock rose from the $30 per share range up to $115 per share. The company was adding approximately 10,000 users per day. Analysts at Zacks Investment Research reached a general consensus rating of "moderate buy" for AOL, expecting the company to continue its growth.

HISTORY

Stephen Case, America Online Inc.'s CEO, was a development manager at Pizza Hut when he became interested in a new online service called Source in the early 1980s. His interest led him to Control Video, a company that ran an online service for those using Atari computer games. In 1985, after financial struggles, the company was renamed Quantum Computer Services and began a new service called Q-Link, an online service for those using Commodore computers. By 1987 Quantum made agreements with Apple and Tandy due to Q-Link's popularity, and a service called America Online was introduced in 1989 for IBM-compatible and Apple computers. Quantum Computer Services changed its name in 1991 to America Online.

Stephen Case became the company's CEO in 1992 and launched an aggressive marketing campaign in an effort to beat competitors like Prodigy and CompuServe. Other features were added to America Online including Time Warner's *Time* magazine, General Media International's *Omni* magazine, and news from Turner Broadcasting's CNN. The company also added a Windows form of its online software.

By 1995 America Online tapped into the Internet, allowing its users access to unlimited information as well. That same year the company introduced Global Network Navigator, a service solely geared toward the Internet. America Online also signed an exclusive marketing deal with Intuit, inventor of Quicken financial software. American Online went on to sign similar deals with AT&T, Netscape, and Microsoft. In an effort to remove some of its competition, the company reduced its rates in 1996, causing its lines to flood with response. As a result, many users were denied access due to busy signals. The company faced law suits and millions in reimbursement costs to customers.

STRATEGY

Since Stephen Case took over as CEO, America Online Inc.'s strategy has been one of continued growth at any cost. He hoped to reach 10 million subscribers by 1998, and actually reached 12 million—14.5 million including the company's acquisition of CompuServe, with 2.5 million additional customers. Another part of his strategy has been the endless searching for ways to increase the company's revenues. Increasing competition and technology have motivated American Online to surge ahead.

In May of 1998, America Online announced it would acquire NetChannel, Inc. a Web-enhanced television company. The company claimed the acquisition would further its "AOL Anywhere" strategy of making the AOL brand available on all emerging interactive platforms. It would also allow them to capitalize on NetChannel's experience and technology to accelerate AOL's own development of a branded service offering interactive content developed for television.

Among other strategies was AOL's drive for increased revenue. In March of 1997 America Online announced it planned to incorporate company-sponsored advertisements in its chat rooms (online discussion areas for individuals and groups of 23 people or less). These chat rooms, called "People Connection," totaled 14,000 possible areas of simultaneous discussion. The hope had been that companies would buy space in these rooms to advertise their various products or services. Ads were being rotated every 60 seconds in windows in these designated discussion areas.

AOL's growth strategy applied to its approach overseas as well. Case hoped to become the leading universal consumer online service some time after 1998. He entered a joint operation with German media master Bertelsmann in 1995. With services operating in France, Germany, and Britain, the two hoped to dominate the European market by 1998. Plans to move into Asia, Japan, Australia, and/or India surfaced as well.

April 15, 1997 marked the day America Online had planned to introduce its online service in Japan using

FAST FACTS:
About America Online, Inc.

Ownership: America Online is a publicly owned company traded on the New York Stock Exchange.

Ticker symbol: AOL

Officers: Stephen M. Case, Chmn. & CEO, 39, $271,250; Bruce Bond, Pres. & CEO, ANS Communications, Inc., 51, $513,216; Robert W. Pittman, Pres. & CEO, AOL Networks, 43, $460,064; Theodore J. Leonis, Pres. & CEO, AOL Studios, 41, $283,125

Employees: 7,371

Chief Competitors: AOL is one of the leading providers of consumer online services. As such, its primary competitors are: AT&T Corp.; MCI; Microsoft; NETCOM; People World; Prodigy; and Time Warner. Other online competitors include: Dow Jones; News Corp.; PSINet; Reuters; Starwave; and Thomson Corp.

Japanese language, content, and customer benefits. America Online aimed to make Japan its biggest international market. Japan held 5.7 million potential online members. Other market figures included the estimated 500,000 America Online members in Europe and the 100,000 members of America Online Canada (AOL Canada). Overall, international subscribers accounted for 750,000 market members.

INFLUENCES

Since Q-Link's popularity in 1985, America Online has geared itself toward expansion. Acquiring business deals with big names like Tandy, Apple, and Commodore, America Online established itself as an online developer. At a time when the market was growing due to increasing technological capabilities, America Online expanded quickly.

America Online created a service for Apple Computers called Applelink Personal Edition, which Apple planned to introduce with the Macintosh and Apple II's. Apple's decision to cancel the deal left America Online (then called Quantum Computer Services) with time,

CHRONOLOGY:

Key Dates for America Online, Inc.

1989: Founded as Quantum

1991: Changes name to America Online

1992: Stephen Case becomes CEO

1995: Introduces Global Network Navigator

1996: Reduces rates and gains 500,000 new subscribers in one month

1998: Acquires NetChannel

money, and energy invested in a new service with no market outlet. The company decided to release the service under the name America Online, but faced financial frustrations concerning marketing its service. With little money to spend on advertising, the company decided to launch its service (1989) by using mailers, exhibiting software at trade shows, and by putting its name on magazine covers.

After five years, America Online acquired 5 million subscribers. The company was growing so fast it was in the number three slot of online service companies, behind Prodigy and CompuServe. America Online soon passed both companies to be the number one online service company in the world. By early 1998, America Online had 12 million subscribers, plus CompuServe's 2.5 million subscribers.

Not only did America Online grow rapidly, but so did the competition, forcing the company to compete with companies like AT&T and Microsoft Corp. In a continuing effort to increase its customer volume, America Online offered free trial offers of software sending diskettes out in the mail all across the country. This direct marketing effort proved to be wildly successful. The company also reduced its prices in 1996 from $9.95 for five online hours, plus $2.95 for each additional hour, to a flat rate of $19.95 for unlimited online hours. No company to date had such competitive prices.

America Online increased its customer volume faster than it anticipated—500,000 new subscribers in the month of December alone joined in. The number of online visits by customers went from 6 to 11 million in a matter of months in late 1996. The company, anticipating some growth, added modems and connection lines, but still was unable to meet customer demand. Busy signals turned signed up customers away, causing attorney generals in 20 states to threaten the company with law suits if it continued to make promises to its customers it couldn't keep. After attempts to fix the overload failed, the company offered refunds to dissatisfied customers, totaling a loss of $24 million. Despite these setbacks, most America Online users stuck through the frustrations for the lower price.

CURRENT TRENDS

America Online continued its aggressive approach to growth by keeping the flat rate price of $19.95. It also made other attempts to increase customer volume by adding new communication lines at a fast pace. In 1996, the company had 143,000 modems in its U.S. "AOLnet"—by the end of 1997, they had 350,000 modems. Also, the company hired Bob Pittman, co-founder of MTV, to devise a strategy to keep new members from turning to another online service, as the turnover rate had reached 25 percent in 1997. He developed plans for the company to feature hot options, similar to his creations with cable channels. These options would include company-generated content as well as agreements with new programmers.

Other attempts by America Online to increase customers and revenue have included joint efforts with big name rivals like Microsoft and AT&T. America Online agreed to boost Microsoft's Internet browser software in exchange for packaging America Online's software with every copy of Windows '95. AT&T agreed to supply a communication link to the company from its WorldNet service. And in 1997 American Online acquired one of its chief competitors, CompuServe. America Online planned to maintain CompuServe as a separate service, primarily due to the two services' separate target audiences—AOL targeted the mass market, while CompuServe targeted the business and professional audience.

PRODUCTS

AOL service includes news, entertainment, information, online shopping, buddy lists, and AOL's web site, which provides AOL NetFind and AOL Instant Messenger services. The newsstand section offers more than 90 magazines accessible to AOL subscribers online. AOL also provides chat rooms for real-time conversations with other members (and sometimes with celebrities) and email service for sending mail, data files, Internet hyperlinks, photos, and sound files to AOL members and worldwide Internet users. As part of its online service, the company provides parental and mail controls and a secure Internet browser.

One of the company's newest products, announced in May of 1998, was "You've Got Pictures!," a joint project with Kodak. According to the company's press release, You've Got Pictures! will "make online pictures as easy to obtain as prints, as easy to send as e-mail and easier to organize, store and personalize than ever before."

CORPORATE CITIZENSHIP

America Online has a philanthropic division named the AOL Foundation. The Foundation's mission is "To pioneer the development of strategies and programs that leverage the power of the emerging global medium to benefit society by improving the lives of families and children, and empowering the disadvantaged." The Foundation's first major grant program was announced in February of 1998. It was called the Interactive Education Initiative and represents an effort to develop and spread effective uses of technology in schools. Another example of the company's charitable activities was its participation in the fight against breast and ovarian cancer as a part of Revlon's Run/Walk for Women.

GLOBAL PRESENCE

Adding local services in Britain, France, Germany, and Canada, America Online's international enterprises have grown by half a million since their 14 month-old beginning. Standing as the largest online service company in the world, America Online Inc. has made tremendous efforts to work out the bugs to open its communication lines aiming to maintain this title. America Online currently offers special versions of AOL for residents of Canada, Germany, France, the United Kingdom, Sweden, Japan, and Australia. Global partnerships for international consumer online services include Bertelsmann AG, Europe's largest media company. In Japan, AOL has forged alliances with Mitsui, one of the world's largest trading companies, and Nikkei, one of the leading Japanese publishing firms.

SOURCES OF INFORMATION

Bibliography

"ABC News Announces Plans to Launch a 24-Hour Online News Service In Partnership With America Online, Netscape and Starwave." *Yahoo!,* 3 April 1997.

Alsop, Stewart. "A Few Kind Words for America Online." *Fortune,* 17 March 1997.

"America Online, Inc." *Hoover's Online,* 20 May 1998. Available at http://www.hoovers.com.

"America Online, Inc. to Acquire NetChannel, Inc." America Online Press Release, 6 May 1998. Available at http://www-db.aol.com/corp/news/press/view?release=348.

"America Online to Launch Service in Japan." *Reuters,* 25 March 1997.

"AOL and Kodak Announce "You've Got Pictures!" America Online Press Release, 19 May 1998. Available at http://www-db.aol.com/corp/news/press/view?release=353.

"AOL Chief Faces the Music." *Cable News Network,* 24 January 1977. Available at http://www.cnn.com.

"AOL Membership Passes 8 Million Mark." *Fox News,* 17 January 1997.

"AOL Plans Ads in Chat Rooms Stock Climbs." *Reuters,* 5 March 1997.

Cortese, Amy. "America Online's Global Push." *Business Week,* 22 April 1996.

Dubrowski, Jerry. "Disney's ABC, AOL, Netscape Form Online News Partnership." *Reutrers,* 3 April 1997.

Eng, Paul. "The Online World of Steve Case." *Business Week,* 15 April 1996.

Gunther, Marc. "The Internet Is Mr. Case's Neighborhood." *Fortune,* 30 March 1998. Available at http://www.pathfinder.com/fortune/1998/980330/aol.a.html.

Himowitz, Michael J. "Cyberspace: The Investor's New Edge." *Fortune,* 25 December 1995.

"Internet Market Changing After AOL's Flat-Rate Troubles." *Fox News,* 7 March 1997.

Jackson, David S. "AOL Buys Some Time." *Time,* 10 February 1997.

Yudkowsky, Chaim, and Terry Brock. "AOL Is Moving Fast to Make Sure It Stays No. 1." *Washington Business Journal,* 30 September 1996.

For an annual report:

on the Internet at: http://www.aol.com/corp/inv/reports **or** write: Secretary, America Online, Inc., 22000 AOL Way, Dulles, VA 20166.

For additional industry research:

Investigate companies by their Standard Industrial Classification Codes, also known as SICs. America Online's primary SIC is:

7375 Information Retrieval Services

America West Airlines, Inc.

FOUNDED: 1981

Contact Information:

HEADQUARTERS: 4000 E. Sky Harbor Blvd.
   Phoenix, AZ 85034
PHONE: (602)693-0800
FAX: (602)693-5546
URL: http://www.americawest.com

OVERVIEW

America West Airlines began service as a regional carrier in Phoenix, Arizona, in 1983. It grew steadily for eight years, endured three years of Chapter 11 bankruptcy (1991-94), then reemerged as a viable nationwide force in the airline industry. The company focused on a strategy of discount prices and alliances with other airlines. The company served 91 destinations, including eight internationally. Some destinations were served through "codesharing" agreements with other airlines. By 1996, America West ranked ninth in revenue among U.S. passenger airlines. However, the airline ranked number one for short flights (500 miles or less) in 1997 and 1998 in a *Frequent Flyer Magazine* J.D. Power And Associates Customer Satisfaction Study.

COMPANY FINANCES

America West's 1997 annual revenues were $1.9 billion, up 7.8 percent from $1.7 billion in 1996. Fourth quarter 1997 revenues alone increased 7.5 percent to $472.9 million from $440.0 million the previous year. Net income rose to $75 million, up 781 percent from $8.5 million in 1996. Of 1997 revenues, the airline's passenger division showed the largest increase, rising from $46.5 million in 1996 to $51.7 million in 1997, an 11.1 percent increase.

The company's stock price was around $29 per share in mid-1998, and ranged from $12 to $31 during the first six months of the year. America West stock's 52-week high was $31.31, and its 52-week low was $12.00. Diluted earnings per share (EPS) for the year were $1.63 versus $.21 in 1996, a 700 percent increase.

The consensus among analysts at Zack's Investment Research was a moderate buy rating for America West, with a few advising a "hold" rating. They did expect stable growth for the company, projecting increased earnings per share of $2.40 for fiscal year 1998, and $2.45 in fiscal 1999.

ANALYSTS' OPINIONS

America West's new prosperity and expansion plans did not go unnoticed by industry analysts. The 1997 edition of *Hoover's Handbook of American Business* described America West as "climbing toward complete recovery" from its bankruptcy years. However, in a *New York Times* article, Adam Bryant suggested that America West might be trying too hard to recover. He predicted that all major airlines in general would soon return to their historic competitiveness; he noted that America West, in particular, had been criticized for resuming its efforts to expand.

After the ValuJet crash in 1996, the U.S. government did a thorough inspection of several discount airlines, including America West. According to Michael A. Dornheim in *Aviation Week & Space Technology,* the inspectors concluded that America West's maintenance staff was too small and was over-worked—a situation that could have resulted from over-ambitious expansion plans. Ambition aside, America West's geographic location should help boost its growth in the years ahead. *Moody's Transportation Manual* noted that both Phoenix and Las Vegas (America West's main hubs) ranked among the world's 25 most popular air travel destinations; both seem poised for significant population growth and both provided ideal connections to popular West Coast destinations.

HISTORY

Airline consultant Edward R. Beauvais founded America West in 1981, following the deregulation of the airline industry in 1978. Beauvais saw a need for better air service between California and other southwestern states, especially for business commuters. After spending two years establishing a financial base and gathering facilities and equipment, America West began airline service in 1983, with 3 aircraft and 280 employees. The company offered flights from Phoenix to 5 southwestern cities. By 1986, it had expanded to 34 cities, and by 1990 it was flying to 62 cities and earning more than $1 billion annually.

From the beginning, America West borrowed large amounts of money to meet ambitious expansion goals.

FINANCES:

America West Airlines Net Sales, 1994-1997 (million dollars)

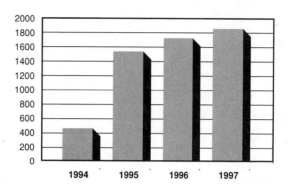

America West Airlines 1997 Stock Prices (dollars)

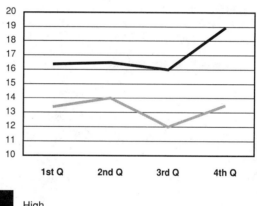

 High

Low

This debt, plus an industry-wide slowdown and an increase in fuel prices led America West to file Chapter 11 bankruptcy in 1991. Chapter 11 bankruptcy allows a company to stay in business without immediately paying all its creditors, as long as it can convince the bankruptcy court that it intends to eventually pay them.

Beauvais resigned as chairman in 1992, during an industry-wide price war. A year later the company hired William Franke to help it recover from bankruptcy, and he soon became the company's president. By 1994, America West had emerged from bankruptcy. And in 1997, America West was the major air passenger carrier

FAST FACTS:

About America West Airlines, Inc.

Ownership: America West Holdings Corporation is a publicly owned company traded on the New York Stock Exchange.

Ticker symbol: AWA

Officers: William A. Franke, Chmn., 59, $584,504; Richard R. Goodmanson, Pres. & CEO, 49; Ronald A. Aramini, Sr. VP, Operations, 51; W. Douglas Parker, Sr. VP & CFO, 35, $211,667

Employees: 11,000

Principal Subsidiary Companies: America West Airlines is a wholly owned subsidiary of America West Holdings Corporation.

Chief Competitors: As a major airline primarily serving North America, America West's competitors include: Alaska Air; American Airlines; Delta; Flight Safety; Mexicana; Northwest; Reno Air; Southwest; TWA; United; and USAir.

in Phoenix. Its other major hub was in Las Vegas, while a smaller hub in Columbus, Ohio, enabled it to serve the eastern United States. In 1997 America West flew to 84 cities in 36 states, as well as 6 cities in Mexico and 1 in Canada. It had a fleet of 101 planes and employed more than 11,000 people.

STRATEGY

According to its 1997 mission statement, America West's goal was to be a "low-cost, full-service, nationwide airline." Its leaders defined four "strategic imperatives" to help it reach that goal. These were to "maintain a low unit cost, focus on the customer, build financial power and market strength, and create a high-performance culture." The first two of those imperatives were reflected in America West's matching the low fares of other discount carriers while still offering "full-service" amenities such as advance seat assignments, first class seating, in-flight meals, in-flight movies, and complimentary copies of the *Wall Street Journal.*

During 1997, America West's on-time performance improved by 10 percentage points as measured by the

U.S. Department of Transportation (DOT) and flight cancellations decreased by 50 percent. The airline ranked number one in baggage handling as recorded in the DOT's *1997 Air Travel Consumer Report.* These and other initiatives were part of America West's focus on customer service and operational reliability throughout the company. Their "Pride in All We Do" campaign was designed to get employees' help defining and meeting company goals. America West employees held sessions known as "WorkOuts" to come up with ideas and make recommendations on how to improve the company's operational performance.

Both before and after its years of bankruptcy protection, America West sought greater "financial power and market strength" by buying or leasing additional aircraft, seeking new routes, and forming alliances with other airlines. Its alliance with Mesa Air Group allowed the company to provide extensive service in the Southwest region, while its alliance with Continental Airlines helped it reach more eastern cities. America West continued its strategic growth by adding service from Phoenix and Las Vegas to Cleveland and Washington Dulles, increasing frequency to key markets, and increasing available seat miles by 9 percent. They also expanded the company's codeshare agreement with British Airways to include connections at its Las Vegas and Columbus hubs—an agreement was already in place for the company's hub in Phoenix. "Codesharing" meant the two companies used the same identifying information for flights they shared. This makes it easier for travel agents to book America West flights, making it more likely that agents would steer customers their way.

A central part of America West's strategic growth plan was the expansion of its Nite Flite service at the Las Vegas hub. This program, whose operations primarily take place between 10 p.m. and 2 a.m., helps the carrier maximize its revenue potential. Approximately 15 percent of the company's revenues came from its Nite Flite service, as it takes place during a time period when most domestic carriers' fleets are not in operation.

To increase the company's profile, America West teamed up with resorts to offer special vacation deals. It sometimes painted its aircraft and gave them names like "Tribute to Nevada," to appeal to specific groups of customers. It signed deals to be the "official airline" of various athletic events. It was also the official airline of the Phoenix Suns professional basketball team and was a corporate sponsor of the team's sports facility, which was therefore named America West Arena.

INFLUENCES

Industry deregulation in 1978 had to do mainly with the business aspects of the airline industry, such as the number of routes available and the price of fares. Such regulations made it hard for newer or smaller airlines to compete. Then, just as the major airlines began using larger jets such as the 747, the energy crisis of 1974 led to skyrocketing fuel costs, which naturally meant higher costs for air travel. Many people felt that a lessening of government control would mean cheaper tickets, so in 1978 the airlines were deregulated. Deregulation enabled entreprenuers like Beauvais to find plenty of financial backing for their new airlines. But it also meant fierce competition right away as the number of interstate airlines increased from less than 40 in 1978 to 125 by 1984.

Deregulation brought several innovations now taken for granted by air travelers, such as "frequent flyer" programs and the "hub" system. Like spokes converging on the hub of a wagon wheel, flights come in to a hub airport from various directions at approximately the same time. Connecting flights then leave in the opposite directions a short while later. The airlines found this arrangement to be more efficient and cost-effective.

Adam Bryant, writing in the *New York Times,* described the years following deregulation as a time when "the nation's skies were viewed as a battleground, and bigger airlines operated on the premise that it was possible to drive their weaker rivals out of business and dominate the industry." By 1997, however, after a decade of bankruptcies and sagging stock prices, airlines were beginning to focus more on cost-effectiveness: lowering travel agent commissions; using electronic ticketing; forming alliances with other airlines; and using computers to analyze when and where people preferred to travel. America West was among those that followed this cost-cutting pattern.

One challenge especially for smaller airlines like America West was obtaining and retaining landing rights at larger airports. The government assigns "slots" to various airlines, which must maintain a certain number of flights at each slot in order to keep it.

CURRENT TRENDS

In 1998, America West Airlines and EVA Airways announced a new codeshare agreement, which, subject to government approval, would connect passengers from EVA's daily nonstop Taipei service to Los Angeles and San Francisco to America West hubs in Phoenix and Las Vegas. Pending U.S. Department of Transportation approval, the agreement was scheduled to begin during the summer of 1998. "This codeshare agreement will enhance service for our customers to Asia making travel to and from popular destinations easier and more convenient," said Mike Smith, senior vice president, marketing and sales, America West Airlines. America West's strong established service from Los Angeles and San Francisco was a key factor in the codeshare arrangement. Expansion through the use of codesharing services appeared to be an adopted strategy for America West's expansion in the late 1990s.

CHRONOLOGY:

Key Dates for America West Airlines, Inc.

1981: Founded by Edward R. Beauvais

1983: Begins service in Phoenix, Arizona as a regional carrier to the southwestern United States

1985: Takes delivery of its first 737; first year to show a profit

1987: Initiates FlightFund, its frequent flyer program

1990: Department of Transportation reclassifies America West as a major airline

1991: Files for Chapter 11 bankruptcy

1992: Beauvais resigns as chairman and William Franke takes the CEO position to help the company recover from bankruptcy

1994: America West emerges from bankruptcy

1996: Western Athletic Conference names America West their official airline

1997: Becomes the major air passenger carrier in Phoenix, Arizona

1998: America West Airlines and EVA Airways announce a new codeshare agreement

Another focus the company adopted was focusing corporate growth on the Phoenix hub, the backbone of its route system. As a result of the downsizing precipitated by corporate restructuring during its bankruptcy period, the Phoenix hub became undersized relative to overall air travel demand, which grew substantially over the same time period (1991-1994). During 1996 alone, daily departures from Phoenix increased from 175 to 188—that number was expected to grow to approximately 200 by 1998. Growth at Phoenix would focus on mid- to long-haul markets.

PRODUCTS

America West's product and service offerings include FlightFund(r), America West Airlines' frequent flyer program, which allows customers to earn at least 750 miles, even on short flights, plus through participating hotel and rental car partners, FlightFund Visa cards, and long distance telephone partners. The Phoenix Club(r), at the airline's main hub Sky Harbor International Airport, provides customers with club-sharing privileges in 15 major cities, domestic and international. Amenities such as private conference rooms, PCs, phones, and fax machines, as well as snacks, beverages, newspapers, and bonus miles were included. Other basic services offered by America West included baggage handling, convention and meeting services, passenger assistance, pet transportation, special needs passenger services, and services for unaccompanied minors.

CORPORATE CITIZENSHIP

America West donates air travel to various charitable organizations. The America West Airlines Foundation, a nonprofit organization funded mainly by employees, provides educational assistance to disadvantaged children and to children of America West employees. Airline employees receive special training for helping physically challenged customers. Special phones are available for the hearing impaired.

America West addresses environmental concerns related to its operations. Scrap metal and waste oil are recycled, and wash water is recycled through the hangar's cooling system. Paper, cardboard, plastic, and aluminum items from offices and planes are recycled. And unused individually wrapped food items are donated to food banks.

EMPLOYMENT

For every pilot and flight attendant it employs, an airline requires nearly a hundred "operational" employees such as ticket clerks, office workers, and maintenance staff. America West trains most of its operational staff to do several jobs, rotating them as needed. Good work is rewarded by incentive bonuses. The company provides prenatal, child, and elder care, as well as mental health,

substance abuse, and legal assistance. It has a medical clinic and a 24-hour child-care facility in Phoenix. *Working Mother* magazine included America West on its list of "Best Companies for Working Mothers" five years in a row.

America West's pilots, flight attendants, mechanics, and dispatchers are represented by labor unions. As of 1997, the company was negotiating with unions to represent its other employees as well.

SOURCES OF INFORMATION

Bibliography

"America West Airlines and EVA Airways Expand Service With New Codeshare Agreement." *PRNewswire,* 21 April 1998.

"America West Holdings Corporation." *Hoover's Online.* Available at http://www.hoovers.com.

"America West Holdings Corporation Reports Best Financial Results in Company History." *PRNewswire,* 20 January 1998. Available at http://prnewswire.com/cgi-bin/stories.pl?ACCT= 105&STORY=/www/story/1-20-98/397179&EDATE=.

Bryant, Adam. "U.S. Airlines Finally Reach Cruising Speed." *New York Times,* 20 October 1996.

Dornheim, Michael A. "America West Undergoes First Post-ValuJet Inspection." *Aviation Week & Space Technology,* 26 August 1996.

Hoover's Handbook of American Business 1997. Austin, TX: Hoover's Business Press, 1996.

Moody's Transportation Manual. New York: Moody Investors Service, 1996.

For an annual report:

on the Internet at: http://prnewswire.com/AREPORTS/121453.6

For additional industry research:

Investigate companies by their Standard Industrial Classification Codes, also known as SICs. America West's primary SIC is:

4512 Air Transportation, Scheduled

American Airlines, Inc.

OVERVIEW

American Airlines, Inc. is the principal subsidiary of AMR Corporation (AMR). In 1982 stockholders voted to approve a plan of reorganization under which they formed a new holding company, AMR Corp., which became the parent company to American Airlines Inc. They took the name "AMR" from the airline's three-letter New York Stock Exchange symbol. For financial reporting purposes, AMR's operations fall within three major lines of business: the Airline Group (American), The SABRE Group, and the Management Services Group. American operates American Eagle, a group of four small regional airlines that connect passengers from smaller markets into American's hub system. AMR also provides leasing; airport ground management; and consulting, information, and telemarketing services. Additionally, the company developed the SABRE reservation system, the world's largest privately owned real-time computer network in the world. Management believes the holding company structure improves the company's ability to manage separate business segments effectively and provides a platform for further expansion of the company's businesses.

American's passenger division is one of the largest scheduled passenger airlines in the world. American provides scheduled jet service to more than 160 destinations throughout North America, the Caribbean, Latin America, Europe, and the Pacific. American's cargo division is one of the largest scheduled air freight carriers in the world. It provides a full range of freight and mail services to shippers throughout the airline's system. In addition, through cooperative agreements with other carriers, it can transport shipments to any country in the world.

ALSO KNOWN AS: AMR Corporation
FOUNDED: 1934 as American Airways, Inc.

Contact Information:

HEADQUARTERS: 4333 Amon Carter Blvd.
    Fort Worth, TX 76155
PHONE: (817)963-1234
FAX: (817)967-9641
URL: http://www.aa.com
    http://www.amrcorp.com

FAST FACTS:

About American Airlines, Inc.

Ownership: American Airlines is a publicly owned company traded on the New York Stock Exchange and Zurich, Basel, and Geneva Stock Exchanges. American Airlines' stocks are also traded unlisted on the Midwest Stock Exchange and the Pacific Stock Exchange.

Ticker symbol: AMR

Officers: Robert L. Crandall, Chmn., Pres., & CEO, 62; Donald J. Carty, Pres., American Airlines, Inc., AMR Airline Group,51; Gerald J. Arpey, Sr. VP & CFO, 38; Anne H. McNamara, Sr. VP & Gen. Counsel, 49

Employees: 113,900

Principal Subsidiary Companies: AMR's selected subsidiaries and affiliates include: American Airlines, Inc., AMR Eagle, Inc. (commuter services), AMR Investment Services, Inc. (investment management), AMR Services Corp. (ground services), SABRE Computer Services (data processing), SABRE Decision Technologies (consulting to travel and other industries), SABRE Interactive (PC-based travel services), and SABRE Travel Information Network (reservations).

Chief Competitors: As a major airline, American Airlines' competitors include: United Airlines; USAir; Continental Airlines; TWA; Delta; Southwest Airlines; Northwest Airlines; America West; and Air France.

On an average day American Airlines receives more than 343,000 reservation calls and flies more than 2,200 flights.

COMPANY FINANCES

In 1997, the AMR Corp. generated revenues of $18.5 billion, up 4.6 percent from $17.7 billion in 1996. Of that, the Airline Group (which consists of American Airlines, Inc., AMR Eagle, Inc., and American's Cargo Division) brought in combined revenues of $16.9 billion in 1997, versus $16.2 billion in 1996 and $15.5 billion in 1995. The Airline Group accounted for 88 per-

cent of 1997 sales. The SABRE group had 1997 sales of $1.8 billion, accounting for 9 percent of total sales, and the Management Services Group accounted for 3 percent of sales with $610 million in sales. In the first quarter of 1998, AMR reported earnings of $290 million, 91 percent growth over first quarter 1997 earnings of $152 million.

From 1990 to 1993, the airline industry experienced unprecedented losses due to high fuel costs, general economic conditions, intense price competition, and other factors. As a result of price competition, American could not raise prices to compensate for the escalating fuel costs. During this period, AMR lost more than $1.3 billion.

AMR's reported earnings per share was $10.90 in 1997, up from $9.92 in 1996. By May of 1998 that figure rose to $12.37 per share. The actual stock price per share has been rising steadily since 1995, when it ranged from a low of $54 7/8 per share to a high of $78 per share. In the second quarter of 1996 that high reached $96 3/4 per share, and in the fourth quarter of 1997 AMR's stock price reached a high of $131 13/16 per share. Stock prices have continued to rise in 1998, ranging from $150 to $153 13/16 per share. It is currently the highest-priced airline stock in the United States. In order to make its stock more accessible to small investors, AMR announced a 2-for-1 stock split. This will reward current shareholders with double the number of shares they currently own, and split the purchase price of AMR stock per share in half.

In 1996 American derived 69.6 percent of its passenger revenues from domestic operations and 30.4 percent from international operations versus 68.9 percent of its passenger revenues from domestic operations and 31.1 percent from its international operations in 1995.

ANALYSTS' OPINIONS

In June of 1997, Standard & Poor's raised the corporate credit ratings and senior debt ratings of AMR Corp. and subsidiary American Airlines Inc. to "investment grade" with an outlook of "stable." The upgrade was based on stronger industry conditions and the company's concentration on core markets and profitable international routes. This resulted in improved earnings and cash flow. AMR's new corporate credit rating was also based on strong revenue and cash flow generation from the airline, an improving balance sheet, and earnings contributions from small, but profitable, nonairline businesses such as the SABRE reservations system. Additional elements cited in American's favor included a revenue edge from its extensive route network—one of three largest domestic carriers, largest in Latin America, and second-largest to Europe. The company's alliance with British Airways PLC also helps form a strong competitor in that market and generate added revenues. Reasons the airline did not get an even higher rating were attributed to the high industry risk of airlines, rising labor costs, and a possible sale of its computerized reservation system unit. The overall ratings for AMR Corp. and American Airlines will likely improve if the company's performance continues at its current trend.

HISTORY

Robertson Aircraft Corporation and about 85 other small airline companies were consolidated in 1929 and 1930 into the Aviation Corporation, which eventually formed American Airways, the immediate predecessor of today's American Airlines. It was in 1934 that the company reorganized American Airways and became American Airlines, Inc. Not long after, American developed an air traffic control system that would later be used by all airlines and administered by the U.S. government. The company also introduced the first domestic scheduled U.S. freight service in 1944. The Douglas 7Aircraft Company and American took the initiative and debuted the first commercial flight with the Douglas DC-3 between Chicago and New York on June 25, 1936. American focused on the innovation and modernization of its fleet and acquired its first McDonnell Douglas MD-11 in 1991, which accommodated 251 passengers. They constructed this type of aircraft for long-hauls, which made it possible for American to venture into the international markets.

In 1989, AMR bought Eastern Air Lines' Latin American routes, the U.S.-London routes from TWA, and Continental's Seattle-Tokyo routes. In addition, they got approval to fly to Manchester, England, from the Department of Transportation. These and other expansion efforts into international markets helped the company's renewed growth and continue to do so throughout the 1990s.

STRATEGY

American maximizes passenger traffic and revenue potential by channeling into or through its hubs, which serve as gateways for the airlines route network. Through its hub-and-spoke system, American serves more markets with greater frequency than would be possible with the same number of aircraft in a point-to-point route system. At American's largest hub, the Dallas/Fort Worth International Airport, they operate more than 750 flights per day to 128 domestic and 17 international destinations. Additional hubs include Chicago, Miami, and San Juan. The company believes these hubs are well positioned as geographically favorable locations for continued growth. American Airlines has many cooperative-service relationships (sometimes called code shares) with selected airlines across the world. These airlines

CHRONOLOGY:
Key Dates for American Airlines, Inc.

1934: American Airways, Inc. reorganizes to form American Airlines, Inc.

1936: American uses Douglas DC-3 for first domestic flight between Chicago and New York

1944: The first domestic scheduled freight service is introduced

1953: An 80-passenger DC-7 makes the first scheduled non-stop transcontinental flight

1959: The first Boeing 707s enter into service for American

1968: President C.R. Smith leaves to join the Johnson Administration

1974: C.R. Smith returns to bring American out of its financial crisis

1981: AADVANTAGE Program is introduced

1989: Expands into Latin America, The United Kingdom, and Japan

1991: Purchases McDonnell Douglas MD-11, which carried 251 passengers

1994: Chemical Product Control Program is initiated

1998: First flight attendant class in which all attendants will be bi- or multi-lingual

service many destinations worldwide that American does not serve itself. Through these relationships, American can offer service to destinations throughout the world. Although tickets show American Airlines' flight numbers, all or part of the journey might be on one of their cooperative partners.

Further efforts toward continued growth for the company include expanding foreign routes in areas such as Latin America, Asia, and Europe and alliances with carriers such as British Airways. In addition, American plans to upgrade its air fleet, and ordered 103 aircraft from Boeing and the right to purchase more than 527 additional jets during the next 22 years. This arrangement would allow the airline to move gradually toward a very high level of fleet commonality, and provide for modest capacity growth in future years.

In a new marketing venture, American Airlines teamed up with the MGM Grand to offer what the MGM

Grand termed an "exclusive and unprecedented agreement." Beginning in May of 1998, the MGM Grand began offering AADVANTAGE members mile points for hotel stays, theatre tickets, and gambling activity. MGM Grand President Dan Wade speculated that the alliance reinforces "the power of global branding among the leaders in the travel industry."

INFLUENCES

American Airlines attributes its recent successes to several factors, including sensible pricing and favorable fuel prices. The company also gave a nod to its employees around the world, adding that it was their dedication and teamwork that gave American's customers the good service that keeps them coming back.

Compared to its competition American has certain advantages. Its fleet is young (average aircraft age—eight years), efficient, and quiet. It has an immense domestic and international route structure, secured by efficient hubs. In addition, the company's AADVANTAGE frequent flyer program is the largest in the industry. American established this program to develop passenger loyalty by offering awards to travelers for their continued patronage. AADVANTAGE members earn mileage credits for flights on American and American Eagle.

Also contributing significantly toward AMR's success is the SABRE reservations system (of which AMR owns 80 percent, and 20 percent is publicly owned). Though it accounted for a small percentage of overall sales in 1997, that percentage is growing—*Fortune* magazine reported in its 1998 Fortune 500 issue that AMR receives 20 percent of its profits from the SABRE system. The system is used by 45 percent of U.S. travel agencies to book reservations, according to *Fortune* magazine.

CURRENT TRENDS

A key element of Americans' strategic growth plan took place in 1996, when the company announced its plans to create a worldwide alliance between American and British Airways. Subject to regulatory approval, the two carriers will introduce extensive code sharing across each other's networks and establish full reciprocity between frequent flyer programs. Additionally, the carriers will combine passenger and cargo activities between the United States and Europe and share the resulting profits on these services. This alliance positions American to compete in thousands of new markets and make them fully competitive with the existing global alliances of other major U.S. carriers, such as that of United with Lufthansa and SAS, Northwest with KLM, and Delta with Austrian, Swissair, and Sabena. As of September

1997, this alliance was under review by the U.S. Department of Transportation.

Due to competition, fares have fallen substantially in the past 10 years, and that trend should continue. To fill seats on weekend flights, for which there is typically little demand and which normally go empty, American is promoting special fares via the Internet. Participants in its NetsAAvers program register through Americans' Web site to receive a weekly E-mail message outlining fare offerings.

PRODUCTS

While focusing on air safety, American is currently equipping its 649 planes with early warning devices called Enhanced Ground Proximity Warning Systems. The new system will give flight crews a map-like display of nearby terrain on all sides of the aircraft. Existing ground proximity systems, by contrast, can only read terrain that is directly below the aircraft.

CORPORATE CITIZENSHIP

Environmental awareness is promoted throughout the company. In the late 1990s the company was committed to developing and carrying out business practices that help safeguard the earth's environment. They started the in-flight recycling program that recycles more than 336,000 pounds of aluminum annually. Also, the Chemical Product Control Program, started in 1994, has reduced the number of various types of chemicals at American from 15,000 to 2,000. The company will invest more than $20 million by the end of 1997 in environmental systems and clean up programs. For example, American is in the process of removing and/or upgrading underground storage tanks. This effort is 95 percent complete. In addition, American was the first airline to receive the Animal Transportation Association's Animal Welfare Award. They recognized the Passenger and Cargo Divisions for "outstanding work" supporting animal welfare projects, including the dramatic rescue of three African lions from a Mexico City zoo.

GLOBAL PRESENCE

American provides service to and from cities in various other countries, across the Atlantic and the Pacific, and also between the United States and the Caribbean, and Central and South America. International travel accounted for 30 percent of American's passenger revenue in 1996. American continues to be the dominant carrier in Latin America with 64 percent of total U.S. airline traffic. The company continues to add to its international

AIRLINE FOOD GETS FIRST CLASS UPGRADE

Everything on the menu sounds so appetizing, it's hard to decide which entree to order: Maple barbecue chicken with sauteed yellow squash served with zucchini and a cornbread pilaf, salmon with Shangdon sauce and stir fried vegetable rice, or penne pasta with balsamic broth and goat cheese garnish. Must be the menu at a fancy gourmet restaurant, right? Guess again. These are just some of the new meals being offered by American Airlines to its first class passengers. American consulted with chefs Larry Forgione of American Place in New York, and Jasper White of Legal Sea Foods in Boston to revamp over half of its first class dinner lineup. Other airlines, including Delta, U.S. Airways, and Continental have redesigned their menus as well. Why the change? Customers want better food.

A survey of 1,000 frequent flyers by LSG-Sky Chefs revealed that 56 percent would consider changing airlines if they could expect better food. Forty-three percent want airlines to come up with new food, while 67 percent desire healthy foods. Other factors relating to customer satisfaction while dining in the sky were frequency and variety of drinks, cloth napkins, and hot towels.

For the most part, airlines have been very responsive to their customers' desires. In addition to the changes to its first class menu, American now offers Bistro service on flights that last two to three hours. The service allows customers to grab their own sack of food from a cooler on the jetway before boarding. Some of the Bistro sacks include Lender's bagels, full-sized deli sandwiches, side salads, and pasta salad to name a few. United Airlines has hired Sheila Lukins, co-author of the Silver Palate cookbooks, to come up with 25 hot meals for coach-class customers. Starting in October 1998, Delta Air Lines' coach fliers will be treated to steak from Michael Jordan's Steak House NYC. Travelers flying in U.S. Airways Envoy class can choose from four entrees and hors d'oeuvres and desserts from Philadelphia's Le BeeFin restaurant. With its Chef on Board program for Business First flights, Continental Airlines has an actual chef on the plane to help serve and prepare food.

Airlines have answered the call for healthier foods as well. In 1997 United was ranked first for the third year in a row in a study conducted by the Physicians Committee for Responsible Medicine (PCRM) to determine the availability of low-fat and vegetarian foods served by airlines. One of United's healthy entrees included cholesterol-free, mushroom-filled ravioli in marinara sauce served with a zucchini, yellow squash, and carrot medley with only 2.5 grams of fat. Numbers two and three in the study were American and Northwest Airlines, respectively. All of the airlines that participated in the study offered cholesterol-free meals with no more than 28 percent of calories coming from fat.

Customers have apparently noticed the difference in airline food quality. In 1997, food satisfaction ratings on United flights featuring Sheila Lukins' meals improved by 27 percent from the previous year among coach fliers. American must be doing something right, too. It announced in 1997 that it was releasing the second edition of the American Airlines cookbook, "A Taste of Something Special," featuring recipes from American's most popular entrees.

---

network by entering into a code share agreement with Chinese Eastern Airlines in March 1997.

American is also the dominant U.S. carrier to Latin America, serving 27 nations in the Caribbean, Mexico, Central and South America, and the number two U.S. carrier to Europe. Current American code share alliances include South African Airways, British Midland Airways, Gulf Air, Quantas Airways, Canadian Airlines, Singapore Airlines, LOT Polish Airlines, China Airlines, El Al Israel Airlines, and TACA Group. The TACA group is composed of TACA International Airlines of El Salvador and its affiliate partners-AVIATECA of Guatemala, COPA of Panama, LACSA of Costa Rica, NICA of Nicaragua, and TACA de Honduras. Current additional partners pending with the TACA Group of Central America carriers include LAPSA of Paraguay, BWIA, Transaero Airlines, EL AL, and Avianca.

EMPLOYMENT

The airline business is labor intensive. American has employees based in the Americas, Asia, the Caribbean, Europe, and the Middle East. In addition, the company has 194 City Ticket Office locations in the United States and Canada. American distributed almost $61 million in profit-sharing and bonus checks to more than 21,700 employees in the Dallas-Fort Worth base in March 1997 for contributions to American's 1996 performance. American launched its profit-sharing programs in 1984.

On March 2, 1998, American Airlines began its first flight attendant training class in the company's history in which all the prospective U.S.-based attendants have either bilingual or multilingual skills. The first class included 52 new hires who were expected to begin work on flights in the spring. This group of flight attendants speak Spanish, French, Japanese, German, Portugese, Italian, and Swedish; all also speak English and some speak additional languages. This is American's way of working towards a goal of 50 percent of the flight staff speaking second or third languages, a goal the company hopes to continue moving toward when hiring 1,600 new employees in 1998. American is looking for diversity in its workforce, and not only in language skills. Recent hires ranged in age from 21 to 52, more than half of whom were men. And they came from places as far as Austria, Ecuador, and Costa Rica.

SOURCES OF INFORMATION

Bibliography

"AAL Signs Pact With China Line." *Travel Weekly,* 10 March 1997.

"American Sees Progress By Regulators In British Airways Alliance Review," 8 September 1997. Available at http://www.amrcorp.com/amr/sep0897b.htm.

"AMR/American Airlines: A Brief History." Dallas, TX: American Airlines, August 1994.

"AMR . . . A Global Company." 4 May 1998. Available at http://www.amrcorp.com/amr/global.htm.

"AMR, American Airlines Ratings Raised to Investment Grade by S&P." *Standard & Poor's CreditWire,* 16 June 1997. Available at http://wwwa.pcfn.com/sitelite/standard/investhelp.htm.

"AMR At A Glance." 4 May 1998. Available at http://www.amrcorp.com.

"AMR Corporation Corporate Facts." Dallas, TX: American Airlines, September 1996.

"AMR Corporation 1997 Annual Report." Dallas, TX: American Airlines, January 1997.

"AMR Corporate Communications," 4 May 1998. Available at http://www.amrcorp.com.

"AMR Corporate Facts." Dallas, TX: American Airlines, September 1996.

"AMR Corporation." *Hoover's Online,* 4 May 1998. Available at http://www.hoovers.com.

"AMR Reports First-Quarter Earnings of $290 Million; 2-For-1 Stock Split Proposed," 15 April 1998. Available at http://www.amrcorp.com.

"AMR's Environmental Programs," 4 May 1998. Available at http://www.amrcorp.com/amr/environ.htm.

Cronin, Mary. "The Travel Agents' Dilemma." *Fortune,* 11 May 1998. Available at http://www.pathfinder.com/fortune/digitalwatch/0511fill.htm.

"Financial Results," 4 May 1998. Available at http://www.amrcorp.com/amr/investor/results.htm.

Kirkpatrick, David. "Microsoft: Is Your Company Its Next Meal?" *Fortune,* 27 April 1998.

"MGM Grand Announces Exclusive Marketing Agreement with American Airlines," 4 May 1998. Available at http://biz.yahoo.com/bw/980504/mgm_grand__1.html.

"Newest AA Flight Attendant Class Is Speaking Your Language," 10 March 1998. Available at http://www.amrcorp.com.

"Stock Price Trends," 4 May 1998. Available at http://www.amrcorp.com/amr/investor/trends.htm.

For an annual report:

on the Internet at: http://www.amrcorp.com/air/investor/investor. htm **or** write: AMR Corporation, Mail Drop 5651, PO Box 619616, Dallas/Ft. Worth Airport, TX 75261-9616

For additional industry research:

Investigate companies by their Standard Industrial Classification Codes, also known as SICs. American Airline's primary SICs are:

4512 Air Transporation Scheduled

4513 Air Courier Services

American Eagle Outfitters, Inc.

FOUNDED: 1977

OVERVIEW

American Eagle Outfitters, Inc. is a specialty retailer of women's and men's casual apparel, footwear, outerwear, and accessories. Its products include denim, khakis, skirts, sweaters, shirts, belts, socks, and bags—all of which are sold in 335 malls and outlet malls in 39 states, principally in the Midwest, Northeast, and Southeast.

COMPANY FINANCES

Business at American Eagle Outfitters has been booming since 1996. In fiscal 1997 sales soared to $405.7 million, up from $326.4 million in fiscal 1996. The company reported net earnings of $19.5 million for fiscal 1997, compared with $5.9 million in fiscal 1996. In the first quarter of fiscal 1998, the company reported net earnings of $5.9 million on sales of $99.7 million; this compared with a net loss of $3.6 million in the first quarter of fiscal 1997. Same-store sales increased 15.1 percent in fiscal 1997.

Shareholders who own American Eagle stock have reason to cheer as well. In June 1998, the company's stock was up nine-fold from the prior year. The company announced one 3-for-2 stock split in January 1998 and another in April 1998. Per-share earnings in fiscal 1997 tripled to $1.28. American Eagle Outfitters stock was listed at $34 in June 1998. As of April 1, 1998, there were 83 shareholders on record. The company has never paid cash dividends and doesn't anticipate paying any in the future.

Contact Information:
HEADQUARTERS: 150 Thorn Hill Dr.
    Warrendale, PA 15086-7528
PHONE: (724)776-4857
FAX: (412)779-5585
TOLL FREE: (888)A-EAGLE5
EMAIL: custsrv@ae-outfitters.com
URL: http://www.ae-outfitters.com

FINANCES:

American Eagle Outfitters
Net Sales, 1994-1997
(million dollars)

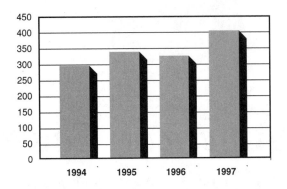

American Eagle Outfitters
1997 Stock Prices
(dollars)

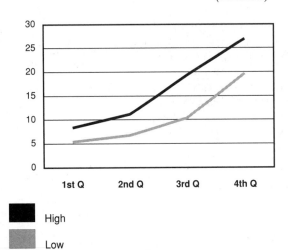

■ High

■ Low

ANALYSTS' OPINIONS

Although the fashion industry is notoriously unpredictable, many analysts like the direction American Eagle Outfitters is going. The company is one of 12 pacesetters chosen by the *Daily News Record* in 1998. The choice was based on the "innovative," "exciting," and "especially creative" things the company is doing in the men's wear scene. According to the article, "with third quarter (fiscal 1997) net tripling to $6.3 million and

same-store sales surging to 18.8 percent in December (1997), it's clear that Warrendale, Pa.-based American Eagle Outfitters has found a winning formula."

The *Bloomberg News* reports that five analysts recommend investors buy American Eagle Outfitters stock. "I'm a big fan of American Eagle," notes stock analyst Thomas A. Filandro in the *Knight-Ridder/Tribune Business News*. Analyst Maria Medaris O'Shea, in a report for Bankers Trust Alex Brown Inc., writes that "longer term, we remain impressed with American Eagle's merchandising initiatives and long-term strategies for sales and earnings growth." Analysts also point to the company's focus on the same core age group and the right mix of casual and fashionable clothes, both of which are keys to its success.

Other analysts feel that American Eagle Outfitters stock cannot continue to post the sharp gains it has in recent months. Caroline Waxler of *Forbes* said in a June 1998 article that the company is about to "hit a wall. . . .There's no way the company can continue its current 70 percent-plus monthly rate of same-store sales growth," she reasons. Waxler predicts that the stock will drop 30 percent as sales growth stalls.

HISTORY

American Eagle Outfitter's first store opened in 1977. The stores originally sold branded men's sports apparel, equipment, and accessories for outdoor sports, including hiking, mountain climbing, and camping. When its first store opened, retail operations were run by Natco through its subsidiary Peatro. In 1991 Peatro was experiencing substantial losses, and the Jerome Schottenstein family acquired the company, along with Retail Ventures, another specialty clothing store operator. (The Schottensteins are heirs of Lithuanian immigrant Ephraim Schottenstein, whose business interests included real estate, clothing, and furniture stores.)

The Schottenstein family reconfigured American Eagle Outfitters' merchandise mix, improved the look of its retail outlets, brought in new management, and expanded the number of store locations. The company repositioned itself to sell its own American Eagle brand clothing in 1992. In November 1993, American Eagle Outfitters was incorporated in Ohio, and in January 1994, the company went public, with the Schottenstein family retaining a 60 percent ownership.

American Eagle Outfitters has two wholly owned subsidiaries, formed in 1995. The first holds the trade name American Eagle Outfitters, and the second is a finance subsidiary set up to provide financing to its parent company. Two years later, American Eagle Outfitters acquired Prophecy, Ltd., an apparel maker based in New York. The majority owner of Prophecy was the Schottenstein family.

American Eagle also launched a line of women's casual clothing in 1995. The company has added 213 new American Eagle Outfitters stores since 1993 and planned to add an additional 50 in 1998.

STRATEGY

By the late 1990s, American Eagle Outfitters began to more clearly define its target customers and began implementing what the company refers to as a "back to basics" approach to merchandising and marketing. American Eagle's target customer is "a collegiate, 20-year-old male or female who desires fashionable, yet affordable, all-American, casual lifestyle apparel." By targeting 20-year-olds, the company hopes to broaden its customer base to include 16- to 34-year-olds. Customers in this age group tend to buy clothes more often than older customers and they spend more money, according to stock analyst Thomas A. Filandro, who was quoted in an April 1998 *Knight-Ridder/Tribune Business News* article.

According to American Eagle Outfitters, company management has adopted five operating strategies to "differentiate the company from its competition, improve profitability, and consistently increase net sales." Building the American Eagle Outfitters brand is first and foremost among the company's strategies. In 1997, American Eagle's three brands made up 99 percent of company sales. Management intends to keep it this way, and it has supported company brands with special marketing and advertising programs that emphasize a wholesome, youthful, outdoor image. Marketing and promotional partnerships with manufacturers of mountain bikes, four-wheel-drive vehicles, and jet skis are among the alliances forged to appeal to American Eagle's core clientele.

Providing value to its target customers is another key American Eagle strategy. "Fashionable interpretations of fundamental wardrobe items," such as jeans, sweaters, khakis, and T-shirts, are offered by American Eagle Outfitters. The merchandise price points are competitive with or lower than comparable mall-based stores.

Designing its own merchandise with an in-house team of designers provides American Eagle a competitive advantage. Designers can quickly interpret fashion trends for its target customers and design garments that can be merchandised at competitive prices.

American Eagle Outfitters integrates its merchandise production and sourcing. When American Eagle purchased Prophecy in May 1997, it gained the ability to monitor the production of its clothing and to improve its sourcing. The company hopes the end result will be lower costs and more timely delivery of clothing to its stores.

Timing is everything to American Eagle Outfitters, especially when it comes to rolling out new seasonal clothing lines. The company plans to display store merchandise closer to the season when it will be worn. Tra-

FAST FACTS:
About American Eagle Outfitters, Inc.

Ownership: American Eagle Outfitters is a publicly owned company traded on NASDAQ.

Ticker symbol: AEOS

Officers: Jay L. Schottenstein, Chmn. & CEO, 42, 1997 base salary $250,050; George Kolber, VChmn. & COO, 46, 1997 base salary $407,692; Saul Schottenstein, 76, VChmn.; Roger S. Markfield, Pres. & Chief Merchandising Officer, 55, 1997 base salary $412,464

Employees: 6,685

Principal Subsidiary Companies: American Eagle has two wholly owned subsidiaries, one of which holds the trade name American Eagle Outfitters and the other is a finance subsidiary whose purpose is to provide financing to the parent company.

Chief Competitors: American Eagle Outfitters competes with retailers of casual apparel and footwear marketed to young customers. Some primary competitors include: Abercrombie & Fitch; The Buckle; The Gap; J. Crew; Lands' End; The Limited; L.L. Bean; and Pacific Sunwear.

ditional merchandising theory calls for rolling out merchandise in advance of the season. However, American Eagle claims that its customer base tends to make its purchases at the time they will be worn. The company also plans to adjust its merchandise mix according to the various climates where its stores are located.

INFLUENCES

In 1996 American Eagle Outfitters launched its own credit card. The company is pleased with the results, with more than 300,000 cardholders by spring 1998. This move has been responsible for increasing the company's total sales per customer. American Eagle Outfitters' credit card sales accounted for more than 8 percent of total sales volume in fiscal 1997. The company has found that holders of store credit cards typically spend nearly 40 percent more than customers using Visa and Mastercard.

CHRONOLOGY:

Key Dates for American Eagle Outfitters, Inc.

1977: The first American Eagle store opens, selling branded men's sports apparel

1991: The Schottenstein family acquires American Eagle

1992: Starts selling American Eagle brand clothing

1993: American Eagle Outfitters is incorporated

1994: The company goes public

1995: Starts selling a line of women's casual clothing

1997: Purchases apparel maker Prophecy, Ltd.

The AE Clear Card was introduced by the company in Spring 1998. Touted as the first of its kind, the card is actually clear; that is, you can see through it. The new credit card was designed to increase brand awareness and strengthen the company's identity. "It's a fun, original concept that looks cool and separates AE from other retailers," said Michael James Leedy, vice president of marketing and creative sevices for American Eagle Outfitters, in a company press release.

CURRENT TRENDS

While American Eagle Outfitters is still positioned to target the 20-year-old male collegian, the company is increasingly focused on attracting women into its stores. Since women shop more frequently than men, the company hopes to capitalize on this sales potential. Dresses have become a bigger part of the stores' merchandise mix. Store design also has been refined to attract a more feminine clientele. Hardwood floors, light-colored wooden fixtures, and off-white walls create a clean and casual ambience. In 1997, additional fitting rooms were added to approximately 100 American Eagle Outfitters stores to accommodate the increase in female clientele. The company tries to maintain a uniform look throughout all of its stores. Regional "visual directors" were added to the company payroll to insure that merchandise displays and selling floor arrangements are kept identical from store to store.

Opening stores in new and existing markets is an effort the company undertook in the early 1990s and continues in the late 1990s. Since 1993, American Eagle Outfitters has added 213 stores. In 1997, it opened 36 more stores and announced plans to add 50 more in 1998. In the years ahead, the company plans to continue expansion at an annual rate of 15 to 20 percent. Since the company is focused on growing its women's apparel business, it has found it necessary to locate stores with 20 percent more floor space in order to better accommodate a full line of both men's and women's merchandise.

In its expansion efforts, American Eagle will continue focusing on increasing the number of stores in regional malls. The company estimates that there are at least 500 additional enclosed mall locations that are suitable for its stores. High traffic street locations in urban and university settings, as well as airports and strip malls, would also be considered attractive opportunities for expansion. The company continues to evaluate the feasibility of expanding in the western United States—in 1997 only one store was located west of the Rocky Mountains.

American Eagle Outfitters has recognized that the Internet offers a unique potential for expanding its customer base, and in 1997, the company launched its interactive web site featuring "The Line," where customers can see samples of American Eagle Outfitters apparel. Customers also may purchase merchandise through the web site. Another web site feature, "The List," is American Eagle Outfitters' guide to current trends in music, media, and travel. Included in the list are the company "picks" of current music CDs, movies, books, and magazines, as well as horoscopes and a question-and-answer feature on a "hot" movie personality. The site also offers corporate information, opportunities to apply for company store credit, and employment openings.

PRODUCTS

American Eagle Outfitters sells casual, outdoor-oriented clothes and accessories to men and women between the ages of 16 and 34. Khakis, denim jeans, shirts, shorts, dresses, wool and cotton sweaters, knit shirts, jackets, shoes, belts, socks, and bags make up American Eagle Outfitters' line of apparel.

The company's three private label brands are American Eagle Outfitters, AE, and AE Supply. American Eagle's in-house design team interprets fashion trends and then incorporates them into apparel design; the clothes are then manufactured using outside vendors.

In 1998, women's wear made up 50 percent of American Eagle's sales. Men's wear accounted for 41 percent of sales and outdoor wear, while accessories and footwear generated 9 percent of sales.

CORPORATE CITIZENSHIP

American Eagle Outfitters was involved in two lawsuits regarding its business practices in 1998. In the first case, clothing retailer Abercrombie & Fitch filed a lawsuit against the company over alleged imitation of its products and operations. American Eagle Outfitters responded to the suit in a company press release, saying it was "meritless, frivolous, and bordering on ridiculous. For example, we're being sued for using primary colors and 'all natural fabrics.'"

The second litigation, filed in federal court, involves two Detroit teenagers who were detained at an American Eagle Outfitters store at an area mall on suspicion of shoplifting T-shirts. The lawsuit, which asks for damages of $21 million, alleges that the store clerks monitored the 18- and 19-year-old African-America customers very closely. After they left the store, they were approached by an American Eagle employee and a mall security guard who took them to an office where police later interrogated and handcuffed them. According to the *Detroit Free Press*, "Because store employees said they were missing some T-shirts, police examined the T-shirts the teens had on under their sweater vests. Police concluded their shirts did not come from the store. But they confiscated their vests, which the teens had bought the previous day, and said they would return them only if the two could produce receipts." The teens alleged that they were singled out because they are African-Americans. Joe Kerin, executive vice president of American Eagle Outfitters, responded in the *Detroit Free Press* by saying that "American Eagle Outfitters has a strong history of nondiscrimination. We hired a law firm that reported to us that what happened in the store had nothing to do with race discrimination."

EMPLOYMENT

In the late 1990s, American Eagle Outfitters employed approximately 6,700 people in its 330 store locations and Warrendale headquarters. An executive vice president of store operations, six regional managers, and 37 district managers—each of whom supervises an average of nine stores—are responsible for store operations. A store manager, two assistant managers, and a mix of 9 to 15 full- and part-time sales associates make up the sales teams in individual stores.

In 1997, the company introduced a new in-store training program to provide on-site training and skills development for the stores' sales and managerial staff members. Called AE University, the user-friendly training system includes a video that employees can use at their own pace. In addition to the training program, in 1997 American Eagle also introduced a new sales incentive program called AE Rewards. In this program, sales associates earn points for achieving sales productivity goals; these points can be redeemed for merchandise from an AE Rewards catalog.

American Eagle Outfitters posts current job openings at its home office, as well as field positions, on its web site. Available positions are coded in the job description, and applications may be made directly from the web site. Medical, dental, and life insurance; short- and long-term disability; six paid holidays and three personal days a year; merchandise discounts; a matching 401(k) program; profit sharing; and an employee stock purchase plan make up the benefits package offered to company employees.

SOURCES OF INFORMATION

Bibliography

"American Eagle Outfitters, Inc." *Hoover's Online,* June 1998. Available at http://www.hoovers.com.

American Eagle Outfitters, Inc. 1997 Annual Report. Warrendale, PA: American Eagle Outfitters, 1997.

Lindeman, Teresa F. "Pennsylvania-Based American Eagle Outfitters Rides High on Youth Wave." *Knight-Ridder/Tribune Business News,* 28 April 1998.

"The New Retail Establishment: Twelve Chains that Are Setting the Pace in Today's Men's Wear Scene." *Daily News Record,* 9 February 1998.

Oguntoyinbo, Lekan. "Teenagers Sue Store, Mall, Claiming Discrimination." *The Detroit Free Press,* 25 April 1998.

———. "Clothier Stands by its Actions in Dispute." *Detroit Free Press,* 31 March 1998.

Palmieri, Jean. "Santa Smiles on Jay Jacobs, American Eagle; Men's Sweaters and Suits Help Chains Register 18% Gains in December." *Daily News Record,* 7 January 1998.

Waxler, Caroline. "Eagle Swoops." *Forbes,* 15 June 1998.

For an annual report:
telephone: (724)776-4857

For additional industry research:
Investigate companies by their Standard Industrial Classification Codes, also known as SICs. American Eagle Outfitters' primary SICs are:

2311 Men/Boys' Suits & Coats

2321 Men/Boys' Shirts

2325 Men/Boys' Trousers & Slacks

2331 Women/Misses' Blouses & Shirts

2337 Women/Misses' Suits & Coats

2339 Women/Misses' Outerwear NEC

2387 Apparel Belts

3143 Men's Footwear, Except Athletic

3144 Women's Footwear, Except Athletic

American Express Company

FOUNDED: 1850

Contact Information:
HEADQUARTERS: 200 Vesey St.
  New York, NY 10285
PHONE: (212)640-2000
FAX: (212)619-9802
URL: http://www.americanexpress.com

OVERVIEW

American Express is a financial institution that provides its customers with various services in the travel, financial, and network services industries. The company's largest division, Travel Related Services (TRS), is home to the American Express cards. American Express TRS also serves as a worldwide travel agency, publishing related magazines as well. TRS is located in 160 countries. Another division, American Express Financial Advisors, offers investment counseling services and markets life insurance, investment funds, annuities, mutual funds, and financial advisory services. A third division, American Express Bank/Travelers Cheque recently took over responsibility for the travelers cheque portion of American Express business, counted as part of the Travel Related Services division until 1998. This division also provides loans and other financial products and services to the company's international clientele.

COMPANY FINANCES

Net revenues for American Express rose 8.4 percent in 1997 to $17.8 billion, compared with $16.4 billion in 1996 and $15.9 billion in 1995. Helping the company to achieve this growth, according to its annual report, were increases in worldwide billed business, growth and wider interest margins in outstanding cardmember loans, and higher management and distribution fees. Of 1997 revenues ($17.8 billion), the majority came from the Travel Related Services division, which earned $12.6 billion. American Express Financial Advisors earned $4.6 billion, and American Express Bank/Travelers Cheque earned $637 million. The Corporate and Other division reported 1997 revenues of $123 million.

First quarter 1998 net revenues were reported as $4.5 billion, up 8.6 percent from first quarter 1997 ($4.1 billion). Growth for 1998 was attributed to the company's Travel Related Services and Financial Advisors divisions. Revenues for TRS were up 18 percent from the previous year, due to factors such as more cardholders and higher cardmember spending, which American Express attributed in part to its Membership Rewards program. The American Express Financial Advisors division also reported 18-percent growth over first quarter 1997, reflecting stock market appreciation, higher sales of mutual funds and other investment vehicles, and an increase in the company's managed assets.

Earnings per share (EPS) for American Express rose 6.7 percent from 1996 to 1997, from $3.90 to $4.16. In previous years, American Express EPS were $3.10 (1995), $2.69 (1994), and $2.93 (1993). Cash dividends of $.90 per share were declared in 1997, equal to those paid in 1996. Earnings per share for the first quarter of 1998 were $.98, up 4.3 percent from first quarter 1997 EPS of $.09. American Express's stock price hovered around $103 per share in mid-1998. The company's 52-week high was $108.63 per share, and its 52-week low was $70.75. This represented significant improvement from its five-year low of $22.38 per share.

ANALYSTS' OPINIONS

As seen by many analysts, American Express was a company pulling itself out of a slump, one limb at a time. The company's early refusal to adopt ideas of joint ventures for issuing credit and charge cards put American Express far behind its chief competitors. However, the company has seen significant improvement under CEO Harvey Golub, who took command of the company in 1993. As reported by John Greenwald in *Time,* American Express raised its share of the $469 billion card market from 18.3 to 18.9 percent in the first half of 1997, reversing a 10-year trend of decreasing market share. Wall Street's opinion has also risen since Golub took over, and American Express stock shares have risen to their highest numbers yet—they were around $103 per share in mid-1998. Recommendations for purchase of American Express stock varied among investment analysts, ranging from "hold" to "strong buy," with roughly equal frequency.

One obstacle facing the company was Visa's refusal to allow American Express to issue Visa cards. This rule applies to banks as well, who cannot conduct joint efforts with American Express to issue Visa cards. Taken to court, Visa's rule still stands. Therefore, most new cardholders are those who have switched from another credit card company due to low introductory percentage rates offered for a limited time. These customers come

FINANCES:

American Express Net Revenues, 1994-1997 (billion dollars)

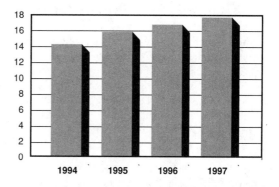

and go as competing companies offer these rates frequently. Despite this and other obstacles, many analysts see American Express as a company with significant advantages. First, it stole market share from Visa and MasterCard in 1997. The Nilson Report for 1996 showed the amounts charged on American Express cards rose 15.6 percent, whereas Visa's rose 15.5 percent and MasterCard's rose only 9.6 percent. Furthermore, 92 of the Fortune 100 companies use American Express corporate cards. Even with this good news, analysts agree American Express must remain assertive in marketing efforts.

One of the company's strengths is its progress in data mining. To simplify, American Express functions as the payment processor for the merchant and the credit card issuer. This puts the company in a very good position to know a lot about its customers' purchases. As CEO Harvey Golub stated in *Forbes,* "Say you go to a lot of northern Italian restaurants on the Upper West Side, and a new one opens up . . . We can get you to try the new restaurant by, say, giving you a bottle of wine when you go in." Most analysts agree this personalizing strategy has great hopes for the company. Data American Express receives about its customers has been far more informative than that acquired by Visa and MasterCard.

HISTORY

Henry Wells formed American Express in 1850 with two of his competitors in the delivery services area. He merged the company with Merchants Union Express in 1868 to create a money order that would compete with those offered at government post offices. Travelers

FAST FACTS:
About American Express Company

Ownership: American Express is a publicly owned company traded on the New York Stock Exchange, Boston Stock Exchange, Chicago Stock Exchange, Pacific Stock Exchange, London Stock Exchange, Swiss Stock Exchange, Dusseldorf Stock Exchange, Frankfurt Stock Exchange, Paris Stock Exchange, and the Brussels Stock Exchange.

Ticker symbol: AXP

Officers: Harvey Golub, Chmn. & CEO, 59, $3,200,000; Kenneth I. Chenault, Pres. & COO, 46, $2,030,769; Richard Karl Goeltz, VChmn. & CFO, 55, $1,160,000

Employees: 73,620

Principal Subsidiary Companies: Among the many subsidiaries of American Express are: American Express Bank International, American Express Financial Corporation, American Express Publishing Corp., American Express Student Funding, Inc., American Express Travel Related Services Company, Inc., and IDS Securities Corporation. Select foreign subsidiaries include: AEB - International Portfolios Management Company (Luxembourg), AllCard Service GmbH (Germany), and Havas Voyages American Express (France—20–percent ownership).

Chief Competitors: As a provider of travel, financial, and investment services, American Express Company's primary competitors include: Accor; Advance Publications; Advanta; Allstate; Banc One; Barclays; Chase Manhattan; Citicorp; Dean Witter; Discover; First Chicago NBD; First USA; General Motors; Household International; John Hancock; MasterCard; MBNA; Merrill Lynch; New York Times; Prudential; Visa; and World Travel.

Cheques were introduced in 1891 after Wells' partner William Fargo experienced currency difficulties in France.

The American Express card was introduced in 1958 with no credit limits, but cardholders were required to pay off the balance each month. Under the guidance of CEO James Robinson, American Express aimed to become a financial services marketplace. Over a period of 10 years, American Express bought the Boston Company, a bank; Balcor, a real estate company; Lehman Brothers, an investment banking company; and three brokerages—Investors Diversified Services (IDS), E.F. Hutton, and Shearson Loeb Rhoades. Each of these financial institutions was eventually sold and brought together (with the exception of IDS) under the name Shearson Lehman Brothers. Also, in an effort to compete with MasterCard and Visa, American Express launched the Optima card (which allowed cardholders to carry balances) in 1987. However, having no former involvement with underwriting, the company incurred many losses.

The financial marketplace strategy failed, and American Express saw a decrease in profits in the early 1990s. It did, however, purchase Lifeco Services Corporation in 1989, giving American Express the fifth largest travel institution in the United States. Unfortunately, the American Express card lost market share in the early 1990s, and Robinson was replaced with a new CEO, Harvey Golub, in 1993. Under Golub's vision, American Express restructured its divisions to work in unison. Golub and company president Kenneth Chenault sold the brokerage institutions and improved the company's travel division by buying U.S. offices and international accounts of Thomas Cook. The Optima card was brought back to life, and the company's credit card market share increased. This was in part due to joint ventures with other companies, and in part to the company's renewed emphasis on increasing the number of vendors offering the American Express card by reducing the company's take on each purchase.

STRATEGY

Offering a strand of new products each year is one part of American Express's strategy to compete with other credit card issuers. It jointly developed cards with Delta Air Lines Inc., ITT Sheraton, Hilton Hotels Inc., and United Airlines Inc. American Express also made deals with the New York Rangers and Knicks involving various benefits like frequent flyer miles and discounts on hotels. In other efforts to expand, the company began offering credit cards in Taiwan, Hong Kong, Britain, and Canada. It has also been targeting the younger market, spending $266 million on advertising, much of which highlights celebrities such as Jerry Seinfeld and Tiger Woods using their cards.

One of the company's key strategies in 1997 was to better meet the credit needs of small business owners. They aggressively targeted the lending business and ended the year with lending balances triple those of a year ago. American Express began offering a Small Business Corporate Optima Platinum Card and later introduced a joint venture with AT&T Capital, providing financing for smaller capital expenditures. At the end of 1997, they began testing an auto leasing service.

American Express's growth strategy focused on three main themes: "opening the American Express network, expanding our presence in financial services, and deepening our penetration of markets outside the United States." "Opening the American Express network" referred to the company's practice of partnering with other credit card issuers, and the company even established a separate organization to manage this business segment. In 1997, they signed agreements with 10 new partners outside the United States. "Expanding our presence in financial services" translated into focusing on increasing brand awareness in the financial marketplace as a trusted provider of financial services—and not just a card and travel services provider. American Express planned to use several avenues to do this, including retail channels, the workplace, and third-party financial institutions.

The third part of the company's strategy was international expansion. Many analysts see credit institutions as a mature business in the United States. Competition in this field is fierce, and many companies have taken their focus overseas. More and more people in developed countries were moving into the middle-class each year, giving markets overseas quite an appeal. During 1997 American Express introduced 20 new consumer and corporate cards in foreign markets, including England, Canada, and Hong Kong. The company also made deals with banks in Portugal, Greece, Israel, South Africa, and Turkey to distribute charge and credit cards. American Express established another division of the company, Global Network Services to further this company goal.

INFLUENCES

American Express's early vision under James Robinson led to a strategy of climbing the ladder of success alone. For example, American Airlines held talks with American Express in efforts to offer a co-branded credit card featuring frequent flier miles. American Express quickly rejected this offer. Similar offers by other companies were turned down as well. American Express stuck to its goal of being an all-in-one, convenient financial institution. Problems arose, however, when customers didn't see a need for an all-in-one finance center. They continued to conduct financial affairs separately with brokers, banks, and mutual funds. Even still, the company refused to conduct joint business deals with other companies. This decision caused American Express's market share to go from 26 percent in the United States in 1985 to 15 percent by 1995. After James Robinson's replacement as CEO in 1993, Golub made great efforts to get back on the competitive track. Since his takeover, American Express's number of cardholders has increased from 26 to 30 million. The measure of charges has increased as well, 37 percent or $162 billion. Income after taxes for the company almost doubled, and the stock more than quadrupled as well.

Although this growth was impressive, a lot of harm had already been done since American Express was behind the times in seeking joint ventures. Even with the

CHRONOLOGY:

Key Dates for American Express Company

1850: Founded

1868: Merges with Merchants Union Express

1891: Introduces Travelers Cheques

1914: Diversifies into the travel industry

1918: American Railway Express Co. subsidiary is created

1929: Chase Securities Corporation acquires control of the company

1944: Ralph T. Reed becomes president

1958: American Express card is introduced

1968: Buys Fireman's Fund American Insurance

1970: Sells freight operations acquired during WWII

1977: James Robinson becomes CEO

1981: Purchases Shearson Loeb Rhoades and the Boston Company

1982: Reorganizes under the holding company American Express Corp.

1984: Purchases Lehman Brothers

1987: Launches Optima card; acquires E.F. Hutton

1989: Purchases Lifeco Services Corporation

1993: Harvey Golub becomes CEO

1996: Launches American Express's Charge Against Hunger

1997: Begins testing an auto leasing service

1998: Offers the Blue Credit Card in the United Kingdom

company's measure of charges growing 15 percent ($21 billion) in 1995, it was slim compared to Visa's growth of $162 billion. However, in 1997 American Express actually raised its share of general card volume to 18.9 percent of the total market. This resulted in the company taking only a small part of Visa's sizeable market away, but it was a marked improvement nonetheless. The company has been able to do this in part because it has increased its volume from being offered at approximately 72 percent of merchants to 92 percent. However, they had to take a cut in the amount of discounts taken from sales in order to convince more merchants to offer the card—they reduced American Express shares of each transaction from 3.22 percent to 2.74 percent (compared to less than 2 percent taken by Visa).

CURRENT TRENDS

Expansion has been one of American Express's most recent strategic shifts. It signed a deal with Microsoft to develop an on-line service where business travelers could make reservations and purchase tickets from personal computers or laptops. Another area of expansion involved the company's interest in purchasing distinguished accounting firms. The purchase of several divisions of Checkers, Simon & Rosner LLP (later renamed Chicago Metro Area office of American Express Tax & Business Services) in early 1997 presented several advantages for American Express. First, the company automatically doubled its tax and business services organization in size. Second, customers' needs were satisfied better with the combined assistance of a major corporation and the personal services of a local firm. Various services offered have included employee benefits, business and technology consulting, tax planning and compliance, retirement assistance, bookkeeping, estate planning, and litigation support.

Another popular trend American Express took advantage of was the practice of associating its business with a charitable cause. For example, American Express's Charge Against Hunger campaign advertised that for every purchase made with American Express credit cards for a certain time period in 1996, the company agreed to donate $.03 to anti-hunger organization Share Our Strength. A recent survey (1995) by a Boston consulting firm asked company executives about the purpose behind such campaigns. The results were: 93 percent said "to build deeper relationships and trust with customers," 89 percent said "to enhance a reputation or image," and 50 percent said "to increase sales," according to Romesh Ratnesar in *The New Republic.*

PRODUCTS

Products offered by American Express include consumer credit cards, corporate card services, Membership Rewards, travel services and publications, and financial investment and banking services. Magazines offered by the Travel Related Services division include *Food & Wine, Travel & Leisure,* and *Your Company.* One new product offering in 1998 was the Blue Credit Card in the United Kingdom, targeted to the country's younger (23-35 age group) market. The card offered a simple cashback reward, appealing to what American Express considers the younger, modern lifestyles.

CORPORATE CITIZENSHIP

American Express's community involvement remains impressive. Areas identified as priorities for funding include community service, cultural heritage, and economic independence. The company has supported United Way organizations across the United States for years and is known for aiding those in need due to natural disasters through the American Red Cross and other agencies. The company also sponsored the AIDS Walks in New York City, Minneapolis, Washington, D.C., and Boston. Other contributions include renovations of housing facilities for low-income families; clean up efforts of parks, schools, and neighborhoods; and involvement in Meals on Wheels, a program designed to aid the elderly.

The company also surrounds much of its community involvement around the environment. Recent grants include: World Monuments Watch, an effort to protect endangered historical sites worldwide; New York City Interactive Cultural Guide and Calendar, an on-line service listing cultural events and institutions in New York City; Czech Greenways, a fund for Central/Eastern Europe to assist in creating a tourism course around Prague; Frederick R. Weisman Art Museum, a display in Minneapolis of paintings by significant African-American artists; and Ontario Heritage Foundation, an effort to persuade youngsters to volunteer preservation activities in Canada.

GLOBAL PRESENCE

American Express conducts business throughout the United States and in more than 160 countries. Sales in 1997 for the United States alone were $13.40 billion (75 percent of total sales for that year). Europe came in second that year with sales totaling $2.20 billion (12 percent of total annual sales). The Asia/Pacific region accounted for $1.37 billion (7 percent of sales), while other regions totaled $1.27 million (7 percent of total sales). Of the company's 73,620 employees, 28,929 were employed outside the United States.

American Express Travelers Cheques are used worldwide, and its international corporate card business is growing. American Express took advantage of co-branding opportunities by introducing joint corporate cards with NatWest in the United Kingdom, Banco Bital in Mexico, Credit Lyonnais in France, and Qantas Airways in Australia. In 1997, the company launched its proprietary Corporate Card for Small Business in Australia and the Canadian Government Card. American Express also launched a global advertising campaign that focused on marketing its financial and travel services to areas around the world, including Asia and Latin America. Despite its best efforts, however, it did not gain overall market share in most international markets. In 1997's fourth quarter, card billings and travel sales in Southeast Asia slowed.

SOURCES OF INFORMATION

Bibliography

"American Express Acquires Accounting Divisions." *Fox News Network,* 19 March 1997. Availble at http://www.foxnews.com.

American Express Annual Report. 3 June 1998. Available at http://www.americanexpress.com.

"American Express Company." *Hoover's Online.* 3 June 1998. Available at http://www.hoovers.com.

American Express Company Web Site. 3 June 1998. Available at http://www.americanexpress.com.

Day, Kathleen. "American Express Recharging Its Image." *The Washington Post,* 29 March 1997.

Greenwald, John. "CHARGE!" *Time,* 12 January 1998.

Levere, Jane. "Microsoft-American Express Pact Shakes the U.S. Travel Industry." *The New York Times,* 3-4 August 1996.

Oliver, Susan. "The Battle of the Credit Cards." *Forbes,* 1 July 1996.

Ratnesar, Romesh. "Doing Well By Doing Good." *The New Republic,* 6 January 1997.

Yang, Catherine. "Are Visa and MasterCard Hogging the Business?" *Business Week,* 17 February 1977.

For an annual report:

on the Internet at: http://www.americanexpress.com/corp/annual_report/annual97/index.shtml **or** write: Corporate Secretary's Office, American Express Co., 200 Vesey St., New York, NY 10285

For additional industry research:

Investigate companies by their Standard Industrial Classification Codes, also known as SICs. American Express' primary SICs are:

4724 Travel Agencies

6189 Asset-Backed Securities

6211 Security Brokers, Dealers, and Flotation Companies

American Greetings

FOUNDED: 1906

Contact Information:
HEADQUARTERS: 1 American Rd.
    Cleveland, OH 44144
PHONE: (216)252-7300
FAX: (216)252-6777
URL: http://www.americangreetings.com

OVERVIEW

American Greetings is the world's largest publicly owned maker of greeting cards and other "social-expression" products. It controls 35 percent of the U.S. greeting card market, a second-place seat behind Hallmark's 43 percent market share. American Greetings is number one in Canada, New Zealand, Australia, and South Africa. Its products appear in approximately 100,000 retail stores in over 75 countries, including all 682 Toys 'R' Us stores in the United States and two out of every three mass-merchandiser stores. Sixty percent of drug-store chains carry American Greetings products, as do one-third of grocery stores. Daily sales total millions. In 1997 general greeting cards accounted for 44 percent of American Greetings' sales, while seasonal cards accounted for 22 percent and wrapping paper and party supplies accounted for 18 percent. The balance represents sales of the company's wide range of other products, including candles, reading glasses, and home-educational materials. Recent years have seen a greater diversification among products offered, though the company has been consistently profitable throughout its history.

COMPANY FINANCES

The year 1997 was American Greetings' ninety-first consecutive year of improved sales. Net sales of general cards rose by 10.3 percent, and sales of seasonal cards rose by 12.5 percent. Sales in 1997 were just over $2.1 billion, an increase of 7.95 percent over 1996, for a net income of $167.1 million. American Greetings' stock price rose by more than 60 percent for the 1997 fiscal

year. Shareholder equity measured $1,361,655, or $18.16 per share. Net earnings per share were $2.23 with dividends of $.67 per share paid. In April 1998, the company paid its 186th straight quarterly dividend.

Utilizing resources from two 1997 divestitures, American Greetings bought back 4.5 million outstanding Class A shares—about 6 percent of the total equity—in 1998. Class B shares are not publicly traded. Class A shares have been moved from the NASDAQ exchange to the NYSE exchange where they have been traded since February 1998. The company expects this move to result in lower volatility and greater liquidity for the stock. Its total market capitalization exceeds $3 billion.

ANALYSTS' OPINIONS

American Greetings is noted both for its perpetual improvement in sales and for diversifying its product lines. In *Supermarket News,* Arthur Andersen's Michael Killeen characterized American Greetings' management as "very astute marketing people."

HISTORY

American Greetings was founded in 1906 by Jacob Sapirstein, a Polish immigrant who had worked in his relatives' hotel card shop. He began by purchasing picture postcards and selling them wholesale out of a horse-drawn wagon. The business became a family tradition when Sapirstein's son Irving became his partner. Shortly thereafter, Irving's brother Morris joined in what came to be called the Sapirstein Greeting Card Company. By 1932 the Sapirsteins were producing their own cards.

In the 1940s the company changed its name to American Greetings Publishers. The company went public in 1952 and was incorporated under the name it retains today. Business continued to thrive, and in 1967 the company introduced the popular character Holly Hobbie. By 1985 it was a billion-dollar operation.

STRATEGY

Demographic research is the core of American Greetings' marketing plan. The company studies the consumer bases of the stores that carry its products, assesses the most viable target markets, and tailors products to factors like age, gender, and ethnicity. In 1991 American Greetings established its own "research council" in order to better understand the purchasing habits of grocery-store patrons. They found that women between the ages of 55 and 64 are the largest consumer group, many of whom buy several dozen cards per year. The research

FINANCES:

American Greetings Net Sales, 1994-1997 (million dollars)

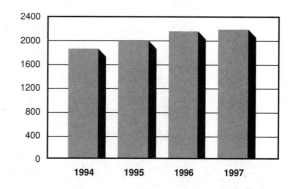

American Greetings 1997 Stock Prices (dollars)

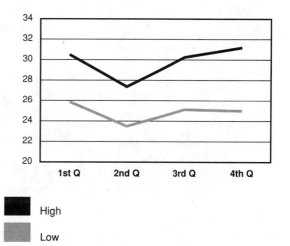

High

Low

council encourages stores to be experimental in matters of marketing and merchandising. In 1997 American Greetings released a three-year study entitled "Winning the Battle of Consumer Perceptions," which focused on maximizing profit by organizing general-merchandise and health- and beauty-product displays.

Identifying new and existing markets, efficiently creating innovative products, and rigorous test marketing can be linked with American Greetings' success. Among a staff of more than 400 artistic personnel, the "Retail Creative Services" group designs themed display units for different seasons and holidays. One example is

A woman reading through American Greetings' large selection of Easter cards to choose the most personal messages for her family members. (Courtesy of American Greetings.)

the popular "Wacky Factory," an eye-catching, 13-foot-tall fixture for shelving Easter-related products. Additionally, electronic touch-screen kiosks with party planning pointers are distributed by this group to be tested and used in U.S. grocery stores to promote supermarkets as places to purchase party products.

In 1997 American Greetings revamped its market strategy with a 16-month in-house campaign called "The All New American Way." It replaced nearly 80 percent of its card designs in approximately 30,000 retail outlets in an effort to accommodate a broader array of today's American lifestyles, but birthday and general cards still form the backbone of the updated collections. Examples

of their emphasized content include multicultural themes and communication across generations in families. According to company president Ed Fruchtenbaum, "This is a magnitude of change in greeting cards seen only once each generation."

As part of "The All New American Way," the company introduced the "Just Because" line in 1998. The collection boasts all-purpose (or "anytime") greeting cards; this category of general cards accounts for about 15 percent of output. The first year of production involved a $20 million marketing campaign, the first of such moves for American Greetings in a decade. Magazine advertisements for the "Just Because" line featured glued-in replicas of cards sent by celebrities for reasons other than special or calendar-based occasions. For example, the ads featured a card from Dr. Ruth Westheimer to a fellow therapist in whom she "can confide [she] stole this card," and one from Joan Rivers to her daughter to report on a sale of shoes. The company expects the line to boost overall sales as consumers realize that they need not observe a special time or event in order to send someone a greeting card.

The company's candle subsidiary, GuildHouse Candles was added in 1997. American Greetings has been a player in the candle market for decades, but it has now allocated considerable resources—including full-time sales and marketing staffs—toward turning what was once just a product line into a business entity in its own right. In a 1997 quarterly report to shareholders, Edward Fruchtenbaum said of the launch, ". . . GuildHouse can compete better if it can think and act like a candle company, not a greeting card company that happens to sell candles." One objective is to place the candles in stores where the company has not traditionally sold greeting cards. In 1996 American Greetings undertook the same type of institutional upgrade for its DesignWare line of party supplies as its first "strategic business unit."

INFLUENCES

Recent consolidations in the U.S. retail sector—such as the closings of F. W. Woolworth and Lechmere, as well as mergers among the pharmacy chains—may pose some challenges to American Greetings if there are fewer outlets in which to sell products, but the risk is difficult to gauge. In 1997 American Greetings sold its Acme (picture frames) and Wilhold (hair care) divisions, which were not profitable enough to remain part of the business from a long-term strategic point of view.

Investment in technology has been a priority for American Greetings. Sales personnel use laptop computers to keep track of information on sales calls, for example. The company's distribution systems are automated, thus facilitating speed and accuracy in filling orders. In addition, printing costs have fallen with the company's use of high-tech Komori presses, which are faster and deliver a higher-quality print job.

CURRENT TRENDS

American Greetings is entering the age of electronic greeting cards. In addition to selling cards through its web site, it has introduced a CD-ROM called *American Greetings CreataCard Plus,* which lets consumers use their home computers to create their own cards. Also in 1997, the company entered into an exclusive, three-year agreement with America Online, through which it will

FAST FACTS:
About American Greetings

Ownership: American Greetings is a publicly owned company traded on the New York Stock Exchange.

Ticker symbol: AM

Officers: Morry Weiss, Chmn. & CEO; Edward Fruchtenbaum, Pres. & COO

Employees: Over 21,000

Chief Competitors: American Greetings' competitors include: Hallmark; Gibson Greetings; and Factory Card Outlet.

DID YOU KNOW THAT. . .

- Americans spend more than $6 billion a year on greeting cards and related social expression products, sending more than seven billion greeting cards to loved ones?

- Christmas, Valentine's Day, and Easter are the top three card-sending holidays?

- "to express friendship" is the second most popular nonholiday reason for people to send a card?

- Father's Day is one of the top three occasions of the year for sales of humorous cards?

- a full 30 percent of American Greeting's Father's Day cards are funny, compared to only 18 percent of Mother's Day cards?

- on Mother's Day 1998, approximately 178 million cards were sent, compared to 100 million for Father's Day?

provide over 10 million subscribers access to more than 1,000 "paperless" cards that can be sent as e-mail messages. Among the points in the company's mission statement is a commitment to "use technology to advance sales, operations and retail partnerships."

CHRONOLOGY:

Key Dates for American Greetings

1906: The Sapirstein Greeting Card Company is founded by Jacob Saperstein

1918: Saperstein's son, nine-year-old Irving, becomes the first partner

1928: A contract worth $24,000 becomes the company's largest order to date

1932: Starts manufacturing its own line of greeting cards

1940: Company is renamed American Greetings Publishers

1944: Incorporates as American Greetings Corporation

1952: American Greetings goes public

1967: Holly Hobbie is introduced

1972: Ziggy is introduced as "the world's most loveable loser"

1977: Holly Hobbie is the most popular female licensed character in the world

1985: Sales pass $1 billion for the first time

1992: American Greetings purchases Custom Expressions, Inc., makers of a video touchscreen customized card creator; Hallmark sues for patent infringement

1997: American Greetings enters into a three-year exclusive agreement with America Online to provide electronic cards that can be sent as e-mails

In 1997, following a successful test-marketing scheme, American Greetings broke into the $630 million market for home educational products by introducing its line of 330 Learning Horizons brand materials. These items include workbooks, flash cards, puzzles, stickers, and audiotapes, which are aimed at children attending preschool through grade six. The average price for the products is $4.00. For its research phase, the company consulted a panel of parents and educational professionals who could provide feedback and advice about the developing products. American Greetings has noticed an upswing in purchases of at-home educational aids by parents and grandparents, whereas teachers had once been the primary buyers. School-supply vendors had been the traditional outlet for such products, but Learning Horizons can be found in grocery stores. In *Supermarket News*, execu-

tive director Mark Schantz describes the products as "a one-stop shopping experience for parents who are interested in helping a child who may be having difficulty in school, or is bored or wants something enriching." Unlike many of the company's other products, Learning Horizons does not involve any licensed images.

The White House has selected American Greetings to design President Clinton's official Christmas card since 1993. The company's other significant presence at the White House is its sponsorship of the annual Easter Egg Roll, in which it has participated through the 1990s. The governors of Ohio, Arkansas, Kentucky, and Tennessee have also selected American Greetings to produce their holiday cards.

PRODUCTS

The mainstay of American Greetings is its card business, which includes general greeting and seasonal cards. The company has diversified into the areas of various consumer products, such as seasonal wrapping paper (under the Plus Mark brand name); supplemental educational products (under the Learning Horizons brand name); nonprescription reading glasses (under the industry-leading Magnivision brand name); candles (under the Guild-House brand name); party supplies (under the Design-Ware brand name); stickers; plush toys; and stationery. The company has also added licensed images of children's characters to its product lines. American Greetings is party to several multiyear agreements, which allow them to use "Rugrats," "Teletubbies," and Richard Scarry's characters on products including cards, balloons, wrapping paper, and stickers.

GLOBAL PRESENCE

American Greetings operates all over the world under various subsidiaries' trade names. A presence has recently been established in the South Pacific, with the acquisition of John Sands in New Zealand and Australia, where it now enjoys a 44 percent market share. In 1998 its British holding company, UK Greetings Ltd., acquired Camden Graphics Group, which it hopes will serve it well in a nation where the annual greeting-card consumption is a staggering 41 per capita. The deal was expected to take American Greetings' British market share from 11 percent to 15 percent. Subsidiary Carlton Cards' products are widely distributed in Great Britain and lead the Canadian greeting-card marketplace as well.

EMPLOYMENT

In the late 1990s, the company started a "Chairman's Award" to salute employees who have shown excellence in "community service, customer service, innovation, personal initiative, and teamwork." The company sponsors a defined benefit health care plan that furnishes postretirement benefits to personnel (65 years or older) who have worked full-time for 15 years and were hired before 1992.

SOURCES OF INFORMATION

Bibliography

Alaimo, Dan. "American Greetings Rewriting 80% of Its Cards." *Supermarket News,* 16 June 1997.

American Greetings 1997 Annual Report. Cleveland, OH: American Greetings Corporation, 1997.

"American Greetings Adds Clifford the Big Red Dog and Teletubbies to Licensed Products." *PR Newswire,* 18 March 1998.

"American Greetings Announces Acquisition of London-Based Camden Graphics." *PR Newswire,* 10 March 1998.

"American Greetings Announces Completion of 4.5 Million Share Repurchase Plan." *PR Newswire,* 5 March 1998.

"American Greetings Corporation." *Hoover's Online.* April 1998. Available at http://www.hoovers.com.

"American Greetings Corporation." *International Directory of Company Histories.* Detroit, MI: St. James Press, 1995.

"American Greetings Declares 186th Consecutive Dividend." *PR Newswire,* 7 April 1998.

"American Greetings Now Listed as 'AM' on the New York Stock Exchange." *PR Newswire,* 11 February 1998.

"American Greetings to Sell Units." *PR Newswire,* 7 July 1997.

Coleman, Calmetta Y. "American Greetings Thinks Time for 'Anytime' Is Now." *Wall Street Journal,* 24 March 1998.

Elson, Joel. "American Greetings Launches DesignWare." *Supermarket News,* 24 February 1997.

———. "Educational Line to Show and Tell at FMI." *Supermarket News,* 5 May 1997.

First Quarter Report to Shareholders. Cleveland, OH: American Greetings Corporation, July 1997.

Mendelson, Seth. "Above the Crowd." *Supermarket Business,* June 1996.

———. "Multimedia Yields Multiple Benefits." *Supermarket Business,* March 1996.

"Profit from Perceptions." *Supermarket Business,* 2 May 1997.

Second Quarter Report to Shareholders. Cleveland, OH: American Greetings Corporation, September 1997.

Snyder, Karyn. "Greetings: Card Company Wants to Help Drugstores Increase Profits." *Drug Topics,* 16 September 1996.

Third Quarter Report to Shareholders. Cleveland, OH: American Greetings Corporation, January 1998.

Troy, Mike. "Home Study Scores Big." *Discount Store News,* 2 June 1997.

Turcsik, Richard. "American Greetings Kiosks Aid Parties." *Supermarket News,* 13 January 1997.

Veiders, Christina. "American Greetings Poised to Grow at Retail." *Supermarket News,* 2 March 1998.

Wildemuth, Scott. "I-Commerce Is in the Cards." *Datamation,* October 1997.

For an annual report:
telephone: (216)252-7300

For additional industry research:
Investigate companies by their Standard Industrial Classification Codes, also known as SICs. American Greetings' primary SIC is:

2771 Greeting Cards

American Stock Exchange, Inc.

ALSO KNOWN AS: AMEX
FOUNDED: 1911 as the American Curb Market Association

Contact Information:

HEADQUARTERS: 86 Trinity Pl.
   New York, NY 10006-1881
PHONE: (212)306-1000
FAX: (212)306-1644
URL: http://www.amex.com

OVERVIEW

The American Stock Exchange is one of three leading U.S. markets in securities, or financial assets, of which stocks are its principal article of trade. Stocks are a form of security whereby individuals can purchase partial ownership and voting power in a publicly owned corporation, and a stock exchange is an environment in which traders buy and sell stocks on behalf of their clients.

The American Stock Exchange, or AMEX, as it is called, has forged its identity in contrast to its two larger rivals, the older and more established New York Stock Exchange (NYSE) and the more dynamic NASDAQ (National Securities Dealers Automated Quotations). It trades a much smaller volume than either. Generally, the AMEX is home to smaller, more entrepreneurial companies than the NYSE, which lists such giants as IBM and McDonnell Douglas. This is because the AMEX has less strict requirements than its older Wall Street neighbor, whose conditions for listing a company include $2.5 million in annual before-tax earnings. Like the NYSE, however, the AMEX is an auction exchange, a traditional stock environment with traders on the floor buying and selling shares in public companies. This is in contrast with the NASDAQ, where trading takes place electronically.

Companies listing on the AMEX include Viacom, IVAX, Forest Laboratories, and Hasbro. When companies list on the AMEX, they choose a "specialist unit" of three or more stock specialists to perform their trading on the floor. The American Stock Exchange is governed by a 25-member board, including 12 representatives from the securities industry, 12 from the public, and a chairman.

In April 1998 the boards of the AMEX and the National Association of Securities Dealers (NASD), the parent of the NASDAQ, announced they had reached a definitive agreement on a plan to merge the AMEX into NASD's family of companies. Under the agreement, the AMEX will continue to operate as a separate specialist-based auction market with its own members and listed companies.

COMPANY FINANCES

At the end of 1997, AMEX listed 783 companies with a market value of $168 billion dollars. This represented the exchange's highest number of new listings this decade, up 30 percent over 1996 listings, as well as record trading volume in equities and options. On February 12, 1998, a regular membership seat sold for $460,000, the highest price ever for an AMEX seat.

ANALYSTS' OPINIONS

When *Investment Dealers Digest* referred to AMEX as "a bit of a poor relation among exchanges," it was echoing a familiar sentiment among observers such as *Barron's,* which had called it "an investment backwater" in a 1995 article. Investment industry observers, initially optimistic about the possibility that AMEX might present a substantial challenge to the NASDAQ, became more skeptical when the company failed to make substantial gains against its rival. Nonetheless, there continued to be hope for the growth of AMEX under the guidance of CEO Richard Syron.

AMEX has attracted interest from the computer industry because it is seen as the more high-tech of the two New York floor exchanges, both in its listings and in its in-house technology. *Wall Street & Technology* magazine in December 1995 praised the AMEX web site for its "winning Web alchemy" because the site promised to bring in new business to AMEX while educating visitors on the stock market.

With the proposed merger of AMEX with NASDAQ, there is much speculation as to how it will effect the industry. Some foresee higher costs and tightened liquidity, while others feel that the merger will make it easier and cheaper for those who trade in smaller stocks.

HISTORY

In the 1700s brokers began gathering in the area of the New York City docks to trade stock. This informal trading arrangement continued throughout the nineteenth century, gaining the nickname "Curb Market" because

FAST FACTS:

About American Stock Exchange, Inc.

Ownership: The American Stock Exchange is a not-for-profit auction exchange for the trading of stock in its nearly 800 listed companies.

Officers: Richard F. Syron, Chmn. & CEO; Anthony J. Boglioli, VChmn.; Max C. Chapman Jr., VChmn.; Thomas F. Ryan Jr., Pres. & COO

Employees: 670

Chief Competitors: Trading in stocks and other financial assets, the American Stock Exchange (AMEX) competes with: New York Stock Exchange (NYSE) and National Securities Dealers Automated Quotations (NASDAQ).

traders conducted their business quite literally on the curb. In 1911 this name was formalized with the formation of the New York Curb Market Association. The Curb Market finally moved indoors with the construction of the American Stock Exchange Building on Trinity Place, which commenced in 1920.

The exchange weathered the 1929 Crash and the ensuing Depression and in 1953 took its present name. Along with the NYSE, it began to make use of computers, and the two companies jointly formed the Securities Industry Automation Corporation (SIAC) in 1972. In the 1980s, AMEX experienced growth along with the rest of the stock market, and in 1987—the year of another October "crash," this one with much less severe impact—the exchange expanded its facilities. However, it continued to lag behind the NYSE and NASDAQ in volume of trade. In 1994 its board named former Boston Federal Reserve Bank President Richard Syron as its chairman and chief executive officer. During the same year, the AMEX board inaugurated a new advertising campaign to increase its business.

During 1995 the AMEX was making its presence known on the World Wide Web. Visitors to the exchange's Internet site could learn about AMEX and its listings, while listed companies could retrieve stock information. Despite some gains in 1997, the AMEX board agreed to merge with the National Association of Securities Dealers (NASD), NASDAQ's parent company, becoming an independent subsidiary of NASD and continuing as a specialist-based auction market and maintaining its members

CHRONOLOGY:

Key Dates for American Stock Exchange, Inc.

1911: Founded as the American Curb Market Association

1920: Moves indoors to the American Stock Exchange building on Trinity Place

1931: Expands its space to accommodate more trading

1953: Becomes the American Stock Exchange (AMEX)

1958: Appoints Mary Roebling governor

1972: Forms the Securities Industry Automation Corporation (SAIC) with NYSE

1977: Women begin trading on the AMEX floor

1985: Is linked electronically with the Toronto Stock Exchange

1986: Opens a European office

1987: Expands its facilities

1994: Richard Syron becomes Chairman & CEO

1995: Begins listing stock information on the World Wide Web

1997: Forms the Institutional Client Group

1998: Announces agreement to merge AMEX into National Association of Securities Dealers' (NASD) family of companies

and listings. AMEX Chairman Richard Syron believes that "this combination builds on our organizational strengths—the Amex's auction market, service orientation, and new jointly developed technology platforms and the NASD's state-of-the-art quote-driven market and strong financial resources. It optimizes value for all concerned—investors, member firms, and listed companies."

STRATEGY

In seeking to differentiate itself from its two rivals, the AMEX has sought to portray itself as more modern and high-tech than the NYSE and as a more profitable trading market than the NASDAQ. Hence it has emphasized the use of computers, becoming in 1995 the first U.S. stock exchange to create an Internet site, something

the more staid NYSE has not yet done. In portraying itself as a more lucrative market than the NASDAQ, the American Stock Exchange released an advertisement in late 1994 touting 301 companies that had switched from NASDAQ to AMEX in the seven years following the 1987 crash. On both fronts, AMEX sought to portray itself, in the words of the slogan governing its massive advertising campaign launched in the early 1990s, as "The Smarter Place to Be."

Also vital to the AMEX image is that of an exchange friendly to mid-range or small entrepreneurial companies, as opposed to the extremely large and highly organized businesses who list on the NYSE. In particular, Arthur Levitt, Jr., exchange chairman in the 1970s and chairman of the Securities and Exchange Commission (SEC) as of 1997, emphasized AMEX interest in individual investors and small, dynamic companies.

In an attempt to make it easier for quote vendors to get the information out to the customer, AMEX delisted 250 index options series. This first of many steps should help cut down on the overwhelming number of quotes with which vendors must deal.

To bring AMEX to the forefront, a 1998 partnership was formed with Reuters America Inc. to broadcast daily from the AMEX television studios. *First Business,* a live 30-minute show, was scheduled to carry 75-second financial reports. Larry Kofsky, Wall Street Business correspondent, will cover the day's stories. Live video of the exchange, as well as market reports, have been available on AMEX's web site since mid-1997.

In a move to attract new listings, the Institutional Client Group (ICG) was formed in 1997. ICG's job is to work with those in investment banking in order to aggressively woo new companies. Though AMEX listings have seen a good rise since 1995, loss of former listings have kept the overall increase minimal.

INFLUENCES

Like all segments of the investment community, the AMEX has been influenced by stock market crashes, most notably the 1929 crash. But whereas the influence of stock market fluctuations comes and goes, the influence of its rivalries continued into the late 1990s.

In the early 1990s, the American Stock Exchange directed most of its advertising efforts against NASDAQ rather than the NYSE. This was not only because NASDAQ, like AMEX, traded in emerging companies and presented less stringent listing requirements but also because the number two competitor was rapidly nearing first place. AMEX seemed to have been presented with a golden opportunity in 1995 when NASDAQ found itself caught up in a trading scandal and a Justice Department investigation. Most observers believed that AMEX would come out the winner, and, indeed, it seemed poised to do so.

Though *Investment Dealers Digest* reported in March 1995 that AMEX had spent only $679,000 on advertising in the first 11 months of 1994, as compared with $32 million for NASDAQ, AMEX appeared to have spent its dollars effectively. In one of its more successful advertisements, a full page in the *Wall Street Journal,* AMEX detailed the 301 companies that had switched from NASDAQ to AMEX in the seven years since the October 1987 crash. This resulted in enormous investor interest, particularly in one company featured in the ad, Organogenesis, which had been attempting to develop a skin substitute to assist in the healing of wounds.

But, as *Barron's* reported in February 1995, Organogenesis stock failed to perform, and a closer examination of the list of the other 300 companies showed that AMEX had in fact lost 113 of them for a variety of reasons, none of which looked good for AMEX. (Some had switched back to NASDAQ or to the NYSE, while others had been delisted because they had fallen into bankruptcy or other types of financial difficulty.)

The failure of AMEX's Emerging Company Marketplace, a venture launched in 1992 and cancelled in May 1995 by the board of directors, was a further blow to the company's confidence. But the April 1994 ascendancy of Chairman Richard Syron, who helped to smooth over difficulties between executives and traders on the floor, gave observers new hope for the future of AMEX as it continued to pursue its tradition of innovation in the market.

CURRENT TRENDS

The American Stock Exchange has tended to present itself as more forward-looking than its NYSE competitor, and as part of this it has been a leader in its use of computer technology in the marketplace. In the 1980s, it became the first stock market to introduce "touch-screen" technology for order placement on the floor. In 1996, traders on the AMEX floor began using wireless hand-held computers linked through a local area network (LAN), which made it possible for them to place orders without using the traditional hand signals that were once a colorful element of stock market trading.

Thus, it was not surprising when in 1995 the AMEX became the first U.S. exchange with a site on the Internet, which according to the company's annual report was getting 30,000 "hits" a day within a year of its establishment. The web site offers users access to general information on stocks and investments, as well as specific data on AMEX-listed companies and on the exchange itself.

PRODUCTS

The American Stock Exchange has typically traded in stocks or options, which represent the option to buy a given number of shares in a certain company over a specified time period. In 1995, several industry publications reported that AMEX would eventually move into trading futures, which involve speculation on the value of a commodity or stock at a set date in the future. Also in that year's annual report, AMEX announced a number of new derivatives, which are customized contracts whose value is derived or based on such indices as interest rates, currency exchanges, or the stock market itself. New products introduced by the AMEX Derivative Securities Division included listing on the Inter@ctive Week Internet Index, an index of 37 Internet-related companies whose name refers to *Inter@ctive Week* magazine.

To better serve its investors, AMEX unveiled a number of products in 1997. The AMEX Institutional Management (AIM) report helps their companies manage their institutional shareholder base. According to John Lafferty, president of JM Lafferty Associates Inc., "with the AIM Report, AMEX is helping companies see in precise, quantitative, and comparable terms how their stock fits with the portfolios of institutional investors. Once a company understands how it is positioned by investors, why some institutional investors hold its shares while others don't, it can articulate its aspirations in terms of the market."

Another service is the use of DIAMONDS, which trade like common stock shares. Used for the stocks in the Dow Jones Industrial Average (DJIA), DIAMONDS, according to CEO Richard Syron, will allow investors to "own a slice of the Dow Jones Industrial Average—representing the bluest of all the blue chip stocks—with a single security that is simple to trade and inexpensive to own." A DIAMONDS web site is accessible via AMEX's home page, providing FAQs, performance charts, price quotes, and other information.

Harnessing the power of the Web, AMEX also held its first online industry conference, ConferenceNet. The service facilitates fund managers' conferences on specific industries such as real estate, health care, or energy right from their desks. Video and audio presentations, graphics, and question-and-answer periods will provide investors with industry-specific information.

SOURCES OF INFORMATION

Bibliography

American Stock Exchange Annual Report. New York: American Stock Exchange, 1997.

"AMEX Boosts New Listings Effort." American Stock Exchange Press Release, 12 June 1997.

"AMEX Equity Options Trading Hits Record Volume in April." American Stock Exchange Press Release, 4 May 1998.

"AMEX Launches First Stock Market Investment Based on the Dow Jones Industrial Average." American Stock Exchange Press Release, 20 January 1998.

"AMEX Seat Sale Record at Highest Level in Exchange's History." American Stock Exchange Press Release, 12 February 1998.

"Amex Takes Action to Stem Flood of Options Quotes." *Investment Dealers' Digest,* 1 September 1997.

Barney, Lee. "Winning Webs." *Wall Street & Technology,* December 1995.

"First Live On-line Video of Wall Street Featured on New AMEX Web Site." American Stock Exchange Press Release, 9 September 1997.

Greco, Matthew. "Amex Introduces ConferenceNet." *Investor Relations Business,* 15 December 1997.

Lohse, Deborah. "Amex's Board Approves Merger Pact, with NASD Board Expected to Follow." *Wall Street Journal* Eastern Edition, 9 April 1998.

———. "Nuptials May Boost Small Caps' Status." *Wall Street Journal,* Eastern Edition, 16 March 1998.

Longo, Tracey. "Too Big For Its Britches?: As the NASD Prepares to Swallow AMEX, What Will Be the Aftertaste for Planners?" *Financial Planning,* 1 May 1998.

Lux, Hal. "Can This Exchange Be Saved?" *Investment Dealers Digest,* 11 December 1995.

Mack, Gracian. "Defining the Playing Field." *Black Enterprise,* June 1995.

Maxey, Daisy. "Merger Would Have an Impact on Funds." *Wall Street Journal,* Eastern Edition, 16 March 1998.

"NASD, AMEX Boards Approve Definitive Merger Agreement." American Stock Exchange Press Release, 9 April 1998.

"Reuters and Amex Team Up For TV!" American Stock Exchange Press Release, 6 January 1998.

Scipio, Philip. "Exchanges Share Holder Information: IROs Are the Target of This Latest Marketing Blitz by Nasdaq, Amex." *Investor Relations Business,* 2 June 1997.

"Trading Places." *The Economist,* 25 March 1995.

"Trading Records, Surge in New Stock Listings, and Promising New Products Mark 1997 as Milestone Year for American Stock Exchange." American Stock Exchange Press Release, 22 December 1997.

Wyatt, Edward A. "Here Today . . . ." *Barron's,* 27 February 1995.

For an annual report:

on the Internet at: http://www.amex.com

For additional industry research:

Investigate companies by their Standard Industrial Classification Codes, also known as SICs. The American Stock Exchange's primary SIC is:

6231 Security & Commodity Exchanges

American Suzuki Motor Corporation

OVERVIEW

Suzuki motorcycles, automobiles, all-terrain vehicles, and marine outboard motors are manufactured and sold in the United States by American Suzuki Motor Corporation (American Suzuki), a subsidiary of Japan's Suzuki Motor Corporation (Suzuki). The parent company was established in 1909 as a manufacturer of weaving machines, but after World War II it began to produce motorized vehicles. In the late 1990s Suzuki was the third-ranking manufacturer of motorcycles worldwide, behind Honda and Yamaha, as well as a prominent international manufacturer of small automobiles and marine recreational vehicles. It manufactures and distributes its products in more than 170 countries. Motorcycles make up only about 15 percent of Suzuki's business, but in the United States it is best-known for its fast racing bikes and rugged motocross bikes, as well as its compact SUV (Sport Utility Vehicle) automobiles. There are more than 1,400 independently owned Suzuki dealers in the United States.

COMPANY FINANCES

In 1997, the Suzuki group posted a drop in both sales and profits for the first time in four years. Demand dropped in its domestic Japanese market due to economic problems in Asia, with sales in Japan falling 10.4 percent to $6.15 billion. However, this was partially offset by strong sales in Suzuki's overseas markets. Buyers took advantage of the favorable exchange rate on the weakened Japanese yen, and overseas sales went up 9.6 percent to $6.75 billion. American Suzuki experienced a

FOUNDED: 1909 (parent company founded as Suzuki Loom Works)

Contact Information:

HEADQUARTERS: 3251 E. Imperial Hwy.
 Brea, CA 92621-6722
PHONE: (714)996-7040
FAX: (714)524-2512
URL: http://www.suzukicycles.com

FAST FACTS:

About American Suzuki Motor Corporation

Ownership: American Suzuki Motor Corporation is a subsidiary of Suzuki Motor Corporation, a Japanese public corporation traded on the Tokyo (Nikkei) Stock Exchange.

Ticker symbol: J.SUZ

Officers: Sokichi Nakano, CEO; Ken Ayukawa, CFO

Employees: 13,873 (Suzuki total)

Principal Subsidiary Companies: American Suzuki Motor Corporation has three divisions: Automotive; Motorcycle and ATV; and Marine.

Chief Competitors: Suzuki competes with other manufacturers of motorcycles and other small motor vehicles, including: Honda; Kawasaki; and Yamaha.

sales drop of 22 percent in the first 10 months of 1997, compared with the previous year.

ANALYSTS' OPINIONS

Several of American Suzuki's 1997 motorcycles received rave reviews from *Cycle World* and *Motorcycle Online*. The Suzuki TL1000S was named *Cycle World's* "Best Superbike" of 1997, and *Motorcycle Online* called the bike "an absolute bargain" in its class.

HISTORY

American Suzuki's position as a premier manufacturer of racing and off-road motorcycles could never have been predicted from its quiet origins. In 1909, Michio Suzuki established the Suzuki Loom Works in Hamamatsu, a small seaside village in Japan that is still the worldwide headquarters of the Suzuki Motor Corporation. He hoped to become successful as a manufacturer of weaving machines. In the early 1930s Suzuki decided to diversify by also building small automobiles. However, the company was taken over by the Japanese government as it poured resources into war production, and instead it became a manufacturer of military equipment.

After the war ended, the Japanese economy was so shattered that the weaving business was impossible to revive. Suzuki returned to his idea of creating new types of motor vehicles, introducing a motorized bicycle, or "moped" in 1952. This vehicle, with its tiny 36 cc two-stroke engine, soon was joined by other, more powerful, two-wheeled vehicles, as well as small automobiles. The first Suzuki motorcycles arrived in the United States in 1963. The focus became and remained production of fast, tough road and motocross bikes.

Suzuki's U.S. presence expanded to the marine market in 1977, with the addition of its line of outboard motors, already proven in the international market. All-terrain vehicles were added in 1982. Finally, the Suzuki automotive line was introduced in the United States in 1985, and the American Suzuki Motor Corporation subsidiary created the following year.

STRATEGY

American Suzuki's motorcycle operations must be viewed within the larger picture of Suzuki Motor Corporation's overall strategy. Within Japan, the company has focused on marketing a variety of specialized minivehicles, finding great competition from leading companies such as Toyota and Honda in the traditional automotive market. The hallmark of Suzuki vehicles has been their compact and fuel-efficient design.

On an international level, Suzuki has often sought new markets in developing countries with growing populations, where smaller, less costly vehicles are likely to find eager buyers. Developing countries in which Suzuki has found a niche have included Cambodia, India, China, Egypt, Hungary, Pakistan, Indonesia, and the Philippines. Within the United States, Suzuki's approach has been to build small, inexpensive, and tough automobiles such as the Sidekick. Its motorcycles are designed for younger buyers, with the emphasis on speed, sleek design, and off-road capabilities.

Suzuki's ambitious U.S. goals include unit sales of 100,000 by 2001, and adding 100 dealers to its current 300. The company planned to accomplish this through new products and an increase in its relatively quiet U.S. advertising presence.

INFLUENCES

Suzuki has frequently found itself battered by global events. Its original weaving operations were cut short by the Japanese government's takeover of its operations to produce military equipment in the 1930s and 1940s. The collapse of the Japanese economy following World War II, plus the dismal state of the textile industry, led Suzuki to transform itself into a manufacturer of vehicles.

In the early 1970s, Suzuki was deeply affected by the international repercussions from the OPEC oil embargo. It responded to the gasoline shortages by introducing tiny fuel-efficient automobiles, but it was beaten to market by its competitors, and found itself constrained by new U.S. trade restrictions on Japanese goods. However, a joint venture with General Motors, which sold Suzuki automobiles through GM under the names Chevy Sprint and GEO Metro, helped it to establish itself in the American marketplace.

A significant low point for Suzuki in the United States occurred in the mid-1980s, when the Suzuki Samurai recreational automobile was judged to be unsafe by *Consumer Reports* magazine, which wrote that the vehicle's high center of gravity made it likely to flip over when taking turns. In an illustration of the potential pitfalls of cross-cultural communication, the apologetic resignation of the entire team of Japanese executives running American Suzuki was widely misinterpreted as an abandonment of the U.S. market. In the 1990s, sales of Suzuki automobiles improved somewhat after changes were made to improve safety, and increased sales of its motorcycles helped to balance the earlier losses. Still, the company found it difficult to compete when other car manufacturers began to offer small sport utility vehicles with newer designs and more marketing muscle behind them.

CURRENT TRENDS

American Suzuki is determined to maintain a niche as a manufacturer of unique products. No longer known as a manufacturer of small two-stroke motorcycles, American Suzuki now concentrates on making and selling four-stroke streetbikes and rugged, high-performance models. Its bikes are noted for speed, a reputation that is aided by the numerous international races won on Suzuki bikes. With the rapidly growing popularity of Harley Davidson motorcycles in the later 1990s, American Suzuki also is placing more emphasis on marketing large cruising motorcycles, particularly the Bandit 1200S.

In its automotive line, American Suzuki continues offering its four wheel drives in the robust U.S. sports utility vehicle market, and added the Esteem subcompact sedan and wagon.

PRODUCTS

In 1997 American Suzuki manufactured over 30 different models of motorcycles and ATVs (All-Terrain Vehicles), all of them far removed from the original "Power Free" 36 cc motorized bicycle introduced in 1952. Engine sizes ranged from 600 to 1200 cc.

Six automotive models are produced, including the Sidekick sport utility vehicle, the Swift coupe, and the Esteem sedan and wagon.

CHRONOLOGY:
Key Dates for American Suzuki Motor Corporation

1909: Parent founded as Suzuki Loom Works

1937: Begins to diversify product lines by building a small automobile

1945: Following the war, Suzuki begins producing looms again

1951: The cotton market collapses and Suzuki again focuses on automobiles and motorcycles

1952: Introduces a moped

1963: First Suzuki motorcycles arrive in the U.S.

1977: Introduces marine outboard motors in the U.S.

1982: Introduces all-terrain vehicles in the U.S. market

1985: Introduces automobiles into the U.S. market

1986: Creates the American Suzuki Motor Corporation subsidary

CORPORATE CITIZENSHIP

American Suzuki, like other motorcycle manufacturers, is concerned about having safe riders on the road. It is a founding member of the Motorcycle Safety Foundation, and encourages both new and experienced owners of its motorcycles to take riding skills courses sponsored by the organization. As of 1997, over 1 million motorcyclists had graduated from these courses. Because so many of its bikes are designed for off-road use, American Suzuki also participates in the national "Tread Lightly" program, which reminds off-road riders to respect the environment and the rights of other trail users.

Suzuki helps fund the Air Bag and Seat Belt Safety Campaign under the auspices of the National Safety Council. The goal of this campaign is to educate the public about proper use of seat belts and child safety restraints in cars with airbags, in order to maximize the effectiveness and minimize the risk of these safety devices.

GLOBAL PRESENCE

Suzuki first marketed its motorcycles in the United States in 1963, soon after the company attracted international attention when one of its small early models won the famous Isle of Man race. Following the oil embargo of the early 1970s, Suzuki also began exporting its motorcycles to other countries in Asia, notably Thailand, Indonesia, and Taiwan. The United States is Suzuki's largest overseas market, and 80 percent of its Suzuki motorcycles are produced outside of Japan.

Suzuki employs almost 14,000 people worldwide, and distributes its products (automobiles, motorcycles, and marine vehicles) in more than 170 countries. One factor which has generated valuable worldwide publicity for Suzuki since the early 1960s has been the many motorcycle races won by Suzuki bikes. According to figures compiled by American Suzuki, Suzuki motorcycles have won 9 World Championships in the Grand Prix roadracing category, 27 World Motocross Grand Prix titles, and numerous victories at American Motorcycle Association championship competitions, LeMans, the Bol d'Or, and the Isle of Man.

EMPLOYMENT

Amercian Suzuki Motor Corporation employs hundreds of staff members in sales, marketing, technical assistance, and distribution at its Brea, California, headquarters.

SOURCES OF INFORMATION

Bibliography

American Suzuki Motor Corporation Press Releases, 1997. Available at http://www.suzukicycles.com.

Fortune, Tom. "Suzuki's 1997 New Model Line Up." *Motorcycle Online,* 25 August 1997. Available at http://www.motorcycle.com.

Halliday, Jean. "American Suzuki Skids as Rivals' Vehicles Improve." *Advertising Age.* 1 December 1997.

Simley, John. "Suzuki Motor Corporation." *International Directory of Company Histories,* Vol. 9. Detroit: St. James Press, 1994.

"Suzuki Group Sales, Profits Dip First Time in Four Years." *Reuters,* 26 May 1998.

"Suzuki Motor Corporation." *Hoover's Online,* 28 May 1998. Available at http://www.hoovers.com.

"Ten Best List." *Cycle World,* August 1997.

For additional industry research:

Investigate companies by their Standard Industrial Classification Codes, also known as SICs. American Suzuki's primary SICs are:

3711 Motor Vehicle & Passenger Car Bodies

3714 Motor Vehicle Parts & Accessories

3751 Motorcycles, Bicycles & Parts

Ameritech Corp.

OVERVIEW

One of the world's 100 largest companies, Ameritech serves customers in the 50 states and 40 countries. Ameritech provides advanced telecommunications services to nearly 12 million customers in Illinois, Indiana, Michigan, Ohio, and Wisconsin. These services include local exchange and toll service, network access and telecommunications products; cellular and other wireless services; leasing; directory and electronic advertising services; and interactive services (including Internet access). Internationally, the company has partnership operations in Canada, Hungary, Belgium, Denmark, Germany, New Zealand, Norway, Poland, and China. Ameritech also owns the world's largest maker of automated library systems (Ameritech Library Services) and the second largest security monitoring company (National Guardian).

Big changes occurred in the telephone service market with the passage of the Telecommunications Act of 1996, which created opportunities for competition in what was once a heavily monopolized industry. Long-distance carriers, such as AT&T (Ameritech's one-time parent) sought to enter the local telephone service market, while local service providers were looking to provide long-distance service. Ameritech offers long-distance service to its cellular customers and is still negotiating the hurdles it must overcome before it can offer long-distance services to the rest of its customer base. Because of the industry's regulatory environment, Ameritech must prove that local-service competition exists within its Midwest territory before it can enter the long-distance business.

Contact Information:
HEADQUARTERS: 30 S. Wacker Dr.
 Chicago , IL 60606-7487
PHONE: (312)750-5000
FAX: (312)207-1601
TOLL FREE: (800)327-9346
URL: http://www.ameritech.com

FINANCES:

Ameritech Corp.
Revenues, 1994-1997
(billion dollars)

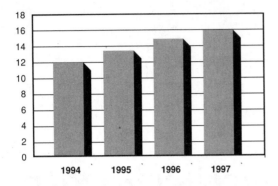

COMPANY FINANCES

First quarter 1998 earnings for Ameritech were $4.1 billion (compared to first quarter earnings of $3.8 billion in 1997 and $3.5 billion in 1996). Total 1997 revenues for Ameritech were $15.9 billion, up 7.2 percent from 1996 revenues of $14.9 billion and 1995 revenues of $13.4 billion. The company's net income rose to $2.3 billion in 1997, compared to $2.1 billion in 1996 and $2.0 billion in 1995. This represents significant improvement over a 1994 net loss of $1.0 billion.

Ameritech's earnings per share rose by 8.3 percent, from $1.91 in 1996 to $2.14 per share in 1997. It was the sixth straight year that Ameritech's earnings per share (EPS) rose: in 1992 the company's EPS was $1.23; 1993, $1.37; 1994, $1.54; and in 1995, $1.71. As of May 1998, the company's EPS was $2.03.

Ameritech's year-end stock price for 1997 was $40.25, up 32.8 percent from $30.32 at year-end 1996. The 52-week high was $50.25 and the 52-week low was $30.12.

ANALYSTS' OPINIONS

The telecommunications business is expected to continue its trend of greater growth and competition, according to industry analysts on Wall Street. 1996 was a year of historic legislation in the industry, including deregulation of the local and long distance phone markets through the passage of the Telecommunications Act of 1996. As the long distance and local carriers cross into one another's markets, analysts predict continued consolidation within the industry. "You'll see more mergers because you've still got several companies hanging out there," said Alex J. Mandl, the former president of AT&T.

The excellent shape of this industry bodes well for Ameritech's continued growth. So far the company has a record 17 consecutive quarters of double-digit growth. However, according to Zacks investment services, 11 out of 24 analysts currently give the company a "hold" rating, recommending that Ameritech investors simply hold on to the stock they own for now. Of those 24, another 6 recommended a "strong buy" rating, 6 a "moderate buy," and 1 analyst rated the company a "moderate sell." Zacks also estimated Ameritech's growth rate for the next year and half between 8.67 and 10.19 percent.

HISTORY

Ameritech was once a property of long-distance giant AT&T, but in 1984 the company was spun-off as part of AT&T's anti-trust settlement. Ameritech was formed from 5 of AT&T's 22 telephone subsidiaries (Illinois, Indiana, Michigan, Ohio, and Wisconsin Bell) and 6 additional subsidiaries (Ameritech Services Inc., Ameritech Communications Inc., Ameritech Credit Corp., Ameritech Development Corp., Ameritech Mobile Communications, and Ameritech Publishing, Inc.). The company began operating on January 1, 1984 and in December of the same year purchased 19.9-percent interest in Cantel, a Canadian cellular phone company.

From the start, Ameritech pushed to become an international player, and over the next four years the company laid the groundwork for the creation of Ameritech International in 1989. In 1987 Ameritech started iNet, a company offering electronic mail and information services in partnership with Bell Canada and Telenet. In 1990 Ameritech was chosen, with Bell Atlantic, to purchase a $2.5-billion interest in New Zealand's public phone system. The next year it joined France Telecom and the Polish government to create a national cellular phone system in Poland. Also in 1991, Ameritech and Singapore Telecom joined to acquire 49.9-percent interest in Norway's NetCom GSM (cellular services).

Not all of Ameritech's growth has taken place overseas, however. In 1991, Ameritech bought Cybertel, a cellular firm in St. Louis; Knowledge Data Systems (data processing systems); and NOTIS (library information software systems). By 1993 the company was ready for a major restructuring—Ameritech was realigned and focused for the next three years on planning the company's future in video, long distance, and wireless services. Seeking to distinguish itself as a new telecommunications entity, Ameritech retired the Bell logo and unveiled its new Ameritech logo. Its first purchase of 1993 was a 15-percent share of MATAV, Hungary's telephone company.

In 1995 Ameritech, seeking to diversify, became the second largest U.S. security monitoring provider with its purchase of National Guardian Corporation. Back on the telecommunications field, Ameritech signed a five-year contract with WorldCom (the fourth largest U.S. long distance provider) in 1996 to sell Worldcom long-distance services. Also in 1996, a group of businesses called DSB Telecommunications (and led by Ameritech) became partners with Belgacom SA, the national telecommunications operator of Belgium. Early in 1997 Ameritech was the first Baby Bell to seek clearance to enter the long distance market, but later withdrew the request.

STRATEGY

Ameritech's primary strategy is to "speed growth in our core business." These core businesses all achieved double-digit growth in 1997. Ameritech's customer base for its cellular services grew 27 percent, paging services grew 31 percent, and the company saw 71 percent growth in sales of ISDN lines. Other core businesses include call management services and directory advertising. The company hopes to propel continued growth for Ameritech in core areas by expanding its sales channels and payment options for those services.

Expansion is a watchword for Ameritech. The company recognizes the enormous opportunities that are available in global competition and has sought to take advantage of those opportunities by creating strategic alliances throughout the world. "Driven by strong customer demand, new services and entry into new markets, Ameritech is entering an era of greatly expanded opportunity," said Richard C. Notebaert, chairman and chief executive officer of Ameritech. "Our success in sustaining double-digit growth while investing in high-potential businesses such as long distance and cable TV demonstrates both our disciplined strategic focus and our proven ability to execute in one of the world's fastest growing industries."

Ameritech's international businesses accounted for more than one-fourth of the company's earnings growth in the first quarter of 1997. Another of Ameritech's primary strategies, to "connect customers around the world," focuses on expanding its market for its core businesses into new international markets. According to its annual report, Ameritech is already the "largest U.S. investor in European telecommunications, with investments valued at more than $6 billion."

Ameritech also uses powerful marketing strategies to propel its growth rate. The company designs its business units around specific market segments and tends to those customers with defined marketing practices. The first of those is its sales force of 25,000-plus people making Ameritech products and services available in more than 1,100 retail stores. The company also relies heavily on "brand leadership," or how recognizable the Ameri-

FAST FACTS:
About Ameritech Corp.

Ownership: Ameritech is a publicly held company traded on the New York Stock Exchange.

Ticker symbol: AIT

Officers: Richard C. Notebaert, Chmn., Pres. & CEO, 50, 1997 base salary $1,047,000; Oren G. Shaffer, Exec. VP & CFO, 55, 1997 base salary $500,000; W. Patrick Campbell, Exec. VP Corp. Strategy & Bus. Dev., 51, 1997 base salary $491,800; Barry K. Allen, Exec. VP Regional & Wholesale Operations, 41, 1997 base salary $417,900

Employees: 74,359

Principal Subsidiary Companies: Ameritech's affiliates include Americast (a joint venture with Bell-South Corp., SBC Corp., and Walt Disney), Belgacom (local, long-distance, cellular, and security services in Belgium), Centertel (cellular service provider in Poland), China Unicom, MATAV (long-distance and cellular service in Hungary), NetCom (cellular services in Norway), Tele Danmark (local, long-distance, cable, and cellular services in Denmark), and Telecom Corporation of New Zealand Ltd.

Chief Competitors: A major communications and regional holding company, Ameritech's most direct competitors include: Bell Atlantic; BellSouth; SBC Communications; and U.S. West Communications Group.

tech brand name is among the general public. The Ameritech name and logo appears on its trucks, directories, pay phones, and products. In addition, they offer a consolidated bill for Ameritech customers, in which all Ameritech services are billed in one location-cellular service, security, Internet access, and phone service. Finally, the company offers round-the-clock service to its customers. Through these mechanisms, Ameritech has achieved (according to its surveys) brand awareness of 95 percent in the Upper Midwest area.

INFLUENCES

Ameritech counts among its successes (and strategies for growth) "new services for customers." The two

CHRONOLOGY:

Key Dates for Ameritech Corp.

1984: Is spun-off by AT&T on January 1

1987: Starts iNet

1989: Ameritech International is created

1990: Buys into New Zealand's public phone system

1991: Begins joint ventures with Poland's and Norway's cellular phone systems; bought Cybertel, Knowledge Data Systems, and NOTIS

1993: Purchases 15 percent of MATAV

1995: Purchases National Guardian Corp.

1996: Signs contract to distribute WorldCom

1997: Applies for and then withdraws an application for clearance to enter the long distance market

1998: Invested in Tele Denmark

most successful have been security services and cable television. The first, SecurityLink, installs, monitors, and services security systems and currently counts one million customers. Ameritech counts itself as the first and only company among its peers to establish such a strong presence in that market. Its cable television service has also proved a successful venture for the company. They currently offer services in Illinois, Michigan, and Ohio and have earned a 36-percent market share in areas where Ameritech's cable services are offered. One area in which Ameritech has not been able to extend its reach remains long-distance services. The company expected to be able to enter this market due to passing deregulatory legislation in 1997. However, regulatory agencies continued to restrict Ameritech from pursuing that goal, one that they hope to be able to reach in 1998.

CURRENT TRENDS

During the first three months of 1997, Ameritech continued making progress toward furthering its growth. The company reached an agreement to purchase Sprint's local communications business in part of Chicago and 10 of its suburbs. The deal adds 136,000 access lines to Ameritech's huge stable of access lines, which now number 19.9 million. The company is also continuing ex-

pansion of its Americast™ enhanced cable television service. It has added 5 cable television franchises since January 1997 and now owns 34 franchise agreements with communities covering more than 1.7 million people. Also, Ameritech signed an agreement with Teleglobe International, expanding the reach of Ameritech's long distance network to more than 240 countries and territories worldwide.

PRODUCTS

Services offered by Ameritech include: local telephone service; interstate network access; long distance; intrastate network access; product leasing (telephones, pagers, etc.); and directory, cellular, and interactive services (such as Internet access). Ameritech also offers its customers selected services including advertising, electronic business services (voice messaging, Caller ID, call waiting, etc.), interactive video, personal communications (wireless services including two-way paging), security monitoring, and managed services.

CORPORATE CITIZENSHIP

In 1996, Ameritech contributed over $25 million of its earnings to selected educational, civic, health and human services, and cultural nonprofit organizations. Of the total, $6.4 million was devoted to research, training, and innovative applications of communications technologies, and to programs for colleges to attract and retain qualified and diverse teachers and students.

In April 1997, Ameritech awarded a $650,000 grant to the Foundation for Independent Higher Education that allows private colleges across the country new opportunities to explore the benefits of telecommunications technology. The Ameritech Distance Collaboration Grant Program will award grants of up to $50,000 to groups of private colleges that propose innovative uses of technology and collaboration to improve their academic programs, business offices, and/or student services. These grants are a continuation of Ameritech's tradition of support for private higher education. Since 1994, Ameritech has contributed over $2.4 million to the state independent college associations in Illinois, Indiana, Michigan, Ohio, and Wisconsin.

Also announced in April 1997 was the awarding of $600,000 to 10 libraries across the United States through a partnership between the Library of Congress and Ameritech. The money will be used to digitize historically significant American collections of art and make them available for the first time on the Internet. This effort is the first to make unique collections from libraries across the United States available online via the Library of Congress to millions of children, students, educators, and teachers.

GLOBAL PRESENCE

Ameritech is the seventh largest communications company in the world. It offers local and long-distance telephone service, cellular service, phone directories, business purchasing guides, and wireless services in Austria, Belgium, Croatia, the Czech Republic, Denmark, Germany, Hungary, Luxembourg, the Netherlands, Norway, Slovakia, Slovenia, and Switzerland. Ameritech's strong global presence includes strategic partnerships with select international companies.

In January of 1998, Ameritech finalized a $3.1-billion investment in Tele Danmark, which will eventually give Ameritech a 42-percent stake in the company. Other alliances include: Atlantic Canada On-Line; Belgacom SA in Brussels and Belgium; Matav (MTA), Hungarian Telecommunications Company in Budpest; NetCom GSM in Oslo, Norway; and China Unicom. Ameritech is also a partner with GE Information Services providing worldwide communications systems. While currently heavily invested in Telecom Corp. of New Zealand, Ameritech announced in late 1997 that they would be selling off shares in that company to the public. They plan to use finances from that sale toward further expansion in North America and Europe.

EMPLOYMENT

According to Ameritech's web site, "Our commitment to employees is to balance our business objectives with employee's needs for security and protection through total compensation." Ameritech does this by offering employees compensation through a base salary, annual bonus, and benefits. In addition, each employee is offered the chance to become a shareholder in the business, an offer of which 75 percent of Ameritech employees take advantage. The company sees its own responsibility to train employees effectively to make smart business decisions. They also trust that the proper training and support will allow employees to make decisions that benefit the company and its shareholders.

The company also sees diversity as one of its primary goals and defines that term as, "the process of recognising, understanding, valuing and utilizing all the ways in which we differ." That definition includes not only hiring practices, but the ways in which employees work, the contributions they make, and the environment and resources they need to achieve company goals.

SOURCES OF INFORMATION

Bibliography

"American History from Across U.S. to Go On-Line Through Library of Congress/Ameritech Awards." *PR Newswire,* April 1997.

"Ameritech Corporation." *Microsoft Investor,* 6 May 1998. Available at http://investor.msn.com/invsub/analyst/recomnd.asp? Symbol3DAIT.

Ameritech Corporation. *Notice of 1998 Annual Meeting and Proxy Statement.* 27 February 1998.

Ameritech Corporation 1998 Annual Report. Chicago, IL: Ameritech Corporation, February 1998.

Ameritech Home Page. 7 August 1998. Available at http://www.ameritech.com.

"Ameritech and Sprint Announce Agreement: Ameritech to Purchase Sprint Chicago Suburb Local Communications Business Assets." *PR Newswire,* April 1997.

"Ameritech Announces National Distance Collaboration Grants for Independent Colleges." *PR Newswire,* April 1997.

"Baby Bell SBC Asks FCC to OK Long-Distance Service in Oklahoma." *Associated Press,* April 1997.

"Benefits," 7 August 1998. Available at http://data.ameritech.com/ame_emp/bene.html.

"Diversity," 7 August 1998. Available at http://data.ameritech.com/ame_emp/diver.html.

Landler, Mark. "Year of Intense Activity Looms for Phone Industry, Experts Say." *The New York Times,* January 1997.

For an annual report:

on the Internet at: http://www.ameritech.com/investor/annuals/1997/index.htm **or** write: Ameritech Shareowner Services c/o First Chicago Trust Company of New York, PO Box 2558, Jersey City, NJ 07303-2558.

For additional industry research:

Investigate companies by their Standard Industrial Classification Codes, also known as SICs. Ameritech's primary SICs are:

3661 Telephone and Telegraph Apparatus

3669 Communications Equipment, NEC

4813 Telephone Communications, Except Radiotelephone

4899 Communications Services, NEC

7319 Advertising, NEC

7382 Security Systems Services

7389 Business Services, NEC

Amoco Corporation

FOUNDED: 1889

Contact Information:
HEADQUARTERS: 200 E. Randolph Dr.
    Chicago, IL 60601-7125
PHONE: (312)856-6111
FAX: (312)856-4883
TOLL FREE: (800)333-3991
EMAIL: info@amoco.com
URL: http://www.amoco.com

OVERVIEW

Amoco Corporation is a diversified company with three main sectors—Oil Exploration and Production, Petroleum Products, and Chemicals. With revenues exceeding $36 billion and total assets exceeding $32 billion, Amoco Corporation is one of the largest publicly traded producers of crude oil and natural gas in the world. Amoco is the thirteenth largest industrial corporation in the United States, the fifth largest oil company, and is ranked twenty-second in the 1998 Fortune 500. It is the largest producer of natural gas in North America. The company's Chemicals division was the largest producer of chemical products in the United States.

COMPANY FINANCES

Amoco's total revenues in 1997 were $31.9 billion, down slightly from 1996 revenues of $32.1 billion. Net income dropped about 4 percent from $2.8 billion in 1996 to $2.7 billion in 1997. Of 1997 revenues, Amoco's Exploration and Production sector earned $7.39 billion; Petroleum Products earned $22.79 billion; Chemical Operations earned $5.94 billion; and Corporate and Other Operations earned $48 million.

Amoco's stock price was around $41.00 per share in mid-1998. Its 52-week high was $49.50, and Amoco stock's 52-week low was $39.63. Stock prices were lower due to a 2-for-1split in 1997. During fiscal year 1997, Amoco stock ranged from $79.25 to $99.00 per share. The company paid approximately $2.80 per share in dividends in 1997—up 8 percent from 1996 ($2.60).

Amoco's net income per share during 1997 was $5.55, slightly lower than 1996 earnings per share of $5.69. As of mid-1998, earnings per share for 1998 were $2.50.

ANALYSTS' OPINIONS

All major U.S. oil companies were expected to see some sort of earnings decline due to dramatic slides in world oil prices. As reported in *Tulsa World,* earnings during the first part of 1998 could drop as much as 40 percent compared to last year. Analysts anticipated a drop not only in production income, but in refining and chemical operations as well. The decline in oil prices was attributed to two factors: a supply increase instituted in November of 1997 by Saudi Arabia just when demand lowered due to the Asian economic crisis; and the El Nino weather phenomenon, which brought unusually warm winter temperatures to the Northern Hemisphere. Amoco, in particular, was impacted by the drop in oil and gas prices; first quarter earnings per share were $.73, compared to $1.36 in the first quarter of 1997. However, they seemed to improve by mid-1998, rising to $2.50.

Even with these difficulties, however, PaineWebber analyst Frank Knuettel upgraded ratings for six major oil companies, including Amoco. "We think oil supply and demand will come into balance before year end which almost inevitably would generate positive earnings surprises." He warned that if that failed to happen, however, earnings would be less likely to rise. He upgraded Amoco's specific rating from "neutral" to "attractive."

Also having a positive impact on Amoco's performance was it success with a new oil well. Located in the Whitney Canyon field near Evanston, Wyoming, production of natural gas began at 60 million cubic feet per day. Amoco reported that rate was higher than any other well in the field in the last 15 years. The company also said the new well meant an increase in plant processing to about 200 million cubic feet per day; the plant was designed to process up to 250 million cubic feet of gas per day. According to Amoco's Michael Poehl, "Our early results to maximize production at Whitney Canyon have been outstanding. We expect to be at plant capacity for Whitney Canyon by year-end."

HISTORY

Amoco Corp. was incorporated on June 18, 1889, as Standard Oil Company when it built its first refinery in Whiting, Indiana. The corporation was exclusively a midwest refiner and marketer of petroleum products in its early years. In 1894 it began an unbroken record of yearly dividend payments. Prior to December 1, 1911, Amoco was a subsidiary of Standard Oil Co. of New Jersey, which distributed the stock to its stockholders under the Sher-

FINANCES:

Amoco Corp.
Revenues, 1994-1997
(million dollars)

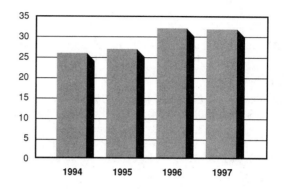

Amoco Corp.
1997 Stock Prices
(dollars)

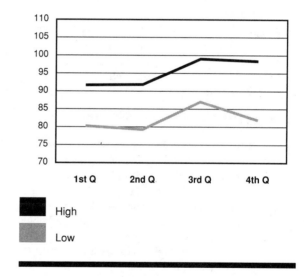

man Antitrust Act. Amoco was thus separated from all the other companies in the Standard Oil Company.

The Amoco name was adopted for the corporation in 1985 to effectively eliminate name confusion and promote a common identification of the parent corporation and its subsidiaries, which market internationally under the Amoco brand. Amoco, however, still retains exclusive legal right to use the Standard Oil name for trademark purposes in certain states in the Midwest.

In 1913 Amoco pioneered an invention of the thermal cracking process, which doubled the yield of gaso-

FAST FACTS:

About Amoco Corporation

Ownership: Amoco Corp. is a publicly held company traded on the New York Stock Exchange.

Ticker symbol: AN

Officers: H. Laurence Fuller, Chmn. & CEO, 59, $1,940,150; William G. Lowrie, Pres., 54, $1,223,047; John L. Carl, Exec. VP & CFO, 50; James E. Fligg, Sr. Exec. VP, Strategic Planning & Int'l Bus. Dev., 61, $1,010,301

Employees: 43,451 (1997)

Principal Subsidiary Companies: Amoco Chemical Co., Amocams/Modular Inc., Amoco Credit Co., Amoco Venture Capital Co., Amoco Technology Co., Amoco Fabrics and Fibers Co., and Amoco Pipeline Co. are some of the subsidiaries of Amoco Corporation.

Chief Competitors: As a producer and marketer of petroleum products and services, Amoco's main competitors include: Arco; Dow Chemical; Exxon; E.I. DuPont Nemours; British Petroleum; Pennzoil; Shell Oil; and Texaco.

---

line from crude oil; that same year also marked the beginning of regular quarterly dividend payments. Amoco experienced dramatic growth from post-World War I to the 1950s through the establishment of substantial crude oil production and transportation operations, additional refineries, extended marketing areas and facilities, and a start in petrochemicals. Exploration in Canada and overseas also began late in this period.

In the late 1950s Amoco consolidated and reorganized its subsidiaries into four groups for easier and more efficient management. This became the basis for the company's structure during the 1990s. In 1978 Amoco had a major disaster when the super-tanker, the Amoco Cadiz, ran on to the bottom of the shore, dumping 120,000 tons of oil off of the French coast. This spill was six times more than the well-publicized Exxon Valdez oil spill that occurred in 1989 and resulted in a $128-million judgment against Amoco in 1990. In 1988, Amoco acquired Dome Petroleum of Canada, a company heavily in debt but rich in resources, making Amoco the largest private owner of natural gas reserves in North America. In the 1990s, the Amoco Corporation formed a large integrated

petroleum and chemical enterprise with three main subsidiaries—Amoco Exploration and Production, Amoco Petroleum Products, and Amoco Chemicals.

STRATEGY

Amoco's primary strategy for continued corporate development was "discovery," not just in terms of finding new oil and gas deposits, but of "discovering" new opportunities, new products, new areas for growth, and new ways of working and exploiting technological challenges. Amoco also sought new business relationships in order to add value to its business, both internally (through its Shared Services organization) and externally through partnerships and alliances with companies worldwide. In 1998, Amoco planned to invest $4.2 billion in corporate capital and exploration, areas it hoped would bring better opportunity for company growth. In order to make sure those efforts would not cost the company too much financially, Amoco sold certain U.S. oil and gas holdings, amounting to approximately 10 percent of domestic production. For example, in June 1998 Amoco announced that Chevron Products Co. was acquiring Amoco's Lubricants business unit. Using these growth strategies, the company hoped to realize a 25-percent increase in exploration and production by 2001 and targeted 4-percent growth in refining and marketing.

INFLUENCES

When compared to its competitors, Amoco's performance was lagging behind. However, the company felt its continued renewal of early 1990s restructuring efforts was helping to bring about significant turnaround. The company did realize some turnaround, specifically in its exploration program, which for five years in a row (1993-1997) added more reserves than it produced. Also, the company averaged 145-percent "reserve replacement" over those same five years. Amoco attributed these favorable results to more focused exploration efforts and better use of new technology.

CURRENT TRENDS

According to the *Hoovers Handbook of American Business,* Amoco shed its weak product lines, including its oil well chemicals business, and invested $1.7 billion in the company's faster-growing and more profitable businesses. One of the profit centers that developed as part of this move was Amoco's polyester business. In 1992, Amoco led the consortium that successfully laid a 255-mile natural gas line in the North Sea. In 1992 Amoco became the first foreign oil company to explore the Chinese mainland.

CHRONOLOGY:

Key Dates for Amoco Corporation

1889: Incorporates as Standard Oil Company (Indiana), a subsidiary of Standard Oil Company (New Jersey)

1894: Begins unbroken record of yearly dividend payments

1911: Standard Oil Company (Indiana) is separated from its parent and all other subsidiaries after Standard (New Jersey) was found to be in violation of the Sherman Antitrust Act

1913: Pioneers a method that doubles the yield of gasoline from crude oil

1921: Purchases a half interest in the Sinclair Pipe Company to improve transportation capacity

1925: Purchases for $37.6 million an interest in the Pan American Petroleum & Transport Co., achieving the largest oil consolidation in the history of the industry

1929: Acquires through a stock swap additional stock of Pan American bringing ownership to 81 percent

1932: Sells Pan American's foreign interests to Standard (New Jersey) for $48 million plus 1.8 million shares of Standard (New Jersey) stock

1935: Standard (Indiana) leased company-owned stations to individual owners to get around a government tax

1942: The Big Inch pipeline, built by several oil companies including Standard (Indiana), carried 300,000 barrels of crude from Texas to the East Coast where it was used for the war effort

1952: Standard (Indiana) is acknowledged as the nation's largest domestic oil company

1955: Re-enters foreign market by organizing Pan American International Oil Corporation

1961: Standard (Indian) began replacing the brand name with Amoco, a derivative of American Oil Company, owned by Pan American

1967: Amoco begins exploration in the Persian Gulf

1970: Lead-free 91-octane gasoline is introduced by Amoco

1978: The *Amoco Cadiz* runs aground off the French coast spilling 730,000 gallons of oil; the French government brings a $300 million lawsuit against Amoco

1985: Standard (Indiana) officially changes its name to Amoco Corporation

1990: Amoco appeals a $128 million judgement brought down in the French lawsuit

1998: Sells the lubricants business unit to Chevron Products Co.

A significant year for Amoco was 1994. Amoco and Norsk Hydro, in a joint effort, evaluated the oil and natural gas exploration opportunities off the Russian Coast. The other big events were two natural gas discoveries off Trinidad and major oil discoveries in Colombia, the North Sea, and the Gulf of Mexico. In 1995, Shell Oil and Amoco announced a limited partnership to handle most U.S. operations. Amoco was the key player in this association, owning about 65 percent of the venture.

PRODUCTS

Amoco has three main subsidiaries that deal with three distinct markets and industries. Amoco Exploration and Production is one of the world's leading producers of energy resources for a growing world economy. Holdings include more than 42 million acres of oil and gas leases on every continent except Antarctica. Worldwide net production in 1996 averaged 662,000 barrels of crude oil and natural gas liquids per day and more than 4 bil-

lion cubic feet of natural gas per day. About 40 percent of oil and natural gas production revenues were from sources outside the United States. The Amoco Exploration and Production sector is made up of eight separate and independent business groups; each focuses on a few select areas in the world where the company expects to grow profitably through exploration, development, new ventures, and acquisitions.

The second sector is the Amoco Petroleum Products, which include refining, marketing, and transportation of fuel and other products throughout North America. In 1996, five refineries processed a total of 1 million barrels of crude oil daily. Amoco Petroleum Products market gasoline in 30 states in the United States through more than 9,000 service stations.

Amoco Chemicals is the third and fastest growing sector of Amoco Corp. Comprised of six business groups, Amoco Chemicals accounted for nearly 45 percent of Amoco's total revenues. Much of Amoco Chemical's growth is due to its status as the world's largest producer of purified terephthalic acid (PTA), the preferred raw ma-

---

THE WHITING FACTORY - A CANDLE IN THE WIND

Few people know about Amoco's candlemaking history, yet from 1893 to 1956 the company operated one of the largest candle factories in the United States. Candles basically consist of paraffin wax, a by-product of the oil refining process. Thus, Amoco's involvement in this business came naturally, and the Whiting Candle Factory was established right next to the company's Whiting, Indiana, refinery.

The factory operated in the nineteenth century, when kerosene, not gasoline, was Amoco's sales leader. The Whiting Factory started producing plain white candles and so-called "pound cakes" of pure, refined wax. These were used for canning and preserving foods. Twenty years later, America's involvement in World War I led to the company's becoming one of the largest candle manufacturers in the country. In 1918 the Whiting Factory's entire production of six- and eight-inch candles was purchased by the Army for use in the trenches. Thirty-eight candle machines produced half a million candles every day. By the end of the war, Amoco had shipped a total of 285 million candles to France.

The postwar years witnessed an even stronger surge in candle demand. This was primarily due to the fact that during the war Americans noticed how candles were used for decorative purposes in Europe, particularly for the holidays. Thus, by the late 1920s, candles for religious observances accounted for fifteen percent of the factory's production. However, the greatest demand was still for the original plain white candles. They were used by plumbers, miners, and dairy distributors as well as for emergency lighting by the general public. The Whiting Candle Factory more than doubled its production capacity between 1923 and 1928 to a million pounds of wax per month. By this time Amoco was the only major oil company in the United States that manufactured candles.

During World War II, approximately 75 percent of the factory's candles were, once again, made for various military purposes. Melted wax, for example, was used to plug tent leaks. After the war, the Whiting Candle Factory accounted for about 10 percent of all candles bought in the United States. More than 150 varieties were produced, while sales were handled by only four representatives. These were the factory's peak years.

The Whiting Candle Factory was closed in 1956, after more than sixty years of operation. The reasons were twofold. First, Amoco had to seek more profitable opportunities through its primary line of products, and secondly, candle production had declined in the later years as more wax was being sold to other producers and manufacturers of wax products. The fact remains that many people, especially former G.I.s, have fond memories of Amoco's candles.

---

terial for the manufacture of polyester. Other chemical products include polybutene (used in cable insulation, fuel additives, and adhesives) and polypropylene (used in synthetic fibers for carpet backing, food and agricultural packaging, and appliances). Amoco Chemicals is well positioned to capitalize on the increasing global demand for polyester products.

CORPORATE CITIZENSHIP

Amoco documents its corporate commitment to health and environmental safety. This policy's primary purpose is "to promote respect and care for people and the environment." Each year, along with its annual report, Amoco publishes an Environmental Health & Safety Report that describes accomplishments that help Amoco meet this corporate goal and changes in environmental policy. In 1997 the Environment, Health and Safety (EH&S) department completed a strategic planning process. As a result, the company reorganized the EH&S department to ensure that all areas of Amoco had access to the resources needed to apply environmental, health, and safety considerations to the corporate planning process and to business decisions.

One of Amoco's major community involvement programs is the Private Sector Initiative's Home Repair Program in Houston, Texas. As part of this initiative, Amoco volunteers join others from the Houston area to repair and paint homes of elderly and disabled homeowners. Family members join employees to replace siding, trim, broken windows, screens, exterior doors, and locks. They also powerwash the homes and repaint. As a result, more than 325 homes were updated in Houston in 1997.

Other company community relations efforts are coordinated and/or funded by the Amoco Foundation, Inc. The Foundation contributed about $21 million to community and educational organizations in 33 countries in 1997. It specifically targets programs and organizations that help Amoco conduct business responsibly. Additionally, on behalf of company employees who volunteered for at least 50 hours in 1997, the Foundation awarded $726,000 in grants to more than 680 organizations across the globe. It also donated $2.2 million in matching grants to educational institutions. Another program, AmoCARES (Concerned Amoco Retirees Engaged in Service), contributed about $600,000 in volunteer services.

GLOBAL PRESENCE

Amoco has operations worldwide in both its petroleum and chemical product sectors. Petroleum exploration took place in about 20 different countries as of 1998. Still, more of Amoco's revenues were derived from sales in the United States, $28.2 billion of total 1997 revenues ($36.3 billion). Canadian revenues were $3.4 billion, and sales in Europe accounted for $2.2 billion. The remaining $2.5 billion came from Amoco's remaining foreign operations.

EMPLOYMENT

As one of its primary goals, Amoco tries to attract, develop, and retain people who match its corporate environment. According to the company, these people are "diverse, global, and must act consistently with our values. In this environment, each employee can use his or her full talent, energy and commitment to meet customer expectations and achieve business objectives." In 1997, 400 employees from around the world attended Amoco's third Diversity Conference. Attendance was almost double that of 1996.

To protect employees, Amoco approved a new operating policy focused on increased corporate commitment to safety. In 1997 the company also spent more than $45 million training employees at every level, including technical training, supervisory training, and a Renewal Series program for top management. In more rural areas around the world, Amoco sponsors medical visits to communities near the company's operations. These doctors provide general medical checkups, vitamins, and general information to area families.

SOURCES OF INFORMATION

Bibliography

"Accord Set to Participate in Kazak Pipeline Project." *The Wall Street Journal,* 14 March 1997.

"Amoco Corporation." *Hoover's Online.* 28 June 1998. Available at http://www.hoovers.com.

Amoco Corporation 1997 Annual Report. Chicago: Amoco Corporation, 1998. Available at http://www.amoco.com/about/ar97/home.html.

"Amoco and Shell Oil Form Partnership." *The New York Times,* 26 February 1997.

"Amoco Wyoming Well Begins Natural Gas Production." *Reuters,* 11 June 1998.

"Big-Oil Earnings Expected to Plummet." *Tulsa World,* 16 April 1998.

"Chevron Acquires Amoco's Lubricants Business." *Chevron Corporation,* 11 June 1998.

Manufacturing USA. Detroit, MI: Gale Research, 1996.

Moody's Company Data Report. Moody's Investor Service, 1996.

"PaineWebber Ups Oils to Overweight." *Reuters,* 12 June 1998.

Wolf, Gillian, updated by David E. Salamie. "Amoco Corporation." *International Directory of Company Histories,* Vol. 14. Detroit, MI: St. James Press, 1996.

For an annual report:
on the Internet at: http://www.amoco.com/about/ar97/home.html **or** write: Annual Report, Attn: N. R. Stevenson, Amoco Corp., 200 E. Randolph Dr., Mail Code 2304, Chicago, IL 60601-7125

For additional industry research:
Investigate companies by their Standard Industrial Classification Codes, also known as SICs. Amoco's primary SICs are:

1311 Crude Petroleum and Natural Gas

2821 Plastics Materials and Resins, NEC

2869 Industrial Organic Chemicals, NEC

2911 Petroleum Refining

4612 Crude Petroleum Pipelines

4613 Refined Petroleum Pipelines

5171 Petroleum Refining

5541 Gasoline Service Stations

6719 Holding Companies

Anheuser-Busch Companies, Inc.

FOUNDED: 1852

Contact Information:

HEADQUARTERS: 1 Busch Pl.
   St. Louis, MO 63118
PHONE: (314)577-2000
FAX: (314)577-7622
TOLL FREE: (800)DIAL-BUD
URL: http://www.anheuser-busch.com
   http://www.budweiser.com

OVERVIEW

Anheuser-Busch Companies, Inc. is a St. Louis-based corporation with subsidiaries that include the world's largest brewing organization, the second-largest U.S. manufacturer of aluminum beverage containers, and one of the largest theme-park operators in the United States. Anheuser-Busch is also involved in producing malt, milling rice, developing real estate, and other business activities. In 1997 Anheuser-Busch Companies had worldwide sales of $12.8 billion.

Anheuser-Busch, Inc. (ABI), a subsidiary of Anheuser-Busch Companies, is the largest brewer in the world. In 1998, ABI accounted for 46.9 percent of all the beer sold in the United States, compared to 22.7 percent for the second largest U.S. brewer, Miller Brewing Company. ABI sold a total of 96.6 million barrels of beer in 1997. The company's Budweiser beer, with it famous "King of Beers" slogan, is by far the best selling brand of beer, with 21 percent of the U.S. market.

COMPANY FINANCES

In 1997, Anheuser-Busch reported gross sales of $12.8 billion, up 1.7 percent from 1996 sales of $12.6 billion. Net sales for 1997 were $11 billion, compared to $10.8 billion in 1996. All divisions performed well and realized increased revenues, including the Busch Entertainment Corp. (theme parks), which exceeded $100 million in operating profits for the first time. Gross sales for the first quarter of 1998 were reported as $2.9 billion, $87 million more than first quarter 1997 sales, an increase of 3.1 percent. The company's theme park operations noticed a loss in earnings over the period from first quarter 1997 to first quarter 1998, however, as did its international beer operations. The decline in international operations was attributed by Anheuser-Busch to 1997's unusually strong first quarter, during which new operations were opened in China, Argentina, and the Philippines. Worldwide beer volume rose 4.4 percent in 1998's first quarter, while domestic beer volume increased by 5.3 percent.

In 1997, Anheuser-Busch paid $1 per share dividends to shareholders, an 8.7-percent increase over dividends paid in 1996 of $.92 per share. Anheuser-Busch stock showed a 52-week high of $49.31 per share, and its 52-week low was $38 1/2. Anheuser-Busch earnings per share were $.54 in the first quarter of 1998, 5.9 percent more than the same period in 1997.

ANALYSTS' OPINIONS

Opinions of stock market analysts on Anheuser-Busch (A-B) Companies have appeared to be somewhat mixed. For example, in a November 1997 report, JP Morgan Securities Inc. recommended Anheuser-Busch stock only as a "long-term buy," citing reasons such as price constraints in the U.S. market (meaning Anheuser-Busch could not raise its prices) and because analysts expected lower earnings per share from 1997-99. JP Morgan did cite some factors that could offset the impact of this on A-B stock, such as better cost containment by the company and more revenue contributions from Grupo Modelo in Mexico.

However, in 1998 Brown Brothers Harriman rated Anheuser-Busch as "outperform/buy," citing expected increases in the company's earnings per share, an expected increase in domestic consumption, and growth in Bud Light sales. The company's growth in international business and increases in overall demand for A-B products prompted other analysts, such as those at CIBC Oppenheimer, to rate the company a "strong buy," while others remained neutral on A-B stock. Analysts at Zacks Investment Research and Morgan Stanley recommended a "hold" rating on Anheuser-Busch stock through 1998, citing a sluggish domestic market for beer and an expected modest 3-percent growth rate for the company.

HISTORY

Anheuser-Busch was founded in 1852 as the Bavarian Brewery in St. Louis by George Schneider, who sold the brewery eight years later to Eberhard Anheuser. Anheuser's son-in-law, Adolphus Busch, joined the company in 1865, eventually becoming a partner and president of the company. In 1876, Busch helped restaurateur

FINANCES:

Anheuser-Busch Net Sales, 1994-1997 (billion dollars)

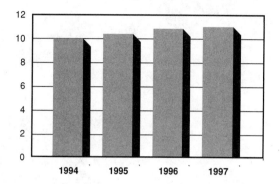

Anheuser-Busch 1997 Stock Prices (dollars)

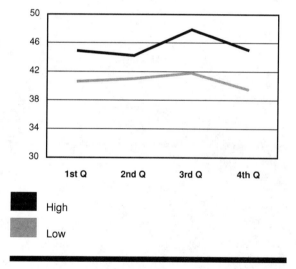

Carl Conrad create Budweiser beer—rights to the name Budweiser had been purchased from another brewery. In 1896, they created the Michelob brand.

When Adolphus died in 1913, his son August took over the company, which was re-named Anheuser-Busch, Inc. in 1919. Anheuser-Busch has grown from its roots as a regional beer company into the largest international brewer/marketer and a leading operator of theme parks. During prohibition, when it could not sell beer, the company nearly went under, but survived by selling other products such as ice cream, ginger ale, malt syrup, and nonalcoholic Budweiser. Once Prohibition was repealed, in the 1930s the firm began a steady ascent toward the

The Anheuser-Busch brewery in St. Louis, Missouri, established in 1852, was declared a national historical landmark in 1967. (Courtesy of Anheuser-Busch Companies, Inc.)

top of the beer business. By 1957, Anheuser-Busch surpassed Schlitz in sales to become the largest U.S. brewer, a title it has held ever since. Busch Entertainment Corp., a theme park operator, was created in 1959 with the opening of Busch Gardens in Tampa, Florida. In 1982, Anheuser-Busch bought Campbell Taggart, a baked goods maker, and also created its Eagle snack foods unit. Both were sold off in 1996, taking the company out of the food business. That same year the company also sold the St. Louis Cardinals, an earlier acquisition. In 1989, Anheuser-Busch acquired Sea World from Harcourt Brace Jovanovich, adding Anheuser-Busch to the ranks of the country's largest theme park operators.

STRATEGY

In the mid-1990s Anheuser-Busch Companies summed up its corporate strategy with four key phrases, which still applied in 1998: focusing on the core businesses of beer, entertainment, and packaging; leveraging resources; thinking differently; and "making friends." The company's focus on core businesses was illustrated by its exit from unrelated businesses (see History above). The company planned to leverage its resources by investing $2 billion in its brewery systems from 1996 to 2001, increasing its quality standards, expanding internationally, and creating new "specialty" beers. They also used aggressive marketing to capitalize on core brands. One of the most successful campaigns was Budweiser Concentration Week, the largest selling promotion in Anheuser-Busch's history, in which employees and wholesalers "hit the streets" selling Budweiser.

"Thinking differently" applied to improving relationships with wholesalers and re-engineering internal management systems. And "making friends" referred to the promotion of the safe use of alcoholic beverages, increasing the company's charitable activities, and promoting environmental conservation. Another corporate strategy, articulated in 1998, focused on reducing costs, improving productivity, and changing the company's pricing strategies in order to increase the profit margin, rather than increasing price.

Global marketing was clearly on the mind of Anheuser-Busch in the late-1990s, since the global beer market was four times larger than the U.S. market. As of 1997 Anheuser-Busch's beer brands were sold in more than 80 countries, either as an imported beer or produced locally under license. While brewing traditionally has been a local industry, Anheuser-Busch was expanding into China, Japan, Mexico, Brazil, and other countries in the mid-1990s. In the early 1990s, Anheuser-Busch bought a 5-percent stake in Tsingtao, China's largest brewery, for $16.4 million and later purchased 80 percent of a large brewery in Wuhan in central China. The company also spent $600 million buying shares of leading breweries in Mexico and Brazil.

FAST FACTS:
About Anheuser-Busch Companies, Inc.

Ownership: Anheuser-Busch Companies, Inc. is a publicly owned company listed on the New York Stock Exchange and other stock exchanges around the world.

Ticker symbol: BUD

Officers: August A. Busch, III, 59, Chmn. & Pres.; W. Randolph Baker, 50, VP & CFO; Patrick T. Stokes, 54, VP & Group Exec.; John H. Purnell, 55, VP & Group Exec.

Employees: 24,326

Principal Subsidiary Companies: Anheuser-Busch Companies, Inc., is the parent company for Anheuser-Busch, Inc. (U.S. brewing); Anheuser-Busch International, Inc. (overseas brewing and marketing); Busch Agricultural Resources, Inc. (raw materials for brewing); Busch Media Group, Inc. (advertising placement); Busch Creative Service Corporation (marketing and business communication); St. Louis Refrigerator Car Company (railroad car maintenance and repair); Manufacturers Railway Company (terminal rail-switching services); Metal Container Corporation (aluminum can manufacturing); Anheuser-Busch Recycling Corporation (collection of recyclable materials); Precision Printing and Packaging, Inc. (labels and cartons); Busch Entertainment Corporation (theme parks); and Busch Properties, Inc. (real estate development).

Chief Competitors: Anheuser-Busch is primarily a maker and distributor of beer. As such, its primary competitors are: Adolph Coors Co.; Bass; Boston Beer Co.; Carlsberg; Guinness; Heineken; Interbrew; Molson; Miller Brewing Co.; Stroh Brewery Co.; and San Miguel. As an owner and operator of theme parks, Anheuser-Busch also includes among its competitors Six Flags; Viacom, Inc.; and Walt Disney Co.

The company established an international division in 1981, but major growth in international sales did not begin until the mid-1990s. One observer noted that Anheuser-Busch's international efforts "were going nowhere" until the company gave up efforts to set up its own overseas operations and began establishing partner-

CHRONOLOGY:

Key Dates for Anheuser-Busch Companies, Inc.

1852: Founded as Bavarian Brewery

1860: Is sold to Eberhard Anheuser

1865: Adolphus Busch joins the company

1876: Purchases the Budweiser beer brand

1896: Creates the Michelob brand

1913: Adolphus Busch dies

1919: Company renamed Anheuser-Busch, Inc.

1920: Prohibition closes the brewery for thirteen years

1934: August Busch dies

1953: Acquires St. Louis Cardinals

1957: Becomes largest U.S. brewer

1959: Opened Busch Gardens in Tampa, Florida

1981: Establishes an international division

1982: Buys Campbell Taggart and creates Eagle snack foods unit

1989: Acquires Sea World

1996: Sells Eagle Snack Foods, Campbell Taggart, and the St. Louis Cardinals; introduces freshness dating and Bud Ice

ships with foreign brewers in the early 1990s. After that, results were more promising. For example, Anheuser-Busch's international volume grew 13.4 percent in 1997, to 7 million barrels. However, this was still a small total compared with its U.S. sales of 89.6 million barrels. In 1997, Anheuser-Busch had an 8-percent share of the worldwide beer market.

Anheuser-Busch planned to grow internationally through a complex web of joint marketing agreements, local brewing, import distribution agreements, joint ventures, contract brewing, and equity investments. In 1997 sales outside the U.S. market increased by 13 percent. The company also planned to build Budweiser as a global brand, focusing on marketing the beer in countries with rising growth rates and standards of living. Sales of Budweiser overseas increased by 18 percent in 1997, mostly in China, the United Kingdom, Ireland, and South America.

INFLUENCES

Today, the company is known as much for its intensive and creative marketing as for its beer. Despite fierce competition, A-B's creative television and print advertising has kept its flagship "Bud" brand on top of the beer market. In the mid-1990s, nearly all A-B beer brands were growing despite slow growth in the overall beer market. Bud Light was particularly successful, growing fast enough to overtake Miller Lite as the nation's number-one light beer.

In 1996 Anheuser-Busch made a major marketing change by using "freshness dating" on its Budweiser beer. The company called the freshness dating a "born on" date to show that its beer is brewed, transported, and sold quickly. The company aggressively focused on this new concept in a major television advertising campaign and continued to use this as a strategy illustrating the beer's high quality in the late 1990s.

CURRENT TRENDS

Even though specialty beers accounted for a small part of the U.S. beer market in the mid-1990s—about 2 percent—large breweries such as Anheuser-Busch began making specialty beers under different labels to appeal to people who like exotic beer. One of the specialty beers introduced by Anheuser-Busch's Specialty Brewing Group was Pacific Ridge Pale Ale, which was launched in California in November 1996. Other brands included Red Wolf, Elk Mountain Amber Ale, ZiegenBock, and Christmas Brew.

At the same time, the company aggressively challenged much smaller specialty brewers. In 1996, the company went so far as to petition the U.S. Bureau of Alcohol, Tobacco & Firearms to require small "contract brewers," which market specialty beers that are actually made at larger breweries, to state the name of the company that brews the beer on labels and advertisements. The petition was supported by some microbrewers who brew beer in their own establishments.

Another major trend Anheuser-Busch faced in the mid-1990s was social and regulatory pressure over its marketing tactics, particularly television advertising. Most of the controversy was concerned with the effect of advertising for beer and other alcoholic beverages on teenagers. While Anheuser-Busch said that its marketing and advertising was geared at an adult audience, many consumer activists claimed that the "spillover" effect of such marketing encouraged underage drinking.

As a result, Anheuser-Busch and other brewers tried to create a more favorable image by funding programs that encourage abstinence for people under 21 and responsible drinking for adults. The company also modified some of its marketing tactics. For example, in re-

sponse to regulatory pressures, Anheuser-Busch removed its beer commercials from the cable channel MTV in 1996 since many MTV viewers were below the legal drinking age. However, MTV Networks planned to transfer most of the ads to its affiliate, VH-1, which is oriented toward adults.

PRODUCTS

Anheuser-Busch extended its product line in 1997, adding new specialty extensions to its Michelob line. These included Honey Lager and Pale Ale, released in the United States. HefeWeizen, another brand, was expanded from select markets to national availability. And Black and Tan was planned for national release in 1998. Seasonal beers were also planned under the Michelob name, including Maple Brown Ale and Winterbrew Spiced Ale.

In Japan, Anheuser-Busch also extended its product line. Through its existing alliance with the Kirin Brewery Company, the company began brewing Kirin Lager, Kirin Ichiban, and Kirin Light at the A-B Los Angeles brewery. The joint venture, the first time Anheuser-Busch has brewed foreign brands for U.S. sale, is 90-percent owned by Kirin.

CORPORATE CITIZENSHIP

Anheuser-Busch and its charitable foundations donated funds to hundreds of charitable organizations in the mid-1990s, helping to provide relief after disasters like the Oklahoma City bombing, flooding, and hurricanes. The company also funded educational opportunities through the United Negro College Fund, National Hispanic Scholarship Funds, and National Korean American Scholarship Foundation. Anheuser-Busch donates to health care institutions, the arts, civic and cultural groups, and social service agencies. The company also participates in alcohol awareness and education, sponsoring programs that send a message of personal responsibility in schools, in the home, and anywhere that sells alcohol. The company's goal is to work with teachers, law enforcement, and community organizations to fight drunk driving and underage drinking. They teamed up with 7-Eleven and created a program promoting "Family Talk About Drinking." 7-Eleven stores post prominent notices to make the public aware of the program, information about which patrons can receive by calling 800-359-TALK.

Anheuser-Busch is also the world's largest recycler of aluminum beverage containers. The company's recycling efforts are coordinated by the Anheuser-Busch Recycling Corporation, which recycled 125 percent of the amount of cans actually sold by Anheuser-Busch in 1997.

GENTLE GIANTS—THE BUDWEISER CLYDESDALES

Working together in eight-horse teams called hitches, the Budweiser Clydesdales are arguably one of the greatest American icons. First introduced in 1933 to celebrate the end of Prohibition, the Clydesdales have risen to immense popularity. However, these horses have to pass strict standards to earn a place on the team. An acceptable horse must be 72 inches tall at the shoulder, be reddish-brown (bay) with a black mane and tail, have white stockings on all four legs, and a white blaze on its face; it must also have passed its third birthday.

Descended from ancient European war horses, the Clydesdales have been bred in North America to be powerful enough to pull a wagon or a plow. Anheuser-Busch is dedicated to preserving the Clydesdales and maintains breeding and training facilities at Grant's Farm in St. Louis, Missouri, and in Romoland, California. From there horses that meet the standards are trained and sent to one of three touring hitches in St. Louis, Romoland, or Merrimack, New Hampshire; or they are sent to one of Anheuser-Busch's theme parks so visitors can see them.

The touring hitches travel all over the world to perform at special events such as the Rose Bowl and other parades. Before a hitch can make an appearance they must be groomed and decorated with red, white, and blue ribbons woven through their manes and tails. The handlers hitch them up to an antique four-ton brewery wagon using a custom made black leather harness. The finishing touch on every hitch is a dalmatian. The Clydesdales are beautiful to watch as they perform "high, graceful strides" while pulling the wagon, and people come from miles around to see them. Thanks to Anheuser-Busch, the next generation will enjoy them, too.

GLOBAL PRESENCE

Anheuser-Busch's two main strategies for global operations were to build Budweiser into an "international premium brand" and to build partnerships with foreign brewers. The company's largest and most profitable foreign market was the United Kingdom, in which the Budweiser brand showed double-digit growth rates—Budweiser had 2.9-percent market share of the U.K. market at the end of 1997. Bud Ice, introduced in 1996, holds 25 percent of the United Kingdom's ice beer market. Through a partnership with Guinness Ireland, Budweiser has been introduced into Northern Ireland and captured 25.4-percent share in the lager market there. Budweiser has also been successfully introduced into Paraguay, Brazil, Colombia, Honduras, China, and the Philippines. Latin America and Asia were still considered "key strategic markets" by the company in 1998.

In 1996 Anheuser-Busch began making beer for Japan's Kirin Brewery, the company's first attempt to make a foreign brand of beer. At the same time it ended talks to obtain the rights to the Budweiser name throughout Europe, which it sold previously. Anheuser-Busch continued the same arrangement it had for decades: it kept the Budweiser name in 11 European countries while Czech brewer Budvar Budejovicky owned it in nine others (in those countries, Anheuser-Busch uses the alternative, "Bud").

SOURCES OF INFORMATION

Bibliography

Anheuser-Busch Companies Annual Report 1997. St. Louis: Anheuser-Busch Companies, Inc.

Anheuser-Busch Companies 1996/1997 Fact Book. St. Louis: Anheuser-Busch Companies, Inc.

"The Beer Barons Raise Their Glasses to the World." *The Economist,* 13 May 1995, 61.

"It's a Small World for U.S. Brewers; International Beer Sales Are Flourishing, Providing a Pleasant Change From a Flat Domestic Market." *Beverage Industry,* May 1996, 10.

Palmer, Jay. "Brewing Storm: New Beer Makers Gain Popularity, But Trouble May Bubble Up." *Barron's,* 28 October 1996, 37.

For an annual report:

The company's annual report is available on the Internet at: http://www.anheuser-busch.com/finhome.htm or call (314)577-3889 or write: Vice President and Secretary's Office, Anheuser-Busch Companies, 1 Busch Pl., St. Louis, MO 63118.

For additional industry research:

Investigate companies by their Standard Industrial Classification Codes, also known as SICs. Anheuser-Busch's primary SICs are:

2038 Frozen Specialties, NEC

2082 Malt Beverages

3411 Metal Cans

7996 Amusement Parks

Apple Computer, Inc.

OVERVIEW

Apple Computer is one of the world's leading computer companies. The company designs, builds, and markets computers, peripheral equipment, and software for homes, businesses, educational institutions, and the government. Apple also provides customers with multimedia and connectivity solutions. Apple was a pioneer in the field of personal computers with its easy-to-use, object-based Apple Macintosh—the bulk of Apple's net sales come from the sale of this line. This user-friendly computer interface "for the rest of us" has since spawned competitive imitations, namely Microsoft's Windows '95. In 1997, Apple was fighting to recapture users lost to dominant IBM-compatible computers running the Windows operating system.

FOUNDED: 1977

Contact Information:

HEADQUARTERS: 1 Infinite Loop
   Cupertino, CA 95014-2084
PHONE: (408)996-1010
FAX: (408)974-2113
TOLL FREE: (800)776-2333
URL: http://www.apple.com

COMPANY FINANCES

Apple reported second quarter revenues for 1998 (ending March 27, 1998) of $1.4 billion and unit sales of 650,000. The company recorded a quarterly net profit of $55 million. This represented significant improvement over performance for the same quarter in 1997, when Apple recorded a net loss of $708 million. First quarter revenues for fiscal year 1998 (ending December 26, 1997) were $1.6 billion, a net profit of $47 million. Unit sales that quarter were 635,000. Overall net sales for 1997 were $7.1 billion, down from 1996 sales of $9.8 billion. Apple incurred overall net losses of $1.0 billion, compared to a net loss of $816 million in 1996. Of the company's sales, half were earned internationally.

FINANCES:

Apple Computer Net Sales, 1994-1997 (million dollars)

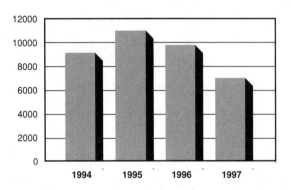

Apple Computer 1997 Stock Prices (dollars)

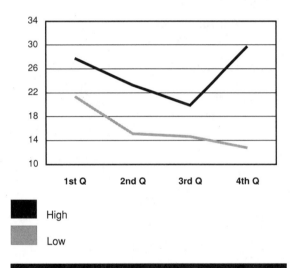

For the second quarter of 1998, Apple earned earnings per share (EPS) of $.38, about the same as it earned in the first quarter ($.37). The company's stock price in mid-1998 was around $28.00 per share. Its 52-week high was $31.63, and the 52-week low was $12.75. For the years 1993 through 1997 Apple stock had a five-year high of $65.25 per share, and $12.75 was its five-year low.

ANALYSTS' OPINIONS

Steve Jobs' return to Apple was applauded by some and criticized by others. Many praise his pioneering work in taking object-oriented technology to the World Wide Web and see this as Apple's salvation, especially as it strives to stay Internet-compatible. Others see him as a power-monger scheming to take over Apple and fear he could bring about the company's demise with ruinous policies. According to Sebastian Rupley of *PC Magazine,* Apple's key goal should be to attract the best software developers.

Analysts seemed to feel it was best to take a "wait and see" attitude on Apple stock and gave it a "hold" rating, though a few did award the company "moderate buy" or even "strong buy" ratings, based on the company's improved performance in the first half of 1998. In June of 1998, Standard & Poor's (S&P) revised its outlook on Apple Computer Inc. from negative to positive. S&P's revision reflected Apple's improved profitability and financial flexibility. Prior negative ratings were based on declining revenues and operating losses in 1996 and 1997, as well as the company's struggle with competitive conditions in the industry and its declining market share. Also, Apple's market presence in the higher-growth corporate and consumer markets was small and still declining.

Cited as positives for the company were its strong position in the education and desktop publishing markets, as well as Apple's significant progress in reducing staff and operating costs. This, and its improved financial position during 1998, helped improve Apple's outlook. The analysts still had long-term concerns about the company's ability to sustain its revenue growth and profitability, however. Overall, S&P reported that, "Ratings could improve if Apple is able to stabilize revenues while maintaining profitability and financial flexibility."

HISTORY

Steve Jobs and Stephen Wozniak, two college dropouts, built the first Apple computer in Jobs' garage in 1976. This microcomputer, the Apple I, was a bare-bones creation with no monitor, casing, or keyboard. These were later added, as were software and ports for third-party peripherals. On January 3, 1977, Apple Computer, Inc. was incorporated. In 1980, with the sale of more than 130,000 Apple IIs and $117 million under its belt, the company went public at $22 per share. After a 1981 plane crash, Wozniak returned briefly but ultimately left the company.

In 1984, Apple revolutionized microcomputing with the introduction of its Macintosh (Mac) personal computer. Unlike other computers on the market, the Mac interface allowed users to forgo the ubiquitous text commands, instead opting for a system whereby the user would control operations by clicking and dragging on-screen "icons."

According to some accounts, Jobs originally opposed the Mac and only embraced it (dismissing its very

The Research and Development offices and corporate headquarters of Apple Computer, Inc. (Photograph by Peter Stember. Courtesy of Apple Computer, Inc.)

proponents and taking the credit himself) after the dismal market failure of his Lisa system. After a volatile power struggle within the company, Apple's board of directors voted unanimously to replace Jobs with former PepsiCo executive, John Sculley. Soon thereafter, Apple entered the desktop publishing market with the Mac Plus and LaserWriter printer. In 1987, Apple founded a software company, later named Claris.

The rise of archnemesis Microsoft took larger and larger bites out of Apple's market share, and the company soon had to contend with a comparable opponent with a similar product. Complicating matters was the fact that Apple would not license its software to other computer manufacturers, a move that did not improve the company's marketability. Widespread competition in the PC market often made IBM clones more economical, with software widely available. In 1994, the company released its Power Mac computer, though sales did not live up to expectations. In 1995, the company was forced to shut down its online service, eWorld. In 1996, Apple brought in a new CEO, Gilbert Amelio.

Widely regarded as the force behind the successful turnaround at National Semiconductor, Amelio immediately announced major changes at Apple. He divided the company into seven divisions, each responsible for its own success or failure. Nonetheless, under this new organizational structure, divisions were more accountable to top management, which would have tighter control over the company's actions. Soon thereafter, Amelio announced the purchase of Jobs' company, NeXT software.

Jobs would return to Apple as a consultant and Apple would replace the Mac OS with NeXT's "Rhapsody" operating system, expected for release in 1998. In another surprise move, the company announced that Wozniak would join Jobs on Apple's executive committee and as a consultant to Amelio.

STRATEGY

Apple's primary strategy during the late 1990s was to maintain and augment its market share in the personal computer industry while developing and expanding similar endeavors such as personal interactive products, client/server systems, on-line services, and the licensing of its Macintosh operating system. The company's original strategy of not licensing the operating system to other developers, or authorizing the production of Mac clones, came back to haunt it. In 1994 the company made an about face, licensing three companies to produce Macintosh clones and, in turn, lost some of its market share. That same year, it released its Power Mac, a much faster computer running on a PowerPC microchip, which allowed users to use software for several different platforms, including Windows. In order to spark the creation of more Mac-compatible software, Apple licensed the rights to its operating system (Mac OS) to IBM and Motorola in 1996. In 1997, interim CEO Steve Jobs announced the company was pursuing an alliance with Microsoft to offer a Mac version of Microsoft Office. Apple

FAST FACTS:

About Apple Computer, Inc.

Ownership: Apple is a publicly owned company traded on NASDAQ, the Tokyo Stock Exchange (under symbol AAPLE), and the Frankfurt Stock Exchange (symbol APCD).

Ticker symbol: AAPL

Officers: Steve Jobs, Interim CEO & Co-founder, 42; Fred D. Anderson, Exec. VP & CFO, 52, $520,311; Timothy D. Cook, Sr. VP, Worldwide Operations; Nancy R. Heinen, Sr. VP & Gen. Counsel

Employees: 10,176 (1997)

Chief Competitors: Apple Computer's main competitors in the electronic computer industry include: Hewlett-Packard; Compaq; Dell; Gateway; Intel; and IBM. Networking and software competitors include: Microsoft; Novell; PowerComputing; and Sun Microsystems.

also revoked one of its licenses for the Mac clones, to Power Computing, in order to regain some of its lost market share.

In 1997, in the interest of long-term viability, the company embarked on a major reorganization and draconian cost-cutting measures, including the layoffs of several thousand employees (almost a third of the company). It also brought Steve Jobs back as interim CEO, replacing Gil Amelio and resulting in yet another strategy shift for Apple Computer. These and other moves resulted in Apple's first profitable quarter in years (first quarter 1998). Jobs streamlined the organization, squelched Mac cloning, bear-hugged old nemesis Microsoft, forged a foothold in network computers costing less than $1,000, and—taking a cue from Dell Computer—started selling built-to-order systems over the Internet. Apple generates sales through catalogs, through regional retailers, and nationally through CompUSA.

In May 1998, Jobs announced Apple was pursuing a new strategy focused on regaining market share in software development—developers who deserted the Macintosh operating system in favor of Windows during the mid- to late 1990s. Toward this goal, Jobs was scrapping the company's Rhapsody operating system except as a transition vehicle to the new Mac OS X (OS "10"). Rhap-

sody would have allowed the Mac's operating system to run software for chips made by Intel, IBM, and Motorola as well as Apple, but would have required software developers to rewrite old Macintosh code from scratch. The new system, OS X, would have features such as hardware memory protection, more efficient multi-tasking, and faster networking. It also would not require programmers to rewrite old code from scratch. Jobs' strategy was supported by Microsoft, Adobe, and Macromedia executives, who were happy to be able to write applications that worked on both the old and new Mac systems. In the wake of Jobs' announcement, Apple's stock price rose to $39.9, the highest it reached in a year.

INFLUENCES

Apple's comfortable advantage was eclipsed in the late 1980s when Microsoft released its Windows operating system. The Windows graphical interface was in many ways similar to the look and feel of the Macintosh—so similar that Apple decided to sue, albeit unsuccessfully. In the mid-1990s, with Windows running on more affordable IBM clones, Apple's earnings began to fall. The company's problems included shrinking revenues, defecting executives, market-stealing clone sales, and troubled products, such as its discontinued Newton handheld computers. However, Apple owners remain the industry's most loyal repurchasers. And Macintosh computers still had a niche in educational institutions and design shops. Designers specializing in Web page design and graphic arts especially liked the Mac systems, making the company a major Internet products provider.

CURRENT TRENDS

While third-party software designed for Windows abounded, Macintosh-compatible software was much harder to come by. However, in 1998, Hewlett-Packard announced that they would make printers compatible with the Mac operating system, which would help with some of Apple Computer's compatibility issues. The 1990s saw a boom in the commercialization of the Internet. Customers by the millions were joining the online market, an area in which Apple hoped to shine. One of the company's major efforts to do so was the forming of its WebObjects Consulting Group, which was formed around WebObjects, Apple's leading Web application development platform. The consulting group provides in-depth consulting for businesses on strategic web-based solutions for database publishing, digital asset management, and e-commerce.

PRODUCTS

New products offered at Apple include the iMac, a new Macintosh computer designed for consumers. Announced on May 6, 1998, "Reception from the Macintosh community and computer industry as a whole to the iMac has been reminiscent of the rollout of the first Macintosh in 1984, which also featured a breakthrough design for its time," said Andy Gore of *Macworld* magazine. Other products developed during 1997-98 included Apple's G3 Powerbooks and the Power Macintosh G3, "Apple's most powerful computer ever." Other hardware offered includes servers, message pads, and "emates." Apple also marketed software, starting with the Mac operating system and networking software. Software products included FileMaker Pro (database software), QuickTime (video, sound, music, 3D, and virtual reality software for both Macintosh and Windows), and WebObjects (a Web development application).

Peripherals offered by the company include scanners, printers, monitors, network interfaces, and CD-ROM drives. The company also produces an extensive array of software applications and utilities. Its two personal digital assistants are the Newton and the MessagePad.

CORPORATE CITIZENSHIP

Apple is an active corporate citizen. Since the early 1980s, the company has donated computer products to schools and nonprofit groups. Its grants have provided for the collaboration of K-12 schools with schools of education to strengthen teacher training. Volunteer organizations are using donated Apple products to serve their communities. At its key sites around the world, the company has established Community Affairs teams to ensure a proactive community presence. In June 1998, Apple pledged up to $1 million in network software and training to Los Angeles County schools through the county Office of Education's Technology Learning program.

GLOBAL PRESENCE

With headquarters in Cupertino, California, Apple has manufacturing facilities in Singapore and Ireland. It also has distribution facilities in the United States, Canada, Australia, Europe, Singapore, and Japan. The company has business, education, government, scientific, and consumer entertainment customers in more than 140 countries. Sales in North America accounted for about half of Apple's revenues. Of remaining sales, $1.6 billion was earned in Europe (24 percent), $1 billion was earned in Japan (15 percent), $490 million was earned in other Asia/Pacific regions (7 percent), and sales to the rest of the world were $347 million (5 percent).

CHRONOLOGY:

Key Dates for Apple Computer, Inc.

1976: Steve Jobs and Stephen Wozniak build the first Apple computer in Jobs' garage

1977: Apple Computer, Inc. is incorporated

1980: Goes public at $22 per share

1984: Introduces the Macintosh personal computer

1985: Jobs leaves Apple and creates a new computer company, NeXT Incorporated

1988: Apple reorganizes into four operating divisions; brought suits against Microsoft and Hewlett-Packard for copyright infringement of its operating system

1991: PowerBook notebook is introduced, gaining 21 percent market share in less than six months

1992: Most of its lawsuit against Microsoft and Hewlett-Packard is dismissed

1994: The Power Mac is released

1996: Apple brings in new CEO Gilbert Amelio

1998: NeXT is purchased, bringing Jobs back to Apple as a consultant

EMPLOYMENT

Ultimately, employees may be the ones who pay the price for Apples' turnaround. In 1996, the company laid off 1,800 workers. In 1997, the company began more major layoffs—this time over 2,000 of its remaining 11,000 full-time employees. The layoffs were a crucial part of Apple's plan to slash operating expenses by 20 percent. The company refocused, however, and in 1998 was hiring employees to fill positions needed to pursue Apple's new technical goals, satisfy customer needs, and identify new markets. In the first half of 1998, the company hired more than 600 new employees and employed 9,049 people worldwide.

As part of its corporate culture, Apple considers the work environment critical. The corporate workspace is open and informal meeting areas are located throughout offices for meetings or just relaxing with colleagues. Some offices are even furnished with pool tables, ping pong tables, and basketball and volleyball courts. At Apple's headquarters, a coffee shop, fitness center, company store, and bookstore are all available onsite. For offices

"THINK DIFFERENT"

On September 28, 1997, Apple Computer, Inc. introduced its first major ad campaign in a decade. The "Think Different" campaign uses photographs of major figures in recent history, along with the simple line, "Think Different." Each person is someone who was considered a "rebel," "misfit," or pioneer. They did things differently and wound up changing the world. Although none of the people in the pictures are identified, they are symbols for change.

The campaign honors creative geniuses who have touched the lives of many people through the things they have done. Figures include Neil Armstrong, Muhammad Ali, Thomas Edison, Joan Baez, Albert Einstein, John Lennon and Yoko Ono, Amelia Earhart, Lucille Ball and Desi Arnaz, Rosa Parks, and Jim Henson. Although many advertising campaigns today use celebrities to promote their products, Apple is using celebrity figures in a way that honors their spirits and accomplishments.

Apple Computer, Inc.'s Interim Chief Executive Officer, Steve Jobs said, "Think Different celebrates the soul of the Apple brand-that creative people with passion can change the world for the better," and with people like Mahatma Ghandi and Pablo Picasso in ads for Apple, who can argue with that?

---

that do not have fitness facilities, reimbursement for fitness memberships is available as a benefit to employees. Other benefits offered by Apple include bonus programs, stock purchase plans, and 401(k) plans. The company also provides health benefits, profit sharing, tuition reimbursement, and substantial discounts on Apple computer equipment.

SOURCES OF INFORMATION

Bibliography
"11-Year Financial History." Cupertino, CA: Apple Computer, Inc., 1998.

"Apple at-a-Glance." Cupertino, CA: Apple Computer, Inc., 1997. Available at http://product.info.apple.com/pr/background/pr.background.glance.html.

"Apple Computer, Inc." *Hoover's Online.* 30 June 1998. Available at http://www.hoover.com.

"Apple Extends WebObjects Consulting Group to Design and Publishing Market." Cupertino, CA: Apple Computer Inc., 17 March 1998.

"Apple Pledges Up to $1 Million in Network Software and Training to Los Angeles County Schools." Apple Computer Inc. Press Release, 3 June 1998. Available at http://www.apple.com/pr/library/1998/jun/3la.html.

"Apple Worldwide Community Affairs: A Letter from Gilbert Amelio." Apple Computer, Inc., 1997. Available at http://www2.apple.com/communityaffairs.

Gruman, Galen. "Apple's Make-or-Break Decision Time." 20 March 1997. Available at http://www.macworld.com/daily/daily.1085.html.

"Mac Faithful Like the New Apple iMac: It's Just Right'." *Macworld,* 10 June 1998. Available at http://macworld.zdnet.com/features/0698/imacsurvey.html.

Markoff, John. "Rhapsody's Out, OS X In, in Shift of Gear at Apple." *The New York Times,* 12 May 1998.

"Report Suggests Ailing Apple Will Eliminate 40% of Work Force." *Dow Jones & Company, Inc.,* 24 February 1997.

Rupley, Sebastian. "Apple's NeXt OS: Steve Jobs Makes an Apple Comeback." *PC Magazine,* 18 February 1997.

Sanford, Glen. "A History of Apple." 1997. Available at http://www.apple-history.pair.com.

For an annual report:
on the Internet at: http://www.apple.com/investor/annualreports.html **or** write: Apple Investor Relations, 1 Infinite Loop, MS 301-4IR, Cupertino, CA 95014 **or** call 408-974-3123

For additional industry research:
Investigate companies by their Standard Industrial Classification Codes, also known as SICs. Apple's primary SICs are:

3571 Electronic Computers

5045 Computers, Peripherals and Software

7372 Prepackaged Software

7379 Computer Related Services, NEC

Applebee's International Inc.

OVERVIEW

Headquartered in Overland Park, Kansas, Applebee's International Inc. develops, franchises, and operates close to 1,100 casual dining restaurants in 48 states and 5 countries. As of early June 1998, Applebee's opened its 1,000th Applebee's Neighborhood Grill & Bar brand restaurant. In addition, it operated about 60 Rio Bravo Cantina brand restaurants, making Applebee's International the largest casual dining restaurant chain in the world. Of the 1,000-plus Applebee's brand restaurants, about 200 are company owned—the remainder are franchised. The company owns about 35 of the Rio Brava Cantina brand restaurants; the rest are franchised.

Further sharp increases in the company's number of restaurants are expected as Applebee's continues to expand aggressively. More than 500 restaurants were added between December 1994 and April 1998. The company opened its 1,000th Applebee's brand restaurant in Aurora, Colorado, on June 9, 1998, the first casual-dining restaurant chain to hit that milestone. The closest casual-dining restaurant competitor has about 700 outlets, according to industry data.

Announcing the company's first quarter 1998 results in late April 1998, CEO Lloyd L. Hill said the company was running well ahead of its target for the period. He said reductions in labor costs and improvements in other controllable expenses during the first quarter resulted in a higher level of earnings than had been expected at the end of last year. "This quarter's performance gives us added confidence that we are well positioned to continue delivering improved results as we move through the balance of 1998."

FOUNDED: 1988

Contact Information:

HEADQUARTERS: 4551 W. 107th St., Ste. 100
   Overland Park, KS 66207
PHONE: (913)967-4000
FAX: (913)341-1694

FINANCES:

Applebee's International Operating Revenues, 1994-1997 (million dollars)

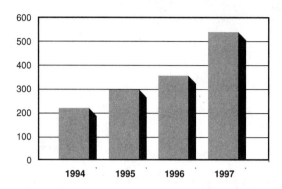

Applebee's International 1997 Stock Prices (dollars)

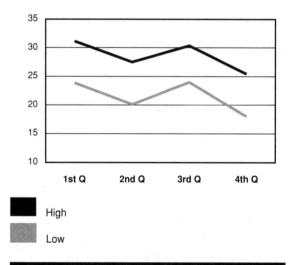

■ High

▨ Low

COMPANY FINANCES

Applebee's International posted net earnings of $45.1 million on revenue of $515.8 million in 1997, compared with a net of $38.0 million on revenue of $413.1 million in 1996. Company-owned restaurants accounted for $452.2 million, or 88 percent of total revenue in 1997. Franchised operations produced $63.6 million, or 12 percent of total revenue. The company reported net income of $12.0 million on revenue of $146.6 million for the first quarter of 1998, compared with net earnings of $10.9 million on revenue of $116.3 million in the first quarter

of 1997. Applebee's posted net income of $27.5 million on revenue of $343.6 million in 1995, compared with net earnings of $16.9 million on revenue of $208.5 million in 1994.

ANALYSTS' OPINIONS

The investment community seemed to be bullish on Applebee's International during the first half of 1998, with a number of analysts and fund managers putting the company's stock high on their "buy" list. Stevin Hoover, chairman and CEO of Hoover Capital Management of Boston, told *Worth Magazine* that the company, "has a few great things going for it. First it serves the right demographic group, the 24- to 55-year-old segment, which makes up almost 40 percent of the U.S. population, and is still growing. This group spends more than $60 billion a year on 'home-meal replacement," the new buzzword for eating out. Its preference is for middle-level casual dining, as opposed to fast-food or high-end restaurants. Second, Applebee's is perhaps the only restaurant in this niche to successfully franchise its name—approximately 80 percent of Applebee's restaurants are franchises, an annuity-style business that has offered the company steady and rising free cash flow." Hoover went on to say that, although Applebee's growth outside the United States had not yet taken off in a big way, he sees enormous potential for such expansion in both Europe and Canada.

Hoover's upbeat view of Applebee's prospects were echoed in early 1998 by analyst John Dorfman of *Bloomberg News.* He said he was impressed by Applebee's growth and management. Dorfman's friend, Jeff Omohundro, a restaurant analyst with Wheat First Union, concurred with Dorfman. He said that the company would have been his number one pick had it not been for the Apple South defections, which he felt raised the risk level in the stock a bit. In June 1998, analyst Eric Wold, of Van Kasper & Co. in Princeton, New Jersey, also added Applebee's to his "buy" list.

HISTORY

Partners John Hambra and Abe Gustin acquired an Applebee's franchise from a subsidiary of W.R. Grace in 1986. Two years later, the two bought out the Applebee's franchisor and formed Applebee's International Inc. Under new management, the franchisor launched into a period of rapid expansion. It grew from just over 50 restaurants in the late 1980s to about 500 by 1994. That same year, one of the company's largest franchisees, Tom DuPree of Apple South, mounted an unsuccessful attempt to take over the parent company.

In 1995 Applebee's acquired Innovative Restaurant Concepts, the company that had developed a small chain of Mexican food restaurants called Rio Bravo Cantinas. By adding a second restaurant brand, Applebee's executives hoped to create an avenue for even greater expansion.

In addition to its restaurants throughout the United States, Applebee's has franchised operations in a handful of foreign countries, including Canada, Curacao, Germany, Greece, the Netherlands, and Sweden. The company hopes to add further franchised operations abroad in the future.

In 1997 Applebee's management tangled again with its biggest franchisee, Apple South, which announced a plan to sell its more than 250 Applebee's brand restaurants. This was due to the franchisor having refused to expand Apple South's franchise territory. In December of 1997 Applebee's announced it had reached an agreement with Apple South. Under this agreement Applebee's would acquire 32 Applebee's restaurants in Virginia from Apple South for $93.4 million in cash. At the same time Apple South announced three letters of intent to sell 61 additional Applebee's restaurants to two existing and one new Applebee's franchisees. The 61 restaurants are in the Washington, D.C., metropolitan area, Mississippi, and Tennessee.

The agreement between the two companies calls for Apple South to divest all of its other Applebee's restaurants as soon as it's practical. Should Apple South fail to sell all of its Applebee's franchises by the end of 1999, the agreement gives Applebee's an option to acquire them according to a pre-determined pricing formula. Under the divestment agreement between the two companies, Apple South will be released from any noncompetition obligations. However, they will be restricted from negotiating with, or acquiring certain competing restaurant concepts for up to a year.

In announcing the divestment agreement with Apple South, Applebee's Chairperson Abe J. Gustin said, "We believe this important agreement reached by Applebee's International and Apple South allows both companies to move forward with their respective long-term strategies. Apple South has been a valued franchisee and an integral part of the success of the Applebee's system throughout the evolution of the concept." He said the plan would allow new and existing franchisees to acquire "strategically important restaurants and territories."

STRATEGY

Applebee's International launched an aggressive expansion strategy in the late 1980s. This increased its chain of Applebee's Neighborhood Grill & Bar restaurants from 55 in 1988 to more than 500 by 1994. That expansion was continuing unabated in the latter half of the 1990s. On June 9, 1998, the company opened its 1,000th Applebee's brand eatery in Aurora, Colorado.

FAST FACTS:

About Applebee's International Inc.

Ownership: Applebee's International is a publicly owned company traded on NASDAQ.

Ticker symbol: APPB

Officers: Abe J. Gustin Jr., Chmn., 63, $610,000; Lloyd L. Hill, Pres., CEO, & COO, 53, $510,000; George D. Shadid, Exec. VP, CFO, & Treasurer, 43, $405,000; Steven K. Lumkin, Sr. VP, Strategic Development, 43, $285,000

Employees: 18,000

Principal Subsidiary Companies: In addition to more than 1,000 Applebee's Neighborhood Grill & Bar locations, the company operates close to 60 Rio Bravo Cantina Tex-Mex restaurants.

Chief Competitors: Applebee's principal competitors include: Bob Evans; Boston Market; Cracker Barrel; Family Restaurants; IHOP; Lone Star Steakhouse; Luby's; Morrison Restaurants; Outback Steakhouse; Quality Dining; Ruby Tuesday; Taco Cabana; and Unique Casual Restaurants.

Applebee's acquired another vehicle for expansion in 1995 when it bought Innovative Restaurant Concepts, developer of the Rio Bravo Cantina chain. In 1997 alone, the company opened 145 new Applebee's restaurants and added 26 restaurants to its Rio Bravo Cantina chain. Plans for 1998 called for the opening of 21 additional Rio Bravo Cantina restaurants. The company acknowledged that its Rio Bravo Cantina restaurants had failed to perform as well as anticipated. Still, corporate strategy calls for continuing expansion of the Tex-Mex chain.

INFLUENCES

The growing appetite among young adults for casual dining at reasonable prices has been a crucial factor in the company's success. The company has captialized on this burgeoning market with aggressive expansion, adding more than 500 restaurants between the end of 1994 and mid-1998. As of year-end 1997, Applebee's owned approximately 5 percent of the $36-billion casual-dining market, and nearly 20 percent of the $10-billion "bar and grill" segment of the market, according to Lloyd

CHRONOLOGY:

Key Dates for Applebee's International Inc.

1980: The first T.J. Applebee's restaurant opens

1983: Creative Food N Fun Co. purchases Applebee's

1988: Abe J. Gustin, Jr. and John Hamra purchase Applebee's and formed Applebee's International Inc.

1995: Applebee's acquires Innovative Restaurant Concepts

1997: Applebee's biggest franchise announces plans to sell its 250 restaurants

Hill, the company's CEO. Hill predicted that system-wide sales, which totaled about $1.8 billion in 1997, would exceed $2.0 billion in 1998.

Speaking at the opening of the company's 1,000th Applebee's-brand restaurant in Aurora, Colorado, on June 9, 1998, Hill said, "We've succeeded in growing to 1,000 neighborhoods through a combination of excellence in menu, neighborhood location, management, overall execution, and dedication of our franchisees and employees, who strive to ensure that every dining experience is a positive one for our guests."

CURRENT TRENDS

Applebee's has tried to use the latest technology to run an efficient operation. In the area of training, the company has utilized a number of cutting-edge technologies, "to employ the most effective training method for a given situation," according to Matt Carpenter, the company's executive director of training.

Video has been widely used by the company in training because it is an efficient way of quickly distributing consistent information from management to a large number of employees, some of whom may be located some distance from corporate headquarters. Applebee's International has developed a library of more than 100 tapes, all of which were scripted internally and produced by an outside contractor. In addition to its program of training tapes, the company sometimes broadcasts live, interactive conferences, most of them occasioned by the roll-out of new products, to its restaurant locations around

the world. Many of these sessions are arranged by Hospitality Television, a Louisville, Kentucky-based company that specializes in satellite television and "interactive, distance learning" for food service operators.

Carpenter, touting the advantages of teleconferencing, said that, "unlike video, which is one-way, this validates that transfer of training occurred, with the opportunity for staff to interact with experts." The company's use of new technologies to expedite the training process does not end with video tapes and teleconferencing. Applebee's has developed CD-ROM programs, including full-motion video clips to train staff, some of whom are in remote locations, in how to prepare new additions to the menu. Participants are led through a series of interactive exercises, which bars progress to the next segment until all questions have been answered accurately. The program prevents trainees from logging off until they have reached a score of 90 percent or better. Carpenter says the program allows managers "to evaluate the length of time staff spends with the exercises and how well they perform."

Carpenter said that when the company rolled out a new, computerized system for forecasting sales and scheduling employees to 135 restaurants, Applebee's training costs were cut in half using computer-based training techniques. The computer-based training was supplemented by on-the-job, in-person coaching.

The company's use of new technology to do business faster, better, and smarter isn't limited to training. All of the company's multi-unit managers have notebook computers while in the field, using e-mail to create a virtual office while traveling.

Outlining the rationale for its use of high-tech training techniques, Steve Lumpkin, senior vice-president said, "Substantial investments in infrastructure allow us to send technology, instead of staff, to restaurants for training. With a shrinking labor pool headed into the future, investment in technology now will pay off in staff production and loyalty later. When you effectively train staff to take care of guests, the profits take care of themselves."

PRODUCTS

Applebee's International operates two restaurant brands: Applebee's Neighborhood Grill & Bar eateries, numbering slightly more than 1,000 as of mid-1998; and Rio Bravo Cantina restaurants, which totaled 58 at the end of April 1998.

GLOBAL PRESENCE

In addition to its restaurants across the United States, Applebee's operated 6 franchised restaurants in Canada,

1 in Curacao, 3 in Germany, 1 in Greece, 1 in Sweden, and 4 in the Netherlands in the 1990s.

EMPLOYMENT

Applebee's is always on the lookout for motivated, ambitious individuals who would like to join the company's team, either at its Overland Park, Kansas, headquarters or in one of the approximately 200 company-owned restaurants around the country. Interested parties are encouraged to send inquiries in writing to Human Resources, Applebee's International Inc., 4551 W. 107th St., Ste. 100, Overland Park, KS 66207.

SOURCES OF INFORMATION

Bibliography

"Applebee's Achieves Industry Milestone Opening 1,000th Restaurant in Aurora, Colorado." *Business Wire,* 8 June 1998.

"Applebee's International Inc." *Hoover's Online,* 29 June 1998. Available at http://www.hoovers.com.

"Applebee's International Rated New 'Buy' at Van Kasper." *Bloomberg Data,* 22 June 1998.

"Applebee's International to Acquire 32 Restaurants as Part of Apple South Divestment Plan." *Business Wire,* 23 December 1997.

"Applebee's Reports Fourth Quarter Earnings of 31 Cents Per Share; Applebee's Concept Exceeds $1.82 Billion in 1997 System-Wide Sales." *Business Wire,* 8 February 1998.

"Applebee's Reports First Quarter Earnings of 39 Cents Per Share." *Business Wire,* 29 April 1998.

Dorfman, John. "A Pair of Restaurant Stocks Whet My Appetite." *Bloomberg News,* 30 June 1998.

Lynch, Peter. "Best of the Best." *Worth Magazine,* March 1998.

For an annual report:

write: Investor Relations, Applebee's International Inc., 4551 W. 107th St., Ste. 100, Overland Park, KS 66207.

For additional industry research:

Investigate companies by their Standard Industrial Classification Codes, also known as SICs. Applebee's International's primary SICs are:

5812 Eating Places

5813 Drinking Places

6794 Franchises, Selling or Licensing

Arby's, Inc.

FOUNDED: 1964

Contact Information:
HEADQUARTERS: 1000 Corporate Dr.
    Fort Lauderdale, FL 33334
PHONE: (954)351-5600

OVERVIEW

Arby's Inc. is the world's largest franchise restaurant system that sells primarily roast beef sandwiches, controlling approximately 73 percent of that market in 1997. Based on company figures, it was the tenth largest restaurant chain in the United States, and had worldwide sales of about $2.1 billion. After sluggish performance in the 1980s and the early 1990s, Arby's changed ownership and its performance improved considerably, helped by an expanded menu, revamping of its restaurants, and expansion of the chain.

Arby's restaurants can be found in 48 states and 10 foreign countries, although the vast majority are located in the United States and Canada. At the end of 1997, the 6 leading states were: Ohio, with 234 restaurants; Texas, with 181; California, with 161; Michigan, with 154 restaurants; and Georgia and Indiana, with 152 restaurants each. The country outside the United States with the most operating units is Canada, with 119 restaurants.

Arby's traditionally has operated chiefly as a franchise chain. Of its 3,100 restaurants in 1997, the company owned only 355, and the rest were franchises. In 1997, Arby's owner, Triarc Companies, Inc. (Triarc), sold those 355 company-owned restaurants to the chain's largest franchisee, RTM Restaurant Group, but retained control of the Arby's brand and management of franchise rights.

COMPANY FINANCES

Arby's sales, system-wide, were approximately $2.1 billion in 1997, up from approximately $1.9 billion in

1995 and $2.0 billion in 1996. Prior to the sale, revenues were principally derived from sales at company-owned restaurants. In 1997, approximately 53 percent of revenues came from sales at company-owned restaurants and approximately 47 percent were derived from royalties and franchise fees. As a result of Triarc's sale of the remaining 355 company-owned restaurants to RTM, the Triarc Restaurant Group now operates solely as a franchisor and derives revenues from two principal sources: royalties from franchisees and franchise fees.

Arby's restaurant revenues decreased $147.9 million (51.3 percent) to $140.4 million, principally reflecting impact of the RTM sale on May 5, 1997. Aside from the effect on sales of the RTM sale, restaurant revenues increased $6.5 million (4.8 percent). Also a result of the sale, first quarter restaurant revenues for 1998 were $18.1 million, down from $47.4 million in first quarter 1997. The decrease in restaurant sales, however, was partially offset by a $4.7-million increase in royalties and franchise fees. RTM now operates the 355 restaurants as a franchisee and pays royalties to Triarc at a rate of 4 percent of restaurant net sales.

FAST FACTS:
About Arby's, Inc.

Ownership: Arby's, Inc. is a wholly owned subsidiary of RC/Arby's Corp. RC/Arby's Corp. is a subsidiary of Triarc Companies, Inc. and CFC Holdings Corp.

Officers: Nelson Peltz, 54, Chmn. & CEO; Peter W. May, 54, Pres. & COO; Fred H. Schaefer, VP & Chief Acct. Off.; John L. Barnes, Jr., Exec. VP & CFO

Employees: 7,035

Chief Competitors: As a franchise restaurant system, Arby's chief competitors are: McDonald's; Burger King; Wendy's; Boston Market; and Subway.

HISTORY

The original Arby's restaurant opened in Youngstown, Ohio, in 1964, by brothers Forrest and Leroy Raffel. The chain grew modestly in its early years, focusing on its trademark roast beef sandwiches. They merged the company with Royal Crown in 1976, and retired in 1979. After several disastrous years under the ownership of corporate raider Victor Posner's DWG Corporation, Arby's was sold to Triarc Companies Inc., which worked hard to rejuvenate the chain.

Under Triarc's ownership, Arby's modernized many of its facilities, began national advertising, and expanded its menu beyond the roast beef sandwich for which it was best known. By 1998 Arby's operated 3,100 restaurants, more than 2,900 in the United States and the remaining in 10 other countries, chiefly Canada. About a quarter of the restaurants were concentrated in 5 states—Ohio, Texas, California, Michigan, and Florida. In 1997 Triarc sold its company-owned restaurants to RTM Restaurant Group of Atlanta. Arby's retained its brand identity and management of the chain, and planned to open 150 more franchises in 1998. In 1997, after the RTM sale, Triarc continued to to develop products under both the Arby's brand name and others that Triarc had acquired.

STRATEGY

During the 1980s and early 1990s, under the ownership of the ill-fated DWG Corporation, Arby's suffered noticeably from a lack of direction and innovation. When it was purchased by Triarc, its new president, Don Pierce, used his experience from the world of fast-food fried chicken (at KFC International) to slowly turn the troubled chain around. The roast beef sandwich remained the cornerstone of Arby's menu, but it was joined by an expanded menu including "home-cooked" foods and international items.

Into the late 1990s Arby's pursued a "multi-branding" strategy, in which one of its restaurants would sell several brand name food items (Arby's, ZuZu's, P.T. Noodle's, and T.J. Cinnamon's brands). Triarc added T.J. Cinnamon to the list of product offerings in 120 stores in 1997, with another 250 expected to add the brand in 1998. Both Triarc and the RTM Restaurant Group planned to continue this multi-branding approach. RTM also agreed, under terms of the sale, to build another 400 Arby's restaurants during the next 14 years. Triarc had its own plans to open new franchises, expecting to open 150 in 1998.

The company's advertising strategy relies primarily on regional television, radio, and newspapers. Owners of local franchised restaurants contribute to the cost of local advertising, and also to the Arby's Franchise Association (AFA), which produces system-wide advertising and promotional materials for all Arby's restaurants. Key competitive factors the company tries to address in its advertising include price, product quality, and service.

CHRONOLOGY:

Key Dates for Arby's, Inc.

1964: Founded in Youngstown, Ohio

1976: Merges with Royal Crown

1979: Founders Forrest and Leroy Raffel retire

1984: DWG takes over Royal Crown

1993: Triarc Companies Inc. takes over DWG holdings

1995: Introduces Roast Town restaurants

1997: Triarc sells its company-owned restaurants to RTM Restaurant Group

INFLUENCES

In the 1980s Arby's unfortunately became swept up in a series of corporate raids typical of the decade. It came under the ownership of the Royal Crown Corporation, which itself was taken over by the DWG Corporation in 1984. DWG was one of many companies under control of the infamous corporate raider, Victor Posner. It was one of Posner's key holdings and it suffered mightily during his tenure. A shareholder suit against Posner revealed that he had flagrantly misused DWG's corporate funds. For example, in 1991 he charged $173,000 in meal expenses (about $474 per day) to DWG. During a five-year period, he received salaries and bonuses of $31 million—more than the company's $26 million in earnings for that time period. At the same time, DWG's creditors went unpaid and employees were under a salary freeze. While many of Posner's companies went bankrupt, DWG did manage to survive. Posner and his son were barred by a federal court in 1993 from ever again acting as officers or directors of any public company.

While owned by Posner, Arby's lost much of its market due to management neglect. Fortunately, in mid-1993 Triarc Companies Inc. took over Posner's DWG holdings, including Arby's and Royal Crown Cola. Arby's new president, Don Pierce (hired from PepsiCo's KFC International), moved quickly to revive the faltering chain. While retaining the "Old West" motif, the new management quickly began to remodel restaurants and introduced a new line of "home-cooked" items (such as, fresh bread and apple pie) at new Arby's Roast Town restaurants. Although sales increased from $223 million (1994) to $273 million (1995) and then $288 million

(1996) under the new management, profits fell each year, and Arby's operated at a loss of $43 million in 1996.

In 1997 Triarc sold the 355 company-owned Arby's restaurants to its largest franchisee, Atlanta's RTM Restaurant Group, which already operated 670 Arby's. Triarc would continue marketing the Arby's brand as a franchisee of the other 3,000-plus Arby's restaurants. As part of the deal, RTM agreed to build 400 more Arby's by the year 2010.

CURRENT TRENDS

Under its new owner as of 1997, RTM Restaurant Group, Arby's planned to continue expanding and upgrading its menu and continued to operate as a franchise-based chain, with former owner Triarc remaining active in marketing and in chain operations. Major expansion of the chain also is anticipated through the first decade of the next century.

PRODUCTS

Arby's key product since its founding has been its roast beef sandwich. Until Triarc took over the chain in 1993, Arby's was slipping in the highly competitive fast food industry. Triarc decided to freshen the Arby's image. While retaining its Old West motif and its roast beef sandwich, Arby's began to expand its fast food menu. In 1995, it introduced a new concept, the Roast Town restaurant, at which customers could buy items such as roast beef slices and apple pies. According to Arby's president Don Pierce, customers were beginning to prefer this type of food rather than the basic fast-food hamburger, noting that, "Some people call them quick comfort foods' because they're something like what Mom used to cook at home." For those who chose to be daring and venture a bit further from home, Arby's also introduced other items such as jalapeno peppers with cream cheese, steak and red bean chili, and "bumbleberry pie."

Arby's also introduced the concept of "multibranding" at some of its restaurants in the mid-1990s. After Arby's entered into several new purchase and franchise agreements, customers at many of its restaurant could choose from ZuZu's Mexican food; P.T. Noodle's Asian, Italian, and American noodle dishes; and T.J. Cinnamon's gourmet cinnamon rolls. Also, after its acquisition of Arby's restaurants from Triarc, RTM, true to its Atlanta roots, also decided to replace Triarc's Royal Crown Cola as the Arby's house beverage, in favor of the much more popular and Atlanta-based Coca-Cola.

GLOBAL PRESENCE

Of the 3,100 company-owned and franchised Arby's restaurants operating as of January 1997, all but 163 were located within the United States. Canada was the home of 111 restaurants, with 52 restaurants scattered in another 9 countries. The restaurants in these 9 countries tended to be larger than those in the United States and Canada, which usually ranged in size from 700 to 4,000 square feet.

EMPLOYMENT

At the beginning of 1997, Arby's employed 7,035 people, 6,110 of them hourly workers in its restaurants. As in most fast food settings, many of these hourly workers were part-time employees and none were represented by labor unions.

SOURCES OF INFORMATION

Bibliography

Kolody, Tracy. "Arby's Chief Hungry for Success." *Chicago Tribune,* 24 April 1994.

RC/Arby's Corporation Annual Report. Fort Lauderdale, FL: RC/Arby's Corporation, 1998.

RC/Arby's Corporation Form 10-Q, 18 May 1998. Available at http://www.sec.gov.

"Switching to Coke." *Atlanta Journal-Atlanta Constitution,* 3 July 1997.

"Triarc Sells Arby's Restaurants to Franchisee RTM." *Business Wire,* 6 May 1997.

Vorman, Julie. "Arby's Turns to Mom's Home Cooking." *Reuter Business Report,* 27 February 1995.

Walsh, Sharon. "Posner, Son Barred From Running Firms." *Washington Post,* 2 December 1993, B11.

For an annual report:

write: RC Arby's Corp., 1000 Corporate Dr., Fort Lauderdale, FL 33334

For additional industry research:

Investigate companies by their Standard Industrial Classification Codes, also known as SICs. Arby's primary SIC is:

5812 Eating Places

Arthur Andersen LLP

FOUNDED: 1913

Contact Information:
HEADQUARTERS: 1345 Avenue of the Americas
New York, NY 10105
PHONE: (212)708-4000
EMAIL: firmwide@arthurandersen.com
URL: http://www.arthurandersen.com

OVERVIEW

Arthur Andersen is a global firm providing economic and financial consulting services; business consulting services; tax and business advisory services; and audit and business advisory services. Arthur Andersen serves the market through a fully integrated organization comprising separate practice entities organized under the laws of the country in which they are based.

COMPANY FINANCES

Global revenues for Arthur Andersen increased 13 percent from 1996 to 1997, rising from $4.6 to $5.2 billion. Of 1997 revenues, $2.6 billion was earned in the United States, $.7 billion in the Asia/Pacific, and $1.7 billion was earned by overall area including Europe, the Middle East, India, and Africa. Revenues for the parent company, Andersen Worldwide, totaled $11.3 billion in 1997 (including Arthur Andersen revenues), $6 billion of which was generated domestically and $5.3 billion of which was generated outside the United States.

HISTORY

Arthur Edward Andersen, the founder and guiding force behind Andersen Worldwide, was born in Plano, Illinois. Andersen displayed a propensity for mathematics at a very young age, and upon graduation from high school he worked in the office of a comptroller while attending classes at the University of Illinois. In 1908 he

received a degree as a certified public accountant (CPA) becoming the youngest CPA in Illinois at the age of 23.

Andersen served as senior accountant for Price Waterhouse from 1907 to 1911. Afterwards, Andersen worked as comptroller for a year before being appointed chairperson of Northwestern University's accounting department. In 1913, Andersen decided to establish his own accounting firm, and at the age of 28 he founded the public accounting firm of Andersen DeLany and Company in Chicago.

Following Congress' establishment of Federal Income Tax and the Federal Reserve in 1913, the demand for accounting services increased dramatically. This resulted in rapid growth for Andersen's small firm. One of Andersen's first clients was Schlitz Brewing. The list expanded rapidly to include International Telephone and Telegraph, Colgate-Palmolive, Parker Pen, and Briggs and Stratton, among many others. The company's primary business, however, consisted of numerous utility companies throughout the Midwest, including Cincinnati Gas and Electric Company, Detroit Natural Gas Company, Milwaukee Gas Light Company, and Kansas City Power and Light Company.

Fifty percent of Andersen's revenues during the 1920s were derived from work generated by utility companies. Andersen's firm was becoming labeled as a "utility firm" in accounting circles. In 1917 Andersen was awarded an honorary B.B.A from Northwestern University. In 1918, when DeLany left the partnership, the firm became known as Arthur Andersen and Company.

The company grew rapidly with many employees becoming licensed as accountants and auditors in many states. Six offices were opened nationwide. Those in New York (1921), Kansas City (1923), and Los Angeles (1926) were the company's main offices. Already serving as an auditor for many industrial corporations, Arthur Andersen began providing financial and industrial investigation services. About 400 people were employed with the company in 1928, and by 1940 that figure had increased to 700. The firm opened more offices in Boston and Houston in 1937 and Atlanta and Minneapolis in 1940.

During World War II, Andersen reached the pinnacle of his success. His numerous writings on accounting related subjects prompted a growing admiration and respect for him in financial, industrial, and academic circles. Andersen served as president of the board of trustees at Northwestern University and as a faculty member in accounting at the school. During this time Andersen groomed his associate, Leonard Spacek, for the company's leadership position. Spacek joined Arthur Andersen and Company in 1928 and was named partner in 1940. After Arthur Andersen died in 1947, Spacek took over the company, remaining committed to the regimented management style of the founder.

By the time Spacek retired in 1973, Arthur Andersen and Company had opened 18 new offices in the United States and over 25 offices in countries through-

FAST FACTS:
About Arthur Andersen LLP

Ownership: Arthur Andersen is a privately owned company.

Officers: W. Robert Grafton, Acting CEO, Andersen Worldwide; Jim Wadia, Managing Partner, Arthur Andersen

Employees: 58,000

Principal Subsidiary Companies: Arthur Andersen, along with Arthur Andersen Knowledge Enterprises and Andersen Consulting, is a division of Andersen Worldwide. Arthur Andersen Franchise Services and Cross Roads Savings and Loan Association are two other subsidiaries.

Chief Competitors: Arthur Andersen is part of one of the largest financial services and consulting companies in the world. As such, its primary competitors are: Ernst and Young; KPMG; Coopers Lybrand; Booz Allen and Hamilton; McKinsey and Company; and Price Waterhouse.

out the world. The company had a staff of over 12,000, and revenues increased from $6.5 to over $51 million between 1947 and 1973. Arthur Andersen had grown into one of the world's preeminent accounting firms, featuring a profitable consulting service that helped large corporations install and use computer systems in the 1950s, and it branched out into production control, cost accounting, and operations research during the 1960s. In the 1970s, the company became involved in a host of consulting activities, including systems integration services, strategic services, developing software application products, and providing a variety of other technological services.

Harvey Kapnick succeeded Spacek, and under him the consulting division expanded and developed rapidly. By 1979, the consulting division's fees represented 20 percent of Andersen's total revenues. Kapnick was succeeded by Duane Kullberg (who originally joined the company in 1954 as an auditor), whose first years at Andersen were wrought with problems. Nevertheless, the company continued to thrive. By 1988, 40 percent of the company's total revenues were generated from consulting fees, making Arthur Andersen the largest consulting

CHRONOLOGY:

Key Dates for Arthur Andersen LLP

1913: Arthur Andersen establishes his own accounting firm at the age of 28 called Andersen DeLany and Company

1918: DeLany leaves the partnership and the firm becomes Arthur Andersen and Company

1938: Arthur Andersen is offered the presidency of the New York Stock Exchange, which he declined

1947: Andersen dies and Leonard Spacek takes over the company

1950: Begins a consulting service, which helped corporations install and use their first computer systems

1960: Adds production control, cost accounting, and operations research services

1970: Begins involvement in technological services such as systems integration and software application

1984: Arthur Andersen & Co. is forced to pay settlements totaling $65 million within two months

1988: Over 40 percent of revenues come from consulting fees, making the company the largest consulting firm in the world

1989: Lawrence Weinbach becomes president and revenues nearly double within four years

1992: The firm is sued by the government's Resolution Trust Corporation for negligence in its audit of a failed financial institution

1998: Arthur Andersen and Specialty Technical Publishers announce publishing alliance to create accounting publications and CD-ROMs

---

firm in the world. Around this time, tension between the auditors of the firm and the consultants was brewing, centering on discrepancies in payscale (auditors were paid more than the consultants) and disagreement over the control of consulting operations. Tensions increased, consultants left the company, and lawsuits were filed. The company was in one of its most confused stages.

In an effort to end the internal discord, Arthur Anderson was restructured into an auditing and tax firm known as Arthur Andersen, and a subsidiary consulting firm was formed called Andersen Consulting. Each be-

came a separate entity with its own management structure responsible only to the parent company, Andersen Worldwide.

Lawrence Weinbach, a graduate of the Wharton Business School, replaced Kullberg in 1989. Known for his diplomacy, Weinbach tried to smooth out the hard feelings between the two divisions of Arthur Andersen. Under his leadership the company's revenues skyrocketed from under $3.0 billion in 1988 to $5.6 billion in 1992. This increase, nearly 50 percent, was generated by the company's increase in consulting activities. During the years 1988-1992, Andersen Consulting's revenues grew by 89 percent while Arthur Andersen's revenues grew by 38 percent. In 1997, Weinback retired from Andersen Worldwide, and W. Robert Grafton was named acting CEO. Andersen Consulting, though still a part of parent company Andersen Worldwide, was in negotiation to break off from the firm.

STRATEGY

In March 1997, a third division of Andersen Worldwide was formed, known as Arthur Andersen Knowledge Enterprises to handle information technology services. According to *The Wall Street Journal,* the new venture based in San Francisco was established to perform such functions as auditing services of electronic commerce transactions over the Internet. It could also be viewed as an attempt by the company to take advantage of the market for information technology (IT) services, which was propelling Andersen Consulting's rapid growth—business that would no longer benefit Andersen Worldwide if a split between its two firms was successfully negotiated.

Toward further expansion of the company's offerings, Arthur Andersen and Specialty Technical Publishers Inc. announced a new publishing alliance in May of 1998. This alliance would provide a "comprehensive line of interpretive accounting publications and CD-ROMs designed for financial reporting professionals," according to Arthur Andersen's press release. The series addresses such matters as international GAAP analysis and U.S. accounting topics including financial assets and liabilities, business combinations, leasing, income taxes, and compensation arrangements.

PRODUCTS

Arthur Andersen offers professional services that provide clients all over the world with "knowledge." The company views its role as the acquisition and sharing of knowledge—of how to improve performance in management, business processes, operations, information technology, finance, and change navigation—so that its clients can grow and profit. Areas of concentration include Assurance and Business Advisory Services—auditing services that assure the integrity and reliability of a client's information; assess the effectiveness of existing processes; and help identify, measure, and control risk. Business Consulting services help companies attain performance improvement and lasting change. Economic and Financial Consulting services apply business and industry knowledge to help clients plan and implement financial strategies that meet corporate objectives and enable companies to improve performance and acquire competitive advantage. Arthur Andersen's Tax, Legal, and Business Advisory Services serve multinational companies, privately held businesses, and individuals to address taxation, regulation, and expansion issues.

GLOBAL PRESENCE

Arthur Andersen is a global organization, with 363 offices in 78 countries. In another move toward increasing its global presence, the company announced in May 1998 that it started discussions with Coopers & Lybrand-Brazil to investigate a possible merger of the two companies' operations in that country. In 1997 Coopers & Lybrand-Brazil produced more than $60 million in revenues. The combined company, as a member firm of Arthur Andersen, would become the leader in Brazil's professional services market. "Our goal in serving clients is to bring the best skills to bear on their problems," said Jose Luis (Checho) Vazquez, area managing partner for Arthur Andersen in Latin America. "This merger of equals will enable us to combine complementary resources, broaden regional coverage and strengthen our industry expertise."

EMPLOYMENT

According to one Arthur Andersen employee, "For me, the people were the draw to Arthur Andersen's CRM ["computer risk management"] practice. Everyone I have worked with has been helpful and nurturing. From the beginning, my colleagues made me feel that this would be a good fit. The position has all the elements I was looking for: challenge; opportunity; a way to stay abreast of leading-edge technologies; and a way for me to apply my systems background in a business environment." The company makes a practice of training and empowering its employees to better help clients. It also invests in professional education and development for employees, as Arthur Andersen views those as important elements in keeping the company ahead of emerging technologies and market shifts. According to Lawrence Weinbach, "Education gives us our competitive edge. Anybody can hire smart people. It's what you do with them that makes the difference. In a professional service organization, all you have to sell are your people's abilities, so we invest in that." Training locations are located in the Netherlands, Spain, the United States, and 10 sites in Asia/Pacific and Latin America. Each share a common core curriculum to ensure a common methodology and approach to training.

SOURCES OF INFORMATION

Bibliography

"Arthur Andersen Announces New Accounting Reference Series." Arthur Andersen News Releases, 21 May 1998.

"Arthur Andersen & Co, SC." *Hoovers Handbook of American Business.* Austin, TX: Reference Press, 1996.

Arthur Andersen Home Page. June 1998. Available at http://www.arthurandersen.com.

"Arthur Andersen Investigating Merger with Coopers & Lybrand Member Firm in Brazil." Arthur Andersen News Releases, 20 May 1998.

Derdak, Thomas. "Arthur Andersen & Company, Société Coopérative." *International Directory of Company Histories.* Vol. 10. Detroit, MI: St. James Press, 1995.

MacDonald, Elizabeth. "Arthur Andersen Starts New Unit, Promotes Officials." *The Wall Street Journal,* 7 March 1997.

Manufacturing USA. Detroit, MI: Gale Research, 1996.

For additional industry research:

Investigate companies by their Standard Industrial Classification Codes, also known as SICs. Arthur Andersen's primary SICs are:

8721 Accounting Auditing and Book Keeping Services

8742 Management Consulting Services

AT&T Corporation

ALSO KNOWN AS: American Telephone and Telegraph
FOUNDED: 1899

Contact Information:

HEADQUARTERS: 32 Avenue of the Americas
    New York, NY 10013-2412
PHONE: (212)387-5400
FAX: (212)841-4715
TOLL FREE: (800)348-8288
EMAIL: att@equiserve.com
URL: http://www.att.com

OVERVIEW

AT&T is a communications company offering long-distance telephone service, among other services. In 1996 the company divided itself into three separate operations: AT&T Corp. (telecommunications), NCR Corporation (computers), and Lucent Technologies Inc. (network products). The two latter divisions were then sold. With increased long-distance competition during the 1990s, AT&T was forced to focus on retaining its market share in that core business area.

Other services offered by AT&T Corporation include WorldNet, an Internet-access service; local phone services; and the AT&T Universal Card, a credit card. The company also provides cable television and wireless phone service in more than 100 cities in the United States. DIRECTTV, a television satellite system, is among the newest of AT&T's innovations.

COMPANY FINANCES

As reported by the company, AT&T's total 1997 revenues were $50.9 billion, a decrease of 2 percent from 1996 revenues of $52.2 billion. Of 1997 revenues, $22.03 billion was generated by the company's business markets division (BMD); $23.52 billion was generated by its consumer markets division (CMD); and $4.43 billion was generated by AT&T wireless services. First quarter revenues for 1998 were $12.63 billion, up slightly from $12.54 billion in the first quarter of 1997.

Net income for 1997 was $4.6 billion, compared to $5.9 billion in 1996. Again, AT&T showed improvement during the first quarter of 1998—net income for the quarter was $1.32 billion, up from $1.12 billion in the first quarter of 1997.

AT&T stock was valued at around $60.00 per share in mid-1998. The company's 52-week high was $68.50, and its 52-week low was $34.00 per share. The company's earnings per share (EPS) in 1997 were $2.79, compared to $3.60 in 1996. As of mid-1998, earnings per share were $2.96.

ANALYSTS' OPINIONS

Analysts tend to view long-distance service as a mature market in the United States, as well as a market characterized by increasing competition due to more cost-focused consumers. Some experts say AT&T's lack of swift reaction to this change accounted for some of the company's problems. For example, while companies such as Sprint offered flat rates for long-distance service early on, AT&T remained at the high end of the price scale. Eventually, the company offered a $.15-per-minute flat rate to compete with the lower prices of smaller companies. AT&T was also struck hard in 1996 by companies that purchased long-distance service in bulk and then resold to consumers and businesses at less expensive rates.

AT&T admitted to being caught off-guard by smaller companies offering fierce competition. This oversight caused AT&T's long-distance services to not perform as expected. As reported by Catherine Arnst in *Business Week,* Jeffrey A. Kagan, president of a consulting firm, commented in late 1996 that "AT&T's ability to move into other areas depends on a healthy core business, and their core business is not healthy right now."

The most recent threat to AT&T was the rise of the Internet, offering faxing, phone calls, live radio programs, and video conferencing—areas in which AT&T hoped to provide services. Many analysts view AT&T's launch of WorldNet as a successful embrace of the competition offered by the Internet in these areas. In fact, analysts say fewer than 50,000 people currently make phone calls using the Internet, giving telecommunications companies like AT&T an edge in the market.

A technological advantage that some analysts believe may be beneficial to the company was AT&T's plan to implement "Project Angel." The project would give customers the option to choose their local telephone provider, which may be enough, some say, to successfully launch such a program. Once in place, this technology could also offer consumers the capability to hook computers up at high speeds for minimal costs. Some analysts believed this technology was AT&T's competitive edge, although many kinks have not yet been ironed out.

From 1988 to 1996, analysts criticized CEO Robert Allen's strategies. During his years of service, the com-

FINANCES:

AT&T Corp. Revenues, 1994-1997 (billion dollars)

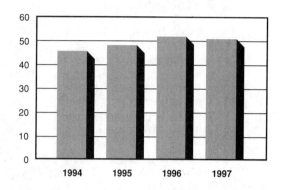

AT&T Corp. 1997 Stock Prices (dollars)

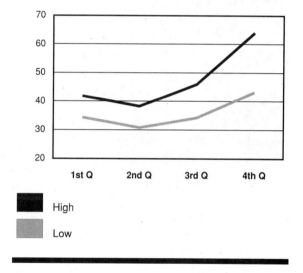

High

Low

pany spent $20 billion on purchases of businesses and $19.0 billion in redesign efforts. Since January of 1996, AT&T's stock has dropped 20 percent. Despite all of this, many analysts agreed that AT&T remained financially strong. AT&T was the number one performing stock on the Dow-Jones index for the third quarter of the 1997 fiscal year. The company brought in over $8.0 billion in annual cash flow. Its assets totaled $56.0 billion and outstanding debt totaled $8.5 billion. Many view AT&T's financial standing, coupled with its strong name-recognition, as its strongest asset for competitive survival.

The AT&T building in New York, designed by Philip Johnson, towers over its immediate neighbors. (Photograph by Richard Payne.)

HISTORY

Alexander Graham Bell's invention of the telephone in 1876 led to the developments of Bell Telephone (1877) and England Telephone (1878), which were later combined to create National Bell Telephone in 1879. After fighting off competitor patents like those of Western Union, in 1882 National Bell acquired Western Electric, the leading electrical equipment manufacturer in the United States at the time. After Bell's patent expired in the 1890s, competing phone companies emerged. The company changed its name to American Telephone & Telegraph (AT&T) and moved from Boston to New York in 1899.

As a result of the company's acquisition of Western Union in 1909, AT&T had control over two markets: communications and electrical equipment manufacturing. Under President Woodrow Wilson, AT&T was forced to sell Western Union and refrain from purchasing other independent phone companies without approval. AT&T was also forced to provide access to its networks to other companies. In other words, the government was forcing AT&T to give up its standing as a monopoly (a situation where one-third of a local or national market is controlled by one supplier). This allowed competitors, such as MCI, to obtain access to AT&T's networks, which created instant long-distance competition.

A lawsuit initiated by the government caused AT&T to sell seven Bell companies in 1984. AT&T was allowed to keep its long-distance services and Western Electric. Many jobs were cut in order for AT&T Corp. to remain competitive in such a rapidly growing industry. AT&T bought the electronic mail service division of Western Union in 1990. AT&T Corp. ranked seventh in the world's computer makers after it bought Teradata and NCR in 1991 (sold along with Lucent in 1996); the company also bought McCaw Cellular in 1995.

STRATEGY

AT&T was organized into divisions and businesses addressing its specific markets. These divisions were: the Consumer Markets Division (CMD), Business Markets Division (BMD), AT&T Solutions (professional services), AT&T Wireless Service, AT&T Local Services Division, and AT&T Universal Card Services (UCS). These are bolstered by two other organizations—Network and Computing Services and AT&T Labs—that provide the company's divisions and businesses with a competitive advantage in serving their customers.

As a result of AT&T's slipping core business—long-distance service—the company revised its corporate strategy for the 1990s. AT&T's new focus was geared toward communications solutions for large and small customers. Included among these solutions were long-distance, wireless, satellite TV, and credit card services. Local calling services emerged as well, along with a push to expand digital wireless networks.

An emphasis on international growth and outsourcing arose during the late 1990s as well. Refining their strategy in 1997, the AT&T Board of Directors announced its intent to sell two of the company's profitable but non-strategic businesses: AT&T Universal Card Services and the Customer Care unit (formerly known as American Transtech) of AT&T Solutions. Another part of the company's new strategy was its plan to cut costs by eliminating up to 17,000 positions by the year 1999.

INFLUENCES

AT&T's primary source of revenue was from its long-distance service. An industry leader, the company ventured into other business areas including computers, wireless services, credit cards, and satellite TV. However, an unfortunate combination of increased competition and AT&T's underestimation of smaller telephone companies caused AT&T's long-distance service to suffer.

AT&T's venture into the computer industry in the 1980s failed. Purchasing NCR Corporation, AT&T hoped to breathe life back into its computer operations. After the company suffered losses totaling $10.1 billion, including several startups in handheld computers and software that were stifled shortly after their unveiling, AT&T decided to sell NCR. Even the company's Universal Card began to suffer due to enormous default rates. AT&T was forced to sell NCR and Lucent Technologies in order to focus on long-distance service and its increasing competition; therefore, AT&T Corp. was the only remaining segment of the previous three AT&T divisions.

Due to increasing cost-consciousness on the part of long-distance customers, new strategies were essential for AT&T's competitiveness. Staying at the high end of the price scale in this market was no longer a practical move for AT&T, a company struggling to maintain its position as the long-distance leader of the nation. AT&T's latest challenge was to maintain market share while growing new services like WorldNet, the Internet access service launched in the late 1990s.

CURRENT TRENDS

WorldNet was one service among many in AT&T's latest strategy called "bundling," according to Catherine Arnst in *Business Week*. The company placed high expectations in its recognizable name to sell "bundles" or packages of products including local and long-distance calling, wireless service, and Internet access. AT&T's goal was to become a convenient one-stop communications services company. Since 1994, the company has been implementing this strategy by acquiring companies like McCaw Cellular. AT&T also seized opportunities in video with its 2.5 percent interest in Hughes Electronics Corp.'s DirectTV, a satellite service being marketed to AT&T customers. AT&T's WorldNet service also ranked as the second largest Internet-access server.

FAST FACTS:
About AT&T Corporation

Ownership: AT&T is a publicly owned company traded on the New York Stock Exchange as well as the Boston, Midwest, Pacific, and Philadelphia exchanges in the United States. AT&T stock is also traded on stock exchanges in Brussels, Geneva, London, and Paris.

Ticker symbol: T

Officers: C. Michael Armstrong, Chmn. & CEO, 59, $291,667; John D. Zeglis, Pres., 50, $1,609,000; Daniel E. Somers, Sr. Exec. VP & CFO, 50; R.C. Mark Baker, Exec. VP International, 51

Employees: 128,000 (1997)

Principal Subsidiary Companies: AT&T's chief subsidiaries include WorldNet, AT&T Digital PCS, AT&T Submarine Systems, Inc., and McCaw Cellular.

Chief Competitors: As a major telecommunications provider, AT&T's chief competitors include: Ameritech; Bell Atlantic; BellSouth; Cable & Wireless; GTE; MCI; Northern Telecom; Pacific Telesis; and US WEST Communications. Competitors in related industries in which AT&T also participates include: AirTouch; America Online; CompuServe; Frontier Corporation; IBM; NETCOM; PSINet; and WorldCom.

PRODUCTS

AT&T runs the world's largest communications network and is the leading provider of long-distance and wireless services. The company also offers online services and cable television and, in the late 1990s, it began to deliver local telephone service.

"Project Angel" was among AT&T's newer developments in the late 1990s. More a "technology" than a product, the company introduced its plans for this new service in the mid-1990s. AT&T planned to use radio technology to deliver local telephone service and high-velocity Internet access without requiring a new wire to be connected to the customer's house. An 18-inch square box was designed to attach to the side of a house or small business, then the box would be connected to the existing. When a call is made, a signal inside the box triggers

CHRONOLOGY:

Key Dates for AT&T Corporation

1899: Founded as American Telephone & Telegraph

1909: Acquires Western Union

1913: AT&T agrees to the Kingsbury Commitment in which it will 1) buy no more independent phone companies without government approval; 2) sell Western Union; and 3) allow independent phone companies to use its networks

1925: Bell Labs is formed

1949: The Justice Department sues AT&T to try to force them to sell Western Electric

1956: A settlement in the Justice Dept. case allows AT&T to keep Western Electric but forbids them to enter any other unregulated markets

1968: FCC takes away AT&T's telephone equipment monopoly

1969: Allows other companies such as MCI to connect to their phone network

1984: The U.S. government forces AT&T to sell seven Bell companies

1990: Buys the electronic mail service division of Western Union

1991: Acquires Teradata and NCR Corp.

1995: Purchases McCaw Cellular

1996: Company is divided into three separate operations: AT&T Corp., NCR Corporation, and Lucent Technologies

1997: Forms a partnership with Bell Atlantic Corp. and Nynex Corp. to provide customers with lower rates

an antenna nearby, which connects to AT&T's network. The intended result was wireless communication for local calling, an increasingly popular market as local telephone markets have been allowing customers choices in local service providers.

The "Renaissance Network" was another technological trend at AT&T. Plans for this new technology were to allow customers to reach anyone anywhere using any means of communication. This technology involved a high-tech digital system able to provide a foundation for these services.

CORPORATE CITIZENSHIP

Through the AT&T Foundation, AT&T awards grants to benefit programs in Education, Arts and Culture, and Civic and Community Service. In the area of education, AT&T has traditionally invested in pre-college and higher education programs with emphasis on math and science, both of which are important to the company's business. They place increasing importance on the use of technology and its role in the enhancement of teaching and learning. In late 1995, AT&T announced a five-year commitment totaling $150 million for its new program, the AT&T Learning Network. Designed to get the nation's schools onto the "Information Superhighway," the program represents AT&T's largest commitment to education thus far.

AT&T also promotes arts and culture around the world by supporting arts programs. The company supports such initiatives by bringing artists and innovative work together with wide audiences. The Arts & Culture program awards between 150 and 200 grants every year. AT&T's efforts in the area of community service are directed toward enhancing life in the communities in which AT&T employees and customers live and work. The company does this by developing programs that address the needs of specific communities through communications and information technology and by encouraging employees to participate in public service.

GLOBAL PRESENCE

AT&T provides long-distance service to every country and territory in the world and direct-dial service is available to more than 270 countries. International growth is of increasing importance to AT&T. Current growth areas include China, where a China-United States cable network was planned by 1998. China Telecom and AT&T Submarine Systems Inc. are among the 10 carriers who signed agreements to construct this first fiber optic undersea telecommunications cable linking the two countries. With technology able to transmit voice, data, and images at eight times today's established capability, more than 1 million calls could be placed at the same time.

A similar undersea cable was planned to connect the United States and the United Kingdom, providing complete service by 1998. And yet another was developed to connect the United States, Germany, and the United Kingdom by 1998 as well.

AT&T Corporation also provides products and services worldwide. However, most of the company's sales are generated in the United States—90 percent of AT&T's total sales. International sales accounted for the remaining 10 percent. In 1997, however, AT&T announced developments to invest up to $9 billion in order to expand its network to new markets, including local phone and Internet services.

EMPLOYMENT

AT&T bills itself as a "demanding and dynamic organization that requires a commitment to our community, environment, people, and most importantly, Our Common Bond." The company seeks people who thrive on challenges, are self-confident, and seek immediate responsibility. It also values previous exposure to international or multicultural environments.

AT&T offers competitive benefits that can be tailored to the needs of individual employees. The company also has a comprehensive corporate education program, providing in-house training courses to help employees improve technical and managerial skills. It also offers tuition reimbursement for those wishing to pursue advanced degrees. AT&T adheres to its policy of equal opportunity for employees, placing value on diversity.

SOURCES OF INFORMATION

Bibliography

Arnst, Catherine, and Amy Barrett. "AT&T?." *Business Week,* 10 March 1997.

Arnst, Catherine, and Peter Coy. "AT&T: Will the Bad News Ever End?" *Business Week,* 7 October 1996.

"AT&T Building the Network of the Future Today." *PRNewswire,* 17 March 1997.

"AT&T Corp." *Hoover's Online.* 30 June 1998. Available at http://www.hoovers.com.

"AT&T to Build First China-U.S. Undersea Cable." *Business Wire,* 30 March 1997.

"AT&T to Build World's Most Powerful Undersea Network." *Business Wire,* 24 March 1997.

Coy, Peter. "Can AT&T Keep Learning to Love the Net?" *Business Week,* 7 October 1996.

Fillion, Roger. "AT&T, Baby Bells Offer Plan to Cut Phone Rates." *Reuters,* 4 April 1997.

Ziegler, Bart. "AT&T Cut Allen's Bonus in '96 Due to Company's Performance." *The Wall Street Journal,* 2 April 1997.

For an annual report:

on the Internet at: http://www.att.com/ir/investorinfo.html **or** write: AT&T Investor Relations, Rm. 3349A2, 295 N. Maple Ave., Basking Ridge, NJ 07920 **or** call (800)972-0784

For additional industry research:

Investigate companies by their Standard Industrial Classification Codes, also known as SICs. AT&T's primary SICs are:

4813 Telephone Communications, Except Radio Telephone

4841 Cable And Other Pay Television Services

7389 Services-Business Services, NEC

Avon Products, Inc.

FOUNDED: 1886

Contact Information:

HEADQUARTERS: 1345 Avenue of the Americas
    New York, NY 10105-0196
PHONE: (212)282-5000
FAX: (212)282-6049
URL: http://www.avon.com

OVERVIEW

Avon Products, Inc. is the world's largest direct seller of cosmetics and a leader in the direct sale of fashion jewelry and collectible gift items. With 2.6 million sales representatives (445,000 in the United States) and almost 35,000 employees in 134 countries, Avon's annual revenue is more than $5 billion dollars. The company constantly expanded its international market by offering sales in new countries and acquiring companies like Avon Lifedesigns, a women's workshop firm, and Discovery Toys, a direct sales toy manufacturer. Avon maintains customer loyalty by creating and offering recognizable brands, including Anew, Skin-So-Soft, Avon Color, Far Away, Natori, Rare Gold, and Millennia. Though the company was expanding its sales avenues, more than 95 percent of Avon's sales were still generated by "Avon Ladies."

COMPANY FINANCES

Avon Products, Inc. earned 1997 sales of $5.08 billion, up from $4.8 billion in 1996. This marked the eighth consecutive year that Avon revenues increased. Of that $5.08 billion, 34 percent ($1.73 billion) was earned in the United States, 16 percent was earned in Europe ($811 million), 15 percent was earned in the Pacific region ($782 million), and remaining revenues ($1.75 billion) were earned in other countries across the world. As of mid-1998, revenues for fiscal year 1998 were already $5.17 billion, increasing for the ninth year in a row. Net income for the same period also rose, from $317.9 million in 1996 to $338.8 million in 1997. As of mid-1998, Avon's net income for the year was $266.5 million.

Earnings per share (EPS) were also on a steadily increasing trend. In 1996 Avon earned $2.38 per share, and in 1997 that increased to $2.54. As of mid-1998, the company's earnings were $1.99 per share, well on their way to another increase for the company's shareholders. Avon's stock price was almost $78.00 per share in mid-1998. Its 52-week high was $79.00, and its 52-week low was $31.50 per share.

ANALYSTS' OPINIONS

Avon's financial record during the 1990s speaks well for itself—the company has good cash flow, consistent sales growth, and its operations are well diversified geographically. Its compound annual average return to stockholders was 29.6 percent (the S&P 500 average was 16.3 percent). Analysts at Zack's Investment Research seemed confident advising investors to buy into the company—half rated the company a "strong buy," while the other half rated it a "moderate buy."

HISTORY

Founded in 1896 as the California Perfume Company, Avon spent its first 10 years building its reputation as a company dedicated to women. By 1900 the company had over 6,000 representatives with sales of more than $200,000. Early in its history, Avon realized the advantage of expanding its sales beyond the United States, and in 1914 the company entered the Canadian market. In 1928 "Avon" was introduced as a brand name for a limited number of products. Proving successful, the name was changed to Avon Products in 1939, and the company went public a mere seven years later in 1946. A 26-year growth spurt began in 1948 when Avon entered more than 10 new countries, introduced 450 products, and its annual sales figure grew to more than $1 billion. By 1978 Avon had more than 1 million representatives; that same year Avon began its sponsorship of women's sporting events.

Avon celebrated its one-hundredth birthday in 1986, as well as the beginning of 10 years of technological advancement in product development. Products developed during that time included those with active ingredients such as retinol, alpha hydroxy acids, and collagen boosters. Avon's first global fragrance, Far Away, was almost immediately a world best seller on the fragrance market. In 1996, Avon served as the exclusive cosmetics sponsor for the Olympics and embarked on a marketing campaign using well known athletes as "Just another Avon Lady." Avon also began offering goal setting seminars and services for women, a program called Avon

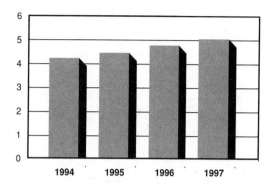

FINANCES:

*Avon Products Inc.
Net Sales, 1994-1997
(billion dollars)*

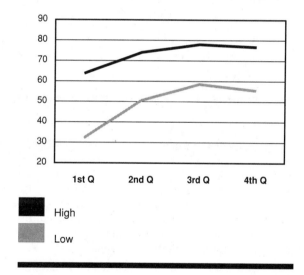

*Avon Products Inc.
1997 Stock Prices
(dollars)*

LifeDesigns. In 1998, Avon launched a new women's magazine, *Athena,* in conjunction with publisher Hachette Filipacchi.

STRATEGY

Avon has three main strategies for growth. The first is a commitment to geographical expansion. During the 1990s, Avon focused on introducing its products to countries with developing economies. Avon focused on emerging economies since there was a big demand for

FAST FACTS:

About Avon Products, Inc.

Ownership: Avon Products, Inc. is a publicly owned company traded on the New York Stock Exchange.

Ticker symbol: AVP

Officers: James E. Preston, Chmn., 64, $1,424,147; Robert J. Corti, Sr. VP & CFO, 48; Charles R. Perrin, CEO, 52; Andrea Jung, Pres. & COO, 39, $520,506

Employees: 34,995

Principal Subsidiary Companies: Avon Products' principal subsidiaries are Avon Lifedesigns and Discovery Toys.

Chief Competitors: As a direct seller of merchandise, Avon counts among its competitors: Mary Kay Cosmetics; Amway; Fuller Brush; and Tupperware. As a manufacturer and marketer of cosmetics, toiletries, and fragrances, additional competitors include: BeautiControl Cosmetics; The Body Shop; Cosmair; Estee Lauder; Procter & Gamble; Revlon; and Unilever.

western products, an underdeveloped retail infrastructure, and a vast pool of entrepreneurial women seeking opportunities as sales representatives. The company entered 18 such markets since 1990—including Brazil, Argentina, the Phillippines, and Malaysia—and was in the midst of making provisions to enter China, Central Europe, and Russia. By 1995, nearly half of Avon's pretax income was generated in developing markets.

The second key strategy employed by Avon Products, Inc. is the leveraging of direct selling channels. In addition to cosmetics and toiletries, which generates over 60 percent of its revenue, Avon uses direct selling as a means to sell clothing, fashion jewelry, home furnishings, home entertainment products, vitamins, licensed products bearing the Olympic logo, and a special edition Barbie. By introducing new products to an already loyal customer base, Avon ensures more sales.

Finally, Avon strives to make its direct selling channels more contemporary. They update service options by using toll-free telephone numbers, fax access, regular mail, and a site on the World Wide Web. Avon also makes marketing alliances with companies such as Reader's Digest to reach a wider customer base. In 1995,

they began testing the use of a catalog allowing customers to order directly from the company rather than through a representative; by 1996, catalogs were used routinely as a sales tool.

In 1998 Avon decided to channel more of its money into advertising and promotional efforts. The company had plans to shift $400 million of its annual costs to these efforts in hopes to make the Avon name more recognizeable—hopefully in the league of brand names such as "Coca-Cola" or "Bacardi." The plan also entailed dropping 30 percent of its existing brands in the process.

Other promotional and marketing strategies were carried out through assistance to Avon sales representatives. Avon did this by providing agents with brochures, product samples, and demonstration products. Other tactics included trial sizes, gift packages, and combination offers. Other aids and promotional pieces were specifically designed for women who did not sell door-to-door, such as flyers and other promotional pieces that could be posted rather than distributed.

INFLUENCES

In the mid-1970s Avon experienced problems due to recessionary conditions and the number of women rejoining the work force—fewer women were home to answer the door. Also, many of its products were priced too high for women with small incomes. In response, Avon began expanding its markets, including targeting younger women and introducing a line called Colorworks, which was specially targeted toward teenagers.

After the recession, Avon pursued a strategy of diversification in order to extend its product offerings. In an effort to enhance its image, Avon acquired Tiffany Jewelry in 1979. Later, the company launched a new clothing line, which was developed with designer Diane Von Furstenberg. Other acquisitions included health care companies such as Foster Medical and the Mediplex Group. Tiffany Jewelry and the health care companies were later sold. However, this diversification left the company with a large amount of debt and in a vulnerable financial position. Three takeover attempts were made, including attempts by competitors Amway and Mary Kay. The takeover bids were held at bay in part by massive letter-writing campaigns undertaken by Avon's sales representatives.

Other ventures focused more on expanding Avon's own product offerings and have proved more successful. The company's new line of women's clothing was introduced in the United States in 1994—it earned more than $500 million by 1997. Its joint venture to market Barbie dolls with Mattel proved Avon's best-selling gift product in the history of the company.

PRODUCTS

Avon's most well known products include Anew, Avon Skin Care, Moisture Therapy, and Skin-So-Soft. The Skin-So-Soft line also offered the insect-repellent products Skin-So-Soft Bug Guard and Moisturing Suncare Plus; the repellents were made without the use of DEET, a chemical used in the repellent products sold by most other manufacturers. Cosmetic and fragrance brands offered at Avon included Avon Color, Beyond Color, Color Bundle, Color Last Plus, Far Away, Incredible Lengths, Millennia, Moisture 15, Natori, Perfect Wear, Rare Gold, and True Color.

CORPORATE CITIZENSHIP

Along with its drive to employ women in an industry pitched to women, Avon exhibits a commitment to women's issues and needs. In 1993 the Avon Breast Cancer Awareness Crusade was first introduced. Working in conjunction with the YWCA, National Alliance of Breast Cancer Organizations, the Centers for Disease Control, and the National Cancer Institute, the Crusade now raises money, runs education programs, and offers early detection screening services to women around the world. Avon Products also started the Worldwide Fund for Women's Health, whose goal is to promote women's health worldwide by developing programs that address the leading women's health issues in each area.

Avon extended its citizenship to include the Avon Products Foundation. According to Avon, "the foundation is dedicated to supporting endeavors that understand and respond to the unique needs of women and their families, and enable women to reach their full potential." The Foundation also identified education as a vital concern to women and children across the world. The Foundation met its goals by giving more than $800,000 in grants annually to programs in health, education, community services, and arts and culture. Recipients of Foundation awards included the United Negro College Fund, the Organization of Chinese Americans, the American Indian College Fund, the National Hispanic Scholarship Fund, the Business and Professional Women's Foundation, and Hostos Community College (Bronx, New York).

GLOBAL PRESENCE

Avon's presence is truly global—its products are available in 134 countries on 6 continents. The company maintains operations in 44 markets. Since its entrance into the Canadian market in 1914, Avon Products have been dedicated to expanding into international markets. The appeal of American products was a major factor in

CHRONOLOGY:

Key Dates for Avon Products, Inc.

1886: Founded as the California Perfume Company

1900: Has 6000 sales representatives

1914: Begins selling products in Canada

1916: Incorporates in New York

1928: Avon is introduced as a brandname

1939: Changes company name to Avon Products

1946: Avon goes public

1948: Introduces 450 new products; sales figures reach $1 billion

1954: Begins selling in Puerto Rico and Venezuela

1959: Begins selling products in Mexico, Brazil, Germany, and the U.K.

1969: Introduces Avon products in Japan

1978: Begins sponsoring women's sporting events

1979: Acquires Tiffany Jewelry

1986: Introduces Far Away fragrance

1993: Avon Breast Cancer Awareness Crusade is introduced

1996: Begins seminars for women called Avon LifeDesigns

1998: Introduces the women's magazine *Athena*

its success, as was its offer of self-employment for women. In many countries, opportunities like those presented to women by Avon were scarce. Although Avon waited another 40 years before expanding beyond North America, it began entering international markets aggressively in 1954, adding Puerto Rico and Venezuela. By 1959 Mexico, Brazil, Germany, and the United Kingdom enjoyed the ability to purchase Avon products. Asia's market was opened to Avon by its entrance into Japan in 1969. During the late 1990s, Avon products were available in 135 countries. Avon was directly present in 44 of those countries, while they sold through specially appointed representatives and local distributors in 90 others. South Africa was added to the growing list in 1996, marking Avon's first presence on the African continent. Avon was also considering ventures that would launch them into Bulgaria, Romania, the Ukraine, and Vietnam.

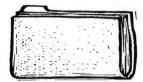

BARBIE TEAMS UP WITH AVON

What could be better than the life of Barbie? Not only is the Barbie doll one of the top-selling toys around the world, but Avon has recently developed a line of cosmetics especially for her!

Teaming up with Mattel, Avon became the sole supplier of special-edition Avon Barbie dolls. With sales of 40 million dolls in 1996, Avon's Barbie dolls were the biggest product launch in the company's history.

Based on the success of the Avon Barbie dolls, Avon created a line of doll cosmetics in 1997. Realizing that the future of the company was with young girls who were enjoying the special-edition Avon Barbie dolls, Avon created a cosmetics line that the girls could use on their Barbies as well as on their own bodies. Ranging from lip balm to cologne spray, the Barbie cosmetics line is a huge marketing ploy by Avon. Knowing that the young girls who are using the Barbie cosmetics will identify makeup with the Avon label, Avon hopes that the cosmetics line will boost future sales.

Targeting girls from the ages of 6 to 9, Avon has pointed out that "Girls are our customers of tomorrow." Since Barbie dolls have always been a popular toy with young girls, it made sense to Avon to develop a cosmetics line exclusively for Barbie. Being a plastic doll named Barbie certainly has its perks!

Avon has 19 laboratories and manufacturing facilities located around the world. Of the company's 34,995 employees, 26,942 were located outside the United States.

EMPLOYMENT

As reported by Betty Morris in *Fortune,* "Avon has no glass ceiling." The company has been on the *Women's Wire* list of the top 100 companies for women since the early 1990s. Four of the company's eight top executives were women and, of Avon managers worldwide, more than 40 percent were women. An example of Avon's sense of corporate responsibility was its interest in maintaining a woman- and family-friendly work environment. According to *Women's Wire,* "Avon offers its employees a wide range of family-friendly services, including child care referrals, adoption aid, and flexible work schedules." Avon's corporate citizenship begins with its own employees.

SOURCES OF INFORMATION

Bibliography

"Avon Products, Inc." *Hoover's Online,* 2 July 1998. Available at http://www.hoovers.com.

Avon Products, Inc. 1996 Annual Report. New York: Avon Products, Inc., 1997.

Avon Products, Inc. 1997 Form 10-K. U.S. Securities and Exchange Commission, 1998.

Avon Products Inc. Home Page, June 1998. Available at http://www.avon.com.

Morris, Betty. "If Women Ran the World It Would Look a Lot Like Avon." *Fortune,* 21 July 1997.

"Top 100 Companies for Women." *Women's Wire Home Page,* 1996. Available at http://www.women.com/work/best/A.html#avon.

For an annual report:

on the Internet at: http://www.avon.com/about/financial/company/annual.html **or** telephone: (888)AVP-FACT **or** write: Avon Shareholder Relations, Avon Products, Inc., 1345 Avenue of the Americas, New York, NY 10105-0196

For additional industry research:

Investigate companies by their Standard Industrial Classification Codes, also known as SICs. Avon's primary SICs are:

2844 Perfumes, Cosmetics, and Other Toilet Preparations

3911 Jewelry, Precious Metal

3961 Costume Jewelry and Costume Novelties, Except Precious Metal

5137 Women's, Children's, and Infants' Clothing and Accessories

5963 Direct Selling Establishments

Bacardi-Martini U.S.A., Inc.

FOUNDED: 1936

OVERVIEW

Bacardi-Martini U.S.A. is a privately held producer and marketer of spirits worldwide, including rum, whisky, beer, brandy, cognac, gin, port, tequila, vodka, and wine. After losing its Cuban assets and operations in 1960, the company moved its headquarters to Puerto Rico and has since spread its wings to span the globe. As U.S. alcohol consumption declines, the company is betting on product diversification and stepped up sales abroad. Its recent acquisition of Martini & Rossi has made it one of the five largest spirit-producing companies in the world, with $350 million in annual sales. Bacardi-Martini U.S.A. is one of the largest Hispanic-owned businesses in the United States.

Contact Information:
HEADQUARTERS: 2100 Biscayne Blvd.
    Miami, FL 33137-5028
PHONE: (305)573-8511
FAX: (305)573-7507
URL: http://www.bacardi.com

COMPANY FINANCES

Bacardi-Martini U.S.A., Inc. earned $598 million in revenues in 1996 as compared to $595 million in 1995. In 1995, parent company Bacardi Ltd.'s total sales were $2.5 billion, with annual profits of $250 million. In 1994 the company's sales dropped to $570 million from 1993's $578 million, which was also down from 1992's total revenue of $580 million.

HISTORY

In 1862 don Facundo Bacardi opened his first distillery in Santiago, Cuba. The building was reportedly full of bats, which explains the company's current em-

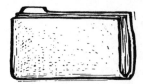

FAST FACTS:
About Bacardi-Martini U.S.A., Inc.

Ownership: Bacardi Limited is a privately held company.

Officers: George "Chip" Reid, Jr., Pres. & CEO, Bacardi Limited; Eduardo Sardina, Pres. & CEO, Bacardi-Martini U.S.A.

Employees: 600

Principal Subsidiary Companies: Bacardi-Martini U.S.A., Inc. is a wholly owned subsidiary of Bacardi Limited.

Chief Competitors: As a marketer of distilled spirits, wine, and beer, Bacardi-Martini's primary competitors include: Anheuser-Busch; Allied Domecq; Diageo; Gallo; Heineken; Pernod Ricard; Seagram; and Southern Wine & Spirits.

---

blem. By 1876, the distiller became known internationally when its Bacardi Rum won a medal of recognition at the Centennial Exhibition in Philadelphia. In 1910, Bacardi extended its bottling operations to Barcelona, Spain. The company later established its two largest distilleries in Mexico and Puerto Rico in 1931 and 1936, respectively. Marking its first physical presence in the U.S. market, Bacardi opened an office in New York City. Bacardi Imports, the predecessor to Bacardi-Martini U.S.A., was formed in 1944.

The revolutionary forces of Fidel Castro and Che Guevara overthrew the dictatorship of Fulgencio Batista in 1959, and the island soon created its own Caribbean brand of locally stilled Communism. In 1960 Bacardi was forced to become a Cuban exile company. Also in 1960, the new Cuban government confiscated Bacardi's assets and operations, then valued at more than $76 million. The exiled company soon opened facilities in south Florida, Puerto Rico, and the Bahamas.

By 1978 Bacardi Rum became the top-selling brand of distilled spirits in the United States. Sales that year exceeded more than 7 million cases. With 14 million cases sold worldwide in 1979, Bacardi Rum surpassed Smirnoff Vodka to become the best-selling spirit brand on the planet. In 1992, the company unified its five strategic operating units by forming Bacardi Limited, which then became incorporated and headquartered in Bermuda. The following year it acquired the sparkling

wine producer Martini & Rossi. In 1995 Bacardi Imports was officially renamed Bacardi-Martini U.S.A., Inc. Bacardi Limited's board of directors chose George "Chip" Reid, Jr. to lead the company as its president and CEO in 1996; he officially took office in 1997.

STRATEGY

Since its establishment, Bacardi has become a global presence with facilities around the world. In a move that allows the company to minimize import duties and their consequent effect on competitiveness, the family-controlled distiller produces its rum in multiple locations. Bacardi soon sought broader options in spirits distribution with a special eye on Europe. A series of joint ventures with Martini & Rossi set the company's strategy on the path of synergy. Bacardi acquired the family-owned Martini & Rossi in 1993. In the late 1990s the new company benefitted from Martini & Rossi's strong standing in the European market, complimented by Bacardi's strong presence in the Americas—particularly in the United States and Mexican markets.

CEO Reid designed an aggressive plan for guiding Bacardi Limited to its goal of "becoming the largest spirits producer in the world." His plan focuses on three areas: continue Bacardi Limited's success in developing new products; capitalize on emerging markets; and develop strategic alliances. Reid's primary goal during the late 1990s was to boost Bacardi Limited's sales by 20 percent to $3 billion by the year 2000. Contributing to this goal was the company's 1998 acquisition of two more premium liquor brands; Bacardi Ltd. bought the Dewar's Scotch whisky and Bombay gin brands from Diageo PLC for $1.9 billion.

In 1997, Bacardi-Martini U.S.A. restructured its marketing department, with improved focus on core Bacardi brands. The changes were announced following the promotion of former marketing controller Stella David to marketing director in September 1997.

INFLUENCES

As a result of the increasing recognition of alcohol as a harmful drug and the risks associated with driving, U.S. consumers were drinking less alcohol. From 1986 to 1996, alcohol consumption dropped from 67 to 55 percent among the adult population. As far as distilled spirits were concerned, brown goods such as whiskey and cognac declined in popularity more than white goods such as vodka, tequila, gin, and rum. Sales of specialty beers and wine eclipsed distilled spirits consumption as a whole. However, when American consumers did drink distilled spirits, they opted for premium varieties. With this drop in domestic consumption, U.S.-based wine and distilled spirits companies increased exports or broadened their sales base, often venturing into non-alcohol related products. Thanks to some improved economies abroad, U.S.-based distillers were able to augment exports by 18 percent in 1994.

CURRENT TRENDS

Fearing a decline in wine consumption in the United States, the Wine Market Council planned an advertising campaign aimed at younger consumers. Until 1996, distillers had a self-imposed ban on broadcast advertising; however, Seagram's decided to break with that ban. Bacardi has already launched an aggressive European print campaign. If the Seagram's decision serves as a precedent, Bacardi and other distillers could consider a move toward broadcast advertising.

In a search for additional tax revenues, forces within the U.S. government have proposed increasing the federal excise tax on distilled spirits. While this move would have little impact on Bacardi's foreign operations, its U.S. sales would be affected. The American distilled spirits industry claims higher taxes would put a bigger dent in already declining domestic sales and actually backfire, yielding fewer tax dollars.

PRODUCTS

For most consumers, Bacardi is synonymous with one product: its best-selling Bacardi Rum, arguably the world's most valuable spirits brand name. With the addition of Martin & Rossi products, however, it can also boast some additional top sellers, namely Martini brand Vermouth and Martini brand Asti sparkling wine. In the 1990s, Bacardi extended its product line, and its Bacardi Breezer refreshers were particularly successful. These products added to the multi-product culture already existent at at Martini & Rossi, whose Italian sparkling wines have been around for close to a century. In the 1980s, Martini & Rossi had already augmented its product line with the acquisition of several private brands of cognac and liqueurs. Eristoff brand vodka and William Lawson's scotch whiskey were among that long list of company products.

Bacardi Limited's portfolio includes a full range of products such as rum, vermouth, Scotch whiskey, cognac, brandy, gin, tequila, vodka, port, wine, and beer. The Bacardi product line became varied and impressive, especially after its 1993 merger with Martini & Rossi. In 1997 trademarks or registered trademarks of Bacardi & Company Limited and affiliates included (among others): B&B, Bacardi 151, Bacardi Black (outside the United States), Bacardi Breezers, Bacardi Gold, Bacardi Light, Bacardi Limon, Bacardi Solera, Bacardi Spice, Benedictine,

CHRONOLOGY:
Key Dates for Bacardi-Martini U.S.A., Inc.

1862: Don Facundo Bacardi opens his first distillery in Santiago, Cuba

1876: Bacardi Rum wins a medal of recognition at the Centennial Expedition in Philadelphia, Pennsylvania

1888: Queen Maria of Spain grants permission for Bacardi to display the royal coat of arms on their label when he cures Prince Alfonso's illness by administering Bacardi Rum

1910: Bacardi opens bottling operations in Barcelona, Spain

1926: Bacardi diversifies into beer

1931: Opens a huge distillery in Mexico

1936: Opens a large distillery in Puerto Rico

1944: Bacardi Imports is formed

1958: Bacardi moves from Cuba to Nassau, The Bahamas

1960: Loses Cuban assets and operations and becomes a Cuban exile company

1978: Bacardi Rum becomes top-selling brand of distilled spirits in the United States

1992: Forms Bacardi Limited

1993: Acquires Martini & Rossi

1994: Establishes The Bacardi Foundation

1995: Company is renamed from Bacardi Imports to Bacardi-Martini U.S.A.

1996: George Reid, Jr. is voted in as president and CEO

1998: Introduces Martini Vermouth in Brazil

Camino Real, Caribbean Classics, Castillo A Ejo, Charles Volner, China Martini, Gaston De La Grange, Glen Deveron, Gran Reserva Especial, Grande Auguri, Eristoff, Estelar Suave, Exshaw, Hatuey By Bacardi, Martini, Martini & Rossi Asti Spumante, Montelera Riserva, Nassau Royale, Natasha, Noilly Prat, Pastis Casanis, Pastis Duval, Ron Bacardi A Ejo, Russian Prince, St. Raphael, Vergel, Veuve Amiot, Viejo Vergel, William Lawson's Finest Blend, and William Lawson's Scottish Gold.

THE BACARDI BAT

When don Facundo Bacardi opened his first distillery in Cuba, it was occupied by a family of bats, which not only delighted him, but prompted his wife, dona Amalia Lucia Victoria, to suggest that he put a "bat" label on every bottle of Bacardi rum.

Although most people would be horrified to discover that they shared their home with bats, Don Facundo Bacardi saw the bat as a sign of success. According to Cuban tradition, the bat brings good fortune, health, and family unity to any home they occupy.

Moreover, both don Facundo and dona Amalia Lucia Victoria were Spanish immigrants to Cuba, and the Spanish have their own beliefs about the bat. Spanish lore has it that in 1238, King James I of Aragon was preparing for battle when a bat perched on his helmet. James believed that the bat was watching over his troops, and the next day he won the battle. The king then included the bat in the coat of arms of Valencia, a nearby province of don Facundo's native home in Spain, and the bat was immortalized as a symbol of watchfulness and family harmony in Spain.

As Bacardi's company grew, so did the stories of his bats. Word of the bats in his distillery spread throughout Cuba, and the Cubans dubbed Bacardi's liquor as "el ron del murcielago," the rum of the bat, and declared that the rum contained good fortune and magical powers because of the prophetic bat.

CORPORATE CITIZENSHIP

In its role as a corporate citizen, Bacardi shows an inclination toward environmental issues. Founded in 1994, The Bacardi Foundation collaborates with environmental, government, and civic groups to promote the protection of the world's coastal waters and beaches. The Foundation helps academic marine scientists studying sensitive coastal areas and educates the public of the environmental importance of these areas. With its flagship "Clean Water Weekends" program, the Foundation works with The Nature Conservancy, Clean Florida Keys, and the Florida Keys National Marine Sanctuary to help volunteer boaters, beach enthusiasts, and divers clean up the waters, beaches, and reefs of the Florida Keys.

As for its political activities, Bacardi's image may not be as clean. According to the report "Squeeze Play:

The United States, Cuba, and the Helms-Burton Act," Bacardi was involved in a larger scheme to trade money for political favors. Between 1981 and 1996, the right-wing Cuban American National Foundation poured $3.2 million into the U.S. political system in exchange for three major policies: the 1980's creation of Radio Marti, a taxpayer-financed program that broadcasts to Cuba; the elimination of trade with Cuba by subsidiaries of U.S. companies; and passage of the Helms-Burton law, which bars U.S. entry to executives of foreign firms who work with the expropriated properties of current U.S. citizens. Bacardi's Cuban properties were confiscated without compensation by the revolutionary government of Fidel Castro; congressional aides intimately involved in designing the Helms-Burton law depended heavily on lobbyists and lawyers with ties to Bacardi.

GLOBAL PRESENCE

While incorporated and headquartered in Bermuda, Bacardi Limited runs manufacturing and bottling facilities in North, Central, and South America; the Caribbean; and Europe. Its two primary rum producing facilities are located in Puerto Rico and Mexico. Bacardi products are marketed around the world. Bacardi-Martini U.S.A. was also promoting Bacardi products abroad by marketing Hatuey Cuban beer more widely and by redesigning the labels for Martini Vermouth bottles before launching them in Brazil in March of 1998.

SOURCES OF INFORMATION

Bibliography

Bacardi Corp. Profile, 12 September 1996.

Bacardi Corporate Information, 1996. Available at http://www.bacardi.com.

"Bacardi-Martini U.S.A., Inc." *Hoover's Online,* 6 July 1998. Available at http://www.hoovers.com.

Clairvoyant, Kethia. "Cash From Miami Group Helped Shape U.S. Cuba Policy, Report Says." *Cox News Service,* 1997. Available at http://www.latinolink.com/news/news97/0123ncub.htm.

Dortch, Shannon. "Grain and Grape Futures (Demographics of Alcohol Consumption)." *American Demographics,* January 1997.

Heuslin, William. "Food, Drink & Tobacco: With Domestic Markets Maturing, the Smart Food, Drink and Tobacco Companies Are Heading Overseas." *Forbes Annual Report on American Industry,* 13 January 1997.

For additional industry research:

Investigate companies by their Standard Industrial Classification Codes, also known as SICs. Bacardi-Martini's primary SICs are:

2082 Malt Beverages

2084 Wines, Brandy, and Brandy Spirits

2085 Distilled & Blended Liquors

Barnes & Noble, Inc.

OVERVIEW

Barnes & Noble, Inc., the largest bookselling chain in the United States, is best known for its book "superstores"—giant, supermarket-style stores that it introduced in the 1970s. These stores, numbering 483 in 1998, offer a wide variety of books at discount prices. Barnes & Noble also operated 528 mall-based bookstores in 1998, under the names B. Dalton Bookseller, Doubleday Book Shops, and Scribner's Bookstores. It also publishes books under its own name, and is a leading seller of books through mail-order catalogs.

Although most of Barnes & Noble's business is carried out in the United States, it also owns part of Chapters, Canada's largest retail book chain, and Calendar Club, a seasonal kiosk operation that operates both within the United States and internationally. In 1997 Barnes & Noble entered the world of online bookselling challenging pioneer Amazon.com in the growing Internet commerce business. Its total sales for the fiscal year ending January 31, 1998, were $2.8 billion. Chairman Leonard Ruggio and his brother Stephen, company vice chairman, hold about 28 percent of Barnes & Noble's stock.

COMPANY FINANCES

From fiscal 1994 through fiscal 1998 Barnes & Noble's total revenues skyrocketed: starting with $1.62 billion in 1994, revenues rose to $1.97 billion in 1995, $2.45 billion in 1996, $2.79 billion in 1997, and $2.8 billion in 1998. (Barnes & Noble's fiscal year runs from February through January.) In the same time period, net

FOUNDED: 1873 (incorporated 1894, as C.M. Barnes Company)

Contact Information:

HEADQUARTERS: 122 5th Ave.
New York, NY 10011
PHONE: (212)633-3300
FAX: (212)675-0413
URL: http://www.barnesandnoble.com

FINANCES:

Barnes & Noble Inc.
Revenues, 1994-1997
(million dollars)

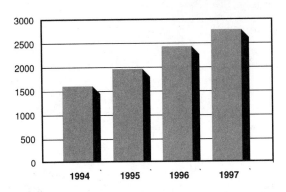

Barnes & Noble Inc.
1997 Stock Prices
(dollars)

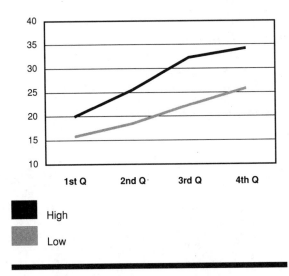

income rose from $8 million in 1994 to $53 million in 1998.

HISTORY

In 1873 Charles Montgomery Barnes opened a second-hand book business in Wheaton, Illinois. Soon afterward he moved to Chicago, where he began to sell new books as well. Within 20 years his C.M. Barnes Company had limited itself to selling schoolbooks. His son, William R. Barnes, joined the family business, but decided in 1917 to move to New York and sold the original business. In its place, he invested in a New York educational bookstore, Noble & Noble, renaming it Barnes & Noble. William R. Barnes stayed with the company only until 1929, but the company name was kept.

Barnes & Noble was a wholesale business, dealing with schools, libraries, and book dealers. Customers who came in looking to purchase a single book were allowed into the building, but not encouraged; eventually a small retail corner was set up for these customers. The demand for a retail textbook store grew, and Barnes & Noble opened its first retail store in New York City, enlarging it in 1941 to serve the students of the many colleges and schools there. Innovations in this store included a multiline telephone service and piped-in "Muzak." The store had a stock of 2 million books—huge for the time. From the 1940s until the 1970s Barnes & Noble steadily grew, adding an import and export division, publishing children's educational books and a series of study guides, and opening an outlet for used books and publishers' remainders—the outlet bought used books from 200 campus bookstores. The *Guiness Book of World Records* for 1972 listed Barnes & Noble as the world's largest bookstore.

By the early 1970s, however, the store was doing poorly. John Barnes, the last family member to run the business, died in 1969, and Barnes & Noble was bought by Amtel, a corporation that also made toys and tools. Business went downhill, and in 1971 Amtel sold the store to Leonard Riggio who as a teenager worked in the New York University bookstore. (Riggio, in 1965, at the age of 25, borrowed $5,000 to buy a college bookstore.) Soon his tiny Waverly Book Exchange was matching the sales of his old employer, and he bought and opened 10 more stores in the next five years. After he bought the Barnes & Noble store, he changed all the stores' names to Barnes & Noble.

Riggio expanded Barnes & Noble, adding nonfiction books and "how-to" books. His philosophy was that more people read for information than for entertainment. Soon new stores were opened in New York, New Jersey, and Pennsylvania, but the centerpiece of Riggio's business was a new concept in bookstores: a book supermarket. He opened a huge three-building annex across from the original New York store, with fiction, best-sellers, and gift books added to the store's stock. But most important of all, even new books and best-sellers were deeply discounted. Riggio targeted a new audience: shoppers who might not even read the books they bought. Riggio's idea was an instant success and customers crowded the stores, pushing shopping carts through the aisles.

In the late 1970s Riggio also began to acquire other retail bookstore chains, including Bookmasters, Marboro Books, Inc., B. Dalton Bookseller (the second-largest chain at the time, behind Walden Books), Doubleday Book Shops, and Bookstop. Many of these stores were located in suburban shopping malls. Riggio also reacquired rights to the Barnes & Noble name for publishing books, which had been sold when John Barnes died in 1969.

By the 1990s Riggio had shifted the focus of his stores. Many "superstores" were added, and prices were still discounted, but the stores were designed as welcoming spaces with cafes and play areas that invited customers to browse and socialize. Each of these stores cost more than $1 million to build; however, even with rapidly rising revenues, Barnes & Noble posted losses in the early 1990s. Riggio decided to raise cash by selling stock publicly in late 1993 (keeping almost one-third of the stock himself). Buyers were so eager to buy the stocks that the initial stock price was driven to almost double what experts had predicted.

In the 1990s competitors frequently complained that Barnes & Noble and its rapid growth were damaging other chains and destroying small, independent booksellers. However, many customers seemed pleased to select from Barnes & Noble's huge stock of books, and to pay less for them as well. Year after year in the later 1990s, Barnes & Noble announced record sales and profits.

STRATEGY

As outlined in its annual report, Barnes & Noble has a multifaceted strategy. One of its main targets is the chief book-buying population in the United States—people between 45 and 64 years old (a segment that is projected to grow in coming years). It clusters its stores in high-traffic areas, convenient to transportation and parking, and offers extended shopping hours. Having a wide variety of titles for customers to select from also is key to the company's strategy; each store features between 60,000 and 175,000 titles, and other books not in stock can be specially ordered. Store employees are expected to be helpful and knowledgeable, and the company strongly encourages promotions to management from the existing pool of employees. Each store is designed to resemble a European library, with comfortable seating, attractive space, and refreshments. The opening of every new store is accompanied by a major campaign, including print and radio advertising, mail, and community events.

Discounted prices are based on a national pricing strategy, with hardcover best-sellers discounted by as much as 30 percent. Barnes & Noble also ties in its other business activities with its store operations. Books published under the Barnes & Noble imprint are prominently featured in the company's direct-mail catalogs, along with publishers' remainders and hard-to-find imported books.

Barnes & Noble book sellers offer a variety of events at their various locations. Here harpist Christine Vivona performs at the Foothills Mall store in Casa Adobes, Arizona. (Photograph by Kevin Lee. AP Photo/Arizona Daily Star.)

INFLUENCES

In addition to the major influences discussed above—notably the arrival of Leonard Ruggio at the helm—Barnes & Noble has been both helped and hindered by its rapid growth. The expansion of the company's network of "superstores" has been accompanied by the inevitable closing of small, independent bookstores. Along with Barnes & Noble, Borders Bookstores (once a single Michigan bookstore) has also became a growing superstore chain in the 1990s, setting off what one columnist in *Fortune* referred to as "bookstore wars."

The superstore concept was highly successful for Barnes & Noble. At the same time, its growth and success earned Barnes & Noble the hostility of many small bookstore owners and some community activists. In addition, publishers also have been displeased with the superstores' high return rate for unsold books. (Publishers often agree to take back unsold books from bookstores, unlike many other businesses in which a store must absorb the cost of unsold items.) In March 1998 a lawsuit was filed in California against both Barnes & Noble and Borders Bookstores by the American Booksellers Association (ABA) and 26 independent bookstores. The stores and the ABA claimed that the giant chains had engaged

FAST FACTS:
About Barnes & Noble, Inc.

Ownership: Barnes & Noble, Inc. is a publicly owned company traded on the New York Stock Exchange.

Ticker symbol: BKS

Officers: Leonard Ruggio, Chmn. & CEO, 57, $1,440,000; Stephen Ruggio, VChmn & COO, 43, $736,000; J. Alan Kahn, COO, 51; Mitchell S. Klipper, Exec. VP, 40, $736,000

Employees: 29,500 (1998)

Principal Subsidiary Companies: Barnes & Noble, Inc. operates through subsidiaries in the United States, including Barnes & Noble Booksellers, B. Dalton Bookseller, Doubleday Book Shops, and Scribner's Bookstores. It is a partial owner of Chapters, a Canadian bookseller, and Calendar Club, which operates internationally.

Chief Competitors: Barnes & Noble has many competitors among traditional retail bookstores, mail-order businesses, and online booksellers. Its chief competitors include: Borders Bookstores; Walden Books; Books-A-Million; and Amazon.com.

in unfair trade practices and competition that had harmed their businesses.

CURRENT TRENDS

In the late 1990s Barnes & Noble placed an increased emphasis on opening more superstores, sometimes as many as 150 in a single year. At the same time, it decided to close or restructure many of its mall-based bookstores, such as B. Dalton Bookseller stores, whose sales had been declining. Ironically, the company itself admitted that the main competitor for these mall-based stores probably was the book superstore. More than 50 of these mall-based stores were closed every year beginning in 1989.

In March 1997 Barnes & Noble launched an online bookselling service through America Online (AOL). AOL agreed to allow Barnes & Noble to be the exclusive bookseller on its site, thus shutting out Amazon.com,

previously the leading online bookseller. Two months later, Barnes & Noble also set up its own web site for online purchases. The online service offers discount prices similar to those in its retail stores. The entry of Barnes & Noble into the online market set off a price war with Amazon.com; with the expected addition of Borders Bookstores close behind Barnes & Noble, competition was expected to be fierce. After nine months of operation, the Barnes & Noble online service had lost $9 million. (Amazon.com also was still losing money, even though it had been operating far longer and had taken in almost $150 million in sales in 1997.) Some analysts suggested that although the online bookselling business showed promise, like many other Internet-based businesses it involved very high startup, marketing, and expansion costs, and profits were not possible in the initial months or even years.

CORPORATE CITIZENSHIP

Barnes & Noble tries to maintain a "community bookstore" atmosphere, even in its giant superstores. Many stores have a cafe, and offer a wide variety of activities ranging from children's story hours to author appearances. On its web site, Barnes & Noble offers visitors an "online community," in which they can discuss works of various authors or literary topics, recommend books to other readers, and even chat online with authors.

In 1990 Barnes & Noble established the Discover Great New Writers Program to give new authors a chance to reach a wider audience. In connection with this program, Barnes & Noble has bestowed an annual Discover Great New Writers Award since 1993. This award is given to a first-time American novelist who has been featured in the Discover Great New Writers Program during the previous year, and includes a $5,000 prize to the winner. A description of each award-winning book is featured on the company web site.

Barnes & Noble supports First Book, a national organization that provides books to children who have difficulty accessing them outside of school. It also is a chief sponsor of Writer's Harvest, an annual series of readings sponsored across the United States by Share Our Strength, an anti-poverty organization.

GLOBAL PRESENCE

Barnes & Noble chiefly operates stores within the United States. It also is a partial owner of Chapters, Canada's largest retail book chain, and Calendar Club, a seasonal kiosk operation that operates both within the United States and internationally. With the advent of its online business as well as its ongoing mail order catalog business, Barnes & Noble is likely to increase its busi-

CHRONOLOGY:

Key Dates for Barnes & Noble, Inc.

1873: Founded

1894: Incorporates as C.M. Barnes Company

1902: William R. Barnes becomes president

1917: William R. Barnes sells the original business, moves to New York, and invests in Noble & Noble-renamed to Barnes & Noble

1929: William R. Barnes leaves the company

1941: Barnes & Noble enlarges its first retail bookstore

1944: Begins publishing educational books for children

1969: John Barnes dies; bookstore is purchased by Amtel; rights to publish under the Barnes & Noble name are sold

1971: Amtel sells the company to Leonard Riggio

1972: The *Guiness Book of World Records* Lists Barnes & Noble as the world's largest bookstore

1979: Acquires Bookmasters

1986: Buys B. Dalton Bookseller

1990: Establishes the Discover Great New Writers Program; purchases Doubleday Book Shops

1991: Reacquires rights to publish under the Barnes & Noble name

1993: Initial Public Offering of stock

1997: Launches an online bookselling service through American Online

1998: American Booksellers Association files a lawsuit against Barnes & Noble and Borders Bookstores

ness outside of the United States. When Barnes & Noble began to sell its stock publicly in 1993, about one third of its stock was retained by CEO Ruggio's financial partner Vendex, a Dutch conglomerate.

EMPLOYMENT

As of early 1998 Barnes & Noble employed 14,500 full-time employees and between 15,000 and 17,000 part-time hourly employees. Because the bookselling business fluctuates widely by season, the part-time employee number varies as well. About 75 percent of Barnes & Noble's store managers were promoted from within its existing group of employees, and none of its employees are represented by unions.

SOURCES OF INFORMATION

Bibliography

"Barnes & Noble, Inc." *Hoover's Online,* 26 July 1998. Available at http://www.hoovers.com.

Barnes & Noble, Inc. Annual Report. New York: Barnes & Noble, Inc., 1997.

Berreby, David. "The Growing Battle of the Big Bookstores." *New York Times,* 8 November 1992.

Nickell, Joe. "Online Booksellers Pay to Win." *Wired,* 16 March 1998. Available at http://www.wired.com.

Norton, Rob. "Why the Bookstore Wars Are Good." *Fortune,* 27 October 1997.

Panepinto, Joe. "Battle in the Online Bookstacks: B&N vs. Amazon." *Family PC,* September 1997.

Symons, Allene. "Barnes & Noble to Buy B. Dalton: Will Become Largest Chain." *Publishers Weekly,* 12 December 1986.

Woodward, A. "Barnes & Noble, Inc." *International Directory of Company Histories,* Vol. 10. Detroit: St. James Press, 1995.

For an annual report:

on the Internet at: http://www.sec.gov/cgi-bin/srch-edgar **or** write: Barnes & Noble, 122 5th Ave., New York, NY 10011

For additional industry research:

Investigate companies by their Standard Industrial Classification Codes, also known as SICs. Barnes & Noble's primary SICs are:

5942 Book Stores

5961 Catalog and Mail Order Houses

6719 Holding Companies, NEC

BASF Aktiengesellschaft

ALSO KNOWN AS: BASF
FOUNDED: 1861

Contact Information:

HEADQUARTERS: Carl-Bosch Strasse, 38
   Ludwigshafen 67056 Germany
PHONE: (212)815-2367
FAX: (212)571-3050
URL: http://www.basf-ag.basf.de/basf/html/e/home.htm
   http://www.basf.com

OVERVIEW

BASF Corporation is the second largest chemical manufacturer in the world. Based in Germany, the company manufactures and markets various chemicals and plastics. BASF has five main operating units: Plastics and Fibers, Colorants and Finishing Products, Health and Nutrition, Chemicals, and Oil and Gas. The company manufactures and markets products in 39 countries and operates business affairs in over 170.

COMPANY FINANCES

In 1997 sales for BASF AG were $31.01 billion; net income was $1.78 billion. Of 1997 sales, $7.99 billion was earned in Germany (26 percent); $10.97 billion was earned in other European countries (35 percent); $6.48 billion was earned in North America (21 percent); $3.73 billion was earned in the Asia/Pacific and Africa (12 percent); and $1.82 billion was earned in South America (6 percent). Sales for BASF Corp. in the United States were $4 billion. Broken down by operating division, the company's Plastics and Fibers division earned the most revenue, $8.04 billion (26 percent of overall 1997 sales). Colorants and finishing products brought in $7.11 billion (23 percent); Health and Nutrition products generated $6.06 billion (19 percent); Chemical brought in $4.86 billion (16 percent); Oil and Gas revenues were $3.47 billion (11 percent); and revenues derived from all other sources totaled $1.45 billion (5 percent).

The company's total earnings per share (EPS) for 1997 were $2.90, a slight decline from 1996 earnings of

$2.93 per share. BASF AG's stock price in mid-1998 was around $46.00 per share. Its 52-week high was $46.25, and its 52-week low was $31.25 per share.

ANALYSTS' OPINIONS

Many analysts view the chemical manufacturing industry as a mature market with too many competitors. This led some analysts to praise BASF's joint efforts with Hoescht and Royal Dutch Shell. Jackie Ashurst, a chemicals analyst, was quoted in the October 10, 1996 issue of *The Wall Street Journal* as saying, "[The joint ventures will] consolidate an industry that has too many players. It will create cost and marketing efficiencies, and raise the possibility of some further restructuring in the industry." Ronald Koehler, chemicals and pharmaceuticals analyst, stated in the same article that the merged efforts of BASF and Hoescht would create the largest polypropylene supplier in Europe, totaling a combined market share of 27 percent. Other experts remain skeptical, claiming BASF's efforts may be in vain as other competitors will arise. Some even question the accuracy of the 27-percent market share, saying it might be closer to 20 percent.

HISTORY

German jeweler Frederick Englehorn founded BASF, initially known as Badische Anilin & Soda-Fabrik, in 1865 to produce coal tar dyes. Demand for dyes was strong, growing in conjunction with the textile industry, and BASF earned a top position in the world dye market by the end of the nineteenth century. BASF set new trends with its development of synthetic dyes, particularly indigo, in 1897. In 1901 BASF pioneered the invention of indanthreme dyes, which were exceptionally lightfast and washfast. These dyes soon overtook indigo's supremacy in the dyeing and printing industry. During the early twentieth century, BASF entered into another product sector with its research into nitrogen and development of the Haber-Bosch process. This process allowed atmospheric nitrogen to be combined with hydrogen at high pressures and temperatures, and with the use of catalysts, to form ammonia. It also led the way to synthetic production of nitrogen fertilizers.

Due to the weakness of the German economy following World War I, BASF, Hoechst, Bayer, and three other companies were merged in 1925, resulting in the founding of I.G. Farbenindustrie AG. With this merger, BASF ceased to exist as an independent company, and the new company's headquarters were moved to Frankfurt. BASF developed polystyrene, PVC, and magnetic tape during this joint operation.

As the motor car proved a runaway success during the 1920s, BASF invested its resources in developing fuels, operating agents, synthetic rubber, and raw materials and sur-

FAST FACTS:
About BASF Aktiengesellschaft

Ownership: BASF is a publicly owned company traded on the OTC (over-the-counter) exchange.

Ticker symbol: BASFY

Officers: Jurgen Strube, Chmn., Pres. & CEO; Hanns-Helge Stechl, Vice-Chmn.; Hans Albers, Chmn. of the Supervisory Board; Harald Grunert, CFO

Employees: 104,979 (1997)

Principal Subsidiary Companies: BASF Aktiengesellschaft's subsidiaries include: Knoll AG, Comparex Informationssysteme GmbH, Knoll Deutschland GmbH, BASF Corp., BASF in east Asia, BASF in southeast Asia/Australia, and BASF in Japan. The company is a publicly traded operating unit of BASF Group.

Chief Competitors: As one of the world's largest chemical manufacturers, BASF's primary competitors include: Akzo Nobel; Bayer; Bristol-Myers Squibb; Dow Chemical; DuPont; Eli Lilly; Exxon; Hoechst; Merck; Pfizer; Rhone-Poulenc; Royal Dutch/Shell; Sony; and Warner-Lambert.

face coatings. The company's first tankers of automobile gasoline were produced in 1927. The development of the first synthetic rubber, "Buna," followed in 1930.

Early in World War II, the first air raids began on BASF's Ludwigshafen and Oppau works. Damage was severe, and when the site became occupied by American troops on March 23, 1945, it was a pile of rubble. After 65 air raids, 33 percent of the factory buildings had been totally destroyed and 61 percent were damaged severely. After World War II, I.G. Farben was dissolved by the Allied Control Council, and BASF began operating alone again in 1952. The company worked to reconstruct its factories after damage from the war.

Due to popular household demand for basic chemicals following World War II, BASF regained its strength. With this newfound strength, the company sought partnerships in other countries. They joined with Dow Chemical in the United States in 1958, which it completely owned by 1978. The company began building production sites all over the world during the 1960s, including Brazil, France, India, Japan, the United States, Australia, Mexico, Argentina, Spain, Belgium, Italy, and the United

CHRONOLOGY:

Key Dates for BASF Aktiengesellschaft

1865: Badische Anilin & Soda-Fabrik (BASF) is founded to produce coal tar dyes

1897: Research into an indigo dye cost the company 18 million gold marks, more than BASF's capital

1901: Indanthrene dyes are developed and becomes the industry leader

1914: BASF paves the way for agricultural chemistry with the opening of the Limburgerhof Agricultural Center

1925: BASF merges with Hoechst, Bayer, and three other German companies to form I.G. Farben

1945: During World War II, 45 percent of BASF buildings are destroyed in bombing raids

1952: I.G. Farben is separated into three large firms: Hoechst, Bayer, and BASF

1961: BASF invents Styropor, a new lightweight packing and insulating material

1968: Purchases Wintersall potash and natural gas company to become Germany's second largest chemical company

1978: Completes ownership of Dow Jones

1991: Signs an agreement with Russia and France to produce natural gas there

1996: Merges with Hoechst and Royal Dutch/Shell

Kingdom. BASF's Antwerp production site was especially important, becoming the second largest European complex.

BASF soon became a leading manufacturer of plastics and synthetic fibers. BASF also began producing petrochemicals and bought Wintershall, a German oil and gas manufacturer, in 1969. Wintershall marketed natural gas to the European market.

Purchasing other companies proved successful for BASF in its goal to expand. Some of the companies it acquired include Wyandotte Chemicals in 1969, Chemetron in 1979, and Inmont in 1985. BASF also bought Synthesewerk Schwarzheide (SYS), a large chemical company in eastern Germany, in 1990. BASF signed agreements with Russia and France in 1991 to

produce natural gas there. The following year, the company bought Mobil's polystyrene-resin business in the United States.

By 1994 BASF became the world's second largest chemical manufacturer after it bought Imperial Chemical's polypropylene business. BASF also purchased the pharmaceutical division of Boots, a U.K. retailer, in 1995. In 1996 BASF saw a need, as did its competitors, to merge in order to avoid drastic market turns. The company signed deals with Hoechst and Royal Dutch/Shell that year. It also planned to sell its audio and videotape businesses to RAKS, a Turkish cassette manufacturer.

STRATEGY

BASF devised a growth strategy it called "Vision 2010." This is the year by which the company aimed to be the number one global chemical manufacturer. The company strives toward improved efficiency and flexibility. It also views change as its foundation for future success.

Although BASF yielded sales in South America, North America, Europe, and Asia/Africa in the late 1990s, its strongest potential for growth was seen in Asia due to its strong market demand compared to other regions. Even though the company is based in Germany, it has placed itself in other countries due to the increasing costs of production and shipment in that country. BASF's European and German facilities serve mostly as production, research, and development sites.

BASF's strongest international markets were for natural gas and oil. Other strong markets included pharmaceuticals, crop protections agents, and vitamins. Foams, other plastics like polystyrene, and colorants gave BASF a strong international presence as well.

Selling off some of its businesses in the late 1990s, BASF aimed to focus on its core business. Businesses sold included its electrical insulation systems business, container coatings business, and subsidiaries Resart GmbH and Critesa SA, Spain, along with PMMA plastics. BASF also reduced its holdings in Kali und Salz Beteiligungs AG, owned through Guano-Werke GmbH, from more than 75 percent to less than 50 percent. The company also agreed to sell Chemag Aktiengesellschaft. BASF reorganized some areas of the company, including the transfer of its building paints operations to newly founded BASF deco GmbH and the transfer of the company's printing system operations to BASF Drucksysteme GmbH.

INFLUENCES

BASF's early success began with its development of synthetic dyestuffs. The chemical manufacturing market following World War II was favorable, allowing BASF to spread its wings to the United States, eastern

Germany, Russia, and France. The purchase of Mobil's polystyrene-resin business gave BASF 10 percent of the U.S. market in 1992. However, the early 1990s also proved to be difficult for the company. BASF sales dropped due to high domestic-labor expenses, slow buyer demand, and a strong Deutschmark. The company was able to remain balanced, however, due to a raised universal need for BASF's chemicals, plastics, and fibers.

CURRENT TRENDS

BASF continued to reach its global goals through expansion. It took advantage of the North American Free Trade Agreement (NAFTA) by developing plans for an industrial manufacturing site on the Gulf Coast. A. Jennings, President of BASF Corporation's Chemical Division said in a January 22, 1997 issue of *The Wall Street Journal,* "This investment is of strategic importance to BASF because it will ensure integrated long-term propylene and ethylene supply for future expansion in the NAFTA region." BASF was expanding its U.S. presence by building a new plastics plant in Texas and expanding plastic-making operations in Alabama, Louisiana, and Illinois. BASF also used acquisitions as a growth strategy in the United States. One example was its signing of a million-dollar deal with Molecular Simulations Inc. (MSI) in October of 1996. This venture allowed BASF scientists and researchers to use the company's new software to further the BASF chemical developments through vivid graphical imitation of molecular structures.

The company's expansion plans included other acquisitions, some of which were premix plants for feeds in Poland and South Africa; a coatings manufacturer; the printing ink businesses of Punch Printing Inks Ltd., Ireland, and Schou Trykfarver A/S, Denmark; the surfactant businesses of Olin Corporation and PPG in the United States; and 50-percent holdings of Hanwha Chemical Corp., Korea, in the joint venture Hanwha BASF Urethane Ltd. (now BASF Urethane Korea Ltd.). Other acquisitions and joint ventures also took place during 1997.

Also part of BASF's expansion was its launch into Asia—China in particular. In late 1996 negotiations were underway with China regarding the building of a manufacturing facility in Nanjing. Negotiations were to be finalized in early 1997. The company established a presence in Hong Kong and also planned to build a new facility in China and Malaysia. New plants were already built in Australia, Indonesia, Japan, and Pakistan. In South Korea, BASF agreed to buy Daesang's profitable chemical unit for $600 million.

Part of BASF's plan to expand also involved getting rid of trouble spots. The company made plans in late 1996 to sell its magnetic division to Turkey's RAKS Holding A.S. In addition, BASF entertained talks of selling its 51-percent share of its potash and rock-salt producer Kali und Salz Beteiligungs AG to Canada's Potash Corporation.

PRODUCTS

Products marketed by BASF's Health and Nutrition division include pharmaceuticals, fine chemicals (especially vitamins), fertilizers, and crop protection products. The Colorants and Finishing Products division offers products such as dyestuffs, dyes for the oil industry, pigments, finishing products, process chemicals, coatings, colorants, graphic systems, dispersions, basic chemicals, catalysts, industrial chemicals, plasticizers, solvents, glues, intermediates, specialty chemicals, surfactant raw materials, and chemicals for motor vehicles and additives. The Plastics and Fibers division offers polyolefins, polyvinyl chloride, polystyrene, engineering plastics, foamed plastics, polyurethane products and systems, PUR elastomers, and fiber products. And the Oil and Gas division markets crude oil, natural gas, and petroleum products such as fuel oil and fuels. Examples of the most well known developments associated with BASF include the synthesis of indigo, Indanthren(r) dyestuffs, and the synthesis of ammonia as a basis for fertilizer production.

CORPORATE CITIZENSHIP

Producing chemicals and other substances, BASF demonstrated its concerns in the area of environmental safety. The company remains active in the Chemical Manufacturers Association (CMA) Responsible Care Program. The company ranks among the best in the U.S. chemical industry after it significantly reduced the amount of chemicals released into the air between 1987 and 1994 by 93 percent.

BASF also developed building plans for a rigid thermoset polyurethane recycling plant. The company picked Detroit for the site since polyurethane is used to make car bumpers and moldings. Set to open in the late 1990s, the plant would use a chemical process that breaks polyurethane plastic to a state at which it can be reused.

Complete accounting of the company's environmental practices are available in its annual *Responsible Care 1997 Environment, Safety and Health Report* and can be ordered online at http://www.basf-ag.basf.de/basf/html/e/mail/ubericht.htm.

GLOBAL PRESENCE

Engaged in business activities in more than 170 countries, BASF has established a strong presence in Europe, North America, Asia, Africa, and South America. The company's largest sales percentages came from various European countries, totaling 64 percent of sales for 1995. North America came in second with a 20-percent hold on sales for that year, while Asia/Pacific & Africa totaled 11 percent; South America claimed 5 percent.

Acquiring the pharmaceuticals business of The Boots Company PLC in Nottingham, England, added to BASF's international strength as well. BASF also continued to enhance its international capacity by developing the BASF East Asia regional division in Hong Kong. To capitalize on the growing Asian market, BASF moved its Textile and Leather Dyes and Chemicals division from Germany to Singapore.

SOURCES OF INFORMATION

Bibliography

"BASF Aktiengesellschaft." *Hoover's Online,* 6 July 1998. Available at http://www.hoovers.com.

"BASF Confirms Plans to Build Ethylene Cracker On U.S. Gulf." *The Wall Street Journal,* 22 January 1997.

"BASF Sells Audio and Video Tape Division as It Focuses on Core Business." *San Diego Daily Transcript,* 15 August 1996. Available at http://www.sddt.com.

BASF Web Site, 19 June 1998. Available at http://www.basf-ag.basf.de/basf/html/e/home.htm.

"Germany's BASF in Ventures to Shore Up Polymers: Amplifier." *The Wall Street Journal,* 10 October 1996.

"Germany's BASF Sells Oilfield Chem. Marketing to U.S. Baker." *The Wall Street Journal,* 29 August 1996.

"Germany's BASF Sees 'Mixed Impression' For 2H Orders." *The Wall Street Journal,* 22 August 1996.

"MSI Signs Million Dollar Agreement With BASF." *Molecular Simulations Homepage,* 2 October 1996. Available at http://www.msi.com.

Welch, Michael. "Philip Environmental, BASF Launch Polyurethane Recycling Venture." *International Environmental Information Network,* 5 November 1996. Available at http://www.envirobiz.com.

For an annual report:
on the Internet at: http://www.basf-ag.basf.de/basf/html/e/investor/investor.htm

For additional industry research:
Investigate companies by their Standard Industrial Classification Codes, also known as SICs. BASF's primary SICs are:

2260 Dyeing And Finishing Textiles, Except Wool Fabrics

2810 Industrial Inorganic Chemicals

2820 Plastics Materials and Synthetic Resins, Synthetic

2833 Medicinal Chemicals and Botanical Products

2834 Pharmaceutical Preparations

2870 Agricultural Chemicals

7371 Services-Computer Programming Services

Bass Hotels & Resorts

OVERVIEW

Bass Hotels & Resorts, the hotel business of Bass PLC, operates or franchises more than 2,600 hotels with about 450,000 guest rooms in 75 countries and territories. Operated under the banner of Bass Hotels & Resorts, previously known as Holiday Hospitality (and Holiday Inn Worldwide before that), are full-service Inter-Continental Hotels and Holiday Inns, as well as the Holiday Inn Express, Holiday Inn Select, Holiday Inn Hotel & Suites, Holiday Inn Sun Spree Resort, Holiday Inn Garden Court, and Crowne Plaza brand hotels.

The original Holiday Inn operation, from which Bass Hotels & Resorts has sprung, was founded by Memphis real estate developer Kemmons Wilson to fill what he saw as an enormous need for decent lodging for the American traveling public. It was an idea whose time had come. The chain quickly grew, spreading across the country through an aggressive franchising program. Before long Holiday Inns began to pop up outside the United States, spreading through Canada, into Mexico, across Europe, and eventually to almost every continent on earth.

COMPANY FINANCES

As a wholly owned subsidiary of Bass PLC, Bass Hotels & Resorts is not required to disclose details of its financial operations. However, it is known that the Holiday Hospitality (before the name change) operation generated revenue of $1.1 billion in fiscal 1996, or 14 percent of Bass's total revenue of $8.0 billion. The Holiday

ALSO KNOWN AS: Holiday Inn
FOUNDED: 1954

Contact Information:

HEADQUARTERS: 3 Ravinia Dr., Ste. 2900
    Atlanta, GA 30346-2149
PHONE: (707)604-2000
FAX: (707)604-5403
URL: http://www.holiday-inn.com

*The historic Chattanooga Choo Choo
Holiday Inn in Chattanooga, Tennessee.*

(AP/Wide World Photos, Inc.)

Hospitality operation posted net earnings of about $305 million, or about 26 percent of Bass's total net income of $1.2 billion.

ANALYSTS' OPINIONS

"As surprising as it was when Timothy Lane resigned last fall from the top spot at Holiday Inn Worldwide after just seven months on the job," wrote Melanie Gibbs in the May 1997 issue of *National Real Estate Investor,* "it was perhaps even more unexpected when Bass PLC tapped hospitality industry outsider Thomas R. Oliver as president, chairman, and CEO of its Atlanta-based hotel division in February. But this move might just be what Holiday Inn needs to upgrade the quality on a brand that the *Wall Street Journal* characterized last fall as having 'a somewhat dowdy image'."

The optimism with which many regarded the appointment of Oliver appears to have been justified. In little more than a year on the job he had restructured management, engineered the acquisition of Inter-Continental Hotels from Japan's Saison Group, and given the company a couple of name changes. The management structure was realigned so that each hotel brand has its own president. Each president reports directly to Oliver. The Inter-Continental acquisition added 187 operating hotels

to the Holiday Hospitality family, as well as another 24 hotels that were in development.

HISTORY

Kemmons Wilson founded the Holiday Inn hotel chain in 1952. Wilson, a Memphis real estate developer, and his family had taken a motor tour of the United States and found less-than pleasant lodging during their journey. He was aware of the Depression-era problems the motel (derived from the words motor and hotel) industry had faced, particularly the negative image the public had of motels. Other issues at that time included the issue of whether women should work in motels and how to deal with the constant bargaining for fees in the absence of set room rates.

The first Holiday Inn opened in Memphis, Tennessee, in August 1952. Each of the 120 rooms had a private bath, air conditioning, and a telephone as well as a host of luxury amenities and attractions such as a swimming pool, dog kennels, free parking, and the now legendary free stays for children under the age of 12. The concept was that each property would be located along major highways, particularly frequently traveled roads, to serve as handy stopovers for road-weary travelers. To build name and brand identities, all of the hotels were basically similar in their appointments and layout, giving customers confidence that they could expect a consistently pleasant stay at any Holiday Inn they might choose.

Holiday Inns of America was incorporated in 1954 to manage the finances and franchising of the properties, as well as to assure uniform quality standards at each property. Kemmons took the company public in 1957 and immediately sold the entire initial public offering—unheard of in those days. Expansion of the chain continued at a dizzying rate through the 1960s with a new property opening every few days. This phenomenal growth was fueled in part by President Dwight D. Eisenhower's massive interstate highway construction program.

Wilson, who is credited within the hotel industry for having created the concept of franchising, began seeking the financing of institutional investors in 1963. The company was also able to improve and eventually grew from a motel concept and image to that of a roadside hotel. The one-thousandth Holiday Inn was opened in 1968. Soon after the company bought Trailways bus company and Delta steamship line, Holidays Inns of America began to offer packaged travel. Wilson retired from the company in 1979.

The advent of affordable air travel, which had begun in the 1970s, eventually had an impact on the corporation. To take advantage of the sharp increase in air travel, Holiday Inn opened locations in close proximity to airports. During this period the company made a number of acquisitions, including Harrah's hotel-casinos. Shortly before the Harrah's purchase, the company dumped Trailways, as bus travel had fallen out of favor with the traveling public.

During the 1980s Holiday Inn attempted to reposition itself in the light of increased competition. Then-CEO Michael Rose, newly appointed in 1981, decided to create two new hotel chains to offset the problems and lure in a new market niche of travelers. These were Embassy Suites, aimed at the upscale business traveler, and Hampton Inns, a budget hotel chain. Both began operations in 1984. Soon after the company acquired two additional hotel chains that were merged into the existing chains.

Still more changes were to come. In 1985 the company issued 6.3 million new shares of stock to be purchased by the corporation. The name of the company was changed to Holiday Corporation and new headquarters offices were opened. A year later real estate mogul Donald Trump announced he had acquired a tiny share in the company, ostensibly to alert management to a possible Trump takeover. Rose decided to recapitalize the corporation to deflect Trump's interest in purchasing Holiday. Now that the company had $2.4 billion in debt, primarily in junk bonds, Trump was no longer interested. The resulting deal left Rose and other managers with a combined 10-percent interest in Holiday Corporation. Most of the other concerns were doing well, but Holiday Inns were badly in need of major renovations, which fueled the public perception that "the chain was past its prime." Rose wanted to dump Holiday Inns regardless of the cost.

In 1988 Holiday Inns International, owner of all the properties outside North American and 13 within the United States, was purchased by Britain's Bass PLC. Two years later Bass completed the $2.23-billion deal by purchasing all the Holiday Inns in the United States from Holiday Corporation. Bass, hearing more and more feedback from travelers that the Holiday Inn chain was getting a little tired looking, embarked on an ambitious renovation campaign.

Holiday Corporation changed its name to Promus Companies after the purchase of the Holiday Inns group by Bass PLC. Promus would continue to oversee its casinos and three chains—Hampton Inn, Embassy Suites, and Homewood Suites hotels. Bass executives attempted to spruce up the aging properties in the United States with a $1-billion renovation campaign that began in 1995. It attempted to create additional market share across the board by expanding Crowne Plaza-branded properties, and in 1991 created the business-like Holiday Inn Express to reach budget and business travelers. By 1995 Crowne Plaza and Holiday Inn Express had about 100 and 350 properties, respectively.

Through the late 1980s and 1990s the company went through numerous restructuring and management changes. Bass was investing capital funds in various updates and renovations, but despite the investment, none

FAST FACTS:
About Bass Hotels & Resorts

Ownership: Bass Hotels & Resorts is the hotel business of Bass PLC. Bass' American Depository Receipts trade on the New York Stock Exchange.

Ticker symbol: BAS

Officers: Thomas R. Oliver, Chmn. & CEO; Andrew MacFarlane, Exec. VP Finance; Cindy Durning, Sr. VP Human Resources

Employees: 10,300 (1997)

Principal Subsidiary Companies: Bass Hotels & Resorts is the parent to Holiday Inn, Crowne Plaza, Holiday Inn Express, Holiday Inn Select, Holiday Inn Garden Court, Holiday Inn Sunspree Resorts, and Staybridge Suites.

Chief Competitors: As a leader in the lodgings industry worldwide, the major competitors of Bass Hotels & Resorts include: Hilton; Hyatt; Marriott International; Ramada; and Westin.

---

paid off for Bass and the Holiday Inn division damaged its bottom line considerably. So much so that in 1992 it filed a lawsuit against Promus, contending that Promus withheld key information from Bass during their negotiations. The result: Bass contended that without that financial information, it obviously had paid an exorbitant price for the chain. In the ensuing years—1993, 1994, and 1995—profits rose. Promus paid $49 million in a settlement in 1995.

Profits for the chain increased 18.9 percent in 1996. However, in December 1996, the company sold ownership and/or management of 61 of its Holiday Inn properties in the United States and Canada to Bristol Hotel Co. for $659 million. Despite the sale to the Dallas-based company, Holiday Inn Worldwide decided to maintain its company-managed Crowne Plaza hotels plus about 100 company-managed Holiday Inn and Crowne Plaza branded hotels in the Asia-Pacific and Europe/Middle East/Africa Division.

The latest of the management changes came in 1997, shortly after the appointment of Thomas R. Oliver, former Federal Express executive, as chairman and CEO in February of that year. Oliver wasted little time in trying to reinvigorate the company. He restructured the com-

CHRONOLOGY:

Key Dates for Bass Hotels & Resorts

1952: First Holiday Inn opens in Memphis, Tennessee

1954: Holiday Inn of America is incorporated

1968: The 1000th Holiday Inn is opened

1979: Founder, Kemmons Wilson, retires

1981: CEO, Michael Rose is appointed

1984: Two new hotel chains, Embassy Suites and Hampton Inns, begin operations

1985: Company name changes to the Holiday Corporation

1988: All of Holiday Inns International are purchased by Bass PLC

1990: Bass purchases all of Holiday Corporation's U.S. holdings

1995: Bass embarks of a $1 billion renovation campaign for its Holiday Inns

1997: Thomas Oliver becomes chairman and CEO of the recently renamed Holiday Hospitality

1998: The name, Holiday Hospitality, is changed to Bass Hotels & Resorts

pany's management so that each hotel brand has its own president, each of whom reports to Oliver. Later in 1997, under Oliver's direction, Holiday Inn Worldwide became Holiday Hospitality. Oliver also embarked on a campaign to give each of the hotel brands under the Holiday Hospitality banner its own distinct personality. In the process of making the changes he felt necessary to make each of the hotel brands a leader in its category of the business, Oliver ruffled a few feathers among Holiday Inn franchisees. That aside, the new chief executive seemed confident he could achieve his goal on time. In an interview with the *Atlanta Constitution and Journal* in April 1998, Oliver explained his rationale for the move: "I needed to have much better clarity of responsibility for people working the brands."

In another bold move in early 1998, Oliver successfully negotiated an agreement for the acquisition of the Inter-Continental hotel chain from Japan's Saison Group. The transaction was valued at $2.9 billion and included Saison's Forum hotel chain as well as an interest in Global Partner, another hotel chain. Under the agree-

ment the world headquarters of Inter-Continental and Forum will move to Atlanta. The Inter-Continental chain has 187 hotels with a total of 65,000 rooms in 69 countries. An additional 24 hotels are under development. Forum operates 20 hotels. In May 1998, to reflect the broadened range of hotel brands, the name of Holiday Hospitality was changed to Bass Hotels & Resorts.

A couple of months after the Inter-Continental acquisition, the company announced it was changing its name from Holiday Hospitality to Bass Hotels & Resorts to better reflect the expansion of the company's hotel brand names.

STRATEGY

In 1997, after the appointment of Thomas Oliver, Bass Hotels & Resorts sought to better position and clarify each of the individual brand identities within the corporation—full-service Holiday Inns, Holiday Inn Express, Holiday Inn Select, Holiday Inn Hotel & Suites, Holiday Inn Sun Spree Resort, and Holiday Inn Garden Court hotels. Each brand was given independent responsibility for sales, marketing, and franchising.

Recognizing that some of its older properties were badly in need of a fresh new look the company embarked on a major renovation campaign. During these renovations, which were completed in the fall of 1997, more than 1,300 hotels were remodeled. Some of the materials needed to finish this massive project included 1.7 million square yards of carpeting, more than 1 million square feet of floor tile, nearly 40,000 gallons of paint, about 650,000 rolls of wallpaper, and 129,000 drapes.

INFLUENCES

Among the trends that has shaped the strategy at Holiday Hospitality in the late twentieth century, probably none has been more significant than the realization that the traveling public is not uniform in their needs. Certain travelers are looking for a certain level of accommodation, while others have different demands. This has given rise to the creation of multiple hotel brands where previously all of a hotel company's properties were essentially the same. Some travelers today want the comfort of apartment-like accommodations if their business or pleasure travel compels to make an extended stay. Other travelers, carefully watching their expenses, are quite content to settle in at a no-frills hotel.

CURRENT TRENDS

Reflecting its expansion beyond the Holiday Inn line of hotels, Holiday Hospitality changed its name to Bass Hotels & Resorts in May 1998. Explaining the company's reasoning behind the name change, Thomas R. Oliver said, "With the recent addition of Inter-Continental to our organization, it became apparent that our previous corporate identity no longer reflected the diverse nature of our global brand portfolio. This change also is an opportunity for us to strengthen the association of our brands with our parent company in investors' and consumers' minds, and reflect a corporate identity consistent with other Bass businesses."

CORPORATE CITIZENSHIP

Bass Hotels & Resorts puts a high priority on community service and undertakes a number of projects each year in an attempt to improve life in the communities in which it operates. One example of such civic-mindedness was the company's donation of $500,000 to Give Kids the World in November 1997. Give Kids the World is a nonprofit organization that has helped to make dreams come true for more than 31,000 children with terminal illnesses by giving them and their families a six-day vacation in central Florida. Each family receives complimentary accommodations, tickets to area attractions including Disney World and Universal Studios, meals, and local transportation.

Bass Hotels CEO Thomas R. Oliver, in presenting the company's check to Henri Landwirth, founder of Give Kids the World, said: "For more than 40 years, families, particularly children, have been very important parts of our lives at this company. No one ever knows what challenges life may present them, and we're more than pleased to play a part in helping make a difference for some very special children and their families."

GLOBAL PRESENCE

As in much of the business world today, consolidation has taken hold in the lodgings industry. For Bass Hotels & Resorts, in particular, this trend is underscored by the company's acquisition in early 1998 of the Inter-Continental hotel chain from Japan's Saison Group. The transaction added more than 200 new hotels to the company's operations. The Inter-Continental properties fall into the luxury, full-service categories of accommodations.

EMPLOYMENT

Holiday Inn Worldwide has had a strong commitment to employee training as far back as the days of founder Kemmons Wilson. "The Holiday Inn University contributed to the consistency of the company's service by providing for the education and professional advancement of its franchisees and property managers, who were offered the opportunity to study management topics, housekeeping systems, and employee relations in short-term, intensive seminars on a college-like campus, completed with sports facilities."

SOURCES OF INFORMATION

Bibliography

Gibbs, Melanie F. "Can Oliver Unleash Holiday's Potential?" *National Real Estate Investor,* May 1997.

Harris, Nicole. "Marketing: Brand Building: Sleepless Nights at Holiday Inn." *Business Week,* 3 November 1997.

Holiday Inn Home Page. 25 June 1998. Available at http://www.holiday-inn.com.

Badaracco, Claire. "Holiday Inns, Inc." *International Directory of Company Histories,* Vol. III. Detroit, MI: St. James Press, 1991.

Roush, Chris. "Accommodating: Holiday Inn CEO Makes First Impression On Troops." *Atlanta Journal and Constitution,* 2 September 1997.

Salamie, David E. "Bass PLC." *International Directory of Company Histories,* Vol. 15. Detroit, MI: St. James Press, 1996.

Saporta, Maria. "Holiday Hospitality's CEO Feels Right at Home." *Atlanta Journal and Constitution,* 21 April 1998.

Saporta, Maria. "Inter-Continental Will Join New Hotel Parent in Atlanta." *Atlanta Journal and Constitution,* 1 May 1998.

Seward, Christopher. "Holiday Inn Parent Buying Luxury Chain." *Atlanta Journal and Constitution,* 21 February 1998.

Shaw, Russell. "Holiday Shuffles Lineup." *Hotel & Motel Management,* 19 May 1997.

Simley, John. "Promus Companies, Inc." *International Directory of Company Histories,* Vol. 9. Detroit, MI: St. James Press, 1994.

For additional industry research:

Investigate companies by their Standard Industrial Classification Codes, also known as SICs. Bass Hotels & Resorts' primary SICs are:

5812 Eating Places

6794 Patent Owners and Lessors

7011 Hotels and Motels

Bausch & Lomb Inc.

FOUNDED: 1853

Contact Information:

HEADQUARTERS: 1 Bausch & Lomb Pl.
  Rochester, NY 14604-2701
PHONE: (716)338-6000
FAX: (716)338-6007
TOLL FREE: (800)344-8815
URL: http://www.bausch.com

OVERVIEW

Bausch & Lomb Inc. is the second largest maker of contact lenses and associated products and is responsible for names like Ray-Ban sunglasses, Curel and Soft Sense skin care products, Miracle-Ear (a recent acquisition of hearing aid products), and others. Facing recent lawsuits and investigations due to questionable sales methods, Bausch & Lomb has undergone a massive reorganization, selling off its oral care, dental-implant, and skin care businesses to focus on its core business—eye care.

COMPANY FINANCES

In 1997 Bausch & Lomb Inc. earned $1.92 billion in total revenues, down 1 percent from 1996 revenues of $1.93 billion. Fifty percent of 1997 revenues ($967 million) were earned in the United States; 25 percent ($482 million) in Europe, the Middle East, and Africa; 19 percent ($357 million) was earned in the Asia/Pacific; and the remaining 6 percent ($110 million) was earned in Canada and Latin America. Broken down by product sectors, the company's vision care segment earned the most revenue with $909 million, 47 percent of sales. The eyewear division earned $492 million, 26 percent of sales; health care products brought in $324 million (17 percent); and pharmaceuticals generated $191 million (10 percent). Bausch & Lomb's eyewear business actually lost money in 1997, significantly impacting the company's overall performance. However, the division was expected to regain profitability in 1998, largely through cost-reduction programs.

First quarter 1998 sales were $553.1 million, a significant increase over the first quarter of 1997 ($451.2 million). Net earnings, however, declined from $3.3 million in the first quarter of 1997 to a deficit of $49.4 million in the first quarter of 1998.

The company's earnings per share (EPS) in 1997 were $.89, significantly down from $1.47 in 1996 and $1.93 in 1995. During the first quarter of 1998, the company earned $.06 per share. Over the 1997 fiscal year, Bausch & Lomb stock ranged in price from $32.50 to $47.88 per share. In mid-1998 the company's stock was selling slightly higher, at almost $50.00 per share. The 52-week high for Bausch & Lomb stock was $52.69, and its 52-week low was $37.00 per share.

ANALYSTS' OPINIONS

Many analysts strongly agree that much of the company's troubles stemmed from questionable practices—such as faking invoices and quietly promising distributors they would not be responsible for payment of goods that were shipped but not ordered. In fact, many analysts wonder why the board kept former CEO Dan Gill on as long as they did. Thinking these practices were the results of isolated incidents, the board kept Gill on as CEO until further investigations raised doubts, leading to his eventual resignation.

Bausch & Lomb's earnings continued to drop over the first three months of 1997. Profits fell to $3.3 million compared to $22.5 million at that time in 1996. Analysts trace many of the company's financial obstacles to inaccurate record keeping, restructuring costs of approximately $80.0 million during 1997 and 1998, and the discontinuation of product lines such as Ray-Ban driving and performance sunglasses.

Overall, analysts recommended either a "hold" or "moderate buy" rating for Bausch & Lomb stock, indicating some confidence in the company's ability to bounce back from previous setbacks.

HISTORY

John Jacob Bausch opened a store in 1853 to sell imported European eyewear. Henry Lomb joined Bausch as a partner after loaning the entrepreneur $60. After Bausch's innovative Vulcanite (a hard rubber) eyeglass frame was developed, the two businessmen opened an office in New York City in 1880. They later began producing microscopes, binoculars, and telescopes. During World War II the company was able to provide the military with lenses for binoculars, searchlights, reflescopes, and telescopes due to William Bausch's (John Jacob's son) optical-quality glass productions in 1912.

FINANCES:

Bausch & Lomb Inc.
Net Sales, 1994-1997
(million dollars)

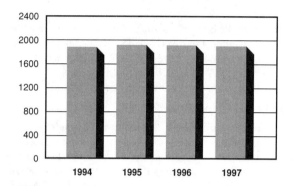

Bausch & Lomb Inc.
1997 Stock Prices
(dollars)

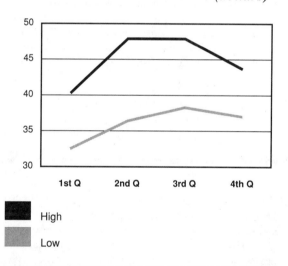

Another big break for the company came when the Army Air Corps asked Bausch & Lomb to invent a product that would diminish sun glare for pilots. From this request, the company produced Ray-Ban sunglasses, still one of Bausch & Lomb's most popular products. During the late 1960s, the company produced lenses used in satellite and missile systems for the government. Buying optical and scientific equipment companies like Ferson Optics and Reese Optical, the company's growth blossomed.

After the Federal Drug Administration (FDA) approved the company's soft contact lenses in 1971, Bausch

FAST FACTS:

About Bausch & Lomb Inc.

Ownership: Bausch & Lomb Inc. is a publicly owned company traded on the New York Stock Exchange.

Ticker symbol: BOL

Officers: William H. Waltrip, Chmn., 60; William M. Carpenter, Pres. & CEO, 45, $1,193,501; James C. Foster, Sr. VP & Pres. & CEO, Charles River Laboratories, 47, $480,764; Dwain L. Hahs, Exec. VP & Pres., Eyewear Division, 45, $501,244

Employees: 13,000 (1997)

Principal Subsidiary Companies: Subsidiaries of Bausch & Lomb include: Arnette Optic Illusions, Inc.; Polymer Technology Corp.; Bausch & Lomb (Bermuda) Ltd.; Bausch & Lomb Lamex, Inc.; Revo, Inc.; BL Industria Otica, Ltda. (Brazil); SPAFAS; Bausch & Lomb de Colombia SA; Charles River Laboratories, Inc.; Operadora de Contactlogia, SA de CV, (Mexico); Wilmington Partners, L.P.; Bausch & Lomb Puerto Rico, Inc.; Dahlberg, Inc.; Bausch & Lomb Canada, Inc.; Bausch & Lomb Venezuela, CA; Charles River Canada, Inc.; East Acres Biologicals; Bausch & Lomb GmbH (Austria); Award PLC (Scotland); Bausch & Lomb Denmark A/S; Bausch & Lomb International, Inc. (Greece); Bausch & Lomb Espana SA (Spain); Bausch & Lomb-IOM SpA (Italy); Criffa, SA (Spain); Bausch & Lomb U.K., Ltd.; Charles River U.K., Ltd.; Madden & Layman Ltd. (U.K.); Charles River Italia SpA; Bausch & Lomb Svenska AB (Sweden); Killer Loop SpA (Italy); Bausch & Lomb BV (Netherlands); Bausch & Lomb Holdings BV (Netherlands); Bausch & Lomb AG (Switzerland); Bausch & Lomb Distops SA (Switzerland); Bausch & Lomb Fribourg SA (Switzerland); Bausch & Lomb Finance SA (Switzerland); OY Bausch & Lomb Finland AB; Bausch & Lomb Norway A/S; Bausch & Lomb France SA; Charles River France SA; Bausch & Lomb Espana SA (Portugal); Bausch & Lomb Ireland; Bausch & Lomb Saglik ve Optik (Turkey); Charles River WIGA GmbH (Germany); Dr. Gerhard Mann, Chem.- Pharm.Fabrik GmbH; Bausch & Lomb South Africa Pty. Ltd.; Bausch & Lomb (Australia) Pty. Ltd.; Bausch & Lomb (Singapore) Private Ltd.; Bausch & Lomb (Malaysia); Bausch & Lomb Far East, P.T.E. (Singapore); Bausch & Lomb (New Zealand) Ltd.; Bausch & Lomb Korea, Ltd.; Bausch & Lomb India Ltd.; Bausch & Lomb China, Inc.; Spafas Jinan Poultry Company, Ltd. (China); B.L.J. Company Ltd. (Japan); Bausch & Lomb Taiwan Ltd.; and Charles River Japan, Inc.

Chief Competitors: One of the world's major manufacturers and marketers of eye care and health care products, Bausch & Lomb's competitors include: Akorn; Allergan; Colgate-Palmolive; Cooper Cos.; Corning; Dep; HEARx; HEI; Hydrion Technologies; Johnson & Johnson; National Vision; NutraMax Products; Oakley; ReSound; Summit Technology; Allegheny Teledyne; and Wesley-Jessen.

& Lomb's sales put the company on the *Fortune* 500 list. Daniel Gill, one of the men responsible for building the soft contact business for the company, became CEO in 1981. His vision led the company to offer optical businesses, such as prescription eyeglass services, and then expand into medical products and research. Related activities included the acquisition of Charles River Laboratories (1984) and Dental Research Corp., maker of Interplak home dental care products (1988).

Gill's focus pushed him to stress double-digit growth rates to top executives. Questionable sales methods were practiced, such as mailing merchandise that had not been ordered, extending credit and payment terms to customers, and pushing buyers into ordering more than they needed. These events were a major reason for the company's record earnings increase in 1990. The purchase of Dahlberg (Miracle Ear hearing aids) and the Curel and Soft Sense lines from S.C. Johnson, as well as overseas expansion, also contributed to the company's growth that year.

An investigation was launched by the Security and Exchange Commission (SEC) in 1995, and shareholders of Bausch & Lomb filed a joint lawsuit. The company also faced a second lawsuit after it marketed one type of contact lens as several different types with varying prices. William Waltrip took over as the company's CEO in 1995; he was replaced by William M. Carpenter in 1997. Bausch & Lomb went to work selling off non-core businesses and signed an agreement to compensate customers filing the product fraud suit. Bausch & Lomb Inc. agreed to pay up to $68 million to make amends with customers.

STRATEGY

After a great deal of reorganization, Bausch & Lomb Inc. established new goals for future growth. First, the company aimed for products introduced no earlier than 1995 to account for 65 percent of revenues. Second, it hoped to increase international sales of eyewear brands other than Ray-Ban by 40 percent. Third, the company began to focus on ways to cut costs and improve delivery services. Overall, Bausch & Lomb organized a comprehensive plan to reduce operating costs by $150 million by the year 2000. By doing so, the company hoped to further the global growth of its core business—eye care.

Continuing to divest itself of non-core businesses, Bausch & Lomb announced in early 1998 that the company had signed a definitive agreement to sell its skin care business (consisting of Curel and Soft Sense) to The Andrew Jergens Company. The deal was subject to regulatory approval, and if obtained, the business would be sold to Andrew Jergens for $135 million in cash, plus the assumption of some liabilities. Strengthening its core business, Bausch & Lomb also made two strategic acquisitions in late 1997—it finalized the $300-million cash purchase of Chiron Vision Corporation and acquired Storz Instrument Company from American Home Products. Together, the acquisitions gave Bausch & Lomb entrance into the cataract, retinal, and refractive surgery markets.

Bausch & Lomb Inc. defines "eye care" as anything that goes in or on the eye. Keeping that definition in mind, the global market for such products has reached some $20 billion. Bausch & Lomb held less than 10 percent of the market share in the late 1990s. With sales of Ray-Ban declining in 1996, the company tried new marketing efforts to launch new styles of Ray-Ban sunglasses. Before the decline, Bausch & Lomb had claimed 40 percent of the sunglasses market. The U.S. market for sunglasses priced over $30 dollars increased by 10 percent in 1996—a major reason for the company's renewed focus on its Ray-Ban products. Asia and Europe continued to be steady regions of growth for Bausch & Lomb as well.

INFLUENCES

Bausch & Lomb's initial success can be attributed to key events in its history. Its first major break was due to Bausch's invention of Vulcanite, which allowed the company to produce and sell its own eyeglasses. A second milestone for the company can be traced back to its 1912 experimentation with optical-quality glass. This allowed for substantial growth during World War II, a period when the military sought out Bausch & Lomb products to better service its soldiers. Another major breaking point for Bausch & Lomb was the Army Air Corps' request for glasses to profoundly reduce glare for its pilots, which became so popular that, in 1936, Ray-Ban sunglasses were then made available to the public. Continual growth allowed Bausch & Lomb to purchase and sell other businesses in related fields, strengthening the company's abilities and making its soft contact lens business flourish.

With company growth slowing in the United States and Europe in the 1990s, former CEO Daniel Gill be-

CHRONOLOGY:

Key Dates for Bausch & Lomb Inc.

1853: John Jacob Bausch and Henry Lomb open a European eyewear store

1890: Bausch & Lomb contract with Carl Zeiss for exclusive rights to his lenses

1907: Zeiss buys 20 percent of Bausch & Lomb

1926: John Jacob Bausch dies and Edward Bausch takes over

1937: Bausch & Lomb goes public

1940: An antitrust lawsuit is brought against Bausch & Lomb's contract with Zeiss

1942: Ray-Ban sunglasses are developed for World War II pilots

1954: The company begins to expand into the electronic optics industry

1966: Bausch & Lomb licenses to make and sell soft contact lenses

1971: Softlens contact lenses are introduced

1983: Tom Cruise wears Ray-Bans in *Risky Business* and sales jump from 16,000 pairs sold to 360,000 pairs

1990: Bausch & Lomb reports record earnings

1995: The Securities an Exchange Commission and shareholders file a joint lawsuit

came desperate for a new game plan. The company's expansions into other health care areas had not been doing as well as anticipated. In fact, many large companies' purchases by Bausch & Lomb were not profitable, and the company had even begun losing contact lens market share to its biggest rival, Johnson & Johnson. Ray-Ban sales were even down. Perhaps the company's largest disadvantage was its refusal to enter the disposable contact lens market, a market captured by Johnson & Johnson in 1987.

Despite all of these factors, company sales records showed adequate growth. An investigation was launched only to discover unethical behavior. Pressures mounted as some executives claimed they were told to ship merchandise even though it wasn't ordered. In an intense effort to meet the numbers established by Gill, many ex-

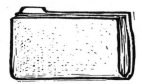

DID YOU KNOW. . .

- Tom Cruise wore Ray-Ban Aviator sunglasses in *Top Gun* and in *Risky Business*?

- Dan Akroyd and John Belushi wore Ray-Ban Wayfarer sunglasses in *Blues Brothers,* and Dan Akroyd and John Goodman wore them in *Blues Brothers 2000*?

- Racecar driver Jeff Gordon only wears Ray-Ban sunglasses?

- Will Smith and Tommy Lee Jones wore Ray-Ban Predator 2 sunglasses in *Men in Black*?

- Cuba Gooding Jr. wore Ray-Ban Sidestreet Metro and Inertia sunglasses in *Jerry Maguire*?

- Julia Roberts wears Ray-Ban Clubmaster sunglasses?

ecutives continued accounting for sold merchandise that was never shipped, but, sources say, allegedly ended up in warehouses.

After the scandal was revealed, Daniel Gill was replaced in 1995. Knowing massive reorganization was needed, new CEO William Waltrip devised a growth strategy centered on cutting costs. Aiming to give shareholders steady earnings and deliver competitive products to customers, Bausch & Lomb's new focus entailed layoffs, sales of non-core businesses, and new plans for obtaining its lost disposable contact lens market share.

CURRENT TRENDS

In line with its recent reorganization strategies, Bausch & Lomb's focus has been on regaining its strength in the contact lens and sunglasses markets. A job cut of 1,900 employees was announced in April of 1997 in efforts to achieve the $150-million savings goal. Almost half of employees who were laid off came from corporate headquarters located in the Rochester, New York. This trend follows a similar layoff count of 2,000 in 1995.

Also characteristic of its restructuring efforts were Bausch & Lomb's recent purchases and sales of related businesses. The company sold Ster-Oss Inc. (a dental-implant business) and its stake in the Oral Care Division

(known for producing Interplak). Bausch & Lomb's new focus aimed at creating new marketing strategies for its Ray-Ban sunglasses. The company purchased Arnette, a small sunglasses company out of California. Other business adventures include a partnership with Porche Design and Insite Vision. These alliances were made to enhance Bausch & Lomb's eye care business in the midst of growing rivals like Oakley Inc. of Irvine, California, which captured consumers between the ages of 16 and 24.

PRODUCTS

Bausch & Lomb is responsible for producing sunglasses under the brand names Ray-Ban, Arnette, Killer Loop, Porsche Design, and Revo. Contact lens products include lenses and solutions under the brands Boston, Sensitive Eyes, SofLens66, ReNu, and ReNu MultiPlus. General pharmaceutical products, such as eye drops, are marketed under brand names Bausch & Lomb and Dr. Mann Pharma. The company's health care division offers products such as biomedical products and hearing aids under the brand names Miracle Ear, Mirage, and Charles River Laboratories. The company's products are available in more than 100 countries worldwide.

CORPORATE CITIZENSHIP

One recent contribution to community involvement made by Bausch & Lomb Inc. involved the adoption of an orphanage in 1996. Following a nuclear accident in Chernobyl, Ireland, Bausch & Lomb employees decided to give time and donations to the Vasilivichi Orphanage for the blind and partially impaired.

According to its annual report, Bausch & Lomb counts corporate diversity as one of its top goals. In 1997, the company was 1 of 5 honored by the U.S. Department of Labor for Exemplary Voluntary Efforts toward increasing employment opportunities for women, minorities, and the disabled.

GLOBAL PRESENCE

Bausch & Lomb has manufacturing or marketing operations in some 30 countries and distributes products in more than 70 other nations. With annual sales totaling almost $2 billion, the company remains focused on its core businesses: soft and rigid gas permeable contact lenses, lens care products, premium sunglasses, and ophthalmic pharmaceutical products. Bausch & Lomb is concentrating on strengthening the leadership position of Ray-Ban in global markets with new product designs and marketing efforts. It is also expanding other brands to new markets.

EMPLOYMENT

Bausch & Lomb employs about 13,000 people in 35 countries. According to the company, they "offer competitive compensation and benefits packages, opportunities for personal growth and development and a stimulating work environment." They also continuously search for employees "who are results oriented, flexible, thrive on challenge and yet are capable of operating in a team environment."

SOURCES OF INFORMATION

Bibliography

"Bausch & Lomb 'Adopt' an Orphanage." *Waterford Today,* 7 February 1996. Available at http://www.aardvark.ie.

"Bausch & Lomb Announces 1st Quarter Results." Bausch & Lomb Press Release, 22 April 1998.

"Bausch & Lomb Completes Acquisition of Chiron Vision Corporation." Bausch & Lomb Press Release, 31 December 1997.

"Bausch & Lomb Completes Acquisition of Storz Instrument Company." Bausch & Lomb Press Release, 31 December 1997.

"Bausch & Lomb Incorporated." *Hoover's Online,* 7 July 1998. Available at http://www.hoovers.com.

Bausch & Lomb: Number One in the Eyes of the World—Bausch & Lomb 1997 Annual Report. Rochester, NY: Bausch & Lomb, Inc., 1998.

"Bausch & Lomb Reports 1997 First Quarter Results and Announces Major Restructuring Plan." Rochester, NY: Bausch & Lomb Inc., 23 April 1997.

"Bausch & Lomb Sells Its Skin-Care Business to the Andrew Jergens Company." Bausch & Lomb Press Release, 8 April 1998.

"Contact Lenses: Settlement of Bausch & Lomb Lens Wearer Class Action." *The Consumer Law Page,* The Alexander Law Firm, 4 February 1997. Available at http://seamless.com.

Dobbin, Ben. "Bausch & Lomb Cuts 1,900 Jobs." *The Associated Press,* 23 April 1997. Available at http://search.washington-post.com.

———. "Bausch & Lomb Posts Sharp Drop in Quarterly Profits." *San Diego Daily Transcript,* 29 January 1997. Available at http://www.sddt.com.

———. "Bausch & Lomb Selling Dental Implant Business." *San Diego Daily Transcript,* 23 July 1996.

Maremont, Mark. "Bausch & Lomb's Board Puts on Its Glasses." *Business Week,* 6 November 1995.

———. "Blind Ambition: Part I How the Pursuit of Results Got Out of Hand at Bausch & Lomb." *Business Week,* 26 November 1996.

———. "Blind Ambition: Part II How the Pursuit of Results Got Out of Hand at Bausch & Lomb." *Business Week,* 26 November 1996.

McCaffrey, Shannon. "Lawsuit Alleges Contact-Lens Wearers Cheated Out of Millions by Makers Who Conspire." *San Diego Daily Transcript,* 19 December 1996.

For an annual report:
on the Internet at: http://www.bausch.com/CorporateInfo/Annual Report/annual1997/welcome.html **or** telephone: (716)338-5757 **or** write: Staff Vice President, Investor Relations, Bausch & Lomb, 1 Bausch & Lomb Pl., Rochester, New York 14604

For additional industry research:
Investigate companies by their Standard Industrial Classification Codes, also known as SICs. Bausch & Lomb's primary SICs are:

2834 Pharmaceutical Preparations

3827 Optical Instruments and Lenses

3851 Ophthalmic Goods

5122 Drugs, Drug Proprietaries, and Druggists' Sundries

Ben & Jerry's Homemade, Inc.

FOUNDED: 1978

Contact Information:
HEADQUARTERS: 30 Community Dr.
    South Burlington, VT 05403-6828
PHONE: (802)651-9600
FAX: (802)651-9646
EMAIL: info@benjerry.com
URL: http://www.benjerry.com

OVERVIEW

Ben & Jerry's manufactures super-premium ice cream, frozen yogurt, sorbet, and ice cream novelties. The company is known for its flavorful ice cream made from fresh Vermont milk and cream, but Ben & Jerry's is also known for its equally colorful names—many of which have been tied to popular culture. For example, some of these include Cherry Garcia (named for the late Jerry Garcia of the band Grateful Dead), Wavy Gravy, Phish Food (named for an alternative band often compared to the Grateful Dead), and Doonsberry Sorbet (named for Garry Trudeau's cartoon). The company meshed ice cream and pop culture and mixed in a healthy amount of planetary and social concern. As of April 1998, *Information Resources Inc.* estimated that Ben & Jerry's held 3.5 percent of the overall market share for ice cream in the United States.

COMPANY FINANCES

Ben & Jerry's net sales for the first quarter of 1998 increased 15 percent to $41.50 million, compared to $36.10 million for the same period in 1997. Net income totaled $380,000, compared to a net loss of $1.00 million in the first quarter of 1997. The company's earnings per share were $.05 in the first quarter of 1998, compared to a net loss of $0.15 per share in the first quarter of 1997. Improved performance was attributed to a 12-percent increase in sales of domestic pint products—Ben & Jerry's Original Ice Cream accounted for most of the increase. In 1997, Ben & Jerry's earned net sales of $174.20 million, compared to $167.10 million in 1996. Net income for 1997 was $3.89 million, just slightly down from its 1996 net income of $3.92 million. 1997's net sales of $174.20 million showed a steady increase since 1993 when sales totaled $140.30 million and rose in 1994 to $148.80 million, in 1995 to $155.30 million, and again in 1996 to $167.2 million.

Ben & Jerry's stock was hovering between $17 and $20 per share in mid-1998. The price ranged over a 52-week period from $12.00 to $22.75 per share. Also as of mid-1998, Ben & Jerry's had earned $.73 per share for the year. In 1997, earnings per share for the year were $.53, compared to 1996 earnings of $.54 per share.

ANALYSTS' OPINIONS

"Growth has probably been the biggest hurdle for management to deal with," according to a 1992 Smith Barney, Harry Upham and Co. analyst report, "from manufacturing in the old renovated gas station and delivering product from the back of an old station wagon to local stores and restaurants, the company has moved to three facilities in which it produces more than 10.6 million gallons per year." Additionally, the company contracts out another 4 to 6 million gallons and distributes through more than 120 franchised Ben & Jerry's "scoop shops" throughout 20 states. Shops are located in New England, New York, the Mid-Atlantic region, Georgia, Florida, Ohio, Indiana, Illinois, and California.

Impacting Ben & Jerry's financial ratings in mid-1998 were unprecedented price increases for fresh cream—the key ingredient in ice cream. Additionally, the price of butter is used as a benchmark to set prices for fresh cream, and the market price for domestic butter, after steadily declining for a decade, reached historically high levels, rising 50 percent between April and June 1998, according to The Motley Fool's *Evening News.* Competitor Dreyer's said the current situation could accelerate consolidation in the ice cream industry and had already increased the wholesale price of its own Dreyer's and Edy's brand products in most markets. The stock market showed the impact in industry stock prices— Friendly stock plunged $5 1/4 points to $15 3/8 per share, while Ben & Jerry's lost $2 3/8 to close at $17.00 per share (June 19, 1998). Investment analysts assigned Ben & Jerry's a "hold" rating for the moment.

HISTORY

Ben & Jerry's Homemade, Inc. was started in Vermont. Founders Ben Cohen and Jerry Greenfield first met in a seventh grade gym class in Merrick, Long Island. The two decided, after many odd jobs and exploits, to go into business together in 1978. The pair took a mail-order correspondence course from Penn State University

FINANCES:

Ben & Jerry's Net Sales, 1994-1997 (million dollars)

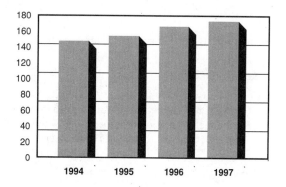

Ben & Jerry's 1997 Stock Prices (dollars)

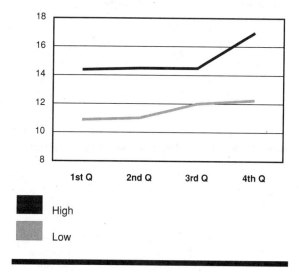

about making ice cream. They scraped together $12,000 and launched Ben & Jerry's, Vermont's Finest Ice Cream and Frozen Yogurt.

The decision to base the company in Vermont occurred after an ice cream parlor opened in Saratoga Springs, New York—the first choice on their location list. Vermont was the only state at the time without a Baskin-Robbins franchise. The store, a renovated gas station in Burlington, Vermont, first opened for business on May 5, 1978. Various intense experimental flavors could be found in the display case. Lore was that the extreme flavorings were a result of Ben's continual allergy and

FAST FACTS:

About Ben & Jerry's Homemade, Inc.

Ownership: Ben & Jerry's is a publicly owned company traded on NASDAQ.

Ticker symbol: BJICA

Officers: Perry D. Odak, Pres. & CEO, 52, $400,000; Ben Cohen, Chairperson & Founder, 46, $183,333; Jerry Greenfield, Vice-Chairperson & Founder, 46, $183,333; Frances Rathke, CFO & Secretary, 37, $207,603

Employees: 736 (1997)

Chief Competitors: As a manufacturer and marketer of premium ice cream, Ben & Jerry's primary competitors include: Dreyer's; Friendly; Haagen-Dazs; Portofino; and Starbucks.

fluent urbanites congregated. These desirable areas include New England, New York, the Mid-Atlantic region, Florida, Texas, the West Coast, metropolitan Chicago, and Denver. According to a 1992 Smith Barney analysis, "The company's marketing strategy has been to focus on innovative, nontraditional methods of promotion and the free advertising it has garnered due to management's unique commitment to the environment and social responsibility."

The company markets its products through supermarkets, grocery stores, convenience stores, and food service operations. They also market products through licensed, franchised, and company-owned "scoop shops." New CEO Perry Odak, in an attempt to improve marketing, redesigned some of the company's packaging. He removed Ben & Jerry's faces from carton tops and replaced them with pictures better displaying the contents of the ice cream, which were not always obvious from product names (e.g., Chubby Hubby is an ice cream containing chocolate-covered peanut butter-filled pretzels). He also began a $2-million advertising campaign.

During 1998 Ben & Jerry's planned to capitalize on its twentieth year in business, building on momentum gained the previous year. New flavor releases were planned, and the company was building up its advertising schedule and scheduled numerous publicity and product sampling events.

sinus problems. Some of these flavors included Honey Almond Mist, Banana Rum, and Oreo Mint. There were, however, some flavors that didn't quite make it, including Lemon Peppermint Carob Chip, and Honey Apple Raisin Oreo.

According to *National Productivity Review,* first-year sales reached nearly $180,000—twice the projected sales, yet the venture did not make a profit. They also sold tubs of ice cream at wholesale to restaurants, but Cohen soon realized that supermarkets and grocery stores were an untapped market. Between 1984 and 1990, Ben & Jerry's sales increased from $4.1 million to $77.0 million. Ben & Jerry's Homemade, Inc. went public on October 30, 1985 at $32.50 per share. The company's sales in the early 1990s were "huge"—$97 million in 1991 and $132 million in 1992. Problems with the super-premium ice cream category began in the mid-1990s when consumer attention to health and frugality began to prevail. According to the *New York Times,* the number of premium ice cream manufacturers were "dwindling."

INFLUENCES

Despite all of Ben & Jerry's good intentions, capitalism and philanthropy did not always blend together as well as a pint of one of the company's "smooth" flavors. After less than two years at the helm, Robert Holland resigned as chief executive officer in late 1995. Apparently, Holland had difficulty working within the company principles while turning a profit. Cohen and Greenfield reportedly objected to Holland's planned market expansion into France because of the country's policies on nuclear testing, as well as his entrance into the sorbet market, citing that the frozen dessert diminished one of the chief missions of Ben & Jerry's—helping Vermont's dairy farmers. Perry Odak, previously chief operating officer of U.S. Repeating Arms Co., was hired by Ben & Jerry's in January 1997 to run the company after Holland's departure.

CURRENT TRENDS

In the late 1990s, Ben & Jerry's found itself correcting past mistakes that had negatively impacted the company's financial performance and resulted in a major net loss for the company in 1994. New CEO Perry Odak was responsible for implementing many of the

STRATEGY

Ben & Jerry's strategy consists of making an exemplary product, earning a fair return, and serving the community. The company sought to place its products in markets with large population bases and also where af-

changes, which were based on applying practical business principles while still retaining the company's "funky" personality. And as reported by *The New York Times,* "Those fearing a sellout, however, should ponder this: Tightening the company's business practices is not only improving the bottom line, but also seems to be promoting worthy causes." Odak took the heat for removing sagging products with devoted fans—such as Peace Pops and Brownie Bars—that were costing the company money. New novelties were introduced, including ice cream on a stick and the Phish Stick. The company also established an alliance with Paul Newman and agreed to manufacture Newman's Own ice cream—Paul Newman donates all proceeds he receives from the sale of these products to charitable and educational purposes.

PRODUCTS

In 1991 Chocolate Chip Cookie Dough sales made Ben & Jerry's number one selling flavor. Also that same year, market testing of eight flavors in the frozen yogurt line was started—sales were kicked off in January 1992. Experimentation with flavors was ongoing and, in the mid-1990s, the company actively sought the help of consumers for new product ideas, one of which resulted in "Cool Britannia"—a flavor suggested by U.K. customers for sale in the United States. Other new flavors included Dilbert's World Totally Nuts, Coconut Cream Pie low fat ice cream, Chocolate Cherry Garcia frozen yogurt, and S'mores low fat ice cream. In 1997 Ben & Jerry's Homemade, Inc. listed more than 50 flavors of ice cream, frozen yogurt, low fat ice cream, and sorbet. About 34 of the flavors are packaged and sold in grocery stores, while the rest are only available in Ben & Jerry's Scoop Shops and for sale to restaurants. In the first quarter of 1998, 14 new products were introduced. The company also sells individual ice cream novelties, such as Ben & Jerry's ice cream on a stick.

CORPORATE CITIZENSHIP

Ben & Jerry's is well known as a company with a serious dedication to corporate responsibility in Vermont, the United States, and around the world. The company gives away 7.5 percent of its pre-tax earnings through the Ben & Jerry's Foundation, employee Community Action Teams, and corporate grants. This concept is called "linked prosperity." The company was awarded America's Corporate Conscience Award for Charitable Giving in 1988 and, that same year, Greenfield and Cohen were named U.S. Small Business Persons of the Year. The company's Ben & Jerry's Foundation supports numerous organizations such as the Citizens Committee for Children of New York, the Environmental Health Coalition, Native American Community Board, Business Partner-

CHRONOLOGY:

Key Dates for Ben & Jerry's Homemade, Inc.

1978: Ben Cohen and Jerry Greenfield found Ben & Jerry's

1979: Ben & Jerry's market expands to include grocery stores and restaurants

1981: The first franchised Ben & Jerry's Scoop Shop opens; *Time* magazine declares their ice cream "the best in the world"

1984: The company goes public

1985: Cohen and Greenfield start the Ben & Jerry Foundation non-profit charity and grant firm

1988: Cohen and Greenfield are given the Corporate Giving Award

1994: Jerry Greenfield steps down as CEO; company looks for a replacement by way of an essay contest: "Why I would be a great CEO for Ben & Jerry's" in 100 words or less

ship for Peace, and other organizations around the United States and the world. It specifically considers proposals relating to children and families, disadvantaged groups, and the environment. All creator royalties from sales of Doonsberry, a blueberry and raspberry fruit sorbet (licensed by Gary Trudeau and Universal Press Syndicate Inc.) are returned to various nonprofit organizations. Phish, Inc.'s shares of the proceeds from ice cream sales goes to environmental efforts in the Lake Champion Region of Vermont.

Founder Ben Cohen clearly articulated this policy in the company's 1990 Annual Report. "The most amazing thing is that our social values—that part of our company mission statement that calls us to use our power as a business to improve the quality of life in our local, national and international communities—have actually helped us to become a stable, profitable, high growth company. This is especially interesting because it flies in the face of those business theorists who state that publicly held corporations cannot make a profit and help the community at the same time, and moreover that such companies have no business trying to do so. The wonderful thing is that despite Ben & Jerry's avowedly and unabashedly populist leanings, you, our shareholders, continue to support us. I am proud to say that the employees of Ben &

A FREE PLANE TICKET (OH, AND ICE CREAM TOO)

When Ben & Jerry's decided to launch a new ice cream flavor named after the comic strip hero Dilbert, they did it in a way that would have made Dilbert proud.

In an effort to introduce their new flavor, "Dilbert's World - Totally Nuts" in a way that was as unique as the flavor of the ice cream, Ben & Jerry's played an April Fool's Day joke on business commuters on select United Airlines flights from New York LaGuardia and Los Angeles International Airports. On April 1, 1998, Ben & Jerry's gave actual airline employees a break from their hectic schedules by teaming up with United Airlines and setting up Dilbert-like office cubicles in the airports. A few lucky and unsuspecting travelers were the targets of the prank.

As passengers checked in at their gates, they were given free samples of the new flavor, as well as a check for the average price of their ticket. Although April Fool's is a day best known for practical jokes, this was no joke. The checks were real and, oh, the ice cream wasn't bad either! It was certainly an off-the-wall April Fool's Day in true Dilbert fashion!

Jerry's are finding ways to help make money and help people at the same time. Once you start figuring out how to put these things together, the old way just doesn't make sense anymore."

On a basic corporate level, Ben & Jerry's created a more environmentally friendly carton (made of un-bleached paper) for its products—the company is expected to start using it in 1998. The company also had a corporate goal of reducing solid waste by 25 percent.

GLOBAL PRESENCE

In 1988 Ben & Jerry's reported the opening of franchised scoop shops in Canada and licensed scoop shops in Israel. While the market in Canada had been slowly growing, the number of Scoop Shops in Israel increased steadily to 14. The company also had a joint venture in Russia called Iceverks, through which it opened four

scoop shops in 1992. Early in 1995 Ben and Jerry's set up an international department and began exploring other markets. They planned to open shops in many European and Asian countries. The company began distribution in the United Kingdom in 1994. In 1998, Ben & Jerry's launched operations in Japan, which contributed to the company's improved financial performance. The company also opened three company-owned scoop shops in Paris.

EMPLOYMENT

Ben & Jerry's is continually cited as an example of one of the more progressive companies for which to work in the United States, particularly because of its clearly articulated corporate policies on a wide array of workplace issues. The company was listed in *Working Mother's* "100 Best Companies for Working Mothers" and also in "The 100 Best Companies to Work for in America"—and not only because of the three, free pints of ice cream allotted each employee on a daily basis, either. In 1990 the highest paid employee, for example, was not able to earn more than seven times the salary of the lowest paid employee. Originally, the ratio had been 5-to-1, but concerns were that the company would be ineffective in courting qualified management in its search for a chief executive officer.

The company makes special efforts to recruit both women and minorities. About 50 percent of Ben & Jerry's senior managers and professional staff are women, including the company's chief financial officer. The company said it made "special efforts to recruit minorities from out of state," due to "the very low number of minorities in the Vermont population."

In addition to a routine array of health and dental coverage, profit sharing, 401K, and other traditional benefits, the company extends its health benefits to same-sex partners. The company also provides up to six weeks of paid leave to all new mothers, including adoptive mothers; fathers are given two weeks of paid paternity leave, with up to 10 weeks unpaid leave. Ben & Jerry's also offers child care benefits and special working arrangements for new mothers, including a "phased return to work" program. And, as an added bonus, the company has a free fitness membership program, "which helps offset the three free pints of ice cream a day available to employees."

SOURCES OF INFORMATION

Bibliography
Ben & Jerry's Home Page, 21 June 1998. Available at http://www.benjerry.com.

"Ben & Jerry's Homemade Inc." *Moody's Investor Service,* 9 January 1997.

"Ben & Jerry's Homemade, Inc. Announces 1997 Fourth Quarter and Year End Results." Ben & Jerry's Press Release, 27 January 1998.

"Ben & Jerry's Homemade, Inc. Announces 1998 First Quarter Results." Ben & Jerry's Press Release, 20 April 1998.

"BJICA." *The Motley Fool Evening News,* 19 June 1998.

De Lucia, M. J. "Ben & Jerry's Homemade Inc. Company Report." Tucker Anthony and R.L. Day, 22 July 1991.

Hays, Constance L. "Getting Serious at Ben & Jerry's." *The New York Times,* 22 May 1998.

"High-Caliber Help for Ben & Jerry's." *Time,* 13 January 1997.

Hitchner, Earl. "We All Scream for Ice Cream." *National Productivity Review,* Winter 1994.

Lewis, Len. "A Cold World." *Progressive Grocer,* November 1996.

Morrow, R.B. "Ben & Jerry's Homemade Inc. Company Report." Smith Barney, Harris Upham and Co., 8 December 1992.

Serwer, Andrew E. "Ben & Jerry's: Corporate Orge(sic)." *Fortune,* 10 July 1995.

For an annual report:

on the Internet at: http://www.benjerry.com/fin/index.html#annuals **or** write: Investor Relations, Ben & Jerry's Homemade, Inc., 30 Community Dr., South Burlington, VT 05403-6828

For additional industry research:

Investigate companies by their Standard Industrial Classification Codes, also known as SICs. Ben & Jerry's primary SICs are:

2024 Ice Cream and Frozen Desserts

5812 Eating Places

Benetton USA Corporation

FOUNDED: 1965

Contact Information:
HEADQUARTERS: 597 5th Ave., 11th Fl.
   New York, NY 10017
PHONE: (212)593-0290
FAX: (212)371-1438
URL: http://www.benetton.com

OVERVIEW

Benetton USA Corp. is the American arm of Benetton Group, which is a family-controlled apparel empire with worldwide presence. The enterprise produces and distributes casual clothing, accessories, and sports equipment for men, women, and children. Benetton is Italy's largest maker of clothes and the world's largest user of carded wool. Its reach spans over 7,000 independently owned stores and five company-owned "megastores," which buy their wares from Benetton. Major sub-brands include United Colors of Benetton, Sisley, and Benetton 012. Benetton Undercolors stores sell lingerie.

COMPANY FINANCES

Excluding figures for Benetton Sportsystem, which was folded into the company during the year, 1997 revenues were $1.75 billion, up 7 percent from 1996. Net income was $185 million, as compared to 1996's $139 million. Operating income for 1997 was $300 million, for an increase of 32 percent over 1996. For the second half of 1997, Benetton Sportsystem's revenues were $312 million. The Asian economic crisis accounts for much of the shortfall between that division's expectations and its results.

In early 1998 Benetton Group split its stock 10-for-1 to raise liquidity and trading volume. That same year the company erased all of its debt for the first time. At the 1998 annual meeting, the dividend was approved to increase five percent to $0.297.

HISTORY

Benetton was started when Giuliana Benetton sold her brother Luciano's accordion and her brother Carlo's bicycle to buy a knitting machine. Luciano had been a delivery boy for a fabric store, dropping off his sister's colorful hand-knit sweaters. He quit his job at the fabric store, and the sibling duo entered the garment business, eventually to be joined by their brothers Gilberto and Carlo. By 1969 they had opened their first shop in the Italian town of Belluno, and a year later a second one opened in Paris. Luciano was an expert at perceiving and exploiting markets with unmet needs; the company has been called "the McDonald's of the fashion industry." By the 1980s the company began to diversify beyond cotton and wool garments and added such items as sunglasses, hats, shoes, watches, and cosmetics. In 1997 the company took over Benetton Sportsytem—an international group of sports equipment producers—from the Benetton family. American business schools now study the development of the company as a case study.

Benetton's Sportsystem division emerged in 1989 when the family's Edizione Holdings put up $182 million to buy Nordica, a privately owned maker of ski equipment. The following year it spent $200 million to buy Prince, a tennis racket manufacturer, which offset the seasonal sales of skis. Subsequent acquisitions included Ektelon, a maker of racquetball equipment, and Kastle, a maker of bicycles and skis. Another strategic purchase, Rollerblade, gave the company a considerable bite of the U.S. in-line skate business.

STRATEGY

A key element in Benetton's operation is its method of filling orders from its stores, since it does not stockpile items in its warehouse. The state-of-the-art, 190,000-square-meter plant in Castrette di Vellorba, Italy, quickly and efficiently produces 100 million garments per year. The facility consists of dual factories—one that makes cotton garments and shirts, and one that makes tailored clothes, skirts, and denim jeans. The automatic distribution system handles more than 30,000 packages each day and is able to function on a skeleton crew of 19, rather than the 400 that a less-advanced setup would require. Order information is received from a central fiberoptic network that manages the company's global needs.

INFLUENCES

The number of Benetton stores in North America dropped from a high point of over 600 in the mid-1980s to about 200 in 1996. Sales during the mid-1990s were sluggish, but in 1994 Benetton instituted a strategic slash in prices—an average of 16 percent in the United

FAST FACTS:
About Benetton USA Corporation

Ownership: Benetton is publicly traded on the New York Stock Exchange and exchanges in Milan, London, and Frankfurt. The Benetton family's Edizione Holdings owns a controlling interest, 71 percent, of the stock.

Ticker symbol: BNG

Officers: Luciano Benetton, Chmn.; Mauro Benetton, Worldwide Marketing Director; Carlo Tunioli, Gen. Manager of Benetton USA

Chief Competitors: Benetton competes in the clothing and sporting-goods industries. Its major competitors include: The Gap, apparel and accessory stores; The Limited, apparel and accessory stores; and K2, sporting and athletic goods.

States—as well as a $157 million stock offering that allowed ownership to migrate outside Italy. In the early 1990s the company invested about $150 million in technology and factories. Benetton is able to keep its raw-materials costs down because it owns cotton farms in Texas and a large sheep farm in Argentina. Moreover, textile dying is done in-house.

Benetton's provocative and highly artistic advertising campaigns, which represent about four percent of the company's operating budget, have created controversy over the years, perhaps because they have depicted overly realistic images and human themes. The ads feature the photography of Oliviero Toscani and have included images of a dead Bosnian soldier, withering AIDS patients, and priests kissing nuns. A recent catalog's cover showed an Israeli man kissing a Palestinian woman. In 1995 Benetton store owners in Germany (the company's second-largest market) withheld franchise fees and merchandise payments, claiming that an advertising campaign was alienating customers and harming their sales. Ultimately, Germany's Supreme Court banned a series of ads (featuring child laborers, an oil-soaked bird, and human buttocks tattooed with "HIV Positive") on the grounds that they were "morally offensive." Luciano Benetton commented on the negative reaction to the ads in *WWD,* "It is very difficult to understand why people got so agitated. If you ask me to analyze it, I honestly have to say I don't know. Benetton's range of products is broad, and is marketed to many cultures," he explained.

CHRONOLOGY:

Key Dates for Benetton USA Corporation

1965: The Benetton Company is formed as a partnership called Maglificio di Ponzano Veneto dei Fratelli Benetton

1969: Benetton opens its first retail store to sell the Benetton line of clothing

1972: Benetton pioneers a dyeing technique that allows minimal inventory and custom garments

1981: Becomes the world leader in knitwear

1986: Makes an initial public stock offering

1989: Benetton's controversial United Colors of Benetton ad campaign begins

1994: Time, Junghans Uhren, and Benetton enter a joint venture to manufacture watches and alarm clocks

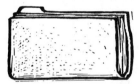

DID YOU KNOW THAT. . .

- Benetton uses over 100 million kilometers of thread each year, which is 2,800 times around the world at the equator?

- the quantity of fabric used each year by Benetton would cover an area twice the size of Belgium?

- the brand names Sisley, 012, United Colors of Benetton, and Zerotondo are all owned by the Benetton Group?

- Benetton sells more than 80 million garments every year in over 120 countries worldwide?

"If we did a pure product campaign, we'd have to do 20 or 30 different campaigns. It would be impossible."

CURRENT TRENDS

Benetton has purchased several large-scale, modern farms in Italy, Argentina, and the United States and is able to produce its own raw materials in the form of cotton and wool. Its flock of 280,000 sheep (Merino and Hereford breeds) is the largest in the world. Although the company reaps over two million pounds of the renewable resource per year, the quantity still fills only about 10 percent of its needs. Investment in research has allowed Benetton to improve the quality of the wool it raises.

In early 1997 the company opened a 12,000-square-foot, three-story flagship store in New York's landmark 1912 Scribner Building at Fifth Avenue and 48th Street, in an attempt to revitalize its presence in the U.S. clothing market. The company spent about $4 million to restore the old building to its original design and condition. In March 1997, Benetton started a bimonthly series of literary readings and arts talks, called "The Salon" since it meets in the store's cafe, in keeping with the locale's rich literary history. In *WWD*, Carlo Tunioli, general manager of Benetton USA, said of the store's opening, "The New York flagship's objective is to send a message to the American market. Here is what we are now in the Nineties. The significance is not only for the U.S. It will be an international presence because Fifth Avenue has become one of the most important malls in the world." The company plans to open similar stores in major U.S. cities if the New York store is successful enough to warrant such expansion.

In 1997 Benetton implemented a new point-of-service (POS) system of tracking sales and inventory across the United States. The system makes financial reporting uniform. Its IBM hardware greatly improves in-store efficiency by reading bar codes.

PRODUCTS

Benetton is primarily a seller of apparel, but it also markets other makers' fragrances, watches, beepers, fashion accessories, and a range of sporting equipment under various high-profile brand names. The United Colors of Benetton line is a collection of colorful, casual garments for adults. Sisley is the company's group of denim clothes. Benetton's children's label is 012, and Zerotundo is marketed to babies and toddlers. Benetton also has several brands of sporting equipment. Asolo makes hiking and rock-climbing shoes. Ektelon is a leader in racquetball equipment. Kastle makes skiing and bicycling equipment. Killer Loop makes snowboards and snowboarding apparel, and the Nordica division is a significant producer of ski boots. Prince is a successful maker of tennis rackets and sportswear. Rollerblade, Inc., now owned by Benetton is the original in-line skate manufacturer.

CORPORATE CITIZENSHIP

Despite the recurring mixed reception of the company's ads, in 1998 the United Nations asked Benetton to design an ad campaign to commemorate the fiftieth anniversary of the United Nations Declaration of Human Rights. The images featured children and excerpts of the Declaration. In *WWD*, John Poerink, director of international marketing and advertising, said "There's a clear, underlying message in all our campaigns—diversity, tolerance, and internationalism."

Benetton has been involved in various humanitarian initiatives over the years. For example, in 1996 Benetton organized the first international conference of SOS Racisme, an organization that promotes ethnic tolerance. Also that year, the United Nations' Food and Agricultural Organization (FAO) asked Benetton to create communications materials for the first World Food Summit in Rome. In 1995 it began an AIDS education initiative in India. Several years earlier, the company had supported a program of distributing condoms and AIDS-prevention information in New York's public schools and had helped the Gay Men's Health Crisis compile a safe-sex guide. Also in 1995, it sponsored a global program called "Colors for Peace," which promoted intercultural awareness in elementary schools.

In 1993 Benetton collaborated with various international relief organizations (such as the International Federation of the Red Cross and the Red Crescent) on the Clothing Redistribution Project. Luciano Benetton, by then a sitting Italian Senator, posed nude in the ad campaign for the program (dignified only by the caption "I want my clothes back"), which called for the public to deliver its unwanted garments to collection sites at Benetton's stores. The charitable effort netted a million pounds of clothing for those in need.

The company sponsors an independent, socially conscious, bimonthly publication called *Colors;* it advocates diversity and takes firm stands on select contemporary issues. Past editions have focused on the global implications of vivisection, war, race, sports, and religion. The award-winning, cutting-edge magazine is distributed in 80 countries (and on the Internet at http://www.colors-magazine.com, as of March 1998) in bilingual editions. Like the company's advertisements, *Colors* communicates its messages with profound photography. Says *Colors* of its mutually respectful relationship with its clothing-giant benefactor, "They don't tell us how to make a magazine, and we don't tell them how to make sweaters." The average age of *Colors'* staff members is 26.

In its tradition of cultivating awareness, Benetton began an educational workshop called Fabrica, which offers specialized artistic training. The school is housed in a seventeenth-century villa near the Italian town of Treviso. Students can receive scholarships to attend Fabrica for a 3- to 12-month period where they can study photography and graphic design.

GLOBAL PRESENCE

Benetton operates all over the world, distributing clothing in 120 countries. The company's largest "mega-store" is in London. In 1995 Benetton opened a factory in Egypt and a store in Sarajevo. In 1997 it added a store in the Romanian capital of Bucharest; at the opening, Luciano Benetton pledged to "maintain acceptable costs across Europe."

SOURCES OF INFORMATION

Bibliography

"Benetton." *Hoover's Online,* 1997. Available at http://www.hoovers.com.

"Benetton Lights Up Landmark." *Chain Store Age Executive with Shopping Center Age,* July 1997.

"Benetton Net up 18.1% As '97 Sales Rise 26.7%." *WWD,* 28 April 1998.

"Benetton Opens Apparel Factory in Egypt; Sees Sales of Over $6M: Annual Capacity of 1.5M Units." *Daily News Record,* 18 July 1995.

"Benetton Plans to Honor Ban on German Ads." *WWD,* 10 July 1995.

"Benetton Raises $157 Million through Sale of Shares in U.S." *WWD,* 3 February 1994.

"Benetton Sees Reassuring Trend in 1998." *Reuters,* 27 May 1998.

"Benetton Sets 10-for-1 Split." *WWD,* 16 April 1998.

Benetton USA Corp. Company Overview, 1997.

"Benetton Website Expands, Colors Magazine Makes Its Internet Debut." *Presswire,* 31 March 1998.

Bernstein, Elizabeth. "Hemingway to Benetton to Sidaris: Historic Scribner Building Renews Its Literary Connection." *Publishers Weekly,* 31 March 1997.

Edelson, Sharon. "Benetton Learns a Lesson." *WWD,* 29 October 1996.

———. "Benetton's U.N. Mission." *WWD,* 3 April 1998.

Fallon, James. "Benetton Opens Megastore in London's Oxford Circus; 17,000-Square-Foot Unit Is Firm's Largest." *Daily News Record,* 26 September 1996.

Forden, Sara Gay. "Luciano Benetton Sees a Rosy Future Despite Cloudy Days." *WWD,* 20 April 1995.

Hye, Jeanette. "Benetton's POS Unites Its Stores." *WWD,* 17 September 1997.

———. "Benetton Unites Stores with Single POS System." *Daily News Record,* 24 September 1997.

Levine, Joshua. "Even When You Fail, You Learn a Lot." *Forbes,* 11 March 1996.

Mussey, Dagmar, and Jeanne Whalen. "Benetton, German Retailers Squabble; Controversial Ads at Heart of Growing Dispute." *Advertising Age,* 6 February 1995.

Palmieri, Jane E. "Benetton Salutes Manhattan: Opening First Flagship Today at Fifth Avenue and 48th St."*Daily News Record,* 29 October 1996.

Ryan, Thomas J. "Benetton Lays Out Plans to Revive U.S. Presence." *WWD,* 29 September 1994.

Sullivan, Ruth. "Balkans United by Colours of Benetton."*The European,* 22 May 1997.

For an annual report:
telephone: (212)593-0290

For additional industry research:
Investigate companies by their Standard Industrial Classification Codes, also known as SICs. Benettton's primary SICs are:

3949 Sporting and Athletic Goods

5699 Apparel and Accessory Stores

Best Buy Co., Inc.

OVERVIEW

Best Buy is the largest consumer electronics retailer in the United States with 290 stores nationwide. The company's growth was based on low pricing and efficiency in operation. Best Buy's sales strategy is a no hassle approach that allows customers to choose their purchases with minimal sales help. Stores have a warehouse look and the size allows for a wide assortment of brand name merchandise. Best Buy's core businesses are home entertainment software, consumer electronics, and PCs/ home office equipment.

Best Buy's most direct competitor is Circuit City. The competition is most intense in entertainment software and computers. Best Buy has also dealt with a changing target market and product mix over the years, and has been successful in adapting to the new trends.

FOUNDED: 1966

Contact Information:
HEADQUARTERS: 7075 Flying Cloud Dr.
   Eden Prairie, MN 55344
PHONE: (612)947-2000
FAX: (612)947-2422
URL: http://www.bestbuy.com

COMPANY FINANCES

Best Buy reported revenues of $8.36 billion for fiscal year 1998 (ended February 28, 1998), an increase of 8 percent over 1997 revenues of $7.77 billion. Net income for the year was $94.5 million, compared to $1.7 million in 1997 (an increase of more than 5,000 percent). Earnings per share were $1.04, compared to $.02 in 1997). For the first quarter of fiscal year 1999, Best Buy reported net income of $15.7 million, or $.16 per share, compared to a net loss in the first quarter of 1998 of $2.6 million.

In 1998, Best Buy's PC and Home Office Equipment product group accounted for the majority of the company's sales, 38 percent—a decrease of 1 percent

FINANCES:

Best Buy Co.
Net Sales, 1994-1997
(billion dollars)

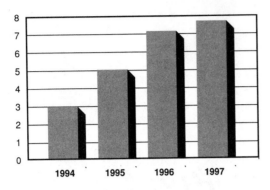

Best Buy Co.
1997 Stock Prices
(dollars)

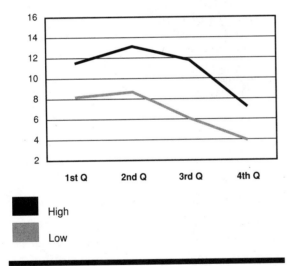

■ High

▨ Low

compared to its share of revenues in 1997. Entertainment Software accounted for 20 percent (up 1 percent from 1997); Appliances accounted for 9 percent; and in the Consumer Electronics Division, the video segment generated 15 percent of sales, while audio generated 11 percent. The remaining 7 percent of sales was generated by other miscellaneous products and services.

ANALYSTS' OPINIONS

Critics believe Best Buy relies too much on computer products and fails to pay attention to profitable areas such

as major appliances and big screen TVs. Best Buy's rapid growth and slim margins have other proponents believing that the company has the potential to become another Phar-Mor, a drug discount chain whose quick expansion caused the company to go bankrupt. Investment analysts were of varying opinions, some seeing the company's growth as cause to grant it a "strong buy" rating, while others were more skeptical and recommended a "hold" rating on Best Buy stock for the moment. Analysts who were skeptical about Best Buy's performance were in part basing their views on the declining numbers in overall consumer sales of personal computers.

HISTORY

In 1966 Richard Schulze opened Sound of Music, a home and car stereo store in Minnesota targeted to teenage boys. Schulze and his partner operated the store for five years, but in 1997 Schulze bought out his partner and began expanding the chain. By 1974, Sound of Music had six stores in Minnesota. In the early 1980s consumer demands were changing. Realizing the need to diversify, Sound of Music began offering other consumer electronic equipment and appliances as part of an effort to target more affluent consumers. In 1983 Schulze changed the company name to Best Buy, and in 1984 he opened the first superstore.

Best Buy grew rapidly with $28.5 million in sales in 1984—compared to $9.9 million in 1983. In 1985, with 9 stores, Best Buy became a public company. By 1987, Best Buy had 24 stores and sales of $240 million, but it was beginning to feel the crunch as other rapidly expanding consumer electronics retailers pushed their way into the market. In order to set his stores apart, Schulze billed Best Buy as a store that allowed consumers to browse without high pressure from sales staff. He reduced employees and eliminated commission-based sales practices.

Best Buy continued to expand during the late 1990s. In 1994 Best Buy decided to expand into the Pacific Northwest where other consumer electronics chains were strong. In 1995, Best Buy became the number three electronic retailer with its 14 stores in Detroit, Michigan. By the end of 1996 the company had 251 stores; that number rose to 272 stores in 1997, and 285 in 1998. The company planned to open another 25 stores during fiscal year 1999. Best Buy operates solely in the United States and by mid-1998 was operating in 32 of them. Most of the stores are located in the Midwest, although Best Buy is expanding elsewhere.

STRATEGY

Best Buy's marketing strategy includes aggressive advertising and competitive pricing, as well as its pursuit of cost saving strategies. The company's Concept II store format was introduced in 1989. Sales people were taken off commission and given straight salary, thereby cutting payroll costs. Also, the store's entire inventory was out on the floor, allowing customers to choose products off the shelf and proceed directly to the cashier. The concept worked so well that a major competitor in Minnesota, Highland Appliance, was forced to close. With this new warehouse atmosphere, however, some vendors were displeased and pulled their products from the stores' shelves. Despite this, Best Buy continued its rapid expansion.

Best Buy also upgrades its facilities and re-organizes its stores to best meet the consumers needs. In 1994, the Concept III store format was introduced, calling for 60,000 square feet of space per store. In keeping with the hands-off attitude, the company installed interactive answer centers offering customers "touch-screen access to product functions, features and prices." In addition, Best Buy increased its assortment of high-end products, added to its parts and accessory departments, and introduced a more appealing color scheme to its stores.

In 1996 Best Buy decided to promote its home video business by ordering direct with Buena Vista, Disney's home video subsidiary. The decision was not only based on cutting costs but also on being more competitive in home video sales. Best Buy would continue to purchase other videos through distribution since distributors are able to offer quick turnaround on orders and are able to warehouse inventory.

Best Buy's new target market is highly-educated, mature, and 36 years old with a household income averaging $50,000 per year. Best Buy has started to market a wider assortment of high quality merchandise. The company's management believed specialty retailers would continue to consolidate during the late 1990s, but that competition from other mass retailers and other sources such as the Internet and mail order companies would continue. To grow in this competitive environment, Best Buy was focused on profit improvement. The company hoped to do this through increased sales of Performance Service Plans (PSPs), more selective use of financing plans, and dedicating more selling space to high profit margin products. Best Buy also hired Andersen Consulting to help further improve corporate systems and strategies.

Customer service at a Best Buy store.
(Courtesy of Best Buy Co., Inc.)

experienced the negative impact of industry downturns. In 1997, there was a notable lack of new products and technology with widespread appeal. Prices of personal computers declined as well. As a result, Best Buy's personal computer revenues were down. Helping the company slightly was increased consumer interest in video products such as digital satellite systems (DSS) and digital versatile discs (DVDs). Even with these new systems, the consumer video segment of Best Buy's sales decreased from 17 to 15 percent of overall sales from 1997 to 1998.

Expansion seemed to be working well for the company. Best Buy attributed its 8-percent increase in sales in 1997 to the opening of 21 new stores, as well as the ability to count a complete year of operations for each of the 47 new stores opened in 1996. However, due to slow industry growth and its impact on profits, expansion was slowed during 1997 and 1998.

INFLUENCES

Best Buy has influenced the electronics industry. Along with Circuit City, it has forced several department stores out of the electronics business or has forced electronic retailers to re-evaluate sales strategies. With its low-cost, low-price, low-margin strategy, Best Buy has set a "new standard for marketing electronic products in a retail environment." However, the company has also

CURRENT TRENDS

In June 1998, Best Buy hired James Damian as Vice President of Visual Merchandising. The company created the new position in which Damian will be responsible for creating a new "in-store visual advertising strategy," according to the company's press release. "Over the past year, Best Buy has focused on incorporating our brand

FAST FACTS:
About Best Buy Co., Inc.

Ownership: Best Buy is a publicly owned company traded on the New York Stock Exchange.

Ticker symbol: BBY

Officers: Richard M. Schulze, Founder, Chmn. & CEO, 56, $750,000; Bradbury H. Anderson, Pres. & COO, 47, $565,000; Allen U. Lenzmeier, Exec. VP & CFO, 53, $435,000; Wade R. Fenn, Exec. VP, Merchandising, 38, $380,000

Employees: 39,000 (1997)

Chief Competitors: Best Buy's most direct competitor is Circuit City. Others include: Tandy Corp. (Radio Shack); Sears (Brand Central); Wal-Mart; CompUSA; Kmart; Target; Office Depot; and Service Merchandise.

CHRONOLOGY:
Key Dates for Best Buy Co., Inc.

1966: Richard Schulze opens a home and car stereo store called Sound of Music

1983: Schulze changes the company name to Best Buy

1984: The first Best Buy superstore opens

1989: Best Buy launches its Concept II stores, with bigger show rooms, fewer sales people, and more self-help product information

1993: Best Buy reports its greatest financial performance

1998: Best Buy has its first $1 million week in movie sales

identity from our inserts, to broadcast ads and into our retail stores," said Julie Engel, senior vice president of advertising. "Damian's specialization in themed envi-

ronments will help create memorable Best Buy in-store elements for our customers."

In addition to refining its advertising tactics, Best Buy found new video technology was helping the store gain market share. In April 1998, Best Buy marked its first $1-million week in movie sales and a significant 35 percent of the DVD movie market. The company attributes its successful sales of DVD products to its "enhanced retail presentation and consumers' continued acceptance of this new product," said Best Buy Merchandise Manager Joe Pagano. Best Buy continued adding DVD movie titles and planned to continue expanding its DVD movie area over 1998.

PRODUCTS

When Best Buy was originally opened as Sound of Music, the store strictly carried audio equipment. As the company's target market (teenage boys aged 15-18) began to decrease in the early 1980s, appliances and VCRs were added to the product mix targeting more mature and affluent customers.

In 1986, Best Buy began to offer entertainment software, adding video rental departments and CDs. Music departments were expanded with each new store that opened, since music proved to be a popular sales item. With sales staggering, Best Buy needed to diversify once again. In 1996, it introduced gourmet kitchen appliances to its outlets offering cookware, small electronics, cutlery, and spices. In addition, Best Buy added several top-end major appliances from such manufacturers as GE, Tappan, Amana, Hotpoint, Roper, White-Westinghouse, Maytag, Sunray, and Gallery. Best Buy also sold personal computers and home office products. It was the first major retailer to sell digital versatile disks (DVDs) and related software beginning in 1998. Plans for the future included products such as flat screen televisions, cellular communications, and the linking of personal computers and consumer electronics.

Additionally, Best Buy offers services such as delivery, installation, and repair of products sold in the store. Computer support and training services are also available on an individual or corporate level.

CORPORATE CITIZENSHIP

Since 1994 Best Buy has sponsored the annual Best Buy Children's Foundation LPGA Golf Tournament. The company is also seeking vendors to participate in a program for at-risk and chronically ill children. The program would provide scholarships for attending summer camps and seminars in order to promote personal growth and instill leadership qualities. Also a supporter of the arts, Best Buy was a sponsor of the 1998 Chicago Blues Festival. There the company presented a check for $2,400 to the Chicago Blues Archives for the "Speakin' of the Blues" Program, a performance series featuring oral histories of remarkable Blues' musicians. In summer of 1997, Best Buy raised funds by donating $1 for each T-shirt sold at the 1997 Chicago Blues Festival.

EMPLOYMENT

Best Buy takes an active interest in its employees. The company recruits through colleges and job fairs. Best Buy offers career development through training practices and offers tuition reimbursement to increase employee knowledge and improve skills. Sales personnel are involved in all aspects of store operations, and the company's policy is to promote from within.

SOURCES OF INFORMATION

Bibliography

Best Buy 1997 Annual Report. Minneapolis, MN: Best Buy Co., Inc., 1998.

"Best Buy Co., Inc." *Hoover's Online,* 21 June 1998. Available at http://www.hoovers.com.

"Best Buy, Circuit City Downsize." *Television Digest,* 23 September 1996.

"Best Buy Presents Check to Benefit 'Speakin' of the Blues' Program." *PR Newswire,* 20 April 1998.

"Best Buy Reports Record Fourth Quarter & Fiscal 1998 Earnings." Minneapolis, MN: Best Buy Co., Inc., 2 April 1998.

"Best Buy Revamps Stores Sales." *Television Digest,* 16 September 1996.

"Best Buy's DVD Marketshare Reaches 35%, Best Buy Hits First $1 Million Post-Holiday Week For DVD Movies." *PRNewswire,* 10 April 1998.

"Career Direction Through Training." *Chain Store Age,* October 1987.

Christman, Ed. "Best Buy, Circuit City a Potent Combo; 2 Chains Change Entertainment Retailing." *Billboard,* 17 June 1995.

Haran, Leah. "Best Buy, Circuit City Raising the Stakes in Electronics Warfare." *Advertising Age,* 27 September 1995.

Hisey, Pete. "Best Buy to Rely on Software, Appliances." *Discount Store News,* 1 July 1996.

"Power Retailers Move Northwest." *Television Digest,* 14 November 1994.

Scally, Robert. "Best Buy Goes Direct with Disney, Blockbuster to Self-Distribute." *Discount Store News,* 2 September 1996.

"Visual Merchandising Exec Joins Best Buy." *PR Newswire,* 9 June 1998.

For an annual report:

on the Internet at: http://www.bestbuy.com **or** write: Best Buy Co., Inc., Investor Relations Dept., PO Box 9312, Minneapolis, MN 55440-9312

For additional industry research:

Investigate companies by their Standard Industrial Classification Codes, also known as SICs. Best Buy's primary SICs are:

5044 Office Equipment

5045 Computers, Peripherals & Software

5064 Electrical Appliances, TV & Radio

5734 Computer and Computer Software Stores

BIC Corporation

FOUNDED: 1958

Contact Information:

HEADQUARTERS: 500 Bic Dr.
   Milford, CT 06460
PHONE: (203)783-2000
FAX: (203)783-2086
URL: http://www.bicworld.com
   http://www.qualitycomesinwriting.com

OVERVIEW

BIC Corporation is a leading manufacturer of stationery products, lighters, and shavers and, as of 1997, was a subsidiary of Societe Bic. With strong profits and annual sales in excess of $500 million ($439.3 million in 1996), BIC Corporation handles all of the company's business in North and Central America. The company has facilities in nine locations in North America, Guatemala, and Mexico. As of 1998, the company manufactured about 3.0 million ballpoint pens, 2.5 million shavers, and 1.0 million lighters per day.

HISTORY

BIC traces its beginnings to 1945, when Marcel Bich, a former production manager for a French ink manufacturer, purchased a factory outside Paris with partner Edouard Buffard to make fountain pen parts and mechanical lead pencils. They founded the company that would later become Bic. Soon after founding the business, Bich began to explore the idea of a reliable, low-cost ballpoint pen. In 1949, Bich introduced the BIC ballpoint pen (shortened from his name) in Europe. The pen was successful in Europe, and in 1958 Bich purchased the Waterman Pen Company, based in Seymour, Connecticut, to gain access to the U.S. market.

In 1959, BIC pens were introduced to the U.S. market with a successful advertising and marketing campaign. A television ad campaign, with the slogan "Writes first time, every time—and for only 29 cents," was credited with creating broad appeal for the BIC pen in the

United States. In 1963 Waterman-BIC, which later became BIC Corporation, moved into new facilities in Milford, Connecticut. In 1967, the BIC Canada division was created, and in 1971, BIC Pen Corp. became a publicly traded company listed on the American Stock Exchange. The name was later shortened to BIC Corporation.

In 1973, BIC Corporation introduced the BIC Lighter, which became the top-selling lighter in North America. Again, a successful advertising campaign was credited with creating strong awareness and demand for the product. The slogan "Flick my BIC" was particularly memorable. In 1976, BIC Corporation continued its string of successful new product launches with the introduction of the BIC Shaver, which became a leading disposable shaver in world markets.

BIC Corporation launched its Specials Markets Division in 1978 to serve the promotional products industry with advertising specialty products. Another division, BIC Sports, was started up in 1981 to market sailboards; by 1996 BIC Sports was the world's leading sailboard company. In 1992 BIC acquired Wite-Out Products Inc. and began selling a complete line of BIC Wite Out correction fluids. During the same year, BIC introduced the BIC Lighter with Child Guard, a lighter with enhanced child-resistant features.

In the early 1990s, BIC Corporation faced major legal challenges to its disposable lighter business in the United States. Many product liability suits were filed against BIC Corporation alleging that its lighters caused personal injury. While almost all of these cases were decided in the favor of BIC Corp., the company had to pay costly bills for its legal defense. BIC Corporation's policy was to litigate rather than settle all product liability claims. According to one market analyst, while this was an expensive process, it helped dramatically reduce the number of new claims filed against BIC Corporation.

In 1998, BIC purchased the Sheaffer Pen Corporation, a Fort Madison, Iowa-based manufacturer. It was the fifth-largest pen manufacturer in the world, and this acquisition added premium writing instruments to Bic's line of product offerings.

STRATEGY

BIC Corporation's basic business strategy in the late 1990s was to produce and market low-cost, high-quality stationery products, lighters, and shavers. The company also pledged to continually seek innovative extensions that distinguished its products from lower-price competitors. For example, while in the early 1990s BIC Corporation was said to have lost market share to cheaper (and lower-quality) imported Asian lighters, the company was able to reverse the trend by implementing more effective marketing and introducing value-added, higher-margin product line extensions. One of Bic's most suc-

The BIC flag waves proudly over the corporate headquarters. (Photograph courtesy of BIC Corporation. BIC is a registered trademark of BIC Corporation.)

FAST FACTS:
About BIC Corporation

Ownership: BIC Corporation is a privately held company and a subsidiary of Societe BIC SA, which is traded on the Paris Stock Exchange.

Officers: Bruno Bich, Chmn. & CEO; Raymond Winter, Pres. & COO

Employees: 2,700

Principal Subsidiary Companies: BIC Corporation's primary subsidiary is the Special Markets Division, which had annual sales of $17 million in 1996.

Chief Competitors: BIC Corporation manufactures and markets writing instruments, razors, and lighters. Competitors in those industries include: American Safety Razor; Gillette; PaperMate; Pentel; Pilot; Sanford; Schick; and Warner-Lambert.

CHRONOLOGY:

Key Dates for BIC Corporation

1945: Marcel Bich and Edouard Bufford start making pen parts in France

1949: Introduces the BIC ballpoint pen

1958: Purchases the Waterman Pen Company located in Seymour, Connecticut, to become Waterman-BIC

1959: BIC pens are introduced into the U.S. market

1963: Moves to Milford, Connecticut

1967: BIC Canada division is created

1971: BIC Pen Corp. becomes a publicly traded company

1973: Introduces the BIC Lighter

1976: Introduces the BIC Shaver

1978: Launches the Special Markets Division

1981: Starts BIC Sports

1992: Acquires Wite-Out Products Inc.

1996: BIC Sports becomes the world's leading sailboard company; introduces the Wite-Out Pen

1998: Purchases Sheaffer Pen Corporation

cessful product introductions was its "wrapped product," which consisted of a BIC disposable lighter with a decorative plastic wrap adhered to the body of the lighter. In 1993, BIC released a new series of limited edition, marble-finish lighters and a line of sports lighters featuring color illustrations of baseball, football, auto racing, boating, and other sports.

Another part of BIC Corporation's strategy was to grow through acquisitions. In June 1992, the company acquired Wite-Out Products Inc., the second-largest manufacturer of correction fluid, for $19.9 million in cash. BIC made modifications in the product—including formula improvements and changing the name of the brand to BIC Wite-Out—and was able to increase its market share in the category. The company's 1997 acquisition of Schaeffer also helped increase Bic's market share by adding premium writing instruments to its product offerings.

INFLUENCES

The enactment of federal rules requiring that all disposable lighters sold in the United States be "child-

resistant" was seen as a beneficial development for Bic. The company developed and patented a child-resistant lighter design said to be superior to those of competitors' products. Since requirements for designing a child-safe lighter were difficult to meet, Bic—with its patented design—had a competitive advantage over other producers.

In the early to mid-1990s, BIC Corporation was also able to revitalize its writing instrument sales by applying the same line extension strategy used for its lighter products (the application of decorative wraps). For example, in the early 1990s, the BIC Wavelengths line of pens and mechanical pencils was broadened to include new designs, including a heat-sensitive pen that changes color as it is held.

In the disposable razor market, BIC Corporation continued to seek new markets by expanding its product line in the early to mid-1990s. The line included the BIC Shaver for Normal Skin, the BIC Lady Shaver, BIC Metal, BIC Pastel Shavers, and twin-blade products. As of 1993, BIC Corporation accounted for 11 percent of the U.S. shaver market measured in revenues and 22.6 percent of the market measured in unit volume (due to the lower price of BIC shavers).

CURRENT TRENDS

New products have long been a growth area for BIC Corporation, and the company continued to roll out many new products in the 1990s. Many of BIC Corporation's writing instruments were tailored for specific age ranges or population categories. For example, Go-Gos were aimed at 10-year-olds, Spring Fever for girls aged 10 to 18, and the Football and Basketball Series for 10 to 14 year old boys. The company's Fashion Rollers included the Bouquet brand, which appealed to young girls, while the Old World brand appealed to businessmen.

PRODUCTS

BIC products include pens, pencils, lighters, and disposable razors. BIC introduced Wavelengths fashion pens and pencils to the United States in 1990, and they soon became very popular. In the mid-1990s, the Wavelengths line in North America was broadened with new designs and the introduction of a series of Fashion Rollers. The company reported strong sales of both its Wavelengths and Classic pens. Also in 1996, BIC rolled out its new Wite-Out Pen, a no-squeeze correction pen. In January 1997, BIC released a line of decorator pens featuring a wraparound PVC shrinkband printed with a universal product code (UPC) that allowed consumers to purchase the pens individually or in packs.

In February 1994, BIC Corporation launched its first-ever line of twin-blade disposable razors, including the BIC Twin Select and Twin Pastel. The new line was designed to compete with Gillette Company's Blue II Plus. In 1996, BIC Corporation introduced its Twin Select Tough Beard Shaver, the first shaver for tough or heavy beards. The company reported strong sales of its twin blade products in 1996.

CORPORATE CITIZENSHIP

In order to further educational development, BIC offers "Quality Comes in Writing," an educational program created for the company by Lifetime Learning Systems. It is available to teachers at no charge on the program's Web site at http://www.qualitycomesinwriting.com. The program is designed to help students in grades 4 through 6 develop strong writing skills through interesting activities. Students practice writing skills as they decode, create, and write their own stories, study and write ballads, and keep a hypothetical journal for a famous person. The program contains four Activity Masters, which can be copied so students can use them as worksheets; a Teacher's Guide that includes a list of the program's objectives, suggestions for introducing activities, and follow-up activities; a poster of writing hints for classroom display; and 30 take-home booklets to promote parental involvement in the writing process outside the classroom.

BIC Corporation's status as a good corporate citizen was on shaky ground in the eyes of some students, however. Students at Bristol Eastern High School tried to curb Bic's product testing on animals. Earthlings, a student environmental group, sponsored a "pen swap" in hopes of encouraging peers to trade in BIC pens (the ink is tested on animals) with those from Pilot, one of the few writing instrument manufacturers that does not do animal testing. The group got the information from the PETA (People for the Ethical Treatment of Animals) Internet site, which contains information claiming BIC tests its ink in the eyes of rabbits and beagles. Pilot donated pens for the product exchange. In response, BIC claimed in March 1997, that animal testing was required by law "... to determine the safety ... of any new formulations for ... inks or correction fluids," as reported in *The Tattoo: A student publication of The Bristol Press.* "There is no ongoing testing," the statement says, contrary to PETA's claims. Students went ahead with the pen swap after hearing that Gillette (owned by Bic) and Pilot were both able to use older test data to get around the law requiring testing.

GLOBAL PRESENCE

BIC Corporation's international operations include subsidiaries in Canada, Mexico, Puerto Rico, and Guatemala. As of 1996, the company did not operate in

WRITING FOR MILES

BIC sells over 14 billion pens in 150 different countries every day. Each of BIC's medium point pens can write for more than two miles, and each fine point pen will write for more than three miles. Combined, that's enough ink to cover the Great Wall of China almost 2 million times per day!

BIC takes great care in making and packaging their world-renowned ball-point pens; each pen gets special attention. The whole process starts with huge 600 gallon tanks of BIC's own ink. They use black ink the most, followed by blue, red, and green. After making the ink, tungsten carbide pellets are ground into finished balls. This process takes more than 60 machine hours, and the balls are then visually inspected using a special screen. In all, 17 quality checks are made during the ball-grinding and point-making process.

The next step in the BIC production process is the cartridge assembly, where the ink is injected into the plastic tubes. Once they are filled, a robotic arm puts them in a centrifuge machine where all excess air is removed. Completed ink cartridges are then transported to the final assembly area by the BIC robot, which looks like the BIC Boy logo and travels throughout the halls just like a regular BIC employee. The robot can transport as many as 100,000 cartridges at a time.

During this time, injection-molding machines, along with plastic extruders, are used to create the barrels and caps for the pens. Caps and barrels start out as plastic pellets and are placed inside machines that run at temperatures of 400 Fahrenheit degrees. The machines shape the outside of the pens. Once the pens are assembled, they are packaged and sealed into boxes. From there they are shipped out all over the world.

Europe or Asia—markets being served by parent company Societe Bic. Sales by foreign subsidiaries accounted for about 20 percent of BIC Corporation's sales in the mid-1990s.

EMPLOYMENT

According to the company, BIC invests heavily in employee training and technology. Employees are able to expand and grow with the company through their

Employee Involvement Program in which individual ideas and suggestions are "recognized, implemented and rewarded."

SOURCES OF INFORMATION

Bibliography

BIC Corporation Company Report. New York: Smith Barney Shearson, 20 August 1993.

BIC Corporation—Quality Comes in Writing Web Site, June 1998. Available at http://www.qualitycomesinwriting.com.

BIC Corporation Web Site, June 1998. Available at http://www.bicworld.com.

"Eastern Students Plan Pen Protest." *The Tattoo: A Student Publication of The Bristol Press,* 7 April 1997. Available at http://ourworld.compuserve.com/homepages/Majerus_Collins/bicpens.htm.

Fox, Harriet Lane. "BIC Launch Sets Off Razor Wars." *Marketing,* 3 February 1994.

Hartman, Lauren R. "BIC Pens a Bestseller with Shrinkbands." *Packaging Digest,* January 1997.

Kaplan, Andrew. "Scorching Demand for Lighters." *Distribution Journal,* 15 April 1996.

Societe BIC 1996 Annual Report. Clichy, France: Societe Bic, 1997.

For additional industry research:

Investigate companies by their Standard Industrial Classification Codes, also known as SICs. Bic's primary SICs are:

3421 Cutlery

3951 Pens And Mechanical Pencils

3999 Manufacturing Industries, NEC

Binney & Smith, Inc.

OVERVIEW

Binney & Smith, Inc. sells many products for creative and practical uses. Each year the Easton, Pennsylvania-based company produces more than two billion Crayola crayons—enough to circle the globe four and a half times. Besides crayons, Binney & Smith cranks out 200 million markers and 100 million sticks of chalk a year. The Hallmark Cards subsidiary also makes Silly Putty, the classic toy that started out as a wartime experimental rubber replacement. Revell-Monogram, the world's largest plastic model kit maker, joined Binney & Smith's toy chest full of creative activity products in 1984. Hobbyists who make those miniature hot rods and fighter planes may even use Liquitex, the world's best selling acrylic paint and another Binney & Smith brand.

Clearly the success of the Crayola brand taught the company the importance and power of cultivating a trusted name in the marketplace. Crayola remains the company's top seller and best known brand. Research shows that at least 98 out of 100 Americans recognize the Crayola brand. The smell of Crayola crayons also scores among the 20 most recognized scents, according to company literature that cites a Yale University study; coffee and peanut butter hold the top two spots, and crayons hold the eighteenth position.

The company continues to add to its carefully crafted mix of quality products. Binney & Smith sells its art supplies through both consumer and educational channels.

FOUNDED: 1902

Contact Information:
HEADQUARTERS: 1100 Church Ln.
 Easton, PA 18044-0431
PHONE: (610)515-8000
TOLL FREE: (800)CRAYOLA
URL: http://www.crayola.com

The original Crayola crayons and packaging, manufactured by Binney & Smith Inc. (Courtesy of Binney & Smith, Inc.)

COMPANY FINANCES

Since Binney & Smith is privately held, they do not release financial data.

HISTORY

In 1864 Joseph Binney founded the Peekskill Chemical Works, a company that produced charcoal and lamp black in upstate New York. In 1880 Binney moved his company headquarters to New York City, where he was joined by his son, Edwin Binney, and his nephew, C. Harold Smith. When Joseph Binney retired in 1885, the younger Binney and Smith formed a partnership called Binney & Smith.

Binney & Smith boasts a long history of coloring America. Exploiting the natural gas deposits found in nearby Pennsylvania, the new company actively developed carbon black. The tiremaker Goodrich slapped Binney & Smith carbon black on formerly white car tires to make them last five times longer and look nicer. The company also made red oxide pigment used in barn paint.

Taking advantage of the region's large slate supply, the partners bought a water-powered stone mill in Easton at the turn of the century and added slate school pencils to their product line. Further responding to classroom needs, Binney & Smith introduced a dustfree chalk stick in 1902. The chalk quickly proved so popular with teachers that it won a gold medal at the St. Louis World Exposition. At the same time, the newly-incorporated company became a worldwide distributor for several carbon black producers.

When Binney & Smith representatives visited local schools to show off their popular wares, they saw a need for affordable wax crayons for students. With that in mind, the company simply reworked its industrial marking crayons by making them smaller and adding pigment to the paraffin. Edwin Binney's wife, Alice, coined the Crayola name by combining the French word for chalk, *craie,* with a corruption of *oleaginous.* The crayons were a hit with teachers and children. In 1903 the first box of eight sticks sold for a nickel. The first colors to roll off the line were black, brown, blue, red, purple, orange, yellow, and green.

Binney & Smith continued to prosper. In a generous move during the Great Depression, the company hired poor local farm families to hand label crayons. Binney & Smith added Artista brand paints and Perma Pressed sharpenable fine art crayons to their product line in the 1920s. In 1936 the company helped found the Crayon, Watercolor, and Craft Institute, which promoted safe products for the art industry. In 1949 Binney & Smith introduced a box of 48 Crayola crayons. The box featured exotic new colors, such as burnt sienna, periwinkle, and bittersweet. To fulfill growing de-

FAST FACTS:
About Binney & Smith, Inc.

Ownership: Binney & Smith, Inc. is a subsidiary of Hallmark Cards, Inc., a privately held corporation.

Officers: Donald J. Hall, Chmn., Hallmark Cards, Inc.; Richard S. Garin, Pres. & CEO, Binney & Smith

Employees: 2,600

Principal Subsidiary Companies: Binney & Smith is a wholly owned subsidiary of Hallmark, which is a privately held company. The Hall Family retains majority ownership while employees own the remainder.

Chief Competitors: Binney & Smith, Inc. competes with a number of companies that offer art supplies and toys. Among its competitors are: American Greetings; Gibson Greetings; Hasbro; IFE; Marvel; Mattel; Time Warner; Viacom; and Walt Disney.

mand, the company opened a plant in Winfield, Kansas in 1952.

America's baby boom brought more change and continued growth for Binney & Smith. In 1958 the 64-crayon box with a built-in sharpener debuted to rave reviews. That same year Binney & Smith bought two smaller crayon-making companies in Canada and England. The private company went public in 1961. By 1963 investors could buy shares of Binney & Smith through the American Stock Exchange. The company bought Cincinnati-based Liquitex in 1964.

Corporate headquarters moved from New York City to Easton in 1976. The next year Binney & Smith acquired the rights to Silly Putty, the popular play stuff that comes in an egg-shaped package. On the 75th birthday of Crayola crayons, Crayola markers debuted. In 1979 the company put all its children's products under the Crayola name and all fine art materials under the Liquitex name.

Hallmark Cards, the world's largest greeting card maker, bought Binney & Smith in 1984. The company introduced washable makers in 1987 and acquired the Magic Marker name in 1988.

The 1990s brought much hoopla and some controversy. Despite protests, in 1990 Binney & Smith retired eight classic colors to make room for brighter shades. In

CHRONOLOGY:

Key Dates for Binney & Smith, Inc.

1864: Joseph Binney founded the Peekskill Chemical Works to produce charcoal and lamp black

1885: Joseph's retires and his son Edwin Binney and nephew C. Harold Smith form a partnership called Binney & Smith

1902: Binney & Smith introduce a dust-free chalk stick, which wins a gold medal at the St. Louis World Exposition

1903: The company produces the first box of Crayola crayons, selling for a nickel

1936: Becomes a founding member of the Crayon, Water Color, and Craft Institute

1948: An in-school training program begins to educate art teachers about the many ways to use the expanding line of Crayola products

1958: The 64-color assortment of Crayola crayons with built-in sharpener debuts

1961: Binney & Smith goes public

1977: The company acquires the rights to Silly Putty

1984: Binney & Smith becomes a wholly owned subsidiary of Hallmark

1990: Eight traditional crayon colors are retired to the Crayola Hall of Fame

1996: The 100-billionth Crayola crayon rolls off the production line

1993 Binney & Smith set up a nationwide contest to name 16 new colors for their upcoming giant box of 96 crayons. Winners included robin egg's blue, macaroni and cheese, denim, tropical rain forest, and razzmatazz. In 1994 Hallmark bought kit-maker Revell-Monogram for Binney & Smith. The company discontinued food-scented crayons in 1995 after only one year on the shelves, citing fewer than 10 reports of kids eating the non-toxic products in batches of cherry, chocolate, and other mouthwatering aromas.

Drawing on other technological innovations in the 1990s, Binney & Smith began to produce crayons that changed color and glowed in the dark. The company invested $2 million in a downtown Easton renovation and development project that surrounded the planned Cray-

ola Factory, a family discovery center. Timed to coincide with the opening of the Crayola Factory, the 100-billionth Crayola crayon rolled off the production line in July 1996, poured by none other than Fred Rogers of *Mister Rogers' Neighborhood.* The company welcomed the 100,000th Crayola Factory tourist just three months later. Binney & Smith started to consolidate manufacturing operations in 1997. It closed down its plant in Kansas and laid off 345 workers in a town of just 12,000 people, while opening a larger plant in Pennsylvania, where the company got a state grant of $800,000. In 1998 the U.S. Postal Service honored Binney & Smith with a stamp depicting the original eight-count box of Crayola crayons.

STRATEGY

From Ty's Beanie Babies to McDonald's hamburgers, top brands often rule. Binney & Smith brands include Crayola, Liquitex, Revell-Monogram, Magic Marker, and Silly Putty.

According to company literature, "The Crayola brand name is recognized by 99 percent of Americans and is ranked 51st of all world brands (1991 Landor Image Power Survey) in terms of the brand's recognizability and consumers' esteem for the brand." While closely guarding its integrity, the company has licensed its registered trademark of Crayola to more than 20 companies that make a variety of products, including costumes, watches, clocks, children's clothes, stuffed animals, and eyeglasses.

Capitalizing on its strong name recognition among adults who grew up coloring with Crayolas, the company has built a growing office products business. It also markets its products to restaurants, hotels, airlines, and specialty promotion companies.

INFLUENCES

Acting on behalf of political correctness, in 1992 Binney & Smith introduced multicultural crayons in deference to the diversity of those using the crayons. The colors, such as tan and mahogany, correspond with many different skin tones in an effort to make children aware and respectful of cultural differences. The company's own sensitivity to such matters began in 1962 when the crayon color "flesh" was changed to "peach."

CURRENT TRENDS

Binney & Smith drew on high-tech innovations in the 1990s, introducing crayons that smelled good, changed color, or glowed in the dark. For the computer generation, the company teamed up with top graphics designer, MicroGrafx, to create an array of multimedia paint programs that are easy enough for kids to use. The software includes sound and animation capabilities.

PRODUCTS

Binney & Smith makes crayons, markers, chalk, colored pencils, paints, activity kits, model kits, accessories, and modeling compounds. The company makes a conscious effort to make safe, high-quality products that appeal to a broad spectrum of consumers.

Under the Crayola name, the company has made more than 100 billion crayons since their creation in 1903. That averages out to approximately two billion crayons each year—and five million each day. Studies show that North American children use about 730 crayons by the time they reach age 10. The two most popular colors remain red and blue. The 24-count box is the company's best seller. Binney & Smith even makes jumbo sized versions that wash off clothes and walls, perfect for toddlers and their parents. The company also makes glueless airplane kits and premium watercolor paints under the Crayola name.

Other branded product lines include: Liquitex, fine art and decorative art supplies; Silly Putty, the play putty that comes in 15 different colors; Revell and Monogram plastic model kits, from miniature classic car replicas to detailed military aircraft; and Magic Markers, including highlighters, permanent ink markers, specialty presentation markers, and a line of dry-erase products.

CORPORATE CITIZENSHIP

According to company literature, "Responsible corporate citizenship is one of our business operating principles that's taken very seriously. In each of our communities where we maintain manufacturing facilities, we provide support for arts, education, human services and civic organizations that work hard to make our regions better places to live."

Binney & Smith also exhibits a strong commitment to arts-in-education initiatives throughout the country. In 1984 Crayola rolled out its Crayola DREAM-MAKERS art education program that showcases the talents of elementary school students.

On the environmental front, the company proudly boasts that "more than 95 percent of our product packaging is made from recycled or recyclable materials. Scrap plastics, corrugated cardboard and other waste materials are kept from landfills through enhanced recycling efforts. Even our pencils use reforested wood, protecting tropical and old-growth forests."

DID YOU KNOW THAT. . .

- kids in North America spend 6.3 billion hours coloring each year?
- North Americans buy 2.5 billion crayons annually?
- most kids spend an average of almost half an hour a day coloring?
- after 37 years of being Crayola's senior crayon maker, Emerson Moser told his co-workers that he was blue-green colorblind and couldn't distinguish all the colors?
- Crayola crayons are made into 96 different colors. . . but there are only 18 different label colors?
- Crayola crayons are translated into 12 different languages?

GLOBAL PRESENCE

Crayola products can be found in more than 80 countries and in 12 languages. In Canada, Crayola is the only brand of crayons sold in the entire country.

The company has manufacturing and distribution facilities around the world. Plant locations include Lindsay, Ontario; Bedford, England; Mexico City, Mexico; and Indonesia. The marketing division has offices in England, Germany, France, Spain, Singapore, and Australia.

EMPLOYMENT

The company employs more than 2,500 people, largely located in Pennsylvania and spread out in manufacturing and distribution facilities around the world.

SOURCES OF INFORMATION

Bibliography

Bennett, Steve and Ruth. "Crayola Amazing Art Adventure, Crayola Art Studio." *Quickspin Software Review,* 1995.

"Bringing Dreams to Life: Crayola Dream-Makers." *Northern Today,* DeKalb, IL: Northern Illinois University, 26 April 1996.

"The Complete List of Crayola Trivia Questions." *Crayola's Home Page,* 5 May 1998. Available at http://www.crayola.com.

"Crayola: A Colorful History." *Crayola's Home Page,* 5 May 1998. Available at http://www.crayola.com.

"The Crayola Factory." *Crayola's Home Page,* 5 May 1998. Available at http://www.crayola.com.

"How are Crayola Crayons Made?" *Crayola's Home Page,* 5 May 1998. Available at http://www.crayola.com.

"News from Crayola." *Crayola Press Release,* April 1997.

For additional industry research:

Investigate companies by their Standard Industrial Classification Codes, also known as SICs. Binney & Smith's primary SICs are:

3952 Lead Pencils and Art Goods

5092 Toys & Hobby Goods and Supplies

Birkenstock Footprint Sandals, Inc.

OVERVIEW

Birkenstock Footprint Sandals, Inc. is famous for its trademark product—bulky but comfortable leather sandals, worn by "hippies" in the late 1960s and by almost everyone else in later years. The California-based company does not manufacture shoes itself; instead, it is the exclusive American importer and distributor of Birkenstock footwear, which is made in Germany by a two-century-old company. The founder of Birkenstock Footprint Sandals, Margot Fraser, discovered the sandals in Germany while on vacation in 1966. Although she had no business experience, she decided to sell the sandals in the United States when she realized how much better her feet felt after wearing them. However, traditional shoe stores had no interest in the admittedly unattractive sandals; Fraser found her original market in health-food stores.

Birkenstock grew from a one-woman company operating out of Fraser's home and selling a few pairs of shoes at a time, to a highly successful company with $82 million in sales in 1997. Almost two million pairs of "Birkenstocks" are sold in the United States every year. In addition to its original brown leather sandals for adults, Birkenstock now sells 300 styles and colors of shoes and sandals for adults and children. Some new products come in bright colors and in synthetic materials, and many celebrities and fashion models were seen wearing Birkenstocks in the 1990s. Birkenstock is noted for its community activism and its excellent employee relations.

FOUNDED: 1966

Contact Information:

HEADQUARTERS: 8171 Redwood Blvd.
  Novato, CA 94945
PHONE: (415)892-4200
FAX: (415)899-1324
TOLL FREE: (800)761-1404
URL: http://www.birkenstock.com

BIRKENSTOCK®

FAST FACTS:

About Birkenstock Footprint Sandals, Inc.

Ownership: Birkenstock is a privately owned company.

Officers: Margot Fraser, Pres. & Founder; Dennis Cutter, CFO; Mary Jones, VP & HR Manager

Employees: 195 (1997)

Principal Subsidiary Companies: Birkenstock is the exclusive importer and distributor of German-made Birkenstock Original Contoured Footbed sandals and shoes in the United States. It maintains two company-owned retail stores, two mall outlet stores, and a large distribution and marketing center at its headquarters in Novato, California.

Chief Competitors: Birkenstock has a host of competitors in the footwear business. Its top competitors include: NIKE; Deckers Outdoor Products; and Wolverine World Wide.

COMPANY FINANCES

Because Birkenstock is a private company, it does not release detailed financial information to the public. Its 1997 sales were $82 million, a 26-percent increase over 1996 sales of about $65 million. However, sales for both 1995 and 1994—$55 and $50 million, respectively) were down from sales in 1993 of $60 million.

HISTORY

Although Birkenstocks have only been sold in the United States since the 1960s, in Germany the Birkenstock family has been manufacturing shoes since the 1700s. In 1774 J.A. (Johann Adam) Birkenstock was registered in the church archives of Langenbergheim, Germany, as "subject and shoemaker." Since that time, the Birkenstock family has continuously made and sold footwear. J.A. Birkenstock's grandson, Konrad Birkenstock, owned two shoe stores and was the person who shaped the family business for the next century. In the late 1800s shoes were made with flat soles and were very uncomfortable since the human foot is curved. In 1897

Konrad Birkenstock invented the first contoured insole, which allowed his cobblers to design custom footwear. However, custom footwear became less popular as cheaper factory-made shoes were more widely manufactured. So Birkenstock turned to another idea: in place of the rigid metal arch supports used in factory-made shoes, he designed a flexible arch support insert.

Around the time that World War I began, Konrad's son Carl joined the business. Soon the company concentrated on developing orthopedic shoes and inserts to be worn by wounded soldiers. By the 1920s Birkenstock orthopedic products were being sold throughout Europe. In the 1930s and 1940s, thousands of people in Europe attended Birkenstock-sponsored educational seminars about the benefits of orthopedic shoes. In 1954 a new family member, Karl Birkenstock (Carl's son) stepped into the leadership role. Karl Birkenstock moved the company back into the shoe manufacturing business, and focused on developing a shoe that was based on the shape and movement of the human foot—a shoe that would provide all of the benefits of walking barefoot. In 1964 Birkenstock presented the result of years of design work: a shoe with a footbed made of latex, cork, and jute, with a raised toe bar and a heel cup to better distribute the body's weight. The following year the sole was attached to two leather straps, and the first Birkenstock sandal was born.

At this point Margot Fraser entered the picture. She was a German-born dress designer who had moved to the United States. While on vacation at a spa in Germany in 1966, Fraser asked for advice about her chronic foot problems. Someone suggested that she try the new Birkenstock sandals; she did, and within months her foot pain had vanished. Fraser decided that she should share the sandals with other American women who experienced constant discomfort and even pain from the high-heeled, pointed-toe shoes that were in fashion. But when she approached the owners of shoe stores, they told her that American women would never wear such ugly shoes, no matter how comfortable they were. So Fraser took a different approach, and brought the sandals to a convention of health-food store owners in San Francisco. Her first customer was the manager of a health food store, whose feet were so sore that she was carrying her shoes around the auditorium. The manager bought three pairs to sell in her store, all in her own size in case nobody bought them.

Sales of the shoes were slow through the early 1970s, with Fraser ordering 20 pairs at a time from Germany and using her garage as a warehouse. Fraser had no business training and no financial resources to build the business. Her marriage broke up in 1969 and she left everything behind, including her business. But the few customers she did have convinced her to start it again, which she did with the financial help of the woman who had bought the first pairs of sandals at the convention. In 1971 Fraser moved the business to a small office above a California health-food store, and incorporated it as

Birkenstock Footprint Sandals, Inc. In the same year, the classic "Arizona" sandal, still a best-seller today, was introduced. The German company made Fraser its sole importer and distributor within the United States, and opened a larger factory to meet the increased demand for its products.

Sales of Birkenstocks dropped during the 1980s, as customers became more interested in athletic shoes and luxury items. In 1988 sales were a mere $8.6 million. In 1989, Birkenstock changed its logo and began to increase the number of styles and colors available, including new sandals for children. An attractive mail-order catalog was launched in 1990, and other catalog sellers, such as L.L. Bean and The Sharper Image, also began to sell Birkenstocks. Sales of Birkenstocks soared through the 1990s, as Baby Boomers who had first worn them in the 1970s returned to their comfortable favorites, along with their children who bought the new designs. In the late 1990s celebrities such as Madonna, Harrison Ford, and even the emergency room staff on the television program ER were seen wearing Birkenstocks. Photographs of models in fashion magazine ads also frequently paired high-fashion clothing with a pair of Birkenstock sandals. By 1995 annual sales had leapt to $55 million, and in 1997 they reached a record $82 million. Margot Fraser still heads the company, but has initiated a plan by which employees will take over ownership.

STRATEGY

Founder Margot Fraser has always followed a simple but incredibly successful strategy. She believes that her product contributes to health and comfort; if her company continues to produce a quality product, people will continue to buy it. Birkenstock does very little advertising, and considers its customers its best salespeople. As she told *Entrepreneur* magazine in 1995, "All we have to do is stay in business and perform."

While Birkenstock continues to produce the sandals that made it prosper in the early 1970s, it has expanded its product line in the 1990s to reach a new generation of customers, still insisting that every product meet a high standard of quality and be orthopedically sound. Fraser also is noted for encouraging employee participation in business decisions of all kinds. She herself had no business training, and believes that a company that treats its employees with respect will encourage creativity and be successful.

CURRENT TRENDS

As Birkenstock celebrated its thirtieth anniversary in 1996, it also went off in several new directions. The company had to face competition from athletic shoes,

Footwear from Birkenstock Footprint Sandals, named Arizonas. (*Courtesy of Birkenstock Footprint Sandals, Inc.*)

sport sandals (such as "Teva" sandals), and cheaper imitations of its own products. Several hundred new customers were approved as Birkenstock retail outlets, bringing the national total to 3,500 by 1998. And Birkenstock itself went into the retail business for the first time, although in a limited fashion. It opened two company-owned retail stores (in San Francisco and Berkeley, California) and two mall outlet stores (in Gilroy, California, and Orlando, Florida).

Birkenstock also sought to reach new customers in addition to its loyal existing customers. New lines of more trendy Birkenstocks, featuring brighter colors and

CHRONOLOGY:

Key Dates for Birkenstock Footprint Sandals, Inc.

1897: Konrad Birkenstock develops the first shoe with a contoured insole

1902: Birkenstock develops the first flexible arch supports

1925: Birkenstock's arch supports are being exported all over Europe

1932: Leading medical specialists support the Birkenstock system in international training seminars

1964: Karl Birkenstock uses his father's arch support as the basis for a shoe and creates the Birkenstock sandal

1966: Margot Fraser begins importing Birkenstocks into the United States

1970: The most recognized Birkenstock, the Arizona, is introduced

1971: Fraser incorporates her company as Birkenstock Footprint Sandals, Inc. and becomes the sole American distributor

1989: Fraser joins with the German designers to expand the product line

1997: Birkenstock USA is entered into the Footwear News Hall of Fame

using synthetic materials, were introduced. But, along with its new and often younger customers, the company still understood the importance of loyalty to its original customers from the "hippie" days. As Margot Fraser told *Entrepreneur,* "Quality of life is back in. Baby boomers are aging and noticing foot problems, and that alone may be enough to give us a 20-year growth curve."

PRODUCTS

As of 1998 Birkenstock sold 300 styles and colors of shoes and sandals, for both adults and children. In addition to offering its traditional leather sandals (such as the ever-popular "Arizona"), Birkenstock was reaching out to the new generation of customers who grew up during the athletic shoe craze, as well as aging Baby

Boomers who wanted more comfortable footwear once again. New product lines include the "Betula" collection, colorful sandals and clogs with lug soles; the "Footprints" collection of walking and trekking shoes; "Tatami" wedge shoes and sport sandals; and an expanded line of "Birkikids" sandals and clogs for children. Even though many of the new models come in fashionable colors and use synthetic materials instead of leather, all of them retain Birkenstock's orthopedic design.

In the late 1990s Birkenstock also began to market a line of professional footwear designed for clinical, medical, and food-service workers. These shoes are water- and grease-resistant, and can be bought in fashionable colors. The "ESD" shoe is another unique professional product—a shoe for computer technicians that prevents the buildup of static electricity.

CORPORATE CITIZENSHIP

Birkenstock is frequently listed as one of the most socially and environmentally responsible companies in the United States. It donates a portion of its annual profits to more than 100 community organizations, particularly those near its Marin County headquarters (such as the Marin Conservation League and the Marin Agricultural Trust). It also has donated generously to national organizations, such as Canine Companions for Independence, which trains assistance dogs for physically challenged people. Since 1991 Birkenstock has had a corporate "Green Team" that educates employees about environmental activities and practices in the workplace, and the company is committed to being environmentally responsible. Its home page describes this overall environmental policy: "At Birkenstock, if we had a choice, we'd leave nothing behind but our footprints."

GLOBAL PRESENCE

Birkenstock Footprint Sandals, Inc. limits its business operations to the United States, in which it is the exclusive importer and distributor of Birkenstock footwear. The shoes and sandals are made in Germany by the company founded over 200 years ago by J.A. Birkenstock. The two operations are totally independent; the German company owns no share of the U.S. operation, and vice versa.

EMPLOYMENT

Although it employs only about 200 people, Birkenstock has received numerous awards based on its innovative employee practices. Internal communication is highly emphasized and openly appreciated. As each fiscal year begins, all employees meet to discuss Birkenstock's future direction. It is not unusual for a clerical employee to rise to high levels; for example, Mary Jones (Vice President and Human Resources Manager) began as a part-time bookkeeper in the company's early years. When a company bonus is distributed, all employees, including executives, receive the same amount. Executives do not receive additional benefits such as company automobiles. Birkenstock's appreciation for its employees has been returned; even during the company's lean years between 1985 and 1990, only one manager left.

Margot Fraser, in her late 60s in 1998, started a transition plan for the time when she no longer heads the company. To assure that the company she founded continues in its present direction, she has instituted a plan through which the employees of Birkenstock will eventually buy the company. In fact, in the late 1990s employees already owned 40 percent of the company.

SOURCES OF INFORMATION

Bibliography
Baber, Bonnie. "Margot Fraser." *Footwear News,* 15 December 1997.

"Birkenstock Footprint Sandals, Inc." *Hoover's Online,* 27 July 1998. Available at http://www.hoovers.com.

Eskenazi, Joe. "Birkenstock Stands on Solid Footing." *Daily Californian,* 9 September 1996.

McGarvey, Robert. "Shoe In." *Entrepreneur,* February 1995.

Patterson, Cecily. "From Woodstock to Wall Street." *Forbes,* 24 August 1992.

Rourke, Elizabeth. "Birkenstock Footprint Sandals, Inc." *International Directory of Company Histories,* Vol. 12. Detroit: St. James Press, 1996.

Scott, Mary, and Howard Rothman. *Companies With a Conscience.* New York: Carol Publishing Group, 1992.

Skorupa, Susan. "Birkies at 30." *Reno Gazette-Journal,* 23 February 1997.

For additional industry research:
Investigate companies by their Standard Industrial Classification Codes, also known as SICs. Birkenstock's primary SICs are:

3100 Leather & Leather Products

3149 Footwear Except Rubber, NEC

The Black & Decker Corporation

Contact Information:
HEADQUARTERS: 701 E. Joppa Rd.
   Towson, MD 21286
PHONE: (410)716-3900
FAX: (410)716-2933
TOLL FREE: (800)54-how-to
URL: http://www.blackanddecker.com

OVERVIEW

The Black & Decker Corporation is the world's largest manufacturer of small power tools and electric lawn and garden tools with sales of $4.94 billion in 1997, compared to $4.91 billion in 1996. Black & Decker is a world leader in the production of specialty fastening systems, glass container-making equipment, steel golf club shafts, and security hardware (deadbolt, locksets, electronic locks). Alligator, Black & Decker, DeWalt, Dynalite, and Dustbuster are a few of the brand names manufactured by Black & Decker. In North America, Black & Decker was also the largest full-line supplier of small household appliances until it sold the home appliance line in 1998.

COMPANY FINANCES

Black & Decker's overall sales have been growing at a slow but steady pace, increasing from $4.76 billion in 1995 to $4.91 billion in 1996 and $4.94 billion in 1997. Of the company's 1997 sales, 42 percent were generated by its power tools division; 14 percent came from commercial and industrial products; 13 percent from household products; 12 percent from security hardware; 7 percent from outdoor products; 7 percent from accessories; and 5 percent from plumbing products. Operating income for the 1995-97 period was more volatile, decreasing from $426.1 million in 1995 to $356.9 million in 1996, but jumping to $489.3 million in 1997.

The company's earnings per share (EPS) also dropped in 1996, from $2.29 in 1995 to $1.66. In 1997 it climbed to $2.35 again, and in May of 1998 was as high as $8.13. Dividends paid to stockholders remained the same from 1996 to 1997, at $.48 per share.

On the stock market Black & Decker was performing well during 1998, with a stock price hovering between $50 and $55 per share. The company's 52-week low was $33 3/4, and its 52-week high was $55 1/16.

ANALYSTS' OPINIONS

Analysts seem to approve of Black & Decker's latest moves. Zacks Investment Research granted the company a "strong buy" rating. Part of this may be due to the company's sale of the home appliance line and return to its roots in the power tool business. Since the announcement of the sale in January of 1998, Black & Decker's stock price has risen close to 15 percent, even more concrete evidence of investor approval.

The American Marketing Association awarded its 1997 Edison Award, the marketing profession's highest honor, to Nolan D. Archibald, chairman, president, and CEO of Black & Decker for making lasting and significant contributions to marketing during his business career. According to the Association, "This man has led the Black & Decker Corporation into a rise of profitability; from his leadership with new product development success, concern for customer service, marketing expertise and strong customer partnerships."

HISTORY

In 1910 two young men in Baltimore, Maryland, S. Duncan Black and Alonzo G. Decker, started The Black & Decker Manufacturing Co. with an initial investment of $1,200. They built specialized machinery, including a milk bottle cap machine, a vest pocket adding machine, a postage stamp splitting and coiling machine, machinery for the U.S. Mint, a candy-dipping machine, and a cotton picker. In 1916 the world's first portable half-inch electric drill was put on the market. This innovation, introducing portability, changed the small tool industry.

The company's first plant opened in Towson, Maryland, in 1917 and remains the company's world headquarters. In 1922 a Canadian subsidiary was formed, and by 1925 the company expanded to include a subsidiary in England (Black & Decker, Ltd.). During the Great Depression of the 1930s the company continued to expand, establishing a subsidiary in Australia and adding on to the Towson plant. The company also began expansion into the consumer housewares market. In 1933 new products were added such as a portable circular saw, an adjustable-clutch electric screwdriver, an electric fender straightener for automotive repair, and an electric heat gun.

Black & Decker went public on the New York Stock Exchange in 1936. During World War II the company

FINANCES:

Black & Decker Sales, 1994-1997 (billion dollars)

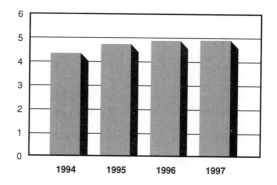

Black & Decker 1997 Stock Prices (dollars)

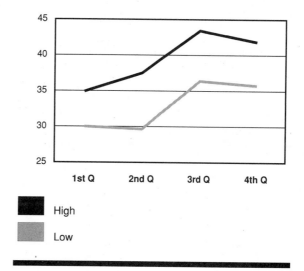

manufactured fuses, gun shells, and other ordinances for the military as part of the war effort. After the war, Black & Decker introduced the Home Utility line of small tools for the do-it-yourself market.

In 1951 Alonzo G. Decker became president after S. Duncan Black, president since 1910, died. Black & Decker continued to expand internationally in 1956 by building plants in South Africa and in Victoria, Australia. In that same year, Alonzo G. Decker died and was replaced by Robert D. Black, S. Duncan Black's brother, as president and chairman of the board.

FAST FACTS:

About The Black & Decker Corporation

Ownership: Black & Decker is a publicly owned company traded on the New York Stock Exchange.

Ticker symbol: BDK

Officers: Nolan D. Archibald, Chmn., Pres. & CEO, 54; Thomas M. Schoewe, Sr. VP & CFO, 45; Leonard A. Strom, Sr. VP Human Resources, 52; Charles E. Fenton, Sr. VP & Gen. Counsel, 49

Employees: 28,600

Principal Subsidiary Companies: Black & Decker Corporation's principal subsidiaries are: Advanced Technology Inc. of Delaware; Black & Decker (U.K.); Black & Decker Canada Inc.; Black & Decker Eletrodomesticos Ltda. (Brazil); Black & Decker G.m.b.H. (Germany); Black & Decker Housewares Ltd. (Singapore); Black & Decker Inc.; Black & Decker (U.S. Pte.) Inc.; Black & Decker Italia S.p.A. (Italy); Black & Decker (Australasia) Pty. Ltd. (Australia); Black & Decker (Belgium) S.A.; Black & Decker, S.A. de C.V. (Mexico); Black & Decker (France) S.A.R.L.; Emhart Corporation; Emhart Deutschland G.m.b.H. (Germany); Emhart Industries, Inc.; Emhart International Ltd. (U.K.); Emhart Scandia AB (Sweden); Planning Research Corporation; and PRC Business Information Systems, Inc.

Chief Competitors: As a manufacturer and marketer of power tools, hardware, and building products, Black & Decker's primary competitors include: Stanley Works; Snap-On; Makita; Bosch; and Sears.

In 1961 the first cordless electric drill was introduced, further bolstering Black & Decker's place in the home tool market. A new concept in household appliance technology revolutionized its industry in 1978 with the introduction of the Dustbuster, a hand-held, cordless vacuum cleaner. Technical sophistication added to the company's product offerings with the introduction of electronic power tools for consumers in 1980, including a drill press with a built-in microcomputer and digital display panel. In 1984 they acquired General Electric Company's small household appliance division and its manufacturing plants. Black & Decker continued to expand globally, buying and leasing manufacturing plants around the world.

In 1988, Black & Decker was inducted into the U.S. Space Foundation's Space Technology Hall of fame for its cordless power tool achievements and its contributions to NASA's Gemini and Apollo programs. In 1968 it developed a unique power head for the Apollo Lunar Surface Drill that removed core samples from the moon; and in 1988 it advanced cordless technology with The Univolt Universal Voltage Charging System, the world's first global battery charger featuring interchangeable energy packs.

STRATEGY

A November 1996 *Washington Times* article reported, "Black & Decker's business strategy in the 1990s has been straight from the business school textbooks: get back to core operations, boost product development, divest extraneous holdings, and cut the fat out of manufacturing processes and management to improve margins." Innovative product development seems to be the lynchpin of Black & Decker's success. As the world leader in small tool and appliance sales, Black & Decker plans to remain in the forefront by continuing to introduce innovative tools and appliances. The tool-buying public's quest for new and innovative products was illustrated by the SnakeLight flexible flashlight, which was so popular when it hit the market in 1994 that supply trailed its enormous demand for over a year. The company vigorously defended the SnakeLight against patent infringement by Catalina Lighting Inc., which was marketing a flexible flashlight under other brand names.

The company's decision in 1998 to sell off the home appliance line is yet another example of this continuing strategy. By divesting itself of its household appliance division, Black & Decker continues its return to core products. The company's plans in 1998 include highlighting its high-end power tools, distributed under the DeWalt brand name. Since starting the line six years ago, DeWalt has come to represent 20 percent of the company's sales.

Black & Decker's research and development efforts to create innovative tools are also a major part of the company's manufacturing and marketing strategy. In marketing products, they emphasize the reputation of quality and reliability of the brand name—part of the tradition of the company for many years. The company's corporate attitude, "the customer is king," is demonstrated by concern with pricing, quality, and service. Another leading component of its marketing strategy is Black & Decker's well-advertised service centers. The company operates 170 service centers, with roughly half located in the United States.

INFLUENCES

Because Black & Decker manufactures not only appliances and tools, but also commands a huge worldwide market for its fastening systems (blind riveting; stud welding, and assembly systems; specialty screws; prevailing torque nuts and assemblies; insert systems), and is diversified in other areas such as security hardware, it was somewhat buffered against the cyclical nature of appliance and tool sales in the United States. However, in late 1996 declining profit margins on the core industry of power tools, economic problems in Europe, and high manufacturing start-up costs in Latin American took its toll on Black & Decker profit margins.

David Leibowitz, an analyst with Burnham Securities in New York, was quoted in the *Washington Post* as saying "Black & Decker has gone through a series of ups and downs in the last seven years, with the downs being largely attributable to Archibald's $2.8-billion purchase in 1989 of Emhart Corp., a manufacturer of door locks, water faucets and computer software." While the purchase gave Black & Decker rights to Kwikset locks and Price Phister faucets, it also gave it a number of incompatible businesses, such as PRC Inc., an information services firm. He also noted that, "A favorable tax adjustment, coupled with the cost savings in Europe, aggressive marketing campaigns in North America and an improving competitive picture in Latin America will help mitigate any earning disappointments."

CURRENT TRENDS

The growth of the "do-it-yourself" and home improvement market after World War II, along with the maturing of the "baby boom" generation (as they began to buy and remodel homes) benefited Black & Decker greatly, and the company situated itself to take advantage of the trend toward home improvement. However, increased competition by tool companies such as Makita and Bosch was impacting strongly upon Black & Decker's hardware sales, and profits in this area were not as great as in earlier years. Renewed focus on the high-end power tool market seems to be helping. The DeWalt brand, one of the company's more expensive lines, seems to appeal to growing numbers of consumers, while the brand was once purchased primarily by contractors and other building professionals.

PRODUCTS

Black & Decker manufactures power tools and accessories, electric lawn and garden tools, glass container-making equipment, security hardware, and many other lesser-known products. These are marketed under vari-

CHRONOLOGY:

Key Dates for The Black & Decker Corporation

1910: The Black & Decker Manufacturing Co. founded

1916: Markets the first portable 1/2" electric drill

1917: Opens first plant in Towson, Maryland

1922: Forms a Canadian subsidiary

1925: Adds a subsidiary in England

1936: Black & Decker goes public on the New York Stock Exchange

1946: Introduces the first power tools for the consumer market

1956: Builds plants in South Africa and Victoria, Australia

1961: Introduces the first cordless electric drill

1968: Creates a tool to remove core samples of the moon for NASA

1978: Introduces the Dustbuster

1984: Acquires General Electric Company's small appliance division

1988: Introduces the Univolt Universal Voltage Charging System

1992: Introduces the DeWalt line

1994: Introduces the SnakeLight

1998: Announces plans to sell home appliance line

ous brand names such as Price Pfister, Kwikset, DeWalt, Brew N Go, and Alligator, among others.

As part of Black & Decker's long-held reputation as an innovator, the company often introduces new tools and appliances that are reasonably priced. These have included the DustBuster cordless hand-held vacuum cleaner, Space Saver "under the cabinet" appliances, the SnakeLight flexible flashlight, the FloorBuster cordless room vacuum with full-length upright handle, and the ScumBuster cordless submersible tub and tile scrubber. A new component-type system was the VersaPak System, which consists of 20 products—each of which run off one or two VersaPak interchangeable batteries.

Black & Decker also is a world leader in the manufacture of fastening and assembly systems products. These

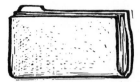

TIM "THE TOOL MAN" TAYLOR WOULD BE PROUD

Looking to add a new deck to the back of the house? Or perhaps just anchoring some screws for that latest picture on the wall? Dewalt, the high-end power tool division of Black and Decker, has become one of the leading choices of today's consumers who are trying to keep up with the Joneses. These high-end power tools, once the domain of professional contractors and tradesmen, have moved into the homes of consumers, who are no longer satisfied with ordinary household equipment. Today, no self-respecting handyman or woman would be caught using anything less than a professional quality power tool for those necessary household chores. So, although the only time these tools may come out of the box is at Christmas to assemble presents, high-end power tools have become a status symbol in many of today's homes.

are marketed under the trademarks and trade names Emhart Fastening Teknologies, Dodge, Gripco, Gripco Assemblies, HeliCoil, NPR, POP, Tucker, Warren, Dril-Kwik, Jack Nut, KALEI, Plastifast, PLASTI-KWICK, POP-matic, POP NUT, WELL-NUT, Parker-Kalon, and others. The principal markets for these products are the automotive, transportation, construction, electronics, aerospace, machine tool, and appliance industries.

GLOBAL PRESENCE

Black & Decker has a major presence in international markets and plans to keep expanding global markets. Its products are currently marketed in more than 100 countries. In 1997, Europe represented 28 percent of Black & Decker's global sales, or $2.85 billion. Other countries outside the United States accounted for 14 percent of worldwide sales, or $716 million. Altogether, foreign operations account for 42 percent of the company's revenues. In 1997, European operations improved despite the impact of currency fluctuation, according the Black & Decker's annual report. Latin America was also performing well; however, Brazil and Asia experienced some difficulties. Black & Decker planned to restructure its global operations in 1998, closing plants in Canada, Singapore, and Italy, and eliminating some design cen-

ters. They also planned to consolidate distribution and transportation operations in Europe, centralize services, and streamline management.

The Black & Decker Manufacturing Company began its development into a global business in the early 1920s. Burgeoning overseas sales towards the end of World War I led the company to expand into Canada, Great Britain, the Soviet Union, Australia, and Japan. With the introduction of the world's first power tools for the consumer market in 1946, the success of this inexpensive Home Utility line was expanded to include a set of circular saws in 1949, in addition to a finishing sander and jigsaw in 1953. The company also continued to market new tools for professional users, such as an impact socket wrench in 1949, and two heavy-duty routers in 1957. By 1969 foreign operations accounted for 43 percent of Black & Decker's sales and earnings. In 1973 the Workmate portable worktable and accessories were first marketed in England, and proved successful around the world.

EMPLOYMENT

Of the 28,600 persons employed by Black & Decker's operations worldwide, approximately 2,000 employees in the United States are covered by collective bargaining agreements. The corporation also has government-mandated collective bargaining arrangements or union contracts with employees in other countries. Black & Decker's operations had not been affected significantly by work stoppages in the 1990s. In the opinion of company management, employee relations were good.

SOURCES OF INFORMATION

Bibliography

Berselli, Beth. "In a Return to Core Products, the Home Appliance Line Will Go." *Washington Post,* 9 February 1998.

Black & Decker 1997 Annual Report. Towson, MD: Black & Decker Corporation, 1998.

Black & Decker Corporation Home Page, 13 May 1998. Available at http://www.blackanddecker.com/.

"The Black & Decker Corporation." *Hoover's Online,* 13 May 1998. Available at http://www.hoovers.com.

Fisher, Eric. "Black & Decker Retools to Rebuild Image, Focus." *The Washington Times,* 11 November 1996.

For an annual report:

telephone: (800)992-3042 or (410)716-2914 **or** write: Black & Decker, Mail Stop TW266, 701 E. Joppa Rd., Towson, MD 21286.

For additional industry research:

Investigate companies by their Standard Industrial Classification Codes, also known as SICs. Black & Decker's primary SICs are:

3546 Power-Driven Handtools

5072 Hardware

Blockbuster Entertainment Group

OVERVIEW

Blockbuster Entertainment Group is predominantly known for its operations as a video rental and sales outlet. In 1997 the company operated 6,470 video and music stores in the United States and abroad. The company also has interest in other ventures, including Spelling Entertainment, a television and film production company; and The Discovery Zone, a commercial playground firm. The company purportedly has 25 percent of the U.S. market for rentals of home videos and video game cartridges, however, the U.S. market during the late 1990s favored purchasing video tapes rather than renting.

COMPANY FINANCES

Blockbuster's revenues have continuously increased over the years. In 1993 revenue was $2.22 billion, and it jumped in 1994 to $3.30 billion. In 1995 and 1996 total revenue rose slightly to $3.33 and $3.54 billion, respectively. Blockbuster's 1997 revenues were $3.91 billion, showing 10.5-percent growth over 1996 revenues. For the first time since the second quarter of 1996, same store sales within U.S. stores increased by 2 percent. In the first quarter of 1998 total video revenues were $930 million, an increase of 13 percent over the first quarter of 1997.

HISTORY

Blockbuster's founder, David Cook, first started a company called Cook Data Services in Dallas, Texas. The company sold software and computer services to the

FOUNDED: 1985

Contact Information:

HEADQUARTERS: 1201 Elm St.
    Dallas, TX 75270
PHONE: (214)854-3000
FAX: (214)854-3241
URL: http://www.blockbuster.com

FAST FACTS:

About Blockbuster Entertainment Group

Ownership: Blockbuster Entertainment Group is a wholly owned subsidiary of Viacom, Inc., a publicly owned company traded on The American Stock Exchange.

Officers: John Antioco, Chmn. & CEO, 47; Thomas Byrne, VChmn., Int'l Operations & Strategic Dev.; Lynn J. Lyall, CFO, 43

Employees: 85,000 (1997)

Chief Competitors: As a retailer of movies and music, Blockbuster's major competitors include: Borders; Camelot Music; Circuit City; Hollywood Entertainment; Barnes & Noble; MTS; and Wherehouse Entertainment.

oil and gas industries until Cook decided to parlay his computer expertise into video rental. The first store was opened in 1985, and in 1986 the name was changed to Blockbuster Video. By 1987 Cook was bought out by Wayne Huizenga.

Huizenga, according to *Fortune,* was worth an estimated $700 million and single-handedly helped professional sports grow in southern Florida. He had healthy interests in the Florida Marlins and Florida Panthers and purchased the Miami Dolphins for $128 million, making him the only owner of teams in three major sports. As the head of another company, Waste Management Inc., Huizenga was known for his aptitude at deal making. He and his cronies, according to one profile of the man, were adept at starting businesses and subsequently bringing friends into these deals. One such pal, John Melk, invested in a Blockbuster store in Chicago. Huizenga purportedly "took one look at the books" in 1987 and "bought control of the whole company—which then was known as Blockbuster Video and owned only 8 stores, with 11 more franchised—for $18 million. And he just kept building," stated the *Fortune* profile. Blockbuster stock grew by more than 3,500 percent in a seven-year period.

Huizenga built the chain by voraciously purchasing smaller video rental companies. First to be gobbled were Southern Video Partnership and Movies to Go; later purchases included Video Library, Major Video, and a franchise owner, Video Superstar MLP. These purchases of regional multi-store video rental companies continued through the 1990s. This strategy even gained a toehold for Blockbuster in Europe, with the purchase of holdings in the United Kingdom beginning in 1992. Acquisitions made in the United Kingdom included the Cityvision, Sound Warehouse, and Music Plus chains.

Huizenga has been credited with making this form of business respectable. "He also did a lot to clean up the image of the video store industry: No more dirty middle-aged men in raincoats. Blockbuster banned X-rated movies and opened big, brightly lit stores with large selections and small prices: three bucks for three nights, while competitors offered just one-night stands." Under his direction, Blockbuster grew to an international chain of 4,300 stores with 1993 revenues of $2.2 billion. Reportedly, Huizenga's aim was to open a new store every day while investing about $150 million each year in advertising.

In 1994 Huizenga reportedly wanted to buy Viacom Inc., a cable provider, which then owned 70 percent of Spelling Entertainment. In January of that year, he attempted to strike a merger deal with Viacom but dropped it due to falling stock prices. Despite that, Blockbuster had purchased $1.85 billion or about 15 percent of Viacom stocks. Later that year the tables were turned. Entertainment conglomerate Viacom purchased both Paramount Communications and Blockbuster Entertainment for $17 billion. The Blockbuster acquisition helped Viacom win over other suitors in the Paramount purchase, which would enable it to compete with the big boys— Time Warner, Disney, and News Corp.

According to a *Newsweek* analysis shortly after the deal, Blockbuster faced, "a couple of headaches. There's too much competition in the video business. The chain has been cutting prices—and thus profits—trying to fend off everyone from mass market retailers to grocery chains that have jumped into the business. . . . Blockbuster, also one of the nation's largest recorded-music retailers, is under attack from rivals in that business, too."

By February 20, 1995, *Newsweek* estimated Blockbuster had captured 20 percent of the video rental market and was growing at the rate of 600 video stores per year. "The chain's 50 million members rent one out of every five of the estimated 4.6 billion videos rented each year." That same article pointed out that the company was having its share of legal problems. Parent Viacom filed suit against Hollywood Video, alleging that it illegally hired Blockbuster employees. Additional suits were pending, one of which resulted in a $124-million judgment. Berrard, company president, was subsequently placed under investigation for perjury in one of those cases.

In 1996 Blockbuster's operating revenues were down 11 percent or $730 million. Part of the decline was attributed to the drying up of the video rental market, thanks to the various flavors of satellite broadcasting and pay-per-view.

The company's next CEO was Bill Fields. He resigned his a position as CEO of Wal-Mart to do so, leaving a company 30 times the size of Blockbuster. According to *Fortune,* Fields led "a full-fledged 'Wal-Martization' of Blockbuster, turning the video-rental outfit into an operator of entertainment variety stores. He's opening Blockbuster outlets in small towns and rural markets. And he's cutting costs the way any good Wal-Mart executive would: by sacking middlemen and by strong-arming suppliers."

In 1996 Blockbuster announced that the company planned to open more than 1,200 new stores in Europe by the year 2000. Also in 1996, parent company Viacom announced it was filing bankruptcy for Discovery Zone, and lost $105-million of pretax income as a result of closing 50 music outlets and moving Blockbuster's headquarters. In 1997 Viacom pulled back on expansion plans for Blockbuster and began to rework the revitalization efforts made by Fields, who resigned as CEO. Viacom hired John Antioco away from Taco Bell in June 1997, and Antioco began his term with Viacom, taking in another $300 million. Under Antioco's lead, Blockbuster's rental sales increased significantly by early 1998, partially due to efforts to stock more copies of hit movies. The company was also able to reduce its debt by $2 billion. Now that the company was once again on solid ground, it was rumored that Viacom CEO Sumner Redstone planned to sell off the company by 2000.

STRATEGY

According to a 1997 press release, parent company Viacom believed that Blockbuster, under the management of John Antioco, would improve its performance by "refocusing on and growing market share in the video rental category through improved marketing and promotion, better store site selection, more targeted tape purchases and a renewed emphasis on operational efficiency and customer service."

Blockbuster was also pursuing a strategy of improved customer satisfaction, hoping to better Blockbuster's performance. Viacom was implementing various programs with major video suppliers to improve selection, convenience, price, and availability of videos, as well as designing new advertising campaigns to highlight these improvements.

An example of Blockbuster's new campaigns for 1998 was a new line of "edgy, innovative television commercials," created by Young and Rubicam. According to Blockbuster, the company's goal was for its commercials to be as captivating as the movies Blockbuster members rent, while also promoting the fact that Blockbuster customers "get your movie . . . and go home happy." Different versions were made of the new commercials to convey various messages, including promotion of Blockbuster's guaranteed new release program, the fact that

CHRONOLOGY:
Key Dates for Blockbuster Entertainment Group

1985: The first Blockbuster opens in Dallas, Texas

1987: Wayne Huizenga buys out Blockbuster

1989: Blockbuster opens its 1,000th store and first in London

1991: Philips Electronics invests $66 million in Blockbuster in exchange for marketing Philips products within the stores

1993: Acquires a majority interest in Spelling Entertainment Group

1994: Viacom acquires Blockbuster

1996: Sears and Blockbuster announce a deal for Blockbuster Music sites in Sears Brand Central locations

1998: Citibank and Blockbuster announce agreement to install Citibank banking machines in 3,000 Blockbuster locations

Blockbuster stores stock more copies of new releases, and Blockbuster's wide variety of movie genres.

INFLUENCES

The standardization of the video recording technology certainly helped propel the growth of the video tape rental market. Too expensive to purchase at one time, video rentals were a welcome alternative to standing in long lines at the movie theatre and braving sticky floors. Trend-watcher Faith Popcorn said the "cocooning" trend—that is in essence staying home rather than going out of the nest for entertainment—was partially predicted by the high number of VCR sales and tape rentals. "By 1988, 60 percent of American homes had a VCR, home-pop microwave popcorn sales were a $300 million business, and restaurant sales were woefully down while take-out restaurant sales were up to an astonishing 15 percent of total food expenditure."

In the mid-1990s the advent of mega-channel cable television, pay-per-view television, and various forms of satellite entertainment took a huge bite out of the video rental market. Viacom believes Blockbuster's slow down

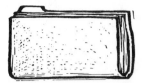

IF THEY DON'T CARRY IT, YOU DON'T NEED TO SEE IT?

Blockbuster is known for having multiple copies of all the latest hit movies, but they tend to shy away from carrying films that potential customers might find objectionable. This means that you will easily find 50 copies of *Titanic* (1997), but you will search in vain for even one copy of director Martin Scorsese's *The Last Temptation of Christ* (1988). If a film is released with an NC-17 rating, such as *Showgirls* (1995), you can expect Blockbuster to carry the R-version of the film; that is, an edited and censored version (although you'll need to check out the fine print to discover this). Blockbuster does what it has to in an effort to maintain their "family" image.

in performance during the late 1990s may also have been affected by factors such as general economic trends in the movie and home video industries, the quality of new titles available, competition, marketing programs, special events, and new technology. The company saw a seasonal pattern to the home video business, with peak rental times mirroring school vacation patterns.

CORPORATE CITIZENSHIP

In June 1998, Blockbuster announced it had entered into an agreement with the American Film Institute (AFI). Blockbuster pledged its support for the Institute's 18-month celebration of the one-hundredth anniversary of American movies. Blockbuster agreed to provide sponsorship of "AFI's 100 Years . . . 100 Movies" celebration with a financial commitment of $2 million. "Blockbuster recognizes the invaluable role of the American Film Institute in preserving and promoting the rich history of American film that is now available on home video," said chairman and CEO John Antioco. "By joining in a long-term relationship with the AFI, and supporting the '100 Years' celebration, we are helping to boost public interest in the timeless films that are the core of Blockbuster's rental library." Blockbuster also agreed to sponsor a related 10-part series of one-hour programs on TNT.

GLOBAL PRESENCE

Blockbuster has franchise and/or development agreements in place in more than 28 international markets. As of December 31, 1997, the company had 2,011 stores operating in foreign countries.

SOURCES OF INFORMATION

Bibliography

"Blockbuster, American Film Institute Launch New Alliance With 'Afi's 100 Years . . . 100 Movies' Celebration." Blockbuster News Release, 15 June 1998.

"Blockbuster Entertainment Group." *Hoover's Online,* 6 July 1998. Available at http://www.hoovers.com.

Loeb, Marshal. "There's No Business Like Show Business." *Fortune,* 8 August 1994.

"Now This is Entertainment . . . Blockbuster Launches New Ad Campaign." *PR Newswire,* 10 June 1998.

Popcorn, Faith. "The Popcorn Report." *HarperBusiness,* 1992.

Roberts, Johnnie L. "Chips off the Block." *Newsweek,* 20 February 1995.

———. "Doing It His Way; Viacom's Sumner Redstone Is Tough. But Sacking His No. 2 Won't Solve His Problems." *Newsweek,* 29 January 1996.

Sellars, Patricia. "Wal-Mart's Big Man Puts Blockbuster on Fast Forward." *Fortune,* 25 November 1996.

"Viacom Expects Blockbuster Second Quarter Revenue and EBITDA Below Analyst Estimates; Company to Take Charges at Blockbuster." Viacom Press Release, 1 July 1997.

For an annual report:
on the Internet at: http://www.viacom.com

For additional industry research:
Investigate companies by their Standard Industrial Classification Codes, also known as SICs. Blockbuster's primary SICs are:

5731 Radio, Television, and Consumer Electronics Stores

5735 Record and Prerecorded Tape Stores

7841 Video Tape Rental

BMW

OVERVIEW

Bayerische Motoren Werke (Bavarian Motor Works, or BMW) is Europe's top auto exporter. Their motorcycle line also competes globally. BMW is one of the world's best-known manufacturers of high-performance automobiles, and the company's sales continue to climb throughout the world. The company truly has a global presence, having 14 subsidiaries in Germany alone and foreign subsidiaries in 20 countries. Expansion has also included the acquisition of U.K. auto manufacturer Rover, as well as an agreement to produce engines with the Rolls-Royce Company. The company's U.S. subsidiary, BMW of North America, has handled the marketing and distribution of BMW products in North America since 1975. In 1994, the company built an assembly plant in Spartansburg, South Carolina. Including the Rover subsidiary, sales exceeded 1 million vehicles in 1995. In 1997, BMW sold almost 1.2 million units, increasing 4.5 percent from 1996 unit sales of 1.1 million.

ALSO KNOWN AS: Bayerische Motoren Werke AG
FOUNDED: 1916

Contact Information:

HEADQUARTERS: Petuelring 130
    Munich   80788 Germany
PHONE: 49-89-38-95-53-8
FAX: 49-89-3-59-36-22
URL: http://www.bmw.com

COMPANY FINANCES

In 1997, BMW sales were up 15 percent from 1996, from 52.265 billion Deutschmarks (DM) to DM 60.137 billion. This was equivalent to an increase from approximately $30.2 billion in 1996 to $34.8 billion in 1997 at late 1997 conversion rates. Net income increased by 52 percent, rising from DM 820 million ($475 million) in 1996 to DM 1.2 billion ($695 million) in 1997. Revenues rose at a faster rate than production and unit sales, however. The company attributed this to a shift in consumer demand for more expensive models and higher revenues

BMW's Fiz Research and Development Center. (Courtesy of BMW)

due to leasing. It was also due in part to the shift in valuation of currencies against the Deutschmark.

The largest part of BMW sales were generated in Europe, about 67 percent. Germany accounted for about 28 percent, the United Kingdom for about 17 percent, and the rest of Europe for the remaining 22 percent of overall sales. North America generated about 16 percent of BMW sales, and the combined market including the Asia-Pacific region, Latin America, and Africa also accounted for about 16 percent of sales. By product sector, BMW automobiles accounted for more than half of the company's sales, about 55 percent. Rover Group products generated about 28 percent of sales, while BMW Motorcycles contributed about 1 percent. Aero engines, financial services, and other BMW subsidiaries generated remaining 1997 revenues.

ANALYSTS' OPINIONS

BMW continues to be touted as one of the world's best automobiles. Mercedes-Benz took the number one spot as the most highly regarded automaker, followed by fellow German automaker BMW, according to the second annual Global Automotive Image Survey conducted by Market Opinion Research of Irvine in 1996. And a new survey indicates that manufacturers are building better-quality vehicles. As reported by the Mercury News

wire service, "For the first time in the three years Strategic Vision has conducted its quality index, a vehicle scored more than 900 points. BMW's 7 series scored 906. A perfect score is 1,000." Analysts believe that BMW's strong product mix is improving, and that profits are on a solid growth track.

HISTORY

In 1916, the Rapp Company was founded as an aircraft engine factory in Munich, Germany; the following year the name was changed to Bayerische Motoren Werke (BMW). At the end of World War I, the Versailles Treaty prohibited German firms from airplane engine production; since the company was already making motorcycle engines, they expanded to motorcycle production in 1923. By 1929, the company began to manufacture the "Dixi," the first BMW automobile. The growing auto and engine company produced vehicles and engines for Germany's war effort in World War II, and in 1943 they developed a jet airplane engine. The following year it went into production as one of the world's first jet engines. The company also tested rockets for use in the war. However, by 1945 and the defeat of Germany by the Allies, the company was in ruins. Plants in four different German cities had been destroyed and the main factory in Munich was dismantled. The Allies imposed a three-year ban on production because of the company's involvement in constructing aircraft engines and rockets.

In 1951, BMW produced its first post-War car—the 501—but it was a financial failure. The following year, their limousine manufacturing operations suffered large losses, and the company was put up for sale. However, BMW's shareholders, workers, and dealers banded together to help the company, and with a new capital structure, it survived and began to grow. In the 1960s, BMW's reputation as a high-performance "prestige" automobile manufacturer was established. BMW of North America, Inc. (BMW NA) was established in 1975 as the U.S. importer of BMW automobiles. The North American subsidiary assumed import and distribution responsibilities for BMW motorcycles in 1980. The next year, BMW became the first European car importer to establish a subsidiary in Japan. In 1994, U.K.-based Rover Group joined BMW.

STRATEGY

BMW's business strategy was capitalizing on its reputation of fine German engineering and its history as a producer of prestigious racing cars and luxury automobiles. BMW is not one of the world's largest vehicle makers, yet it is large enough for efficient, high-quality production even as it maintains its position as a premium, exclusive make. BMW's product philosophy has never been directed at the masses, and the company has weathered poor economic environments in many of the countries to which it exports. In the 1960s, the company began producing small family-style sedans, but included the company's well-designed engines. BMW's reputation for a practical but high performance auto withstood the test of time. In the economic doldrums of the 1990s in the United States, sales continued to climb. This was testament to BMW's philosophy: to manufacture cars that appeal to the luxury-conscious, but never lose sight of the mundane details of auto ownership.

In the words of Chairman of the Board Bernd Pischetreider, "Adding the BMW and Rover sales together, the BMW Group has retailed substantially more than 1.1 million vehicles in 1996. As these sales figures indicate, BMW has evolved into a true global player in just a few short years. While sales volume is gratifying, it is not our primary goal, and we do not chase short-term sales results. We do expand carefully and strategically, and have made changes that make sense for us in the long term."

"To elaborate just a bit on how much we have changed, consider these facts: (1) 80 percent of our sales are now outside of Germany; (2) only 50 percent of our work force is German; and (3) we are the only European car company with an operational U.S. plant. Of course, BMW must—and will—be in the right place, at the right time, with the right products. And integral to this strategy is our belief that the various brands within the BMW

FAST FACTS:
About BMW

Ownership: BMW stock can be purchased over-the-counter (OTC); it is also publicly traded on stock exchanges in Frankfurt, Dusseldorf, Vienna, and Geneva.

Ticker symbol: BYMTF

Officers: Bernd Pischetscrieder, Pres., CEO, & Chmn. of the Board of Management; Eberhard von Kuenheim, Chmn. of the Supervisory Board; Volker Doppelfeld, CFO; Hagen Luderitz, Exec. Director

Employees: 117,600

Principal Subsidiary Companies: At least 48 percent of BMW is owned by the Quandts, a German family with many holdings in various industrial operations. BMW's U.S. subsidiary is BMW of North America, Inc. BMW also owns the British-based Rover automotive manufacturing company; nonautomotive subsidiaries include Softlab (information systems) and Kontron Elektronik (computers).

Chief Competitors: An international manufacturer of luxury, high-performance automobiles and motorcycles, BMW's competitors include: Daimler Benz; Acura; Ford (Jaguar); Harley-Davidson Motorcycles; Honda; Rolls-Royce; and Toyota.

family must always maintain their clear and distinct identities. A BMW will always perform and handle like a BMW. That is why we will not serve certain market segments with BMW products but with other products. We think this is a very smart strategy."

INFLUENCES

BMW's car sales in the last few decades have continued to increase, along with the demand for higher-priced models. In 1996, there was a 9-percent increase in sales over 1995 (for products with the BMW name brand). Sales in the United States continue to rise. Motorcycle sales, however, have been falling, owing to the decreased purchasing power of younger Europeans, who make up the largest part of BMW's motorcycle market. Unemployment among this group, coupled with increased com-

CHRONOLOGY:

Key Dates for BMW

1916: The Rapp Company, an aircraft engine factory, is founded in Munich, Germany

1917: Rapp becomes Bayerische Motoren Werke (BMW)

1923: The first BMW motorcycle is introduced

1928: BMW buys a car factory and the rights to build a small car called the Dixi

1932: The 3/20 is the first car to be developed at the Munich factory

1934: Aircraft engine manufacturing becomes an independent business unit

1943: The world's first jet engine successfully flies

1945: After World War II, the Allies impose a three-year ban on BMW production because of its involvement in the war effort

1951: BMW introduces its first post-war car

1959: BMW goes up for sale; shareholders, dealers, and workers band together to keep the company alive

1965: The company ceases building aircraft engines for the next 25 years

1970: BMW's second car factory is constructed

1979: The world's first digital engine electronics are developed by BMW

1984: BMW makes the first European cars with catalytic converters

1993: The 5-millionth car rolls off the BMW production line

1994: The U.S. car plant starts up; the U.K.-based Rover Group joins BMW

1995: The Z3 roadster is the first BMW car not produced in Germany

1998: BMW gains the rights to the name and marques of Rolls-Royce

petition from Japanese motorcycle manufacturers, has influenced this drop in sales. BMW's takeover of Rover in 1994 was promising, even though that subsidiary did not show a profit in 1995 and 1996. As BMW acquires various subsidiary automobile companies that cater to dif-

ferent markets, its overall sales figures should continue to increase. The company was introducing several new product models, such as a 5-Series station wagon to appeal to those growing yuppie families.

CURRENT TRENDS

As of first quarter 1998, BMW sales continued to progress nicely, as in years before. Delivery of new cars was expected to decline, however, compared to the first quarter of 1997. The company anticipated the slip as a result of model changeover in its 3 Series. Deliveries in the Rover Group were expected to remain at about the same level as in 1997. Internationally, demand was expected to temporarily decline during 1998. This reflected volatile markets in east Asia and a slight downward trend in the North American automobile purchasing market. BMW was also anticipating weakened demand in southeast Asia, due to the region's financial difficulties, which would hopefully be offset by sales in western Europe and North America. At Rover Group, demand was already found for Rover's new Freelander, which was hoped to increase business volume in 1998. In addition to restructuring the model range, BMW investments during 1998 were focused predominantly on its Birmingham and Oxford plants and international sales.

In what would become another unique addition to its product offerings, BMW announced a $572-million deal, subject to shareholder approval, that it would acquire Rolls-Royce from its parent company, Vickers PLC. The announcement was made on March 30, 1998. In April, however, the *New York Times* reported that Rolls-Royce had instead decided to consider a higher purchase offer from Volkswagon. As of May 9, 1998, BMW had announced they would not be making any additional offers to top Volkswagon's bid for the company, but had already claimed that if Vickers PLC sold Rolls-Royce to anyone but BMW, they would stop delivery of BMW engines to Rolls-Royce. Finally, in July 1998, BMW gained the rights to the name and the marque for Rolls-Royce. BMW granted Rolls-Royce a license to manufacture and distribute Rolls-Royce vehicles until December 31, 2002.

PRODUCTS

James Bond drove the new M3 Roadster in the film "Goldeneye" and introduced the world to the latest BMW model. This model is produced exclusively in South Carolina (the company's sole U.S. assembly plant), and owners can "build their own" by ordering custom components to make their roadster unlike any other. The new 318ti three-door coupe has been called an "entry luxury car"—a lower-priced high performance sedan for younger, more savvy buyers. The 7 Series luxury sedan

BMW's Z3 Roadster made an appearance in the James Bond film "GoldenEye." (AP Photo/HO.)

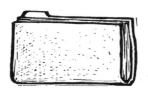

BOND'S BMW'S

James Bond, also referred to as Agent 007, first drove a BMW in the movie *GoldenEye* in 1996; Bond's choice: a BMW Z3 Roadster in Atlanta Blue. Of course, this "Beemer" didn't just come with the standard equipment. The Roadster featured a cell phone that allowed 007 to drive the car remotely. Intruders were deterred by an electrifying shock if they touched the car even slightly. The car was also modified with a rear parachute, an inboard satellite tracking system, and two stinger missiles. These options are only available to secret agents, though.

For his promotion of BMW in the movie *Golden-Eye*, the company gave Pierce Brosnan, who played James Bond, a BMW 850 CSI. A short time after, police caught him doing 120 mph. However, the suave Irish-born actor was not given a speeding ticket but was in-

stead interrogated about specifics of the bungee jump stunt in the movie.

The next Bond movie, *Tomorrow Never Dies,* featured a BMW K 1200 RS Custom Cruiser motorcycle and a BMW 750il. The Aspen Silver BMW 750il reaches speeds of 0 to 60 mph in 6.7 seconds, which actually made it faster than the Roadster Bond drove in *Golden-Eye.* Both of these movies helped to increase BMW's sales. The year *GoldenEye* was released, the BMW Z3 was in high demand even before it went on sale. Automobile aficionados may feel that if it's up to James Bond's standards then it must be a high-class product, or just maybe there's a secret agent hiding deep down in all of us.

with an 8-cylinder engine includes an on-board navigation system, which determines your actual position using signals from up to six navigation satellites, a magnetic compass built into the rear shelf, and data transmitted from the front ABS wheel sensors. The new R1100RS motorcycle, which costs over $15,000, is a lux-

ury-loaded touring bike. BMW plans to broaden its appeal to other markets by introducing a station wagon model, as well as producing the engine for the "Mini," a British economy car that will offer BMW engineering, but under a different brand name to protect the exclusivity of the BMW name.

GLOBAL PRESENCE

The company has a global presence, having 14 subsidiaries in Germany alone and foreign subsidiaries in 20 countries. Sales outside Germany comprise 80 percent of total sales, and only 50 percent of BMW's work force resides in Germany. BMW has entered into several joint ventures with other companies, one of which was Chrysler, with whom they were building an engine plant in South America to produce small engines for non-BMW brands.

BMW's global engine strategy entails building several new manufacturing plants in different areas of the world. After the company acquired part of Rolls Royce, a plan for producing a small four-cylinder engine in England was announced. This engine will be incorporated into the new generation of the Mini, a small car almost ubiquitous in the United Kingdom, which attracts a very different market than luxury BMW models. This was BMW's entrance to a completely new market and, more importantly to a new marketing strategy. The Mini already has an established reputation in Europe. The offering of a low-priced economy model was not expected to compromise the "high end" status of BMW, since it would be sold under a different name brand. The Mini engine would also be produced in a joint venture with Chrysler in a South American plant. A BMW news release reports: "This enables us to reach two strategic targets: First, we are creating a very favorable cost structure for the new generation of the Mini, which will certainly be an advantage in such a fiercely contested segment of the market. Second, by producing engines in South America, we are opening up the local markets for the sale of BMW and Rover cars. This strategy is creating an interesting partnership for the concerned parties." Latin America, with its expanding economy, is an appealing market for high-end BMW cars also; Latin America is the world's fastest growing car market.

The Asian market proved more difficult to break into, however. They began marketing Land Rovers in Korea, and sales in Singapore, Indonesia, and Malaysia showed double-digit growth. Assembly plants were started up in Vietnam and the Philippines, and in the market in which BMW has the greatest penetration, Hong Kong, the company's market share was 12 percent.

EMPLOYMENT

BMW believes in starting employees with its "value orientation" program, which has been in place since 1983. Additional human resources efforts were directed toward the continued training, development, and promotion of those same employees, a policy that benefits both employees and the company. In 1998, a more comprehensive training program was launched, focusing on the recruitment and development of highly qualified young employees. By the year 2000, up to 3,000 apprenticeships will be underway at BMW. All who successfully complete the internships are subsequently offered full-time employment with the company.

Continuing education and qualification was another approach taken by BMW, developing the potential and capabilities of employees already employed by the company. Individual responsibility taken by each employee played a large part in this effort, but such efforts were well supported by BMW "in the form of comprehensive advice and an individual range of courses." BMW Learning Management and Training added new courses to its offerings to allow for BMW's technical and economic requirements. In 1997 additional focus was placed on information technology.

In 1997 BMW created more new jobs. During the year, the total number of employees increased by 1,500 to 117,600—a new high for the company. Between 1995 and 1997, more than 8,000 new employees were hired worldwide.

SOURCES OF INFORMATION

Bibliography

"Bayerische Motoren Werke AG." *Hoover's Online,* June 1998. Available at http://www.hoovers.com.

BMW 1997 Annual Report. Munich, Germany: Bayerische Motoren Werke AG, June 1998 Available at http://www.bmw.com/bmwe/enterprise/gb97/index.shtml.

BMW Home Page, June 1998. Available at http://www.bmw.com.

"International Business; VW Is Set to Win Rolls-Royce as BMW Drops Out of Bidding." *New York Times,* 9 May 1998.

MacLeod, Alexander. "A German Rolls-Royce? Or a British BMW?" *The Christian Science Monitor,* 1 April 1998.

Mercury News Wire Services—Auto News in Brief: *Owners Report Fewer Problems in New Vehicles,* 25 April 1997. Available at http://www.sjmercury.com/business/drive/docs/009652.htm.

Miller, Scott. "New Models Boost BMW to Record 1996 Sales." *Reuter Business Report,* 30 January 1997.

For an annual report:

on the Internet at: http://www.bmw.com/bmwe/enterprise/gb97/index.shtml

For additional industry research:

Investigate companies by their Standard Industrial Classification Codes, also known as SICs. BMW's primary SICs are:

3711 Motor Vehicles and Passenger Car Bodies

5012 Automobiles and Other Motor Vehicles

The Body Shop International PLC

OVERVIEW

The Body Shop is a manufacturer and retailer of natural cosmetics and health care products. However, the company embodies two distinct philosophies. It is a capitalist enterprise, but one with an extremely well articulated plan to strike out for worthy causes, whether that cause is animal testing or acid rain. *Time* captured the essence of The Body Shop, stating that, "Visiting a Body Shop is like walking into the headquarters of a political cabal-albeit one scented with dewberry perfume. There are slogans and messages scattered among the fruit-scented soaps and peppermint foot lotions. Exhortations to save the whales and fight for human rights shout from store windows, countertops, and recycled shopping bags. Even Body Shop trucks are employed as rolling billboards for pithy slogans."

FOUNDED: 1976

Contact Information:
HEADQUARTERS: Watersmead Littlehampton
 West Sussex, BN17 6LS United Kingdom
PHONE: 44-1-90-373-1500
FAX: 44-1-90-372-6250
URL: http://www.the-body-shop.com

COMPANY FINANCES

The Body Shop went public in 1984. The first day of trading, the value per share increased from $1.30 to $2.30. This meant that first day the company became valued at more than $11 million and the net worth of Anita and Gordon Roddick increased to $2 million. In 1997, the company's per share price ranged from an average low of $8 3/4 per share to average high of $15 7/8 per share, and yielded a .56 per share dividend. As of April 27, 1998, the per share price was $10.25 per share.

Over the past three years, The Body Shop International's worldwide sales have increased at a conservative

FAST FACTS:

About The Body Shop International PLC

Ownership: The Body Shop is a publicly owned company traded OTC (over-the-counter).

Ticker symbol: BDSPY

Officers: Anita L. Roddick, Co-founder & Chmn., 55; T. Gordon Roddick, Co-founder & Chmn. 55; Patrick Gournay, CEO; Stuart A. Rose, Managing Director, 47

Employees: 2,426

Chief Competitors: As a shop specializing in healthy and/or organic cosmetics and personal care products, The Body Shop's most visible competitors in the United States include: Bath & Body Works, owned by The Limited and Origins, owned by Estee Lauder. Foreign competitors include: Applewoods and Red Earth. Near competitors include those in the general cosmetics and personal care industry, such as Amway; Avon; L'oreal; and Mary Kay.

rate, from 500.1 million pounds in 1995 to 577.5 million pounds in 1996, and up to $622.5 million pounds in 1997. These sales figures represented 8-percent growth for the company from 1996 to 1997. Net assets rose slightly more slowly, from 110.6 million pounds in 1995 to 122.6 million pounds in 1996, and reaching 130.1 million pounds in 1997.

The company's earnings per share were slightly more volatile, dropping from 11.5 pence (18.6 cents) in 1995 to 9.8 pence (15.8 cents) in 1996. Earnings bounced back almost to the 1995 level in 1996, reaching 11.4 pence per share. Dividends paid per share over the same period were 2.4 pence per share in 1995, 3.4 pence in 1996, and 4.7 pence in 1997.

ANALYSTS' OPINIONS

"It's going to take years to tell whether the new marketing and sales strategies can turn around the company's fortunes," stated a 1996 *Fortune* article, "and to know to what extent Roddick will let her professional managers run the business at the expense of her beloved environmentalism. In the meantime, the fact that there's hardly

a financial analyst who has much positive to say about the company's prospects suggests that, for now, investors should probably stick to buying the Body Shop's soap-but not its shares." In the past two years since that report, The Body Shop has continued to be a rather risky investment, performing at times so shakily as to generate rumors that Anita Roddick was going to buy back the company. Due to poor performance, The Body Shop has already purchased 25 stores from franchisees. In February of 1998, Steen Kanter, head of U.S. operations resigned, leading to speculation that The Body Shop International would sell off the stores. Adding weight to the rumor, according to an article in *Investor's Chronicle,* was the fact that the company's stock price has dropped to its lowest levels in almost ten years. In May of 1998, it was announced that not only would Anita Roddick not be buying back her company, but she was stepping down as CEO. Patrick Gournay from the French food company Groupe Danone was appointed as her replacement, and Mrs. Roddick will act as co-chairman along with her husband. It was yet to be determined what sort of effect this would have on The Body Shop.

HISTORY

Anita Roddick, founder of the company with her husband, Gordon, was born to Italian immigrants to the United Kingdom. She trained to be a teacher, but, after getting kicked out of a kibbutz in Israel, decided instead to travel the world. It was on a visit home in 1968 that she met Gordon Roddick.

In her travels, Roddick saw women using all sorts of natural potions for cleansing and self-care. She thought a storefront shop offering natural self-care products would do well in her funky neighborhood, so she and Gordon took out a 4,000-pound bank loan to open the first Body Shop. At one point, Gordon Roddick went off on a horse trek in South America. Upon his return, he found not one, but two shops and an ever-increasing demand for the products. When Roddick wanted to open a second store in Chichester, the bank refused her loan request for $8,000. A friend introduced her to a local businessman. Ian McGlinn, who has been billed by Roddick as the ultimate silent partner, was prepared to invest the full amount in return for a half share in the business. Since Gordon was unable to respond with his advice in a timely fashion, Anita made the deal. That $8,000-investment has since grown to more than $145 million.

The Body Shop has aggressively pursued foreign expansion. However, the United States, the company's second largest market, has proved particularly difficult. The company first opened a storefront in 1988 in Manhattan. Among its travails were continued controversy over store posters, which continually surfaced through 1997, and the United States' litigious nature, which Roddick says has halted some of her ideas from coming to fruition.

However, despite The Body Shop's difficulties, American entrepreneurs seemed to think she was on to a good thing: in 1993 Roddick claimed there were at least 33 copy cat stores in the United States.

A rocky year in 1992 frustrated investors more than the Roddicks. Stockholders dumped shares after a bad earnings report and price per share slid from $5.20 to $2.70. That alone put the company atop the *Financial Times* list of Top 10 corporate losers of 1992. In 1996, the share price was reported as having dropped 65 percent—from $6.55 in 1992 to an estimated $2.29 in early 1996. Yet, in 1993 *People* hailed Roddick as "one of the five richest women in England." That year she had more than 950 shops in 42 countries, over 130 of them in the United States.

More than 20 years after its birth, The Body Shop had more than 1,600 retail stores worldwide (as of May, 1998). In 1996 the company was hailed as "Britain's most successful international retail business." Sales in 47 countries in 1997 combined for a total of 622.5 million pounds in retail sales. Of the company's shops, 39 percent are located in the United Kingdom, and 27 percent are located in the United States.

Unfortunately, not all aspects of the company's performance have done so well. Despite booming sales in Asia, in the critical U.S. market it actually lost money. Rather than working on increasing sales in existing shops, the company pursued a rapid expansion policy, opening stores in top malls in the United States over the past two years with hopes of gaining a foothold against the fast-expanding Bath & Body Works. It has not been working. U.S. operations lost $3.7 million in the first six months of fiscal 1996 on sales of $46 million. Same-store sales fell by 8 percent. Bath & Body Works, by contrast, opened 412 stores in five years and is showing a profit. Unfortunately, since then The Body Shop's profits have slipped an additional 2.6 million pounds.

The Body Shop, however, is a scrappy, survivalist retailer. As *Management Today* observed, the company "has survived two recessions, a fluctuating exchange rate, a bout of rapid expansion and a host of those business-of-the-year-style awards that are guaranteed to put the hex on any firm." In that same article, speculation was made that Anita and Gordon Roddick might buy back The Body Shop as a result of dropping share price, poor U.S. performance, and a general discontent with the way the company must operate. However, Anita Roddick stepped down as CEO in mid-1998, and her corporate activities will be limited to her duties as co-chairman of the company. It will be left to the new CEO, Patrick Gournay to try to reverse the company's downward slide.

CHRONOLOGY:

Key Dates for The Body Shop International PLC

1976: Anita Roddick opens a stand-alone shop of natural-ingredient cosmetics

1977: Roddick begins licensing franchises

1984: The Body Shop goes public

1988: The first stores open in the United States

1990: Opportunities to franchise in the United States prompts more than 2,000 applicants

1996: The Body Shop is hailed as "Britain's most successful retail business"

1998: Anita Roddick steps down as CEO

cate our business to the pursuit of social and environmental change." Whether fighting animal testing, environmental pollution, or promoting the rights of indigenous peoples, the company publicizes these activities, not its products. Slogans and messages touting these and other causes are the primary focus of in-store decor and The Body Shop's revamped web site. Basic information about products is available, but Anita Roddick relies on her personal publicity and that surrounding the company's adopted causes to promote the company.

Recently, however, minimal attempts have been made at adopting some sort of marketing plan. In fall of 1997, The Body Shop launched an ad campaign featuring "Ruby," a more realistic model the company hoped would promote diverse images of beauty and combat use of the stereotypical model. And due to declining sales in the United States, U.S. stores were redesigned with new colors and store layouts. Other store improvements included brighter lighting, a more coordinated decor, and better use of in-store promotional materials (such as signs). Finally, in 1997 The Body Shop created a "brand council" to handle strategic brand development and global marketing. They also hired an agency to handle U.K. advertising and launched the first major advertising campaign in the company's history.

STRATEGY

The Body Shop's primary strategy is clearly defined in the first sentence of its mission statement—"to dedi-

CURRENT TRENDS

In March of 1998 The Body Shop announced the release of its new hemp line. The line's initial five products, designed to combat dry skin, are Hemp Elbow Grease, Hemp Soap, Hemp 3 in 1, Hemp Lip Conditioner, and Hemp Hand Protector. In a press release, Anita Roddick described hemp as "a traditional natural ingredient with a fantastic history." She claims her new line will not only launch a new product line for the company, but help educate others and rehabilitate the market for industrial grade hemp.

PRODUCTS

The Body Shop's ever-changing line of products includes soaps, perfumes, hair care products, potions for expectant/new mothers, men's personal care items, skin care items, home fragrances, and cosmetics. Specialty areas include: aromatherapy products (Relaxing Body Lotion), products for hands and feet (Peppermint Foot Lotion), and its sensitive skin care line (includes items such as sensitive skin-lip balm, blemish stick, freshener, and body wash).

CORPORATE CITIZENSHIP

Is The Body Shop actually a corporate good citizen or simply looking to generate publicity? For some observers and customers, there's an extremely thin line between the two. More often than not, Roddick doesn't care to tow any one line, save her own agenda, which is carried out as corporate policy. Roddick has championed a host of high-profile causes—a boycott of Shell and support for organizations such as Greenpeace and Friends of The Earth, to name a couple. In the last few years, however, Roddick has defined very specific goals for the company. An example of one of The Body Shop's goals, taken from the 1997 Values Report, reads "Our future planning will be balanced between the environmental implications of our business and economics. We will devote increasing efforts to establishing nonexploitive trading arrangements with communities in less developed countries as a means to protecting their cultures and their environments." The company has invested in "Trade, Not Aid" enterprises in the United Kingdom and abroad, where, "they search the world for indigenous people willing to squeeze oil from Brazil nuts, make paper from water hyacinths, weave back scrubbers out of cactus fiber-anything that could provide the natives with income and the Body Shop with sales." These include a soap factory in Easterhouse, Glasgow, which was established in a high unemployment region in 1988. Roddick has also funded a Boys Town for orphans in India and assisted in funding the rebuilding of Romanian orphanages.

Roddick claims consumers want to feel good about the products they purchase and will pay more if they per-

ceive that money is going to a good cause. She backed that ideology further when she and more than 30 other firms, including Ben & Jerry's and Stride Rite shoes, created a group called Businesses for Social Responsibility, which *Time* called "a politically correct alternative to the Chamber of Commerce." Ultimately, Roddick states in the '97 Values Report that she hopes to ". . . forge a new and more sustainable ethic for business." She wants The Body Shop to establish precedents that other companies can follow and serve as an educational resource on environmental issues.

A 1996 *Management Today* article offered the following observation. "It seems far more likely that she simply wants to put Body Shop money behind causes she personally believes in and is not the slightest bit interested in whether investors think they are getting value or not. The idea that profit should be the only corporate goal is, she says, just bunkum. And many would support her on that. 'Who wants another bloody faceless cosmetics company?' she asks. 'If I thought I had worked 20 years in this company and it would end up an Estee Lauder, I would pack up and go home today.' Quite right."

GLOBAL PRESENCE

Based in the United Kingdom, The Body Shop counts the United States as a foreign market. With extensive franchises around the globe, as well as suppliers around the world, in 1993 it was written that "the biggest question about Roddick's future now seems to be what she'll do when she runs out of countries." That same year The Body Shop expanded into Mexico, with plans to open retail stores in Cuba and Vietnam. Roddick and company generally look in each country or area for native products to be incorporated into the product line prior to opening retail stores in a country. Roddick projected that there would ultimately be between 500 to 1,000 Body Shops in the Americas, primarily in the United States (as of late 1997, there were 287). After the United Kingdom and United States, The Body Shop's third largest market is in Japan, whose imported natural cosmetics market is rapidly expanding and where The Body Shop is the major brand. There were 105 Body Shop outlets in Japan by fall of 1997.

EMPLOYMENT

The Body Shop has made efforts to improve employee development programs. In June 1997, the company broadened its pension and investment offerings to employees. They have modeled specific career paths and have adopted a strategy of diversity. Further improvements included more flexibility in working hours, a commitment to hiring more women in senior management positions, and employing more people from minority backgrounds and disabled persons. The company offers training for its employees at a center in London. Anyone in the company, including franchisees and their employees, can attend at no cost. According to one account, the emphasis is on the products themselves rather than selling the products. By the end of 1998, one of Roddick's goals was to "have implemented equality of opportunity monitoring systems that reflect best practices in relevant industries."

Roddick is the company's culture and its conscience. It is she who sets the tone for the entire company, including its political agenda, which some employees have, according to one 1993 article in *People* have found disagreeable. When Roddick announced the Body Shop's collective opposition to the Gulf War in 1991, she bigfooted a protest within the company. Indeed, when asked if there's room for political diversity at the Body Shop, Roddick replies, "Not much. If you don't want to be part of this kind of social activism, you can work for Coors beer."

SOURCES OF INFORMATION

Bibliography
"Body Shop Chief to Step Down." *The New York Times,* 13 May 1998.

Brock, Pope. "Anita Roddick." *People Weekly,* 10 May 1993.

Davidson, Andrew. "Anita Roddick." *Management Today,* March 1996.

Elmer-Dewitt, Philip. "Anita the Agitator." *Time,* 25 January 1993.

Fallon, James. "Body Shop's Operating Deficit Grows." *WWD,* 9 May 1997.

Lee, Julian. "Body Shop Axes Top Global Role." *Marketing,* 31 July 1997.

Masako Fukuda. "Cosmetics Put on a More Natural Face." *Nikkei Weekly,* 15 September 1997.

Roell, Sophie. "US Headache as Boss Quits." *Investors Chronicle,* 13 February 1998.

Wallace, Charles P. "Can the Body Shop Shape Up?" *Fortune,* 15 April 1996.

For an annual report:
on the Internet at: http://www.the-body-shop.com/values/values97.pdf **or** write: The Body Shop, Sharon Sims, Watersmead Littlehampton, West Sussex BN176LS

For additional industry research:
Investigate companies by their Standard Industrial Classification Codes, also known as SICs. The Body Shop's primary SICs are:

2844 Perfumes, Cosmetics, and Other Toilet Preparations

5999 Miscellaneous Retail Stores, NEC

The Boeing Company

FOUNDED: 1916

Contact Information:
HEADQUARTERS: 7755 E. Marginal Way S
    Seattle, WA 98108
PHONE: (206)655-2121
FAX: (206)655-7004
URL: http://www.boeing.com

OVERVIEW

The Boeing company has been the leading aircraft manufacturer in the world for 30 consecutive years. It was also among the top three U.S. exporters for five consecutive years beginning in 1990. The company's primary businesses are commercial aircraft construction, defense and space, and computer services. The company successfully juggled the continuing need for commercial passenger airliners with its defense contracts, which account for an estimated 30 percent of its business as a result of the company's merger with McDonnell Douglas in 1997. Boeing works with companies such as Lockheed Martin, Sikorsky, and Bell Helicopter Textron, and is the leading contractor for NASA.

COMPANY FINANCES

Operating revenues for 1997 were $45.8 billion, compared with $35.5 billion in 1996 and $33.0 billion in 1995. The higher revenues for 1997 reflect increased deliveries in both the Commercial Aircraft and the Information, Space, and Defense Systems segments, as well as 1997 operations of the aerospace and defense units acquired from Rockwell International Corporation in December 1996. Of 1997 revenues, commercial aircraft generated $26.9 billion, or 59 percent of the company's total, compared to 56 percent ($19.9 billion) in 1996 and 53 percent ($17.5 billion) in 1995. Information, Space, and Defense Systems segments accounted for $18.1 billion in 1997 sales, compared to $14.9 billion in 1996 and $14.8 billion in 1995. Remaining sales were accounted for by Boeing's customer and commercial financing divisions among others.

Boeing stock was trading around $48.00 per share in mid-1998. The company's 52-week high was $60.50, and its 52-week low was $42.81. Boeing's five-year high was also $60.50, but its five-year low was $16.69. Boeing's earnings per share were down, at $.63 per share by year end 1997, compared to $1.92 in 1996.

ANALYSTS' OPINIONS

Analysts were divided over what rating to grant Boeing Company stock, some recommending shareholders simply hold onto what they own, an equal number recommending a "moderate buy" rating, and just as many recommending the company as a "strong buy." While the company realized net losses of $178 million in 1997, some of that loss was due to outlays needed to fund Boeing's acquisition of the McDonnell Douglas Long Beach commercial aircraft division, a venture not nearly as successful as its aerospace operations. Boeing also had to absorb $1.6 billion in losses as a result of production problems. Sales and operating revenues still rose by $10 billion, however, and the company was successfully addressing recent production issues.

HISTORY

Bill Boeing and Conrad Westervelt built an airplane at Seattle's Pacific Aero Products in 1916. The next year, the company became the Boeing Airplane Company. Throughout its history The Boeing Company has successfully provided air power for decades of defense contracts, beginning in World War I when the company built flight trainers for the United States Navy.

To bide its time between world wars, the company embarked on air mail service. It established the first international air mail route between Seattle and neighboring British Columbia. Other routes were developed starting in 1927. Boeing purchased several companies in the late 1920s, all in aviation-related businesses. Bill Boeing and Frederick Rentschler combined their businesses in 1929 into a firm called United Aircraft and Transport. The advent of regulations for air mail services led to the formation of United Airlines, and Boeing Airplane continued as an aircraft manufacturer.

Boeing has also seen American consumers through the birth and adolescence of commercial passenger airline travel. The company built many of the most popular commercial airliners between 1935 and 1965 including the PanAm 314 Clipper and the 747 Jumbo Jet. Boeing also brought the first pressurized cabin to market, the Model 307 Stratoliner.

The downsizing and consolidation within the modern aircraft industry has affected Boeing, which has integrated competitor companies into its operations. Boeing

FINANCES:

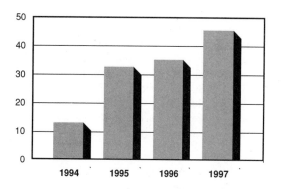

Boeing
Sales, 1994-1997
(billion dollars)

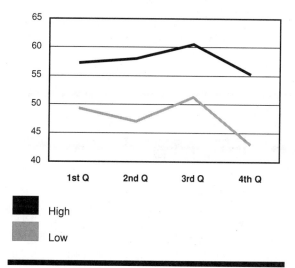

Boeing
1997 Stock Prices
(dollars)

and Rockwell completed a merger of their defense and aerospace units in 1996, and Boeing completed its merger with McDonnell Douglas Corp. on August 1, 1997.

Boeing experienced some difficulties getting approval from Europe on its merger with McDonnell Douglas. The European Union was concerned about Airbus Industrie, a French consortium and Boeing's only major competitor, and its continued viability if the merger went through. Boeing did finally get approval from the European Union Commission. However, the company had to sign nonexclusive contracts for the next decade in order to do so.

FAST FACTS:
About The Boeing Company

Ownership: Boeing is a publicly owned company traded chiefly on the New York Stock Exchange. Additional U.S. exchanges that trade Boeing stock are the Boston, Chicago, Cincinnati, Pacific, and Philadelphia Stock Exchanges. Boeing common stock is also listed on the Amsterdam, Brussels, London, Swiss, and Tokyo stock exchanges.

Ticker symbol: BA

Officers: Philip M. Condit, Chmn. & CEO, 57; Harry C. Stonecipher, Pres. & COO, 61; Theodore J. Collins, Sr. VP, Gen. Counsel, & Secretary, 61; Boyd E. Givan, Sr. VP & CFO, 61

Employees: 238,000

Chief Competitors: Boeing is a manufacturer of commercial jetliners and military aircraft and is one of the largest aerospace companies in the world. Its primary competitors include: Airbus; Bombardier; Daimler-Benz; Lockheed Martin; Raytheon; Rockwell International; and Thiokol.

STRATEGY

One of Boeing's primary goals, according to its 1997 annual report, was to "build a position of leadership in information, space, and defense markets comparable to the one we have long held in commercial aircraft." The company went after that goal using substantial internal investment and through strategic acquisitions and mergers. During 1997, Boeing's Information, Space & Defense Systems Group (ISDS) accounted for 40 percent of total company sales, partially due to contributions of a full year of revenues from the aerospace and defense operations acquired from Rockwell International in December 1996.

In order to meet incredibly high demand from the industry (which more than doubled), Boeing also had to create and maintain a focus on work process improvements and the flow of parts and materials. The company was building a major initiative to vastly simplify the aircraft configuration process for customer specifications. Its new system was also designed to simplify processes used to schedule and order parts and manage inventory.

INFLUENCES

Competitive pressures and lower fares for personal travel caused a long-term downward trend in passenger revenue yields worldwide. And in Asia, recessionary economies, reduced business travel, and devalued currency contributed to sharply reduced revenues. One example occurred in Indonesia, where three Boeing 737s built for Garuda Indonesia Airlines remained grounded in the United States until the Indonesian government could pay for them. As a result of these factors, and price pressure on the Boeing products, the company needed major productivity gains to ensure a favorable market position.

Another factor influencing Boeing's performance in 1997-1998 was the sudden increase in demand for Boeing commercial jets, just as Boeing executives were concentrating instead on the company's expansion of its aerospace division, and its related acquisitions of Rockwell and McDonnell Douglas. The problem was so bad, that as it was stated in the *Wichita Business Journal,* "The Boeing Co. has so many manufacturing orders, that if each airplane were built one at a time, the last would be completed by people not yet born." Not only were Boeing's production methods an area for needed improvement, but parts shortages were as well. To rectify the problem, Boeing began working with vendors on improved production processes, helping to alleviate further shortages.

In May of 1998, Boeing was experiencing additional difficulties, this time as a result of damaged wiring in its 737s. According to *The New York Times,* half of all Boeing 737s inspected on May 11 alone showed wear in the fuel pump wiring. The identified flaw not only resulted in grounded planes pending inspection, but opened up the possibility of investigation of Boeing's role in the explosion of a Philippine Airlines aircraft on a Manila runway in 1990, and TWA Flight 800 as well. The TWA flight, however, was on a 747, and the identified flaws were found only on Boeing's 737s.

CURRENT TRENDS

Boeing's direction for the late 1990s and into the next millennium was greater diversifaction as a company. What has helped the company to do this is improved balance between aerospace products. Prior to the McDonnell Douglas merger, Boeing had a 3-to-1 ratio between commercial jetliners and all of its other products in revenue generation. In 1997, that ratio became 3-to-2. Boeing equates this better balance with "greater stability and agility." When one market is down, the company could somewhat rely on another to be up. This gave Boeing more latitude to deploy people from one sector to another, wherever the need arose.

Boeing identified "fast growth" as its new motto in the commercial aircraft business, as a result of strong growth in airline traffic, record airline profits, and the need to replace aging aircraft. The outlook for military aircraft and missiles business also looked promising, and Boeing hoped to capitalize on development of next-generation aircraft and missile programs for the U.S. military agencies.

PRODUCTS

The Boeing Company has a line of planes designed for customer and cargo uses ranging from the 737 to the 777—the best selling jetliner of this line was the Boeing 737. The company also manufacturers defense and space aircraft such as the CH-47 Chinook helicopter and the F-22 fighter (built with Lockheed Martin) and the V-22 Osprey tilt-rotor aircraft (built with Bell Helicopter Textron). It also provides information systems and management services. Other aerospace products Boeing builds include electronic and defense systems, missiles, rocket engines, launch vehicles, and advanced information and communication systems.

CORPORATE CITIZENSHIP

The Boeing Company feels strongly about corporate citizenship, and focuses its efforts on education, health and human services, the arts, and civic participation. 1997 company contributions totaled $51.3 million. Including contributions from Boeing employees, total contributions were more than $90 million. Boeing employees also donated time and service to local communities.

Of company contributions, $16 million was given to promote education. Boeing works with educational institutions and students at all levels, and places special emphasis on enhancing engineering curricula at U.S. colleges and universities. Boeing also offers internships to students starting at the eleventh grade level.

Boeing is an environmentally conscious company. In 1997 it was testing alternative paint primers that did not contain toxic chemical compounds. And in September of 1997, the EPA honored Boeing with its Region IX Pollution Prevention Award for "reducing and eliminating the generation of pollutants at their source." Boeing also worked with the United Nations Environmental Programme, sponsoring a conference in India that focused on ozone-depleting gas emissions in the aviation industry.

GLOBAL PRESENCE

The Boeing Company serves customers in 145 countries. The company has endured its share of criticism from its increase in outsourcing parts and assemblies to Chinese companies despite continued tension between the United States and China. Boeing operates one of the

CHRONOLOGY:
Key Dates for The Boeing Company

1916: Founded

1917: Names the company the Boeing Airplane Company

1927: Starts establishing air mail routes

1929: Combines with another company to form United Aircraft and Transport

1933: Introduces the first all metal airliner

1934: Antitrust laws split company into United Air Lines, United Aircraft, and Boeing Airplane Company

1941: First B-17s see combat

1945: The *Enola Gay,* a B-29, drops the world's first atomic bomb on Hiroshima

1954: Develops the Dash 80

1958: First passenger jet, the 707, is introduced

1962: Two 707 models begin to serve as "Air Force 1"

1967: The first flight of the 737 takes place

1969: The 747 flies for the first time

1970: Establishes Boeing Computer Services

1987: Buys some of ARGOSystems

1989: First V-22 Osprey flies

1990: Announces plans to build the 777

1993: NASA choooses Boeing Defense & Space Group as a contractor for the Space Station

1994: Boeing becomes number one U.S. aerospace firm in total sales; first flight of the 777

1995: A 69-day labor strike is waged against Boeing

1996: Acquires aerospace and defense units from Rockwell International

1997: Merges with McDonnell Douglas

world's largest aircraft spare parts centers at Beijing Capital Airport. Comparable to Boeing facilities in London and in Singapore, they are able to ship urgent orders from among 35,000 parts in just 2 hours. According to Boeing's web site, "In addition to Boeing parts, the center stocks parts from 25 suppliers, provides support for com-

TO BOLDLY GO. . .

The Starship Enterprise must have been built by Boeing. Who else would Starfleet trust to build the vessels needed for "exploring strange new worlds" and "seeking out new life and new civilizations"? Who else has Boeing's track record of developing space systems? From almost the very beginnings of the American space program, Boeing has been there.

Boeing's involvement began in earnest in 1960 when its Delta II rocket was launched, carrying the Echo 1A satellite into orbit. Then in 1966 and 1967, the Boeing-built Lunar Orbiters circled the moon, photographing the surface in order to help NASA choose a safe landing site for the Apollo 11 astronauts. The astronauts reached the moon with the help of the 363-foot-tall Saturn V rocket. Its development was integrated by Boeing, which also made the first stage booster. It was 138 feet high and had 7.5 million pounds of thrust—the equivalent of 130 of today's most powerful jet engines. The Saturn V was used 13 times—not once failing.

But Boeing did not just help the astronauts get to the moon, it also helped them get around once they got there. The Lunar Roving Vehicles, built by Boeing in only 17 months, were used on the last three Apollo missions. The rovers looked like modified dune buggies and enabled the astronauts to travel more than 20 miles from the landing site. The vehicles operated without a problem in temperatures that ranged from minus 200 to plus 200 Fahrenheit degrees. To this day the rovers are still parked on the lunar surface.

Boeing's involvement in the lunar missions might have been its most spectacular moment, yet it remains heavily involved in the space program to this day. It continues to launch Delta rockets, and it has a large role to play in the Space Shuttle operations—Boeing processes all space suits and equipment, and McDonnell Douglas, with which it merged in 1997, developed the aft propulsion pods and structural parts of the boosters used to get the shuttles into orbit.

But probably the most exciting and interesting project that Boeing was involved in in the late 1990s was the International Space Station, the largest peacetime international scientific venture ever undertaken. Sixteen countries were participating. Boeing was the main contractor of the station that, when completed, will have a total area covering two football fields. It is scheduled to be completed in 2003 and will take more than 40 launches to complete. This massive undertaking is truly a venture that requires international cooperation. Says Doug Stone, Boeing Space Station program manager, "Space Station is about people of all walks, all races, many political systems all coming together to reach outside ourselves and accomplish something far greater than any of us could accomplish alone. To attempt what seems impossible, to reach beyond your grasp, to dare great deeds—this is an important part of being human." James T. Kirk couldn't have said it better himself.

ponent repair and overhaul, and provides logistics training for airlines." These policies, of course, have been decried by United States labor unions. However, Boeing sees China as a market with incredible growth potential. The Chinese economy has been growing more than twice as quickly as North America or Europe, and was expected to be the world's largest within 20 years. Air travel within China has also been growing rapidly, at a rate of approximately 20 percent each year. Given those numbers, Boeing foresees a market worth $124 billion (and for 1,900 commercial aircraft) over the next 20 years, and hopes to capitalize on that growth.

EMPLOYMENT

Boeing has had its share of labor problems, including a bitter strike that lasted 69 days in 1995, resulting in $2 billion in financial losses to the company as well as substantial trickle-down losses to the numerous subcontractors and communities in which Boeing operates.

The cyclical nature of aircraft manufacturing is notoriously hard on workers, as evidenced by a suit brought against the company in 1995 by 18 former Boeing employees accusing the company of employment fraud. These people, hired in 1988 and 1989 at the end of the Boeing boom, contended Boeing misled job applicants the promised of secure new careers in the Puget Sound area as pre-flight mechanics and electricians in the Everett division. These people had, according to newspaper accounts, left homes in locations as distant as Georgia, Texas, and New York to work for the aircraft manufacturer. They contend they were promised at least five years of work; none worked for more than three years. Boeing contended none of these employees were provided with a contract or written statement promising them long-term employment, nor did they ask for a written guarantee.

Changes in technology have also resulted in worker woes. When Boeing shifted to using advanced design software, for example, that translated into the need for thousands fewer machinists to build each plane.

Once again on an upswing, at the end of 1996 Boeing was hiring at such a rapid pace that its suppliers' employees were being drained. According to the *Puget Sound Business Journal,* "One wag said the company will hire anyone who can pronounce 'machinist'." Worldwide employment was up to 238,000 at the end of 1997, compared to 211,000 in 1996 and 169,000 in 1995.

SOURCES OF INFORMATION

Bibliography

1997 Current Market Outlook. Seattle, WA: The Boeing Company: 1997.

Banks, Howard. "Slow Learner." *Forbes,* 4 May 1998.

The Boeing Company 1997 Annual Report. Seattle, WA: The Boeing Company, 1998.

"Boeing Corp. Moving Ahead and Flying High." *The Online Investor,* 4 August 1997. Available at: http://www.investhelp.com/ba_spotlight.shtml.

Brown, Leslie. "Former Boeing Workers Accuse Washington Jetmaker of Employment Fraud." *Knight-Ridder/Tribune Business News,* 16 May 1995.

Company Profile. Seattle, WA: The Boeing Company, 1995.

Dove, Laurie. "Boeing Turns Dilemma Into Success Story." *Wichita Business Journal,* 16 March 1998.

Hackney, Holt. "Boeing: Back on Course." *Financial World,* 18 January 1994.

Homes, Stanley. "Boeing's Dangerous Liaison." *Seattle Times,* 22 March 1998.

Ropelewski, Robert. "Boeing Keeps Sharp Focus on China." *Interavia Business & Technology,* November 1996.

Wald, Matthew L. "Checks of 737's Show More Damaged Wiring." *The New York Times,* 12 May 1998.

Wilhelm, Steve. "Boeing: Commercial Side Still the Growth Engine." *Puget Sound Business Journal,* 3 January 1997.

For an annual report:

on the Internet at: http://www.reportgallery.com/Boeing97 **or** telephone: (800)457-7723 **or** write: The Boeing Company, Mail Code 3T-33, PO Box 3707, Seattle, WA 98124-2207

For additional industry research:

Investigate companies by their Standard Industrial Classification Codes, also known as SICs. Boeing's primary SIC is:

3721 Aircraft

Borders Group, Inc.

FOUNDED: 1995

Contact Information:

HEADQUARTERS: 500 Washington St.
Ann Arbor, MI 48104
PHONE: (313)913-1100
FAX: (313)913-1965
URL: http://www.borders.com

OVERVIEW

Borders Group, Inc. owns two of the nation's top bookstore chains. Since 1992 Borders has been the number two bookseller in the nation, second only to Barnes & Noble. In 1998 Borders' consolidated sales reached $2.26 billion. This number represented a 15-percent increase over 1997 sales of $1.95 billion.

Each Borders Books & Music superstore stocks and sells hundreds of thousands of books, music, movies, foreign language tapes, and CD-ROMs. In addition, each superstore provides customers with coffee bars where they can read and socialize. Sales for the superstores in 1998 were up, rising to $1.26 billion. In contrast, sales for Waldenbooks were down to $968 million. The three retail stores under Borders Group, Inc. include Waldenbooks, Borders, and Planet Music, a CD superstore. As of 1998 there were 923 Waldenbooks, 203 Borders stores, and 3 Planet Music stores.

COMPANY FINANCES

Borders Group, Inc. earned 1997 revenues of $2.26 billion, up from 1996's $1.9 billion. The company's net income rose from $58 to $80 million over the same period. Approximately 56 percent of the company's revenues were generated by its Borders Books & Music superstores; 43 percent was generated by the company's mall stores; and the remaining 1 percent was derived from miscellaneous "other" sources. Sales for the first quarter ending April 26, 1998 were $545.3 million, an increase of 17.6 percent over sales of $463.6 million during the same period in 1997. Sales at Borders stores increased to $335.0 million, 27.1 percent more than first quarter revenues of $263.5 million in 1997. Waldenbooks sales were down from $197.3 million in the first quarter of 1997 to $191.7 million in first quarter 1998.

Borders stock was priced around $36.00 per share in mid-1998. Its 52-week high was $37.63, and the 52-week low for Border's stock was $21.88 per share. In fiscal year 1997 (ended January 31, 1998), Borders earned $.98 per share, a significant increase from 1996 earnings per share (EPS) of $.70. Analysts expected the company's earnings for the current fiscal year to rise to $1.22 per share and up to $1.52 per share in 1999, according to Zack's Investment Research. First quarter earnings for 1998 were $.05 per share, compared to $.04 per share for the same period during 1997.

ANALYSTS' OPINIONS

"What started as a 5,000-square-foot secondhand bookshop in 1971," wrote John Marks in *U.S. News & World Report,* "has grown into a $412-million chain of superstores that has profoundly altered the $17.5-billion book business. Big booksellers like Walden, B. Dalton and Crown have occupied real estate in shopping malls for years, but Borders and its chief rival, Barnes & Noble, offer readers massive selections in larger retail spaces. Borders's huge operations have become anchors for malls nationwide, a destination for shoppers rather than a digression. And alongside bestsellers, they display just about any title a book lover could want—from obscure works of religion by mystics like Meister Eckhardt, to new poetry by unknown authors, to a host of works from university presses."

However, this same company, with its origins as an independent bookseller, has been lambasted for the "chaining" of national book retailing, as small independents are unable to compete against the corporate giants that Barnes & Noble and Borders Books & Music have become. Regardless of the criticism, investment analysts were confident in Borders ability to earn profitable returns for shareholders. As reported in *The Detroit News* in 1997, "Book industry analysts on Wall Street have been issuing a stream of glowing recommendations. Amongst the most startling is the Borders' stock price, now near $44, will jump to as high as $69 within 12 months." "We consider Borders to be in the very elite group of high-quality retailers," said Linda Farquhar, a securities analyst for Alex Brown in New York. While stock has not risen quite that high in the year since that report, the company was performing well and was still considered a good investment by industry analysts. At least half of the analysts at Zack's Investment Research recommended a "strong buy" rating for the company, with remaining analysts recommending a rating of "moderate buy."

FINANCES:

Borders Group Sales, 1994-1997 (billion dollars)

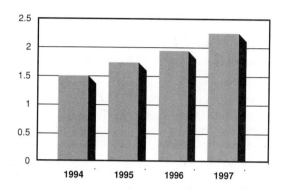

Borders Group 1997 Stock Prices (dollars)

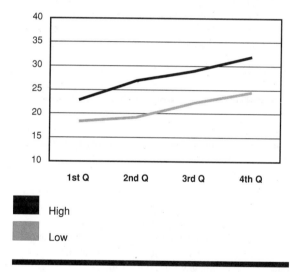

■ High

■ Low

HISTORY

Borders Books was founded in 1971 as a used and "serious" bookstore by Louis and Tom Borders in Ann Arbor, Michigan. The store evolved into a funky iconoclastic bookstore with a reputation for a wide and deep selection of books, as well as knowledgeable staff and excellent service. Fueled by the Ann Arbor store's success, Borders expanded into new markets, targeting the untapped suburban market. Eventually the company was opening stores nationwide. The company also founded Book Inventory Systems to assist them and other inde-

FAST FACTS:

About Borders Group, Inc.

Ownership: Borders is a publicly owned corporation traded on the New York Stock Exchange.

Ticker symbol: BGP

Officers: Robert F. DiRomualdo, Chmn. & CEO, 52; Bruce A. Quinnell, Pres. & COO, 48; George R. Mrkonic, VChmn., 44; Kenneth E. Scheve, Sr. VP Finance & CFO, 51

Employees: 24,300

Principal Subsidiary Companies: Subsidiaries of Borders Group, Inc. include Borders Online, Inc. (Borders.com); Borders Inc.; Waldenbooks; Planet Music; Borders Singapore PTY, Ltd.; and BGI (UK) Ltd.

Chief Competitors: As a major retailer of books, video, audio, and other education and entertainment media, Border's primary competitors include: Amazon.com; Barnes & Noble; Blockbuster; Books-A-Million; Camelot Music; Crown Books; Media Play; and Musicland.

pendent booksellers in tracking stock, but abandoned the software to concentrate on the opening of more retail stores in 1985.

In 1992 Borders was acquired by Kmart Corporation and consolidated with Waldenbooks, which Kmart had purchased in 1984, and Planet Music (purchased by Kmart in 1994 as CD Superstores) under the Borders Group. In April 1995, Borders bought its stock back from Kmart and took the company public as Borders Group, Inc.

The U.S. Justice Department began investigating Borders Group, as well as competitor Barnes & Noble, in the late 1990s on the grounds that both companies were conspiring to renegotiate contracts in malls where they had stores so that these two chains would be the only bookstores allowed in the mall.

STRATEGY

Borders reportedly owes its success to "one man's hard work and vision [that] had irrevocably stamped the store's bibliophilic culture." The manager of the original

Borders, Joe Gable, is credited with infusing his passionate love of books, dedication to his customers, and business acumen into a standard retailing practice employed now throughout Borders stores. As of 1995, Gable had managed the Ann Arbor bookstore for 21 years.

"To this day, Gable's ideas about marketing books resonate throughout the Borders chain," says Rich Flanagan, Borders president and CEO, according to a 1995 *U.S. News & World Report* article. "Gable doesn't like to display books face out on the shelf, for example. He believes that just one cover of a bestseller should be sufficient to let the customer know what the book is about. And he likes to place a table at the front of the bookstore and fill it with as many obscure books as bestsellers, so that lesser-known authors get a shot at the reader's attention, too."

The company's overall strategy during the late 1970s was to continue its growth and profitability through expansion of its superstores (in the United States and internationally), focusing on core operations and cost reduction in Waldenbooks stores, and strategically combining certain books and music operations. In the early 1990s Borders expanded stock to include music. Customers are able to listen to samples of selected items before purchasing. Also added to Borders stock were CD-ROMs and software programs. And for customers' pleasure, the company provides in-store coffee bars and hosts in-store appearances by authors, musicians, and artists.

INFLUENCES

A good deal of Borders' success, and why it continues to grow, is its focus on customer service. As syndicated columnist Jeffrey Gitomer reported about his experience at the bookseller, "What Ms. McCarter [sales associate] did in all three situations was select the option that was the most trouble for her—the most work for her—and the most satisfying for me. There's a correlation there, a Law of Service that should be the credo of every service driven organization in America: The more you do for the customer, the harder it is on you, but the more pleasing and the more memorable it will be to the customer. And the more loyal the customer is likely to be, the more they are likely to tell positive stories about you, read word-of-mouth advertising."

CURRENT TRENDS

Borders Books is at the crux of Borders Group Inc.'s operations. The company opened 41 of its superstores in 1995, another 41 stores in 1996, and 40 more in 1997. Each of these has an average of 30,000 square feet of both books and music.

Waldenbooks, still surviving in the 1990s, also had its own publishing company, Longmeadow Press. The 175 classics, special-interest books, and calendars published by the company each year generates about 2 percent of Waldenbooks' sales because of the high profit margins on these products, according to a 1995 report by *Knight-Ridder/Tribune Business News.* Waldenbooks also had better name branding that year than Borders Books and Music, which was predicted to help its sales. Despite this, the company closed 110 Waldenbooks in 1995 and an additional 31 stores closed in 1996. Additional closings were planned—by the year 2000, the company expected to run between 800 and 850 stores. As of 1998, there were 923.

Borders latest venture, scheduled for full-scale launch in Summer 1998 was Borders.com, run by subsidiary Borders Online, Inc. This web site, the company's online book store, was launched in direct competition with established online booksellers Amazon.com and chief rival Barnes & Noble. Amazon and Barnes & Noble had been offering online services for more than a year when Borders finally made its unofficial debut on the Web in May 1998, with its official "opening" scheduled for a couple of months later. According to Joe Nickell in *Wired,* analysts at Forrester Research attributed the delay to the company being caught "with its pants down." He implied the company was not ready with the technology necessary to compete or it would not have waited so long to do so. Scott Wilder, Borders.com's director of online services, seemed confident that the company would be able to compete on a level playing field despite its late entrance to the industry. He claimed that Borders.com would, by the time of its official launch, bring together more titles in many different media than its competitors, specifically referring to the ability to search the books, movie, and audio databases simultaneously for titles that could be found in all three areas.

CHRONOLOGY:

Key Dates for Borders Group, Inc.

1971: Borders is founded by Louis and Tom Borders as a single used book store in Ann Arbor, Michigan

1985: The Borders brothers open the first prototype superstore

1988: Robert DiRomualdo joins Borders to help the store expand

1992: Kmart Corporation purchases Borders

1994: Waldenbooks, another Kmart subsidiary, and Borders join to form Borders Group, Inc.

1995: Borders buys back its stock from Kmart and goes public

nizations—to assist their fundraising efforts. And all Borders stores schedule Borders Benefit Days through which Borders donates to a nonprofit group a portion of sales to its members." Also in support of education, Borders offers additional discounts to teachers of students from pre-school though high school. Additionally, in 1995 Borders contributed $1,000 to the National Endowment for the Arts for every new Borders store opened.

PRODUCTS

Products sold by Borders Group, Inc. include books, music, videos, and other media. Products are marketed through Borders Books & Music, Waldenbooks, Planet Music, and Borders.com.

CORPORATE CITIZENSHIP

Borders works to support the arts and education. Each store has a staff member committed to community relations. They provide children's programs, educational lectures, readings, and music performances. According to the Borders, Inc. site on the World Wide Web, "Community Relations Coordinators also work with local groups on projects to benefit their communities. For example, each CRC works with local nonprofit organizations—particularly schools, libraries, and literacy orga-

GLOBAL PRESENCE

Borders was shifting its focus during the late 1990s to international expansion. As of mid-1998, the company had operations in the United Kingdom and Singapore. The store in Singapore opened November 1, 1997, and met with a level of success the company did not anticipate. Though the country had been experiencing an economic slump and retail sales were at historic lows, Borders found itself faced with a different problem. The 130 employees hired to run the store weren't enough to cope with the new store's business volume. According to Ben Dolven, "The place was usually packed by the afternoon, lines lengthened in front of the cash registers, and by the end of most evenings, staff were scrambling to reshelve the piles of perused books scattered all over the 31,000-square-foot store." Borders hired 70 new employees, including a "shelving crew" to handle the volume, which has since stabilized but remains higher than Borders stores in the United States.

EMPLOYMENT

Since opening, Borders has hired educated and knowledgeable book and music lovers who can offer exceptional service to their customers, including help locating hard-to-find titles and free gift wrapping. The company's hiring process includes initial considerations of education, experience, and customer service abilities. However, Borders also analyzes applicants' performance on a written examination testing their knowledge of material found in the stores.

Borders Books has had its share of problems in attempting to keep a uniform, yet independent corporate culture intact, evidenced perhaps best by its union woes. Attempts by various retail stores to unionize labor have been met with varying degrees of success. Similar organizing efforts at a Borders Books & Music store in Chicago under the auspices of United Food and Commercial Workers International Union (UFCW) in the fall of 1996—and with the support of *Roger & Me* director and *TV Nation* creator Michael Moore—met with success. A total of three stores were unionized as of 1997.

SOURCES OF INFORMATION

Bibliography

"Borders Group Announces First Quarter Results." Borders Group, Inc. Press Release, 13 May 1998.

Dolven, Ben. "Find the Niche: Borders and Starbucks Find Success in Singapore." *Far East Economic Review,* 26 March 1998.

Elmer, Vickie. "Borders Plays Hero, Waldenbooks the Victim in Bookstore Suspense Story." *Knight-Ridder/Tribune Business News,* 14 May 1995.

Ewell, Christian. "Workers Accuse Borders Books & Music Workers of Firing Union Supporter." *Knight-Ridder/Tribune Business News,* 28 June 1996.

Gitomer, Jeffrey. "When Confronted With Service Options, Go For the Hardest Way," June 1997. Available at http://www.BordersGroupInc.com/4.0/index.html.

Kinsella, Bridget. "Borders Chicago Store Goes Union." *Publishers Weekly,* 7 October 1996.

Marks, John. "How Borders Reads the Book Market." *U.S. News & World Report,* 30 October 1995.

———. "Union Drive Grows at Borders - with Push from Author Moore." *Publishers Weekly,* 25 November 1996.

Nickell, Joe. "Quietly Opening the Borders." *Wired,* 4 June 1998. Available at http://www.wired.com/news/news/business/story/12718.html.

Preddy, Melissa. "Borders Is a Best Seller on Wall St.: Analysts Wild About Retailer." *The Detroit News,* 16 February 1997. Available at http://www.BordersGroupInc.com/4.0/1997/4.3.1.html.

For an annual report:

email requests to: cpadxp@borders.com **or** fax to: (734)477-4538 **or** write: Borders Group, Inc. Investor Relations, 100 Phoenix Dr., Ann Arbor, MI 48108

For additional industry research:

Investigate companies by their Standard Industrial Classification Codes, also known as SICs. Border's primary SICs are:

5735 Book Stores

5942 Record and Prerecorded Tape Stores

Bristol-Myers Squibb Company

FOUNDED: 1887

OVERVIEW

Bristol-Myers Squibb is one of the largest pharmaceutical companies in the United States. The company has three core business groups: Worldwide Medicines, Nutritionals and Medical Devices, and Worldwide Beauty Care. The pharmaceutical division (part of the Worldwide Medicines group) accounted for 60 percent of the company's revenues in 1998. That division focused on the development of cardiovascular, anti-infective, and anticancer drugs during the late 1990s.

Bristol-Myers Squibb competes with many pharmaceutical companies, such as Merck, Ciba-Geigy, and Pfizer, and with consumer product companies, such as Procter & Gamble and Gillette. The company's strength is attributed to its wide range of products and competitive positioning in the market. The company's future lies in maintaining and expanding its core product lines, developing new products, and expanding through licensing, partnerships, collaborations, and acquisitions.

Contact Information:
HEADQUARTERS: 345 Park Ave.
New York, NY 10154-0037
PHONE: (212)546-4000
FAX: (212)546-4020
URL: http://www.bms.com

COMPANY FINANCES

Bristol-Myers Squibb earned 1997 revenues of $16.7 billion, up from $15 billion in 1996. The company's net income also rose, from $2.8 billion in 1996 to $3.2 billion in 1997. Almost 60 percent of sales—approximately $11 billion—were generated in the United States. By product segment, the company's pharmaceuticals earned the largest percentage, 60 percent of revenues ($9.9 billion); nutritional products earned $1.9 billion (11 percent); medical devices earned $1.8 billion

FAST FACTS:

About Bristol-Myers Squibb Company

Ownership: Bristol-Myers Squibb is a publicly owned company traded on the New York Stock Exchange.

Ticker symbol: BMY

Officers: Charles A. Heimbold, Jr., Chmn. & CEO, 64; Michael F. Mee, Sr. VP & CFO, 55; Charles G. Tharp, Sr. VP, Human Resources, 46; Kenneth E. Weg, Exec. VP & Pres., Worldwide Medicines Group, 59

Employees: 53,600

Principal Subsidiary Companies: Bristol-Myers Squibb's principal subsidiaries are: Bristol-Myers Products; Bristol-Myers Squibb Co. Industrial Div.; Bristol-Myers Squibb Co. Mead Johnson Nutritionals; Calgon Vestal Laboratories; ConvaTec; Clairol Inc.; Maxtrix Essentials; Edward Weck Inc.; Mead Johnson Pharmaceuticals; Westwood-Squibb Pharmaceuticals Inc.; and Zimmer Inc.

Chief Competitors: As a manufacturer and marketer of pharmaceuticals and healthcare products, Bristol-Myers Squibb's competitors include: Abbott Labs; American Home Products; Amgen; Ballard Medical; Bayer; Biogen; Biomet; Chiron Corp.; Ciba-Geigy; Danek Group; Dial; Dow Chemical; DuPont; Eli Lilly; Genentech; Gillette; Glaxo Wellcome; Glycomed; Hoechst; Immunex; Johnson & Johnson; L'Oreal; Merck; Mitek Surgical; Monsanto; Novo Nordisk; Pfizer; Pharmacia & Upjohn; Procter & Gamble; Rhone-Poulenc; Roche; St. Jude Medical; Sandoz; Schering-Plough; SmithKline Beecham; U.S. Surgical; and Warner-Lambert.

(11 percent); beauty care earned $1.7 billion (10 percent); and consumer medicines earned $1.3 billion (8 percent).

In 1997, Bristol-Myers Squibb earned $3.14 per share, up from earnings per share (EPS) of $2.80 in 1996. According to the company's first quarter reports, 1998 earnings per share (as of mid-1998) were $3.58. The company's stock was priced around $115 per share in mid-1998. Its 52-week high was $117, and its 52-week low was $71 per share.

ANALYSTS' OPINIONS

Analysts at Zack's Investment Research reported increased earnings per share for the company in mid-1998 (at $3.57 per share), and they expected the company's growth to continue even more rapidly. The firm projected earnings of $4.06 per share for Bristol-Myers Squibb during fiscal year 1999. However, recommendations for stock transactions were mixed, with about one-third of analysts recommending a "strong buy" rating for the company, another third recommending a "moderate buy," and remaining analysts recommending a "hold" rating. While the company's performance was clearly not expected to falter, stock prices were at historic highs, and some felt the company would not be able to sustain its growth rates.

HISTORY

Upon developing a plan for producing pure ether and chloroform, Dr. Edward Squibb founded Squibb in 1858. Dr. Squibb did fairly well, passing the business on to his sons in 1891. Squibb provided penicillin and morphine to troops during World War II. Mathieson Chemical bought the company in 1952, and Olin Industries bought Mathieson in 1953. Olin Mathieson Chemical was formed but Squibb retained its identity. During the late 1960s and early 1970s, Olin Mathieson Chemical reorganized and the company's name was changed to Squibb Corporation. During the late 1970s, Squibb introduced Capoten, a major cardiovascular drug; Capoten was the first drug to attack a specific disease-causing agent and was an important product for Squibb.

William Bristol and John Myers bought the Clinton Pharmaceutical Company in 1887. The company originally sold pharmaceuticals in bulk quantities. In 1900, the company incorporated and changed its name to Bristol-Myers. Some of the company's early products included Sal Hepatica, a mineral salt laxative, and Ipana, a toothpaste containing a disinfectant. During World War II, Bristol-Myers manufactured penicillin for the Allied armed forces. Bristol-Myers continued to grow and began to expand internationally during the 1950s. The company expanded partially through acquisition, obtaining companies such as Clairol, Mead Johnson, and Zimmer. New drugs for treating cancer and anxiety were introduced in the 1970s and 1980s.

In 1989, Bristol-Myers acquired Squibb Corporation, forming Bristol-Myers Squibb. Together, the companies offered a strong consumer health product line, an expanding prescription drug line, biomedical research facilities, and a large budget for further research. When formed, the new company became the second largest pharmaceutical company in the world. Since then, the company has met with more success in product development.

In 1996, Bristol-Myers Squibb introduced Pravachol, a drug that lowers cholesterol, and it became the company's second drug to earn more than $1 billion in sales. In 1997, Bristol-Myers Squibb acquired the rights to develop two protease-inhibitor compounds as possible treatments for HIV and AIDS from Novartis. It also began offering Excedrin Migraine—the first and only over-the-counter migraine medication to get FDA approval.

STRATEGY

Bristol-Myers Squibb's strategy is to focus on the customer. New products are researched and new partnerships are formed to offer customers the broadest line of health and personal care products possible. The company has also developed a policy called "segment selling." Sales teams are structured to offer a diverse mix of products to meet customers' needs. Segment selling has achieved cost-saving benefits and has given sales representatives more time to promote other products.

Bristol-Myers Squibb represents its products to customers as "answers." For example, the company was committed to working with Medicaid programs, and to facilitate that effort, it developed an econometric matrix demonstrating cost-effective answers to healthcare dilemmas. Presentations were made to Medicaid officials to illustrate how the use of pharmaceuticals could control healthcare costs and how budgets would be affected. As a result, both Florida and Texas decided not to put restrictions on monthly per patient spending on prescription drugs.

In 1998, the company expanded its line of beauty aids with the purchase of privately held Redmond Products, maker of Aussie natural hair care products.

INFLUENCES

Bristol-Myers Squibb has faced many challenges throughout its history. The company was challenged in the early 1960s when Johnson & Johnson introduced the over-the-counter nonaspirin pain reliever, Tylenol. Bristol-Myers Squibb fought back with its introduction of Datril and priced it below Tylenol. Still, during the late 1960s, growth was slow and many new products were not selling. The company decided to concentrate on advertising its core brands and increasing its healthcare products line. This line was expanded with the acquisitions of Zimmer Manufacturing, an orthopedic and surgical products company, and Unitek Corporation, a supplier of dental equipment.

In the mid-1970s, there was growing concern for the amount of flourocarbons being emitted into the atmosphere with the use of aerosol sprays. Bristol-Myers Squibb responded by stepping up advertising of its Ban roll-on type deodorant. Subsequently, Ban became the

CHRONOLOGY:

Key Dates for Bristol-Myers Squibb Company

1858: Dr. Squibb establishes Squibb, producing pure ether and chloroform

1887: William Bristol and John Myers buy a failing pharmaceutical company in New York called Clinton Pharmaceutical Company

1898: Clinton Pharmaceutical becomes Bristol-Myers Company

1900: Bristol-Myers incorporates

1928: Bristol-Myers and other drug companies become a part of Drug, Inc., a newly formed holding company

1933: Drug, Inc. folds

1952: Mathieson Chemical buys Squibb and Olin Industries buys Mathieson

1959: Bristol-Myers acquires Clairol

1984: Upjohn and Bristol-Myers sign an agreement allowing Bristol-Myers to develop Nuprin, a nonprescription form of ibuprofen

1989: Bristol-Myers merges with Squibb Corporation to form Bristol-Myers Squibb

1997: Bristol acquires the rights to develop possible treatments for HIV and AIDS; releases Excedrin Migraine

number one selling deodorant. Similarly, in 1977, the National Cancer Institute discovered a link between a common hair colorant ingredient, 2-4 DAA, and cancer in laboratory rats. Bristol-Myers responded by offering a new line of hair-coloring products and removed the questionable ingredient from its original line of products.

Product-tampering became a problem in the early 1980s, and Bristol-Myers Squibb's Excedrin was one such product that was affected. In 1983, Bristol-Myers introduced tamper-resistant packaging for its capsule products in response to the new Food and Drug Administration regulation. Tampering occurred again in 1986, this time causing two deaths. Bristol-Myers recalled the Excedrin capsules and pulled all of its nonprescription capsules from shelves. Capsules were replaced with caplets, a capsule-shaped pill with a special coating. The company became the second in its industry to discontinue the use of capsules in the over-the-counter market.

One of Bristol-Myers Squibb's most successful drugs was Taxol, the company's brand name for paclitaxel, a trace compound found during the 1970s that National Cancer Institute researchers discovered stops the growth of some cancerous tumors. Though the company did not discover the drug, it finished clinical studies for the Institute in cooperation with Hauser, Inc., a Colorado lab that worked out issues related to extracting the drug from its source—yew trees. Though the company couldn't get a patent since it did not invent the drug, it received five years of exclusive marketing from the government as a reward for its efforts in product development. Since its release, Taxol has turned into an incredibly successful method of treatment for ovarian and breast cancer—as well as a cash cow for Bristol-Myers Squibb. In 1997, the drug had worldwide sales of $941 million and became the company's second-largest seller. It was estimated that Taxol accounted for up to 15 percent of 1997 profits of $3.2 billion.

CURRENT TRENDS

The demand for hair color and hair care products increased throughout the 1980s and 1990s as a result of the expanding middle-aged market. Taking advantage of a burgeoning market, the company's Clairol subsidiary stepped up advertising and revamped its Nice 'n Easy and Ultress brands. The Ultress brand featured a more contemporary package and supermodel Linda Evangelista as its spokesperson.

Bristol-Myers Squibb's subsidiary Zimmer, Inc. was approved by the Food and Drug Administration in 1998 to manufacture and market a new formula for "cross-linked polyethylene." The formula, developed at the Massachusetts Institute of Technology (MIT), would improve wear performance on joint replacement components. Also in the medical arena, the company was sponsoring a public awareness initiative for diabetes. As part of this effort, Bristol-Myers Squibb was hoping to get at least 1 million Americans to get their blood sugar levels tested, as well as their level of risk for type 2 diabetes.

In mid-1998, Bristol-Myers Squibb also expected to launch a new "pharmaceutical robot" designed to mix compounds, perform experiments, and measure reactions. Named the "Haystack," this robot was expected to perform one month's worth of human experimentation in a single day. Bristol-Myers Squibb would join the ranks of Glaxo Wellcome, Smithkline Beecham, and Zeneca Agrochemicals, all of whom already use similar automation in product research and development.

PRODUCTS

Bristol-Myers Squibb has four product categories in three core business areas: prescription drugs and consumer health products (Worldwide Medicines group), medical devices and toiletries (Medical Devices group), and beauty aids (Worldwide Beauty Care and Nutritional group). In 1998, prescription drugs accounted for 60 percent of the company's total sales. The company's major pharmaceutical drugs include cardiovascular drugs such as Capoten, Corgard, Monopril, and Pravachol; cancer drugs such as Platinol, TAXOL, and VePesid; an antibiotic drug called Azactam; an antidiabetic drug named Glucophage; a cholesterol reducer called Questran; and an AIDS treatment drug named VIDEX. The consumer health products sector includes such products Bufferin, Excedrin, Comtrex, and Nuprin.

Popular brands of toiletries and beauty aids include Herbal Essences (shampoo and conditioner), Ban (deodorant), Keri (lotion), Miss Clairol (hair coloring), Nice 'n Easy (hair coloring), Theragran (vitamins), and Vavoom (hair sprays). Medical devices offered include products for minimally invasive surgery, as well as orthopedic and surgical instruments.

In 1995, Bristol-Myers Squibb's Mead Johnson Nutritionals subsidiary launched its Boost nutritional drink. The drink was targeted at active adults seeking quality calories in the quest to stay physically fit. Boost was a milk-based, lactose-free drink that was high in calcium and low in saturated fat with 25 vitamins and minerals. In 1998, Mead Johnson again sought to capitalize on this trend, introducing "Choice dm" nutrition bars and through its purchase of "Choco Milk," one of Mexico's leading nutritional supplements.

CORPORATE CITIZENSHIP

Bristol-Myers Squibb has always strongly supported medical research. In 1977, what is now known as the Bristol-Myers Squibb Unrestricted Biomedical Research Grants Program was established. The plan awarded grants to medical schools, hospitals, and research centers in the United States and around the world. The medical research community praised the program since it supported scientific research in a time of limited government assistance. The program also forged a better relationship between academic scientists and the pharmaceutical industry. Since 1984, the company has also offered its Fellowship Program in Academic Medicine for Minority Students. Through the program, more than 280 students were awarded grants of up to $6,000, which enable the students to spend 8-12 weeks studying under biomedical researchers.

Bristol-Myers Squibb also made concentrated efforts to "prevent and minimize pollution, to reduce accidents, conserve resources, and promote EHS [Environmental Health and Safety] protection, education, and technology transfer around the globe." Employees from varying disciplines within the company worked together to develop business improvements that would also prove beneficial to the environment.

GLOBAL PRESENCE

Bristol-Myers Squibb has a very strong global presence. With international sales representing almost 50 percent of its business, Bristol-Myers Squibb remains deeply committed to strengthening current and establishing new business relationships in the international market. The company's largest markets are in the United States, France, Japan, Germany, and Canada. Since growth has been slowing in mature markets such as the United States and Europe, Bristol-Myers Squibb continues its expansion plans to Eastern Europe, Latin America, and Asia. In some cases, Bristol-Myers Squibb has established warehousing systems, and in other cases the company has formed alliances with local or competing companies.

In China, the only means to conduct business was through the establishment of plant operations, and Sino-American Shanghai Squibb was formed as a result. The joint pharmaceutical venture made Bristol-Myers Squibb the first western pharmaceutical company to break into the Chinese market. Bristol-Myers Squibb's subsidiary Zimmer opened a teaching facility in Shanghai in 1994. The facility, located at the Shanghai Academy of Sciences, provided ongoing education in orthopedic surgery to Chinese surgeons.

Japan is the second largest market for Bristol-Myers Squibb. In 1994, the company opened a new research laboratory in Kanagawa to unite research efforts.

In 1994, a European market research study led Bristol-Myers Squibb to acquire A/S GEA Farmaceutisk Fabrik, a Scandinavian manufacturer of generic brand pharmaceuticals. The purchase increased Bristol-Myers Squibb's generic brand market share in Europe. With business opportunities continuing to grow in Russia and Eastern Europe, Bristol-Myers Squibb's subsidiaries have opened plants in Poland, Hungary, and the Czech Republic.

EMPLOYMENT

At Bristol-Myers Squibb, diversity was a clearly stated value. In 1996, the company produced a full re-

port devoted to the issue titled, "Diversity and Equal Opportunity at Bristol-Myers Squibb Company." Among efforts made by the company to further that corporate goal were minority fellowships, college and graduate internship programs, high school programs, minority recruitment, community program support, and financial assistance.

SOURCES OF INFORMATION

Bibliography

Barrett, William P. "Delaying Tactics." *Forbes,* 23 March 1998.

Bristol-Myers Squibb Company 1997 Annual Report. New York: Bristol-Myers Squibb Co., 1998.

"Bristol-Myers Squibb Company." *Hoover's Handbook of American Business 1996.* Austin, TX: The Reference Press, 1995.

"Bristol-Myers Squibb Company." *Hoover's Online,* 25 June 1998. Available at: http://ww.hoovers.com.

Bristol-Myers Squibb Company Home Page, 25 June 1998. Available at: http://www.bms.com.

Dennis, Kathryn. "Girl Talk: Bristol-Myers Squibb's Product Bias Shows Through Its Cyberclub for Women." *ADWEEK Eastern Edition,* 26 February 1996.

Gillis, Chris. "Pharmaceuticals, Shampoo and Logistics." *American Shipper,* October 1995.

Kuchinskas, Susan. "Drug Needle in the Haystack." *Wired News,* 17 February 1998.

Mirabile, Lisa, ed. *International Directory of Company Histories.* Detroit, MI: St. James Press, 1990.

Morrison, Shauna, ed. *Standard & Poor's 500 Guide.* New York: The McGraw-Hill Companies, Inc., 1996.

For an annual report:

on the Internet at: http://www.bms.com/financial/index.html **or** write: Secretary, Bristol-Myers Squibb Co., 345 Park Ave., New York, NY 10154-0037

For additional industry research:

Investigate companies by their Standard Industrial Classification Codes, also known as SICs. Bristol-Myers Squibb's primary SICs are:

2834 Pharmaceutical Preparations

2844 Perfumes, Cosmetics, and Other Toilet Preparations

3842 Orthopedic, Prosthetic, and Surgical Appliances and Supplies

Brunswick Corporation

FOUNDED: 1845

Contact Information:
HEADQUARTERS: 1 N. Field Ct.
    Lake Forest, IL 60045
PHONE: (847)735-4700
FAX: (847)735-4765

OVERVIEW

Brunswick Corporation is a leading multinational company in outdoor and indoor active recreation markets. Brunswick has a market presence in billiards, bowling, marine power, pleasure boating, fishing, camping, biking, and exercise equipment. Some of the best-known Brunswick brand names are Sea Ray and Bayliner boats, Force and Mariner outboard engines, Brunswick billiards tables and bowling products, Zebco fishing tackle, American Camper and Remington camping equipment, Igloo coolers, Roadmaster and Mongoose bicycles, Boston Whaler fishing boats, and LifeCycle, Hammer Strength, and ParaBody exercise equipment. Brunswick is the largest manufacturer in the United States of leisure and recreation products and the world's leading manufacturer of pleasure boats and equipment.

Brunswick is divided into six groups. These are BORG, BIRG, the Mercury Marine Group, the Sea Ray Group, and the U.S. Marine Division. The sixth division, Life Fitness, was acquired in 1997. The Marine segment has the largest dollar sales volume of recreational marine engines and pleasure boats in the world. Brunswick also operates one of North America's largest bowling chains.

Brunswick ranked as the largest corporation in the transportation equipment industry in *Fortune's* Fortune 500 Largest U.S. Corporations. In the late 1990s company revenues were $3.16 billion, ahead of the number-two ranking Harley-Davidson. Brunswick also ranked number one in boat building and repair in the 1990s. Brunswick was considered one of the top 10 most profitable public-recreation equipment companies in the late 1990s, competing with such companies as Harley-Davidson and K2. In 1996 the company was ranked one

BRUNSWICK

of the top leisure-time companies in the S&P 500. Those companies were ranked by sales growth, profit growth, returns, and profit margins. Brunswick was joined in the top five by Disney and Marriott, among others.

Brunswick has a leading position in 7 of the 10 most popular sports in the United States, based on participation. These include motor boating, billiards, fishing, bowling, camping, exercise with equipment, and bicycling. The only three in which Brunswick did not participate were basketball, swimming, and exercise walking.

COMPANY FINANCES

In 1997 Brunswick had a 16-percent increase in sales, a 21-percent increase in operating earnings, and a 15-percent increase in net earnings. Net earnings reached $214.2 million, with sales in recreation rising significantly with the acquisition of new companies. In 1996 operating earnings had risen 18 percent to $304.8 million, on sales of $3.2 billion (an increase of 9 percent). Large pleasure boats also had higher margins and strong sales due to extensive marketing. Brunswick's recreation segment added $113.8 million in 1996 and $397.6 million in 1997 to its sales. (Some of the increase was due to higher bowling center revenues.) The marine divisions posted increases in sales of $140.2 million in 1996 and $99.5 million in 1997. Brunswick's stock price ranged from $24 to $37 in 1997.

ANALYSTS' OPINIONS

The Federal Trade Commission dropped a four-year investigation into allegations of antitrust in the company's engine business in the late 1990s. Analysts had watched Brunswick struggle through some extremely rough water. In the 1980s, a hostile takeover was averted as Brunswick shed some of its divisions, but the corporation was left with much to adjust. By expanding into related recreational and leisure industries, Brunswick was able to offset losses when the marine segments hit a low point in their cycle.

HISTORY

John Brunswick came to the United States in 1834 when he was not quite 15 years old. He made his way to Cincinnati, where in 1845 he built one of the first billiard tables in the country. He founded the John M. Brunswick company that same year. Famous billiards players who played on Brunswick tables included Mark Twain, the Rockefeller family, Abraham Lincoln, Teddy Roosevelt, and the Vanderbilt family. Brunswick family members led

FINANCES:

Brunswick Corp. Net Sales, 1994-1997 (billion dollars)

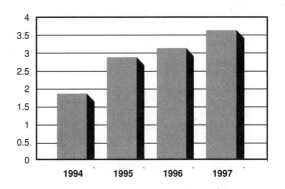

Brunswick Corp. 1997 Stock Prices (dollars)

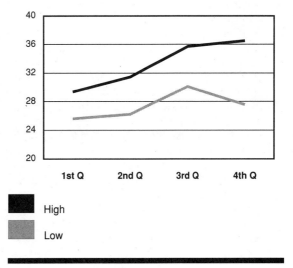

the company until 1966, priding themselves on the fine craftsmanship and dedication of John Brunswick. When John brought his half-brothers from Switzerland, he changed the name of the firm to J.M. Brunswick and Brothers. In 1872 they changed the name to J.M. Brunswick Billiard Manufacturing Company, welcoming son-in-law Moses Bensinger into the business. Moses Bensinger orchestrated a merger with the rival Julius Balke, and in 1884 the company was renamed Brunswick-Balke-Collender Company. They began making bar furnishings and bowling equipment toward the turn of the century. Moses Bensinger's son, Benjamin, led the com-

FAST FACTS:

About Brunswick Corporation

Ownership: Brunswick is a publicly owned company traded on the New York, London, Chicago, and Pacific Stock Exchanges.

Ticker symbol: BC

Officers: Peter N. Larson, Chmn. & CEO, 58, 1997 base salary $800,000; Peter B. Hamilton, CFO & Sr. VP, 51, 1997 base salary $400,000; Richard S. O'Brien, VP & Treasurer, 48; Kathryn J. Chieger, VP Corporate & Investor Relations, 49

Employees: 25,300

Principal Subsidiary Companies: Under the Brunswick umbrella are diverse companies. The Brunswick Outdoor Recreation Group (BORG), headquartered in Tulsa, Oklahoma, includes Zebco fishing equipment, Igloo coolers, Roadmaster and Mongoose bicycles, and American Camper and Remington camping equipment. The U.S. Marine Division, headquartered in Arlington, Washington, makes Bayliner, Maxum, Trophy, and Robalo boats. The Sea Ray Group, headquartered in Knoxville, Tennessee, includes Boston Whaler, Sea Ray, and Baja boats. The Mercury Marine Group, headquartered in Fond du Lac, Wisconsin, includes Mariner outboard motors, MerCruiser sterndrives and inboards, Force outboards, and Mercury outboards. The Life Fitness Division, headquartered in Franklin Park, Illinois, includes Life Fitness and Hammer Strength fitness equipment. The Brunswick Indoor Recreation Group (BIRG), headquartered in Lake Forest, Illinois, makes bowling and billiard equipment and owns/operates the Brunswick Recreation Centers.

Chief Competitors: Because of its diverse product mix, Brunswick competes with multinational companies in industries across the field of indoor and outdoor recreation. Primary competitors include: Outboard Marine, manufacturer of outboard motors and boats; K2, manufacturer of outdoor recreational goods; and Huffy Corp., bicycle manufacturer in a top market position. Since Brunswick is a leader in the leisure industry, some analysts would also consider these companies competitors: Walt Disney Company and Marriott International. A competitor in the public recreation equipment industry is Harley-Davidson, manufacturer of motorcycles.

pany into the burgeoning city of Chicago, where their factory north of the Chicago River filled a city block.

In the early 1900s Brunswick experimented with rubber tires, phonograph cases, and phonographs. Cab Calloway and Duke Ellington were among the recording stars who were recorded on the Brunswick label, which appeared on records into the 1950s. Eventually Brunswick sold the recording company to Warner Brothers. Benjamin's son Bob kept the company going from 1930 through the Great Depression.

The 1950s were marked by the tremendous success of bowling's Automatic Pinsetter. Earnings in 1954 were $700,000 on sales of $33 million, while in 1961 earnings were $45 million on sales of $422 million. Bob Bensinger's younger brother, Ted, started a period of acquisition, purchasing the boating and fishing giants Mercury and Zebco. In 1960 the company became Brunswick Corporation. Again new fields beckoned, and some brought turbulence to Brunswick. Sherwood Medical Industries became a leader in the manufacture of medical and laboratory supplies, but after a 1982 takeover battle Brunswick disposed of its medical business. Chairman Jack Reichert moved the focus back to leisure. In 1986 the company bought Bayliner marine and Ray Industries, (maker of Sea Ray) for nearly $1 billion.

Brunswick's leaders met with difficulties, not the least of which was the tremendous downturn in yachts in the 1980s. By 1996 the company's tides turned with its move into both camping and bicycling with the purchase of American Camper and Roadmaster Bicycles. In 1997 Brunswick bought Life Fitness for $314.9 million. Soon after Life Fitness bought Hammer Strength and Para Body Inc. Other successful Brunswick acquisitions include Igloo Products, manufacturer of ice chests and coolers; Flexible Flyer, maker of sleds; and Mongoose, bicycle maker.

Only 10 men have led the Brunswick Corporation in its 150 years. For most of its history the company was under family ownership. Peter N. Larson was named CEO in April 1995, and added the title of chairman that October. Larson had previously spent close to 20 years at Johnson & Johnson, following a period at Kimberly-Clark. Larson doubled capital spending between 1995 and 1997 and brought Brunswick to a comfortable lead in many of its markets.

STRATEGY

Brunswick met with success when its multilevel business was kept in close rein. When boat sales are weak, bowling, billiards, and fishing seem to pick up some of the slack in earnings. Brunswick began opening stores-within-stores at mass retailers including Kmart and Wal-Mart. Its aim was to group camping and fishing equipment together with related products, such as coolers.

INFLUENCES

Brunswick was an innovator that kept its finger on the pulse of society. Its billiards tables were among the first manufactured, and its automatic pinsetter changed the game of bowling forever. Brunswick made records in the industry's infancy, and even had success in the medical field. Ultimately, Brunswick found that a focus on its core of recreation kept the company on track. The economic downturn in the 1980s and the resulting steep decline of luxury boat purchases forced the company to spread out, seeking corporate income from other areas. Adapting to changes meant being willing to change even its core business. The introduction of cosmic bowling brought renewed strength to the sport and to Brunswick's role.

CURRENT TRENDS

Brunswick CEO Peter Larson aimed to increase sales in his recreation divisions to compensate for any weakness in the marine divisions. His goal was to have half of Brunswick's sales come from recreation by the year 2000, while in the late 1990s these sales accounted for less than 30 percent of the total. Strong and creative marketing improved results for 1998, despite lower demand for smaller boats and outboard engines. The Environmental Protection Agency mandated emissions for marine engines that were significantly lower beginning in 1998. As a result, Brunswick's 1997 costs were higher as the company changed over to direct-fuel-injection engines.

In 1997 some of Brunswick's advertisements emphasized the company's experience rather than each product's selling points. For example, a television advertisement for Bayliner boats mentioned nothing about the boat, and contained no dialogue. Instead, the spot showed a family in a Bayliner boat, video of exotic tropical fish, and the suggestion that this is a family experience at its best. In the fishing division, Zebco's web site aimed for multigenerational appeal. It encourages parents and grandparents to teach their children to fish, while attracting youngsters with a fishing game. Brunswick also strengthened its alliance with the Disney Company. Official boats of Disney World include Boston Whaler, Sea Ray, and Bayliner, as well as Water Mouse, a two-seat mini runabout.

PRODUCTS

Brunswick Indoor Recreation Group (BIRG) makes and sells billiards tables and accessories and bowling supplies. Brunswick Outdoor Recreation Group (BORG) makes camping, fishing, and bicycling equipment under the Igloo, Zebco, Remington, Ridehard, Hoppe's, Road-

CHRONOLOGY:
Key Dates for Brunswick Corporation

1845: Founded

1872: Company is renamed J.M. Brunswick Billiard Manufacturing Company

1884: Renamed again as Brunswick-Balko-Collender Company

1930: Bob Bensinger becomes president

1960: Becomes Brunswick Corporation

1977: Wins an innovation award at the International Marine Trades Exhibit and Conference

1986: Buys Bayliner marine and Ray Industries

1995: Peter N. Larson becomes Chairman and CEO

1996: Purchases American Camper and Roadmaster Bicycles; becomes an official sponsor of the Olympics

1997: Acquires LifeFitness

master, and Mongoose brands. The Mercury Marine Group makes outboard engines, such as Mariner and Force. The Sea Ray group makes pleasure boats and fishing boats, and jet and high-performance boats known as Baja, Boston Whaler, and Sea Ray. The U.S. Marine Division is known for saltwater fishing boats Trophy and Robalo, Bayliner pleasure boats, and Maxum pleasure boats. In 1977 Brunswick won an innovation award at the International Marine Trades Exhibit and Conference for its voice-activated Lazer trolling motor. The motor allows the angler to keep his hands occupied with fishing rather than driving the boat.

CORPORATE CITIZENSHIP

As a participant in the many communities that are home to Brunswick plants and headquarters, the corporation has been a good neighbor. Brunswick is best known in this arena as a sponsor of athletic events. In 1984 the company sponsored an international amateur bowling tournament in Las Vegas, Nevada, with competitors from 14 countries. In 1988 bowling was included as a demonstration sport at the Summer Olympic Games in Seoul, Korea, with Brunswick's sponsorship. In

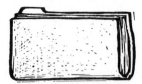

BOWLING—SPORT OR STATE OF MIND?

In the past few years, Brunswick has invested approximately $1 billion in "strategic acquisitions." What's their game? It's all in the numbers—the population numbers, that is. As far as disposable income is concerned, the 35-54 age group accounts for 51 percent of all consumer spending. In addition, Brunswick knows that it's the 45-64 age group (which includes some of the Baby Boom generation) that spends the most money on recreation gear and that is going to have the highest population growth in the next decade. So, just how many more bowling alleys will there be? How many more beer frames? How many more pairs of two-toned bowling shoes? Only time will tell.

Barcelona's 1992 summer games, Brunswick supplied recreational bowling and billiards for the athletes, and in the 1995 racing of America's Cup the company supplied support boats. As an official sponsor of the 1996 Olympics in Atlanta, Brunswick supplied 200 support boats for use in Savannah and Lake Lanier, Georgia.

For many years Brunswick has been involved in clean air requirements for pleasure boats. Mercury Marine developed the Optimax, an outboard engine that reduces emissions with quiet, smoke-free operation, direct fuel injection, and fuel economy that improved by 45 percent. The engine was developed to meet Environmental Protection Agency standards.

GLOBAL PRESENCE

BORG has a manufacturing plant in Mexico, BIRG has an active plant in Germany, and Brunswick operates joint ventures in Brazil, Hong Kong, Korea, Singapore, and Thailand. Mercury Marine has manufacturing facilities in Belgium and Mexico as well as joint ventures in Japan and China. Brunswick also has a 50-percent inter-

est in Nippon Brunswick K.K. International sales are primarily of marine products and bowling equipment. Most of Brunswick's international commerce is with Europe and the nations of the Pacific Rim. Foreign sales were $509 million in 1995, $438 million in 1996, and $506 million in 1997.

EMPLOYMENT

The 25,000 employees of Brunswick Corporation have vastly different working lives depending on the division of the company that employs them. Manufacturers of fishing and pleasure boats in Tennessee and makers of cardiovascular training equipment in Illinois may never see the workings of the Brunswick billiards equipment that led to the founding of the company.

SOURCES OF INFORMATION

Bibliography

Clemans, John. "Tarpon Time." *Motor Boating & Sailing,* December 1995.

"Forbes 500s." *Forbes,* 2 April 1997.

"Fortune 500 Largest U.S. Corporations." *Fortune,* 28 April 1997.

Janssen, Peter. "Sea Ray's Better Idea." *Motor Boating & Sailing,* January 1998.

Kogan, Rick. *Brunswick: The Story of an American Company.* Lake Forest, IL: Brunswick Corp., 1995.

Melcher, Richard A. "Brunswick Wades into New Waters." *Business Week,* 2 June 1997.

Rudeen, Louisa. "Behind the Scenes." *Motor Boating & Sailing,* August 1996.

Samuels, Gary. "After the Storm." *Forbes,* 3 July 1995.

"Sea Ray 370." *Yachting,* April 1995.

For an annual report:
write: Brunswick Corp., 1 N. Field Ct., Lake Forest, IL 60045

For additional industry research:
Investigate companies by their Standard Industrial Classification Codes, also known as SICs. Brunswick's primary SICs are:

3519 Internal Combustion Engines, NEC

3732 Boat Building and Repair

3949 Sports and Athletic Goods, NEC

7933 Bowling Centers

Bugle Boy Industries Inc.

OVERVIEW

Founded in 1977, Bugle Boy Industries Inc. enjoys annual sales of nearly $500 million. The company produces sportswear, jeans, and assorted products in no-wrinkle, 100 percent cotton fabrics. The company sells its lines to more than 7,000 leading American department stores and retailers including J.C. Penney, Kohl's, and Sears. Bugle Boy apparel can also be found at various family stores and at Bugle Boy Factory Outlets.

COMPANY FINANCES

Bugle Boy's 1997 sales were $470 million, with an estimated net income of $11 million. The company ranked number 466 on *Forbes'* 1997 list of The Top 500 Private Companies.

ANALYSTS' OPINIONS

Many analysts had a favorable view of Bugle Boy Industries Inc.'s financial picture during the 1990s. CEO William Mow had a revenue goal of $1 billion by the year 2001, which was seen as fairly conservative. Potential growth and profits for the company remained favorable over the decade, on an international scale as well as within the United States. Among the company's competitive advantages was its inventory system, which is accessible to sales and management personnel from laptop computers. The company also claims to have a price

FOUNDED: 1977

Contact Information:
HEADQUARTERS: 2900 Madera Rd.
    Simi Valley, CA 93065
PHONE: (805)582-1010
FAX: (805)582-5236
EMAIL: customerservice@bugleboy.com
URL: http://www.bugleboy.com

FAST FACTS:

About Bugle Boy Industries Inc.

Ownership: Bugle Boy Industries Inc. is a privately owned company.

Officers: Dr. William C.W. Mow, CEO, 62; Rosa Mow, Pres. & COO; Michael Seyhun, Sr. VP & CFO; Ken Sekella, Human Resources Mgr.

Employees: 2,200

Chief Competitors: Bugle Boy is a manufacturer and marketer of jeans, sportswear, and other casual apparel. As such, its primary competitors include: Calvin Klein; Farah; Fruit of the Loom; Guess?; Haggar; J. Crew; Jordache Enterprises; Levi-Strauss; Liz Claiborne; Osh Kosh B'Gosh; Oxfor Industries; Polo; The Gap; Tommy Hilfiger; and VF Corp.

advantage over chief competitor Levi-Strauss in international markets.

Among analyst concerns was the celebration of Bugle Boy's success in the young men's division. Some say this notoriety could cause serious marketing difficulties for the company's conservative men's division, arguing that men entering their mid-20s tend to prefer jeans to trendy clothes. This, they say, was at the root of Levi's solid 65 percent market share on men's clothing. Due to Levi's market standing, it has widespread admittance to a variety of department stores, whereas Bugle Boy has been bound to stores like Sears and May Company. Therefore, many analysts say an improved image is needed for Bugle Boy's men's division to sustain its growth.

HISTORY

Dr. William Mow (born Mow Chao Wei), CEO of Bugle Boy Industries Inc., founded the company in 1977. Launched as Buckaroo International, Mow and partner Stanley Buchthal were convinced they could sell men's pants. Mow's computer and technological background, however, provided him with few advantages and little knowledge of the industry. The first four years of the business proved difficult. In 1981, Bugle Boy moved to cut its products down to include casual men's slacks.

Having realized success with its "parachute pant" line in 1983, the company began to produce a boys clothing line the following year.

The 1980s proved to be a changing decade for Bugle Boy. The company signed its first U.S. licensee agreement in 1986, one that allowed Bugle Boy to expand its product lines. By 1988, the company had established Jeans and Missy divisions and signed its first foreign licensee agreement with Canada. By 1989 Japan and Eastern Asia were added to the list of regions with which the company had licensee agreements.

By 1990 Bugle Boy's sales passed the $500 million mark, allowing the company to better serve buyers by implementing Electronic Data Interchange (EDI) services, laptop computer systems that provide up-to-date inventory and pricing information for Bugle Boy salesmen and management. With increased success, the company introduced numerous clothing lines in the 1990s, such as wrinkle-free products (1994), the Black Label and Gold Crest line (1995), and the Classics line (1996).

STRATEGY

Bugle Boy Industries Inc. has held on to a simple fundamental principle: to offer genuine value and quality while increasing company profits. In other words, by offering fashionable, comfortable clothing at an affordable price, the company believed itself capable of competing with big names like Levi-Strauss. To best assist its buyers, Bugle Boy has heavily relied on its high-tech laptop inventory system.

Targeting the average American family, Bugle Boy Industries Inc. has consistently sought to increase its name recognition. One example was expansion of its product line to include newborns, infants, toddlers, and sized 4-16 boys and girls clothing. Also in an effort to make its name more recognized globally, the company pursued license agreements with choice merchandisers as a strategic means of expansion. As of the late 1990s, Bugle Boy Industries Inc. enjoyed 98 percent brand awareness and had firmly established itself as a family brand for "middle America." The company continued its national advertisements in 1998 focusing on "Americana." The theme uses red, white, and blue colors and depicts an "All-American Bugle Boy(r) family" in everyday life.

Bugle Boy held market share of 50 percent in the young men's division and 45 percent of the boy's division in the U.S. market. Bugle Boy's biggest concern was competitor Levi-Strauss, which held 65 percent of U.S. market share in the men's division and boasted global sales of more than $3.6 billion. Bugle Boy has not yet obtained licensees in Europe, a major international playing field. The company has an office in Tokyo's Shibuya district in Japan and has a licensing agreement with the giant grading company Itohman to sell Bugle Boy jeans in 500 stores given a two-year time frame.

INFLUENCES

The first season Bugle Boy clothing was offered for sale, the company lost $250,000. Putting up his house as collateral, William Mow was able to secure more credit. His peers thought he was a business failure. Anxious to prove himself, he bought out partner Buchthal for $2,000 in 1981 and renamed the company Bugle Boy. The company's designer at that time, Vincent Nesi, agreed to head sales and marketing if Mow would reduce the company's lines to just pants. Mow agreed, and the strategy proved successful when the company sold $960,000 worth of merchandise between May and August of 1981. Sales jumped to $2.6 million by the spring of 1982, earning the company's first time profit of $200,000. The company continued to grow and remain profitable.

By 1984, sales had doubled to $43 billion. The company used parachute material to produce a new line of pants known as "parachute pants." Unfortunately, the company overestimated the sale potential and manufactured too many parachute pants, forcing the company to sell them all in 1984 for 25 cents a pair.

Desperate to produce a successful product, the company launched its cargo pant line in November of 1984. These pants were made from pigmented canvas and were the only winner in the apparel industry during Christmas of that year. The company more than bounced back from an almost total disaster to become instantly popular. Its cargo pants' success, however, did not outweigh the company's losses from the parachute pants line.

By 1986, the company rebounded, earning $6 million in profits while sales remained steady. The parachute pants catastrophe left retailers with many doubts, and the company's focus was shifted to regain their trust. Proving itself, the company's sales reached $189 million in 1987, with continued growth of more than 40 percent in 1988. The company learned its lesson and began consolidating efforts before growth got out of control.

Among the company's most successful campaigns was its denim promotion in 1988, the television commercial that introduced the phrase, "Excuse me, are those Bugle Boy jeans you're wearing?" By 1990, Bugle Boy enjoyed 70 percent growth as well as substantial profits. Since then, the company has aimed at continuing growth of 20 percent per year. William Mow has stated he expects to be doing $1 billion worth of sales by the year 2001.

CURRENT TRENDS

During the late 1990s, Bugle Boy Industries Inc. focused on expanding its product lines and launching new advertising campaigns, both as a means to increase the company's global name recognition. Among the results of Bugle Boy's efforts was its 1997 title as the Official

CHRONOLOGY:

Key Dates for Bugle Boy Industries Inc.

1977: Dr. William Mow launches Buckaroo International to sell men's pants

1981: Mow renames the company Bugle Boy

1983: Introduces the "parachute pant" made from parachute material

1986: The company signs its first licensing agreement

1988: Introduces the "Excuse me, are those Bugle Boy jeans you're wearing?" ad campaign; signs its first foreign licensing agreement

1990: Bugle Boy sales pass $500 million for the first time

1994: Introduces wrinkle-free pants

1997: Bugle Boy begins pursuing the golf attire market

Clothier of the Indy Racing League. In a signed agreement, Bugle Boy provided travel sportswear and uniforms for all 21 teams and maintained privileges to sell Indy 500, Indy Speedway, United States Auto Club, and Indy Racing League trademark clothing. Also, in late 1997, the company began heavy pursuit of a new market—the golf business. Bugle Boy golf apparel was introduced in the spring of 1997, and the company was working to sign contracts with some Professional Golf Association (PGA) touring professionals in late 1997. The company's line of golf apparel was available at Mervyn's and Sears in northern California and slotted for sale in southern California by 1998.

Other trends toward expansion included Bugle Boy's license agreements with merchandisers: Topsville, Inc. (a trendsetting producer in children's clothing); Chano International (an elite men's and boys' underwear manufacturer); Timestar, Inc. (an international manufacturer of stylish watches); and Vision Eyewear International, Inc. (maker of elite protective sunglasses). According to the signed agreement, these merchandisers entered into joint efforts with Bugle Boy to market and sell Bugle Boy merchandise. Apparel and accessories added to Bugle Boy's line of merchandise included bikinis, boxers, classic briefs, flannel wear, watches, sunglasses, and children's wear and accessories.

Bugle Boy Industries Inc. also signed an agreement with Lollytogs Ltd., a clothing manufacturer based in

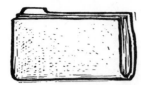

A MAN WHO DOESN'T NEED TO BLOW HIS OWN HORN

Bugle Boy is the brainchild of Mow Chao Wei, a Chinese national who fled the country in 1949 before the Communist takeover. Reputedly, his family got the last Pan Am Flight out of Shanghai before the Communists shut the airport down. Arriving in the United States, Mow Chao Wei reinvented himself as William Mow, and subsequently went on to get a Ph.D. in electrical engineering from Purdue University. An early researcher in microchip technology, Dr. Mow made the unlikely jump to fashion by founding Bugle Boy in 1977. As he said, "I had invented machines with millions of wires that measured time to a billionth of a second. I thought I could make a pair of pants."

New York. Under the terms of the agreement, Bugle Boy allowed the company to use the Bugle Boy name to manufacture and sell school uniforms. Strategically, Bugle Boy saw this as an opportunity to increase its share of the children's clothing market and not be excluded due to the increasing popularity of school uniforms.

PRODUCTS

Bugle Boy makes and markets men's, women's, and children's clothing. Most product lines focus on casual clothing such as jeans and khaki pants, T-shirts, and polo shirts. The company also sells swimwear, outerwear, and accessories such as belts, socks, underwear, and sunglasses. Bugle Boy also distributes clothing under the Vincente Nesi and Vincente labels.

GLOBAL PRESENCE

Over the years, Bugle Boy's business has expanded to include 22 domestic and international licensees in the United States, Japan, Canada, Mexico, Central America, and the Caribbean. Manufacturing for the company takes place in 40 countries worldwide, but it is concentrated in Taiwan, Hong Kong, and China. One of the largest privately owned apparel companies in the United States, Bugle Boy Industries Inc. relies heavily on its strategy of high-quality production at an affordable price to increase its global presence. Its most recent expansion efforts have been directed toward China.

SOURCES OF INFORMATION

Bibliography

Bugle Boy Home Page, 26 April 1998. Available at http://www.bugleboy.com.

"Bugle Boy Industries Inc." *Hoover's Online,* June 1998. Available at http://www.hoovers.com.

"Chairman Mow." Transpacific Media Inc., 1995 Available at http://www.tmiweb.com.

Smith, Leo. "Bugle Boy Aims to Sew Up School Share with Line of Uniforms." *Los Angeles Times,* 29 April 1997.

"The Top 500 Private Companies." *Forbes,* 1 December 1997.

Wilcox, Gregory. "Teeing Up—Company Eyes Whole New Market with Golf Apparel." *Daily News,* 3 October 1997.

For additional industry research:

Investigate companies by their Standard Industrial Classification Codes, also known as SICs. Bugle Boy's primary SIC is:

5699 Apparel and Accessory Stores

Burger King Corporation

OVERVIEW

Burger King Corporation operates the second largest fast food restaurant in the United States, with 9,400 locations in all 50 states and 53 countries around the world. It is a leader in the fast food industry, with sales reaching $9.8 billion in 1997. The company operates in a mature U.S. market, meaning there is little new business being generated in the United States, and competitors continue to battle for existing business. Burger King promotes its products aggressively in the United States, while also continuing its expansion into foreign markets.

Burger King was troubled for a while by a lack of corporate direction. Franchises operate independently, and many times differently from one another, creating an image of inconsistency in food and service. With innovative ideas and aggressive advertising, Burger King managed to pull through, remaining second in its industry only to McDonald's.

COMPANY FINANCES

In 1997 Burger King's worldwide system sales reached $9.8 billion, up 8 percent from 1996. The company's sales growth in the United States was just over 20 percent, and 866 new restaurants were opened worldwide.

HISTORY

The Burger King Corporation was founded in 1954 in Miami, Florida, by entrepreneurs James McLamore and David Edgerton. McLamore and Edgerton targeted

FOUNDED: 1954

Contact Information:
HEADQUARTERS: 17777 Old Cutler Rd.
　　Miami, FL 33157
PHONE: (305)378-7011
FAX: (305)378-7262
URL: http://www.burgerking.com

FAST FACTS:

About Burger King Corporation

Ownership: Burger King Corporation is a wholly owned subsidiary of Diageo PLC, formed by the merger of Grand Metropolitan PLC and Guinness.

Officers: Dennis Malamatinas, CEO, 42; Colin Heggie, Sr. VP & CFO; Paul E. Clayton, Pres., Burger King North America, 39

Employees: 26,000 (1997)

Chief Competitors: Burger King is a fast-food chain. Its primary competitors include: McDonald's; Wendy's; and Hardee's.

the post-war generation by offering fast food at a reasonable price. With drive-ins popping up all over the United States and offering cheap fast food, the concept was not unique. However, Burger King tried to give its restaurant a special edge, being the only fast-food chain at the time to offer comfortable eat-in dining rooms.

The Whopper—a hamburger made with sauce, cheese, lettuce, pickles, tomato, and onion—was introduced in 1957 as the burger for the bigger appetite. At that time it cost $.37, while the company's original hamburger was $.18; McDonald's hamburger was only $.15.

In 1959 McLamore and Edgerton decided to franchise the business. They acquired national and international franchising rights in 1961, and Burger King soon became a national chain. In 1967 Minneapolis-based Pillsbury Company acquired the company. At that time, it had 274 restaurant locations and 8,000 employees.

Pillsbury purchased the 274-store chain for $18 million in 1967. However, franchises were still operating independently. Franchisees, such as Billy and Jimmy Trotter, began buying as many stores as they could, and individual franchisees were becoming more powerful than the parent company. Pillsbury curtailed the expansion of the Trotter brothers through a lawsuit, but this didn't prevent other franchisees from doing the same. In 1977 Pillsbury hired Donald Smith, a former top executive with McDonald's. Smith began to apply the same management techniques used at McDonald's to organize and control the franchises of Burger King. He set ownership rules for the franchises, which made it nearly impossible for an individual franchisee to become more powerful than the parent company. Smith also replaced 8 out of 10 managers

with people from McDonald's and ordered routine monitoring of each franchise with unscheduled visits.

In 1988 Grand Metropolitan PLC bought out Pillsbury in a corporate takeover. In response, Burger King franchise owners formed the National Franchise Association (NFA). The NFA revised the franchise agreement, including a process for resolving encroachment disputes and policies pertaining to the spending of national advertising funds. Originally formed out of panic, the NFA eventually formed a strong relationship with the Burger King Corporation. This relationship was important since in 1996, only 758 of Burger King's then 8,250 restaurants were operated by the company.

STRATEGY

Burger King's success was due largely to its ability to anticipate and keep up with consumer trends. In 1974 multiple lines were added to speed up service. Drive-thru windows were re-introduced in 1975 after being eliminated in the 1950s when dining rooms were added. (Drive-thru windows account for 60 percent of the company's business.) In 1978 specialty sandwiches such as fish, chicken, ham and cheese, and steak were introduced and targeted to the adult consumer. A breakfast menu was added during the early 1980s; salad bars and a "light" menu were introduced for the health-conscious crowd in 1985.

Burger King later adopted a "back-to-basics" attitude, concentrating on its original burgers, fries, and soft drinks. When McDonald's introduced its Arch Deluxe for the "grown up" taste, Burger King fought back with its "Still the One" campaign, offering the Whopper for only $.99, resulting in a significant increase in traffic for the hamburger chain. Burger King considers advertising an important element of its success and has used memorable campaigns such as "Have It Your Way" and "We Do It Like You'd Do It."

INFLUENCES

When Donald Smith left in 1980, management at Burger King became inconsistent and unstable. With the lack of an identifiable image, several advertising campaigns failed miserably. Burger King fought back with continued expansion abroad and attempts to meet consumer demands by adding and changing menu items. For example, in August 1997 the company introduced the Big King, and in December Burger King launched its new french fries, directly challenging McDonald's dominance with its advertising.

CURRENT TRENDS

Despite setbacks, Burger King was competing fiercely for the number one spot in the fast food hamburger business. Even with the loss of their marketing link with the Walt Disney Company to McDonald's, Burger King reported an 8-percent increase in sales—a record $9.8 billion for fiscal year 1997. This increase and a 1.5-percent rise in same-store sales indicated that Burger King had not been significantly affected by this major loss.

PRODUCTS

In 1990 Burger King introduced the BK Broiler, a grilled chicken sandwich that sold up to a million sandwiches a day following its launch. However, the Whopper sandwich, an immediate hit since its introduction in 1957, remains one of the best known hamburger sandwiches in the world, selling more than 1.5 million every year. The Bacon Double Cheeseburger was introduced in 1982; the Croissan'wich, a breakfast sandwich, debuted nationally in 1985; and Chicken Tenders and French Toast Sticks, a new breakfast product, was introduced in 1986. In addition to its Whopper and BK Broiler sandwiches, the company offers the standard extras such as french fries and soft drinks.

Instead of introducing new products, the company decided to zero in on its core products—hamburgers, fries, and soft drinks—emphasizing their quality and value. Increased competition from supermarkets and home meal replacement outlets forced Burger King and other fast food restaurants to re-evaluate products, pricing, and service. While McDonald's intended on changing its menu, Burger King opted to plan new promotions and open more restaurants.

CORPORATE CITIZENSHIP

Burger King takes an active interest in the improvement of inner cities. CEO Robert Lowes teamed up with African-American entrepreneur La-Van Hawkins to develop Burger King franchises placed in inner city neighborhoods under the Enterprise Communities and Empowerment Zones program instituted by the Clinton Administration. The program aims to improve neighborhoods by offering jobs, along with the opportunity for workers to become owners of their own franchises. Burger King is the largest fast food franchisor participating in this program.

GLOBAL PRESENCE

Burger King continues to expand internationally at a steady rate. The restaurant's largest international market is the United Kingdom, with over 350 units. The Asia/Pacific area has 254 units, and Latin America has

CHRONOLOGY:
Key Dates for Burger King Corporation

1954: James McLamore and David Edgerton co-found Burger King of Miami

1957: The Whopper makes its debut

1963: Burger King opens its first international restaurants

1967: Pillsbury acquires Burger King

1975: The first European Burger King opens in Madrid, Spain

1977: The 2,000th Burger King opens in Hawaii, putting locations in all 50 states

1988: Grand Metropolitan PLC acquires Pillsbury and its subsidiaries

1997: Burger King establishes the Welfare-to-Work program with assistance from the White House

1998: Guiness and Grand Metropolitan merge to form Diageo PLC

272 units. Burger King adapted regionally by observing local food customs, such as complying with the kosher rules in Israel.

Throughout the 1990s international expansion continued with restaurants opening in the former East Germany, Hungary, Mexico, Poland, Saudi Arabia, Israel, Oman, Dominican Republic, El Salvador, Peru, New Zealand, and Paraguay. The biggest challenge Burger King faced globally was the careful planning and distribution of restaurants. According to Burger King's Head of Worldwide Development, David Fitzjohn, Burger King must do even more "intensive analysis of the intricacies of each country, each city, and each site."

In 1996 Burger King began aggressive expansion into Japan when it teamed up in a joint venture with Japan Tobacco Inc. The target market was teenagers with free time and extra cash. In early 1997 Burger King bought Morinaga Love, a Japanese fast food chain, planning to replace salmon and eggplant burgers with hamburgers. Burger King hoped to attract customers to the nostalgic American decor of the restaurants. Burger King plans to further develop in all areas, but anticipates considerable growth in the Middle East. Other expansion plans include Russia and China.

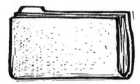

HOLD THE PICKLES?

In an effort to differentiate its product from that of arch-rival McDonald's, Burger King emphasizes its "Have It Your Way" philosophy in its ad campaigns, and Burger King statisticians have revealed that the Whopper can be ordered in no less than 1,024 different variations.

From its humble beginnings in Miami in 1954, Burger King now boasts approximately 10,000 restaurants worldwide, bringing in $10 billion a year in sales from 1,400 customers per restaurant per day (and 60 percent of this business is drive-thru). These customers wolf down 1.6 billion Whoppers and 1.7 billion orders of fries a year (napkin consumption, however, remains a closely guarded company secret). A Whopper is now available in all 50 states, and if the local food mystifies or terrifies you while on vacation, be assured that a Whopper can be had in 56 other countries, including Peru, Singapore, and Saudi Arabia.

For the first time, in 1997, Burger King reported profits in the international marketplace. The company's performance was significantly improved in Europe (particularly the United Kingdom and Germany), where profits grew by 9 percent. Also performing well were stores in Latin America (comparable store sales for 1997 were up 6.4 percent) and the Asia/Pacific region (comparable sales rose 4 percent).

EMPLOYMENT

More than 600 people are employed by Burger King at its corporate headquarters in Miami, Florida. There are also 10 regional offices throughout the continental United States. Hiring is done through various departments, and recruiting is done through colleges and through newspaper and trade journal ads. When hiring new employees, the company seeks those with backgrounds in data processing, finance, and marketing. Burger King also hires temporary summer interns and offers a work-study program for students.

Employees are trained on the job. To support on-the-job instruction, formal classroom lectures and in-house and outside seminars are offered. Burger King continues to upgrade its training procedures. While restaurant chains were realizing the need for interactive

training programs, Burger King introduced an interactive compact disc for training its employees. Through CD-player-television hookups, the compact disc enables trainees to interact with the program using wireless or hard-wired control devices.

Periodic evaluations are given to assess employees' career developmental potential. Employees are given opportunities for advancement through trade and association participation, management training, and skills training. Burger King promotes from within, leading to higher level professional or management positions. The company offers its employees numerous benefits including life, medical, health, and dental insurance. They also offer pension, stock, and hospitalization plans, along with tuition reimbursement.

SOURCES OF INFORMATION

Bibliography

Bernstein, Charles. "Fitzjohn Navigates Careful BK International Growth." *Restaurants & Institutions,* 15 May 1995.

"Burger King Corporation." *International Directory of Company Histories,* Vol. II. Detroit, MI: St. James Press, 1990.

Dun & Bradstreet Information Services, North America. *The Career Guide 1997: Dun's Employment Opportunities Directory.* Bethlehem, PA: Dun & Bradstreet, Inc., 1996.

Dun & Bradstreet Information Services, North America. *Dun & Bradstreet Million Dollar Directory: America's Leading Public & Private Companies.* Bethlehem, PA: Dun & Bradstreet, Inc., 1996.

"Grand Metropolitan 1997 Interim Announcement." Diageo PLC, 1998. Available at http://www.diageo.com/ReportsAccounts/index.htm.

"Grand Metropolitan 1997 Preliminary Statement of Annual Results." Diageo PLC, 1998. Available at http://www.diageo.com/ReportsAccounts/index.htm.

Kramer, Louise. "BK Franchisee Association Comes of Age." *Nation's Restaurant News,* 10 June 1996.

———. "Burger King, Hawkins Tap into the Inner-City Market." *Nation's Restaurant News,* 4 March 1996.

Pollack, Judann. "Burger King Sizzles in Wake of Arch Deluxe." *Advertising Age,* 17 June 1996.

———. "The Struggle for the Next Helping." *Advertising Age,* 7 October 1996.

For an annual report:
on the Internet at: http://www.diageo.com/ReportsAccounts/index.htm

For additional industry research:
Investigate companies by their Standard Industrial Classification Codes, also known as SICs. Burger King's primary SICs are:

5812 Eating Places

6794 Patent Owners & Lessors

Calvin Klein Inc.

OVERVIEW

As the fashion industry has progressed, it has grown and transformed into an icon. One of the most influential designers in that movement is Calvin Klein. His designs and ideas brought fashion into a new realm that took on its own personality. With products ranging from clothing to bed linens to perfume, people around the world are familiar with Calvin Klein, and his name has become synonymous with couture fashion. Calvin Klein's products are high quality and have price tags that reflect it. His products are displayed and sold in top notch department stores such as Dayton Hudson's and Saks Fifth Avenue, as well as in the 30 Calvin Klein retail stores operating worldwide.

COMPANY FINANCES

Calvin Klein's approximately 400 in-store shops earned $5.1 billion in revenue during 1997, approximately 28 percent of which was earned in Europe. The company expects revenues to increase 15 percent during 1998. Calvin Klein hoped to add between 650 and 700 new shops in department stores during 1998 in order to better compete with rivals DKNY Jeans and Tommy Hilfiger.

HISTORY

Calvin Klein started his self-titled company in 1968 with company Chairman Barry Schwartz. He began designing coats and later ventured into sportswear. Intro-

FOUNDED: 1968

Contact Information:
HEADQUARTERS: 205 W. 39th St., 5th Fl.
 New York, NY 10018
PHONE: (212)719-2600
FAX: (212)730-4818

A 1980's Calvin Klein jeans advertisement featuring model Brooke Shields. (AP/Wide World Photos, Inc.)

duced in 1980, Calvin Klein jeans helped lead the company to success during the designer blue jeans craze. His unique designs were appealing to the population at large and brought in a substantial profit. It was during the early 1980s that the company made the decision to adopt a form of advertising that would really grab the attention of consumers. Klein hired Richard Avedon to head up the campaign, and it was he who filmed the famous television ads featuring Brooke Shields. Klein continued to utilize provocative advertising since it generated a tremendous amount of revenue. During the late 1980s, the company released several ads for its Obsession perfume as well as for Calvin Klein's underwear line. The ads were pretentious and erotic but were always discussed among consumers and store buyers. Klein usually disregarded attacks by those who disagreed with the ads because it was these displays that turned Calvin Klein into a household name.

The ads brought in profits for Calvin Klein and also helped accelerate the careers of several actors and models, including musician Marky Mark and model Kate Moss. Even with the popularity of the ads and products, Calvin Klein experienced a loss at the expense of lower-priced retailers such as The Gap. In order to ease some of the financial strain, record producer David Geffen purchased $60 million of the company's junk bond debt in 1992. In 1993, Calvin Klein was the subject of a biography that portrayed him as a drug addict during the Studio 54 designer jeans years. This book, titled *Obsession,* was disputed by many within the company but published

nevertheless. The controversy surrounding Calvin Klein ads did not cease. In August 1995 the company decided to withdraw ads shot by Steven Meisel; these television and print ads were seen as possible child pornography. This was looked into extensively, but no formal charges were pressed against Calvin Klein or the company, and the company continued its provocative advertising.

STRATEGY

Advertising used by the company was influential in circulating its products. Ads usually showed scantily clad men and women wearing only certain pieces of Calvin Klein clothing. Whether it was underwear or a simple pair of blue jeans, the billboards and magazine ads were eye catching. The most famous clothing ad was one of the company's first—a television ad featuring actress Brooke Shields uttering the statement, "You know what comes between me and my Calvins? Nothing." Ads like these helped increase sales worldwide. The company continued to enjoy much success and continued to release new products for the public to devour.

During the late 1990s, Calvin Klein was planning to build up its brand's "tops" business, adding fleece tops, woven shirts, T-shirts, and active wear in a wider range of colors than was offered in previous years. It also added more styles to its jean line, including "skateboard" and "carpenter" styles, dark denim, and stretch denim. New products and new shops would be launched with extensive advertising campaigns focused on depicting healthy adults in active, outdoor lifestyles.

Another strategy used by Calvin Klein to extend its product reach was the licensing of the Calvin Klein name to foreign companies. One such example was its agreement to license its home furnishings line to Crown Crafts, Inc. Another example was Calvin Klein's latest deal to extend its menswear partnership with GFT, SpA. The two companies signed a long-term international licensing agreement covering Europe, the Middle East, and the Asia/Pacific region (excluding Japan). The two companies have worked together since the early 1990s building a highly successful men's line in the United States with hopes of extending it to other major regions of the world. The product line is planned for launch in Europe in the spring of 1999, supported by advertising and public relations campaigns. A complete lifestyle collection is to be designed and sold under the Calvin Klein label; distribution will be limited to high-end specialty retailers, department stores, and Calvin Klein Collection stores.

INFLUENCES

Much opinion concerning Calvin Klein, as an individual and about his advertising strategies, was negative. Critics saw Klein as a fiendish drug addict with little self-control, and controversy surrounding his advertisements was intense. In the beginning, there was some argument regarding the sexual undertones in the ads, and the problems grew. In 1996, Calvin Klein Industries produced a series of television commercials showing a series of baby-faced models wearing very little clothing, usually just a tee shirt and a pair of Calvin Klein blue jeans. Models were then questioned by a person the viewer never saw but sounded as though he was a mature, older man. According to writer Carolyn Christenson, Calvin Klein exploited the sexuality of the younger generation in order to sell his products. Christenson felt that Klein was completely aware of the controversy that would surround his ads but went ahead with them anyway. In the mid-1990s the company continued to draw criticism for using models that looked anorexic, underaged, and drugged. New advertising in 1998 focused on a more wholesome lifestyle and included healthier looking models in outdoor settings.

Calvin Klein was also impacted significantly by counterfeiting in the fragrance industry. The company, along with the Colombian government, participated in an ongoing investigation into the problem. More than 6,000 counterfeit units of CK One, Escape, Eternity, and Obsession were found in an April 1998 seizure alone. The problem was also uncovered in September of 1997 in Panama, where another seizure took place. Counterfeit containers were made so that those purchasing the bot-

FAST FACTS:
About Calvin Klein Inc.

Ownership: Calvin Klein Inc. is a privately owned company.

Officers: Barry K. Schwartz, Chmn. & CEO; Calvin Klein, VChmn., 50; Gabriella Forte, Pres. & COO; Lawrence C. DeParis, Sr. VP, Finance & CFO

Employees: 900

Chief Competitors: Calvin Klein is one of the most recognized designers and marketers of apparel and fragrances. Primary competitors include: Donna Karan; The Gap; Gucci; Guess?; J. Crew; Jordache Enterprises; Liz Claiborne; Nautica; Nike; Levi Strauss Associates; OshKosh B'Gosh; Oxford Industries; Polo/Ralph Lauren; and Tommy Hilfiger.

tles believed they were buying authentic Calvin Klein products. According to Jennifer Owens' article in *Women's Wear Daily,* Calvin Klein was one of the fragrance industry's leaders in attacking the counterfeiting problem.

CURRENT TRENDS

Calvin Klein adopted a strategy in the late 1990s that made its clothing and fragrances as recognizable in Europe as they were in the United States. Moving toward this goal, in mid-1998 the company announced a summer 1999 menswear collection. The collection included a new couture line for the European market that was produced and distributed by GFT, SpA, an Italian manufacturer that has produced the company's black-on-black label in the United States since 1992. It would be the first time a top-of-the-line Calvin Klein line was made widely available to the European market—until the agreement with GFT, the Calvin Klein men's couture collection was only available in a Calvin Klein store in Paris. The new line was scheduled to be in stores in the spring of 1999 for distribution to upmarket retailers through GFT showrooms in Milan, Madrid, Paris, Dusseldorf, and London. A roll-out across the Middle East and Asia was planned sometime after the line's initial release in Europe.

Calvin Klein not only introduced several new clothing lines, cosmetics, perfumes, and eyewear but also de-

HE'S HIP, HE'S COOL

He started designing and selling women's apparel in 1968, and now Calvin Klein sits upon the fashion-world throne like a king of coats, a top-dog of tank-tops, an undisputed ruler of underwear. Whereas he once sold clothes, he now sells a lifestyle.

His clothing fashions are generally noted for their clean, simple, minimalistic styles, and this stands in direct contrast to the often controversial advertising campaigns designed to sell those clothes. The designation "designer" is used to sell anything from jeans to fragrances, and it is intended to make Calvin Klein customers stand out from the crowd. As Calvin Klein says, "People who wear cK (Calvin Klein) are very real. . . they're about today."

Calvin Klein is about attitude, techno detail, hip packaging, and complexion enhancing colorations. It is, in a nutshell, the celebration of style. And it sells like hotcakes.

veloped products outside of the fashion realm. In November 1996, in conjunction with Mattel, Inc., the company produced a Calvin Klein Barbie doll. This collector's edition doll was dressed from head to toe in Calvin Klein apparel. She wore a denim skirt with the company's logo and a gray crop top covered by a denim jacket. The doll also wore Calvin Klein undergarments. Also included with this edition were several accessories featuring the Calvin Klein name, including a windbreaker, baseball cap, and sneakers. The Barbie originally retailed for $70 and was sold exclusively at Bloomingdale's.

Calvin Klein's latest scent, Contradiction, became one of the best-selling women's scents in the United States (ranked fourth in sales), according to a May 1998 article in *Women's Wear Daily*. It also received The Fragrance Foundation's FiFi award as one of the industry's top perfumes. Building on the new product's success, Calvin Klein planned to add a line of body and bath products, as well as Contradiction for men. Aggressive marketing campaigns were planned for both new product areas. The men's campaign targeted the "virile young father," according to the company. The ads feature a 26-year old model and father of three, portrayed wearing a suit and appearing "healthy and happy" and "full of self-confidence." Since Escape was launched in 1993, Contradiction was Calvin Klein's first introduction of a men's

scent—the company would reportedly spend $11 million on advertising and marketing for the product's launch.

PRODUCTS

Calvin Klein produces several items that are extremely popular with the public. The company's clothing line includes blue jeans, tee shirts, blouses, skirts, dress pants, and men's dress shirts. All of its items are high in quality and priced at the higher end of the spectrum. The company also put its name on eyewear and an extensive line of cosmetics. (Formed in 1985, the Calvin Klein Cosmetics Company was a division of the Unilever Corporation.) Calvin Klein consistently develops innovative products that have significant impact on the fragrance industry, such as Obsession, Eternity, Escape, CK One, CK Be, and Contradiction. Each fragrance has its own line of body products. These brands are honored several times for the success of the fragrance as well as for the advertising, design, and marketing campaign.

CORPORATE CITIZENSHIP

Though the company did not discuss its donation publicly, the Calvin Klein Foundation provided $5,000 toward a controversial exhibit on the history of garment sweatshops at the Smithsonian's Museum of American History. Other apparel companies and associations have reportedly declined sponsorship fearing they may be too closely associated with the sweatshop image as a result.

GLOBAL PRESENCE

In March 1998 Calvin Klein opened a new store in Rome's shopping district near the Spanish Steps. Located in a former Gianfranco Ferre boutique, the company restored the building and preserved its entire exterior—the building is a historic site protected by the Italian government. Following its opening, Calvin Klein planned to move south, opening shops in Sicily and Catania, and already has one shop in Milan. Overall, Italy represents approximately 25 percent of the company's business in Europe. Calvin Klein also operates shops in London, Barcelona, Lisbon, Moscow, Tel Aviv, Kuwait City, and the Saudi Arabian cities of Jeddah, Riyadh, and Dubai.

Calvin Klein has offices in Asia and Europe. In May 1998, it was announced that Crown Crafts, Inc. entered into a long-term international licensing agreement with Calvin Klein, Inc. to manufacture and distribute Calvin Klein soft home furnishings. The agreement included the Calvin Klein Home bed, bath, and table linen collections and the company's new Home Khakis line entitling the company to distribute products in the Americas, Europe, and the Middle East. According to Calvin Klein president Gabrielle Forte, "With our Calvin Klein businesses growing around the world, we are confident that this new partnership with Crown Crafts will help us to realize the full worldwide potential for our Home Collection in the coming years." Design and marketing activities, including advertising and public relations, continued to be administered by Calvin Klein, Inc. in New York and Milan. The company's most recent agreement, signed in June 1998, will also extend its international reach—Calvin Klein's licensing agreement for its menswear line with GFT, SpA was extended to Europe, the Middle East, and the Asia/Pacific (excluding Japan). The deal was expected to complement the company's existing international licenses, such as those with Stefanel SpA for cK Calvin Klein apparel in Europe and the Middle East and The Fratini Group for cK Calvin Klein Jeanswear in Europe, the Middle East, and Asia.

SOURCES OF INFORMATION

Bibliography

Aktar, Alev. "Contradiction Adds a Bath and Body Line." *Women's Wear Daily,* 1 May 1998.

Born, Pete. "Calvin's New Contradiction." *Women's Wear Daily,* 12 June 1998.

Calvin Klein Barbie—Limited Edition Exclusives, 1 April 1998. Available at http://www.barbie.com.

"Calvin Klein, Inc. Signs Letter of Intent With GFT S.p.A. to Launch Menswear Collection in Europe Beginning Spring 1999." Calvin Klein Inc. Press Release, 30 June 1998.

Christenson, Carolyn. "Calvin Klein Ads: Art or Pornography?" *The Bucknellian Online,* 14 September 1995.

Clark, Jennifer. "Calvin Klein Unveils New European Line in Milan." *Reuters,* 1 July 1998.

Conti, Samantha. "Buon Giorno, Roma, from Calvin Klein." *Women's Wear Daily,* 6 April 1998.

"Crown Crafts Enters International Agreement With Calvin Klein, Inc. for Calvin Klein Home." *PR Newswire,* 26 May 1998.

"FiFi Honours the World's Fragrant Stars." *Cosmetics International,* 25 June 1998.

Owens, Jennifer. "Klein Fakes Seized." *Women's Wear Daily,* 24 April 1998.

Ramey, Joanna. "Smithsonian Gets $5,000 from Calvin for Exhibit." *Women's Wear Daily,* 18 November 1997.

Socha, Miles. "Rebuilding Calvin's Jeans." *Women's Wear Daily,* 5 March 1998.

For additional industry research:

Investigate companies by their Standard Industrial Classification Codes, also known as SICs. Calvin Klein's primary SICs are:

2844 Perfumes, Cosmetics, and Other Toilet Preparations

5136 Men's and Boy's Clothing and Furnishings

5137 Women's, Children's, and Infants' Clothing and Accessories

Campbell Soup Company

FOUNDED: 1869

Contact Information:

HEADQUARTERS: Campbell Pl.
  Camden, NJ 08103-1799
PHONE: (609)342-4800
FAX: (609)342-3878
URL: http://www.campbellsoups.com

OVERVIEW

Campbell is the world's largest producer and marketer of soups, vegetable juices, and sauces. Its soups account for about 80 percent of all canned soup sold in the United States. Other products include Godiva Chocolates, Great Starts breakfasts, Pepperidge Farm cookies and crackers, and Swanson frozen foods.

COMPANY FINANCES

In fiscal 1997 (ending August 3, 1997), Campbell Soup Company achieved record net sales of $7.96 billion, up 4 percent from 1996 sales of $7.68 billion. In company reports, growth was attributed to a 3 percent increase from new products, 2 percent from higher selling prices, and 2 percent from acquisitions, while it was offset by a 3 percent decline attributed to divestitures. Overall, net sales from ongoing businesses increased 7 percent in 1997 and 1996. By division, soups and sauces accounted for $4.1 billion in sales; biscuits and confectionary products accounted for $1.5 billion; foodservice revenues were $459 million; and other miscellaneous products and services accounted for remaining revenues. The company's Pepperidge Farm and Godiva brands were solid contributors to company performance, both experiencing double-digit growth in 1997.

Net earnings for 1997 were $713 million, down 11 percent from 1996 earnings of $802 million. The company's earnings per share declined 6 percent, from $1.61 in 1996 to $1.51 in 1997. The company attributed the drop to "special charges" the company recorded in the first quarter of 1997—before the charge, net earnings increased 9 percent and earnings per share increased 15 percent.

The company's stock price as of mid-1998 was around $54 per share. Its 52-week high was $62.88, and its 52-week low was $46 per share.

ANALYSTS' OPINIONS

In early 1997, several market analysts were enthusiastic about Campbell Soup Company's financial performance and its management. A February 1997 report by Deutsche Morgan Grenfell noted that Chairman David Johnson's goal was to make Campbell Soup a world-class consumer goods company. "The company has proven that it can successfully rejuvenate and leverage its core brand strengths, innovate with new product introductions, drive volumes through new marketing campaigns, and discover significant cost-saving opportunities by divesting underperforming assets," the report said. Deutsche Morgan Grenfell recommended that its clients buy Campbell stock, saying that "Campbell's strategy seems like a textbook case for good management."

Another report produced in February 1997 by Credit Suisse First Boston was equally enthusiastic about Campbell and its management. "Campbell is a company on a roll," the report said. "The focus on returns on invested capital and improving the leading businesses has never been higher, and the company is enjoying the benefits of significant (higher) pricing in its flagship soup business."

Fortune also reported the health of the "comfort-food" industry as a whole in early 1998. As stated by Jeanne Lee, "After all, what could be more reassuring now than the stable cash flow, predictable double-digit growth, and minimal emerging-market exposure offered by the edibles you grew up with, like Campbell Soup and Sara Lee? We mean it. Packaged-food stocks make an exciting opportunity today precisely because they aren't too exciting." Investment analysts expected the industry to continue showing annual growth rates between 12 and 14 percent for the next several years.

HISTORY

Campbell Soup Company was founded in Camden, New Jersey, in 1869 as a partnership between Abram Anderson (an icebox manufacturer) and Joseph Campbell (a fruit merchant) to produce canned tomatoes and vegetables, jellies, soups, condiments, and minced meats. In 1876, Anderson left the partnership and Arthur Dorrance and Joseph Campbell formed a new partnership, beginning a long-term association between the Dorrance family and the company.

FINANCES:

Campbell Soup Co. Net Sales, 1994-1997 (million dollars)

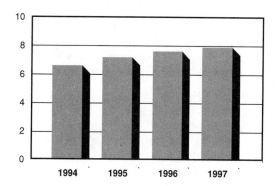

Campbell Soup Co. 1997 Stock Prices (dollars)

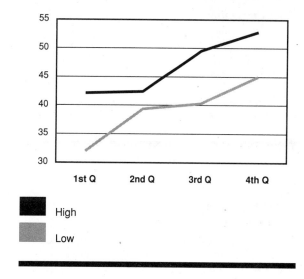

In 1891, the name of the company became The Joseph Campbell Preserve Company. Campbell retired in 1894 and was succeeded by Dorrance. In 1897, Dorrance's 24-year-old nephew, Dr. John T. Dorrance, joined the company. Trained as a chemist, he developed the process for producing condensed soup. The elimination of water resulted in lower packaging, shipping, and storage costs for the company. As soup sales accelerated, the Campbell Soup Company grew rapidly. In 1904, the company developed its "Campbell Kids" campaign as a marketing device to sell soup and, in the same year, 16

FAST FACTS:

About Campbell Soup Company

Ownership: Campbell Soup Company is a publicly owned company traded on the New York Stock Exchange and other stock exchanges around the world.

Ticker symbol: CPB

Officers: Dale F. Morrison, Pres. & CEO, 48; David W. Johnson, Chmn., 65; Basil L. Anderson, Exec. VP & CFO, 52; Robert F. Bernstock, Exec. VP & Pres., Specialty Foods

Employees: 37,041

Principal Subsidiary Companies: Campbell Soup Company has three major divisions: U.S.A. (soups, sauces, condiments, frozen dinners, and juices); Bakery and Confectionery (Pepperidge Farm and Godiva chocolate); and International Grocery.

Chief Competitors: A manufacturer and distributor of food products such as soups, sauces, and convenience foods, Campbell's competitors include: ConAgra; General Mills; Diageo PLC; H.J. Heinz Co.; Hershey Foods; Hormel; Kellogg Company; Nestle; PepsiCo Inc.; The Quaker Oats Co.; Philip Morris Cos. Inc.; RJR Nabisco; Sara Lee Bakery Co.; and TLC Beatrice.

million cans of Campbell soup were sold. Campbell bought Franco-American in 1915. In 1922, the company changed its name to the Campbell Soup Company.

Campbell depended on its core soup products for growth in the first half of the twentieth century. In 1948, however, the company expanded through its acquisitions of V8 Vegetable Juice and C.A. Swanson & Sons in 1955. In 1966, Campbell's bought Godiva Chocolatier, Inc., and in 1978, Vlasic pickles. Mrs. Paul's Seafood, Prego, and LeMenu were all added during the early 1980s.

In 1993, the company took a $300-million restructuring charge to reduce staffing and close and consolidate various operations in order to renew the company's solid financial status. Under the leadership of Robert W. Johnson, Campbell sold several of its food lines in 1993 and 1994, and in 1995 it sold the Mrs. Paul's frozen seafood product line to VDK Holdings, maker of Van de Kamp's frozen seafood. In 1995, Campbell purchased Pace Foods in San Antonio, the leading U.S. producer of

salsa, for $1.1 billion. The next year, the company went through another restructuring that reduced operating costs and cut employment by 6 percent.

STRATEGY

In the 1990s, Campbell Soup Company's single-minded goal was to dramatically increase total return to its shareholders. Other goals included increasing profits and boosting the company's stock price. As of 1996, the company was succeeding through its use of cost-cutting methods and improved marketing efforts. Overall marketing support for its products increased—advertising spending was expected to be up 30 percent through the late 1990s.

Like other food companies, Campbell Soup's basic strategy is to develop new products while investing in its established "core" brands. Campbell's soups and sauces accounted for $4.1 billion in sales in 1997, most of which came from three varieties—tomato, chicken noodle, and cream of mushroom. The company planned to make an enhancement to one of these top sellers every year during the late 1990s. For example, in 1996 the company added 33 percent more chicken to its chicken noodle soup. In addition to the strong sales of the top-selling soups, Campbell's line of Fat-Free Cream soups saw 48 percent growth from 1996 to 1997.

In 1996, Campbell's Pepperidge Farm unit "relaunched" its Milano cookies and Goldfish crackers with new marketing strategies. Sales of both products increased dramatically. The company's Franco American unit increased marketing support for its core Spagettios brand in 1996, leading to a 15 percent sales increase. In 1998, Campbell's revamped its successful "M'm! M'm! Good!" campaign (first launched in the 1930s) to air during the Winter Olympics. The company's largest campaign in its history, "M'm! M'm! Good For The Body, Good For The Soul" was launched in February 1998 and focused on the "nurturing and nourishing" qualities of Campbell's soup. All the company's soup lines—such as Red and White, Home Cookin', and Healthy Request—were featured in the campaign.

Another part of Campbell's strategy in the 1990s was to sell businesses outside its "core areas." For example, Campbell's sold its interests in tomato processing and poultry processing, and in 1996 the company considered selling its can-making operations. By selling these assets, reducing its employment by 6 percent, and establishing a global purchasing operation, Campbell planned to reduce operating costs by a total of $200 million in 1996 and 1997. In September 1997, the company announced a plan to spin off seven non-core businesses, including Swanson frozen foods, Vlasic pickles, Swift Armour meats, and other international specialty foods businesses. The spin-off would provide significant cost reductions for Campbell and allow the company to focus on businesses with the highest growth potential—soup and sauces, biscuits and confectionery, and foodservice—all of which grew 10 percent in sales and 15 percent in earnings during 1997. The Vlasic spin-off was completed March 30, 1998, creating a new $1.4-billion company called Vlasic Foods International.

In the late 1990s, Campbell Soup was also trying to increase sales by eliminating hundreds of lower-profit products (including many soups) and directing investment dollars to top-selling, higher-profit products, such as Pepperidge Farm Goldfish crackers, V8 Juice, Prego spaghetti sauce, and chicken noodle soup. The company also expanded into non-soup food areas by acquiring Fresh Start Bakeries, makers of buns and muffins for McDonald's, and by developing a potpie filling and crust for KFC.

INFLUENCES

In the late 1980s, Campbell Soup Company was said to be struggling due to falling profits, weak marketing, and a bitter feud within the Dorrance family, which owned the majority of the company's stock. (As of mid-1998, the family still owned about 44 percent of the Campbell Soup Company.) In January 1990, a company outsider, Robert W. Johnson, was named president. He began a turnaround that made the company a solid financial performer and an innovative marketer. From 1990 to 1995, Campbell's profits multiplied at an average annual rate of nearly 18 percent, to $698 million in the fiscal year ending July 31, 1995. According to a report in *Fortune* magazine, Johnson's success was due to his unusual combination of talents, including strong control of company finances; effective communication with and motivation for employees; and an "obsession" with beating Campbell's competitors in profits.

CURRENT TRENDS

During the mid- to late 1990s, Campbell Soup Company was involved in the development of "functional foods," also called "nutraceuticals." This product category, which was first developed in Europe, involved creating food/pharmaceutical hybrids. Functional foods promise benefits such as lowering blood pressure and boosting the immune system. Before manufacturers of functional foods could make health claims for their products in the United States, however, they needed the permission of the U.S. Food and Drug Administration.

In the mid-1990s, Campbell Soup Company invested five years and more than $20 million to develop a line of functional foods called Intelligent Quisine. Aiming the products at older consumers with health problems treatable through better nutrition, Campbell tested 40 dif-

CHRONOLOGY:
Key Dates for Campbell Soup Company

1869: Company founded as a partnership between Abram Anderson and Joseph Campbell to produce canned goods

1876: Andersen leaves the partnership and Campbell forms new partnership with Arthur Dorrance

1891: The company officially becomes the Joseph Campbell Preserve Company

1894: Campbell retires and Dorrance takes over

1899: Dr. John T. Dorrance develops a method for canning condensed soup

1904: Introduces the Campbell's Kids

1915: Purchases Franco-American

1922: Company name becomes Campbell Soup Company

1948: Campbell begins expanding beyond soups by acquiring V8 Vegetable Juice

1955: Acquires C.A. Swanson & Sons

1966: Acquires Godiva Chocolatier, Inc.

1971: Sales top $1 billion for the first time

1978: Purchases Vlassic Foods

1982: Acquires Mrs. Paul's Kitchens

1993: Takes a $300 million restructuring charge to reduce staffing and consolidate operations

1995: Sells Mrs. Paul's Kitchens and purchases Pace Foods

ferent "healthy" meals, from french toast and sausage to grilled chicken dijon. In clinical trials, people eating three of these meals per day had reduced blood pressure and cholesterol, according to Campbell. In January 1997, Campbell was test marketing Intelligent Quisine in Ohio.

PRODUCTS

The company was still actively introducing new products during the late 1990s. One market analyst credited them with introducing truly new products, not just recycled versions of old ideas with minor changes. Some of these new products included premium soup in glass

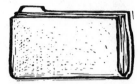

WORLDWIDE APPEAL

"M'm! M'm! Good!" is that famous jingle known to Campbell's soup fans far and wide. The Campbell Soup Company, created by Joseph Campbell and Abraham Anderson in 1869, has grown to become the number one wet soup company in the world. Campbell's soups, more popular than cold cereals, coffee, or bath tissue, are found in 93 percent of American households. Three soups, including tomato, introduced in 1897, along with cream of mushroom and chicken noodle, which debuted in 1934, are some of the more popular ones enjoyed by Americans. Combined, there are roughly 2.5 billion bowls of these three soups consumed in the United States each year.

But America isn't the only place people are slurping up great quantities of soup. Known worldwide, Campbell's has introduced soups such as watercress, duck gizzard, Chinese borsch, pork, fig, and date soups to Hong Kong and China. In Mexico, people can purchase cream of chili poblano soup, and in Australia, pumpkin soup is a best-seller.

jars, which had estimated sales of $15 million in 1997; frozen restaurant-style soups; the Healthy Request Creative line of 98 percent fat-free soups, which had estimated fiscal 1997 sales of $75 million; a brand of premium canned pasta; and new fat-free Swanson broth.

In 1996, Campbell and its Swanson Frozen Foods unit launched "Swanson Lunch and More Casseroles." The Lunch and More product line included seven frozen, single-serve casseroles based on famous Campbell Soup recipes, such as Chicken Noodle Casserole and Tuna Noodle Casserole, and six two-compartment meals. In 1997, new products such as V8 Splash and Franco-American Superiore all-family pastas contributed to the company's sales growth. Campbell's goal for the year 2000 was to derive 25 percent of its sales from products introduced in the last five years.

GLOBAL PRESENCE

Campbell and market observers agreed that the international grocery business held a great deal of promise for the company in the late 1990s. In 1997, international volume and market share gains were achieved in all countries, with exceptional growth realized in Australia, Canada, and Japan. The company's goal was to increase international revenues to 50 percent of sales. Campbell's products were sold in 120 countries around the world.

As of 1996, Campbell held only 10 percent of the non-U.S. market for soup, which amounted to $5 billion in retail sales. However, when it acquired Erasco, Germany's number one soup company in 1996, Campbell increased its international soup sales by almost 40 percent. Campbell planned to continue its international expansion through acquisitions. Also in 1996, Campbell Soup Company made several other significant changes in its international business. These included setting up joint ventures in Malaysia with Cheong Chan and with Helios Foods (through its Arnotts unit) in Indonesia. Campbell also acquired Homepride Sauces, the leading cooking sauce in the United Kingdom.

Campbell was focusing heavily on Asia in the late 1990s, where disposable income was increasing and soup was a favored food. Targeted markets included Japan, Malaysia, Indonesia, and Hong Kong. Campbell's international strategy in soups was to customize its brands to local tastes. For example, Campbell's cream of pumpkin was Australia's top-selling canned soup in 1996, while Hong Kong's favorite was watercress and duck gizzard soup.

EMPLOYMENT

Campbell's firmly believes that in order for the company to succeed, diversity is an integral part of its corporate culture. Diversity in ideas, background, experience, and personality all contributed to "bringing forth the best from each and every team member, and the best from Campbell's itself." The company dedicated itself to developing employees through the support of training and encouragement, as well as by challenging employees with responsibility, variety, and growth. Campbell's Professional Development Programs were offered to recent college graduates, as were internships, and co-op programs were made available for undergraduates. Specific professional development programs include: Marketing Leadership Program, Financial Leadership Program, MBA, Information Technology Leadership Program, Corporate Audit Leadership Program, and Sales Leadership Program.

The company offers a comprehensive benefits package to employees, including health coverage (medical, dental, and vision), various insurance options (such as long-term disability and life insurance), and flexible spending on benefits as defined by the needs of the individual employee.

SOURCES OF INFORMATION

Bibliography

"Campbell Launches New Soup Campaign: M'm! M'm! Good For The Body, Good For The Soul." Campbell Soup Company Press Release, 9 February 1998.

"Campbell Soup Co. Debuts First Ever Co-Branded Product Partnering Swanson Frozen Foods with American's Favorite Soup." *Frozen Food Digest,* December 1995.

Campbell Soup Company 1996 Annual Report. Camden, NJ: Campbell Soup Company, 1997.

Campbell Soup Company 1997 Annual Report. Camden, NJ: Campbell Soup Company, 1998.

Donlon, J.P. "Top Spoon Stirs It Up." *Chief Executive,* November 1996.

Grant, Linda. "Stirring It Up at Campbell." *Fortune,* 13 May 1996.

Lee, Jeanne. "Comfort Stocks." *Fortune Investor,* 2 March 1998.

McCarthy, Michael J. "Food Companies Hunt For a 'Next Big Thing' But Few Can Find One." *The Wall Street Journal,* 6 May 1997.

Ono, Yumiko. "Campbell Outlines Broad Reorganization; Plans Include Cutting Jobs and Brands, Buying Firm and $160 Million Charge." *The Wall Street Journal,* 6 September 1996.

"Van de Kamp's Buys Mrs. Paul's." *The Wall Street Journal,* 8 May 1996.

For an annual report:

on the Internet at: http://www.campbellsoups.com/financialcenter/1997AR

For additional industry research:

Investigate companies by their Standard Industrial Classification Codes, also known as SICs. Campbell's primary SICs are:

2032 Canned Specialties

2038 Frozen Specialties, NEC

2051 Bread and Other Bakery Products, Excluding Cookies and Crackers

2052 Cookies and Crackers

2066 Chocolate and Cocoa Products

Canon U.S.A., Inc.

FOUNDED: 1965

Contact Information:
HEADQUARTERS: 1 Canon Plz.
   Lake Success, NY 11042-1198
PHONE: (516)328-5000
FAX: (516)328-5069
TOLL FREE: (800)OKC-ANON
URL: http://www.usa.canon.com

OVERVIEW

Canon U.S.A., Inc. is a leader in professional and consumer imaging equipment. Some of its products include copiers, printers, micrographics, imaging filing systems, facsimile machines, word processors, typewriters, calculators, cameras and lenses, camcorders, and optical equipment among many others. Canon holds about 25 percent of the U.S. photocopier market. The company is renowned for its innovations, and is consistently one of the top 10 companies in terms of U.S. patents issued. With revenues of $1.9 billion in 1997, Canon continued to show solid sales growth throughout the 1990s. Canon employs more than 9,800 people at more than 30 facilities throughout North, Central, and South America and the Caribbean.

COMPANY FINANCES

Canon U.S.A., Inc.'s 1997 revenues increased 43.7 percent to 221,036 million yen ($1.9 billion) or 8.6 percent of net sales from fiscal 1996 earnings of $7.5 billion. This compares with 7.1 percent in 1995 and 5.7 percent in 1994. Canon's net income in 1996 was 94,177 yen ($812 million), a 71.1-percent increase over 1995, representing a 3.7-percent return on sales. Net income in 1995 and 1994 was 55,036 and 31,024 million yen, respectively.

In fiscal 1997 Canon reported record sales for the second consecutive year in both consolidated net sales and net earnings. The company's net sales increased by 7.9 percent to 2,761.0 billion yen ($21.2 billion), and net earnings increased by 26.2 percent to 118.8 billion yen ($914 million) over fiscal 1996. Net income per common and common equivalent share for fiscal 1996 was 106.96 yen ($0.92), and the annual dividends per share increased by 2.00 yen ($0.02) to reach 15.00 yen ($0.13) per share.

Canon's increase in revenue was the direct result of earnings incurred by its business machines; in particular, digital and color-copying machines. In fact, Canon's business machines accounted for 83 percent of the company's overall earnings. Cameras, on the other hand, accounted for 9 percent of overall net sales, representing strong demand for the Advanced Photo System-based cameras. Canon's optical and other products contributed 8 percent of overall earnings.

ANALYSTS' OPINIONS

In 1996 Canon's broadcast lenses earned Canon U.S.A. an Emmy Award, the highest honor in the U.S. television industry. In 1997 Canon's GP200F was named Multifunction Product of the Year in the annual office machine dealer survey conducted by Marketing Research Consultants, Inc. (MRC). In fact, dealers have recognized Canon for the past 12 years with an award by MRC.

Canon's ELPH camera was awarded a gold medal at the 1997 Industrial Design Excellence Awards (IDEA) design competition. First introduced in 1996, the ELPH camera has won many other awards and has been called "a timeless design destined to become a classic."

The 1998 Value Line Investment Survey reported that several Japanese companies will have a decrease in earnings due to the financial collapse in southeast Asia. In addition, it also stated that "foreign chipmakers have been hurt by low prices since 1996." However, Value Line predicts that increase in demand for the video disk technology will compensate for the other less-profitable business areas. Nevertheless, in their opinion, "These stocks are not timely in 1998 and investors should research them carefully."

HISTORY

In 1933 Takeshi Mitarai and Saburo Uchida formed "Seiki Kogaku Kenkyusho" (Precision Optical Research Laboratory) in Tokyo to build Japan's first 35mm camera. Two years later the camera was introduced under the brand name "Kwanon," after the Buddhist goddess of mercy; later they renamed the company "Canon." U.S. GIs stationed in Japan after World War II were avid customers for the cameras. In 1955 Canon established a small branch office in New York City, believing that the North American market could become a major part of their operations.

FAST FACTS:
About Canon U.S.A., Inc.

Ownership: Canon U.S.A., Inc. is a subsidiary of Canon, Inc., which is a publicly owned company traded on NASDAQ.

Ticker symbol: CANNY

Officers: Haruo Murase, Pres. & CEO; Seymour Liebman, Exec. VP, Finance & Administration; John Bollock, VP Human Resources

Employees: 9,800

Principal Subsidiary Companies: Canon U.S.A., Inc.'s many subsidiaries include: Astro Business Solutions Inc., Astro Office Products Inc., Canon Computer Systems Inc., Canon Information Systems Inc., Canon Research Center America, Canon Virginia Inc., SELEX Div., and Visual Communications System Div.

Chief Competitors: Canon competes for market share domestically and overseas. Some primary competitors include: Casio; Compaq; Dell; Eastman Kodak; Fuji Photo; Lam Research; Hewlett-Packard; Kodak; Minolta; NEC; Nikon; Seiko; Sharp; Siemens; Sony; Texas Instruments; Toshiba; Zerox; Olympus; Tokyo Electron; Varian; and Advantest.

In 1964 Canon diversified into business equipment, introducing the first 10-key electronic calculator, and then in 1968 it developed a plain-paper photocopier, independent of Xerox's patented technology. However, Canon's advances in the business equipment field were not matched by innovations in its photography sector, and thus Canon was surpassed by Minolta and Pentax as Japan's leading camera exporters. Canon's managing director in the early 1970s, Ryuzaburo Kaku, turned the company around, promoting the electronic AE-1 in a media blitz that in 1976 included the first television commercials for a 35mm camera. By automating almost every feature, Canon made 35mm cameras accessible to even the clumsiest camera operator. Its success catapulted Canon past Minolta as the world's number-one camera maker.

In 1979 Canon produced the first copier to use a dry developer. Canon Virginia, Inc., Canon's primary production facility in the United States, was opened in Newport News, Virginia, in 1987. In 1992 Canon announced

CHRONOLOGY:

Key Dates for Canon U.S.A., Inc.

1933: Takeshi Mitarai and Saburo Uchida form Seiki Kogaku Kenkyusho (Precision Optical Research Laboratory) to build Japan's first 35mm camera

1935: They introduce the "Kwanon" camera named after the Buddhist goddess of mercy

1937: Incorporates under the name Precision Optical Company

1941: Precision Optical develops Japan's first indirect x-ray camera

1947: The company is renamed Canon Camera Company Limited

1955: The American subsidiary opens in New York

1964: Introduces the world's first ten-key keypad electronic calculator

1968: Introduces the world's first plain-paper copier to rival Xerox's xerography procedure

1976: Canon develops a 35mm camera that uses a microprocessor to focus automatically and set exposure length

1982: Introduces the world's first personal copier

1992: Announces joint venture with IBM to create portable personal computers with built-in printers

1997: Receives *Discover* magazine's Technology Innovation Award for its solar shingles

a joint venture with IBM to produce portable personal computers with built-in bubble-jet printers, and has since cooperated with IBM in other joint ventures. In 1996 the company established a research and development center for its bubble-jet printers and peripheral products in Costa Mesa, California.

STRATEGY

Canon's strategy of introducing cutting-edge technology in a myriad of products has served the company well. More than 10 percent of its annual head-office sales are funneled into the research and development of original technologies, and the company patents numerous in-

novations every year. Canon has also diversified its products as part of its strategy; for example, when the plain-paper copier market matured in the early 1980s, Canon shifted to manufacturing other automated office machines, including laser printers and fax machines.

Canon continues to produce innovations that make advanced cameras easy to use, and has introduced a camcorder that lets users operate the focus and other functions by eye movement. One of Canon's newest technological breakthroughs and one that may be its entree into new markets is ferroelectric liquid display for flat-panel high-resolution display screens. Canon expects this product to replace cathode ray tubes in computer and TV screens as the industry standard. If Canon can position itself as a leading producer in this burgeoning market, the company can open a new sector of its production and marketing in TV screen production.

Canon also continues to introduce new standards for consumer electronics, including Elph, the world's smallest compact camera, and the first solar-powered camera. Canon plans to spend the balance of the decade focusing on multimedia technologies and clean-energy products such as solar cells. United Solar, an American joint venture between Energy Conversion Devices, Inc. and Canon Inc., developed a flexible solar shingle product— a thin-film solar cell in the form of a lightweight roofing shingle that employs proprietary thin-film photovoltaics. The shingle can be incorporated aesthetically into the roof to provide electrical energy to the household by converting sunlight directly into electricity. The UNI-SOLAR shingle was judged the best innovation in the environment category by a panel of experts from *Discover* magazine and was awarded the magazine's 1997 Technology Innovation Award.

INFLUENCES

A healthy demand for personal computers has helped Canon's sales in Japan. The falling price of personal computers worldwide allows consumers to spend more on peripherals, such as printers and copiers. To avoid the effects of a slowing U.S. economy, stagnant growth in Europe, and weak consumer spending at home, Canon has cut costs by shifting production outside Japan and buying more parts overseas.

Canon's strategy for product introduction is to meet the needs of each geographic location. For example, the demand for digital technology exists in Japan, North America, and Europe. However, in southeast Asian nations the demand is for black-and-white analog machines. Therefore, Canon's products are developed and marketed accordingly. This strategy has proven successful for Canon.

CURRENT TRENDS

In 1988, a year after its 50th anniversary, Canon instituted a new corporate philosophy. According to the CEO, this is "the achievement of corporate growth and development, with the aim of contributing to global prosperity and the well-being of humankind . . . *kyosei*." The Japanese word *kyosei* means living and working together for the common good. However, some critics of Japanese mega-industries believe this concept is used as a justification for the formation of cartels.

Canon continues to introduce new products to remain competitive within the industry. For example, the company launched a new XL1 computer video camera, the Hybrid digital-video camcorder, and the $3.7-million I-line stepper, among other products. The company also formed a partnership with competitor Hewlett-Packard to build laser printers. An article in the *Far Eastern Economic Review,* referred to Canon as "one of a number of companies that have managed to perform well despite Japan's economic difficulties." However, the article also commented on the future growth of Canon: "The company will have to develop more extremely successful products if it is to continue growing at its current rate." Some analysts believe that Canon is not developing any such products at this time. On the contrary, the company continues to be committed to research and development. Canon believes it will succeed in the new market of digital networked systems and, therefore, continue its growth.

PRODUCTS

Canon manufactures many diverse products. Business machines are its best-sellers; these include bubble-jet printers, computers, electronic typewriters, fax machines, full-color copiers (Canon Color Laser Copier 800S), office copiers, personal copiers, and word processors. Computer peripherals include image scanners, printers, and laser-beam printers. The new printer pushes digital color laser output quality and reliability to new heights.

In its photography sector Canon continues to innovate, especially in the field of digital cameras. The Power Shot 350 is Canon's easy-to-use digital camera. The ES6000 Hi8 Camcorder allows the user to control the functions of the camcorder (focus, start/stop, fade in/out, etc.) simply by using eye movement. The EOS IX 35mm camera is Canon's top-of-the-line camera. The Canon ELPH has won many awards since its official introduction in February 1996, including a Gold Medal in the 1997 Industrial Design Excellence Awards design competition, sponsored by *Business Week* magazine and the Industrial Designers Society of America. *Photographic Trade News* named it "Camera of the Year" and *Popular Science* listed it among the "Best 100 Products of 1996." *Good Housekeeping* rated it a "good buy." The Canon ELPH 490Z is the world's smallest 4x power zoom camera. The Photo-Video Player IP-100 is designed for use with any Advanced Photo System-format film (also made by Canon). Using this player, photographs taken with Canon ELPH, ELPH 490Z, or EOS IX cameras can be viewed on a regular television. Canon also produces lenses for the movie industry and binoculars for personal use.

In its medical equipment division Canon's newest offerings are a high-speed film scanner for X-ray film filing and teleradiography, the world's first full auto-alignment tonometer (for ophthalmologic use), the CF-60UD fundus camera, the RK-3 auto refractor/keratometer, and the Communicator CC-7P and CC-7S (a compact communication aid for people with speech disorders). Canon manufactures optical drives and cards; the Read/Write drive RW50 is used in a range of applications, including health care, and to offer secure identification cards for travel and immigration. Canon has introduced its new silicon wafers (SOI wafers) called ELTRANTM (Epitaxial Layer TRANsfer). The new process of manufacturing its silicon chips has been patented by Canon.

CORPORATE CITIZENSHIP

In 1990 Canon introduced its "Clean Earth Campaign" with a toner recycling program, and it has since expanded the program to include work with major environmental organizations. In the United States, Canon has given major financial contributions to the National Park Foundation; has sponsored the National Wildlife Federation's "NatureLink" program, which provides nature visits inner-city families; and sponsors the widely acclaimed PBS television program "Nature." Canon also operates several public art-related programs, including ARTLAB, a laboratory that aims to create new artistic fields by applying digital technologies to artistic pursuits. ARTLAB consists of an office and a factory that are staffed full-time by Canon's computer engineers. The Canon Foundation provides funds for scientific research and grants to promote mutual understanding between European countries and Japan. The company also supports the United Nations Environmental Programme photo contest, an international event that heightens people's awareness environmental issues. At the local level it supports arts and sports programs in communities where their corporate subsidiaries and plants are located. Finally, the company participates in Yellowstone National Park's wildlife conservation program.

GLOBAL PRESENCE

Canon is truly a global corporation, with subsidiaries in Europe, South America, North America, the United

Kingdom, and Asia, and with sales agents in most countries. Canon's expectations for growth hinge on other markets in the Asia/Pacific region. It plans to set up joint ventures in the Philippines, Vietnam, and India in response to growing demand for printers and copiers there. As the business-machine market matures in the United States and Europe, Canon continues to expand into other technologies, usually through joint ventures with small innovative companies. Industry trend spotters consider Canon's effort to move into "clean" technology to be a smart move, as the company offers more products for the growing environmentally conscious market.

EMPLOYMENT

Canon seeks employees on its web site. The company's message to potential employees is, "If you're motivated, upbeat and show real team spirit—and you're eager to explore our vision of the future—find out more about jobs we currently have available and the benefits they provide. Be sure to fill out our mini-resume!" The company offers complete benefits, including profit sharing and an annual bonus program. Because of its diversity and global presence, Canon is always seeking employees in its various business segments. The company posts available positions on its web site, along with a brief description of each.

SOURCES OF INFORMATION

Bibliography

Canon Annual Report. Tokyo, Japan: Canon, Inc., 1997.

Canon, Inc. Home Page, 20 May 1998. Available at http://www. canon.com.

"Canon Reports Results for Fiscal 1997." *Canon Corporate Public Relations.* New York, 1998.

Canon, USA. Home Page, 27 July 1998. Available at http://www. usa.canon.com/.

Desmone, Edward W. "Can Canon Keep Kicking?" *Fortune,* 2 February 1998.

"Friendly Enemies: Canon and Hewlett-Packard Have a Fruitful Marriage Building Laser Printers, Even While They Duke It Out In Other Markets." *Fortune,* 2 February 1998.

"Foreign Electronics/Entertainment." *The Value Line Investment Survey,* 13 February 1998.

"Hybrid Digital-Video Camcorder." *Electronics Now,* January 1998.

Landers, Peter. "Quality Counts." *Far Eastern Economic Review,* 5 February 1998.

McGrath, Dylan. "$3.7M I-line Stepper Introduced by Canon." *Electronic News (1991),* 30 March 1998.

Mitchell, Keith. "Not for the Camera-Shy." *Macworld,* February 1998.

For an annual report:

write: Canon U.S.A., Inc., 1 Canon Plz., Lake Success, NY 11042-1198

For additional industry research:

Investigate companies by their Standard Industrial Classification Codes, also known as SICs. Canon's primary SICs are:

3577 Computer Peripheral Equipment

5043 Photographic Equipment and Supplies

5044 Office Equipment

5045 Computer, Peripherals, and Software

5047 Medical and Hospital Equipment

5048 Ophthalmic Goods

Carnival Corporation

OVERVIEW

The Miami-based Carnival Corporation, also known as the "Fun Ships," is the world's largest and most profitable cruise company, holding approximately one-third of the North American cruise market. As a whole, the cruise corporation has interests in seven cruise brands including Carnival Cruise Lines, Holland America Line, Windstar Cruises, Cunard Line, Seabourn Cruise Line, Costa Crociere, SpA, and Airtours' Sun Cruises. Together, these lines operate a total of 42 cruise ships sailing to destinations such as the Caribbean, Bahamas, Mexico, Alaska, South Pacific, and Europe. The corporation has become the most affordable and popular line among families looking for a unique vacation experience. With cruise ships named "Tropicale," Fantasy," and "Sensation," the line focuses on budget minded individuals who are interested in participating in several activities and, at the same time, enjoy a relaxing holiday.

Carnival is the industry leader, with an estimated North American market share of 38 percent, maintaining a solid lead over its nearest competitor, Royal Caribbean, who acquired Celebrity Cruises. This increased Royal's market share to an estimated 27 percent. In addition, in 1998 the Walt Disney Co. entered the cruise market with the introduction of the first of two cruise ships. As reported in Carnival's 1997 Annual Report, "The U.S. Bureau of Economic Analysis predicts that by year 2000 there will be a 30-plus percent growth in the 41-59 age group, a prime demographic group for cruising, and a very positive indication for the cruise industry."

FOUNDED: 1972

Contact Information:

HEADQUARTERS: Carnival Pl., MSEO 1000
    3655 NW 87th Ave.
    Miami, FL 33178-2428
PHONE: (305)599-2600
FAX: (305)406-4700
URL: http://www.carnival.com
    http://www.carnivalcorp.com

CARNIVAL
CORPORATION

FINANCES:

Carnival Corp.
Revenues, 1994-1997
(billion dollars)

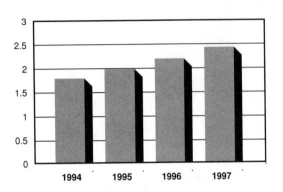

Carnival Corp.
1997 Stock Prices
(dollars)

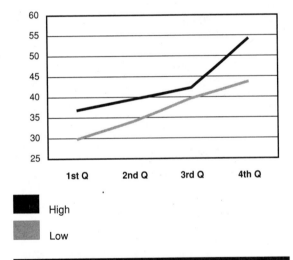

■ High

▨ Low

Carnival's Board of Directors approved a two-for-one stock split of its Class A common shares. Also, the Board reported a regular quarterly dividend of $.15 per share. In 1997 Carnival stock ranged from a low of $34.38 to a high of $76.50 over a 52-week period. The annual dividend was $2.32 and Carnival's price-earnings ratio was 29.08.

ANALYSTS' OPINIONS

In 1997 William Blair & Co. reported, "the cruise industry will be one of the faster-growing segments of consumer spending over the next 5-10 years, as major demographic changes dramatically shift consumer spending from goods to services, especially leisure." In fact, on March 23, 1998, *The Wall Street Journal* reported "strong demand for cruises" as Carnival's profits increased by 29 percent. The 1997 Value Line Investment Survey reported that the recreation industry would experience growth in 1998 and, therefore, many shares within the industry are expected to perform well. Some analysts believe Carnival, Princess Cruises, and Royal Caribbean Cruises will control 80 percent of the North American market share by the year 2000.

On April 3, 1998 Standard & Poor's Credit Rating Co. revised the outlook of Carnival Corporation to positive from stable. *Standard & Poor's* referred to Carnival as "reflecting continued strong operating results, improving credit measures, and favorable industry fundamentals." T. P. Razukas of Duff & Phelps Credit Rating Co. agreed and wrote, "The addition of new ships has driven company's growth and market share gains, as the North American cruise market continues to consolidate." Also, Carnival Corporation's "modern and cost-efficient fleet has enabled the company to attract customers and reduce prices when necessary without a significant adverse impact on earnings." Many analysts believe consolidation within the industry helps to strengthen it by removing the weaker players. In the same way, less competition should reduce price wars and make the industry more profitable for everyone.

COMPANY FINANCES

Carnival Corporation reported net income of $109.9 million on revenues of $557.8 million for its first quarter 1998, which ended February 28, compared with net income of $85.4 million on revenues of $521.1 million for the same quarter in 1997—a 7.1-percent increase. Net income increased 28.8 percent for the first quarter in 1998, marking the twenty-seventh consecutive quarter in which Carnival has reported year-over-year earnings improvement.

HISTORY

Carnival Cruise lines began in 1972 when Ted Arison persuaded his friend, Meshulam Riklis, to lend him $6.5 million to purchase the ship "Empress of Canada." Arison, formerly with Norwegian Cruise Lines, and Riklis, owner of Boston-based American International Travel Service, set up Carnival as a subsidiary of AITS. They renamed the ship the "Mardi Gras," and it unfortunately ran aground on its maiden voyage. This sent the company into the red for the next three years. Arison bought out Riklis in 1974 for $1, and assumed the company's $5-million debt.

Arison wanted to create a cruise line that offered affordable vacations to young, middle-class customers. He invented an innovative way to cruise by offering live entertainment, gambling, and other activities on cruises. Within a month of this creation Carnival was profitable, the debt was paid off, and Arison bought a second ship. A third ship was purchased in 1977.

In 1978 fuel and shipbuilding costs were high, but Arison stunned the industry by announcing that Carnival would be building a ship that would set sail in 1982. In 1979 Arison's son Micky took over as CEO, and it was his motivation and Carnival's success that led the company to build three more ships. Carnival continued to grow and became the number one cruise line, and in 1987 the company went public.

During the course of the company's growth, the line added three- and four-day cruises to the Bahamas. In 1988 Carnival opened the Crystal Palace Resort in the Bahamas, and after purchasing Holland America Line (HAL) in 1989, began offering luxury cruises. HAL offered cruises to Alaska and the Caribbean. Carnival also acquired Windstar Cruises, which offered trips to the Caribbean and the South Pacific. During this time, the corporation also ran Westours and the Westmark hotel chain.

Carnival continued to add new ships in the 1990s, and in 1991 purchased Premier Cruise Lines. That same year the company started a joint venture with Seabourn Cruise Line. They sold one of the Crystal Palace Resort hotels to the government-owned Hotel Corporation of the Bahamas, and put the rest of the resort up for sale in 1992. A total of 82 percent of the resort/casino was sold in Nassau in 1994. That year the company changed its name to Carnival Corporation to distinguish between the entire company and the cruise line of the same name. Carnival also announced that it would merge with Continental Companies to form Carnival Hotels and Casinos, which increased Carnival's land interests. Besides these business endeavors, Carnival and HAL planned to launch seven new ships—three in 1996, one in 1997, and three in 1998.

STRATEGY

The company markets the Carnival Ships as the "Fun Ships" and incorporates themes such as "Carnival's Got the Fun" and "The Most Popular Cruise Line in the World." Carnival's strategic approach to advertising is directed to consumers on network television and through extensive print media. Carnival believes its advertising generates interest in cruise vacations generally and results in a higher degree of consumer awareness of the "Fun Ships" concept and the "Carnival" name in particular.

FAST FACTS:
About Carnival Corporation

Ownership: Carnival Corporation is a publicly owned company traded on the New York Stock Exchange.

Ticker symbol: CCL

Officers: Micky Arison, Chmn. & CEO, 47, 1997 base salary $1,211,000; Gerald R. Cahill, Sr. VP Finance & COO; Howard S. Frank, VC & COO, 56, 1997 base salary $897,000; Roderick K. McLeod, Sr. VP Marketing

Employees: 18,100

Principal Subsidiary Companies: Carnival's principal subsidiaries include Holland America Line Westours Inc. and Crystal Palace Hotel Corp.

Chief Competitors: Carnival Corp.'s primary competitors include: Accor; Canadian Pacific; Carlson; Club Med; Costa Cruise Lines; Overseas Shipholding; Peninsular and Oriental; Princess Cruises; Royal Caribbean Cruises; Sea Containers; Thomson Corp.; Trafalgar House; Vard; Viad; and Walt Disney.

INFLUENCES

To attract other cultures to Carnival, the company began FiestaMarina cruise line for Latin travelers. This turned out to be a difficult venture because of marketing and equipment problems—the project was discontinued in 1994. Even with this disappointment, Carnival purchased a stake in United Kingdom's Airtours, which consisted of airplanes, cruise ships, hotels, and travel agencies.

In 1996 Carnival Corporation announced that it would be participating in a joint venture with Hyundai Merchant Marine to create "Carnival Cruises Asia." This would develop the Asian cruise market and would begin with Carnival Cruises' MS "Tropicale" in the spring of 1998. Initial cruises were to be from Inchon, Korea, to China, and possibly Japan. The "Tropicale" was a 1,022-passenger ship scheduled to undergo a multimillion dollar renovation before entering the Asian service. The 36,674-ton vessel was also set to be repositioned to other ports throughout southeast Asia. Scheduled cruise operations were set for the spring of 1998, however, the joint venture was dissolved in September 1997.

The "Carnival Destiny" cruise ship, one of the largest in the world, is taller than the Statue of Liberty. It can accommodate 3,400 passengers and 1,000 crew members.

(*Reuters/Str/Archive Photos.*)

CURRENT TRENDS

From 1995 to 1996 Carnival experienced a slow period, but in 1997 the cruise industry outlook seemed to improve. CEO Micky Arison felt that demand was actually the strongest he had witnessed since he entered the industry in the early 1980s. Some analysts felt that the extensive advertising by Disney Cruise Lines for their spring 1998 launch heightened industry awareness among consumers. Due to the success of the "Rotterdam," introduced in November 1997, Holland America Line announced it had contracted for a sister ship for delivery in the year 2000. The company's confidence in the future led them to undertake the largest passenger shipbuilding program ever, with new ships planned for each of their major cruise brands. Additionally, Carnival was expected to debut the world's first smoke-free cruise ship, the "Paradise," in November 1998.

In 1997 Carnival Cruises announced it would be starting a new advertising campaign to attract individuals who were looking for a fun vacation. The television advertisements focused on a combination of real and animated imagery. The commercials, created by HMS Partners, were 30 seconds long and aired nationally. Both consisted of music and visuals until the end, when television personality Kathie Lee Gifford made

an endorsement. (Gifford is a longtime spokesperson for Carnival.) The first spot was entitled "Fish," and contained underwater scenes of different species of fish, swimming around a Caribbean reef. The fish hear Mambo music coming from a nearby Carnival cruise ship, and the fish begin to dance. The voice-over by Gifford begins and the phrase "I guess some vacations are just more fun than others" is heard. The second commercial was similar, but the dancing fish are replaced by dancing palm trees on a deserted Caribbean island.

The intended function of the commercials was to promote an idea of fun. Carnival's president, Bob Dickinson stated, "We were seeking a fresh approach to advertising yet one that continued our efforts to convey the single most outstanding feature of a Carnival cruise vacation-fun." They designed the commercials so the viewer would draw their own conclusions regarding the type of fun they would experience on a Carnival cruise. Many cruise lines showed how they would pamper their guests, but Carnival wanted the spots to induce a personal response. They showed the commercials during "Good Morning America," the "Today" show, "CBS This Morning," and "The Tonight Show." They also showed the commercials during prime time throughout the week.

PRODUCTS

Primarily, the Carnival Corporation offers fun as its most lucrative product. Its ships offer a variety of activities ranging from shuffleboard to swimming and exercising in their famous Nautica Spas. Carnival has 3-, 4, and 7-day cruises to the Bahamas and the Caribbean. There is also a Walt Disney package available that includes lodging at a Disney World Resort, admission to the theme park, and a 5-, 6-, or 7-day cruise. In 1996 Carnival added an 11-day cruise to Hawaii, 10- or 11-day cruises to the southern Caribbean, and 10- or 11-day cruises to the Panama Canal. Seven-day cruises to Alaska are also available. Each cruise ship offers an around-the-clock buffet that includes several different edibles. They also offer 24-hour room service. The chefs are masters at preparing several varieties of international cuisine and traditional favorites. The food is included in the price of the cruise, so the travelers can indulge at no extra cost.

Each ship has live entertainment, dancing, and casinos. Gambling is available throughout the day and evening, and Carnival boasts the world's largest cruise ship jackpot. The ships have Las Vegas-type shows that consist of singing and dancing. Airfare, accommodations, meals, entertainment, ports of call, and activities are all included in the price of the cruise. In 1996, to guarantee satisfaction, Carnival offered a program to passengers who were dissatisfied with their trip. A first in the industry, this program would reimburse those individuals who were unhappy with their cruise. To make it easier for consumers to take a cruise, Carnival incorporated Princess Cruises' policy and started a financing program in 1997. In addition, to attract more business the company launched a new site on the World Wide Web in April 1998.

Carnival also tries to accommodate younger passengers. To do this, they started "Camp Carnival," which offers activities that appeal to children and teens. A children's pool and slide, teen club and video game room, and a special children's menu are some of the items available with "Camp Carnival." This program also offers babysitting at a nominal fee.

CORPORATE CITIZENSHIP

CEO Mickey Arison set up the Arison Foundation under the "corporate umbrella." The foundation contributes heavily to the arts, an area in which he exhibits extreme interest. Through the Carnival Cruise Line, the company set up the Carnival Cruise Foundation, which funds many charitable organizations.

GLOBAL PRESENCE

Originally, Carnival Corporation had a market presence primarily in North America. In 1996 the company

CHRONOLOGY:
Key Dates for Carnival Corporation

1972: Ted Arison borrows $6.5 million from Meshulam Riklis to buy a cruise ship and start a company; Carnival Cruise is formed as a subsidiary of Riklis' company American International Travel Service

1974: Arison buys Riklis share of Carnival for $1, but also got its debt of $5 million

1979: Ted Arison's son Micky becomes president and CEO of Carnival

1984: Carnival initiates the "Fun Ship" advertising campaign featuring Kathy Lee Gifford

1987: Carnival goes public

1990: Ted Arison steps down as chairman and Micky takes over

1994: Carnival Cruise becomes Carnival Corporation and merges with Continental Companies to form Carnival Hotels and Casinos

1997: A joint venture with Hyundai Merchant Marine to create Carnival Cruises Asia is dissolved

began to expand into Europe and partnered with U.K.-based, Airtours. Airtours sells packaged tours in the British, Belgian, French, Dutch, Scandinavian, and North American markets. In 1997 Carnival expanded its global presence with its 50-percent interest in Costa Cruises, headquartered in Italy, which sells most of its cruises in southern Europe, primarily Italy, France, and Spain. In addition, The Holland America Westours offers cruises in the Caribbean, Alaska, Panama Canal, Europe, the Mediterranean, Hawaii, the South Pacific, South America, and the Orient. Carnival hoped to acquire Cunard Line, which operates five luxury cruise ships, by July 1998. Carnival entered this agreement with a group of Norwegian investors, however, Carnival would be the majority shareholder. This acquisition was an attempt to further Carnival's global expansion.

SOURCES OF INFORMATION

Bibliography
Anderson, Chris. Carnival Corporation Telephone Conversation, 26 May 1998.

"Carnival Corporation." *Hoover's Handbook of American Business 1998.* Austin, TX: The Reference Press, 1997.

"Carnival Corporation." *Hoover's Online,* May 1998. Available at http://www.hoovers.com.

Carnival Corporation Annual Report. Miami, FL.: Carnival Corporation, 1997.

"Carnival Corporation Launches Web Site." *PR Newswire,* 1 April 1998. Available at http://www.marketguide.com.

Carnival Corporation Home Page, 23 August 1998. Available at http://www.carnival.com.

"'Carnival Cruises Asia' Selected as Name for New Carnival/Hyundai Joint Venture Company." Carnival Cruises Press Release, 25 February 1997.

"Carnival Cruise Lines to Introduce New Television Advertising Campaign Featuring Computerized and Special Effects." Carnival Cruise Lines Press Release, 2 January 1997.

"Carnival to Add Loan Program." *Travel Weekly,* 17 April 1997.

de la cruz, Jennifer. Carnival Corporation Telephone Conversation, 27 May 1998.

Razukas, T.P., et al. "Carnival Corporation-Company Report." *Duff & Phelps Credit Rating Co.,* 29 September 1997.

"Recrestion Industry." *The Value Line Investment Survey,* 28 November 1997.

Simonson, R.J., et al. "Carnival Corporation-Company Report." *William Blair & Co.,* 12 May 1997.

"Strong Demand for Cruises Fuels 29% Profit Increase." *The Wall Street Journal,* 23 March 1998.

For an annual report:

telephone: (305)599-2600, x-10850

For additional industry research:

Investigate companies by their Standard Industrial Classification Codes, also known as SICs. Carnival Corp.'s primary SICs are:

3731 Ship Building and Repairing

4481 Deep Sea Transportation of Passengers, Except by Ferry

4724 Travel Agencies

7011 Hotels and Motels

7991 Physical Fitness Facilities

Cartier, Inc.

FOUNDED: 1847

OVERVIEW

Cartier is one of the world's leading luxury goods companies. The company designs, manufactures, and distributes jewelry, watches, fragrance, pens, lighters, silver, and crystal. The House of Cartier is identified with quality, prestige, and history, and has served as crown jeweler to 19 royal houses.

Since its beginning in 1847, Cartier has been closely identified with jewels and other objects of exceptional quality. Cartier is known for its use of rare materials, unique designs, and timeless creations representing status and mystique. Its customers range from members of royalty and celebrities to young women seeking a distinctive engagement ring. Cartier's success was founded in family tradition, loyalty, and the quest for innovative objects. Writing in *Vogue,* Joan Juliet Buck asserted that "Cartier has set the standard of luxury."

Contact Information:
HEADQUARTERS: 5th Ave. and 52nd St.
    New York, NY 10022
PHONE: (212)753-0111
FAX: (212)753-7250

COMPANY FINANCES

Cartier is a family business that has no intention of ever going public. In 1989, President of Cartier International Alain Perrin explained: "I consider a luxury company going public a big risk, unless you need the money to fund an acquisition," adding that "if you are well managed, you can fund your expansion yourself." In 1998 Cartier did in fact expand with its own resources and remained a private company.

According to Perrin, the company's annual sales have increased an average of 20 to 25 percent over the past 10 to 12 years, and most sales are in jewelry and

FAST FACTS:
About Cartier, Inc.

Ownership: Cartier is a privately held company.

Officers: Main-Dominique Perrin, Chmn. & CEO of Cartier International; Micheline Kanoui, Director of Design; Simon J. Critchell, Pres. & CEO of Cartier, Inc.

Employees: approximately 300

Chief Competitors: Cartier, Inc. competes with other designers within the luxury jewelry industry. Some primary competitors include: Dior; Chanel; Tiffany & Co.; Goldman, Sachs & Co.; and House of Winston.

watches. It is estimated that the company's annual sales are $120 million. Cartier's high-end jewelry represents about 22 percent of the group's revenues.

HISTORY

The House of Cartier was established in 1847 by Louis-Francois Cartier, who took over Maitre Adolphe Picard's jewelry workshop in Paris at the age of 31. The establishment was moved in 1853, and Cartier began developing a private clientele. During the rule of Napoleon III, a period of unrest ended in Paris with the resumption of many elaborate celebrations and balls that widened the market for luxury goods and further helped the house of Cartier to expand. The Emperor's first cousin, Princess Mathilde, also contributed to Cartier's growth, resulting in another move to a more prestigious Paris location in 1859. Louis-Francois attracted the notice of several members of royalty, including Empress Eugenie. His friendship with Worth, the great couturier, helped establish many other influential and long-lasting connections.

Cartier turned over the business in 1874 to his son Louis-Francois Alfred, who then made his eldest son Louis a partner in 1898. In 1899 Cartier made its final move in Paris to the prestigious 13 rue de la Paix, where Alfred entrusted the House of Cartier to his three sons— Louis-Joseph, Jacques-Thedule, and Pierre-Camille. Recognized as the world's premier jewelry retailer, Cartier continued to cultivate an elite clientele, and the three brothers began searching worldwide for innovative products and materials.

At his brother Louis's request, Pierre traveled to Russia in search of the finest enamels and hard stone animals in an attempt to compete with Peter Carl Fabérge. Relationships with the United States were strengthened in 1910 when Cartier sold the "Hope" diamond to Mrs. Evalyn McLean of New York. That sale aided in establishing connections with wealthy financiers and industrialists such as the Rockefellers, Vanderbilts, Goulds, and Fords. From London, Jacques searched for the finest pearls in the Persian Gulf and traveled to India to fulfill orders from Indian maharajahs who wanted their multicolored treasures reset by Cartier.

Although wristwatches had been in stock since 1888, they became popular only with Cartier's introduction of the Santos watch in 1911. The prototype model was a gift from Louis Cartier to Brazilian aviator Alberto Santos-Dumont. Other products introduced by Cartier were the Tank watch and the "Love Bracelet." Cartier was extremely creative during Louis's management. He revolutionized the industry until his death in 1942, the same year his younger brother Jacques also died. The company was then taken over by Robert Hocq, who developed new product lines of watches, leather goods, and perfumes.

STRATEGY

Cartier introduces many objects that reflect contemporary ideas and trends, as well as the demands of its exclusive clientele. In 1902 Cartier workshops operated at fever pitch to accommodate orders from royal courts all over the world for the coronation of Edward VII. In 1930, an Indian maharajah bought 250 Cartier clocks and watches and hired someone whose sole responsibility was to keep them all wound. Inspired by a watch that had been damaged in an apparent car wreck, in 1967 Cartier created the Crash Watch, which exhibited a distorted dial and subsequently became a collector's item. The introduction of Cartier's Tank Française Watch in 1996 prompted watchmaker Jean-Charles de Castelbajac to say, "If all tanks were made by Cartier, we would have the time to live in peace!"

Cartier introduces new collections every two years at a showing or premiere. For its "Jewels of the Nile" exhibition in New York, the store was completely decorated in an Egyptian theme, complete with a pyramid and two live peacocks. This jewelry collection was a more modern version of Louis Joseph Cartier's designs from the early 1900s.

Cartier's boutiques are as luxurious as its products. The Beverly Hills boutique features a limestone and Vermont verde marble facade with windows framed in brass. Features include a fine jewelry salon with oak panels, carved moldings, and soft peach ceiling lights. During the boutique's opening in 1992, clients were invited for champagne.

In 1995 Cartier introduced So Pretty de Cartier, the first perfume offered since its very first fragrance, Les Must, was launched in 1981. Although Cartier has historically avoided advertising, CEO Simon Critchell promoted the new product with an extensive $2-million campaign.

INFLUENCES

Cartier credits its success to "talented colleagues"—in particular, Jeanne Toussaint, whom Louis referred to as a "trend watcher, a style setter, a woman who understood luxury and how to make it synonymous with Cartier." As a closely held company, Cartier guards its proprietary secrets closely and deals decisively with counterfeiters, once crushing fake Cartier watches on a Los Angeles street with a steamroller. Roberta Naas reported that "Cartier is so often emulated by others that it has imposed strict locked-door policies in its design houses and has started stringent anticounterfeit efforts in the watch world." Cartier has two jewelry design houses, one for the more modern line and the other, whose location is top secret, for the "important" jewelry.

Cartier's most timeless pieces are made of platinum, whose use in fine jewelry it pioneered in 1898. In February 1997, The Consumer Benchmark Survey revealed that "platinum has become the metal of choice for most innovative and sought-after luxury jewelry designers and the high-end jewelry purchaser . . . Of manufacturers polled, 96 percent had increased the use of platinum in their top lines, and 94 percent added new platinum designs to their lines within the past nine months."

In 1997 Cartier celebrated its 150th Anniversary with the introduction of several new product lines. As evidence of Cartier's standing as the most famous French jeweler, the company became a member of the "Vendome Luxury Group" in 1993. The group was presided over by Joseph Kanoui, who joined Cartier after Robert Hocq's death in 1979, and included Cartier, Alfred Dunhill, Montblac, Piaget, Baume and Mercier, Karl Lagerfeld, Chloe, Sulka, Hackett, Seeger, and James Purdy and Sons.

CURRENT TRENDS

In the late 1990s signature lines were keeping Cartier's traditions alive. Often found in necklaces, bracelets, and watches, its Panther motif (known as la Panthere in French) brings together the most luxurious metals, precious stones, and artistic creations in some of the rarest pieces of jewelry in the world. The famous Panter design was a tribute to Jeanne Toussaint and her influence in the company.

CHRONOLOGY:
Key Dates for Cartier, Inc.

1847: The House of Cartier is established by Louis-Francois Cartier

1859: Cartier moves to a more prestigious Paris location after gaining several members of the royalty as customers

1874: Louis-Francois Alfred, Cartier's son, takes over the company

1899: Alfred passes the company, recognized as the world's premiere jewelry retailer, to his three sons: Louis-Joseph, Jacques-Thedule, and Pierre-Camille

1910: Sells the "Hope" diamond to Evalyn McLean of New York, establishing contacts with the wealthy American elite

1911: The Santos watch is introduced and popularizes the Cartier watch line

1942: Louis and Jacques both die; Robert Hocq takes over the company

1967: Cartier designs a watch inspired by a watch damaged in a car crash called the Crash Watch; it becomes an instant collector's item

1981: Les Must, the company's first perfume, is introduced

1993: Cartier becomes a member of the Vendome Luxury Group

1997: Cartier celebrates its 150th anniversary by releasing Cartier Privé

PRODUCTS

Throughout the years, Cartier has introduced several limited-edition specialty items. In honor of its 150th anniversary, the company released three successful series of unique, rare objects inspired by its private archives. Editions began in late 1996 and continued through 1997, with pieces released in quantities of 3, 150, and 1,847 to represent the 3 bands of its popular "Rolling Ring," the 150th anniversary, and the year that Cartier was founded, 1847. This collection, called Cartier Privé, includes jewelry, watches, pens, spectacles, and a broad range of chain purses with jeweled clasps.

CORPORATE CITIZENSHIP

In 1993, Cartier objects were displayed as part of an auction of singer Elton John's personal collection organized by Sotheby's; proceeds were donated to the Elton John AIDS Foundation. Perrin administers the Cartier Foundation for Contemporary Art, which supports, collects, and exhibits contemporary art from around the world annually. Proceeds from a showing of Cartier's jewels from the 1920s and 1930s at the Metropolitan Museum of Art in New York City were donated to the Society for the Advancement of Education. In 1997 Cartier donated $25,000 to the Crystal Charity, a children's philanthropy. In addition, Cartier donated a $26,600 watch to be raffled off at the annual Charity Ball. Cartier often makes substantial contributions to many other charitable organizations.

GLOBAL PRESENCE

Cartier has 165 boutiques on five continents. The company markets its products through a global network of 179 Cartier stores and 8,000 authorized dealers in 123 countries. In addition to 6 stores in Paris, there are 21 stores in the United States, 3 in Canada, and 6 throughout the Caribbean. The newest stores are in Barcelona; Buenos Aires; Moscow; Taiwan; and Boca Raton, Florida.

SOURCES OF INFORMATION

Bibliography

"150 Years of History and Romance." Cartier's 1997 Press Kit, 1997.

Buck, Joan Juliet. "Cartier: The Jewel in the Crown . . ." *Vogue,* February 1986.

"Cartier Launches Jewels of the Nile." *WWD,* 30 June 1989.

Denny, Godfrey. "Pierre Haquet Resigns as Cartier Director." *WWD,* 9 February 1993.

"Fabulous Jewelry from the House of Cartier." *USA Today,* May 1997.

Fallon, Jim. "Cartier Explores Growth Outside the Jewelry Label." *WWD,* 4 August 1989.

Haber, Holly. "Cartier Reopens in Dallas." *WWD,* 27 October 1997.

Larson, Soren. "Cartier's New Look: So Pretty." *WWD,* 8 September 1995.

Meadus, Amanda. "Cartier Keeps on Fighting." *WWD,* 17 October 1994.

Okun, Stacy. "The Legend and the Legacy: The House of Cartier Celebrates 150 Years of History and Romance." *Town & Country,* March 1997.

"Platinum Gains Ground with Designers and Consumers." February 1997. Available at http://www.hauer-international.com.

"Power Players in the Luxury Market," 9 May 1998. Available at http://www.robbreport.com.

Thompson, Michael. "Louise Cartier's Lasting Imprint." *Jewelers Circular Keystone,* February 1997.

Trujillo, Kerting. "Cartier Opens Jewelry Store in Boca Raton, Fla." *Knight-Ridder/Tribune Business News,* 11 February 1997.

Weideger, Paula. "Is the British Museum Falling Down?" *New Statesman,* 3 October 1997.

For additional industry research:

Investigate companies by their Standard Industrial Classification Codes, also known as SICs. Cartier's primary SICs are:

5094 Jewelry, Watches & Precious Stones

5944 Jewelry Stores

Caterpillar Inc.

OVERVIEW

Caterpillar Inc. manufactures construction, mining, and agricultural machinery. It also manufactures diesel and gas engines for trucks, locomotives, and ships, as well as electrical power generation systems. Caterpillar is a top manufacturer of earthmoving machinery, construction equipment, natural gas engines, and industrial gas turbines. The company also provides financial services for its customers. Caterpillar's focus on quickly bringing new products to market and expanding its clientele has helped increase company profits.

Chairman and CEO Donald V. Fites has stated that the "fundamental building blocks for continued success and future growth are in place." These building blocks consist of modern factories, new technology, an effective organizational structure and culture, and new products to reach expanding markets. The financial results from 1993 through 1997 demonstrate the effectiveness of the company's strategy: sales grew 63 percent, profit increased 155 percent, and profit per share increased 176 percent. Caterpillar exported a record $6.12 billion worth of products during 1997, marking an 11-percent increase over 1996. Caterpillar anticipates sales growth to customers outside the United States to increase to 75 percent of total sales and anticipates sales and revenues to climb to $30 billion by the year 2010.

COMPANY FINANCES

Profits for 1996 totaled $1.36 billion, or $3.54 per share of common stock, compared to 1995 profits of

ALSO KNOWN AS: Cat
FOUNDED: 1925

Contact Information:

HEADQUARTERS: 100 NE Adams St.
   Peoria, IL 61629
PHONE: (309)675-1000
FAX: (309)675-4457
TOLL FREE: (800)228-7717
EMAIL: CATir@CAT.e-mail.com
URL: http://www.caterpillar.com
   http://www.cat.com

CATERPILLAR®

The second fiscal quarter of 1998 was the company's second-best quarter ever for revenues and profits. Revenues totaled $5.6 billion and profits reached $446 million. As of second quarter 1998, the company had recorded profits in 16 of the previous 18 quarters.

FINANCES:

Caterpillar Sales, 1994-1997 (billion dollars)

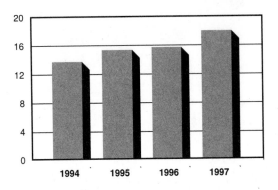

Caterpillar 1997 Stock Prices (dollars)

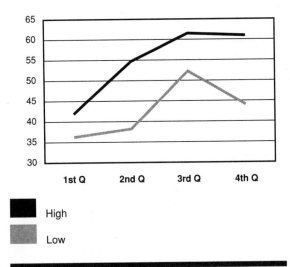

ANALYSTS' OPINIONS

Some financial analysts have expressed surprise over Caterpillar's financial success in the late 1990s. The 11-percent sales increase in 1996 was achieved with only a 2-percent increase in prices. However, some analysts have cautioned investors to remember that they closely link Caterpillar's financial success to the health of the economy.

Other analysts and investors have expressed concern over the labor issues at Caterpillar in the late 1990s. Labor strikes by the United Auto Workers (UAW) and legal action taken against the company for various workers' rights issues have plagued Caterpillar. The dispute ended in March 1998 with a six-year ratified agreement that gave UAW represented employees some of the best wages and benefits in the industry.

Another area of possible concern is Caterpillar's $1.8 billion capital-investment program. The company has been investing in new equipment in order to increase the flexibility of its manufacturing operations. While this may be a wise strategic move, some say such an expenditure is risky and the company could feel a negative impact if the health of the economy takes a turn for the worse.

HISTORY

In 1904 Benjamin Holt sought to create a machine that moved over dirt easily. He altered a tractor by replacing its steam engine with a gas engine and replacing its iron wheels with crawler tracks. He called his invention a "caterpillar." During World War I, the British armed forces imitated these adaptations when they designed their armored tanks.

Holt merged his operation with Best Tractor in 1925, and in 1928 the company was renamed Caterpillar. Its headquarter was located in Peoria, Illinois. In an effort to expand, the company sought foreign markets in the 1930s and formed an international dealer network. Caterpillar continued to grow in the 1940s, and the company supplied its earthmoving machinery to the U.S. Army during World War II. Sales more than tripled at this time. Even after the war, the company continued to enjoy large profits and increasing demand for its machinery. The company's first overseas plant was established in the United Kingdom in 1951. By 1963 Caterpillar had also established a joint venture with the Japanese giant, Mitsubishi.

$1.14 billion, or $2.86 per share. Revenues for 1996 were $16.52 billion, which was an increase of $450 million over 1995 revenues.

Caterpillar reported that 1997 was a "record setter" for the company. Revenues for 1997 were $18.93 billion, up 15 percent from 1996. Profits were $1.67 billion, up 22 percent from 1996. Profit per share of common stock was $4.44, up 25 percent from 1996 and recorded as the best ever in Caterpillar's history. This reflected the impact of the higher profit and the company's ongoing share repurchase program.

By 1981 Caterpillar's sales had reached nearly $9.2 billion. However, the company's 50-year span of ceaseless profits ended when it racked up $953 million in losses between 1982 and 1984. Demand for the company's products had fallen while the level of foreign competition had risen to an all-time high. Caterpillar expanded its product line in order to remain competitive with such global players as Japan's Komatsu, and in 1987 Caterpillar launched a $1.8 billion program to update its factories.

STRATEGY

Chairman Fites has put in place a strategy designed to make Caterpillar globally competitive using predominately United States-based manufacturing operations. One element of this strategy includes implementing a six-year capital-investment program aimed at cultivating more flexible manufacturing operations. Another strategic ingredient is a focus on new product development. Also, the company is a strong supporter of the General Agreement on Tariffs and Trade (GATT) and the North American Free Trade Agreement (NAFTA), which stands to reason since a large portion of Caterpillar's revenues come from its exports to foreign countries. Through these international trade agreements, governments define their rules for exporting and importing products to and from foreign countries. The ultimate goal is to reduce or eliminate government restrictions on imports and exports.

Caterpillar has also expanded its operations by acquiring other companies that strategically fit into its own line of business. One such move was the acquisition of Perkins Engines—Perkins is one of Caterpillar's major suppliers. Caterpillar acquired Kato Engineering from Rockwell Automation in 1998, which will further Caterpillar's growth in the electric power generation business. Since 1991 Caterpillar has entered into 38 acquisitions and joint ventures ranging from partial to 100 percent ownership.

To emphasize its focus on customer needs, Caterpillar began offering financial services to its customers in the late 1990s. Caterpillar Financial Services now serves customers in 60 countries. The company has instituted profit centers as well. These aim to mold the company into a more flexible organization that is able to do whatever is necessary to meet customer demands.

INFLUENCES

Caterpillar's upward climb to success dates back to World War I, when Benjamin Holt's track-type tractors were in high demand since they could pull artillery and supply vehicles through rough terrain. The company's profits and recognition grew tremendously during this time, as well as during World War II.

FAST FACTS:
About Caterpillar Inc.

Ownership: Caterpillar Inc. is a publicly owned company traded on the New York, Pacific, and Chicago Stock Exchanges in the United States and on stock exchanges in Belgium, France, Germany, Great Britain, and Switzerland.

Ticker symbol: CAT

Officers: Donald V. Fites, Chmn. & CEO, 63, 1997 base salary $3,356,650; Glen A. Barton, Group Pres., 57, 1997 base salary $1,116,299; Gerald S. Flaherty, Group Pres., 58, 1997 base salary $1,119,600; Richard L. Thompson, Group Pres., 57, 1997 base salary $920,233

Employees: 65,947

Principal Subsidiary Companies: Caterpillar Inc. has operations and subsidiary companies around the world. Caterpillar's chief subsidiaries include: Balderson Inc., Caterpillar Financial Services Corp., Caterpillar China Investment Co., Caterpillar Inc. Engines Div., Caterpillar Insurance Services Inc., Caterpillar Investment Management Ltd., Caterpillar Paving Products Inc., Caterpillar World Trading Corp., Engine Service Specialists Inc., Solar Turbines Inc., and Caterpillar Logistics Services, Inc.

Chief Competitors: Primary competitors include: AGCO; Allied Products; Case; Core Industries; Cummins Engine; Daimler-Benz; Deere; Ford; Krupp; Hitachi; Hyundai; Ingersoll-Rand; Isuzu; Komatsu America; Penske; Peterson Tractor; Rolls-Royce; Stewart & Stevenson; Terex; Thermo Power; and Volvo.

The company's expansion into foreign markets began in the postwar period. In 1950 Caterpillar Tractor Co. Ltd. was established in the United Kingdom, marking the first of many operations abroad. By choosing strategic locations around the world for its manufacturing operations, the company was less disadvantaged by tariffs, foreign exchange deficiencies, and import restrictions.

Caterpillar's overseas success reached new heights when the company signed an agreement with Mitsubishi in 1963 to conduct joint manufacturing operations in Japan. This joint venture, renamed Shin Caterpillar Mitsubishi Ltd. in 1987, has grown to become the number-

CHRONOLOGY:

Key Dates for Caterpillar Inc.

1904: Benjamin Holt invents the first Caterpillar by modifying a tractor

1915: British armed forces imitate his track designs in creating their armored tanks

1925: Holt merges his company with Best Tractor, renaming the company Caterpillar Tractor Company

1942: Caterpillar equipment and designs are used in the M4 tanks during World War II

1961: The first Diesel Sixty tractor rolls off the assembly line

1950: Establishes the first overseas plant in the United Kingdom

1963: Mitsubishi and Caterpillar form a joint venture

1981: Caterpillar Financial Services Corporation is formed to offer equipment financing

1997: The company acquires Perkins Engines and becomes the world leader in diesel engine manufacturing

two manufacturer of construction and mining equipment in Japan and one of the most successful United States-Japanese joint ventures to date. However, not all of Caterpillar's overseas ventures are so successful. Caterpillar's joint venture with China's Shanghai Diesel Engine Company Ltd. lost $3.6 million in 1996. By the end of 1997, Caterpillar was considering pulling out of the venture.

The economic recession and globally competitive environment of the 1980s forced Caterpillar to cut costs. The company cut jobs and analyzed how to restructure itself in order to avoid similar economic impacts in the future. In 1987 the company underwent a $1.8 billion modification program aimed at making its manufacturing plants flexible enough to produce various types of products. By doing so, the company could offer double the amount of products offered a decade earlier.

CURRENT TRENDS

One of Caterpillar's strategic moves is its trend toward setting up more joint ventures and acquisitions, par-

ticularly involving foreign markets. Among these joint ventures is Caterpillar's involvement with the Asian Strategic Investments Corporation (ASIMCO) and CITIC Machinery Manufacturing Incorporated (CMMI). Initiated in early 1997 and located in Ahanxi Province in north central China, this joint operation, called Shanxi International Castings Co., Ltd., produces engine-related castings for medium- and heavy-duty diesel engines. Caterpillar provides its casting technology and expertise, while ASIMCO and CMMI provide the funding, operation sites, machines, supplies, and staff.

In response to growth in the agricultural equipment industry, Caterpillar has established a joint venture with a German company, Claas KgaA, to manufacture and sell combine harvesters and rubber-belted agricultural tractors in Europe and North America. The manufacturing facility for this venture is under construction and set to be completed in 1999. By combining their products and efforts, the two companies seek to better serve the growing need for efficiency on large farms.

Another foreign venture for Caterpillar is its acquisition of the Swedish manufacturer, Skogsjan AB. This company manufactures forestry machinery and supplies that compliment Caterpillar's line of forestry equipment. Skogsjan markets its products in Sweden, Norway, Germany, Austria, Switzerland, and the United Kingdom.

PRODUCTS

The mining industry also plays an important role in Caterpillar's business—Caterpillar is the world leader in sales of mining trucks. The company is designing a greater-capacity mining truck and plans to introduce the first mechanical-drive mining truck with a capacity of more than 150 tons.

A joint venture between Caterpillar and Finland's Tamrock Corp. was established in March 1998. The new company, Caterpillar Impact Products Limited, is located in Slough, England. According to Seppo Karkkainen, managing director of the partnership, "By combining Tamrock's hydraulic hammer expertise with Caterpillar's position as a world leader in construction and mining equipment, they will ideally position the new company to develop new business and new products." Also in early 1998, Caterpillar introduced a new line of compact construction equipment at a trade show in Germany.

CORPORATE CITIZENSHIP

In the late 1990s Caterpillar assisted the Pines of Carolina Girl Scout Council with repair costs incurred by Hurricane Fran. The Clayton Caterpillar plant is near the Girl Scout camp that suffered almost $200,000 in damages, and Caterpillar donated $10,000 for repairs.

A Caterpillar frontloader releasing dirt into a dump truck. (*Courtesy of Caterpillar Inc.*)

Caterpillar was named 1996 Employer of the Year by the Industry-Labor Council. The award recognizes the company for its efforts to integrate disabled workers into its workforce. Caterpillar was cited for its "barrier-free, cost-effective initiatives to return injured workers [to the job], and active outreach to recruit workers with disabilities."

GLOBAL PRESENCE

Caterpillar is the leading U.S. exporter in its industry. With about half of its sales coming from outside the United States, Caterpillar is highly dependent upon international markets. The markets in developing countries are especially important to the company—they accounted for 36 percent of Caterpillar's 1997 sales. The machinery and equipment that Caterpillar manufactures are used by these developing countries to improve their infrastructure and industrial capacity. In the Asia/Pacific region, Africa, and the Middle East, combined sales rose 37.7 percent in 1995.

Caterpillar continues to have a strong presence in Australia, Belgium, Brazil, China, France, Germany, Hungary, India, Indonesia, Italy, Japan, Mexico, Poland, Russia, and the United Kingdom. The company has 197 dealer networks that together service almost every country in the world. Caterpillar is one of the world's top three manufacturers of diesel engines. The company also ranks as a leader in many of its other businesses, including construction and mining machinery, natural gas engines, and gas turbines.

EMPLOYMENT

Caterpillar values teamwork among its employees. The company's many divisions (engineering, manufacturing, marketing, distribution, finance, product support, and customer service) operate on a "pay for performance" philosophy. In other words, rewards are given to those who do outstanding work. The company hired more than 200 college graduates in both 1996 and 1997 to fill full-time positions in such areas as engineering, information services, accounting, and marketing.

However, discord between Caterpillar and its blue-collar workforce has had a negative impact on the company. Between 1992 and 1996 the National Labor Relations Board (NLRB) found Caterpillar to be guilty of unfair labor practices a total of 230 times. This stemmed from a long-term labor dispute between the United Auto Workers (UAW) and Caterpillar. The union and the company eventually hammered out a new agreement, which is effective until April 1, 2004.

In 1996 the Occupational Safety and Health Administration (OSHA) recommended that Caterpillar be fined $27,125 for health and safety violations. According to UAW Vice President Richard Shoemaker, Caterpillar's top management had been "putting production and other considerations before the lives and the health of workers."

SOURCES OF INFORMATION

Bibliography

"About Caterpillar." *Caterpillar Home Page.* 28 May 1998. Available at http://www.caterpillar.com.

"After Long Struggle, UAW-Caterpillar Workers Ratify a New Contract." *News from the UAW,* 22 March 1998. Available at http://www.uaw.org.

"Cat-Claas Connection." *Implement & Tractor,* March-April 1997.

"Caterpillar and Claas Announce Intention to Form Large Agricultural Equipment Joint Venture." *Caterpillar Home Page,* 13 February 1997. Available at http://www.caterpillar.com.

"Caterpillar Announces Sponsorship for the NASCAR Winston Cup Series in 1997." *Caterpillar Home Page,* 7 September 1996. Available at http://www.caterpillar.com.

"Caterpillar, ASIMCO and CMMI Announce Joint Venture in Shanxi Province, China." *PR Newswire,* 3 April 1997. Available at http://www.newsalert.com.

"Caterpillar Developing Larger Mining Truck." *PR Newswire,* 14 March 1997. Available at http://www.newsalert.com.

"Caterpillar Employment." *Caterpillar Home Page,* 28 May 1998. Available at http://www.caterpillar.com.

"Caterpillar Exports Set New Record in 1996." *Caterpillar Home Page,* 28 February 1997. Available at http://www.caterpillar.com.

"Caterpillar Inc." *Hoover's Online,* 28 May 1998. Available at http://www.hoovers.com.

"Caterpillar Leaders Cite Record 1995 Performance, Preview Significant Worldwide Opportunities at Annual Stockholders' Meeting." *Caterpillar Home Page,* 10 April 1996. Available at http://www.caterpillar.com.

"Caterpillar Provides $10,000 for Girl Scout Camp Repair." *PR Newswire,* 31 March 1997. Available at http://www.newsalert.com.

"Caterpillar Selected as 1996 Employer of the Year by Industry-Labor Council." *Caterpillar Home Page,* 1 October 1996. Available at http://www.caterpillar.com.

"Caterpillar Strategy Ensures Long-Term Profitability." *PR Newswire,* 9 April 1997. Available at http://www.newsalert.com.

"Caterpillar to Expand Forest Products Business." *PR Newswire,* 24 February 1997. Available at http://www.newsalert.com.

"Caterpillar to Supply $36 Million of Equipment to Russia's Largest Diamond Producer." *Caterpillar Home Page,* 11 September 1996. Available at http://www.caterpillar.com.

"Caterpillar Today." *Caterpillar Home Page,* 28 May 1998. Available at http://www.caterpillar.com.

Elstrom, Peter. "This Cat Keeps On Purring." *Business Week,* 20 January 1997.

"A Good Place to Work." *Caterpillar Home Page,* 28 May 1998. Available at http://www.caterpillar.com.

"New College Graduate Hires at Caterpillar to Number over 200 in 1997." *Caterpillar Home Page,* 24 September 1996. Available at http://www.caterpillar.com.

"NLRB Judge Rules Caterpillar Bargained in Bad Faith; Violated Union Members' Rights." *News from the UAW,* 31 October 1996. Available at http://www.uaw.org.

Osenga, Mike. "Caterpillar Buys Perkins-Wow." *Diesel Progress North America Edition,* January 1998.

Quintanilla, Carl. "Caterpillar's Profit Surges 33%, Exceeding Analysts' Forecasts." *The Wall Street Journal Interactive Edition,* 16 April 1997. Available at http://interative6.wsj.com.

"UAW Blasts Caterpillar for Pattern of Repeated Health/Safety Violations." *News from the UAW,* 5 December 1996. Available at http://www.uaw.org.

"U.A.W. Members Back Contract with Caterpillar, First Since '91." *New York Times,* 23 March 1998.

Yatsko, Pamela. "Rethinking China." *Far Eastern Economic Review,* 18 December 1997.

For an annual report:

on the Internet at: http://www.CAT.com **or** telephone: (800) 228–7717 **or** write: Secretary, Caterpillar Inc., 100 NE Adams St., Peoria, IL 61629-7310

For additional industry research:

Investigate companies by their Standard Industrial Classification Codes, also known as SICs. Caterpillar's primary SICs are:

3272 Concrete Products Manufacturing, except Block and Brick

3511 Turbines and Turbine Generator Sets Manufacturing

3519 Internal Combustion Engine Manufacturing

3523 Farm Machinery and Equipment Manufacturing

3531 Construction Machinery and Equipment Manufacturing

3537 Industrial Truck and Tractor Manufacturing

3563 Air and Gas Compressor Manufacturing

5082 Construction and Mining Machinery Wholesaling

CBS Corporation

FOUNDED: 1927

Contact Information:
HEADQUARTERS: 51 W. 52nd St.
New York, NY 10019
PHONE: (212)975-4321
FAX: (212)975-8714
URL: http://www.cbs.com

OVERVIEW

CBS Corporation, founded in 1927, is the world's second-oldest broadcasting company and is colloquially referred to as the "Tiffany Network." It owns and operates 76 AM and FM radio stations in 17 markets in the United States; owns and operates 14 television stations in 7 of the 10 largest markets in the United States; distributes news and other programming to more than 200 affiliated television stations in the United States and abroad; and owns and operates several cable television networks, including The Nashville Network (TNN), Country Music Television (CMT), Eye on People, TeleNoticias (a Spanish-language network that reaches 22 countries), and two regional sports networks.

COMPANY FINANCES

Revenues from 1995 to 1997 were $1.1 billion, $4.1 billion, and $5.4 billion, respectively. The company had a net loss of $10 million in 1995 and a net income of $95 million and $549 million in 1996 and 1997, respectively.

ANALYSTS' OPINIONS

The CBS television network has faced fierce competition in the mid- to late 1990s from NBC's top series, *Friends, Seinfeld,* and *ER.* Analysts have pegged CBS as being in need of turnaround, and some have recognized that the network is coming out of its slump thanks to the company's aggressive efforts to remain competitive.

The cable network launched by CBS in 1997, Eye on People, has received mixed reviews. Richard Zoglin, writing for *Time* magazine, stated, "With dozens of channels fighting for a limited amount of space on the cable dial, a fuzzily conceived network like Eye on People lacks the gotta-have-it factor."

CBS's acquisition of the Spanish-language cable network, TeleNoticias, was seen as a smart strategy, since the U.S. Hispanic market has been growing faster than any other segment of the market. One in ten Americans is of Hispanic origin, and that number is expected to increase to one in four by the year 2050. Mark Levin, an analyst with Dabney/Resnick, said in *The News Times,* "it puts CBS in a wonderful position to dominate the Spanish-language international news market." CBS's minority investment in SportsLine USA, which publishes several online sports sites, was also seen as a wise move.

HISTORY

William Paley, owner of Columbia Broadcasting System in 1928, was responsible for establishing the company as a broadcasting trend setter. Paley had set his sights on CBS becoming the number-one broadcasting network, and he lured big-name stars like Jack Benny, George Burns, and Gracie Allen from NBC. He also instituted daytime dramas on the network and established a reputable news operation.

From 1955 to 1968 CBS ranked number-one in television ratings. However, its programs were targeted towards older viewers, and CBS's ratings dropped in the early 1970s. Seeing a need for a new strategy, the company bought cable television operations, but the Federal Communications Commission (FCC) later prohibited such activity by broadcast networks. (This prohibition has since been reversed.)

Next, the company attempted to expand its lines of business. Between the 1960s and the 1980s, CBS bought several companies—including the New York Yankees baseball team, the Fender guitar company, and the Steinway piano company—only to sell them shortly afterward. In 1982 CBS formed an alliance with Twentieth Century Fox Video and created CBS/Fox, a videocassette distribution operation. Another venture was Tri-Star Pictures, which was a joint effort between CBS, the cable television network HBO, and CPI Film Holdings. CBS sold Tri-Star Pictures in 1985.

The company faced some major obstacles in the 1970s and 1980s. One such hurdle was the absence of a company head; William Paley had failed to name a successor upon his departure. Additionally, Walter Cronkite's retirement and the company's struggle to fend off takeover efforts by Ted Turner in 1985 resulted in decreased ratings. Loews Corp., headed by Laurence

FINANCES:

CBS Corp.
Revenues, 1995-1997
(billion dollars)

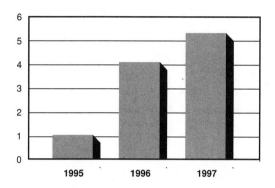

CBS Corp.
1997 Stock Prices
(dollars)

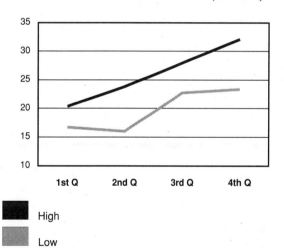

Tisch, bought 25 percent of CBS stock, but the investment was later reduced to 18 percent. Tisch became the CEO of CBS in 1987. Ratings then soared and CBS was in the number-one slot by 1991, even though the company's financial situation was looking grim. During Tisch's years at the helm, CBS offered David Letterman $14 million per year to move his popular late night show from NBC to CBS. He accepted. *The Late Show with David Letterman* is still a very popular and profitable series for CBS.

As the longstanding broadcaster of National Football League (NFL) games, CBS was hurt when it lost

FAST FACTS:

About CBS Corporation

Ownership: CBS Corp. is a publicly owned company traded on the New York, Philidelphia, Boston, Chicago, and Pacific Stock Exchanges.

Ticker symbol: CBS

Officers: Michael H. Jordan, Chmn. & CEO, 61; Louis J. Briskman, Sr VP & Gen. Counsel, 49; Mel Karmazin, Chmn. & CEO of CBS Station Group, 54; Leslie Moonves, Pres. of CBS Television, 48

Employees: 51,444 (46,113 located in the United States)

Principal Subsidiary Companies: The company's primary operations include CBS Cable Networks, Inc.; CBS Communications Services, Inc.; Group W Broadcasting, Inc.; Group W Television Stations, Inc.; Home Team Sports Limited Partnership; Infinity Broadcasting Corp.; CBS Broadcasting, Inc.; and Westinghouse Holdings Corp.

Chief Competitors: The television and radio broadcasting industries are highly competitive. Some primary competitors are: NBC; ABC; Fox; A&E Television; BET; Clear Channel; Discovery Communications; Gaylord Entertainment; IFE; News Corp.; Sony; Time Warner; Viacom; and Walt Disney.

---

the broadcasting rights to the Fox television network in 1994. CBS was sold to Westinghouse Electric Corp. in 1995 for $5.4 billion, and in 1997 Westinghouse Electric Corp. changed its name to CBS Corp. In 1998 CBS reached an agreement with the NFL to broadcast its American Football Conference games starting with the 1998 season.

STRATEGY

Many of CBS's initial strategies in television and radio have paid off, as evidenced by the longevity of some of its programs. The daytime drama *Guiding Light* marked its sixtieth anniversary in 1997, making it the longest-running program in broadcast history. In addition, *The Young and the Restless* completed 13 years of programming, during nine of which it maintained the position as daytime's number-one program. Other CBS milestones include the twenty-fifth anniversary of Chicago's WXRT-FM; the twenty-fifth anniversary of New York's oldies station, WCBS-FM; and the thirtieth anniversary of New York's news radio station, WCBS. Also, the television program *60 Minutes* has finished among the top 10 prime time programs for an unprecedented 20 consecutive seasons.

CBS's programming has attracted older viewers than its chief competitors, ABC and NBC. Its strategy has involved targeting viewers between the ages of 25 and 54. These viewers, according to CBS, are generally more educated, have higher incomes, more prone to city life, and more likely to have children living at home. However, in the mid- to late 1990s, some CBS radio and television stations were losing listeners and viewers, which did not bode well for revenues. KCBS in Los Angeles lost 36 percent of its afternoon viewers between 1994 and 1997. Women aged 25 to 54—the target audience—were tuning in less than previously. The local news program on WCBS radio in New York lost 26 percent of its listeners in 1996 and has not been competitive for more than 14 years. Chicago radio station WBBM has lost 36 percent of its afternoon listeners since 1990.

Laurence Tisch's strategy during his reign as CEO has been seen as a tight-fisted approach to business, which is a questionable strategy in such as competitive business. This frugality caused CBS to let its broadcasting agreement with the National Football League slip away, which then resulted in losing several CBS-affiliated stations to the other networks. Tisch was also reluctant to financially support the growth of its news and cable operations, which was something its competitors were doing.

After CBS was sold to Westinghouse, Peter Lund, who took over after Tisch, began to change the prevailing strategy at CBS. A major problem for the television network had been its failure to dominate prime time on any night of the week. An attempt to target the younger generation failed, and Lund decided it was best to build on the established reputation of CBS in hopes of bringing about a turnaround.

Since Westinghouse's purchase of CBS, the company has moved into cable television and Internet operations. It has also become the nation's largest radio group in terms of revenue with its purchase of Infinity Broadcasting Corp., home of Howard Stern and Don Imus. And it once again has the broadcasting rights to NFL games.

The 1998 Morgan Stanley, Dean Witter report on CBS suggests the company may be on the road to recovery. "We believe that advertising demand for the radio and TV industries, and for CBS in particular, has picked up substantially since December, increasing the likelihood of relatively dramatic improvements at the CBS station groups and reducing the risk of widening losses at the CBS network."

CURRENT TRENDS

CBS has ventured into new businesses in an effort to get back on the competitive track. Unlike its competitors, CBS's television network is still targeting the older audience and has been paying heavily for prime time programming. Says CEO Michael Jordan, "[Television is] a low-margin to break-even business. . . . Radio is the best media business that we're in." The *New York Times* has reported that media analysts are encouraged by the growth of CBS's broadcasting business.

Two new lines of business for CBS are cable television networks and the Internet. In March 1997, CBS launched its cable network, Eye On People. This marked the first cable venture for the company in 14 years. This network is available on cable systems in 62 markets, including New York, Los Angeles, and Chicago, and reaches more than seven million households. Also, CBS purchased several established cable networks, including The Nashville Network (TNN), Country Music Television (CMT), and TeleNoticias. TNN, reaching more than 70 million households in the United States and Canada, is the second-largest North American network and the eighth-largest advertiser-supported cable network in the United States. CMT has nearly 40 million subscribers in the United States. TeleNoticias, a Spanish-language network available in 22 countries, gives CBS access to the powerful Hispanic market in the United States, as well as access to Latin American markets. It also marks CBS's entrance into the 24-hour news industry.

CBS entered the Internet arena with its investment in SportsLine USA, which publishes online sports sites offering game scores, radio broadcasts, video segments, statistics, written narratives, and live conversations. The chief competitor of this venture is ESPNet SportsZone.

PRODUCTS

CBS News and *Time* magazine joined forces in June 1997, to produce "People of the Century: The Time 100." This two-year project consists of prime time television broadcasts and special issues of the magazine celebrating the lives and legacies of 100 people who helped shape the twentieth century.

In October, 1997, CBS News and Data Broadcasting Corporation, a provider of online financial and market information, announced the creation of CBS MarketWatch. This 50-50 joint venture offers online stock prices, business news, and financial information at no charge. In November 1997, the company launched CBS HealthLine, a 24-hour phone-in health information service produced in conjunction with *This Morning*. Like CBS MarketWatch, CBS HealthLine provides consumers with information beyond what television broadcasts can offer.

CHRONOLOGY:
Key Dates for CBS Corp.

1927: Arthur Judson founded the United Independent Broadcasters

1928: Columbia Phonograph buys rights to UIP's operations only to sell them back in frustration because of lack of advertiser loyalty; UIP becomes Columbia Broadcasting System

1933: The Columbia News Service, the first radio network news operation, is formed

1938: CBS purchases the American Record Company, which becomes the Columbia Recording Corporation

1940: The world's first color television broadcast is made from a CBS transmitter on the Chrysler Building to its offices a few blocks away

1946: The FCC rejects CBS's color broadcast system calling it "premature"

1956: CBS's *$64,000 Question* game show was found to be rigged

1968: *60 Minutes* makes its debut

1972: Both *M*A*S*H* and *The Waltons* make their debut

1983: CBS, Columbia Pictures, and HBO join forces to create Tri-Star Pictures, a motion picture production and distribution company

1994: Fox wins rights to broadcast NFL football's National Football Conference games, a longstanding CBS staple

1995: Westinghouse Electric Corp. buys CBS and changes the company name to CBS Corp.

1998: CBS wins the rights from NBC to broadcast NFL football's American Football Conference

CORPORATE CITIZENSHIP

In a newsletter to CBS employees, CEO Michael Jordan expressed his personal thoughts about philanthropy. "It has been a long held belief of mine that there is a correlation between corporate performance and a sense of responsibility to society at large. The active support of a wide range of national and local organizations, as well as the volunteer activities of employees, ultimately separate a great company from a merely successful one." To that end, the company is involved in several philanthropic efforts, including the CBS Foundation, which was created by CBS founder William S. Paley in 1953. Also, the company has an Employee Matching Gifts Program in which the company matches dollar-for-dollar any charitable contributions from its employees. CBS also offers scholarships to the children of its employees.

SOURCES OF INFORMATION

Bibliography

Baker, Stephen, and Elizabeth Lesly. "Westinghouse Gets a Little Twang for Its Buck." *Business Week,* 24 February 1997.

Baker, Stephen, and Michael O'Neal. "Too Big A Stretch?" *Business Week,* 11 November 1996.

"CBS Corporation." *Hoover's Online,* 27 April 1998. Available at http://www.hoovers.com.

CBS Corporation 1997 Annual Report & 10-K. New York: CBS Corporation, 1998.

"CBS Corporation Company Report." *Morgan Stanley, Dean Witter,* 25 February 1998.

CBS Home Page, 27 April 1998. Available at http://www.cbs.com.

Elber, Lynn. "CBS Network Not Looking at News Channel; Football a Goal." *San Diego Daily Transcript,* 23 July 1996.

Gunther, Marc. "Turnaround Time for CBS." *Fortune,* 19 August 1996.

Kramer, Farrell. "CBS Buys 22% Stake in SportsLine." *The New York Times,* 6 March 1997.

La Franco, Robert. "Tarnished Tiffany." *Forbes Today,* 10 February 1997.

Lesly, Elizabeth. "Good Morning, CBS." *Business Week,* 3 June 1996.

Whitefield, Mimi. "CBS Buys 24-Hour Spanish Language Newscast." *The News-Times,* 28 June 1996.

Zoglin, Richard. "Does the Eye Have It?" *Time,* 7 April 1997.

For an annual report:
telephone: (888)NYSE-CBS

For additional industry research:
Investigate companies by their Standard Industrial Classification Codes, also known as SICs. CBS's primary SICs are:

4832 Radio Broadcasting Stations

4833 Television Broadcasting Stations

4841 Cable & Other Pay Television Services

The Charles Schwab Corp.

OVERVIEW

Charles Schwab is the largest discount broker in the United States. Unlike a full-service brokerage firm, a discount broker makes trades for clients without suggesting what stocks to buy. Nevertheless, in 1997 Charles Schwab was moving toward providing investors with more financial information and counseling, as well as financial products. Indeed, the company became a major provider of a full range of financial services. It is a leading distributor of mutual funds and offers several of its own funds, known as SchwabFunds. It provides consumers with banking services such as check-writing and a debit card. It offers both personal and company retirement accounts. In addition, through its Mayer & Schweitzer subsidiary, Schwab offers trade execution services to broker-dealers and institutional investors in the over-the-counter market and NASDAQ. As of March 1998, through its principle operating subsidiary Charles Schwab & Co., Inc., Schwab provided financial services for 5 million active accounts with $407 billion in assets through 275 branch offices.

Charles Schwab has been a market leader and innovator in both products and distribution. The company has a strong track record of growth with a net income increasing at an average annual rate of 22 percent over the last 10 years, 36 percent over the last five years, and 35 percent in 1997. In comparison, some of the larger brokerage firms' earnings per share increased at an average annual rate of 21 percent over the last five years. Schwab's primary goals are to continue growth by leveraging its brand name through marketing and advertising, continued development of products and services, expansion and development of its delivery channels, and investment in technology.

FOUNDED: 1971

Contact Information:
HEADQUARTERS: 101 Montgomery St.
San Francisco, CA 94104
PHONE: (415)627-7000
FAX: (415)627-8538
TOLL FREE: (800)435-4000
URL: http://www.schwab.com

Charles Schwab

FAST FACTS:

About The Charles Schwab Corp.

Ownership: Charles Schwab is a publicly owned corporation traded on the New York, Boston, Cincinnati, Chicago, Pacific, and Philadelphia Stock Exchanges.

Ticker symbol: SCH

Officers: Charles R. Schwab, Chmn. & Co-CEO, 60, 1997 base salary $10,187,229; David S. Pottruck, Co-CEO & COO, 49, 1997 base salary $7,150,039; Timothy F. McCarthy, Pres. & COO, 46, 1997 base salary $1,708,291; Luis E. Valencia, Exec. VP & Chief Administrative Off., 52, 1997 base salary $1,286,061

Employees: 12,700

Principal Subsidiary Companies: Charles Schwab's principal subsidiaries are Charles Schwab & Co., Inc., a securities broker-dealer; Mayer & Schweitzer, Inc.; Charles Schwab Investment Management, Inc., an investment advisor; Charles Schwab Trust Company, which provides custody services for independent investment managers; and Charles Schwab Europe (formerly known as ShareLink), a retail discount securities brokerage firm.

Chief Competitors: The discount brokerage industry is very competitive and the level of competition is expected to increase. Discount brokers can also expect competition from other related industries such as full-service brokers, banks, mutual funds, software development companies, insurance companies, and others. Primary competitors include: Merrill Lynch; Smith Barney; Dean Witter; Paine Webber; Quick & Reilly; Fidelity Brokerage Services; AmeriTrade; Waterhouse Securities; and Olde Discount.

COMPANY FINANCES

In 1996 Schwab posted record earnings for the sixth consecutive year. Earnings increased 35 percent to $234.0 million, or $1.30 per share, up from $173.0 million, or $.97 per share, in 1995. Schwab handled over 97 million calls and more than 21 million trades. The trend continued into 1997 with reported net income of $270.3 million, or $.99 per share, on revenues of $2.3 billion. A

contributing factor for the increase was the 1.2 million new accounts opened in 1997.

The Charles Schwab Corporation reported net income of $68.0 million, or $.25 per share, on revenues of $604.4 million for the quarter ended March 31, 1998. Net income for the first quarter of 1997 was $66.7 million, or $.25 per share, on revenues of $535.7 million. In the first quarter of 1998 trading activity reached record levels.

Attracting new customer accounts is important in generating revenues. Schwab added 358,000 new customer accounts during the first quarter of 1998, an increase of 20 percent from the 297,000 new accounts added during the first quarter 1997. During the first quarter 1998, 48 percent of total customer trades were executed through online channels, versus 33 percent in 1997.

ANALYSTS' OPINIONS

Charles Schwab's consistently powerful earnings and revenue growth make it a favorite among analysts. In early 1997, many analysts remained skeptical about long-term prospects for the stock. Nevertheless, the brokerage business tends to have sharp ups and downs. With the market due for a downturn and Charles Schwab's stock price already quite high, some analysts were expressing caution about near-term outlook for shares.

Charles Schwab continues to be recognized as a leader. In January 1998 *Forbes* ranked Charles Schwab among the best companies in its Fiftieth Annual Report on American Industry. The report also referred to Charles Schwab as the "entrepreneur who took advantage of technology to build a giant business from scratch." Also in 1998, Charles Schwab was named the overall winner of the Global Information Infrastructure (GII) Commerce Award. The company was recognized for its use of the Internet and network technology, which produced impressive results.

HISTORY

After some early mishaps in the mutual fund business, Charles Schwab set up a small money-management firm in San Francisco in the early 1970s. In 1975 Congress deregulated the stock brokerage industry, thus ending the power of the New York Stock Exchange to set commission rates. With fixed commissions gone, the door opened for Charles Schwab to start a discount brokerage firm, which took orders to buy and sell securities but did not maintain a large research staff to make specific stock recommendations.

By 1980 Charles Schwab was by far the largest discount broker. In 1983 Bank of America acquired the firm for $55 million. Founder Charles Schwab and a group of investors bought the company back in 1987 for $238 million. In 1991 Schwab acquired Mayer & Schweitzer, which provided trade execution services to broker-dealers and institutional customers in the over-the-counter market. In 1993 Charles Schwab opened its first overseas office in London. The company continued to grow and prosper during the mid-1990s. According to *Forbes,* in 1995 Charles Schwab ranked fifth among brokerage firms in total assets. Moreover, its 36-percent return on equity was the highest among leading brokerage firms.

STRATEGY

Traditionally, discount brokers offer services for the "do-it-yourself" investor. By eliminating overhead for investment research performed by security analysts, discount brokers have been able to offer trading services at lower costs. But the brokerage industry was changing rapidly. In 1996 Charles Schwab found that some 50 percent of its new accounts had never traded stocks before, compared with just 5 percent in 1987. Since so many investors were inexperienced, Charles Schwab believed it had an obligation, as well as a business opportunity, to provide them with the investment counseling they needed. Thus, Charles Schwab began to offer its customers education and guidance through both computer software and its customer representatives. In February 1997 the company inaugurated Market Buzz, an information service on its web site that offered market news, data, and research. Charles Schwab also provided greater incentives to employees to refer customers to the company's network of 5,000 independent investment advisers. Clients who signed on with these independent investment advisers accounted for nearly one-third of Schwab's assets.

Schwab also distinguished itself through technological innovations. Management estimated that some 40 to 50 percent of all its trades were done through technology-based distribution channels. Some 25 percent of all trades are conducted through Telebroker, an automated, touch-tone telephone service that allows clients to get stock prices and place orders. Charles Schwab also offers trading on the Internet through e.Schwab and other services. Another innovation was VoiceBroker, a telephone system that uses voice-recognition technology to conduct broker services.

Finally, through its nationwide advertising and marketing programs, Charles Schwab worked to create a strong brand name in the stock brokerage business. The company continues to use the positive image of founder Charles Schwab extensively in its advertising, which conveys an image of confidence and reliability. The company uses national and local advertising to expand its client base and relies on referrals by existing clients. The majority of Schwab's ads appear in financial newspapers and periodicals and on national and local cable television and radio stations.

CHRONOLOGY:
Key Dates for The Charles Schwab Corp.

1971: Founded

1975: Begins offering discount brokerage services

1980: Becomes the largest discount brokerage firm

1983: Bank of America acquires the company

1987: Charles Schwab and some investors repurchase the firm

1990: Opens the first central service center

1991: Acquires Mayer & Schweitzer

1993: Opens first overseas office, in London

1995: Employees participate in the AIDS Walk

1997: Launches Market Buzz

1998: Company is named the winner of the Global Information Infrastructure Commerce Award

INFLUENCES

One of the most influential strategies in terms of overall market growth was Charles Schwab's implementation of central servicing centers. The initial service center opened in Indianapolis, Indiana, in 1990 and handled overflow calls from the branches in the eastern United States. In 1991 the company opened a second central servicing center in Denver, Colorado, which managed overflow calls from branch offices in the Midwest and the western United States. The service centers handle Charles Schwab's toll-free numbers, which represent a majority of the company's calls. The brokers in the service centers are available 24-hours-a-day to accept trade orders or answer investors' questions. Approximately 40 percent of the trades executed by Schwab are through the calling center, about 50 percent are done electronically, and less than 10 percent are done through the branches. The company's facilities are strategically located across the United States to offer effective broad geographic coverage for customers.

While discount brokerage was taken for granted in recent years, the service was considered unusual when it first appeared in 1975. Charles Schwab successfully used advertising to establish the credibility of the business, and by 1980 it was the largest discount broker. But the costs for these campaigns, as well as spending for ad-

SCHWAB RECEIVES PRAISE AND CRITICISM ALL IN THE SAME DAY

Charles Schwab had to deal with a lot of angry customers when their system went down for two hours in the early morning of April 20, 1998. Traders were unable to make stock trades through the Schwab web site or through the company's telephone system. Schwab employees couldn't access user accounts or stock information. Customers, however, were able to place free-of-charge, time-stamped trades with operators by telephone or in person at Schwab's 275 branches nationwide. A Schwab spokesperson said the network problems were caused by the crash of a central hub. Ironically, these problems happened on the same day that Schwab's web site was honored with a Global Infrastructure Commerce Award at the Comdex Spring 98 computer trade show in Chicago. Schwab received the award for helping make online stock trading easy and inexpensive.

vanced computer systems, caused cash shortages that eventually resulted in the sale of the company to Bank of America in 1983. That sale, however, caused its own problems. For example, Charles Schwab wanted to offer its own line of mutual funds, but federal law at the time prohibited banks and their subsidiaries from engaging in this business. While Charles Schwab wanted to challenge the laws, Bank of America was reluctant, since it didn't want to antagonize banking regulators. The tension between Charles Schwab and its parent company was apparent, and in 1987 Charles Schwab and a group of investors bought the company back for $238 million. That year the firm had sales of $465 million and profits of $26 million; it had 1.6 million customers—five times as many as its nearest competitor. It was spending $15 million a year on advertising.

In October 1987, however, the market crashed, and by mid-1988 trading volume had fallen by some 40 percent. Schwab cut costs and executive salaries so that the firm could be profitable on only 8,000 trades a day, compared with 12,000 before the cost-cutting measures took effect. But even with these steps profits fell 70 percent to $7.4 million, based on revenues of $392 million. Unlike the crash of 1929, however, the crash of 1987 did not have a major impact on the economy, and the brokerage business recovered relatively quickly. By 1992

Charles Schwab had 175 branch offices with 2,500 brokers; revenue for the year was $909 million, with profits of $81 million.

The bull market of the 1990s attracted hundreds of thousands of new investors, which greatly benefited Charles Schwab. For the five-year period beginning in 1991, earnings expanded at an annual rate of 36 percent, reaching $234 million in 1996. Revenues grew at a 27-percent pace to $1.85 billion; and customer assets more than doubled between 1994 and 1997 to $253 billion. The stock market rewarded this excellent performance. Between late 1994 and early 1997 Charles Schwab stock rose 275 percent, compared with 160 percent for the industry as a whole. The company continued to spend large amounts on advertising to attract additional new investors—$84 million in 1996, compared with $53 million in 1995.

CURRENT TRENDS

In 1997 Wall Street was focusing its energies on attracting and servicing the small investor who was the mainstay of Charles Schwab's business. The company strived to maintain its edge by delivering innovative products that would keep it a step ahead of the competition. Charles Schwab was particularly successful in the area of mutual funds, where it became one of the leading distributors in the industry. The company expanded the outlets for its distribution of mutual funds to banks and small brokerage firms.

The growth of the Internet was also having a powerful effect on the brokerage business. The Internet has a large amount of financial information available for free, and online brokerages sprang up to service the "do-it-yourself" investor. In an interesting reversal of its traditional role in the industry, in 1997 Charles Schwab was the old, established firm being undercut by young upstarts. When Charles Schwab introduced its e.Schwab service for Internet trading, the basic charge of $29.95 was still twice that of the pioneering E-Trade Group of Palo Alto, California. Indeed, Charles Schwab was moving toward providing more counseling to investors partly because it was losing some of the "do-it-yourself" market to E-Trade and other cheaper Internet brokers.

PRODUCTS

Charles Schwab continued to create new offerings in order to enhance its product line and enhance customer service. In 1996 alone it added SchwabNOW (Internet trading), SchwabPlan (401(k) retirement accounts), SchwabLife (life insurance), and StreetSmart Pro (investment services). Schwab was also considering introducing other deposit and credit services, such as mortgages.

Schwab continued to invest in technology throughout the first quarter of 1998. It increased overall trade processing capacity by nearly 70 percent and enhanced web site capabilities with The Analyst Center™. The latter provided customers with access to investment information and research companies such as Dow Jones, Standard & Poor's, First Call, and Big Charts on individual stocks and industries at no cost. The IRA Analyzer™ is an online investment tool designed to educate investors about retirement planning choices. Also, during the first quarter 1998 the Schwab MoneyLink™ service was expanded to allow customers to use the Charles Schwab web site automated telephone system. Schwab representatives could use the MoneyLink to transfer money between Schwab and other financial institutions.

CORPORATE CITIZENSHIP

The Charles Schwab Corporation Foundation, founded in 1993, is extensively involved in supporting nonprofit programs in local communities. Charles Schwab employees were involved in the 1995 AIDS Walk in more than 20 cities. Coupled with the company's corporate sponsorships, Charles Schwab raised over $125,000 to fight the disease. In an effort to encourage employees to become active in the community in which they live, Schwab implemented a program called Assisting Society through Schwab Employee Teamwork and Service (A.S.S.E.T.S.). Every year one employee is awarded a Community Service Award; Schwab then makes a contribution to the organization of the employee's choice. In the summer of 1995 over 650 Charles Schwab employees in 22 cities helped raise money for breast cancer research by participating in the Race for the Cure. Charles Schwab also double-matched employee contributions to relief funds in Oklahoma City following the bombing of the federal building.

GLOBAL PRESENCE

Charles Schwab's global presence is still relatively small. The great majority of Schwab's business is in the United States; however, it does have a branch office in the United Kingdom. The company also offers multilingual services through Asia Pacific Services and Latinoamericano.

EMPLOYMENT

Charles Schwab has a reputation for agility and technological innovation. As demonstrated by its revolutionary move into the discount brokerage business, it is happy to take on the traditional leaders of an industry and fight for its turf. The company's customer representatives are known for offering excellent service.

SOURCES OF INFORMATION

Bibliography

Calway, Mark. "Schwab's New Strategy: Discount Brokerage, Premium Advice." *San Francisco Business Times,* 29 November 1996.

Charles Schwab. *10-K and Annual Report.* San Francisco, CA: The Charles Schwab Corp., 1996.

Charles Schwab. *10-K and Annual Report.* San Francisco, CA: The Charles Schwab Corp., 1997.

Charles Schwab Corporation. *The Corporate Directory of U.S. Public Companies.* San Mateo, CA: Walker's 1998.

Charles Schwab Home Page, 27 April 1998. Available at http://www.schwab.com.

Hersh, James S., and Vanessa O'Connell. "Rise of Mass Market in Mutual Funds Fuels Schwab-Fidelity Feud." *Wall Street Journal,* 23 September 1996.

Hilder, D.B. "Charles Schwab - Company Report." *Morgan Stanley & Co.,* 1 November 1996.

O'Connell, Vanessa. "Schwab's Fund Supermarket' Weighs a Move to Banks." *Wall Street Journal,* 24 October 1996.

Schultz, Ellen, and Bridget O'Brian. "Schwab Plans Custom Advice, Roiling Advisers." *Wall Street Journal,* 30 May 1996.

For an annual report:

write: The Charles Schwab Corp., Investor Relations, 101 Montgomery St., San Francisco, CA 94104

For additional industry research:

Investigate companies by their Standard Industrial Classification Codes, also known as SICs. Charles Schwab's primary SICs are:

6211 Security Brokers & Dealers

6282 Investment Advice

Chevron Corporation

FOUNDED: Incorporated in 1926 as Standard Oil Company of California. The company adopted the name Chevron Corporation in 1984.

Contact Information:

HEADQUARTERS: 575 Market St.
    San Francisco, CA 94105
PHONE: (415)894-7700
FAX: (415)894-0348
URL: http://www.chevron.com

OVERVIEW

Chevron Corporation is one of the largest oil refiners in the United States. It owns and operates many operations that are central to oil production, from exploration to refining to distribution. It is the fifth-largest oil company in the world (based on revenues), the largest U.S. marketer of petroleum products, one of the largest marketers of liquefied petroleum gas worldwide, and the third-largest U.S. producer of natural gas. The company operates in the United States and approximately 100 other countries, and owns net reserves of nearly 4.2 billion barrels of oil and natural gas liquids. Overall, Chevron is the tenth-largest producer of oil and holds approximately 9 percent of the gasoline market share.

Chevron owns six U.S. refineries and markets products through 7,750 retail outlets, also in the United States. In addition, the company owns interests in 14 refineries and 8,500 outlets in primarily the Asia Pacific region through Caltex, its 50-percent-owned affiliate. Chevron has a tanker fleet of 52 vessels, either owned or chartered, and a pipeline more than 13,000 miles long. The company produces petrochemicals in 10 plants worldwide, and operates or markets in more than 80 countries. (Petrochemicals are chemical substances obtained from petroleum or natural gas, such as gasoline, kerosene, or petroleum.)

COMPANY FINANCES

Chevron's goal was to achieve $3 billion in earnings by 1998, which it reached one year ahead of schedule in 1997. In fact, that year Chevron's net income was a record $3.25 billion, up 25 percent from $2.60 billion in 1996 and 250 percent from $930 million in 1995. Net income for 1994 was $1.70 billion and $1.26 billion for 1993. Chevron has increased its cash dividend every year since 1987, and in 1997 paid $2.28 per share.

Chevron reported first quarter 1998 net income of $500 million ($.77 per share), a decrease of 40 percent from the 1997 first quarter net income of $831 million ($1.27 per share). Chairman and CEO Kenneth Derr commented, "First quarter 1998 earnings were affected adversely by lower crude oil prices, lower natural gas prices, and foreign currency losses." Total revenues for the quarter were $7.7 billion, a decrease of 31 percent from $11.1 billion in the first quarter of 1997.

Chevron's assets total approximately $35.0 billion. The company's annual capital and exploration expenditures total nearly $1.5 billion. There are 166,000 Chevron stockholders holding about 325 million shares of common stock. The company has declared a dividend for the past 10 years. This pattern continued in 1998 when the company declared a quarterly dividend of $.61 per share.

ANALYSTS' OPINIONS

Some experts are predicting oil prices to be flat over the next 15 years and that oil demand will increase to nearly 100 million barrels per day. The 1998 Value Line Investment Survey reported that petroleum industry profits are expected to fall 10 percent in 1998 because of overproduction and a mild winter. Morgan Stanley, Dean Witter reported in late 1997 that "the outlook for earnings and dividends growth is positive, with gains expected to approximate 6-7 percent during 1998-99 and profit growth is expected to remain firm in 1998-99."

According to CEO Kenneth Derr, *The Oil & Gas Journal* reported that the oil industry is continually being charged with "pollution, greed, discrimination and disregard for any value other than profit." Derr argues, "Our industry invests a lot of money protecting the environment." After all, Chevron did receive the 1997 National Health of the Land Award, the 1997 Governer's Award, and an Emerald Award for its educational radio program in Alberta, Canada.

HISTORY

In 1938 Standard Oil Co. of California (now Chevron) made a huge oil discovery in Saudia Arabia, which eventually led to the discovery of 52 oil fields. After World War II, the company began a major effort to market Arabian crude oil, which was probably the single most important factor in establishing Chevron as a major multinational company. The company acquired

FINANCES:

Chevron Corp. Sales, 1994-1997 (billion dollars)

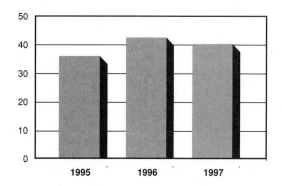

Chevron Corp. 1997 Stock Prices (dollars)

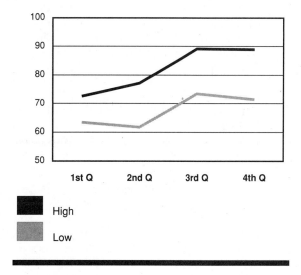

thousands of service stations and terminals on the East Coast and part ownership of many more throughout Europe, East Africa, and Asia. The Chevron discovery changed the course of history throughout the world.

STRATEGY

Since 1989 Chevron has instituted cost-cutting initiatives in the upstream (exploration and production) and downstream (refining and marketing) businesses of the

FAST FACTS:

About Chevron Corporation

Ownership: Chevron Corporation is a publicly owned company traded on the New York, Chicago, Pacific, London, and Swiss Stock Exchanges.

Ticker symbol: CHV

Officers: Kenneth T. Derr, Chmn. & CEO, 61, 1997 base salary $3,618,604; Martin R. Klitten, VP & CFO, 53, 1997 base salary $1,127,885; James N. Sullivan, Vchmn, 60, 1997 base salary $1,920,158; Peter J. Robertson, VP & Pres. of Chevron Production Co., 51, 1997 base salary $1,122,308

Employees: 40,820 (approximately 30,000 located in the United States)

Principal Subsidiary Companies: Chevron is a fully integrated petroleum giant, and as such, operates many subsidiaries that are related to oil production and refining. Chevron's principal subsidiaries are Chevron U.S.A. Products Company Inc.; Chevron Chemical Company; Chevron USA; PLEXCO (polyethylene pipe manufacturer); Chevron Overseas Petroleum, Inc. (COPI); Chevron Products Company; Chevron Canada Resources (CCR); Gulf Oil (Great Britian) Limited; and the Pittsburg & Midway Coal Mining Co. (P&M). Chevron also holds a one-quarter interest in the NGC Corporation, which is the largest natural gas and gas liquids wholesaler in North America.

Chief Competitors: The oil industry has undergone a major transition in the area of competition. In response to the industry's inherent risks, Chevron now seeks out competitors in order to form partnerships. Its primary competitors include: Amoco Corporation; Exxon Corporation; British Petroleum; Mobil Corporation; Marathon Oil Co.; Shell Oil Co.; Arco; Phillips Petroleum Co.; Texaco; Dow Chemical; Pennzoil; and Union Carbide.

company, and these have had good results. Chevron's current strategy to improve financial performance has nine components: (1) Build a committed team to accomplish the corporate mission. (2) Accelerate exploration and production growth in international areas. (3) Accelerate total growth in the Caspian region, where the countries are in a period of rapid economic growth.

(4) Generate cash from North American exploration and production operations while maintaining value through sustained production levels. (5) Achieve top financial performance in U.S. refining and marketing. (6) Caltex (Chevron's 50 percent-owned affiliate, a leading competitor in the Asian/Pacific regions) should achieve superior competitive financial performance, while growing in attractive markets. (7) Continue to improve competitive financial performance in chemicals while developing and implementing attractive opportunities for growth. (8) Be selective in other businesses. (9) Focus on reducing costs across all activities.

INFLUENCES

First and foremost the oil industry is strongly influenced by government regulation and environmental issues. When an oil spill occurs or the natural habitat is threatened, there is a negative impact on the industry at large. This negative impact will prohibit growth for the industry and, as a result, affect earnings across the board. To cut down on such risks, Chevron and other oil companies are forming partnerships. These partnerships also offer the companies operational and financial advantages. As a result of this trend, oil companies do not feel threatened by competitors, because they are viewed as potential new partners. In 1998 Chevron developed a corporate mergers and acquisitions group specifically for this purpose. As a result, Chevron and Texaco are planning to establish a joint venture of their global marine and industrial fuels and marine lubricant businesses, which operate in more than 100 countries worldwide.

Although sluggish oil markets depressed prices in the early 1990s and forced Chevron to cut costs and improve efficiency, the company is pursuing an aggressive exploration and production strategy outside the United States. In 1996 the company's average sales price per barrel of refined product in the United States was $29.96 per barrel, an increase of $3.75 per barrel over 1995. However, margins were squeezed because prices did not fully recover higher crude oil feedstock and fuel costs. The added cost of producing federal- and state-mandated cleaner-burning gasolines was an additional factor.

CURRENT TRENDS

Perhaps the most important asset in Chevron's upstream portfolio is the Tengiz field in the Republic of Kazakstan. In 1993 Chevron entered into a joint venture with Kazakstan to develop the more than six-billion barrel field. By midyear 1997 approximately 166,000 barrels of oil were being produced per day, the major constraint being the lack of export facilities. This figure should be dramatically higher when the Caspian Pipeline connecting Tengiz with the Russian Black Sea is completed in 1999 or 2000. Other projects that could produce significant results in the early part of the next century include Papua New Guinea, Java, and the Britannia field in the North Sea. The company's Genesis project in the Gulf of Mexico is not expected to reach full production until about 2000.

Regarding oil prices, Chevron's 1997 annual report stated, "The short-term price outlook is not strong. Crude oil and natural gas prices started down in late 1997, and in the first quarter 1998 oil prices hit their lowest level in nearly four years." However, CEO Kenneth Derr reported in an April 1998 press release that "Chevron has established a strong foundation for future growth in spite of the recent downturn in oil prices." Derr feels Chevron has better long-term growth opportunities and he expects oil prices will bounce back later this year.

PRODUCTS

Chevron explores for and extracts crude oil, natural gas, and natural gas liquids. These natural resources are then sold as is or are refined into gasoline and lubricants. Through its subsidiary Chevron Chemical and its International Group, the company produces and markets petrochemicals for industrial use throughout the world. These chemicals include: benzene, cumene, cyclohexane, paraxylene, ethylene, propylene, normal alpha olefins, polyethylene, styrene, and polystyrene.

The company offers customers a variety of Chevron credit cards. These include gas cards with no annual fee; a Premium Card that offers savings on airline tickets, hotels and car rentals; and a no-fee Chevron business card that helps companies organize their records and track expenses. The Chevron Travel Club provides towing services, trip routing and other travel services. Chevron is in the process of installing approximately 6,000 ATM machines at its service stations in the United States. It plans to have 450 machines installed by the end of October 1998.

CORPORATE CITIZENSHIP

Chevron participates in the American Business Collaboration for Quality Dependent Care program, which provides day care for its 9,000 employees in the San Francisco Bay area. The program trains local child-care providers to be more accessible to working families by extending the hours that child care is available, increasing the flexibility of care schedules, and improving the availability of back-up care. "Companies are recognizing that their employees have a life outside of work and they should honor that," said Sue Osborn, work and family coordinator for San Francisco-based Chevron.

CHRONOLOGY:
Key Dates for Chevron Corporation

1926: Incorporates as Standard Oil

1938: Makes a large oil discovery in Saudi Arabia

1940: Discovers the Abquaic Field which has produced more than 7.5 billion barrels of oil

1951: Safaniya, the world's largest offshore field, is discovered

1957: California Shipping Co. is formed

1965: Chevron Shipping Co. is formed

1969: The first very large crude Carrier, the S.S. John A. McCone, begins service

1976: Chevron switches their tankers from steam to diesel power

1984: Changes name to Chevron Corporation

1991: Institutes condensed work week program

1993: Enters into joint venture with Kazakstan

1998: Donates to American Red Cross Disaster Relief Fund to help flood victims

"We've been able to work other companies, leverage our funds and do something more significant."

Chevron has also been active in AIDS-related philanthropy, perhaps as a result of its Bay Area connection with the devastation AIDS has wrought in that part of the United States. The company was cited by several organizations as an example of how corporations can approach this subject. Chevron sponsors the "AIDS Corporate Update," which encourages public-private partnerships to fund HIV research and community education, and to ensure that members of the working community remain healthy and productive.

In late 1997 Chevron formed an alliance with Freedom Fund Inc., an African-American nonprofit organization based in Oakland, California, to provide management, employment, and training opportunities to African Americans. Chevron provided an existing service station and funding for a technology institute to the project. If this venture proves to be successful, Chevron's contribution could surpass $10 million.

In 1998 Chevron donated $75,000 to the American Red Cross Disaster Fund to aid victims of floods and tornadoes in Florida and California. In fact, the company has a long history of helping people in disaster situations; it has given nearly $500,000 toward disaster relief in the two states. In addition, Chevron Global Lubricants, a business unit of Chevron Products Co., set up a toll-free hotline to answer flood victims' question on water-related damage to gasoline- and diesel-powered engines. It also compiled a fact sheet containing tips on how to protect or repair water-damaged equipment.

GLOBAL PRESENCE

Chevron operates in the United States and approximately 100 additional countries. Petroleum activities are widely distributed geographically; major operations are located in the United States, Canada, Australia, the United Kingdom, Congo, Angola, Nigeria, Papua New Guinea, Indonesia, China, and Zaire. Chevron markets its products in more than 60 countries, primarily through its Caltex affiliate. Through its subsidiaries and affiliates, Caltex conducts exploration, production, and geothermal operations in Indonesia, and refining and marketing activities in Asia, Africa, the Middle East, Australia, and New Zealand. Major operations are found in Korea, Japan, Australia, Thailand, the Philippines, Singapore, and South Africa. Chevron's Tengizchevroil affiliate conducts production activities in Kazakstan. Chemical operations are concentrated in the United States, but also include facilities in France, Japan, and Brazil. Chemical manufacturing facilities are under construction or planned for construction in Singapore, Saudi Arabia, and China. Chevron's coal operations are located in the United States.

EMPLOYMENT

Chevron's philosophy is that the best global companies have managed their human resources based on skill, talent, experience, and merit—without regard to race or national origin. "The Chevron Way," a document containing the company's mission and vision statements, sets up a standard of excellence for each employee. Chevron also makes good use of employee surveys to measure employees' attitudes about the company and then carries through on its findings. The company's leadership training, diversity training, upward feedback, and job selection programs have been set up in response to employee concerns.

In 1991 Chevron implemented a condensed work week program in which employees can put in longer workdays in exchange for an extra day off every week or two. The decision to offer the program was made, in part, based on employee surveys. Other benefits were instituted after surveys indicated employee needs. These include family leave for up to six months to care for the

sick or elderly (before it was federally mandated), prorated benefits for part-time workers, an increased lifetime maximum for mental health benefits, and greater choice in structuring profit-sharing plans. Finally, Chevron's strategy is to make employees feel empowered as "stakeholders" in the company, as well as to build employee commitment. A program called "Chevron Success Sharing" provides eligible employees with a percentage of their annual salary as a cash bonus if the company achieves certain financial goals. In most companies such bonuses are offered only to senior management; however, as CEO Kenneth Derr noted, "Everyone is working harder and companies need to recognize that. Employees who are working as a committed team share with stockholders a sense of ownership."

SOURCES OF INFORMATION

Bibliography
Bole, Kirsten. "Chevron Inks $2B Agreement." *San Francisco Business Times,* 15 July 1996.

———. "Chevron Set to Sack 200 Researchers." *San Francisco Business Times,* 5 August 1996.

"Chevron and Texaco Intend to Form Joint Venture of Marine Lubricant Bussinesses." *PR Newswire,* 30 March 1998.

Chevron Corporation Annual Report. San Francisco, CA: Chevron Corporation, 1997.

"Chevron Corporation." *The Corporate Directory of U.S. Public Companies.* San Mateo, CA: Walker's, 1998.

Chevron Home Page, 1 May 1998. Available at http://www.chevron.com.

"Chevron Launches M&A Unit." *The Oil Daily,* 3 February 1998.

McAuliffe, Don. "Chevron's Nationwide ATM Network will be Satellite-Linked." *Knight-Rider/Tribune Business News,* 24 October 1997.

Mellow, Craig. "Big Oil's Pipe Dream." *Fortune,* 2 March 1998.

Morgan Stanley, Dean Witter. *Company Report,* 3 December 1997.

"Petroleum (integrated) Industry." *The Value Line Investment Survey,* 27 March 1998.

Symanovich, Steve. "Taking Baby Steps to Improve Child Care." *San Francisco Business Times,* 17 February 1997.

For an annual report:
on the Internet at: http://www.chevron.com **or** write: Comptroller's Dept., 575 Market St., Rm. 3519, San Francisco, CA 94105-2856

For additional industry research:
Investigate companies by their Standard Industrial Classification Codes, also known as SICs. Chevron's primary SICs are:

1311 Crude Petroleum and Natural Gas

2911 Petroleum Refining

Chiquita Brands International Inc.

OVERVIEW

Thanks to its very successful Chiquita Banana ad campaign and a jingle that most baby-boomers know by heart, Chiquita Brands is a household name that almost everyone associates with bananas. The company likes to point out that although bananas are still a huge chunk of its business (60 percent of annual sales), there is much more to it than bananas. Chiquita markets and distributes a variety of other fresh and processed food products. It markets these products under a number of brand names, including Chiquita Jr., Amigo, Chico, Frupac, Pacific Gold, and Consul.

Chiquita has worked hard to be a good citizen wherever it operates. In countless communities around the world, Chiquita strives to make a positive contribution, particularly on social issues and the environment. Some neighborhoods provide the local infrastructure Chiquita needs to do business efficiently. Yet all of these benefit the citizens of the communities where the company is located.

FOUNDED: 1870

Contact Information:

HEADQUARTERS: 250 E. 5th St.
 Cincinnati, OH 45202
FAX: (713)784-8030
PHONE: (513)784-8000
URL: http://www.chiquita.com

COMPANY FINANCES

In 1997 Chiquita Brands posted net earnings of $300,000 on revenue of $2.43 billion, compared with 1996's net loss of $50.0 million on revenue of $2.44 billion. For the first quarter of 1998, Chiquita reported net income of $41.1 million on sales of $717.2 million. In 1995 the company reported net income of $9.0 million on revenue of $2.57 billion, compared with 1994's net loss of $72.0 million on revenue of $3.96 billion. In 1997

FINANCES:

Chiquita Brands International Inc. Net Sales, 1994-1997 (billion dollars)

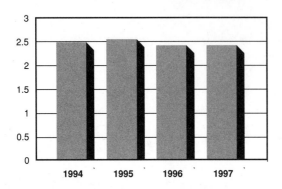

Chiquita Brands International Inc. 1997 Stock Prices (dollars)

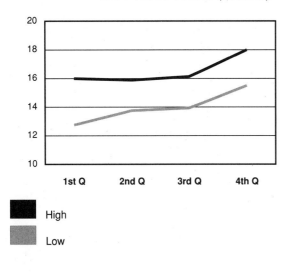

bananas accounted for 60 percent of Chiquita's total sales, with other products generating the remaining 40 percent. Sales in North America accounted for 55 percent of total revenue, while sales in Central and South America brought in 2 percent, and sales to Europe and other regions generated 43 percent.

HISTORY

Chiquita had its origins in the Boston Fruit Company, founded in 1870 by partners Captain Lorenzo

Baker and Andrew Preston. The idea for the enterprise came to Captain Baker after a voyage to Jamaica during which he purchased 160 bunches of bananas. Sailing back to the port of Jersey City, New Jersey, the captain arranged to sell the bananas through Boston produce broker, Andrew Preston. Fifteen years later, Baker and Preston, along with Preston's partners, formed The Boston Fruit Company.

The Boston Fruit Company eventually became Chiquita Brands International, a far-flung international corporation with about 40,000 employees, or associates as they are known within the company in the late 1990s. More than 30,000 of those associates live and work in Latin America, where the company grows the majority of its bananas. Other associates work in the company's Cincinnati headquarters and offices and plants around the world, as well as on ships carrying Chiquita's fruit to global markets.

Chiquita's history also includes Minor C. Keith who traveled in 1871 to Costa Rica where he contracted to build a railroad. Desperate for both cargo and passengers for the new railroad, he planted bananas along the railroad's rights of way to provide paying fares to inland destinations as well as back to the sea. Twenty-eight years later in 1899, Keith's rail companies and Boston Fruit Company merged to create the United Fruit Company. The new company began importing bananas from a number of Central American plantations to expand its distribution network in the United States. Also in 1899, Fruit Dispatch Company was formed to distribute bananas throughout the United States, pioneering a number of new techniques in the transportation of perishable produce to inland destinations.

In the early 1900s United Fruit built the first refrigerated cargo ship, which soon was part of what became known as the "Great White Fleet." The ships were painted white to reflect the heat of the tropical sun and help maintain optimal temperature for the fruit in transit. That containerized fleet today numbers more than 20 vessels, all of which are owned, operated, or chartered by Chiquita. In 1903 United Fruit Company's stock was first listed on the New York Stock Exchange, and a year later the company put together an unbroken line of wireless communications between company headquarters and South America.

It was not until 1944 that the Chiquita brand name was introduced. To help promote the brand throughout the United States, the company also introduced its Miss Chiquita character and jingle the same year. Three years later, in 1947, the name "Chiquita" was registered in the United States as a trademark.

United Fruit Company was purchased in 1970 by Eli Black, who changed its name to United Brands. Seventeen years later, Carl H. Lindner acquired the company. He changed the company's name in 1990 to Chiquita Brands International. Already a major global player, Chiquita expanded its marketing and distribution to eastern Europe, Asia, and the Middle East in the early 1990s. The company also expanded its product line to include other fresh fruits. In the late 1990s the company was still the world leader in the production, distribution, and marketing of branded fresh bananas.

Chiquita won a face-off with its hometown newspaper in the summer of 1998. The *Cincinnati Enquirer* published a front-page apology for an "untrue" May 3 story lambasting Chiquita business practices. The newspaper also agreed to pay Chiquita $10 million. The story was based on company voice-mail messages that allegedly were obtained illegally by lead reporter Michael Gallagher. On July 2, 1998, Chiquita sued Gallagher, accusing him of stealing the voice-mail messages. The company's suit sought damages for defamation, trespassing, conspiracy, fraud, and violations of electronic-communications privacy laws.

STRATEGY

Fearful of relying too heavily on bananas for its fortunes, the company, known then as United Fruit, launched a program of diversification in the 1960s. In 1966 United Fruit purchased the A&W product line, which included bottled soft drinks and drive-in restaurants. The following year, the Baskin-Robbins ice cream empire was added to the company's holdings. The diversification process was reversed somewhat during the 1970s and 1980s after the company's acquisition by Eli Black, founder of AMK Corporation, which included the John Morrell meat packing business. Black changed the company's name to United Brands and sold off many of the diversified holdings United Fruit had acquired during the latter half of the 1960s. Baskin-Robbins was sold in 1973. The A&W restaurant chain was sold in 1982. Five years later, United Brands sold off the A&W soft drink product line.

In 1987 United Brands was acquired by Carl H. Lindner's American Financial Corp. In 1990, Lindner changed the company's name to Chiquita Brands International in an attempt to capitalize on the worldwide brand name recognition. In 1992 Chiquita diversified once again with the acquisition of Friday Canning Corporation, a leading private label vegetable canner. The company's expansion into canning operations accelerated in 1997 with the acquisition of Owatonna Canning Company and American Fine Foods. The company also announced that it had agreed to acquire Stokely USA Inc., a leading producer of canned vegetables, for $110 million in a stock-and-debt deal. The Stokely acquisition was formally completed in 1998.

Although the emphasis has been on diversifying its product line under Lindner, Chiquita began to move out of the meat processing business in 1992. By 1995 the company had completed the sale of the John Morrell meat packing operation.

A line of bananas is being moved through a Costa Rican packing plant at a subsidiary plantation of Chiquita Brands International, Inc. (AP Photo/The Cincinnati Enquirer.)

INFLUENCES

One of the key influences on Chiquita has been the progression to global business. The company's decision to change its name in 1990 from United Brands to Chiquita Brands International reflected the importance the company attached to the worldwide recognition of the company's Chiquita brand name. Born in 1944, the company's Miss Chiquita character and jingle have won friends for the company's products around the world. In 1994 the company celebrated the 50th anniversary of Miss Chiquita and held a national casting call to select a Miss Chiquita. Three years later, the company decided its catchy jingle could probably use some updating and held a contest to see who could come up with the best new lyrics. The rules stipulated, however, that the tune of the jingle and its opening line ("I'm Chiquita Banana, and I've come to say . . .") had to remain the same.

CURRENT TRENDS

Chiquita Brands continues to diversify, moving slowly and deliberately to find businesses that fit with the company's existing divisions. Even as it has moved into

FAST FACTS:

About Chiquita Brands International Inc.

Ownership: Chiquita Brands International Inc. is a publicly owned company traded on the New York Stock Exchange.

Ticker symbol: CQB

Officers: Carl H. Lindner, Chmn. & CEO, 78, $215,000; Keith E. Lindner, VChmn., 38, $380,000; Steven G. Warshaw, 44, Pres. & COO, 44, $1,150,000; Robert W. Olson, Sr. VP, Secretary, & Gen. Counsel, 52, $765,000

Employees: 40,000

Principal Subsidiary Companies: Friday Canning Corporation of New Richmond, Wisconsin; Solar Aquafarms Inc. of Sun City, California; and Chiquita Banana Group of Cincinnati, Ohio, are subsidiaries of Chiquita Brands.

Chief Competitors: Chiquita's principal competitors include: Bestfoods; Cadbury Schweppes; Coca-Cola; Del Monte; Dole; Fresh America; General Mills; Goya; Smucker; Ocean Spray; PepsiCo; RJR Nabisco; Seagram; TLC Beatrice; United Foods; and Universal Foods.

markets a number of other fresh and processed foods. Its fresh produce line includes peaches, pears, plums, peppers, tomatoes, cucumbers, kiwifruit, citrus, and mangoes. Among the processed products the company markets include canned vegetables, fruit and vegetable juices, candy, cookies, milk, ready-to-eat salad, and teas. These products are distributed under a number of brand names other than Chiquita including, Amigo, Consul, Chico, Frupac, Pacific Gold, and Chiquita Jr.

CORPORATE CITIZENSHIP

Chiquita has taken significant pride in its contributions made in the communities where it operates. With more than 75 percent of its employees, also known as associates, based in Latin America, the company has done a great deal in this region to improve the quality of life. Prominent among its contributions throughout these countries has been the building of hospitals, schools, and power plants. It has also built ports and railroads to assist in doing business more efficiently. These additions to the local infrastructure have proven beneficial to local residents as well.

In the United States, Chiquita has been a strong supporter of efforts to protect the environment. It also has contributed generously to domestic programs to fight hunger, such as Second Harvest, the nation's largest hunger relief organization with a national network of 187 regional food banks. At Second Harvest's annual Hunger's Hope awards dinner in June 1998, the company was one of several U.S. corporations presented with a Hunger's Hope Partnership Award for their contributions of food, funds, services, technical assistance, or personal commitments.

other product lines, the banana, which gave the company its start, is certain to remain the heart of its business.

The growing worldwide trend away from trade protectionism was considered likely to help Chiquita increase its international sales more vigorously than in the past. In the late 1990s trade barriers were falling at an increasing rate. Countries would continue to band together in trade blocs, and under international trade agreements. In 1997 Chiquita won an important trade victory. The World Trade Organization (WTO) ruled that the European Union's (EU) trade policy giving preferential treatment to bananas from former European colonies, such as Jamaica, was illegal. The EU policy, introduced in 1993, was challenged in a 1996 filing by Chiquita, Guatemala, Mexico, and Honduras to the WTO.

GLOBAL PRESENCE

Chiquita Brands has been generally viewed as an international company, with 40,000 employees and a variety of operations in every continent except Antarctica. Until the late 1990s, the company owned or leased nearly 150,000 acres of land, primarily in the Central American countries of Costa Rica, Honduras, and Panama and the South American country of Colombia. Most of this land has been used for growing, packing, and shipping its bananas. Marketing operations are located around the world.

PRODUCTS

Best known for its bananas, which continue to generate about 60 percent of total annual sales, Chiquita also

EMPLOYMENT

The company has always considered its employees its most important asset, providing many opportunities for career advancement. According to 1998 Chiquita company literature, "our multi-tiered operations allow us

CHRONOLOGY:

Key Dates for Chiquita Brands International Inc.

1899: The United Fruit Company is created to produce and ship bananas in the United States

1903: United goes public; begins using refrigerated vessels for shipping

1910: Initiates research to develop disease-resistant bananas

1944: The name Chiquita and the Miss Chiquita character are introduced

1947: Chiquita is registered as a trademark in the United States

1958: Scientists recommend new disease-resistant varieties of bananas

1963: Chiquita begins the biggest branding program ever undertaken by a produce company; the blue sticker is introduced

1970: Merges with ATK corporation and the company name becomes United Brands Company

1984: American Financial Corporation becomes the majority shareholder

1998: Acquired Stokely USA Inc.

---

to offer rewarding positions with global opportunities. Our philosophy is to develop high-potential associates and provide them the broadest path for success. Each year, Chiquita sets it sights on a new level of excellence. For this, we have our associates to thank. For they are the people who have made us what we are today and what we will be tomorrow."

Chiquita looks for ambitious people who are results-oriented. Because it is a global company with opportunities in a number of disciplines, including administration, finance, field operations, information systems, marketing, production management, purchasing, quality control, and human resources, Chiquita needs people with a variety of skills, educational backgrounds, and interests.

The company insists on excellence from its associates, and it is generous in the rewards it has offered for such excellence, including an outstanding compensation and benefits package. Chiquita has been dedicated to the concept of promotion from within, which has given employees an opportunity to advance based on their abilities and their contributions to the company.

SOURCES OF INFORMATION

Bibliography

"Chiquita Brands International Inc." *Hoover's Online,* 1 July 1998. Available at http://www.hooovers.com.

"Chiquita Buying Stokely for $110 million in Stock." *Reuters,* 18 September 1997.

"Chiquita History." *Chiquita Brands International Inc. Home Page,* 1 July 1998. Available at http://www.chiquita.com/discover/oshistory.html.

"Chiquita Sues Ex-reporter, Alleging Theft." *Minneapolis Star Tribune,* 3 July 1998.

"Chiquita Today." *Chiquita Brands International Inc. Home Page,* 1 July 1998. Available at http://www.chiquita.com/discover/ostodayhtml.

For an annual report:
on the Internet at: http://www.chiquita.com/ **or** write: Investor Relations, Chiquita Brands International, 250 E. 5th St., Cincinnati, OH 45202

For additional industry research:
Investigate companies by their Standard Industrial Classification Codes, also known as SICs. Chiquita's primary SICs are:

0161 Vegetables and Melons

0172 Grapes

0174 Citrus Fruits

0175 Deciduous Tree Fruits

2032 Canned Specialties

2033 Canned Fruits and Vegetables

2037 Frozen Fruits and Vegetables

5148 Fresh Fruits and Vegetables

Chrysler Motors Corporation

FOUNDED: 1925 as Chrysler Corporation

Contact Information:
HEADQUARTERS: 1000 Chrysler Dr.
   Auburn Hills, MI 48326-2766
PHONE: (248)576-5741
FAX: (248)512-2912
TOLL FREE: (800)992-1997
URL: http://www.chryslercorp.com

OVERVIEW

Chrysler Corporation is the number three automaker in the United States behind General Motors and Ford Motor Company. It markets cars and light trucks under the Chrysler, Dodge, Eagle, Jeep, and Plymouth brands. Chrysler Corporation, which formally became Chrysler Motors Corporation on April 1, 1998, announced a proposed merger in 1998 with Daimler-Benz, which would result in the creation of DaimlerChrysler, a new German company. Both companies have very distinct product lines, and compete in different markets for different customers (except in the sport utility vehicle category). DaimlerChrysler plans to expand into global markets where only one of the former companies may have previously been competing. The largest proposed industrial merger in history—valued roughly at $92 billion—will combine two companies with similar corporate cultures to create a single entity capable of becoming one of the world's leading designers and producers of cars and trucks. The merger, if approved by regulators, shareholders, and unions, will be completed by the end of 1998.

COMPANY FINANCES

For the second quarter of 1998, Chrysler Corporation reported net earnings of $1.0 billion ($1.55 per common share), compared to the same period in 1997 when net earnings were $483 million ($.71 per common share). Increased earnings reflected increases in vehicle shipments, improved product mix, and decreased warranty costs, which were partially offset by an increase in average sales incentives and higher profit-based employee compensation. Chrysler reported total revenues of $61.1 billion for 1997, compared to $61.4 billion in 1996. Pretax earnings in 1997 were $4.6 billion, and net earnings were $2.8 billion. Net earnings per common share were $4.15 and the dividend declared per common share was $1.60. In 1996 pretax earnings were $6.1 billion, net earnings were $3.5 billion, net earnings per common share were $4.83, and the declared dividend per common share was $1.40. Revenue in 1997 was affected by a very costly 29-day strike at the Mound Road Engine Plant located in Detroit, Michigan.

HISTORY

In 1925 the Chrysler Corporation was incorporated by Walter Percey Chrysler. Chrysler was a former vice president of General Motors who had resigned over policy differences and had gone on to restore the Maxwell Motor Corporation to solvency. He designed Maxwell's first Chrysler automobile and exhibited it in 1924 in the lobby of the Hotel Commodore in New York City, since a vehicle not yet in production could not be displayed at the New York Auto Show. The car was a major success—the company sold 32,000 vehicles at a profit of $4 million before the year's end.

Following the success of his first car, Chrysler designed four more automobiles—the 50, 60, 70, and Imperial 80—named for their maximum speeds, which surpassed the 35 mph top speed of the Ford Model T. By 1927 the Chrysler Corporation had firmly established itself with sales of 192,000 cars, becoming the fifth largest company in the industry.

Chrysler realized the need to build his own plants in order to exploit his firm's manufacturing capabilities. Dillon Read of the New York banking firm of Dillon Read and Company had bought the Dodge Corporation of Detroit from the widows of the Dodge Brothers and reached an agreement with the now well-known Walter Chrysler. In 1928 the Dodge Corporation became a division of the Chrysler Corporation, and the size of the company increased fivefold.

The manufacture of Chrysler, Plymouth, and Dodge cars was suspended during World War II while Chrysler converted to war production. Chrysler's wartime service earned it a special Army-Navy award for reliability and prompt delivery. Some of its main war products included the B-29 bomber engines and anti-aircraft guns and tanks.

The company began experiencing three significant problems in the immediate postwar period: a loss of the initial enthusiasm and drive that had helped its constant innovation and experimentation in the early days; an exhaustion of engineering breakthroughs; and changes in American tastes and the increased demand for sleeker, less traditional models of cars. In addition, Chrysler did not focus on marketing, which was then an emerging trend in the auto industry.

FINANCES:

Chrysler Corp. Revenues, 1994-1997 (billion dollars)

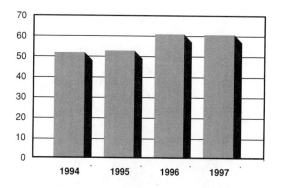

Chrysler Corp. 1997 Stock Prices (dollars)

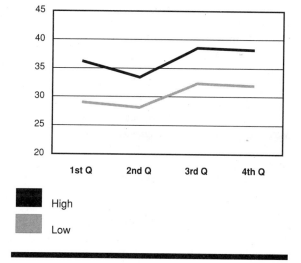

High

Low

L.L. Colbert, a lawyer, became the president of Chrysler in 1950 and hired McKinsey and Company, a management consulting firm, to put Chrysler back on track. The result was three reforms—development of international markets, centralized management, and a redefined engineering department—but Colbert's reforms did not significantly improve Chrysler's competitiveness.

Lynn Townsend was hired to be the new corporate head in 1952. He consolidated the Plymouth and Chrysler car divisions, closed some unproductive plants, reduced the workforce, installed an IBM computer system to replace 700 clerical staff workers, and enhanced sales by

The Dodge Viper, which premiered in 1993. (Courtesy of American Automobile Manufacturers Association.)

providing the best warranty in the industry. Within five years Lynn Townsend had revitalized the corporation. A Space division was formed that became the prime contractor for the Saturn booster rocket. By the end of the 1960s Chrysler had plants in 18 different countries.

Before the end of the decade, the domestic market was undergoing major changes—inflation was taking a toll, imports of foreign vehicles had increased, and crude oil prices had risen steadily. Chrysler, intent on fighting domestic competition, lost pace in the rapidly changing market and did not produce enough of its popular compact cars to meet consumer demand. In addition, with an overstock of larger vehicles, Chrysler reported a $4-million loss in 1969 in sharp contrast to its profit of $122 million the previous year.

John J. Ricardo succeeded Townsend as president and immediately began cutting expenses by reducing salaries, workforce, and the budget, and experimented with the marketing of foreign cars. However, Chrysler was not reading the public mood. The company continued manufacturing large gas-guzzling cars even during the 1973-74 Arab oil embargo in a market already dominated by Cadillacs and Lincolns. In 1974 losses totaled $52 million, and the following year's deficit was five times that amount. The company experienced a brief respite in 1976-77.

In 1978 Chrysler reported a loss of $205 million, causing great concern among the company's financiers. Chrysler saved itself from bankruptcy through highly charged negotiations with the federal government, which guaranteed loans up to $1.5 billion on the condition that Chrysler raise $2.0 billion on its own. Under the leadership of Lee Iacocca, an ex-Ford executive with a flair for marketing and public relations, Chrysler recovered in spite of plant closures, layoffs, and a company-wide restructuring worth $577 million. The dedication and hard work of Chrysler's employees played a key part in the resurgence of the corporation.

The 1980s brought exciting changes to the corporate structure as well as to the product lines. General Dynamics bought Chrysler Defense, and the loans that the government had guaranteed were paid back seven years early. The K-car debuted in the 1981 model year, and minivans, a category Chrysler pioneered and continues to dominate, were introduced in 1983. A merger with American Motors put the Jeep and Eagle brands in dealers' showrooms. The Dodge Viper concept car excited crowds at the North American Auto Show in 1989 and revived interest in Chrysler's products.

In 1992 Chrysler introduced the concept of Cab-Forward design. This concept made the wheels appear to be pushed forward, back, and out, creating greater stability and enlarging the passenger compartment. The 1990s saw the reporting of record net earnings for multiple quarters and the dedication of the world headquarters building in Auburn Hills, the European headquarters in Brussels, and the Chrysler Japan office in Tokyo.

The $1.5 billion Chrysler Motors world headquarters building in Auburn Hills, Michigan. After the proposed merger with Daimler-Benz, this site will remain as one of the two DaimlerChrysler world headquarters buildings. *(Photograph by Carlos Osorio.* *AP/Wide World Photos, Inc.)*

FAST FACTS:
About Chrysler Motors Corporation

Ownership: Chrysler Motors Corp. is a publicly held company traded on the New York Stock Exchange.

Ticker symbol: C

Officers: Robert J. Eaton, Chmn. & CEO, 57, $4,612,500; Thomas P. Capo, VP & Treasurer, 46; Thomas T. Stallkamp, Pres., 51; Gary C. Valade, Exec. VP & CFO, 55, $1,412,503

Employees: 121,000

Principal Subsidiary Companies: Chrysler Motors Corporation oversees many subsidiaries. Some of the most well-known are Chrysler Financial Corporation, Chrysler Insurance Corporation, New Venture Gear, Chrysler International Corporation, and Pentastar Aviation.

Chief Competitors: Chrysler Motors Corporation's mission is to be the premier car and truck company in the world by the year 2000. Achieving this is no easy task, given the other automotive manufacturers Chrysler faces in the marketplace. Competitors include: General Motors; Ford Motor Company; Toyota; Volkswagen; Nissan; Fiat; Honda; Kia; Hyundai; and Mazda.

STRATEGY

According to Robert J. Eaton, chairman of the board and CEO, Chrysler's strategy is simple. It consists of sticking to its core business, following through on an aggressive product development program, focusing on quality, continuously improving their operations and developing their international markets, and reducing costs.

The corporation was restructured in 1991 into platform teams in order to facilitate product development. In this team approach, engineers, designers, marketers, accountants, suppliers, and factory workers cooperate simultaneously on a specific product line. In the old system, each functional group independently did its own work and then passed it on to the next department.

INFLUENCES

In the 1930s Chrysler's farsightedness helped the company survive the Great Depression far better than oth-

ers in the industry. Chrysler realized the dangers associated with rapid growth and the importance of maintaining flexibility in his vehicle models and designs. Although he had to pay more for car parts than other companies, he discontinued his policy of manufacturing as many parts as possible for his cars. On more than one occasion Chrysler did not keep pace with the rapidly changing industry and suffered massive losses. Restructuring the organization, its processes, and strategies maneuvered the company to its current position in the industry.

CURRENT TRENDS

Chrysler has been working to reduce the amount of time it takes for a vehicle to get from concept to market, and has provided a benchmark for others in the industry. Chrysler has a program in place for its suppliers to submit ideas for saving costs that resulted in identified sav-

CHRONOLOGY:

Key Dates for Chrysler Motors Corporation

1925: Walter Percey Chrysler, a former GM vice-president, incorporates the Chrysler Corporation

1928: Dodge becomes a division of Chrysler

1942: Production of cars comes to a halt as Chrysler concentrates on war machine production

1957: Chrysler's space division is formed and Chrysler becomes the main contractor for the Saturn booster rocket

1963: Chrysler revolutionizes the industry with a 5-year, 50,000 mile power train warranty

1974: Chrysler continues manufacturing gas guzzlers through the Arab oil embargo; losses totaled $52 million

1978: Lee Iacocca becomes the head of Chrysler

1980: Iacocca secures a federal loan worth $1.2 billion to keep Chrysler alive

1983: Chrysler pays off loan seven years ahead of schedule

1984: The company boasts record earnings of $2.4 billion

1987: Chrysler takes over the American Motors Corporation, getting the prized Jeep line along with it

1992: Cab-Forward Design, for greater stability and handling, debuts

1998: Chrysler proposes merger with Daimler-Benz

HEMI RULES NASCAR CIRCUIT

With the 1964 introduction of the 426 Hemi motor at the Daytona 500, Chrysler proved itself as an automobile producer that could dominate the NASCAR circuit. Initially, this engine's singular purpose was to put Chrysler ahead of the pack on the nation's stock car tracks, as the 426 was produced strictly as a racing engine, but eventually the Hemi dominated the streets of America as well.

In its first year of production, Hemis powered four Mopars to sweeping victories at Daytona, with these stock cars finishing in the top four. This single event caused NASCAR officials to eventually impose tighter production rules on Chrysler. As a result of such rules, Chrysler began producing Hemi engines for not only the stock cars, but for normal production cars as well.

With 426 cubic inches producing 425 horsepower and 490 foot-pounds of torque, the slightly lower-powered street version of the Hemi was not for the weak of heart. Produced by Chrysler from 1966 to 1971, 426 Hemi-powered street cars ruled many back-road drag races before emissions laws and high production costs, among other factors, caused them to be phased out. At the same time, their race version counterparts were reigning on the NASCAR circuit. Today, nearly 30 years after the last 426 Hemi came off the assembly line, car enthusiasts still regard this engine a classic. Bringing astronomical prices for restored versions, the Hemi-powered cars are considered among the most legendary of the muscle car era.

ings of more than $1.2 billion during the 1997 model year.

With the 1998 proposed merger with Daimler-Benz, Chrysler may stimulate a global realignment of the automotive industry.

PRODUCTS

The Chrysler Corporation is known for many of its historical vehicles, which include the Imperial, New Yorker, Valiant, Barracuda, and the Viper, among many others. In 1997 Chrysler introduced the all-new Dodge

Durango sport utility vehicle, which was recognized as "Sport-Utility Vehicle of the Year" by *Four Wheeler's* magazine. The Dodge Intrepid and Chrysler Concorde were also completely redesigned. The Dodge Ram Quad Cab and the 5.9 Liter Jeep Grand Cherokee Limited also made their debuts. A new 1998 Chrysler 300M and Chrysler LHS were also planned.

CORPORATE CITIZENSHIP

Chrysler invests heavily in the people and communities that surround its corporate facilities and plants. The Chrysler Fund has spent $177 million through 1996 for cultural, educational, and community improvement initiatives. An example of this was when Chrysler and the UAW donated a total of $25,000 to the American Red Cross Disaster Relief Fund to help the Orlando, Florida, area when it was hit by tornadoes. Chrysler encourages employee and dealer involvement in charitable projects as well.

GLOBAL PRESENCE

While North America accounts for the majority of Chrysler's sales, the company sells its cars, minivans, and trucks in more than 140 countries. In 1997 the United States accounted for 80 percent of vehicle unit sales; Canada for 9 percent; Asia, Taiwan, Brazil, Australia, and the Middle East for 5 percent; Europe for 4 percent; and Latin America for 2 percent. Chrysler has assumed distribution in several countries around the world, including Japan, Taiwan, Korea, Argentina, Brazil, Austria, France, Italy, Germany, the Netherlands, and Belgium. In 1997 Chrysler Asia Pacific established its new headquarters in Singapore. Chrysler also assembles vehicles in Austria, Venezuela, Argentina, Egypt, China, Thailand, Indonesia, and Malaysia.

SOURCES OF INFORMATION

Bibliography

"Chrysler Corporation." *Hoover's Online,* 28 July 1998. Available at http://www.hoovers.com.

Chrysler Corporation Times, 12 March 1998.

Chrysler Corporation Times, 14 May 1998.

Chrysler Home Page, 22 April 1998. Available at http://www.chrysler.com.

Covell, Jeffrey L. "Chrysler Corporation." *International Directory of Company Histories,* Vol. 11. Detroit, MI: St. James Press, 1995.

Ryckebusch, Michele. *Chrysler through the Years.* Auburn Hills, MI: Chrysler Communication Programs Department, 1996.

For an annual report:

on the Internet at: http://www.investor-rel.com/chrysler **or** write Investor Relations, Chrysler Motors Corp., 1000 Chrysler Dr., Auburn Hills, MI 48326-2766

For additional industry research:

Investigate companies by their Standard Industrial Classification Codes, also known as SICs. Chrysler's primary SICs are:

3679 Electronic Components, NEC

3711 Motor Vehicles and Car Bodies

3714 Motor Vehicles Parts and Accessories

6159 Miscellaneous Business Credit Institutions

6399 Insurance Carriers

Circuit City Stores, Inc.

FOUNDED: 1949 (as Wards Company)

Contact Information:

HEADQUARTERS: 9950 Mayland Dr.
   Richmond, VA 23233
PHONE: (804)527-4000
FAX: (804)527-4194
URL: http://www.circuitcity.com

OVERVIEW

Circuit City, a Fortune 500 company, is the nation's largest retailer of major brand-name consumer electronics and appliances and a leading retailer of personal computers and music software. The company operates 512 "Superstores," 50 Circuit City Express (mall-based) stores, and 4 consumer electronics-only stores in the United States. Many Superstores range from 18,500 to 43,300 square feet. Plans for 1998 included an additional 60 Superstores with a total of 80 by the end of the decade. More importantly, the company has a presence in all the top 50 U.S. markets and nearly all the top 100. Still, Circuit City, with a presence in 65 percent of the U.S. market, has the option of expanding. The company plans to expand its store base 13 to 14 percent per year.

Circuit City's core product categories are audio, video, and appliances. Over the years the company has introduced many key products such as the IBM PS/1 computer in 1991, making Circuit City the first superstore to sell it. Circuit City offers exclusive or semi-exclusive brands, unlike its competitor, Best Buy. This allows the company to raise margins and reduce attention to low-profit items. Circuit City is the only nationally franchised Sony XBR and Alpine dealer.

COMPANY FINANCES

In 1998 net earnings were $104 million, compared with 1997's $136 million. Circuit City Stores total sales for the year ending February 28, 1997 increased 16 percent to $8.87 billion from $7.66 billion in the prior fiscal year. In fiscal 1996 total sales were $7.03 billion, a 26-percent increase from 1995's $5.58 billion.

Over the last 11 years, Circuit City has also shown a steady increase in profits. The company's stock ranged from a low of $31.00 to a high of $49.63 over a 52-week period. The annual dividend was $.14 per share and Circuit City's price-earnings ratio was 10.97.

ANALYSTS' OPINIONS

Some critics contended that Circuit City is at a disadvantage by having a commissioned sales force. In response, Circuit City contracted with an independent research firm in 1994 to find out customer opinion of the level of service provided by electronics retailers. The result was that Circuit City's level of service was right where other retailers were—scored with too little attention paid to the customer.

Other critics believe that Circuit City is a "loss-leader" merchant in the music business. They claim that Circuit City and competitor Best Buy attract customers to their stores with low-priced music and then try to sell them higher priced merchandise. Other music retailers fear they could be squeezed out of the market by this tactic and there has been pressure on music manufacturers to stop selling to Circuit City and Best Buy.

On January 12, 1998, D. H. Toung of Argus Research Corp. compared Circuit City to Best Buy, in reference to earnings: "The CC Circuit City shares are trading at 23-times our EPS estimate for fiscal year 1999. We believe that the company's improving earnings and growing market share support this evaluation. Historically, the shares have traded in a P/E range of 10-28 times earnings. We believe the shares can trade into the upper end of this range. With its price having declined 23 percent from a 52-week high (compared with a 7.6 percent decline for the BBY shares Best Buy), we view the CC shares as more attractively valued than the BBY shares."

HISTORY

In 1949 Samuel Wurtzel started a small retail television business in Richmond, Virginia, called Wards Company, which eventually expanded to include small appliances. In the 1960s the focus shifted to selling stereos, as consumer demand dictated. Wards began to acquire several appliance retailers to strengthen its presence in the marketplace and became a public company in 1961.

In 1966 Alan Wurtzel, Samuel's son, joined the business and changed the stores into full-line electronics retailers. Wards opened its first electronics superstore in 1975 and it was an instant success. That same year the company spent half its net worth to start its first electronics superstore in Richmond. The move was such a success that in 1981, Wards moved into the New York

FINANCES:

Circuit City Net Sales, 1994-1997 (million dollars)

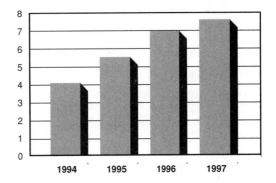

Circuit City 1997 Stock Prices (dollars)

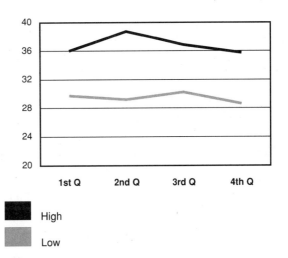

market by acquiring Lafayette Radio Electronics. The company then decided to refocus attention on the market in Los Angeles and pulled out of New York. After this experience, Wards began to hit single markets with a large number of stores. This strategy proved to be successful. The company continued to expand and, in 1984 Circuit City was established as the company name.

STRATEGY

Circuit City's marketing strategy emphasizes a broad selection of products, price ranges, and new prod-

FAST FACTS:

About Circuit City Stores, Inc.

Ownership: Circuit City Stores, Inc. is a publicly owned company traded on the New York Stock Exchange.

Ticker symbol: CC

Officers: Richard L. Sharp, Chmn. & CEO, 50, 1997 base salary $890,488; Alan W. McCollough, Pres. & COO, 47, 1997 base salary $466,165; Richard S. Birnbaum, Exec. VP Operations, 44, 1997 base salary $589,450; Michael T. Chalifoux, Sr. VP & CFO & Corporate Secretary, 50, 1997 base salary $475,193

Employees: 42,312

Chief Competitors: Circuit City's competitors include other full-service retailers, self-service retailers, general merchandise retailers, and local independent operators. Over the years the company's competition has shifted to include more self-service retailers, who offer a more limited product selection but at highly competitive prices. Some primary competitors include: Best Buy; CompUSA; Wal-Mart; Sears; Service Merchandise; The Wiz Inc.; Kmart; Office Depot; Montgomery Ward; Costco Companies; Sun Television and Appliances; Tops Appliance City; Tandy Corporation; and Media Play.

---

ucts. Merchandise pricing and selling strategies vary by market to reflect competitive conditions. The target market is baby boomers, and the company's strategy is to keep prices low and provide exceptional service. The company sells top-line, multi-feature merchandise requiring knowledgeable salespeople. New salespeople go through extensive training and are required to pass a test before they go out on the job. According to *Forbes*, Circuit City keeps from 20 to 70 sales people per store.

Circuit City attributes its success to the use of key prices and commissioned sales personnel, and the ability to regionalize its stores to fit the target market. Despite low pricing and high overhead, Circuit City is still able to turn a generous profit. This is due to the fact that Circuit City sells top-of-the-line merchandise with high margins. The company prides itself in its efficient operations, and learned that price wars were not the answer to gain market share. "There is no competitive advantage to lowering prices," CEO Richard Sharp commented, "the easiest thing is to match price." Therefore, as part of its com-

petitive strategy, Circuit City provides each customer with a low-price guarantee. In short, the company will beat any legitimate price from a local competitor.

Since 1993 Circuit City has followed a "showroom" format, in which only one model of each product is displayed. The company has an automatic replenishment of inventory, which keeps stock neither too high nor too low. Before entering a new market, Circuit City first conducts a market survey to determine demand. From the results of its findings, the company then chooses an appropriate store format. Also, to make certain the consumers are satisfied with their purchase and service, Circuit City conducts more than 25,000 telephone surveys each month.

The ability to choose its business partners wisely is another Circuit City strong point. In 1993 Circuit City chose to end its partnership with Mitsubishi, claiming that the company's products were "uncompetitive in pricing and technology." Some of the company's partnerships that have proven successful are General Electric, Hewlett-Packard, Hitachi, JVC, NEC, Packard Bell, Panasonic, Sony, Thomson, and Whirlpool. The company also relies on considerable amounts of advertising to stimulate Superstore and electronics-only store sales. Because of their presence in most major metropolitan markets, Circuit City has begun to take advantage of national broadcast and print advertising opportunities.

INFLUENCES

Market trends have influenced Circuit City. When consumer spending dropped in 1990 and the electronics industry was failing to introduce new products, Circuit City earnings decreased. In response, the company decided to expand to malls and opened its first Impulse store (currently called Circuit City Express). Circuit City has also been influenced by its competitors' moves. In 1993 Circuit City installed music departments in its stores as a reaction to Best Buy's success in its sale of music. The strategy was aimed at putting pressure on Best Buy rather than adding to profits.

In 1993 Circuit City expanded to Chicago where Best Buy had the largest market. Also in 1993 Circuit City opened a used car dealership in Richmond, Virginia, called CarMax. CarMax offers a good selection, reasonable prices, and high quality vehicles priced $1,000 under list, including warranties and other enhancements. The idea was to apply power retailing to auto dealing. In 1994 the company opened a second CarMax in Raleigh, North Carolina. Plans for 1997 included opening 8 to 10 more stores and 15 to 20 after that. Circuit City intends to have 80 to 90 CarMax units by 2001.

Expansion to the Northwest started in 1994 with Circuit City opening its first stores in Portland, Oregon. In 1995 Circuit City opened stores in Connecticut, Denver,

Buffalo, Rochester, and Salt Lake City. In 1996 the company entered two new markets, Pittsburgh and Detroit, expanding more high-price items like personal computers and home theater systems. Plans for 1997 included opening stores in New York City.

CURRENT TRENDS

Circuit City has responded to trends successfully. In 1996 the company downsized, opening smaller stores in response to a lapse in sales. The smaller stores cut costs since they were less expensive to operate. In response to an increase in appliance sales, Circuit City installed an on-line system providing approximately half its stores access to GE and Amana product specifications and also enabling them to manage special orders. By 1997 approximately 17 percent of Circuit City's sales came from major appliances.

Circuit City predicts that sales will reach $104.3 billion by the year 2000. There are plans for rapid expansion into new markets and increases in store size. Higher productivity will also be key to reaching this goal. Circuit City's entry into the New York market could not have come at a more opportune time, as Nobody Beats the Wiz, which had been the largest electronics retailer in this region, closed 17 of its 53 New York-area stores. The Wiz filed Chapter 11 and was subsequently purchased by Cablevision Systems.

In fiscal 1998 Circuit City expects to open approximately 60 Superstores, replace 10 to 15 stores, and add Circuit City Express stores. New market entries will comprise 35 to 40 of the new Superstores, including approximately 15 in the New York City market and entries into Indianapolis, Indiana; Dayton and Columbus, Ohio; and many smaller markets. According to CEO Richard Sharp, "Circuit City's goal is to maximize profitability in each market it serves by capturing large market shares that produce high sales volumes across a broad merchandise mix."

PRODUCTS

Circuit City sells video equipment including televisions, digital satellite systems, video cassette recorders, and camcorders; audio equipment including home stereo systems, compact disk players, tape recorders, and tape players; mobile electronics including car stereo systems and security systems; home office products including personal computers, peripheral equipment, and facsimile machines; other consumer electronics products including cellular phones, telephones, and portable audio and video products; entertainment software; and major appliances including washers, dryers, refrigerators, microwave ovens, and ranges.

Circuit City is reluctant to invest in too many computer software titles because they become outdated so

CHRONOLOGY:
Key Dates for Circuit City Stores, Inc.

1949: Samuel Wurtzel starts a small television retail business called Wards

1960: Wards expands into licensed television departments with larger mass merchandisers around the country

1961: Wards offers stock to the public selling 110,000 shares

1970: Samuel Wurtzel steps down as president and Alan Wurtzel, Samuel's son, takes over as president

1977: Wards becomes Circuit City when the stores expanded into full-service electronics stores

1987: Sales reach $1 billion for the first time

1993: Circuit City begins to sell used cars under the name CarMax

1998: Digital Video Express and Circuit City join together to develop a new format of DVD

quickly. In 1996 Circuit City expanded more high-price items, like personal computers, which accounted for one-fourth of overall sales in 1997, and home theater systems. As a result, the Circuit City brand grew. The company believes that software will soon be distributed electronically instead of through retail channels.

Future products include Digital Video Discs (DVD) that are the same size as audio disks and provide excellent quality and sound for home theater first-run films. Digital Video Express (Divx) has joined with Circuit City to create an enhancement of the current digital video disc, or DVD, technology and will compete directly with video rental and pay-per-view. This new technology could cause consumers to wonder whether the DVD players without the Divx enhancement will quickly become obsolete. Even though you can view DVD disks and Divx disks on the Divx players, Divx disks will not work on standard DVD players. Circuit City has invested about $100 million in the two-thirds owned partnership with Digital Video Express and plans to launch the product by mid-1998. However, much controversy is surfacing with the launch of this new format of the current DVD standard. Some analysts believe this gives consumers a choice. When all is considered, *Discount Store News* believes it will "ultimately depend on the consumer" whether Divx succeeds in the marketplace. Best Buy will not be supporting Divx.

CORPORATE CITIZENSHIP

According to Morgan Stewart, spokesperson for Circuit City, the company operates the Circuit City Foundation, which contributes generously to various charitable organizations. In addition, the company's associates volunteer for different causes. Top management does not include their corporate citizenship in their annual report, press releases, etc. Morgan Stewart went on to say that the company donates because "it is the right thing to do, and not for publicity."

GLOBAL PRESENCE

Circuit City has more than 500 stores in the United States, with the largest number being in California. Originally started in Virginia, Circuit City developed stores in the South and West, and were very successful. In 1991 the company entered the Texas market and opened superstores in Dallas, Houston, and Austin. Texas is where the stores first offered electronic office products such as computers, copiers, fax machines, and software. With its entry into New York, Circuit City now operates in nearly all the top 50 markets. Circuit City has considerable expansion opportunities and plans to operate 800 stores by 2001. Circuit City operates exclusively in the United States, and there is no indication that the company will go international.

EMPLOYMENT

Circuit City recruits through college campuses, trade journals, and newspaper advertising, and new employees require five weeks of training. Circuit City promotes from within and conducts routine evaluations. Employees may attend seminars and workshops to improve skills. The company operates an internal training and development program to help employees in their career direction. They also offer summer internships to students. Due to rapid expansion, Circuit City is always seeking employees.

SOURCES OF INFORMATION

Bibliography

Andreoli, Teresa. "New Markets, Service, Ads Lead Circuit's Growth Charge." *Discount Store News,* 3 July 1995.

"Best Buy and Circuit Sales Rise." *Television Digest,* 9 March 1998.

"Best Buy, Circuit City Downsize." *Television Digest,* 23 September 1996.

Christman, Ed. "Best Buy, Circuit City a Potent Combo; 2 Chains Change Entertainment Retailing." *Billboard,* 17 June 1995.

"Circuit City Fires Back at Critics." *Discount StoreNews,* 19 September 1994.

"Circuit City Projects $15B by Year 2000." *Discount Store News,* 4 December 1995.

"Circuit City Stirs DVD Brouhaha: Will its New Format Jeopardize Holiday Sales?" *Discount Store News,* 6 October 1997.

"Circuit City Stores Inc." *The Corporate Directory of U.S. Public Companies.* San Mateo, CA: Walker's, 1998.

"Circuit City Stores, Inc." *Hoover's Handbook of American Business 1996.* Austin, TX: The Reference Press, 1995.

Circuit City Stores, Inc. Annual Report. Richmond, VA: Circuit City Stores, Inc., 1997.

Dun & Bradstreet Information Services, North America. *The Career Guide 1997: Dun's Employment Opportunities Directory.* Bethlehem, PA: Dun & Bradstreet, Inc., 1996.

Haran, Leah. "Best Buy, Circuit City Raising the Stakes in Electronics Warfare." *Advertising Age,* 27 September 1995.

Moukheiber, Zina. "Retailing: Annual Report on American Industry." *Forbes,* 1 January 1996.

"Power Retailers Move Northwest." *Television Digest,* 14 November 1994.

"Retailers Aim to Avert Price War." *HFD-The Weekly Home Furnishings Newspaper,* 22 November 1993.

Rubinstein, Ed. "Sharp Touts Potential of CarMax." *Discount Store News,* 4 November 1996.

Stewart, Morgan. Circuit City Telephone Conversation, 27 May 1998.

Toung, D.H. "Circuit City/Best Buy-Company Report." *Argus Research Corp.,* 12 January 1998.

For an annual report:

on the Internet at: http://www.circuitcity.com **or** write: Office of the Corporate Secretary, Circuit City Stores, Inc., 9950 Maryland Dr., Richmond, VA 23233-1464

For additional industry research:

Investigate companies by their Standard Industrial Classification Codes, also known as SICs. Circuit City's primary SICs are:

5722 Household Appliance Stores

5731 Radio, Television, and Consumer Electronic Stores

Citicorp

FOUNDED: 1812 as City Bank of New York

OVERVIEW

Citicorp, also known as Citibank, is the second-largest U.S bank. Citicorp, along with its subsidiaries and affiliates, is a financial service institution serving approximately 3,000 locations, offering retail and corporate products in 100 countries worldwide. It is the world's largest credit card issuer and the sole provider of global consumer banking. Its services include savings and checking accounts, credit cards, and consumer loans. Because Citicorp operates as a local bank, many of its competitors are, in fact, other local banks. Citicorp conducts business within two franchises, Global Consumer and Global Corporate Banking. Though Citicorp is second to Chase Manhattan Corporation on the U.S. bank asset ranking, Citicorp has the larger global presence. Worldwide Citibanking accounts numbered 20 million as of March 31, 1998, up 6 percent from 1997.

Citicorp's operations span 37 countries in central/eastern Europe, the Middle East and Africa; 26 countries in Latin America; 16 countries in Asia; 19 countries in western Europe, as well as Canada and the United States. The company's goal is to have 1 billion customers worldwide by 2010, up from about 60 million today.

Contact Information:
HEADQUARTERS: 399 Park Ave.
   New York, NY 10043
PHONE: (212)559-4822
FAX: (212)559-5138
TOLL FREE: (800)285-3000
URL: http://www.citicorp.com

COMPANY FINANCES

Global Consumer net income in the first quarter of 1998 was $458 million, compared with $493 million in 1997. The increase primarily reflects strong performance in the North America, Europe, and Japan Citibanking businesses. Global corporate banking net income was

Federal Reserve, the combined company would dominate the banking industry with $150-billion market capitalization. Citicorp's earnings per share were $2.23, exceeding analysts' estimates.

FINANCES:

Citicorp
Revenues, 1994-1997
(billion dollars)

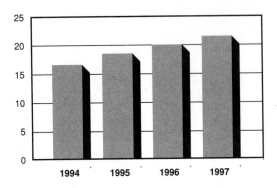

Citicorp
1997 Stock Prices
(dollars)

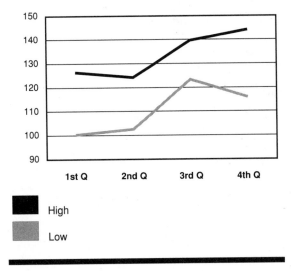

$753 million in the first quarter, up $104 million or 16 percent from 1997. Citicorp's stock ranged from a low of $109 to a high of $182 over a 52-week period.

Citicorp's earnings increased 7 percent for the first quarter of 1998 to 1.1 billion while chief rival, Chase Manhattan, reported a 22-percent decrease for the same period. Citicorp's increase was the result of a recent announcement of the company's plans to merge with Traveler's Group. Following this announcement Citicorp's market value increased to $81.9 billion on April 6, 1998. Providing the merger is approved, in particular by the

ANALYSTS' OPINIONS

Although some analysts were more than doubtful of Citicorp's recovery after 1991, many see a company whose fourth-quarter earnings in 1996 were better than the per share increase anticipated by Wall Street analysts. By 1997 Citibank repurchased $820 million of its stock. By doing this, Citicorp was showing investors it had great prospects for the future.

Citicorp's strategy of selling brand recognition for customer loyalty is questioned by some critics. First, as Carol J. Loomis pointed out in the April 29, 1996, issue of *Fortune,* advances in technology might not allow for that kind of loyalty. Why, she asks, should customers remain loyal to Citicorp when they can surf the Web and compare financial institutions? Also, she continues, what value does sticking to high premium prices have when Citicorp's competitors are lowering theirs? CEO John Reed claims the competition for this strategy hasn't been shaped yet.

HISTORY

Colonel Samuel Osgood founded City Bank of New York in 1812, later renamed National City Bank of New York. It became the first commercial bank to offer consumer loans and by 1939 had more than 100 offices in foreign lands. In 1955 it merged with First National (New York) and was again renamed First National City Bank, only to change to Citicorp in 1974.

Growth continued in the late 1970s when Walter Writson, the company's CEO at that time, launched Citicorp's international business. Citibank entered the credit card market and became the largest issuer in the United States by 1977. It was also the first bank to present ATMs (automatic teller machines). John Reed, the individual behind the creation of these machines, became Citicorp's chairman in 1984.

By the 1980s Citibank was the largest bank in the United States, spreading into San Francisco, Chicago, Miami, and Washington, DC. However, the 1980s proved to be difficult times for the company due to defaulted loans overseas, which cost the company $4 billion in 1987 and 1989. Following this loss Citibank faced the decline of the commercial real estate market in the United States. Struggling to regroup, the company acquired $2.6 million by recapitalizing in 1991 and 1992. Selling assets and eliminating dividends also proved necessary for survival. In 1992 the U.S. government put a limit on the number of loans the company was permitted to make.

STRATEGY

Citicorp's goal is to expand earnings by 10 to 12 percent per year. Seeing a need for impressive growth, John Reed brought in new management from outside of the company in an attempt to improve the company's image. These efforts reflected Reed's goal to establish Citicorp as a well-recognized and well-respected name. Citicorp continues to seek alliances that provide broader physical distribution. The company's early entry into the international market has proven successful and profitable. Many other banking institutions are just beginning to enter foreign markets, due to the saturated market in the United States (in particular, credit cards).

Citicorp is known for positioning itself to gain the business of customers early in their lives. Citicorp may initially provide a student loan or credit card and later provide a mortgage, car loan, or investment product. This is what Citicorp refers to as a "life cycle" approach to marketing. The company targets the "twentysomething" market to invest in Roth IRAs. Citicorp developed a brochure titled "Get a Roth Rolling . . . and Other Ideas On How to Fund Your Retirement," which is designed to encourage young people to think ahead.

Citicorp's credit card market share in Asia is twice that of its largest rival. Citicorp was the first bank to offer 24-hour-a-day, 7-day-a-week service, multicapability ATMs, and credit cards to the Asian region.

INFLUENCES

Citicorp's initial struggles in the late 1980s and early 1990s revolved around two major setbacks: overseas financial difficulties and a decline in the commercial real estate market. The 1990s proved to be times of slow-gaining strength for such a prosperous company one decade earlier. By 1991 the company had lost $457 billion, and fears of total failure plagued the minds of investors and analysts. Although Citicorp's international difficulties continued in the late 1980s, particularly in Brazil and Argentina, the company was not quick to shy away from other promising, arising markets. In fact, the company's willingness to continue to invest in foreign markets is what later proved to be a saving factor. Citicorp also avoided having to sell part of its credit card business during the difficult times. Credit cards, in turn, churned up $1.2 billion for the company in 1995. That year Citicorp returned to a prosperous state, with profits totalling $3.5 billion and a record-setting return on equity of 18 percent. By 1996 Citicorp was operating in over 96 countries. Herein lies John Reed's strategic shifts of aiming for 10 to 12 percent return on equity.

FAST FACTS:
About Citicorp

Ownership: Citicorp is a publicly owned company traded on the New York, Chicago, Pacific, London, Amsterdam, Tokyo, Zurich, Geneva, Basle, Toronto, Dusseldorf, and Frankfort Stock Exchanges.

Ticker symbol: CCI

Officers: John S. Reed, Chmn., 58, 1997 base salary $31,100,792; Paul J. Collins, VChmn. Emerging Markets, 60, 1997 base salary $13,993,188; H. Onno Ruding, VChmn., 57, 1997 base salary $1,348,000; Victor J. Menezes, Exec. VP & CFO

Employees: 93,700 (including 54,800 outside the United States)

Principal Subsidiary Companies: As a global company with approximately 3,000 locations and affiliate offices worldwide, Citicorp's principal subsidiaries include: Citibank Mexico (SA Grupo Financiero Citibank); Citibank, NA; Citibank Overseas Investment Corporation; Citibank Privatkunden AG (Germany); Citicorp Holdings, Inc.; Citicorp Mortgage, Inc.; Citicorp North America, Inc.; and Court Square Capital Ltd.

Chief Competitors: The company is subject to competition from both bank and non-bank insititutions that provide financial services. Citicorp's primary competitors in the United States include: Chase Manhattan Corp. and BankAmerica.

CURRENT TRENDS

Citicorp diligently sought to develop and implement a $700 million database business undertaking called the Relationship Banking System (RBS). The idea here was to improve the relationship between the customer and Citicorp via a computerized database. In essence, customers would be able to track their financial status using their Citicards or home computers. Also involved in this project was a plan to increase the customer information on file, allowing the company to track the lives of its customers and send information appropriate to their experiences.

Citicorp cut its fees to remain competitive within the electronic trades (in particular Fidelity Brokerage Services and Charles Schwab & Co.). Citicorp now charges

CHRONOLOGY:

Key Dates for Citicorp

1812: Founded as City Bank of New York

1914: Company is renamed National City Bank of New York

1955: Merges with First National (New York); renamed First National City Bank

1961: Offers high-interest specified-term CDs

1967: Incorporates in Delaware

1968: First National City Corp. is created as a holding company

1974: Company is renamed Citicorp

1977: Becomes largest issuer of credit cards

1978: Acquires Carte Blanche

1981: Acquires Diners Club; surpasses Bank America to become the largest U.S. bank

1984: John Reed becomes chairman

1985: Introduces Direct Access

1986: Introduces touch-screen automated teller machines

1987: Acquires Great Western Leasing and Great Western Credit companies

1992: U.S. government sets limits as to the number of loans a company could make; begins issuing Photocards

1993: Merges their savings banks and creates Citibank, FSB

1994: Opens the first foreign-owned commercial bank in Russia; sells Quotron Systems, Inc.

1997: Becomes first U.S. bank to conduct yuan-based transactions in China

1998: Acquires AT&T Universal Card Services; Citicorp and Travelers Group announce plans to merge and form Citigroup Inc.

$19.95 for electronic trades and $29.95 for trading with a live representative. With its new fees Citicorp undercuts the discount brokerage leader, San Francisco-based Schwab, which charges a $29.95 fee for electronic trades. Although Citicorp does not offer Web-based trading, it plans to add the capability early in 1999.

Citicorp and Travelers Group are planning to combine their resources with what is being called a megamerger. The new organization, which will be named Citigroup Inc., will serve over 100 million customers in 100 countries around the world. The April 20, 1998 issue of *Business Week* stated, "The Citicorp-Travelers Group merger will create a global financial services giant with $700 billion in assets. Previous financial supermarket models have failed, but changing investor demographics could make this deal the model for a financial services revolution." CEO John Reed stated in *Fortune* magazine that the ability to cross-market and globalize was a major attraction in the merger of the two companies. The projected target date is the third quarter 1998.

PRODUCTS

Citicorp's newest product offering is the CitiFreedom Annuity Plus, which is underwritten by Citicorp Life Insurance Co. The CitiFreedom program for retirement is aimed at investors aged 35 to 55. In particular, it is trying to capture baby boomers during their prime investment years. The annuity guarantees a return of at least 4.25 percent and requires customers to invest at least $150 a month for 10 years.

On April 2, 1998, Citibank completed the acquisition of AT&T Universal Card Services. This acquisition strengthens Citibank's position as the leading credit card issuer. Citibank also launched the DriversEdge card, which enables customers to accumulate rebates toward the purchase or lease of a new car.

CORPORATE CITIZENSHIP

One obvious way Citicorp provides services to the community is by assisting those in financial need. For example, in La Paz, Bolivia, the company helped fund local businesses—even street vendors—who have come across resistance when seeking loans. By doing so, the company has helped develop international markets.

Other contributions include Citibank's sponsorship of a fund-raising event in Hong Kong. More than 750 employees participated in the Community Chest's Walk for Millions, collecting donations over $335,000. In the United States, Citicorp sponsored "The Glory of Byzantium," an art exhibit at the Metropolitan Museum of Art in New York. Citibank's efforts to support the arts include grants to symphony orchestras, theater and dance companies, performing-arts centers, libraries, museums, festivals, and exhibitions. The company also provided grants in Germany, Brazil and Mexico.

Citicorp also involved itself in supporting low- and middle-income housing structures. The company invests in low-income housing tax credits, aiding the financing of the construction of these sites. St. Edmund's Corner in New York is a typical example. Here, four- and five-bedroom units are made available at an affordable price for households with incomes less than 50 percent of the region's average.

GLOBAL PRESENCE

Citicorp planted itself into international markets early in its history. It operates in more than 96 countries and territories, including western Europe, Asia/Pacific, and Latin America. The Asia Pacific region remained a prosperous area of growth for Citicorp, reaping profits in 1994 of $781 million, more than one-fifth of the company's total profits.

By 1997 Citicorp obtained more than half of its profits from new, developing international markets. Commercial banking revenues earned by Citibank in countries other than the United States were trading—29 percent, transaction service—32 percent, lending—10 percent, and capital markets/other—21 percent.

EMPLOYMENT

Citibank employs approximately 93,700 individuals worldwide. The company continues to improve its employee evaluation system to ensure a person's qualifications best suit his/her job description. Citicorp emphasizes leadership, teamwork, and building effective control environments for managing cooperatively.

Recently two black Citibank employees filed a lawsuit claiming white co-workers had been sending racist e-mail back and forth. The lawsuit claimed that the plaintiffs were not provided the same work environment as whites, had been denied promotions, received less pay, and witnessed racially stereotypical conversations by supervisors. Citicorp continues to investigate the situation.

SOURCES OF INFORMATION

Bibliography

Aley, James. "John Reed Speaks." *Fortune,* 11 May 1998.

Chase, Brett. "Chase Profits Down 22% Slim 7% Rise for Citicorp." *American Banker,* 22 April 1998.

"Chemical, Chase Post Strong Earning Gains." *FOX News Network,* 21 January 1997. Available at http://www.foxnews.com.

"Citicorp." *Hoover's Online,* 12 May 1998. Available at http://www.hoovers.com.

Citicorp Annual Report. New York: Citicorp, 1997.

"Citibank Describes Byzantium Exhibit as Major Event in Arts-Support Programs." *News from Citicorp,* 3 March 1997. Available at http://www.citibank.com.

Citibank Home Page, 18 May 1998. Available at http://www.citibank.com.

"Citibank Is Voted 'Best Bank' for Second Year Running in Euromoney's 1996 Excellence Awards." *News from Citicorp,* 11 July 1996. Available at http://oak2.citicorp.com.

"Citicorp Marketing Roth IRAs to Gen X." *American Banker,* 30 March 1998.

"Employees Sue Citibank Over Racist E-Mail." *FOX News,* 19 February 1997. Available at http://www.foxnews.com.

Glasgall, William. "Just the Start?" *Business Week,* 20 April 1998.

Holland, Kelley. "The CEO Who Never Sleeps." *Business Week,* 29 January 1996.

Loomis, Carol J. "Citicorp: John Reed's Second Act." *Fortune,* 29 April 1996.

Malkin, Elisabeth, et al. "No Deposit, No Return." *Business Week,* 23 September 1996.

Marcial, Gene G. "Irate at a Miserly Student Loan." *Business Week,* 27 May 1996.

Matthews, Gordon. "Citi Leads in Market-Cap Derby; Top 100 Gained 10% in Quarter." *American Banker,* 13 April 1998.

Quittner, Jeremy. "Citicorp Testing Unusual Variable Guaranteed To Return at Least 4.25%." *American Banker,* 22 January 1998.

Ring, Niamh. "Citicorp Cuts Trade Fees to Compete with Discounters." *American Banker,* 2 February 1998.

Schmeltzer, John. "'Equity' Loans May Boost Funds for Communities." *Chicago Tribune,* 25 October 1996.

"Stock Focus: Citicorp." *The Tampa Tribune,* 19 February 1997. Available at http://www.tampatrib.com.

For an annual report:

on the Internet at: http://www.citibank.com or write: Citicorp, Corporate Affairs, 850 3rd Ave., 13th Fl., New York, NY 10043

For additional industry research:

Investigate companies by their Standard Industrial Classification Codes, also known as SICs. Citicorp's primary SICs are:

6021 National Commercial Banks

6035 Federal Savings Institutions

6712 Bank Holding Companies

The Clorox Company

FOUNDED: 1913

Contact Information:
HEADQUARTERS: 1221 Broadway
   Oakland, CA 94612-1888
PHONE: (510)271-7000
FAX: (510)832-1463
EMAIL: info@clorox.com
URL: http://www.clorox.com

OVERVIEW

The Clorox Company manufactures and markets household grocery products and products for institutional markets in the United States and internationally. Though the Clorox name adorns only the company's bleach products, Clorox is a diversified manufacturer and marketer of a variety of consumer products ranging from household cleaners to salad dressings.

COMPANY FINANCES

The Clorox Company continued to improve its financial performance in 1997 earning revenues of $2.5 billion, up 14.2 percent from 1996 revenues of $2.2 billion. The company's net income also rose 12.3 percent from $222 million in 1996 to $249.4 million in 1997. Approximately 85 percent of 1997 sales were generated in the United States ($2.1 billion), and remaining sales of $389 million were earned from foreign operations. The company was on track for additional revenue increases in 1998—revenues for the first nine months of fiscal 1998 were $1.9 billion, up from $1.8 billion for the same period in 1997. Net income rose 14 percent from $175 million in 1997 to $200 million as of third quarter 1998.

Earnings per share (EPS) also rose, from 13 percent from $2.14 in 1996 to $2.41 per share in 1997. As of third quarter 1998, the company's earnings were $1.93 per share, compared to $1.63 for the same period in 1997. The Clorox Company's stock traded at around $95.00 per share in mid-1998. Its 52-week high was $98.75, and its 52-week low was $61.88 per share. The company's price/earnings ratio was $35.30.

ANALYSTS' OPINIONS

Clorox stock has been performing well since late 1997. Investment analysts have been upgrading the company's rating and forecast continued growth in Clorox earnings per share. As of third quarter 1998 (ended March 31, 1998), the company's EPS were $2.69, and analysts at Zack's Investment Research anticipated 1999 earnings of $3.02 per share. DCJ direct upgraded the company's status from "market perform" to "buy" in June 1998—and Prudential had already done so in October of 1997. Reasons for increased confidence in The Clorox Company's financial performance include a solid 8.8-percent annual growth rate and record earnings during the late 1990s, especially during the third quarter of fiscal 1998. For that period, net sales were $680.5 million, up 5 percent from $649.2 million for the same period in 1997.

HISTORY

Clorox was founded in 1913 as the Electro-Alkaline company by five Oakland, California, entrepreneurs who invested $100 a piece to establish America's first commercial liquid bleach factory. With a business plan to convert brine from nearby salt ponds of the San Francisco Bay into sodium hypochlorite bleach, they purchased a plant site in August of 1913. The bleach was packaged in five gallon returnable containers and delivered by horse drawn carriage to local breweries, dairies, and laundries for cleaning and disinfecting purposes.

An initial stock issue of 750 shares priced at $100 each was fully subscribed by the end of 1914 and provided the company with $75,000 in start-up capital. By 1916, a less concentrated household version of the bleach was available for sale in amber tinted glass bottles. Free distribution and door-to-door salesmen helped gather orders for the household bleach and local grocers helped with the distribution. By the 1920s, Clorox's manufacturing plant produced about 2,000 cases or 48,000 bottles of bleach per day. As demand for Clorox bleach grew, the company expanded its manufacturing and distribution capabilities nationwide. By the 1930s, Clorox was the best selling liquid bleach in the country.

During World War II, because of the decreased availability of chlorine, bleach manufacturers were required to decrease the concentration of sodium hypochlorite in bleach. William J. Roth, then CEO of the Clorox Chemical Company, refused to compromise on the quality of the bleach and jeopardize customer satisfaction, and so he decreased Clorox production instead. He also terminated a number of contracts for chlorine that were negotiated before the war because the agreements paid suppliers too little for a substance now in such short supply.

By the mid-1950s, Clorox Chemical Company had garnered the largest share of the U.S. chemical bleach

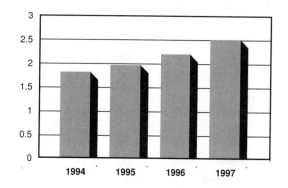

FINANCES:

Clorox Co.
Net Sales, 1994-1997
(billion dollars)

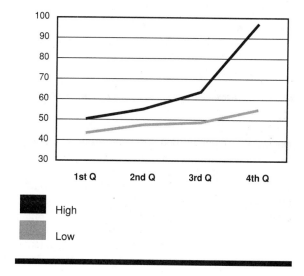

Clorox Co.
1997 Stock Prices
(dollars)

market. Procter & Gamble considered Clorox a valuable addition and acquired the company in 1957, changing its name to The Clorox Company. Within three months of the purchase Clorox gained its lost independence. The Federal Trade Commission (FTC) challenged the acquisition on the grounds that it might lessen competition or create a monopoly in household liquid bleaches, a violation of the Clayton Act. After 10 years of litigation, on January 2, 1969, The Clorox Company regained full formal autonomy as a publicly held corporation.

With this independence came a new commitment to growth and diversification. Clorox management imple-

FAST FACTS:

About The Clorox Company

Ownership: Clorox is a publicly held company traded on the New York Stock Exchange.

Ticker symbol: CLX

Officers: G. Craig Sullivan, Chmn., Pres. & CEO, 57, $1,655,350; Edward A. Cutter, Sr. VP, Secretary & Gen. Counsel, 58; Karen M. Rose, Group VP & CFO, 48

Employees: 5,500

Principal Subsidiary Companies: The Clorox Company has several subsidiaries including Clorox International Co., Clorox Sales Co., Kingsford Products Co., The Hidden Valley Mfg., Clorox Professional Products, Brita Products Co., American Sanitary Company, and Armor All Products Corporation.

Chief Competitors: A manufacturer of household and institutional products, Clorox's competitors include: Colgate-Palmolive; Dial; Procter & Gamble; S.C. Johnson; and Unilever.

---

mented a three-pronged strategic plan aimed at acquiring and developing a food specialty business, a line of institutional food products, and a line of cleaning products. They identified a list of potential targets, many of which were purchased within the year. The first companies acquired were chemical companies, including Jiffee Chemical Corporation, manufacturer of Liquid-Plumr drain opener; Shelco, manufacturer of Jifoam Aerosol Oven Cleaner; and the 409 division of Harrell International, producer of Formula 409 spray cleaners. Internally, the Clorox Company introduced Clorox-2, a dry non-chlorine bleach in September, 1969.

As part of the second step of its strategic plan, Clorox acquired McFadden Company, makers of Litter Green cat litter; Grocery Store Products Company, manufacturer of specialty food products such as B & B Mushrooms, Kitchen Bouquet gravy thickener, and Cream of Rice cereal; and a year later the company purchased Hidden Valley Ranch Food Products. In the early 1970s, the company's chlorine bleach sales rebounded as concerns arose over the health and environmental effects of enzyme and phosphate detergents.

In 1972, Clorox met the third objective of its strategic plan with the acquisition of Martin-Bower Corpora-

tion, a manufacturer and supplier of disposable packaging and paper goods for the food service industry; and Nesbitt Food Products, a manufacturer and distributor of soft drink concentrates. The following year Clorox acquired Kingsford Charcoal. Following this string of acquisitions was a growing stream of new products from the company's new Technical Center, which opened in 1973.

In the mid- to late 1970s, Clorox met with several setbacks and had to sell its Martin-Bower subsidiary, at a loss, to the H.J. Heinz Company. This was followed by the sale of its Cream of Rice product, which was not performing as well as expected. Many factors, including consumers' fear of recession, were affecting sales at Clorox. Efforts to generate and rapidly build an international business base were also stymied by heavy competition.

In 1981 Clorox acquired Comerco, a Tacoma, Washington-based producer of stains and wood preservatives marketed under the Olympic brand. Two years later they acquired Lucite Paints from E.I. DuPont de Nemours and Co. However these two product lines also did not meet the company's sales expectations and were sold to PPG Industries in 1989.

Clorox had to face one of its toughest challenges in 1982, when Procter and Gamble decided to challenge the company that had retained leadership of its laundry bleach product for so many years, with the test marketing of it's new product Vibrant. Clorox's response strategy was to launch another new bleach product at the same time, called Wave. Vibrant never made it past the test market. However, this event set the stage for numerous attempts by each company to invade markets for products long dominated by the other.

Starting in 1987, Clorox targeted a new set of companies to purchase in an effort to enter the bottled water industry. Deer Park Spring Water Company, Deep Rock Water Company, Aqua Pure Water Company, and Emerald Coast Water Company were included in this phase of Clorox acquisitions, which ended in 1988.

STRATEGY

The Clorox Company had ambitious goals for itself to meet by the year 2000. These included achieving company-wide sales of $3.5 billion. The company also wanted to grow its international business to represent 20 percent of company sales by that year. As part of its work toward meeting those goals, Clorox was focusing on improvement in its laundry and household cleaning businesses, as well as its insecticides.

Efforts were also made to enhance performance in the company's Food Products division. Prices were reduced on K.C. Masterpiece, its new Honey Steakhouse flavor was launched, and distribution gains were made in several club store accounts. These efforts resulted in record shipments for K.C. Masterpiece in 1997. Also, shipments of Hidden Valley bottled dressings were up, though slightly. As a result of increased competition, Clorox boosted spending on advertising and sales promotions and introduced two new flavors (Garden Vegetable Ranch and Fat-Free Roasted Garlic Italian). Overall, the Food Products Division reduced its cost structure by bringing contract-manufactured products in-house and simplifying its product lines.

Dollars spent on advertising Clorox products were up in 1997 as a result of the company's commitment to better marketing of its products. In 1995, Clorox spent $217.7 million on advertising; by 1996, that number reached $285 million, and in 1997 $348.5 million was targeted toward product marketing.

INFLUENCES

After several years of uneasy coexistence, the war between Clorox and Procter & Gamble erupted in 1988. It began with the company's introduction of the Clorox Super Detergent brand of laundry soap powder. Procter & Gamble responded with its own version of detergent with bleach. This was followed by the introduction of more products placed in direct competition with each other. Meanwhile, a shift in consumer preferences from powdered detergent to liquid detergent was adding to the company's marketing problems. This and an attempt to inject new life into its consumer products business motivated Clorox to acquire the Pine-Sol cleaner and Combat insecticide lines of American Cyanamid Company in 1990.

During 1998, the company's investment in its food products was paying off. The Hidden Valley line of bottled salad dressings saw increased volume and contributed substantially to The Clorox Company's financial growth. Also helping sales was record numbers of shipments of its K.C. Masterpiece barbecue sauces. International expansion also contributed toward improved financial results in 1998. Shipments in the company's most aggressively targeted area, Latin America, rose due to the acquisition of Super Globo in Brazil and the introduction of seven new products in the area during 1998's third quarter alone.

CURRENT TRENDS

By the mid-1990s Clorox was marketing many of the best known retail brands in America. The great majority of its brands were either market leaders or a strong second. The company also operated a professional products unit, which focused on expanding many of its successful retail franchises in cleaning and food products into new channels of distribution. Craig Sullivan became

CHRONOLOGY:
Key Dates for The Clorox Company

1913: Founded as the Electro-Alkaline Company

1914: Issues initial stock of 750 shares to get start-up capital

1922: Electro-Alkaline becomes the Clorox Chemical Company

1928: Goes public

1957: Procter & Gamble acquires the company and changes the name to The Clorox Company

1967: The Supreme Court orders Procter & Gamble to divest itself of Clorox because it could create a monopoly of liquid household bleaches

1975: A civil antitrust lawsuit against Clorox and Procter & Gamble by Purex Corp. is brought to trial; it is later thrown out of court

1982: Procter & Gamble begins marketing their own bleach products to challenge Clorox

1987: Clorox begins to diversify into the bottled water market by purchasing several companies within that industry

1998: Clorox begins focusing on their food products division and are rewarded with record sales of K.C. Masterpiece barbeque sauce and increased sales of Hidden Valley Ranch salad dressing

the CEO of Clorox in 1992. His corporate strategy was to change the focus of Clorox from simple acquisition to a balanced approach involving both acquisitions and new product introductions. This approach was in stark contrast to the company's previous eight years, when Clorox had considered about 200 acquisitions but did not follow through with any of them.

PRODUCTS

Clorox retail brands include: Armor All and Rain Dance automobile cleaning products, Formula 409 spray cleaner, Liquid-Plumr drain cleaner, Tilex mildew remover, S.O.S. steel wool soap pads, Pine-Sol cleaner, Black Flag insecticides, Fresh Step cat litter, Brita water filtration systems, Kitchen Bouquet browning and seasoning sauce, Hidden Valley salad dressings, Kingsford and Match Light charcoal briquettes, Combat Insect Control Systems, and PowerPack professional dilution-control spray cleaners, among others.

CORPORATE CITIZENSHIP

In its home town of Oakland, California, Clorox announced that the company was sponsoring the East Bay Habitat for Humanity's 1998 Build-A-Thon on June 27, 1998. The company was contributing $3,500 to Habitat for Humanity and would also be represented by a crew of company volunteers. About 60 Clorox employees planned to spend the day working on foundations and framing walls. This effort by the Clorox Company was part of the company's commitment to improving the quality of life in communities where Clorox employees live and work. Community programs are implemented through The Clorox Company Foundation, a strategic program of grantmaking, employee volunteer activity, and collaborative efforts with community leaders and other charitable organizations and companies.

In another of its charitable activities, Clorox was providing an education grant from Combat (part of its Kingsford Products Company) to help promote "Fight Asthma Now!," a program designed to send more than 14,000 volunteers to distribute 500,000 bilingual educational brochures in New York, Los Angeles, Houston, and Miami—cities where roach problems are most severe. The program, coordinated by Combat Insect Control Systems, the Allergy and Asthma Network/Mothers of Asthmatics (AAN/MA), and HOPE for Kids, came after a study confirmed that the spread of asthma among inner-city children was a result of roach infestation and the resulting allergens. The campaign planned to work with community groups to spread its simple three-step message of Prevent, Kill, and Clean.

GLOBAL PRESENCE

Clorox products are sold in over 70 countries and manufactured in more than 35 plants in North America, South America, Europe, Africa, and Asia. The Clorox Company's international strategy hinged primarily on establishing joint ventures with local businesses in developing countries where a strong demand for liquid bleach as a household cleaner and disinfectant was present. The company's international business realized double-digit growth in profits in 1997, growth attributed to Clorox's core business, new product introductions, and acquisitions.

The Latin America region represents the largest part of the company's international business. In 1997, 19 new products were introduced there and 3 acquisitions were made, including: Limpido (Colombia's leading maker of liquid bleach); Pinoluz (Argentina's leading pine cleaner); and the Shell Group's cleaners and insecticides group in Chile. The region was also targeted for aggressive development in 1998.

Other foreign ventures included the Asia-Middle East region, where the company ran businesses in the Republic of Korea, Japan, China, Malaysia, Hong Kong, Singapore, and Australia. The region also includes joint ventures in Saudi Arabia, Egypt, Yemen, and central Europe. The company had long-term plans for growth in the region, while immediate activity included launching S.O.S. floor cleaner in Indonesia, S.O.S. sponges and Yuhanrox liquid bleach in the Republic of Korea, Clorox Gentle bleach in Malaysia, and Combat insecticide in China. Combat's increasing popularity actually required expansion of the company's plant in Korea. The 1997 acquisition of Armor All marked The Clorox Company's first entrance into the Australian market.

EMPLOYMENT

The Clorox Company expressed a commitment to "having the very best people in all our positions, driving the business" in its 1997 Annual Report. In 1997, it adopted an initiative called "Organizational Effectiveness" to address concerns about simplifying company processes so that employees would be free to work on issues that truly affected Clorox business performance. Organization Effectiveness was a step following its existing work simplification effort. Themes the company focused on included improving the decision making process by putting decision making power in the hands of those closest to the issue, streamlining company planning and forecasting, and standardizing activities carried out on a regular basis. As stated by Clorox CEO G. Craig Sullivan, "We want Clorox people to put the creativity in the content, not the form."

SOURCES OF INFORMATION

Bibliography

"The Clorox Company." *Hoover's Online,* 4 July 1998. Available at http://www.hoovers.com.

The Clorox Company 1997 Annual Report. Oakland, CA: The Clorox Company, 1997.

Davids, Meryl. "Clorox Brightens Its Outlook." *Journal of Business Strategy,* July-August 1994.

Manufacturing USA. Detroit, MI: Gale Research, 1996.

Moody's Company Data Report. Moody's Investor Service, 1996.

"New Campaign Targets Asthma Awareness in Cities." *PR Newswire,* 7 May 1998.

"Raising Walls! The Clorox Company Sponsors East Bay Habitat's Build-A-Thon." *Business Wire,* 22 June 1998.

Schusteff, Sandy. *International Directory of Company Histories,* Vol. III. Detroit, MI: St. James Press, 1991.

For an annual report:

on the Internet at: http://www.clorox.com/invest.html **or** write: Investor Relations, The Clorox Company, 1221 Broadway, Oakland, CA 94612

For additional industry research:

Investigate companies by their Standard Industrial Classification Codes, also known as SICs. Clorox's primary SICs are:

2035 Pickles, Sauces, Salad Dressings

2841 Soap and Other Detergents

2842 Polishes and Sanitation Goods

2899 Chemical Preparations, NEC

3295 Minerals, Ground or Treated

Club Mediterranee SA

ALSO KNOWN AS: Club Med
FOUNDED: 1950

Contact Information:

HEADQUARTERS: 11 rue de Cambrai
   Paris 75019 France
PHONE: +33-1-53-35-35-53
FAX: +33-1-53-35-36-16
TOLL FREE: (800)Club Med
URL: http://www.clubmed.com

OVERVIEW

Club Mediterranee SA, commonly known as Club Med, operates around 130 vacation villages in some 50 countries on 6 continents. These villages offer guests a unique, all-inclusive (one-price food-and-fun package) vacation experience. In addition, the company operates two luxury sailing ships, Club Med 1, which was sold in 1997 and Club Med 2. Club Med 1 sails on the Caribbean and Mediterranean, while Club Med 2 cruises the South Pacific and French Polynesia, but will be taking on Club Med 1's itinerary in 1998. Both are some 600 feet in length and have 8 decks, a 400-person capacity, spacious windows, two restaurants, four cocktail lounges, piano bars, nightclubs, and 24-hour medical care.

COMPANY FINANCES

In 1998 Club Med's total revenue was $1.05 million, down from 1997's $1.42 million, which was also down from 1996's total revenue of $1.56 million. 1994 saw revenue at $1.70 million, and in 1995 total revenue reached a five-year high of $1.73 million.

HISTORY

Club Med was founded in 1950 by Gerard Blitz, an Olympic water polo champion from Belgium, who later partnered with Gilbert Trigano. Blitz offered the concept of a vacation escape that emphasized sports and friendships to Europeans who were tired of post-war life. Trigano's family supplied the tents used as guest quarters at

the first Club Med village on the shores of Alcudia, Majorca, Spain. The guests lived communally, helping to cook meals and wash dishes.

The idea behind the club, according to the company, was "to create an environment completely different from daily life, where guests could partake in a full range of recreation options without worrying about money. Out of this concept grew the all-inclusive vacation package where vacationers pay one price for transportation, lodging, three meals per day, wine and beer with lunch and dinner, most sports and leisure activities with lessons, and evening entertainment." Guests are given the freedom to choose the activities in which they wish to participate, or they can choose not to participate in any organized activities.

STRATEGY

Club Med's "secret," according to the company, is its "ability to stay ahead of the changing desires and needs of the vacationing public, while maintaining the spirit of the village lifestyle." The company has added single rooms and intimate restaurant settings, as well as televisions and telephones "to make rooms at the Club's facilities more comfortable and individualized." However, one industry publication noted that this was anathema, "quite a revolution for a hotel group that began its existence as a haven of peace for urban dwellers seeking to escape to greener pastures."

Club Med hosts 1.3 million guests annually and anticipates that number to reach 2 million by the year 2000. In part, the company attributes this to the shift from being seen as a vacation destination for single people to attracting couples, families, and senior citizens as well. Of the more than 1.5 million guests at Club Med in the mid-1990s, more than 250,000 of them were children; about 50 percent of the guests were married couples.

INFLUENCES

In order to combat competition from the large hotel chains opening copycat facilities and making takeover gestures, Club Med began a massive investment program in the late 1990s. The company intended to invest $50 to $80 million annually for several years to renovate its properties at a rate of 4 to 5 updates per year. The company plans to complete 15 such renovations by the year 2000, in addition to the construction of some 20 new villages. Club Med hires architects and designers for these renovations and additions, including Christian Liaigre, a Parisian designer who was responsible for redesigning Club Med villages at Gregolimano and Kos in Greece. Club Med plans to have some 117 villages around the world by the end of the century.

FAST FACTS:
About Club Mediterranee SA

Ownership: Club Mediterranee SA is publicly owned and traded OTC (over-the-counter).

Ticker symbol: CLMDY

Officers: Philippe Bourguignon, Chmn. & Pres., 49; Yves Martin, Director General Marketing Worldwide; Henri Giscard d'Estaing, Assistant Director General, Finance, Development, & International Relations; Claude Ravilly, SEVP Finance & Informatique

Employees: 20,000 (1996)

Principal Subsidiary Companies: Club Med's primary subsidiaries include Club Aquarius, Club Med, Inc., and Club Med Sales, Inc.

Chief Competitors: Club Med's major competitors include: Accor SA, a worldwide hospitality company, hotel operator, travel agency, and auto rental company and Carnival Corporation, a top overnight cruise, hotel, and tour operator.

CURRENT TRENDS

Club Med is a customer-driven company that listens carefully to what guests want. In fact, the idea for Baby, Mini, and Teen Clubs came from customer requests. Originally the Club catered primarily to singles and couples. As these people aged and had children, they wanted to vacation as a family. Thus, the first Mini Club opened in 1967 and the first Baby Club opened in 1971. The Club Med in Sandpiper, Florida, was named the "Best of '97" family resort in an America Online poll. Yet each village has its own unique style, some providing conditions more appropriate for a family environment, while others are geared to the singles lifestyle.

In 1994 Club Med launched its own Internet site, becoming one of the first travel organizations to do so. The site was completely redesigned and re-launched after a year and a half of experimentation, and new features are continually added, including graphics, photography, audio, weather reports, weekly updates, and promotions. By partnering with Reality Studio and Live Picture, Club Med's web site offers a virtual reality tour of its vacation spots.

CHRONOLOGY:

Key Dates for Club Mediterranee SA

1950: Gerard Blitz brings the 2,300 charter members of the club together in a small village in Spain to escape from the daily life of postwar Europe

1957: Club Mediterranee is incorporated

1961: The Rothschild Group becomes the largest shareholder and begins financing further expansion

1968: Club Med signs a preferential agreement with American Express to attract U.S. clients

1980: Copper Mountain, Colorado, the first full-scale Club Med village in the United States, opens

1984: Club Med, Inc. opens in New York to take over operations in North and Central America, Asia, and the Pacific and Indian Oceans

1987: The first full-scale village opens in Japan

1990: Club Med extends its agreement with American Express; the world's largest sailing ship, *Club Med 1* is launched

1997: Club Med 1 is sold

CORPORATE CITIZENSHIP

Club Med states that its top priority in developing and operating its destinations is to respect local ecological environments and to fully integrate the architecture of any new villages into existing surroundings.

The company also began offering "environmentally conscious" sailing packages aboard luxury ships in the Caribbean, Polynesia, and Mediterranean in response to the success of the cruise industry. Launched in 1990, Club Med 1 was touted as the world's largest computer-operated sailing ship. According to the company, "Sail power helps conserve the dwindling fossil fuel supply. When she must run her engines, Club Med 1 utilizes a light, high-grade oil, free of most impurities. Solid wastes are incinerated; cans/glass compacted, stored and off-loaded for recycling at the end of each voyage."

In the mid-1990s, French authorities reportedly offered Club Med officials the option of locating one of its new villages on Muruoa Atoll, a French nuclear test site that was closed in 1996. According to an article in *Hotel and Motel Management,* a spokesman for the French Foreign Ministry said the location on the blast site would be "an excellent means of demonstrating that French tests had never in any way polluted the area." "If the offer is serious," said Serge Trigano, then chairman of Club Med, "it'll be a pleasure to go and visit the site and see what can be done."

GLOBAL PRESENCE

Club Med operates all-inclusive vacation resorts and hotels around the world and is continually looking for new pieces of paradise to develop. This expansion meets the growing needs of a diverse global clientele.

In the late 1990s Club Med built its one-hundred and fifth village, located on Cuba's Varadero peninsula 90 miles east of Havana. Construction was financed by the Cuban government. The company has also made significant progress towards expansion in Asia, such as the first Club Med resort in China—located on Lake Yang Zhong Hai in the city of Dunming—as well as developing locations in Singapore and Indonesia. In 1996 the company announced that it intended to increase its presence in Spain and Italy and form a management group for its southern European operations.

EMPLOYMENT

Hosts and hostesses are called GOs, which stands for Gentils Organisateurs, or gracious organizers. They are recruited from more than 20 countries. Job requirements are a "sense of organization and a sense of humor" along with "administrative skills and a talent for managing sports, for creating the space people need to relax, have fun and enjoy themselves." An average 600-bed village is staffed with 90 to 100 of these employees, whose average age is 28. They have the opportunity to move to a new village every 6 to 12 months. GOs participate in the daily life of the village when not working as sports instructors, entertainers, chefs, or administrators. Unlike the usual uniform-clad hotel employee, GOs do not wear uniforms, and they do not accept tips.

SOURCES OF INFORMATION

Bibliography

"Beauty and 'Beast' of Kunming." *South China Morning Post,* 31 March 1998.

Club Med Home Page, 5 April 1998. Available at http://www.clubmed.com.

"Club Med Moves into Cuba." *Euromarketing,* 30 January 1996.

Club Med Trident. New York: Club Med, Inc., 1996.

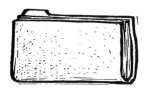

VACATIONS FOR JOCKS

Into sports and adventure? Gotta little extra money to spend? Then a Club Med vacation is the thing for you. Club Med is Sports Central. At a Club Med village, you can work out before breakfast, play a set of tennis afterwards, waterski and windsurf until lunch, and snorkel and sail until dinner. Or maybe you prefer aerobics followed by a round of golf, or archery followed by a rugged mountain-bike ride. Or perhaps you'd rather do a little scuba diving and then some horseback riding. Club Med has got it all. The possibilities are endless. Activities are available all day long, from dawn until dusk. By land, air, or sea, in summer, fall, winter, or spring, Club Med has got the activity for you.

Like to explore under the sea? Dive the exotic waters off Bora Bora in French Polynesia and discover exotic new worlds and sea life. Rather be on top of the water? Windsurf the waters surrounding the Greek isle of Kos or waterski the azure sea off of Kemer, Turkey. Always wanted to run away and join the circus? Visit the Club Med in Ixtapa, Mexico, and master the tightrope and trampoline, and sail through the air with the greatest of ease on the trapeze. Or just clown around if you want. Crave the excitement and thrills of the Great Outdoors? Visit the French Pyrenees and try your hand at canyoning, rappelling, rock climbing, rafting, and the challenging "Indiana Jones" course. Looking for something a little more relaxing? Ride horseback along the rolling hills near Sonora Bay, Mexico, or tee it up on Lindeman Island in Australia. More into cold weather sports? Shred the Rockies on a snowboard at a Club Med in Copper Mountain, Colorado, or do some serious schussing at the village in St. Moritz, Switzerland. And after a hard day of play, relax with an "anti-stress" massage and a hot water soak.

In addition to these adventurous activities, Club Med villages have your more mundane sports also: fishing, tennis, weight lifting, aerobics, in-line skating, squash, basketball, volleyball, softball, soccer, ping-pong, billiards, yoga, and more. And you don't have to worry about being inexperienced at an activity—Club Med caters to all levels of expertise and offers expert instruction to help you along. If some days you feel like doing nothing, you can do exactly that—just relax on the beach and catch some rays. But if nonstop action and adventure are what you mainly crave, a Club Med village is the place for you.

"Club Mediterranee SA." *Hoover's Online,* 6 July 1998. Available at http://www.hovers.com.

"Family Travel Network Announces Winners of 'Best of '97' Poll." *PR Newswire,* 7 January 1998.

MacDonald, John. "Club Med, Not Wanting to Resort to Its Old Image, Broadens its Appeal." *Seattle Times,* 27 October 1996.

Michaud, Paul. "Competition Sparks Club Med Restructure." *Hotel & Motel Management,* 3 July 1996.

"Online Travel Industry Experiences Interactive Revolution Fueled by Live Picture Reality Studio." *PR Newswire,* 23 March 1998.

Sidron, Jorge. "Club Med Finds Success Sticking to Key Formula: Fun, Relaxation." *Travel Weekly,* 25 November 1996.

For additional industry research:

Investigate companies by their Standard Industrial Classification Codes, also known as SICs. Club Med's primary SIC is:

7011 Hotels & Motels

The Coca-Cola Company

FOUNDED: 1892

Contact Information:
HEADQUARTERS: 1 Coca-Cola Plz.
   Atlanta, GA 30313
PHONE: (404)676-2121
FAX: (404)676-6792
URL: http://www.cocacola.com
   http://www.coke.com

The Coca-Cola Company

OVERVIEW

The Coca-Cola Company is the largest soft drink marketer in the world, holding 47 percent of the global market for soft drinks. It also produces other beverage and food products. About 90 percent of the company's revenues come from sales of beverages and 10 percent from food products. The Coca-Cola Company is very active internationally. While the company has very strong sales in the United States, 68 percent of its soft drink products are sold outside of North America. The Coca-Cola Company is regarded as one of the best managed companies in the world: in *Fortune* magazine's fifteenth Annual Survey of corporate reputations, published in March 1997, The Coca-Cola Company was ranked first based on its strong marketing skills, the quality of its products and services, financial soundness, corporate and environmental responsibility, and overall business performance.

COMPANY FINANCES

In its earnings statement, Coca-Cola reported another year of record volume and earnings per share in 1997. Earnings per share increased 19 percent in 1997. Revenue for 1997 totaled $18.87 billion and has risen steadily over the years. In 1993 total revenue was $13.96 billion, and rose in 1994 to $16.17 billion. In 1995 total revenue jumped to $18.02 billion and 1996 saw total revenue at $18.55 billion.

Worldwide, Coca-Cola's unit case volume increased 14 percent and gallon shipments grew 15 percent in the first quarter of 1998. Some revenue increases were off-set significantly by the impact of a stronger U.S. dollar. The U.S. dollar in 1997-98 was about 10 percent stronger than a weighted average of foreign currencies in 1996.

Excluding the impact of non-recurring items, oper-ating income grew 10 percent. Additionally, on a local currency basis, Coca-Cola continued to invest aggres-sively in volume-building marketing initiatives.

Coca-Cola purchased approximately 20 million shares of its own common stock in 1997. In the first quar-ter of 1998 it purchased another 4 million shares. Since January 1984, Coca-Cola has repurchased 31 percent of its outstanding common shares to create a cumulative to-tal of more than 1 billion shares, at an average cost of approximately $11 per share.

ANALYSTS' OPINIONS

The Coca-Cola Company has long been a favorite of stock market analysts, and many were recommending that investors buy its stock in the mid-1990s. Prudential Securities stated that the company was "being extremely aggressive in certain markets in an effort to capitalize on PepsiCo's vulnerability and overall strategy of shrinking its international soft drink business."

Wheat, First Securities also recommended that clients buy Coca-Cola stock (as of October 1996), citing the continued strength of its marketing programs, partic-ularly the Olympics, innovative packaging initiatives, and the introduction of new products worldwide. Wheat, First Securities also said that The Coca-Cola Company also benefited from strong volume growth produced by solid increases in unit sales of its major brands. The in-creases were the result of innovative packaging and ef-fective promotional support.

HISTORY

As a company Coca-Cola has grown consistently for more than 100 years. From one soft drink sold in an At-lanta pharmacy, The Coca-Cola Company has grown into an enormous worldwide marketer of many brands of soft drinks and food products. If all the Coca-Cola ever pro-duced were placed in regular size bottles and lined up to form a four-lane highway, that road would wrap around the earth more than 81 times.

Coca-Cola was first produced in Atlanta, Georgia, on May 8, 1886, when pharmacist Dr. John Styth Pem-berton mixed a caramel-colored syrup in a three-legged brass kettle in his backyard. After it was combined with carbonated water, Pemberton began selling the product as a fountain drink at Jacob's Pharmacy in Atlanta. The

FINANCES:

Coca-Cola
Net Revenues, 1994-1997
(billion dollars)

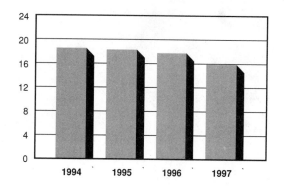

Coca-Cola
1997 Stock Prices
(dollars)

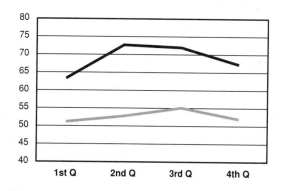

 High

Low

famous "Coca-Cola formula" has been a closely-guarded secret ever since, held in a bank vault.

In 1891 Asa Candler acquired total control of Coca-Cola. The following year Candler and several partners formed The Coca-Cola Company. The new company used advertising and promotion to make Coca-Cola avail-able everywhere, a strategy still used today.

In 1894 the first bottled Coca-Cola was sold. Bot-tling operations were soon established throughout the United States. Since then The Coca-Cola Company has sold its products in two main ways: through fountain

A look at the development of and changes made to the Coke bottle's shape since its original creation. (Courtesy of The Coca-Cola Company.)

(post-mix) operations, such as those found at movie theaters and fast food restaurants, and through sales of bottled and canned products in stores and vending machines.

In 1919 The Coca-Cola Company was sold by the Candler group for $25 million to Atlanta banker Ernest Woodruff. Four years later Ernest Woodruff's son, Robert Woodruff, was elected president of the company. He would lead the company for more than six decades.

The Coca-Cola Company first moved outside the soft drink industry when it bought the Minute Maid Company in 1960. Other food companies were acquired and merged into what is now Coca-Cola Foods. Today the company is still based in Atlanta, where in 1996 it opened a new tourist attraction, "The World of Coca-Cola Pavilion."

STRATEGY

The Coca-Cola Company's business strategy is simple: make its products available everywhere in the world and trigger purchases (through advertising and promotion) as often and in as many ways as possible. This strategy is clearly successful: in the late 1990s Coca-Cola was one of the world's most recognized brand names and was available in almost 200 countries. The company is famous for its advertising, which has always followed new trends.

As a global company, Coca-Cola adjusts its advertising and marketing programs for different regions of the world. For example, in new markets such as Poland and India, the company focuses on setting up bottling systems. In emerging markets, the company works to build enough bottling plants to meet the rapidly growing demand for its products. In highly developed markets, such as Europe and North America, the company focuses on developing new products, such as low-calorie and "alternative" beverages.

The heart of the Coca-Cola business strategy is its bottler system, which the company says is the single factor most responsible for the global popularity of its products. Many Coca-Cola bottling plants are locally owned and operated by independent business people who hold licenses to bottle and sell Coca-Cola products. However, the largest U.S. bottler—Coca-Cola Enterprises—is 44-percent owned by The Coca-Cola Company. Coca-Cola Enterprises controls 2,500 local bottlers and accounts for about 55 percent of all U.S. bottling volume.

INFLUENCES

The Coca-Cola Company has enjoyed an almost continuous history of success and growth. From 1886 to 1960 it marketed only Coca-Cola, but did so very successfully. In 1960 it introduced its first non-cola products, the Fanta line of flavors, which were followed by other new soft drinks in the 1960s and 1970s. In 1982 it launched diet Coke, the first extension of the Coca-Cola brand name. Diet Coke was extremely successful, and within one year of being introduced was the largest selling low-calorie soft drink in America.

Even Coca-Cola's biggest marketing mistake turned into a success. In 1985, after extensive taste testing, the company announced that it had reformulated its main Coca-Cola brand. Thousands of Coca-Cola drinkers protested the change, and after extensive publicity and media coverage, the company re-introduced the "old" Coca-Cola as Coca-Cola classic. The new product was re-named Coke II. Coca-Cola classic continues to be the top selling soft drink in the United States.

It took 22 years for the Coca-Cola Company to sell the first billion servings of Coca-Cola. In 1998 they were selling a billion drinks a day.

CURRENT TRENDS

Nearly 775 million servings of Coca-Cola products are consumed around the world each day. The company's goal is to increase that number in three ways: by bringing Coca-Cola products to the few places on earth where it is not available; increasing consumption of Coca-Cola products where they are available; and developing new products. While North America still accounts for one-third of the company's business, in the mid- to late 1990s much of the company's sales growth has come from overseas.

To expand global distribution of its products, the company is aggressively developing bottling networks worldwide through new agreements and joint ventures. The Coca-Cola Company has also developed new products to challenge rivals in other beverage areas. For example, in 1994 the company introduced Fruitopia to compete with Snapple's successful "new age" beverages, and its POWERade beverage competes with Quaker's Gatorade brand.

The result of all these trends is that The Coca-Cola Company continues to expand not only in international markets, but in the United States as well. For example, in the first six months of 1996, the company accounted for 80 percent of the total soft drink industry expansion in the United States, according to an analysis by the Morgan Stanley Company. The Coca-Cola Company's goal is to account for 50 percent of the U.S. soft drink market by 2001.

PRODUCTS

Products of The Coca-Cola Company include: Coca-Cola classic, caffeine free Coca-Cola classic, diet Coke,

FAST FACTS:
About The Coca-Cola Company

Ownership: The Coca-Cola Company is a publicly owned company traded on the New York Stock Exchange.

Ticker symbol: KO

Officers: M. Douglas Ivester, Chmn. & CEO, 50, $2,856,250; Charles S. Frenette, Senior VP, Chief Marketing Officer, 45; James E. Chestnut, Sr. VP & CFO, 47

Employees: 29,500 (1997)

Principal Subsidiary Companies: The Coca-Cola Company operates subsidiaries including Coca-Cola Foods and Coca-Cola Enterprises.

Chief Competitors: Because of its global approach to the beverage market, Coca-Cola competes with a variety of companies. Some primary competitors include: Chiquita Brands; Cadbury Shwepppes; Cott; Philip Morris; Ocean Spray; PepsiCo Inc.; Seagram; Procter & Gamble; Triarc; and Unilever.

caffeine free diet Coke, Sprite, diet Sprite, Cherry Coke, diet Cherry Coke, Barq's, Coca-Cola, Fanta, Fresca, Fruitopia, Hi-C fruit drinks, Mello Yello, Minute Maid and diet Minute Maid soft drinks, Minute Maid juices, Mr. PiBB, Powerade, Surge, and TAB.

The Coca-Cola Company was also able to breathe new life into its older products in the mid-1990s. In 1996 Sprite was the fastest-growing soft drink brand in the United States and became the fourth best selling brand, due mostly to a sarcastic ad campaign that made fun of the "hype" in other soft drink ads. Sprite's slogan was "Image is nothing. Thirst is Everything. Obey your thirst."

In early 1997 The Coca-Cola Company introduced Surge, a highly caffeinated citrus beverage designed to compete with Pepsi's Mountain Dew. As of April 1997 the company had spent $13 million to advertise the product. However, R.J. Corr Naturals Inc. was suing Coca-Cola over its advertising theme, "Feed the Rush." Corr said that the advertising infringes on one of its products, Ginseng Rush.

Citra, a thirst-quenching citrus soft drink, was nationally launched after successful initial regional market

CHRONOLOGY:

Key Dates for The Coca-Cola Company

1886: John Pemberton invents Coca-Cola

1891: Asa Candler buys Coca-Cola from Pemberton

1899: Candler sells bottling rights to Benjamin Thomas and John Whitehead

1894: The first bottled Coca-Cola is sold

1916: Candler retires

1919: Company is sold to Ernest Woodruff for $25 million

1923: Ernest's son Robert Woodruff becomes president

1928: Coca-Cola begins supplying Coke to the Olympic Games

1940: Coca-Cola is bottled in 45 countries

1941: Introduces the slogan "It's the Real Thing"

1960: Buys Minute Maid Company; introduces Fanta

1961: Introduces Sprite

1963: Introduced Tab

1967: Forms the Coca-Cola Company Foods Division

1972: Introduces Mr. PiBB

1979: Introduces Mello Yello

1981: Roberto Goizueta becomes president

1982: Introduces Diet Coke; acquires Columbia Pictures

1984: Creates the Coca-Cola Foundation

1985: Changes the Coca-Cola recipe; introduces Cherry Coke

1990: Introduces POWERaDE

1994: Introduces Fruitopia

1995: Buys Barq's root beer

1996: Opens "The World of Coca-Cola Pavillion"

1997: Introduces Surge; Goizueta dies and is replaced by Douglas Ivester

1998: Company sells one billion drinks per day

testing, and is available in nearly 50 percent of the United States. A multi-dimensional marketing campaign featuring Citra's "No Thirst is Safe" theme was launched at the beginning of 1998.

CORPORATE CITIZENSHIP

The Coca-Cola company believes it is appropriate to give back to the communities in which they do business. This concept of mutual benefit has resulted in cultural exchanges, sports sponsorships, financial support, and technological support in developing nations.

In all of Coca-Cola's sports affiliations, its support for the International Olympic Games is most visible and historic. Coca-Cola has been supplying its products to the Olympics since 1928, and is the official soft drink supplier.

In 1984 The Coca-Cola Company created the Coca-Cola Foundation to increase its ongoing aid for educational excellence. The Coca-Cola Foundation's mission is to nurture and promote a favorable environment by globally supporting educational and related community needs. Through its scholarships and minority education, the Foundation helps students to increase their chances of getting a college education. And because Coca-Cola believes the arts add value to a total public school curriculum, the Foundation also supports education in the arts for both teachers and students. The Foundation also supports interdisciplinary educational programs that provide multilingual and multicultural experiences. Some of the global programs provided by the Coca-Cola Foundation include the Coca-Cola World Fund at Yale, the King Juan Carlos I Center for Spanish Studies at New York University, and a consortium of three universities: Clark Atlanta University, University of Nairobe in Kenya, and the University of Zimbabwe in Harare.

Concerned with the environment, the Coca-Cola Company has adopted a set of environmental policies. An environmental management system ensures implementation of the policies to protect and preserve the environment in such areas as recycling, source reduction, water and energy conservation, and wastewater quality.

Coca-Cola introduced the first two-liter plastic bottle made with 25 percent recycled plastics after winning rare FDA approval to package food in recycled packaging. Coca-Cola also uses recycled aluminum; both are important practices that reduce waste and conserve energy.

Coca-Cola was criticized in the early 1990s for its plan to construct plantations for its Minute Maid products on land that was a tropical rain forest in Belize. Immediately Coca-Cola sold some of the land and set aside the rest for environmental conservation.

GLOBAL PRESENCE

Global markets are key to The Coca-Cola Company's continued growth. The company's first venture into international markets was in the early 1900s, when Coca-Cola was introduced in Canada. In the 1920s the company made its first serious effort to expand sales of Coca-Cola around the world. Overseas sales climbed rapidly and by 1940 Coca-Cola was botled in more than 45 countries. Coca-Cola's global business was helped greatly by the company's commitment to supply U.S. servicemen with Coca-Cola during World War II. After the war, distribution systems were in place in many countries to market Coca-Cola. By the mid-1970s more than half of Coca-Cola's global sales came from outside the United States.

The Coca-Cola Company's global presence is strong and growing. Unit case sales increased 10 percent in 1993, including strong growth in China and Mexico. The company's international soft drink operating income was up 18 percent in 1994. In 1997 The Coca-Cola Company was propelled to a strong worldwide unit case volume gain of 8 percent, which amounts to over 600 million additional cases. Sprite also continued its explosive global growth with worldwide unit case sales advancing 13 percent.

In the mid-1990s Coca-Cola expanded further into Central China, forming a partnership with several private and state-owned Chinese firms to build a new bottling plant in Zhengzou. That plant opened in 1996. Coca-Cola products were available to 80 percent of China's 1.2 billion people as of 1996. In 1997 Coca-Cola's sales volume grew 30 percent.

Much of Coca-Cola's international success in the mid-1990s came at the expense of its biggest rival, PepsiCo, which in 1996 suffered large declines in its soft drink product sales. In 1996 The Coca-Cola Company scored a major gain when it convinced the Cisneros Group in Venezuela to stop bottling Pepsi products and begin bottling Coca-Cola products.

Volume growth is a primary measure of the health of Coca-Cola's global business. In Latin America, unit case volume increased 12 percent and gallon shipments grew 9 percent in 1997. In the Middle East and Far East, unit case volume increased 10 percent and gallon shipments grew 14 percent in 1997. In eastern Europe the company expanded its market share in the mid-1990s, and in 1996 it controlled 65 percent of the market in Romania, more than 50 percent in Hungary, more than 30 percent in the Ukraine, and 37 percent in Poland.

EMPLOYMENT

The Coca-Cola Company maintains a long-standing commitment to equal opportunity and affirmative action. The company values the diversity of its employees and strives to create a working environment that is free from discrimination and harassment with respect to race, sex, color, national origin, religion, age, and sexual orientation. Coca-Cola also makes reasonable accomodations to qualified individuals with disabilities.

FLUID INTAKE STRATEGIES

By the mid-1990s, the average American was drinking 343 eight-ounce servings of Coke products per year. Mexico followed, with 322 Cokes per year, and Australia beat out Norway by gulping down 292 Cokes per year. At the other end of the spectrum, the average Chinese person drank only four Cokes, and the average Indian drank only two Cokes annually. It's easy to see why Coke has targeted China and India as areas where the company can expand significantly. In their 1995 annual report, Coke sketched out their corporate strategy by asking the question, "What's our most underdeveloped market?" Their answer is quite simple, "The human body." As Coke explained to its shareholders, "We're focused on expanding our share of every human being's fluid intake . . . as long as people consume approximately 64 ounces of fluid per day, our growth opportunities will be virtually unlimited."

A COKE BY ANY OTHER NAME?

Coca-Cola is a company whose products are known and sold throughout the world; in fact it is probably one of the most recognizable "symbols" of America. However, for all its marketing and distribution efforts, it has run into some problems in overseas markets. For example, when Coca-Cola was first shipped to China, the company wanted to name the product something that, when pronounced, sounded like "Coca-Cola." The only problem was that the characters they decided to use meant "bite the wax tadpole," in Chinese. The company later changed to a set of characters that translates to "happiness in the mouth." It wasn't pronounced like Coca-Cola, but at least it meant something a bit more pleasant.

Coca-Cola fosters the growth of minority and women-owned businesses through its targeted purchasing programs. Two women and 2 people of color sit on the 14 member board of directors. Also, there are 4 women and 6 people of color among the top 38 officers at Coca-Cola.

SOURCES OF INFORMATION

Bibliography

Coca-Cola Company 1995 Annual Report. Atlanta, GA: The Coca-Cola Company, 1996.

Coca-Cola Company 1997 Annual Report. Atlanta, GA: The Coca-Cola Company, 1997.

Coca-Cola Company 1998 First Quarter Financial Statement. Atlanta, GA: The Coca-Cola Company, 1998.

Gleason, Mark. "Sprite Is Riding Global Ad Effort to No. 4 Status." *Advertising Age,* 18 November 1996.

McBride, Sandra. "News from China: The World's Largest Population Meets the World's Two Greatest Soft Drink Marketers." *Beverage World,* September 1996.

Sellers, Patricia. "How Coke Is Kicking Pepsi's Can (Competition Between Coca-Cola and PepsiCo)." *Fortune,* 28 October 1996.

Prendergast, Mark. *"For God, Country and Coca-Cola: The Unauthorized History of the Great American Soft Drink and the Company That Makes It."* New York: Scribners, 1993.

For an annual report:

on the Internet at: http://www.cocacola.com/profile/report/index.html **or** write: The Coca-Cola Company, 1 Coca-Cola Plz., Atlanta, GA 30313

For additional industry research:

Investigate companies by their Standard Industrial Classification Codes, also known as SICs. Coca-Cola's primary SICs are:

2033 Canned Fruits, Vegetables, Preserves, Jams & Jellies

2086 Bottled & Canned Soft Drinks and Carbonated Waters

2087 Flavoring Extracts and Flavoring Syrups, NEC

Colgate-Palmolive Company

OVERVIEW

Colgate-Palmolive is the nation's leading manufacturer of toothpaste, with a strong presence in the personal care, household cleaning, and pet food sectors as well. The company's Colgate brand toothpaste moved into the number one position in 1997, displacing Procter & Gamble's Crest brand, while Palmolive leads in the liquid dishwashing detergent field. Ajax, the company's longtime abrasive cleanser, is literally a household word, and various Colgate-Palmolive brands such as Murphy Oil cleaning products and Irish Spring soap have benefited from popular advertising campaigns. Fab laundry detergent and Mennen deodorant (a brand acquired in 1992) are also among the leading competitors in their areas, and Science Diet is the top seller among premium pet foods.

The company has an enormous global presence with plants in 75 countries and products available in virtually every nation in the world, including Australia, Brazil, Canada, China, Colombia, France, Italy, Mexico, Thailand, and the United Kingdom.

COMPANY FINANCES

Colgate-Palmolive posted a net income of $740 million on revenue of $9.06 billion in 1997, compared with a net of $635 million on sales of $8.75 billion in 1996. Net income rose more than 16 percent between 1996 and 1997. Colgate reported net earnings of $172 million on worldwide sales of $8.36 billion in 1995, compared with net income of $580 million on sales of $7.14 billion in 1994. The company reports that it has paid dividends on

FOUNDED: 1806

Contact Information:

HEADQUARTERS: 300 Park Ave.
  New York, NY 10022
PHONE: (212)310-2000
FAX: (212)310-3405
URL: http://www.colgate.com

FINANCES:

Colgate-Palmolive
Net Sales, 1994-1997
(billion dollars)

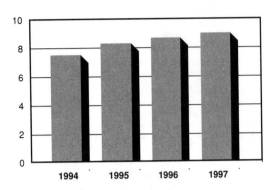

Colgate-Palmolive
1997 Stock Prices
(dollars)

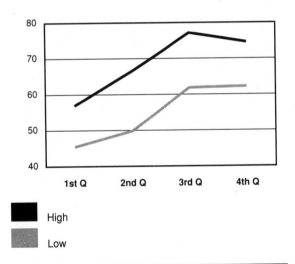

its common stock since 1895 with the size of dividends paid per share increasing for the past 35 years.

ANALYSTS' OPINIONS

Market observers are positive about Colgate-Palmolive, given its stability and its continued growth. The company overcame negatives associated with its rampant acquisitions in the 1970s divesting itself of many of the holdings in the following decade. In August 1995, how-

ever, *Business Week* sounded an ominous tone when it described Colgate as having been "caught off-guard" by competing specialty toothpaste brands bearing a higher price tag and greater status. That same year *Barron's* reported that investors were disappointed by slower growth in earnings for a number of companies, including Colgate-Palmolive; but as the magazine reported, optimism for the company's future remained high.

HISTORY

Colgate-Palmolive was formed by the merging of two companies. William Colgate established the Colgate Company, manufacturer of starch, soap, and candles, in New York City in 1806. B.J. Johnson entered the soap business in Milwaukee in 1864 with the first factory for what would eventually become the Palmolive Company. The two did not merge until 1928, when Colgate was already more than a century old.

By its 100th anniversary, Colgate's product line included more than 600 types of perfume and almost 200 types of soap. Although it began life as a soap distributor and would ultimately merge with Palmolive, the company made its name with toothpaste, which it first produced in 1873. In 1896 Colgate became the first toothpaste brand to be packaged in tubes.

Two years later, the B.J. Johnson Soap Company introduced Palmolive, a "floating" soap. It opened its first overseas facility; a factory in Toronto, Canada, in 1913; and began selling in England during the same year. In 1916, the Johnson company incorporated and changed its name to Palmolive in recognition of its popular brand. It remained Palmolive until 1926 when it merged with Peet Brothers to form Palmolive-Peet.

Colgate became a publicly traded company in 1908 and saw duty in World War I by producing protective coatings to counteract the effects of poison gas. In 1928 Colgate merged with Palmolive-Peet. The new company, Colgate-Palmolive-Peet, might have proceeded with a proposed merger involving Hershey and Kraft, but the 1929 stock market crash put an end to those plans.

The company introduced Fab laundry detergent and one of its best-known products, Ajax cleanser, in 1947. Six years later it became the Colgate-Palmolive Company and in 1956 established its headquarters on Park Avenue in New York. The company introduced a series of innovative products in the 1960s, and endured troubled times in the 1970s with a series of unprofitable acquisitions. It sold off most of its questionable acquisitions during the 1980s. With the acquisition of the Mennen Company in 1992, Colgate added a deodorant/antiperspirant line to its already established lines of personal care and household products.

STRATEGY

Colgate-Palmolive has long been an innovator in products and packaging. Just as Colgate was the first toothpaste brand to be packaged in tubes, in 1984 Colgate-Palmolive introduced the first toothpaste pump. The company introduced a series of firsts, including the first cold-water laundry detergent (Cold Power, 1965), cosmetic toothpaste (Ultra Brite, 1968), concentrated detergent (Fresh Start, 1980), and automatic dishwashing liquid (Palmolive, 1986.)

Like many other consumer product manufacturers, Colgate-Palmolive has relied heavily on extensive and repetitive advertising. In the fall of 1996, *Advertising Age* predicted that the company would spend $32 million on advertising a new whitening toothpaste and $15 million on a campaign for the new Lady Speed Stick Invisible Dry deodorant. Palmolive's success in the 1970s could partially be attributed to the well-known series of advertisements depicting Madge the manicurist, who regularly placed her clients' hands in bowls of Palmolive—thus emphasizing that the detergent was gentle on hands. Also highly effective was the Irish Spring commercial from the same era, which played on gender identification with certain brands, using the slogan (delivered by a woman with an Irish accent), "Manly, yes, but I like it too."

The company has emphasized oral hygiene and good health in its marketing campaigns for Colgate toothpaste, leaving the "sex appeal" to its Ultra Brite whitening toothpaste. (In the 1970s when Ultra Brite first used that phrase in its advertising, it was considered somewhat daring.) From there the toothpaste manufacturer concentrated on products that fight cavities, plaque, and tartar. For instance, in 1986 Colgate-Palmolive introduced tartar-control Colgate, a contrast with specialty brands that, as *Business Week* observed in an August 14, 1995 aritcle, "[focus] on things other than the therapeutic benefits of toothpaste."

INFLUENCES

Colgate-Palmolive seems to have fared best when it stayed closest to its core product line of personal care, laundry, and household cleaning items. In the 1970s, management attempted to diversify, purchasing not only Helena Rubenstein, whose cosmetic line might have seemed in keeping with the company's personal care items, but such wide-ranging enterprises as Ram Golf and Maui Divers. These endeavors did not prove to be successful, and Colgate-Palmolive divested itself of these properties, as well as its Etonic shoe line, in the 1980s.

In late 1996, Colgate-Palmolive met its leading rival, Procter & Gamble (P&G), in court over a dispute involving a Colgate ad that P&G claimed was a copy of its own Crest commercial. This was not the only time that year the company faced advertising difficulties. The

FAST FACTS:
About Colgate-Palmolive Company

Ownership: Colgate-Palmolive Co. is a publicly owned company traded on the New York Stock Exchange.

Ticker symbol: CL

Officers: Reuben Mark, Chmn. & CEO, 59, 1997 base salary $1,222,500; William S. Shanahan, Pres. & COO, 57, 1997 base salary $756,167; Lois D. Juliber, Exec. VP & COO, Developed Markets, 48, 1997 base salary $450,000

Employees: 37,800

Principal Subsidiary Companies: Colgate-Palmolive has 237 subsidiaries worldwide, including Hills Pet Nutrition Inc., Mennen Company, Murphy Phoenix Company, and Softsoap Enterprises Inc.

Chief Competitors: Colgate-Palmolive's competitors include: American Home Products; Amway; Avon; Gillette; and Procter & Gamble.

company was forced to withdraw an Australian sunscreen ad because it received criticism for alleged racial overtones. Generally, though, advertising has been a strong suit for Colgate-Palmolive, as it must be for marketers of personal care products.

CURRENT TRENDS

The year 1994 marked a milestone for Colgate-Palmolive marketing strategy. In that year, the company made a shift from its traditional pricing structure, based on special promotions, to the more low-key "everyday low pricing," which emphasized purchasing on the basis of need rather than high-powered promotions.

In 1994 the company launched its largest series of new products in a decade: Colgate Toothpaste with Baking Soda & Peroxide, Irish Spring Waterfall Clean Soap, Palmolive Antibacterial Dishwashing Liquid, and the Murphy Kitchen Care line. In the mid-1990s it also introduced Colgate Plus Ultra Fit Compact Head toothbrushes, and in December 1996 it introduced Lady Speed Stick Invisible Dry Deodorant. With concerns over germs growing in the 1990s, antibacterial soaps became popular, and in 1996 Colgate announced the introduction of

CHRONOLOGY:

Key Dates for Colgate-Palmolive Company

1806: Founded by William Colgate in New York to make and sell soap, starch, and candles

1820: Colgate expands it manufacturing to a New Jersey factory to produce soaps and starch

1857: William Colgate dies and Samuel Colgate takes over; company name is changed to Colgate & Company

1864: B.J. Johnson opens a soap factory in Milwaukee, Wisconsin

1872: The Peet Brothers open a soap factory in Kansas City, Kansas

1873: Colgate begins selling toothpaste in a jar

1898: Johnson's company creates Palmolive soap

1908: Colgate goes public

1916: Johnson's company incorporates and officially becomes Palmolive Company

1926: Palmolive merges with the Peet brothers to become Palmolive-Peet

1928: Colgate and Palmolive merge to form Colgate-Palmolive-Peet

1947: Introduces Fab laundry detergent and Ajax cleaner

1953: The company name changes to Colgate-Palmolive Company

1963: Colgate-Palmolive expands by introducing Baggies, a new food wrap

1973: Cosmetics manufacturer Helena Rubenstein is acquired

1981: Colgate loses a suit brought by United Roasters for breach of contract

1982: Colgate is sued by the federal government for job discrimination

1992: Mennon Co. is purchased

1993: S.C. Johnson Wax's liquid hand and body soap brands are purchased, making Colgate-Palmolive the worldwide leader in liquid soap

1997: Colgate brand becomes the number one selling toothpaste

Irish Spring Sport, an antibacterial product intended to compete with a "body wash" produced by Procter & Gamble. The company anticipates continued global success with present and future products.

PRODUCTS

Colgate-Palmolive has a wide line of products in the following areas: personal care, household and fabric care, pet nutrition, and assorted specialty items. Colgate-Palmolive's personal care line includes Colgate toothpaste; Mennen, Speed Stick, and Lady Speed Stick deodorants; Skin Bracer after shave; and Irish Spring deodorant and Palmolive cosmetic soaps. Palmolive is also a brand in the household/fabric care area with its dishwashing liquids and powder. Also included in this area are Ajax, Fab laundry detergent, Murphy Oil soap, and Handi Wipes. With the acquisition of Hills Pet Products in 1976, Colgate-Palmolive entered the pet food business, with specialty dietary management products HealthBlend and Science Diet, as well as Prescription Diet, a line available only through veterinarians. Finally, through its subsidiary, Princess House, Colgate-Palmolive manufactures crystal and giftware.

CORPORATE CITIZENSHIP

Colgate-Palmolive has pursued an outstanding program of corporate citizenship, both globally and locally. In 1987 the company announced plans for a significant redevelopment of the Jersey City, New Jersey, waterfront plant. The revitalization plan, for which ground was broken in 1990, included proposals for offices, parks, housing units, a hotel, and a marina. Throughout the world the company has devoted millions of dollars and thousands of person-hours to education, health, sports, and community programs, mostly targeted toward young people.

In 1987 Colgate-Palmolive helped fund the revitalization of Wadleigh School in New York City, a junior high with a crumbling infrastructure and a disastrous academic record. In addition, a "friendship school" in Cali, Colombia, built with Colgate money, provides education to children between the ages of 6 and 12. Outside Johannesburg, South Africa, is a pioneering multiracial day-care center called the Wonderland School, operated by Colgate-Palmolive. In the Philippines and many other developing countries, the company sends dentists into villages and barrios to treat underprivileged children. The company also sponsors sporting events throughout the world, most notably the Colgate Women's Games, which involve 15,000 women, and a Colgate Sports & Activity Day on the island of Fiji gives disabled participants an opportunity to compete.

GLOBAL PRESENCE

Colgate has an enormous global presence. The list of countries where no Colgate-Palmolive products are sold (North Korea, Mongolia, Iran, Cuba, Somalia, and a handful of others) is far shorter than the one listing the 194 (at last count) nations in which its products are available. By contrast, the United Nations in 1997 had only 185 members. The company's global expansion began in the early part of the twentieth century, and by 1997 it had plants in 75 countries.

Although Colgate-Palmolive has established itself in most parts of the world, it continues to seek new segments of international markets, especially in developing countries. In 1996, the company undertook a remarkable promotional activity that combined corporate citizenship with a forward-thinking strategy of marketing. Colgate "video-vans" throughout India began distributing free toothpaste samples to rural villagers. The Indian villagers, the vast majority of whom were not exposed to Western-style oral care (including toothpaste), represent a potential market of more than 600 million people. In the Western world, Colgate-Palmolive continues to develop new variations on traditional soap and toothpaste products.

EMPLOYMENT

Colgate-Palmolive's public relations presents the company work force in a glowing light, emphasizing diversity and stability. Its 1995 annual report, for instance, listed numerous top management personnel who had served the company for one, two, and even three decades, along with in-depth commentary from a wide range of managers. While diversity was a popular buzzword in corporate America in the 1990s, it seems to have come naturally to a company with offices and plants on every continent except Antarctica. As the 1990s neared an end, optimism for the company's future remains high.

Colgate-Palmolive's recruiting and employment practices have received praise from *Personnel Journal,* which awarded the company's human resources department its "Global Outlook Award" for 1995.

As for stability, although the corporation has gone through numerous mergers, acquisitions, and divestitures since its founding, the core entity has existed since 1806,

an impressive record in the ever-shifting world of corporate America. In 1995 the company announced plans to downsize 3,000 jobs and either close or reconfigure 24 of its facilities over the next three years.

SOURCES OF INFORMATION

Bibliography

Bary, Andrew. "Ear to the Ground." *Barron's,* 25 September 1995.

"Colgate Aligns HR With Its Global Vision." *Personnel Journal,* January 1995.

The Colgate-Palmolive Company. New York: Colgate-Palmolive Company, n.d.

"Colgate Readies $32 Mil. Launch." *Advertising Age,* 28 October 1996.

Collins, Glenn. "P. & G. Sues Colgate on TV Commercial." *New York Times,* 5 December 1996.

Edgar Database, 6 June 1998. Available at http://www.edgar-online.com.

Our History. New York: Colgate-Palmolive Company, September 1995.

Schiller, Zachary. "The Sound and the Fluoride." *Business Week,* 14 August 1995.

Sloan, Pat. "Colgate Sets Dec. Launch For New Lady Speed Stick." *Advertising Age,* 30 September 1996.

Worldwide Community Activities: Working Together For a Better World. New York: Colgate-Palmolive Company, n.d.

For an annual report:

on the Internet at: http://www.colgate.com/Investor/index.html

For additional industry research:

Investigate companies by their Standard Industrial Classification Codes, also known as SICs. Colgate-Palmolive Company's primary SICs are:

2047 Dog and Cat Food

2841 Soap and Other Detergents

2842 Polishes and Sanitation Goods

2844 Toilet Preparations

3229 Pressed and Blown Glass, NEC

3991 Brooms and Brushes

Columbia Records

FOUNDED: 1886

Contact Information:
HEADQUARTERS: 51 W. 52nd St.
   New York City, NY 10019
PHONE: (212)445-4321
FAX: (212)445-5523
URL: http://www.columbiarecords.com

OVERVIEW

Columbia Records has come a long way from its beginning at the end of the nineteenth century, although its product remains basically the same. From the 1880s to the present, the company has sold prerecorded sound. A music industry pioneer in both technology and content, Columbia Records continues operating as one of the four label groups of Sony Music Entertainment Inc. (SMEI), a global recording company. The other three label groups within SMEI are Epic Records Group, Sony Classical, and Relativity Entertainment Group.

Columbia Records originated in the late 1880s as the Columbia Graphophone Company of Bridgeport, Connecticut. The original company was built upon the experiments of scientist Charles Sumner Tainter and Chichester A. Bell. Bell, a cousin of telephone inventor Alexander Graham Bell, was an engineer. In 1886 the two received a patent for a wax-coated cardboard cylinder on which sounds could be recorded. Their machine, the Graphophone, made its official debut in Washington, D.C., three years later.

The relationship between Sony Corporation and Columbia Records dates back to 1968, when CBS, which then owned the Columbia label, joined with Sony in order to expedite its expansion into the Asian market. Twenty years later, Sony acquired the CBS Records Group. Sony Music Entertainment Inc., including the Sony division of which Columbia Records is a part, is a truly international recording company boasting more than 9,000 employees.

COMPANY FINANCES

As one of four label groups within Sony Music Entertainment Inc., Columbia Records does not independently report its financial results; they are included in the Sony Corporation's posted net earnings. For fiscal 1998, ended March 31, 1998, SMEI reported net earnings of $1.67 billion on revenue of $50.73 billion, compared with net income of $1.13 billion on revenue of $45.7 billion in fiscal 1997. In fiscal 1996, Sony's reported net earnings of $512 million on revenue of $43.3 billion, compared with a net loss of $3.3 billion on revenue of $44.8 billion in fiscal 1995.

ANALYSTS' OPINIONS

"What I have learned over the years is that with patience comes success," Columbia Records President Don Ienner told *Billboard Magazine*. "I've learned that desperate people do desperate things, and we're not desperate, and our artists are not desperate. Desperation is easy—to be wild and crazy and run the sprint—but I want to be here for the long-distance run. I'd rather run the marathon than the 50-yard dash."

HISTORY

The Columbia Records of today can trace its roots to the Columbia Graphophone Company and the nineteenth century experiments of Chichester A. Bell and Charles Sumner Tainter. Their invention, the Graphophone, which came nearly 10 years after Thomas Edison's tinfoil phonograph, employed a recording stylus that traced sound vibration-induced sound patterns onto a cylinder of wax-coated cardboard.

The North American Phonograph Company, a maker of office dictating machines, was spawned by the purchase of controlling interests for both the Graphophone and Edison's phonograph. Regional subsidiaries across the United States received rights. However, once the invention entered the entertainment field, a clear leader emerged. The Columbia Phonograph Company, a subsidiary for the Washington and Baltimore area, led the pack with its recordings of popular tunes, speeches, military marches, and other sounds.

In 1895, Columbia already was producing hundreds of cylinders a day. In 1891, Columbia offered its first catalog, and in 1900, it boasted a recording collection that surpassed the 5,000 mark. The cylinder, however, was a platform destined to be obsolete. By 1901, the Gram-O-Phone, an invention by Emile Berliner, which opted for flat discs with a lateral-cut track, had proven itself as the better quality, longer-lasting platform. That same year, Columbia released its first seven-inch discs. By 1904, the company was producing 78 rpm discs, as

Ownership: Columbia Records is a division of Sony Music Entertainment Inc., which is a division of Sony Corp.

Officers: Don Ienner, Pres.

Employees: 9,000 in Sony Music Entertainment, Inc., which includes Columbia Records

Chief Competitors: Columbia Records' major competitors include: EMI Group; Philips Electronics; PolyGram; Universal Studios; and Viacom.

well as double-sided records. Three years later, the company obtained the Velvet Tone record, an indestructible disc commissioned to Guglielmo Marconi. By 1914, Columbia had stopped producing cylinders and had become the Columbia Graphophone Company. The next technological advance came in 1948; Columbia released the 33 1/3 rpm long-playing record, which quickly became the industry standard for sound reproduction.

In addition to its role as a technological pioneer, Columbia led the way in terms of musical achievement. Stars of the Metropolitan Opera in New York saved their voices for posterity in Columbia recordings as early as 1903. The company contributed to the ragtime dance phenomenon with its 1911 release of "Alexander's Ragtime Band," by Irving Berlin. In 1916, Columbia set an American precedent of recording symphony orchestras when it captured the sounds of the New York and Chicago orchestras. The following year, New Orleans' Original Dixieland Jazz Band recorded at Columbia Studios in New York. By 1919, the record industry was worth $150 million, with Americans buying more than 25 million 78 rpm records a year. To strengthen its hold, Columbia acquired the Otto Heinemann Phonograph Corporation (Okeh) in 1926 and brought on board such stars as Louis Armstrong, Bix Beiderbeck, Clarence Williams, and Mamie Smith.

The 1930s saw further mergers and acquisitions within this industry. In 1934, the American Record Company-Brunswick Record Company (ARC-BRC) purchased Columbia and Okeh. Four years later, William Paley's Columbia Broadcasting System (CBS) bought ARC-BRC. Columbia soon began to sign recording contracts with artists, including the biggest names in jazz.

CHRONOLOGY:

Key Dates for Columbia Records

1886: Chichester A. Bell and Charles Sumner Tainter receive a patent for their Graphophone

1891: Columbia Phonograph Company sends out a catalog of its popular tunes, speeches, and other sounds recorded onto Graphophone cylinders

1901: Columbia releases its first seven inch disc when the Gram-O-Phone flat proves to be the better product

1904: Columbia begins producing 78 rpm discs as well as two-sided discs

1913: Columbia stops producing cylinders and becomes the Columbia Graphophone Company

1926: Columbia takes over the Otto Heinemann Phonograph Corporation bringing over stars such as Louis Armstrong and Clarence Williams

1934: American Record Company-Brunswick Record Company (ARC-BRC) purchases Columbia

1938: CBS buys ARC-BRC

1948: Columbia releases the 33 1/3 rpm long-playing record, which becomes the industry standard

1953: CBS launches Epic Records

1968: CBS forms a joint venture with Sony— CBS/Sony—to market American records in Japan

1978: CBS Records becomes the first U.S. record company to pass $1.2 billion in worldwide sales

1988: Sony Corporation acquires CBS Records to become Sony Music Entertainment Inc.; CBS/Sony becomes Sony Music Entertainment (Japan) Inc.

1994: Sony reorganizes into four labels: Columbia Records, Epic Records, Relativity Records, and Sony Classical

1998: Columbia adopts the "developing-artists retail program" to encourage consumers to try lesser-known artists

---

Count Basie, Duke Ellington, Benny Goodman, and Billie Holiday were just a few of the many artists on the Columbia Recording Corporation's high profile roster.

CBS Records saw tremendous growth throughout the 1960s and 1970s. The Columbia House Company emerged as the company's direct mail order club, and by the end of the 1990s, it was operational as part of a joint venture with Time-Warner Inc., the world's largest direct marketer of music and videos. In an effort to expand into the Asian market, CBS joined the Sony Corporation to form CBS/Sony in 1968. Ten years later, CBS Records became the first U.S. record company to pass the billion-dollar mark, with worldwide sales of $1.2 billion.

In 1988, Sony Corporation acquired the CBS Records Group. Ten years later, Sony Music Entertainment Inc. was a massive global recording company with more than 9,000 employees worldwide. In 1994, Sony regrouped into four labels. One of these labels was the Columbia Records Group, made up of Columbia and the WORK Group, which in turn has its own family of labels. The other three label groups within SMEI are Epic Records Group, Sony Classical, and Relativity Entertainment Group.

STRATEGY

Columbia's strategy for success, in one word, is "innovation." Since its inception, the company has been in the forefront of technological innovation. At the end of the twentieth century, as a member of the technologically inclined Sony family, this trend remained unchanged. Likewise, it continues its role as a pioneer in the music industry.

In 1998, in a market saturated with new, high-priced musical products, the company adopted a new strategy: the "developing-artists retail program." With this approach, prices for albums by lesser-known, newer bands would be reduced until a certain quota were sold. Once the albums passed the targeted sales threshold, the price per recording would be raised to that of better known artists. This strategy encourages consumers to try unknown artists without having to spend the same mount of money they traditionally would have spent on an established artist.

Don Ienner, president of Columbia, has attributed his company's success to its commitment to developing its artists, its careful selection of a new management team, and a more open-minded outlook. "Two years ago, I started thinking we needed a new face," he told *Billboard* in 1996. "I felt we needed to get people in here who believed as strongly as I did in the artists at Columbia Records and in Columbia Records itself."

INFLUENCES

Columbia Records was among a number of record labels that had expressed unhappiness with what they saw as an unwelcome trend in the industry's Grammy nominations and awards. In recent years, industry insiders have increasingly complained that the nominations and awards seemed out-of-step with what was really happening within the U.S. recording business.

Responding to the Grammy's sensitivity to the industry's discontent, Columbia Records President Don Ienner said of the Grammys in early 1998: "They certainly have made an effort and a lot of it has paid off in a more well-rounded and responsible way of getting nominations and awards." Ienner admitted that key nominations for several Columbia artists accounted for at least some of his enthusiasm.

CURRENT TRENDS

The 1980s saw two revolutionary developments in the recorded music industry. The 33 1/3 rpm long-playing record, or LP, was on its way out. Sony, with help from CBS, introduced its compact disc in 1982. The new, laser driven medium, with its crystal-clear tonal quality, would spell the demise of the record-turntable paradigm that had dominated the industry for so long. At the same time, the music video was born. An artist could not succeed only on the merits of his or her music alone; no self-respecting pop musician could expect to hit the charts without releasing an accompanying promotional video.

The final decade of the twentieth century brought a number of changes for Columbia Records and the recording industry as a whole. Consolidation efforts that had brought Columbia Records and other labels into the Sony fold continued at a rapid pace throughout the business. In order to better compete, in 1994 Sony Music Entertainment Inc. reorganized its holdings into four label groups: Columbia Records Group, Epic Records Group, Relativity Entertainment Group, and Sony Classical.

PRODUCTS

Since 1994 Columbia Records Group has seen a number of chart successes. In 1996, the company managed to push the dormant band Journey back to Top 40 success. While Columbia continued to earn solid money with mainstay musicians such as Neil Diamond, Mariah Carey, and Alice in Chains, it also managed the successful debut of many new bands, including the Fugees, the Presidents of the United States Of America (which disbanded by 1998), dog's eye view, Nas, and Stabbing Westward. In addition to rock and pop music, the company boasts artists in many popular genres, such as rap, hip hop, country, and Latin.

At the end of 1997, Columbia Records released *Diana, Princess of Wales: Tribute,* a two-CD collection of recordings by some of the world's best known singers and groups. The collection raised money for The Diana, Princess of Wales Memorial Fund, and recordings represented an industry-wide collaboration between major record companies and top international artists.

CORPORATE CITIZENSHIP

Columbia Records and Sony Music Entertainment Inc. believe they have a responsibility to the communities in which they operate and attempt to give back to those communities whenever possible. In the spring of 1992, as part of the national "I Attend" be-in-school program, Columbia announced a series of surprise appearances by its recording artists at high schools across the United States. The program attempts to provide students with an incentive to attend school every day. For its part, Columbia awards a private concert (by a Columbia artist) to the participating school in each designated area that records the biggest overall percentage increase in attendance between January 26 and May 1, 1998.

GLOBAL PRESENCE

While Columbia Records is based in the United States, it is part of a huge international conglomerate operated by Japan's Sony Corporation. It draws talent and business from around the world. Columbia's recordings are sold around the globe, and its artists reflect the international diversity of Sony.

SOURCES OF INFORMATION

Bibliography

"Columbia Records." *Company ProFiles,* 10 October 1990.

"Corporate Fact Sheet." Sony Music Entertainment Inc., 1997. Available at ttp://www.music.sony.com/Music/PressInfo/corpfact.html.

"A History of Columbia Records and Epic Records." Sony Music Entertainment, Inc., 1997. Available at http://www.music.sony.com/Music/PressInfo/hist.html.

"Sony Corporation." *Hoover's Online,* 20 May 1998. Available at http://www.hoovers.com/premium/profiles/41885.html.

Verne, Paul. "Columbia Thriving Across the Board." *Billboard,* 7 September 1996.

"World of Sony Music: A Thumbnail History of Sony Music." Sony Music Entertainment Inc., 1998. Available at http://www.music.sony.com/world/aboutus/history.html.

For an annual report:

on the Internet at: http://www.sony.co.jp/soj/CorporateInfo/AnnualReport97/index.html

For additional industry research:

Investigate companies by their Standard Industrial Classification Codes, also known as SICs. Columbia Records' primary SICs are:

6794 Patent Owners And Lessors

7389 Business Services, NEC

Columbia Sportswear Company

FOUNDED: 1938

Contact Information:

HEADQUARTERS: 6600 N. Baltimore
    Portland, OR 97203
PHONE: (503)286-3676
FAX: (503)289-6602
TOLL FREE: (800)MA-BOYLE
EMAIL: consumer_services@columbia.com
URL: http://www.columbia.com

OVERVIEW

Columbia Sportswear, a major marketer of outerwear and sportswear, does everything from designing and manufacturing to marketing and distribution. From a small regional hat distributor, the company has grown to become one of the world's largest outerwear brands and the leading seller of skiwear in the United States. A family-owned business in existence for 60 years, Columbia Sportswear distributes products to more than 10,000 retailers in 30 countries.

Formerly focusing on durable outdoor hunting and fishing gear, Columbia Sportswear's new product development efforts in the 1990s resulted in its expansion into additional merchandise categories and, ultimately, the development of its "head-to-toe" outfitting approach.

Columbia Sportswear's merchandise can be broken down into four main product lines: sportswear, rugged footwear, accessories, and outerwear—all suitable for either casual wear or various outdoor activities, including snowboarding, golf, hunting, and fishing. Specific items include rainwear, T-shirts, sleeveless shirts, hiking shorts, and polo shirts. Some of the company's trademarks include Columbia Sportswear Company, Columbia, Bugaboo, and Bugabootoo. The company plans to continue growth by distributing to a wider international market and expanding categories of merchandise.

COMPANY FINANCES

In the 10-year period between 1987 and 1997, Columbia Sportswear's sales went from $18.8 to $353.5

million, an increase of 30.6 percent; operating income increased from $1.6 to $44.3 million in that same time period, representing a 35.1-percent increase. In 1997, Columbia Sportswear's sales outside of North America comprised 10 percent of total net sales, increasing from $9 million to over $35 million in the four-year period between 1993 and 1997. In that same time frame, sportswear sales went up by 221.5 percent, while outerwear sales increased by 43.7 percent. Rugged footwear, a new product in 1993, went from $1.2 million in sales that year to $24.3 million in 1997.

In the spring of 1998, Columbia Sportswear, a privately held company throughout its 60-year history, offered 5.6 million shares of stock to the public at an initial offering of $18.00 per share. After the offering, senior management owned nearly 77 percent of the outstanding common stock of the company.

ANALYSTS' OPINIONS

At the time of the stock offering in March 1998, analysts were uncertain whether an active trading market would result. Columbia Sportswear acknowledges that price fluctuations could occur as a result of competitive pressures, either through product development or financial strategies. In addition, its products are largely seasonal- and weather-based, causing fluctuations in sales and operations. Consequently, the financial data for any given quarter does not necessarily indicate a trend for future quarters. For example, Columbia Sportswear's skiwear line obviously suffers a decline in summer months or during unseasonably warm winter weather. Additionally, the 1997 upset in the Asian market could have an effect on the company's success in that part of the world.

HISTORY

In 1937 Paul and Marie Lamfrom left their native Germany for the United States. They settled in Portland, Oregon, and bought a small hat distributorship. But after a few years, the Lamfroms were having difficulty getting products from suppliers and made the decision to manufacture the products themselves.

The Lamfroms' daughter, Gertrude, best known to all as Gert, got married in 1948 to Neal Boyle, who ultimately became president of Columbia Sportswear. When Neal died unexpectedly in 1970, Gert found herself at the head of a company that was "near bankruptcy." In the decade that followed, the company continued to struggle. Son Tim, who was about to finish his studies at the University of Oregon, left college to join his mother in the management of the company. Together they led the company out of its financial morass and put it on the road to profitability. As of 1998, the 74 year-old Gert re-

FAST FACTS:

About Columbia Sportswear Company

Ownership: Columbia Sportswear became a publicly traded company in the spring of 1998 with its stock traded on NASDAQ.

Ticker symbol: COLM

Officers: Gertrude Boyle, Chmn., 74, 1997 base salary $153,920; Timothy P. Boyle, Pres., CEO, Treasurer, & Secretary, 48, 1997 base salary $323,733; Don Richard Santorufo, Exec. VP & COO, 51, 1997 base salary $286,946

Employees: 1,234

Principal Subsidiary Companies: Columbia Sportswear owns subsidiaries in Japan and Canada; a Canadian holding company called Columbia Sportswear Holdings Limited (CSHL); and GTS, Inc., a holding company in the United States. All of the subsidiaries are wholly owned by Columbia Sportswear.

Chief Competitors: Columbia Sportswear's major competitors include: Nike; L.L. Bean; Timberland; Patagonia; Marmot; Nikwax; Royal Robbins; and Woolrich.

mained chairman of the board, while son Tim served as president and chief executive officer.

In 1984 Columbia Sportswear developed an advertising campaign, which has endured through the 1990s. The ads portray Columbia Sportswear's infamous matriarch, Gert Boyle (or "Ma Boyle"), as a stern taskmaster who is tyrannizing her son, Tim. In the ads, Gert is having Tim test Columbia Sportswear products in ways that are dangerous or risky. For instance, in an ad from the mid-1990s, Gert is shown driving a 4 x 4 through rough terrain while son Tim is strapped to the roof—wearing Columbia Sportswear outerwear.

Columbia Sportswear's diverse outerwear and sportswear product lines evolved from a focus on producing durable hunting and fishing gear. In the 1990s, Columbia Sportswear aggressively pursued the diversification of product lines; this is also when Columbia Sportswear developed the concept of "head-to-toe" outfitting so that consumers could rely on Columbia Sportswear to supply them with a coordinated and complete line of apparel and footwear.

CHRONOLOGY:

Key Dates for Columbia Sportswear Company

1938: Founded by Paul Lamfrom

1948: Gert Lamfrom, Paul Lamfrom's daughter, marries Neal Boyle

1964: Neal Boyle takes over the company after Paul Lamfrom dies

1970: Neal Boyle dies unexpectedly and his wife Gert Boyle—Paul Lamfrom's daughter—takes over

1982: Interchange System is created; Bugaboo parka is introduced

1984: Launches "Mother Boyle" ad campaign

1994: Gert Boyle's son, Tim, takes over the CEO position

1996: Launches golfwear line; opens flagship retail store in Portland, Oregon

1997: Begins participating in Start Making a Reader Today

1998: First public offering of stock

The 1990s also marked the opening of Columbia Sportswear's flagship store in Portland, Oregon, as well as the success of the store-within-a-store concept. These "concept shops" are areas within a retail store that are dedicated to Columbia Sportswear merchandise. By the end of 1997, Columbia Sportswear had 164 concept shops; plans called for doubling the number of these shops by the end of 1998.

STRATEGY

The company's strategy focuses on increasing sales to distributors and increasing concept shops located in larger retail outlets, such as department stores. Columbia Sportswear also initiated an inventory management system in the mid-1990s to reduce excess inventory. The strategy involved limiting the time between a customer order and the production cycle. The 1996 budget reflected Columbia Sportswear's cost-containment strategy by reducing the spending for advertising and discretionary projects and enacting a temporary hiring freeze.

Future strategies involve an aggressive focus on developing specific high-opportunity markets. Columbia Sportswear will target sales increases in its footwear and sportswear lines. For instance, MTV's popular "Road Rules" features a cast entirely outfitted by Columbia Sportswear. "Road Rules 5," which premiered in January 1998, featured the five participants involved in cattle driving, ski jumping, and caddying at a golf tournament. Columbia Sportswear has been supplying "Road Rules" with apparel since 1995.

Another strategic idea was to sign professional golfer Steve Jones to a three-year endorsement contract, beginning in 1998. Jones was named the PGA "Comeback Player of the Year" when he won the U.S. Open at Oakland Hills Country Club after recovering from a near-disastrous off-road motorcycle accident. As of January 1998, Jones began wearing Columbia brand sportswear and rainwear on professional golf tournaments. Tim Boyle, Columbia Sportswear's president, explained the rationale behind the company's agreement with Jones. "Golf has become a staple of today's active outdoor lifestyle, which also may include activities like hiking, fishing, and skiing. Steve Jones is an avid outdoorsman, which makes him the perfect representative for our company." Columbia Sportswear launched a line of golfwear in 1996 and is hoping the affiliation with Jones will boost its sales along with other merchandise lines.

However, Columbia Sportswear has no plans to change its ongoing award-winning advertising strategy featuring a cranky Chairman of the Board Ma Boyle putting son Tim through the mill.

INFLUENCES

Columbia Sportswear strives to create merchandise that is both functional and durable. By emphasizing these classic traits over faddish looks, Columbia Sportswear minimizes dated clothing that can occur from varying consumer tastes in fashion trends. Many products are actually a variation on existing designs.

Columbia Sportswear avoids high production costs by having independent manufacturers produce merchandise. These manufacturers are, however, under the control of Columbia Sportswear employees, who have authority over the selection process. This combination of independent manufacturers and Columbia Sportswear employees helps the company exercise flexibility and reduce expenditures. In fact, more than 85 manufacturers in 12 countries provide manufacturing for Columbia Sportswear, resulting in a total of over 85 percent of the company's products being produced outside the United States.

In the 1990s, Columbia Sportswear experienced an increase in expenses as a result of increased personnel costs. More staff was needed to handle the company's steady growth in the domestic market and its expansion in foreign markets.

In addition, this growth prompted the company to build a new distribution center in Portland, Oregon. Inventory had been previously handled by paper, through accounting ledgers. Technologically state-of-the-art, the new distribution center was 99 percent accurate in inventory and shipping. Within three weeks after becoming operational, shipping increased by 50 percent.

CURRENT TRENDS

Columbia Sportswear continues to build its hold on the domestic market, particularly in the area of outerwear. Future commitments include expanding international markets and diversifying product lines with particular emphasis on rugged footwear and sportswear. Columbia Sportswear believes the existing trend to dress casually and for an active outdoor-oriented lifestyle will continue to benefit sales.

Columbia Sportswear's management information system is scheduled to be phased out and was expected to be totally replaced by 1999 with a more technologically advanced system that is more focused on inventory control.

Columbia Sportswear intends to capitalize on specific regions of foreign markets where the popularity of outdoor activities should boost sales, in particular France, Spain, Italy, Sweden, Germany, the Netherlands, and the United Kingdom. In addition, sales counters were established in 15 stores in South Korea and the company will have full control of its product distribution in Japan by the end of 1998.

PRODUCTS

Some of Columbia Sportswear's products include Interchange System outerwear, Radial Sleeve designs, and high-performance Omni-Tech waterproof/breathable fabrics. All of these products are worn by professional golfer Steve Jones under his agreement to endorse Columbia Sportswear products on professional golf tours.

Hunters provided Columbia Sportswear with an interesting problem: When going outdoors in the very early hours of the morning on a hunt, temperatures would be low, but would increase significantly through the day making their traditional hunting garb impractical. They needed clothing that could be adapted to temperature fluctuations and would, at the same time, provide camouflage. In response, Columbia Sportswear created the Interchange System. The Interchange System, originally designed in 1982, has a waterproof outer shell with a warm zip-out lining. Hunting garments containing the Interchange System are camouflage, and in some products a reversible liner is offered. For skiers, these innovations were incorporated into the Bugaboo Parka, which has outsold all other ski jackets on the market.

The company's Omni-Tech waterproof/breathable fabrics, which rival Gore-Tex in their effectiveness, are treated with a water-repellent finish and can be found in a wide range of Columbia Sportswear merchandise, including footwear.

CORPORATE CITIZENSHIP

Columbia Sportswear began participating in Start Making A Reader Today (SMART) in 1997. Contributing $60,000 to the SMART program, which helps teach children to read and guides them from kindergarten through second grade, the company also provides volunteers from different departments. The program helps about 5,000 children in Oregon and was used as a prototype for national reading programs.

In 1996 Gertrude Boyle, chairman of Columbia Sportswear, was a recipient of the Astra Award, granted by Gateway to the Women's Market, which is a resource and support organization for businesswomen. The Astra Awards were given to 15 outstanding women achievers in Oregon. Also, the company is involved in local fund-raisers and contributes to nonprofit organizations and local schools.

GLOBAL PRESENCE

Columbia Sportswear markets to more than 10,000 retailers in 30 countries and plans to aggressively market products to those that exist in Europe and Asia. The company opened an office in Tokyo in the late 1990s and expanded existing markets in Russia and South Korea, including a 1,600-square foot retail store in Seoul. Columbia Sportswear also plans to seek expansion in Italy, Spain, France, and Germany. Outside of North America, sales rose from $9 million in 1993 to over $35 million in 1997, but as of 1997 those sales were only 10 percent of total net sales. Of the 5.6 million shares of common stock offered in 1998, 1.12 million shares were offered in a concurrent international offering.

EMPLOYMENT

As of December 31, 1997 Columbia Sportswear, employed 1,234 total full time employees, 863 of whom were located in the United States, 62 in Canada, 23 in Europe, and 286 in Asia.

SOURCES OF INFORMATION

Bibliography

"Columbia Sportswear." *Hoover's Online,* April 1998. Available at http://www.hoovers.com.

"Columbia Sportswear-Acucobol Partners in Success." *Acucorp Home Page,* April 1998. Available at http://www.acucobol.com/Partners/Success/ColumbiaSports.html.

Columbia Sportswear Home Page, April 1998. Available at http://www.columbia.com.

FreeEDGAR Home Page, April 1998. Available at http://www.FreeEdgar.com.

"Gertrude Boyle." *Gateway to the Women's Market,* April 1998. Available at http://www.womensmarket.com/gateway/astra/1996/astra_gertrude_boyle.html#top.

"Oregon's Private 150: 18. Columbia Sportswear Co." *Oregon Business Channel,* April 1998. Available at http://www.oregonbusiness.com/Channel05/companies/P150-018.html.

Reseller's Source Kit Home Page, April 1998. Available at http://www.rs-kit.com/Camp5.htm.

Rose, Michael. "Columbia Sportswear Ramps Up Foreign Sales Push." *The Business Journal, Portland,* 22 September 1997. Available at http://www.amcity.com/portland/stories/092297/story7.html.

Round Rocks Home Page, April 1998. Available at http://www.roundrocks.com/others/dist/columbiasportsw.html.

"The Somerset WMS and Columbia Sportswear." *Somerset Home Page,* April 1998. Available at http://www.somersetwms.com/columbia.html.

For an annual report:

on the Internet at: http://www.columbia.com/columbia/investor/default.htm

For additional industry research:

Investigate companies by their Standard Industrial Classification Codes, also known as SICs. Columbia Sportswear's primary SIC is:

5130 Apparel, Piece Goods, and Notions

Comedy Central Inc.

OVERVIEW

Comedy Central was developed as a marriage of Time Warner's HBO and Viacom's MTV Networks. Both HBO and MTV had developed comedy channels, and neither of them was reaching a critical mass of subscribers. The union of the HA! and Comedy Channel efforts was named Comedy Central Inc. when it was launched in April 1991. By 1998 Comedy Central was reaching about two-thirds of the U.S. households that were equipped with cable television. Comedy Central was ranked second by millions of subscribers in 1996 after The Learning Channel, which had 54 million subscribers to Comedy Central's 44 million. In 1997 Comedy Central's subscribers numbered 49 million.

COMPANY FINANCES

Comedy Central spent its first five years as a money-losing venture. The channel's 1994 losses were not quite as steep as those in 1992 and 1993, but they were still a relatively significant $16.5 million. In 1995 Comedy Central lost around $11.0 million, and a year later it lost less than half that much. In 1997 Comedy Central earned its first profit. Profits were under $10.0 million, with advertising sales generating most of the station's revenues. Cable operators were not required to pay a large fee to carry Comedy Central, whereas they had to make significant investments to carry such channels as ESPN.

In 1991 the $8.0 million brought in through advertising represented 45 percent of the company's total revenues. In 1994 the $34.0 million in advertising revenues

FOUNDED: 1991

Contact Information:
HEADQUARTERS: 1775 Broadway
   New York, NY 10019-1903
PHONE: (212)767-8600
FAX: (212)767-4257
EMAIL: mail@comcentral.com
URL: http://www.comedycentral.com

FAST FACTS:

About Comedy Central Inc.

Ownership: Comedy Central is a 50–50 joint venture of Time Warner Entertainment Company, a publicly owned company traded on The New York Stock Exchange, and Viacom International, a publicly owned company traded on the American Stock Exchange.

Ticker symbol: VIA (Viacom); TWX (Time Warner)

Officers: Doug Herzog, Pres. & CEO, 39; Eileen Katz, Sr. VP, programming

Chief Competitors: Comedy Central's competitors are other cable channels. In some ways, the networks are Comedy Central's competitors, as well. The top tier of cable channels is said to include: CNN; TBS; and The Learning Channel.

accounted for more than half of the company's total revenues. Advertising revenues came close to $60.0 million in 1996, with anticipated yearly increases of nearly $20.0 million. Viacom reported to shareholders that Comedy Central's improved performance could be seen in the price of advertising on the hit show South Park. Advertisers including AT&T, Snapple, and Calvin Klein paid up to $80,000 for a 30-second spot during the show.

ANALYSTS' OPINIONS

Television and cable have been extremely competitive industries in the late twentieth century. Many cable companies fold soon after they open shop. Industry analysts were largely skeptical that Comedy Central would find success where others had failed. Three years after the venture began, Comedy Central had a subscriber base of around 31 million and 10 million more than that had signed on within a few years. The skyrocketing success of South Park also brought kudos to Comedy Central. In 1998, 5.2 million viewers were counted watching the show during a two-week period. Almost one quarter of the show's audience was under 18, and close to 60 percent were in the 18 to 34 age range. Advertisers were eager to reach this market, knowing that during the airing of a popular episode, the advertisers could reach a potential 7-percent share of the market.

HISTORY

In 1991 executives at Viacom's MTV Networks and Time Warner's HBO decided to join forces rather than suffer as they both saw losing numbers in their attempts to add comedy cable channels. Thomas Freston of MTV and Michael Fuchs of HBO merged their networks into Comedy Central in 1991 and hired Robert Kreek as CEO. Kreek, a veteran at Fox, revamped programming, trimmed staff, and even gave away some national advertising. Comedy Central's forbears were Comedy Channel, which HBO had developed beginning in 1989, and HA! from Viacom's MTV Networks. Both of these channels ran into trouble getting subscribers. After initial outlays of close to $50 million, both stations were primarily featuring reruns of classic comedy, and both were losing money.

In the fall of 1990 Freston and Fuchs put together a joint venture, launching Comedy Central in April 1991. Putting some effort into original programming led to the early success of the topical show Politically Incorrect. The show was Comedy Central's flagship until it defected to ABC in the fall of 1996.

The two primary goals of Comedy Central were to get cable companies to offer the channel to their subscribers and to get advertising revenue. By the end of 1991 the cable giant Tele-Communications, Inc. (TCI) signed on and Comedy Central's subscribers numbered 22 million. This was the beginning, however, of a continuous effort by Comedy Central executives to keep their channel available through cable offers. TCI and other cable companies regularly add and remove channels from their service and viewers often resort to letter-writing and telephone campaigns to reinstate their favorite channels.

Things started turning around in 1995 when Doug Herzog was recruited away from MTV to become president and CEO of Comedy Central. Herzog spent 11 years at MTV where he was a programmer focused on changing MTV's video-only format. He replaced Kreek and developed new shows including The Daily Show, which focused on current events in the way Politically Incorrect had.

Herzog had a huge hit on his hands with the debut in the fall of 1997 of South Park, a raunchy animated comedy starring four third graders from a Colorado town of the same name. The eight- and nine-year-olds who talk like truck drivers soon developed a loyal audience, even in areas where Comedy Central was not available. Through the Internet and successful merchandising, the characters and vocabulary of South Park were everywhere.

STRATEGY

In its brief history Comedy Central had a distinct goal of making niche in cable television. The officers and executives wanted to reach more viewers in homes. They used animated comedy shows to compete with game shows, and kept their programming lineup varied. In 1992 the cable industry was re-regulated by the federal government so until 1994, when the government relaxed its rules, the potential subscriber base for the channel was limited. Bob Kreek, Comedy Central's first president and CEO, worked within the limits of the regulations and also found innovative programming to add to the existing library of reruns the channel was showing. The Federal Trade Commission was also investigating Time Warner as it acquired Turner Broadcasting Systems and there was talk in 1996 that Viacom might purchase Time Warner's stake in Comedy Central. The commission's review came and went, however, and there was no change in the joint venture ownership of Comedy Central.

During the Republican National Convention in 1996 in San Diego, Comedy Central proved itself an able medium for yet another kind of programming. The network news coverage of the convention was limited and relatively uninteresting. Comedy Central dispatched correspondents Al Franken and Arianna Huffington, who provided humorous coverage of the convention. The hit show Politically Incorrect was also broadcast live from the convention site in San Diego. Not long thereafter, the show moved to ABC, and there was concern that Comedy Central was losing its flagship show. Bill Maher and the show became the weeknight post-Nightline show, but Comedy Central found success with other shows. The Daily Show became the network's place for topical humor. At the web site http://www.thedailyshow.com, the day's biggest stories are also promoted.

In 1997 Comedy Central's advertising agency, Holland Advertising, created an April Fool's spoof that was distributed as an Advertising Age circular. It included imaginary news events such as an article that changed the name of Time Warner to Turner Time, and an article on a new fragrance named for the advertising executive Jerry Della Femina. The circular also featured an advertisement showing Newt Gingrich eating crow, a broad parody of the milk mustache campaign.

Comedy Central strives to create original programming that is both irreverent and cutting edge. The channel's shows have been rewarded by the industry. Jonathan Katz won a 1995 Emmy for Outstanding Voiceover performance for his work on Dr. Katz. The series Win Ben Stein's Money won two Emmy awards for daytime television shows in May 1998. South Park won a CableACE Award for the Best Animated Series in 1998, and the show was on the cover of such varied publications as *Newsweek* and *Rolling Stone*. The show's creators, Trey Parker and Matt Stone, were awarded a NOVA Award from the Producers Guild of America for the most promising producers on television in 1998.

CHRONOLOGY:

Key Dates for Comedy Central Inc.

1991: Founded

1994: U.S. government relaxes cable industry programming rules

1995: Doug Herzog becomes president & CEO; launches Radio Active

1996: Politically Incorrect moves to ABC; starts the Daily Show

1997: Earns its first profit; introduces South Park

1998: South Park wins CableACE Award for Best Animated Series

INFLUENCES

Larry Divney, the executive vice president of advertising sales, was Ted Turner's friend from Divney's days in advertising sales at CNN. Turner, the vice-chairman of Time Warner, knew that Divney was the man behind advertising sales and that advertising sales were the way Comedy Central would earn money. As for programming, Comedy Central was willing to take risks and discovered that aggravating some of their viewers was worthwhile if it got them the attention they hoped for.

CURRENT TRENDS

The popularity of Comedy Central's South Park has led to a multitude of merchandising opportunities. The licensed product line was worth $30 million in the late 1990s and South Park t-shirts, hats, and bumper stickers could be found across the country. The Internet provided Comedy Central with a way to reach viewers whose local cable providers did not carry the channel's programming. Many Comedy Central enthusiasts became fans of certain shows through Internet sites. For example, there are 250 unofficial web sites only for the show South Park. Comedy Central also made it a priority to have closed captioning available for much of its programming day. Reruns of such standard classics as Saturday Night Live and The Odd Couple are closed-captioned, and all of South Park's existing episodes are also closed-captioned.

PRODUCTS

In 1998 the best-known product of Comedy Central was its show South Park. While its cutout animation was not considered particularly clever or stylish, the characters are drawn in such a way that they are universally recognized by viewers young and old. South Park's creators are Trey Parker and Matt Stone, 20-something film-school classmates from University of Colorado at Boulder, who made a short video as a Christmas present commissioned by a Hollywood executive. The Spirit of Christmas was just the kind of twisted story that led to South Park. Comedy Central took a risk and hired them and made a huge success of these third grade characters from a Colorado mountain town. Stan, Kyle, Cartman, and Kenny (who gets killed on each episode), look cute with their big eyes and round faces, until the dialogue starts, and the plots begin to revolve around bathroom humor. But despite objections and outcry from parents and schools, the show posted some Nielsen ratings of 1.7 for the Wednesday night time slot at 10:00 PM, which previously averaged 0.5.

Some of the other popular programs on Comedy Central include Absolutely Fabulous, a British import with a cult-like following; Viva Variety, which gives a European spin to the variety show format; and Make Me Laugh, a television game show with contemporary comedians taped in front of a live audience.

The Daily Show started in 1996 and moved into the 11 PM time slot after the departure of Politically Incorrect. Dr. Katz: Professional Therapist was the first animated series about a therapist. In 1995 Comedy Central launched Radio Active, a live remote program that radio stations around the country used. Comedy Central gained a reputation through this show as source for comedy as well as a cable channel. The office lobby at Comedy Central headquarters became a lounge area used by dozens of stations in the first two years of the show.

GLOBAL PRESENCE

Comedy Central's International Business Development Division is responsible for oversees expansion. The division distributes original programming such as The A List, London Underground, and Two Drink Minimum. In mid-1998 Comedy Central announced new markets for some of its most popular shows. South Park will be seen in Argentina, Germany, New Zealand, and the Middle East. Dr. Katz will be available in Argentina, Australia, Belgium, New Zealand, The Netherlands, and Portugal. Viewers in New Zealand and Australia will be able to see Viva Variety.

EMPLOYMENT

Television and cable television are notorious industries for the people trying to build careers from within. Some of Comedy Central's employees began at HBO, some began at MTV, and many were hired along the way. The self-contained sales force from HBO's Comedy Channel had 20 members who started a new management team at the new entity. Larry Divney is the head of advertising sales and became one of the longest-remaining executives at Comedy Central. Those who work for him say there is a sense of freedom and self-direction at the company that encourages members of the sales force to achieve results at their own pace and that confidence and motivation extends to other areas of the company. Even the Comedy Central web site invites potential summer interns to submit resumes for a variety of positions at the company.

SOURCES OF INFORMATION

Bibliography

Bellafante, Ginia. "Bob Dole is So Old That . . ." *Time,* 26 August 1996.

Borgi, Michael. "At Comedy Central, It's Divney World." *Mediaweek,* 14 April 1997.

Carter, Bill. "As Their Dominance Erodes, Networks Plan Big Changes." *The New York Times,* 11 May 1998.

———. "Comedy Central Makes the Most of an Irreverent, and Profitable, New Cartoon Hit." *The New York Times,* 10 November 1997.

Clash, James M. "Mr. Hatfield, Meet Mr. McCoy." *Forbes,* 30 January 1995.

The Comedy Central Home Page, 27 May 1998. Available at http://www.comedycentral.com.

Elliott, Stuart. "Warning: The Merry Pranksters of Madison Avenue Are Out Today." *The New York Times,* 1 April 1997.

Flint, Joe, and John Dempsey. "Herzog at Center of Comedy." *Variety,* 19 June 1995.

Grover, Ronald. "If These Shows Are Hits, Why Do They Hurt So Much?" *Business Week,* 13 April 1998.

Hamilton, Kendall. "Meanwhile, Back at HQ." *Newsweek,* 23 March 1998.

Horak, Terri. "Comedy Central Keeps Radio Active." *Billboard,* 16 August, 1997.

Luscombe, Belinda. "Eye of Newt, Mouth of Crow." *Time,* 7 April 1997.

Marin, Rick. "'Peanuts' Gone Wrong." *Newsweek,* 21 July 1997.

———. "The Rude Tube." *Newsweek,* 23 March 1998.

Peers, Martin, and John Dempsey. "Viacom May take TW's Comedy Central Stake." *Variety,* 26 February 1996.

Richmond, Ray. "Changing of the Off-Guard on Tap at Comedy Central." *Variety,* 4 November 1996.

———. "Comedy Central Finally Parks Itself in the Black." *Variety,* 6 October 1997.

For additional industry research:

Investigate companies by their Standard Industrial Classification Codes, also known as SICs. Comedy Central's primary SIC is:

4841 Cable and Other Pay Television Services

Compaq Computer Corporation

FOUNDED: 1982

Contact Information:
HEADQUARTERS: 20555 State Highway 249
   Houston, TX 77070
PHONE: (281)370-0670
FAX: (281)374-1740
TOLL FREE: (800)345-1518
URL: http://www.compaq.com

OVERVIEW

Compaq Computer Corporation ranks as the world's largest supplier of personal computers (PCs) and shipped its 30 millionth PC in 1997. The company has been recognized as one of the 100 best employers in the nation. Its product line includes: desktop, portable, and notebook computers; servers; peripherals and monitors; software; and entertainment and multimedia products. Compaq achieved $1 billion in sales faster than any other computer company in the United States. Focusing on fast growth, the company has worked to outshine the only four companies larger than itself: IBM, Fujitsu, Hewlett-Packard, and NEC. In fact, Compaq's goal is to be one of the top three computer companies in the world by the year 2000.

COMPANY FINANCES

Compaq reports that in 1997 its North American sales constituted 55 percent of total sales. Sales in Europe, the Middle East, and Africa represented 32 percent. The remaining 13 percent of sales accounted for its Asia/Pacific, Japan, Greater China, and Latin America divisions. Sales in 1997 reached $24.58 billion as compared with $20.01 billion in 1996.

Listed on the New York Stock Exchange under the symbol CPQ, its first-quarter 1997 high was $17.35 and its low $14.40; its second-quarter high was $21.63 and low $14.40; third-quarter high was 39.13 and low 20.38; and fourth quarter high was 38.63 and low was 26.66.

ANALYSTS' OPINIONS

Compaq's operating profits of 9 percent are higher than those of any other personal computer company, making it the leader in the computer industry's most financially rewarding area. This area is also comprised of servers that connect to other personal computers and entertainment software applications. Compaq holds a 36 percent server market share, while IBM has only 14 percent of this market. The most serious criticism that has surrounded Compaq is that it has been so intent on becoming one of the top three PC companies that it has spread itself too thin. As a result, some analysts have feared, Compaq would begin losing customers and stock value. Eckhard Pfeiffer, the company's chief executive officer, intends on competing by maintaining low-cost, high-volume products in the business, which is a strategy questioned by many. Still, analysts have been impressed by Compaq's financial picture. By generating new customer sales while expanding existing customer sales, the company increased its international PC market share from 10 percent to 12 percent.

Some analysts have predicted that Hewlett-Packard and Compaq would eventually compete for leadership in the industry. Compaq's competitive edge rests on the idea of using the Wintel server, combining Microsoft Windows and Intel to develop a computing network. In fact, 67 percent of Wintel servers sold by way of computer resellers come from Compaq.

HISTORY

Compaq was founded in 1982 by Joseph A. "Rod" Canion and two other former Texas Instrument employees. Based in Houston, Texas, Compaq was designed to produce and sell portable IBM-compatible computers. After shipping its first computer in 1982, the company quickly generated unmatchable sales of $111 million by 1983. That growth continued when Compaq released the first 28-pound portable computer in 1983. A successful strategy for Compaq has been selling rights to dealers and suppliers of the IBM personal computer in order to move its stock quickly. By 1990 Compaq had 3,800 retailers in 152 countries. In 1992 the company released the Compaq SYSTEMPRO/XL, the fastest PC server in the world at that time. By the following year, Compaq had bypassed IBM as the world's leading manufacturer of personal computers.

Joseph Canion resigned in 1991 when the company faced tough times due to economic decline. A former marketing executive of Texas Instruments, Eckhard Pfeiffer, took over as chief executive officer.

The company attempted to increase business by introducing many new models of personal computers in 1995. The following year, Compaq slashed prices as

FINANCES:

*Compaq Computer
Sales, 1994-1997
(billion dollars)*

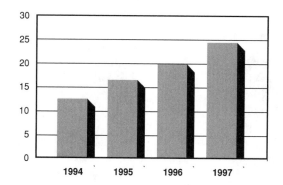

*Compaq Computer
1997 Stock Prices
(dollars)*

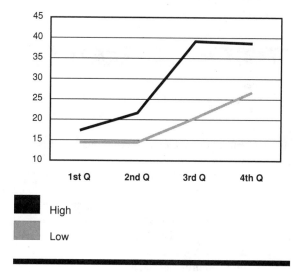

much as 51 percent on some models in an effort to increase consumer appeal. That same year it teamed up with Fisher-Price to introduce Wonder Tools, a line of computer toys for children.

Compaq followed these changes with an internal restructuring. It organized four groups centered on enterprise computing, consumer products, communications products, and desktop and portable personal computers. Compaq also entered the workstation market at this time, producing high-powered computers with a sales price ranging from $6,000 to $15,000.

The latest Compaq Presario 4240ES computer. (Courtesy of Compaq Computer Corporation.)

STRATEGY

When Eckhard Pfeiffer took over leadership for Compaq, he set the goal that the company become one of the third-largest computer companies worldwide, which could have explained the company's passion for speed. Compaq aims for great success in all of these areas: revenue growth, market share gains, new business development, and manufacturing. This kind of strategy has greatly benefited Compaq. Another element in Compaq's strategy has been the idea of partnerships in business. The company has formed alliances with such companies as Intel, Fisher-Price, Microsoft, Digital Equipment, Novell, and Cisco Systems. Compaq based its decision to form partnerships on this philosophy, as stated in an April 1996 issue of *Fortune* magazine. Gary Stimac, former vice president of the systems division was quoted as saying, " . . . if we can't do it ourselves, we need to find out who is best in each category and bring them into the solution . . . ."

INFLUENCES

Since Compaq's drop in revenue in 1991, Pfeiffer made it his mission to send the company to new heights. Previously, Compaq was a computer company that manufactured quality products at high prices, welcoming

gross margins of 37 percent. With Pfeiffer's plan, the company sacrificed those margins down to 23 percent in order to produce volume. Pfeiffer cut sales and administrative costs in half from 22 percent of sales to 11 percent of sales, which has led Compaq to be the leading low-cost manufacturer in the industry. In fact, cost cutting has proven less stressful for Compaq than its competitors.

Again in the spring of 1996, Compaq faced analysts with the news that the company was not likely to produce the earnings predicted, which caused company stock to take a deep plunge. Eckhard Pfeiffer saw a need to create greater profits along with growth, and he quickly revised his strategy to include price reductions of 20 percent for dealers. This proved successful, and its March quarter for 1996 jumped 42 percent. This incident, however, caused Compaq to change its vision.

Soon following price reductions came an internal reorganization. Nine new divisions were created to focus on areas of rapid growth. These included Internet products and services, small-business systems, and engineering workstations. Many analysts feared that Compaq could not operate efficiently with its growing number of divisions. Nonetheless, Pfeiffer continued to shift the company's focus. He brought in managers from the competition such as those from Unisys Corp. and Digital Equipment. Because Compaq's own employees were overlooked, many executives quit in late 1996.

According to Pfeiffer, another area requiring expansion was the options business, which included monitors, networking cards, and modems. These areas eventually produced great profits for Compaq, giving the company an edge over its competitors by not remaining simply a PC company. Analyst Lee Sullivan has likened this to Mattel's strategy in manufacturing Barbie. That is, the company made a large amount of money from the outfits, not just the doll. After 1995 PC options became a successful line of business for Compaq.

CURRENT TRENDS

Compaq continued to focus on aggressive profit and growth into the late 1990s. The company developed new partnerships with many companies, allowing for advancement without great expense. For example, Compaq relied on Andersen Consulting and software producer SAP to set up and maintain systems in the manner of the Hewlett-Packard/IBM partnership. In forming these alliances, Compaq launched itself onto the major playing field without incorporating the extensive costs of operating its own services or software business.

Compaq's focus has always been highly consumer-oriented. One of the projects receiving funds at Compaq has been the startup of Intellon Corp., which creates computer chips for use in such products as stereos and refrigerators. Eckhard Pfeiffer sees this as the wave of the future. He believes that computers will eventually control air-conditioning, heating, and security systems in homes and businesses.

PRODUCTS

Compaq's theory of being fast to yield success carries over to its product development as well. The company is organized in five product groups. Its PC Products group accounted for 47 percent of company sales in 1997. Its Compaq Deskpro was reportedly the most popular PC in the world during this time. This group has introduced a line of portable computers, including the Armada 1500 and Armada 7700. Compaq's Enterprise Computing Group focuses on server products, workstations, and storage and options. It accounted for 36 percent of sales in 1997. From this area has come Compaq's ProSignia 200 servers and ProLiant 7000 with PCI Hot Plug technology. It was hoped that the group's new E2000 Platform Architecture would enable more powerful and flexible solutions for the needs of enterprise customers.

Compaq's Consumer Products Group, which focuses on computers and peripherals for the consumer and home office market, brought in 16 percent of 1997 company sales. In 1997, this group introduced its low-cost (under a $1,000) Presario 2000 series to attract the 60 percent of U.S. families without personal computers at the time. Later that year, its consumer line was expanded to include new processor technologies with easier Internet access, digital video disk (DVD) capabilities, and a creative imaging center.

In August of 1997 Compaq merged with California-based Tandem Computers, forming a division that served to expand its enterprise product line into the mission-critical computing space. During this year, Tandem launched its ServerNet NonStop Himalaya S-series system and continued to work on its UNIX system products and wireless applications. The following year brought closer partnering with Compaq's Enterprise Computing Group.

Compaq's Communication Products Group focuses on local area network (LAN) products such as network interface cards and hubs and switches providing a range of network systems for businesses. It also provides a wide range of remote access products such as modems and ISDN routers. With the acquisition of Microcom in 1997 came the availability of modem pools and remote access concentrators.

CORPORATE CITIZENSHIP

Compaq has stood as a leader in the environmental, health, and safety arenas. The company was recognized

FAST FACTS:
About Compaq Computer Corporation

Ownership: Compaq is a publicly owned corporation traded on the New York Stock Exchange.

Ticker symbol: CPQ

Officers: Eckhard Pfeiffer, Pres. & CEO, 1997 base salary $1,250,000; Earl L. Mason, Sr. VP & CFO, 1997 base salary $475,000; Gregory E. Petsch, Sr. VP Manufacturing & Quality, 1997 base salary $425,000

Employees: 32,565

Principal Subsidiary Companies: Compaq's principal subsidiaries are PC Products Group, Enterprise Computing Group, Consumer Products Group, Communications Products Group, and Tandem Computer Group.

Chief Competitors: In a highly competitive industry, Compaq strives to maintain its market share. Some primary competitors are: Fujitsu; Hewlett-Packard; IBM; NEC; Dell; and Gateway 2000.

by the World Environment Center in January of 1997 as the recipient of the WEC Gold Medal for International Corporate Environmental Achievement. Compaq was praised for establishing an Environmental Policy in its early years, and it continues to show great care in assessing environmental issues at each stage of a product's life cycle. It also was the first in the industry to develop energy-efficient computers, with the capability of CO_2 emission reductions. Compaq also showed leadership in the environmental field by introducing manufacturing methods that did away with the use of chlorofluorocarbons (CFCs). Environmental, health, and safety education and training have remained standard operations for Compaq among senior management, employees, suppliers, vendors, and school children. The company is also a member of the Industry Cooperative for Ozone Layer Protection.

In June of 1996 Compaq was chosen as "PC Partner of the Year" by the U.S. Environmental Protection Agency. This award acknowledged Compaq's efforts to move forward in environmental concerns of its products, to promote the Energy Star Program, and to offer Energy Star-compliant computer products. Compaq also participates in the Green Lights Program, which promotes en-

CHRONOLOGY:

Key Dates for Compaq Computer Corporation

1982: Former Texas Instruments employees create Compaq Computer Corporation in Houston, Texas

1983: Compaq sets the standard for portable PCs with the release of its Compaq Portable

1987: Intel and Compaq collaborate to release the DESKPRO 386, twice as fast as any IBM PC

1991: Compaq restructures, laying off 12 percent of its workforce

1993: Compaq beats IBM as the world leader in PC manufacturing

1995: Fisher-Price and Compaq team up to create a line of computer toys for children

ergy-efficient lighting. In addition to this, the company has worked to advance recycling. It has pursued various methods for product design that relieve the disassembly and recycling process at the end of a product's life. Called the "Design for Environment," this attempt expanded to new product designs.

Waste disposal operations also continued to be evaluated at Compaq. The objective was to ensure that the company uses waste treatment facilities that function in a safe, environmentally responsible manner. Compaq developed an onsite audit of commercial waste treatment, storage, disposal, and recycling facilities. In all of its environmental operations, the company conducted formal audits internally, as well as through the International Standards Organization certification specifications.

GLOBAL PRESENCE

Products manufactured by Compaq are sold and supported in more than 100 countries by way of a network of Compaq partnerships. The company has continued its efforts to meet current and future needs of customers. It has supplied Internet and enterprise computing solutions, networking products, as well as commercial PC products and consumer PCs.

Compaq engages in a wide range of marketing, sales, and customer support programs through its North Amer-

ican Division. These programs focus on pricing, new channel development, customer satisfaction and support, and marketing in the United States and Canada. Compaq ventured into the European market in 1994. It currently owns subsidiaries in Germany, the United Kingdom, France, Austria, Bahrain, Belgium, Czech Republic, Denmark, Finland, Greece, Hungary, Italy, the Netherlands, Norway, Scotland, Spain, South Africa, Sweden, Switzerland, Portugal, and Poland. In addition, the company's European division includes the Middle East and Africa.

In 1991 Compaq incorporated Compaq Computer Asia/Pacific Pte. Ltd. To take advantage of the great potential for the company in the Asia/Pacific region. With headquarters in Singapore, Compaq has subsidiaries in Australia, Hong Kong, Malaysia, New Zealand, Taiwan, and Thailand. Other Compaq offices are located in China, Korea, India, Brunei/Indonesia/Philippines, and Indochina.

Japan allowed Compaq to design a line of desktop, portable, and notebook computers and PC systems exclusively for the Japanese market. Compaq also operates sales in Latin America and houses subsidiaries in Argentina, Brazil, Chile, Columbia, Venezuela, and the Caribbean/Central American region. Compaq has remained highly dependent upon international markets for its desktop, portable, and server products. Due to increased demands throughout Europe, the Middle East, and Africa, Compaq has built a manufacturing facility in Erskine, Scotland, which produces a full range of Compaq desktop, server, and portable products. The company also opened a manufacturing facility in Singapore in May of 1990, which expanded in 1994 due to new customer demands in the Asia Pacific locale. China and Brazil house manufacturing plants as well to meet the increased needs for PCs.

EMPLOYMENT

Compaq believes its employees are critical to its success. In 1997 the company had 32,565 full-time employees and 8,878 temporary and contract workers. It reports that it has developed competitive human resources policies consistent with its business strategies.

SOURCES OF INFORMATION

Bibliography

Compaq Computer Corporation Annual Report, 10 June 1998. Available at: http://www.edgar-online.com.

Compaq Computer Corporation Home Page, 10 June 1998. Available at http://www.compaq.com.

"Compaq Computer Corporation." *Hoover's Online,* 10 June 1998. Available at http://www.hoovers.com.

Kirkpatrick, David. "Fast Times at Compaq." *Fortune,* 1 April 1996.

——. "They're All Copying Compaq." *Fortune,* 25 November 1996.

McWilliams, Gary. "Compaq: There's No End to Its Drive." *Business Week,* 17 February 1997.

Sullivan, R. Lee. "Compaq's Barbie-Doll Strategy." *Forbes,* 4 November 1996.

For an annual report:

on the Internet at: http://www.edgar-online.com

For additional industry research:

Investigate companies by their Standard Industrial Classification Codes, also known as SICs. Compaq's primary SIC is:

3571 Electronic Computers

CompuServe Interactive Services, Inc.

FOUNDED: 1969 as Compuserve Inc.

Contact Information:

HEADQUARTERS: 5000 Arlington Centre Blvd.
    Columbus, OH 43220
PHONE: (614)457-8600
FAX: (614)457-0348
URL: http://www.world.compuserve.com

OVERVIEW

With more than 2.5 million members, CompuServe Interactive Services is one of the world's largest online service providers and is a world leader in the field of data communications and computer-based interactive services. In February 1998 CompuServe became a subsidiary of America Online Inc. (AOL) after experiencing trouble attracting and retaining subscribers. The deal reportedly would lessen the frequency of busy signals for AOL subscribers, and would also reduce episodes of being disconnected midstream. CompuServe still operates as a separate brand, with its own e-mail, content, and other features. The company focuses on small business, professional, and technical users.

COMPANY FINANCES

Over the years CompuServe's revenues have increased steadily. In 1993 revenues were $315.4 million; in 1994, $429.9 million; in 1995, $582.8 million; in 1996, $793.2 million; and in 1997, $841.9 million. Revenues rose due to an increase in subscribers desiring consumer online and Internet services. Of 1997's sales, 71 percent came from the United States, and the remaining 29 percent from other countries such as France, Germany, the Netherlands, Switzerland, and the United Kingdom. In addition, 66 percent ($556 million) came from online services, 31 percent ($258 million) from network services, and 3 percent ($28 million) from other services. In the fourth quarter of 1997 CompuServe's stock reached a high of $13.63 and the low was $8.88, as compared to the fourth quarter of 1996 when the high was $35.50 and the low was $27.75.

ANALYSTS' OPINIONS

CompuServe's objective is to "lead in the development and implementation of personal and commercial applications with computer-based interactive technology." By increasing its subscriber base for online and Internet services, and stressing technology both to individuals and businesses, the company seeks growth domestically and internationally. Because technology is changing rapidly, there are opportunities with corporations needing to outsource their data communications. The changing work environment including home-based and increased travel provide other growth sources.

HISTORY

What is now a worldwide service had its humble beginnings in Jeffrey Wilkins' 1969 move to computerize his father-in-law's insurance company. In 1977 Wilkins developed a mainframe computer time-sharing network called MicroNet. This simple arrangement was a precursor to today's online services. Only three years later, CompuServe was acquired by the tax preparation firm of H&R Block, giving it the monetary boost needed to build up its online technology. Wilkins left the company in 1985, but not without seeing the birth of several now-standard staples of the online world, namely online forums and e-mail.

In 1995, as competition in the online arena became more fierce, CompuServe bought SPRY, an Internet software developer, and soon offered subscribers access to the World Wide Web through a Web browser built into the CompuServe software. This proprietary Web browser was later dropped, however.

In 1996, an effort was launched to transform CompuServe from "a privately held, proprietary technology-driven company to a publicly held, market-driven company." On April 19, 1996, H&R Block put CompuServe up for its initial public offering. The $454 million raised was well below analysts' expectations. At about the same time, CompuServe's subscriber growth had come to a standstill, prompting its stock price to plummet. In 1997 Robert Massey, president and CEO, resigned. Frank Salizzoni took over as acting chairman, CEO, and president, dividing his time between CompuServe and H&R Block.

In the late 1990s CompuServe struggled to obtain and keep subscribers. As a result, in February 1998, H&R Block sold its controlling interest in CompuServe to WorldCom Inc., a large telecommunications company, for $1.2 billion in stock. WorldCom, in turn, paid America Online $175 million in cash and gave it CompuServe Interactive in exchange for AOL's networking subsidiary ANS Communications Inc. The deal allowed AOL to add CompuServe's 2.6 million subscribers to its own base, increasing its total to 11.6 million. CompuServe, however, continues to operate as a separate brand with its

FINANCES:

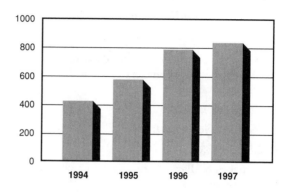

CompuServe Interactive Services, Inc. Revenues, 1994-1997 (million dollars)

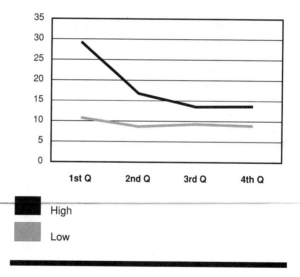

CompuServe Interactive Services, Inc. 1997 Stock Prices (dollars)

■ High
▨ Low

own content, e-mail, features, and functionality. Mayo S. Stuntz, Jr., former executive vice president and CEO of Century 21 Real Estate Corporation, was named president of CompuServe.

STRATEGY

After years of peddling its own incompatible proprietary technology, CompuServe began the drive toward Web-based technology. In May 1996, the company an-

FAST FACTS:

About CompuServe Interactive Services, Inc.

Ownership: CompuServe is owned by America Online, a publicly owned company traded on The New York Stock Exchange.

Ticker symbol: AOL

Officers: Mayo Stuntz Jr., Pres.

Employees: 3,050 (1997)

Principal Subsidiary Companies: CompuServe Interactive Services, Inc. is a subsidiary of America Online (AOL).

Chief Competitors: CompuServe competes in the online services industry as well as in the Internet and networking services industries. Major competitors include: AT&T; Microsoft; and Prodigy.

---

nounced it would adopt Internet-based open standards, which means that subscribers would be allowed to use either the CompuServe proprietary interface or standard browser software to access the online service. The rationale given for this decision was that it would reduce time dedicated to marketing and would make the service more user-friendly. Moreover, with an eye on considerable cost reduction, it would simplify content development by allowing the company to purchase existing Web technology instead of constantly creating its own content. CompuServe announced that it would allow its users to use the Netscape Navigator to browse the World Wide Web, and would get rid of its own proprietary CompuServe browser.

In order to recapture market shares lost to its major competitors, CompuServe padded its management team. It invested heavily in infrastructure. In the fiscal year ending April 30, 1996, the company spent $219 million on doubling its network capacity, in addition to speeding up connections with modem upgrades.

In 1996, the H&R Block board of directors announced three actions toward a split with the CompuServe Corporation to create two separate, publicly traded firms. First, the board authorized the spin-off of its remaining 80.1 percent of CompuServe shares to H&R Block shareholders. Second, the board reduced the H&R Block quarterly cash dividend. Finally, the board allowed open market repurchase of up to 10 million of its Com-

puServe shares in the two years following the spin off of the company. Upon completion of the initial public offering in April 1996, more than 18 million CompuServe shares were sold.

The company continued to strive toward its goal of market segmentation and online services customization. In 1997, after the failure of one of its family-oriented online service endeavors, the company put its focus on users in the world of business.

In 1997, CompuServe had the ability to reach more than 90 percent of the U.S. population living in metropolitan areas of 25,000 or more. At the price of a local telephone call, these users had high-speed connections to local CompuServe Information Service (CIS) nodes. Of the previous year's sales of $793 million, CompuServe's online services accounted for 71 percent of total sales. Network services accounted for 25 percent.

"In the consumer market," said the company's former CEO, Robert Massey, "CompuServe's future lies in vastly expanding its reach by eliminating the access restrictions our proprietary architecture once imposed. With our migration to open standards, tens of millions of Internet users will have direct access on a subscription basis to our unique content and the many benefits we bring. Furthermore, CompuServe is pursuing opportunities to generate profits from the unique characteristics of the Internet and its massive global reach. Our strategy calls for the development of several additional sources of revenue including online advertising, electronic commerce and transaction fees. We see the coming commercialization of the Internet as a wealth of opportunity."

INFLUENCES

For years, CompuServe enjoyed a comfortable position in the relatively small world of online services. When the mass-commercialization of the Internet arrived in the 1990s, however, it was electronic archrival America Online that raced to the front of the pack. Whereas America Online captured novice users with an easy-to-use, graphically sophisticated interface, CompuServe bungled with its harder-to-use software, lackluster marketing strategy and lack of aggressiveness with the competition. In late 1996 CompuServe finally released CompuServe 3.0, an advanced, user-friendly interface that imitated America Online's use of graphics and speech technology. But this was too little, too late. CompuServe became a subsidiary of AOL in February 1998 through a buyout with long-distance provider WorldCom Inc.

CURRENT TRENDS

CompuServe offers a variety of services to its subscribers, including e-mail, online chats, and forums.

Through SPRYNET, subscribers enjoy many services including local and global news, financial, sports, and links to other databases. In addition, the development of software to facilitate their services allows the company to be a leader as a value-based and customer oriented organization.

PRODUCTS

The company's interactive services include the CompuServe Information Service (CIS), an online service aimed at 3.4-million home and office users. The service features access to scores of information features, such as Business Database Plus (a compendium of business articles); Executive News Service (clips from the major wire services); Knowledge Index (access to more than 100 databases and 50,000 journals); and many more. For consumers interested in Internet-access-only service, the company responded by unveiling its SPRYNET service, which had close to 200,000 subscribers by the end of 1996. CompuServe's network services include system management, connectivity, and wide area network (WAN) applications. In a bid for the home market, the company launched its WOW! consumer online service for novice users. The service failed, however, and CompuServe was forced to cancel it in 1996. CompuServe also offers services worldwide. In Japan, for example, 1.5 million consumers have access to NiftyServe, a domestic CIS counterpart.

CORPORATE CITIZENSHIP

The company claims to be progressive—environmentally conscious, health and fitness oriented, with flexible time schedules for its employees. While trying to provide access to both proprietary and Internet services, however, the company has actually restricted access to certain Internet material. This move toward censorship came in late 1995, after a German prosecutor accused CompuServe of defying local law by providing subscribers access to sex-related newsgroups and materials. The company subsequently banned some 200 such groups and soon began offering Microsystems' Cyber-Patrol software as a means of controlling access to sexually explicit material on the Internet.

GLOBAL PRESENCE

CompuServe was the first online service to go global. In a 1987 joint venture with Fujitsu and Nissho Iwai, the company unveiled its NiftyServe online service in Japan. In 1991 the first European office opened in the United Kingdom. With close to 1 million European sub-

CHRONOLOGY:
Key Dates for CompuServe Corporation

1969: CompuServe is established by Jeffery Wilkins

1977: MicroNet is launched to provide computer time-sharing services

1979: The online service, CompuServe Information Service, is introduced

1980: CompuServe becomes a wholly owned subsidiary of H&R Block

1985: Wilkins leaves the company

1989: CompuServe becomes the first general videotex service to get 500,000 subscribers

1991: A U.S. District Court finds that CompuServe need not be responsible for the content of the information sent through their services

1996: H&R Block puts CompuServe up for an initial public offering

1997: AOL acquires CompuServe

scribers, CompuServe is the biggest online service provider on the continent. Throughout the 1980s and 1990s, access was established in other parts of Europe, as well as in Australia, Africa, Asia and Latin America. While global access to CompuServe nodes is far-reaching, this is often at the cost of speed. In 1997, nodes in some major capitals were accessible at a modem speed of no greater than 9,600 bauds per second.

EMPLOYMENT

The company tells potential employees, "At CompuServe, you will find long-term professional and personal growth in an appealing atmosphere. The customer is our purpose. The associate is our foundation and future. A better society is our legacy." The company says employees have open and direct, hands-on participation in an informal but high-tech setting where situations are changing continually. A dynamic, challenging environment means expectations of, and reward for creativity. The company therefore provides its employees with training for "professional, technical and personal growth."

SOURCES OF INFORMATION

Bibliography

"CompuServe Corporation." *Hoover's Handbook of American Business 1998.* Austin, TX: The Reference Press, 1997.

CompuServe Corporation 1996 Annual Report, April 1998. Available at http://www.edgar-online.com.

Compuserve Home Page, 27 April 1998. Available at http://world.compuserve.com.

"H&R Block to Spin Off Remaining CompuServe Shares: Dividend Reduction and Stock Repurchase Plan Announced." H&R Block, Inc. Press Release, 16 July 1996. Available at http://www.handrblock.com/press_releases/spinoff.html.

Lazarus, David. "Rumored AOL-CompuServe Deal Seen as Good Fit." *Wired News,* 2 April 1997. Available at http://www.wired.com/news/.

For an annual report:

on the Internet at: http://www.edgar-online.com

For additional industry research:

Investigate companies by their Standard Industrial Classification Codes, also known as SICs. Compuserve's primary SICs are:

6719 Holding Companies, NEC

7375 Information Retrieval Services

Continental Airlines, Inc.

OVERVIEW

Continental Airlines is the fifth largest airline in the United States, flying to more than 120 domestic and about 70 international destinations. The company has recovered from years of financial struggles. In fact, the company's last year to turn a profit since CEO Gordon Bethune stepped in and rescued the company was 1986. With a new strategy in place he changed the way the airline operated, getting rid of many unprofitable businesses.

COMPANY FINANCES

In 1997 Continental posted net income of $385 million on revenues of $6.66 billion, as compared to 1995's net income of $319 million on revenues of $6.36 billion and 1995's net income of $224 million on revenues of $5.82 billion.

Trading on the New York Stock Exchange, Continental reports that there were "approximately 3,133 and 17,956 holders of record of its Class A common stock and Class B common stock, respectively." The company does not intend to pay out any cash dividends, but "may consider repurchase of its common stock under certain market conditions."

Continental reports that revenues increased in 1997 as compared to 1996 in the following areas:

- Passenger revenue increased 13.4 percent, $789 million
- Cargo revenue increased 13.6 percent, $21 million

FOUNDED: 1934 (as Varney Speed Lines)

Contact Information:

HEADQUARTERS: 2929 Allen Pky., Ste. 2010
   Houston, TX 77019
PHONE: (713)834-2950
FAX: (713)834-2087
URL: http://www.flycontinental.com

FINANCES:

Continental Airlines Operating Revenue, 1994-1997 (billion dollars)

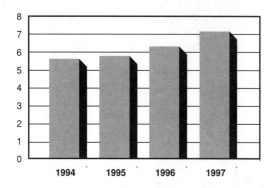

Continental Airlines 1997 Stock Prices (dollars)

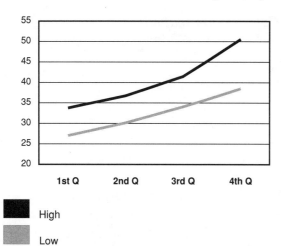

■ High

■ Low

- Mail and other revenue increased 12.8 percent, $43 million

- Wages, salaries, and related costs increased 16.3 percent, $236 million

- Employee incentives increased 29.9 percent, $29 million

- Aircraft fuel expense increased 14.3 percent, $111 million

- Commissions expense increased 11.2 percent, $57 million

- Aircraft rentals increased 8.3 percent, $42 million

- Maintenance, materials, and repairs increased 16.5 percent, $76 million

- Other rentals and landing fees increased 12.9 percent, $45 million. The company also reported that its financial and operating performance improved significantly in 1996 compared to 1997. This includes the strategic plan to strengthen operations and improve customer satisfaction and employee relations.

ANALYSTS' OPINIONS

While analysts have been impressed with Continental's comeback, most know it will take time for the company to cast off its old reputation for slow, poor service. With tremendous profits in comparison to previous years, most experts have remained hopeful. In February 1998 Continental's annual report stated that a five-year collective bargaining agreement with the company's pilots was met. Previous records have indicated that the company's average salary for its pilots, including pension, benefits, and payroll taxes, totaled $113,000 per pilot in the 12-month period ending September 30, 1996. This average wage falls short by 38 percent in comparison to other wages paid by major carriers such as Delta Air Lines, American Airlines, USAir, United Airlines, and Northwest Airlines. Continental intends to be wage competitive by the year 2000.

HISTORY

After Texas Air, a holding company for Texas International, bought Continental Airlines in 1982, the company faced financial losses exceeding $500 million between 1978 and 1983. Owned by Frank Lorenzo's Jet Capital Corporation, the company was forced to file bankruptcy, but came out of its heavy debt in 1986. It was the lowest-fare airline with the cheapest labor costs in the industry.

Texas Air moved on to buy other airlines in 1986, including Eastern Air Lines, People Express Airlines, and Frontier Airlines. Escalating financial difficulties forced bankruptcy court to replace Texas Air from Eastern's management in 1990 with Martin Shugrue as the trustee. It was then that Texas Air became Continental Airlines Holdings.

Due to high fuel prices and low flying traffic, Continental was also plunged into bankruptcy in 1990. It recovered in 1993 and appointed Gordon Bethune as CEO the following year with a new strategy in place, the company sought out a code-sharing agreement (an agreement between airlines to purchase regular flights on each others' planes) with CSA Czech Airlines, allowing Continental to enter new flight markets like Newark, Cincinnati, Norfolk, and Cleveland.

STRATEGY

With new CEO Gordon Bethune in the company's driver's seat, Continental launched a new growth strategy. First, the company aimed to increase its services in its three United States hubs: Cleveland, Houston, and Newark. Second, it set its sights on expansion efforts in markets other than the United States, particularly where it has historically been strong. Lastly, Continental Airlines sold its businesses that were causing monetary losses, like Continental Lite.

Bethune has also restructured many operations to make flights more convenient for customers. Continental has made great efforts to improve baggage handling, clean planes more thoroughly, including scheduling additional paint jobs, and add more food on several flights. An employee bonus incentive program has been established to help the company better serve its customers and, in turn, increase its traffic.

INFLUENCES

The company's long history of financial struggles has prompted drastic changes. Trying to benefit from the cost advantages it had over other airlines, Continental's former CEO Frank Lorenzo did away with labor contracts and drove the company into bankruptcy. Customer service was deemed less important than turning a profit, ultimately causing the company to suffer.

Under the leadership of CEO Gordon Bethune, Continental strives for better business practices. Quality is an important factor, as the airline continues to work toward improving customer satisfaction. Additional earlier flights have better accommodated business travelers, along with additional domestic and international flights which strengthen alliances. Money-losing businesses were dropped, with increased attention to creating more traffic in its existing hubs.

A survey done in June 1996 showed Continental to be first among other airlines in customer service for flights longer than 500 miles. The previous year it had ranked last among nine major carriers. Former analysts stated the company's new image will take time to develop. 1996's net income of $319 million was a 42.2 percent increase from 1995. In 1997 the company reported a net income of $385 million with $1 billion in cash and cash equivalents.

FAST FACTS:
About Continental Airlines, Inc.

Ownership: Continental Airlines, Inc. is a publicly owned company traded on the New York Stock Exchange.

Ticker symbol: CAIB

Officers: Gordon M. Bethune, Chmn. & CEO, 56, 1997 base salary $755,750; Lawrence W. Kellner, Exec. VP & CFO, 39, 1997 base salary $427,172; Gregory D. Brenneman, 36, base salary $583,410

Employees: 39,300 (17,100 customer service agents, reservation agents, ramp, and other airport personnel; 7,000 flight attendants; 6,300 management and clerical employees; 5,500 pilots; 3,300 mechanics; and 100 dispatchers)

Principal Subsidiary Companies: Continental Airlines, Inc.'s wholly owned subsidiaries are Continental Express, Inc. ("Express") and Continental Micronesia, Inc. ("CMI"), serving 191 airports globally.

Chief Competitors: The airline industry vies with its competitors who may have more resources and lower cost structures. Some primary competitors include: Air France; Alaska Air; and All Nippon Airways.

CURRENT TRENDS

In keeping with its newfound strategy, Continental has been operating in ways to increase business. Acquisitions, merger talks, and an intensive focus on customer satisfaction have all composed more recent trends for the company. In the late 1990s the company was using its proven strategy for growth opportunities. Intending to increase traffic, Continental announced a bid made in April 1997 for a 20-percent interest in Argentine carrier Aerolineas Argentinas. The company's interest in the airline exemplifies its efforts to expand in profitable markets.

Another interest Continental has shown has been for a possible merger with Delta Air Lines in late 1996. If the merger were to come full circle, the two companies would form the largest airline in the world. Sources have said Continental initiated the merger talks with Delta. With Delta's stronger presence in Europe, Continental would gain greater access there, while Delta would ben-

CHRONOLOGY:

Key Dates for Continental Airlines, Inc.

1937: Robert Forman Six purchases 40 percent interest in Varney Speed Lines and changes the name to Continental Airlines

1945: Continental acquires numerous aircraft through military surplus

1955: Service rights between Chicago, Denver, and Los Angeles bring the company into competition with other national carriers for the first time

1964: Forms Continental Air Services to transport U.S. troops to and from southeast Asia

1980: Continental attempts to merge with Western Airlines

1981: Texas Airlines acquires Continental

1983: Continental files for Chapter 11 bankruptcy

1990: Texas Airlines changes their name to Continental Airlines Holdings, Inc.

1996: A survey shows Continental to be first in customer service for flights longer than 500 miles

efit from Continental's strengths in South and Central America.

Continental has formed a significant alliance with Northwest. The joint venture includes the KLM Royal Dutch Airlines. The alliance includes schedule and airport facility coordination and other activities.

The company has aimed to maintain its high ratings with customers as it has implemented a new frequent flier policy. In an attempt to attract other airlines' customers, Continental has targeted elite passengers with the automatic enrollment of its One Pass frequent-flyer program if customers have existing elite status from another airline. Looking to capitalize on the business travel market, the company has hoped to attract business passengers who often purchase last-minute tickets at much higher rates.

CORPORATE CITIZENSHIP

The company's recent success has brought much attention and praise. Since 1995 Continental Airlines, Inc.

has received numerous awards for its performance. In 1995 it was named *Business Week's* NYSE "Stock of the Year." *Fortune* also name its stock "Best Investment" of 1995. The following year it earned the J.D. Power/ Frequent Flyer award for Best Airline for Customer Satisfaction for Flights 500 Miles or More. Two other awards were given to the company in 1997 as well. In February the company was called "Airline of the Year" by *Air Transport World,* and in April, *Smart Money* magazine named Continental's Business First the top business class among U.S. Airlines.

GLOBAL PRESENCE

As of 1998, Continental Airlines, Inc. provides service to 125 cities in the United States. It also services 66 international destinations to Asia, Australia, Europe, and Latin America. The company's hubs are in Cleveland at Hopkins International Airport; Houston at George Bush Intercontinental Airport; and Newark at Newark International. With the company's recent alliance with Northwest, Continental will "connect with Northwest's hubs in Minneapolis, Detroit, and Memphis." With its new code-sharing agreement with CSA Czech Airlines, Continental has increased its service in Newark and Cleveland as well.

Upgrading its reputation, as of March 1998 Continental has commitments to purchase 154 jet aircraft from Boeing Co., estimated to be a $6.7-billion investment. Awaiting board approval, Continental's decision stems from its plans for international expansion.

EMPLOYMENT

Continental believes their employees are its greatest resource, with strengths in reliability and providing customer satisfaction. The company utilizes a varied communication process with its employees, which includes updates on company oriented bulletins, publications, and videotapes.

SOURCES OF INFORMATION

Bibliography

Boisseau, Charles. "Continental's Net Income Soars; Pilots to Seek Big Wage Increases." *Houston Chronicle,* 21 January 1997. Available at http://www.chron.com.

"Continental Airlines." *AeroWorldNet,* 27 January 1997. Available at http://www.aeroworldnet.com.

"Continental Airlines, Inc." *Hoover's Online,* 23 August 1998. Available at http://www.hoovers.com.

Continental Airlines, Inc.'s Home Page, May 1998. Available at http://www.flycontinental.com.

"Continental Airlines Interested in Buying Stake in Aerolineas Argentinas." *San Diego Daily Transcript,* 9 April 1997. Available at http://www.sddt.com.

"Continental to Fly Solo with Boeing?" *MSNBC,* 1997. Available at http://www.msnbc.com.

Graczyk, Michael. "Continental Airlines Shows Improved Earnings." *San Diego Daily Transcript,* 22 April 1996. Available at http://sddt.com.

Levere, Jane L. "Continental Airlines Is Wooing Elite-Level Frequent Fliers From Its Competitors." *The New York Times,* 31 January 1996. Available at http://search.nytimes.com.

Schwartz, Karen. "Delta, Continental Holding Merger Talks." *San Diego Daily Transcript,* 4 December 1996. Available at http://www.sddt.com.

For an annual report:

on the Internet at: http://www.edgar-online.com

For additional industry research:

Investigate companies by their Standard Industrial Classification Codes, also known as SICs. Continental's primary SIC is:

4512 Air Transport Scheduled

Converse, Inc.

FOUNDED: 1908

Contact Information:

HEADQUARTERS: 1 Fordham Rd.
   North Reading, MA 01864
PHONE: (508)664-1100
FAX: (508)664-7258
URL: http://www.converse.com

OVERVIEW

Converse, Inc. manufactures athletic shoes and sells them at its 31 company-operated retail stores. Converse led the athletic footwear market for many years with the Chuck Taylor All Star basketball shoe, but when the company encountered brisk competition in the 1980s and 1990s, its sales dropped below those of companies such as Nike, Reebok, and Fila. Nonetheless, Converse still ranks among the six leading athletic footwear producers in the United States. Converse remains well below Nike and Reebok, which in 1997 held 47 and 15 percent of the U.S. athletic shoe market, respectively. In the 1990s Converse Inc.'s revenues fluctuated in part because of the fickle nature of the athletic shoe market, much of which is made up of male adolescents under age 17. In 1997 sales totalled a record $450.2 million, a 28.9 percent increase from 1996. The company registered sales of $349.0 million in 1996, a 14 percent increase over 1995 revenues of $300.0 million. Converse also performed well in 1994 with revenues of $437.0, a 15 percent climb from sales of about $371.0 million in 1993. To remain competitive and increase its share of the sportswear market, Converse plans to continue introducing new shoe lines fortified by endorsements from professional athletes and to enhance its athletic apparel presence.

COMPANY FINANCES

Converse's 1997 sales totalled $450.2 million, a 28.9 percent increase from 1996. Domestic sales represented

63.0 percent of the company's net sales. Non-U.S. net sales accounted for 36.7 percent of total revenues in 1997, compared to 44.4 percent in 1996.

FINANCES:

Converse
Net Sales, 1994-1997
(million dollars)

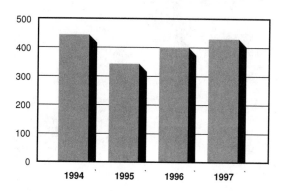

ANALYSTS' OPINIONS

Industry observers expressed mixed feelings about Converse Inc.'s efforts to hasten its turnaround. Some maintain that changing the company logo to the Chuck Taylor patch will not inspire the double-digit growth Converse expects. According to Mark Tedeschi in *Sporting Goods Business,* analysts believe the company's reliance on Dennis Rodman's endorsement is poor, since the endorsement may fail to drum up substantial new sales because of waning consumer interest in Rodman and competition from Nike's Jordan collection. Even though many observers feel the company lacks a broad enough product focus, they contend that Converse will experience new growth, but at a moderate rate.

Converse
1997 Stock Prices
(dollars)

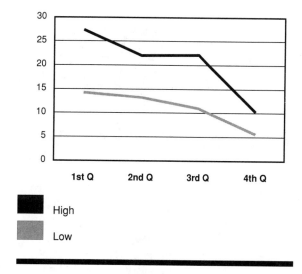

HISTORY

In 1908 Marquis M. Converse established Converse Inc.'s ancestor, Converse Rubber Co., in Malden, Massachusetts. After two years of operation, Converse Rubber generated an average of 4,000 boots per day. In 1917 the company launched its most popular shoe of all time, the All Star basketball shoe. The All Star led the company to popularity and prosperity, especially when it received the endorsement of basketball player Chuck Taylor in 1921.

However, in 1929 financial troubles hit Converse and the company went bankrupt. Mitchell B. Kaufman took over Converse in 1929 and ran it until he died just a year later. At that point, Albert Welchsler became the company's owner, but by 1933 Welchsler could no longer afford to run the company, which had experienced poor profits due to the Great Depression. In 1933 the Stone family bought Converse and operated it for 39 years, watching it grow into a major footwear contender. During World War II Converse supplied the U.S. military with footwear and outerwear. After the war Converse shifted its focus back to the consumer market, opening two new plants for large scale production.

In the 1970s Converse began to diversify, adding hockey pucks, boots, and teethguards to its repertoire of products. Converse also created three sales divisions—sporting goods, footwear, and industrial products—to oversee its assorted products. In 1972 Converse changed hands again when Eltra Corporation purchased the company from the Stone family. Eltra held on to the company through most of the 1970s as Converse expanded and acquired other companies. However, when the economy soured in the late 1970s, Eltra's parent company, Allied Corporation, took control of Converse. In 1982 Allied abandoned the consumer market and sought a buyer for Converse, which by then was the leading producer of basketball shoes, manufacturing 12 million pairs of shoes a year. Executives at Eltra eventually bought Converse from Allied for $100 million and took the company public in 1983.

The company's next owner, Interco, acquired Converse in 1986 and sales rose to $315 million the follow-

A pair of authentic Converse All Star hightop athletic shoes. (Courtesy of Converse.)

FAST FACTS:

About Converse, Inc.

Ownership: Converse, Inc. is a publicly owned company traded on the New York Stock Exchange.

Ticker symbol: CVE

Officers: Glenn N. Rupp, Chmn. & CEO, 53, 1997 base salary $476,538; Donald J. Camacho, Sr. VP & CFO, 47, 1997 base salary $192,837; James E. Solomon, Sr. VP Marketing, 42, 1997 base salary $285,577

Employees: 2,249

Principal Subsidiary Companies: Converse has 17 international subsidiaries in France, Netherlands, Belgium, Germany, Portugal, Spain, Italy, Japan, Scandinavia, Mexico, Brazil, and Barbados.

Chief Competitors: Competition in the athletic footwear market considers fashion, price, quality, performance, and durability. Some primary competitors include: Reebok International, Inc.; adidas AG; and Nike Inc.

ing year. However, its new parent company suffered from a series of financial problems and filed for bankruptcy in 1991. Converse remained an Interco subsidiary until November 1994 when the ailing company sold its shares of Converse, spinning off the shoe maker as an independent company.

STRATEGY

From its entrance into the athletic shoe market, Converse has used endorsements of famous athletes to promote its products. Basketball player Chuck Taylor promoted the company in the 1920s and 1930s, and basketball stars such as Earvin "Magic" Johnson and Dennis Rodman carried the company's banner in the 1990s. Converse has sought to diversify its footwear offerings and expand its product line to include more athletic apparel. In 1996, apparel represented $9 million of the company's total sales, and the company projected a 10-percent increase for apparel in 1997.

In the mid-1990s, Converse removed its star and chevron logo of the 1980s and 1990s, replacing it with the Chuck Taylor patch. In 1996 Converse introduced a new line of basketball shoes, the All Star 2000, as part of its campaign to increase new product offerings. Furthermore, Converse eliminated its baseball and football shoes and tightened its focus on basketball, cross-training, leisure, and children's shoes. Converse also renovated a North Carolina production plant so it could produce more shoes in the United States, thereby expediting the company's shoe deliveries.

INFLUENCES

Because of the initial success of the All Star shoes, Converse relied on them to drive its sales. This strategy helped the company become the leading basketball-footwear provider for many years. Eventually this success eclipsed the company's vision. Consequently, Converse failed to continue developing innovative shoes as competition in the athletic footwear market started to intensify in the 1970s. Companies such as Nike and Reebok introduced leather performance shoes (previous models had been canvas), which received a strong response from both consumers and players. However, in the 1980s Converse followed this trend and launched numerous new athletic shoe styles, boosting its sales by 400 percent.

Converse Inc. also learned some lessons from its disastrous 1995 acquisition of Apex One Inc., a producer of licensed athletic apparel from professional sports teams. Converse quickly attempted to increase its presence in the apparel market by purchasing the nearly bankrupt Apex One, but Apex had fallen so far behind in delivering products to retailers that the retailers scaled back business with Apex or severed their connections completely. As a result, Converse lost $41 million from the purchase and closed the apparel manufacturer just three months after buying it.

CURRENT TRENDS

With the 1997 emergence of two professional women's basketball leagues as part of the Women's Professional Basketball Association (WNBA), athletic-shoe producers expanded their basketball shoe lines to target women for what some analysts predicted may be the fastest growing product area. As of 1997, only Nike and Reebok sold women's basketball shoes, but others (including Converse) planned to introduce them in 1998.

PRODUCTS

Part of Converse Inc.'s plan to improve its sales included the introduction of new high-performance and athlete-endorsed shoes. In 1996 Converse rolled out its All Star 2000 shoes, which proved popular and helped the company improve its sales. To compete with Nike's

CHRONOLOGY:
Key Dates for Converse, Inc.

1908: Marquis M. Converse establishes the Converse Rubber Company

1917: Converse introduces the Converse canvas All Star, one of the first basketball shoes

1921: Charles "Chuck" Taylor becomes the brand's first endorser

1929: Converse Rubber Company files for bankruptcy

1933: The Stone family purchases Converse

1953: Converse establishes the Coastal Footwear Corporation in Puerto Rico

1972: Eltra Corporation purchases Converse ending the Stone Family's 39 years of ownership

1977: Converse is contracted as the official shoe of USA Basketball

1979: Allied Corporation takes over control of Converse from Eltra

1982: Allied abandons the consumer market and seeks a buyer for Converse

1983: Eltra buys back Converse and takes it public

1986: Interco Incorporated acquires Converse

1994: Interco spins off Converse and it becomes an independent public company

1996: Converse introduces the All Star 2000 in an effort to increase new product offerings

Air Jordan concept, Converse decided to launch a series of four shoes designed around the styles of Dennis Rodman. The first style released featured splashy colors, while the remaining were planned to be more conservative, given the lukewarm response to the first. In addition, Converse continued to manufacture and market its classic Chuck Taylor All Star canvas athletic shoe, which sold more than 560 million pairs since its introduction.

Recently Converse used its tag and marketing statement "Stay True." The reasoning behind this slogan is that athletes should "stay true" to themselves, be proud of their success, and appreciate those who have helped them succeed.

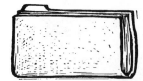

THESE SHOES WERE MADE FOR BASKETBALL

One of Converse, Inc.'s greatest accomplishments came early in its history, in 1917. That year brought Converse its most successful product, its trademark All Star basketball shoes. At that point, basketball was still in an embryonic stage, invented fewer than 30 years earlier in 1891 by James Naismith at the International YMCA Training School.

Nonetheless, with the endorsement and marketing abilities of basketball star Charles "Chuck" Taylor, the shoes' success soared to great heights. Taylor joined the company in 1921 and his signature was added to the shoe in 1923, helping launch Converse All Stars as the standard for basketball players for many years. Since no professional teams had been established, Taylor built his reputation as a basketball player in high school and adult leagues. While working for Converse, Taylor traveled around the country, hosting basketball clinics, meeting coaches, and promoting his signature Chuck Taylor All Stars.

Eventually, Taylor was inducted into the Naismith Memorial Hall of Fame. The shoe has a kind of "hall of fame" status as well—the Chuck Taylor All Star canvas athletic shoe has sold over 560 million pairs since its introduction.

CORPORATE CITIZENSHIP

Federal, state, and local laws monitor companies regarding possible environmental contamination, such as waste disposal and emission of various materials. The main materials used in Converse's shoes are canvas, linen, and rubber. The company believes any negative environmental claims they may incur will not affect its business.

Converse maintains a state-of-the-art biomechanics research laboratory that supports an ongoing search for new technology and enhancements to shoes geared for specific sports. The company's patented REACT shock absorption technology acts as a cushion in certain areas of the shoes' construction to protect athletes' feet from high impact.

From 1936 to 1984 Converse sponsored the Summer Olympic Games and provided footwear for the ath-

letes. In addition, Converse has funded an abundance of basketball organizations and events around the world. The sportswear company supported USA Basketball, which organizes basketball teams to represent the United States in worldwide basketball tournaments. Converse also has sponsored international basketball organizations including the World Association of Basketball Coaches and Federation Internationale de Basketball, an organization composed of members from 176 countries.

GLOBAL PRESENCE

Converse products are marketed in 90 countries outside the United States. Foreign sales in 1997 were 36.7 percent of total earnings, compared with 44.4 percent in 1996. Although the majority of the company's footwear is sourced from various Far East factories, most of the athletic originals products are manufactured domestically. In 1997, 16 manufacturers in China, Taiwan, Macau, Vietnam, and the Philippines sold over 13.3 million pairs of shoes to Converse.

EMPLOYMENT

Converse has a 38-member sales force that markets its footwear through approximately 4,200 active retail accounts. In 1997 domestic sales represented 63 percent of the company's net sales. The 13 account executives who service national and regional accounts are paid salaries plus bonuses. The company has a non-contributory pension plan for domestic salaried employees based on years of service and final annual compensation. Hourly employees also have a non-contributory defined contribution plan. Converse also sponsors a savings plan and offers stock options to key employees. In addition, the company has a Non-Employee Director's Plan, which encourages non-employees of outstanding ability to enter and remain with the company as directors.

SOURCES OF INFORMATION

Bibliography

Cohen, Kerstan. *International Directory of Company Histories.* Detroit, MI: St. James Press, 1994.

Gaffney, Andrew. "Glenn Rupp: Chairman/CEO, Converse Inc." *Sporting Goods Business,* September 1996.

Galaraza, Pablo. "Converse: Walk, Don't Run." *Financial World,* 29 August 1995.

Maremont, Mark. "How Converse Got Its Laces Tangled." *Business Week,* 4 September 1995.

Tedeschi, Mark. "Converse, Following Sluggish Spring Sales, Draws Mixed Review with 1998 Focus." *Sporting Goods Business,* 7 August 1997.

For an annual report:

on the Internet at: http://www.edgar-online.com

For additional industry research:

Investigate companies by their Standard Industrial Classification Codes, also known as SICs. Converse's primary SICs are:

5136 Men's/Boys' Clothing

5137 Women's/Children's Clothing

5139 Footwear

Dayton Hudson Corporation

FOUNDED: 1969

Contact Information:
HEADQUARTERS: 777 Nicollet Mall
   Minneapolis, MN 55402
PHONE: (612)370-6948
FAX: (612)370-5502
URL: http://www.dhc.com

DAYTON HUDSON CORPORATION

OVERVIEW

Dayton Hudson Corporation is a general merchandise retailer that may be more commonly known by its subsidiaries: The Department Store Division, Mervyn's California, and Target. The Department Store Division consists of 67 Dayton's, Hudson's, and Marshall Field's stores spread over nine states. The 295 Mervyn's California stores offer name brand casual apparel and home goods, and operate in 16 states. Target is a discount chain consisting of over 700 stores in 33 states. Customers are typically families and merchandise is varied, from trendy clothing to household goods. All of Dayton Hudson's customers are referred to as "guests." Overall, Dayton Hudson owns over 1,140 stores in 39 states.

COMPANY FINANCES

In fiscal year 1997 (ending January 31, 1998), revenues were $27.76 billion, a nine-percent increase over the previous fiscal year. Financial data for the past five years is as follows (all amounts shown are in millions): Revenue for 1997, $27,757; 1996, $25,371; 1995, $23,516; 1994, $21,311; and 1993, $19,233; net earnings for 1997, $751; 1996, $463; 1995, $311; 1994, $434, and 1993, $375; earnings per common share for 1997, $1.80; 1996, $1.05; 1995, $0.67; 1994, $1.70; 1993, $1.00. Of 1997 revenues, 74 percent were from Target, 15 percent were from Mervyn's, and the Department Store Division contributed 11 percent of revenues.

ANALYSTS' OPINIONS

Many industry analysts consider Dayton Hudson stock a stable or growth-oriented investment. Zacks research analysts, overall, recommend Dayton Hudson stocks. Of 14 brokers surveyed, seven call Dayton Hudson stock a "strong buy," four recommend it as a "moderate buy," and three recommend holding existing stocks. None suggested selling the Dayton Hudson stocks. Dayton Hudson stocks are ranked 11 of 24 within its industry. Zacks analysts further predict an increase in per share price from fiscal year 1997 to fiscal year 1998.

Dayton Hudson itself was "comfortable" with estimates conducted by median analysts for fiscal year 1998; a 16-percent growth for the year was predicted. Additionally, on May 19, 1998, Merrill Lynch announced that it had raised its estimates for Dayton Hudson based on first-quarter earnings exceeding earlier expectations.

HISTORY

The Dayton Hudson Corporation has its origins in companies founded more than 100 years ago and has a long history of acquisitions and expansions. In 1881 the J.L. Hudson Company was founded in Detroit. Over 20 years later, in 1902, the Dayton Company was founded in Minneapolis. The two companies didn't actually merge until 1969. In the meantime, however, the Dayton Company acquired J.B. Hudson, a jeweler in Minneapolis, in 1929. In 1956 Dayton opened Southdale, marking the origins of the mall concept—Southdale was the world's first completely enclosed two-tier shopping center. In 1954, J.L. Hudson opened Northland Center in Detroit, and it was the world's largest shopping center at that time. Entering its foray into discount chain stores, Dayton opened the first Target store in 1962. In 1966 Dayton created B. Dalton Bookseller and made its stock publicly available in 1967. Also in 1967, J.B. Hudson and Shreve and Co. merged to form Dayton Jewelers. A merger of Dayton Department Store, Lipmans, and Diamond's occurred in 1968, and in 1969 the Dayton Hudson Corporation was formed when Dayton Corporation and J.L. Hudson Company merged. Dayton Hudson continued to acquire companies including Lechmere, a hardgoods retailer out of Boston, and J.E. Caldwell, a jewelry chain based in Philadelphia. In 1971 revenues reached the $1 billion mark. In 1978 Dayton Hudson Corporation acquired Mervyn's; this made the company the seventh-largest merchandise retailer in the United States. In 1982 revenues reached the $5 billion mark. Annual revenues exceeded $10 billion in 1987, $20 billion in 1994, and $25 billion in 1996.

STRATEGY

Dayton Hudson's financial strategy involves keeping capital markets liquid, managing the amount of float-

FINANCES:

Dayton Hudson Corp.
Revenues, 1994-1997
(billion dollars)

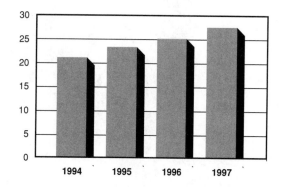

Dayton Hudson Corp.
1997 Stock Prices
(dollars)

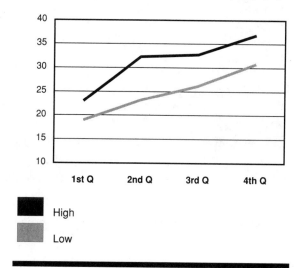

ing-rate debt, and maintaining a balanced range of debt maturities. The Target proprietary credit card, called the Target Guest Card, asserts the subsidiary's brand identity and elevates shoppers to a status usually associated with non-discount chains or upscale department stores. Mervyn's' individual strategy involved offering more national brands, such as Union Bay, Dockers, Villager by Liz Claiborne, and Haggar City Casuals. In a more focused marketing effort, Mervyn's vacated its Florida and Georgia markets in 1997 and closed seven other stores. Mervyn's also remodeled existing stores and invested in new fixtures and vendor merchandise shops for approx-

Marshall Field's store in Chicago, Illinois, as it appeared in 1879. (*Courtesy of Dayton Hudson Corporation.*)

imately 175 stores. Strategies for 1998 include installing vendor shops and completely renovating 10 store locations. The Department Store Division expanded its merchandise line for both vendor products and its own merchandise. In 1997 Hudson's of Port Huron, Michigan, and Marshall Field's in Columbus, Ohio, opened while two stores under the Department Store Division that were under-performing were closed.

Dayton Hudson continues to focus strategic efforts in the direction of the Target Guest Card to build customer loyalty. Strategies also involve consolidating operations and distributing data regarding key trends among

its divisions. Dayton Hudson's long-range earnings growth objective is 15 percent or better.

Perhaps Dayton Hudson's biggest strategic undertaking is the implementation of its common information systems. Formerly, all of the finance, credit, sales processing, inventory management, and personnel systems were on a mainframe and handled independently through Dayton Hudson's three main divisions. Distribution centers and stores used client/server systems. Dayton Hudson is switching to an IP-based wide area network; the goal is to improve inventory management, which could result in a potential savings of $100 million annually.

Also, the three divisions will be better able to facilitate the exchange and distribution of key trends and best practices. It is too soon to tell whether or not the strategy will pay off; if it fails, customer service would likely suffer, earnings may drop, and the system could turn out to be just too complex to handle. Dayton Hudson feels it's a risk worth taking because its ultimate success could result in a revolution in the 150-year-old retail industry. The control of labor and merchandise and a clear picture of consumers' needs are among the possible changes that could result. The way Dayton Hudson is handling the three-year project is by dividing it into hundreds of smaller projects with shorter turnaround times of six to twelve months in length.

INFLUENCES

Dayton Hudson's strategies have been influenced by pressure to improve financial performance or consider a merger. In 1996 Dayton Hudson rejected J.C. Penney's proposal to buy Dayton Hudson at what was then a substantial increase in per share price. J.C. Penney offered a stock-and-cash proposal of $90 to $95 per share while Dayton Hudson's stock was at $76. The bid would have been worth $6.82 billion. Although Target is Dayton Hudson's primary revenue producer, it is somewhat offset by the marginal profits of the mid-line Mervyn's. Thomas Buynak, an analyst at Society Asset Management, said, "This offer ups the pressure to deliver results and focus on their overall game plan." Dayton Hudson's Target chain represents about two-thirds of total sales and profits, so it is an attractive takeover choice.

CURRENT TRENDS

Besides the three-year plan to consolidate its systems operations, Dayton Hudson plans to continue its growth primarily through expansion and acquisition. In 1997 60 new Target stores were opened, including the retailer's first stores in Cincinnati, Philadelphia, and New York City. In April 1998 Dayton Hudson acquired Rivertown Trading, a direct marketing firm based in Minnesota. In October 1998 Dayton Hudson's Target division plans to open 23 new stores over 12 states, including its first store in Delaware. The stores will be opening in Exton, Pennsylvania; Wilmington, Delaware; Altoona, Pennsylvania; Princeton, Milltown, and Brick, New Jersey; Copiague, New York; College Point, Henrietta, and Victor, New York; Roanoke, Virginia; Kansas City, Missouri; Marietta and Douglasville, Georgia; Loveland, Colorado; Niles, Arlington Heights, and Highland Park, Illinois; Austin, Coon Rapids, and Fergus Falls, Minnesota; Watsonville, California; and Irving, Texas.

FAST FACTS:
About Dayton Hudson Corporation

Ownership: Dayton Hudson is a publicly owned company traded on the New York Stock Exchange.

Ticker symbol: DH

Officers: Robert J. Ulrich, Chmn. & CEO, 53; James T. Hale, Sr. VP, Gen. Counsel, & Sec., 56; Douglas A. Scovanner, Sr. VP & CFO, 41

Employees: 230,000

Principal Subsidiary Companies: Dayton Hudson Corporation owns and operates Dayton's, Hudson's, Marshall Field's, Target, and Mervyn's.

Chief Competitors: Dayton Hudson's primary competitors are both retail department stores and retail discount stores including: Ames Department Stores; Bradlees, Inc.; Dillard's, Inc.; J.C. Penney Company, Inc.; Kmart Corp.; Neiman-Marcus Group, Inc.; Sears, Roebuck & Co.; Strawbridge & Clothier; The Bon-Ton Stores, Inc.; The Caldor Corporation; Value City Department Stores; Wal-Mart Stores, Inc.; and Woolworth Corporation.

PRODUCTS

Dayton Hudson's Department Store Division has been focusing on expanding its own brands of merchandise in order to better penetrate the retail market and enhance company identification through product label. Products include Field Gear, Field Manor, 111 State, and Indeed. The Department Store Division has also been expanding its upscale merchandise to re-establish itself as a "fine" department store. The Division now offers Anne Klein II, Dana Buchman, Tommy Hilfiger, and Nautica. The Department Store Division also features a key trend or product in each of its stores. For example, in spring 1996 it introduced "The Player's Shop" to capitalize on the golf season. The shop was helped by the Dayton's Challenge Golf Tournament. Sales from golf equipment and apparel doubled over 1995.

Target competes with stores like K-Mart and Walmart by offering department-store quality merchandise at competitive discount prices. In 1996 Target launched a new line of its own products called Cherokee, consisting mainly of high quality casual wear such as t-shirts and sweatshirts. In its first six months, the Cherokee line exceeded the 18-month sales plan by $50 million.

CHRONOLOGY:

Key Dates for Dayton Hudson Corporation

1881: The J.L. Hudson Company is founded in Detroit, Michigan

1902: The Dayton Company is founded in Minneapolis, Minnesota

1938: Dayton's founder George Draper Dayton dies

1944: Dayton becomes one of the first stores to offer its workers a retirement policy

1954: Hudson opens the world's largest shopping center, Northland Center, in Detroit

1956: Dayton opens Southdale, the world's first completely enclosed, two-tier shopping center

1962: Dayton opens the first Target store

1967: The Dayton Corporation goes public

1969: Hudson and Dayton merge to become the Dayton Hudson Corporation

1978: Dayton Hudson acquires Mervyn's

1987: Dayton Hudson survives a hostile takeover attempt by Dart Group as well as a bogus counteroffer from an investor who, it was later revealed, had no financial backing

1997: Dayton Hudson receives the President's Service Award for its community service programs

---

Mervyn's plans to continually increase the name brands offered and to enhance product presentation in its stores. For example, Mervyn's added Fila and adidas to its athletic footwear merchandise offered and implemented in-store shops to increase brand recognition.

CORPORATE CITIZENSHIP

Dayton Hudson sponsors many community involvement programs through grants and volunteer work. In 1997 Dayton Hudson received the nation's highest honor for community service, the President's Service Award, for its Family Matters program. In June 1997 Dayton Hudson held a "Week of Giving," which involved thousands of volunteers committed to improving their communities. Dayton Hudson held the Week of Giving again in May 1998 and more than 10,000 youths were involved. Dayton Hudson's goal is to conduct a Week of Giving initiative in all of the markets it occupies. The company predicts as many as 1,000 of these projects may be completed.

Wherever Dayton Hudson opens a Target store, it establishes a Good Neighbor Volunteer Program, targeting the resolution of a specific community issue through volunteerism; over $1 million a week will be donated to the communities totaling over $57 million in grants in 1998. Target has given five percent of pretax dollars to communities having a Target store since its founding in 1962. In 1997 Dayton Hudson made over $46 million in donations to art, social, and education groups. It donated $2.8 million in corporate contributions to United Way organizations, and Dayton Hudson employees were responsible for an additional $10.2 million given to the United Way. Over $2.6 million in scholarships were provided by Dayton Hudson and over half a million dollars was raised for local schools by the Target Guest Card initiative; this program, called School Fundraising Made Simple, provided one percent of purchases made on Target Guest Cards to a school of the customer's choice.

Although Target makes the most donations and boasts the most revenue of the Dayton Hudson divisions, Mervyn's is also involved in community service. In 1997 its Childspree program provided 14,000 needy children with school supplies and clothes. Mervyn's also provides funding for workshops where parents learn to work with their children to help them succeed in school. Over 50,000 parents and children are involved in the program.

The Department Store Division initiated a fundraising effort for ten art and cultural groups through Hudson's, which provided a grant of $0.5 million, plus an additional $1 million to match community donations.

EMPLOYMENT

Dayton Hudson stresses a fast-paced environment in its recruitment efforts. It also holds numerous on-the-job training programs. Dayton Hudson had 230,000 employees as of the end of fiscal year 1997; of those, 166,000 were employed at Target, 29,000 at Mervyn's, and 35,000 in the Department Store Division.

SOURCES OF INFORMATION

Bibliography

"Company News On Call." *PR Newswire,* 13 July 1998. Available at http://www.prnewswire.com/AREPORTS/342677.6.

"Dayton Hudson Corp." *Yahoo! Finance,* 10 July 1998. Available at http://biz.yahoo.com/p/d/dh.html.

Dayton Hudson Home Page, 13 July 1998. Available at http://www.dhc.com.

"Hoovers Top Employers." *Hoover's Online,* 10 July 1998. Available at http://www.hoovers.com/browsetop/topd.html.

For an annual report:

on the Internet at: http://www.prnewssire.com/AREPORTS/342677.6 **or** write: Dayton Hudson Corporation, Investor Relations, 777 Nicollet Mall, Minneapolis, MN 55402-2055

For additional industry research:

Investigate companies by their Standard Industrial Classification Codes, also known as SICs. Dayton Hudson's primary SIC is:

5311 Department Stores

Deere & Co.

FOUNDED: 1836

Contact Information:
HEADQUARTERS: 1 Deere Pl.
  Moline, IL 61265-8098
PHONE: (309)765-8000
FAX: (309)765-5772
URL: http://www.deere.com

OVERVIEW

Despite some tough sledding during the recession of the early 1990s and a period of low farm prices, Deere remains the world's largest manufacturer of farm equipment. The company has also remained a top manufacturer of industrial and lawn-care machinery. Equipment produced by the company includes tractors, harvesters, sprayers, and crop-maintenance machinery. It also manufactures construction equipment, diesel engines, chain saws, snowblowers, and lawn trimmers. Deere & Co. has also added financial services to its growing list of operations, offering insurance and leasing to its customers worldwide.

Founded in 1836 by John Deere, the company has come a long way from its origins in a blacksmith shop in a tiny Illinois village to become a huge diversified corporation reaching most of the world's major markets. Sales from its worldwide operations totaled $12.6 billion in 1997 and produced net earnings of $960 million.

The company's involvement in overseas markets, begun when it launched its first foreign operation in Canada in 1931, has grown substantially. In 1996, 25 percent of the company's total revenue was derived from overseas operations. With operations and sales in most regions of the world, Deere is better able to weather a sale slump in one area by concentrating its selling efforts in other regions not affected by the slump.

Throughout its long history Deere & Co. has placed a high priority on giving something back to the communities in which it operates. Through its John Deere Foundation, the company has contributed substantially to such causes as human services, community development, education, and cultural enrichment. Such contributions in 1997 exceeded $11 million.

COMPANY FINANCES

Deere & Co. posted net earnings of $960 million on revenue of $12.6 billion in 1997, compared with $817 million on revenue of $11.1 billion in 1996. Per-share earnings of $3.78 in 1997 were up substantially from $3.14 in 1996. Per-share earnings in 1995 and 1994 were $2.71 and $2.33, respectively. By far the biggest share of Deere's sales came from farm equipment, which generated 56 percent of total revenue. Sales of construction equipment accounted for 18 percent of total revenue, followed by 14 percent from sales of commercial and consumer equipment, 6 percent from credit operations, and 6 percent from insurance and health care.

ANALYSTS' OPINIONS

Many analysts have been impressed with Deere's rebound since its struggles in the early 1990s. With its global presence expanding and worldwide opportunities emerging, many experts remain hopeful. However, some point out that the company has not completely emerged from danger. Analysts contend that Deere's markets are slow-growing in nature. Some also anticipate fierce competition with companies like Case.

Other controversies surrounding Deere, which have concerned analysts, have included contract talks between the company and the United Auto Workers (UAW) in the late 1990s. Although it was known for its unusually good employee relations, the company faced tough talks, raising fears of a strike. Eventually, Deere and the union were able to hammer out an agreement, but analysts say the UAW still has concerns about some issues, including the company's tendency to outsource much of its work, which could threaten current employees with the loss of their jobs. Deere, however, believes its employee relations have remained positive.

HISTORY

In 1896 John Deere opened a blacksmith shop in Grand Detour, Illinois. Soon after, Deere began searching for a way to plow black Midwestern soil, since the plows used at the time caused the soil to stick to the blades. In 1837 he designed a circular saw that moved so fast it was called "the whistling plow." By 1838 he had sold only 3, but by 1842 he was making 1,300 per year.

Charles Deere (John's son) came aboard in 1853, starting a long-running custom of family management. Looking to expand, Charles Deere established a distribution system to dealerships and broadened product lines. In fact, in the 1900s the company bought other agricultural equipment manufacturers and produced internal

FINANCES:

Deere & Co.
Net Sales & Revenues, 1994-1997
(billion dollars)

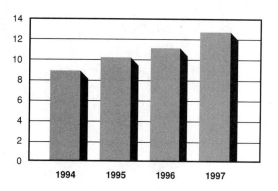

Deere & Co.
1997 Stock Prices
(dollars)

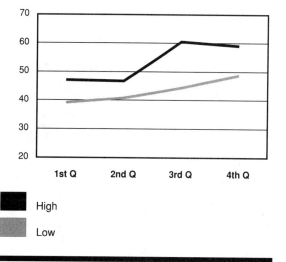

■ High

▨ Low

combustion engines for its harvesting equipment and tractors.

Deere & Co. launched its first foreign operations in Canada in 1931. After 1958, when the company surpassed International Harvester, Deere & Co. was the biggest agricultural equipment manufacturer in the United States; it became the largest in the world by 1963. Eventually, overseas business grew to include Mexico, Argentina, France, and Spain.

The industry was hit hard in 1986 and 1987, causing Deere's financial losses to reach $328 million.

The John Deere Model 9400 tractor. (Courtesy of Deere & Co.)

Nonetheless, it was the only company in the industry to maintain its ownership and not shut down factories during the financial strain of the 1980s. Shifting gears, Deere CEO Robert Hanson (the first company head not related to the family) invested more than $2 billion in research and development segments. By doing so, Deere & Company was able to produce its largest-ever new product line in 1989.

In the early 1990s Deere began expanding its lawn care equipment business to include Europe. By 1991 it had purchased a large interest in SABO Maschinenfabrik, a German producer of commercial lawn mowers. Deere & Co. also obtained distribution rights to Zetor tractors and Brno diesel engines from the Czech Republic, with the plan to sell them in Latin America and the Far East.

Expansion also occurred on Deere's home front. With an all-new tractor line introduced in 1994, Deere aimed to stay a jump or two ahead of the competition. The company purchased Homelite in 1994, thereby expanding its lines to include other hand-held outdoor power equipment.

Early in 1998 Deere reached a joint venture agreement with Springfield Remanufacturing Corporation of Springfield, Missouri. Under the agreement, a new organization will be formed to remanufacture diesel engines for Deere's agricultural and construction equipment divisions. The limited-liability joint venture, which will be named ReGen Technologies LLC, will also remanu-

facture engine-related components. ReGen Technologies was expected to begin operations before the end of 1998 in a newly constructed manufacturing facility in Springfield.

STRATEGY

Deere & Co. has based much of its business practices on the strategy of pursuing genuine value through constant improvement and profitable growth. Within these strategic goals, Deere has aimed for all of its businesses to emerge as leaders in their respective markets, while performing above customers' expectations. Deere also has sought out new markets for its exports from the United States, which led to the introduction of new products. Finally, Deere has expanded its financial services subsidiary, John Deere Credit, to include foreign markets for the first time in the company's history.

INFLUENCES

To enhance manufacturing and production, in 1993 the company used its hourly workers to make sales presentations and help market the company's products. This unique approach appears to have been beneficial, since profits have been on the rise since 1994. Deere adopted its approach as a result of a recession that took its toll on the company in the early 1990s. Also, competition from big companies like Caterpillar Inc. and declining farm incomes were reflected in Deere's $20-million loss in 1991. The company's CEO, Hans Becherer, sought to diversify into the financial services arena by offering the company's health maintenance programs to nonemployees. His move resulted in a 43-percent increase in this operation's profits in 1995.

CURRENT TRENDS

In recent years, encouraged by the dynamic growth in many of the world's economies, Deere & Co. has taken an increasingly global outlook, utilizing foreign acquisitions and licensing agreements to expand its worldwide network of businesses. In 1997 Deere acquired the assets of Maschinenfabrik Kemper GmbH, a German farm equipment manufacturer. This purchase has allowed Deere to expand its headers used with forage harvesters. Kemper, a major European manufacturer of farm machinery, continues to develop and manufacture its other products.

Licensing agreements have also allowed Deere to extend its name globally. Signing a deal with the Florsheim Company of Chicago in late 1996, Deere & Company agreed to allow Florsheim to use the Deere name on quality outdoor footwear and work boots. The company also planned to launch women's and children's footwear lines.

Finally, the company has added sponsorship of the PGA Tour and the Quad City Classic to its lineup of recent ventures. An agreement was signed in 1997 designating Deere as the title sponsor of the Quad City Classic for the period of 1998-2006. The PGA Tour was appointed to design, build, and operate a new Tournament Players Club golf course, named TPC at Deere Run, marking the home of the Quad City Classic. Deere also was designated as the Official Golf Course Equipment Supplier of the PGA Tour. With this title, the company assumed responsibility for supplying golf and turf equipment, construction supplies, and utility transportation.

PRODUCTS

As the world's largest manufacturer of farm equipment, Deere & Co. has a product line that, despite the company's ventures into other sectors, is still heavily weighted toward agricultural equipment. Its major tractor lines range from the 5000 TEN series and the 6000 TEN series through the 7000 TEN and 8000/8000T series to the 9000 series. Deere also offers CTS and Maximizer model combines, the PRO-Series cotton picker and the 7455 cotton stripper, a wide variety of baling

FAST FACTS:
About Deere & Co.

Ownership: Deere & Co. is a publicly owned company traded on the New York Stock Exchange.

Ticker symbol: DE

Officers: Hans W. Becherer, Chmn. & CEO, 62, $2,200,000; Joseph W. England, Sr. VP, Worldwide Parts & Corporate Administration, $740,000; John K. Lawson, Sr. VP, Engineering, Technology, & Human Resources, $690,000; Bernard L. Hardiek, Pres., Worldwide Agricultural Division, $840,000

Employees: 34,000

Chief Competitors: Deere & Co., a major diversified corporation with extensive operations in agricultural, construction, and commercial equipment as well as such financial services as credit and insurance, faces stiff competition in all the sectors in which it operates. Some of its major competitors include: Aetna; Black & Decker; Blue Cross; Case; Caterpillar; CIGNA; FMC; Ford; General Electric; Honda; Hyundai; Ingersoll-Rand; Kubota; Mitsubishi; Navistar; New Holland; Prudential; Toro; and Volvo.

equipment, sprayers, planting and seeding equipment, and tillers.

Deere & Co. also manufactures and markets a wide variety of construction equipment, including backhoes, excavators, motor graders, landscape loaders, scrapers, forklifts, skidders, crawler dozers, and crawler loaders. The company's John Deere Lawn & Garden division offers a full range of home-scale equipment for the maintenance of private lawns and gardens.

CORPORATE CITIZENSHIP

Deere & Co. has a long tradition of using its resources to benefit society, stretching back to the company's founding in 1836. Through the years the company has supported a wide variety of worthwhile nonprofit causes through direct corporate gifts and through the contribution of the time and talents of people and organizations associated with Deere & Co.

CHRONOLOGY:

Key Dates for Deere & Co.

1836: Founded by John Deere

1837: John Deere develops the circular plow blade

1853: Charles Deere begins to run the company

1868: Company is incorporated as Deere & Company

1874: The Gilpin Sulky Plow, which could plow three acres in 12 hours, is introduced

1898: The Deere Gang Plow, which could plow six acres in 12 hours, is introduced

1907: Charles Deere dies and William Butterworth succeeds him as president

1911: Acquires Van Brunt Manufacturing Company

1918: Waterloo Gasloline Engine Company, a tractor maker in Iowa, is bought

1928: Charles Deere Wiman, John Deere's great-grandson, becomes president

1931: Begins its first foreign operation in Canada

1963: Becomes the largest agricultural equipment manufacturer in the world

1969: Company begins running John Deere parts and service centers through the 3,700 independent dealers

1972: The John Deere bicycle is introduced to take advantage of the rapidly expanding market

1976: A six-week strike reduces inventory when demand for equipment remained strong

1982: Acquires Central National Life Insurance Company and expands into leasing operations

1986: Wins an $11 million military contract to develop an implement for repairing bomb-damaged runways

1994: Purchases Homelite

1996: Begins licensing agreement with Florsheim

1998: Begins joint venture with Springfield Remanufacturing Corp.

The company works through the John Deere Foundation to deliver its philanthropic support to those in need. According to company literature, the objective of the foundation is "to enhance the ability of the communities we serve to meet their growing needs and to pro-

vide the company with an established forward-looking program of charitable giving." In 1997 the company and its employees, through payrolls deductions, contributed more than $11 million to help support a variety of worthy causes. Among the areas addressed by Deere contributions were human services, community development, education, and cultural enrichment.

GLOBAL PRESENCE

Deere & Co. has made continuing efforts to expand its global presence selling agricultural equipment in more than 110 countries. In 1996 its overseas sales were responsible for one-fourth of the company's combined equipment sales. The company has been able to make greater inroads in a number of foreign markets with the easing of trade barriers. This has allowed Deere to manufacture tractors in Brazil—the biggest Latin American market. Deere also opened an office in Beijing and continues to seek production and marketing of agricultural equipment there. All in all, a rise in worldwide farm incomes coupled with flourishing economic climates in North America have contributed to the company's global expansion.

Consistent with its strategic goals, Deere & Company has been anxious to capitalize on growing economies around the world that have a higher demand for agricultural goods. The company recently expanded its international sales to include the Ukraine and Kazakhstan. These growing economies have also produced strong markets for industrial and construction equipment. Many of these nations are also looking for diesel engines with clean emissions and economic fuel consumption.

The popularity of golf in parts of Asia has resulted in increased sales of golf and turf equipment in that region. The rise in demand for golf course maintenance equipment has boosted Deere's financial assistance programs, particularly John Deere Credit, which has expanded to include Canada, Mexico, and the United Kingdom.

For Deere & Co., 1996 was a financially rewarding year for overseas operations. Sales leaped to $2.7 billion, an increase of over $500 million from the previous year. The company has cited sales increases in Europe, Australia, and Argentina as contributing factors for such growth. Deere also experienced a 30-percent increase of exports in the first quarter of 1997 due to healthy agricultural economies in Europe, Australia, and South Africa. It also signed a deal with the former Soviet republic of Ukraine to sell 1,049 combines—the biggest business deal in Deere's history. With overseas sales on the rise, Deere & Co. also increased its share of ownership in its Mexican and Brazilian businesses.

In late April 1998 Deere CEO Hans Becherer and Turkmenistan President Saparmurat Niyazov signed an agreement to establish long-term cooperation. The agreement calls for Deere to be the principal supplier of agricultural equipment to Turkmenistan, a former republic of the Soviet Union.

EMPLOYMENT

Deere & Co. offers a broad range of job opportunities in both technical and nontechnical disciplines. The company's steady growth ensures a continuing demand for qualified personnel to fill openings in both Deere's core equipment businesses and its subsidiary financial services operations.

SOURCES OF INFORMATION

Bibliography

Becherer, Hans W. "Letter to Stockholders." *1996 Annual Report.* Moline, IL: Deere & Company, 1997. Available at http://www.deere.com.

"Deere Announces 9-Year PGA TOUR Agreement." Deere & Co. Press Release, 2 April 1997. Available at http://www.deere.com.

"Deere & Co. and Springfield Remanufacturing Corporation Announce Joint Venture." Deere & Company Press Release, 15 January 1998. Available at http://www.deere.com/news/regen.htm.

"Deere & Company." *Hoover's Online,* 10 May 1998. Available at http://www.hoovers.com.

Deere & Company Home Page, 10 May 1998. Available at http://www.deere.com.

"Deere Signs Agreement with Turkmenistan." Deere & Company Press Release, 27 April 1998. Available at http://www.deere.com/news/turksign.htm.

"Deere to Acquire German Farm Machinery Company." Deere & Co. Press Release, 28 February 1997. Available at http://www.deere.com.

Elstrom, Peter. "Heavy Equipment Gets Into Gear." *Business Week,* 5 August 1996. Available at http://bwarchive.businessweek.

"John Deere Licenses Florsheim to Market Footwear Line." Deere & Co. Press Release, 8 April 1996. Available at http://www.deere.com.

Kelly, Kevin. "Deere's Surprising Harvest in Health Care." *Business Week,* 11 July 1994. Available at http://bwarchive.businessweek.

———. "The New Soul of John Deere." *Business Week,* 31 January 1994. Available at http://bwarchive.businessweek.

———. "Why the Talks at Deere Hit Bedrock." *Business Week,* 31 October 1994. Available at http://bwarchive.businessweek.

Magnusson, Paul. "How Badly Will the Dollar Whack the U.S.?" *Business Week,* 5 May 1997.

For an annual report:

on the Internet at: http://www.deere.com/aboutus/finpub/ **or** write: Stockholder Relations Dept., 1 John Deere Pl., Moline, IL 61265-8098

For additional industry research:

Investigate companies by their Standard Industrial Classification Codes, also known as SICs. Deere & Co.'s primary SICs are:

3519 Internal Combustion Engines, NEC

3523 Farm Machinery and Equipment

3524 Lawn and Garden Equipment

3531 Construction Machinery

Dell Computer Corporation

FOUNDED: 1983

Contact Information:

HEADQUARTERS: 2214 W. Braker Ln.
   Austin, TX 78758-4053
PHONE: (512)338-4400
FAX: (512)728-3330
TOLL FREE: (800)474-3355
URL: http://www.dell.com

OVERVIEW

Dell is the world's leading direct seller of computer systems. Head-to-head with chief rival Gateway 2000, the company's direct marketing allows it to offer products at a price lower than computers purchased through traditional sales channels, namely retailers or value-added resellers. The company sells computers assembled to order and does so in the higher margin markets. The company sells predominantly to corporate accounts, with less than 10 percent sold to individuals or home computer users.

Dell has grown rapidly, sometimes faster than the company could control. Doing well selling directly to customers, in the early 1990s Dell tried selling in retail stores and expanded product lines, both of which were unsuccessful. Refocusing on its core strategy and hiring experienced managers helped put Dell back on the right track. In mid-1998 Dell's stock reached a high of $114.25 per share; in 1990 it could have been purchased for $0.23 per share.

Michael Dell founded the company in his dorm room as a freshman at the University of Texas. He bought excess components from companies, built and sold computers, and noticing computer sales people weren't necessarily knowledgeable, offered over-the-telephone support. Dell figured that customers wanted technologically current, low-priced computers with good service. To save consumers money, Dell sells and ships directly to the customer. Dell also builds its computers to order, eliminating the need for customers to buy more than they need.

The Internet is made for a direct seller like Dell. Customers can place orders online and the product will be shipped out, just as if they had called. Internet sales reached $6 million per day by mid-1998. The company is also using the Internet to boost sales overseas by offering web sites targeted to 42 specific countries.

COMPANY FINANCES

Dell's 1998 fiscal year ended February 1, 1998. Sales were $12.3 billion, up 57.7 percent from 1997 sales of $7.8 billion. Net income rose 82.2 percent, from $518 million in 1997 to $944 million in 1998. Sales in the United States were $8.5 billion, and accounted for 69 percent of total sales. Sales in Europe were $3.0 billion (24 percent), and sales in Asia were $840 million (7 percent). In 1998 Dell's web site generated $6 million per day in sales.

Dell went public in 1984 and since 1996 the stock has soared. In fact, from 1990 to May 1998 the stock price went from $0.23 per share to $68.00, an increase of 29,600 percent. For a 52-week period in 1997-98, the company's stock reached a high of $114.00 (and a low of $35.00). The company does not pay dividends, preferring to reinvest in the company. When Dell offers stock splits, as it did on July 25, 1997 and March 6, 1998, the splits were paid in stock, not cash.

ANALYSTS' OPINIONS

Corporate leaders, investors, analysts, and industry watchers alike keep track of Michael Dell and Dell Computer Corporation. Since the company invented the direct marketing plan in the industry, some are waiting to see whether the company will continue to lead or will be lead. Some analysts downright gush when they speak of the company and its simple yet radical idea. As one analyst said, who wouldn't want to sell directly to the customer?

With computer and technology companies reporting less than expected sales and revenues in 1997 and 1998, some are waiting for the bump in Dell's road. By mid-1998, it was said that except for Dell and Gateway, Inc., every personal computer (PC) manufacturer was losing money. Some, however, expect Dell to remain a leader, noting that other PC makers, such as IBM, are trying to emulate Dell's approach. Dell is moving on, however, to invent the next model for computer sellers.

HISTORY

Michael Dell was a freshman at University of Texas when he began selling computer components from his dorm room. Soon life in business seemed more practical than another three years on campus as a pre-med student.

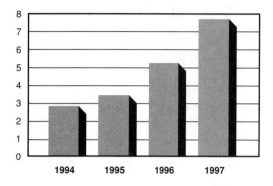

FINANCES:

Dell Computer Corporation
Net Revenues, 1994-1997
(billion dollars)

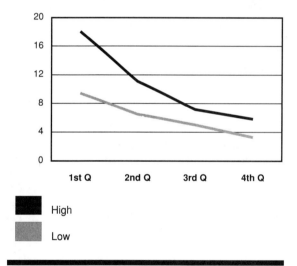

Dell Computer Corporation
1997 Stock Prices
(dollars)

He went into business for himself as a reseller of IBM PCS. At that time dealers were forced to make huge purchases from IBM, so Dell offered to take their excess stock and sell it for them. His discounts of 10 to 15 percent were a healthy amount below retail. Soon the nascent, burgeoning market for personal computers transformed Dell's dorm space into more office than living quarters and he dropped out of college to devote his time to making IBM clones.

Dell was no ordinary company and Michael Dell was no ordinary entrepreneur. Dell Computer Corporation was not the first time Michael reinvented a way to sell a

FAST FACTS:

About Dell Computer Corporation

Ownership: Dell Computer is a publicly held company trading on NASDAQ. Michael Dell owns slightly more than 16 percent of the company.

Ticker symbol: DELL

Officers: Michael S. Dell, Chmn. & CEO, 33, 1998 base salary $788,462, bonus $2,000,000; Morton L. Topfer, VChmn., 61, 1998 base salary $616,346, bonus $2,000,000; Thomas J. Meridith, Sr. VP & CFO, 47, 1998 base salary $408,288, bonus $1,020,719

Employees: 16,000

Chief Competitors: Dell competes with other computer companies, both direct marketing and retail. Some primary competitors include: Compaq Computer Corporation; Gateway, Inc.; and International Business Machines Corporation.

---

product. When he was 12, Michael held an auction to sell stamps; it netted him $1,000. As a senior in high school he sold newspapers, making $18,000. His secret was the old business adage: know your customer. Since new residents and newlyweds were the most likely subscribers, Michael researched marriage licenses and real estate transfers to solicit customers. At college, Michael decided he could give computer owners better service via telephone than the original sales people could. His experience taught him that customers often knew more about computers than the people selling them did. Eventually, Michael formulated his goal: to compete head-to-head with IBM.

Dell, the man and the company, was a pioneer in direct marketing of computer system. Despite management problems in the mid-1980s, the fledgling company plodded on. The Dell Computer name was not affixed to the operation until about 1987, when it started adding staff to sell to government and corporate accounts. A year later, the company went public with a $34.2-million initial public offering.

The company's growth was rapid—from $546 million in fiscal 1991 to $2 billion in 1993. In 1993, however, the inexperience of top management, especially Michael, began to show and become a liability. New products and ideas put forth failed. With sales of about

$3 billion, Texas-based Dell Computer posted a loss of nearly $36 million that year. More important, Dell lost ground to rival computer makers Packard Bell and Gateway 2000, dropping from fifth to sixth place in the market. Dell's stock began to fall: in January 1993 it was worth $49 per share, by July it hit a low of $16.

Many entrepreneurs burn out when little companies expand. It is to Michael's credit that he looked for the problems, diagnosed them, then fixed them. The biggest problem facing Dell in 1993 was not being able to track profit and losses by product type: the company had no idea which products were bringing in money and which were losing money. Michael brought in more experienced managers and high-level executives and put the company back on track. The company returned to their core products and customers, and was rewarded with soaring sales, income, and stock prices.

STRATEGY

Bell's strategy is simple: the customer deserves the best product at the best price, with the best service. Not only that, the customer deserves the product he wants. Dell computers are made to order, so customers get exactly what they want. This is in direct contrast to many retail computer stores, where customers end up buying more computer than they need. Since Dell knows what the customer wants, it can more accurately predict future needs and develop products based on those needs. Dell also offers superior customer service, providing on-site service for its computers for one year and offering extended warranties.

Dell runs its procurement, manufacturing, and distribution processes in the most efficient manner possible. By selling direct and making computers to order, Dell keeps on hand a minimum of component parts, reducing inventory and the risk of the parts becoming obsolete. (The company only keeps about eight days of inventory on hand, versus the industry average of 8 to 12 weeks.) This strategy allows Dell to be one of the first to reap the benefits when prices fall at the wholesale level. Unlike retailers, Dell doesn't need a network of wholesalers and distribution centers. It can sell at lower prices because there is no middleman, no need to carry a high inventory, and no need to waste time or money in competing for shelf space in retail stores.

Dell maintains good working relationships with the top technology companies. Receiving input from these companies allows Dell to design computers with the best technology available. The company has programmers, engineers, and project managers who design products, allowing for the most efficient manufacturing, best reliability, and performance. Dell spent $204 million on research and development in 1998, up from $126 million in 1997.

In February 1998 Compaq Computer announced it would buy Digital Equipment, turning it into a $38-billion-a-year company, and vaulting it ahead of Dell. Compaq's acquisition allows it to offer consulting services as well as hardware to corporations. Far from panicking, Dell has not backed away from its core strategy; the company feels it will acquire even more business from consulting firms, such as Andersen Consulting. Dell had been bidding against Compaq for this business, but with Compaq competing against the consulting firms, the company feels assured of winning their business.

INFLUENCES

After making a tremendous start, the company faltered in the early 1990s. Direct selling worked so well, Dell decided to offer retail units to capture more sales. Customers didn't bite, however, and Dell withdrew from the retail market. Dell aggressively expanded its product line, but found little success, as well. Spread too thin and trying to manage and maintain a fast growing company, Dell's computers dropped in quality. To make matters worse, service on these subpar units also dropped.

Michael learned from the experience and refocused his efforts on making all of the company work together. He also hired more experienced executives to help him run the company. By 1994 Dell returned to its core strategy of quickly delivering the best technology to suit the needs of its customers, at a low price with excellent service.

CURRENT TRENDS

Dell set the trend for direct sale, made-to-order computers. While the industry averages a growth rate of 15 percent for shipped units, Dell's growth rate is 58 percent. While the industry seems to be trying to catch the wave Dell created, the company is busy making the next business model. This includes cutting even further the number of days inventory sits on the self, offering even better service, tapping into Internet market, and turning customers into repeat customers.

Dell jumped on the Internet bandwagon with enthusiasm. A natural extension of customer direct selling, the Internet offers customers a place to look at Dell products and offerings at their leisure. In 1997 sales through the Internet topped $1 million per day; a year later daily sales reached $6 million. In addition, Dell is using the Internet to increase international sales; the company has designed more than 42 country-specific web sites. In 1998, Internet sales were $1 million per day in Europe alone.

To keep customers coming back, Dell offers a lease program on some of its computers. This program has proved popular among those afraid of their computer be-

CHRONOLOGY:
Key Dates for Dell Computer Corporation

1984: Michael Dell drops out of the University of Texas to found Dell Computers

1988: Dell goes public, opens a London office, and forms a Canadian subsidiary

1990: Subsidiaries in Italy and France are set up; Dell ranks number one in J.D. Powers & Associates' first survey of PC-customer satisfaction

1993: Digital Equipment Corporation surpasses Dell to become the biggest computer mail order company

1998: Dell and Gateway, Inc. are announced as the only PC companies to turn a profit

coming obsolete not long after spending a large amount of money for them. The program is also a hit with customers who have sticker shock; for less than $65.00 per month, they can lease a Dell computer. Working just like a car lease, the Dell Personal Lease program lasts from 2 to 3 years, has no up-front costs, and allows the customer to buy the computer at the end of the lease. The price is 15 percent of the computer's original price after a three-year lease or 22 percent after a two-year lease. Gateway, Dell's direct-selling competitor, went even further. Gateway's program offers free Internet access during the lease term and allows the customer to trade the computer in after two years for a newer one.

PRODUCTS

Dell offers two models of desktop computers—the OptiPlex and Dimension. The OptiPlex is for larger companies and institutions needing network capabilities, allowing for remote manageability and control. The Dimension line is tailored for small businesses and individuals. This line ranges from top-of-the-line technology, with prices to match, to lower-end technology with value pricing.

Dell also sells two lines of notebook computers. The Latitude is for business customers and has networking capabilities, and the Inspiron—introduced in late 1997—is for users needing the latest in technology and multimedia capabilities.

During 1998 the company expanded to high-performance workstations, forming a special business unit to take care of this new market. The Workstation 400 runs the Microsoft Windows NT operating software and is for businesses needing advanced technology to run sophisticated programs. The Workstation 400 is for those who work in industries such as computer-aided design and software development.

Dell also offers network servers, software, and accessories. The company will install off-the-shelf software, such as Microsoft Office or a company's own, specifically designed software. Dell has many different service and support options, customized to the customer's needs.

CORPORATE CITIZENSHIP

Dell believes in investing in the community, especially its home base of Austin, Texas. The Dell Foundation, through cash and non-cash donations, partners with non-profit organizations, especially those dealing with children. The company provides corporate sponsorship of various programs in the community. Dell also encourages charitable donations and the volunteer efforts of its employees. In addition to charitable efforts, Dell tries to maintain a positive economic impact in communities and to be an environmentally aware company.

GLOBAL PRESENCE

Dell's international sales were $4.3 billion in fiscal 1998, with sales expected to reach over $6.0 billion in 1999. Its products are sold in more than 170 countries, covering 3 geographic regions. The Americas include the United States, Canada, and Latin America. The European region covers European countries, as well as some in the Middle East and Africa. The Asia-Pacific/Japan region includes the Far East, Japan, Australia, and New Zealand.

In addition to its manufacturing facility in Austin, Texas, Dell has facilities in Limerick, Ireland, and Penang, Malaysia. By the end of 1998, Dell planned to open another plant in Limerick and one in Xiamen, China. In all, Dell has 38 subsidiaries in 33 countries. In 1998 the company held a 7-percent share of the world-wide market; the company wants to increase that to 20 percent.

SOURCES OF INFORMATION

Bibliography

Corcoran, Elizabeth. "The Direct Approach." *Washington Post*, 1 July 1998.

"Dell Computer Corporation 10-K Form." 14 April 1998. Available at http://www.sec.gov.

The Dell Computer Home Page, 19 July 1998. Available at http://www.dell.com.

"Dell Computer Corporation." *Hoover's Guide to Computer Companies*. Austin, TX: The Reference Press, 1997.

"Dell Internet, Overseas Sales Up." *Reuters*, 17 July 1998.

Einstein, David. "Dell, Gateway Use Payment Plans to Attract Buyers." *San Francisco Chronicle*, 10 July 1998.

Jacob, Rahul. "The Resurrection of Michael Dell." *Fortune*, 18 September 1995.

Kirkpatrick, David. "No Big Deal Why Michael Dell Isn't Afraid of the New Compaq." *Fortune*, 2 March 1998.

———. "Why Compaq Envies Dell: The Leading Maker Alters Course." *Fortune*, 17 February 1997.

McGraw, Dan. "The Kid Bytes Back." *U.S. News & World Report*, 12 December 1994.

Serwer, Andy. "Michael Dell Rocks." *Fortune*, 11 May 1998.

For an annual report:

on the Internet at: http://www.dell.com **or** write: Investor Relations, Dell Computer Corp., 2214 W. Braker Ln., Austin, TX 78758

For additional industry research:

Investigate companies by their Standard Industrial Classification Codes, also known as SICs. Dell's primary SICs are:

7371 Computer Programming Services

7372 Prepackaged Software

7373 Computer Integrated Systems Design

7376 Computer Facilities Management

7378 Computer Maintenance & Repair

7379 Computer Related Services, NEC

Delta Air Lines, Inc.

FOUNDED: 1924

OVERVIEW

Suffering from four years of financial loss, Delta Air Lines, Inc. rallied and became profitable in 1996. Cutting costs is among the priorities at Delta in an effort to remain competitive with the low-budget airlines, whose popularity is rising. Delta Air Lines, Inc. flies to 153 cities in the United States and 51 cities in 31 countries abroad. In an effort to boost air traffic to Europe, the company has increased service out of JFK International Airport.

Contact Information:
HEADQUARTERS: Hartsfield Atlanta International Airport
    Atlanta, GA 30320-6001
PHONE: (404)715-2600
FAX: (404)765-2233
URL: http://www.delta-air.com

COMPANY FINANCES

Delta states that for the quarter ending March 31, 1998, unaudited operating income of $336 million and net income of $195 million were recorded. For the quarter ending March 31, 1997, unaudited operating income of $336 million and net income of $195 million were recorded. The company also stated that its operating margin (operating income divided by operating revenue) was 9.9 percent for the quarter ending March 31, 1998 compared to 10.1 percent for the quarter ending March 31, 1997. Further, with Delta's 1998 alliance with United Airlines, Inc., an estimated $600 million in annual gross revenue benefits was expected.

ANALYSTS' OPINIONS

Many analysts agree that Delta Air Lines, Inc.'s restructuring plans were a necessity. Once known for its

▲ Delta Air Lines

FINANCES:

Delta Air lines Operating Revenues, 1994-1997 (billion dollars)

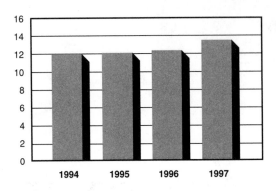

Delta Air lines 1997 Stock Prices (dollars)

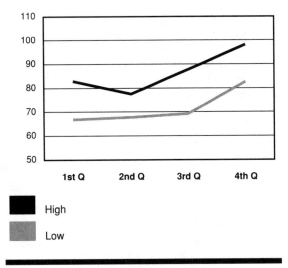

■ High

■ Low

ing the company back to profitable margins. Many critics were skeptical of his goal of 7.5 cents per airplane seat per mile of flight by June 1997, yet Allen had gone on to show an 8.4-cents per mile expense by the end of 1995—two years away from the target date. By early 1997 that cost was 8.69 cents per mile.

HISTORY

Founded in Macon, Georgia, in 1924, Huff-Daland Dusters (renamed Delta Air Service in 1928) was established as a crop-dusting service to treat boll weevils that were overrunning cotton fields. The company began offering passenger flights in 1929 from Dallas to Jackson, Mississippi. Delta contracted with the United States Postal Service in 1934 to fly from Fort Worth to Charleston, South Carolina, using Atlanta as a hub. The company relocated to Atlanta in 1941.

Over the years, Delta Air Lines, Inc. added flight destinations to include Cincinnati, New Orleans, Chicago, and Miami. When the company bought Southern Airlines in 1952, other destinations included cities in the South, the Midwest, Texas, and the Caribbean. Almost instantaneously the company has become the fifth largest airline in the United States. International service increased when the company bought Northeast Airlines in 1972 and offered service to New England, Canada, and London.

In 1983 the company reported its first financial loss due to a poor economy. Having become profitable once again by 1985, Delta purchased Western Air Lines the following year, and also used its profits to begin flights to Asia in 1987. International flights accounted for 11 percent of Delta's passenger revenues by 1989, and during this time the company made deals with Swissair and Singapore Airlines. Delta also conducted a joint venture with TWA and Northwest to create WORLDSPAN, a computer service that managed reservations.

Delta witnessed a financial setback in 1990 as a result of fuel and labor increases coupled with reduced fare rates. Delta followed this disappointment with the purchase of gates, planes, and three Canadian routes from Eastern. The company also purchased Pan Am's New York-Boston shuttle, European routes, and a Frankfurt hub. These purchases made the company the largest airline in the world based on the cities it served and its fruitfulness.

Once again the company began to see financial difficulties due to price wars and a weak economy, and by 1992, Delta was forced to evaluate cost-cutting possibilities. The company reduced planes and short-distance routes. In 1995 the company decided to cease its flights to Bangkok, Hong Kong, and Taipei, since they had not been financially rewarding. ValuJet's disastrous flight crash and grounding in 1995 was expected to increase

lavish in-flight services, Delta had become a high-priced airline when faced with competition from airlines offering lower fares. Although Delta's profits rose in the fourth quarter of 1996 by $55 million compared to the fourth quarter in 1995, several analysts said the company's operational costs remained high. Compared to the $2.78-billion operational costs of 1995, analysts remained watchful as Delta's operational costs rose to $2.97 billion in 1996. Delta cited the 1996 Olympics as the source for increased operational expenses, since Delta's hub is located in Atlanta, where the event took place that year.

Analysts have been impressed by former CEO Ronald Allen's efforts to reduce expenses while bring-

Vacationers and business travelers taking off aboard a Delta Air Lines airplane. (Courtesy of Delta Air Lines.)

Delta's passengers. Delta aimed to boost passenger volume by offering Delta Express, an inexpensive service flying to 15 cities in the eastern United States.

STRATEGY

Since Ronald Allen's cost-cutting plans went into effect in 1994 the company has remained focused on profitability. Delta's interests have included forming creative partnerships and overhauling everything from baggage handling to maintenance. Allen's goal was to reduce spending to the point that only 7.5 cents per airplane seat per mile of flight would be spent by June of 1997—a plan he called "Leadership 7.5." In other words, the company was seeking to cut costs by $2 billion. Cost-cutting goals were established for specific categories: $400 million from marketing, $300 million from layoffs, and $310 million from in-flight services.

INFLUENCES

Changes in the industry began in the early 1990s. The rising popularity of low-cost, low-fare airlines forced Delta to make continual cutbacks yielding less profits. In fact, by the end of 1995, 60 percent of Delta's domestic flights were in competition with other low-cost carriers'

flights. Customers had begun looking at cost as the top consideration when purchasing a ticket versus luxury or in-flight service.

Delta's Leadership 7.5 plan was implemented in 1994 as a result of a changing industry. Even changes in European markets demanded Delta to make revisions. In 1995 improved economies in the United States and parts of Europe accounted for Delta's increased European market share. A new European advertising campaign was partly responsible for a five-percent increase in European air traffic as well.

European markets received increased attention as competing airlines added new flight times and non-stop services. Delta had begun looking to other companies for code sharing agreements as a means of increasing profitability, flight availability, and competitiveness. Code sharing simply means airline companies agree to purchase regular flights on each others' planes, which allows them to establish or increase their presence in strategic international markets. By 1995 Delta was able to provide service to Brussels from Chicago and Boston, to many German destinations, to London, to Vienna from New York, and to Geneva from Washington, D.C.

The 1996 Summer Olympics held in Atlanta proved beneficial for Delta Air Lines, Inc., since its largest hub is based in Atlanta. The company had filled an average of almost 75 percent of its seats. Since off-peak flights generally carry a small group of people, this figure indi-

FAST FACTS:

About Delta Air Lines, Inc.

Ownership: Delta Air Lines, Inc. is a publicly owned company traded on the New York Stock Exchange.

Ticker symbol: DAL

Officers: Maurice W. Worth, COO, 57, $539,076; Harold C. Alger, Exec. VP Operations, 59, $539,076; Gerald Grinstein, Chmn., 65; Leo F. Mullin, Pres. & CEO, 54

Employees: 63,441 (1997)

Principal Subsidiary Companies: Delta Air Lines, Inc.'s chief subsidiaries include: Delta Express, the Delta Shuttle, the Delta Connection, and Delta's Worldwide Partners.

Chief Competitors: Competition among airlines is strong. Delta states that it competes with many major airlines on its principal routes as well as with regional, national, and all-cargo carriers. Some primary competitors include: Continental Airlines; Alaska Air; and British Airways.

cated Delta's flights were full a majority of the time during the Olympics.

CURRENT TRENDS

Due to new strategies being developed by the competition to better service European-bound customers, Delta Air Lines, Inc. devised new plans for its transatlantic flights. First on the agenda have been plans to add non-stop flights from Kennedy International Airport to Istanbul, Madrid, and Manchester. Expansion plans have included year-round service to Athens and an additional daily flight to Rome. Other added flights have included Stuttgart and Zurich, both cities being reached via Atlanta.

As well as adding flights, Delta has also implemented plans for discontinuations. Among those have been the doing away with non-stop flights from Los Angeles to Frankfurt and Frankfurt to Athens, Bucharest, Istanbul, Warsaw, Moscow, and St. Petersburg.

The European service changes revolve around Delta's goal of cutting costs by $62 million per year. Fol-

lowing the purchase of Pan Am's European operations in 1991, Delta's financial losses mounted, causing a need for a change. Although the company made a profit on transatlantic flights in 1996, the competition from United Air Lines and Lufthansa had been fierce. Delta has chosen to take a one-time restructuring fee of $60 million in order to increase its European service.

The company reports that in 1998 a marketing alliance was formed with United Air Lines, Inc. The two airlines plan to code-share (subject to both airlines' pilots' unions) and reciprocate with frequent flyer programs and other areas of marketing.

New purchases are also a part of Delta's strategic direction. In March 1997 the company announced plans to purchase jets from Boeing Company totaling up to $12 billion. In hopes of replacing its 55 L-1011s by the end of the 1900s, Delta has agreed to buy 24 Boeing 767s, 777s, and newer 737s as its first purchase.

The airline industry, many analysts agree, is a mature one in the United States and abroad. The European market has been one of increasing demand, especially since competing airlines have begun service improvements. Delta's efforts to improve its European operations have included code-sharing, which subject to government approval, could allow Delta enormous European expansion.

One code-sharing agreement has produced increased exposure in China for Delta Air Lines, Inc. Under the signed agreement with China Southern Airlines, Delta would be able to provide service between Los Angeles and Guangzhou. China, in turn, would purchase seats on Delta's flights to include cities like Atlanta, Boston, Cincinnati, Detroit, Las Vegas, New York, Orlando, Philadelphia, Phoenix, Portland, Salt Lake City, San Francisco, and Washington D.C.

CORPORATE CITIZENSHIP

Delta Air Lines, Inc.'s community involvement has revolved primarily around two organizations: United Way of America and the Crested Butte Ski Weekend, an event held for at-risk inner-city teens. In conjunction with United Way of America, Delta has agreed to offer round trip travel tickets to people suffering from life-threatening illnesses in order to allow them access to the best treatment available. A new program called SkyWish permits travelers to donate their frequent flyer miles to United Way of America, helping those in need of medical treatment.

Delta was also the leading sponsor of the Crested Butte Ski Weekend where inner-city teenagers are brought together to meet successful, inspirational role models like Hank Aaron. A Winter Weekend auction has been held there, where various vacation packages and do-

CHRONOLOGY:

Key Dates for Delta Air Lines, Inc.

1924: Huff-Deland Dusters is established as a crop dusting service

1928: Renames company to Delta Air Service

1929: Begins offering passenger flights from Dallas, Texas, to Jackson, Mississippi

1941: Delta relocates to Atlanta, Georgia

1953: Merges with Chicago and Southern Airlines

1967: Delta Air Lines becomes the company name after a merger with Delaware Airlines

1972: Northeast Airlines is purchased

1982: Delta forms two computerized marketing subsidiaries to coordinate and sell tickets on Delta flights

1991: Purchases a package of assets from Pan Am giving Delta a hub in Frankfurt, Germany, as well as dozens of European routes

1998: United Air Lines and Delta forms a marketing alliance

nated items are auctioned off. The proceeds go to FutureForce, an Atlanta Project program where at-risk teens between the ages of 12 and 19 are taught how to set and achieve goals through personal development. Delta's contributions have included air transportation, auction items, and volunteers.

In regard to environmental issues, Delta reports that it has a program in place to investigate and remedy, if necessary, any air pollution, soil, and/or ground water contamination issues.

GLOBAL PRESENCE

Delta states that as part of its plans to expand in Latin America, it recently set up service between Atlanta and Caracas, Guatemala City, Panama City, San Jose, and San Salvador. In addition, the company purchased a 35-percent equity interest in Aeroperu.

EMPLOYMENT

The company states that the outcome of its collective bargaining agreement it entered with its 8,600 airline pilots in 1996 could not be determined in 1998. The bargaining agreement covers issues of pay rate, rules and working conditions, and obligation to fly to new equipment.

Delta feels that its executives' salaries are below their peers' at other airlines, so they have developed an Incentive Compensation plan (pay for performance) aligned that with the company's strategic objectives. In addition, safety, customer satisfaction, and on-time performance are continually stressed.

SOURCES OF INFORMATION

Bibliography

"Air France Joins Delta's SkyMiles Program." *PR Newswire,* 2 April 1997.

"Airlines End Talks." *Cable News Network,* 16 December 1996.

"Delta Air Lines and China Southern Announce Code-Sharing Agreement." *PR Newswire,* 2 April 1997.

"Delta Air Lines Helps Carter Center Bring High Hopes to Inner-City Teens." *Delta News,* 6 February 1997.

"Delta Air Lines, Inc." *Hoover's Online,* 11 April 1997. Available at http://www.hoovers.com.

Delta Air Lines, Inc. Home Page, 21 April 1997. Available at http://www.delta-air.com.

"Delta Earnings Better Than Expected; Operating Costs Still High." *Fox News,* 23 January 1997. Available at http://foxnews.com.

"Delta Shuffles Flights in Europe." *United Press International,* 7 April 1997.

"Delta Talks Merger with Continental." *Associated Press,* 4 December 1996.

"Delta to Move Cincinnati/Paris Flight to Charles de Gaulle Airport." *PR Newswire,* 2 April 1997.

"Delta Will Revamp European Service." *Cincinnati Enquirer,* 8 January 1997.

Edgar Database Web Site, 6 June 1998. Available at http://www.edgar-online.com.

"FAA Developing Checks in Response to Delta Problem." *Reuters,* 30 March 1997.

Greising, David. "It Hurts So Good at Delta." *Business Week,* 11 December 1995.

Greising, David, and Wendy Zellner. "Delta Express or 'Delta Distress?'" *Business Week,* 26 August 1996.

———. "No Wind Beneath Its Wings." *Business Week,* 16 December 1995.

"Official: Delta to Agree to Long-Term Commitment to Boeing." *Fox News,* 20 March 1997.

Reed, Dan. "Delta Reports Sixth Straight Quarter of Record Profits." *Arlington Online,* 24 October 1996. Available at http://www.arlington.net.

Stern, Willy. "WARNING!—Bogus Parts Have Turned Up in Commercial Jets. Where's the FAA?" *Business Week,* 10 June 1996.

"United Way of America and Delta Air Lines Announce Sky-Wish," 21 April 1997. Available at http://www.Invalley.org.

Walker, Karen. "Delta's History," 21 April 1997. Available at http://www.airapps.com.

For an annual report:

on the Internet at: http://www.edgar-online.com

For additional industry research:

Investigate companies by their Standard Industrial Classification Codes, also known as SICs. Delta's primary SIC is:

4512 Air Transportation Scheduled

Dole Food Company, Inc.

OVERVIEW

Dole Food Company, Inc. is widely known as a pioneer in providing tropical fruit products to the United States. Since its founding in Hawaii in 1851 as Castle & Cooke, Dole (now headquartered in California) has grown into the world's largest grower and supplier of fresh fruits and vegetables. In addition to tropical fruits such as pineapples and bananas, Dole grows and distributes other fruits from apples to oranges, as well as over 20 vegetables. Dole claims to be the premier North American supplier of grapes, lettuce, celery, cauliflower, and dried fruits and nuts. Other Dole products include canned products, pre-packaged salads, and pre-cut vegetables.

Dole products are sold throughout the United States and in over 90 other countries. Although Dole also operated other types of businesses, in the mid- and late 1990s it decided to refocus on its best-known food products. It sold its juice-producing operations, except for pineapple juice, to The Seagram Company in 1995, and in that year also spun off its real estate and resort operations in Hawaii to a separate company, Castle & Cooke. In 1997 Dole's sales were over $4.3 billion.

COMPANY FINANCES

Dole's sales figures from 1993 through 1997 show constant growth. According to the company's 1997 annual report, its sales were: $3.10 billion in 1993; $3.50 billion in 1994; $3.80 billion in 1995; $3.84 billion in 1996; and $4.30 billion in 1997. During these five years,

FOUNDED: 1851 as Castle & Cooke

Contact Information:

HEADQUARTERS: 31365 Oak Crest Dr.
  Westlake Village, CA 91361
PHONE: (818)879-6600
FAX: (818)879-6618
URL: http://www.dole.com

FINANCES:

Dole Food Co. Revenues, 1994-1997 (billion dollars)

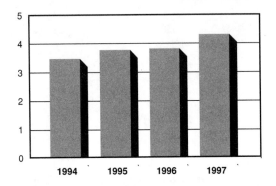

Dole Food Co. 1997 Stock Prices (dollars)

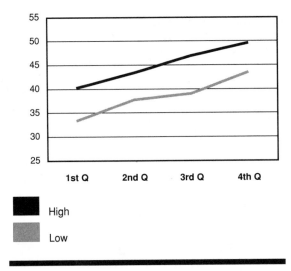

Dole's net income doubled, from $78 million in 1993 to $160 million in 1997. (This figure doubled even though there was a $97-million loss in 1995 from the discontinued operations.)

HISTORY

The history of Dole Food Company, Inc. is actually the story of two companies whose paths crossed in Hawaii early in the twentieth century. Castle & Cooke had been founded by missionaries in 1851 to provide posts in that part of the world with staple items. Samuel Castle and Amos Cooke had formed an alliance to manage the church's depository. Seven years later they became agents for sugar concerns in Hawaii. As the nineteenth century brought growth and investors to Hawaii, Castle & Cooke eventually became a prosperous land development and real estate company.

Meanwhile, James Drummond Dole came to Hawaii in 1899, after graduating from Harvard. His cousin, Sanford B. Dole, was a politician who became governor of Hawaii, which had been recently acquired as a U.S. territory. He urged James to try to develop a commercial market for pineapple. James took his cousin's advice and bought 60 acres of land near Honolulu. James Dole built a cannery to process his fruit for shipping, and in 1903 his newly formed Hawaiian Pineapple Company successfully shipped and sold 2,000 cases of canned pineapple. Within only a few years, this number had jumped to 25,000 cases.

In its early years, Dole's company sold pineapple largely to the California region, and many people in the United States had never seen or tasted a pineapple. Dole began a national advertising campaign for his canned fruit, hoping to entice new customers by giving the canned fruit appealing brand names like "Ukulele." The company also employed a new advertising concept, publishing recipes in the newly popular "ladies' magazines." By the end of World War I, production had risen to a million cases of pineapple a year, and the Hawaiian Pineapple Company was a world leader in processing pineapple. In 1922 Dole bought the island of Lana'i and established a huge plantation. His company's biggest investor turned out to be Castle & Cooke, now a profitable land development firm that bought one-third of Dole's company.

Dole's company lost millions of dollars in the early 1930s. Castle & Cooke bought a controlling share of the Hawaiian Pineapple Company and, although Dole remained as chairman of the board until 1948, Castle & Cooke was in charge, and was responsible for restoring the company to financial health.

In 1961 Castle & Cooke purchased the remainder of the Hawaiian Pineapple Company. It also began expanding its operations beyond Hawaii, by establishing plantations in the Philippines to continue to supply markets with both pineapple and bananas. The banana business expanded further in 1964 with the purchase of Standard Fruit of New Orleans. Because the Dole brand was already well known to the public from sales of pineapple products, it was also added to new products. Television advertising became a key component of Castle & Cooke's marketing efforts. In the 1970s and 1980s the company emphasized the health benefits of its products. A huge media campaign in the early 1990s encouraged consumers to eat more fruits and vegetables, of course emphasizing pineapples.

However, the 1980s and early 1990s brought added financial difficulties to the company. Castle & Cooke was carrying a huge amount of debt, and it had to struggle through two unsuccessful takeover attempts in the mid-1980s. To protect itself, Castle & Cooke merged with Flexi-Van, a container leasing firm operated by David H. Murdock. Under Murdock's direction, the company was reduced to its most basic ventures: fruit and real estate. In 1991, Castle & Cooke changed its name to the Dole Food Company, Inc. Murdock unexpectedly announced that Dole would end its pineapple growing operations on Lana'i, and instead would develop resort properties there through its Castle & Cooke subsidiary.

In the mid-1990s Dole decided to expand its operations in many directions. In 1994 it acquired a share of Jamaica Fruit Distributors, bought Dromedary (the date company), and acquired Made in Nature, an organic produce and food supplier that at the time was the largest in that sector of the organic foods industry. Dole had hoped to capture a part of the organic food market, which was then posting double-digit growth each year. However, only a little over a year later, Dole decided to make another sharp change of direction. It sold Made in Nature back to its original owners, and spun off its Castle & Cooke real estate and resorts division to its shareholders in order to focus on its food-related businesses. Dole also finalized the sale of its global juice business to Seagram's Tropicana juice division. Dole retained its canned pineapple juice unit, entering into a long-term supply contract arrangement with Tropicana. This arrangement allowed Dole to keep active in the juice market, since pineapple juice is a base ingredient for many blended juices. In 1996 Dole expanded its juice operations once again, by purchasing the controlling share of Pascual Hermanos, Spain's leading citrus fruit and vegetable producer. It also decided to close its California dried fruit facility, which had suffered losses for a prolonged time.

STRATEGY

James Drummond Dole founded his company on a commitment to "quality, quality, and quality," as he said in the company's original statement of principles. Aside from this basic principle, Dole also has been perceptive in its choice of manufacturing and marketing techniques. In its early days Dole took advantage of new technology (fruit canning), which led to its initial success. In the mid-twentieth century, the company turned to another new form of technology, television advertising, to greatly increase its sales. Its advertising campaign of the early 1990s ("How'd You Do Your Dole Today?") capitalized on the growing public awareness of the need to eat more fruits and vegetables. Dole also repeatedly expanded its product line and then cut back to its basic operations in times of difficulty. International expansion also has played a key role in the company's operations, especially in the 1990s.

FAST FACTS:
About Dole Food Company, Inc.

Ownership: Dole Food Company, Inc. is a publicly owned company traded on the New York Stock Exchange.

Ticker symbol: DOL

Officers: David H. Murdock, Chmn. & CEO, 74, $1,369,842; David A. DeLorenzo, Pres. & COO, 51, $823,231; Gregory L. Costley, Pres., Dole North America Fruit, 44

Employees: 44,000 worldwide

Principal Subsidiary Companies: Dole Food Company, Inc. operates numerous subsidiaries in Asia, Latin America, and Europe, as well as the United States, grouped as Dole Holdings, Inc., and Castle & Cooke Worldwide Limited. Its real estate and resort operations were spun off in 1995 as Castle & Cooke, Inc., and all of its juice operations (except pineapple juice) were sold to The Seagram Company Ltd. in the same year.

Chief Competitors: Dole Fruit Company, Inc.'s top competitors include: Chiquita Brands; Del Monte; and Tri Valley Growers.

INFLUENCES

Previous efforts to ship fresh pineapple to the U.S. mainland from Hawaii had failed miserably, since the trip took weeks by boat and there was no way to refrigerate the fruit during the journey. However, James Dole decided to try a different approach, and built a cannery to process his fruit for shipping. In 1903 he successfully shipped and sold 2,000 cases of canned pineapple.

The combination of the Great Depression and the initial failure of a new product, pineapple juice, led to Dole losing millions of dollars in the early 1930s. Ironically, it was the initially unsuccessful pineapple juice that helped the company to recover. With the end of Prohibition, it advertised pineapple juice as a great mixer with liquor.

CURRENT TRENDS

Dole has placed an increased emphasis on marketing a wide variety of products that are nutritious, tasty,

CHRONOLOGY:

Key Dates for Dole Food Company, Inc.

1851: Founded as Castle & Cooke in Hawaii

1899: James Drummond Dole comes to Hawaii

1903: James Dole forms the Hawaiian Pineapple Company

1922: Dole buys the island of Lanai

1961: Castle & Cooke purchases the rest of the Hawaiian Pineapple Co.

1964: Purchases Standard Fruit of New Orleans

1989: Establishes the "Shark Shootout"

1991: Castle & Cooke changes its name to Dole Food Company Inc.

1994: Dole acquires part of Jamaica Fruit Distributors, all of Made in Nature, and Dromedary

1995: Sells juice-producing operations (except pineapple juice) to Seagram Company; sells Made in Nature

1996: Purchases Pascual Hermanos

1998: Dole distributes products in 90 countries

and convenient. As of 1998 it sold more than 70 varieties of fruits and vegetables, as well as over 100 processed and packaged fruits, juices, and nuts. Dole recognized the consumer trend toward convenient packaged foods that also are healthy. To address this rapidly growing demand, it introduced a line of pre-cut vegetable and salad mixes. Following its rapid series of acquisitions and sales of operations in the mid-1990s, Dole seems to have regrouped itself around its founder James Drummond Dole's original statement of principles, a commitment to "quality, quality, and quality."

PRODUCTS

Produce under the Dole brand includes dried fruits and nuts (almonds, prunes, raisins, and packaged trail mixes); fresh fruits (bananas, pineapples, coconuts, stone and tree fruits, grapefruit, lemons, oranges, tangelos, tangerines, kiwifruit, pears, and raspberries); fresh vegetables (artichokes, asparagus, bell peppers, broccoli, car-

rots, lettuce, onions, peas, potatoes, and radishes); and packaged foods (canned fruits and vegetables, freshly cut packaged salad mixes, and other freshly-cut salad ingredients). The company also distributes date products under the Dromedary label.

CORPORATE CITIZENSHIP

Dole is a sponsor of the "Shark Shootout," an annual golf tournament held in California and hosted by golfer Greg "The Shark" Norman. Established in 1989, the tournament raises funds for children's charities. Dole also donates funds and products to community health-oriented programs, particularly in the area of nutrition education for children, and to food programs for the needy. It created the first CD-ROM multimedia program designed to teach elementary school students about nutrition, using characters such as Bobby Banana and Pamela Pineapple. In addition to its corporate web site, Dole also maintains a nutrition education web site, accessible at http://www.dole5aday.com.

GLOBAL PRESENCE

As of early 1998 Dole distributed its products in 90 countries. It maintained the position of industry leader within the United States, Canada, Mexico, and Japan. However, in the 1990s significant expansion of the company's international operations took place. Key marketing efforts have been targeted at Europe (particularly eastern Europe), South Korea, Thailand, the Philippines, and the Middle East. In 1997 about 40 percent of Dole's sales (after accounting adjustments) were in North America; the remaining sales were divided almost equally among its Latin American, Asian, and European operations. Critics of the company have included labor and consumer groups that take issue with its international operations.

Because Dole maintains such a strong international presence, it is often subject to unanticipated changes in the laws, tariffs, and political conditions of the countries in which it does business. For instance, its banana sales in Europe have been significantly disrupted by the European Union's banana regulations, which were challenged by several countries (the United States, Ecuador, Mexico, Honduras, and Guatemala), but were still in effect in 1998. These regulations set up quotas and tariffs for bananas that are imported into Europe. The World Trade Organization issued a report in 1997 in response to complaints from countries outside of the European Union. It agreed that the regulations unfairly favor banana imports into Europe from countries in Africa and the Caribbean that used to be European colonies.

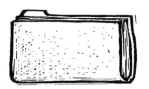

THE PINECONE FRUIT

The Dole Food Company got its start with pineapples, so it's no surprise that it's the top product sold by and closely associated with the company.

Originating in Central and South America, the pineapple got its name from Spanish explorers who called it "pina," which is Spanish for pinecone—the seed they thought the fruit resembled. The English later added "apple" to the word. In 1493, Christopher Columbus found pineapples in Guadeloupe and brought them back to Queen Isabella of Spain. They became popular in Europe and were even grown in seventeenth-century greenhouses.

Although pineapples grow in many tropical areas worldwide, most people associate pineapples with Hawaii, where they have been grown since the early 1800s. It is believed that Captain Cook may have brought the pineapple to Hawaii, or some were washed ashore from Spanish shipwrecks.

The pineapple is a good source of vitamin C and is also used as a symbol of welcome and hospitality in many areas of the world.

SOURCES OF INFORMATION

Bibliography

Blamey, Pamela. "Seagram Buys Most Dole Juice Units." *Supermarket News,* 19 June 1995.

Carlsen, Clifford. "Dole Plucks Marin Organics Giant; Acquisition of Made in Nature Plants Seed for Golden Harvest." *San Francisco Business Times,* 2 September 1994.

"Dole Food Company." *Hoover's Handbook of American Business 1997.* Austin, TX: The Reference Press, 1996.

Dole Food Company, Inc. Annual Report. Westlake Village, CA: Dole Food Company, Inc., 1997.

"Dole to Spin Off its Real Estate and Resorts Division to Its Shareholders." *Knight-Ridder/Tribune Business News,* 17 October 1995.

Dubovoj, Sina. "Dole Food Company, Inc." *International Directory of Company Histories,* Vol. 9. Detroit, MI: St. James Press, 1994.

"Tropicana + Dole = International No. 1." *Beverage World,* June 1995.

For an annual report:

on the Internet at: http://www.dole.com **or** write: Office of the Corporate Secretary, Dole Food Co., Inc., 31365 Oak Crest Dr., Westlake Village, CA 91361

For additional industry research:

Investigate companies by their Standard Industrial Classification Codes, also known as SICs. Dole's primary SICs are:

0174 Citrus Fruits

2033 Canned Fruits & Vegetables

2034 Dried & Dehydrated Fruits & Vegetables

5149 Groceries & Related Products, NEC

Domino's Pizza, Inc.

FOUNDED: 1960

Contact Information:
HEADQUARTERS: 30 Frank Lloyd Wright Dr.
    Ann Arbor, MI 48106-0997
PHONE: (313)930-3030
FAX: (313)668-4614
EMAIL: webmaster@www.dominos.com
URL: http://www.dominos.com

OVERVIEW

As of 1997 Domino's Pizza, Inc. was the largest pizza delivery company in the world and the world's second largest pizza chain, behind Tricon Restaurant Group's Pizza Hut. Domino's had 4,431 pizza delivery stores in the United States and more than 1,521 units in 59 foreign countries by the end of 1997. Its 1997 sales were $3.16 billion, earning Domino's a place as the two-hundredth largest private company on the *Forbes* Private 500 list. Domino's sells a variety of pizza products, including deep-dish, pan, and thin-crust pizzas, as well as specialty items such as flavored-crust pizzas.

In 1997 Domino's sold over 325 million pizzas, with pepperoni being the most popular topping. The chain used over 27 million pounds of pepperoni that year, as well as over 174 million pounds of part-skim mozzarella cheese and over 3 million pounds of pizza sauce, among other ingredients.

COMPANY FINANCES

Following several difficult years, Domino's annual sales have risen steadily since 1993: $2.2 billion in 1993; $2.5 billion in 1994; $2.6 billion in 1995; and $2.8 billion in 1996. In 1996 the firm saw a 2-percent increase in sales at stores open more than one year. By the end of 1997 Domino's had achieved record sales of almost $3.2 billion, a 14.3-percent increase over 1996. (Because Domino's is a privately held company, it does not issue stock to the public.)

HISTORY

Domino's traces its roots to 1960, when Tom Monaghan and his brother, James, purchased "DomiNick's," a pizza store in Ypsilanti, Michigan. Monaghan borrowed $500 to buy the store, and in 1961 James traded his half of the business to Tom in exchange for a Volkswagen Beetle automobile. Tom Monaghan established the pizza business to support himself while he studied to be an architect. Soon after, however, he dropped out of school to build the business.

By 1965 Tom Monaghan was the sole owner of the company, and he renamed the enterprise Domino's Pizza, Inc. As Domino's grew, its success was attributed to a simple but powerful idea: Monaghan, who had been raised in Catholic orphanages and foster homes, believed that people who ordered pizzas were hungry. To keep them happy a company must not only deliver pizzas, but promise fast delivery. Domino's went on to guarantee pizza delivery in 30 minutes or less.

That 30-minute delivery philosophy began to blossom in the mid- to late 1970s. In 1967 the first Domino's Pizza franchise store was opened in Ypsilanti, Michigan. The franchising concept helped to dramatically accelerate the company's growth. In 1978 the two-hundredth Domino's store opened, and in 1983 Domino's opened its first international store in Winnipeg, Canada. In that same year the 1,000th Domino's store opened. In 1985 Domino's opened 954 new units, making a total of 2,841.

In 1989 Monaghan stepped down as Domino's president for two years to devote himself to philanthropic work. According to some press reports, the company did not do well during that time, but after Monaghan's return the company was able to restore profitability. In 1992 Domino's began the national roll-out of bread sticks, the company's first national non-pizza menu item. In 1993 Crunchy Thin Crust Pizza was introduced nationwide. In that same year the company dropped its 30-minute delivery guarantee in corporate stores following highly publicized accidents involving Domino's delivery drivers.

In 1994 the first Domino's store in eastern Europe opened in Warsaw, Poland. In that same year the first agreement to develop Domino's in an African country was signed by Specialized Catering Services, Inc. In 1995 Domino's Pizza International division opened its one-thousandth store.

STRATEGY

Domino's basic business strategy has been to offer a limited menu through carryout or delivery only. Until 1992 the company's outlets offered just two products: Domino's Traditional Hand Tossed Pizza and Coca-Cola. Beginning in 1992, however, Domino's began to expand its menu options; during the next five years it added bread

FAST FACTS:
About Domino's Pizza, Inc.

Ownership: Domino's Pizza, Inc. is a privately owned company.

Officers: Thomas Monaghan, Pres. & Chmn.; Cheryl A. Bachelder, VP, Marketing & Product Development; Harry Silverman, CFO & VP, Finance & Administration

Employees: 170,000 (1997 est.)

Principal Subsidiary Companies: Domino's Pizza, Inc. operates about 6,000 stores in the United States and 60 other countries. Its main subsidiary is Domino's Pizza International, Inc.

Chief Competitors: Major competitors include the many other pizza chains and fast food operations in the United States and elsewhere, such as: Bertucci's; Little Caesar's; Papa Gino's; Pizza Hut; and McDonald's.

sticks, Ultimate Deep Dish Pizza, Crunchy Thin Crust Pizza, Buffalo Wings, Roma Herb Crust Pizza, Garlic Crunch Crust, and Pesto Crust Pizza.

In addition to its corporately owned stores, Domino's operates an extensive franchise network, with independent owners operating Domino's stores. According to the company, over 90 percent of its 1,200 franchisees started with the company as drivers. The company's franchising system provides ownership opportunities only to qualified internal candidates, as of the late 1990s. A candidate is required to have successfully managed and/or supervised a Domino's store for one year, and must have also completed required training courses. External candidates are not considered for full franchise status; however, external investors, approved by Domino's, can become 49-percent owners in a franchise supporting an internal candidate.

Another key part of Domino's business strategy is the distribution of pizza store products to both corporately owned stores and franchise stores. In the late 1990s the distribution division of Domino's Pizza, Inc. (DPD) operated a network of 18 domestic distribution centers, supplying over 4,200 Domino's pizza stores with more than 150 products, from basic food items to pizza boxes and cleaning supplies. DPD's equipment and supply division also offers items such as counters and ovens. DPD

CHRONOLOGY:

Key Dates for Domino's Pizza, Inc.

1960: Tom and James Monaghan buy a DomiNicks pizza store

1961: James sells his part of DomiNicks to Tom

1965: Company is renamed Domino's Pizza Inc.

1967: First Domino's Pizza franchise opens in Ypsilanti, Michigan

1978: 200th Domino's store opens

1982: Establishes Domino's Pizza International, Inc.

1983: Opens first international store in Winnipeg, Canada

1985: Opens 954 new stores

1986: The Partners Foundation is founded

1992: Domino's introduces bread sticks on their menus

1993: Crunchy Thin Crust Pizza and Ultimate Deep Dish Pizzas are introduced nationwide

1994: Opens store in Warsaw, Poland; eliminates 30-minute delivery guarantee; adds buffalo wings to the menu

1995: Opens 1000th international store

1996: Adopts a new logo and new uniforms; introduces flavored crust pizzas

1997: Becomes the largest pizza delivery company in the world

is also a major pizza dough producer, averaging 175 million pounds of dough per year.

A key part of Domino's business strategy in the mid-1990s included intensive lobbying of Congress over tax legislation that affected its operations. In 1996, Domino's and other pizza delivery firms faced a mandated increase in their costs when the U.S. Congress passed legislation raising the minimum wage. Domino's delivery drivers, for example, were frequently paid the minimum wage. However, another bill providing a tax credit for tips collected by delivery drivers was also passed in 1996 by Congress, helping offset the cost of the minimum wage measure. The tax credit, which was strongly promoted by the pizza industry, was an extension of a tax credit already enjoyed by traditional restaurants.

The passage of the tax cut was seen as evidence of the "vast influence" that pizza firms such as Domino's had developed on Capitol Hill and within a national trade group, the National Restaurant Association, according to Glenn Simpson, writing in the *Wall Street Journal.* The special tax break was expected to cost the U.S. government about $6 million in lost revenue in 1997. Domino's encouraged dozens of its franchisees to lobby for the tax credit, according to Simpson.

INFLUENCES

In the mid-1990s Domino's began to experience some financial difficulty, and in 1993 the company reported a 4.3-percent decline in total sales to $2.2 billion and a 1.2-percent decrease in the number of operating units. According to John McLaughlin, writing in *Restaurant Business,* Domino's experienced sharp losses in the mid-1990s due to Monaghan's "previous financial excesses," but added that more prudent financial management helped the company regain profitability.

Domino's began to restructure its product and marketing operations, adding new products and changing some of its long-time practices. In 1994 Domino's eliminated its 30-minute delivery guarantee after a jury in St. Louis, Missouri, awarded $78 million to a woman who was injured in a collision with a Domino's delivery van. Other accidents involving Domino's delivery vehicles had led to fatalities. Critics charged that the company's guarantee caused safety problems, and while Domino's denied the charges, the negative publicity prompted the company to abandon its policy.

While Domino's distribution division was a key part of its strategy, some franchisees challenged its business practices in a 1995 anti-trust lawsuit, charging that the company was allegedly overcharging for supplies, including raw pizza dough. The 11 franchisees who filed the suit said they were prevented from contracting with outside raw dough suppliers. The lawsuit claimed that Domino's was charging franchisees five times the market price for pizza dough, and also claimed that Domino's practices added between $3,000 and $10,000 in costs annually to each franchise's costs. Domino's denied the charges in the suit.

CURRENT TRENDS

In 1996 Domino's announced that it was planning a new image for the company. Along with adopting a new logo, Domino's began to upgrade its stores' appearance, and its employees began to sport light khaki pants instead of their traditional navy uniforms. With ever increasing competition from both traditional pizza chains and sellers of gourmet pizzas (such as California Pizza

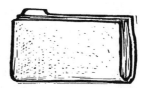

Kitchen), Domino's decided both to build up its existing product line and to test some new concepts, such as the flavored crusts introduced in 1996 and 1997. International expansion remained a priority. Founder Monaghan, firmly in control once again, had no plans of retiring after over 35 years with the company.

DOMINO'S SLICE OF PIE IN THE WOODS

PRODUCTS

While Domino's' traditional operating strategy had been based on offering a very limited menu, in the mid-1990s the company began expanding its product offerings to meet the changing tastes of its customers. In 1992 it added bread sticks; the next year it introduced Ultimate Deep Dish Pizza and Crunchy Thin Crust Pizza. Buffalo Wings, a chicken product, was added in 1994. In 1995 Domino's (and other pizza chains) began offering these chicken wings as appetizers, in mild, hot, and barbecue flavors.

Domino's also pursued another product trend in the mid-1990s: flavored pizza crusts. Domino's successfully introduced its Roma Herb Crust Pizza in June 1996 and its Garlic Crunch Crust in November 1996, although both were billed as limited-time promotions. In 1997, Domino's expanded its crust offerings with a new Pesto Crust Pizza.

CORPORATE CITIZENSHIP

Domino's has been known as a supporter of many volunteer organizations, and its chairman, Tom Monaghan, has been a major supporter of many Catholic charities. As of 1997 Domino's has been a national sponsor of Project Safe Place, a network of "safe places" where young people in trouble can go to request help. Employees at such safe places offer a secure place to wait while the local youth shelter is contacted. Domino's outlets in cities implementing the program are "safe place" sites. The company also pays for the cost of Safe Place materials.

Domino's also operates its own "Partners Foundation," which provides financial support for Domino's franchisees and employees with special needs caused by natural disasters, on-the-job accidents, family emergencies, and other problems. In 1995, the Partners Foundation addressed 600 cases, of which 579 received support. Funding for the Partners Foundation, which was founded in 1986, was derived mostly from voluntary payroll deductions, functions sponsored by Domino's, and special events. In 1995 Partners assisted Domino's franchisees and employees affected by the Mississippi River flooding in New Orleans, Louisiana, and by Hurricane Opal in Florida and the Caribbean.

Located one mile off the eastern tip of Michigan's Upper Peninsula and 50 miles east of the Mackinac Bridge, Woodmoor Resort on Michigan's largest island, Drummond Island, was purchased in the mid-1980s by Domino's Pizza as a corporate retreat. The resort, which is now locally owned and operated, contains a large waterfront cottage designed for Domino's Pizza founder, Tom Monaghan. The Monaghan home is built in the Frank Lloyd Wright style, with wood, natural stonework, and glass. The cottage has five bedrooms that each include a private bathroom, a large combination dining and living room, and a full kitchen and mini washer/dryer. The cottage features views of the bay, and a children's "playcottage" connected to the building.

GLOBAL PRESENCE

As of 1997 Domino's operations outside of the United States were handled by Domino's Pizza International, Inc. (DPI), a wholly owned subsidiary of Domino's Pizza, Inc. established in 1982. With 150 franchise members, DPI operated 1,521 stores in 59 international markets as of 1997. DPI contributed $440 million to the company's $2.6 billion in sales in 1995.

When Domino's first went international in the mid-1980s, it used the same menu—dominated by large size pizzas—that was successful in the United States. However, that approach was not successful in some international markets such as Germany, where small, individual pizzas were popular. At first, international sales were minimal—amounting to just $16 million in 1986.

However, in the early 1990s, Domino's began modeling its international business on successful overseas operations such as its Japanese franchisee, which was run by a local businessman who experimented with toppings such as squid and sweet mayonnaise. As a result, Domino's began selling international "master franchise" rights to operations that understood local markets. As of 1996 international sales had risen to more than $500 million annually.

Under the "master franchising" system, Domino's Pizza, Inc. sells the rights to develop Domino's in a country or territory. Domino's stores outside the United States are all franchise-owned. In addition to creating new international franchises, Domino's was also promoting the conversion of local pizza chains to the Domino's Pizza brand in the mid-1990s. For example, in 1994 an agreement was signed with an 88-unit Australian pizza company to convert its units to the Domino's brand. The conversion brought Domino's store count in Australia from 25 to over 100 in two years.

Toppings used by Domino's operations vary considerably in different parts of the world. In the late 1990s pepperoni was the number one topping in the United States, but squid was the leading topping in Japan. Tuna and corn were popular in England, while eggs in Australia and guava in Colombia were leading sellers.

SOURCES OF INFORMATION

Bibliography
Benezra, Karen. "Domino's Bachelder Backs Up to Basics." *Brandweek*, 2 September 1996.

"Franchisees File Antitrust Suit Against Domino's Pizza." *Nation's Restaurant News*, 10 July 1995.

Grant, Paul J. "Slice of Life." *Quality*, February 1994.

Horovitz, Bruce. "Domino's Theory: Toss Old Image, Get Back to Top." *USA TODAY*, 13 June 1996.

Kramer, Louise. "Franchisee Group Hits Domino's With Antitrust Suit." *Nation's Restaurant News*, 11 September 1995.

Lang, Joan. "Lust for Crust." *Restaurant Business*, 10 December 1996.

McGinn, Daniel. "Here's to Pie In the Sky." *Newsweek*, 13 January 1997.

McLaughlin, John. "Is There Life After Thirty?" *Restaurant Business*, 1 March 1994.

Norton, Frances E., updated by Paula Kepos. "Domino's Pizza, Inc." *International Directory of Company Histories*, Vol. 21. Detroit, MI: St. James Press, 1998.

Oneal, Michael. "'God, Family, and Domino's - That's It'." *Business Week*, 30 January 1995.

Rubel, Chad. "Pizza Chains Winging It." *Marketing News*, 27 March 1995.

Simpson, Glenn R. "Special Delivery: Pizza Makers' Success On Tax Break Reveals A Slice of Political Life." *The Wall Street Journal*, 9 September 1996.

"Think Globally, Bake Locally." *Fortune*, 14 October 1996.

"Thomas S. Monaghan." *Nation's Restaurant News*, February 1996.

For an annual report:
on the Internet at: http://www.dominos.com **or** write: Domino's Pizza, Inc., 30 Frank Lloyd Wright Dr., Ann Arbor, MI 48106-0997

For additional industry research:
Investigate companies by their Standard Industrial Classification Codes, also known as SICs. Domino's primary SICs are:

5812 Eating Places

6794 Patent Owners And Lessors

Dow Jones & Company, Inc.

OVERVIEW

Dow Jones is a multinational media company specializing in business news. It is best known for the Dow Jones Industrial Average, an index of stock prices based on leading companies traded on Wall Street. Print publications include the company's flagship newspaper, *The Wall Street Journal,* and *Barron's* magazine. An international empire with offices in the financial centers of Europe and Asia, Dow Jones & Company Inc. is divided into three industry segments: financial information services, business publishing, and general-interest community newspapers.

COMPANY FINANCES

In early 1998 stockholders on record included 12,100 common stockholders and 4,600 holders of non-traded class B common stock. Dividends of $.96 per share were paid in 1996 and 1997. In 1997 the company's stock ranged from a low of $33 3/8 to a high of $55 7/8. A 1997 net loss of $802.1 million was incurred ($8.36 per common share) compared to 1996 earnings of $190 million ($1.96 per common share). Revenue in the same period increased 4 percent to $2.6 billion.

ANALYSTS' OPINIONS

In its February 1997 exposé on the rift within the family who owns the governing shares in Dow Jones, *Fortune* magazine enumerated numerous mistakes made

FOUNDED: 1882

Contact Information:
HEADQUARTERS: 200 Liberty St.
   New York, NY 10281
PHONE: (212)416-2000
FAX: (212)416-4348
URL: http://www.dowjones.com

will be enhanced by television operations and IDD Enterprises, a Dow Jones wholly owned subsidiary.

FINANCES:

Dow Jones Revenues, 1994-1997 (million dollars)

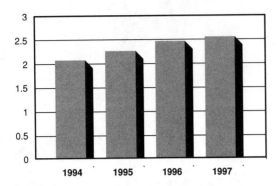

Dow Jones 1997 Stock Prices (dollars)

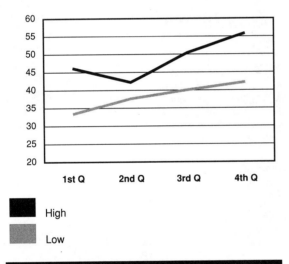

HISTORY

In 1882 reporters Charles Dow and Edward Jones formed a financial news agency in a small basement office near the New York Stock Exchange. Dow and a third reporter, Charles Bergstresser, wrote the news, and Jones edited it; the handwritten stories were then delivered to Wall Street subscribers. Within a year they had named their newspaper the *Customer's Afternoon Letter.* Charles Dow had meanwhile developed a stock price index called the Dow Jones Average, and the paper soon ran the daily average as a standard feature. In 1889, when the paper was renamed *The Wall Street Journal,* Dow Jones opened its first out-of-town bureau, with Clarence Barron, founder of *Barron's* magazine, as its head. In 1902, Barron purchased the company, and his descendants continued to own a sizable portion of its stock in 1997.

The turn of the century brought the Dow Jones News Service or "broadtape," a ticker stock market information service delivered to subscribers over telegraph lines. In the 1920s the ticker would become a symbol of Wall Street and its rapid growth. During that era Dow Jones grew too, with the establishment of *Barron's* in 1921 and the spread of broadtape service through the nation's major cities. Thus Dow Jones was in a position to be hard hit by the crash of 1929 and the ensuing Depression, a period when the *Wall Street Journal*'s subscription rate plummeted.

After weathering the 1930s and entering the 1940s with strategic changes in its methods of operation, Dow Jones continued to grow steadily. In 1967 it entered a joint venture with the Associated Press, creating the AP-Dow Jones Economic Report, which enabled it to extend its financial information to larger markets around the globe. During the decades that followed, the world of Dow Jones was dominated by two apparently conflicting themes: progress in technical innovation and conservatism in corporate strategy. In 1997 a rift among Clarence Barron's heirs brought these concerns to the forefront again.

STRATEGY

Although Dow Jones began in New York, its leadership clearly understood that the term Wall Street does not simply refer to the street in New York, but to the whole world of finance. Thus, the business community throughout the nation would need up-to-date information on activities in the stock markets of New York and, in turn, New York's financial leaders needed updates on what was going on in the rest of the world. These needs

by the company's management in the 1980s. The list included a number of previously missed opportunities in the area of television, an arena the company entered in the 1990s. Observers in the financial world have sounded tones of amazement and sometimes disgust at what is perceived as the overly cautious management style at Dow Jones; hence *Fortune* observed that Dow Jones "has seemed for years to operate in a world utterly unlike the one judged in [*The Wall Street Journal*'s] pages."

Dow Jones is optimistic regarding earnings from its business publishing segment, primarily from advertising rate increases. The company stated that its 1998 results

led to the rapid spread from its Wall Street origins to the Boston branch headed by Clarence Barron and subsequent widespread use of broadtape in the 1920s, which linked the nation's market centers in a network of information. In the 1940s *The Wall Street Journal*'s managing editor Bernard Kilgore adopted a strategy that the paper continued to follow five decades later—offering a national perspective on the news, rather than one confined to a specific area. Thus under Kilgore's guidance the paper's Pacific Coast Edition, which had featured entirely different stories than its Eastern parent, was brought into alignment with the national edition.

Dow Jones' clientele, business people around the world, required continual attention to innovations in information technology. In 1971, long before widespread access to what became known as the information superhighway, the company introduced the Dow Jones News/ Retrieval Service, which made it possible for subscribers to obtain current information via their computers.

INFLUENCES

Perhaps the single greatest influence on the fortunes of Dow Jones has been the family that inherited a large share of the company from their forebear, Clarence Barron. (In 1997 the Barron heirs owned 42 percent of the company.) For years the heirs maintained what *Fortune* in February 1997 called "the coziest partnership between a family and a publicly held company in America." The heirs of Clarence Barron maintained a conservative strategy in both daily operations and in financial management. Thus, unlike other well-known newspaper families, they seldom interfered in the daily affairs of *The Wall Street Journal,* leaving it to the journalists to run. Likewise, when it came to the boardroom the family trusted management to make the decisions.

In many ways, the influence of the Barron family (few family members still carried Clarence's surname) was a positive one. In the case of the newspaper, their hands-off ownership style permitted it to become one of the leading national dailies—a paper that, unlike many competitors, tends to take the side of business and free enterprise on its editorial page. Also, the patriarchal control of the larger enterprise helped keep Dow Jones safe in the 1980s, when many other venerable old companies fell victim to hostile takeovers.

Barron's heirs reigned with caution and stability, but the negative side of their strategy was apparent in the company's growth from 1986 to 1996. In that decade, sales increased from $1.13 billion a year to almost $2.48 billion—more than double—but profits stayed almost the same: $183 million in 1986 and $190 million ten years later.

When Barron's great-granddaughter Bettina Bancroft died in May 1995, leadership passed to a new generation led by Bancroft's daughter Elizabeth "Lizzie"

FAST FACTS:
About Dow Jones & Company, Inc.

Ownership: Dow Jones is a publicly owned company traded on the New York Stock Exchange.

Ticker symbol: DJ

Officers: Kenneth L. Burenga, Pres., COO, & Director, 53, 1997 base salary $590,000; Carl M. Valenti, Sr. VP, 59, 1997 base salary $453,000; Peter G. Skinner, Sr. VP, 53, 1997 base salary $435,000

Employees: 12,300 (approximately one-quarter based outside the United States)

Principal Subsidiary Companies: Dow Jones has a vast base of affiliates, licensees, and subsidiary companies including Dow Jones Markets; IDD Enterprises, L.P.; and a worldwide television alliance with NBC.

Chief Competitors: Competitors of Dow Jones include: Bloomberg L.P., a financial news and data company, magazine publisher, and operator of national television, radio, and newspaper wire services; New York Times, a media and communications conglomerate with interests in newspapers, magazines, broadcasting, and information services; and Reuters Group PLC, a general news agency and financial information distributor.

Goth, who was born in 1965. Goth and her cousins wanted to know why stocks were performing so poorly, and they began to challenge the governing philosophy of Dow Jones. No longer did they see the company as (in the words of one past statement to shareholders) "a quasi-public trust." They were determined to see the company become more profitable, and if that meant getting rid of ambitious and ultimately unsuccessful enterprises, they were willing to do so. Goth's strategy made plenty of enemies in the family, but it also brought her some allies. In 1997 market analysts began to closely watch this family feud for signs of the company's future direction.

CURRENT TRENDS

With the ascendancy of Lizzie Goth and her faction, the Dow Jones board of directors is more aggressive and

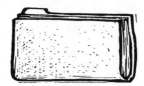

THE WALL STREET SHUFFLE

What exactly is the Dow Jones Industrial Average (DJIA)? The DJIA is an index computed by totaling the stock prices of 30 major U.S. industrial companies and dividing it by a number that accounts for stock-split distortions over the years. Want to know what happened to the price of the 30 stocks in the DJIA today? Don't look at the average itself but at the percentage change in the Dow on a specific day. Over 100 years old, the DJIA is the best-known market indicator in the world. The industrial average started out using 12 companies in 1896, and it was upped to 20 companies in 1916. The 30-stock average appeared in 1928, and although the number has since remained the same, companies are added and deleted from time to time. When choosing a new company to add, they look for a history of successful growth along with interest among investors. The most common reason for changing a stock is that something significant is happening to the company, such as being bought out by another company. In 1991 Walt Disney replaced USX Corp., J.P. Morgan replaced Primerica Corp., and Caterpillar replaced Navistar. Some stocks have bounced in and out of the DJIA, particularly General Electric, which has been included three times, and taken out twice. Similarly, U.S. Rubber and Du Pont have been included in the average more than once. So, just how high can the DJIA climb? There is no limit to how high it can go.

more oriented toward growth than in the mid-1990s. *Fortune* magazine, notable for its coverage of the dispute between the heirs of Charles Barron, offered speculation in February 1997 as to possible choices for future boards; most of the named individuals came from information industry leaders such as Microsoft and Intel.

The company, always a leader in the field of electronic information, has continued to offer new electronic products such as *The Wall Street Journal* Interactive Edition, introduced in 1996. During 1997 Dow Jones, along with the National Broadcasting Company (NBC), entered into an international business alliance. In the United States the company reported that a multiyear licensing agreement to supply business news programming had been made with CNBC, an overseas operation. In 1998 Dow Jones, along with primary exchanges in France, Germany, and Switzerland, began a series of indexes that track the performance of certain European equities, as well as gauge the market performance of countries that are expected to join the European Monetary Union.

PRODUCTS

Dow Jones' products include the following information services: Dow Jones Markets, Dow Jones News Service, Dow Jones 90-Day News/Retrieval, AP-Dow Jones News Service, Capital Markets Report, Asian Equities Report, and Emerging Markets Report. Among its business publications, the most prominent is *The Wall Street Journal,* which also has international editions, *The Wall Street Journal Europe* and *The Asian Wall Street Journal,* as well as *The Wall Street Journal Classroom Edition,* used in 3,600 schools nationwide. The *Journal* offers new regional coverage in New England. Magazines include *Barron's, Far Eastern Economic Review,* and *American Demographics.* The company owns a number of smaller enterprises, including Ottaway Newspapers Inc., a group of 19 local dailies that make up Dow Jones' "community newspapers" division.

The company's business unit, Dow Jones Interactive Publishing is a leading publisher of electronic business and financial news, delivering to customers via personal computers, fax machines, and radio. Two radio programs are offered: The Wall Street Journal Report on AM and The Dow Jones Report on FM.

GLOBAL PRESENCE

Seventy-three percent of Dow Jones' income in 1997 came from the United States. Europe, the Middle East, and North Africa made up 14 percent; Asia and the Pacific, 9 percent; and other regions, 2 percent.

Dow Jones has operations in Canada, Panama, the Bahamas, Chile, and other parts of the Americas; the United Kingdom, Ireland, and much of western Europe; Hong Kong, Singapore, and Malaysia; Australia, New Zealand, and other parts of the Pacific; and South Africa.

EMPLOYMENT

Dow Jones began a cost-reduction program, which resulted in the firing of 200 to 300 employees, primarily at its subsidiary, Dow Jones Market. Nevertheless, the company has a strong employee benefits package, and lists available jobs at its web site. Full-time employment of 12,309 employees in 1997 was an increase of 3.9 percent from 1996 when employees totaled 11,844.

SOURCES OF INFORMATION

Bibliography

Baumohl, Bernard, et. al. "More Bad News for Dow Jones." *Time,* 31 March 1997.

Carvell, Tim. "The Owners Are Restless." *Fortune,* 17 February 1997.

"Dow Jones." *Hoover's Online,* 8 June 1998. Available at http://www.hoovers.com.

"Dow Jones: A Brief History" and "A Guide to Dow Jones' Business Segments." New York: Dow Jones & Co., 1997. Available at http://www.dowjones.com.

Nocera, Joseph. "Heard on the Street." *Fortune,* 3 February 1997.

For an annual report:

on the Internet at: http://www.dowjones.com

For additional industry research:

Investigate companies by their Standard Industrial Classification Codes, also known as SICs. Dow Jones' primary SICs are:

2711 Newspapers

2721 Periodicals

4832 Radio Broadcasting Stations

4833 Television Broadcasting Stations

6289 Security/Commodity Services, NEC

7372 Prepackaged Software

7383 News Syndicates

Dr Pepper/Seven Up, Inc.

FOUNDED: 1885 (Dr Pepper); 1936 (The Seven Up
   Company); 1988 (Dr Pepper/Seven Up, Inc.)

Contact Information:

HEADQUARTERS: PO Box 869077
   Plano, TX 75086-9077
PHONE: (972)673-7000
FAX: (972)673-7980
TOLL FREE: (800)527-7096
URL: http://www.drpepper.com

OVERVIEW

Dr Pepper is a 113-year old company, the oldest major soft drink brand in the United States; Seven Up is almost 70 years old. The two merged in 1988 after they were both bought by Hicks and Haas, a Dallas investment firm. The new company, Dr Pepper/Seven Up, Inc. was acquired in 1995 by Cadbury Schweppes PLC, a British candy and beverage company. Cadbury Schweppes looks at Dr Pepper as a leading brand and hopes changes to the formula and packaging of 7Up will make it a major player in the soft drink industry.

The greatest challenge to Dr Pepper/Seven Up is solving its distribution problem. In the United States the company relies mainly on Coke and Pepsi bottlers to make and distribute its products. Understandably, the big two would rather have their bottlers concentrate on their own brands, even though Pepsi retains the non-U.S./Puerto Rico rights to 7Up. Dr Pepper/Seven Up's plans for the future include a joint venture company that will distribute its products to parts of the United States.

The other challenge to the company is positioning 7Up as an alternative to Sprite. In early 1998 the formula for 7Up was changed and was met with increased volume sales in areas where the company heavily advertised.

COMPANY FINANCES

Although Cadbury Schweppes began as a candy company, by 1995 beverages accounted for half of its total sales. The beverage division, which includes Dr Pepper/Seven Up, had worldwide sales of $4.9 billion in

1996, 56 percent of Cadbury Schweppes' $8.8 billion in sales for the year. In 1997 the division's worldwide sales of $3.3 billion accounted for 47.4 percent of Cadbury Schweppes' $6.9 billion in sales. The total decrease in sales for the beverage division was $1.6 billion, or 32.7 percent, from 1996 to 1997. Profits of the Cadbury Schweppes beverage division also fell from $752 million in 1996 to $567 million in 1997, a decline of 24.6 percent. During a 52-week period in 1997-98, the company's stock sold for a high of $63.50 per share and a low of $34.63.

While worldwide sales of the Cadbury Schweppes division fell 32.7 percent from 1996 to 1997, sales rose 116.1 percent in the United Kingdom, 7.0 percent in Africa, and 1.4 percent in the United States. Sales declined in Europe (13.0 percent) and in the Pacific Rim (2.6 percent).

ANALYSTS' OPINIONS

Some analysts noted that Dr Pepper/Seven Up handled the takeover by Cadbury Schweppes smoothly. Although sales of Dr Pepper declined slightly in 1995, it remains a popular brand with consumers and distributors. While Dr Pepper is perceived as a strength to the company, Seven Up is seen as a weakness, as it never seems to beat out its competitor Sprite.

Some analysts say Dr Pepper/Seven Up needs to distinguish itself in the marketplace—giving consumers a reason to choose its products. Others say if Seven Up doesn't do something to set it apart from Sprite, it will probably fade into obscurity.

HISTORY

In 1885 Charles Alderton, a pharmacist, poured the first Dr Pepper at Morrison's Old Corner Drug Store in Waco, Texas. Dr Pepper (which dropped the period in "Dr" in the 1950s) was named after Dr. Wade Morrison's first employer, Dr. Charles Pepper, but it was also called "Waco" for a brief period of time. Of all major soft drinks in the United States, Dr Pepper is the oldest brand and the oldest manufacturer of concentrates and syrups.

The popularity of Dr Pepper spread beyond Waco, and soon others wanted to buy the syrup to sell at their soda fountains. A ginger ale bottler, Robert S. Lazenby, agreed to produce Dr Pepper syrup for sale. Lazenby engineered the first mass introduction of Dr Pepper at the 1904 St. Louis World's Fair. Lazenby and Morrison eventually formed the Artesian Manufacturing & Bottling Company, adopting the name Dr Pepper Company in 1924. In 1946 Dr Pepper went public and was listed on the New York Stock Exchange.

FAST FACTS:
About Dr Pepper/Seven Up, Inc.

Ownership: Dr Pepper/Seven Up is owned by the British firm, Cadbury Schweppes PLC, which is publicly traded on the London, Australian, and New York Stock Exchanges.

Ticker symbol: CSG (NYSE)

Officers: Todd Stitzer, Pres. & CEO; Michael McGrath, COO

Employees: 42,911 (1996, for Cadbury Schweppes)

Chief Competitors: Dr Pepper/Seven Up competes against all beverage makers, especially carbonated-beverage makers. The principle competitors are: Coca-Cola and PepsiCo.

Dr Pepper remained a fairly obscure regional soft drink through its early years and on into maturity. Despite more than a century of existence, Dr Pepper did not become a truly national product until the mid-1980s, having been introduced nationally in the 1970s.

In 1984, management, attempting to avert a hostile takeover of the company, sold Dr Pepper for $416 million. The buyer was Forstmann Little, a multibillion-dollar partnership based in New York. Forstmann Little & Company privatized the company and took it off the New York Stock Exchange in February 1984. According to one long-term company executive, the Forstmann Little purchase was made merely to raise quick money for the investors. The partnership sold Dr Pepper in 1986.

C. L. Grigg, owner of The Howdy Company, developed 7Up in 1929. Grigg created the lemon-lime soda to go with the Howdy Orange drink. The popularity of the new soda led Grigg to change the company name to The Seven Up Company in 1936. By the late 1940s 7Up was the third-best-selling soda in the world. During this time the Grigg family maintained private ownership, but took the company public in 1967.

In 1978 tobacco giant Philip Morris purchased The Seven Up Company, looking to diversify from its tobacco holdings. Sales of 7Up began to decline, and a decade later Philip Morris was looking for a buyer. It thought it had a buyer in PepsiCo until the Federal Trade Commission ruled the sale anticompetitive. At the same time, the FTC ruled another sale anticompetitive—that of Dr Pepper by Forstmann Little & Company to Coca-Cola.

CHRONOLOGY:

Key Dates for Dr Pepper/Seven Up, Inc.

1885: Pharmacist Charles C. Alderton develops "Dr. Pepper's Phos-Ferrates"

1891: Dr Pepper becomes available in bottles for the first time

1904: Dr Pepper's marketers demonstrate their soft drink at the St. Louis World's Fair

1929: The Howdy Company introduces its lemon-lime beverage "Bib-Label Lithiated Lemon-Lime Soda," later renamed "7Up"

1936: The Howdy Company becomes the Seven Up Company

1946: Dr Pepper goes public

1967: The Seven Up Company goes public

1978: Philip Morris purchases the Seven Up Company

1984: Forstmann Little & Co. purchases Dr Pepper and privatizes it

1986: Hicks & Haas, an investment firm, purchases both Dr Pepper and Seven Up

1988: The two firms merge to become Dr Pepper/Seven Up, Inc.

1995: Cadburry Schweppes buys Dr Pepper/Seven Up

1998: 7Up changes its formula and bottle design

A Dallas investment firm, Hicks and Haas, stepped in and bought both companies in 1986. The two companies were merged in 1988, creating Dr Pepper/Seven Up, Inc.

Cadbury Schweppes, a British candy and beverage maker, acquired Dr Pepper/Seven-Up in March 1995 for $1.7 billion. The company's goal is to have "global leadership in the non-cola sector of the soft drinks market." The acquisition tripled Cadbury Schweppes' share of the soft drink market, making it an industry leader overnight.

STRATEGY

One of Cadbury Schweppes' strategies is to focus on key brands, especially Dr Pepper. The company wants to expand markets, be an innovator in flavors and packaging, and develop an efficient way of delivering its soft drinks to consumers.

Dr Pepper/Seven Up has distribution agreements with Coke and Pepsi bottlers. Coca-Cola and PepsiCo have exerted pressure on bottlers to dump Cadbury beverages from their lines, as well as at venues such as stadiums and athletic facilities, and to sign exclusive agreements for sales of their products. It has, therefore, become important for Dr Pepper/Seven Up to have its own distribution network, instead of relying on competitors.

Dr Pepper/Seven up continues to offer and promote special incentive programs for the various beverages in its line. In the first quarter of 1997 Dr Pepper sent a trade mailer to bottlers and managers in its various distribution channels as a "thank you" and reminder about the brand. The mailer was also sent to the media and investment brokers. A consistent strategy has been the company's sponsorship of various sporting events and participation in events such as the Tournament of Roses Parade.

New marketing plans and product designs were launched in 1997. Dr Pepper's "This Is The Taste" campaign led to record sales of the soft drink—brand sales grew almost double the industry rate. Also new for 1997 was Dr Pepper's new angle bottle. The company added top soda fountain accounts as well.

In 1998 7Up was made from a new formula and sold in a new splash bottle. Backing the changes was a new advertising campaign that included frequent samples to consumers.

INFLUENCES

Dr Pepper/Seven Up continues to plan long-term for its own distribution system—currently, Coke and Pepsi bottlers account for over half of the company's distribution. A new joint venture called The American Bottling Company was formed in February 1998. The new company will buy two independent bottling groups and distribute Dr Pepper/Seven Up in the midwestern United States. Cadbury Schweppes extended its licensing agreement with Coca-Cola Enterprises through December 2005 for distribution of its soft drinks in other areas of the United States.

PRODUCTS

Dr Pepper/Seven Up's market analysis of its customers' consumption habits shows that Dr Pepper drinkers tend to be heavy soft drink consumers. They also drink Dr Pepper in larger quantities than those who primarily drink other brands. At the end of 1997, Dr Pepper's U.S. market share had increased to a record 6.3 percent. Sales declined throughout 1997 for 7Up, but at a slower rate than previous years; fourth-quarter sales were in line with fourth-quarter 1996 sales. In the first quarter of 1998, in which the new formula received strong support, the volume of 7Up sold was up between 7 and 21 percent.

The conglomerated Dr Pepper/Seven Up offers numerous beverages as a result of its purchase by Cadbury Beverages. These include (in order of 1996 sales) Dr Pepper, 7Up, Canada Dry, Diet Dr Pepper, Diet 7Up, Sunkist, Squirt, A&W Root Beer, Schweppes, Crush, Welch's, Sun-drop, Vernors, IBC Root Beer, Country Time, A&W Cream Soda, Cherry 7Up, Diet A&W, Hines, Caffeine Free Diet Dr Pepper, Diet Cherry 7Up, and Caffeine Free Dr Pepper. In terms of overall market share in 1997, Dr Pepper placed fourth among soft drinks; 7Up placed seventh, just behind competitor Sprite. The top three drinks—Coca-Cola, Pepsi-Cola, and Diet Coke—remain the top sellers.

GLOBAL PRESENCE

Because parent Cadbury Schweppes is based in the United Kingdom, Dr Pepper/Seven-Up classifies as a "foreign" holding. The company enjoys a healthy presence in an estimated 200 markets outside the United States. In 1996 Dr Pepper was introduced in Australia, Mexico (the second-largest soft drink market in the world), and Russia, and was re-launched in the United Kingdom. Company market research showed a 41 percent brand awareness prior to the launch and a 93 percent brand awareness after the aggressive introduction.

SOURCES OF INFORMATION

Bibliography

Benezra, Karen. "Dr Pepper Seem Closer To Forging Bottler Deal." *Brandweek,* 10 November 1997.

The Cadbury Schweppes Home Page, 1 May 1998. Available at http://caburyschweppes.com.

Demaret, Kent. "'Foots' Clements, Master of the Soft-Drink Sell, Makes a Hot Deal." *People Weekly,* 8 September 1986.

The Dr Pepper Clock Dial. Dallas, TX: Dr Pepper, Spring 1997.

"History of Dr Pepper." *Dr Pepper Museum and Free Enterprise Institute,* 4 June 1998. Available at http://www.drpepper.com.

Rodengen, Jeffrey L. "The Legend of Dr Pepper/Seven-Up." Fort Lauderdale, FL: Write Stuff Syndicate, Inc. 1995.

Theodore, Sarah. "Breaking New Ground; Dr Pepper/Seven Up Recreates Itself for Its New Role in the Soft Drink Industry." *Beverage Industry,* January 1997.

"The Top 10 Soft Drink Review." *Beverage World,* March 1997.

For an annual report:
on the Internet at: http://www.cadburyschweppes.com

For additional industry research:
Investigate companies by their Standard Industrial Classification Codes, also known as SICs. Dr Pepper/Seven Up's primary SICs are:

2087 Flavoring Extracts Etc., NEC

6719 Holding Companies, NEC

DreamWorks SKG

FOUNDED: 1994

Contact Information:
HEADQUARTERS: 100 Universal Plz., Lakeside Bldg.
   Universal City, CA 91608
PHONE: (818)733-7000
FAX: (818)733-6153
URL: http://www.dreamworksrec.com/

OVERVIEW

Founded in 1994 by three of the entertainment world's biggest names, DreamWorks SKG is a huge multimedia conglomerate with interests in motion pictures, interactive game software, music, toys, and television programming. Given the resumes of the Hollywood giants who launched it, it is hardly surprising that the expectations for DreamWorks have been inordinately—perhaps unrealistically—high. The founding partners are Steven Spielberg, Jeffrey Katzenberg, and David Geffen. Spielberg, the extremely successful director of such blockbuster films as *Schindler's List, Jurassic Park,* and *E.T.,* is charged with managing DreamWorks' motion picture operations. Katzenberg, who is credited with Walt Disney's successful return to the animated features that first gave it fame, is responsible for DreamWorks' animation and television divisions. Long a powerhouse in the music industry, Geffen leads DreamWorks Records, the fledgling company's music division.

It was nearly three years after the founding of DreamWorks before the company rolled out its first motion picture. The film, *The Peacemaker,* was followed in quick succession by *Amistad* and *Mouse Hunt,* all of which were released in 1997. Perhaps because such big things were expected from DreamWorks, the three films' lukewarm reception at the box office was considered a major disappointment. In 1998, DreamWorks released *Deep Impact,* a story of a giant comet on a collision course with Earth. Early box office returns indicated the company's fourth film was likely to be fairly successful, if not a blockbuster, but again, it didn't quite fulfill the company's expectations.

DreamWorks was still without a studio in 1998, so it operated out of offices and facilities scattered over greater Los Angeles. The huge Playa Vista land development on the west side of Los Angeles, where DreamWorks had indicated it might wish to build a studio, seemed likely to get a green light in mid-1998 after years of delay.

COMPANY FINANCES

DreamWorks is a privately owned company and is not required to disclose details of its financial operations.

ANALYSTS' OPINIONS

Perhaps out of envy, or perhaps out of a genuine conviction that a better performance could be expected, many in Hollywood have enjoyed criticizing DreamWorks during its relatively short life. According to *Entertainment Weekly,* one Hollywood agent said of DreamWorks, "Based on a billion dollars and those three minds, what a completely unimpressive start." Another lamented that, "This studio was supposed to be talent-driven. This looks like a very suit-driven [company] so far."

Others have urged critics to give the DreamWorks team some time to get its act together. Arnold Rifkin, president of the William Morris Agency, was quoted by *Entertainment Weekly* as saying, "Given who [the founders] are, there was a level of expectation far greater than anyone could have achieved. But they are capable of achieving that." Further, others contended that Spielberg, Katzenberg, and Geffen have done quite well, considering that a major new Hollywood studio had not been launched in decades. *Entertainment Weekly* quoted Harold Vogel, an entertainment analyst with Cowen and Co., as saying, "To do what they've done in three years is remarkable."

HISTORY

The 1994 announcement that Steven Spielberg, one of Hollywood's most successful film directors, was teaming with Jeffrey Katzenberg, former Walt Disney executive, and music guru David Geffen to launch the first new studio in decades stunned and excited Hollywood. It was almost inevitable that the expectations generated by this announcement would be difficult to achieve.

Spielberg, Katzenberg, and Geffen each put up about $33 million to get the company started, but even more was needed. Fortunately, there was no shortage of investors willing to take a chance on DreamWorks. Paul

FAST FACTS:
About DreamWorks SKG

Ownership: DreamWorks SKG is a privately held company.

Officers: David Geffen, Partner; Jeffrey Katzenberg, Partner; Steven Spielberg, Partner; Ronald L. Nelson, CFO

Employees: 1,700

Chief Competitors: DreamWorks' major competitors include: Activision; All American Communications; Carsey-Werner; CBS; Creative Technology; Electronic Arts; Film Roman; KingWorld; LucasArts; NBC; News Corp.; Nintendo; PolyGram; Rank; Sony; Spelling Entertainment; Time Warner; Viacom; and Walt Disney.

Allen, cofounder of Microsoft, chipped in half a billion dollars, and Microsoft Corp. itself invested at least $30 million. Additionally, South Korea's One World Media came through with $300 million.

Three years passed before the company released its first film, *The Peacemaker.* The film, starring George Clooney and Nicole Kidman, was a disappointment at the box office, giving rise to more criticism. *Amistad,* which was critically acclaimed, failed to catch on at the box office, and *Mouse Hunt* followed. All three films were released without much success in the final months of 1997. The public seemed much more receptive to *Deep Impact,* the story of a comet hurtling toward Earth, and *Paulie,* the story of a slick-talking parrot. Both were released in the spring of 1998. *Saving Private Ryan* and *The Prince of Egypt,* both slated for late 1998 release, held even higher hopes for DreamWorks.

Although DreamWorks started slowly on the film front, a good deal was accomplished in other areas. DreamWorks and Microsoft set up a joint venture to develop interactive entertainment software, and DreamWorks and Silicon Graphics cofounded a $50 million animation studio. In addition, the company negotiated a television programming partnership with ABC, as well as a 10-year licensing agreement with Home Box Office, which was estimated to be worth $1 billion. The acquisition of ABC by Disney in 1996, however, cast some doubt on the viability of DreamWorks' partnership with ABC. Further complicating the ABC deal was a $250

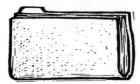

LET US ENTERTAIN YOU

The idea was simple. Take three talented and rich people and combine forces to create a mega-company called DreamWorks, the first new major Hollywood studio to appear in some time. Is this an original idea? Not really. Long before Steven Spielberg, Jeffrey Katzenberg, and David Geffen formed DreamWorks, silent film stars Charlie Chaplin, Mary Pickford, and Douglas Fairbanks founded United Artists with a similar philosophy: to create a talent-friendly movie company. With the recent folding of companies such as Carolco, Cinergi, and Savoy Pictures, there appears to be a need for organizations that have the ability to buy, produce, and distribute entertainment products. DreamWorks has the talent and the money to fulfill all those functions.

storytelling, but the stories are made, distributed, and exhibited in different formats. On top of that, the technological revolution of the last decade has had a profound effect on each and every one of the disciplines. What does it mean? That in many respects companies that were built out of bricks and mortar 65 years ago are hobbled in their ability to embrace and/or catch up with the opportunities being offered by today's new tools and technologies."

The cofounders feel comfortable with the strategy they adopted when launching DreamWorks in 1994, according to Katzenberg. Each one brings to the company his individual strength, and the company has endeavored to put these strengths to the best possible use. For example, Spielberg, who has amassed a long list of successful film credits, is concentrating on motion picture production. Geffen, already a major force in the music business, is looking after that end of DreamWorks' operations. He is also, Katzenberg said, "sort of the guiding business leader, and he makes sure the entrepreneurial instinct remains our overriding spirit." Geffen acts as a liaison with the company's investors and monitors DreamWorks' strategic alliances with other companies and groups.

million suit filed against Disney by Jeffrey Katzenberg, one of the founders of DreamWorks.

The company's early offerings for television failed to generate much excitement. Among DreamWorks' failed TV series were *Champs, Ink, Arsenio,* and *High Incident.* One sitcom that managed to survive beyond a single season was *Spin City,* starring Michael J. Fox.

On the music front, DreamWorks was also a slow starter. Two of the company's top recording artists were Randy Travis and George Michael, performers considered by many to be past their prime. Michael's debut album on the SKG label was far less successful than some of his earlier releases. One of the music division's hottest releases was comedian Chris Rock's *Roll with the New.* Despite the success of this release, many observers said the company's music division was out of step with the times and needed to get in touch with current trends in the business.

STRATEGY

The basic concept behind DreamWorks, according to cofounder Jeffrey Katzenberg, is storytelling, which is distinct from the rationale behind the movie studios of the past. Katzenberg said these other studios were driven first and foremost by production for a single outlet, movie theaters. In an interview Katzenberg said, "Contrast that with the studio of today, which is engaged in a host of different enterprises. They all revolve around

INFLUENCES

Among the influences that have helped shape DreamWorks' strategy is the growing appetite of the American public for well-produced, feature-length animated films. Katzenberg, who brings to DreamWorks years of experience with animation at Disney, is spearheading the development of animated features for the company. The first of these features, *The Prince of Egypt,* was scheduled for release during the 1998 Christmas season.

Another trend, successfully exploited by many Hollywood film studios, is the growing market for spin-off products from successful film projects. DreamWorks is certainly not overlooking such marketing opportunities. Of the market for spin-off products, Katzenberg told IBM's *Think Leadership,* "When great properties are created these days, the enterprises are surrounded by very valuable, very compelling, and equally creative ancillary opportunities. When a *Jurassic Park* comes along, there is a *Jurassic Park* the movie, the video game, and the soundtrack. There's *Jurassic Park* publishing, t-shirts, toys, and other types of merchandise."

CURRENT TRENDS

All three cofounders of DreamWorks are dedicated to keeping the company small enough to ensure that all parties are always operating on the same wavelength. It is large enough to be able to demand full market value for its product and for the creativity of the people who put out that product. It is also important, according to Katzenberg, that the company be, "smart enough to make sure we all synergistically feed on one another and create values for each other. To make it all work takes state-of-the-art technology that allows us to take advantage of the opportunities that exist."

PRODUCTS

DreamWorks is involved with a wide variety of products, including the production of live and animated motion pictures, television programming, music recording, and interactive entertainment software. In addition to its own product lines, the company has entered into joint venture agreements with several other companies. These include the production of computer-animated films with Pacific Data Images, digital film recorders with Kodak, interactive CD-ROMs with Microsoft, and toys and games with Hasbro.

GLOBAL PRESENCE

Although DreamWorks' headquarters and its production facilities are all located within the United States, the entertainment business has become increasingly international in nature. Many of the industry's motion pictures are filmed at overseas locations, and the international distribution of a film often produces a large percentage of its overall revenue. Additionally, the talent that goes into these film projects is drawn from all around the world.

SOURCES OF INFORMATION

Bibliography

Bates, James, and Patrice Apodaca. "Stalking the King of Animation." *Los Angeles Times,* 20 June 1996.

"DreamWorks." *Morning Edition (National Public Radio,* 20 November 1997.

"DreamWorks SKG." *Hoover's Online,* 11 June 1998. Available at: http://www.hoovers.com.

"DreamWorks Signs Dennis Leary." *Business Wire,* 29 April 1998.

"How the Dream Works." *Think Leadership.* IBM Corporation, 1997.

Pringle, Paul. "Mouse Hunt: After Decades of Ruling the Movie-'Toon Roost, Disney Faces an Animated Flock of Competitors." *Dallas Morning News,* 16 November 1997.

Young, Josh, and Willman, Chris. "Needs Improvement: A Special DreamWorks Report Card: DreamWorks Created by Hollywood's Best and Brightest." *Entertainment Weekly,* 17 October 1997.

For additional industry research:

Investigate companies by their Standard Industrial Classification Codes, also known as SICs. DreamWorks' primary SICs are:

3652 Prerecorded Records and Tapes

7810 Motion Picture Production and Allied Services

7812 Motion Picture & Video Production

7822 Motion Picture Distribution Services

7824 Film or Tape Distribution for Television

The Dun & Bradstreet Corporation

FOUNDED: 1841 as the Mercantile Agency

Contact Information:

HEADQUARTERS: 1 Diamond Hill Rd.
Murray Hill, NJ 07974
PHONE: (908)665-5000
FAX: (908)665-5524
URL: http://www.dnbcorp.com

OVERVIEW

The Dun & Bradstreet Corporation (D&B) is a holding company for Dun & Bradstreet, Reuben H. Donnelley, and Moody's Investor Service. Dun & Bradstreet is one of the world's largest credit reporting agencies. Their service covers over 48 million businesses in nearly 40 countries. Moody's Investor Service publishes debt ratings on corporate and government securities, as well as other business and financial information. Reuben H. Donnelley publishes yellow pages directories.

Previously a much larger company, D&B reorganized and spun off A.C. Nielsen (their marketing information services) and Cognizant (their market research and high-tech advisory services) into independent, publicly held companies in 1996. In 1998 the company announced a plan to split off Reuben H. Donnelley as well.

COMPANY FINANCES

In 1995, the last full year before the split, worldwide sales totaled $5.4 billion. In 1997 worldwide sales totaled $2.15 billion. Of this, 74 percent of revenues are from U.S. sales and 22 percent are from European sales. Approximately 64 percent of revenues came from The Dun & Bradstreet operating company, 18 percent from Moody's, and 18 percent from R.H. Donnelley.

As of February 20, 1998, more than 171 million shares of The Dun & Bradstreet's common stock were outstanding. The total market value of the common stocks held by non affiliates (i.e., people not considered officers of the company) was approximately $5.63 billion. The stock price ranged from $23.75 to $31.25 per share over the prior 12-month period.

ANALYSTS' OPINIONS

In a 1995 *Money* article, seven leading money managers offered advice for poor stock performers, with Dun & Bradstreet leading the list. They warned that the company was due for a major restructuring. Yet when Dun & Bradstreet formally announced their restructuring, it created very little excitement among market analysts. According to *Business Week,* if Dun & Bradstreet's leadership hoped to thrill investors with their announcement, they were headed for a disappointment, or a "deafening silence." Likewise *Barron's* reported in the same month that in spite of the good news, the market had not responded. But six months later, the same publication speculated that, because of the restructuring, good things lay in Dun & Bradstreet's future.

Standard & Poor's includes Dun & Bradstreet in their S&P 500 index. Their Feburary 1998 Stock Report lists D&B as a "secure investment," with yield of 2.7 percent, and a price earnings ratio of 18.3. They expect a 9 percent "earnings per share" growth in 1998.

HISTORY

In 1841, Lewis Tappan founded the Mercantile Agency for the purpose of "obtaining, in a proper manner, intelligence of the responsibility of merchants visiting the market." The first company of its kind, it helped New York store owners to evaluate credit applications and determine potential bad-risk customers. John Bradstreet of Cincinnati, Ohio, formed a similar company after he obtained a large store of credit information from the liquidation of a client's estate in 1849.

The growing Mercantile Agency hired attorneys and other observers in communities throughout the United States to help prepare credit reports on local businesses. These observers included four future U.S. presidents: Abraham Lincoln, Ulysses S. Grant, Grover Cleveland, and William McKinley.

Robert Graham Dun headed up the Mercantile Agency from 1859 to 1900, after which the company assumed the name R.G. Dun & Company. Two other subsidiaries of Dun & Bradstreet, R.H. Donnelley and Moody's, were also formed around the turn of the century. Reuben H. Donnelley of Chicago published his first telephone directory in 1886, and John Moody put out the first of his industrial manuals in 1900.

R.G. Dun & Company's chief rival in the credit reporting business was the Bradstreet Company, and for many years the two fought a costly feud. In 1933 Dun's

FINANCES:

Dun & Bradstreet Corp. Operating Revenues, 1994-1997 (billion dollars)

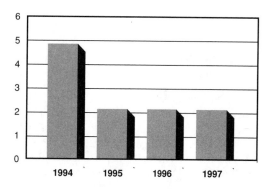

Dun & Bradstreet Corp. 1997 Stock Prices (dollars)

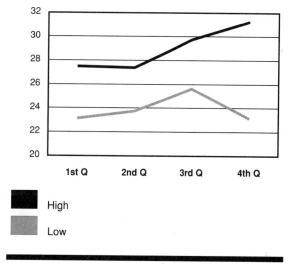

■ High

▨ Low

president, Arthur Whiteside, proposed merging the companies to save them both from economic ruin. Thus Dun & Bradstreet was born. The company merged with the R.H. Donnelley Company in 1961, and with Moody's Investors Service in 1962. Throughout the 1960s and 1970s, the company progressed in innovative uses of information technology. In the 1970s and 1980s, it acquired other information companies, most notably television ratings giant A.C. Nielsen in 1984.

In 1995, Dun & Bradstreet did $5.4 billion in business worldwide. However, poor stock performance led to the company's divesting itself of many of its holdings.

FAST FACTS:

About The Dun & Bradstreet Corporation

Ownership: Dun & Bradstreet is a publicly owned company traded on the New York Stock Exchange.

Ticker symbol: DNB

Officers: Volney Taylor, Chmn. & CEO, 58, $2,147,449; Frank S. Sowinski, Sr. VP & CFO, 41, $701,746; John Rugherford, Jr., Pres.—Moody's Investor Service; Frank R. Noonan, Sr. VP & Pres.—Reuben H. Donnelley, 55, $693,913

Employees: 15,100

Principal Subsidiary Companies: The Dun & Bradstreet Corporation is composed of the Dun & Bradstreet operating company, Moody's Investor Service, and Reuben H. Donnelley.

Chief Competitors: Dun & Bradstreet's primary competitors are: American Business Information; Dow Jones; Hoover's Inc.; Morningstar Inc.; Reuters; and Thomson Corp.

In 1996 Dun & Bradstreet separated from two of its biggest holdings, Nielsen and Cognizant, splitting them off into independent publicly held companies. In 1998 the company announced a plan to split Reuben H. Donnelley as well.

By narrowing its scope, Dun & Bradstreet returned to the elements on which its business was built: credit reporting and business information.

STRATEGY

In a pamphlet with which it introduced "The New Dun & Bradstreet" to the public in 1996, the company proclaimed, "We've been working on the Information Highway for 155 years." Similar statements at its web site emphasize Dun & Bradstreet's tradition of innovation. Given that Lewis Tappan's Mercantile Agency was the first of its kind, it should not be surprising that the company would stress its history of innovation. But Dun & Bradstreet's image as a long-standing provider of business information has been just as important. Longevity implies reliability, and reliability is even more important in the information industry than in many other businesses.

INFLUENCES

The technology of information gathering and storage has influenced Dun & Bradstreet from its beginnings. Mercantile Agency partner Benjamin Douglass in 1847 helped his firm become one of the first to make use of the telegraph, invented only three years before; and in 1874 the agency became the first commercial customers of the Remington typewriter. In the 1970s the company established its National Business Information Center, a large computer network and one of the first intranets, a computer network internal to a specific company. Dun & Bradstreet continued to stay abreast of information-age innovations in the 1990s.

In the 1990s Dun & Bradstreet, known for its reports on other businesses, was ironically forced to undergo rigorous self-analysis. In 1933, when it came to settling the long-standing feud between the Dun and Bradstreet companies, a merger had been a perfect cure. But like many companies in the 1970s and 1980s, Dun & Bradstreet succumbed to a mania for rapid growth and diversification. This led to the purchases of Technical Publishing in 1978, National CSS (a computer company) in 1979, McCormack & Dodge software in 1983, A.C. Nielsen in 1984, pharmaceutical market-research giant IMS International in 1988, and Management Science America in 1989.

Dun & Bradstreet would have also purchased Information Resources Inc., a competitor of Nielsen, but a 1987 antitrust suit stopped it from doing so. What ultimately quashed merger mania at Dun & Bradstreet, however, was not legal action but the bottom line. In the early 1990s the company started selling off unprofitable subsidiaries, consolidating its worldwide data centers, and downsizing its work force. Still, profits did not improve. Like competitor Dow Jones, Dun & Bradstreet had seen its revenues grow dramatically in a decade, but net income had stayed the same despite a few high years. The company's stock, as *Barron's* reported in August 1995, was still trading at the same price as in 1989, $56 per share.

In 1996 management decided to spin off Nielsen and Cognizant, and to return the core Dun & Bradstreet Corporation to its original focus: business information services.

CURRENT TRENDS

The biggest trend at Dun & Bradstreet is its renewed focus on its core business, which is information. The company continues to develop new products, particularly ones that are computer-based. In a move linked with its reorganization, in August 1996 the company increased its available line of credit, a back-up to its bonds, to $1.2 billion; hence the money should be there for innovation as needed.

CHRONOLOGY:

Key Dates for The Dun & Bradstreet Corporation

1841: Lewis Tappan founded Dun & Bradstreet as the Mercantile Agency

1849: John M. Bradstreet Company is founded

1859: Robert Dun takes over the Mercantile Agency and changes the name to R.G. Dun & Co.

1869: The firm opens an office in San Francisco

1896: Robert Dun Douglass becomes general manager of the firm

1900: The firm begins operation as a common-law trust with Douglass in charge as an executive trustee

1931: R.G. Dun acquires National Credit Office and reorganizes into the holding company R.G. Dun Corporation

1933: R.G. Dun Corporation merges with Bradstreet Company

1942: Acquires Credit Clearing House

1961: Dun & Bradstreet merges with R.H. Donnelley

1962: Merges with Moody's Investors Service; introduces a nine digit numbering system called Data Universal Numbering system (D-U-N-S) to identify companies in their databases

1978: Purchases Technical Publishing

1979: Acquires National CSS; first edition of Dun's Financial Profiles is published

1983: Purchases McCormack & Dodge

1984: Acquires A.C. Nielsen

1988: Buys IMS International

1996: Dun & Bradstreet spins off both A.C. Nielsen and Cognizant

1997: Sells NCH Promotional Services

PRODUCTS

Dun & Bradstreet Information Systems' most important product is its database of information on 48 million businesses worldwide. Its Data Universal Numbering System or D-U-N-S™, a nine-digit designation for individual businesses that has proven more efficient than alphabetical cataloging, helps the company keep track of the multitudinous enterprises in its database. Parts of this database, which is updated continually, go into a wide variety of books and electronic products such as the D&B regional Business Directory, a CD-ROM introduced in October 1996. In addition, Dun & Bradstreet provides custom credit reports on specific businesses, similar to the reports Equifax and TRW provide on individuals.

Moody's Investor Service likewise produces a number of business guides, including a debt rating service that analyzes corporate and government securities. At the end of 1997, Moody's had outstanding ratings on approximately 85,000 corporate and 62,000 public finance obligations. R.H. Donnelley's yellow page advertising and directory business has clients throughout the United States, including NYNEX, Cincinnati Bell, and Sprint.

GLOBAL PRESENCE

Dun & Bradstreet maintains offices in 36 countries including the United States, and has independent corre-spondents in over 150 other countries worldwide. Moody's also has offices in the United States, Canada, the larger countries of western Europe, and Oceania. R.H. Donnelley's business is confined to the United States.

EMPLOYMENT

Downsizing will continue to be a part of Dun & Bradstreet's strategy, but that downsizing is turning the company into a more focused and profitable enterprise.

SOURCES OF INFORMATION

Bibliography

Bary, Andrew. "Going Separate Ways." *Barron's,* 15 January 1996.

Byrne, John. "Why D & B is Glued to the Ticker." *Business Week,* 19 February 1996.

Dorfman, Dan. "Cranky Money Managers Try to Light a Fire Under These 10 Big Stocks." *Money,* June 1995.

"Dun & Bradstreet." *Standard and Poor's Stock Report,* 21 February 1998.

Dun & Bradstreet Corporation. *Introducing The New Dun & Bradstreet.* Murray Hill, NJ: Dun & Bradstreet, 1996.

"The Dun & Bradstreet Corporation." *Hoover's Online,* 23 June 1998. Available at http://www.hoovers.com.

Dun & Bradstreet's Home Page, April 1998. Available at http://www.dnbcorp.com.

The Launch: The New Dun & Bradstreet. Murray Hill, NJ: Dun & Bradstreet, 1996.

Norris, James. *R.G. Dun & Co. 1841-1900 The Development of Credit Reporting in the Nineteenth Century.* Greenwood Press, 1978.

For an annual report:

write: Dun & Bradstreet, 1 Diamond Hill Rd., Murray Hill, NJ 07974

For additional industry research:

Investigate companies by their Standard Industrial Classification Codes, also known as SICs. Dun & Bradstreet's primary SICs are:

2741 Miscellaneous Publishing

7323 Credit Reporting Services

7375 Information Retrieval Services

E.I. du Pont de Nemours and Co.

OVERVIEW

Du Pont is the largest chemical company in the world. The company manufactures and sells thousands of products to many markets through 80 business units. Products produced include textiles, agricultural products, specialty chemicals, fibers, automotive and engineering polymers, and pharmaceuticals. The petroleum industry contributed to nearly half of Du Pont's sales, yet the company announced in 1998 that it would sell its wholly-owned petroleum subsidiary, Conoco, Inc. Du Pont is choosing to focus on its Life Science industry.

Du Pont and its subsidiaries conduct business in some 70 countries worldwide. Du Pont has about 175 manufacturing and processing facilities, which include 140 chemical and specialty plants, 8 petroleum refineries, and 27 natural-gas processing plants. The company operates research and development labs in 18 states in the United States and more than 11 foreign countries.

COMPANY FINANCES

In 1997 Du Pont's worldwide sales were $45.1 billion, a gain of 2.9 percent over 1996 sales of $43.8 billion. The company's profits were down by $1.2 billion—$2.4 billion in 1997 as opposed to $3.6 billion in 1996—due mainly to nonrecurring charges in the amount of $1.7 billion taken in 1997. Excluding the nonrecurring charges, in 1997 Du Pont reported its fourth consecutive year of record earnings. The company also raised dividends 10.3 percent, from $1.12 per share in 1996 to $1.23 per share in 1997. During a 52-week pe-

ALSO KNOWN AS: Du Pont
FOUNDED: 1802

Contact Information:
HEADQUARTERS: 1007 Market St.
  Wilmington, DE 19898
PHONE: (302)774-1000
FAX: (302)774-7321
TOLL FREE: (800)441-7515
EMAIL: info@dupont.com
URL: http://www.dupont.com

FINANCES:

E.I. du Pont de Nemours Sales, 1994-1997 (billion dollars)

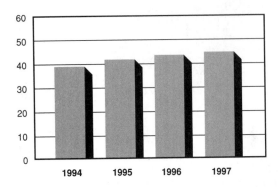

E.I. du Pont de Nemours 1997 Stock Prices (dollars)

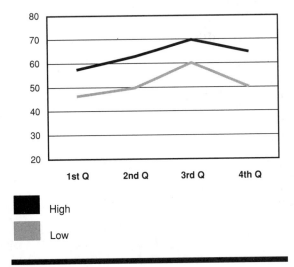

riod in 1997 Du Pont's stock ranged from a high of $69 to a low of $46.

All industry segments showed gains in sales from 1996 to 1997, except Life Sciences, which remained the same, and Diversified Businesses, which was down by 9.7 percent. In 1997 Petroleum contributed 46.6 percent of Du Pont's total sales, followed by Fibers with 17.1 percent, Polymers with 15.1 percent, Chemicals with 9.5 percent, Diversified Businesses with 6.2 percent, and Life Sciences with 5.5 percent.

Although lower petroleum prices, unfavorable currency rates, a rapid pace of acquisitions, and the Asian economic crisis could point to a downturn in 1998, Du Pont fully expects to continue with record sales and earnings. Although Asia is in turmoil, Europe and the United States, which account for 80 percent of the company's sales, are projected to have healthy economies. Like many other companies, in 1997 Du Pont was hard hit by the strong U.S. dollar, so the company has raised prices overseas to compensate for currency rates. Petroleum and natural gas prices have declined, which translates into lower raw-material costs for Du Pont's Chemicals industry.

HISTORY

E. I. Du Pont De Nemours and Company began as a family-owned gunpowder and explosives partnership in 1802. Eleuthere Irenee Du Pont de Nemours, the founder, was born to French nobility, emigrated to Delaware in 1800 after the French Revolution, and set up a gunpowder plant on Delaware's Brandywine Creek. The plant grew to be the largest of its kind, and within a couple of decades it was also producing dynamite, nitroglycerine, and guncotton. About a century after it was founded, the senior partner Eugene Du Pont died. The surviving partners decided to sell the company to the highest bidder, who turned out to be Alfred I. Du Pont, a distant cousin of the founder.

Alfred Du Pont and two cousins, Coleman Du Pont and Pierre Du Pont, expanded the company to command the entire explosives market by 1907. The company was so dominant that the U.S. government initiated antitrust proceedings against it. In 1912 Du Pont was deemed a gunpowder monopoly and was ordered to divest itself of a substantial portion of its business.

Modernization, diversification, good management, and a command of the market characterized Du Pont's industrial-era phase. The outbreak of World War I generated about $89 million in business, and the company diversified into paints, plastics, and dyes. Numerous fiber-related discoveries made Du Pont a strong contender in that market. Du Pont chemists' experiments with a product called guncotton led to the company's entry into the textile business. In the 1920s Du Pont acquired rights to produce cellophane. Du Pont made it moisture-proof, transforming cellophane from a decorative wrap to a packaging material for food and other products. Du Pont introduced the clothing fiber Rayon in the 1920s. The company's most important invention, Nylon, was created in 1938. A large number of plastics and synthetic fibers followed.

The demand for artificial fibers collapsed in the mid-1970s, bringing the company's bread-and-butter business to a halt. Increased cost of raw materials and declining demand continued to depress the market in 1979. The collapse compelled Du Pont to concentrate exclusively on repairing its older businesses, thereby reducing its commitment to research and development.

Continued reliance on fibers made Du Pont one of the worst-hit companies in the 1980 recession. However, the company's continued attention to the fibers business resulted in the discovery of a very important material called Kevlar in 1980. The revolutionary material was light yet strong, possessing a tensile strength five times that of steel. Du Pont made the largest financial gamble in history when it invested $250 million in a Kevlar plant expansion. However, Kevlar's true success ultimately depended on the price of its raw material, oil.

The largest merger in history occurred when Du Pont took over Conoco Oil Company, the second-largest oil company in the United States. The company enjoyed greater growth and financial security when it acquired Remington Arms, a manufacturer of sporting firearms and ammunition. By 1982 Du Pont had also acquired New England Nuclear Corporation and Solid State Dielectrics.

By the mid-1980s Du Pont had approximately 90 major businesses selling a wide range of products to different industries, including petroleum, textile, transportation, chemical construction, utility, health care, and agricultural. Du Pont had business operations in more than 50 nations, and was organized into 8 principle business segments—biomedical products, industrial and consumer products, fibers, polymer products, agricultural and industrial chemicals, petroleum exploration and production, coal, and petroleum refining, marketing, and transportation.

FAST FACTS:
About E.I. du Pont de Nemours and Co.

Ownership: Du Pont is a publicly owned company traded on the New York Stock Exchange.

Ticker symbol: DD

Officers: John A. Krol, Chmn., $2,169,668; Charles O. Holiday, Pres. & CEO, $1,576,400; Gary M. Pfeiffer, Sr. VP & CFO; Archie W. Dunham, Exec. VP, $2,117,500

Employees: 98,000 (1997)

Principal Subsidiary Companies: Du Pont is organized into six industry segments: Chemicals, Fibers, Polymers, Petroleum, Life Sciences, and Diversified Businesses.

Chief Competitors: Du Pont's diversity means it has worldwide competitors, both large and small. The company competes against chemical companies, oil and gas producers, and agribusiness companies. Some competitors are: BASF; Imperial Chemical Industries; Dow; Amoco Corp.; Exxon; Arco; Room and Haas; Courtaulds; and RPM.

STRATEGY

Du Pont's growth strategy contains four elements: research and development (R&D), acquisitions and expansions, focus on core businesses, and concentration on Life Sciences.

Du Pont's philosophy is staying ahead of competition by investing in research and development. The purpose of R&D is to make existing products better, find new applications, and develop new products and technologies. In 1997 the company spent $1.1 billion on R&D, up 8.1 percent from 1996; this amounted to 2.4 percent of the company's 1997 sales. While most of the company's R&D facilities are located in the Wilmington, Delaware, area (Du Pont's headquarters), there are 75 R&D sites worldwide, including more than 40 sites in 18 states in the United States.

The company is expanding the divisions it believes fits into its core industries. Acquisitions, joint ventures, and partnerships are used to strengthen Du Pont's industries. In 1997, Chemical made an offer to purchase ICI's foreign titanium dioxide business, subject to governmental approval. The deal would allow Du Pont to manufacture titanium dioxide in Asia and Africa, something the company had been looking to do. Du Pont announced a total of $7 billion in acquisitions in 1997. At the same time, the company began expanding its current businesses by adding manufacturing plants and upgrading facilities around the world.

While Du Pont adds to and expands its core businesses, it also sells off companies and joint ventures in industries not related to the core focus. For example, the company sold printing, publishing, and graphic arts businesses, as well as some medical products companies. Reflecting Du Pont's belief that alternatives to petroleum will be found, in May 1998 the company decided to sell 20 percent of its wholly-owned subsidiary Conoco, Inc.

Du Pont's newest focus is the Life Sciences industry. Du Pont Merck, the company's 50/50 joint venture with pharmaceutical maker Merck, had been developing drugs. In May 1998 Du Pont announced it would buy out Merck's portion of the venture, renaming the company DuPont Pharmaceuticals. The company is also pushing hard into the biotechnology market, developing alternatives for foods and petro-based fibers. Du Pont expects the Life Sciences industry to contribute 30 percent of the company's income by the year 2002.

CHRONOLOGY:

Key Dates for E.I. du Pont de Nemours and Co.

1802: Eleuthere Irenee du Pont de Nemours founds the company

1811: U.S. president Thomas Jefferson endorses du Pont

1902: Three cousins of the founder buy the company and reorganize

1909: The company begins investigating synthetic fibers

1912: DuPont is deemed a gunpowder monopoly and forced to divest itself of portions of its business

1931: Freon refrigerant is discovered

1938: DuPont invents Nylon fiber and Teflon

1955: DuPont starts expanding into Europe helping to rebuild the war-torn continent

1960: The company invents Lycra spandex

1976: DuPont makes a public commitment to stop CFC production

1981: Acquires Conoco and Consolidation Coal

1990: Merck and DuPont merge to form DuPont-Merck Pharmaceutical Company

1993: The company forms alliance with Asahi of Japan to grow Nylon business in Japan

1998: DuPont announces plans to buy Merck's portion of DuPont-Merck and rename the company DuPont Pharmaceuticals

INFLUENCES

With the inventions of Nylon, Rayon, and other fibers, Du Pont began focusing on the fiber industry, to the detriment of others. In the 1970s the company nearly collapsed after the cost of raw materials increased and demand plunged. The lesson learned was to diversify. Du Pont expanded its scope with many acquisitions. The company decided to risk becoming a leader in the Life Sciences by delving into development and production of biomedical products and agricultural chemicals.

Du Pont also became heavily involved in joint ventures worldwide. The company supported these businesses with large amounts of capital investment and research and development expenditures. Du Pont entered diverse fields, including genetic engineering, drugs, agricultural chemicals, electronics, fibers, and plastics. Du Pont also had the multinational marketing capability and the resources to become a major influence in the Life Sciences.

Although diversification put the company at less risk if one product failed, by 1985 Du Pont was bloated with its numerous businesses. The company undertook a massive restructuring, eliminating non-core businesses and investing heavily in the industries thought to bring future growth. Du Pont began to move away from commodity production, concentrating instead on oil, health care, electronics, and specialty chemicals.

CURRENT TRENDS

Lycra, a stretch polymer invented in 1959, became a big hit in the 1980s and 1990s after being adapted for biking clothes and other exercise outfits. Lycra clothing became fashionable, and big-name designers started incorporating Lycra (generic name spandex) in their fashions. Lycra profits topped $200 million per year. Even though Du Pont's patent on Lycra expired, Du Pont continued to improve the fabric and was its only major manufacturer. To maintain its dominant position, Du Pont announced that it would spend $500 million over the next three years to build or expand Lycra plants.

Even though the Gulf War temporarily drove up oil prices, leading to profits of more than $1 billion for Conoco, the worldwide recession was hurting most of the rest of the company. Du Pont reduced its focus on electronics and pharmaceuticals and refocused on its core businesses. As part of this initiative Du Pont acquired ICI's worldwide Nylon business in 1993. In January 1995 Du Pont and Dow Chemical announced their intention to form a joint venture for the discovery, development, production, and sale of thermoset and thermoplastic elastomer products. The venture was expected to have initial annual sales of about $1 billion.

In 1996 Du Pont streamlined its Nylon business by eliminating about 3,000 employees and launching a major restructuring program for its worldwide Nylon operations. The company continued to focus on its fiber division, developing new technologies that could cut polyester fiber production costs by up to 20 percent in the year 2000.

PRODUCTS

Some of Du Pont's most significant inventions include neoprene synthetic rubber (1931), Lucite (1937), and Nylon and Teflon (1938).

In 1997 the Nonwoven's division of Fibers introduced Xavan, a polypropylene for industrial packaging, furniture, and bedding. Fibers also developed new applications for existing products; Kevlar will be used to make concrete stronger, and Teflon will be used to produce low-friction socks.

CORPORATE CITIZENSHIP

Du Pont was one of the country's biggest air polluters, and the company spent more than $1 billion on pollution control and clean-up in the early 1990s. The firm spent another $1 billion to replace its chlorofluorocarbon business with chemicals less harmful to the ozone layer. Du Pont was also creating safer herbicides and expanding into the growing recycling market. Partly because of these changes, Du Pont's sales of agricultural chemicals tripled between 1985 and 1990 to $1.7 billion.

GLOBAL PRESENCE

Du Pont is one of the most diversified companies globally. With plans to increase its presence in high-growth areas of the globe, Du Pont has embarked on several undertakings in the Asia-Pacific region. Forming alliances and investing in product research and development was expected to enable Du Pont to double its market value in South America, Europe, and Asia. The company was expected to invest about $300 to $400 million on growth opportunities in Europe, which account for 25 percent of the company's earnings and sales. More than 35 percent of Du Pont's workforce is outside the United States.

SOURCES OF INFORMATION

Bibliography
Chapman, Peter. "Nylon Producers Completing Year of Record Output." *Chemical Market Reporter,* 6 January 1997.

Chirls, Stuart. "Du Pont: Technology May Slash Polyester Fiber Costs by 2000." *WWD,* 27 February 1997.

The Du Pont Home Page, 21 May 1998. Available at http://www.dupont.com.

"E. I. Du Pont De Nemours." *Hoovers Handbook of American Business 1996.* Austin, TX: The Reference Press, 1995.

"E.I. du Pont de Nemours and Company." *General Business File.* Ann Arbor, MI: University of Michigan, 1997.

E. I. du Pont de Nemours and Company 10K Filing, 21 May 1998. Available at http://www.sec.gov.

Hess, Glenn. "Du Pont Vows to Double Value Within Five Years; Company Plans to Improve Presence in High Growth Areas of the Globe." *Chemical Market Reporter,* 3 March 1997.

Lewis, Scott M. "E. I. du Pont de Nemours & Company." *International Directory of Company Histories,* Vol. 11. Detroit, MI: St. James Press.

Manufacturing USA. Detroit, MI: Gale Research, 1996.

Sherrid, Pamela. "Please Pass the Bioengineered Butter." *U.S. News and World Report,* 2 March 1998.

For an annual report:
on the Internet at: http://www.dupont.com **or** telephone: (302)744-4994 **or** write: Investor Relations, N9420, 1007 Market St., Wilmington, DE 19898

For additional industry research:
Investigate companies by their Standard Industrial Classification Codes, also known as SICs. Du Pont's primary SICs are:

1311 Crude Petroleum and Natural Gas

2221 Broadwoven Fabric Mills—Manmade

2819 Industrial Inorganic Chemicals, NEC

2869 Industrial Organic Chemicals, NEC

2899 Chemical Preparations, NEC

Duracell International Inc.

FOUNDED: 1935

Contact Information:
HEADQUARTERS: Berkshire Corporate Pk.
  Bethel, CT 06801
PHONE: (203)796-4000
FAX: (203)796-4187
URL: http://www.duracellusa.com

OVERVIEW

Duracell is the leader in the battery market, continuing to dominate its chief competitor, Eveready—the maker of Energizer batteries. The company, famous for its "Copper Top" products with their distinctive gold-and-black coloring, manufactures batteries for ordinary consumer use, as well as ones made especially for cameras, hearing aids, and other items. In 1997 Duracell had sales of $2.5 billion worldwide, and its stocks performed well. The company was purchased by Gillette in early 1997 for $7.0 billion. This move was seen by many analysts as an "ideal marriage" that would boost the performance of both companies. With approximately 70 percent of Gillette's sales coming from overseas, compared to about 50 percent for Duracell, the merger was expected to make Duracell even more of a presence in world markets.

COMPANY FINANCES

From 1992 to 1997 Duracell recorded an annual average growth rate in profits of 12.2 percent, rising from $296 million in 1992 to $526 million in 1997. Revenues performed almost as well, rising at an average annual rate of 9.3 percent over the same period, from $1.6 billion in 1992 to $2.5 billion in 1997. Total sales for parent company Gillette amounted to $10.1 billion in 1997. The Duracell acquisition played a major role in boosting Gillette's quarterly dividends which, as of June 1998, stood at 12.75 cents per common share, representing a 19-percent increase from the previous rate of 10.75 cents and establishing a new annual rate of 51 cents per share, compared with the former rate of 43 cents.

ANALYSTS' OPINIONS

When Gillette announced its plans to acquire Duracell, Wall Street reacted positively. According to *Business Week,* the effect of the announcement was an increase in the value of both companies' stock. Even before the buyout, *Fortune* had judged Duracell (along with Gillette) a company with outstanding growth prospects in the global market. Following the merger, sales and profits for both companies jumped. Though some analysts felt that Gillette stocks were overpriced, others were betting that Gillette would continue to perform above expectations now that Duracell was in the fold. Goldman Sachs Inc., for example, added Gillette to its recommended list, while PNC Institutional Investments Inc. raised its rating from "market perform" to "outperform."

HISTORY

In 1935 Philip Rogers Mallory established P.R. Mallory & Co., which produced a number of items for industry, including batteries. One of his leading technicians was Samuel Ruben. The two are generally credited as the minds behind Duracell as a business, and a product. The company entered the consumer products market in 1947 with the production of a hearing-aid battery. The trademark name Duracell did not appear until 1964. In 1971 the company became the first to sell alkaline cell batteries to consumers, beginning with a 9-volt model. (An alkaline battery has less tendency to corrode than an ordinary zinc battery, giving it a longer life.)

In 1978 P.R. Mallory became Duracell Inc., and was purchased by Dart Industries. Two years later, food marketing giant Kraft merged with Dart. When the two split in 1986, Kraft took Duracell with it. The changes in Duracell's ownership, however, were not over. In 1988 Kohlberg Kravis Roberts (KKR), famous for their leveraged buyouts, or LBOs, purchased the corporation. Duracell was clearly on the rise: the $1.9 billion paid by KKR (one of the biggest LBOs in Wall Street history) was more than nine times what Dart had paid for it only a decade earlier.

In 1991 KKR took the company public. With new products introduced, as well as a strong marketing campaign, Duracell's fortunes grew—from $1.25 billion in sales in 1989 to $2.08 billion in 1995. In the latter year, KKR sold a large portion of its shares, reducing its ownership to one-third. Then, on September 12, 1996, the Gillette Company announced plans to purchase Duracell for $7.00 billion, a transaction completed in early 1997.

The merger proved a boon to both companies, with the combination of the two marketing and distribution organizations helping boost sales of both batteries and razor blades. "You frequently see the Sensor Excel (razor) right next to the Duracell batteries at the checkout

FINANCES:

Duracell International Revenues, 1994-1997 (billion dollars)

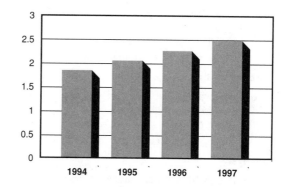

Duracell International 1996 Stock Prices (dollars)

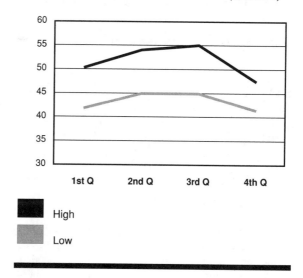

counter," said analyst Tony Vento, in a *Business Wire* article. "The merchandising possibilities are tremendous."

STRATEGY

As a maker of consumer products, Duracell has naturally pursued a strategy of widespread exposure to the public through advertising, particularly on television. In 1974 it became the first consumer battery advertised on television. In the mid-1990s Duracell launched a clever

FAST FACTS:

About Duracell International Inc.

Ownership: Duracell is a publicly owned company traded on the New York Stock Exchange.

Ticker symbol: DUR

Officers: Edward F. DeGraan, Exec. VP; Edward A. Battocchio, Sr. VP, Manufacturing & Technical; Robert C. Giacolone, Sr. VP, Management; Ronald V. Waters, VP, Finance

Employees: 7,900

Principal Subsidiary Companies: Duracell is a subsidiary of the Gillette Company.

Chief Competitors: Duracell's largest competitor is Eveready, a Ralston Purina subsidiary and maker of Energizer batteries. Other competitors include: Matsushita; Rayovac; Sanyo; Toshiba; and Utralite Batteries.

---

marketing campaign, with television commercials featuring the Copper Top family. They resembled the typical family of a television sitcom, except that they all happened to be battery-powered, which resulted in some predictably funny situations. The company sent out buses resembling enormous batteries in the summer of 1996, to promote its then-newly introduced PowerCheck line.

Equally unsurprising, given its product and its consumer-driven market, is Duracell's emphasis on product innovation. Such innovation is itself almost another form of marketing. It involves a strategy of "creating" a need in the consumer, then filling it. Hence the introduction of what parent company Gillette calls "consumer-perceptible advantages" such as freshness dating, or the visible gauge on the PowerCheck batteries. Duracell pioneered the development of environmentally friendly alkaline batteries in 1992. In 1996, the company announced plans to extend its research into new alkaline technologies that could revolutionize the battery by extending its capabilities.

INFLUENCES

In the late 1990s, the two leading influences on Duracell were its famous rivalry with Eveready, makers of Energizer, and its purchase by Gillette. As successful as

Duracell's marketing campaign with the Copper Top family was, the Copper Tops were hardly a match for the sometimes bitingly satirical Energizer Bunny ads. Still, Duracell remained ahead in this competition, with a 42-percent market share of the worldwide battery market and 45 percent of the U.S. market, as opposed to 24 percent for Energizer and Eveready combined. According to *Financial World,* Duracell was worth more as a brand than its competitor, due to its lowered costs, themselves a product of its overseas strategy. If anything, Duracell's competition with Energizer has helped to keep the company's leadership on its toes, always forging ahead into new markets.

Duracell's public relationship with Gillette began in September 1996, when the latter announced plans to purchase the battery maker. Although Gillette refers to the buyout as a "merger," it is clear which company has the upper hand. Both entities were pursuing an aggressive overseas growth strategy even before the sale of Duracell. These common goals played a part in Gillette's decision to purchase the smaller company. As *USA Today* pointed out, Gillette offered Duracell an opportunity to widen the scope of its overseas marketing, and Duracell, in turn, gave Gillette a broadened product line.

CURRENT TRENDS

A leading trend with Duracell as an independent company, and one which continued following its purchase by Gillette, was overseas expansion. In its 1996 annual report, Gillette marked this as an outstanding trend at Duracell, citing its establishment of operations in Brazil, China, and eastern Europe. The establishment of facilities in China and India, and acquisitions of battery makers in South Africa and South Korea, were moves considered particularly promising. China and India, which together contain half the world's population, consume some 5 billion household batteries—one-quarter of the global total—per year.

Another trend that will continue to have a significant impact on the Duracell product line is the proliferation of new electronic items that require more and different types of batteries. Among appliances that have already led to growth for Duracell are digital pagers, an increasingly popular item in the 1990s, as well as cellular phones and portable CD players.

PRODUCTS

Duracell makes alkaline batteries in several major sizes, including AAA, AA, C, and D. AA is the largest and most popular category. In 1996 the company introduced Duracell PowerCheck AA Batteries, which include a heat-sensitive strip that shows how much energy is remaining in the battery. In its 1996 annual report, Gillette announced plans to introduce similar AAA, C, and D batteries in 1997. According to *Forbes,* the company planned to introduce a standard portable computer battery into a market swelled with some 200 different varieties. The response from computer manufacturers, however, was not strong. In 1998 the company introduced DURACELL Ultra, the first alkaline battery specifically designed for "high-drain" devices.

Besides alkaline batteries, the company produces photo batteries, alkaline lantern batteries, watch batteries, special application batteries, hearing aid batteries, and Mallory super heavy duty plus batteries.

CORPORATE CITIZENSHIP

In 1982 Duracell USA initiated the Duracell/NSTA Scholarship Competition, a nationwide program to promote science education in American schools. It was administered under the auspices of the National Science Teachers Association (NSTA). The company has also made enormous efforts to reduce the harmful impact of its products on the environment and to promote recycling. Steady improvements to the service life of DURACELL AE alkaline batteries have helped reduce the production of solid waste due to consumers throwing away batteries less often. The company has also promoted the use of longer-lasting zinc air batteries for hearing instruments and discontinued the sale of mercury cells in the United States.

From 1993 to 1997, Duracell's manufacturing facilities around the world reduced their generation of hazardous waste by more than 59 percent, and increased the amount of materials recycled by approximately 45 percent. The company also uses recycled material in its packaging, and is leading an international battery industry effort to develop an environmentally beneficial and economically feasible recycling process for its other batteries.

GLOBAL PRESENCE

In the five years between 1992 and 1997, Duracell spread to almost 20 countries, including some of the largest markets in the world: India, China, and Russia. Two of its most notable purchases were the South African facilities of its competitor, Eveready, and the South Korean Sunpower Company, which gave Duracell a 45-percent share in that country's battery market.

Prior to its purchase by Gillette, Duracell conducted 80 percent of its business in North America and Europe. Then, with the wide geographic spread of Gillette, makers of various manual and electric shaving instruments as well as the Oral-B toothbrush, Duracell had an opportunity to experience rapid global expansion. This was particularly true in Third World markets, where the com-

CHRONOLOGY:

Key Dates for Duracell International Inc.

1935: Philip Rogers Mallory establishes P.R. Mallory & Co. to produce industrial items including batteries

1947: Mallory enters the consumer market by producing a hearing-aid battery

1964: The trademark name Duracell appears for the first time

1971: Mallory becomes the first company to sell alkaline cell batteries to consumers

1978: P.R. Mallory becomes Duracell Inc. and is purchased by Dart Industries

1980: Kraft merges with Dart

1986: Kraft and Dart part ways and Kraft keeps Duracell

1988: Kohlberg Kravis Roberts buys Duracell in a leveraged buyout

1991: Duracell goes public

1997: Gillette Company purchases Duracell

pany expected to "upgrade" consumers from lower-value zinc carbon batteries to the Duracell alkaline brand. As expected, Duracell performed exceptionally well in international markets following its acquisition by Gillette.

Duracell's regional brand names include: Superpila, Italy; Daimon, Germany; and Sunpower, South Korea. The Hellesens and Tudor lines are both sold in Scandinavia. Duracell opened factories in China in 1994, and in India in 1995. The company has subsidiaries in Canada, Denmark, Italy, France, and Belgium. It also has operations in Poland, Russia, Morocco, Turkey, and South Africa.

EMPLOYMENT

Duracell has pension and savings plans for its employees. When the company was bought out by Gillette, employees experienced a windfall from their stock options. Additionally, Gillette invests approximately $125 million annually in worldwide employee training and development programs.

SOURCES OF INFORMATION

Bibliography

Capell, Kerry. "At Duracell, An Early Christmas." *Business Week,* 30 September 1996.

"Duracell." *Hoover's Online,* May 1998. Available at http://www.hoovers.com

"Duracell Corporate Information," May 1998. Available at http://www.duracell.com/news/.

"Duracell Energizes Gillette." *Financial Post,* 18 September 1996.

"Duracell Merger Pays Off for Gillette." *Financial Post,* 3 February 1997.

Gillette Company 1996 Annual Report. Boston, MA: Gillette Company, 1997.

Gillette Company 1997 Annual Report. Boston, MA: Gillette Company, 1998.

"Gillette-Duracell Union Seen As Ideal Marriage." *Financial Post,* 16 September 1996.

Lamonica, Paul. "Battling Batteries: Why Duracell and Eveready Are Neck and Neck in Market Share, But Not In Brand Value." *Financial World,* 30 January 1996.

Maremont, Mark. "How Gillette Wowed Wall Street." *Business Week,* 30 September 1996.

Oliver, Suzanne. "Batteries Not Included." *Forbes,* 11 March 1996.

For an annual report:

on the Internet at: http://www.gillette.com/financials/gar.pdf

For additional industry research:

Investigate companies by their Standard Industrial Classification Codes, also known as SICs. Duracell's primary SICs are:

3691 Storage Batteries

3692 Primary Batteries—Dry and Wet

5063 Electrical Apparatus & Equipment

Eastman Kodak Company

OVERVIEW

Eastman Kodak is one of the leading image photography businesses in the United States. The company is constituted by eight major divisions: Consumer Imaging; Kodak Professional, Digital and Applied Imaging; Entertainment Imaging; Health Imaging; Commercial and Government Systems; Business Imaging Systems; Office Imaging; and Global Customer Service and Support. In 1997, Eastman Kodak was the top U.S. manufacturer of 35 millimeter (mm) film, capturing 65 percent of the U.S. market. Worldwide, Kodak shares the lead in film sales with Fuji Photo. Kodak also manufactures cameras, information systems (including writable CDs and software), and X-ray and medical imaging technology.

Like many giants in American industry in the 1990s, including Chrysler, Texaco, and IBM, Kodak found itself weighed down by an outdated business model and in need of extensive renovations to compete in the changing business world. For years, Kodak relied heavily on the hefty—70 percent—profit margins available in the consumer film business. Due in part to pressure from consistent underpricing by competitor Fuji Photo, these profit margins have been rapidly dwindling. With the likelihood that the future for the photographic industry will be digital, Kodak is under extreme pressure to produce digital imaging technology and products. To retain its eminent position in the world of photographic equipment and supplies, Kodak hired maverick George Fisher, former CEO of Motorola, as Chairman and CEO in 1993 and began plans to streamline its business concerns, update its products to keep pace with new technologies, and attempt to penetrate and secure new foreign markets.

FOUNDED: Eastman Kodak Company was founded in 1884 as the Eastman Dry Plate and Film Company.

Contact Information:

HEADQUARTERS: 343 State St.
    Rochester, NY 14650
PHONE: (716)724-4000
FAX: (716)724-1089
URL: http://www.kodak.com

FINANCES:

Eastman Kodak Co.
Sales, 1994-1997
(billion dollars)

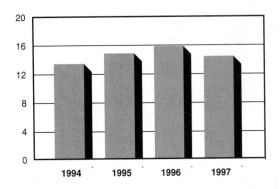

Eastman Kodak Co.
1997 Stock Prices
(dollars)

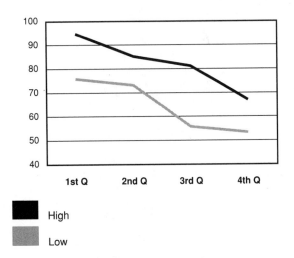

COMPANY FINANCES

In 1997, Eastman Kodak had worldwide sales in excess of $14.5 billion, a decrease of 9 percent from the year before. (In 1996, Kodak's sales reached almost $16 billion.) Over half of Kodak's 1997 sales came from Consumer Imaging, the company's largest business unit, which provides film and other photographic products to consumers. Over half of Consumer Imaging's sales, about $4.2 billion, came from outside the United States; about $3.5 billion of the unit's sales came from inside the United States. Kodak's Commercial Imaging sales reached $6.8 billion in 1997, a decline of 17 percent from the previous year. After deducting costs for restructuring and asset impairments, Kodak's total earnings from operations for 1997 totaled just $130 million dollars, down 93 percent from 1996. Because Kodak failed to meet earnings targets and stock slumped dramatically in the second half of 1997, falling from $80 in mid-June to $58 in mid-December, the company cut CEO George Fisher's bonus.

From April 1995 to April 1998, Eastman Kodak stock fluctuated from a low of about $55 to a high of almost $95. From April 1997 to April 1998, the stock ranged from $54 to a high of $84. By May of 1998, the stock had reached about $73.50—up 10 points from January. In 1997 Kodak's earnings per share was about $3.52. Jonathan Rosenzweig of Salomon Smith Barney says the brokerage firm expects Kodak's price-earnings (P/E) ratio at December 1998 to be 17.7. On April 15, 1998, due to greater than expected savings associated with Kodak's restructuring, decreasing losses in the digital area, positive growth in Kodak's Advanced Photo System products, and evidence that Kodak's prices are moderating in certain consumer and commercial areas, Salomon Smith Barney upgraded its rating of Eastman Kodak stock to 1M ("Buy, Medium Risk"), up from a 3M rating ("Neutral, Medium Risk").

ANALYSTS' OPINIONS

Surviving in the photographic industry into the twenty-first century will likely require Kodak to shift toward newer technologies, like digital imaging technologies. In this arena, however, Kodak faces fierce competition from U.S. and Japanese companies like Sony and Canon who are accustomed to the quick pace of change in digital technology. With regard to digital camera manufacturing, many hold that Kodak's chances of making a profit are slim. Aside from the Instamatic, Kodak has little past success with conventional cameras, and profit margins on new digital devices are marginal. Some suggest that trying to grow in both the analog and digital photography worlds at once may be Kodak's greatest current challenge. As head of the consumer group at Hewlett-Packard, Antonio M. Perez asks, "Can Kodak balance the needs of their revenue- and profit-generating film business with their new investments in digital technology?" Some, like industry reporter Ilan Greenberg, suggest that, "The company will ultimately fail to reinvent itself . . . it will never make it into the ranks of America's leading digital corporations." Robert I. Krinsky, principal at IdeaScope, a Cambridge, Massachusetts consulting firm, says that "[t]o win at this game will require speed and flexibility—and that's not what I think of when I think of Kodak."

A *close-up of the upper levels of the Kodak corporate headquarters historic building in* Rochester, New York. *(Courtesy of Eastman Kodak Co.)*

HISTORY

In the late 1870s, when 24-year-old George Eastman, a bank clerk in Rochester, New York, told a coworker he was planning a vacation to Santo Domingo, the co-worker suggested Eastman make a photographic record of his trip. Interested in the idea, Eastman purchased the necessary photographic equipment—a camera, film, and wet-plate developing equipment and supplies—only to find they were much too bulky for travel. Rather than leaving the equipment behind, Eastman cancelled his vacation and turned his attention to investigating how to make photographic equipment more convenient. For several years, Eastman experimented with a dry-plate developing process he'd read was being used by British photographers. After just three years, Eastman obtained a U.S. patent for a product he was satisfied with and began making dry plates to sell to photographers. On January 1, 1881, local businessman Henry A. Strong joined Eastman to form the Eastman Dry Plate Company.

At first, the quality of the dry plates the company produced was uneven and, because Eastman insisted the company replace defective plates free of charge, Eastman Dry Plate nearly collapsed. But continued research resulted in better product and the company grew. Determined to develop a camera that would be "as convenient as the pencil," Eastman experimented to try to find a light, flexible replacement for the glass plate. In 1883,

Eastman produced a film system consisting of a gelatin-coated paper packed in a roll holder that could be used in almost any dry-plate camera. The following year, the company became known as Eastman Dry Plate and Film Company, and Henry Strong served as its president while George Eastman was treasurer. In 1888, the company introduced its first camera, which came loaded with enough film for 100 photographs. Customers sent the entire camera filled with the exposed film back to the company for processing. For $10, the company developed the film, printed the photographs, and refilled the camera with a new roll of film.

In 1889, Eastman changed the company's name to Eastman Company. Apparently still not satisfied with the name, Eastman experimented with many combinations of letters starting and ending with "k," which he thought was a "strong, incisive sort of letter." Finally, Eastman came up with the name "Kodak" and, in 1892, he renamed the company Eastman Kodak Company. When Henry Strong died in 1919, George Eastman became president of Eastman Kodak. Committed to making photography convenient and inexpensive, Eastman launched the Folding Pocket Kodak Camera in 1897 and, in 1900, introduced the first Brownie camera, an easy-to-operate, inexpensive model that sold for $1.00 and used film that cost $.15 a roll. For the next two decades, Kodak continued introducing new products and technologies: in 1902, it offered a machine that developed film without a

The first Kodak camera introduced in 1888. (Courtesy of Eastman Kodak Co.)

darkroom; in 1913, the company introduced sheet film for use for professional photographers; and in the 1920s, in its newly developed research center (one of the first industrial research centers in the United States) Kodak developed 16 mm motion picture film, a 16 mm Cine-Kodak motion picture camera, and the Kodascope projector. Kodak also developed products specifically to support the United States' involvement in World War I, like aerial cameras and unbreakable lenses for gas masks.

In 1932, ailing and claiming in a note that he believed his work was done, George Eastman committed suicide. Despite this tragedy, Kodak continued to thrive. The year Eastman died, the company introduced the first 8 mm motion picture system for amateur photographers. Within three years, the company introduced 16 mm Kodachrome film, the first commercially successful amateur color film. In the 1940s, Edwin Land (who would go on to found Polaroid Corporation) offered Kodak the opportunity to market the instant camera he had invented, but Kodak declined. After expending energy and resources producing equipment and film for the United States military during World War II, Kodak brought out an inexpensive Brownie hand-held movie camera in 1951; the following year, the company offered the Brownie's projector. In 1953, Kodak formed the Eastman Chemical Products Company to produce chemicals, plastics, and fibers used in film production. Kodak had always incorporated the price of film processing in the cost of its film, but in 1954, it was forced to give up this practice. With its Chemical Products Company, however,

Kodak was now positioned to serve a new market, the burgeoning photofinishing market, by supplying it with chemicals and equipment for film developing and processing. Having made important progress in color slide technology, Kodak introduced the first fully automatic slide projector, the Kodak Calvalcade, in 1958; three years later, the company introduced the Carousel line of projectors that became extremely successful.

In 1963, Kodak would revolutionize amateur photography with its introduction of the easy-to-use Instamatic camera that used a film cartridge instead of a roll, eliminating the need to load film in the dark. In 1965, the company introduced a cartridge system for its super-8 Instamatic movie camera and projector. By 1972, Kodak had launched five different, immediately successful pocket models of the Instamatic camera; by 1976, Kodak had sold about 60 million Instamatic cameras—about 50 million more cameras than all its competitors combined. In 1972, Kodak formed a subsidiary it called Eastman Technology to develop new products in areas unrelated to photography. The following year, Eastman Technology purchased Spin Physics, a San Diego-based manufacturer of magnetic heads used in recording equipment.

In the early 1970s, Kodak became the defendant in antitrust lawsuits filed by several smaller companies, alleging that Kodak had illegally monopolized the photographic industry. The most famous of these cases involved Berky Photo, who charged Kodak with conspiring with Sylvania Companies and General Electric Company in developing two photographic flash products. The case was eventually settled out of court in 1981 for $6.8 million. In the mid-1970s, after meticulous research and planning, Kodak introduced its Ektaprint Copier-Duplicator thereby directly challenging Xerox and IBM, two firmly entrenched competitors. Not only did the Ektaprint produce numerous copies at high speed, but it also collated them, a unique feature at the time. Although initially considered a success, and surely one of Kodak's most successful products of that decade, the Ektaprint lost about $150 million over its first five years due to its late market entry. In 1976 Kodak challenged Polaroid Corporation's hold on the instant photography market by introducing its own line of instant cameras that developed film into photographs outside of the camera within minutes of taking the pictures. Although Kodak secured 25 percent of the instant camera market in the United States in its first year, quality problems and Polaroid's introduction of another new instant camera squelched sales.

In the late 1970s, several Japanese competitors and U.S. suppliers, including Fuji Photo and 3M Company, challenged Kodak's dominance in the photographic paper market. The Japanese had the additional advantage of competing against a strong U.S. dollar, which was substantially reducing Kodak's profits in foreign markets. Through the 1980s and 1990s, Fuji Photo began capturing a substantial share of the U.S. photographic film market by offering a similar quality product at a much lower price.

STRATEGY

For years, Eastman Kodak preferred its products' long-term quality over quick market entry. The company's cautious product-development process cost it dearly on several occasions. For example, in 1975, after years of development, Kodak finally introduced the Ektaprint copier to serve businesses with large-scale copying needs. The copier did its job well, but largely due to its slow entry into the market, the Ektaprint lost an estimated $150 million in its first five years. Another product that stalled then failed in this way was Kodak's instant camera, introduced in 1976, about four years after Kodak decided to develop it. Unfortunately, by the time of the product's launch, the company was riddled with production problems and faced a lawsuit filed by Polaroid claiming patent infringement.

Early on, Kodak branched out into related non-photographic concerns. In 1920, the company founded Tennessee Eastman to produce chemicals for Kodak's film manufacturing and processing. In 1953, Kodak merged its Tennessee Eastman with its Texas Eastman chemical business to form Eastman Chemical Products, which would sell alcohol, plastics, and fibers for industrial pur-

FAST FACTS:
About Eastman Kodak Company

Ownership: Eastman Kodak Co. is a publicly owned company traded on the New York Stock Exchange.

Ticker symbol: EK

Officers: George M. C. Fisher, Chmn. & CEO, 56, 1997 pay $3,725,000; Daniel A. Carp, Pres., COO, & Director, 48, 1997 pay $1,167,309; Harry L. Kavetas, CFO, Exec. VP & Director, 59, 1997 pay $1,047,692; Carl F. Kohrt, Exec. VP & Asst. COO, 53, 1997 pay $886,538

Employees: 97,500

Principal Subsidiary Companies: Eastman Kodak Company has operations worldwide and manufacturing plants in Australia, Brazil, Canada, France, Germany, Ireland, Mexico, the United Kingdom, the United States, and elsewhere. The company is parent to Eastman Software, Inc.; Fox Photo, Inc.; and an equal co-owner with Sun Chemical Corporation of Kodak Polychrome Graphics, a global graphic arts supply company with operations in more than 40 countries.

Chief Competitors: Eastman Kodak's competitors include: Fuji Photo Film Co., Ltd.; Hewlett-Packard; Nikon Corporation; and Minnesota Mining and Manufacturing Co.

poses. Later, in 1972, Kodak formed a subsidiary it called Eastman Technology to develop new products in areas unrelated to photography. The following year, Eastman Technology purchased Spin Physics, a small company that manufactured magnetic heads for use in recording equipment. In 1980, Kodak entered the health sciences field with its Ektachem 400 blood analyzer, supplementing its then current position as supplier of X-ray film to hospitals and medical facilities. Unfortunately, the Ektachem proved unable to match competitors in terms of reliability and speed. In 1984, Kodak introduced two improved versions of the blood analyzer. In 1988, when drug stocks were at their peak, Kodak purchased Bayer aspirin manufacturer Sterling Drug for $5.1 billion. It later sold the company in 1994.

By the early 1980s, it had become clear to Kodak that it needed to enter the electronics industry, which was defining the future for image and print. In an effort to do

CHRONOLOGY:

Key Dates for Eastman Kodak Company

1884: Founded as the Eastman Dry Plate and Film Company

1888: Eastman introduces its first camera

1889: Changes name to Eastman Company

1892: Company is renamed Eastman Kodak Company

1897: Introduces the Folding Pocket Kodak Camera

1900: Introduces the Brownie Camera

1913: Introduced sheet film for professional photographers

1919: Henry Strong dies; George Eastman becomes president

1932: George Eastman commits suicide; Kodak introduces 8mm motion picture system

1951: Introduces hand-held movie camera

1952: Offers the Brownie projector

1953: Forms Eastman Chemical Products Company

1958: Introduces the Kodak Calvacade slide projector

1963: Introduces the Instamatic camera

1972: Introduces five models of the Instamatic camera; forms Eastman Technology

1975: Introduces the Ektaprint copier

1981: Berkey Photo lawsuit is settled

1982: Purchases Atex

1984: Purchases Verbatim

1988: Purchases Sterling Drug

1990: Sells Verbatim

1992: Sells Atex; launches Photo CD

1993: George Fisher is hired as chairman and CEO

1994: Sells Sterling Drug

1996: Launches Advanced Photo System (APS)

1997: Loses claim with the World Trade Organization that Japan was denying fair access to its market

1998: Enters joint venture with Kodak Polychrome Graphics; holds Imaging Expo at the Olympic Games in Nagano, Japan

so, in 1982, Kodak purchased Atex, a supplier of electronic word-processing systems for newspaper publishers. The following year, Kodak formed its electronics division. Two years later, Kodak moved further into electronics with its purchase of Verbatim, maker of floppy disks and other electronic storage systems. But Kodak was unable to keep pace with the quickly changing computer industry, and soon its Atex word processing systems were outdated. After five years of lackluster sales, Kodak sold Verbatim in 1990. Although Kodak had paid more than $80 million for Atex in 1982, a decade later, it sold the company for a mere $5 million.

With increasing pressure from its competitor Fuji Photo, which throughout the 1990s undercut Kodak's prices and eroded its market share, Kodak was forced to further streamline its operations, selling off its Eastman Chemical division in late 1993 and its Sterling Drug business in 1994. Another part of its response to Fuji was to form strategic alliances with other companies. In 1991, Kodak joined with Canon Inc., Fuji Photo, Minolta Co., Ltd., and Nikon Corporation in a research and development project to investigate technologies for a new photo system. As a result of this endeavor, in 1996, Kodak launched its Advanced Photo System (APS), "user friendly" photo system and its Advantix line of cameras and film.

In 1993, George Fisher came to Kodak as chairman and CEO from Motorola Inc., in which he had turned an ailing electronics company into a telecommunications powerhouse. As CEO of Motorola, Fisher had developed a tremendously successful two-pronged strategy, which he believed he could apply immediately to Kodak. First, he would produce high-tech products; in this case, digital photographic equipment producing images that could be stored on disk. And second, he would use diplomacy to win in the global arena. As CEO at Motorola, Fisher had successfully lobbied Washington to help open Japan's market for Motorola; now, Fisher hoped to convince the U.S. government and the World Trade Organization to open the Japanese film market to U.S. film competitors like Kodak. By late 1997, it appeared that neither approach was working. Kodak's digital offerings, like its Photo CD, hadn't caught on with the majority of consumers. By November, Kodak's 1997 loss on the Photo CD reached $400 million. And, according to Prudential Securities, from November 1996 to November 1997, Fuji's share of the U.S. photo film market rose from 14.0 to 19.4 percent, while Kodak's share slipped from 71.4 to 65.0 percent. Moreover, Fuji further increased its distribution in the United States by taking over photo finishing laboratories for Wal-Mart and by spending more than a billion dollars from the mid- to late 1990s to start up six factories in South Carolina.

In response to Kodak's dismal performance and the company's lack of success with the World Trade Organization, which in the fall of 1997 rejected Kodak's claim that Japan had denied the company fair access to its film market, Kodak president and COO Daniel Carp announced in November 1997 that Kodak would be changing its business model. Carp claimed that Kodak would become much more competitive and capable of achieving profitable growth by spending $100 to $150 million less on research and development in 1998; by changing its approach to equipment manufacturing, possibly by employing outsourcing; by entering into joint ventures like Kodak Polychrome Graphics, the global graphics art supply company Kodak co-owns with Sun Chemical Corporation; and by laying off 10,000 employees worldwide and reducing Kodak's costs by $1 billion by the end of 1999. (The company planned to cut almost 20,000 workers from its payroll by the year 2000.) Carp added that instead of reducing prices, Kodak would come back from its share loss by increasing spending on advertising, by working with retailers to strengthen Kodak's retail presence, and by continuing to support Kodak's relaunch of its Advantix line of photo products. Some have been skeptical about how these moves could help Kodak to recapture sales against Fuji given Fuji's consistently lower prices. (In the summer of 1997, Fuji's products often cost as much as 30 percent less than Kodak's in the United States.)

INFLUENCES

Some of the most profound influences on Eastman Kodak came in the last quarter of the twentieth century. The late 1970s economic recession in the United States caused Kodak's consumer photographic equipment and film sales to plummet. In response, Kodak shifted its focus and emphasized sales in other areas, such as chemicals, business systems, and professional photo finishing services. Probably the single biggest influence on Kodak began in the late 1970s when Japanese competitors like Fuji Photo and U.S. suppliers such as 3M Company were starting to offer products, in this case paper products, of nearly the same quality as Kodak's for much less. As the dollar grew stronger, Kodak's profits suffered in foreign markets and Japanese underpricing finally began to erode Kodak's share of the U.S. market as well.

Under this increasing competitive pressure, Kodak cut its workforce by 5 percent in 1983. The following year, Kodak lost the title of "official film of the 1984 Summer Olympics" to Fuji, further evidence of its declining status. In 1986, a federal appeals court ordered Kodak to leave the instant camera business and Kodak was forced to offer its customers a trade-in option for the cameras that it had been producing for a decade. To offset this financial burden and to try to boost earnings, Kodak reduced its work force by another 10 percent. Since his arrival from Motorola in 1993, George Fisher has had a tremendous influence on the company, cutting funding for research and development and reducing the work force by another 10,000 positions. Finally, perhaps one of the most profound current influences on Kodak, and on the photographic industry as a whole, has been the Internet and the trend toward digital imaging.

CURRENT TRENDS

The extraordinary, continuing growth of the Internet has produced tremendous interest in digital photography, photography creating images that can be put on disk. Many see digital imaging as the future for today's photography businesses, which could derive their future revenues from digital cameras, Internet-based photo services, software for image enhancement, and digital peripherals for home and office. In an effort to produce the digital imaging technology that could be necessary to its future, Kodak made some striking moves: in the summer of 1997, for example, the company appointed Willy C. Shih, former Silicon Graphics vice president of marketing, as president of Kodak's Digital and Applied Imaging business. Also in 1997, Kodak bought Wang Laboratories' document management software operations for $260 million thereby creating a new subsidiary it called Eastman Software.

Kodak made another move toward the digital arena when it entered into a joint venture with Sun Chemical Corporation, the world's largest manufacturer of printing ink and organic pigments and a large part of the Japanese company Dainippon Ink & Chemicals, Inc. The joint venture combines Kodak's Graphics Systems Markets business, part of its Professional Division, with Sun Chemical Corporation's Polychrome Division to form Kodak Polychrome Graphics, a worldwide supplier of graphics arts products and services. This partnership was well positioned to supply over $1 billion in goods to the market and to provide a transitional route to existing and future digital solutions. In March of 1998, Eastman Software, Inc. announced its launch of a line of collaborative work management products for Microsoft Exchange, the leading business messaging platform. To further solidify its entrance into the world of digital photography, Kodak held a "trade show" for the public it called its "Imaging Expo" at the Winter Olympic Games in Nagano, Japan, in 1998. There, Kodak displayed products and services, offered live interactive exhibits, and introduced its Picture Network, an Internet-based picture-sharing service.

PRODUCTS

From the start, George Eastman's goal was to produce convenient, easy-to-use, inexpensive photographic equipment so that virtually anyone in the United States who wanted to own a camera could. Eastman introduced his first commercial camera in 1888: it was small, inexpensive, and easy to use. From then on, the company produced a long line of inexpensive photographic equipment. In 1982, Kodak introduced a line of small cameras that it considered a modern replacement for the Instamatic, a wildly successful camera that dominated the market in the 1960s and 1970s. These new cameras, called disc cameras, used film discs instead of cartridges,

COSMIC CAMERAS

When you think Kodak, you probably think of a little yellow Instamatic, four-inch color prints, and "Kodak moments." But Kodak is also associated with more otherworldly ventures—when NASA has had a need for quality, high-tech space imaging, remote sensing, and optical systems, it has turned to Kodak.

Kodak's space heritage dates back to the mid-1960s, when NASA sent the five Lunar Orbiters to the moon in order to map its surface in preparation for the first lunar landing. Each orbiter had a Kodak-built photographic system and processing laboratory that photographed the lunar surface, processed and scanned the film, and sent a video signal back to Earth. By the end of the mission, over 1,600 pictures were taken and 99 percent of the moon's surface was photographed. But most importantly, the pictures helped NASA identify the Sea of Tranquility as the landing site for the Apollo 11 mission in 1969.

To record that historic mission, the Apollo astronauts took 33 rolls of Kodak film, plus a special stereoscopic color camera used to take extreme close-ups of the moon's surface. Today, thanks in great part to Kodak, we have a better understanding of the geology of the moon.

And Kodak "cameras" have also helped us learn more about the geology of the red planet. In July 1997, the Pathfinder lander descended upon the Martian surface and released the Sojourner surface rover. Kodak developed the imaging sensors that functioned as the rover's "eyes," helping Sojourner successfully maneuver the rocky Martian terrain. Kodak also developed the sensors set to be used in the orbiter and lander for the December 1998 Martian mission. These sensors, though, will provide 2.5 times better resolution then the ones used in Sojourner.

Kodak has also played a large role in aiding the development of the biggest and best telescopes. The camera company produced the backup mirror for the Hubble Space Telescope. The mirror weighs 1,700 pounds and, as Kodak is quick to point out, does not contain the "spherical aberration" found in the original. Kodak also developed the world's largest segmented mirror. In 1997 this mirror was place in the Hobby-Eberly Telescope at the McDonald Observatory in Texas. It captures the light from objects that are 100 million times fainter then what the unaided human eye can see. And in the fall of 1998, the space shuttle was scheduled to take up the Kodak-built Advanced X-ray Astrophysics Facility (AXAF). This telescope system will focus X-rays with a resolving power that is equivalent to eyesight that can read a newspaper from half a mile away—"Superman eyesight", as Kodak boasts. With AXAF, scientists will be able to better study the fantastic phenomena in the backwaters of the cosmos.

Kodak has been instrumental in humanity's quest to discover the wonders beyond our little blue globe, and it will continue to help us peer into the farthest reaches of our universe as we continue the quest to unravel the mysteries of its beginnings.

---

but they were not successful. In 1984, Kodak teamed up with Matsushita Electric Industrial Company of Japan to produce its first electronic product, an 8 mm camcorder.

In 1992 Kodak launched its Photo CD, a writable compact disk with the ability to store photographs. The product failed with general consumers but achieved some success with small businesses and desktop publishers. Kodak relaunched the Photo CD in 1995, this time directly to the desktop publishing market. In October of that year, at the Photo and Imaging Expo in London, Kodak introduced the Advanced Photo System (APS), which resulted from its 1991 joint research and development project with four other major photographic companies: Canon, Fuji Photo, Minolta, and Nikon. Cameras in the Advanced Photo System use film that permits "magnetic information exchange"—that is, the film is coated with a special magnetic layer that allows cameras and other writing devices to add information (about the scene photographed, for example) to the film. APS cameras also permit three format choices for photos and allow the changing of a roll of film midway through shooting and the reloading of a partially used roll. Kodak named its line of APS cameras and film "Advantix" and originally launched the line in February 1996. But poor product availability and an advertising campaign that never told consumers why they should purchase the Advantix made for an unsuccessful launch. In 1997 the company relaunched the product.

Along with launching several digital cameras in 1997, Kodak also entered into partnerships with computer-industry companies like Picture Works Technology to try to revitalize its networked PC applications. In March of 1998, by way of Eastman Software, Inc., Kodak launched a line of collaborative work management products for Microsoft Exchange, the leading business messaging platform.

Michael D. McCreary, director of operations of Eastman Kodak's Microelectronics Technology division, claimed in 1998 that the division was making the highest-resolution color image sensors available on the market. Like regular computer chips, the image sensors process information but the information is received in the form of light instead of electrical signals.These image sensors can be used in cutting edge products such as digital cameras.

In early 1998 Kodak announced that it was launching seven new Advantix APS products: two color films, a 400-speed black and white film, a zoom camera, two personal film scanners, and a single-use camera that allows customers to choose between two of Kodak's APS formats. At the winter Olympics in Nagano, Japan, Kodak introduced its Picture Network, an Internet-based picture-sharing service that allows consumers to share picture with other Web users by posting them on the Internet.

Kodak Business Imaging Systems introduced a high-performance scanner in March of 1998 at the CeBIT information technology conference in Hanover, Germany. The Kodak Digital Science Scanner 3500 is a mid-volume scanner intended to bring simple, high-performance scanning to the general office for traditional scanning as well as Internet-based applications. In April 1998, Kodak Polychrome Graphics, Kodak's joint venture with Sun Chemical, announced its Digital Science DCP 9500 desktop color proofer, a digital continuous-tone proofing system that can create professionally accurate color proofs from a host computer in about five minutes. Available worldwide in June 1998, the DCP 500 was to be marketed largely to pre-press customers like trade shops, advertising agencies, and commercial printers.

GLOBAL PRESENCE

As the company's first venture outside of the United States, Kodak opened its Eastman Photographic Materials Company in London in 1889. In 1891, Kodak constructed a manufacturing plant outside London to accommodate increasing European product demand. By 1900, Kodak established distribution points in Italy, France, and Germany. Throughout the century, as the European and world markets grew, so did Kodak's presence in them.

In 1995, Kodak opened a distribution center in Moscow, Kodak AO, which received Kodak products from plants in the United Kingdom, France, and Germany. From 1996 to 1997, Kodak's 35 mm roll volume grew 61 percent in Russia. In the early 1990s, Kodak established two facilities in China to manufacture 35 mm cameras, electronic components, and photo processing equipment. Within several years, Kodak founded a software development center in Shanghai. In March of 1998, Kodak announced plans to invest more than $1 billion over several years to expand its presence in China, increasing its manufacturing and marketing capabilities there by acquiring several ailing Chinese film manufacturers, building a new plant, and overhauling its existing facilities. Kodak thus became the first foreign company to work with the Chinese government and China's current state-owned businesses to build a large, world-class industry. China is now Kodak's third-largest color film and paper market.

Nonetheless, Kodak has only secured 10 percent of the Japanese market, which is the second-largest photographic film and paper market in the world. Fuji has a 70 percent share of that market. Moreover, while Fuji's share of the U.S. photo film market has been increasing to nearly 20 percent, Kodak's share has fallen to 65 percent.

SOURCES OF INFORMATION

Bibliography

"As Kodak Advantix System Gains Momentum, Kodak Unveils Plans to Drive Future Growth with Seven New Products." *Business Wire,* 20 January 1998.

"Carp Says Changes to Create Far More Competitive Kodak." *Business Wire,* 10 November 1997.

Cary, Peter. "Loser Layoffs: Kodak Offers an Object Lesson in the Perils of Downsizing." *U.S. News & World Report,* 25 November 1996.

"Eastman Kodak Company." *Hoover's Online,* 10 April 1998. Available at http://www.hoovers.com.

"Eastman Kodak: Collaborative Work Management Solutions for MS Exchange from Eastman Software." *M2 PressWIRE,* 18 March 1998.

Ebersole, Phil. "Kodak Keeps Edge with Color Image Sensors." *Gannett News Service,* 25 March 1998.

Gillis, Chris. "Kodak's Experience in Russia." *American Shipper,* October 1995.

Greenberg, Ilan. "The Bleak Picture." *The Red Herring Online,* January 1998.

Holstein, William J. "Imperfect Picture: Kodak's Continuing Woes." *US News & World Report,* 14 November 1997.

"Imaging Expo Creates Kodak Moments for Olympic Fans in Nagano." *Business Wire,* 27 January 1998.

"Kodak and Polychrome Joint Venture Will Create New Global Organization to Serve Graphics Arts Market." *Business Wire,* 14 October 1997.

"Kodak Expands Investments to Manufacture Film and Paper in China." *Business Wire,* 23 March 1998.

"Kodak Polychrome Graphics Announces New Desktop Color Proofing Solution." *Business Wire,* 5 April 1998.

Laver, Ross. "An Image Problem." *McLean's,* 5 February 1996.

Mirabile, Lisa, ed. *International Directory of Company Histories,* Detroit: St. James Press, 1990.

"New Kodak Document Scanner Emphasizes Ease of Use, Signals Company's Aggressive Move into Mid-Volume Market." *Business Wire,* 13 March 1998.

Nulty, Peter. "Corporate Performance: Kodak Grabs for Growth Again." *Fortune,* 16 May 1994.

Reingold, Jennifer, Richard A. Melcher, and Gary McWilliams. "Executive Pay." *Business Week,* 20 April 1998.

Roberts, Dexter, Joyce Barnathan, and Robert J. Dow. "Now, It's Reform or Bust in Beijing." *Business Week,* 6 April 1998.

Smith, Geoffrey, William C. Symmonds, Peter Burrows, Ellen Neuborne, and Paul C. Judge. "Can George Fisher Fix Kodak?" *Business Week,* 20 October 1997.

Standard & Poor's Register of Corporations, Directors and Executives. New York: The McGraw-Hill Companies, Inc., 1997.

For an annual report:

on the Internet at: http://www.kodak.com **or** write: Literature & Marketing Support, Eastman Kodak Company, 343 State St., Rochester, NY 14650-0532

For additional industry research:

Investigate companies by their Standard Industrial Classification Codes, also known as SICs. Eastman Kodak's primary SICs are:

2843 Surface Active Agents

2865 Cyclic Crudes & Intermediates

3081 Unsupported Plastics Film & Sheet

3861 Photographic Equipment & Supplies

Eddie Bauer Inc.

FOUNDED: 1920

OVERVIEW

Launched with a single store in Seattle in 1920, Eddie Bauer Inc. has grown into an international retail marketing giant. The company is famous around the world for its product line of sportswear, accessories, and home furnishings, all designed for the casual lifestyle. The company markets through four different outlets: Eddie Bauer Sportswear, Eddie Bauer Home, AKA Eddie Bauer, and Eddie Bauer Outlets.

Eddie Bauer Sportswear, the heart of the company's business, is retailed through a network of more than 400 stores across the United States and Canada. Outlets are also operated under joint venture arrangements in Germany, Japan, and the United Kingdom. The company's sportswear line, best known for its outerwear, also features a full range of casual apparel and accessories, footwear, and travel gear marketed through nearly a dozen annual catalog mailings, as well as over the Internet.

The company has embarked on an ambitious expansion program, which has as its goal the opening of 70 to 80 news stores every year. If successful, the company's total retail outlets will come close to doubling in five or six years.

Contact Information:
HEADQUARTERS: 15010 NE 36th St.
   Redmond, WA 98052-5317
PHONE: (425)861-4851
FAX: (425)882-6383
TOLL FREE: (800)426-6253
URL: http://www.eddiebauer.com

COMPANY FINANCES

As a wholly owned subsidiary of Spiegel Inc., Eddie Bauer does not report independently on its financial operations. Eddie Bauer generates estimated annual sales in excess of $1.5 billion, which indicates that the chain accounts for slightly more than half of Spiegel's total rev-

FAST FACTS:
About Eddie Bauer Inc.

Ownership: Eddie Bauer Inc. is a wholly owned subsidiary of Spiegel Inc., a publicly owned company traded on NASDAQ.

Ticker symbol: SPGLA

Officers: Richard T. Fersch, Pres. & CEO; Carolyn Swearingen, Sr. VP; James R. Cannataro, CFO; Julie Cosser, Sr. VP, Merchandising

Employees: 1,500 at corporate headquarters

Chief Competitors: Among Eddie Bauer's major competitors are: The Gap; J. Crew; Land's End; L.L. Bean; Neiman Marcus; Nordstrom; and Polo.

enue, which totaled $3.06 billion in 1997. Spiegel reported net losses of $33 million in that same year. This compared with a net loss of $13 million on revenue of $3.02 billion in 1996. In 1995, Spiegel registered a net loss of $10 million on revenue of $3.18 billion, compared with net earnings of $25 million on revenue of $3.02 billion in 1994.

HISTORY

Eddie Bauer, founder of the billion-dollar-plus retail empire that bears his name, was born on October 19, 1899, the child of Russian immigrants. A lover of the outdoors, Bauer's hunting and fishing exploits often landed his name in the Seattle newspapers. A story, perhaps untrue, suggests that he was moved to launch his own line of outerwear when he came down with hypothermia after the woolen clothing he wore on a fishing trip failed to perform as advertised.

Bauer's original store, dubbed quite simply, Eddie Bauer's Sporting Goods, opened in downtown Seattle in 1920. Two years later, Bauer set a retailing precedent when he introduced his unconditional guarantee that pledged that "every item we sell will give you complete satisfaction or you may return it for a full refund." Introduced at the same time was the company creed: "To give you such outstanding quality, value, service and guarantee that we may be worthy of your high esteem."

In 1927, shortly after his marriage to Christine "Stine" Heltborg, Bauer added women's apparel to the product line at his Seattle store. When the company se-

cured the U.S. and Canadian patents for the Bauer Shuttlecock in 1934, it helped to popularize the game of badminton in North America. Two years later, Bauer shook up the sportswear industry when he introduced his patented Skyliner jacket, the first garment insulated with goose down; this was an immediate hit with customers. A year later, the company began marketing the Downlight vest.

The company got a boost in 1941 in the form of an order from the U.S. Army Air Corps for the Eddie Bauer B-9 Flight Parka. More than 50,000 of the jackets were produced for use by airmen during high-altitude flights. Near the end of World War II in 1945, Eddie Bauer Inc. mailed out its first catalog. During the period between 1953 and 1968, the company outfitted a number of scientific and exploratory expeditions. These expeditions included the American assault on K-2 in the Himalayas, a 1957 scientific expedition to Antarctica, and the American Antarctic Mountaineering Expedition of 1966.

In 1968, Eddie Bauer retired, selling his business to William Niemi, a longtime friend and partner. That same year the company opened a store in San Francisco, its first store outside Seattle. Three years later, in 1971, Eddie Bauer Inc. was sold to General Mills Inc. This kicked off an aggressive drive to expand the company's retail outlets nationwide. By the end of 1988, the chain had expanded to a network of 61 stores with more than $250 million in annual sales. Eddie Bauer was sold to Spiegel Inc. that same year. This further accelerated the company's expansion of retail outlets, which numbered close to 400 in 1996.

The 1990s brought continued expansion for Eddie Bauer Inc. and the beginning of its expansion beyond North America. In 1993, the company launched its first mail-order catalog in Germany. The following year, a catalog was introduced in Japan, and three retail outlets were opened in Tokyo. In 1995, the company launched a joint venture in Germany, which would open stores in Germany and elsewhere in Europe. In addition, these stores would handle mail-order catalog operations. Eddie Bauer UK, the company's joint venture in the United Kingdom, was launched in 1996 to develop and operate stores and mail-order operations.

Eddie Bauer Inc. suffered a public relations setback in 1997. A jury awarded $1 million to three young African-American men who accused the company of "consumer racism" when it detained them on suspicion of shoplifting. One of the plaintiffs in the suit claimed store security personnel forced him to take off his shirt.

STRATEGY

Eddie Bauer experienced extremely strong growth from the late 1980s through the mid-1990s. However, there was no sign that the company would be resting on its laurels. The company set for itself the ambitious goal of opening 70 to 80 new stores every year. Retail outlets are not the only arena in which the company planned to keep busy. Its direct mail operations were sending out more than 100 million catalogs every year. The company's demographic profile was a broad one, focusing on the 18- to 34-year-old market segment.

The company expanded on the popularity of its casual sportswear and successfully translated that into a line of dressier apparel appropriate for the business setting. Talking about the success of its AKA Eddie Bauer stores, Julie Cosser, senior vice president of marketing, told CNNfn's "Biz Buzz" that since most of their loyal customers "obviously have other days in their week, it seems only natural to take our casual foundation and actually roll that out into products that are appropriate for the office. So it's a business that's based still in comfort and casual wear but a little bit more dressed up."

INFLUENCES

One of the keys to the success of Eddie Bauer Inc. has been its executives' recognition that the nature of retail marketing was evolving continually. This evolution dictated a sometimes drastic periodic revamping of its strategy. The company has managed to build itself into an international retailing giant with annual revenues of about $1.5 billion by staying ahead of the wave of change, especially in the areas of direct mail and the Internet.

CURRENT TRENDS

The growing American and worldwide appetite for doing business in cyberspace has not been lost on Eddie Bauer Inc. The company launched its World Wide Web site (http://www.eddiebauer.com) in 1996 and opened up a whole new world of marketing possibilities. Cyber-shoppers are able to order almost any product the company offers through its web site.

PRODUCTS

Eddie Bauer Inc. markets a wide range of sportswear, accessories, and home furnishings through four basic outlets. Eddie Bauer Sportswear, the company's core retailing operation, sells men's and women's sportswear designed for the casual lifestyle of the late twentieth century. Eddie Bauer Sportswear stores, numbering more than 400 by the close of the 1990s, also markets accessories, footwear, and travel gear. The sportswear product line is also available through direct mail and the Internet.

CHRONOLOGY:
Key Dates for Eddie Bauer Inc.

1920: Eddie Bauer's Sports Shop opens in downtown Seattle

1927: Eddie Bauer adds women's apparel to its product line in his store

1936: Bauer introduces the Skyliner jacket, the first to be insulated with goose down

1945: Bauer issues the company's first mail-order catalog

1953: Eddie Bauer outfits the American K-2 Himalayan Expedition

1968: Eddie Bauer retires; the first store outside Seattle opens in San Francisco

1971: General Mills buys Eddie Bauer

1983: Ford and Eddie Bauer join to produce Eddie Bauer Edition Ford vehicles

1988: Spiegel purchases Eddie Bauer

1994: Spiegel launches Distribution Fulfillment Services, Inc., one of the most technologically advanced mail-order fulfillment facilities in the United States

1997: The 500th Eddie Bauer store in North America opens

AKA Eddie Bauer targets the market for those wanting apparel that offers the comfort and styling of the company's traditional sportswear yet is dressy enough to be worn in a work setting. There were approximately 30 AKA Eddie Bauer stores across the country by 1998. The AKA Eddie Bauer line is also marketed by direct mail and online.

The company's venture into the home furnishings market, Eddie Bauer HOME, sells a line of wood and upholstered furniture, home decorating accessories, gift items, tableware, bed linens, and products for the bath in its 30 to 40 U.S. stores. The goal of its HOME stores was to bring to home furnishings the same comfort and relaxed feel that made the company's sportswear line popular throughout the years of its existence.

Acting as the company's clearinghouse, Eddie Bauer Outlets offers regular Eddie Bauer merchandise at prices marked 30 to 70 percent below regular retail. There were

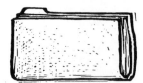

SPORTS DUDE DUDS FOR ALL

Eddie Bauer was a man's man—a hunting, fishing, shooting whiz—a man who created the kind of clothes worn by the U.S. Army Air Corps in World War II, as well as various mountaineering and Antarctic expeditions. Today, of course, we live in a different world. You can climb into your four-wheel drive sport utility vehicle and make the dangerous trek to an Eddie Bauer store in your local climate-controlled mega-mall. Once there, you can purchase the latest offerings from Eddie Bauer; that is, such items as bed linens, designer eyewear, and upholstered furniture. Most recently, Eddie Bauer has made a foray into the alternative medical field of aromatherapy. There may not be much of a need for aromatherapy on an Arctic expedition—yet.

about 50 Eddie Bauer Outlets in the United States by the end of the 1990s.

CORPORATE CITIZENSHIP

Eddie Bauer Inc. always felt a strong responsibility to the communities in which it operated. The company has taken particular pride in its Global ReLeaf Tree Project, a joint venture with American Forests, the nation's oldest citizen conservation group. Eddie Bauer's headquarters in the Pacific Northwest also has been home to extensive forestry operations. The tree planting campaign, however, extends throughout the United States.

The company announced in June 1998 that the project had planted its 1.25 millionth tree, halfway to its ultimate goal of planting 2.5 million trees by 2000. Under the company's "Add a Dollar, Plant a Tree" campaign, customers are encouraged to add a dollar or two to their purchases to be used for the planting of trees. Each dollar donated pays for the planting of a single tree. In addition to donations from customers, Eddie Bauer employees, known as associates, can contribute to the tree planting project through payroll contributions.

Accepting the Natural Resource Council of America's 1998 Award of Achievement, Adam Schoenberg, American Forests' director of corporate development, said much of the credit for the project's success can be traced to "the commitment of the Eddie Bauer associates.

Last autumn for the first time Global ReLeaf became a part of the Associates Pledge Drive. More than $70,000 was pledged for planting trees in 1998."

GLOBAL PRESENCE

Eddie Bauer began expanding outside the United States in 1993 when it launched its first mail-order catalog into the German market. This was followed two years later by the inauguration of Eddie Bauer Japan, which opened three retail outlets in Tokyo and mailed out the first Japanese catalog.

The globalization of Eddie Bauer Inc. continued in 1995 when the company launched its Eddie Bauer Germany joint venture. The venture's announced goal was the development and operation of Eddie Bauer retail outlets and catalogs in Germany and elsewhere in Europe. The following year, the company launched a joint venture in the United Kingdom to develop and oversee stores and catalog operations in that country.

In 1996, the number of Eddie Bauer stores in Japan rose to 14, plus they had 3 discount outlets. Eddie Bauer Germany opened its first 2 stores in that country during the same year. The next year, an additional 11 stores were opened in Japan. The total in Germany rose to 7 that same year. Eddie Bauer UK opened its first 2 stores in Cardiff and in Kent.

EMPLOYMENT

Eddie Bauer has always sought ambitious, energetic people who want to work for a company that could offer integrity, opportunity, and excitement. For the right candidates, the company has promised challenging career growth as well as the training and support needed to succeed.

Eddie Bauer Inc. employed about 1,500 people at its Seattle headquarters in 1998. Thousands more work in the company's retail outlets across the United States and overseas. Plans to open between 70 and 80 new stores each year would mean that opportunities in retail sales would continue to grow steadily.

The company's boast in its literature has been that as an employer, they are "one of the best in the business—a fact proven by our industry-leading education and training program, our excellent benefits package, and our team-oriented approach to doing business. As we continue to achieve impressive sales growth and open more stores across North America and internationally, we offer you a future full of possibilities. Eddie Bauer's future holds the promise of explosive expansion."

SOURCES OF INFORMATION

Bibliography

Bessonette, Colin. "Q&A on the News." *Atlanta Journal and Constitution,* 30 December 1997."

"Eddie Bauer Company History: A Legend for 78 Years." *Eddie Bauer Home Page,* February 1998. Available at http://www.eddiebauer.com/eb/EBhq/companyoverview.asp.

Eddie Bauer Global ReLeaf Tree Project Reaches Halfway Mark." *Business Wire,* 17 June 1998.

"Eddie Bauer Inc." *Hoover's Online,* 28 June 1998. Available at http://www.hoovers.com.

"Employment@Eddie Bauer." *Eddie Bauer Home Page,* 28 June 1996. Available at http://www.eddiebauer.com/eb/EBhq/employmentcenter.asp.

Loviglio, Joann. "Plaintiffs in Eddie Bauer Suit Awarded $1 Million." *Columbian,* 10 October 1997.

"Spiegel Inc." *Hoover's Online,* 28 June 1998. Available at http://www.hoovers.com.

For additional industry research:

Investigate companies by their Standard Industrial Classification Codes, also known as SICs. Eddie Bauer's primary SICs are:

2321 Men's/Boys' Shirts

2325 Men's/Boys' Trousers and Slacks

2329 Men's/Boy's Clothing, NEC

2339 Women's/Misses' Outerwear, NEC

2369 Girls'/Children's Outerwear, NEC

2511 Wood Household Furniture

2512 Upholstered Household Furniture

2519 Household Furniture, NEC

5311 Department Stores

Esprit de Corp.

ALSO KNOWN AS: Esprit
FOUNDED: 1968

Contact Information:

HEADQUARTERS: 900 Minnesota St.
   San Francisco, CA 94107
PHONE: (415)648-6900
FAX: (415)550-3951
TOLL FREE: (800)4-ESPRIT
URL: http://www.esprit.com

OVERVIEW

In the rag trade, as some call the clothing business, today's hot look can be tomorrow's thrift store remnant. No company knows that better than Esprit de Corp., which, in its tumultuous history, has had to reinvent itself time and again in order to stay current and keep its products in America's closets. Esprit designs, produces, and distributes sportswear, children's wear, shoes, accessories, and eyewear. It sells its products through department stores and mail-order catalogs in the United States and 350 of its own retail stores in 44 countries. The company has recently launched an effort to reposition its line of clothing to appeal to more mature customers.

COMPANY FINANCES

Esprit's 1997 sales reached $350 million, which was a 16.7 percent increase over 1996 sales. Of this, 65.2 percent was derived from retail sales and 33.5 percent from wholesale sales.

ANALYSTS' OPINIONS

In a 1997 *WWD* article, Michael Steinberg, chairman of Macy's West, claimed that Esprit's fortunes had been turned around under chairman Jay Margolis' direction. "The strength of the company is that they have a very solid leader and experienced management . . . . The product looks better and is selling at retail." Steinberg had initially placed a new line of Esprit's sportswear in 12 Macy's stores, then rolled it out to 18, then expanded it into 30 stores. Said Steinberg, "We are rolling them out more aggressively as their performance improves . . . . It is a slow rebuilding process, and we weren't going to start them off in 60 or 70 stores until they proved themselves, and they are proving themselves. . . . They have a better understanding of who the customer is and how it translates into the Nineties."

In a 1996 poll conducted by Fairchild Publications, publisher of *WWD,* which is the leading apparel trade newspaper in the United States, Esprit was named as the twenty-eighth most-recognized brand in the United States.

HISTORY

Esprit de Corp. was an outgrowth of Plain Jane, a company that was founded by Susie Tompkins and her friend Jane Tise. Doug Tompkins, then Susie's husband, joined that company in 1968 after he sold North Face, his skiing and climbing apparel and equipment company. Tise and the Tompkinses parted ways in the mid-1970s and the Tompkinses became sole owners of the company. In 1978 the name of the company was changed from Plain Jane to Esprit de Corp.

For its first several years, the line was especially popular with teenagers. Fashions reflected their tastes with easy-to-wear casual clothes in durable fabrics and engaging colors. Eventually, Esprit clothing would represent both youthful style and career-minded fashion— that is, playful looks that can be worn in more "adult" settings such as the casual office.

Shopping, of course, has been the prime way to gain access to Esprit fashions. Ironically, retailing was nearly the downfall of the Esprit de Corp. organization. In the early 1980s the company was a leading sportswear manufacturer, selling in all the major department stores and boutiques. But, as *Working Woman* writer Ellie McGrath described it, "The company's decision [in 1981] to create boutiques within major department stores . . . was akin to booking passage on the *Titanic.* Retail giants like Macy's and Bloomingdale's are struggling under the weight of heavy debt and poor sales. Meanwhile, Esprit faced big-time competition from the Gap and the Limited, which invested in freestanding stores and now dominate the very niche that Esprit pioneered."

The rejuvenation of Esprit came about in spite of— or perhaps because of—the turmoil occurring in Tompkins' personal life. According to a 1990 article in *WWD,* "Conflicts between [Doug and Susie Tompkins], in addition to an uncertain retail climate and lackluster junior market, prevented Esprit from becoming domestically the billion-dollar company that many observers thought it could be. Although worldwide sales reportedly topped $1

FAST FACTS:
About Esprit de Corp.

Ownership: Esprit de Corp. is a privately held company whose controlling partners include Oaktree Capital Management, Cerberus Partners, and Jay Margolis.

Officers: Jay Margolis, Chmn. & CEO; Alison May, COO & CFO

Employees: 5,000 (about 1,350 in the United States)

Chief Competitors: Key competitors include: Tommy Hilfiger; Gap; The Limited; Calvin Klein; and Guess.

billion, much of that was from international sales, which, except for southern Europe, is owned and operated by a series of partnerships, in which the Tompkinses have various stakes." The company first suffered a loss in 1986. About this time, the Tompkinses became estranged, and the company was torn by divergent views as to its fashion focus.

In the spring of 1988 a new board of directors was formed to replace the Tompkinses and another board member. Mr. Tompkins was demoted from chief executive officer to chief operating officer. Susie Tompkins was demoted from creative director to consultant. She even resigned for a time and then later returned to the company.

Power struggles for ownership of the company continued and, in 1989, Doug Tompkins was granted an exclusive, 120-day option to purchase the 50 percent of Esprit de Corp. owned by Susie Tompkins. Additional problems ensued because the company, valued at $380 million, was said to have been valued too low. Finally, in December 1989, the company was put up for sale.

In June 1990, the Tompkins' joint ownership of Esprit de Corp. was dissolved, and the two-year struggle over leadership of Esprit ended when the company announced that Susie Tompkins was heading an investment group to buy out Doug Tompkins. Susie Tompkins also lent $10 million to the company to create an employee stock ownership plan, which she said was a gesture to thank loyal employees.

The company's U.S. revenues dropped from $400 million in 1990 to $250 million in 1996. Jay Margolis,

CHRONOLOGY:

Key Dates for Esprit de Corp.

1968: Plain Jane dress company is founded by Susie Tompkins and Jane Tise; Doug Tompkins, Susie's husband, joins the company as a partner

1976: The Tompkinses become sole owners of Plain Jane

1978: Plain Jane becomes Esprit de Corp.

1986: Corrado Federico becomes the company's new president; the Tompkinses remain with the company as board members

1988: A new board of directors is hired to replace the Tompkinses

1997: Esprit is placed on the U.S. Department of Labor's "Trendsetter List"

---

formerly an executive with such companies as Liz Claiborne and Tommy Hilfiger, joined Esprit as its chairman and chief executive officer. Later in 1996 it was decided to restructure Esprit. Oaktree Capital Management and Cerberus Partners, as well as Margolis, became controlling shareholders in exchange for equity in the company. Soon after, Susie and Doug Tompkins sold their remaining interests in Esprit's worldwide operations to Michael Ying, Esprit's partner in Hong Kong.

STRATEGY

In an effort to revive its fortunes, the company announced in 1997 that it would open 10 new Esprit stores and 100 new in-store shops within department stores. As of early 1997, Esprit had approximately 90 of these so-called "shop-in-shops;" in 1996 they had only 10 such stores.

Other plans included the shifting of the customer demographic to attract the college and career markets in addition to their mainstay market, junior girls. The company aimed to reposition its products to appeal to women from 17 to 30 years of age and older by showing more attention to detail, using higher quality fabrics, and bringing closer collaboration with Esprit's European and Asian operations. The hoped-for result was to develop attractive new collections that would "possess a modern and sophisticated, yet distinctly fun Esprit feel."

Jay Margolis, in a 1997 *WWD* article, said, "The history of Esprit is great patterns, colors and little sundresses and T-shirts, and we went there for spring. It is back to looking like Esprit. . . . With Esprit U.S., we think the void is somewhere between the Gap and Banana Republic. . . . Ours will be more contemporary than Gap, and older, but not as old as Banana Republic." Under Margolis' leadership, sales rebounded in 1997 to $350 million, a 16.7 percent increase over 1996's disappointing results.

One of Esprit's most innovative sales tactics has been its mail order catalog. Launched in the 1980s, the catalog was hailed as ground breaking and was subsequently regarded as a predecessor of the lifestyle catalogs of the 1990s. The catalog went out of print in the late 1980s but was re-launched by Margolis in 1997. The new catalog, according to an Esprit press release, would promote "Esprit's renewed image and promises innovative approaches to graphic design and photography." Margolis viewed the catalog as "one facet of a comprehensive plan to revitalize Esprit's image, clothing design and retail presence, while targeting customers' contemporary apparel needs."

CORPORATE CITIZENSHIP

In the spring of 1992, the company initiated the Ecollection line of clothing. The line is notable for being produced in the most environmentally friendly way possible. From organically grown cotton, to recycled wool, to biodegradable enzyme washes and metal-free dyes, this line of casual sportswear supported the more environmentally conscious lifestyle of the 1990s. Even the accessories were earth-friendly and socially conscious; reconstituted glass for jewelry, hand painted buttons, and recycled sea shells were part of Esprit's Ecollection.

Esprit's advertising also has a history of social consciousness. A full-page installment was placed in its 1987 catalog titled "AIDS: A Global Epidemic." The text advised consumers to practice safe sex, contained current facts that served to dispel rumors about AIDS, and provided a national hotline.

In 1997 Esprit de Corp. was placed on the U.S. Department of Labor's "Trendsetter List," which is a roster of companies that meet criteria that prevent retailers from purchasing goods made in "sweatshop" conditions. According to *WWD*, "To get on the list, an apparel maker or retailer must demonstrate a commitment to labor laws and cooperate with those who enforce the laws. List members must also educate contractors about labor laws and routinely inspect these suppliers for compliance."

In this same *WWD* article, Kathleen Anderson, vice president of administration at Esprit de Corp., said, "It just reflects what we've been doing for a long time. Esprit has been conscious of these issues since the early Nineties. . . . One new addition to Esprit's anti-sweat-shop program is the posting of posters at contractors' [facilities] with toll-free numbers that workers can call with complaints. The company already routinely inspects its contractors and has an outside company also conducting inspections."

GLOBAL PRESENCE

In 1997 the Esprit brand was sold in more than 350 free-standing Esprit stores in 44 countries around the world. The company maintained creative offices in Hong Kong, Dusseldorf, and San Francisco. The international arm of the company, Esprit International, functions as a separate entity and employs nearly 5,000 people world-wide. It posted sales of approximately $1.6 billion in 1997. Esprit de Corp. owns about 35 percent of Esprit International.

SOURCES OF INFORMATION

Bibliography

Carlsen, Clifford. "Esprit Dressed to Thrill." *San Francisco Business Times,* 24 January 1997.

———. "Esprit Told to Sell Fast or Lose Company." *San Francisco Business Times,* 5 January 1996.

Ellis, Kristi. "Esprit de Corp.'s Marching Orders." *WWD,* 9 January 1997.

"Esprit de Corp." *Hoover's Online.* May 1998. Available at http://www.hoovers.com.

Esprit Holdings Ltd. Annual Report 1996/97. San Francisco, CA: Esprit de Corp., 1997.

"Esprit Relaunches its Revolutionary Catalog: San Francisco-Based Clothing Manufacturer Esprit de Corp. Will Reinstate Its Mail Order Division for Fall '97." *Esprit Home Page.* May 1998. Available at http://www.esprit.com/new/pr/pr970710_right.html.

Marlow, Michael. "Susie Buys Out Doug, Prepares to Lift Esprit." *WWD,* 4 June 1990.

McGrath, Ellie. "Esprit, the Sequel." *Working Woman,* September 1991.

Ramey, Joanna. "Labor Adds to Trendsetter List." *WWD,* 26 March 1997.

White, Constance C. R. "Susie Tompkins: Crossing a New Bridge." *Women's Wear Daily,* 10 March 1993.

For an annual report:

on the Internet at http://www.esprit-intl.com/company/

For additional industry research:

Investigate companies by their Standard Industrial Classification Codes, also known as SICs. Esprit's primary SICs are:

2331 Women's & Misses' Blouses & Shirts

2335 Women's & Misses' Dresses

2361 Girls' & Children's Dresses & Blouses

2369 Girls' & Children's Outerwear, NEC

The Estee Lauder Companies Inc.

FOUNDED: 1946 as the Estee Lauder Cosmetic Company.

Contact Information:

HEADQUARTERS: 767 5th Ave.
  New York, NY 10153
FAX: (212)572-3941
PHONE: (212)572-4200

OVERVIEW

The Estee Lauder Companies Inc. is one of the largest cosmetics companies in the world, selling about 700 different skin care, makeup, and fragrance products under brand names that include Aramis, Bobbi Brown essentials, Clinique, Estee Lauder, Origins, and Prescriptives. Until late 1995 the company was the largest privately owned cosmetics company in the United States. By 1997 its products accounted for about 40 percent of all cosmetic sales in U.S. department and specialty stores.

Through the years Estee Lauder grew substantially, expanding its product line by developing its own companies (like Origins Natural Resources Inc. in 1990), acquiring new companies (like Bobbi Brown essentials in 1995), obtaining licensing agreements (like the one it secured with American fashion designer Tommy Hilfiger in 1994), and by entering into joint ventures (such as that with perfumer Herbert Frommen in 1996). By the late 1990s the company was selling its expanded line of products not only throughout the Americas, Europe, Belgium, Canada, Japan, Switzerland, the United Kingdom, Venezuela, and South Africa, but it was entering or making plans to enter new areas like India and China.

COMPANY FINANCES

In 1997 total sales reached $3.38 billion, which was 6 percent higher than the previous year's sales of $3.19 billion. Of that, 39 percent came from sales of skin care products, 37 percent from makeup, and 24 percent from fragrances. Of this, 57 percent of net sales and 53 percent of operating income came from the United States alone. The Europe/Middle East/Africa region represented 27 percent of net sales and 34 percent of operating income. The Asia/Pacific region represented 16 percent of net sales and 13 percent of operating income.

Total revenue for both 1996 and 1997 showed a consistent trend of revenues increasing. For example, 1993 saw sales of $2.45 billion and 1994 sales were $2.58 billion. By 1995 sales jumped to $2.90 billion. Net income also rose steadily during the same period, from $58 million in 1993 to $70 million in 1994, reaching $121 million in 1995, and jumping once again to $160 million in 1996 and $198 million in 1997.

HISTORY

In the 1930s Josephine Esther Mentzer, now known as Estee Lauder, began her career by selling skin care products (an all-purpose face cream and a cleansing oil) that her uncle, John Schotz, originally formulated. Later she packaged these formulations and began selling them. Her line was comprised of six products—three skin care products and three color cosmetics including a face powder, a lipstick called "Just Red," and a turquoise eye shadow. In the mid-1940s, Estee Lauder convinced department store Bonwit Teller to take her products, and she sold them there herself on Saturdays. At that time, a hallmark of success for a cosmetics company in New York was to be carried by Saks Fifth Avenue, then considered the most elegant department store, and shortly after the end of World War II Estee Lauder made her way in.

From the mid-1940s until the mid-1950s Estee Lauder traveled across the United States selling her products. In 1946 she founded her company as the Estee Lauder Cosmetic Company. In the early 1950s she came out with Youth Dew, a product that would catapult her into fame and wealth. Marketed as a bath oil that doubled as a perfume, Youth Dew was an attempt to provide everything the American women wanted in a fragrance: it was bold yet inexpensive—and it was a huge success. Soon, Youth Dew accounted for 80 percent of Estee Lauder's sales at Saks. By 1960 the company passed the $1 billion mark in sales, and Estee Lauder was incorporated.

In the late 1950s and the early 1960s, European skin care products became exceedingly popular in the United States, and cosmetic companies—including Estee Lauder—were quick to capitalize on this. Some companies got into trouble with the U.S. Food and Drug Administration because of their bizarre and sometimes morally questionable ingredients (placental creams briefly gained some popularity at this time) and because of their outlandish claims (for example, Revlon alleged that its Ultima cream would penetrate "into the living cells"), but Estee Lauder was more cautious with the product she brought out at this time, a cream she called

FINANCES:

Estee Lauder Net Sales, 1994-1997 (million dollars)

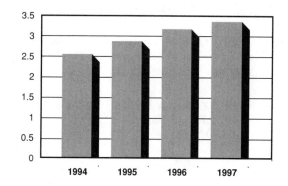

Estee Lauder 1997 Stock Prices (dollars)

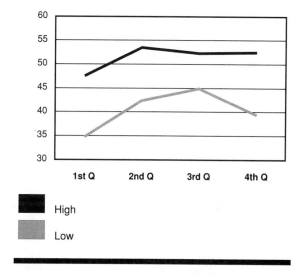

Re-Nutriv. As the writer Lee Israel rightly noted, it was "a name that said nothing and everything." The cream was extraordinarily expensive, selling for $115 a pound, which drew attention to, and created publicity for, the product and the company.

In 1964 Estee Lauder introduced a perfume for men called Aramis. The following year, she brought out 21 additional products in the Aramis line. The line was enormously successful. So successful that soon, cosmetics giant Charles Revson of Revlon copied its strategy and the tortoise shell packaging, launching his own rival male fragrance called Braggi. This move, which came at the

FAST FACTS:

About The Estee Lauder Companies Inc.

Ownership: The Estee Lauder Companies Inc. has been publicly owned since 1995 and is traded on The New York Stock Exchange.

Officers: Leonard A. Lauder, Chmn. & CEO, 64, $4,453,500; Robert J. Bigler, Sr. VP & CFO, 49; Fred H. Langhammer, Pres. & COO, 53, $3,150,000; Andrew J. Cavanaugh, Sr. VP, Human Resources, 50

Employees: 14,700 (1997)

Principal Subsidiary Companies: The Estee Lauder Companies Inc.'s subsidiaries include Estee Lauder Inc., which is privately owned and whose subsidiaries include: Aramis Inc., Clinique Laboratories, Inc., Estee Lauder International Inc., Estee Lauder U.S.A., and Origins Natural Resources, Inc.

Chief Competitors: As one of the world's leading manufacturers of prestige skin care, makeup, and fragrance products, Estee Lauder's competitors include: Avon; L'Oreal; Chanel; Coty; Helene Curtis; Mary Kay; Revlon; Procter & Gamble; and Unilever.

same time as the demise of Estee Lauder's two other rivals, Helena Rubenstein in 1965 and Elizabeth Arden in 1966, would fuel an already unpleasant competitiveness between Charles Revson and Estee Lauder.

An interview in the late 1960s with a renowned New York dermatologist, Dr. Norman Orentreich, appeared in *Vogue* magazine that would greatly influence the future of skin care claims and would provide inspiration for Estee Lauder's Clinique line of cosmetics. Estee Lauder hired the writer of the article, *Vogue* managing editor Carol Phillips, to develop and oversee a new cosmetic line catering to the younger, more health- and fitness-conscious woman—an allergy-tested, fragrance-free line with another "name that said nothing and everything": Clinique. When Charles Revson learned that Estee Lauder had put out her Clinique line, he quickly slapped together a hypo-allergenic line of his own (something he claimed he'd had in mind for years), which he called Etherea. The line was a flop, in part because of its careless and hasty development, and in part because of waning department store interest in carrying Revson's lines.

In 1972 Estee's son Leonard Lauder, who had joined the company in 1958, was made president and Estee Lauder remained chief executive officer. Leonard would come to be regarded by many as the reason for the company's great and lasting success. He was tremendously dedicated and hardworking and had an extraordinary business sense; his plans were systematic, long-term, and goal-oriented, and he demonstrated enormous patience in waiting for them to come to fruition. In 1973, Estee's younger son Ronald was made executive vice president of Clinique Laboratories at age 29, and her husband Joseph Lauder oversaw production at the Lauder's plant in Melville, Long Island, as he'd done from early on.

By 1978 Estee Lauder's sales were enormous. Sales of the Estee Lauder line reached about $170 million, Clinique sales were steady at about $80 million, and the Aramis line reached about $40 million with Aramis cologne and aftershave accounting for 50 to 80 percent of men's fragrance sales in some department stores. That same year, Estee Lauder launched two women's perfumes, White Linen and Cinnabar. The latter, originally planned as a toned-down version of Youth Dew, was to be called Soft Youth Dew. But when Yves Saint Laurent hit it big with his wildly successful Opium perfume, introduced in Paris in 1977 and in the United States in the fall of 1978, Estee Lauder quickly changed gears—and product name, packaging, and marketing—to produce Cinnabar. When the product came out (looking a lot like Opium with its box and tasseled bottle) many of the bottles still read "Soft Youth Dew."

In 1979 Estee Lauder launched an upscale, medical-sounding cosmetic line for professional women called Prescriptives. The line did not enjoy an immediate success, however. In 1982 Leonard Lauder was made chief executive officer and Ronald Lauder was named chair of international operations. Estee Lauder maintained her position as chairman of the board and Joseph Lauder continued to oversee company plant operations. In January of the following year, Joseph Lauder collapsed and died. Later in 1983, Ronald Lauder left the company to serve as Deputy Assistant Defense Secretary in the Reagan Administration, and for the first time, Estee Lauder sales reached the $1 billion mark. The only product Estee Lauder launched in 1983 was a night cream called "Night Repair," which the company claimed was the strongest treatment item in its history. The cream, advertised as a "breakthrough" in skin care was phenomenally successful. By 1988 Estee Lauder had captured a third of the prestige cosmetics market in the United States.

In 1989, after losing a bid to become mayor of New York City, Ronald Lauder returned to the company. The following year, Robin Burns, former president of Unilever's Calvin Klein Cosmetics Corporation, was hired to head Estee Lauder's domestic branch, Estee Lauder U.S.A. Burns, who had played key roles in the successful introductions of Obsession and Eternity perfumes, began her tenure with an attempt to update and re-vamp the image of several Estee Lauder fragrances, overseeing advertisements featuring the model Paulina Porizkova who had represented the entire Estee Lauder line since 1988.

Also in 1990 the company formed a new subsidiary, Origins Natural Resources Inc., targeting young, environmentally conscious consumers. Origins products were packaged in recycled paper, no animal products were used in the cosmetics, and color cosmetic shades appeared in natural tones. In 1991 Prescriptives introduced its All Skins makeup for women of different ethnic backgrounds and within two years, the product was attracting almost 4,000 new customers monthly. By 1992 Prescriptives was bringing in an annual $70 million in sales.

In 1995 Leonard Lauder became chairman of the company. Estee Lauder was now chairwoman emeritus of her company, earning $3.82 million in 1995, making her the fifth highest-paid woman in corporate America that year. On November 17, 1995, The Estee Lauder Companies Inc. went public, selling 13 percent of its stock and thereby raising an estimated $365 million. Early in 1997, Leonard and Ronald Lauder sold an additional 7.2 million shares, leaving the Lauder family with about 78 percent of outstanding shares and 95.9 percent of the combined voting power.

The late 1990s brought new challenges for The Estee Lauder Companies by way of the courtroom. Estee Lauder won a judgment against Gap Inc. for its use of "100%" in its "100% Body Care" toiletry products in 1996, alleging that consumers might confuse Gap's line with its own new "100% Time Release" line. A federal appeals court, however, overturned the ruling in early 1997. In the meantime, a former Estee Lauder employee filed a multimillion-dollar lawsuit against the company claiming racial discrimination and retaliatory discharge. In a separate, unrelated case, another person still employed by the company filed a $2 million sexual harassment suit against the company and one of its top executives.

CHRONOLOGY:

Key Dates for The Estee Lauder Companies Inc.

1944: Estee Lauder begins selling her own cosmetics from behind the counter in various New York department stores

1946: Estee and husband Joseph found the Estee Lauder Cosmetic Company

1948: The first department store account is established with Saks Fifth Avenue

1953: Estee Lauder launches the first dual bath oil and perfume called Youth Dew

1960: The Neiman Marcus award for Distinguished Service in the Field of Fashion is presented to Estee Lauder

1968: Estee Lauder launches Clinique Laboratories, Inc.

1979: Estee Lauder products become available in Moscow, Leningrad, and Kiev, Russia

1989: The Beauty Boutique is opened in Budapest, Hungary; the first freestanding perfume store in Moscow is opened

1994: The American Society of Perfumers offers Estee Lauder their first Living Legend Award

1995: Estee Lauder goes public selling 13 percent of its stock

1996: Estee Lauder joins with European fragrance designer Herbert Fromman to start Palladio Fragrances International

STRATEGY

Estee Lauder was herself a brilliant marketer of cosmetics, early on handing out free samples and later introducing the "gift with purchase" strategy. But Estee Lauder didn't just sell cosmetics, she sold a look, a dream. One advertising strategy for doing this involved the use of same elegant model in distinct posh settings to personify the company over a period of time.

The first woman to embody the "Estee Lauder look" was Chicago housewife Phyllis Connors; but it was Karen Graham, who began her 15-year tenure with Estee Lauder in 1971, who was perhaps the most successful of the Lauder models. Graham was beautiful, lean, refined, seemingly wealthy, and seemingly at home in elegant surroundings—a full-bodied personification of Estee Lauder's vision of "the good life" for women. Karen Graham became so identified with the company that people often thought she was Estee Lauder herself. In 1988 the company chose Paulina Porizkova with her friendlier face and, therefore, presumably broader consumer appeal. Model Elizabeth Hurley took over the role in the early 1990s.

INFLUENCES

The Estee Lauder Companies' marked success owes much to its ability to respond to the changing social climate. When European skin care and beauty products came into vogue in the United States, Estee Lauder responded with her Re-Nutriv cream, which was extremely successful. Another enormous influence on the young Estee Lauder company in the late 1960s was the new emphasis placed on health and science. It came by way of *Vogue* magazine's famous interview with New York skin specialist Dr. Norman Orentreich, which had him stating that skin care would provide a template for the basic three-product line of Clinique skin care products.

In 1979 this same scientific emphasis would help inspire the Prescriptives line, whose products were supposedly even more cutting edge and high-tech—and were certainly more costly—than the products in the Clinique line. In the early 1990s, after extensive marketing research, the company started its Origins Natural Resources Inc. in response to the consumer's growing concern about the environment. The products were sold in packages made of recycled materials and printed with the words "Origins Commitment: Preservation of earth, animal and environment."

CURRENT TRENDS

In the mid-1990s Estee Lauder began a new trend toward what might be called "external expansion": acquiring new companies, obtaining licensing agreements, and entering into joint ventures to produce new products. For example, in 1995 Estee Lauder acquired a majority interest (51 percent) in the Canadian cosmetic company M.A.C. Two years later, it increased its majority ownership position to 70 percent. Similarly, in October 1995, Estee Lauder purchased another popular skin care and color cosmetic company, Bobbi Brown essentials, which had a distinct customer profile from that of M.A.C. Both companies went on to enjoy considerable success. In 1994, Estee Lauder obtained a licensing agreement with American fashion designer Tommy Hilfiger to market Tommy perfume. Two years later, the company began to discuss a licensing deal to produce men's and women's fragrances for Milan-based fashion house Prada.

During this time Estee Lauder entered into a joint venture with Herbert Frommen, the highly respected former president of the fragrance company Lancaster, to develop and market fragrances primarily for the European market. The joint venture was called Palladio Fragrances International, and in the fall of 1996, it launched its first fragrance, Kiton, for the upscale Italian men's label of the same name.

PRODUCTS

A key Lauder strategy has been the continuous introduction of new products. Each year, about a third of the company's sales volume has come from products introduced within the previous three years. In the 1990s,

successful new products included Prescriptives' All Skins makeup; Clinique's Moisture On-Call, Long Last Soft Shine Lipstick, and Stay the Day Eyeshadow; Estee Lauder's Fruition Extra, Thigh-Zone Body Streamlining Complex, Indelible Lipstick, and Double Wear Stay-in-Place Makeup, along with Estee Lauder's Pleasures fragrance. By the late 1990s, Estee Lauder's fragrance line had expanded to over a dozen distinct scents, still including Estee Lauder's own original Youth Dew, as intense and persistent as when it first appeared four decades earlier. Early in 1996 The Estee Lauder Companies purchased a single-item skin care line called "Creme de la Mer" from Max Hubner. In the summer of 1997 it launched its Pleasures fragrance for men.

Throughout the 1990s, demand continued to be strong for established products like Clinique's Dramatically Different Moisturizing Lotion, Prescriptives' Virtual Skin, Estee Lauder's Advanced Night Repair, and classic Estee Lauder fragrances like Beautiful and White Linen.

GLOBAL PRESENCE

By the end of the 1990s about half of The Estee Lauder Companies' sales came from outside of the United States. Its products accounted for about 20 percent of the $15 billion in prestige cosmetic sales worldwide, and the company was committed to continued international expansion. During the first half of the 1990s international net sales increased at a compound annual rate of 8.8 percent. In its 1996 fiscal year, the company launched Clinique in Russia, with a free-standing store in Moscow and Budapest. Estee Lauder also opened in locations in Poland, Hungary, and the Czech Republic. In its 1997 fiscal year Estee Lauder began selling in Romania and planned to continue expanding into Bulgaria and Latvia, as well. The Estee Lauder Companies had been represented in Asia since the late 1960s, first entering Japan in 1968, South Korea in 1988, and China via Shanghai in 1993.

By the end of the decade, the company had a truly global presence, selling its products throughout North and South America, Europe, eastern Europe, Russia, several Baltic states, Africa, the Middle East, China, and the Asia/Pacific region including Korea, Singapore, Japan, New Zealand, Australia, Malaysia, and Thailand. Furthermore, it was focusing on new territory, considering moving into Serbia and Slovenia and expanding into the potentially enormous markets of Brazil and India.

SOURCES OF INFORMATION

Bibliography

Bender, Marilyn. "Estee Lauder: A Family Affair." *At the Top.* New York: Doubleday & Company, Inc., 1975.

Born, Peter. "Lauder Scores a Hit in Romania." *Women's Wear Daily,* 30 May 1997.

———. "Lauder's Zen-like China Plan." *Women's Wear Daily,* 31 May 1996.

"Employee Suing Estee Lauder." *Women's Wear Daily,* 16 January 1997.

"Estee Lauder Companies Reports 36% Increase in Fiscal 1997 Third Quarter Earnings; Worldwide Net Sales Up 7% on Constant Currency Basis." *PR Newswire,* 29 April 1997.

"Estee Lauder Co's: Net Income Climbed 19% in Fiscal Second Quarter." *The Wall Street Journal,* 29 January 1997.

"Estee Lauder: New Launches Drive Growth." *Cosmetics International,* 25 March 1997.

"Estee Lauder Wins '100%' Case with Gap." *Women's Wear Daily,* 23 July 1996.

"Gap Blocked from Using '100%' in Body-Care Line." *The Wall Street Journal,* 23 July 1996.

Hammond, Teena. "Court Rules for Gap in Appeal of Lauder Suit on '100%' Mark." *Women's Wear Daily,* 26 March 1997.

Hammonds, Keith, ed. "Glossy Finish." *Business Week Online,* 4 December 1995.

Israel, Lee. *Estee Lauder: Beyond the Magic.* New York: Macmillan Publishing Company, 1985.

"Joint Adventure." *Women's Wear Daily,* 9 February 1996.

Larson, Soren. "Lauder Shines on Fifi Night (24th Annual Fragrance Foundation Awards)." *Women's Wear Daily,* 7 June 1996.

Lauder, Estee. *Estee Lauder: A Success Story.* New York: Random House, 1985.

"Lauder is Working on Plans for Creme de la Mer Line." *Women's Wear Daily,* 22 March 1996.

"Lauder Said to be in Talks with Prada." *Women's Wear Daily,* 17 March 1996.

"Launches and Acquisitions Help Lauder to Global Growth." *Cosmetics International,* 10 December 1996.

Norton, Frances E. "Estee Lauder." *International Directory of Company Histories.* Vol. 9. Detroit: St. James Press, 1994.

Ono, Yumiko. "Estee Lauder Expects Earnings to Soar on Strong Sale of Perfumes, Makeup." *The Wall Street Journal,* 26 July 1996.

Ono, Yumiko, and Robert Berner. "Estee Lauder Says Gap Line Infringes on Trademark." *The Wall Street Journal,* 6 June 1996.

"Pay Day." *Women's Wear Daily,* 18 October 1996.

Raper, Sarah. "Helmut Lang May Be the Next Designer in Lauder's Stable." *Women's Wear Daily,* 29 February 1997.

Rutberg, Sidney. "Tommy Scents Push Lauder Net Up 36%." *Women's Wear Daily,* 30 April 1997.

"Secondary Offering." *Women's Wear Daily,* 11 February 1997.

"USA's Highest-Paid Women: Magazine Tallies Top Compensation for '95." *USA Today,* 17 December 1996.

Young, Vicki M. "Ex-employees File Suits Against Lauder, Karan." *Women's Wear Daily,* 30 August 1996.

Zinn, Laura. "At Estee Lauder, the Sweet Smell of Survival." *Business Week Online,* 14 November 1992.

For an annual report:

telephone: (800)308-2334 **or** write: Investors Relation Dept., The Estee Lauder Companies Inc., 767 5th Ave., New York, NY 10153

For additional industry research:

Investigate companies by their Standard Industrial Classification Codes, also known as SICs. Estee Lauder's primary SICs are:

2844 Toilet Preparations

6719 Holding Companies, NEC

Exxon Corporation

FOUNDED: 1882

Contact Information:
HEADQUARTERS: 5959 Las Colinas Blvd.
   Irving, TX 75039-2298
PHONE: (972)444-1000
FAX: (972)444-1882
URL: http://www.exxon.com

OVERVIEW

Exxon stands as the number three company in the United States after General Motors and Ford, according to Fortune 500, and the number two oil and gas producer in the world. It owns 4 U.S. refineries and 8,500 gas stations. It also runs 31 refineries in 17 countries and is involved in selling and producing petrochemicals, and mining coal and other minerals.

The 1989 "Exxon Valdez" oil tanker spill in Prince William Sound, Alaska, caused the company financial headaches after being levied a punitive damages fine of $5 billion. Recovering from that disaster, the company has been looking to expand its power generation business in China. It also has been sinking massive funds into its refining and retail businesses in the Asia/Pacific region, while expanding operations in Japan, Malaysia, Singapore, and Thailand.

COMPANY FINANCES

Exxon had over $135 billion in sales as of fiscal year end 1997 (December). Gross profit was $43 billion for 1997, up from just under $41 billion in 1996 and $40 billion in 1995. The gross profit margin was 35.8 percent in 1997, 35.1 percent in 1996, and 37.2 percent in 1995. Total net income was $8.46 billion for 1997, up from $7.51 billion in 1996, and $6.47 billion in 1995. Sales of $135.0 billion in 1997 compare with $131.5 billion in 1996, $121.8 billion in 1995, $112.0 billion in 1994, and $109.5 billion in 1993. High price per share averaged $67.25 for fiscal year 1997, while the average low price for the same period was $48.25. This compares with an average high price of $48.25 per share for 1996 and an average low of $38.81. As of June 8, 1998, the stock closed at $71.19. There were 642,466 holders of record of Exxon common stock as of January 31, 1998.

ANALYSTS' OPINIONS

In 1997 analysts predicted that Exxon would increase dividends at a faster rate than the annual 2 percent forecast for S&P (Standard & Poors) companies over the next three years. In fact, Exxon exceeded the return on the S&P 500 with a total return of 26 percent in 1996 and 74 percent over two years. Analyst Paul Ting of Salomon Brothers noted, "These are the kinds of returns other companies have been targeting for years." Analyst John Hervey of Donaldson, Lufkin, & Jenrette said, "The company offers one of the best and most consistent return records in the oil industry." Exxon's U.S. refining operation earned $57 million in 1997, gaining 43 percent and exceeding the S&P 500, which was 29 percent. Analyst Paul Ting said he believed the company's stock would reach an all-time high, perhaps reaching into the high $60 range. That prediction has already come true, as Exxon stock reached over $70 per share in June 1998. According to Zack's, brokers recommended buying or holding Exxon stock.

Much of the controversy surrounding the Exxon Corporation has not been its financial condition, but rather its handling of the Exxon Valdez oil spill. The 1989 mishap resulted in a $5-billion fine. The National Transportation Safety Board found that the cause of the spill was neglect of the third mate to appropriately manipulate the ship due to extreme exhaustion and his heavy workload. The cause was also due to the intoxication of the master on board. The controversy surrounding the case has largely been due to the company's attempts to compensate seafood processors in Alaska with $70 million. Publicly announcing its good faith gesture, Exxon was later rebuked by U.S. District Judge H. Russel Holland when it was discovered the company required the Alaskan businesspeople to give back any compensation they might win in court. He ruled that Exxon would not be allowed to receive any of the punitive damages funds, which meant Exxon would lose a total of $700 million. Due to an appeal announced in February 1997 by Exxon, no damage funds have been paid as of mid-1998.

HISTORY

After forming the Standard Oil company in 1870, John D. Rockefeller created the Standard Oil Trust, which enabled the firm to establish new, independent companies in various states by dissolving existing Stan-

FINANCES:

Exxon Revenues, 1994-1997 (billion dollars)

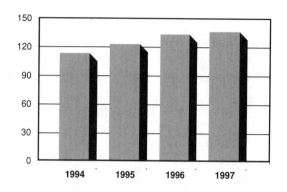

Exxon 1997 Stock Prices (dollars)

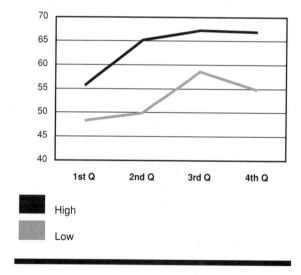

dard Oil associates. The Supreme Court, however, ordered these companies to be split into 34 entities since the Trust owned 90 percent of the petroleum industry. One of the split companies was New Jersey's Standard Oil (Jersey Standard). When Walter Teagle was president of Jersey Standard in 1917, he quietly bought half of Humble Oil of Texas and moved operations into South America. The company also participated in the Red Line Agreement in 1928, which designated most Middle East oil to selected companies. Other overseas ventures included the 1948 purchase of a 30-percent ownership in Arabian American Oil Company along with a 7-percent

FAST FACTS:

About Exxon Corporation

Ownership: Exxon Corporation is a publicly owned company traded on the New York Stock Exchange.

Ticker symbol: XON

Officers: Lee R. Raymond, Chmn., Pres. & CEO, 59, $3,250,000; Robert E. Wilhelm, Sr. VP, 57, $1,307,001; Harry J. Longwell, Sr. VP, 56, $1,280,001

Employees: 80,000 (1997)

Principal Subsidiary Companies: Exxon's chief subsidiaries include: Natuna gas field (50–percent ownership); Exxon China, Inc.; Exxon Coal and Minerals Company; Exxon Company, International; Exxon Company, U.S.A.; Exxon Computing Services Company; Exxon Exploration Company; Exxon Production Research Company; Exxon Research and Engineering Company; Exxon Upstream Technical Computing Company; Exxon Upstream Development Company; Exxon Ventures Inc. (CIS); Exxon Chemical Company; Imperial Oil Limited; SeaRiver Maritime Financial Holdings

Chief Competitors: Some of Exxon's primary competitors are: Amerada Hess; Amoco; Ashland; ARCO; British Petroleum; Broken Hill; Caltex Petroleum; Chevron; Dow Chemical; Eastman Chemical; Elf Aquitaine; FINA; Huntsman; Imperial Oil; Koch; Mobil; Norsk Hydro; Occidental; PDVSA; PEMEX; Pennzoil; Petrobras; Phillips Petroleum; Royal Dutch/Shell; Sun; Texaco; Tosco; Total; and Union Carbide.

interest of Iranian production purchased in 1954. These two moves deemed Jersey Standard the biggest oil company in the world. When oil companies still using the Standard Oil name protested Jersey Standard's use of the name Esso, the company became Exxon in 1972. This change cost the company $100 million.

Other financial difficulties hit Exxon after the oil crisis of the 1970s, which quickly reduced its oil reserves. Exxon was hit hard again in 1989 when the Valdez oil tanker spilled 11 million gallons of oil into Alaskan waters. Shoveling out billions in cleanup costs, the company was called "reckless" by a federal jury in Alaska. The 1990s were characterized mostly by expansion for

the Exxon Corporation. The Natuna gas field was developed after Exxon and Pertamina, the Indonesia state oil company, agreed to terms. The company also agreed to a $15-billion development of three oil and natural gas fields near Sakhalin Island in Russia, and was able to entertain further expansion plans after it announced a large oil discovery in the Gulf of Mexico in 1996.

STRATEGY

In 1997 Exxon's chairman, Lee Raymond, referred to the company's strategy in *Forbes* as "the relentless pursuit of efficiency." Reducing operating costs and focusing on return on capital have been core strategies for the company. Exxon's exploration and production businesses have revolved around the following strategies as well: to make existing oil and gas production sites as profitable as possible, to invest only in projects that produce returns, and to profit from strengthening natural gas markets.

Exxon's refining and marketing businesses have had strategies of their own. One ingredient has been the expansion in profitable, growing markets, like Asia-Pacific, eastern Europe, and Latin America. A second strategy involved the company's restrictions on refining investments in markets that do not produce high growth. A third element has been the company's constant efforts to lower operating expenses and to refine production. Lastly, Exxon has aimed to remain focused on research investment activities.

INFLUENCES

Although Exxon has filed an appeal to $5 billion in damages assessed against it for the Valdez oil spill, the company has stored away that amount in case the appeal is lost. Additionally, falling oil prices may cause Exxon to cut its prices, which should eventually result in lower profits. Energy demand is decreasing, partially because of the unusually mild winters, while at the same time, oil supplies are increasing. Exxon estimates that crude oil use in Asia is going to increase dramatically, perhaps to exceed the combined use of crude oil in the United States and Europe; as a result, the company is pursuing expansion efforts in the Asian market, including developing a $2-billion petrochemical facility in Singapore. The facility is expected to be operable by 2000.

CURRENT TRENDS

Formerly, Exxon stayed away from large investments in liquefied natural gas (LNG). As of 1997, however, the company began pursuing LNG projects in

Yemen and Indonesia. It also developed natural gas fields in Russia. Still recovering from a marred reputation after the Valdez disaster, the company launched a request to be allowed back into the same Alaskan waters it polluted in 1989, Prince William Sound. The ship, now renamed the SeaRiver Mediterranean, was prohibited from entering the waters after the spill by the Oil Pollution Act. The company's motivation for such a request stemmed from the fact that it was losing money operating the ship in Europe and Egypt, where less expensive ships are readily available.

Another strategic move by Exxon has been the introduction of its Tiger Express retail stores. The first store was opened in Houston, where Tiger Express offers customers a one-stop gas station shopping experience. Employees wear khaki pants and specially designed polo shirts. Other conveniences include a Taco Bell Express drive-thru, a Check Express check-cashing service, a service that allows customers to pay at the pumps, indoor bathroom facilities, diaper changing tables in men's and women's restrooms, and recorded music playing at the pumps and inside the store.

PRODUCTS

Exxon's primary products are oil and gas, however, its chemical division also manufactures and sells plastics, synthetic rubbers, performance fluids, plasticizers, basic chemical building blocks, and lubricant and fuel additives.

CORPORATE CITIZENSHIP

Exxon Corporation has launched several efforts in aiding the community and its environment. One such effort has been the financial contributions aimed at preventing the tiger, the company's symbol, from becoming extinct. It planned to donate approximately $5 million to support breeding efforts and zoo information displays and tiger projects in Siberia and Sumatra. Controversy surrounding Exxon's efforts has stemmed from accusations that the company has not addressed the real threats facing the extinction of tigers: poaching, illegal trade in tiger parts, and annihilation of the animals' prey by hunters. Some have said the company has no plans to enter anti-poaching efforts since such activities have been touchy in Asia, a large market for Exxon. Critics have said that without attention to the real dangers, the company's contributions will be of little value.

Other efforts to incorporate community involvement have included Exxon's efforts in education. Through the Exxon Education Foundation, it has offered $13.5 million in grants to 885 colleges and universities. Under the Foundation's Educational Matching Gift Program, all

CHRONOLOGY:
Key Dates for Exxon Corporation

1882: Incorporates as the Standard Oil Company of New Jersey

1899: Standard Oil (New Jersey) becomes the sole holding company for all Standard Oil interests

1911: The Supreme Court orders Standard Oil (New Jersey) to separate from its subsidiaries

1919: Standard (Jersey) purchases 50 percent of Humble Oil & Refining, the biggest of Standard's suppliers

1926: Standard (Jersey) introduces the Esso brand name

1943: Several Venezuelan interests are consolidated into the Creole Petroleum Corporation

1948: Purchases 30 percent ownership of Arabian American Oil Company

1954: Purchases a 7 percent interest of Iranian production, making Standard (New Jersey) the largest oil company in the world

1972: Exxon Corporation becomes the official name of the company

1989: The *Exxon Valdez* crashes off the coast of Alaska spilling 260,000 barrels of crude oil

1996: Exxon announces a huge oil discovery in the Gulf of Mexico

employees' donations would be matched by Exxon 3-to-1, the largest matching gift program in the nation.

Exxon has also provided assistance in the Ambassador Franklin Williams Scholarship Program from the Stevens Institute of Technology. Exxon gave $1.5 million in grants within an eight-year period to award scholarships for minority students.

GLOBAL PRESENCE

Exxon operates in more than 100 countries. Exxon China Inc. is headquartered in Beijing. Activities there include exploration, refining, and marketing. Chemical and electric power businesses have been established there as well. Exxon's Coal and Minerals Company is located in Colombia, the United States, and Australia. Also accountable for electrical generation capabilities in Hong Kong, the company conducts business in power generation and coal and mineral exploration. Europe, offshore Malaysia, and Australia serve as oil and gas production cites for Exxon. Exxon Company International and its associates produce gas and oil in 12 countries. This makes up over half of the company's petroleum liquids production and two-thirds of its gas production. One subsidiary, Exxon Ventures Inc., manages exploration and production activities in the former Soviet Union. The company runs offices in Baku, Azerbaijan; Almaty, Kazakstan; and Moscow, Yuzhno-Sakhalinsk, and Arkhangelsk, Russia. Another subsidiary, Imperial Oil Limited, stands as a leading member of the Canadian petroleum business. It has been Canada's largest crude oil producer and the biggest refiner and marketer of petroleum products.

EMPLOYMENT

Statistics show that Exxon makes efforts to hire, retain, and promote minorities and women. In 1997 Exxon hired a total of 1,073 employees in the United States. Women comprised 36 percent of that total, and minorities another 26 percent. Forty-five percent of co-op assignments and internships were given to women out of a total of 289 participating students; another 38 percent were minorities. Exxon allies itself with the National Action Council for Minorities in Engineering (NACME), the Texas Alliance for Minorities in Engineering (TAME), and the National Society of Black Engineers. Exxon also participates in university programs, scholarship programs, and internship programs.

SOURCES OF INFORMATION

Bibliography

Carey, John. "Help or Hype from Exxon?" *Business Week,* 28 August 1995.

Clarke, Jim. "Exxon to Appeal $5 Billion Oil Spill Judgment." *San Diego Daily,* 13 February 1997.

Drago, Mike. "Exxon Wins $250 Million Claim Against Insurers." *San Diego Daily,* 10 June 1996.

Edgerton, Jerry, and Jim Frederick. "Build Your Own Wealth Drip by Drip." *Money,* 1 August 1997.

"Exxon Corporation." *Hoover's Online,* 13 July 1998. Available at http://www.hoovers.com.

The Exxon Corporation Home Page, 13 July 1998. Available at http://www.exxon.com.

"Exxon Says Earnings Rise 15 Percent." *Reuters Limited,* 21 April 1997.

"Exxon's Tiger Express Now Open; Called Gas Station of the Future." *Houston Chronicle,* 12 February 1996.

Fitch, Malcolm. "Why Strong Earnings Aren't Enough For This Tiger." *Money,* 1 March 1998.

France, Mike. "Commentary: Corporate Litigation: Playing Hardball Is One Thing . . ." *Business Week,* 1 July 1996.

Galvin, Kevin. "Exxon Wants Exxon Valdez Allowed Back in Prince William Sound." *San Diego Daily,* 16 January 1997.

Mack, Toni. "The Tiger Is on the Prowl." *Forbes,* 21 April 1997.

Patty, Stanton H. "Prince William Sound Rebounds." *The Columbian,* 29 March 1998.

"Stevens Institute of Technology Honors Exxon for Its Support of The Ambassador Franklin Williams Scholarship Program." 13 May 1997. Available at http://biz.yahoo.com.

Teitelbaum, Richard. "Giants of the Fortune 5 Hundred: Exxon: Pumping up Profits for Years." *Fortune,* 28 April 1997.

For an annual report:
on the Internet at: http://www.exxon.com

For additional industry research:
Investigate companies by their Standard Industrial Classification Codes, also known as SICs. Exxon's primary SICs are:

1311 Crude Petroleum and Natural Gas

1382 Oil and Gas Exploration Services

2911 Petroleum Refining

Fannie May Holdings

OVERVIEW

The Archibald Candy Corporation, the privately owned parent company of Fannie May Candies and Fanny Farmer Candies, has sold confections since the 1920s through its retail candy chain stores. Fannie May and Fanny Farmer Candy have a combined number of over 330 stores and are located in 22 states, primarily in the Midwest and the East. Archibald Candy manufactures approximately 75 percent of its products and obtains the remainder from outside vendors. Its product line consists of over 125 items, including chocolates, mints, toffee, and eggnog creams (all made by Archibald Candy); products such as ice cream, nuts, gift items, and novelties are purchased from vendors. In addition to its own stores, Archibald Candy provides confections to approximately 6,000 other retailers. Archibald also sells through catalogues and fundraising events.

In 1996 Archibald Candy Corporation sold chocolates for an average of $10.50 per pound. As such, *Consumer Reports* rated its chocolates the best value of 11 chocolates tested. The main factors were taste and texture, and Archibald Candy's chocolates were described as "very tasty, at about one-third the price of the top three" and having "good taste at a very good price." The chocolate ranking number one overall went for $38.00 per pound, by comparison.

COMPANY FINANCES

Archibald Candy is a privately held company selling a diverse line of confectionaries through its own

ALSO KNOWN AS: Archibald Candy Corporation
FOUNDED: 1920

Contact Information:
HEADQUARTERS: 1137 W. Jackson Blvd.
   Chicago, IL 60607
PHONE: (312)243-2700
FAX: (312)243-5806
TOLL FREE: (800)333-FMAY
EMAIL: fannie@fanniemaycandies.com
URL: http://www.fanniemaycandies.com

FAST FACTS:
About Fannie May Holdings

Ownership: Fannie May Holdings, a privately held firm, is controlled by affiliates of TCW Capital and Jordan Industries.

Officers: Thomas H. Quinn, Chmn. & CEO; Ted A. Shepherd, Pres. & COO; Joseph S. Secker, CFO; Donna Snopek, VP Finance & Accounting, & Secretary

Employees: 2,050

Principal Subsidiary Companies: Fannie May Holdings wholly owns Archibald Candy Corporation, which is the parent company of Fannie May Candies and Fanny Farmer Candies.

Chief Competitors: Fannie May Candies and Fanny Farmer Candies are primarily met with competition from: Godiva; Burdick; Whitman's; Russell Stover; and Teuscher.

day. By the mid-1930s Fannie May had expanded outside of Illinois and had a total of 47 shops. Sticking to the company philosophy of quality, Fannie May sold less candy during World War II rather than substitute cheaper ingredients and sell the same amount. When candy would run out each day, the store would close until more could be manufactured. Fannie May Candy factories now manufacture 40 million pieces of candy each year.

In 1919 Frank O'Connor started Fanny Farmer Candies in Rochester, New York, and he named the company after Fannie Merritt Farmer. Fannie Farmer, known as the "mother of measurements," is famous for *The Boston Cooking School Cookbook,* now known as the *Fannie Farmer Cookbook,* which she wrote in 1896. She had her own cooking school and was reputed to be the first woman to lecture at Harvard Medical School. Mr. O'Connor owned the largest retail candy company in Canada, Laura Secord Candy Shops, when he decided to open Fanny Farmer Candies in Rochester four years after Farmer's death. He later opened stores throughout New York and, in the 1920s, expanded into other states. Mr. O'Connor's mission was markedly similar to H. Teller Archibald's, that is, "Make the finest, freshest chocolate available."

stores and other retailers in the United States. Annual sales at fiscal year end August 1997 were $121.9 million. This reflects an increase over August 1996 sales of $117.3 million, and $115.6 million in August 1995. However, net income dropped from $5.6 million in 1995 to $1.4 million in 1996 and $1.2 million in 1997.

HISTORY

Oddly enough, Fannie May Candies and Fanny Farmer Candies were both started only one year apart, by two different men in two different cities. Fannie May Candies was founded in Chicago in 1920 by H. Teller Archibald and Fanny Farmer Candies was founded in 1919 by Frank O'Connor in Rochester, New York.

No one knows why H. Teller Archibald named his company Fannie May, but he founded it on a philosophy to "make the best quality candy possible and always sell it fresh." After Archibald started the first store, he created a candy kitchen on West Madison Street that remained until the end of the 1930s, at which time Fannie May bought property at 1137 West Jackson Boulevard in Chicago, which is the company's headquarters to this

STRATEGY

H. Teller Archibald and Frank O'Connor had a simple strategy for success—quality. The Archibald Candy Corporation to this day lays claim to that single philosophy, which, for H. Teller Archibald, was to "make the best quality candy possible and always sell it fresh." Frank O'Connor's goal for Fanny Farmer Candies, to "make the finest, freshest chocolate available" fit easily into the overall Archibald Candy Corporation philosophy.

In 1996 Archibald Candy launched an advertising campaign through The Walden Group, an Illinois-based ad agency. According to Walden, Fannie May presented little challenge; most of Walden's customers require the resolution of some kind of problem, but Fannie May's ad campaign needed only to focus on pleasure. Walden focused on the Fannie May line of summer candies, which are designed to fare well in hot temperatures. The ad agency created a poster of these candies in the form of a harvest. Later Robert Redford, filming on location in Chicago, was in a Fannie May store and asked if he could get a copy of the poster, which has proven to be a popular item in itself. In addition, Walden created a television campaign for Archibald, which features the Easter Bunny's ears drooping sadly as she discovers that being responsible for delivering Fannie May Candies means being unable to eat any.

In 1997 Archibald Candy created a new specialty division with the purpose of launching and marketing a new product line, the Fannie May Candies Celebrated

Collection. The specialty division is an addition to the existing sales division, and markets the new product line to upscale department stores, gift shops, and specialty retailers. The product consists primarily of seasonal assortments, and is marketed only at the company's three peak seasons: Christmas, Valentine's Day, and Easter.

INFLUENCES

When Fannie May Candies opened its first store in Chicago in 1920, its mission of selling quality candy at affordable prices was rewarded with overall success. As a result, H. Teller Archibald opened another store, again in Chicago, which was met with similar success. Subsequently, Archibald expanded within the city, throughout Illinois, and ultimately outside of Illinois into other states. It seemed only natural, in 1994, that Archibald Candy Corporation purchase Fanny Farmer Candies, bringing the number of stores to over 330.

CURRENT TRENDS

In 1997 Archibald Candy executed the biggest retail expansion in its history. The plan was to break out of its traditional markets, which were franchises located in the Midwest, and move into 30 new markets with state-of-the-art retail merchandising units (RMUs). To launch its products outside of areas where Fannie May Candies were traditionally sold, Archibald Candy licensed the brand to kiosk vendors in malls and shopping centers across the nation. The company focused on seasonal sales during its three peak holidays—Christmas, Valentine's Day, and Easter. According to Thomas Vitacco, national sales director for Archibald Candy, Fannie May and Fanny Farmer Candies produce approximately 60 percent of revenues during those three holidays. "Everyone agreed that if we could simply focus on those seasonal spikes in business, we would optimize our profitability in our expansion effort," Vitacco said. "Why incur the expense of rent and labor during the moderate times when you can avoid doing that with temporary, seasonal retail?"

In partnership with Schutz International, Archibald created the Fannie May kiosk. The kiosk is of modular construction and allows flexibility to comply with any restrictions developers may have imposed. Vitacco explained, "What we've created is a very modular device that expands horizontally and vertically, so we can adjust it to fit a 10 ft. x 12 ft. pad all the way up to a 10 ft. x 18 ft. pad. Therefore, when developers tell us their measurement requirements, we are able to fit within their range."

Ted Shepherd, Archibald's chief executive officer, was primarily responsible for devising the licensing strategy. Shepherd felt that licensing "was a cleaner

CHRONOLOGY:
Key Dates for Fannie May Holdings

1919: Fannie Farmer Candies founded in Rochester, New York by Frank O'Connor

1920: Fannie May Candies founded in Chicago, Illinois

1935: Fannie May begins expanding outside of Illinois

1937: Refrigeration is developed, allowing Fannie Farmer to build stores farther away from production facilities

1994: Archibald Candy purchases Fannie Farmer and becomes nation's largest candy retailer

1997: Executes biggest retail expansion in its history, licensing the brand to vendors and shopping centers across the nation

proposition and a faster way to market than traditional franchising." Licensing has its benefits over franchising, as owners don't have to pay the franchise fees or royalties to the parent company. Seasonal or temporary kiosks provide new retailers an opportunity to sell products and gauge results without a long-term commitment to a lease. The candy was sold at Houston's The Galleria, Greenspoint Mall, Town & Country Center, West Oaks Mall, Memorial City Mall, Willowbrook Mall, and Sharpstown Center. In addition, seasonal kiosks were opened in Las Vegas's major retail facilities and operated between November 1997 and April 1998 in Las Vegas's Meadows Mall, Boulevard Mall, the Fashion Show, the Peccole Ranch Town Center, and the Galleria at Sunset. In addition, at least 10 kiosks were opened in Atlanta and other areas.

In order to increase efficiency and handle the company expansion as effectively as possible, Archibald streamlined its production process through Infinium Process Manufacturing. Infinium provides Archibald with a "P/ERP" system, a real-time Process Enterprise Resource Planning system, which automates production while ensuring compliance to environmental regulations. P/ERP is an information system that combines Infinium's financial management, human resources, and materials management. According to Richard Pawlicki, Information Systems Director at Archibald, ". . . Infinium's P/ERP solution stands out because it is engineered and designed explicitly for process manufacturers. Infinium will allow us to effectively manage our future growth and

DECODING A BOX OF CHOCOLATES

Have you ever opened up a box of chocolates and bit into half a dozen pieces before you found the one for which you were looking? Or perhaps you're the type of person who sticks their finger into the bottom to see what it is, and then you put it back in the box because it's not the right flavor! Do you know that there is an easier way to tell what's inside the chocolate piece without breaking, biting, or guessing? Each piece has a "code" written into it, and if you know the "code" for you favorite type of chocolate, you'll never again be disappointed when choosing a piece of chocolate.

There are three ways to identify each piece of candy in a box of chocolates: by its unique shape, by the type of chocolate used, and by the squiggle mark on top of the confection. Based on whether the chocolate is round, rectangle, square, or oblong, and the type of chocolate used, you can make an educated guess about what's inside. However, the only sure-fire way to determine the contents of the candy is through the squiggle mark on top of each piece. The squiggle identifies the candy's contents. In order to be sure what is contained in every chocolate in your box, you must be able to "decode" the squiggles.

provide us with the opportunity to move into new distribution channels."

Fannie May has taken steps to improve its packaging procedures. Although the company still performs some tasks by hand, such as hand coating its chocolate-covered raisins, peanuts, almonds, and bridge mix, it has focused on improving automation in other areas in order to increase productivity and to reduce the cost of labor and the potential for injury from heavy lifting. For instance, the case packaging process was done manually until the purchase of an A-B-C Packaging Machine, which partially automated the case packaging process. The cases are erected and sealed mechanically while loading remains a manual process. Quality control has also been a focus. Fannie May recently began using Hi-Speed Cornerstone checkweighing systems. Checkweighers help to find overfill problems. The checkweighers contain a Micromate control system, which are linked to Fannie May's computers, allowing the company to analyze statistics. The statistics are helpful in identifying and resolving overfill patterns. This system also makes recordkeeping easier so the Food and Drug Administration can easily review them during a possible audit.

PRODUCTS

In 1998 Fannie May Candies introduced new product lines and gift ideas. It also refurbished the look of its traditional boxes. One of the new product lines was the introduction of the individually wrapped product as a single-serve piece suitable for individual consumption. Focusing on the more popular, mainstream candies, Fannie May created single-serve pieces for its Chews, which include coffee, caramel, chocolate, and cherry flavors.

In January 1997, at the International Fancy Food and Confection Show in San Francisco, Archibald Candy introduced a new product line called Fannie May Candies Celebrated Collection. The product is sold only during the peak seasons and features a collection of various miniatures and seasonal novelties in fancy, seasonal packaging. Specific items include Miniature Pixies and the Mint Meltaway Combination. Assorted Chocolates are sold in sizes ranging from 3.7 ounces to 19 ounces and prices are between $4.00 to $20.00, respectively. To launch the Celebrated Collection, Archibald Candy formed an addition to its existing sales division. Called the Specialty Sales Division, its function was to launch and market the product to card and gift shops, upscale department stores, and specialty retailers during the peak seasons.

Fannie May and Fannie Farmer Candies offer a large assortment of chocolates and other confections, including what they call "The Confectionary Concoction." These include respective candies from Fannie May and Fanny Farmer such as: Pixies and Pecan Dixies, a combination of pecans and caramel in milk chocolate; Trinidads and Capris, a pastel coating mixed with toasted coconut surrounding a chocolate cream center; Mint Meltaways and French and Frosted Mints, a mint-flavored chocolate center in milk chocolate or coated in a pastel; Debutantes and Miniatures, bite-size pieces of popular candy; and Sweet Persuasions Truffle and Truffles, candies featuring untraditional cream centers, such as Amaretto, Pina Colada, Creme De Menthe, French Vanilla, and White Russian. Fannie May and Fanny Farmer also sell their standard lines of products, which include Eggnog Creams for the holidays; vanilla buttercreams in milk or dark chocolate; Truffle Petites, which are chocolate mixed with crushed almond pieces around a chocolate cream center; Raspberry Creams; Carmarsh, a marshmallow and caramel center; Chocolate Toffee; and Buttercrisp.

SOURCES OF INFORMATION

Bibliography

"Archibald Candy Corporation." *Hoover's Online,* 15 July 1998. Available at http://www.hoovers.com.

"Archibald Candy Corporation." *Infinium Software in Action.* 15 July 1998. Available at http://www.s2k.com/html/archibald.html.

"Consumer Reports is Sweet on Fannie May Candy." *USA Today,* 12 February 1996.

Elder, Laura. "Chicago-based Archibald Candy Corp. Is Sweet on Houston." *Houston Business Journal,* 30 June 1997.

The Fannie May Home Page, 15 July 1998. Available at http://www.fanniemaycandies.com.

Forcinio, Hallie. "A Packaging Wish List." *CandyIndustry,* February 1998.

Gramig, Mickey H., and Chris Roush. "Sweets On The Way." *Atlanta Journal and Constitution,* 3 May 1997.

"Hoover's Top Employers." *Hoover's Online,* 15 July 1998. Available at http://www.hoovers.com.

"In Brief: Chicago Candy Maker Plans Retail Kiosks." *Las Vegas Review-Journal,* 23 May 1997.

Pollock, Will. "Store Fronts." *National Real Estate Investor,* 1 June 1997.

The Walden Group Home Page, 15 July 1998. Available at http://www.waldengroup.com/ads/index.htm.

For additional industry research:

Investigate companies by their Standard Industrial Classification Codes, also known as SICs. Archibald Candy's primary SICs are:

2064 Candy and Other Confectionery Products

2066 Chocolate and Cocoa Products

2096 Potato Chips and Similar Snacks

5441 Candy, Nut and Confectionery Stores

FAO Schwarz

FOUNDED: 1862

Contact Information:

HEADQUARTERS: 767 5th Ave.
   New York, NY 10153
PHONE: (212)644-9410
FAX: (212)753-1797
URL: http://www.fao.com

OVERVIEW

In uniquely designed stores encouraging playfulness and interaction, FAO Schwarz offers everything from toy trains to Barbie dolls to action figures to remote-control vehicles. FAO Schwarz is widely regarded as the premiere specialty toy retailer in the United States with 39 stores nationwide, including flagship stores in New York City, Chicago, Las Vegas, Orlando, and San Francisco. In a $20-billion industry whose growth from 1995 to 1996 was a modest 3.6 percent, FAO Schwarz and other toy retailers began making a graceful expansion into the candy market, which experienced an exceptional sales and growth rate in the late 1990s by reaching more than $21 billion in 1996, up 8 percent from the previous year. For FAO Schwarz, this expansion meant creating a candy division and a series of stores called FAO Schweetz.

COMPANY FINANCES

FAO Schwarz is a privately held company owned by Koninklijke Bijenkorf Beheer (K.B.B.), a private Dutch retailer. Along with FAO Schwarz, K.B.B. owns Bijenkorf department stores in the Netherlands. In February of 1998, K.B.B. agreed to be purchased by Vendex International, owner of rival department store chain Vroom & Dreesman, for 1.7 billion guilders (about $793 million dollars). As the result of the merger, Vendex would become the largest nonfood Dutch retailer and would control virtually all of the country's department stores. Though from 1996-97, K.B.B. reported profits of 61.7 million guilders, in January 1998 the company announced a 141.3 million guilder loss for 1997-98. This came after K.B.B. took an after-tax charge of 200 million guilders to try to restructure its specialty chains. K.B.B. then cut its dividend from 3 to 2 guilders per share.

In the early 1990s, FAO Schwarz had yearly sales of about $53 million. Toward the end of the decade, the company was expanding, planning to open a flagship store in Honolulu, Hawaii, by the fall of 2001 and to announce six more store openings by 1999. From 1992 to 1997, FAO Schwarz tripled in volume.

HISTORY

Six years after Frederick August Otto Schwarz arrived from Westphalia, Germany, he opened his first toy store in Baltimore, Maryland, which he operated for eight years. In 1870, Schwarz moved himself and his business to New York City and opened his "Schwarz Toy Bazaar" on Broadway. With the help of his three brothers, Schwarz's business prospered. By 1876 he published his first catalog, which offered customers outside of New York City access to the business' toys. The business grew, and in 1880 Schwarz moved the store to a larger space in Union Square, which was at that time a fashionable shopping area. After opening two more stores, in 1931 Schwarz moved his flagship store uptown to 745 5th Avenue where the business remained until 1986 when it moved across the street to its current address at 767 5th Avenue.

STRATEGY

Anyone who has seen the movie *Big,* starring Tom Hanks, will not be surprised to see a giant clock tower and to hear the company theme song "Welcome to Our World" immediately upon entering any FAO Schwarz store. These two aspects of the FAO Schwarz experience are carefully crafted to make customers feel they have indeed entered another "world"—the FAO Schwarz world. In the 1990s the company began tailoring its clocks to the locality of the stores in which they reside. For example, in FAO Schwarz's Orlando, Florida, store the face of the clock on the clock tower is sporting sunglasses and sipping orange juice. The clock tower in FAO Schwarz's Las Vegas store features Elvis "Pez-ley" and a bear called LiBEARaci.

Part of FAO Schwarz's winning strategy has been designing stores that are exciting and interesting in decor and filled with an abundance of toys. One facet of this strategy is making sure the toys are unique. Seventy percent of FAO Schwarz's merchandise is exclusive to the company or narrowly distributed and unavailable to FAO Schwarz's competitors. Moreover, the company tries to make its stores animated and interactive, welcoming cus-

FAST FACTS:
About FAO Schwarz

Ownership: FAO Schwarz is a privately held company owned by Dutch retailer K.B.B.

Officers: John Eyler, Chmn.; Bud Johnson, COO; Carolyn Morrison, Exec. VP Store Operations; David Niggli, Exec. VP Merchandising

Employees: 600

Chief Competitors: FAO Schwarz's main competitors include: Toys 'R' Us, the world's leading toy retailer with over 20 percent of the toy-buying market; Wal-Mart Stores, with about 15 percent of the toy market; and Costco Companies, a chain of warehouse clubs.

tomers to touch, examine, and play with the toys. Another aspect of FAO Schwarz's strategy is to provide excellent customer service, including toy authority hotlines, an infant and children's gift registry, and delivery anywhere in the world.

In addition to the company's innovative, fun, and unique store designs and inventory, two interesting facts about FAO Schwarz separate it from most every other toy company—indeed, most every other major retailer. First, FAO Schwarz never advertises. And second, FAO Schwarz never has a sale—not after the holidays, not when sales are slow, not when inventories are bloated.

INFLUENCES

In 1995 candy consumption in the United States reached an annual rate of 23.4 pounds per person. The following year, that number grew to about 25 pounds of candy consumed per person. With flat toy sales, many toy makers have been creating their own lines of candy. In 1997 Mattel licensed Russell Stover to make a Barbie line of candy. Hasbro introduced an extensive line of candy products: a Barrel of Monkeys game made from Gummy candy; a Mr. Potato Head filled with tangy candy; and Monopoly money made of bubble gum. In the mid- to late 1990s, FAO Schwarz developed its own candy retailing division to sell interesting, exclusive candy.

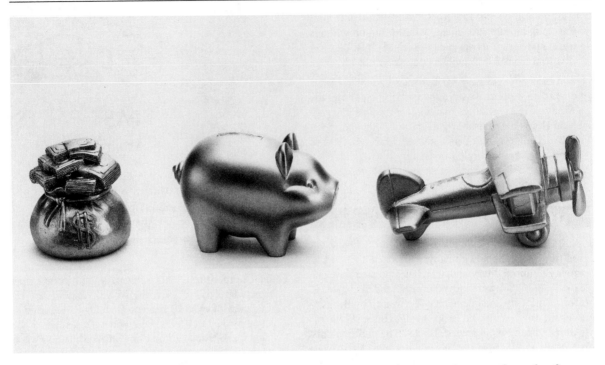

The FAO Schwarz store in Manhattan kicked off a nationwide campaign to elect the first addition to the Monopoly game tokens since 1942. The candidates are a sack of money, a piggy bank, and a bi-plane. (AP Photo/Hasbro.)

DA' BEARS—NOT CHICAGO

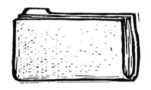

What weighs 6,112 pounds, stands 12 feet high, and is 10 feet wide? Why the FAO Schwartz bear in Boston of course—believed to be the world's largest teddy bear!

Unveiled in 1991 at FAO Schwartz's flagship store in Boston, the bear guarding the front of the store is a city landmark. Dozens of teddy bears were studied in order to create the bronze bear, which was developed as a special gift to the children of Boston. FAO Schwartz chairman/CEO said, "Teddy bears traditionally represent playfulness and the spirit of love and wonder found within the child in everyone." By studying the teddy bears, the New York City design firm that created the bear came up with the perfect expression, shape, face, and personality.

Through the imaginations of 10 artists, a 12-foot plaster model of a teddy bear was produced, and then cut into almost 30 sections. Sand casts of the sections were then made and bronze was poured into each individual piece. The artists then assembled the pieces to form the awesome bear. For the finishing touches, the artists used a mixture of wax and pigment to give the bear a unique coloring and bring it to life. It took the 10 artists more than 1,500 hours over the course of one year to design and develop the bear.

Like other retailers, FAO Schwarz found a lucrative market in mail order business. Along with its "Ultimate Toy Catalogue," FAO Schwarz creates and sends out specialty catalogs. In 1995 the company distributed its first "Collectible Toy Catalogue" featuring classic toys, rare toys, and reproductions of favorite toys from years past. Other FAO Schwarz specialty catalogs include a Barbie catalog and an FAO Schweetz catalog. In 1997 the company distributed more than 6 million copies of its "Ultimate Toy Catalogue."

With the explosive growth of the Internet, many businesses and retailers began to utilize this new avenue for reaching potential customers by creating web sites and offering online shopping. FAO Schwarz was one of these companies, setting up its web site in the mid-1990s. The colorful and attractive site has been called "beautifully crafted" by Michael Gebiki of *The Sydney Morning Herald,* and "as bright and exciting as a child's smile on Christmas morning" by *PC Magazine Online.*

In December 1997, iMALL, Inc., the leading independent shopping mall on the Internet, announced that it would feature 150 of FAO Schwarz's products at the Park Avenue center on its web site. At this location, iMALL also showcases upscale products by Coca-Cola, Disney, and Hanes, among others.

CURRENT TRENDS

Two stores the company opened in 1997 are particularly noteworthy for their innovation and creativity. Guarding the entrance to the Las Vegas store at the Forum Shops at Caesar's Palace is a fully animated Trojan Horse that stands 43 feet high (in keeping with the ancient Greco-Roman theme of the mall). The horse's head moves up and down, steam blows out its nostrils, and its eyes change color. The horse also contains a small shop and a balcony looking out over the rest of the store. From the second floor visitors can enter the horse and get a closer look at its inner workings. This unique store also houses a Monopoly Cafe in its games department, which features a giant Monopoly game board complete with audio. For example, you hear a chugging sound when you step on "Reading Railroad" and police sirens when you step on "Go to Jail." The cafe's tables are shaped like dice and its menu cards are Lease Deeds. The entranceway to FAO Schweetz stars a Jelly Belly Chorus Line and a Godiva Chocolate Vault. The store is also the site of the Temple of Barbie boutique. The store has three floors totaling 56,000 square feet, which is twice the size of the average FAO Schwarz store.

The exterior of the Orlando, Florida, FAO Schwarz store was designed to resemble a giant overturned toy box with toys strewn all about. A 30-foot-high Plexiglas Raggedy Ann waits at the store's main entrance. Other giant Plexiglas figures including a top, a dog, and a pair of 6-foot-tall Barbie shoes sit along the store's perimeter. Popular features in this store include a lifesized doll house, a Lego submarine, a vehicles department with a remote-control car testing area, and a *Star Wars* department.

The late 1990s saw a renewed popularity of the Star Wars films—in part because of the twentieth anniversary of *Star Wars* in 1997 and in part because of publicity surrounding the 1999 release of another *Star Wars* film. FAO Schwarz met this revived interest by featuring *Star Wars* departments in its stores. In Las Vegas, this department includes a *Star Wars* Cantina that serves nonalcoholic beverages like a Yoda Colada. The department also features a to-scale R2D2, a to-scale Storm Trooper, and a Rebel Fighter overhead. The Orlando FAO Schwarz store's *Star Wars* department also features an animated Darth Vader.

Since her introduction in 1959, the Barbie doll has enjoyed tremendous popularity. In an average week in 1995, more than 1 million Barbie dolls were sold. By the late 1990s the average American girl between the ages of 3 and 10 years old owned 8 Barbie dolls. From 1987 to 1995 Barbie sales more than tripled. Because of all this, FAO Schwarz developed a partnership with Mattel and created its "pretty in pink" Barbie Boutiques, which feature Barbie dolls; Barbie apparel for dolls, children, and adults; Barbie fashion accessories and health and beauty aids; animated displays including three-foot rotating Barbies; and limited edition Barbies that include NASCAR Barbie, George Washington Barbie, "Talk with Me" Barbie (who even moves her lips), and *X-Files* Barbie and Ken as Agents Scully and Mulder. Every flagship FAO Schwarz contains a Barbie Boutique, and by the end of the 1990s, there were Barbie Boutiques in 29 FAO Schwarz stores.

PRODUCTS

As toy sales grew flat toward the end of the 1990s, candy sales were booming and FAO Schwarz began its FAO Schweetz candy division. In 1996, FAO Schweetz began testing a 250-foot candy counter in its flagship toy store in Manhattan. Soon, the candy division became the highest-grossing department per square foot, and the company began making plans to increase the candy store's space tenfold.

In 1997 FAO Schwarz opened candy stores in its new Las Vegas and Orlando toy stores. FAO Schweetz stores are intended to be as unique and exciting with regard to candy as FAO Schwarz toy stores are with regard to toys. FAO Schweetz stores contain attractions like an animated Gummy aquarium; a "Chocolate Mint," which is a vault filled with Godiva chocolates; a gumball machine so large children can walk inside it; a dancing chorus line of Jelly Belly jelly beans; a lollipop tree; and selections of M&Ms in 24 colors, including black, gold, and silver. FAO Schweetz vice president Jeff Rubin says, "We take the same approach to candy as to toys . . . it's not just a candy store—it's a candy world."

The FAO Schweetz in Chicago, Illinois, has its own storefront that is unattached to an FAO Schwarz toy store. The candy shop is located in Water Tower Place, one of the city's most popular tourist areas. Within a year of opening, this FAO Schweetz became the most popular candy store in the country. The only other free-standing FAO Schweetz store was opened in February 1998 in Westbury, New York. Along with a Barbie Boutique,

FAO Schwarz intends for every one of its stores to contain an FAO Schweetz in the near future.

GLOBAL PRESENCE

In an interview on CNN at the end of November 1997, FAO Schwarz chairman John Eyler said that in the year 2001, the company would begin opening stores internationally. Eyler added that FAO Schwarz had not yet announced the international locations.

SOURCES OF INFORMATION

Bibliography

Cram, Gordon. "KBB Puts off Vendex Merger Meeting." *The Financial Times (London),* 6 April 1998.

"Dutch Deal for Parent of FAO Schwarz." *The New York Times,* 10 February 1998.

"FAO Schwarz." *Yahoo! Internet Life,* 8 August 1996. Available at http://www.yahoo.com/Business_and_Economy/companies/Toys/Retailers/FAO_Schwarz/.

"FAO Schwarz Gets New Parent in Takeover Deal." *The Orlando Sentinel,* 10 February 1998.

FAO Schwarz Home Page, 3 June 1998. Available at http://www.fao.com.

"FAO Schwarz Joins Other Upscale Merchants in iMALL's Park Avenue." *Business Wire,* 9 December 1997.

"First Award, Store Design: FAO Schwarz." *Playthings,* February 1998.

Gebiki, Michael. "Site Seeing: New York on the Net." *The Sydney Morning Herald,* 22 March 1997.

Hopkins, Jen. "Interview on Moneyline with the Chairman & CEO of FAO Schwarz." *Moneyline with Lou Dobbs (CNNfn),* 27 November 1997.

Horovitz, Bruce. "Discovering Candyland Toymakers Spy Sweet Success in Confections." *USA Today,* 4 March 1997.

McCloud, John. "INProfile: A Trojan Welcome at FAO Schwarz Las Vegas." *Shopping Center World,* 1 November 1997.

"Tall Stories Captivate Customers' Imaginations." *Chain Store Age Executive with Shopping Center Age,* November 1997.

"Top 100 Web Sites." *PC Magazine Online,* February 1997. Available at http://www.zdnet.com/pcmag/special/web100feb97/faoschw.htm.

"Toys 'R Us." *Hoover's Online,* June 1998. Available at http://www.hoovers.com.

Van De Mark, Donald, and Beverly Schuch. "FAO Schwarz Chairman." *Biz Buzz (CNNfn),* 28 November 1997.

For additional industry research:

Investigate companies by their Standard Industrial Classification Codes, also known as SICs. FAO Schwarz's primary SICs are:

2064 Candy & Other Confectionery Products

5092 Toys & Hobby Goods & Supplies

5945 Hobby, Toy & Game Shops

Federal Express Corporation

OVERVIEW

Federal Express Corporation is an express delivery service providing overnight, same-day, and 48-hour services. Daily, FedEx handles more than 3 million shipments of documents, packages, and heavy freight, and provides customers with more than 43,000 package drop-off sites, utilizes 600 aircraft and 39,500 vehicles, and operates in 211 countries worldwide. In January of 1998, FedEx acquired Caliber System Inc., a company offering nonexpress business-to-business delivery and logistics and distribution solutions, and parent company of package carrier RPS, Inc. Caliber System and FedEx came together to form shipping and logistics giant FDX Corporation, a holding company comprised of six major companies as subsidiaries, the largest of which is Federal Express.

COMPANY FINANCES

With its huge networks of information systems and aircraft and ground vehicles, FedEx is an enormously expensive business to run costing between $2.0 and $2.5 billion annually. Interest and depreciation charges from the investments in the company's extravagant networks have, at times, threatened to erase profits altogether. From 1993 to 1997, return on revenues ranged from less than 1.0 percent to a feeble 3.1 percent. CEO Fred Smith hopes to prop up these profit margins to a still slim 6.0 percent.

From 1991 to 1995 revenue per package dropped from $17.33 to $14.62. Profits increased, however,

ALSO KNOWN AS: FedEx
FOUNDED: 1971 by Frederick W. Smith

Contact Information:
HEADQUARTERS: 2005 Corporate Ave.
   Memphis, TN 38132
PHONE: (901)369-3600
FAX: (901)395-2000
URL: http://www.fdxcorp.com
   http://www.fedex.com

positioning the company's resources so as to capitalize on emerging markets for expedited delivery services.

FINANCES:

Federal Express Corp. Revenues, 1994-1997 (billion dollars)

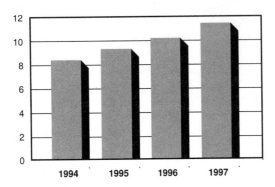

Federal Express Corp. 1997 Stock Prices (dollars)

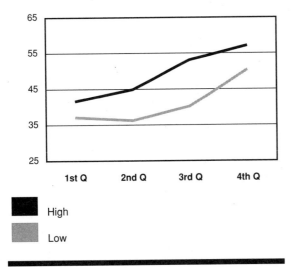

■ High

▨ Low

thanks to an almost doubling of the number of average daily shipments. By 1997 per package revenue increased to $15.11. Net revenues increased 12 percent from $10.2 billion in 1996 to $11.5 billion in 1997. From 1996 to 1997, net income increased 17 percent from $308 to $361 million and earnings per share rose from $2.69 to $3.12. FedEx's price-earnings (P/E) ratio increased from 16.7 in 1996 to 27.1 in 1997. From 1995 to 1998, United Parcel Service of America, Inc.—or UPS—stock more than doubled, rising from $29 to $68, with a surge to $80 during the summer of 1997s UPS strike. FedEx's long-term goal is to achieve sustained earnings growth in part by

ANALYSTS' OPINIONS

Many hold that the future bodes well for FedEx. According to leading research and consulting firm Colography Group, the expedited cargo business should fare well over the next decade with increased demand as businesses try to limit the risk of overproducing, cut enormous inventory costs, and speed product delivery to consumers. According to Julius Maldutis at Salomon Smith Barney, Federal Express's emphasis on cost reduction and yield management improvements should result in earnings growth that is steady and sustainable. Moreover, as the world's economies become increasingly globalized, Maldutis says, FedEx is well-position to provide service to the future marketplace. Some are skeptical about the possibility of serious profits for express services in the expanding global markets in the short term, however. Overnight service requires good roads and reliable communication systems—features that are seriously lacking in many growing regions, like in parts of China and South America.

Many think that the future marketplace will include the Internet and what some call "Web commerce" or online retail, which is expected to capture up to 55 percent of consumer sales worldwide by the year 2010. And FedEx, in Maldutis's opinion, is positioned so as to become the first real logistics company by becoming the airline of the Internet. Some analysts think that 30 percent of documents will be sent over the Internet by the year 2000, throwing the expedited delivery service into a rapid decline. UPS is preparing for that possibility, as it announced in March 1998, by offering a new Internet service that will send documents over the Internet securely and in seconds.

According to Jeffrey E. Garten at Business Week, by 1998, FedEx had become "the global logistical backbone for many of its corporate customers . . . [managing] their worldwide inventory, warehousing, distribution, and customs clearance." Garten sees FedEx as a major force behind globalization. He claims that the heart of FedEx's global strategy is using information technology to aid clients in taking advantage of international markets. "In fact," Garten says, "FedEx sees itself more as an information-technology company than as a transporter of goods."

HISTORY

CEO Fred Smith originally presented his idea for an overnight delivery business in the 1960s in a term paper he wrote for an economics class at Yale University. Famously, the paper received a "C" but Smith was not deterred. While serving as an officer in the U.S. Marine Corps., Smith began collecting money to start up an express delivery company. By 1971, a year after he had left the Marines, Smith had amassed $90 million—$40 million from investors, $8 million of his own money, the rest from banks—to launch his company, making Federal Express the largest startup ever funded by venture capital. And he needed the money to start up this company: before operations could begin, a nationwide network had to be in place. In 1973, with a fleet of 14 Dassault Falcon planes and 389 employees, Federal Express began providing over-night and second day delivery service to 25 U.S. cities. Using Smith's hometown of Memphis as a hub, the planes collected parcels from airports every night and flew them to Memphis where the packages were sorted and then flown to airports close to their destinations. The following morning, the packages were delivered by Federal Express trucks. In 1975, FedEx began an expensive advertising campaign. Within its first two years, the company had lost $29 million.

Briefly, investors considered removing Smith from the company's helm, but FedEx president Arthur Bass defended him and improved the delivery schedule. Soon, the company's volume increased and FedEx began to show a profit. By the end of 1976, FedEx was carrying about 19,000 packages daily and was $3.6 million in the black. The following year, profits reached $8.0 million on $110 million of sales and FedEx was servicing 75 airports and 130 U.S. cities. At this time FedEx had 31,000 regular customers including IBM and the U.S. Air Force, which used FedEx to ship spare parts. The company also found a niche shipping items requiring expedited delivery like blood, transplant organs, and drugs. While FedEx's competitors, like Emery Air Freight, used commercial airlines giving FedEx stiff competition on major passenger routes, the company had an important time advantage with routes between smaller cities and with its flexible time schedule.

In 1978, FedEx went public. The following year, the company made $21.4 million on sales of $258.5 million. By the end of 1980, FedEx had 6,700 employees, 32 Falcons, 15 727s, and 5 737 aircraft. The company was growing at a rate of about 40 percent annually. At this time, a decline in the U.S. Postal Service's reliability prompted more businesses to turn to FedEx for important parcel deliveries. In 1980 FedEx's envelopes, boxes, or tubes, known as Courier-Paks, cost $17 to ship, but overnight delivery was guaranteed. This service became the fastest-growing part of the company's business and in 1980, accounted for 40 percent of FedEx's revenue. In 1981, FedEx introduced its overnight letter, a product that would for the first time bring the company into direct competition with U.S. Postal Service. That year, FedEx had the largest sales of any U.S. air freight company. Unlike its competitors, FedEx targeted shipments of small packages and documents and stressed speed of delivery, which lured many customers away from the company's competitors.

FAST FACTS:

About Federal Express Corporation

Ownership: Federal Express Corporation is a subsidiary of FDX Corporation, a publicly owned company traded on the New York Stock Exchange.

Ticker symbol: FDX (FDX Corp.)

Officers: Frederick W. Smith, Chmn., Pres. & CEO FDX Corp., 53, 1997 pay $1,018,000; Theodore L. Weise, Pres. & CEO Federal Express Corp., 53, 1997 pay $717,601; David J. Bronczek, Exec. VP & COO Federal Express Corp., 43; Tracy G. Schmidt, Sr. VP & CFO Federal Express, 40

Employees: The companies of FDX Corporation together employ about 170,000 people; approximately 140,000 of them work for Federal Express Corp.

Principal Subsidiary Companies: Federal Express is the world's largest express transportation company and has as subsidiaries such related businesses as FedEx Aeronautics Corp., Federal Express Aviation Services Inc., Federal Express International Telecommunications Corp., and Tiger Trucking Inc. In January 1998, Federal Express acquired Caliber System Inc. and together they formed a new holding company called FDX Corporation, now the parent company of Federal Express and five other subsidiary companies.

Chief Competitors: Federal Express is a worldwide express delivery service and has as competitors many multinational express shipping companies including: Airborne Freight, a domestic and international airfreight carrier and the third-ranked domestic airfreight shipping company in the United States; DHL, an international shipping company with a dominant (41 percent) share of the international shipping market; United Parcel Service of America, Inc.; and UPS, the world's largest package-delivery company.

Soon, FedEx's competitors were copying the company's strategy: Emery secured its own planes and began pushing overnight delivery service. Airborne and UPS also moved into the small package air-express delivery service. When FedEx's Courier-Pak began eroding its revenues, the U.S. Postal Service began offering its own overnight mail service at only about half FedEx's price; however, the service wasn't available at all locations. In 1983 FedEx reached $1 billion in annual revenues.

CHRONOLOGY:

Key Dates for Federal Express Corporation

1971: Founded by Frederick W. Smith

1973: Begins providing over-night and second day delivery to 25 U.S. cities

1978: FedEx goes public

1981: Introduces overnight letter

1983: Reaches $1 billion in annual revenues

1984: Buys Gelco Express

1985: Opens a hub at Brussels airport

1988: Provides service to 90 countries

1989: Purchases Tiger International Inc.

1992: Restructures European operations

1996: FedEx pilots join the Air Line Pilots Association

1998: Acquires Caliber System Inc.

The following year, the company acquired a Minnesota-based delivery business serving 84 countries called Gelco Express in hopes of bringing its business overseas. As the 1980s progressed, FedEx acquired companies in Great Britain, the Netherlands, and the United Arab Emirates and UPS began its overseas business operations. In 1985, FedEx opened a European hub at the Brussels airport. By the late 1980s, competition had led to a price war that began to eat into FedEx's profits, reducing them from 16.9 percent of revenue in 1981 to 11.0 percent in 1987. In 1988, FedEx had about 54,000 employees, provided service to about 90 countries, and shipped approximately half of the overnight packages in the United States.

While FedEx was developing its business in the United States, becoming the leader in America, DHL Worldwide Express was building a similar service abroad. When FedEx began expanding its overseas operations, the two companies became major competitors. Between 1985 and 1989, FedEx's international business lost $74 million. Toward the end of the 1980s, FedEx made several additional overseas acquisitions, including Island Courier Companies and Cansica, SAMIMA (Italy), and three Japanese freight carriers. In 1989, FedEx purchased Tiger International, Inc. and so obtained its Flying Tiger heavy-cargo airline and Tiger's

delivery routes and landing rights in Paris, Frankfurt, three Japanese airports, and cities in east Asia and South America. FedEx paid $883 million for Tiger, which increased the company's debt to $2.1 billion. During this time the price wars with competitors continued, and some, like UPS, made inroads into the overnight market—between 1984 and 1988, UPS's overnight service business rose 63 percent and its revenues tripled. FedEx was still the overnight delivery service leader in the United States, but its growth was slowing. In 1984, FedEx's U.S. shipment volume grew 58 percent; in 1988, that growth slowed to 25 percent.

As the company labored to integrate its Tiger acquisition and to develop its European business, in 1989, FedEx's international operations lost $194 million. In April 1990, to help pay for these losses, FedEx finally ended the seven-year price war by raising its domestic prices. In the early 1990s, UPS had become FedEx's main domestic competitor and began luring some FedEx customers away by offering volume discounts. FedEx responded by conducting customer-by-customer price adjustments, consolidating subcontractor truck routes, and streamlining pickup and delivery routes. FedEx also offered enhancements to express-service customers including earlier-in-the-day service, Internet tracking of shipments via FedEx's homepage, and a greater availability of FedEx dropboxes. By mid-1992, FedEx's domestic package business began to rally with revenues increasing to $7.8 from $7.6 billion the previous year.

In 1992 restructuring operations in Europe cost FedEx $254 and $114 million in losses. Though overall sales increased from $5.20 billion in 1989 to $7.69 billion in 1991, over the same period operating income plummeted from $424 to $279 million, while carrying $2.15 billion in long-term debt. To help ease this financial blow, the company was forced to eliminate 7,000 jobs and to scrap European domestic pickup and delivery service. To reduce waste and overhead and increase efficiency, FedEx began implementing cost-cutting policies company-wide but employee-related expenses rose when the company became bogged down in two years of contract negotiations with the Air Line Pilots Association (ALPA). FedEx's 3,100 pilots had so far been nonunion employees; in 1996, the pilots joined the ALPA.

Smith held that when FedEx's international volume increased, its international service would become profitable. To try to boost that volume, FedEx expanded its equipment and service, trading its 727s for larger Airbus Industrie jet aircraft for its three daily European-destination flights. By 1995, international service accounted for 12 percent of FedEx's business and FedEx was linked by more than 200 countries. By 1997, FedEx had sales of more than $11.5 billion against operating income of $699 million.

On January 27, 1998, FedEx completed its acquisition of Caliber System Inc., a business-to-business

ground transportation and logistics and distributions solutions company. The two companies came together to
form holding company FDX Corporation, a worldwide
delivery and logistics powerhouse. FDX has six subsidiaries: Federal Express, RPS, Inc., Viking Freight,
Caliber Logistics, Roberts Express, and Caliber Technology. In the first half of 1998, FDX employed about
170,000 people.

STRATEGY

By the late 1970s, FedEx CEO Smith realized that
much of what the company was carrying in its small
packages was information and that with advances in telephone and computer technology, this information would
eventually be digitally transmitted. So Smith spent $100
million to develop ZapMail, a satellite network that delivered documents electronically in two hours or less. But
ZapMail was plagued by technological problems—fax
machines broke down, light originals failed to transmit,
small telephone line disturbances interrupted transmissions—and it was expensive, $35 for documents 5 pages
or less. Soon, customers discovered it was far less expensive to install their own fax machines. In 1986, FedEx
abandoned ZapMail, taking a $340-million charge
against earnings.

Almost from the start, Frederick Smith stressed the
importance of collecting knowledge about the cargo the
company was transporting, knowledge about its origin,
present location at almost any time, destination, estimated arrival time, price, and cost of the shipment. To
amass and maintain such information for each delivery,
Smith erected a network of information systems—including laser scanners, bar codes, and software—along
with his air and vehicle network. (Boston consultant
Michael Treacy estimates that FedEx is so far ahead with
its information technology that it would take UPS and
FedEx's other competitors at least a year to catch up.)
By installing computer terminals at 100,000 customers
and by giving proprietary software to an additional
650,000, FedEx has enabled shippers to label their own
packages (by the end of 1997, shippers labelled 60 percent of their own packages); then FedEx receives electronic notification to pickup; then the company ships and
delivers the package—all without phone calls, and little
by way of paperwork or personnel.

INFLUENCES

In the 1970s and 1980s, as passenger service grew
explosively, parcel delivery service became much less
important to commercial airlines so there was a new demand for delivery service like that provided by Federal
Express. In 1974, workers at UPS helped contribute to
FedEx's initial success by going on strike. In the sum-

mer of 1997, FedEx enjoyed a brief explosion in business when UPS workers again went on strike. At this
time, FedEx handled an additional 850,000 packages
daily. Some predicted that the strike would permanently—and positively—affect FedEx. By year's end,
Morgan Stanley analyst Kevin Murphy estimated that
FedEx had already swiped 2 percentage points of UPS's
market share, leaving FedEx with a mighty 43 percent of
the express transportation market.

Early on, stiff airline regulations had forbidden
FedEx's using larger planes to carry larger payloads so
that the company was often required to fly multiple Falcons at once on a single route when a larger aircraft would
have saved money. The 1977 deregulation of the airline
industry meant that the company could now fly large aircraft anywhere in the United States at any time.

In the 1980s, a great number of businesses turned to
overnight service. Many companies realized that "just-
in-time" inventories were a way of greatly reducing costs
and keeping prices down and they looked to FedEx to
provide the means for doing this. FedEx soon began
billing itself as a "500-mile-an-hour warehouse."

In the second half of the 1980s as the use of fax machines grew, FedEx experienced a decline in overnight
mail volume and began providing warehousing service
for customers. The company began using its hubs as
warehouses, storing packages there until clients needed
them, then shipping them out overnight.

CURRENT TRENDS

In January 1998, when FedEx purchased Caliber
System, the two companies together formed holding
company FDX, comprised of six subsidiaries: FedEx;
RPS, the second-leading ground carrier of packages under 150 pounds in the United States; Viking Freight, a
"less-than-truckload" or "LTL" freight service serving
the western United States; Roberts Express, the world's
largest surface expedited carrier offering time-critical delivery; Caliber Logistics, which designs and implements
integrated logistics solutions; and Caliber Technology,
Inc., which provides access to information technology.

In acquiring Caliber System, FedEx put itself in a
position to grow more quickly than it could alone. Caliber's RPS subsidiary with its fleet of 13,500 trucks allows FedEx, as FDX, to compete more successfully with
UPS. Since ground fleets are much less expensive to operate than FedEx's system of aircraft and vehicles, the
merger should make FDX more profitable than FedEx
could be alone.

PRODUCTS

In 1996, FedEx expanded its service by introducing
interNetShip, an online shipping service that allows cus-

tomers to print out the necessary shipping codes on a standard laser printer. That same year, FedEx also developed BusinessLink, a software program enabling businesses to create online catalogs and sell merchandise over the Internet, using FedEx's service to deliver the sold goods.

In early 1998 Federal Express and American Express agreed to provide automatic discounts of 10 to 20 percent on many FedEx delivery services to small business owners who are American Express Small Business Corporate Card customers. On February 2, 1998, FedEx introduced FedEx International Economy Freight service providing customers with cost-effective five-business-day service from the United States to key markets in Asia, Europe, and Latin America.

CORPORATE CITIZENSHIP

FedEx has donated its logistic and distribution services to aid several causes around the world. In 1996, the company joined Heart to Heart International to ship $12 million worth of pharmaceutical and medical supplies to Calcutta, India. FedEx has also joined forces with the American Red Cross and has donated $1 million annually in free distribution, logistics, and other services assisting the Red Cross in managing its supplies and delivery of emergency equipment. The March of Dimes Team Walk campaign has been on the company's agenda as well, accounting for the FedEx's ranking as one of the top 15 national organizations to participate.

GLOBAL PRESENCE

Over the next decade, as companies scramble to capture a share of the world's expanding wealth, the world express-transportation market is expected to boom from about $12 billion in 1997 to more than $150 billion by 2007. FedEx is strategically situated to connect the parts of the world predicted to have the greatest future economic prosperity and growth. In 1995, FedEx initiated direct flights to China and introduced a next-business-day service between Asian countries and the United States that it called AsiaOne. Though FedEx had planned to erect an extensive delivery service network in the Far East using a hub in the Philippines, in 1996 the Japanese government suddenly limited FedEx's flying rights from Japan to other Asian countries. Nevertheless, in 1996 FedEx was the only U.S.-based cargo service authorized to do business in China and with its hub in the Pacific Rim area, FedEx is well-positioned with regard to one of the fastest-growing economic centers in the world. In 1997 FedEx launched international flight operations in Moscow, located in a market where exports are expected to grow about 30 percent by the year 2000.

In October 1997, FedEx announced its selection of Miami International Airport as the site for its new hub for Latin American and Caribbean business. FedEx created its Latin American and Caribbean division in 1995 to integrate services within the world's second-fastest economic growth region.

EMPLOYMENT

In 1998, FedEx had about 140,000 workers. The company's employees are famous for their enthusiasm and loyalty, which some consider a strong competitive weapon. This loyalty was evident during the 1997 UPS strike when FedEx was suddenly overwhelmed with more than 800,000 additional packages daily. Thousands of employees voluntarily showed up at the hubs at around midnight, after their shifts were over, to sort for hours. After the strike ended, Frederick Smith ordered special bonuses for his employees and thanked them with 11 full-page newspaper ads that all ended with: "Bravo Zulu!" a military honorific that employees had learned during training. As the employees knew, this was the highest compliment.

SOURCES OF INFORMATION

Bibliography

"Airborne Freight Corporation." *Hoover's Online,* 1 April 1998. Available at http://www.hoovers.com.

"American Express and Federal Express Launch Discounts On Express Delivery Services for Small Businesses." *Business Wire,* 19 January 1998.

Blackmon, Douglas A. "Federal Express Pilots Vote Out Bargaining Unit, Set New Union." *The Wall Street Journal,* 28 October 1996.

———. "Federal Express, UPS Scramble for Footholds in Asian Markets." *The Wall Street Journal,* 22 January 1997.

———. "FedEx to Adopt Rate Structure Based on Distance Package Goes." *The Wall Street Journal,* 23 January 1997.

Brady, Diane. "U.S. Fed Express Sees Double-Digit Growth in Asia; Cites Performance of Philippines Hub - Sr VP." *Dow Jones News Service,* 13 August 1996.

Carson, Teresa. "Federal Express Corp Sees Latin Hub in Miami." *Reuters,* 21 April 1997.

"DHL Worldwide Express." *Hoover's Online,* 1 April 1998. Available at http://www.hoovers.com.

"FDX Corporation." *Hoover's Online,* 1 April 1998. Available at http://www.hoovers.com.

FDX Home Page, 1 April 1998. Available at http://www.fdxcorp.com.

Federal Express Corporation 1997 Annual Report. Memphis, TN: Federal Express Corporation, 1997.

"Federal Express Creates New Transportation Powerhouse." *Business Wire,* 27 January 1998.

"Federal Express to Offer New Delivery Services to Europe." *Dow Jones News Services,* 10 September 1996.

"FedEx Announces New Miami Hub for its Latin America and Caribbean Flights." *Business Wire,* 30 September 1997.

"FedEx Service to China Enhanced." *Xinhua English Newswire,* 10 April 1997.

"FedEx to Acquire Caliber System, Inc. Including RPS Subsidiary." *Business Wire,* 5 October 1997.

"FedEx to Revise U.S. Rates, Offer New Service." *Business Wire,* 5 January 1998.

Garten, Jeffrey E. "Why the Global Economy is Here to Stay." *Business Week,* 23 March 1998.

Grant, Linda. "Why FedEx is Flying High." *Fortune,* 10 November 1997.

Greising, David. "Quality—How to Make It Pay." *Business Week,* 8 August 1994.

Lappin, Todd. "FedEX: The Airline of the Internet." *Wired Magazine,* December 1996.

Lewis, Scott M., updated by Pamela L. Shelton. "Federal Express." *International Directory of Company of Histories,* Vol. 18, Detroit, MI: St. James Press, 1997.

O'Keefe, Terry. "An Inside Look at the Magic Behind Federal Express' Flight." *Atlanta Business Chronicle,* 13 January 1997.

"S&P Description: FDX Corp." *Standard & Poor's,* 9 April 1998.

"The Selling of Subic." *AsiaWeek,* 19 July 1996. Available at http://pathfinder.com.

"United Parcel Service of America, Inc." *Hoover's Online,* 1 April 1998. Available at http://www.hoovers.com.

"U.S. Fedex Announces $3 Mln Expansion Plan in Ireland." *Dow Jones News Services,* 26 September 1996.

"U.S. FedEx Launches Int'l Mail Service in Taiwan." *Dow Jones News Service,* 20 December 1996.

Wechsler, Pat, ed. "UPS: We Also Cyber-Deliver." *Business Week,* 16 March 1998.

For an annual report:

telephone: (901)395-3478 **or** write: Manager, Investor Relations, Federal Express Corp., Box 727, Dept. 1854, Memphis, TN, 38194

For additional industry research:

Investigate companies by their Standard Industrial Classification Codes, also known as SICs. Federal Express Corp.'s primary SICs are:

4212 Local Trucking, Without Storage

4513 Air Courier Services

4731 Arrangement of Transportation of Freight & Cargo

Fila USA

FOUNDED: 1926

Contact Information:

HEADQUARTERS: 14114 York Rd.
  Sparks, MD 21152
PHONE: (410)773-3000
FAX: (410)773-4969
TOLL FREE: (800)787-FILA
EMAIL: andrea.nacmias@filasport.it
URL: http://www.fila.com

OVERVIEW

Fila USA designs, manufactures, and markets apparel and footwear that is unique in both style and performance. In the early 1990s Fila USA emerged as one of the leading companies in the worldwide athletic footwear and apparel business largely because of its ability to enhance its brand image and increase its market share in the largest U.S. product category, men's basketball footwear. By year-end 1996 Fila had become the third-largest athletic footwear brand in the United States behind Nike, Reebok, and Adidas. Fila also claimed the second-largest share of the overall basketball market, and had significantly closed the gap between itself and its three major competitors in worldwide markets.

The company's success was in part based on the implementation of a highly focused product and marketing strategy centered around Grant Hill of the Detroit Pistons, and a select group of other up-and-coming basketball stars. While the effectiveness of marketing is generally difficult to gauge, Fila's sales growth and success on Wall Street are strong indicators of its success.

COMPANY FINANCES

Fila's revenue has markedly increased over its last few fiscal years. Revenue for fiscal year ending December 1996 was $1.23 billion, up from $934 million in 1995 and $616 million in 1994. While gross profit has increased significantly, gross profit margin has remained steady. Gross profit was $516.3 million for fiscal year 1996, $389.3 million in 1995, and $251.6 million in 1994, with a gross profit margin of 41.8 percent in 1996, 41.7 percent in 1995, and 40.8 percent in 1994. Operating income more than doubled from 1994 to 1996, at $150.6 million in 1996, $110.1 million in 1995, and $74.1 million in 1994. Total net income was over two-and-a-half times as much in 1996 as in 1994; $104.5 million in 1996, $62.9 million in 1995, and $41.9 million in 1994.

ANALYSTS' OPINIONS

Fila was named Company of the Year in 1996 by *Footwear News Magazine* due to its emergence as a major force in the athletic footwear market. The company grew from $250 million in sales in 1993 to sales in excess of $1 billion in 1996. Analysts believe the key to the company's success includes its ability to adapt and create changes in the industry, offering retailers new products and strong support. Fila has benefited from its marketing ties to basketball star Grant Hill.

In 1997 analysts recommended stocks in the athletic shoe industry in general, although some were concerned about Fila handling its fierce competitors. According to Zacks, of four brokers surveyed, one recommended strong sell and three recommended holding Fila stock.

HISTORY

The company was founded in 1923 by two brothers who manufactured knitwear in Biella, in northern Italy. When Enrico Frachey joined the company in 1969 as controller, he saw an opportunity to branch into sports apparel. The company grew rapidly and began licensing the Fila name by signing endorsement contracts with celebrity athletes like Bjorn Borg, the former tennis star.

In 1973 the Fila brand of athletic sportswear was launched. From 1984 until the early 1990s Fila's U.S. footwear was produced under a licensing agreement. When Frachey left the company in 1980 Fila underwent a change of ownership. It was acquired by Gemina, an Italian financial institution, which now owns 70 percent of the company. Enrico Frachey returned to Fila in 1987 and made the decision to reacquire the license in the U.S. market. In 1991 Fila regained direct control of the U.S. footwear line, buying back its license. Fila Sports Inc., which distributed sports apparel, and Fila Footwear USA were consolidated into Fila USA and relocated to Maryland. The move allowed the two units to capitalize on design synergies, thereby producing a more integrated Fila collection.

STRATEGY

Keys to the company's success include the ability to adapt and create changes in the industry, offering re-

FAST FACTS:
About Fila USA

Ownership: Fila is a publicly owned company traded on the New York Stock Exchange.

Ticker symbol: FLH

Officers: Gianni Bulgari, Chmn.; Enrico Frachey, CEO; Enzio Bermani, Secretary; Jon Epstein, Pres. & CEO, Fila USA

Employees: 3,448

Principal Subsidiary Companies: Fila Holding S.p.A.

Chief Competitors: Some of Fila's primary competitors are: Nike Inc.; Reebok International; Adidas; Converse; Tommy Hilfiger Corporation; Nautica Company; Asics Tiger Corporation; Polo Sport; and J. Crew.

tailers new products and strong support. Besides capitalizing on its marketing ties to basketball star Grant Hill, Fila plans to put more resources into marketing to women. The company targets a high-end customer by distributing only to specialty stores. For example, its number one customer is Foot Locker, a division of the Kinney group, which is owned by the Woolworth Corporation.

The Fila athletic roster includes: basketball's Grant Hill, Jerry Stackhouse, Chris Webber, and Hersey Janzen; skiing's Alberto Tomba; track & field's Mike Powell; two-time New York City Marathon winner German Silva and Boston Marathon champion Moses Tanui; soccer's Claudio Reyna, Carla Overbeck, and Juergen Sommer; and beach volleyball's Olympic Gold Medalist Kent Steffes.

Fila previously had designers scattered around the United States until the company opened the Fila Agora Footwear and Activewear Design Center in New York. The company is also planning to open a second design center in Santa Monica, California, that will focus on outdoor product offerings. These centers will give designers a gathering spot for a more unified design effort. Equally important is the designers' choice of fabrics, which plays a key role in their approach to style. Performance fabrics are used in all of their apparel, from active wear to outdoor wear. These include technology-advanced materials such as Supplex, Lycra, and Gore-Tex.

CHRONOLOGY:

Key Dates for Fila USA

1923: The Fila brothers found a knitwear manufacturing company in Biella, Italy

1969: Enrico Frachey joins the company and Fila begins to branch into sports apparel

1973: The Fila brand of athletic sportswear is launched

1980: Frachey leaves Fila and the company is acquired by Gemina, an Italian financial institution

1987: Frachey returns to Fila

1991: Fila regains direct control of the U.S. footwear line; Fila Sports Inc. and Fila Footwear USA are consolidated into Fila USA

INFLUENCES

Fila got its big break in the U.S. sports apparel market in the 1970s by having the then immensely popular and famous tennis star Bjorn Borg wear apparel sporting the Fila logo. After a decade, when both tennis and Borg's popularity had somewhat dimmed, Fila turned its attention elsewhere. Rap stars, the company noticed, like Heavy D, were wearing such Fila casual wear as the sweatsuit line. Capitalizing on what looked to be an up and coming trend, Fila's ads became geared to urbanites who wished they were suburbanites. Peter DePasquale, advertising executive for Fila at FCB in New York, said Fila's ads turned "edgy, dark, a little threatening." Another decade or so later, Fila needed to turn its approach around again; both urban and suburban kids were choosing basketball players as their idols.

Fila introduced a new advertising campaign in 1994. The result was the biggest launch for a sports shoe since the introduction of Nike's Air Jordan's, which saw a 60-percent sell-through in its first 10 days. Fila's Grant Hill shoe hit a sell-through of 50 percent after four days, with 1.5 million pairs of shoes sold. By 1996 the athletic shoe manufacturer had gone from eighth in market share to third, right behind giants Nike and Reebok. The campaign included "Rookie's Journal" advertisements for shoes on television and during events watched by younger target audiences such as ESPN, the NCAA basketball tournament, and MTV. Another successful marketing strategy was to arrange for Fila to restore 1,000

basketball backboards to boost the brand's name recognition among young consumers.

The American image and look of the brand is strategic. Because the U.S. market is growing just 5 to 8 percent a year, Fila has tried to respond to changes in consumer tastes. For example, in 1994, when the sales of basketball shoes in the United States fell 30 percent, Fila switched to cross-training and running shoes. Fila stands out as one of the few apparel firms able to make a successful transition into footwear design.

CURRENT TRENDS

Fila increased its advertising budget to $80 million in 1997 in order to keep up with Nike and Reebok, who together spend approximately $200 million yearly on media. Fila realizes it has plenty of unexplored territory in focused market categories, for instance, the women's and children's market, which comprise only a small percentage of the company's business. In addition, the company has been focused on specific footwear lines but is moving to expand the product line. In 1997 the women's market became one priority for Fila, with a multi-million dollar integrated campaign. Accordingly, Fila began seeking endorsements from female professional athletes.

PRODUCTS

Fila introduced its German Silva shoes in March 1997, named for the marathon runner German Silva. The company will be introducing a women's specific walking shoe and a women's-only model in running and cross training. As part of the fall 1997 line, Fila debuted its collection of soccer footwear. Fila's offerings include the Signature Claudio Reyna and Franco Baresi shoes and the Milanello. These will complement the company's current soccer apparel introduction. Fila launched its Signature Stack II basketball shoe and apparel, also in 1997. Like Nike, Fila is bringing its clothing and footwear to the outdoor market. Fila introduced its new line of snowboarding apparel and its full line of outdoor apparel, including trail-running shoes for women. The company also revealed plans to launch a full line of hiking boots. Lastly, new product initiatives include sunglasses, in-line skates, and hard goods such as soccer balls, basketballs, and golf equipment.

CORPORATE CITIZENSHIP

Fila and Grant Hill jointly contributed $120,000 for a Grant Hill Summer Basketball League in Detroit, Michigan, which also offered tutoring in math, English, and science. In addition, Fila sponsors world-class events that support athletics on all levels. Also, The Fila Sky-Marathon, a unique worldwide circuit, is part of the Fila Peak Performance Project in which medical professionals, researchers, and psychologists participate in field testing of Fila performance apparel and footwear prototypes. Skyrunners are chosen to compete in long distance endurance races on some of the world's most rugged peaks. Fila is also the title sponsor of the Fila Summer Pro Basketball League, an annual basketball competition featuring NBA stars and free agents.

GLOBAL PRESENCE

Fila's products are sold at more than 9,000 retail stores in over 50 countries. These include the United States, France, and the United Kingdom. The Italian sportswear is gaining recognition in Hong Kong, Taiwan, Japan, Indonesia, and the Philippines. Although the United States continues to post impressive sales, Korea holds the second largest market, followed by Italy. According to Fila, "The Group's best performance in 1996 came from Europe . . ." For example, footwear is up 99 percent as well as apparel, which is up by 46 percent across all markets in Europe. For this reason, new for 1997 was an initiative to develop and design concept shops for stores in Europe and South America.

In addition to its Maryland headquarters, Fila USA has design and sales offices in New York City: three distribution centers; a research and development center in Massachusetts; a design and product development center in Portland; and outdoor and winter sports and soccer offices in Boulder and Los Angeles, respectively. Also, Fila operates six retail boutiques around the country.

In footwear, Fila has capitalized on the global demand for U.S. athletic shoes. Its shoes are made in China and Indonesia but they are designed in the United States with specific colors and designs. Though its roots are in Italian design, all of Fila's footwear and most of its apparel comes from designers based in New York and Newburyport, Massachusetts. The company is identified as a U.S. brand because of its endorsement strategy and the growing popularity of basketball worldwide.

Fila's 1996 growth came from all major markets worldwide. The United States accounted for 57 percent of the group's net direct sales, compared with 59 percent in 1995. Footwear sales jumped 32 percent (72 percent of U.S. sales), while apparel sales increased 54 percent, reaching a share of 28 percent of total sales in this market. For the second consecutive year, Korea ranked as Fila's second largest market, accounting for 12 percent of total net direct sales. Italy, Fila's third largest market, grew 19 percent overall as a result of a 52-percent and 4-percent increases in footwear and apparel, respectively.

SOURCES OF INFORMATION

Bibliography

The Corporate Directory of U.S. Public Companies. San Mateo, CA: Walker's Research, LLC, 1997.

Crowley, Kevin. "New Fila Think Tank Sports Exotic Designers." *Footwear News,* 5 August 1996.

Feitelberg, Rosemary. "Fila: Success, American-Style." *WWD,* 20 July 1995.

"Fila Development Center Set for Portland, Ore." *Daily News Record,* 4 December 1996.

"Fila Holding S.p.A," June 1998. Available at http://www.marketguide.com/MGI/SNAP/A0560-CS.ohtml.

"Fila Holding S.p.A." *Hoover's Online,* 10 July 1998. Available at http://www.hoovers.com.

Fila Holding S.p.A. 1996 Annual Report. Biella, Italy: Fila, February 1997.

Fila Home Page, June 1998. Available at http://www.fila.com.

Geisler, Meredith. "Fila Footwear Continues Focus on Performance and Growth for Fall 1997." Fila Press Release, 14 February 1997.

Jensen, Jeff. "Shoe Giants Put New Emphasis on Performance." *Advertising Age,* 24 February 1997.

"Jon Epstein Named President & CEO of Fila U.S.A." *Business Wire,* 2 June 1998.

Lefton, Terry. "Fila, Reebok Enforce Jock Legitimacy with Upcoming Tech Campaigns." *Brandweek,* 24 February 1997.

Levine, Joshua. "Badass Sells." *Forbes Magazine,* 21 April 1997.

Peltz, James F. "Miles to Go? Sneaker Stocks are Still on the Fast Track." *Los Angeles Times,* 18 March 1997.

Sanders, Lauren. "Nibbling Away at Nike." *Shoot,* 24 January 1997.

For an annual report:

write: Fila USA, 14114 York Rd., Sparks, MD 21152

For additional industry research:

Investigate companies by their Standard Industrial Classification Codes, also known as SICs. Fila USA's primary SICs are:

2329 Men/Boy's Clothing, NEC

2339 Women/Misses' Outerwear, NEC

3149 Footwear Except Rubber, NEC

5651 Family Clothing Stores

6719 Holding Companies, NEC

6794 Patent Owners and Lessors

Fisher-Price, Inc.

FOUNDED: 1930

Contact Information:

HEADQUARTERS: 636 Girard Ave.
  East Aurora, NY 14052
PHONE: (716)687-3000
FAX: (716)687-3508
TOLL FREE: (800)828-4000
URL: http://www.fisher-price.com

OVERVIEW

Fisher-Price, Inc. is one of the foremost companies in the highly competitive market of toys and furnishings for infants and young children and the world's leading manufacturer of infant and preschool toys. From modest beginnings in 1930 as a manufacturer of simple wood and metal pull toys, Fisher-Price grew into a major corporation with about $1 billion in sales in 1996 and accounting for about 16 percent of Mattel's total revenues (about $770 million) in 1997. The company has endured repeated changes of ownership. In 1969 it was purchased by the Quaker Oats Company; in 1991, when it was an independent public company; and then in 1993, when it became a wholly owned subsidiary of Mattel Inc., thereby making Mattel the largest U.S. toy company.

After several disappointing forays into manufacturing toys for other age groups, in the mid-1990s Fisher-Price refocused on the market that had made it famous and successful: toys and games for children ages five and under. Some of its new products include educational software programs for pre-kindergarten aged children and a line of action figures for preschoolers based on characters that intended to be positive role models.

HISTORY

Fisher-Price began in 1930 in East Aurora, New York, 20 miles southeast of Buffalo, as a joint effort by three partners: Irving L. Price and Helen M. Schelle, who had worked in retail businesses that sold toys among other products, and Herman G. Fisher, who had advertised and sold games. Though none of the partners knew anything about toy manufacturing, they shared an enthusiasm and a common belief that the public would value high quality toys; "gay, cheerful, friendly toys with amusing action, toys that do something new and surprising and funny!" as they wrote in their first catalogue. During its first year in operation, Fisher-Price produced 16 toys, including two quacking wooden pull toys, Granny Doodle and Doctor Doodle. The Doodles were made of splinter-resistant Ponderosa pine and decorated with non-toxic finishes. Even though the Doodles were popular toys, the young company struggled through the Depression years, losing about two-thirds of its capital in the first four years of operation. The company did not actually start to make a profit until after it introduced a new toy, Snoopy Sniffer, in the late 1930s. During World War II, the Fisher-Price plant was temporarily converted to manufacture medicine chests and other war-related goods.

In the early 1950s, plastic was a relatively new material gaining in popularity and Fisher-Price decided to try using it to manufacture toys. Plastic had the advantage of retaining color and decorations longer than wood or metal, and by the end of the decade over half of the toys Fisher-Price was producing were composed at least in part of plastic. Through the 1950s and 1960s, Fisher-Price expanded rapidly, focusing on pre-school toys and introducing new concepts such as musical toys shaped like radios and televisions. In 1966, Herman Fisher retired as president of the company and was replaced by Henry Coords who had been recruited from Western Electric. After Herman Fisher retired and the Little People series of toys was introduced, the Quaker Oats Company acquired Fisher-Price in 1969. In 1970, Quaker Oats' advertising agency, Waring and LaRosa, launched the largest advertising campaign in Fisher-Price's history, spending upward of $1.25 million on television and print advertisements for Fisher-Price toys. By 1976, the company diversified into three areas: products for children 18 months to 4 years (its largest unit), toys for children ages 4 to 9, and a line of products for infants less than 18 month old. Although Quaker Oats consistently increased Fisher-Price's advertising budget—in 1975, for example, it spent almost $2.15 million on network advertising for the toy company—it allocated far less than its top competitors like Hasbro and (then competitor) Mattel. In 1993 Quaker Oats decided to sell Fisher-Price and it was eagerly grabbed by Mattel Inc. Under Mattel's ownership, Fisher-Price refocused on the infant and pre-school market that had made it a leader in the toy industry.

STRATEGY

From its inception in 1930, Fisher-Price's strategy was to make toys with "intrinsic play value, ingenuity, strong construction, good value for the money," as stated

FAST FACTS:
About Fisher-Price, Inc.

Ownership: Fisher-Price Inc. is a wholly owned subsidiary of Mattel Inc., a publicly traded company listed on the New York Stock Exchange.

Ticker symbol: Fisher-Price's parent Mattel Inc.'s ticker symbol is MAT.

Officers: Gary Baughman, Pres.; Gerald V. Cleary, Exec. VP of Sales, Fisher-Price & Tyco Preschool; Jerry Perez, Exec. VP of Marketing; Kevin Curran, Sr. VP Research & Development

Employees: 800

Principal Subsidiary Companies: Fisher-Price is a wholly owned subsidiary of Mattel, Inc., the largest toy maker in the United States.

Chief Competitors: Fisher-Price's main competitors include: Century Products Company, manufacturer of baby furniture and accessories; Galoob Toys, Inc., the third-ranked U.S. toy maker; Gerry Baby Products Company, maker of infant and toddler furniture and accessories; and Hasbro, Inc., the second-ranked U.S. toy manufacturer and maker of Playskool toys.

in the company's first catalogue. Sixty-six years later, the overall strategy of Fisher-Price's parent Mattel as expressed in its annual report for 1996, was "to focus on those brands which have fundamental play patterns and worldwide appeal, are sustainable, and will deliver consistent profitability." For Fisher-Price, this has led to an abandonment of its earlier efforts to expand into manufacturing toys and furnishings for older children, in favor of concentrating on its product lines for infants and pre-school children.

In 1998, Fisher-Price launched a new advertising campaign for its spring line of toys, which it called the "Its a Great Age" campaign aimed at parents, with 85 percent of its television advertising in "parent time." The strategy behind the campaign is to get parents to view Fisher-Price toys as more accessible, as represented not by an authoritative figure, but by someone "right there with Mom as kind of the voice of an experienced Mom helping her through raising her children and getting them developed and out to school," according to Fisher-Price Executive Vice President of Marketing, Jerry Perez.

CHRONOLOGY:

Key Dates for Fisher-Price, Inc.

1930: Founded

1938: Company starts to show a profit

1952: Begins fashioning new toys out of plastic instead of wood

1966: Herman Price retires as president

1968: Little People are introduced

1969: Company is purchased by Quaker Oats Co.

1972: Opens plants in Texas and Mexico

1975: Introduces the Adventure Series

1987: Founded Toy Town Museum

1991: Becomes an independently traded company

1993: Mattel Inc. buys company

1998: Introduces Rescue Heroes

INFLUENCES

After weathering the Great Depression of the 1930s and the temporary rerouting of its plants into wartime production in the 1940s, Fisher-Price shared in the huge growth of the toy industry during the 1950s and 1960s. By the time Quaker Oats bought the company in 1969, Fisher-Price had reached annual sales of over $30 million.

In the 1970s, declines in the birth rate led to stagnant preschool toy sales and Fisher-Price broadened its focus to include manufacturing toys for older children. In 1974, the company introduced a line of dolls and in 1975, it presented its Adventure Series line of toys, including Adventure People for early elementary school aged children. It also obtained the highly profitable license for Sesame Street characters.

In the mid-1980s, a shift in demographics included a rise in the birth rate and a revival of the preschool market, and Fisher-Price suddenly found its position as leader challenged. While established toy companies like Kenner Products, Hasbro, and Mattel expanded into the rejuvenated market, other companies like Matchbox Toys Ltd., Panosh Place, and Schaper Mfg. Co., entered the market with new lines of products including baby exercise tapes and washable vinyl plush toys. In the face of this competition, in 1986 Fisher-Price increased its ad-

vertising budget by 90 percent and changed its advertising strategy to include year-round (not just Christmas-seasonal) promotion of at least 75 of its new toys. At this time, Fisher-Price's new line included its Gummi Bear toys, based on a popular Walt Disney Productions cartoon series. The mid-1980s also saw the introduction of what would become the most successful new product in Fisher-Price's history, a line of toys called Puffalumps, exceedingly soft stuffed animals, which in its first year brought the company sales of about $25 million and helped Fisher-Price to sustain itself in what was becoming a much more competitive industry. However, in 1986, the company overextended itself by expanding production of toys in its four-year-old audiovisual toy division, which included a tape recorder, a phonograph, and a highly popular AM-FM radio with a sing- along microphone. The following year, Fisher-Price introduced its $200 video camcorder for children, which was well received at the American International Toy Fair. Although the camcorder and other (so-called) "promotional products" like a battery-powered sports car enjoyed initial success, by 1988, the company had to divert resources from its infant, preschool, and juvenile lines to support them and by the end of the decade, Fisher-Price was losing money.

In the early 1990s, Fisher-Price discontinued its line of products for older children, hired a new president, Ronald Jackson, and began efforts to recover from record losses of 1990 and early 1991. The company closed 4 of its 13 plants and 2 of its distribution centers, cut its work force by more than 3,000, moved production of some of its lines abroad, and reduced advertising and selling costs by about $17 million. By the end of 1991, Fisher-Price was again making a profit. Earlier that year, Quaker Oats had decided to spin off Fisher-Price and in June 1991, Fisher-Price became an independent publicly traded company listed on the New York Stock Exchange. Meantime, Fisher-Price refocused on infant and preschool products and began to expand its international markets. In November 1993, the stockholders of Fisher-Price and Mattel approved a merger plan under which Fisher-Price became a wholly owned subsidiary of Mattel, making Mattel the largest U.S. toy company.

James A. Eskridge replaced Jackson as president of Fisher-Price in 1993 and, while keeping the company's focus on infant and preschool products, in 1994 he pushed the company into the production of games, dolls, and electronic toys. Eskridge also was in charge when Fisher-Price began to achieve new sales records and became the first toy company to be awarded the Vendor of the Year Award by *Discount Store News* magazine in 1993. In the spring of 1997, Mattel merged with Tyco Toys, Inc. By mid-1997, under Eskridge's successor Byron Davis, Fisher-Price began suffering a decline in sales; within a year, Gary Baughman replaced Davis as president of Fisher-Price.

CURRENT TRENDS

In 1994, Fisher-Price introduced its new outdoor play yard toys, opening two new factories to produce this line. In the same year it also ventured into three new product lines for its target market: games, dolls, and educational electronic toys. With the explosive growth of the Internet came increasing interest in computers, and in the late 1990s Fisher-Price began developing computer products for children ages 2 through 7, including preschool software like Fisher-Price Ready for School Kindergarten, which was one of the top-selling pieces of home education software in the spring of 1998.

With the greying of the Baby Boomers, many older Fisher-Price toys have become highly desirable as collectibles. Several books, such as *A Historical, Rarity, and Value Guide: Fisher-Price 1931-1963,* list the toys produced by the company over the years. Fisher-Price has participated in this nostalgic trend, by setting up the Toy Town Museum, Fisher-Price Toystore, and Fisher-Price Resource Library at the company headquarters in East Aurora, New York.

PRODUCTS

In early 1994, Mattel acquired Kransco, manufacturer of Power Wheels battery-operated ride-on vehicles, which were then marketed under the Fisher-Price brand and brought an additional $200 million in sales to the company. In the later 1990s, Fisher-Price continued to refocus on its core market: infants and young children. However, it began to develop a new approach to this market. In 1996, in partnership with software developer Davidson & Associates, Fisher-Price introduced "Ready for Preschool," a CD-ROM set designed to teach children from 2 to 4 years old basic computer skills through a musical circus game. It also teamed up with computer manufacturing giant Compaq to produce the "Wonder Tools" series of computing products for children aged 3 through 7. "Wonder Tools" included CD-ROM software, a keyboard with oversized keys, and interactive software for children and their families to share. Other products released in 1997 included "Little People" accessories, a Little People Roadside Rescue vehicle set, a two-child wagon, and "Hideaway Hollow" playsets with bunny figures. (In May 1997, Fisher-Price had to recall about 17,000 of the toy police cars in its Little People Roadside Rescue vehicle set, sold since February, because of the possibility of choking hazard due to construction.)

In the spring of 1997, Mattel completed a merger with Tyco Toys, Inc., formerly the third-ranked U.S. toy maker and manufacturer of such toys as Matchbox, View-Master, Magna Doodle, and Tickle Me Elmo. As a result of the restructuring of the Mattel, Fisher-Price, and Tyco lines, Tyco's View-Master and Magna-Doodle brands have become part of the Fisher-Price line of products.

PLAY IS THE WORK OF CHILDREN

When you think of Fisher-Price, you probably think of brightly colored plastic toys that can withstand a nuclear blast or the day-to-day activities of a two-year old. But Fisher-Price is much, much more than that. While you may have had to make do pushing the classic Corn Popper from room to room, today's youngsters can get a medical kit, cameras, in-line skates, a cash register, clothing, backpacks, and yes, even eyewear. Do you have an especially imaginative youngster running around the house? Why not check out Fisher-Price's many playsets? Makes you wish you were still a toddler, doesn't it?

In 1998, Fisher-Price introduced more than 125 new products. At the 1998 American International Toy Fair in New York city in February of that year, the company showcased several of its new toys, including a battery-powered car, the Wild Thing, that can spin around and is operated with a foot pedal and two steering levers. Fisher-Price also introduced its Rescue Heroes line of action figures for preschoolers, figures based on everyday people that encourage nonviolent, positive, rescue-themed action. Alliance Communications signed an agreement with Fisher-Price to produce an animated adventure pilot and in-store video based on the central four Rescue Heroes—a firefighter, a construction expert, a scuba diver, and a mountain ranger—scheduled for completion in June 1998. Fisher-Price intended to back the campaign with over $4 million in advertising. The company claimed that during the first month at market, sales of the Rescue Heroes figures skyrocketed.

CORPORATE CITIZENSHIP

In early 1997 Fisher-Price took the initiative on an important child safety issue. The National Highway Traffic Safety Administration (NHTSA) was in the process of devising regulations requiring a universal child car seat design that would eliminate accidents caused by incorrect installation or by seat designs that were incompatible with car hardware. Before the proposed regulations were released, Fisher-Price already had created a new child car seat with built-in clips that eliminated the problem and had already planned to bring the car seat to market later in 1997. John Rhein, Fisher-Price's Director of

Product Engineering, explained that it could take 10 years for any new regulations to reach even half the cars on the road, so Fisher-Price had moved ahead to address the problem immediately.

GLOBAL PRESENCE

Due in part to Mattel's strong network of affiliates in Europe, Latin America, and Asia, Fisher-Price's late 1993 merger with Mattel sparked tremendous growth for Fisher-Price in international markets. Fisher-Price's parent company, Mattel, markets products in more than 140 countries, with overseas sales accounting for almost 40 percent of the company's total sales. Mattel maintains offices and manufacturing facilities in 37 countries, including the United States, China, Indonesia, Italy, Malaysia, Mexico, and the United Kingdom. It also hires independent contractors in the United States, Mexico, the Far East, and Australia. As with many large companies, Mattel's primary long-term goal included increasing penetration into emerging markets like those of China, India, and Brazil, as well as augmenting its presence in European countries.

SOURCES OF INFORMATION

Bibliography
"Authorities Recall Fisher-Price Little People Police Car." *Air Force News,* 27 May 1997.

"Davidson & Associates, Inc. Ships Fisher-Price Ready for Preschool." *PR Newswire,* 18 October 1996.

"Fisher-Price, Inc." *The Baby Net,* May 1998. Available at http://babynet.ddwi.com/manufacturers.shtml.

"Fisher-Price Rescue Heroes Sales Explode with Aggressive, Multi-Tiered Marketing Campaign." *Business Wire,* 6 April 1998.

"Galoob Toys, Inc." *Hoover's Online,* May 1998. Available at http://www.hoovers.com.

"Gerald Cleary Named Executive Vice President Sales Fisher-Price and Tyco Preschool." *Business Wire,* 26 March 1998.

"Graco Children's Products, Inc." *The Baby Net,* May 1998. Available at http://babynet.ddwi.com/manufacturers.shtml.

Grant, Tina, ed. *International Directory of Company Histories,* Vol. 12. Detroit, MI: St. James Press, 1996.

Hampton, Stuart. "Industry Snapshot: Toys & Games." *Hoover's Online,* May 1998. Available at http://www.hoovers.com.

"Hasbro, Inc." *Hoover's Online,* May 1998. Available at http://www.hoovers.com.

"Mattel Earnings Up Despite Fisher-Price Declines." *Reuters News Service,* 22 July 1997.

"Mattel, Inc." *Hoover's Online,* May 1998. Available at http://www.hoovers.com.

Mattel Inc. Annual Report. El Segundo, CA: Mattel, Inc., 1996.

McRee, Lisa, and Charles Gibson. "New Toy Preview." *ABC Good Morning America,* 20 February 1998.

"New Car Seat From Fisher-Price Takes the Lead in Responding to Proposed New Federal Regulations." *PR Newswire,* 17 January 1997.

"New Wonder Tools Family." Compaq-Fisher-Price Joint Press Release, 4 January 1996.

"'PC World' Magazine's Top Home Computers." *USA Today,* 1 April 1998.

"Retransmission: Alliance Communications Signs Production Deal with Fisher-Price for Rescue Heroes Animated Adventure Pilot and In Store Video." *Business Wire,* 4 February 1998.

"S&P Description: Mattel, Inc." Standard & Poor's, 16 April 1998.

Schuch, Beverly, and Donald Van De Mark. "Fisher- Price President." *Biz Buzz (CNNfn),* 10 February 1998.

For an annual report:
telephone: (310)252-2000 **or** write: Mattel, Inc., 333 Continental Blvd., El Segundo, CA 90245-5012

For additional industry research:
Investigate companies by their Standard Industrial Classification Codes, also known as SICs. Fisher-Price's primary SICs are:

2511 Wood Household Furniture

3942 Dolls & Stuffed Toys

3944 Games, Toys & Children's Vehicles

Foot Locker

OVERVIEW

Foot Locker is the leading retailer of athletic footwear in the United States and the flagship store of the Venator Group (formerly Woolworth Corporation). With more than 7,200 stores in 12 countries and combined sales of $6.6 billion in 1997, the Venator Group's specialty stores have played a major role in reviving the fortunes of the once-struggling department store chain. Venator's Athletic Group includes Foot Locker U.S. and international, Lady Foot Locker, Kids Foot Locker, Champs, and Sports Authority. Together, these stores make the Athletic Group the largest retailer in terms of stores and sales of athletic footwear in the world, owning approximately 45 percent of the U.S. athletic footwear market in 1996.

Foot Locker is a brand-name footwear and apparel specialty store chain. Merchandise includes athletic footwear, apparel, and accessories for men, women, and children. Woolworth Corporation underwent dramatic changes between 1994 and 1997, not least of which was the final closing of the last 400 F.W. Woolworth stores in 1997. Of these, 100 were converted to Foot Locker or other speciality stores, and the rest were closed down permanently. A year later, Woolworth Corporation announced it was abandoning the Woolworth name and as of June 1998 would be known as the Venator Group.

COMPANY FINANCES

The Venator Group has been in the process of restructuring under the new leadership of Roger N. Farah,

FOUNDED: 1974

Contact Information:

HEADQUARTERS: 233 Broadway
 New York, NY 10279-0003
PHONE: (212)553-2000
FAX: (212)553-2018
TOLL FREE: (800)991-6681
EMAIL: customer_service@footlocker.com
URL: http://www.footlocker.com

FAST FACTS:

About Foot Locker

Ownership: Foot Locker is a publicly owned company traded on NASDAQ.

Ticker symbol: Z

Officers: Roger N. Farah, Chmn. & CEO; Dale W. Hilpert, Pres. & COO; Reid Johnson, Sr. VP & CFO

Employees: 75,000 (Venator Group)

Principal Subsidiary Companies: Foot Locker is a wholly owned subsidiary of the Venator Group, formerly Woolworth Corporation.

Chief Competitors: As the number-one athletic footwear retailer in the United States, Foot Locker faces intense competition. Competitors include: Footaction; Niketown; Nordstrom; Modell's Sporting Goods; Footstar; Herman's Sporting Goods; and New Balance.

chairman and CEO. The company made substantial improvements in its financial position in 1996. For example, net income was $169 million, compared to a net loss of $164 million in 1995. Since 1994 the company's operating results, internal support systems, merchandising strategies, and financial position have improved dramatically. The company has also eliminated old inventory and consolidated its distribution facilities. Now with profitability up 260 percent, the company's capital expenditures for 1997 were targeted at $285 million, primarily in the Athletic Group. On the downside, in 1997 a maturing market and stagnating sales of sneakers hurt Foot Locker, which saw same-store sales drop in 12 of the last 13 quarters through January 1998. While Woolworth's total 1997 revenues fell to $6.6 from $7.0 billion in 1996, the Athletic Group, led by Foot Locker, enjoyed a modest increase in revenues, from 3.6 billion in 1996 to $3.7 billion in 1997. Operating profits, on the other hand, dropped to $375 million from $461 million.

ANALYSTS' OPINIONS

According to Jeanne Dugan, in *Business Week,* "Foot Locker is facing increasing competition from superstores and a market whose growth is slowing significantly." Larry Schwartz of JSSI, distributor of British Knights, stated, "They helped create the industry, and all they know is growth. Now they are faced with something they don't have experience with—a mature industry. The sneaker business used to grow 20 to 30 percent a year; now it's only growing 3 to 4 percent a year. They're trying new things. The store format is pretty old and new formats are creating more excitement." In short, in order for Foot Locker to experience growth, the company will need to concentrate on superstores with huge assortments. But, according to John Shanley, a retail analyst with Genesis Merchant Group, "They should have done this three or four years ago and they would have had a shot at it. Now all the competition is there—it's too little, too late in conjunction with the overall slowdown in the athletic marketplace."

By 1998 the soft market for athletic footwear and increased competition were beginning to take their toll on Foot Locker. Venator moved to increase its share of the athletic market and increase distribution by acquiring a competitor, Sports Authority. The acquisition was seen as having the potential to increase operating efficiencies. However, Sports Authority also suffered from weak footware sales and analysts expected a slightly negative impact on financial coverage measures and new difficulties for management. Following the acquisition, Standard and Poor revised its rating of the company from stable to negative. While most analysts felt the company would prosper in the long term, the short term had them worried.

HISTORY

Woolworth Corporation's origins date back to 1879 when Frank W. Woolworth opened the very first "five and dime" in Lancaster, Pennsylvania. Over the century, Woolworth's grew into an $8.1 billion multinational company with over 7,500 stores and related facilities located in 12 countries on 3 continents.

In the 1920s the Kinney company launched its own manufacturing operations, through which they were better able to meet the varied fashion demands of increasingly style-conscious customers. In the 1950s it opened freestanding stores along highways and "strip" stores in small shopping centers close to new housing developments. Kinney made retailing history in the 1960s as the only family shoe store in America's first enclosed shopping mall. In 1963 Woolworth acquired Kinney, and in the 1970s, the company took a major step into athletic footwear retailing with Foot Locker, which became the leader in the business. The first Foot Locker store opened in City of Industry, California, in 1974. By the 1980s Foot Locker was developing innovative partnerships with vendors, pioneering in sports-event marketing, and spinning off into speciality formats such as Lady Foot Locker for women and Kids Foot Locker for children.

By the 1990s Foot Locker and its sister stores were responsible for the bulk of Woolworth's revenues. As for the old "five and dime" stores, they were being squeezed out of the market by specialty stores on the one hand and superstores on the other. In July 1997 Woolworth chairman and CEO Roger N. Farah announced that the company would be permanently shutting down all F.W. Woolworth stores in the United States. "We made the very difficult decision to close our domestic F.W. Woolworth general merchandise operations to help assure the continuing profitable growth of the Woolworth Corporation and to better serve all of our constituencies," Farah said in a press release. "This will enable us to focus on growing our profitable athletic and specialty retailing formats, including Foot Locker, Lady Foot Locker, Kids Foot Locker, Champs Sports, and the Northern Group of apparel stores." Indeed, 100 of the closed Woolworth stores were to be converted to Foot Locker or other specialty stores. At the same time, Farah announced that the company would be changing its corporate name to "better reflect its global specialty retailing formats." The new name, announced in the spring of 1998, was the Venator Group. The new name became official on June 12, 1998. No longer a struggling five-and-dime operation, Woolworth's had become a sportswear giant that was leading the rest of the industry into the twenty-first century.

STRATEGY

Venator pursues growth by seeking strategic acquisitions, such as the recent purchases of the Eastbay Company (a leading catalog retailer of athletic merchandise) and Sports Authority (a major competitor of Foot Locker). Eastbay provides the company with an additional channel of distribution—direct marketing—through which to reach customers, whether under the Foot Locker, Champs Sports, or Eastbay names. In short, the Athletic Group will be able to increase its array of product offerings. In addition, Eastbay will be able to build on its existing strengths by taking advantage of the strong vendor relationships and product development capabilities of the Athletic Group. Management will continue to look to explore other potential acquisitions in 1997 and beyond.

Domestic strategic marketing programs for 1997 included "Hoop-It-Up," a grassroots three-on-three basketball tournament. The company sponsors the "Foot Locker Athletic Club," which consists of world-class track and field athletes, as well as the "Foot Locker Cross Country Championships." In addition, the company is associated with the National Basketball Association, the National Football League, Major League Baseball, and Major League Soccer sponsorships. European marketing programs include the sponsoring of "World League Football" and "Converse 3-on-3 Basketball," a youth basket-

CHRONOLOGY:
Key Dates for Foot Locker

1974: Kinney Shoe Corp. opens its first Foot Locker store in City of Industry, California

1982: The first Lady Foot Locker opens

1986: Kids Foot Locker is launched

1991: Foot Locker expands to 1,352 stores, surpassing the 1,312 Kinney stores

1998: Woolworth, Kinney's parent company, closes its Woolworth stores to focus solely on its sports apparel and specialty retailing ventures

ball program in Italy, Germany, Spain, and England. Lastly, Foot Locker was the first official "UEFA" retailer during the European Champions League Soccer Final—one of the largest sporting events in the world.

As part of its strategy to continue its growth trend, the Athletic Group is introducing new store designs combining trend-setting assortments with exciting and entertaining retail environments. The company said it would be spending $154 million in 1998 to open approximately 275 new stores and remodel approximately 375 existing stores.

Perhaps the most critical strategic move was the company's decision to change its name to Venator Group. "Venator" means sportsman or hunter in Latin. According to Venator Group's chairman and CEO Roger Farah, "The new corporate name positions the company as a high-performance merchandiser that is invigorated and inspired by the ever-changing marketplace as it strives to win the global retail game."

The name change was a clear signal that the old Woolworth's was gone and the new company wanted changes. In March 1998 it announced that it was investing $1 billion through the year 2000 to open or remodel 4,300 stores, mostly in the core business of athletic shoes and clothing, so that half of its stores will be less than three years old. Of the 400 or so Woolworth stores shut down in 1997, 130 were to be transformed into larger Foot Locker, Champs, or Triplex stores, each averaging 12,500 square feet of floor space. Triplex stores feature Foot Locker, Lady Foot Locker, and Kids Foot Locker all under one roof. These were the company's equivalent to the competition's athletic superstores.

INFLUENCES

The Athletic Group is essentially generating all of the Venator Group's profits. While the core U.S. Foot Locker chain is highly mature, with an average store age in excess of 12 years, domestically the chain continues to have numerous opportunities to open additional Lady Foot Locker and Kids Foot Locker stores, thereby not only more effectively targeting specific sub-segments of the market, but enlarging its overall store presence within America's major malls.

At the same time, however, just about all of Foot Locker's competitors were planning to expand in 1998 in spite of the fact that the athletic footwear and apparel industry was enduring a slowdown that had already affected the retailers and manufacturers. Nike, a major supplier to Foot Locker stores, suffered a 69 percent decline in earnings during its fiscal third quarter. Another leading manufacturer of athletic footwear, Reebok, faced a similar, though less severe, slide. As the investor newsletter, *The Motley Fool* put it, "bad times for the shoemakers means bad times for the shoesellers."

Another problem facing Foot Locker was the fact that most of its competitors had built superstores that were 35 to 50 percent larger than the average Foot Locker store. Venator's plan to convert some of its old Woolworth department stores into Foot Locker superstores looked like a good strategy on paper, but in fact was beset by problems. The most pressing was the fact that the best locations had already been grabbed by the competition. In addition, many of the old Woolworth stores were poorly located. In the face of a contracting market, it seemed likely that Foot Locker might find itself closing more stores than it opened. Venator, however, was confident it could weather the storm and that when the slump in the footwear industry subsided, its new name, new look, and new attitude would lead to prosperity in the next century.

CURRENT TRENDS

Overall, Venator sees Footlocker as its real opportunity to expand. Under the restructuring Foot Locker stores will be made much larger and will include more apparel. The company is planning to renovate and expand 300 Foot Locker stores per year; in addition, they also plan to add 250 new Lady Footlocker, Kids Foot Locker, Champs, and European Foot Locker stores.

Foot Locker plans to open a 40,000-square-foot store in Disney's Wide World of Sports Complex at Walt Disney World Resort in Orlando, Florida, in early 1999. The company refers to this as its "superstore" because it will offer activewear, athletic footwear, and accessories for more than 30 sports. Foot Locker is also the sponsor of the facility's track and field complex and will sponsor track meets at the site.

To expand its market share, Woolworth Corporation purchased 27 Koenig Sporting Goods stores from Koenig Sporting Goods, Inc. for approximately $10 million. Koenig, a Cleveland-based privately held company, was a mall-based sporting goods retailer that operated 40 stores in 6 states, primarily in the Midwest. The acquisition gave Venator stores a presence in key metropolitan markets—including the Cleveland/Akron area, Pittsburgh, and Buffalo—where its Champ's Sports Division operated a limited number or no stores. Venator planned to convert the acquired stores to the Champs Sports format and anticipated that the acquisition would increase earnings.

Consumer desires regarding shopping locations have changed, and many now shop outside the mall. Consumers enjoy more retail options than ever before, from megastores to catalogs to computer shopping. Therefore, focusing on convenience, in December 1997 Woolworth opened a new Foot Locker that combined the Foot Locker, Lady Foot Locker, and Kids Foot Locker format under one roof. The new "Triplex" store was specifically designed to compete with the superstores operated by Woolworth's rivals. In addition, in November 1996 the company joined with Toys 'R' Us to sell children's footwear within the toy store chain's KidsWorld, which was another opportunity for Foot Locker to establish itself outside of a mall-based setting. In another move, Venator acquired Sports Authority, another major retailer of athletic footwear and apparel.

In mid-1998 the Venator Group announced plans for a web site that would enable shoppers to price, view, and purchase athletic footwear and apparel over the Internet. The site was to be a fully integrated online entertainment and retail environment featuring a database engine providing users with the largest selection of athletic footwear, apparel, and sporting goods in the world. Customers would be able to purchase styles that are in stock and receive them within 24 to 48 hours. "This is a paradigm shift in retailing," said Robert Landes, chief executive officer of Guidance Solutions, the company developing the site.

PRODUCTS

The Athletic Group purchases footwear and apparel merchandise from vendors worldwide. For example, Nike, Inc. supplied approximately 25 percent of the company's merchandise purchases in 1996. The major brands of merchandise Foot Locker carries include Nike, Reebok, Adidas, Fila, Converse, New Balance, Asics, L.A. Gear, Champion, Starter, and Air Walk. Foot Locker also distributes athletic footwear for most sports, including running, basketball, tennis, aerobics, fitness, track, baseball, football, and soccer. In addition, the company sells licensed team (NBA, NFL, MLB, and MLS) and fitness apparel. Accessories such as socks, athletic bags and hats, and foot-care products are also sold.

CORPORATE CITIZENSHIP

Foot Locker sponsors a National stay-in-school program whereby middle- and junior-high students create a video with a stay-in-school message. In addition, Foot Locker and Fila have replaced, refurbished, and maintained basketball backboards in public school playgrounds in five cities for the past three years. All billboards bear inspirational messages such as "Winners Never Quit." Foot Locker and Nike, Inc. collect and recycle old athletic shoes to reconstruct play courts in cities across the country. All Foot Locker Club athletes adopted a middle school in their hometown to share trials and tribulations of training for competition.

Most important, Foot Locker was one of the sponsors for "The Silent March Against Gun Violence" in 1994. The company offered shoes-for-guns exchanges in six cities throughout the United States. The march was an effort to influence Congress to support two bills that were to be introduced in 1995 that would increase gun licensing and registration requirements for owners as well as dealers.

GLOBAL PRESENCE

The Athletic Group, Venator's largest and most profitable business, operates 3,394 stores in North America, Europe, Asia, and Australia. Europe has 228 Foot Locker stores in the Netherlands, Belgium, England, Germany, France, Italy, Spain, and Luxembourg. In the United States, this division operates the Foot Locker businesses including Foot Locker, Lady Foot Locker, Kids Foot Locker, and World Foot Locker, as well as Champs Sports and Going to the Game. The 2,914 stores are located primarily in regional malls throughout the United States. In Canada, the division operates 188 Foot Locker and Champs Sports stores, located primarily in regional malls. The company believes that the overseas markets offer potential growth opportunities, and is beginning to probe the Asian market.

EMPLOYMENT

In 1995 Woolworth implemented a cost-reduction program through which it saved more than $100 million by reducing staffing levels, occupancy costs, and overhead at both the corporate and divisional levels. Furthermore, the company has targeted an additional $300 million in savings through 1998.

Foot Locker's parent company, Venator, offers most of its employees benefit pension plans based on years of service and career-average compensation. The company also sponsors post-retirement medical and life insurance plans, which are available to most of its U.S. employees.

In order to be eligible for these plans, employees must retire from the company and be covered under the company's active medical or life insurance plan. However, the level of benefits available depends on the year of retirement and the plan in effect at that time.

In January 1996 the company established the Woolworth Corporation Savings Plan. This plan allows eligible employees to contribute 1 to 15 percent of their income on a pre-tax basis to this savings plan, and the company matched 25 percent of the first 4 percent of the employees' contribution. The company also offers employee stock plans to corporate officers and other key employees.

SOURCES OF INFORMATION

Bibliography

Dugan, Jeanne. "Why Foot Locker Is In a Sweat."*Business Week,* 27 October 1997. Available at http://sbweb2.med.iacnet.com/infotrac/session/813/783/9861446/109/ismap4/01?79,9.

Edelson, Sharon. "Retail Wrap." *WWD,* 26 January 1995. Available at http://sbweb2.med.iacnet.com/infotrac/session/813/783/9861446/126/ismap4/11/11?7 5,17.

Emert, Carol. "Shoes Get Protest Role Versus Guns." *Footwear News,* 3 October 1994. Available at http://sbweb2.med.iacnet.com/infotrac/session/813/783/9861446/130/ismap4/13/13?8 2,21.

"Foot Locker Fact Sheet." New York: Foot Locker, 13 November 1997.

Malone, Scott. "Kids Foot Locker Joins Forces with Toys R' Us." *Footwear News,* 25 November 1996. Available at http://sbweb2.med.iacnet.com/infotrac/session/813/783/9861446/94!xrn_1&bkm_94.

———. "Woolworth GM Review Could Boost Shoe Biz." *Footwear News,* 16 June 1997. Available at http://sbweb2.med.iacnet.com/infotrac/session/813/783/9861446/117/ismap4/4/4?78, 34.

"Mickey's Locker." *WWD,* 6 November 1997. Available at http://sbweb2.med.iacnet.com/infotrac/session/813/783/9861446/108!xrn_1&bkm_108.

Palmieri, Jean. "Farah Weight Fate of U.S. Woolworth Chain; Athletic Group Is Seen As Primary Growth Vehicle." *Daily News Record,* 13 June 1997. Available at http://sbweb2.med.iacnet.com/infotrac/session/614/583/4618412/31/ismap4/2/2?26,2 3.

"Woolworth Corporation." *Hoover's Handbook of American Business 1997.* Austin, TX: The Reference Press, 1996.

Woolworth Corporation 1996 Annual Report. New York: Woolworth Corporation, 11 March 1997.

Woolworth Corporation 1997 Annual Report. New York: Woolworth Corporation, 21 April 1998.

"Woolworth Corporation to Close Its U.S. General Merchandise Operations Plans Include Conversion of Approximately 100 Locations to Its Foot Locker And Champs Athletic Formats." New York: Woolworth Corporation, 17 July 1997.

"Woolworth: New Moniker Sheds Old Image." *The Online Investor,* 6 April 1998. Available at: http://biz.yahoo.com.

"Woolworth Outlook Now Negative, Sports Authority On S&P Watch Positive." *Newswire,* 17 July 1997. Available At http://www.pathfinder.com/money/latest/press/PW/1998May08/270.html.

"Woolworth Posts US$100m Profit, Plans 400 New Stores." *Financial Post Daily,* 8 March 1998.

For an annual report:

write: Corporate Secretary, 233 Broadway, New York, NY 10279

For additional industry research:

Investigate companies by their Standard Industrial Classification Codes, also known as SICs. Foot Locker's primary SICs are:

5331 Variety Stores

5611 Men's/Boys' Clothing Stores

5632 Women's Accessory & Specialty Stores

5651 Family Clothing Stores

5661 Shoe Stores

Ford Motor Company

OVERVIEW

One of the "big three" car companies in the United States, Ford has a rich history and heritage. Ford has been responsible for some of the largest contributions to the U.S. economy and its growth. Aside from its status as a car company, Ford also had considerable stakes in the financial services area. The company manufactures car parts and accessories in various divisions like the Body and Assembly Operations, Casting Division, Climate Control Operations, Glass Division, Parts and Services Division, Plastics Products Division, and Transmission and Chassis Operations.

Ford held the number two position among U.S. car companies with 1997 sales of $153.6 billion. Ford also ranked second on the Fortune 500 list of the largest U.S. industrial corporations based on sales, and it was the leading exporter of cars and trucks from the United States and Canada.

FOUNDED: 1903

Contact Information:
HEADQUARTERS: The American Rd.
   Dearborn, MI 48121
PHONE: (313)322-3000
FAX: (313)323-2959
URL: http://www.ford.com

COMPANY FINANCES

Ford's 1997 worldwide net income was $6.9 billion, a 56 percent increase from 1996. Of that, $4.0 billion was generated in the United States, and $2.9 billion was generated internationally. Total revenues for the company were $153.6 billion, $122.9 billion of which was generated by automotive sales, while $30.6 billion was derived from the company's financial services.

Ford's total earnings per share (EPS) for 1997 were $5.62, up 54 percent from 1996's EPS of $3.64. The com-

FINANCES:

Ford Motor Co. Automotive Sales, 1994-1997 (billion dollars)

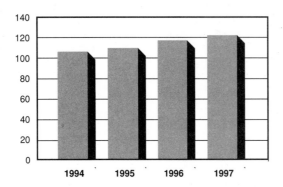

Ford Motor Co. 1997 Stock Prices (dollars)

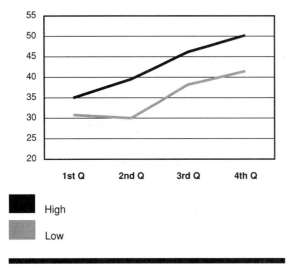

pany's stock price rose from $32 1/4 at year-end 1996 to $48 9/16 at year-end 1997. As of mid-1998, stock was trading at around $58.00 per share. Ford stock's 52-week high was $59.13, and its 52-week low was $26.15 per share.

Ford continued to show improvement during the first quarter of 1998, earning $1.7 billion, or $1.36 per share. The 1998 results compare with earnings of $1.5 billion, or $1.20 per share during the same period in 1997 and beat the company's record for highest first quarter earnings of $1.6 billion, set in 1989.

ANALYSTS' OPINIONS

Ford's Atlanta Assembly Plant, maker of the Ford Taurus and Mercury Sable, was rated by J.D. Power and Associates as the highest quality automobile factory in the world serving the North American market. According to Alex Taylor in the June 22, 1998 issue of *Fortune* magazine, "Ford, the 95-year-old family business that has traditionally been a solid but never dazzling performer, has remade itself into the global powerhouse the rest of Motown would love to be." In 1997, Ford earned $6.9 billion in profits, more than any car company in history. The article also reports that while many doubted Trotman's Ford 2000 initiative, the company was making significant progress toward its goal of merging the Ford's engineering and manufacturing operations in the United States and Europe. The company has gone further than the other big three auto makers toward changing its "old ways." The company had a record first quarter in 1998 and announced that second-quarter results would exceed analyst estimates and beat the previous year's earnings. During May and June of 1998, Ford stock rose 21 percent.

HISTORY

Henry Ford founded the Ford Motor Company in 1903. Born on a farm near Dearborn, Michigan, he made his first rudimentary car, the *Quadricycle,* in a shed behind his home. With $28,000 and a lot of faith and courage, Henry Ford and 12 associates incorporated the Ford Motor Company in 1903 in Lansing, Michigan. Between 1903 and 1908, Henry Ford and his engineers used the first 19 letters of the alphabet to designate their creations, although many of these cars were experimental and never reached the public.

The first production Ford car, the *Model A,* was sold a month after its incorporation to a Chicago dentist named Pfennig. By this time, the company's bank balance had dwindled to $223.65. During the next five years Henry Ford graduated from being chief engineer to president, acquired a majority of the stock, and directed a development and production program that began in a converted wagon factory. In the first 15 months, 1,700 Model A cars chugged out of the old wagon factory.

By the year 1913, Ford had established the world's first moving automobile assembly line production operation and began sales operations in Argentina, China, Indonesia, Siam, and Brazil. By 1915, Ford had built 1 million cars, and by 1922 that number had reached 10 million. Ford production reached 20 million, and the company built its first V-8 automobile in 1931. A new line, Mercury, was introduced in 1938, and the Lincoln Continental was introduced the same year. However, at the start of World War II, Ford was forced to halt civil-

This man is checking vehicle doors at one of Ford's assembly facilities. *(The Bettmann Archive/Newsphotos, Inc.)*

ian production and shift to total military production. By the time the second World War ended, Henry Ford died at the age of 83, in 1947.

Henry Ford II, the oldest grandson of Henry Ford assumed presidency of the company in 1945. As he drove the first post-war car off the assembly line, Henry Ford II made plans to reorganize and decentralize the company. At the time, Ford Motor Company was losing several million dollars a month and was in a critical condition to resume its pre-World War II position as a major force in the now fiercely competitive auto industry.

Henry Ford II turned out to be the ideal individual to tackle the job of leading the family business to becoming a modern, publicly owned corporation. His genius was in his ability to find the most talented people and bring them into leadership positions in this rapidly growing organization. Those hired by Henry Ford II brought quantitative analysis and the science of modern management to the company.

In 1956, the Ford Motor Company took a major step and went public. In the largest stock issue of all time, 10,200,000 shares of the Ford Motor Company were put up for sale and 250,000 investors rushed to pay $657 million for 20 percent of what, until then, had been a family business. In 1958, Ford announced its entry into the heavy and extra-heavy truck market (it had entered the light truck market in 1917), and by 1959, Ford had produced 50 million vehicles.

STRATEGY

Ford started as a domestic company and capitalized on domestic demand. However, this did not detract from the company's focus on globalization. Henry Ford's policy was to become a contributing citizen in every country where Ford sold cars. His slogan was, "Build them where you sell them." In the same vein, Ford believed in equal employment opportunity throughout his company.

Henry Ford II continued his grandfather's equal employment policies, predating federal civil rights legislation. In the late 1970s, when American workers were criticized for producing poor quality, Henry Ford II said, "there is no such thing as a bad employee, only bad managers." Company leadership accepted responsibility, and Ford was the first American auto company to make quality "Ford's number one operating priority."

Ford continued to believe in improving quality via its employees, as opposed to the rest of the industry, which was moving on to the use of high-tech robots. "Teamwork" became the norm from in-plant participatory groups to a new way of developing cars based on cross-functional teams. The idea was to bring in representatives from all engineering and management specialties together into each vehicle development team, then give them the authority to make as many decisions as possible. The first team effort was on a bold new car—the Taurus. The immensely successful effort en-

FAST FACTS:

About Ford Motor Company

Ownership: The Ford Motor Company is a publicly held company traded on the New York Stock Exchange.

Ticker symbol: F

Officers: Alex Trotman, Chmn., Pres., & CEO, 64; W. Wayne Booker, Vice-Chmn., 63; Edward E. Hagenlocker, Vice-Chmn., 58; John M. Devine, VP & CFO, 53

Employees: 363,892

Principal Subsidiary Companies: Ford Motor Company has many subsidiaries. Some of the better known include: Ford Motor Credit Co., Hertz Corp., Lincoln Mercury Division, and Jaguar Ltd.

Chief Competitors: As a major automobile manufacturer, Ford's competitors include: Chrysler; General Motors; Toyota; Honda; Daimler-Benz; BMW; Mitsubishi; Nissan; Hyundai; Kia; and Volkswagon.

couraged management to give the teams more authority and independence.

In efforts to increase profitability, Ford continued restructuring its business and reducing process costs. The company discontinued low-volume, low-profit vehicles such as the Aerostar, Aspire, Thunderbird, Cougar, and Probe; sold its heavy truck operations; reduced excess car capacity; and added capacity for its best-selling light trucks. In 1997, Ford announced financial goals for its automotive business, including targeting a return on sales of 4 percent in North America; in Europe, they hoped to break even; in South America, the company sought reduction in losses compared with 1996. Overall, Ford hoped to reduce total costs by $1 billion and reduce capital spending. The company was able to exceed all of those goals, as stated in its 1997 Annual Report.

The company's latest strategy was its "new edge." The company defined this as an inclusive concept that meant a commitment at Ford to focus on improved quality, cost, and speed; great new products; new design styles with "smooth, sculpted surfaces" and "clear, crisp intersections;" and sharp focus on shareholder value.

INFLUENCES

Ever since its beginning, world events have shaped the Ford Motor company. World War II played a major role in the company's prominence and growth. Also important were the influence of Henry Ford in the pre-World War II period and his oldest grandson, Henry Ford II in the post-war period. The success of the Ford Motor Company was in the fact that Ford grew and adapted to the changing times, while at the same time anticipating industry events and setting trends and milestones of its own.

In the 1960s, for instance, Ford leaders anticipated a weakening of trade barriers and moved to regional trading way ahead of the pack. Ford of Europe was established in 1967, 20 years ahead of the European Economic Community's arrival. Similarly, Ford established the North American Automotive Operations (NAAO) consolidating the United States, Canada, and Mexico in 1972, more than a decade ahead of the North American Free Trade Agreement (NAFTA).

CURRENT TRENDS

In 1994, with the consolidation of Ford's North American and European operations, Ford 2000 was initiated. The Ford 2000 commitment was to bring the entire Ford global organization into a single operation by the year 2000. Ford 2000 created a single global management team to allow the company to eliminate duplication, initiate best practices, use common components and designs for the advantage of scale, and allocate resources to wherever they are needed to best serve market needs.

Ford expected to save billions with the Ford 2000 initiative, but Ford's profit margins fell 60 percent during the 1994-1996 phase because of tough competition. With heavy competition from foreign and other domestic auto makers in the mid-1990s, Ford was going through a difficult period trying to remain profitable. New product introductions and aggressive marketing were results of this effort. In February of 1997, Ford announced its decision to quit the heavy truck business after launching the much publicized HN80 model introduced in fall 1996; this move reflected the importance that Ford company executives placed in a company wide strategic review. "Industry analysts said that Ford's decision to drop out of the heavy truck business recognizes it wouldn't easily have caught the market leaders," according to the *Knight Ridder/Tribune Business News*.

In another move expected to improve performance, Ford planned its launch of its new 1999 Cougar sports coupe. Sold by Mercury, the company utilized the first North American application of Ford's "New Edge" design and side air-bag technology. The car will also be sold in Europe and arrived at dealer showrooms in May

1998. Mercury was hoping to lure new buyers to the brand, in part by moving its headquarters to Irvine, California, in 1998. Ford hoped that southern California's "innovative, trendsetting culture and strong automotive market will foster development of unique vehicles and creative new looks for both brands."

PRODUCTS

Ford has always been a trend setter with its new products. In 1904, Henry Ford set the first speed record driving his "999" race car 91.37 miles per hour on frozen Lake St. Clair, near Detroit, Michigan. Ford introduced the first V-8 engine. In the fall of 1954, the Thunderbird, an American classic, joined the Ford car family as a 1955 two-seater sports car. The original Thunderbird was offered with a 160-horsepower V-8 engine with a three-speed manual transmission and had a new and unique feature—a convertible canvas roof for fair and sunny weather and a detachable plastic hardtop for foul weather.

Ford changed the direction of the American auto industry forever on April 17, 1964, when it unveiled the *Mustang* at the world's Fair in New York. The Ford Mustang caused a sensation that confirmed the theories of Ford product planners who thought a car with a youthful touch would appeal to World War II baby boomers. Dealers were swamped with some 22,000 orders on the car's first day.

In 1980, Ford introduced the 1981 Escort in its first attempt at a world car. CDW27 was Ford's genuine global car. Named Mondeo in Europe, Taiwan, and the Middle East, slightly modified versions went on sale in North America with the names Ford Contour and Mercury Mystique. Ford's CDW27 became a new way of thinking about product development for the Ford Motor Company. It proved that true globalization was possible and that customer focused teams were the way of the competitive future. Runaway successes during the 1990s included the company's sports utility vehicles and F-series pick-ups. The F-series pick-ups outsold any other car in the world during the 1980s and 1990s. In the late 1990s, Ford sold cars under the brands Ford, Lincoln, Mercury, Aston Martin, and Jaguar.

CORPORATE CITIZENSHIP

Ford announced that beginning with 1999 model year cars, all of its sport utility vehicles (SUVs) will be low-emission vehicles, as clean as new cars. And, along with the other major automakers, Ford planned to produce cars with 70 percent lower emissions nationally by 2001. The company also made sure that its production facilities had a minimal impact on the environment. Ford was the first large company in the world to commit globally to ISO 14001 certification, the international environmental management system standard covering all of

CHRONOLOGY:
Key Dates for Ford Motor Co.

1903: Henry Ford establishes the Ford Motor Company

1908: Ford introduces the Model T

1909: Henry Ford applies his assembly line concept to Model T production

1918: Henry Ford retires naming his son, Edsel Ford, as president

1919: Edsel and Henry Ford buy out the other stockholders and incorporate

1922: Acquires the Lincoln Motor Company

1937: Ford produces its 25 millionth automobile

1943: Edsel Ford dies

1945: Henry Ford II is named president

1949: Henry Ford I dies

1956: Ford Motor Company goes public

1958: The Ford Edsel debuts and flops horribly

1962: The Mustang makes its debut and sells 500,000 in 18 months

1979: Henry Ford II relinquishes his position to Philip Caldwell

1986: Ford's income passes General Motors' for the first time since 1924

1993: Ford products are five of the top eight best-selling vehicles in the United States

1999: All Ford sport utility vehicles are manufactured as low-emission vehicles

a factory's environmental efforts, such as energy use, water treatment, waste disposal, and air quality. In the United Kingdom, Ford's Bridgend Engine Plant just began operating the largest solar power installation at any manufacturing site in Europe. Over a 30-year period its solar panels were expected to reduce the amount of carbon dioxide emitted at the plant by more than 4,000 tons.

GLOBAL PRESENCE

While Ford was growing domestically, parallel growth was occurring as part of a foreign expansion pro-

The Ford Expedition, Mustang, and F-150 pick-up that are featured in the "Team Knight Rider" syndicated television show. (Photograph by Blake Little. Reuters/Archive Photos.)

METHOD ACTING FOR PICK-UP TRUCKS

As Batman would tell you, you can't fight crime unless you have a cool set of wheels. That's the concept behind the syndicated television show *Team Knight Rider,* which debuted in the fall of 1997. The stars of the show are Ford vehicles: a Ford Expedition (which goes by the name Dante), a Mustang (Domino), and a F-150 pick-up truck (Attack Beast). If you're wondering why the vehicles have names, it's because the vehicles are really the stars of the show, and all of the vehicles can talk.

The show is a spin-off of the 1980s television series *Knight Rider,* which ran for four seasons and starred David Hasselhoff and his talking car "KITT." Hasselhoff was soon off for the sunnier climes and the beach crowd of *Baywatch,* but the concept of talking vehicles had

caught hold of the public imagination. After all, when conventional law enforcement and national security agencies have failed, that's exactly when you need a talking car to hammer out justice. Thus far, episodes have included "The Blonde Woman," "Angels in Chains," and "Spy Girls."

Usually, manufacturers have to settle for what is called "product placement" when it comes to getting their cars, beer, or soda into films and television. The product is used as a prop and is incidental to the plot or story. Ford has scored a real hit with *Team Knight Rider,* in that their product isn't merely a part of the show, it is the show. The actors and even the stories are incidental to what is largely an advertisement for Ford products.

gram that began in 1904, a year after the company was formed. On August 17, 1904, Ford Motor Company of Canada was formed in the small town of Walkerville, Ontario. From this small beginning grew a large overseas organization of manufacturing plants, assembly plants, parts depots, and dealers. Ford is represented in

some 200 countries and territories around the world, and over 60,000 companies worldwide supply Ford with goods and services.

Markets Ford targeted during the late 1990s included Asia, where the company saw great long-term growth opportunities despite the area's economic turmoil. They aimed for 10 percent market share by 2007. Also as part of its Asian expansion, Ford began manufacturing the Ford Transit in Belarus, China, Malaysia, and Vietnam. The company was also expanding manufacturing opportunities and investing in areas like central and eastern Europe and South America. In Brazil, where Ford planned a new plant, the company's market share increased from 10.7 to 14.5 percent between 1996 and 1997.

EMPLOYMENT

Ford values diversity in its employees and states that "Our global workforce is a competitive strength." The company believes diversity in its workforce helps it better understand and serve customers. Once hired, the company strives to educate and develop its employees. The company's overall goal was for each employee to receive at least 40 hours of training each year.

SOURCES OF INFORMATION

Bibliography

Evanoff, Ted. "Ford to Exit Heavy Truck Business." *Knight-Ridder/Tribune Business News,* 20 February 1997.

"Ford Motor Company." *Hoovers Online,* 1997. Available at http://www.hoovers.com.

Ford Motor Company Annual Report 1997. Ford Motor Company, 1998.

Ford Motor Company Web Site, 30 June 1998. Available at http://www.ford.com.

"Improving Automotive Operations Drive Ford to Record First Quarter Earnings of $1.7 Billion, Up 15%." Ford Motor Company Press Release, 16 April 1998.

International Directory of Company Histories. Vol. 11. Detroit, MI: St. James Press, 1995.

Moody's Company Data Report. Moody's Investor Service, 1996.

Taylor, Alex. "The Gentlemen at Ford Are Kicking Butt." *Fortune,* 22 June 1998.

For an annual report:
on the Internet at: http://www.ford.com/finaninvest/stockholder/stock97/index.htm **or** write: Ford Motor Company, Shareholder Relations, The American Road, PO Box 1899, Dearborn, MI 48121-1899

For additional industry research:
Investigate companies by their Standard Industrial Classification Codes, also known as SICs. Ford's primary SICs are:

3711 Motor Vehicles and Car Bodies

3714 Motor Vehicle Parts and Accessories

6035 Savings Institutions Federal Chartered

6141 Personal Credit Institutions

6159 Miscellaneous Business Credit Institutions

6331 Fire, Marine and Casualty Insurance

7515 Passenger Car Leasing

Fox Broadcasting Co.

FOUNDED: 1986

Contact Information:

HEADQUARTERS: 1211 Avenue of the Americas
   New York, NY 10036
PHONE: (212)556-2400
URL: http://www.foxworld.com

OVERVIEW

In 1986 Keith Rupert Murdoch launched Fox Broadcasting Company, the first new television network in the United States since 1948. Within a decade, what started as an apparently risky broadcasting endeavor became a network capable of reaching almost 96 percent of U.S. homes through 20 stations and more than 176 affiliates. By 1996, Fox was the top-ranked television group in the United States, with 34.8 percent of market coverage. And the collection of U.S. broadcasting networks that used to be called "The Big Three" came to be known as "The Big Four": ABC, CBS, NBC, and Fox. During the "sweeps" of early 1998, for the first time ever, Fox Broadcasting rose from its fourth place position capturing 12.2 million prime time viewers dislodging ABC from its third place spot with 11.7 million viewers.

COMPANY FINANCES

Financial information about a company like Fox Broadcasting—a subsidiary of a subsidiary (Fox Inc.) of a giant corporation (News Corporation Limited)—is very difficult to obtain. Consider that News Corp. is one of the largest media empires in the world and along with owning Fox Broadcasting Company, it owns newspapers (the *New York Post,* four major British newspapers, dozens of Australian newspapers) *TV Guide,* a movie company (Twentieth Century Fox), a book publisher (HarperCollins), a 40-percent stake in a U.K. satellite pay-TV service (British Sky Broadcasting), a majority interest in STAR television, an Asian satellite TV network, an airline, the Los Angeles Dodgers, and a sheep farm. It's not surprising that details of Fox Broadcasting's financial costs and contributions are largely buried or entirely obscured in the enormous network of numbers and facts that make up News Corporation's financial statements.

Nonetheless, a couple of vague details are available. In 1996, News Corp.'s revenues from television totalled $3.35 billion; in 1997, this number grew to $3.70 billion. Operating income from television was $549 million in 1996 and $573 million the following year. From 1996 to 1997, News Corporation's identifiable assets in television grew tremendously, from $7.10 billion to $13.46 billion. Exactly what portion was contributed by Fox Broadcasting cannot be ascertained from the report or from the company itself.

ANALYSTS' OPINIONS

When Fox Broadcasting began delivering programming in 1986, many were skeptical about its chances of success. Brandon Tartikoff, president of NBC Entertainment, called Fox the "coat-hanger network," referring to the fairly weak UHF TV stations Fox had collected. ABC programming master Fred Silverman referred to Fox as "The Mickey Mouse network," and added that "Fox will fail."

Famously, Fox didn't fail—by 1998, for the first time, Fox bumped one of "The Big Three," ABC, for the spot of third-ranked network in the sweeps of early 1998. Sweeps are considered important for broadcasters because networks use ratings to determine advertising charges. But some, like Christopher Dixon, analyst at Paine Webber, think that network broadcasters are fighting the wrong battle. "Whether or not these broadcasters are number one or number three is a little like shuffling deck chairs on the Titanic," Dixon said. Then he added, "To me, the most interesting thing is the shift between broadcast networks as a whole and the cable industry."

HISTORY

Soon after buying the 20th Century Fox film studio in 1985 and six U.S. [Metromedia] television stations in 1986, Rupert Murdoch announced his decision to launch the Fox Broadcasting Company. In a landscape dominated by broadcast giants CBS, NBC, and ABC, Murdoch wanted Fox to become truly competitive, the country's fourth broadcast television network. Many, including the other three networks, were skeptical about Fox's chances of succeeding. Some, like then-ABC Entertainment president Brandon Stoddard, felt the television market was already too saturated for another network. "There probably is a two-network economy as it stands, so I don't know if [a fourth network] can be economically feasible," Stoddard said at the time.

FAST FACTS:
About Fox Broadcasting Co.

Ownership: Fox Broadcasting Co. is a subsidiary of Fox Inc., which is a subsidiary of News Corporation Limited, a publicly owned multinational corporation traded on the New York Stock Exchange.

Ticker symbol: Fox Broadcasting's ultimate parent's ticker is NWS.

Officers: K. Rupert Murdoch, Chmn. & CEO News Corporation Ltd., 67; Chase Carey, COO & Exec. VP Fox Inc., 44; David Hill, Pres. & CEO Fox Broadcasting

Employees: more than 500

Principal Subsidiary Companies: Fox Broadcasting's subsidiaries include Los Angeles-based FNM Films Inc.

Chief Competitors: Fox Broadcasting Co. has as its main competitors the three other major television networks: National Broadcasting Company, Inc. (NBC), the top-ranked television network in the late 1990s, owned by industrial giant General Electric Company; CBS Corporation, formerly Westinghouse Electric, the second-ranked network toward the end of the twentieth century; and Capital Cities/ABC, Inc., subsidiary of entertainment and media behemoth Walt Disney Corporation.

On October 9, 1986, Fox broadcasted its first program, the premiere of *The Late Show With Joan Rivers* with guests Elton John, Cher, Pee Wee Herman, and David Lee Roth. By mid-1987, Joan Rivers left the show, which was then hosted by several guest hosts before being hosted by Arsenio Hall. Then Fox abandoned the late night slot to begin concentrating on prime time programming. In early April 1987, Fox offered its first full night of prime time shows that included an outrageous (and, to many, also hilarious) dysfunctional family, the Bundy's, in a show Fox called *Married . . . With Children*. The show became a subject of controversy when a Michigan woman campaigned to have it removed from the air; the free publicity helped bring the show national attention. By July of 1987, Fox added a second full night of prime-time shows.

More controversial than other networks, Fox attracted an audience and a collection of popular shows,

CHRONOLOGY:

Key Dates for Fox Broadcasting Co.

1985: Rupert Murdoch purchases the 20th Century Fox film studio and announces his plans for a television network

1986: Fox broadcasts its first program, *The Late Show With Joan Rivers*

1987: Fox offers its first full night of prime time shows

1990: The Academy of Television Arts & Sciences gives Fox a three-year contract to broadcast the Emmy Awards; The Simpsons debuts

1993: Fox is offering a full weeks worth of prime time programming

1994: Murdoch purchases New World Communications Group Inc. and switches most of the company's stations from CBS to Fox

1996: Fox Television Station Group becomes the single largest group of television stations in the United States

including *21 Jump Street, The Tracey Ullman Show, America's Most Wanted,* and, in 1990, *The Simpsons.* In 1990, the Academy of Television Arts & Sciences voted to give Fox a three-year contract to broadcast the Emmy Awards, breaking with the show's traditional rotation between the three networks. In an effort to expand its share of the youth market, Fox launched the Fox Children's Network in 1990. The partnership with affiliate stations provided younger viewers with both animated and live-action programming. By 1997, the renamed Fox Kids Network enjoyed its fourth year as the top-rated children's program on broadcast television.

By June of 1993 Fox was offering an entire week's worth of prime-time programming. In May of the following year, the network took a serious step toward achieving a significant presence in major cities throughout the United States: the network bought a minority stake in New World Communications Group Inc. and then switched most of the company's stations from CBS to Fox, unquestionably the largest affiliation switch in the history of television broadcasting. As a result, in many of the areas in which Fox had been broadcasting on a UHF signal, the network could now transmit on a stronger VHF platform, providing a better channel posi-

tion and the ability to reach a larger audience. Two years later, in July of 1996, Rupert Murdoch acquired the remaining 80 percent of New World Communications Group Inc. for $2.5 billion. With 22 owned-and-operated television stations, the Fox Television Station Group became the single largest group of television stations in the United States, reaching 10 of the 11 largest markets—at least 35 percent of the nation's television audience.

STRATEGY

From its early days, Fox showed it would not be like the other networks. When it launched its first night of prime time television on April 5, 1987, Fox did not offer traditional family television. Instead, its first night of prime time programming marked the debut of *Married . . . With Children* and *The Tracey Ullman Show.* Instead of representing a conventional, wholesome household, *Married . . . With Children* introduced viewers to an uncouth, dysfunctional family called the Bundys. The show would go on to win several Emmy Awards and would become the longest-running situation comedy on American television. That same night, *The Tracey Ullman Show* debuted, introducing the brash young comedienne and an animated segment called "The Simpsons." With its teen cop series *21 Jump Street,* the network demonstrated it wasn't afraid to take on serious life issues such as drugs, prostitution, and child abuse, and it perhaps gained some respect for the public service spots that ended most of its *21 Jump Street* shows. This aggressive approach to television programming paid off. By mid-1987, 113 affiliates joined the network and Fox attracted some major advertisers like Bristol-Myers, General Foods, and Johnson & Johnson.

In 1990, the network expanded its blunt, irreverent take on American home life with its debut of *The Simpsons.* Spun off from *The Tracey Ullman Show, The Simpsons* became the first Fox show to beat out its competition on the other networks. In the fall of 1990, Fox moved its animated sitcom to a Thursday night slot to take on NBC's top-rated comedy, *The Cosby Show.* While *The Simpsons* didn't beat out *The Cosby Show* in ratings, it did hurt NBC's ratings and helped establish Fox's image as a major force—especially with the youth market. Fox has become a main vehicle for advertisers wishing to reach the 18 to 34 age group. Many of its shows are youth-targeted or youth-oriented like *The Simpsons, Beverly Hills 90210, The X-Files, Mad-TV,* and *Melrose Place.*

INFLUENCES

Since the early 1980s when only about 25 percent of U.S. homes subscribed to cable services, the cable tele-

AY, CARAMBA!

He's an underachiever and "proud of it," as he (and thousands of T-shirts) will tell you. He gets himself into a lot of trouble and is a perpetual prankster. Once he filled the school groundkeeper's shack with creamed corn to get back at him for taking his skateboard. Another time he cut off the head of the statue of the town founder. You can often find this little good-for-nothing after school writing one of several admonishments on the blackboard: I will not belch the national anthem; I will not call my teacher "hot cakes;" the principal's toupee is not a Frisbee; spitwads are not free speech; I will not bury the new kid. Prank phone calls to the local watering hole are one of his bad habits—"Is Oliver there? Oliver Clothesoff?" If you make an issue of his less-than-perfect behavior, he'll tell you to "don't have a cow, man!" or perhaps "Eat my shorts!" His father, a rather slow-witted chap, is often driven to choking the boy because of his misbehavior. This 1990's Dennis the Menace was once tried for killing his principal and once made the unfortunate miscalculation of selling his soul for $5.

Lisa, the little brat's sister and the brain of the family (but then, considering the family, that's not saying much), believes she has an explanation for her brother's delinquent deeds: "That little hell-raiser is the spawn of every shrieking commercial, every brain-rotting soda pop, every teacher who cares less about young minds

than about cashing their big, fat paychecks." But, as *Time* magazine points out, "the kid knows right from wrong; he just likes wrong better."

Despite of all his misdeeds and bratty behavior (or maybe because of it) *TV Guide* named him one of the top 50 greatest TV stars of all time, and *Time* named him one of the twentieth-century's most influential artists and entertainers—putting him next to Picasso, T.S. Eliot, James Joyce, Frank Sinatra, and the Beatles.

By this time you've probably figured out that the above-mentioned scalawag is none other than Bart Simpson, the impish star of Fox's hit animated series of the 1990s, the *Simpsons,* a cartoon tale about a dysfunctional family living in a dysfunctional town in a dysfunctional universe. Bart became the cultural icon of 1990s—he was the role model of slackers everywhere ("I will not fake my way through life" he was once forced to write on the blackboard). He was also a big boost to Fox, helping propel it to full-fledged network status. The *Simpsons* became the longest running prime time cartoon in history and also won several Emmy's. Eventually it became no longer cool to shout "Cowabunga, man!" or "Ay, caramba!", and Bart's popularity gave way to the likes of Beavis and Butthead and the foul-mouthed tykes of *South Park,* but one suspects that the little yellow rascal from Springfield will outlast them all.

---

vision industry experienced incredible growth. By the late 1980s, the percentage of U.S. homes with cable services more than doubled. By 1997, cable reached 70 percent, or about 65 million U.S. homes. To compete with the expanding reach of cable television, some think network broadcasters need to increase sports coverage, particularly of high profile events like National Football League events and the Olympics. Indeed, when CBS covered the Nagano Winter Olympics in 1998, it dominated the Nielsen Media Research ratings. For Fox, an increase in major sports broadcasting came in 1993, when, to the shock of the industry, it succeeded in luring the National Football League from CBS. For almost $1.6 billion, the network bought four years' worth of broadcast rights. The following year Fox Sports signed a five-year contract with the National Hockey League, and in 1996 it began a five-year deal with Major League Baseball.

Fox also began making inroads into cable when, in October 1996, the Fox News Channel began cable broadcasting with its News Channel. Unfortunately for the company, their earlier distribution plans with Time

Warner Inc. fell through a month earlier—the media monolith backed out of plans for Fox distribution on its New York City cable services. Time Warner was then in the process of merging with Turner Broadcasting, whose Cable News Network (CNN) was a direct competitor to Fox News. CNN was to be carried on Time Warner's cable along with the new 24-hour news station, MSNBC. This meant a loss of more than 1 million homes for Fox. Fox quickly filed a federal anti-trust lawsuit against Time Warner, requesting the court block the merger of Time Warner and Turner Broadcasting and award Fox $1 billion in damages. In spite of the unexpected reduction in distribution, that year Fox News Channel was ranked twelfth among the top cable channels.

CURRENT TRENDS

In September 1997, Fox Broadcasting and Miller Brewing Company reached an unusual agreement. Each week during an NFL game's two-minute-warning, Fox will broadcast an "NFL/Miller Lite vignette," which will take a behind-the-scenes look at unusual NFL fans. Miller Brewing's vice president in charge of marketing, Jack Roony, explained that "[t]hese vignettes will be a celebration of the super fan, the die-hard 'take-your-shirt-off, paint-your- face' fanatic." Moreover, throughout the season Miller will air weekly features on Fox at prime-time. The multi-year agreement specifies that Miller, in conjunction with Fox, will create the weekly features incorporating the "Miller Time" theme while promoting Fox's upcoming programming. Fox has given Miller exclusive beer advertising for all Major League Baseball games broadcasted by Fox, including the 1998 and 2000 World Series games and the 1999 American League Championship series.

PRODUCTS

In addition to news, sports, and children's programming, Fox offers some of the most successful shows on television. Fox's 1997 lineup included tremendously popular shows like *Ally McBeal* and *The X-Files.* Other top-rated prime time Fox programs have included *America's Most Wanted, COPS, Beverly Hills 90210,* and *Melrose Place.* Some of Fox's more controversial programs include specials like "When Stunts Go Bad" and "Breaking the Magician's Code: Magic's Biggest Secrets Revealed." When Fox planned to air its third show revealing magicians' secrets on May 5, 1998, a coalition of over 1,000 magicians from the Society of American Magicians, the International Brotherhood of Magicians, and elsewhere, filed legal action, urged a viewer boycott, and organized free magic shows at public venues around the country at the time of the broadcast. The coalition denounced the program's host, who was dubbed "the Masked Magician," because he wears a costume concealing his face while he exposes secrets behind magic tricks. According to the magicians, the Fox specials threaten the careers of some magicians—since the specials started airing in November 1997, some magicians have lost jobs and some have had to give up elaborate illusions that cost them a tremendous amount of time and money to learn. Magician Andre Cole went to court in Los Angeles in late April 1998 to try to obtain a temporary restraining order to keep Fox from exposing the secret behind his patented "Table of Death" illusion. Cole's request was denied. Veteran magician Chuck Jones said,

"This has not affected me personally. But I worry about the amateur magicians who spend $1,000 or so on one prop, and then it's exposed on these specials. Now they can't use it anymore."

SOURCES OF INFORMATION

Bibliography

Braxton, Greg. "Magicians Wish Fox Special Would Vanish." *Los Angeles Times,* 1 May 1998.

Business Rankings Annual. Detroit, MI: Gale Research, 1998.

Fox Broadcasting Home Page. 1 June 1998. Available at http://www.foxworld.com.

"Fox Sweeps ABC Aside." *CNNfn,* 6 March 1998.

Fox Tenth Anniversary: A Decade of Revolutionizing Television. New York: Fox Broadcasting Co., 31 March 1997. Available at http://www.foxworld.com/presroom.htm#tenth.

Frank, Allan Dodds. "TV Titans Square Off." *CNNfn,* 9 October 1996. Available at http://www.cnnfn.com.

Lazich, Robert S., ed. *Market Share Reporter- 1998,* Detroit, MI: Gale Research, 1997.

"Miller Brewing Teams With Fox in Groundbreaking Agreement." *Business Wire,* 28 August 1997.

"The News Corporation Limited." *Hoover's Online.* 1 June 1998. Available at http://www.hoovers.com.

Paeth, Greg. "Fox in the Penthouse After 10 Years, the 'Coat-Hanger Network' Is Sitting Pretty." *Rocky Mountain News,* 5 April 1997.

Schwartz, Shelly. "ABC Shelves Ellen." *CNNfn,* 24 April 1998.

"S&P Description: New Corp. Inc." *Standard & Poor's,* 7 April 1998.

Wian, Casey. "Murdoch Enters New World." *CNNfn,* 17 July 1996.

For an annual report:
on the Internet at: http://www.newscorp.com

For additional industry research:
Investigate companies by their Standard Industrial Classification Codes, also known as SICs. Fox Broadcasting's primary SIC is:

4833 Television Broadcasting

Frigidaire Home Products

OVERVIEW

White Consolidated Industries (WCI), a subsidiary of Sweden's AB Electrolux, is a holding company for the group's North American operations. The Electrolux Group owns approximately 530 companies in more than 60 countries. The company is the world's largest producer of large appliances (refrigerators, washing machines, and freezers). There were 105,950 Electrolux employees worldwide in 1997 engaged in the manufacturing and sales of more than 55 million household appliances.

Frigidaire Home Products company was established on January 1, 1997 by uniting three sister companies in the WCI/AB Electrolux family: American Yard Products, Frigidaire, and Poulan/Weed Eater and Frigidaire. Combined they are one of the leading North American manufacturers of gas, electric, and battery powered handheld outdoor power equipment, lawn mowers, and lawn and garden tractors. They are also a significant producer of major appliances for the home including refrigerators, freezers, ranges, dishwashers, washers, dryers, room air conditioners, and dehumidifiers. The company has sales and administrative offices in Augusta, Georgia; Mississauga, Ontario; and Shreveport, Louisiana.

Frigidaire Home Products' brand names are some of the best known and respected in the nation including Frigidaire, Tappan, White-Westinghouse, Gibson, and Kelvinator in major appliances. Many of their products proudly bear the Sears Craftsman and Kenmore labels. They also manufacture products for other leading retailers like Lowes, Home Depot, Wal-Mart, and Kmart. The merger of the three companies allowed them to draw on the strengths of each organization and to create new and more efficient ways to serve their customers. It also en-

FOUNDED: 1916

Contact Information:
HEADQUARTERS: 250 Bobby Jones Expy.
  Augusta, GA 30907
PHONE: (706)651-1751
FAX: (706)860-2274
URL: http://www.frigidaire.com

A modern, ergonomic kitchen complete with stainless steel Frigidaire appliances. (Courtesy of White Consolidated Industries.)

ables the company to fully utilize its seven manufacturing plants in the United States and two in Canada to produce products in both indoor and outdoor categories rather than segmenting them into specific ones.

COMPANY FINANCES

Although revenues for the Electrolux Group rose steadily through the 1990s, the company's profits were less satisfactory, prompting the launch of a restructuring program aimed at achieving its goal of an operating margin of 6.5 to 7.0 percent and an aftertax return on equity of 15.0 percent. Sales for the group as a whole reached nearly $16.0 billion in 1996, but fell back to $14.3 billion for 1997.

ANALYSTS' OPINIONS

Frigidaire's Professional Series range and Pure-Source refrigerator ice and waterfilter won the prestigious "Good Housekeeping" magazine "Good Buy" award in 1996 and 1997, respectively. The Precision Wash dishwasher received "Today's Homeowner's" Best new product award in 1996 and 1997 and "Kitchen and Bath Business" recognized the PureSource filter and Warm and Serve range warming drawer with its "Product Innovator" awards.

The company's outdoor products units, freezer factory, and room air conditioner factory have been consistently recognized by Sears as recipients of Partners in Progress awards. Also, the Weed Eater VIP Robotic Solar Mower was the world's first automated, emission free, solar power, lawn maintenance system. Poulan/Weed Eater was global runner-up for the Electrolux Engineering Excellence award for development of the Featherlite gas trimmer, which is 30-percent lighter than standard gas trimmers and the quietest on the market.

In 1996 Frigidaire received the Incentive Manufacturers Representatives Association Gold Key award for outstanding marketing incentive programs, which generated greater than anticipated sales increases and dealer participation.

HISTORY

Frigidaire commemorated its 80th anniversary in 1996, although some of its many companies, which have since consolidated, trace their origins to the 1870s. Frigidaire has its roots in the Guardian Frigerator Co. formed in 1916 to manufacture the first household electric refrigerator, invented by Alfred Mellowes in Fort Wayne, Indiana. General Motors purchased the company in 1919, giving it the capital to grow. In 1921 General Motors moved the company to Dayton, Ohio, as a subsidiary of its Delco-Light unit and later as Frigidaire Division. WCI acquired Frigidaire in 1979 and it became part of AB Electrolux in 1986 with the latter's purchase of WCI. Electrolux invested millions of dollars to upgrade Frigidaire's manufacturing facilities, as well as to revitalize its design group. The Hillard design center was built in 1989 and Electrolux changed the White Consolidated Industries name to Frigidaire in 1991.

STRATEGY

Frigidaire's momentum began in 1995 when the company introduced the Frigidaire Gallery Professional Series, which brought to consumers the popular commercial look of stainless steel appliances at affordable prices. It also earned Frigidaire the Incentive Manufacturers Representatives Association Gold Key award in 1996 for its successful marketing strategy. In 1998 the Gallery Professional Series accounted for approximately 20 percent of total sales under the Frigidaire brand.

Frigidaire has shifted to overseas suppliers of steel and aluminum parts. The reason for the change was the size and scope of the European operations of its parent company, AB Electrolux, and the potential for high-volume discounts on parts purchased internationally.

The company increased its advertising and promotional budget in 1995 to support the introduction of its new Frigidaire Gallery and Gallery Professional introductions, sustaining the increased spending level through 1996. The multimedia program included broadcast and print advertising, in-store materials, theme campaigns, consumer rebates, and special offers.

Frigidaire's plans for the future reflect Electrolux's focus on developing products that are increasingly environmentally friendly, economical, and innovative. The company's latest dishwashers, for example, feature lower water consumption and noise levels than comparable American products.

INFLUENCES

For many years, Electrolux's different operations functioned more or less independently with no coordination among the different factories. To remedy this and facilitate the exchange of ideas and design information between Europe and North America, Electrolux began using CATIA three-dimensional design software developed by Dassault Systemes of France. CATIA provides a joint platform for Electrolux and Frigidaire to use in creating new products since designers in the United States and Europe are in daily contact via the Internet. Electrolux also operates a design center in Pordenone, Italy.

A Weed Eater riding lawn mower manufactured by Frigidaire/White Consolidated Industries. (Courtesy of White Consolidated Industries.)

In 1996 Frigidaire continued its innovative business practices by introducing a number of appliance "firsts" to consumers nationwide. These included a new line of dishwashers, refrigerators with the Frigidaire PureSource built-in ice and water filter, ranges with a convenient Warm & Serve Drawer, and the water- and energy-saving Frigidaire Gallery Tumble-Action Washer, a front-loading machine, which produces a gentler and more thorough wash. Frigidaire gambled that North Americans would abandon their preference for the less efficient, but more affordable, top-loaders. The new front-loader uses 40-percent less water than a typical top-loader, saving about $90 a year in energy costs. "We don't expect it to take over the market overnight, but we do know it is a better machine," said Bob Russell, Frigidaire's vice-president of marketing. Added Russell, "It gets fabrics cleaner, your clothes last longer, and it's much more economical and environmentally friendly."

Indeed, innovative new products are a key component of Frigidaire's strategy in the highly competitive "white goods" market. Even under the best market conditions, competition is stiff, and high internal efficiency and continuous product improvements are required to achieve good profitability.

FAST FACTS:

About Frigidaire Home Products

Ownership: Frigidaire Home Products is division of AB Electrolux, a publicly owned company traded on the New York Stock Exchange and the Stockhom Stock Exchange.

Ticker symbol: ELUXY

Officers: Robert E. Cook, Pres. & CEO; Wayne Schierbaum, VP, Finance

Employees: 15,000 in the United States

Principal Subsidiary Companies: AB Electrolux

Chief Competitors: Frigidaire Home Products is the fourth largest producer of household appliances in the United States. Its main competitors include: Whirlpool; General Electric Appliances; Maytag; Amana; Viking Range; Siemens, and Targa Energy.

CURRENT TRENDS

Consumers assume that appliances have changed in the past 20 years, but most significant improvements occurred only in the 1990s. According to Russell, vice president of marketing at Frigidaire, "Energy and water saving are a growing concern for Americans. We're the first U.S. appliance manufacturer to introduce a full-size horizontal-axis washing machine that washes more gently without an agitator, while using 40-percent less water."

The success of Gallery and Gallery Professional showed that there was a gap in the market. Therefore, Frigidaire's parent company is prepared to invest heavily from now on in product development. In the last few years, it has concentrated on building new, efficient plants in western Europe and the United States, spending about $800 million a year on capital investment. While in the last 3 or 4 years about 75 percent of that investment was on new industrial structures, more than 85 percent will go into new product development in the future.

The trend in white goods manufacturing is towards larger companies with increasingly more global operations. Cost efficiencies obtainable by large producers through international coordination of product development, product platforms, and purchasing were expected to put smaller and local companies under even more severe competitive pressure. In response, Electrolux im-

plemented an acquisition strategy in order to build leadership in the global market and obtain sufficient volumes in its core areas. The company also focused on streamlining its operations to concentrate its resources and better utilize its competitive advantages. Electrolux faced challenges from declining demand in Europe, competition from Whirlpool in the United States, and an inefficient structure.

PRODUCTS

Frigidaire's major appliance product range includes refrigerators, food freezers, ranges, wall ovens, cooktops, washers, clothes dryers, laundry centers, dishwashers, microwave ovens, room air conditioners, and dehumidifiers. Their outdoor product range includes lawn and garden tractors, garden tillers, lawn mowers, chain saws, lawn trimmers, and power blowers.

Feature enhancements and new product introductions in 1997 included the Warm & Serve Zone on select models of the Frigidaire Gallery and Gallery Professional Series electric ranges. Another new product enhancement in early 1997 was the introduction of the remaining four dishwasher models in the Gallery Series.

CORPORATE CITIZENSHIP

Electrolux, Frigidaire's parent company, earned an award as the most environmentally minded company in Sweden in 1993. The company produces a separate environmental annual report in addition to its standard annual report. In response to consumers' concerns about clean, odor-free water, the company introduced the PureSource Filter, which removes lead, chlorine, and other impurities. Statistics revealing that the $3 billion bottled-water industry is growing at 20 percent annually point to significant market potential.

Electrolux is prepared to meet the requirements in the area of energy consumption. It initiated a ban on ozone-depleting CFC (chlorofluorocarbons) and HCFC (hydrochlorofluorocarbons) in its products in 1996, and introduced the first CFC-free products in 1997. In 1995, while focusing on production with low environmental impact, the Group started a certified environmental system recommended under ISO 14001 quality standards in all production units. By the end of 1997, 24 plants had been certified in Europe, with introduction of the program in North America expected within a few years. The Group hopes to have the system fully implemented by year 2000.

Frigidaire recently completed a $750,000 project to reduce energy consumption at its Edison, New Jersey, manufacturing facility by 4.3 million kilowatt hours annually. The company intends to continue this practice by addressing energy management opportunities within its facilities.

GLOBAL PRESENCE

Europe accounted for just over half, or 54.4 percent, of overall Electrolux sales in 1998. North America was the next largest market, at 31.6 percent. Latin America accounted for 7.1 percent; Asia, 4.8 percent; Africa and Oceania, 2.1 percent.

The two-year restructuring program inaugurated by Electrolux in 1997 will entail staff cutbacks worldwide of about 12,000, or 11 percent, along with the shutdown of some 25 plants and 50 warehouses. That is out of a total of about 150 plants and 300 warehouses.

EMPLOYMENT

Frigidaire's holding company, White Consolidated Industries, received the "Best of Show" award in the personalized correspondence category of the 1996 Business Insurance Employee Benefits Communication awards competition. WCI employee benefits spending was $177 million in 1995. The company also sponsored a two-day seminar for workers on maintaining high safety levels within the workplace.

Electrolux established the Electrolux University in 1995. The areas of training include leadership, administration, project management, and quality control. The company is taking the initiative to decentralize its structure through a network of regionally based development centers within the Group. With recruitment of managers a major concern for the company, it is seeking students from universities and institutes, and it also hoped to increase employee movement between countries.

SOURCES OF INFORMATION

Bibliography

Beatty, Gerry. "Stretching a Name; Electrolux Dubs Home Unit Frigidaire." *HFN The Weekly Newspaper for the Home Furnishing Network,* 3 February 1997. Available at http://sweb3.med. iacnet.com.

Carter, Ron. "Frigidaire Soon Will Close Doors on Dublin [Ohio] Operations." *Columbus Dispatch,* 1 April 1998. Available at http://wsj.com.

Ceniceros, Roberto. "Appliance Maker's Statement Solid." *Business Insurance,* 28 October 1996. Available at http://sbweb2. med.iacnet.com.

Elkin, Tobi. "Product Pampering: Appliance Makers May Be About to Reap the Payoff From a New-Product Revolution That Is Yielding New Features That Consumers Actually Want." *Brandweek,* 16 June 1997. Available at http://sbweb2.med.iacnet. com.

Fallon, James. "Electrolux: Merger Is First Step." *HFN The Weekly Newspaper for the Home Furnishing Network,* 30 December 1996. Available at http://sweb2.med.iacnet.com.

Fallon, James. "Frigidaire Soars But Fails to Lift Division." *HFN The Weekly Newspaper for the Home Furnishing Network,* 5 May 1997. Available at http://sweb2.med.iacnet.com.

"Frigidaire Company Receives Gold Key Award." Frigidaire Company News Release, 22 April, 1996. Available at http://www.frigidaire.com/NEWS/7news16.html.

"Frigidaire Home Products." 2 August 1998. Available at http:// www.frigidaire.com.

"Leading Consumer & Trade Publications Applaud Frigidaire Product Innovations." 2 November 1997. Available at http:// www.frigidaire.com/applaud.html.

Nelson, Kessel L. "Frigidaire Project Cuts Elec. Use by 4.3 Million kwh." *Energy User News,* April 1997. Available at http:// sbweb3.med.iacnet.com.

"US Set to Wwitch to European-style Washers." *Financial Post Daily,* 1 October 1996.

"WCI Holds Worker's Compensation/health and Safety Seminar." *Appliance Manufacturer,* August 1996. Available at http://sbweb2.med.iacnet.com/infotrac/session.

For an annual report:

on the Internet at: http://www.electrolux.se/corporate/group/business.html **or** call Investor Relations in Stockholm at: int + 46 8 738 60 03 **or** fax: int +46 8 656 60 90

For additional industry research:

Investigate companies by their Standard Industrial Classification Codes, also known as SICs. Frigidaire's primary SICs are:

3524 Lawn & Garden Equipment

3631 Household Cooking Equipment

3632 Household Refrigerators & Freezers

3633 Household Laundry Equipment

3634 Electric Housewares & Fans

Frito-Lay, Inc.

FOUNDED: 1932

Contact Information:
HEADQUARTERS: 7701 Legacy Dr.
   Plano, TX 75024
PHONE: (972)334-7000
FAX: (972)334-2019
URL: http://www.fritolay.com

OVERVIEW

As the maker of Lay's, the leading potato chip brand (which in 1996 accounted for almost 21 percent of the potato chip market) and of 5 of the 6 leading tortilla chip brands—Doritos, Tostitos, Baked Tostitos, Santitas, and Doritos Thins (which together accounted for over 76 percent of the tortilla chip market 1996)—Frito-Lay is indeed king of the U.S. snack food industry. According to *U.S. News & World Report* in 1996, 94 percent of all households in the United States contain a product made by Frito-Lay. The company's 40 manufacturing plants together produce about 30,000 snack packages every minute and about 40 million bags of potato chips weekly. Frito-Lay's sales account for about 50 percent of parent PepsiCo's total sales annually.

COMPANY FINANCES

In the early 1990s Frito-Lay was losing market share. By 1991, Frito-Lay's profit was only $617 million and the company's share of the market had slid to 38 percent. But when Roger Enrico (now chairman and CEO of Frito-Lay's parent PepsiCo) was put in charge of Frito-Lay in 1991, he turned the company around. By 1995, Frito-Lay's net sales totalled $8.6 billion and the company had an operating profit of $1.43 billion. From the mid- to late 1990s, Frito-Lay continued to grow steadily—net sales reached $9.75 billion in 1996 and in 1997 about $10.37 billion. By 1997 Frito-Lay's net sales accounted for about half of PepsiCo's total net sales of about $20.92 billion. During that time, operating profit continued to increase as well, growing to about $1.61 billion in 1996 and almost $1.70 billion in 1997.

At the end of 1997, PepsiCo's price/earnings (P/E) ratio was 32.1 with estimated earnings per share of $1.15, up from $0.93 in 1996. In the first quarter of 1998, PepsiCo's profit rose 19 percent on increased Frito-Lay sales, but flagging beverage sales and a rise in potato prices lowered the company's share price at the end of April to $39.63 from $43.06. The higher potato price was expected to cut Frito-Lay's profit growth. Still, PepsiCo hoped Frito-Lay would carry the company's beverage division while PepsiCo focussed on updating its soft drinks so as to better compete with rival Coca-Cola Co. Frito-Lay seems to have the might to carry the beverage division; by the end of the 1990s, four of Frito-Lay's products—Lay's, Doritos, Ruffles, and Chee-tos—were each selling over $1 billion retail annually.

ANALYSTS' OPINIONS

Because Frito-Lay is so dominant in the salty-snack foods industry, with primarily only small, regionally-based competitors, like Chicago manufacturer Jay's and Granny Goose Foods, Inc. in California, some allege that Frito-Lay is guilty of anti-trust violations. Peter Sprecker, president of Kentucky-based food manufacturer Louisa's, says that Frito-Lay "is a company that makes Microsoft really look like a pussycat." Others allege that without competition, Frito-Lay will be able to raise prices with impunity. The company is already able to outbid competitors for shelf space (buying shelf space is a widely accepted practice in grocery retailing) and to undercut prices in regions where real competition exists. William Leach, who follows the food industry for investment firm Donaldson, Lufkin Jenrette, claims that Frito-Lay appears to be doing nothing unethical. "They've driven all their competitors out of business by being too successful," Leach says. "They're just better at product development, marketing and execution. But there is no law against doing well."

HISTORY

In 1932, in separate parts of the southern United States, Elmer Doolin and Herman W. Lay each started a snack food business with a loan of about $100. Doolin, who was living in San Antonio, Texas, was inspired by a lunch he had in a small cafe. After ordering a sandwich, Doolin happened to notice a $.05 package of corn chips on the counter and he ordered it. The chips were made from a corn dough that had been developed and used for centuries by Mexicans in the Southwest. Doolin was so impressed with the chips that he sought out the inventor and for $100, bought the recipe, a healthy number of retail accounts, and a hand-cranking potato ricer converted to make the product. Soon, Doolin set up production in his mother's kitchen, making about 10 pounds

FAST FACTS:
About Frito-Lay, Inc.

Ownership: Frito-Lay, Inc. is a subsidiary of PepsiCo, Inc., a publicly owned company traded on the New York Stock Exchange. PepsiCo, Inc. is also listed on the Amsterdam, Chicago, Swiss, and Tokyo Stock Exchanges.

Ticker symbol: PEP

Officers: Steven S. Reinemund, Chmn. & CEO, 49, $1,768,774; Brock H. Leach, Pres. & CEO Frito-Lay North America, 39; James H. O'Neal, Pres. & CEO Frito-Lay International, 60; William R. McLaughlin, Pres. Frito-Lay Europe, Middle East, & Africa Region, 49

Employees: 30,000 (1997)

Principal Subsidiary Companies: Frito-Lay's parent company is beverage and snack-food giant, PepsiCo. Frito-Lay operates approximately 40 manufacturing plants in 26 states and counts among its subsidiaries: Frito-Lay Inc. Council Bluffs; Frito-Lay Inc. North Div.; Frito-Lay of Hawaii Inc.; and Smartfoods Inc.

Chief Competitors: One of the largest snack food companies in the world, Frito-Lay produces potato chips, tortilla chips, pretzels, cookies, and Cracker Jack. The company's competitors include: Nabisco Biscuit; The Proctor & Gamble Company; The Cape Cod Potato Chip Company; Snyder's of Hanover, Inc.; Jay's Foods LLC; and Granny Goose Foods, Inc.

of Fritos (Spanish for "fried") Corn Chips per hour. He sold between $8 to $10 of product daily, with profits sometimes reaching as much as $2 per day. In 1933, Doolin moved the Frito Company to Dallas in order to take advantage of better distribution possibilities. There the business continued to grow, gaining new accounts, but Doolin was not yet able to pay himself a salary.

Meanwhile, in Nashville, Tennessee, in 1932, Herman Lay had begun distributing potato chips for manufacturers, hauling product in his Model A. By 1934, Lay had six routes and was becoming a primary distributor for an Atlanta potato chip manufacturer. Four years later, in 1938, this manufacturer began having difficulties. Lay collected funds from friends and business associates and was able to purchase the failing company, which he re-

CHRONOLOGY:

Key Dates for Frito-Lay, Inc.

1932: Elmer Doolin and Herman Lay founded separate companies that would later become Frito-Lay

1933: Doolin moves the Frito Company to Dallas

1938: Lay buys a failing potato chip manufacturer and renames it H.W. Lay & Company; introduces Lay's Potato Chips

1945: Frito Company grants Lay the right to produce and distribute Fritos

1948: Introduces Cheetos

1959: Elmer Doolin dies

1960: Frito Company and H.W. Lay & Company merge to form Frito-Lay, Inc.; acquires Rold Gold pretzels

1965: Merges with Pepsi-Cola Company to form PepsiCo, Inc.

1966: Introduces Doritos

1982: Anheuser-Busch begins manufacturing Eagle Snacks to compete with Frito-Lay

1989: Frito-Lay restructures into four regional business divisions—North, South, Central, and West

1991: Richard Enrico is assigned to Frito-Lay

1996: Anheuser Busch sells Eagle Snacks name to Proctor & Gamble and its factories to Frito-Lay

1997: Introduces Baked Lays; acquires Borden Foods, which owns Cracker Jack

named H.W. Lay & Company. That year, he introduced Lay's Potato Chips.

Through the late 1930s and the early 1940s both the Frito Company and H.W. Lay & Company grew, and by World War II H.W. Lay & Company, with its Lay's brand of potato chips, had become one of the largest snack food companies in the Southeast. Similarly, the Frito Company, with its Fritos Corn Chips, had grown into one of the largest Southwestern snack food companies. World War II slowed expansion for both companies until about 1945. It was then that the Frito Company granted H.W. Lay & Company one of the first franchises to make and distribute Fritos Corn Chips in the Southeast. By the 1950s, the Frito Company had become a leader in the snack food industry and Frito's Corn Chips were one of the most popular snack foods in the country. Elmer Doolin died in 1959; two years later, the Frito Company and H.W. Lay & Company merged to form Frito-Lay, Inc. That same year, the company acquired Rold Gold Pretzels, firmly establishing itself as a major force in the burgeoning snack food industry.

In 1965 soft drink giant Pepsi-Cola Company and Frito-Lay, Inc. merged to form beverage and snack food giant PepsiCo, Inc. The following year, Frito-Lay introduced Doritos brand tortilla chips and for the next decade and a half, Frito-Lay was the indisputable and largely unopposed leader of the salty-snack food market.

In 1982, in a direct challenge to Frito-Lay's stronghold on salty snack foods, Anheuser- Busch began manufacturing Eagle Snacks and so started a battle, which in the snack foods industry became known as "the Great Potato Chip War." By 1996, the war was over. Never having captured more than 10 percent of the market in almost 15 years, Anheuser-Busch admitted defeat and closed down its Eagle Snacks division. Frito-Lay had won. The following year, Frito-Lay introduced Baked Lays, which enjoyed an immediate success bringing the company an additional $250 million in sales. In late 1997, Frito-Lay announced its further expansion in the area of sweet snack foods with its acquisition from Borden Foods of the then 104-year old snack brand Cracker Jack. At the end of the 1990s, Frito-Lay still ruled the salty-snack foods market.

STRATEGY

In 1991 sales in almost every Frito-Lay category were falling, but because Frito-Lay kept hiking the prices of its products, the company's profits were stable. As John Greenwald rightly noted in his June 10, 1996 article in *Time* magazine, "Raising prices while losing share is a recipe for disaster in an era in which value is a driving force in consumer behavior." In the meantime, in the early 1990s, Anheuser-Busch's Eagle Snacks had begun to claim market share. More, results from Frito-Lay focus group surveys showed that people preferred Eagle Snack chips to Lay's, which they found "too greasy, too bland, and too boring."

In 1991 Roger Enrico, chairman and CEO of Frito-Lay's parent PepsiCo, was assigned to head Frito-Lay and he began a major restructuring, quickly cutting about half a billion dollars from operating expenses by laying off more than 1,000 workers. Then, with Enrico at the helm, Frito-Lay invested about $90 million in researching, redesigning, and repositioning its products, going so far as to assign geneticists the task of creating "the perfect potato," one that would be flavorful but low in sugar. Soon, Frito-Lay introduced new snacks, including a line of baked snacks, began improving existing products, and initiated a serious cost-cutting campaign.

Apparently, the strategy worked. By 1993, Frito-Lay had sales of $4.4 billion; by 1995, sales topped $8.0 billion. Frito-Lay increased its market share from 38 percent in the late 1980s to 55 percent by the mid-1990s. By 1996, Frito-Lay's main competitor Eagle Snacks was defunct and Anheuser-Busch then sold the Eagle Snacks name to Proctor & Gamble and 4 of the snack division's 5 factories to Frito-Lay. Before the end of 1996 Frito-Lay employed about 13,000 delivery workers equipped with hand-held computers capable of following buying trends daily.

INFLUENCES

By the mid-1990s, Frito-Lay so completely dominated the salty snack foods market that virtually all other competitors had dropped out—either by stopping manufacture of salty snack foods, like the Keebler Foods Company, or by closing down altogether. While monitoring Frito-Lay's purchase of Anheuser-Busch's Eagle Snacks factories in the mid-1990s, the U.S. Justice Department became interested in Frito-Lay and in the salty-snack food industry. Soon, the Justice Department began an investigation of anti-trust activity in the industry, focussing on Frito-Lay and on the practice of buying shelf space in supermarkets. This buying of shelf space, a common practice in grocery retailing, can be very lucrative for the retailer: manufacturers sometimes pay up to $100,000 for a foot of desirable shelf space. The Justice Department's investigation was also attempting to determine whether, in order to shut out competitors, Frito-Lay had been buying up more space than it needs. Toward the end of the 1990s, the investigation was still underway.

CURRENT TRENDS

In the 1990s, Frito-Lay's research revealed tremendous growth opportunities in the area of low-fat snacks: almost half of consumers taking part in the research (47 percent) admitted that they felt they should limit their fat intake, but felt they couldn't; another 53 percent claimed that they limited their salty-snack intake because of concerns about good nutrition. In response to these trends, Frito-Lay began introducing low-fat versions of its products, the most successful of which has been a line of low-fat potato crisps called Baked Lays, which are made from dried potato flakes instead of fresh potatoes.

While initial controversy surrounded the early use of Proctor & Gamble's fat-substitute olestra in food products (much was made about reports of gastric distress allegedly caused by the "fake fat") later studies, like one sponsored by Proctor & Gamble published in 1998 in the

BREAKING THE FRITOS CODE

If you have a good eye for detail, you might have noticed that certain Frito-Lay products have either a "K" inside a triangle or a "U" inside a circle somewhere on the package. Just what does this secret code mean? It's pretty simple. The "K" designation is used to identify products that are Kosher; that is, permissible for consumption under Jewish Dietary Laws. Rabbis Ralbag and Genack from New York certify Kosher products for Frito-Lay. "U" is a code assigned to products by the Union of Orthodox Jewish Congregations of America. Check for it on your next bag of Fritos.

Journal of the American Medical Association, concluded that consumers suffered no greater gastric distress after consuming potato chips made with olestra than they endured after eating traditional potato chips. But the study also found that consumers did not like the taste of chips made with olestra as much as that of "regular" potato chips. The chips used in the study were Frito-Lay's new WOW brand; as a result of the study, Frito-Lay decided to change its recipe.

PRODUCTS

Frito-Lay has more than 100 product lines. Some of its more well-known salty-snack food brands include: Chee-tos, Doritos, Fritos, Funyuns onion rings, Lays, Baked Lays, Ruffles, Smartfood popcorn, Sun Chips, Tostitos, and Baked Tostitos. Frito-Lay also makes GrandMa's cookies and Cracker Jack candy-coated popcorn. The company caused a big stir with its 1998 introduction of its WOW brand potato chips, made with Proctor & Gamble's controversial "fake fat" product, olestra, trademarked "Olean." Frito-Lay has also been developing a "three-dimensional tortilla chip," Doritos 3Ds.

GLOBAL PRESENCE

Worldwide, principal salty snack food markets include Brazil, Mexico, the Netherlands, South Africa, Spain, and the United Kingdom. While there is much room for Frito-Lay to expand in the international arena, the challenge for the company is to match flavor with culture. In Asia, where most consumers prefer steak- and cuttlefish-flavored snacks, Chee-tos are sold without cheese. And though potato chips are popular around the world, in Latin America, they don't sell well unless they are flavored with lime and chili. In 1997, Frito-Lay changed its snack food packaging worldwide to create a more uniform, and uniformly recognizable, look. That year, the company also acquired snack food operations in Argentina, Australia, Europe, and the United States.

SOURCES OF INFORMATION

Bibliography

1997 PepsiCo. Annual Report. Purchase, NY: PepsiCo, Inc., 1997.

Angrisani, Carol. "Frito-Lay's Olestra Chips Selling Well in Test Markets." *Supermarket News,* 22 July 1996.

"Anheuser-Busch Companies, Inc." *Hoover's Online.* May 1998. Available at http://www.hoovers.com.

Business Rankings Annual. Detroit, MI: Gale Research, 1998.

"Campbell Soup Company." *Hoover's Online,* May 1998. Available at http://www.hoovers.com.

"Cape Cod Chip's Founder Back in Charge Wages Shelf-by-Shelf War to Rebuild Sales." *St. Louis Post-Dispatch,* 23 February 1997.

"Frito-Lay Company." *Hoover's Online,* May 1998. Available at http://www.hoovers.com.

"Frito-Lay Company to Acquire Cracker Jack." *Business Week,* 7 October 1997.

"Granny Goose Foods, Inc." *Hoover's Online,* May 1998. Available at http://www.hoovers.com.

Greenwald, John. "Frito-Lay Under Snack Attack." *Time,* 10 June 1996.

Harrington, Jeff, Robert McNatt, and Larry Light, eds. "Proctor & Gamble's Chip Upgrade." *Business Week,* 16 March 1998.

"Higher Sales of Snacks Boost PepsiCo Profits but Stock Drops." *The Denver Post,* 29 April 1998.

"Justice Department Taking a Look at Frito-Lay." *All Things Considered (NPR),* 3 June 1996.

"Keebler Foods Company." *Hoover's Online,* May 1998. Available at http://www.hoovers.com.

Lazich, Robert S., ed. *Market Share Reporter-1998.* Detroit, MI: Gale Research, 1997.

McGraw, Dan. "Salting Away Big Profits: Frito-Lay Launches a Powerful Snack Attack and Crunches the Competition." *U.S. News & World Report,* 16 September 1996.

"Nabisco Holdings Corp." *Hoover's Online,* May 1998. Available at http://www.hoovers.com.

"PepsiCo, Inc." *Hoover's Online,* May 1998. Available at http://www.hoovers.com.

"The Proctor & Gamble Company." *Hoover's Online,* May 1998. Available at http://www.hoovers.com.

Schreiber, Paul. "Muffin Men." *Newsday,* 29 December 1997.

"The Story of Frito-Lay, Inc." *Frito-Lay Company Info.* May 1998. Available at http://www.fritolay.com.

Weinstein, Steve. "Frito-Lay Inquiry Spurs Debate." *Progressive Grocer,* July 1996.

For an annual report:
on the Internet at: http://www.pepsico.com **or** write: Investor Relations, PepsiCo, Inc., Purchase, NY 10577

For additional industry research:
Investigate companies by their Standard Industrial Classification Codes, also known as SICs. Frito-Lay's primary SICs are:

2052 Cookies & Crackers

2096 Potato Chips, Corn Chips & Snacks

Fruit of the Loom, Inc.

OVERVIEW

Fruit of the Loom is a vertically integrated international apparel company, one of the leading U.S. manufacturers of basic apparel and boys'-and-men's and girls'-and-women's underwear and the top supplier to the U.S. screen print T-shirt market. In 1996, Fruit of the Loom was the fourth largest U.S. apparel company and the fourth largest licensed apparel maker. That same year, it was the seventh most admired apparel company as ranked by *Fortune* magazine. With a total of 98 offices and manufacturing and warehouse facilities in over 50 locations worldwide, Fruit of the Loom makes products under brand names that include Fruit of the Loom, BVD, Gitano, Wilson, and Pro Player. In the 1990s mismanagement left the company in bad shape and investors were outraged. Fruit of the Loom's efforts to move manufacturing offshore were intended to improve the company's production efficiency and cost position, but increased foreign competition, intense price pressure, and mounting debt have left the company with profound operating challenges. Trying to salvage the company in early 1998 at least enough to prepare it for sale, Fruit of the Loom's chairman of the board and CEO, William F. Farley, proposed to move operations to the Cayman Islands.

FOUNDED: 1926

Contact Information:

HEADQUARTERS: 5000 Sears Tower, 233 S. Wacker Dr.
  Chicago, IL 60606
PHONE: (312)876-1724
FAX: (312)993-1749
TOLL FREE: (800)447-8761
URL: http://www.fruit.com

COMPANY FINANCES

Fruit of the Loom struggled through the second half of the 1990s, losing ground to fashion underwear brands like Calvin Klein and yielding its number one position to Sara Lee Corporation's Hanes. In 1995, Fruit of the

FINANCES:

Fruit of the Loom
Net Sales, 1994-1997
(billion dollars)

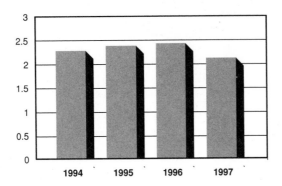

Fruit of the Loom
1997 Stock Prices
(dollars)

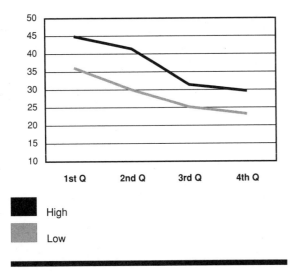

and a net income of negative $487 million. Fruit of the Loom's price-earnings (P/E) ratio was 41.7. At the end of 1997, Fruit of the Loom's total outstanding debt reached $1.2 billion, and the company announced that it was taking another after-tax charge, this time for $372 million, to help make the company more competitive. The sum would be used to help pay for Fruit of the Loom's worldwide restructuring efforts, including the closing and disposal of several domestic manufacturing and distribution facilities.

ANALYSTS' OPINIONS

In early 1998, Fruit of the Loom's chairman and CEO, William Farley, announced his plan to move Fruit of the Loom offshore to the Cayman Islands where foreign income is not subjected to corporate tax—Fruit of the Loom's tax rate would fall from 28 to 11 percent. Though presented as a plan to help the company come back from years of debt and failed attempts at restructuring, some held that Farley was largely interested in preparing Fruit of the Loom for sale. In May 1998, Credit Suisse First Boston analyst Dennis S. Rosenberg suggested that two years of solid performance and free cash flow of at least $300 million could indeed put Fruit of the Loom in a good position for a sale.

HISTORY

Polish immigrant Jacob Goldfarb began his clothing business in 1926 with the goal of producing low priced, quality undergarments—most notably, the popular one-piece men's underwear known as the "unionsuit." Appropriately, Goldfarb called his business The Union Underwear Company. Originally, Goldfarb operated without a factory, buying fabric from a supplier, delivering it to a cutter, then sending the cut pieces to a shop for sewing and finishing. In 1930 promoters from Frankfort, Kentucky, looking for a business to provide employment and money for their town during the Depression, offered to donate a plant for Goldfarb's Union Underwear Company, thereby uniting all the manufacturing operations in one location. By the end of the decade, Goldfarb purchased a 25-year license to use the Fruit of the Loom trademark, hoping the brand would help make his products nationally known. In 1952 Goldfarb opened a Union Underwear plant in Campbellsville, Kentucky, that stood in marked contrast to his earliest approach to manufacturing. This facility provided for on-site knitting and bleaching, in addition to cutting, sewing, and finishing, thereby providing even greater vertical control.

In 1955 a newly formed holding company called the Pacific & Reading Corporation, formerly the Philadel-

Loom recorded an after-tax charge of $287 million to pay for worldwide restructuring efforts to improve operations and reduce the company's cost structure. That year, the company closed 9 plants in the United States and laid off more than 6,000 employees. The following year, Fruit of the Loom returned to profit with net earnings of $151.2 million despite flat sales totaling about $2.44 billion. In 1997 the company reported disappointing earnings, which were largely attributed to price discounting and significant promotional activity. That year, Fruit of the Loom's operating cash flow was a negative $94.9 million; the company had sales of only about $2.14 billion

phia & Reading coal railroad and mining operation, took over Union Underwear, providing it with additional financial resources and enabling it to expand its operations. By this time, Union Underwear was Fruit of the Loom's most prominent licensee—in fact, Union Underwear had grown much larger than Fruit of the Loom—and people had come to identify the brand more with underwear than with fabric. In 1961, to ensure future availability of the Fruit of the Loom trademark, Philadelphia & Reading purchased the Fruit of the Loom Licensing Company. In 1968 Northwest Industries acquired Pacific & Reading, and so, also, Union Underwear. A year later, in an effort to perk up the advertising for its underwear, Union hired well-known and somewhat controversial sportscaster Howard Cosell to appear in five of its television advertisements over the following three years.

In 1975 Union Underwear began its "Fruit of the Loom Guys" campaign, which would be tremendously successful, greatly increasing Union Underwear's market share and brand awareness with consumers. The year after that campaign was launched, Union purchased the 100 year old BVD trademark, which the company used for a separate line of underwear targeted at a more upscale market. Union branched out from men's and boys' underwear and, in 1978, began making "Underoos" decorated underwear for both boys and girls. Also in the 1970s, Union began supplying undecorated T-shirts to the screen print market. Soon this enterprise developed into an enormous business supplying plain T-shirts, sweatshirts, and sweat pants to wholesalers. The business was called Screen Stars.

The 1980s was a heady time of leveraged buyouts, and in 1984, William Farley purchased Northwest Industries for $1.4 billion, thereby acquiring Fruit of the Loom. Farley privatized Northwest Industries and renamed it Farley Industries. The following year Farley restructured the company, sold about $260 million in shares, and changed the name of Union Underwear to Fruit of the Loom, Inc. Farley focused on maximizing profits of Fruit of the Loom, then the top U.S. undergarment company with about 35 percent of the market.

Farley cut costs at Fruit of Loom, sold off many of Farley Industries' other businesses, and used asset sales and revenues from bond issues to modernize domestic operations and expand into Europe. Over the course of the 1980s, Fruit of the Loom expanded into men's fashion underwear, women's underwear, socks, and sportswear. During this time, the activewear market tripled in sales while the underwear market only increased by about 6 percent per year. By the end of the 1980s, Farley Industries was a worldwide textile and clothing corporation bringing in about $4 billion in sales annually. Capital improvements left Fruit of the Loom strapped with debt, and interest expenses consumed huge portions of annual sales revenues—10 percent in 1989. In the late 1980s, low-priced imports began to erode Fruit of the Loom's market share of basic men's undergarments. In 1987 the company went public and changed its name to

FAST FACTS:
About Fruit of the Loom, Inc.

Ownership: Fruit of the Loom, Inc. is a publicly owned company traded on the New York Stock Exchange.

Ticker symbol: FTL

Officers: William F. Farley, Chmn. & CEO, 54, $2,850,000; Larry K. Switzer, Sr. Exec. VP & CFO, 53, $1,085,000; Richard D. Davis, Sr. VP & General Manager Activewear; Robert F. Heise, Sr. VP & Chief Information Officer

Employees: 32,900

Principal Subsidiary Companies: Some of Fruit of the Loom's principal subsidiaries include: Brundidge Shirt Corp.; Camp Hosiery Inc.; Fruit of the Loom Inc. South Carolina Div.; Gitano Group Inc.; Jeanerette Mills Inc.; Panola Mills Inc.; Pro Player Inc.; Salem Sportswear Corp.; and Union Underwear Company Inc.

Chief Competitors: Fruit of the Loom not only manufactures about 35 percent of all male and 15 percent of all female underwear sold in the United States, but it is also the top supplier to the U.S. screen print T-shirt market. The company's principal competitors include: Sara Lee Corporation, manufacturer of Hanes products and Champion athletic knitwear products and the top U.S. maker of intimate apparel, women's and girls' underwear, boys' and men's underwear, and socks; Jockey International, manufacturer of men's, women's, and children's underwear and activewear; and Calvin Klein Inc., maker of haute couture and ready-to-wear apparel including underwear, jeans, and sportswear

Fruit of the Loom. The following year, Fruit of the Loom phased out its Fruit of the Loom Guys in favor of a modern campaign with the slogan "We fit America like we never did before." This campaign emphasized Fruit of the Loom as a basic apparel brand for all ages and both sexes and featured family scenes, as well as ads showing the first woman in panties on network TV.

In 1988, for the first time since Farley acquired Northwest Industries, Fruit of the Loom showed a profit. In 1990 the company again used male celebrities to sell underwear, this time on network TV. The following year, Fruit of the Loom launched the "It's your time" cam-

CHRONOLOGY:

Key Dates for Fruit of the Loom, Inc.

1851: B.B. & R. Knight Brothers create a cloth trademark called "Fruit of the Loom"

1926: Jacob Goldfarb begins a low-priced, high-quality undergarments business called The Union Underwear Company

1930: Investors in Frankfort, Kentucky, offer to donate a factory to Union to bring jobs to the town

1938: Goldfarb purchases a 25-year license for the Fruit of the Loom trademark

1948: Begins marketing Fruit of the Loom in a printed cellophane bag with three pairs of underwear inside, now an industry packing standard

1955: Philadelphia & Reading Corporation buys Union

1961: Philadelphia & Reading acquires the Fruit of the Loom Licensing Company

1968: Goldfarb steps down as the company chairman

1975: Union introduces the "Fruit of the Loom Guys"

1976: Acquires BVD

1984: William F. Farley acquires Union's parent company

1985: Union Underwear is renamed to Fruit of the Loom, Inc.

1998: Farley announces plans to move Fruit of the Loom to the Cayman Islands

---

Farley angered investors by selling about 900,000 of his shares of Fruit of the Loom stock, raking in over $30 million just prior to announcing a 51-percent fall in second quarter earnings. Fruit of the Loom took a $101-million charge in 1997 to pay for a legal judgment from a suit filed by a business sold in 1986. Also in 1997 the company announced layoffs of 7,700 employees at seven plants, two of which it would be closing. Despite Fruit of the Loom's two restructuring efforts, and its layoffs and plant closings, in 1997 operating results had fallen to a $283-million loss. Moreover, by this time Fruit of the Loom had lost market share to Calvin Klein and Tommy Hilfiger, who captured part of the market by defining men's underwear as fashionable. With its production license for Ralph Lauren, Hanes elbowed Fruit of the Loom out of its number one spot in the undergarment industry. By 1998 Fruit of the Loom's debt stood at 50 percent of capital, and the company had average annual interest payments of $100 million. At this point, Farley announced plans to move Fruit of the Loom to the Cayman Islands where foreign income is not subject to corporate taxes.

STRATEGY

Jacob Goldfarb employed several marketing strategies with tremendous results. In the 1940s, he developed the idea of bundling three pairs of underwear in one cellophane package; this idea permanently changed the way most basic underwear were sold in the United States. In 1955 Goldfarb launched extensive nationwide advertising employing banners, posters, signs, and admission tickets, and broke new marketing ground in the industry by becoming the first company to advertise underwear on network television. At about the same time, mass merchandisers were beginning to appear on the retail scene, and Union began to ally itself with them; by the early 1990s, 45 percent of men's basic underwear would be sold in discount stores.

As early as 1969, Union Underwear began the then-unusual move of using celebrities to promote its underwear. First, Howard Cosell appeared in five of the company's TV commercials. Then the company hired British comedian Terry Thomas, hoping his "Englishness" would lend an air of superiority to the product. In 1990 Fruit of the Loom would return to this strategy, this time actually showing celebrities like Ed Marinaro, Patrick Duffy, and David Hasselhoff, for example, in their Fruit of the Loom underwear in commercials on network television.

Union Underwear launched an extremely successful advertising campaign in 1975 when it introduced its Fruit of the Loom Guys. The Fruit of the Loom Guys campaign featured three men dressed as three of the items composing the companies trademark: an apple, a bunch of grapes, and a leaf. The campaign doubled Union Un-

paign for its line of casual wear, now expanded to include infant and toddler apparel. At this time, Fruit of the Loom became a top company in underwear for infants and toddlers and in 1994, it purchased the Gitano brand. Farley continued efforts to restabilize the company, reducing its debt by over $332 million with increased sales reaching $1.4 billion. In 1995 Fruit of the Loom closed 9 plants in the United States, laid off over 6,000 employees, and began moving operations to Central America and the Caribbean.

With the stated goal of more than doubling Fruit of the Loom's revenues to $5 billion, Farley had bought smaller apparel companies and had soon built a virtual empire, as well as a virtual mountain of debt—$1.2 billion by 1997. Some of the companies lost money and none yielded the hope for profit. In May and June of 1997

derwear's share of the men's and boys' underwear market and increased public recognition of the brand to 98 percent.

A less successful campaign was launched in response to Hanes Knit Products' 1982 "Inspector 12" advertising campaign. Hanes' campaign featured a quality control character who would always judge Hanes brand superior to Fruit of the Loom. Fruit of the Loom responded with a series of advertisements all ending with the tagline, "Sorry Hanes. You lose!" Eventually, this "underwar" resulted in a legal battle that was settled out of court with the requirement that both companies withdraw their advertisements.

Fruit of the Loom anticipated the value of developing licensing partnerships to expand its line and boost sales. Its partnerships included agreements with Warnaco, manufacturer of slips and bras, and Wilson, who agreed to Fruit of the Loom's manufacturing a complete line of athletic activewear under the Wilson label. Other licensing partnerships included some with major U.S. professional sports leagues like the National Basketball Association and the National Football League, as well as large entertainment companies like Time Warner and Walt Disney. Fruit of the Loom acquired it own sportswear companies including Salem Sportswear in 1993, and Artex Manufacturing Inc. and Pro Player in 1994.

In September 1997, to promote its newly designed men's briefs, Fruit of the Loom ran an ad in over 1 million subscription issues of *Rolling Stone* magazine featuring an actual 3-inch pair of men's briefs made from the same fabric and including the same improved features as the full-sized briefs. The tiny briefs prompted such a large and enthusiastic consumer response that Fruit of the Loom distributed another 200,000 ad inserts the following month. Consumers used them as soda can holders, golf club covers, and as apparel for stuffed animals.

CURRENT TRENDS

In the 1990s Fruit of the Loom began laying off employees, closing plants, and moving manufacturing operations overseas. In early 1998, chairman and CEO William Farley announced plans to relocate the company to the Cayman Islands. To some, it wasn't clear whether Farley was interested in saving the company or in saving his own investment as the largest shareholder since a move to the Caymans wouldn't go far toward solving Fruit of the Loom's fundamental operating problems. Farley claimed that the move would eventually save the company about $100 million annually by trimming the tax rate from 28 to 11 percent, and this money could be used to pay off debt.

But apparently, the relocation would provide more than a corporate tax break for the company. Fruit of the Loom's filings with the Securities & Exchange Commission (SEC) revealed that the Cayman move had been structured so Farley would receive a huge personal tax break not available to other investors. In the first half of 1998, Farley owned 10 percent of the company, or 7 million shares—82 percent were class B shares worth 5 votes each, giving him a 30-percent voting stake in the company. The relocation was structured to keep Farley's voting majority, and under the terms of the relocation, he would have an opportunity to purchase preferred shares in a Fruit of the Loom subsidiary called FTL-Delaware, the first Fruit of the Loom shares to offer dividends since the company went public in 1987.

PRODUCTS

Fruit of the Loom offers basic, value-priced clothing for infants to senior citizens. Active wear, athletic sportswear, casual wear, children's wear, hosiery, sports-licensed apparel, and underwear are its leading products. The company sells products principally under the brand names Best, Botany 500, BVD, Fruit of the Loom, Funpals, Gitano, John Henry, Kangaroo, Lofteez, Munsingwear, Pro Player, Salem Sportswear, Screen Stars, and Wilson.

In the 1980s, Fruit of the Loom began its evolution from being a basic underwear manufacturer to being an apparel company producing socks, sweatshirts, men's fashion underwear, and women's underwear. Within four years of launching its women's underwear division in 1984, Fruit of the Loom led that category with a 10-percent market share. By the late 1980s brand extensions made up over 40 percent of revenues. In 1991, Fruit of the Loom began offering infants' and toddlers' apparel and Warnaco started to produce and market bras under the Fruit of the Loom name. In 1993 Fruit of the Loom struck a deal with Wilson Sporting Goods to manufacture and sell Wilson athletic wear in the United States. Also in 1993, Fruit of the Loom acquired Salem Sportswear. The following year, the company purchased Artex Manufacturing, which licensed sports leagues and famous cartoon characters from Disney, Peanuts, and Looney Tunes. Fruit of the Loom's three-year licensing agreement with Walt Disney Co. allowed Fruit of the Loom to manufacture and sell apparel sporting Disney characters in the Middle East, Europe, and eastern Europe.

GLOBAL PRESENCE

Fruit of the Loom's main market is the United States, which in 1996, accounted for 85 percent of the company's total sales and 86 percent of the company's total operating income. In 1995 Fruit of the Loom began moving operations to Mexico, the Caribbean, and Central America, hoping to reduce operating costs. Fruit of the Loom maintains 47 manufacturing facilities in Canada, El Salvador, Honduras, Ireland, Jamaica, Morocco, the United Kingdom, and the United States and hopes to move its headquarters to the Cayman Islands by the end of the decade.

EMPLOYMENT

During the 1990s, Fruit of the Loom shut down many U.S. plants and facilities. Some operations it moved abroad; some it simply closed. In 1995 the company closed nine U.S. plants and laid off upwards of 6,000 workers. In 1997 it laid off more than 7,700 employees at seven plants, two of which it closed altogether. In April 1998, the company announced that it would close its Campbellsville, Kentucky, plant and thereby lay off more than 800 more workers. All told, from 1994 to early 1998, Fruit of the Loom laid off 16,355 employees.

By the start of 1998, Fruit of the Loom had almost entirely eliminated its U.S. sewing operations, moving them to cheaper locations abroad. The incentive for U.S. garment makers to move manufacturing operations abroad is powerful. On average, U.S. apparel workers are paid $8 an hour, plus benefits; minimum wage in Mexico is $1 an hour; in Haiti, the minimum hourly wage is $.29. Larry Martin, president of the American Apparel Manufacturers Association observes that "[l]abor costs are 40 percent of making a garment, so it's pretty difficult to compete at $8 to $10 an hour."

SOURCES OF INFORMATION

Bibliography

1997 Fruit of the Loom Annual Report. Chicago, IL: Fruit of the Loom, Inc., 1997.

Aran, Kimberly. "Fruit of the Loom to License Disney, But Europe's No Magic Kingdom." *Crain's Chicago Business,* 31 October 1994.

Business Rankings Annual, Detroit, MI: Gale Research, 1998.

"Calvin Klein Inc." *Hoover's Online,* 18 May 1998. Available at http://www.hoovers.com.

Dougal, April S. "Fruit of the Loom, Inc." *International Directory of Company Histories,* Vol. 8. Detroit, MI: St. James Press, 1994.

"Fruit of the Loom Ratings Placed on Watch Neg by S&P." *Business Wire,* 12 February 1998.

"Fruit of the Loom to Cut 800 Jobs in Another Plant Closing." *New York Times,* 16 April 1998.

"Fruit of the Loom, Inc." *Hoover's Online,* 28 July 1998. Available at http://www.hoovers.com.

Hunt, Nigel. "Fruit of the Loom Cuts about 3,000 US Sewing Jobs." *Reuters Business Report,* 11 November 1997.

"Jockey International." *Hoover's Online,* 18 May 1998. Available at http://www.hoovers.com.

Lazich, Robert S., ed. *Market Share Reporter- 1998,* Detroit, MI: Gale Research, 1997.

Poole, Shelia M. "Kentucky Town in Despair Over Losing Apparel Plants." *The Atlanta Journal and Constitution,* 27 November 1997.

"S&P Description: Fruit of the Loom." *Standard & Poor's,* 15 April 1998.

"Sara Lee Corporation." *Hoover's Online,* 18 May 1998. Available at http://www.hoovers.com.

"Tiny Briefs Mean Big News for Fruit of the Loom." *Business Wire,* 28 September 1997.

Weimer, De'Ann. "Fruit of the Loom: A Killing in the Caymans?" *Business Week,* 11 May 1998.

For an annual report:

on the Internet at: http://www.fruit.com **or** write: Corporate Communications Center, Inc., 400 S. Jefferson, Ste. 303, Chicago, IL 60607

For additional industry research:

Investigate companies by their Standard Industrial Classification Codes, also known as SICs. Fruit of the Loom's primary SICs are:

2252 Hosiery, NEC

2322 Mens/Boys' Underwear & Nightwear

2329 Mens/Boys' Clothing, NEC

2341 Women/Children's Underwear

Fuji Photo Film Co., Ltd.

FOUNDED: 1934

OVERVIEW

Fuji Photo Film is best known as one of the largest photo film producers in the world. The company makes many other products, however, which it divides into three segments. Products in the Information Systems segment include floppy disks, medical imaging systems, and office automation systems. The Photofinishing Systems segment includes instant color print systems and photographic papers, equipment, and chemicals. The Imaging Systems segment includes photo film, cameras, optical products; and motion picture film. Fuji also produces copiers through its Fuji Xerox joint venture.

Contact Information:
HEADQUARTERS: 26-30, Nishiazabu 2-chome
   Minato-ku
   Tokyo 106-8620, Japan
PHONE: 81-3-3406-2444
FAX: 81-3-3406-2173
URL: http://www.fujifilm.co.jp

COMPANY FINANCES

In the year ended March 1997, Fuji Photo Film recorded sales of 125.21 trillion yen, up 15.4 percent from the prior year. Domestic sales totaled 677.3 billion yen, and overseas sales 574.8 billion yen. Net income rose 17.1 percent to 85.3 billion yen, or 166 yen on a per-share basis. Cash dividends for the period were declared at 22 yen per share. Between April 1997 and April 1998 the company's stock traded on the NASDAQ exchange from a low of $33 to a high of $43.

HISTORY

Dainippon Celluloid, a Japanese company, established Fuji Photo Film in 1934 near Japan's famous Mount Fuji. Fuji Photo Film initially produced motion

FAST FACTS:

About Fuji Photo Film Co., Ltd.

Ownership: Fuji Photo Film is a publicly owned corporation traded on the Tokyo and other Japanese stock exchanges. In the United States, it is traded on NASDAQ.

Ticker symbol: FUJIY

Officers: Minoru Ohnishi, Chmn.; Masayuki Muneyuki, Pres.

Employees: 29,903

Chief Competitors: Fuji Photo Film's competitors include: Canon; Minolta; Hitachi; Sony; Sharp; and Toshiba.

---

picture film, dry plates, and photographic paper. By the early 1940s the company was operating four factories and a research facility in Japan. In the 1950s it began to make large amounts of film for the amateur consumer market. Following the creation of an export division in 1956, the company began to sell more film overseas. Fuji Photo Film added magnetic tape to its product line in 1960. In 1962 it formed the joint venture Fuji Xerox with Rank Xerox of the United Kingdom to sell copiers. (Rank Xerox is an affiliate of America's Xerox and the United Kingdom's Rank Organisation).

In the 1970s Fuji emerged as a more serious challenger to Eastman Kodak, the market leader in photo film. Minoru Ohnishi became president of the company in 1980 and started a sustained attack on the U.S. market. Fuji Photo Film was a sponsor of the 1984 Olympics in Los Angeles, which helped give it a stronger presence in the United States. The company's market position in the United States continued to strengthen in the late 1980s and 1990s.

STRATEGY

During its first few years of operation in the 1930s, Fuji Photo Film was plagued by a reputation for poor quality and high prices for its photographic products. In 1936 it brought in a German emulsion specialist who helped the company produce quality black-and-white photo film and motion picture negative film. The im-

proved offerings raised the company's standing in the domestic market. World War II delayed any further development of consumer products, however, as all sensitized materials were dedicated to the Japanese war effort.

In 1947 Japan was allowed to resume normal trade, and Fuji Photo Film began exporting its products to South America and Asia. Most of these shipments were cameras and binoculars, Japanese products that enjoyed a good reputation. But film exports were low, because the company's technology lagged behind those of U.S. and European producers. In the early 1950s licensing agreements with Kodak enabled Fuji Photo Film to produce high-quality black-and-white amateur roll film. With the continuing expansion of the Japanese economy in the 1950s and 1960s, demand for the company's film products grew at a steady pace. Fuji Photo Film also benefited from tariffs on film imports, which gave the company a protected home market.

At the same time, the company worked to expand overseas sales. It entered the North American market in 1955, and by 1958 it had reached 27 export agreements in Asia. However, Fuji Photo Film faced one major obstacle in foreign markets: its film and paper products were not compatible with the most commonly used processing systems in the world. By 1969 Fuji had eliminated this problem, and its film, photo paper, and chemicals were fully compatible.

During the 1970s Fuji Photo Film further expanded its presence in overseas markets, opening manufacturing operations in Brazil, Korea, and Indonesia. The company also spent heavily to generate more sales in the United States, but had difficulty building customer loyalty. While its U.S. market share did double during the 1970s, it still stood at only 4 to 5 percent at the end of the decade. The company had better success, however, at developing new products related to the photographic process. It developed new technology for x-rays and other electronic systems for the medical industry. Fuji Photo Film also was able to enter new markets related to its magnetic research; in 1977 the company introduced Japan's first eight-inch floppy computer disks.

In 1980 Minoru Ohnishi became Fuji Photo Film's youngest president at the age of 55. Ohnishi was determined to reduce Fuji Photo Film's dependence on the Japanese market and increase sales in the United States. In 1979 the company sold film in only 30 percent of U.S. film outlets; by 1984, the level had increased to 60 percent. A major boost to Fuji's fortunes in the U.S. market was its sponsorship of the 1984 Olympics held in Los Angeles. After those games, Fuji Photo Film's U.S. market share in photo film had grown to 8 percent. The company's share of the European film market was also growing, reaching 15 percent by the mid-1980s. The magnetic products division was doing nicely too: between 1978 and 1982, worldwide sales rose fivefold. In fact, by 1983 film sales represented only half of Fuji Photo Film's revenues.

During the second half of the 1980s Fuji Photo Film enjoyed continued success in its U.S. operations. By 1988 its U.S. market share in the film segment was 10 percent. It became the first company to offer a disposable camera in the United States. It built a plant for making printing plates in South Carolina, where it continued to expand local production of other products throughout the 1990s. Fuji Photo Film also managed to increase use of its processing systems in the United States, which helped boost demand for its papers and chemicals.

INFLUENCES

Fuji Photo Film has built its business on price, quality, and strong marketing. Its film has a strong following among professional photographers, and their loyalty gives Fuji prestige among amateur camera buffs. The company is tightly managed with a lean staff: while Fuji's sales doubled between 1987 and 1997, the number of white-collar employees remained about the same. Fuji Photo Film is also an aggressive competitor, which has led to charges of unfair trading practices. It tries to portray itself as a technologically advanced company that is hipper and less stodgy than its main competitor, Kodak.

In the American market, Fuji Photo Film's strategy centers on opening local film and paper production facilities. Building plants in the United States reduces costs, lessens trade friction, and makes Fuji more responsive to changes in the local market. With a net cash position of $4.5 billion in 1997, Fuji was well able to afford new capital investment. The company also has consistently spent 7 percent of its sales on research and development.

CURRENT TRENDS

In the mid-1990s Fuji Photo Film's rivalry with Kodak grew into a major trade dispute between the United States and Japan. In a case before the World Trade Organization (WTO), the U.S. government charged that unfair barriers kept Kodak from expanding its share of the Japanese film market. In 1995 Kodak had 9 percent of this market, versus 70 percent for Fuji Photo Film. Kodak's primary complaint was that Fuji Photo Film had a lock on the Japanese distribution system which, in effect, prohibited competitors from penetrating the Japanese market. Kodak film was sold in just 15 percent of retail outlets in Japan, mostly in large cities. In contrast, Fuji Photo Film sold its film in outlets that accounted for 70 percent of the U.S. market.

In its defense, Fuji Photo Film said that its distributors were not prevented from selling the film of competitors, and that Japan places no tariffs on imported film. The company contended that Kodak's low market share was due to marketing mistakes. Independent observers

CHRONOLOGY:
Key Dates for Fuji Photo Film Co., Ltd.

1934: Fuji Photo Film is established by Dainippon Celluloid

1947: Begins exporting to South America and Asia

1955: Enters the North American market

1956: Creates an export division

1962: Begins joint venture with Rank Xerox (U.K.) to sell copiers

1977: Introduces Japan's first 8-inch floppy computer disk

1984: Sponsors 1984 Olympics in Los Angeles

1997: Opens $300 million dollar paper plant in Greenwood, South Carolina

1998: World Trade Organization rules in favor of Fuji Photo Film in suit filed by Kodak

had mixed views about the case. While noting that Kodak made some good arguments, several analysts pointed out that some of its domestic marketing practices were very similar to those of Fuji Photo Film in Japan. In 1995 Kodak's share of the American film market was 70 percent, compared with 11 percent for Fuji Photo Film. Ultimately, in early 1998, the WTO ruled in favor of Fuji Photo Film. It found that the United States and Kodak had not proved its case that Japan's government had unfairly protected Fuji from foreign competition.

Meanwhile, Fuji Photo Film was taking important steps to boost its U.S. market share. The company scored a significant coup in 1996 by winning contracts to provide supplies to all of Wal-Mart's in-store one-hour labs. Wal-Mart was the largest photofinishing supplier in the United States, with about 2,250 stores. As part of the agreement, Fuji Photo Film bought six off-site wholesale finishing plants from Wal-Mart.

In April 1997, Fuji Photo Film opened a $300 million photographic paper plant in Greenwood, South Carolina, and further capacity enhancements were planned. Some analysts believed the new capacity would give the company added pricing and supply flexibility. According to some estimates, by the end of 1997 Fuji's share of the American market reached 14 percent, significantly above the 1995 level. Kodak attributed much of the increase in the Japanese company's share to aggressive pricing practices. Fuji countered that its low pricing was a "temporary" measure to trim excess inventories.

In the late 1990s Fuji Photo Film faced significant challenges in its home market. Traditionally, profit margins in color film had been high in Japan—as much as 12 percent compared with 6 percent overseas. By year-end 1997, retail prices of film in Japan were 30 to 40 percent below those in the United States. Overall, Fuji Photo Film estimated that its share of the Japanese market had fallen to 67 percent in 1997 against 74 percent in the early 1990s. The company attributed the decline to increased penetration of foreign brands as well as "own-label" film sold by supermarkets and discount stores. During the 1998 Winter Olympics held in Nagano, Japan, Fuji Photo Film and Kodak battled for the loyalty of the consumer. Kodak enjoyed the advantage of being a sponsor of the Games, but Fuji matched Kodak's price cuts and erected big billboards near the Olympic site.

A major threat facing Fuji Photo Film is the rise of the digital camera. Some analysts estimated that in 1997 1.8 million digital cameras were sold, and that number was expected to grow sharply. In this sphere Fuji Photo Film faces competition from not only Kodak, but also companies such as Sony, Canon, and Casio. The company also faces competition in the photographic paper and processing business from Canon, Epson, and Hewlett-Packard, whose newest ink-jet printers produce high-quality prints of digital images on plain and coated paper.

PRODUCTS

In 1996 Fuji Photo Film and four other large film-equipment makers (including Eastman Kodak) launched an "Advanced Photo System," or APS. The collaboration among such bitter rivals was itself unusual, since in the past major innovations had been introduced by one company working on its own. In February 1997 Fuji Photo Film announced its new top-of-the-line APS camera, the Endeavor 400ix Zoom MRC. Using this camera, pictures on the same roll of film can be taken in three formats: C (standard), H (high-vision), and P (panorama). Moreover, photographic data are recorded on the film's magnetic layer when the picture is taken, so that photofinishing labs can determine the optimum color balance and density for each photo. The MRC (Mid-Roll Change) fea-

ture on the Endeavor allows amateur photographers to remove and reinsert a partially exposed roll of APS film, so they can use the most appropriate film for the shooting conditions. And in conjunction with other equipment Fuji Photo Film offers, users can display their photos on a TV or scan and input them into a PC.

GLOBAL PRESENCE

In 1987 only 3.5 percent of Fuji Photo Film's production was outside Japan, compared to 31 percent in 1997. Fuji Photo Film has significant overseas facilities in the United States, Canada, Brazil, and Europe.

SOURCES OF INFORMATION

Bibliography

Desmond, Edward. "What's Ailing Kodak?" *Fortune,* 27 October 1997.

Johannes, Laura. "A Film War Breaks Out in Nagano." *Wall Street Journal,* 3 February 1998.

———. "Fuji Photo Ties Price Cuts to Inventories." *Wall Street Journal,* 25 August 1997.

Maremount, Mark. "Next, A Flap Over Film?" *Business Week,* 10 July 1995.

Nakamoto, Michiyo. "Fujifilm Snaps Up Market Share in the U.S." *Financial Times,* 9 December 1997.

Nelson, Emily. "Fuji, Challenging Kodak, to Make Film in U.S." *Wall Street Journal,* 8 May 1997.

"Negative Vibes." *The Economist,* 26 August 1995.

Ryan, Ken. "P-O-P Goes Fuji: The Computer Products Division Takes Merchandising, Brand Strategy to Higher Levels." *HFN The Weekly Newspaper for the Home Furnishing Network,* 20 February 1995.

"Shuttered." *The Economist,* 5 August 1995.

For additional industry research:

Investigate companies by their Standard Industrial Classification Codes, also known as SICs. Fuji's primary SICs are:

3695 Magnetic and Optical Recording Media

3861 Photographic Equipment and Supplies

The Gap, Inc.

OVERVIEW

In 1998 The Gap, Inc. operated about 2,200 casual clothing stores in the United States, Canada, France, Japan, and the United Kingdom. The company markets its clothes to men, women, and children under a variety of different brands and through several different retail chains including The Gap, GapKids, babyGap, Banana Republic, and the Old Navy Clothing Company. The Gap, with 1997 sales of more than $6.5 billion, was one of the world's most successful and fastest-growing clothing retailers. The company built international brand name recognition and market clout in an industry considered one of the toughest and most competitive in the world. Its continuous efforts to broaden its market and introduce products that would appeal to a wide range of consumer tastes resulted in consistently high annual growth. One example of The Gap's market-widening strategies was its development of the Old Navy Clothing Company in the mid-1990s. This particular subsidiary was aimed at teens and young adults. It provided quality apparel at low prices. From 1997 to 1998, the Old Navy chain grew by nearly half, from 180 stores to 262 stores. Ventures like this, along with the continued release of new products, helped The Gap, Inc. to become one of the country's leading fashion retailers.

COMPANY FINANCES

Over the decade from 1987 to 1997, The Gap recorded steady annual sales growth averaging around 20 percent a year. Sales rose 23 percent in 1997 to more than $6.5 billion from just less than $5.3 billion in 1996. Net earnings also climbed, up from $1.09 per share in

FOUNDED: 1969

Contact Information:

HEADQUARTERS: 1 Harrison St.
San Francisco, CA 94105
PHONE: (650)952-4400
FAX: (650)427-2795
URL: http://www.gap.com

FINANCES:

The Gap, Inc.
Net Sales, 1994-1997
(billion dollars)

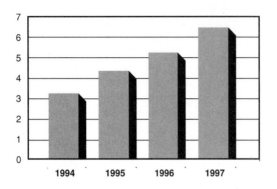

The Gap, Inc.
1997 Stock Prices
(dollars)

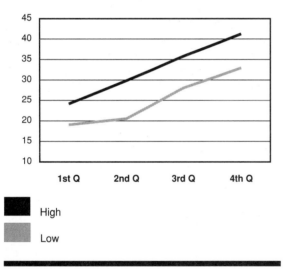

24 percent over sales for May 1997. With total sales of $2.33 billion for the 17 weeks ended May 30, 1998, an increase of 42 percent over sales of $1.64 billion for the same period in 1997, The Gap's growth strategy seemed to be well on track.

ANALYSTS' OPINIONS

While The Gap's consistent and broad-based success caused many analysts to look favorably on the company, the high price of Gap stock in 1997 and 1998 occasionally led to extremes in evaluations. Analysts pointed to the company's strong back-to-school sales and the success of Old Navy in attracting the fast-growing teen and young adult market—a market that showed strong trends in disposable income and consumption spending.

The Gap's extraordinary growth in sales and profits, combined with a level of stability virtually unheard of in the retail industry, led some to refer to it as the blue chip of specialty retailers. *The Online Investor* called The Gap a "hot apparel company whose stock was trading at big premiums," and more analysts began upgrading the company in 1998.

HISTORY

The Gap, Inc. was founded in 1969 by Donald and Doris Fisher in San Francisco, California. The Fishers opened a small store that concentrated on selling Levi's Jeans. They decided to name the store "The Gap" as a reference to the "generation gap." Eight months later a second store was opened in San Jose, California, and by 1970, six Gap stores had been opened. In its beginning, The Gap focused its attention on teenagers; but by the mid-1970s the decision was made to expand into active wear that would appeal to a broader range of consumers. Even with these efforts, by the 1980s "the Gap was still dependent upon its largely teenage customer base," according to *Hoover's Online*.

In 1983 Fisher hired Mickey Drexler as the company's president in an effort to update the company's image. Drexler, a former president of women's clothing manufacturer Ann Taylor, had a spotless record in the apparel industry. His preliminary efforts involved a complete overhaul in the company's mundane clothing style. He introduced apparel that was sturdy, brightly colored, and made from cotton. Drexler also consolidated the Gap's private clothing label into the Gap brand. By 1991 any merchandise sold in the Gap stores was the exclusive Gap brand, made specifically for the stores. The new president also removed many of the typical circular clothing racks and replaced them with white shelving. This decorating move not only made the clothing readily available for customers to try on, but it also created a more attractive, less cluttered shopping environment.

1996 to $1.35 per share in 1997. The company attributed its consistent sales growth to the continuous increase of retail selling space, both through the opening of new stores and the expansion of existing stores. In 1996 and 1997, increases in comparable store sales also contributed to net sales growth. By the end of 1997, Gap stock had quadrupled in value over its mid-1995 worth.

Sales continued to climb in 1998, with the company reporting sales of $609 million for the four-week period ended May 30, 1998, an increase of 47 percent over sales of $413 million for the same period the previous year. Comparable store sales for May 1998 also increased by

In 1983 The Gap, Inc., which already owned and operated well over 550 stores, acquired Banana Republic—a move that dramatically extended the company's reach and exposure. Banana Republic's line of clothing featured a safari motif. The Gap expanded upon this idea, creating a development team to add innovative fashions and accessories. Unfortunately, the novelty eventually wore off and by the late 1980s, Banana Republic's profits were declining. Drexler decided to downplay the jungle image, and introduced a broader range of clothing, including higher-priced leather goods. By the 1990s Banana Republic was in good shape and once again able to contribute to The Gap's rapid growth.

Another Gap subsidiary, GapKids, was introduced in 1985 after Drexler experienced several unsuccessful shopping trips with his own children. He found that many stores offered poorly designed and uncomfortable clothing for children. Added to this was the reality that basic apparel for children was often hard to find. GapKids offered clothing that was fashionable and appealing to parents who shopped at Gap stores themselves. The new chain was enormously successful. In 1990, GapKids introduced a line of clothing exclusively for infants and toddlers. Called babyGap, the new brand was available in most GapKids stores.

In 1994 The Gap launched Old Navy Clothing Company. Originally tested under the name Gap Warehouse, the new store focused on the youth market, offering trendy casual wear at affordable prices. In 1995, Banana Republic opened its first stores outside of the United States in Edmonton and Toronto, Canada. The company also launched a line of bath and body products at Banana Republic the same year.

The Gap continued its expansion in the following years, opening 298 new stores in 1997 and closing 22, for a net gain of 276. The newly opened stores included 98 Gap stores with 18 international locations; 76 GapKids and babyGap stores, with 21 international locations; 34 Banana Republic stores, including 1 store in Canada; and 90 Old Navy stores. The company completed construction of a 189,000 square foot building in San Bruno, California, which serves as part of its headquarter facilities. Meanwhile, the company continued its phenomenal growth, yielding sales 23 percent higher than in 1996, and was showing continued growth into 1998.

STRATEGY

The Gap believes that its brands are among its strongest assets. Its growth strategy is focused on developing and growing those brands. One of the keys to strengthening brand loyalty is advertising. In 1997 the company boosted its investment in advertising and marketing as a percentage of sales by 0.8 percent over the prior year. The company's biggest advertisement was a coordinated print and television campaign for "Khakis," which were becoming increasingly popular among men

FAST FACTS:
About The Gap, Inc.

Ownership: The Gap, Inc. is a publicly owned company traded on the New York Stock Exchange.

Ticker symbol: GPS

Officers: Millard S. Drexler, Pres. & CEO, 1997 base salary $1.9 million; Robert J. Fisher, Exec. VP; Pres., The Gap, GapKids, 1997 base salary $848,548; Warren R. Hashagen, Sr. VP, CFO, 1997 base salary $328,100; Donald G. Fisher, Chmn., 1997 base salary $499,274

Employees: 81,000

Principal Subsidiary Companies: The Gap, Inc.'s principal subsidiaries are Banana Republic, Baby-Gap, GapKids, and Old Navy Clothing Company.

Chief Competitors: Clothing retailing is one of the world's most highly competitive businesses. The Gap's many competitors include: Benetton; Federated; J. Crew; Bugle Boy; Calvin Klein; Dayton Hudson; Dillard's; Esprit de Corp.; Guess?; Gymboree; J.C. Penney; L.A. Gear; Lands' End; The Limited; L.L. Bean; May; Nautica Enterprises; Nike; Nordstrom; OshKosh B'Gosh; Polo/Ralph Lauren; Reebok; and Spiegel.

and women. Sales began growing at a much faster pace than jeans.

In 1997 The Gap also began to explore the possibility of store label credit cards, additional flagship stores, and more extensive television advertising to complement its in-store marketing programs. New product offerings such as home accessories and personal care items were also used to increase brand recognition.

Along with increasing brand recognition, the other main focus of The Gap's strategy for success has been store expansion and development of new distribution channels. Moves in this direction included adding new store formats such as Gap/GapKids combined stores, large flagship stores, men's/women's-only stores, baby-only stores, airport locations, and a wholesaling arrangement with duty-free stores in Hong Kong, Guam, Singapore, Australia, and New Zealand. The company also began integrating its Gap and GapKids field organizations to strengthen brand focus. In addition, it launched an electronic retailing operation on the Internet.

CHRONOLOGY:

The Gap, Inc.

1969: Donald and Doris Fisher found The Gap Stores, Inc. in San Francisco, California

1971: The fishers take The Gap public but retain a majority of the stock

1976: The Gap makes its first major stock offering

1983: Micky Drexler is named as the company's president

1985: GapKids is introduced

1991: The Gap's clothing label is consolidated into Gap brand

1995: Old Navy Clothing Company is launched by The Gap

INFLUENCES

The Gap's continued success has depended largely on its ability to increase sales at existing store locations, to open new stores, and to operate stores on a profitable basis. The company has always been searching for new ways to attract customers. One way of doing this was by consulting the public directly. Between 1992 and 1994 The Gap retained the services of the market research company Prophet to conduct surveys to determine what consumers wanted to see in the stores. The primary source for this information was derived from in-store surveys using portable data entry templates. Those who decided to take part in the survey were directed to Prophet employees on the basis of purchases. They were also given clothing incentives for answering surveys. The data was collected on a nightly basis to obtain the most accurate information.

The surveys provided The Gap, Inc. with reports on areas such as credit card preference, store impressions, and shopping experiences. All of the information aided the company in providing its customers with the quality service and merchandise they wanted.

Nothing breeds imitation like success—and The Gap's success has spawned a host of imitators, all of whom, as the company points out, "make the retail environment in which the Company operates more competitive." The Gap has so far weathered recessions and economic downturns, yet as a retailer, it remained vulnerable to future declines in consumer spending on apparel.

Like many other companies, The Gap faced the need to ensure that its operations would not be adversely affected by software or other system failures related to the year 2000. In 1997 it established a program to identify and implement any necessary changes to its computer systems, applications, and business processes.

CURRENT TRENDS

The Gap has always been willing to venture into new areas in an effort to keep up with current trends and consumer desires. It has rejuvenated its product lines and catered to as many different types of consumer as possible. Besides expanding into the children's clothing market in the late 1980s, the company launched the Old Navy Clothing Company in 1994 to capture a growing, high-spending youth market with funky casual clothes at value prices. Because traditional Gap stores appealed to an older, more upscale market, the move paid off. It helped to quickly expand the company's market.

Old Navy provided extras such as toys, accessories, trendy layouts, and special displays that would attract young shoppers. Stores featured a stripped-down warehouse look with concrete floors and exposed pipes, adding to their hip appeal. Old Navy was able to compete on price while offering a much lighter ambience well-suited to young shoppers who didn't want to spend a lot of money, but were too brand-conscious to shop at the mass market discounters. All of these factors were introduced at a time when discounters such as Target and Wal-Mart were becoming increasingly popular.

PRODUCTS

The Gap's focus has always been to stay on top of current fashion trends while providing the products its customers wanted. When the company was first launched, its primary target was teens and young adults. Although it has diversified its customer base over the years, The Gap remains committed to offering comfortable, casual clothing. Denim was always a mainstay of the youth market, and it was not long before its appeal spread throughout the community. At the end of the 1990s, The Gap retained its youth-oriented focus as it continued to diversify its range of offerings through stores like Old Navy and Banana Republic. With everything from jewelry and accessories to T-shirts and leather jackets, The Gap's range of products has something for everyone—including children, who can be outfitted in miniature versions of popular Gap items at GapKids and babyGap.

CORPORATE CITIZENSHIP

As a modern, youth-oriented company, The Gap has always made a point of trying to behave as a responsible citizen. It has often been quick to provide aid to those in need. One such act of philanthropy occurred in 1997 when The Gap announced that it would be donating $10,000 to the American Red Cross to help flood relief efforts in Kentucky. In addition to the monetary donation, The Gap provided clothes to flood victims who were forced to leave their personal possessions behind due to rising water levels.

Some Gap employees who worked at the company's distribution center in Erlanger, Kentucky, were also affected by the disaster, with at least five of them being forced to leave their homes during the flood. Like the other victims, the Gap employees also received assistance from the Red Cross. According to Molly White, senior director of Gap, Inc. Community Relations, "When employees are affected by a natural disaster, it really brings the tragedy close to home. Because the Red Cross is there for them, we as a corporation want to be there for the Red Cross."

On the environmental front, The Gap is one of eight organizations, including the Natural Resources Defense Council, that manages the Recycled Paper Coalition, which encourages recycled paper purchasing and paper recycling. In 1996, The Gap used environmentally certified, sustainable harvested tropical hardwood for flooring in two of its new Banana Republic stores and later built an experimental "green" Banana Republic store in Texas using primarily recycled materials. A full-time environmental staff oversees manufacturing operations and coordinates programs to recycle shipping and packaging materials at Gap stores throughout the United States. The Gap was also a leading sponsor of the San Francisco area's "Spare the Air" campaign for 1998.

GLOBAL PRESENCE

Although most of The Gap's more than 2,200 stores are located in the United States, the company has opened stores throughout the world, including Canada, France, Japan, Germany, and the United Kingdom. The company also planned to open affiliates in Japan and Germany. The first European store was opened in 1987, and by 1997 the company owned more than 60 stores in Europe.

The Gap built a 129,000 square foot warehouse and distribution center in Roosendaal, the Netherlands, in order to strengthen its European base. While the European stores performed well, they remained unprofitable as of 1997 due to a soft retail market, low brand awareness, and company investments in infrastructure.

EMPLOYMENT

The Gap regards its employees as its most valuable resource. The company offers a comprehensive benefits package that was used to improve quality of life and assist employees in meeting their responsibilities at work and home. Benefits include dental and medical coverage, as well as savings plans. Vacations and paid holidays are also a standard part of employee compensation packages.

SOURCES OF INFORMATION

Bibliography

"The Blue Chip of Specialty Retailers." *The Online Investor,* 3 December 1997. Available at http://fnews.yahoo.com/oli/98/05/13/stock_971203.html.

"Corporate and Government Leaders Join Forces to Launch Spare the Air '98 Campaign in Bay Area." San Francisco: The Gap, Inc., 29 May 1998.

Cuneo, Alice Z. "Gap's 1st Global Ads Confront Dockers on a Khaki Battlefield." *Advertising Age,* April 1998.

"Gap Inc. Announces May Sales." San Francisco, CA: The Gap, Inc., 4 June 1998.

"The Gap, Inc." *Prophet Case Studies.* Prophet Marketing Research, Inc., 1997. Available at http://www.prophet.com/prophet-services/cases/the gap.html.

The Gap, Inc. Annual Report 1998. Available at http://www.sec.gov/Archives/edgar/data/39911/0001012870-98-000890.txt.

"Gap, Inc. Brings Casual Style to Europe." *Netherlands Investment News.* Winter 1995. Available at: http://www.nfa.com/news/archive/winter95/gap.html.

"Gap, Inc. Donates Money and Clothing to Help Kentucky Flood Victims." *Yahoo on the Money,* 1997. Available at http://biz.yahoo.com/bin/jump?/97/03/07/gps_y0029_1.html+gps+97+03.

"The Gap, Inc." *Hoover's Online,* 1998. Available at http://www.hoovers.com.

Tagliabue, John. "International Business; Enticing Europe's Shoppers." *The New York Times,* 24 April 1996.

For an annual report:

on the Internet at: http://www.sec.gov/Archives/edgar/data/39911/0001012870-98-000890.txt

For additional industry research:

Investigate companies by their Standard Industrial Classification Codes, also known as SICs. The Gap's primary SICs are:

5136 Men's/Boys Clothing

5137 Women's/Children's Clothing

5699 Misc. Apparel & Accessory Stores

Gateway, Inc.

FOUNDED: 1985

Contact Information:
HEADQUARTERS: 610 Gateway Dr.
North Sioux City, SD 57049-2000
PHONE: (605)232-2000
FAX: (605)232-2023
TOLL FREE: (800)846-2000
URL: http://www.gateway.com

OVERVIEW

Gateway, Inc. is the number two manufacturer of IBM-compatible personal computers in the United States behind Dell in direct computer marketing. Gateway sells its products to customers through its web site or by phone, rather than resellers. By doing this, the company is able to release new technology faster and cut markup costs. In addition, Gateway manufactures big screen PCTVs, software, and peripherals.

Gateway, Inc. has computer buyers seeing spots—cow-like spots, that is—and executives and shareholders seeing green. Gateway, Inc. spends about $90 million on advertising each year to keep those spots in front of consumers' eyes. This has resulted in 80 percent of consumers and 95 percent of business customers recognition of the company by name. The Gateway, Inc. box is easily recognized by its black-and-white cowhide pattern. The distinctive trademark is homage to the cattle country in which founder Ted Waitt grew up

The company shipped almost 2.6 million computers in 1997 and, in 1998 stepped up its contracting of equipment to the federal government. In addition to its hardware business, Gateway, Inc. was the first personal computer (PC) seller to function as a national Internet Service Provider (ISP), a role accomplished by means of its Gateway.net.

COMPANY FINANCES

Revenue for 1997 was $6.3 billion, up 25 percent from 1996's $5.0 billion, despite a third-quarter slowdown in deliveries that resulted from a United Parcel Service strike. Gross profit was slightly over $1 billion, for a result of $.71 per share. CEO Ted Waitt called this, in the 1997 annual report, "respectable," though he cautioned that "overall it wasn't a great year for us." However, revenue for Gateway has shown a steady increase over the years. In 1993 total revenue for the company was $1.7 billion; in 1994, $2.7 billion; and in 1995, $3.7 billion.

ANALYSTS' OPINIONS

Many magazine articles painted a rosy, yet flawed, picture of Gateway, Inc. in the mid-1990s. Some publications even made Waitt a cover boy in 1997. In 1995 *Financial World,* for example, closely examined the phenomenon of Gateway, Inc.'s seemingly unbridled post-IPO climb: "At the end of its first year as a public company, $1.7 billion-in-sales Gateway Inc., now based in North Sioux City, S.D., is off to a flying start. The shares, offered at $15, are up 50 percent, to $22.50, on strong numbers. In the third quarter, Gateway earned $28 million, up 17 percent from a year ago, on a 61 percent gain in sales, to $644 million. Following similar sales gains of 56 percent in 1993, and 77 percent the year before—at a time when worldwide PC sales were growing just over 15 percent and 11 percent, respectively—you have to say that's impressive." But, " . . . Growth like that is really hard to sustain without gaskets popping somewhere." That article called for better control at the helm: "Waitt has his hands full at Gateway at the moment. He has got to get a handle on its recent expansion, and to keep the company's future growth rate up. He also has to broaden the product line, expand geographically and fight off a resurgent Dell. Oh yes, and he has to cope with the fallout from Intel's flawed Pentium chip."

HISTORY

In 1984, Ted Waitt dropped out of the business-management program at the University of Iowa to work in a Des Moines computer store. After nine months of learning the business, he quit to start his own computer-retail business. Waitt and two partners founded the TIPC Network, which sold upgrades and peripherals for Texas Instruments computers. Mike Hammond was the "techno-nerd" of the founding partners, who also included Ted's brother, Norm Waitt. The TIPC Network began running ads, with a phone number, in computer magazines, to attract business. Waitt borrowed $10,000 from his grandmother to start the company in a house across from a barn on the Waitt farm. Both Waitt and Hammond lived above the office and took phone orders for merchandise. Not far along into their entrepreneurial adventure, the trio determined that they could easily sell complete computer systems by way of the same direct sales channel. The

FINANCES:

Gateway Inc.
Net Sales, 1994-1997
(billion dollars)

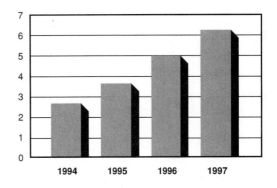

Gateway Inc.
1997 Stock Prices
(dollars)

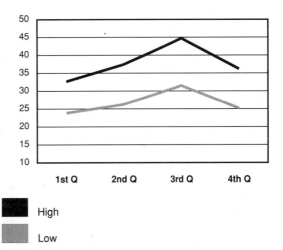

first Gateway 2000 computers—two floppy drives, color monitor, and increased memory—sold in 1987 for about $2,000. At the time, that was the same amount consumers were paying for a bare-bones system.

The Waitt brothers and Hammond christened their new firm Gateway 2000 (re-named Gateway, Inc. in 1998) because they saw the PC to be the gateway to the next century. Cows permeated the company culture. In fact, the company's next move was to Sioux City's Livestock Exchange building, where the scent of cows wafted through the building on particularly hot days. Gateway's aim was to target computer buyers who were eagerly

FAST FACTS:

About Gateway, Inc.

Ownership: Gateway, Inc. is a publicly owned company traded on the New York Stock Exchange.

Ticker symbol: GTW

Officers: Theodore W. Waitt, Founder, Chmn., & CEO, 35, $854.850; Jeffrey Weitzen, Pres. & COO, 44; David J. Robino, Exec. VP & Chief Administrative Officer, 38

Employees: 13,300

Chief Competitors: Some major competitors are: Compaq; CompUSA; Dell; Hewlett-Packard; IBM; Packard Bell; Tandy Corporation; and Texas Instruments.

---

seeking a bargain, and who were not afraid to rifle through the pages of a computer magazine for that deal. The company kept margins low by assembling computers from other companies' components. Since there were no research and development fees, and little overhead, the company splurged on advertising.

In 1990 the company moved to new a home in South Dakota, where there was no state income tax. It soon began shipping 225 PCS per day from there. The following year, Gateway, Inc. was at the top of the *Inc.* 500 list of the fastest-growing companies. Gateway, Inc. made its first billion in 1992, $3.7 billion in 1995, and about that same amount in the first nine months of 1996 alone. In 1993, the company started marketing internationally and opened a manufacturing plant in Ireland. It went public right before Christmas that same year. During late 1994 a sales and customer support center opened in Kansas City. In 1995, the company entered the Australian market when it purchased Osborne Computer of Sidney. In order to seize Asia/Pacific demand, Gateway opened a manufacturing plant in Malacca, Malaysia. The young Waitt's estimated personal net worth was $1.7 billion by 1997.

STRATEGY

Gateway, Inc. had a core strategy of selling computers at the lowest possible price by having minimal overhead and by selling directly to the customer. Although the company has had to diversify beyond this channel, it has remained true to direct selling. It continues to amplify its advertising efforts. Close ties with its customer base allow Gateway to be efficiently responsive to customer needs.

INFLUENCES

Gateway, Inc. had its difficulties, primarily as a result of its extreme growth in the mid-1990s. Many *PC Magazine* readers responded to the company's distinction as an "Editors' Choice" in 1995 with criticism. Some complained, for example, that the toll-free number was impossible to reach, and that assistance-request faxes to the company were not answered promptly. Gateway, Inc. responded, according to the magazine, by stating that its sales had grown faster than its support services. The company experienced difficulty keeping up with demand.

Gateway, Inc. also had challenges in selling its products abroad, prompted by cultural differences. Europeans, for example, were reluctant to purchase expensive consumer goods directly. The same concern was expressed in the United States: how effective was the big-ticket direct sell? In 1995 Gateway, Inc. began to branch out to other means of advertising in the United States. These included placing kiosks in airports and expanding its print-media campaign beyond computer publications.

CURRENT TRENDS

In April 1998, Gateway, Inc. announced that it would open a new administrative office in San Diego, yet would keep South Dakota as its base. The company also planned to open Internet-service headquarters in New York. Gateway Business, based in Irvine, California, was begun, in order to focus more attention on educational, governmental, and commercial customers' technical needs. Education and government accounted for 20 percent of 1997's sales. Another 30 percent of the sales were made to businesses, and 15 percent were outside the United States. On November 6, 1997, Mir-24 cosmonauts Anatoly Solovyev and Pavel Vinogradov used the Internet to order two Gateway G6-233 multimedia PCS, the first two computers sold to customers in space.

In the late 1990s, Gateway, Inc. announced a new technology shopping concept called "Gateway Country Stores." These outlets are unique as they allow customers to go in and test out a product, and then place an order—but not to make a direct purchase on the spot since there is no inventory on hand. These showrooms, of between 8,000 and 10,000 square feet, began to appear in 1996. By the end of 1997 there were 37, with plans for as many more in 1998. Their decor is consistent with the company's prairie theme, and include John Deere tractor seats (underwritten by the tractor company itself) and authentic silos. Such a store has even opened in Auckland, New Zealand.

PRODUCTS

Gateway's products include personal computers, from desktop PCs to PC/TVs to sub-notebooks. The company also sells add-ons, such as CD-ROM drives, fax-modems, monitors, and printers. In April 1998 it announced that it would provide systems with Pentium(R) II processors, based on Intel's 440BX AGPset, in addition to coupons for free upgrades to Windows 98, in anticipation of its introduction, to purchasers of PCs with Windows 95.

CORPORATE CITIZENSHIP

Gateway, Inc. has been a sponsor of the Nike Dakota Dunes Open. In 1996, the event raised over $275,00 for children's charities. In 1997 the Gateway Foundation gave money to over 280 U.S. charities.

GLOBAL PRESENCE

Gateway, Inc. opened a manufacturing and services facility in Ireland in 1993. The company also has locations in Australia, France, Germany, Japan, and Malaysia. European operations became profitable in the third quarter of 1994, when business on that continent contributed to 6 percent of the company's total sales. International sales traditionally account for about half of a computer firm's business, according to *Financial World*. However, of 1997's total sales of $6.3 billion, Europe accounted for 10 percent or $635 million and the Asia/Pacific region accounted for 6 percent or $355 million. The United States accounted for the remaining 84 percent, or $5.3 billion.

EMPLOYMENT

Gateway, Inc. is South Dakota's largest employer, with about half its personnel working inside the state. Globally, the company's employee base grows at an annual rate of over 130 percent. The number of employees rose from approximately 2,800 in 1993, to more than 5,400 in 1994, and then to 9,300 employees in 1995. An estimated one-third of those employees work the telephones in sales and support each day. In 1998 the North Sioux City, South Dakota, work force alone was slated

CHRONOLOGY:
Key Dates for Gateway, Inc.

1985: Ted Waitt founds TIPC Network

1987: TIPC offers their Gateway 2000 computer through their direct sales channel

1988: TIPC changes its name to Gateway 2000

1990: Gateway relocates to South Dakota

1993: Gateway goes public

1998: The company name changes from Gateway 2000 to Gateway, Inc.

to grow by over 250. However, the company has emphasized the need to keep its overhead low, pointing directly to the low hourly wages paid to, as stated in *Forbes,* "hourly employees happy for the work." Gateway, Inc. is a company in which employees have a hand in advertising campaigns as well.

SOURCES OF INFORMATION

Bibliography

"98 Upgrade Opportunity."*Business Wire,* 2 April 1998.

1996 Gateway Annual Report. North Sioux City, SD: Gateway, Inc., 1997.

1997 Gateway Annual Report. North Sioux City, SD: Gateway, Inc., 1998.

"Gateway Announces Further Expansion." *PR Newswire,* 7 April 1998.

"Gateway, Inc." *Hoover's Handbook of American Business 1997.* Austin, TX: The Reference Press, 1996.

"Gateway, Inc." *Hoover's Online,* 20 August 1998. Available at http://www.hoovers.com.

Gateway, Inc. Home Page, May 1998. Available at http://www. gateway.com.

"Gateway to Expand California Operations." *Reuters,* 7 April 1998.

"Gateway 2000 Announces Aggressive Introduction of Latest Technologies." *Business Wire,*15 April 1998.

"Gateway 2000 Signs Agreement with Pulsar Data Systems." *Business Wire,* 25 March 1998.

Haugen, Doris. "Gateway to Move Offices to California." *AP,* 8 April 1998.

Howard, Bill. "The Gateway Phenomenon."*PC Magazine,* 28 March 1995.

Noer, Michael. "New Kid on the Block." *Forbes,* 14 February 1994.

Reidy, Chris. "Gateway 2000 Subsidiary to Open Store in Boston Area." *The Boston Globe,* 6 September 1997.

Ward, Judy. "Little Stock on the Prairie: Gateway 2000, South Dakota's Computer Company, Experiences Growing Pains." *Financial World,* 17 January 1995.

Warshaw, Michael. "Guts and Glory—From Farm Boy to Billionaire: Ted Waitt's Inspiring Story of Incredible Growth." *Success,* March 1997.

For an annual report:

telephone: (800)846-4503

For additional industry research:

Investigate companies by their Standard Industrial Classification Codes, also known as SICs. Gateway, Inc.'s primary SICs are:

3571 Electronic Computers

5961 Catalog and Mail-Order Houses

The Gatorade Company

OVERVIEW

Gatorade is the leading sports drink in the United States and adhered to its slogan, "Life is a sport. Drink it up," by drinking up close to $2 billion in the sports beverage market in 1997. According to Quaker Oats Co., the drink had an 82-percent market share in 1997. The company's goal is to ensure that every hot, sweaty workout concludes with generous gulps of Gatorade.

COMPANY FINANCES

Gatorade is one of Quaker Oats' most successful divisions, accounting for close to a third of the company's total sales. In 1997, overall Gatorade sales worldwide increased 10 percent to $1.52 billion, reflecting an 8-percent increase in the United States and Canada, and 19-percent growth in international sales. Gatorade sales that year topped the billion dollar mark in July, well in advance of company expectations and three months earlier than in 1996. "1997 was an outstanding year for Worldwide Gatorade," said Quaker CEO Robert Morrison, commenting on the results in a company press release. Total revenues for Quaker Oats in 1997 were $5.02 billion, down 4 percent from 1996's $5.20 billion.

ANALYSTS' OPINIONS

"Gatorade defines the category," said Jesse Meyers, publisher of *Beverage Digest,* in a 1992 article about the sports drink market, which appeared in *Time.* "There is

FOUNDED: 1965

Contact Information:
HEADQUARTERS: Quaker Tower
321 N. Clark St.
Chicago, IL 60610-4714
FAX: (312)222-8323
PHONE: (312)222-7111
TOLL FREE: (800)884-2867
URL: http://www.gatorade.com

FAST FACTS:

About The Gatorade Company

Ownership: The Gatorade Company is a division of The Quaker Oats Company, which is a publicly owned company traded on the New York Stock Exchange.

Ticker symbol: OAT

Officers: Robert S. Morrison, Chmn., Pres., & CEO, 1998 salary $950,000, bonus $1 million

Employees: 2,600

Principal Subsidiary Companies: The Gatorade Company is a division of The Quaker Oats Company.

Chief Competitors: Competing sports drinks include: PowerAde,; All Sport,; 10-K,; Exceed,; Cytomax,; Hydra Fuel,; Quickick; and HY-5.

---

not a beverage category in any country in the world that is so dominated by one producer."

Competition was keener and greater for Gatorade in the mid-1990s. "Under twin challenges from Coke's PowerAde and Pepsi's All Sport," according to *Brandweek,* "Gatorade has experimented more with off-beat flavors and packages, including the sports bottles, to broaden consumption occasions of the $1.1 billion brand. Frost's flavors are the first from Gatorade to eschew actual fruit names; they're described simply as light-tasting fruit-flavor blends." Quaker Oats experienced increasing problems in its beverage sales in the mid-1990s following the acquisition of Snapple. "Gatorade parent Quaker Oats has been in turmoil, with high-level execs such as . . . Phil Marineau, making hasty exits as the company scrambled to deal with the consequences of its so-far-disastrous acquisition of Snapple for $1.7 billion." This leads to speculation as to how the company would solve the problem. Discussion among analysts was that perhaps a package deal for the sale of Gatorade and Snapple would be tried as "Gatorade, with an 80% market share and strong international growth potential, could garner closer to 15 times cash flow."

In yet another *Brandweek* article, it was stated that "Rumors have swirled for months that the company may end up dismembered, with Gatorade packaged for sale as a sweetener to unload Snapple." However, *Brandweek* speculated in a 1996 article that "Pepsi wouldn't likely score with Wall Street by paying too hefty a price, yet the prospect of a Snapple spinoff to Cadbury could soften

the blow to '97 earnings. It would also keep Snapple focused within its independent bottling system, among other distributors. "With Gatorade in its pocket, Procter [& Gamble] would gain the ability to ride a marquee brand into the direct-store delivery system beside its Hawaiian Punch and Sunny Delight drinks. Sunny D alone is pegged to become one of P&G's top five brands within the next two years."

Gatorade was given a reprieve when Snapple was acquired in early 1997. It was a lucky thing too. Unloading the failing Snapple left Quaker's beverage division to Gatorade, resulting in immediate positive cash flow. Worldwide, Gatorade reported a 20-percent increase in operating income that year with 10-percent sales growth—a big plus in what was otherwise a stagnant year for Quaker Oats.

HISTORY

Gatorade was the creation of a team of researchers at the University of Florida, including nephrologist, Dr. Robert Cade, in the early 1960s. It was designed to aid athletes by acting as a hydrating replacement for body fluids lost in physical exertion in hot weather. Ten players on the football team tested the liquid during practices and games in 1965.

The tests proved successful. The team had a winning season and, according to company lore, the team "became known as the 'second-half team' by outplaying their opponents during the final half of their games." The team's coach recognized the advantages of having his players drink Gatorade Thirst Quencher: They had fewer problems with dehydration and showed increased efficiency and greater endurance. In fact, on January 1, 1967, when the Gators beat Georgia Tech 27-12 in the Orange Bowl, Georgia Tech Head Coach Bobby Dodd told *Sports Illustrated* magazine the reason for his team's loss was that, "We didn't have Gatorade. That made the difference."

Stokley-Van Camp was given the rights to produce and sell the beverage in the United States in 1967. The company gained permission from the National Football League to offer the drink to teams and contact their trainers. The two parties soon signed a licensing agreement.

This agreement marked the genesis of a trend. Gatorade is often seen on the sidelines at sporting events from little league baseball to professional tennis. It is the official drink of sports organizations including Major League Baseball and the National Hockey League.

So integrated is the drink in the day-to-day business of professional sports, that it soon became a part of victory celebrations, demonstrating its assimilation into sports culture through sideline antics. As *Sports Illustrated* noted, "This business of dousing the coach began when the New York Giants took to pouring a large coolerful of the beverage over Bill Parcells's head during their Super Bowl-winning 1986 season."

Certainly, the added attention brought to the brand-name sports drink didn't hurt its image or market share. And just as teams at many levels have Gatorade on the sidelines, so too have they adopted the ceremonial soaking.

Stokley-Van Camp and Gatorade were purchased by Quaker Oats in 1983. In that year, its sales were about $120 million. Over the following decade, sales increased by more than 100 percent. Quaker Oats company literature states that the company's "research scientists and independent sports-science professionals have continued testing Gatorade to re-affirm its optimum formulation."

The sports drink market continued to grow, prompting a 1992 *Time* article stating, "What they're all worked up about is the U.S. sports-drink market, a billion-dollar retail segment that has been growing about 10% annually. It will take world-class contenders . . . to unseat the defending champion, Quaker Oats Co.'s Gatorade, which accounts for some 90% of nationwide sales. Like Kleenex in the tissue market and Xerox among copiers, Gatorade has become the generic word for sports drinks."

In 1996 the company had sales of about $1.4 billion. That figure continued to grow as Gatorade, in 1996 and 1997, began to target the regular consumer who may or may not participate heavily in sports training or competition. Sales in 1997 rose another 10 percent to more than $1.5 billion.

STRATEGY

Under the direction of the Quaker Oats company, Gatorade's distribution was increased and new flavors have been added. This also included an advertising and promotion campaign held in conjunction with the NBA (National Basketball Association) Championship.

Another innovation was the "Availability" initiative that aimed at increasing distribution and consumption in hot and thirsty "on premise" channels. In other words, the company was pushing to extend Gatorade's reach beyond the traditional sports market and put it in direct competition with traditional soft drinks. In 1997 the Availability team put the drink into 7,200 new locations, prompting David B. Williams, vice president and chief customer officer for Gatorade North America, to say, "As we look at 1998 and beyond, this initiative will drive significant dollar growth."

In parallel with this new strategy, in January 1997 Gatorade launched a new sub-line, Gatorade Frost, to broaden the brand's appeal beyond traditional team competitive sports. Aimed at what the company described as the 'active thirst' category, a market 10 times the size of the sports drink segment, Gatorade Frost proved enormously successful, far exceeding company expectations.

CHRONOLOGY:
Key Dates for The Gatorade Company

1965: Players for the University of Florida begin testing Dr. Cade's hydrating drink

1967: Stokley-Van Camp is given the rights to produce and sell Gatorade; a licensing agreement is reached with the NFL to use Gatorade

1983: Quaker Oats purchases Stokley and Gatorade

1986: The New York Giants begin an NFL tradition by dumping Gatorade on the coaches head following their Super Bowl victory

1990: Michael Jordan signs on as company spokesman

1997: Gatorade launches Gatorade Frost

INFLUENCES

The biggest influence on Gatorade has been the Quaker Oats company's relentless marketing. Sue Wellington, vice president of marketing for Gatorade, told *Brandweek* "that she still views tap water as the toughest competitor—'and we're kicking their butt!'"

That relentless marketing was key to the success of Gatorade Frost. "Gatorade knows the active consumer better than anyone," said (former) Quaker Oats executive James F. Doyle. "We know how to formulate beverages that truly quench to the core, and we understand what it takes to attract the attention of young, active and thirsty consumers. These two elements have been the cornerstone of Gatorade's success for three decades, and Gatorade Frost is no exception."

CURRENT TRENDS

Despite aggressive competition, Gatorade was able to maintain its market share in 1997 and make further inroads into foreign markets. The company cited the addition of new flavors in addition to packaging changes, promotions, and scrutinized distribution. Among these were the Cherry Rush, Strawberry Kiwi, and M'mmmandarina flavors, added in 1996. Prior to that, three new flavors, aimed at women athletes, were introduced—Alpine Snow, Glacier Freeze, and Whitewater Splash.

New package concepts included the introduction of sports bottle four-packs, a "big grip" gallon, and the new

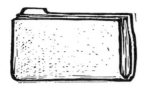

SPORTS DRINK?

Gatorade is marketed not merely as a tasty drink, but as a carbohydrate-electrolyte beverage designed to provide rapid rehydration. How does it work? Well, all food and beverages are absorbed by the small intestine, and Gatorade claims that its 6-percent carbohydrate level and small amount of sodium are ideal for rapid fluid absorption. By comparison, beverages with a higher percentage of carbohydrates, such as fruit drinks and soft drinks, are said to slow the absorption rate of fluids. Gatorade points out that the salt and sugar in Gatorade "stimulates people to drink more fluid voluntarily."

container for its powdered drink mix in the shape of a cooler. The company plans to continue research and development on new flavors into 1997.

The biggest success of 1997 was Gatorade Frost. After only six months in the market, it hit the $100-million sales mark—a figure the company had originally projected for the entire year. It turned out to be the most successful introduction in Gatorade's 30-year history. In making the announcement, Doyle commented, "We knew Gatorade Frost was a very cool idea, but this significant milestone comes far earlier than we'd expected. It's encouraging to see consumers react so positively to what we believed was a hot growth opportunity for Gatorade."

PRODUCTS

Gatorade's original product is a sports drink in a lemon-lime flavor. In the late 1990s, the product was sold in liquid and powdered form and came in a wide range of new flavors including the Gatorade Frost flavors: Alpine Snow, Glacier Freeze, and Whitewater Splash. Boasting the same formulation and fluid replacement benefits as the flagship product line, the new Gatorade Frost drinks feature what the company described as "lighter, more crisp taste profiles."

CORPORATE CITIZENSHIP

Quaker Oats has its own charitable foundation, the Quaker Oats Foundation, which donates money to a va-

riety of causes and funds. In 1998 the foundation presented a $50,000 check to the National Hispanic Scholarship Fund (NHSF). It was the largest single donation to Hispanic education in the Foundation's 50-year history, and provides $3,000 to each of the recipients identified through NHSF.

GLOBAL PRESENCE

For many years, Gatorade was primarily a United States phenomenon. In 1992 Quaker Oats decided to distribute the beverage worldwide. The theory was that the drink would be equally successful outside the United States because "no other sports beverage because of its distinct scientific formulation and market position, is more poised to take advantage of a worldwide opportunity."

The company continues to work at expanding distribution beyond the United States, particularly in Latin America and the Pacific Rim countries. More than $20 million was spent on expansion in 1996, resulting in sales of $283 million in more than 45 nations. The number of countries in which the drink was sold increased by 10 over the previous year. Worldwide sales increased 19 percent internationally, reflecting growth in both Latin America and Italy. In 1997 international sales climbed 18.7 percent to $335.2 million.

By 1998 the company was the world's leading manufacturer of sports beverages, with Gatorade being sold in 47 countries around the world. The number one sports drink in the United States, Canada, Mexico, Italy, Argentina, Brazil, Venezuela, Colombia, Indonesia and the Philippines, Gatorade is also one of the leading sports drink brands in Korea and Australia.

EMPLOYMENT

In 1998 the Quaker Oats Company's Gatorade beverage plant in Kissimmee, Florida, received ISO 9002 certification from the International Organization of Standardization. ISO certification identifies a facility as having demonstrated the highest and most consistent quality practices in its industry. To obtain the certification, Gatorade employees spent two years collecting information, documenting work processes, installing and implementing a computer document control system, and training team members.

SOURCES OF INFORMATION

Bibliography
Brown, Warren. "Quaker Oats Reducing the Chaff." *Washington Post,* 29 March 1988.

"Gatorade Frost Delivers Hot Results: New Line Hits $100 Million in Sales in Just Six Months." *PRNewswire,* 22 July 1997.

"Gatorade Plant Gets World-Class Quality Certification." *PRNewswire,* 26 January 1998.

"Gatorade Sets New Sales Record . . . Again." *PRNewswire,* 17 September 1997.

Gatorade Thirst Quencher: Beverage Comparison Chart. Chicago, IL: The Gatorade Company, 1995.

"The History of Gatorade Thirst Quencher." Stokley-Van Camps, 1992.

Jaroff, Leon. "A Thirst for Competition." *Time,* 1 June 1992.

Khermouch, Gerry, and Karen Benezra. "Gator Wrestler." *Brandweek,* 9 December 1996.

Khermouch, Gerry et. al. "Marketing's Most Wanted: A New Breed Whose Influence Will Impact 1997 Markets." *Brandweek,* 4 November 1996.

Kirshenbaum, Jerry. "Douse It." *Sports Illustrated,* 1 February 1993.

"The Quaker Oats Company and Subsidiaries 10-K Filing." May 1998. Available at http://www.sec.gov.

"Quaker Oats Foundation Gives $50,000 In Hispanic Scholarships." *PRNewswire,* 17 September 1997.

"Quaker Reports 42% Earnings Increase for 1997 Before Unusual Items; Fourth-Quarter Earnings $0.22 Before Unusual Items." *PRNewswire,* 5 February 1998.

"Reynolds Named VP of Availability for Gatorade." *PRNewswire,* 3 February 1998.

For an annual report:

telephone: (800) 685-6566

For additional industry research:

Investigate companies by their Standard Industrial Classification Codes, also known as SICs. Gatorade's primary SIC is:

2086 Bottled & Canned Soft Drinks

Geffen Records, Inc.

FOUNDED: 1980

Contact Information:

HEADQUARTERS: 9130 Sunset Blvd.
   Los Angeles, CA 90069
PHONE: (310)278-9010
URL: http://www.geffen.com

OVERVIEW

Geffen Records is a major record company, which includes imprints Geffen/DGC Records and ALMO Sounds. The company also distributes labels such as DreamWorks SKG Records and Outpost Records.

ANALYSTS' OPINIONS

In 1994 *Billboard* wrote that, "Geffen/DGC's recent conquest of the top three slots on *Billboard's* Modern Rock Tracks chart could be just the beginning for the label, which plans to unleash a heavily alternative-oriented slate of releases in the next quarter. The label is planning to maximize the impact of its new and still-developing acts with marketing, sales, and promotion campaigns custom-tailored to its baby bands needs."

Geffen's 1994 chart trifecta with its DGC acts is an unprecedented feat. The week of January 29, Nirvana's "All Apologies," Beck's "Loser," and Counting Crows' "Mr. Jones" held Nos. 1, 2, and 3 on the Modern Rock Tracks chart, respectively. The following week, "Loser" hit No. 1, "Mr. Jones" climbed to No. 2, and "All Apologies" slipped to No. 3.

It marked the first time a single imprint held the top three slots on the chart since its inception in September 1988, although companies in the Warner family—Warner Bros., Sire, and Reprise—collectively pulled off hat tricks in 1989 and 1992.

HISTORY

Geffen Records was founded in 1980 when David Geffen, previously the founder of superlabel Asylum Records, resumed working in the music business after a four-year absence. The company, then a three-person operation, was located in the original Asylum offices on Los Angeles' famed Sunset Strip. Among its first artists were John Lennon and Donna Summer. Summer had the first single and album for the label, which in turn became its first gold single and first gold album. The John Lennon/ Yoko Ono recording *Double Fantasy,* was the first Geffen Records album to hit number one. This also became its first million-selling album. In its first year of operation, Geffen Records reported its gross to be $25 million.

At the end of the decade, Geffen Records claimed to be "the most successful independently owned record company in history." The label had struck platinum, time and again, with a host of artists including Peter Gabriel, Tesla, Cher, and Aerosmith. One of the biggest of these was newcomer Guns N' Roses. The band's first recording, *Appetite For Destruction,* sold 13 million albums domestically and 5 million internationally. The company reportedly has had 41 albums that have sold more than 500,000 copies, with 22 of those having sold more than 1 million copies.

According to a 1996 *Forbes* interview with David Geffen, "Geffen Records lost money in every quarter for its first six years. Then in 1989 it was worth $500 million."

Geffen Records was purchased by MCA in 1990, ending its reign as the "last major independent" recording label. David Geffen remained chairman of the board and chief executive officer. The company's product distribution was moved to Uni from WEA in 1991. That same year, the company reported that it had grossed $225 million and had released 33 albums.

Also in the 1990s, Geffen Records started DGC Records, an imprint designed for new artists outside the mainstream. One of the first artists on the label was Nirvana. Their debut recording, *Nevermind,* sold more than 12 million worldwide. Other successful recordings by the imprint in the 1990s included The Counting Crows' *August and Everything After;* Hole's *Live Through This;* and Beck's *Mellow Gold.*

In an interview with *Billboard,* Ed Rosenblatt, then head of Geffen Records, discussed where Geffen/DGC Records fit into the label, "We, up to this point, are a rock 'n' roll record company," Rosenblatt explained. "We are not in the urban business . . . We are not in the country business. We're not in the classical music business. We are in the rock 'n' roll business. We're just taking advantage of some excellent signing that our A&R [artist and repertoire] department was fortunate enough to get, and some excellent records that those artists have made." Elaborating on Rosenblatt's theme, Geffen's A&R executive Tom Zutaut adds, "Historically, Geffen Records has always been great about bringing various styles of rock

FAST FACTS:
About Geffen Records, Inc.

Ownership: Geffen Records, Inc. is a privately held company.

Officers: David Geffen, founder; Ed Rosenblatt, chairman & CEO

Employees: 200

Chief Competitors: Geffen Records competes with other records labels including: Sony Music; Warner Music; BMG; PolyGram; and EMI.

music into the mainstream. When hard rock/metal bands were having their day, we were heavy in that business, and we saw it coming before it happened."

Geffen/DGC Records grossed $505 million worldwide in 1994, a year touted in the trade press as its most successful, and certainly the best to date in its then 15-year history. Both Geffen and DGC had a total of 28 albums on the *Billboard* 200 chart in 1994, compared to 18 in 1993. Its recording artists received numerous awards that year as well. The total awards for Geffen Records through 1996 included 76 gold albums, 48 platinum albums, 22 multi-platinum albums, 19 gold singles, 1 platinum single, and 23 Grammy awards.

"When we started the label, we started with people who put us in business right away, but the intention of the label has always been to find and encourage and develop new artists, and that is what we have done from the very beginning," said David Geffen in a 1995 interview with *Billboard.* "From 1985 until 1993, we had three guys that were responsible for a lot of the signings, but not all of them," he says. "Now we have a very full, very active, and very talented A&R staff that is responsible for signing a lot of the acts that have happened this year." Acts signed in 1994 included Veruca, Salt, Beck, and Weezer.

In 1995 Seagram purchased 80 percent of Geffen Records' parent company MCA for $5.7 billion. MCA had purchased Geffen in March 1990, prior to MCA's sale to Matsushita. David Geffen left the company soon after. In April 1995, he parted company with the label he had founded, in order to work exclusively with DreamWorks SKG, an entertainment company he founded with Steven Spielberg and Jeffrey Katzenberg. Ed Rosenblatt, who had been with the company since its formation, took the helm as chairman and chief executive officer. In June 1995, Geffen Records and DreamWorks SKG reached an agreement in which Geffen Records would distribute recordings on that company's newly formed recording labels. The first artist signed to SKG Records was George Michael.

In 1996 the company rolled out its Geffen Gold Line, an array of previously released works to be sold at lower prices, including XTC's *Nonsuch* and the *Days of Thunder* soundtrack. At the end of 1996, MCA, the parent company of Geffen Records, had a 12 percent share of the domestic recording market, and a 6 percent share of the global market. Bill Bennett was named president of both Geffen Records and DGC Records in July 1996. He had been the director of promotion and the general manager, having joined DGC in 1991. Bennett is the second person to hold the title of president in Geffen's 16-year history.

INFLUENCES

Geffen Records, along with its parent company and Virgin Records, ceased distribution with record clubs in 1995. The National Association of Recording Merchandisers found that 74 percent of record club members are also heavy music retail consumers. Music executives contend that the clubs "cannibalize" or eat into retail distribution. These clubs license albums from labels at about half the price that retailers pay, and therefore are able to offer deep discounts and promotional offers.

Geffen Records, in 1995, was the first recording company to use the Internet to release a song. Aerosmith put a "never-before-released" song online for fans to download, *Head First.*

CURRENT TRENDS

In 1998, Geffen started an imprint called Delinquent Records primarily to release soundtracks of movies produced by Jane Hamsher and Don Murphy as JD Productions. Its first offering, the music from *Permanent Midnight,* was released in the third quarter of 1998.

PRODUCTS

Geffen Records' recording artists have included Aerosmith, Beck, Cher, Counting Crows, Peter Gabriel, Guns N' Roses, Hole, Elton John, John Lennon, Pat Metheny, Nirvana, Slash, Donna Summer, Tesla, Weezer, Whitesnake, and White Zombie.

GLOBAL PRESENCE

MCA, the parent company of Geffen Records had a 6-percent share of the $37 million-plus global recording market at the end of 1996. It has affiliates in 89 percent of the world's record markets, and wholly owned MCA record companies in such countries as Australia, New Zealand, Ireland, and Portugal. In 1996 the company began to plan for similar operations in Mexico, Brazil, Argentina, and Thailand. BMG had been responsible for Geffen Records' global distribution, beginning in 1991.

SOURCES OF INFORMATION

Bibliography

Christman, Ed. "MCA, Geffen Defect from Record Clubs." *Billboard.* 4 November 1995.

Geffen Records: An Abridged History. Los Angeles, CA: Geffen Records, 1996.

Gubernick, Lisa. "California Dreamin'." *Forbes,* 29 July 1996.

Morris, Chris. "Geffen Launches Delinquent." *Billboard,* 24 January 1998.

Morris, Chris. "Geffen's Modern Rock Methodology Pays Off." *Billboard,* 12 February 1994.

Reece, Douglas. "Geffen Launches Budget Gold Line." *Billboard,* 9 March 1996.

"Report for the Fiscal Year Ended January 31, 1996." *The Seagram Company Ltd.* Quebec, Canada: 1996.

Rosen, Craig. "Bennett Becomes 2nd Prez in Geffen's History." *Billboard,* 20 July 1996.

Rosen, Craig. "For Geffen's Rosenblatt, Intriguing Power Transfer." *Billboard,* 22 April 1995.

Rosen, Craig. "Geffen Records Enjoys Best Year." *Billboard,* 21 January 1995.

"The Trail Blazing." *Billboard,* 6 May 1995.

For additional industry research:

Investigate companies by their Standard Industrial Classification Codes, also known as SICs. Geffen's primary SIC is:

3652 Prerecorded Records & Tapes

General Electric Company

ALSO KNOWN AS: GE
FOUNDED: 1892

Contact Information:
HEADQUARTERS: 3135 Easton Tpke.
  Fairfield, CT 06431-0001
PHONE: (203)373-2211
FAX: (203)373-2071
URL: http://www.ge.com

OVERVIEW

General Electric (GE) is the fifth-largest and most valuable company in the United States. It is a global conglomerate with business interests in manufacturing, technological services, financial services, network and cable television, and household appliances. It was the world's most profitable corporation in 1997, with revenues of $90.8 billion. The company's financial-services unit, GE Capital Services, has accounted for nearly one-third of the corporation's total profits. GE also owns the National Broadcasting Company (NBC), which includes cable networks CNBC and MSNBC, and profits and ratings alike have soared under the company's control. In 1998, over two-thirds of revenue derived from the company's financial, product, and information services. Jack Welch, GE's chairman, has structured the company to operate according to his own basic business strategy: focusing resources on the company's business units that are the leaders in their respective markets. Business units that have not met that criterion have been sold off or closed.

COMPANY FINANCES

Revenues for 1997 were $90.8 billion. International sales accounted for $39.0 billion of the total—about 40 percent. Net earnings were $8.2 billion, for a result of $2.50 per share, up 14 percent from 1996. In 1996 net earnings were $7.3 billion on revenues of $79.2 billion. Total return per share in 1997 was 51 percent. In 1998 the quarterly dividend was $.30 per share. This dividend has been paid every quarter since 1899, and has increased annually since 1975. Between 1994 and 1998, the com-

FINANCES:

General Electric Co.
Revenues, 1994-1997
(billion dollars)

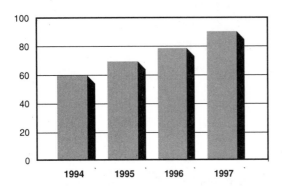

General Electric Co.
1997 Stock Prices
(dollars)

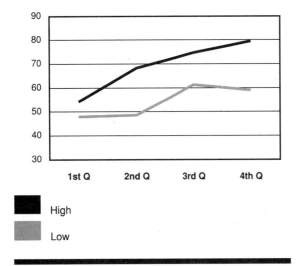

company has been a front-runner in every industry where it is involved. As investment manager Steve Leeb stated in *Business Week,* "One very impressive thing about GE is that it's hard to find any fundamental benchmark on which it doesn't excel." Industry experts have been concerned over the impending retirement of CEO Jack Welch in the year 2000. Welch is considered to be one of the most effective CEOs in the world. Under his guidance, GE has grown into one of the world's most powerful corporations. Much of the company's success can be attributed to his management style. "This guy's legacy will be to create more shareholder value on the face of the planet than ever—forever," said Nicholas P. Heymann, of Prudential Securities, in *Business Week.* Experts have wondered if GE will continue its remarkable prosperity under the guidance of a new CEO.

HISTORY

General Electric was established in 1892 after a merger between the Edison General Electric Company and the Thomson-Houston Electric Company. Thomas Edison was one of the company's first directors. GE's emphasis on research resulted in the development of innovative products such as elevators, light bulbs, toasters, and other household appliances. These products fueled the company's growth during the early 1900s. Diversification continued to increase GE's profit margins throughout the years.

Throughout its history, GE was involved with various ventures. In the 1920s GE, along with Westinghouse, became part of a radio broadcasting venture. In the 1950s, GE became involved with the computer industry but sold that part of the business to Honeywell in 1970. The 1980s were a period of reconstruction for the company.

Jack Welch was named the company's CEO in 1981. Over the next 10 years, GE sold off many of its business interests in order to focus primarily on high-return offerings, such as financial services, medical systems, and aircraft engines. The company acquired NBC in 1986, and entered the lighting industry as a manufacturer and supplier in the early 1990s.

pany has bought back $17 billion worth of its stock. The most recent stock split was in 1997 (2 for 1). GE's market capitalization (the total value of all its stock) is the highest in the world, at more than $245 billion.

ANALYSTS' OPINIONS

GE has received high praise from many analysts for its conviction that resources should go mainly to business units that dominate their respective markets. The

STRATEGY

GE's enormous success is due primarily to its strict adherence to CEO Jack Welch's doctrine of sticking with proven business winners. Welch believes that resources should not be wasted on businesses that are not leaders in the global market. "Don't play with businesses that can't win," he says. "Businesses that are number 3, number 5 in their market—Christ couldn't fix those businesses. They're going to lose anyway." The company's corporate decisions have consistently displayed a Darwinian outlook.

INFLUENCES

By the early 1980s, GE's emphasis on expansion and industrial diversity had created a mammoth organization with multiple levels of bureaucratic management. The company's corporate direction shifted dramatically in 1981, when Jack Welch became CEO. Within the next 10 years, GE dropped business units that had totaled a quarter of the company's sales in 1980. By 1988 the company's restructuring efforts had resulted in the downsizing of 100,000 employees. Management responsibilities had been redefined, resulting in more efficient business practices. The corporate-reengineering efforts paid huge dividends for the company. Profits grew from $1.65 billion in 1981 to $7.28 billion in 1996. By 1997, analysts acknowledged GE to be among the most profitable companies in the world. Market value grew from $12 to $280 billion under Welch.

GE aggressively moved into the investment banking field in 1987 with the purchase of Kidder, Peabody. This acquisition became a business unit of financial services division, GE Capital. The brokerage unit was ultimately a losing investment, and in 1993 a false-profit scandal came to light. In the wake of the turmoil, Michael Carpenter was terminated as Kidder's chair, and the company was sold to Paine Webber in 1994. Analysts criticized GE for its aggressive purchase of the investment banking company due to its limited experience in the industry.

The purchase of NBC in 1986 proved to be a more successful experience for GE. Jack Welch named Robert Wright, a lawyer by trade, with no prior television or entertainment experience, the network's CEO. Welch's decision met with widespread criticism from industry experts at first, but Wright has since silenced his critics by applying GE's business philosophy to network television. Under his guidance, NBC has broadened its business interests into the cable industry with CNBC, as well as into the global television marketplace. NBC experienced four consecutive years of record profits from 1993 to 1997, and, aided by such hit shows as *ER* and *Seinfeld,* consistently dominated the primetime television ratings by the mid-1990s.

GE was faced with several controversies in early 1997. The company had to pay Fonar Corporation almost $100 million as a result of a court order for violating the latter's MRI scanner patents. Furthermore, Dow Chemical sued GE in 1997, claiming that GE had marked, recruited, and hired former Dow workers who had knowledge of Dow's trade secrets. GE was also faced with the possibility of its first labor strike since 1969 when Jack Welch and Edward Fire, the president of the International Union of Electronic Workers (IUE), became involved in an intense war of words over the job security of union workers.

FAST FACTS:
About General Electric Company

Ownership: General Electric is a publicly owned company, traded on the New York Stock Exchange, the Boston Stock Exchange, and The Stock Exchange, London.

Ticker symbol: GE

Officers: John F. Welch Jr., Chmn. & CEO, 62, $8,000,000; Paolo Fresco, VChmn. & Exec. Officer, 64; John D. Opie, VChmn. & Exec. Officer, 60, $2,600,000; Dennis D. Dammerman, Sr. VP Finance & CFO, 52, $2,325,000

Employees: 276,000 (1997)

Chief Competitors: Some of General Electric's competitors include: Allstate; Caterpillar; Cooper Industries; Electrolux; Krupp; General Motors; GTE; Hitachi; ITT Industries; Maytag; Merrill Lynch; Mitsubishi; Polaroid; Philips Electronics; Raytheon; Rockwell International; Rolls-Royce; State Farm; Time Warner; Walt Disney; Westinghouse; and Whirlpool.

CURRENT TRENDS

Never content with its past successes, GE has continually reinvented itself in order to stay ahead of its competition. "We've just got to be faster," says Welch. "We come to work every day on the razor's edge of a competitive battle." An emphasis on product quality and statistical process control was introduced as a company-wide goal in 1997. GE adopted "Six Sigma," a quality-assurance methodology developed by Motorola, Inc., to focus on "defining, measuring, analyzing, improving, and controlling" each process that takes place in the company. Trained GE employees called "Black Belts" and "Master Black Belts" oversee personnel's training in this philosophy. Says Welch of the concept in *Forbes,* "This is not about sloganeering or bureaucracy or filling out forms. It finally gives us a route to get to the control function, the hardest thing to do in a corporation." Welch projected the program's benefits to GE in 1998 to be worth $750 million.

GE firmly believed it could not rely solely on its manufactured products. The concept that enormous revenue could be obtained by supplying services linked to

CHRONOLOGY:

Key Dates for General Electric Company

1892: Edison General Electric Company merges with Thomson Houston Electric Company to form General Electric Company

1901: GE manufactures a high speed turbine for greater electricity production

1905: GE moves into the realm of household appliances

1918: Pacific Electric Heating Company, Hughes Electric Heating Company, and GE merge

1919: At the request of the government, GE creates Radio Corporation of America (RCA) to develop radio technology

1924: Antitrust action is brought against the company causing GE to leave the utilities business

1932: Irving Langmuir, who developed the electron tube for GE, receives the Nobel Prize

1939: GE develops a new mode of radio transmission called Frequency Modulation (FM)

1945: The United States' first turboprop airplane engine is developed by GE

1955: GE develops the reactor for the *Seawolf*, the world's first nuclear-powered vessel

1961: Twenty-nine companies, including GE, are indicted by the federal government for price fixing on electrical equipment

1976: GE pays $2.2 billion for Utah International, the largest corporate purchase at the time

1986: GE purchases RCA and its NBC subsidiary

1997: GE becomes the first company in the world to exceed a market value of $200 million

GE's core businesses, such as assisting clients' business operations in a consulting capacity, was established as the company's ethos. Everything from running airline-engine service shops to giving management-training classes to clients were considered vital keys to GE's future success. The company planned to share its extensive business experiences and lessons learned, as a service to its customers. Industry experts praised this approach. "This is the next big wave in American industry," reengineering expert Michael Hammer said in *Business Week*.

"The product you sell is only one component of your business."

PRODUCTS

General Electric is involved in a broad array of industries. It builds everything from the most mundane lightbulbs to the most sophisticated power systems to hi-tech plastics. Each unit operates on a grand scale. The GE Aircraft Engines division, for example, is the world's largest builder of jet engines for military and commercial planes. Its GE90 engines, for example, power Boeing's 777 aircraft. In a joint venture with French manufacturer Snecma, GE fills engine orders for many major airlines. GE Appliances make familiar household equipment like the GE SmartWater faucet system. Also through this division, it continues to perfect its designs of items such as dishwashers, ovens, and clothes dryers.

GE Capital comprises 27 separate business, which operate all over the world. They include the Penske Truck Leasing company, various specialty insurance entities, and a financial services company in Ireland called Woodchester. The division has enjoyed more than 20 years of increased profits. It attributes its success to its "three-pronged strategic focus": globalization, a commitment to providing value-added services, and adherence to the Six Sigma principles of quality control.

NBC is a leader in television broadcasting. Its programming, from evening news to prime-time situation comedies, which included the perennially popular *Seinfeld* in the 1990s, to political talk shows, consistently scores high in the ratings. 1997 marked NBC's fifth straight year of record earnings.

CORPORATE CITIZENSHIP

GE has long been active in community involvement, primarily through an entity called Elfun (derived from "Electrical Funds"), which the company established in 1928 to provide a vehicle whereby GE employees could fund charitable activities. The organization has expanded its outreach over the years to include volunteer work in the communities where GE is present, and in assisting in educational activities for underprivileged youth. Elfun's membership grew to 35,000 active and retired GE employees in 1997, with local affiliates in 10 countries. In 1992 GE was given The National Science Foundation's first National Corporate Achievement Award, in observance of its support for minority students, educators, and professionals in science and mathematics. GE received the President's Volunteer Action Award in 1994, and in 1995, it was recognized with the Council for Aid to Education's Leaders for Change Corporate Award in recognition of its College Bound program. In 1996 the com-

THE WIZARD OF MENLO PARK

It's safe to say that without Thomas Alva Edison, there would have been no GE. True, Edison was with the company for only two years, but the Edison General Electric Company was GE's predecessor, and it was Edison's inventions and discoveries that paved the way for GE's success.

Edison got his start at inventing and experimentation when he built his first laboratory at age 10. By age 16 he had invented a transmitter and receiver for the automatic telegraph—enabling him to sleep and send messages at the same time (his boss was not too appreciative.) In 1869, Edison invented the Edison Universal Stock Printer and sold the rights for $40,000 (he was only hoping for $4,000). With that money Edison, started a business to build stock tickers and telegraphs, and he also used it to help him continue his experiments.

In 1876 Edison built his laboratory in Menlo Park, New Jersey. There 60 employees worked on 40 projects at a time. Out of the Menlo Park factory came the phonograph, the Edison dynamo, and the invention that Edison is most remembered for, a practical incandescent lamp. It took Edison more than $40,000 and over 1,200 experiments before he succeeded at producing an effective light in 1879. In 1882, Edison set up the first light-power station, helping to illuminate part of New York City.

In 1887 Edison moved to a larger factory in West Orange, New Jersey. Out of that factory came an electrical storage battery, the motion picture camera, and silent and sound movies. In all, Edison was issued 1,093 patents for his inventions—more than anyone else in history. Edison applied for as many as 400 patents in a year. For 65 consecutive years, from 1868 to 1933, Edison had a least one patent issued to him in every year.

Edison attributed his success to hard work and perseverance. He is famous for saying, "Invention is 99 percent perspiration and 1 percent inspiration." He often worked up to 112 hours a week. He saw his failures as learning experiences. The story goes that Edison failed 10,000 times in his experiments to develop a storage battery. But of it he said, "Why, I have not failed. I've just found 10,000 ways that won't work." Edison kept on going where others might have given up. Because of his tenacity, he changed the world and lit the way for scientists working for companies like GE, enabling them to take up where he left off. In 1931, when Edison died, electric lights were dimmed for one minute across all the United States—a fitting tribute to the man who helped to transform the century.

pany and its employees donated more than $75 million to charitable organizations all around the world.

GLOBAL PRESENCE

Most investment analysts have agreed that the Asian market promised the most potential for growth in the 1990s. General Electric, however, began a large-scale investment in Europe. Between 1989 and 1997, the company invested more than $10 billion in European industrial plants and companies. GE's investment gamble yielded profits of $1.41 billion in 1996, as compared to its Asian profits of $585 million. "Investing in Europe today requires guts," London business school professor Sumantra Ghoshal said in *Fortune.* GE views the late 1990s Asian financial crisis as an opportunity so it can position itself for the new millennium.

General Electric's influence has been felt everywhere. It has been conducting business in more than 100 countries, which accounted for 40 percent of the company's business in 1996. A focus on expansion has prompted the company to target such markets as India and China. According to analyst Nicholas P. Heymann, in *Business Week,* "GE is now well positioned to outmaneuver its less flexible and more entrenched global competitors." Markets for GE products outside of the United States have included Asia, Europe, Mexico, and South America.

GE's brand name has not wielded the same clout in Europe as it has in the United States. Its European household-appliance business returned disappointing profit margins throughout the 1990s. GE has experienced its greatest success on the continent with GE Capital Services Europe, however. The European branch of the company's financial services group accounted for almost 13 percent of GE Capital Services' net income in 1996.

EMPLOYMENT

GE offers college students hundreds of internships and co-op programs each year that allow students to explore job opportunities with the company, In addition, recent graduates can begin a career with the company in two ways—Leadership Development Programs offer intensive programs in which participants undergo technical training, and Direct Hires, in which GE businesses hire graduates in positions and into business-specific leadership programs. Career opportunities can be explored at the company's web site and resumes can be sent online.

SOURCES OF INFORMATION

Bibliography

Bernstein, Aaron. "High Tension at General Electric." *Business Week,* 24 March 1997.

Byrne, John A. "How Jack Welch Runs GE." *Business Week,* 8 June 1998.

Conlin, Michelle. "For GE's Jack Welch, Cost-Cutting Isn't an Event, It's a Process." *Forbes,* 26 January 1998.

"Dow Chemical Sues GE over Plastics Secrets." *Reuters,* 1 April 1997. Available at http.pathfinder.com.

"Exxon and General Electric Top Forbes List." *Reuters,* 7 April 1997. Available at http.pathfinder.com.

"GE Posts Profits for Quarter, Year." *Fox News,* 16 January 1997.

"General Electric." *Hoover's Online,* 23 August 1998. Available at http://www.hoovers.com.

General Electric Company 1997 Annual Report. Fairfield, CT: General Electric Company, 1997.

General Electric's Home Page, 23 August 1998. Available at http://www.ge.com.

Greenwald, John. "Jack in the Box." *Time,* 3 October 1994.

Gunther, Marc. "How GE Made NBC No. 1." *Fortune,* 3 February 1997.

Koenig, Peter. "If Europe's Dead, Why Is GE Investing Billions There?"*Fortune,* 9 September 1996.

Marcial, Gene. "You Can't Go Wrong with GE." *Business Week,* 22 July 1996.

Morris, Betsy. "Roberto Goizueta and Jack Welch: The Wealth Builders." *Fortune,* 5 February 1996.

Smart, Tim. "GE's Efficiency Doctor Is In." *Business Week,* 28 October 1996.

Smart, Tim. "GE's Welch: Fighting like Hell to Be No. 1." *Business Week,* (international edition), 8 July 1996.

Smart, Tim. "Jack Welch's Encore." *Business Week,* 28 October 1996.

Smart, Tim. "Who Will Fill Jack's Shoes?" *Business Week,* 28 October 1996.

Swoboda, Frank. "Talking Management with Chairman Welch." *Washington Post,* 23 March 1997.

For an annual report:

telephone: (203) 373-2211 **or** for an audio version, telephone: (203)373-2020

For additional industry research:

Investigate companies by their Standard Industrial Classification Codes, also known as SICs. Generald Electric Company's primary SICs are:

3621 Motors & Generators

3639 Household Appliances, NEC

3724 Aircraft Engines & Engine Parts

4911 Electric Services

General Mills, Inc.

OVERVIEW

General Mills is a producer of packaged consumer foods and ranks second (behind Kellogg) as the nation's leading cereal producer. Forty-five percent of the company sales are in cereals. Its Cheerios brand is the country's most popular cereal. General Mills is the leading producer of flour (Gold Medal), dessert and baking mixes (Betty Crocker and Bisquick), dinner and side-dish products (Hamburger Helper, Suddenly Salad) and fruit snacks (Fruit Roll-Ups). The company's yogurt brand, Yoplait, is ranked second in sales. In addition to Kellogg, the company's chief competitors are Philip Morris and Procter & Gamble.

General Mills has focused on international expansion, recently entering joint ventures with Cereal Partners Worldwide, Snack Ventures Europe, International Dessert Partners, and Tong Want in China.

In 1997 General Mills made the largest acquisition in the company's history with its $570-million purchase of the branded cereal and snack mix lines of Ralcorp Holding, Inc., including Chex cereals and Chex Mix snacks.

COMPANY FINANCES

Company sales for 1997 were $5.6 million. In that year earnings fell, due in part to cereal price cuts and in part to the acquisition of the Chex snack and cereal lines. The company's major cereal competitors reduced their prices and cut marketing spending levels in 1996. In June that year General Mills implemented its own price cuts, which reduced sales by approximately $100 million. In 1997 prices increased 2.6 percent, which was the first in-

FOUNDED: 1928

Contact Information:
HEADQUARTERS: 1 General Mills Blvd.
    Minneapolis, MN 55426-1348
PHONE: (612)540-2311
FAX: (612)540-4925
URL: http://www.generalmills.com

FINANCES:

General Mills Inc.
Sales, 1994-1997
(billion dollars)

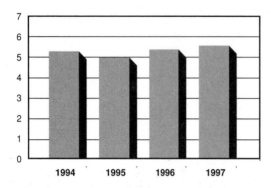

General Mills Inc.
1997 Stock Prices
(dollars)

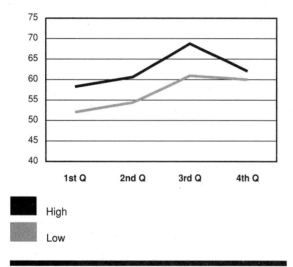

■ High

▨ Low

crease in three years. General Mills' stock value ranged from a low of 56 7/8 to a high of 71 11/16 over a 52-week period. Net earnings per share for the first half of 1998 before unusual items were $1.88, an increase of 4 percent.

ANALYSTS' OPINIONS

General Mills firmly expects its earnings growth to improve in 1998, following the flat figures posted in 1997. Many analysts would agree with this prediction.

The *Value Line Investment Survey* reported that it expects "General Mills' earnings growth to accelerate in the second half of the current fiscal year (ending May 1998). Earnings increases out to 2000-2002 should come close to management's target of 12 percent a year." *Value Line* also states that the company's joint ventures look very promising and should begin to help the bottom line. Stronger and more steady profit growth should become a reality in 3 to 5 years.

HISTORY

General Mills traces its history to the establishment of the Washburn-Crosby Company. This flour miller was awarded a gold medal at an 1880 exhibition, giving rise to its newly named Gold Medal Flour. The company continued operations under this name through the 1920s, primarily selling flour, but in 1924 introduced a ready-to-eat cereal called Wheaties.

In 1925 company president James Bell began a program of consolidation with other mills. The result was General Mills, which became the world's largest miller by 1928. In the 1930s the company began developing so-called convenience foods for consumers. With the advent of World War II, the company produced war goods, including ordnance equipment, and established new divisions in chemicals and electronics. The company paid dividends to its stockholders steadily throughout the 1930s and 1940s.

Diversification of the company began in the 1960s under Edwin Rawlings, then chief executive officer. Rawlings closed half the company's flour mills and divested from unprofitable ventures, a strategy that cost the company $200 million in sales. In the late 1960s Rawlings began acquiring other companies, a practice that continued into the early 1970s. His purchase of both Kenner Products and Parker Brothers ultimately made General Mills the leading toy company worldwide. Rawlings also bought jewelry companies and clothing companies (David Crystal, makers of Izod; Eddie Bauer; Talbots), and purchased Red Lobster in 1970. The latter purchase encouraged the company to form Olive Garden restaurants.

When some of these divisions faltered in the 1980s, they were promptly spun off into other companies or sold. In 1995 General Mills spun off its restaurants as Darden Restaurants to resume its focus on its consumer foods business.

One of the most important parts of the General Mills, Inc. corporate story has been its creation of American pop-culture icons. The most visible of these has been Betty Crocker. Arguably the most important household icon in the United States, Betty has been a fixture on baking mixes since 1936. Her name first appeared on William G. Crocker baking products in 1921. In 1945 Betty was voted the second-most-admired American woman, after Eleanor Roosevelt. Betty's appearance changed only once from 1936 to 1965. As women's roles began to change in the late 1960s, Betty's image was updated five times in a span of 20 years.

The current Betty Crocker, the eighth such recreation, was introduced in 1996 to mark Betty's 75th birthday. The company created a new "look" for Betty Crocker in which the 75 faces of customers who won an essay contest were combined by computer into a composite image representing a wide cross-section of Americans.

STRATEGY

Since the spin-off of its restaurant business in May 1995, General Mills has refocused its attention on its consumer foods business. With the addition of the newly acquired Chex and Cookie Crisp brands and the introduction of three new cereals, the company expected to renew earnings growth in 1998. Following marketing spending cuts in 1997, the company's 1998 marketing expenditures are balanced across the full year. The company's sponsorship of the 1998 Winter Olympics was one of the key elements of its renewed marketing efforts.

Ongoing cost-cutting moves by General Mills included the restructuring of its North American cereal operations. In September 1997 the company closed its two smallest plants in south Chicago, Illinois, and Etobicoke, Ontario, and a cereal production line at its Lodi, California, plant.

According to the company's annual report, General Mills' success over the long term "depends on building unit volumes across our domestic business, increasing our productivity, expanding our international presence and leveraging the benefits of our strong cash flow."

Long-term financial goals for the company have remained essentially unchanged since 1995 when General Mills focused its business on its consumer foods. Those goals, according to the company's annual report, are: 12 percent average annual earnings per share growth; a minimum 25 percent return on capital; balance sheet strength that merits an "A" bond rating; and a 50-60 percent dividend payout.

INFLUENCES

The most significant influence on General Mills' recent operations came in the spring and summer of 1996 when the company's major competitors in the U.S. ready-to-eat cereal market lowered prices up to 20 percent. Big G followed suit in June 1996 and also cut spending for its marketing programs. The company expected this move to reduce its fiscal 1997 sales by approximately $100 million.

FAST FACTS:
About General Mills, Inc.

Ownership: General Mills is a publicly owned company traded on the New York Stock Exchange.

Ticker symbol: GIS

Officers: Stephen W. Sanger, Chmn. of the Board & CEO, age 51 salary, $1,062,050; Raymond G. Viault, VChmn., age 53, salary, $1,040,000; Charles W. Gaillard, Pres., age 56, salary, $930,700.

Employees: 10,200 (1997)

Chief Competitors: General Mills' chief competitors in the ready-to-eat cereal business are Kellogg, the number-one cereal company; Post, the number-three cereal company (owned by Philip Morris); Quaker Oats, Dannon competes with General Mills' Yoplait brand. The company's primary competitors in the dinner, side-dish, and snack lines include: RJR Nabisco; Procter & Gamble; Hershey; Mars; and Nestle.

CURRENT TRENDS

General Mills plans to continue building its brands through increased marketing activity in 1998, particularly in the area of advertising. The company's sponsorship of the U.S. Winter Olympic Games kicked off its renewed marketing effort. Colombo yogurt was the sponsor of the women's hockey team, and the snowboarding and curling events were sponsored by Frosted Cheerios. The Wheaties brand cereal box cover featured the gold medal-winning U.S. Women's Ice Hockey Team. Three additional Wheaties packages featured top-ranked golfer Tiger Woods, who also appeared in the company's television commercials.

PRODUCTS

General Mills' product line includes cereals such as Cheerios, Cocoa Puffs, Kix, Lucky Charms, Total, Trix, and Wheaties; desserts and baking mixes under the trade names Betty Crocker, Bisquick, and Gold Medal; Sweet Rewards reduced-fat and fat-free frostings, cake mixes, and snack bars; snack products and other foods such as Pop Secret popcorn, Bugles, Bac*O's, and Yoplait yo-

Golfer Tiger Woods was named the eighth permanent spokesperson for Wheaties and is shown here on three different cereal box covers. (AP Photo/HO.)

gurt; and dinner and side-dish products including Hamburger Helper, Tuna Helper, and Suddenly Salad.

The company's limited-time-offer products tied to the 1998 Winter Olympic Games were Betty Crocker Team USA (TM) muffin, cake, brownie, and cookie mixes; and USA Olympic Crunch cereal. New products for 1988 included Homestyle Pop Secret popcorn and the Stir 'n Bake dessert mixes, Italian Herb Hamburger Helper, Tuna Melt Tuna Helper, and Betty Crocker seasoned mashed potato side dishes in roasted garlic, sour cream and chives, and butter and herb flavors. New cereals included Team Cheerios, Cinnamon Grahams, and French Toast Crunch. Snack products introduced in 1997 included Fun 'n Games Fruit Roll-Ups, Golden Grahams Treats, and Pop Secret Jumbo Pop.

CORPORATE CITIZENSHIP

Innovation, speed, commitment, and citizenship are the key values General Mills emphasizes in its effort to create a better future for its consumers and communities. The General Mills Foundation demonstrated this commitment with 742 grants totaling $13.1 million targeted to hundreds of organizations in fiscal 1997. The General Mills Foundation also committed more than $2.9 million in matching grants for individual employee contributions, bringing its total grantmaking to nearly $16 million. Its commitments in 1997 included grants to Ohio State Uni-

versity to build a General Mills Cereal Chemistry Lab, the United Negro College Fund for scholarships, Morehouse School of Medicine for physician training, and seven grants funding various educational programs.

General Mills employees and retirees have been actively involved as volunteers in their communities. In 1997, 80 percent of all General Mills employees and 40 percent of retirees gave freely of their time. The company's numerous volunteer projects include a mentoring program for at-risk children, relief efforts for the victims of the record floods of 1997, and Camp Sunrise, a youth employment and camping program for urban youth.

As a food manufacturer, General Mills demonstrates its responsibility to help provide food to hungry Americans through the donation of more than 70 million pounds of food. Grants from the General Mills Foundation also support the Harvesters Community Food Network in Kansas City, Missouri, and other local food banks and meal programs. More than $9 million in product donations were made to Second Harvest, the country's largest food distribution network.

General Mills' community participation as a corporate citizen extends to its involvement in meeting the challenges and problems of our complex society. Challenge U is General Mills' comprehensive student achievement and school improvement program, the goal of which is to reduce the incidence of teenage pregnancy and the high-school dropout rate by providing scholar-

CHRONOLOGY:

Key Dates for General Mills, Inc.

1928: Founded as General Mills

1933: Creates the slogan "Wheaties. The Breakfast of Champions."

1941: Introduces Cheerios

1945: Betty Crocker is voted second most admired American woman

1947: Betty Crocker cake mixes are introduced

1961: Edwin Rawlings becomes CEO

1967: Kenner Products is acquired

1968: Acquires Parker Brothers and Gortons

1970: Purchases Red Lobster

1971: Acquires David Crystal and Eddie Bauer

1977: Buys rights to Yoplait yogurt

1983: Starts Olive Garden restaurant chain

1985: Spins off Kenner Parker Toys and Crystal Brands

1989: Sells Eddie Bauer and Talbots

1995: Spins off restaurants to form Darden restaurants

1997: Purchases Ralcorp Holding, Inc.

BETTY CROCKER, AN AMERICAN LEGEND

From baking mixes and cookbooks, to housewares and appliances, Betty Crocker has long been a household name in America—appearing on more than 250 products. The red spoon logo bearing her name is recognized throughout the world as a symbol of quality.

Betty was "born" in 1921 when General Mills mailed thousands of flour-sack pin cushions to consumers as a reward for completing a promotional puzzle. Each recipient was also mailed a congratulatory letter, and General Mills wanted to sign the letter with a friendly name. The last name of a company director, William G. Crocker, was used, and the first name Betty was chosen for its approachable feel. Consumers liked the name so much that it soon appeared on cooking and baking information to answer the demand for dependable cooking advice.

In 1924, Betty made her radio debut on "Betty Crocker Cooking School of the Air," a program broadcasted in Minneapolis. The show was so popular that it became part of NBC's network lineup soon after. She made an important contribution to America during the Great Depression and World War II through the publication of meal-planning booklets and radio broadcasts. Betty Crocker became a brand name in 1947 when Betty Crocker Ginger Cake mix was released. Until that point, her name had only been used for cooking and baking advice. Since then, consumers have come to recognize the Betty Crocker name and image as well. In the 1950s,

Betty hosted her own television show and appeared on several others.

Throughout the years, Betty underwent many changes to her appearance, but none as big as her alteration in 1996, the year of her 75th birthday. To celebrate, General Mills used a computer to combine 75 women's faces into one to create a more ethnically diverse Betty. This was the eighth version of Betty since her creation.

Today, General Mills continues to vigorously promote Betty Crocker. The company announced in 1998 that it would combine Betty Crocker and its Gold Medal division into a new integrated Betty Crocker division that was projected to produce about one-third of the company's total sales. The same year, General Mills reported that it would open a Betty Crocker Experience store at the Mall of America in Bloomington, Minnesota. Betty Crocker also played a part in the 1998 Olympic Winter Games at Nagano, Japan. General Mills, the sponsor of the US Olympic Team that year, launched a host of Betty Crocker Team USA products such as blueberry muffin and cookie mixes.

With more than 200 cookbook titles, and 250 other cooking and baking-related products carrying her name, Betty Crocker is one of the most popular names among consumers today, and General Mills has taken steps to ensure that she will keep her status for years to come.

ship assistance and school improvement grants. The Power Hour program, funded by the General Mills Foundation, is designed to help increase student academic achievement and improve social interaction for youth in crime and poverty-plagued areas of Southern California. General Mills is addressing the growing problem of violence in communities via grants to the National Coalition of Survivors for Violence Prevention.

GLOBAL PRESENCE

In 1997 General Mills' goal was to raise revenues from international product sales from 4 to 10 percent by the year 2000. The company functions in Europe under the umbrella of Snack Ventures Europe, a joint venture established in 1992 with PepsiCo that combined six existing snack companies. Snack Ventures Europe is the largest snack company on the continent. A similar venture with Nestle, Cereal Partners Worldwide, makes General Mills the second-largest cereal maker in the world.

In 1994 General Mills joined with CPC International to create International Dessert Partners, which expanded baking and dessert mix business to Latin America. The company operates in Mexico, Argentina, Colombia, Brazil, Uruguay, Peru, and Chile.

General Mills Canada holds the number-one market position in desserts, dinner mixes, and fruit snacks in that country. It also ranks as Canada's third-largest cereal company, boasting a gain of two share points in 1997.

Tong Want is General Mills' newest joint venture, located in the People's Republic of China. This 50-50 partnership with Want Want Holdings Ltd. joins General Mills with China's number-one manufacturer of rice crackers in an effort to focus on snack products, including Bugles and other grain-based snacks.

EMPLOYMENT

The modernization of General Mills' breakfast cereal plants in the mid-1990s was part of an ongoing capital improvement plan; however, labor union officials say automation and restructuring have cost employees their jobs. Capital improvement spending at General Mills food division totaled $208 million in 1993. At the company's Buffalo, New York, facility more than $30 million has been spent on improvements since 1981. General Mills Inc. closed its Woodland, California, temporary manufacturing plant in 1994. The breakfast cereal plant had been opened in 1991 to augment cereal

production until a new facility in Albuquerque, New Mexico, could be constructed.

The closing of General Mills' two smallest plants and one cereal production line cost 235 employees their jobs in September 1997.

SOURCES OF INFORMATION

Bibliography

1997 U.S. Public Companies, Directory of Corporate Affiliations, Vol. III. Providence, New Jersey: National Register Publishing, 1997.

1998 American Big Business Directory, Vol. I. Omaha, NE: American Business Directories, 1998.

"General Mills Dismissing Workers and Closing 3 Plants."*The New York Times,* 30 September 1997.

General Mills Home Page. 8 April 1998. Available at http://www.generalmills.com.

"General Mills, Inc." *Hoover's Handbook of American Business 1998.* Austin, TX: Hoover's Business Press, 1998.

"General Mills, Inc." *Market Guide Inc.* 9 April 1998. Available at http://www.marketguide.com/MGI/INDUSTRY/INDUSTRY.htm.

Moody's Handbook of Common Stocks. NY: Moodies Investors Service Inc., 1997.

Sanborn, Stephen. "General Mills." *Value Line Investment Survey.* Value Line Publishing Co. 13 February 1998.

Waxler, Caroline. "Breakfast Champion." *Forbes,* 24 February 1997.

For an annual report:
General Mills' annual report is available on the Internet at: http://www.generalmills.com/financial/report/ **or** write: Investor Relations, General Mills Inc., PO Box 1113, Minneapolis, MN 55440 **or** telephone: (800) 245-5703 **or** (612) 540-2444.

For additional industry research:
Investigate companies by their Standard Industrial Classification Codes, also known as SICs. General Mills' primary SICs are:

2024 Ice Cream & Frozen Desserts

2026 Fluid Milk

2043 Cereal Breakfast Foods

2045 Prepared Flour Mixes and Doughs

2099 Food Preparations NEC

5099 Durable Goods NEC

5141 Groceries-General Line

General Motors Corporation

OVERVIEW

General Motors Corporation is the largest U.S. industrial corporation and the world's leading manufacturer of cars and trucks. GM designs, manufactures, and markets one out of every three cars and trucks produced in the United States. Its nameplates include Chevrolet, Pontiac, GMC, Oldsmobile, Buick, Cadillac, and Saturn. Overseas, the company is involved in the manufacturing and marketing of Opel, Vauxhall, Holden, Isuzu, Saab, Chevrolet, GMC, and Cadillac vehicles. Although the major portion of its business is derived from the automotive industry, GM has substantial interests in telecommunications and space, aerospace and defense, consumer and automotive electronics, financial and insurance services, locomotives, automotive systems, and heavy-duty transmissions.

FOUNDED: 1908

Contact Information:

HEADQUARTERS: 100 Renaissance Center
   Detroit, MI 48243-7301
PHONE: (313)556-5000
FAX: (313)556-5108
URL: http://www.gm.com

COMPANY FINANCES

Since 1992, GM's financial picture has brightened considerably. When John Smith took over as CEO that year, GM owed its pension fund $22 billion, its core North American operations were losing money, and its net liquidity, or cash minus debt, was negative $2 billion. In 1997, according to Daniel Howes in a November 1997 *Detroit News* article, "North American operations are driving the corporation's profitability—though overall, profit margins are still shy of Smith's 5 percent goal—the pension fund is fully funded, and the cash hoard stands at $14.6 billion."

At the end of 1997, GM had a swelling cash flow of $13.9 billion and said that it is committed to return-

FINANCES:

General Motors Corp.
Net Sales & Revenues, 1994-1997
(billion dollars)

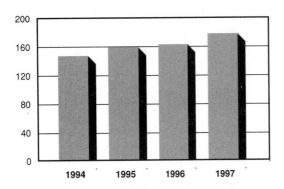

General Motors Corp.
1997 Stock Prices
(dollars)

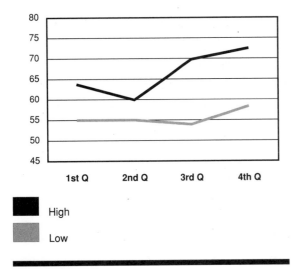

High

Low

ing value to its stockholders. GM announced a third stock repurchase program for $4 billion; this follows a $2.5 billion repurchase program started in August 1997. When the repurchase program is complete, roughly by the year 2000, GM will have reduced its outstanding shares by 20 percent. *The Value Line Investment Survey* reasons that GM management decided on a stock repurchasing program (rather than increasing the dividend) because dividends are taxed twice, at both corporate and personal levels. In addition, GM's dividend yield is already well above the market average. A March 1998 *Fortune* magazine article explains that GM's rationale in funneling

money directly to shareholders is based on the company's reducing its outstanding shares and boosting its stock price. By reducing its outstanding shares, GM makes its earnings per share look better and this attracts investors' attention.

In 1997, GM had sales of $166 billion, compared with sales of $158 billion in 1996, and its net income rose 34 percent to a record $6.70 billion from $4.96 billion in 1996. GM stock ranged from a low of $52 to a high of $72 in 1997. The annual dividend for 1997 was $2.00 per share, and GM's price-earnings ratio was 9.5 in May 1998. In addition, earnings per share in 1997 were $8.62.

ANALYSTS' OPINIONS

The year 1997 was the best earnings year in General Motors' history. Despite this success, *The Value Line Investment Survey* does "not believe that GM will be able to improve earnings in 1998." According to this survey, the launch of GM's C/K light truck platform in North America will result in lost volume and associated launch costs when this changeover occurs. Since the C/K platform makes up almost one-third of GM's North American production, *Value Line* thinks bottom line gains will be hard to come by," but "the eventual positives from the launch should allow GM to increase earnings in 1999."

HISTORY

Though General Motors was formed in 1908, its history can be traced to 1892 when R.E. Olds founded the Olds Motor Vehicle Company to manufacture horseless carriages, according to the *International Directory of Company Histories*. Within a couple of years, Olds managed to convert this factory into the first American factory in Detroit devoted exclusively to the production of automobiles.

At the turn of the century, an engineer named David Buick founded the Buick Motor Company in Detroit. At the same time, Henry Leland founded the Cadillac Automobile Company, also located in Detroit. All three companies were setting their own milestones and performing well. However, in 1903, at a time of market instability, these three companies were forced to form a consortium, and General Motors was thus formed. William Durant, a self-made millionaire, son of a Michigan governor, and a director of the Buick Motor Company, brought together Oldsmobile and Buick, and in 1909, Cadillac and Oakland (later renamed Pontiac) joined the union. Even though this merger drew very little attention, immediate positive financial results were seen.

In 1911, a central staff of specialists was put together to monitor and coordinate the activities in GM's different units and factories, and a testing laboratory was set up to serve as additional protection against costly factory mistakes. The research and development system adopted by GM became one of the largest and most complex in private industry. Additionally, Chevrolet became part of GM in 1918. By 1920 more than 30 companies had been acquired, including Ewing, Marquette, Welch, Scripps-Booth, Sheridan, Elmore, and Rapid and Reliance trucks.

During World War I, General Motors turned to wartime production. Ninety percent of GM's truck production between 1917 and 1919 was for the war effort. Cadillac supplied Army staff cars and V-8 engines, while Buick built airplane motors, tanks, trucks, ambulances, and automotive parts.

The Great Depression created suffering for GM. The company emerged, however, with a new and aggressive management and coordinated policy control, which replaced the undirected efforts of prior years. Alfred Sloan Jr., who had converted a $50,000 investment into assets of $3.5 million in 24 years, joined the corporate management of GM. Sloan helped guide GM through the Depression and built a new management policy that was adopted by many other businesses. By 1941, GM accounted for 44 percent of total U.S. automotive sales, compared to 12 percent in 1921. During World War II, GM's factories were retooled in preparation for war, and between 1940 and 1945, GM produced defense materials valued at an estimated $12 billion.

The 1950s were marked by automotive sales records, innovations in styling, and new engineering discoveries. By 1950, all models built in the United States were available with an automatic gear-box. Between 1951 and 1955, the five divisions of GM—Buick, Chevrolet, Pontiac, Oldsmobile, and Cadillac—started offering a new V-8 engine, power steering, brakes, the first air-conditioning systems, and front seat safety belts. The look of the car from the windows to the interior was redesigned. Overall car sales in the 1950s were good, with growing American families creating a demand for a second family car. However, small European cars were gaining popularity, and American car companies were gradually losing market share to their foreign competitors. In 1957, despite a recession, the United States imported more cars than it exported. In 1959, GM's market share slipped to 42 percent of the year's new car sales.

The 1960 Detroit riots forced GM management to recognize urban poverty. As a result, many minority workers were hired, thanks to the expansionist policies of Presidents Kennedy and Johnson. This move helped GM prosper and diversify; GM's interests included home appliances, insurance, locomotives, electronics, ball bearings, banking, and financing. By the late 1960s, GM's returns on investment increased from 16.5 percent to 25.8 percent. The 1970s were marked by heavy expenditures because GM had ignored the importance of pollution control for so long. The oil embargo sent sales of GM's luxury gas-guzzlers plummeting, but the com-

FAST FACTS:
About General Motors Corporation

Ownership: General Motors is a publicly owned company traded on the New York Stock Exchange.

Ticker symbol: GM

Officers: John F. Smith Jr., Chmn., CEO, & Pres., 59, 1997 base salary $3,350,000; Harry J. Pearce, VChmn., 55, 1997 base salary $1,790,000; J. Michael Losh, Exec. VP & CFO, age 51; Louis R. Hughes, 49, Exec. VP & Pres., International Operations, 49

Employees: 608,000

Principal Subsidiary Companies: General Motors has more than 160 subsidiaries, joint ventures, and affiliates. Its major subsidiaries include Delphi Automotive Systems, General Motors Acceptance Corporation, Hughes Electronics Corporation, General Motors Electro-Motive Division, and Allison Transmission.

Chief Competitors: General Motor's principal competitors in passenger cars and trucks in the United States and Canada include: Ford Motor Company; Chrysler Corporation; Toyota Corporation; Nissan Motor Corporation Ltd.; Honda Motor Company Ltd.; Mazda Motor Corporation; Mitsubishi Motors Corporation; Fuji Heavy Industries Ltd. (Subaru); Volkswagen A.G.; Hyundai Motor Company Ltd.; Daimler-Benz A.G. (Mercedes); Bayerische, Motoren Werke A.G. (BMW); and Volvo AB.

pany's compact and sub-compact cars gained a 40 percent market share by 1974.

Between 1985 and 1992, GM reported declines in earnings. An accounting change in 1987 provided a respite and created an increase in earnings. Since the early 1980s, GM had spent more than $60 billion redesigning many of its cars and the plants that built them. GM also made two expensive purchases in the 1980s: Hughes Aircraft and Electronic Data Systems (EDS). The EDS purchase provided GM with better, more centralized communications and backup systems, as well as a vital profit center. In 1987 for the first time in 60 years, Ford's profits exceeded those of GM.

From 1990 to 1992 GM suffered losses totaling $30 billion. Manufacturing costs that exceeded those of its

CHRONOLOGY:

Key Dates for General Motors Corporation

1903: General Motors is formed by the joining of the Oldsmobile and Buick companies

1909: Cadillac and Oakland (later renamed Pontiac) join GM

1912: Cadillac cars introduce the electric self-starter replacing the hand crank

1918: Chevrolet joins GM

1924: Assembles first GM vehicle abroad in Denmark

1938: Introduces the column mounted gearshift, setting the industry standard

1940: Produces its 25 millionth automobile

1948: Introduces the first torque-converter automatic transmission available in passenger cars

1950: Introduces the Chevrolet Corvette

1961: Introduces the first V-6 for an American passenger car

1969: GM manufactures the guidance systems for the Apollo 11 spacecraft

1974: First company to offer air bags in production vehicles

1987: Wins the inaugural solar car race with its Sunracer

1995: First company to install daytime running lights as standard equipment

1996: Introduces the first electric car for consumers, the EV1

competitors because of high labor costs, overcapacity, complicated production procedures, and competition from 25 companies all contributed to these losses. GM's market share fell from 50 to 35 percent. In 1992, Jack Smith Jr. became CEO of GM, and in 1993, he simplified North American operations, cut the corporate staff, pared product offerings, and divested GM's parts operations. He also negotiated with the United Auto Workers, planned to close more than 24 plants by 1996, and pledged $3.9 billion in jobless benefits, raising blue-collar payroll costs more than 16 percent over three years.

In the early 1990s, GM entered the van, truck, and sports utility vehicle markets. Saturn Corp. was launched at this time, and the weak dollar caused the price of imported cars to increase much faster than domestic prices. All of this helped GM to recapture market share from Japanese manufacturers. In 1993, GM recorded a net income of $2.47 billion on sales of $138.22 billion. Increased 1994 sales totaled $154.95 billion, and 1995 sales were $168.83 billion with profit margins of 3.5 and 4.5 percent, respectively.

On June 7, 1996, GM announced the splitting off of EDS. EDS entered into a 10-year agreement with GM to be its principal provider of information technology services. In December 1996, GM's CIO Ralph Syzgenda announced plans to install 300 of his peers in similar posts at various GM business units to face the challenges of cutting costs, entering new markets, and managing a vast outsourcing arrangement with EDS.

STRATEGY

When GM chairman Jack Smith began his tenure, he introduced a series of "strategy boards" for each sector and region of the company, as well as a "global strategy board" for the company overall. "Each board draws together top executives in manufacturing, finance, purchasing, or various regions, among others, in an effort to manage business together—not as separate fiefdoms," said Daniel Howes in a November 1997 *Detroit News* article. According to Howes, these strategy boards have had a tremendous impact on GM as they have served to foster debate, evaluate data, and generally bring consensus.

The "strategy boards" are but one element in GM's ongoing restructuring efforts since 1992. Among the most significant has been the restructuring of parts operations. GM's parts plants were renamed Delphi Automotive Systems, and 33 operations that were either unnecessary or too expensive were sold or closed, which created profitable independent suppliers. Delphi also opened 104 parts facilities worldwide, with only one in the United States.

In 1994, GM combined all its stamping plants in North America, each with its own set of processes, controls, and management style, into a single Metal Fabricating Division. The following year, according to Howes, "GM appointed a series of 'vehicle line executives' responsible for all facets of car and truck programs. Insiders say the change has dramatically improved the way cars and trucks are developed by injecting accountability into a once-confused web of overlapping responsibilities. The result has been fewer launch glitches and improved quality."

Another one of GM's restructuring moves has been what the company calls the "Hughes Transactions." This

An aerial view of the 1963 Corvette Sting Ray. *(Courtesy of American Automobile Manufacturers Association.)*

was a strategic restructuring of GM's Hughes Electronics subsidiary and included the spin-off and merger of Hughes' defense unit with Raytheon Company. In 1997, GM sold the defense end of this business to Raytheon for nearly $10 billion. At the same time, Delco Electronics, the automotive subsidiary of Hughes, was transferred from Hughes to Delphi Automotive Systems.

According to General Motors' 1997 annual report, the corporation concentrated on four business priorities: "run common, think lean and run fast, compete globally, and grow the business." For GM, getting common involves its processes, parts, and vehicle platforms worldwide. It is an effort that redirects the company's old strategy of independent, stand-alone companies to one of eliminating duplication, confusion, and waste. Global car platforms allow different varieties of the same car to be built in many different countries and marketed globally.

"Thinking lean" translates into cost reductions by streamlining its vehicle development process, for example. In 1997, GM spent $4 billion on a study of cost competitiveness. "Running fast" refers to the need to make changes in a timely fashion—from the construction of new plants to the launch of new models. Competing on a global basis is a strategic priority, as GM is undergoing the largest international production capacity expansion in the company's history. GM's strategy is to build cars and trucks in the location where it wants to sell them. Finally, GM would like to reestablish itself as a growth company, and it plans to spend $21 billion in the United States between 1997 and 2000 investing in emerging markets.

INFLUENCES

In 1997 several strikes by local unions, including two long work stoppages in the United States, influenced GM's market share. Another factor is the seasonal nature of the automotive business. During a changeover to a new model year, sales are affected by the disruption in car production. Strong competition in the already crowded sport-utility market was also a factor in 1997. Finally, due to the weakened currencies in Japan and Germany in 1997, these car manufacturers took advantage of the cost savings in these countries and increased their sales volume. The launch of several new vehicles— including the Saab in Europe—and the higher associated costs led to increased operating costs for GM.

CURRENT TRENDS

One trend in the automotive industry that has had particular significance for GM is the growing consumer demand for trucks. Truck sales were up 10.8 percent in April 1998 from the previous year. It was the sixth straight month of year-over-year truck sales increases.

Truck sales that month were the highest ever for one manufacturer in the history of the industry.

mission is the world's largest designer and producer of heavy-duty automatic transmissions.

PRODUCTS

General Motors divides its business into seven global operating groups and major subsidiaries. General Motors North American Operations (GM-NAO) makes Chevrolet, Pontiac, GMC, Oldsmobile, Buick, Cadillac, and Saturn cars and trucks. In 1997, GM-NAO introduced a record 14 new models. In 1998, GM introduced six new cars and light trucks in North America.

General Motors' subsidiaries produce various products that are important to the company. GM's Delphi Automotive systems is a diverse supplier of automotive systems and components. Delphi's products and services include chassis, interiors, lighting, electronics, power and signal distribution, energy and engine management, steering and thermal systems. In August 1998, GM announced plans to establish Delphi as an independent company so that it could focus on its core business of building cars and trucks. General Motors International Operations (GMIO) makes cars outside of North America, including Opel, Vauxhall, Holden, Isuzu, Saab, Chevrolet, GMC, and Cadillac. General Motors Acceptance Corporation (GMAC) provides a broad range of financial services, including consumer vehicle financing, car and truck extended service contracts, residential and commercial mortgage services, and vehicle and homeowners insurance.

Hughes Electronics Corporation, another subsidiary, designs, manufactures, and markets advanced technology electronic systems, products and services for the telecommunications and space, automotive electronics, and aerospace and defense sectors. Hughes is the largest producer of commercial communications satellites in the world and the leader in distribution networks for cable television and private business networks worldwide. In the telecommunications and space segment, Hughes' products include satellite design and construction and DIRECTV, a direct broadcast satellite television system that had 2.3 million household subscribers in 1996. In 1997, it attracted 1.0 million new U.S. subscribers and was launched in Japan. Hughes' automotive electronics products include air bag electronics, anti-lock brake modules, remote keyless entry, audio systems, climate controls, ignition electronics, pressure sensors, and spark controls. In its aerospace and defense segment, Hughes makes missile systems, radar and communication systems, air defense, training and simulation systems, and guidance and control systems.

General Motors Locomotive Group designs, manufactures, and markets diesel-electric locomotives, medium-speed diesel engines, locomotive components, power generation units, locomotive maintenance services, and light-armored vehicles. Finally, Allison Trans-

CORPORATE CITIZENSHIP

General Motors contributes millions of dollars to a variety of charitable organizations all over the world. GM employees and retirees nationwide volunteer their time and talent by collecting food and clothing, aiding victims of violence and sexual assault, working at homeless shelters, mentoring at-risk students, and sponsoring youth programs and other activities.

The GM Foundation was founded in 1976 to guide the company's philanthropic efforts. In 1996 alone, the GM Foundation donated $27 million to a variety of activities and organizations in the areas of education, health and human services, arts and culture, civic and community, public policy, and environment and energy.

In addition to the GM Foundation, partnerships with community organizations are an important element in GM's philanthropic efforts. GM has had a 46-year commitment to the United Way and is the largest U.S. corporate contributor to this organization.

In 1978, GM formed the GM Cancer Foundation to recognize and reward scientists who have significantly contributed to the treatment and prevention of cancer. GM presents three awards annually: the Charles F. Kettering Prize for the most outstanding recent contribution to the diagnosis or treatment of cancer; the Charles S. Mott Prize for the most outstanding recent contribution related to the causes or ultimate prevention of cancer; and the Alfred P. Sloan Jr. Prize for the most outstanding recent basis science contribution to cancer research. Each prize consists of a gold medal and $100,000.

GLOBAL PRESENCE

General Motors is the largest U.S. exporter of cars and trucks and has manufacturing, assembly, or component operations in 50 countries. GM has a global presence in more than 190 countries. About one-third of GM's sales are generated outside North America, and the company hopes to draw half of its annual revenues that way by 2006. Major markets for exports are Latin America and the Middle East, but exports to the Asia-Pacific region are increasing.

General Motors International Operations, based in Zurich, Switzerland, operates 34 manufacturing and assembly facilities outside of North America. Its 44 sales and marketing operations are located on five continents. GM's international operations are organized into General Motors Europe, Latin America, Africa, Middle East Operations, and Asia-Pacific Operations.

GM would like to dominate the emerging consumer markets in eastern Europe and Russia. Company plans call for the opening of an assembly plant in late 1998 in Poland. GM is also opening plants in Russia, Argentina, China, India, Indonesia, and Thailand. In Russia, Chevrolet Blazers, Cavaliers, and Transports are on the road. The company will invest $2.5 billion in expanding its Asian manufacturing operations and continues to expand in India, with GM, Delphi, Hughes Electronics, GMAC, and GM's Locomotive Group. Under GM chairman Jack Smith, "GM has launched the largest manufacturing expansion in company history—all outside the United States," according to a November 1997 *Detroit News* article.

EMPLOYMENT

General Motors is one of the largest employers in the world. In addition, GM also offers a Global Intern Program and a Global Cooperative Education Program. The intern program offers college students on-the-job experience through temporary full-time positions during college and university summer break periods. College students work throughout the year in GM's co-op program, with work sessions arranged to accommodate class schedules.

General Motors offers its employees one of the most comprehensive benefits programs in the country. GM benefits include a choice of health care plans, life and disability insurance, a savings-stock purchase program, retirement program, product discounts, and paid holidays/vacations.

SOURCES OF INFORMATION

Bibliography
Blumenstein, Rebecca. "GM Doubles Net on Strong Factory Sales." *The Wall Street Journal,* 27 January 1998.

General Motors 1997 Annual Report. Available at: http://www.gm.com/cgi-bin/shareholder/sh_page.cgi?e600.

"General Motors Corporation." *Hoover's Handbook of American Business 1998.* Austin, TX: The Reference Press, 1997.

"General Motors Corporation." *Moody's Handbook of Common Stocks.* New York: Moody's Investor's Service, Inc., 1997.

"General Motors." *Standard & Poor's Stock Reports.* New York: Standard & Poor's, 1998.

Howes, Daniel. "GM Now Running Leaner, Faster." *Detroit News,* 2 November 1997.

Morris, Thomas V. *If Aristotle Ran General Motors: The New Soul of Business.* New York: Henry Holt and Co., 1997.

Paul, Anthony. "Indonesia: Life Under the Volcano." *Fortune,* 13 April 1998.

Shnayerson, Michael. *The Car That Could: The Inside Story of GM's Revolutionary Electric Vehicle.* New York: Random House, 1996.

Taylor, Alex, III. "The Big Three's Dilemma." *Fortune,* 16 March 1998.

Tenreiro, Michael. "General Motors." *The Value Line Investment Survey.* 13 March 1998.

For an annual report:
telephone: (313)556-2044 **or** (800)331-9922

For additional industry research:
Investigate companies by their Standard Industrial Classification Codes, also known as SICs. General Motors' primary SICs are:

3711 Motor Vehicles and Car Bodies

3714 Motor Vehicles Parts and Accessories

6159 Miscellaneous Business Credit Institutions

7374 Data Processing Services

General Nutrition Companies, Inc.

ALSO KNOWN AS: GNC
FOUNDED: 1935

Contact Information:

HEADQUARTERS: 300 6th Ave.
 Pittsburgh, PA 15222
PHONE: (412)288-4600
FAX: (412)288-2099
TOLL FREE: (888)462-2548
URL: http://www.gnc.com/

OVERVIEW

General Nutrition Companies, Inc. (GNC) is a specialty retailer of vitamin and mineral supplements, sports nutrition products, and other health-care items. As of January 1998, the company had 3,435 retail outlets, of which about 60 percent were owned by the company and 40 percent were franchised. The stores are located in all 50 states, Puerto Rico, and 18 foreign countries. Most of the company's stores are called General Nutrition Centers; its other retail outlets are variously named Health & Diet Centres, Amphora, Nature's Fresh Northwest, and GNC Live Well. The company makes many of its own products at its Greenville, South Carolina, plant. According to the company's management, in 1998 GNC held about a 14.2 percent share of the total retail supplement market, which includes the vitamins, minerals, herbs, and sports nutrition categories. In 1993, its share was 9.7 percent.

COMPANY FINANCES

Sales in fiscal 1997 (ended January 31, 1998) totaled almost $1.2 billion, up more than 20 percent from fiscal 1996. Operating earnings (as adjusted by the company to make comparisons meaningful) were $195 million, up from $152 million in fiscal 1996. Between May 1997 and May 1998, the company's stock traded in a range of $22 to $41. The stock did not pay a dividend.

For the first quarter of fiscal 1998 (ended April 30, 1998) the company reported continued strong results. Compared with the first quarter of fiscal 1997, revenues were up 20 percent and net income rose 27 percent. In fiscal 1998, the company planned to open 525 new U.S. stores and 80 new Canadian stores.

HISTORY

In 1935, company founder David Shakarian opened his first health food store in Pittsburgh, Pennsylvania. During the next three decades, he continued to open outlets in Pittsburgh and expanded the concept to other cities, including New York. He also added vitamins and other health food supplements to the product line. In the 1970s, Shakarian opened factories in Pennsylvania, North Dakota, South Carolina, and Minnesota to manufacture his own products. By the early 1980s, the company had more than 1,300 stores.

In 1984, Shakarian died, and the following year Jerry Horn was brought in to run the company. A franchising program started in 1987. In 1989, the company was purchased by Thomas H. Lee Company, a Boston investment firm. GNC made a new public stock offering in 1993. In the mid-1990s, the company became more active in overseas markets, expanding operations to western Europe, the Far East, and the Middle East.

STRATEGY

GNC offers consumers vitamins, minerals, herbs, health foods, and similar products to promote a healthier, more active life. The company tries to capitalize on the latest health trends—some might say "health fads"—and merchandise them to the public in innovative ways. For instance, when herbal supplements became popular in the early 1990s, GNC put them into gel-coated capsules and they became best-sellers. Additionally, in 1995 there was positive press coverage (including a cover story in *Newsweek*) about the possible benefits of melatonin to promote sleep and fight jet lag. GNC, which was already making small amounts of the hormone, quickly ramped up production sevenfold and had the product in its stores within two weeks.

The medical benefits of many of the products GNC sells remain unproven, however. As Christine Rosenbloom, a professor of nutrition at Georgia State University, told *The Wall Street Journal,* "If Vitamin C cured the common cold, do you think anyone would have one?" The company therefore tries to give shoppers a great deal of information about its products without making claims that can't be defended. Indeed, GNC had to be careful; as of 1996 it operated under three consent decrees with the Federal Trade Commission because of false advertising claims on some products. Each item in its stores has a carefully worded sign describing the product— an unusual strategy for a retailer.

There were several other aspects to GNC's strategy in the mid-1990s. First, as indicated earlier, GNC made

FINANCES:

General Nutrition Companies, Inc. Net Revenues, 1994-1997 (million dollars)

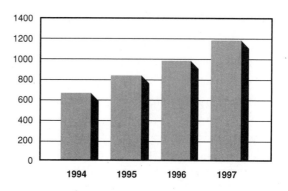

General Nutrition Companies, Inc. 1997 Stock Prices (dollars)

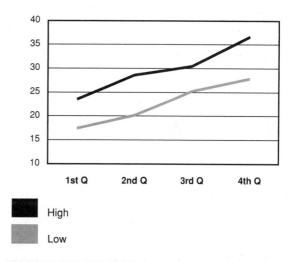

many of its own products, which eliminates middlemen and thereby increases profit. In fact, GNC brands, such as Ultra Mega, Solotron, and National Brand, dominated the company's product mix, although some national labels were also available.

Second the company has vigorously pursued its franchising program. Much of GNC's growth has come from its franchised stores, where sales increases have been better than for company-owned outlets. Franchising has also helped the company expand its operations to other countries, which offer new, untapped markets for GNC products. The growth in both company-owned

FAST FACTS:

About General Nutrition Companies, Inc.

Ownership: General Nutrition Companies (GNC) is a publicly owned company traded on NASDAQ.

Ticker symbol: GNCI

Officers: Jerry D. Horn, Chmn., 60 William E. Watts, Pres. & CEO, 45

Employees: 13,800

Chief Competitors: GNC's competitors include: Amway; CVS; Eckerd; Enrich; Heinz; Herbalife; Natural Alternatives; NBTY; NutraMax Products; Rite Aid; Wal-Mart; and Whole Foods.

and franchised stores has been dramatic. The total number of GNC stores at the end of January 1998 was 3,435, more than double the level of four years earlier.

INFLUENCES

During the 1970s, more Americans began buying health foods, as well as vitamins and other supplements to their diets. GNC grew strongly during this period and greatly expanded its product line. It also started to open outlets in malls, which bolstered sales and gave the company a more upscale image.

By the early 1980s, however, the big retail chains were giving GNC serious competition. Items like rice cakes and tofu, which were once a rarity in supermarkets, became commonplace, and the large drug chains vastly increased their vitamin offerings. Thus GNC's product mix became less unusual, and profitability fell. Moreover, the company had made some decisions that in retrospect seemed unwise. It was offering too many products that cannibalized one another; in other words, additional sales of one item merely stole sales from another. GNC had too many stores—about 1,300—that were too close to each other. The space dedicated to low-margin foods was disproportionately large. The company was also a regular target of federal regulators who accused the company of making false claims about its products.

Perhaps most detrimental, GNC had a healthy, earthy image that was out of place in the 1980s. As in-

dustry analyst Gary Giblen told the *Pittsburgh Post-Gazette,* "You went in and everybody looked unhealthy. The biggest joke about health stores was that the help there looked like they were dying from starvation." By the time founder David Shakarian died in 1984, the company was in bad shape.

GNC's fortunes improved when Jerry Horn took over as president in 1985. He closed stores, streamlined and reorganized the product mix, spruced up packaging, and changed floor plans for a cleaner and less cluttered appearance. He added sections to exploit a growing demand for nonfood health products, such as skin and hair-care items. Horn also beefed up offerings for body builders and other serious athletes with over-the-counter energy and weight-gain supplements. He also tried to appease federal regulators by cleaning up the company's reputation for false advertising.

Horn's most important initiative may have been the creation of a franchising program in 1987. Many of the franchisees were former employees, and they helped to give the company an entrepreneurial spirit. Existing stores that were converted to franchises typically showed sales increases of 60 percent during their first year of private ownership. Although the company struggled to regain profitability, by the end of the 1980s, the company was well on its way to a turnaround.

In 1989, GNC was purchased by the Boston investment firm of Thomas H. Lee in a leveraged buyout, or LBO. In this type of acquisition, the buyer uses mostly borrowed funds that are secured by the assets of the firm to be purchased. As would be expected in an LBO, the acquisition left the company heavily in debt with large interest charges. By 1992, however, the company was again profitable. Lee made a new public stock offering in 1993, which improved the company's financial position substantially. With the new capital, GNC was able to pursue a more aggressive growth strategy. It opened hundreds of new stores, which brought the total number of outlets to 1,553 by the end of fiscal 1993. New lines of apparel and exercise equipment were introduced, and the advertising budget was increased significantly. GNC also began its Gold Star program, which for a $15 annual fee gave customers the right to a 20 percent discount on the first Tuesday of each month. By 1996, the number of Gold Card holders had grown to about 2.4 million, and 7,000 new card holders were being added each week.

CURRENT TRENDS

In the mid-1990s, GNC benefited greatly from the increased interest in vitamins and nutritional supplements among the country's aging Baby Boomers. As consumers of all age groups were becoming more health conscious, increasingly they were seeking out nontraditional health-care products like herbs for their medical benefits. A booming economy also meant that consumers could afford to spend more on self-care products. GNC was capitalizing on these trends by offering high-margin products in attractive stores. In 1995, vitamins and minerals accounted for 40 percent of GNC's sales, while 28 percent came from sports nutrition products and 10 percent from herbs. The balance of its sales came from diet, fitness and apparel, food, and personal care products. The product mix had therefore changed greatly from the early 1980s, when the company focused on commodity-like health foods and vitamins. The new product lineup was popular with consumers, who pushed up the company's sales from $673 million in 1994 to $846 million in 1995, $990 million in 1996, and almost $1.2 billion in 1997.

PRODUCTS

In 1996, GNC created a prototype store called *Alive by GNC,* featuring a new marketing concept. Customized products that are tailored to the consumer's preferences have become increasingly popular in certain retail categories, such as clothing. Alive by GNC sought to extend that trend to the personal health-care market. Visitors to the store are greeted by an information center where they are profiled by computer and receive personalized information on nutrition, exercise, and relaxation. While the store does have prepackaged "vitapaks," a visitor can also start from scratch and devise a personal vitamin regimen. In addition, shoppers can use a computer program to design their own shampoos, conditioners, and lotions. The packaging for these personalized products includes the customer's name as well as the specific ingredients. Visitors can also get fitted for their own personal insoles, have their posture checked, or take a body-fat test.

In late 1997, GNC concluded an agreement with Monsanto to develop and sell a line of nutritional supplement products. These offerings would be based on Monsanto's SeaGold Oil, an algae-derived compound rich in docosahexaenoic acid (DHA). The products would come in gel caps, powders, and food supplement forms.

GLOBAL PRESENCE

In 1994, GNC created an international franchise division to spur growth in overseas markets. As of January 1998, GNC operated 20 Health and Diet Centres and 19 General Nutrition Centres in the United Kingdom, 34 General Nutrition Centres in Canada, and 1 store in New Zealand. There are also 151 franchise stores in 15 international markets.

EMPLOYMENT

GNC is an equal opportunity employer and offers jobs in a wide variety of fields, including accounting finance, art design, construction, customer service, franchising, information systems, legal, logistics/distribution, loss prevention, manufacturing, nutritional research and development, purchasing, and retail sales and marketing. In addition to its nearly 3,500 retail outlets, GNC offers employment opportunities at its corporate headquarters in Pittsburgh, its manufacturing facility in Greenville, South Carolina, and regional administrative offices and distribution centers across the United States. Anyone interested in learning more about employment opportunities and current job openings at GNC may do so by visiting the company Job Opportunities Web page at http://www.gnc.com/index.cfm?todisplay=clients/gnc/moregnc&location=jobs.html&title=GNC%20%2D+Job +Opportunities.

SOURCES OF INFORMATION

Bibliography

"Boomers Boost GNC to Top of the Vitamin Heap." *Stores,* November 1995.

Brookman, Faye. "GNC's New Angle: Do-It-Yourself Beauty." *WWD,* 10 May 1996.

Lerner, Matthew. "Monsanto Increases Stake in Nutriceuticals Market." *Chemical Market Reporter,* 17 November 1997.

Murray, Matt. "GNC Makes Ginseng, Shark Pills Its Potion for Growth." *Wall Street Journal,* 15 May 1996.

Tascarella, Patty. "New, 'Softer' GNC to Convert 55 More Stores to 'Live Well Retail Concept.'" *Pittsburgh Business Times,* 6 April 1998.

Wilson, Marianne. "GNC Targets Health and Wellness with Alive." *Chain Store Age Executive,* April 1996.

For an annual report:

on the Internet at: http://www.gnc.com **or** write: GNC, Inc., 921 Penn Avenue, Pittsburgh, PA, 15222

For additional industry research:

Investigate companies by their Standard Industrial Classification Codes, also known as SICs. GNC's primary SICs are:

2834 Pharmaceutical Preparations

5499 Miscellaneous Food Stores

Georgia-Pacific Corporation

FOUNDED: 1927

Contact Information:

HEADQUARTERS: 133 Peachtree St. NE
   Atlanta, GA 30303
PHONE: (404)652-4000
FAX: (404)230-7008
URL: http://www.gp.com

OVERVIEW

Georgia-Pacific Corporation is one of the world's leading manufacturers and distributors of building products. The company is also a major force in the production of pulp and paper. In 1997 the company's net sales were $13.09 billion, up from 1996's $13.02 billion.

As of 1997 Georgia-Pacific was the number one U.S. producer of structural and other wood panels, and was number two in the production of lumber. Much of the company's wood production comes from its own property. In 1997 the company owned or controlled 6 million acres of timberland and Georgia-Pacific operated the second-largest gypsum wallboard company in North America. The company also controlled the world's largest building products distribution system in 1997, with 100 distribution centers across the country. Georgia-Pacific operates a growing specialty chemicals business based on its propriety technology in wood products resins and pulp- and paper-related chemicals.

In addition to building products, Georgia-Pacific's other major business segment is pulp and paper production. In 1997 the company had the capacity to produce 9.4 million tons of pulp, paper, and paperboard. The company produced containerboard and packaging, communications papers, market pulp, and tissue.

To improve its competitive position, Georgia-Pacific invested $3.5 billion in capital projects and acquisitions between 1994 and 1996, primarily in building products facilities. This was $2-billion more than the investment required for maintenance and environmental compliance, according to the company.

COMPANY FINANCES

The corporation reported consolidated net sales of $13.1 billion and net income of $69 million for 1997, compared with net sales of $13.0 billion and net income of $156 million for 1996. Georgia-Pacific's building products division's net sales of $7.5 billion were up slightly from $7.4 billion the previous year. Sales in its pulp and paper division of $5.6 billion were the same as 1996, but operating profits of $174 million were down from $390 million in 1996. These declines were driven by higher wood costs in the company's manufacturing business, lower average lumber prices, and continued losses in its distribution division. The total debt for Georgia-Pacific Corporation, including both Georgia-Pacific Group and The Timber company, was $5.5 billion at the end of 1997.

Georgia-Pacific set a goal in 1996 of improving earnings by approximately $400 million by reducing overhead costs and improving efficiencies. In 1997 the corporation said it had achieved about $219 million in reductions, about half of its goal.

Georgia-Pacific stock ranged from a low of $70 to a high of $108 through December 16, 1997, when the company reorganized. Over the past five years the stock has traded from a low of $48 to a high of $108. On December 17, 1997, the new Georgia-Pacific Group began trading at $60 and in April 1998 it was selling at $66. The Timber Company opened at $26. Georgia-Pacific stock's price-earnings ratio estimate for 1998 was 15.4. Earnings per share in 1997 were $2.26.

ANALYSTS' OPINIONS

Market analysts note that the financial performances of forest products companies such as Georgia-Pacific tend to be highly cyclical. When prices for paper and wood products are high, so are company sales and profits. When those prices are low, the opposite occurs.

An April 1998 report by *The Value Line Investment Survey* noted that Georgia-Pacific should show improvement in 1998 due to its cost containment efforts and a strengthening of commodity prices. However, the spin-off of The Timber Company may "increase volatility," the report said, since the "G-P Group is unable to rely on cash flow from G-P Corp.'s timber operations during tight periods. But the company may benefit from a more rational capital spending policy."

A January 1998 stock report by *Standard & Poor's* remains "neutral" on Georgia-Pacific's shares. The report looks favorably on the company's move to separate its timber business and the modest upturn in paper and packaging, but is cautious about slowing wood markets.

FAST FACTS:
About Georgia-Pacific Corporation

Ownership: Georgia-Pacific Corporation is a publicly owned company traded on the New York Stock Exchange under its "letter" stocks, Georgia-Pacific Group and The Timber Company. Georgia-Pacific options are traded on the Philadelphia Stock Exchange.

Ticker symbol: GP (Georgia-Pacific Group) and TGP (The Timber Company)

Officers: Alston D. "Pete" Correll, Chmn., CEO, & Pres., 57, $1,050,000; Donald L. Glass, Exec. VP-Timber / Pres., & CEO, The Timber Company, 48, $455,600; John F. McGovern, Exec. VP-Finance & CFO, 50, $540,500

Employees: 46,500

Chief Competitors: Georgia-Pacific Corporation's primary competitors are: Boise Cascade Corporation; Bowater Incorporated; Champion International Corporation; Consolidated Papers, Inc.; Fort James; International Paper; Kimberly Clark; Mead; Owens Corning; Procter & Gamble; Stone Container; Union Camp; USG; and Weyerhaeuser.

HISTORY

The company now known as Georgia-Pacific was founded as a hardwood lumber wholesale company in Augusta, Georgia, by Owen Cheatham in 1927. By 1938 the company also operated five sawmills in the southern United States. The company moved into the northwest U.S. market in 1947 when it purchased a plywood mill in Bellingham, Washington. In the 1950s the company purchased large tracts of land that provided a base of timberlands for wood production—by 1960 the firm owned 1 million acres of timberland. In 1954 the company moved its headquarters to Portland, Oregon, and in 1957 changed its name to Georgia-Pacific. That same year, it established a presence in the pulp and paper industry by building a new mill in Toledo, Oregon.

In the 1960s Georgia-Pacific purchased several forest products companies and also invested in new facilities. As a result, the company was able to move into new lines of business, such as containers, paperboard, tissue, and chemicals. By 1972 the company had grown so large

CHRONOLOGY:

Key Dates for Georgia-Pacific Corporation

1927: Owen Cheatham opens the Georgia Hardwood Lumber Company in Augusta, Georgia

1948: Changes the company name to Georgia-Pacific Plywood & Lumber Company

1951: Name changes again to Georgia-Pacific Plywood Company

1956: Name changes once again to Georgia-Pacific Corporation

1960: Georgia-Pacific becomes the number three company in the industry

1972: Georgia-Pacific is ordered to divest 20 percent of its interests

1987: Paper products becomes more profitable than wood products for the company for the first time

1990: Purchases Great Northern Nekoosa Corp.

1997: Reorganizes as two independent units of timber divisions and manufacturing and distributing divisions

that the U.S. Federal Trade Commission forced it to sell 20 percent of its business assets.

In the 1970s Georgia-Pacific continued to develop its chemical business and introduced inexpensive substitutes for plywood, such as waferboard. In 1979 the company purchased Hudson Pulp and Paper, and in 1982 moved its headquarters to Atlanta.

In 1988 Georgia-Pacific purchased Georgia-based Brunswick Pulp and Paper and its extensive southern timber holdings. In 1990 the company made another major acquisition with its purchase of Great Northern Nekoosa for $3.74 billion. The purchase, which was initially opposed by Great Northern, greatly increased Georgia-Pacific's pulp and paper production capacity but also increased its debt load. To pay off some of that debt, the company sold $1 billion in assets in 1990, including 19 container plants and more than 500,000 acres of timberland.

In 1991 Georgia-Pacific sold a large portion of its interest in Great Northern Paper to Bowater Incorporated. In 1996 the company made a major move to increase its position in the gypsum market by purchasing nine wallboard plants from Domtar Incorporated for $350 million.

In December 1997 Georgia-Pacific instituted a fundamental change in the way it does business. The company reorganized as two independent units to separate the performance and cash flows of Georgia Pacific's timber business from its manufacturing and distribution divisions. The corporation's existing common stock was redesignated as Georgia Pacific Group, representing Georgia-Pacific Corporation's pulp, paper, and building products businesses. The Timber Company was created to represent Georgia-Pacific Corporation's timber holdings. Georgia-Pacific issued stock in the newly formed Timber Company and the newly named Georgia-Pacific Group, which trade independently on the New York Stock Exchange.

STRATEGY

In 1995 Georgia-Pacific Corporation began to use a new operating standard called EVA, the acronym for "economic value added." EVA is a plan for measuring a company's performance and compensation plan. EVA measures a company's progress in economic terms by making sure that management's goals are synchronized with its shareholders' financial objectives. Rather than measure a company's financial success by its level of production or assets, EVA gauges a company by its capacity to produce real after tax profits.

To improve its EVA ratings, Georgia-Pacific's goal in 1995 was to streamline its work processes by establishing precise operating targets and incentives for its management team. The company also planned to "aggressively control costs."

Several strategies came into play when Georgia-Pacific Corporation separated its timber business into a new operating group, The Timber Company, in 1997. From an investment standpoint, the company claims the move should allow The Timber Company stock to be valued higher because of its stable, growing cash flows. Before the split, cash flows from timber operations were redirected into low return investments in plant and equipment. These cash flows can now be paid directly to shareholders in the form of share repurchases.

In addition to investor benefits, the company sees clearer timber pricing as a benefit of the separation of the two companies. The Timber Company supplied 83 percent of its output to the Georgia-Pacific Group in 1998, and its prices were based on an average of The Timber Company's outside sales and Georgia-Pacific Group's own purchases from other suppliers.

Finally, the separation allows company managers the flexibility to make financial and strategic decisions for their own businesses independently, giving them greater responsibility and accountability for the performance of their company.

A three-year investment program, totaling $3.2 billion, was undertaken by Georgia-Pacific from 1994 to

1996. These investments in property, plants, and equipment have been reduced to $750 million annually and the company expects to continue this level of investment for the foreseeable future. Georgia-Pacific says it limits its investments either to businesses with higher returns, such as gypsum and tissue, or to projects that dramatically lower costs or improve efficiency. In 1997 The Timber Company invested $51 million in timber and timberlands. The company says it is committed to maintaining its annual investment at approximately $50 million.

INFLUENCES

Both of Georgia-Pacific's primary businesses are highly cyclical in that prices for building products and pulp and paper tend to rise and fall sharply based on supply and demand. The company's building products business is affected primarily by the level of U.S. housing starts; the level of repairs, remodeling and additions; commercial building activity; the availability and cost of financing; and changes in industry capacity. The performance of the company's pulp and paper business depends on national and international demand for its products, production capacity levels at Georgia-Pacific and its competitors, and the levels of product inventory carried both by the company and its customers. Also, Georgia-Pacific Group's earnings are especially volatile because it manufactures a significant percentage of the worldwide volume of several key products. When prices fluctuate, even in a minor way, Georgia-Pacific's operating income is influenced significantly.

According to the company's annual report, 1997 saw a 10-percent increase in lumber prices as well as a 10-percent increase in gypsum prices. On the other hand, prices for oriented strand board were 22 percent lower. Although average timber prices have remained stable since 1996, prices for hardwood and softwood timber used to make lumber and plywood have increased. Georgia-Pacific expects prices it pays for timber and wood fiber to increase over the foreseeable future.

The Asian economic crisis that began in October 1997 impacted the world pulp market by the end of the year. Orders from Asia dropped sharply, which combined with low pulp and paper prices, forced the company to take 165,000 tons of downtime between October 1997 and April 1998.

CURRENT TRENDS

Reorganization, restructuring, and cost reduction are three key trends for Georgia-Pacific in a three-year effort to improve efficiency throughout the corporation. The separation of the company's timber business from its other operations reflects an effort to make it an independent profit center for management purposes and to make its value more apparent to investors.

The company's restructuring efforts have been felt in all divisions of Georgia-Pacific. To reduce costs in its distribution division, the company sold 13 of its 70 distribution centers in 1998. These closings resulted in a loss of 1,500 of its 5,100 distribution-area employees. The company also announced plans to sell 8 of its 9 major millwork-fabrication plants, which assemble doors, windows, and similar products. Reducing overhead, cutting administrative expenses, and reassessing "administrative activities to eliminate nonessential work and related salaried positions," according to Georgia-Pacific's annual report, are ongoing efforts in the company's cost reduction drive.

Using technology in managing its timber business is one way Georgia-Pacific is facing the Information Age. Developed over a three-year period and at a cost of about $6 million, the Integrated Forest Management System involves Georgia-Pacific's proprietary computerized models, which provide information for planning and financing The Timber Company's forest resources. These computerized models project growth from the forest and predict future inventory estimates based on various management and harvesting scenarios. Georgia-Pacific says that this system will be used on all company properties by the end of 1998.

PRODUCTS

Georgia-Pacific is the largest manufacturer and distributor of building products in the United States. The Georgia-Pacific Group produces wood panels, lumber, gypsum products, chemicals, and other products at 150 facilities in the United States and 7 in Canada. Accounting for 20 percent of domestic production, the company's wood panels include plywood, OSB (oriented strand board) panels, hardboard, particleboard, panelboard, softboard, decorative panels, and medium-density fiberboard.

Annually the Georgia-Pacific Group manufactures 2.7 billion board feet of lumber. The Group's 39 mills make lumber products from southern pine, a variety of Appalachian and Southern hardwoods, cypress, redwood, cedar, spruce, hemlock, and Douglas fir.

The gypsum products manufactured by Georgia-Pacific are wallboard, Dens specialty panels, fire-door cores, industrial plaster, and joint compound. The Group is also the leading supplier of wood resins, adhesives, and specialty chemicals.

In the pulp and paper business, Georgia-Pacific Group produces container-board and packaging, corrugated containers, kraft paper, communication papers, market pulp, and tissue. Its growing tissue products business makes napkins, bath tissue, and paper towels, marketed under the consumer brand names Angel Soft,

Sparkle, Coronet, MD, and Delta. Communication paper, also known as uncoated free-sheet, is used in office copy machines and commercial printing, business forms, stationery, tablets, books, envelopes, and checks.

Georgia-Pacific's six mills make it the world's second-largest market pulp producer. Wood pulps are used in the manufacturer of many paper grades. Fluff pulp is used for disposable diapers and other sanitary items.

The Timber Company, created in 1997 to manage Georgia-Pacific Corporation's timber assets, grows and sells timber and wood fiber. It sells softwood sawtimber, softwood pulpwood, hardwood sawtimber, and hardwood pulpwood to the Georgia-Pacific Group and other industrial wood users.

CORPORATE CITIZENSHIP

As a forest products company that cuts trees to produce its primary products, Georgia-Pacific has to manage the ongoing controversy that surrounds the use of forest resources. The company has responded by developing a comprehensive environmental policy.

In the mid- to late 1990s, Georgia-Pacific was using a set of principles to guide its environmental stewardship efforts. These 18 principles covered 4 main areas including management focus, conservation and sustainable use of resources, protection of health and the environment, and community awareness. The company was also participating in the Sustainable Forestry Initiative (SFI), sponsored by the American Forest & Paper Association, an industry trade group. The SFI established broad forest principles and detailed guidelines for managing forest lands for the future.

In addition to complying with its own environmental rules, in the mid-1990s Georgia-Pacific was providing assistance to its private timber suppliers to help them responsibly manage their land holdings. This company-wide forest management assistance program, called MAP, included reforestation of harvested timber stands and the use of best management practices (BMPs) to help protect water and soil quality during harvesting and replanting operations. One example of a BMP is the creation of buffer zones that limit tree harvesting close to lakes, rivers, and streams.

Georgia-Pacific has also worked with non-profit groups to manage and protect ecologically sensitive land. For example, through a cooperative effort announced in January 1997, The Nature Conservancy's North Carolina Chapter and Georgia-Pacific worked to restore longleaf pine forests and manage 21,000 acres of southeastern coast forest lands along North Carolina's lower Roanoke River. Georgia-Pacific helped the Conservancy's staff in Wilmington, Delaware, create a 20-year forest management plan for these properties through the MAP program. In 1993 Georgia-Pacific signed an agreement with the U.S. Fish and Wildlife Service to conserve the habitat of the red-cockaded woodpecker on its timberlands. Other wildlife that has become a focus of Georgia-Pacific's protection programs are spotted owls, gopher tortoises, bald eagles, and many rare plants.

In 1995 Georgia-Pacific introduced its Environmental Excellence Awards to recognize the company's environmental successes and to encourage ongoing progress. The 1996 awards recognized 20 finalists in the categories of pollution prevention, community service, scientific research and technological innovation, and the Chairman's Award for Environmental Excellence.

GLOBAL PRESENCE

Georgia-Pacific derives most of its sales in the United States. It had a relatively small but growing position in international markets in the mid- to late-1990s. Sales to foreign markets in 1997 made up 8 percent of company sales.

The majority of the market pulp the company produces is exported. (Market pulp, used to make paper, is pulp that is sold on the open market. Pulp produced and used by the same company is not considered market pulp.) As of 1997 the company produced market pulp at six mills with a combined annual capacity of 2.1 million tons. The group exports approximately 65 percent of its market pulp, primarily to Europe, Asia, and Latin America.

EMPLOYMENT

A hiring freeze on salaried employees and a voluntary early retirement program were among the cost-cutting measures instituted by Georgia-Pacific in 1997. The company also began a reassessment of its administrative activities to eliminate nonessential positions. In addition, in late 1997 the company sold or closed a number of its distribution centers and its millwork fabrication facilities nationwide, causing approximately 1,500 employees to loose their jobs.

In May 1998 the company listed openings for experienced professionals in the fields of engineering, finance and accounting, information systems and sales, marketing, and distribution. In addition, Georgia-Pacific recruits for entry level, co-op, and intern positions. Candidates seeking temporary or supplemental jobs are referred to Georgia TEMP, Inc., a wholly owned subsidiary of Georgia-Pacific Corporation, which provides administrative and information systems professionals to Georgia-Pacific's Atlanta headquarters, as well as other Atlanta-area companies.

Among the benefits offered to salaried employees are several different options for health care plans, as well as life insurance, a retirement plan, stock purchase plans, paid holidays and vacations, an educational assistance program, a credit union, and a matching gift program.

SOURCES OF INFORMATION

Bibliography

"Alston D. Correll of Georgia-Pacific." *Corporate America's Most Powerful People, 1997,* 21 May 1998. Available at http://www.forbes.com.

"Facilities To Be Sold, Staff to Be Cut in Restructuring." *The Wall Street Journal,* 15 January 1998.

Fisher, Anne. "Danger Zone." *Fortune,* 8 September 1997.

"Georgia-Pacific." *Forbes 50th Annual Report on American Industry, 1998,* 1 January 1998. Available at http://www.forbes.com.

"Georgia-Pacific." *Hoover's Handbook of American Business 1998.* Austin, TX: The Reference Press, 1997.

"Georgia Pacific." *Standard & Poor's Stock Reports.* New York: Standard & Poor's, 10 January 1998.

"Georgia-Pacific to Split Up Interests in Timber and Paper." *New York Times,* 18 September 1997.

Russo, David A., and others. "Paper & Forest Products Industry." *The Value Line Investment Survey (Part 3 - Ratings and Reports),* 16 January 1998.

Sharav, Ben. "Georgia-Pacific GP." *Value Line Investment Survey,* 17 April 1998.

For an annual report:
telephone: (404)652-5555 **or** write: Investor Relations, Georgia-Pacific Corp., PO Box 105605, Atlanta, GA 30348

For additional industry research:
Investigate companies by their Standard Industrial Classification Codes, also known as SICs. Georgia-Pacific's primary SICs are:

2411 Logging

2421 Sawmills and Planing Mills, General

2426 Hardwood Dimension and Flooring Mills

2435 Hardwood Veneer and Plywood

2611 Pulp Mills

2621 Paper Mills

2631 Paperboard Mills

2653 Corrugated and Solid Fiber Boxes

2657 Folding Paperboard Boxes

2861 Gum and Wood Chemicals

Gerber Products Company

FOUNDED: 1901

Contact Information:
HEADQUARTERS: 445 State St.
   Fremont, MI 49413
PHONE: (616)928-2000
FAX: (616)928-2408
TOLL FREE: (800)4-GERBER
URL: http://www.gerber.com

OVERVIEW

Since 1928 Gerber Products Company has been a major developer, manufacturer, and marketer of baby food. In the United States, it is the leading baby food manufacturer with more than 70 percent of the market. Gerber also has a strong presence in Mexico, Costa Rico, Venezuela, and Poland.

More than 190 varieties of fruits, vegetables, juices, cereals, meats, snacks, and main meals are manufactured by the company. Gerber also sells baby care products in 80 nations.

COMPANY FINANCES

Since Gerber Products Company is a wholly owned subsidiary of Novartis, separate financial statements are not published for the company. However, the 1997 Novartis annual report states that overall sales for Gerber increased 6 percent. Outside the United States the company experienced "double-digit" growth, according to Novartis, through launches of infant formula and cereals.

ANALYSTS' OPINIONS

Environmental groups issued a report in 1997 charging that pesticide residues in baby food brands pose a possible health risk to children. Although the levels of pesticide were below government limits, the groups' report claimed the level of pesticide residues was unsafe for infants.

The Environmental Working Group and the National Campaign for Pesticide Policy Reform reported that 16 pesticides were found in 8 different baby foods from Gerber and its competitors, Heinz and Beech-Nut.

In an Associated Press article, a Gerber spokesman said the company's baby foods were safe, and defended its pesticide elimination program. Gerber and its competitors also disputed the environmental groups' claim that federal pesticide standards didn't adequately protect children.

Meanwhile, a nutrition advocate with the Center for Science in the Public Interest blasted Gerber Products Company's baby food. In March 1997 Michael Jacobson accused the company of exaggerating its baby foods' nutritional quality. He charged that Gerber diluted products with starch, sugar, and water—nearly a year after the company introduced products with no added starch or sugar. A Gerber Products Company spokesman called the claims irresponsible and inaccurate.

HISTORY

In 1927 Dorothy Gerber's pediatrician recommended that she introduce her two young daughters to strained fruits and vegetables. Months after taking her doctor's advice, Gerber had grown tired of peeling, scraping, and straining food. Why, she asked husband Dan, couldn't infant foods be strained and canned at the Fremont Canning Company? Her father-in-law, Frank Gerber, was president of the 26-year-old cannery. Eventually, Dorothy Gerber's conversation with her husband led to talks with Frank Gerber. One year after Dorothy Gerber began the arduous task of straining her daughters' fruits and vegetables, five varieties of Gerber baby food—vegetable soup, carrots, spinach, peas, and prunes—had been created. Six months later the company's baby foods were being sold in grocery stores throughout the United States.

In 1938 Dorothy Gerber started personally answering letters received by the company. In the late 1990s more than 45,000 letters were answered annually by trained correspondence specialists. In May 1986 Gerber began its toll-free information service (1-800-4-GERBER) and in 1991 made that service available 24-hours a day, 7-days a week in the United States and Canada. This information service handles more than 803,000 calls a year about infant feeding and care.

Building on the success of its baby food business, Gerber started making baby care products in 1960. Those products numbered 350 in the late 1990s and include Gerber and NUK brand products such as bottle feeding systems, nipples, pacifiers, teethers, eating utensils, breastfeeding accessories, safety items, and toys.

In 1967 Gerber Life Insurance Company was formed as a subsidiary of Gerber Products Company. It is a di-

FAST FACTS:
About Gerber Products Company

Ownership: Gerber Products Company is a wholly owned subsidiary of Novartis AG, which is a publicly owned company traded over-the-counter.

Ticker symbol: NVTSY

Officers: Alfred A. Piergallini, VChmn., Pres., & CEO; Kurt Furger, Exec. VP & CFO; Mike Lawton, Senior VP & COO

Employees: 4,500

Principal Subsidiary Companies: Gerber Life Insurance Company was formed as a subsidiary of Gerber Products Company in 1967.

Chief Competitors: Chief competitors of Gerber Products Company are manufacturers of baby food and baby care products. They include: Beech-Nut; Heinz; and Playtex.

rect response marketing insurance company and a producer of juvenile life insurance. Gerber Life Insurance Company has more than $9 billion of life insurance in force and insures more than 2 million people throughout the United States and Puerto Rico.

In August 1994 Gerber was acquired by Sandoz Ltd. and in the late 1990s was a part of the Novartis group of companies formed in December 1996 by the merger with Ciba-Ceigy Ltd. Novartis is a leading life science company with core businesses in health care, agriculture, and nutrition.

STRATEGY

Gerber Products Company has maintained its commitment to research and development (R&D)—perhaps the single reason for the company's dominance of the baby food market. Gerber says it has the world's largest private research facility dedicated to infant nutrition. Its baby-focused R&D staff of 80 constantly studies young consumers, whose responses help the staff refine the company's products.

Gerber Products Company's redesign of its Table Teaching 3rd Foods Baby Foods line illustrates just how baby-focused its product development process is. The

CHRONOLOGY:

Key Dates for Gerber Products Company

1901: Founded as an adult food cannery

1928: Begins canning five varieties of baby food

1931: Adopts the Gerber Baby sketch as the company's trademark

1938: Dorothy Gerber starts answering letters from consumers personally

1941: Company is renamed the Gerber Products Company

1956: Gerber is listed on the New York Stock Exchange

1960: Gerber starts making baby care products

1967: Gerber Life Insurance Policy is formed

1977: The company survives a hostile takeover attempt by Anderson, Clayton, and Company

1986: Begins toll-free information phone line: 1-800-4-GERBER

1994: Is Acquired by Sandoz Ltd.; redesigns 3rd Foods product line

1996: Becomes part of Novartis group of companies; begins removing starch and sugar from baby food

line of foods was originally developed for older babies. Its larger jar sizes contained thicker, chunkier food textures. Though the line eventually offered more varieties, it evolved into a product not much different from the Variety Building 2nd Foods Baby Foods line and was redesigned.

INFLUENCES

In 1994 Gerber Products Company began redesigning the Table Teaching 3rd Foods Baby Foods line. Its research showed a need for more variety, thicker and chunkier textures, and more interesting flavors than those consumed by younger babies. Identifying and combining the right tastes and textures became a crucial part of the reformulation. To accomplish it, researchers used a computerized mathematical model to find the right mixture of taste and texture in each product. Once optimal formulations were created, consumer testing commenced.

Consumer testing centered on interpreting and evaluating sensory perceptions. The company used a panel of 8,000 parents and babies to evaluate and help develop the product. In the first stage of testing, adult panelists evaluated sample formulas. Their responses to questions about the samples were incorporated into the mathematical model for analysis. Then a computer generated an equation for the optimal product that yielded the highest *liking* score. Next, researchers generated several prototype formulas. Finally child panelists tasted the formulas and their parents provided evaluations based on the babies' responses to the foods. Scientists also studied the young consumers' nonverbal clues. Turning away from the product, spitting it out, or pushing it off the tray indicated that something was wrong with the food.

The redesign of Table Teaching 3rd Foods Baby Foods produced foods with textures ranging from slightly coarser than pureed to small, tender pieces. The company also added five products to the line. Two years after redesigning its 3rd Foods Baby Foods, Gerber responded to adult customers' demands for baby food with no added starch or sugar by reformulating its core line of products without these two ingredients.

CURRENT TRENDS

In 1997 Gerber designed and implemented various restructuring programs to increase efficiency and profit. The company closed its plant in Asheville, North Carolina, to streamline production capacities. The company also revamped its headquarters/sales organization in Fremont, Michigan, in order to improve operations. The company plans to introduce a new manufacturing technology for jarred baby food designed to improve quality and taste in 1998.

A national trend of lower birth rates translated into a slightly reduced market for Gerber in 1997. However, Novartis claims in its annual report, that Gerber increased its share of this market despite the trend.

PRODUCTS

Juice, cereal, 1st Foods, 2nd Foods, 3rd Foods, and Graduates make up the six principal Gerber baby foods. The entire line of Gerber Products Company's baby foods includes: Gerber Formula, in low-iron, iron, and soy form; "Single Beginnings" 1st Foods Baby Foods, featuring dry cereals, juices, fruits, and vegetables.

"Variety Building" 2nd Foods Baby Foods, feature dry cereals, juices, cereals with fruit, fruit juice with yogurt, fruits, vegetables, dinners, Simple Recipe Dinners, Veggie Recipe Dinners, meats, and desserts.

A 70-YEAR-OLD BABY

On July 28, 1998, Gerber celebrated its 70th birthday, as well as the anniversary of when the company chose the now famous "baby face" for its symbol. Gerber was looking for a baby face for their ad campaign, and they invited leading artists to submit entries. Artist Dorothy Hope Smith sent in a charcoal sketch of her neighbor's five-month-old-baby, inquiring if she was the right age and size of the baby they were seeking. The executives at Gerber thought the sketch was perfect and accepted it as it was. The image was so popular that the company adopted it as its trademark. It is now recognized all over the world and has appeared on every Gerber advertisement and package since 1931.

Over the years the public has pondered over the identity of this famous baby. One of the most circulated rumors was that the baby was Humphrey Bogart. The rumor started because his mother was an accomplished artist and sold drawings for commercial use. However, Humphrey Bogart would have been 29 years old in 1928. There have been speculations that Elizabeth Taylor or Bob Dole were the model, yet the real model was Ann Turner Cook, who turned 72 in 1998; she was two years old when Gerber chose the sketch.

Cook had to defend her Gerber baby identity when a lawsuit was filed challenging the baby's identity. She agreed to appear in court, but that proved unnecessary once the judge saw her baby picture and automatically recognized her from the jars. Cook is not employed by Gerber and receives no royalties for her image, but she does make public appearances for the company and welcomes the semi-celebrity status. A retired English teacher and mystery novel writer, she says, "if you're going to be a symbol for something, what could be more pleasant than a symbol for baby food?"

In December 1996, Gerber unveiled its first new label in more than 40 years. Ann Turner Cook was present for the ceremony, and though the label had changed, her face still remains. "The CEO of the company has assured me they'll never change that part of the label," said Cook in the *Chicago Sun-Times*. She has only seen the original drawing once, but the company gave her a reproduction that hangs in her living room. The original remains locked in a vault at the company's headquarters in Fremont, Michigan, to preserve it for posterity.

"Table Teaching" 3rd Foods Baby Foods include desserts, sauces, and bakery products such as biscuits and Zwieback toast. The Tropical Baby Foods category offers juices such as mango with mixed fruit, and tropical fruits such as papaya with tapioca.

Gerber Graduates Foods for toddlers range from instant oatmeal to meat sticks, microwavable dinners, and fruit snacks.

In October 1997 Gerber introduced a new line of baby food called Tender Harvest. The line features commercially produced organic baby food with approximately 20 products. Initially 10 products were available when the line was introduced, including Apple Mango Kiwi, Chicken & Wild Rice, and Spring Garden Vegetable.

In addition to food Gerber offers a comprehensive line of products to clothe and care for babies. Disposable and reusable nursing systems, nipples, pacifiers, teethers, sterilizers, bottle warmers, feeding dishes, cups, utensils, breast pumps, and safety items such as the bi-fold door lock, auto mirror, and drawer and cabinet latches are carried under the Nuk and Gerber brand names.

CORPORATE CITIZENSHIP

Beginning in June 1997 Gerber's cereal boxes displayed a message to adults about the dangers of allowing babies to sleep on their stomachs. The goal of the national *Back to Sleep* campaign is to reduce the number of infant deaths caused by SIDS, or Sudden Infant Death Syndrome. SIDS, also called *crib death,* kills 4,000 babies in the United States each year. Though the causes of SIDS are unclear, the American Academy of Pediatrics recommends that, to lessen the chance of SIDS, babies should be placed on their backs when they sleep.

Tipper Gore, wife of Vice President Al Gore, led the public education effort to reduce SIDS deaths. "Placing babies on their backs to sleep is one of the most important steps that caregivers can take to reduce the risk of Sudden Infant Death Syndrome, but too many people still don't know this important, simple message," Gore was quoted as saying in a U.S. Department of Health and Human Services press release.

Gerber displayed the message about SIDS and the *Back to Sleep* campaign on 3 million of its cereal boxes.

The company also included the message in mailings to 2.7 million mothers of newborns over a year. A message recorded by Tipper Gore has played on the Gerber toll-free information number (1-800-4-GERBER) 7-days a week, 24-hours a day, for a year. The company estimated it would reach 80 percent of parents with infants across the country.

GLOBAL PRESENCE

Gerber Products Company's production facilities are located throughout the United States, Mexico, Costa Rica, Venezuela, and Poland. According to Gerber's parent company's annual report, Gerber launched its infant formula and cereals in eastern Europe, Latin America, and the Far East in 1997. The labels on its products are printed in 16 languages.

SOURCES OF INFORMATION

Bibliography
"Clinton Administration Announces Expanded *Back To Sleep* Campaign, Tipper Gore To Lead New Effort," 19 May 1997. Available at http://www.gerber.com.

Gerber Corporate Background, 19 May 1997. Available at http://www.gerber.com/corpback.html.

"Gerber Products Company Announces Major Move: New Formulations Free of Starch and Sugar Introduced to Core Line of Baby Food," 19 May 1997. Available at http://www.gerber.com/starchfree.html.

"Gerber, Tipper Gore Say Babies Should Sleep On Backs." *USA Today,* 1 April 1997.

Novartis Home Page, 14 May 1998. Available at http://www.novartis.com/textsite/nutrition/gerber/t-corporate.html.

"Pesticides Common In Baby Food, Report Says." *USA Today,* 1 April 1997.

For an annual report:
telephone: (908)522-6898

For additional industry research:
Investigate companies by their Standard Industrial Classification Codes, also known as SICs. Gerber's primary SIC is:

2032 Canned Specialties

Gibson Greetings, Inc.

OVERVIEW

Gibson Greetings makes and sells over 24,000 different "relationship communication" products ranging from greeting cards to plush toys. Frank O'Connell, Gibson's CEO, sees the company as being "not in the greeting card business [but rather] in the relationship business." Its wares can be found in over 50,000 stores on almost 95 miles of shelf space throughout the United States and Europe, as well as on the Internet. Sixty percent of the company's sales of tangible goods derive from grocery stores, 35 percent from mass merchants, and the rest from drug stores—mostly discount merchants. With a 7-percent share of a $7.1 billion market, Gibson Greetings ranks a distant third among American greeting card makers after Hallmark and American Greetings. In addition to selling its products on others' shelves, Gibson owns a nationwide chain of approximately 190 party-supply stores called The Paper Factory of Wisconsin, Inc., located mostly in manufacturers' outlet malls. Gibson makes its own bows, ribbons, and candles, and outsources most of its other products.

COMPANY FINANCES

In 1997 total revenues were $397 million, and net income was $21.6 million, for a total of $1.27 earned per share. Sales growth for the year stood at 2 percent. In 1997 the return on the average stockholder's equity was 89 percent, and Gibson began a move to buy up to a million shares from its stockholders. The company ended 1997 with $114 million in cash and is pondering using some of it to fund advantageous acquisitions.

FOUNDED: 1850

Contact Information:
HEADQUARTERS: 2100 Section Rd.
Cincinnati, OH 45237
PHONE: (513)841-6600
FAX: (513)758-1692
TOLL FREE: (800)345-6521
EMAIL: emorgan@gibsongreetings.com
URL: http://www.gibsongreetings.com

FINANCES:

Gibson Greetings, Inc.
Net Sales, 1994-1997
(million dollars)

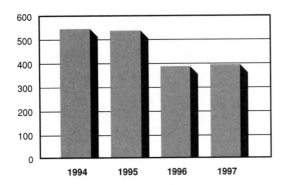

Gibson Greetings, Inc.
1997 Stock Prices
(dollars)

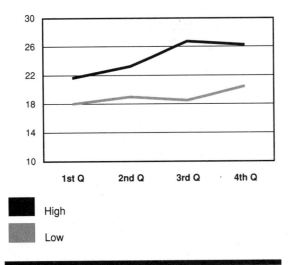

While total revenue for 1997 was up from 1996's $389.4 million, both 1997 and 1996 revenue were down quite a bit from earlier years. For 1993 total revenue was $546.9 million. In 1994 revenue reached an all time high of $548.8 million, but was down a bit in 1995 to $540.1 million. Also, the stock closing prices for the same period fluctuated a bit—from $21.13 in 1993, down to $14.74 in 1994, up to $16.00 in 1995, and continuing to rise in both 1996 and 1997 to $19.63 and $21.88, respectively.

ANALYSTS' OPINIONS

Gibson's stock has soared since O'Connell took over in 1996, propelling Gibson from a $46.5-million loss in 1995 to a net income of $21.6 million in 1997. Industry experts support his ambition to stop making advance payments in order to secure retail display space. The Cleveland-based institutional equity research firm Midwest Research/Maxus Group Ltd. includes Gibson's stock on its "buy" list and has indicated that it is "extremely impressed with the new Gibson." Others, however, are skeptical that his cost-cutting and innovative product lines can permanently improve the company's prospects of competing against industry giants who control a combined 75-percent share of the market.

HISTORY

In 1850 George Gibson, a Scottish engraver and printer, emigrated with his family to the United States along with his own lithographic press. His sons settled in Cincinnati and soon founded Gibson & Company Lithographers, which printed stock certificates, bonds, business cards, and checks, though later they would be bought out by their brother Robert, the company's business manager. On Robert's death, the enterprise was incorporated as The Gibson Art Company, and ownership passed to his four children. The company eventually diversified to print items for retail stores, such as stationery and Civil War prints, and in the 1880s it became a pioneer in the printing of Christmas cards.

By the early 1960s, the company's name had changed again to Gibson Greeting Cards, Inc. Its common stock was listed on the New York Stock Exchange in 1962, but in 1964 it became a privately owned company again when CIT Financial Corporation purchased its assets. Gibson returned to public ownership in 1980 when it was sold to RCA Corporation, which took it over as a subsidiary and substantially expanded it. Two years later, it was sold to a group consisting of Gibson executives and the Wesray Corporation, and in 1983 it was named Gibson Greetings, Inc. The company now holds the distinction of being the oldest greeting card producer in the United States.

STRATEGY

Financially, the mid-1990s were a difficult period at Gibson. In 1994 the company reported a loss of $23 million from a soured derivatives investment, and its stock fell into a slump. One of O'Connell's most significant ideas was to end Gibson's participation in an industry-wide contracts system in which greeting card companies pay retailers advanced cash in order to win premium shelf space for a set time period. O'Connell sees this convention as tying up valuable company resources that could be put toward more productive purposes, such as developing new merchandise lines—a fundamental part of Gibson's new focus. In addition, he wants retailers to assign shelf space according to sales.

Target marketing is an important part of Gibson's current approach. It tries to form special product lines to fit as many demographic types as possible. Various target social groups include sports fans, grandparents, and young adults. For example, in 1998 it launched "Snaps," the first large-scale greeting-card brand to be directed specifically toward "Generation X" consumers. This line of 108 cards uses bold, contemporary graphics and trendy lettering, which were chosen after an extensive market survey of Generation X consumers around the United States. A brand of 3-D wall art called "Cool Stuff for Kids" is aimed at the child market, and "buzzcuts" cards are intended for the Baby Boomer generation. An active sales force consults with store management to gain insight into the consumer base and marketplace.

Gibson is trying to broaden the range of retail markets in which its products appear in an attempt to increase market share, which dropped from 10 percent in 1993 to 7 percent in 1998. According to O'Connell, a key goal is to increase the proportion of revenue that it earns in drugstores, where he sees an untapped market, by setting up mutually advantageous selling arrangements with "a select number of drugstore chains that want to partner with us and do something different."

By the end of 1998, Gibson will have outsourced most of its production away from its Cincinnati headquarters in an effort to reduce its fixed costs. An extensive economic study showed that such a change was imperative in order for the company to remain competitive. Savings from outsourcing are expected to cut $12 million in annual costs by the year 2000, some of which will be the result of providing fewer employee benefits.

INFLUENCES

Among the first tasks the new CEO undertook was to divide the company into specialized units: everyday counter cards, "alternative markets," wrapping paper and partyware, licensing, seasonal, and candles and gifts, so that it could maximize the company's creative and sales talent. Management personnel has become more diverse, and members were brought in from a number of other industries in order to provide broader marketing insight. Gibson also performs extensive market research. Its studies showed that the card-buying public was tiring of the more staid, traditional cards that contained tame, rhyming poetry, so it brought its collections up to date by infusing them with much-needed humor.

The Internet has revolutionized the way Gibson distributes its products. As a further effort to lure new cus-

FAST FACTS:
About Gibson Greetings, Inc.

Ownership: Gibson Greetings, Inc. is publicly held and traded on NASDAQ.

Ticker symbol: GIBG

Officers: Frank J. O'Connell, Chmn., Pres., & CEO, 54, $370,833; James T. Wilson, Exec. VP Finance & Operations & CFO, 49

Employees: 6,600

Chief Competitors: Gibson competitors include: American Greetings and Hallmark.

tomers from new settings, the company invested several million dollars for a minority stake in electronic greeting industry leader Greet Street, on whose web site (http://www.greetst.com) personalized Gibson cards ("e-greetings") can now be bought for $.50. Their cards can be purchased, inscribed, and sent online through Firefly Greetings's site (http://www.fireflygreet.com), as well. A goal for 1998 was to have more than 1,000 card designs available online. A centralized outlet such as the Internet lets Gibson quickly and effectively monitor its cards' progress in order to determine which ideas are selling and which ones aren't.

CURRENT TRENDS

As a sharp departure from the conventional merchandising scheme of aisles and shelves, Gibson has introduced a "Theme Park" prototype concept in stores throughout the United States. This radical in-store concept, which underwent heavy trial research, has been a great success at improving sales so far. Placed among the products, a "theme park" center includes an attractive, wooden design and ongoing feature videos playing on TV screens, all combining to form a miniature attraction right in the store. Moreover, this format makes more efficient use of space. Sales rose by over 20 percent in the Gibson section of a Kroger grocery store where the idea was tested. A similar presentation is Gibson's "boutique" model display, which concentrates a range of products on a common theme, such as anniversaries or a certain holiday. The company intends to add hundreds of these showcases to stores.

CHRONOLOGY:

Key Dates for Gibson Greetings, Inc.

1850: The Gibson Brothers establish Gibson & Company Lithographers

1866: Oversees the production of the first line of American holiday cards

1883: Robert Gibson buys out the brothers and becomes the sole owner

1885: Upon Robert's death, Gibson & Company is incorporated as Gibson Art Company

1960: The company name changes to Gibson Greeting Cards, Inc.

1964: CIT Financial Corporation buys Gibson and privatizes it

1980: RCA acquires CIT

1982: Gibson executives and Wesray Corp. purchase Gibson

1983: Name is changed to Gibson Greetings, Inc. and goes public

1994: Gibson hires its first outside advertising agency

1998: Snaps, the first line of cards aimed at Generation X, is launched

---

Licensing accounts for 13 percent of Gibson's total business, but the company is working to increase that amount. It has expanded the number of licensed themes to more than 75 and expects to continue that trend. In 1997 Gibson entered into a lucrative, long-term licensing deal with Universal Studios Consumer Products Group under which it will market products inspired by that partner's television shows and feature movies. A licensing deal with Viacom demonstrates Gibson's move toward diversification: it provides for the selling of movie-inspired stress balls and magnets in addition to cards. Some of Gibson's licensed products incorporate popular icons such as Garfield and Sabrina the Teenage Witch as well as images from the movies Men In Black, Batman, Space Jam, and Godzilla. The Godzilla-related line, licensed from Sony Corp., will include make-your-own-card kits, wax figurines, and candles.

The innovative Gibson is constantly developing and introducing clever new product concepts. In 1998 it released "Chef'n Around"—all-purpose greeting cards fea-turing recipes from more than a dozen celebrated chefs. Each card contains a color photo of a chef's creation on the front, a recipe inside, and a personal profile of the chef on the back. Featured chefs all belong to an organization called Chefs Collaborative 2000, which advocates organic farming techniques and the purchase of locally grown produce.

Another new line of cards, called "Woof. Meow. Whatever," is aimed at the pet-loving public. In order to capture as wide a market as possible, they will also be offered in pet-care aisles and may soon appear in pet-care specialty stores. In 1998 Gibson introduced a new toy line called "Silly Slammers," miniature bean-bag characters that utter or mutter something when they hit the floor. The Company has developed more than 80 Silly Slammers characters, with shipments totaling more than 7 million units. For Gibson, novel entertainment clearly transcends the greeting-card medium. Silly Slammers are available in toy stores and convenience stores, as well as greeting-card outlets.

As it experienced double-digit growth for its "inspirational products" line in 1997, Gibson decided to invest more resources in its Helen Steiner Rice Collection, which includes prayer cards, bookmarks, plaques, stationery, and magnets featuring the words of their namesake, a poetic Gibson veteran who contributed prolifically to the company's products throughout much of the twentieth century.

PRODUCTS

The company's products comprise a wide range of greeting cards—including "alternative market" and traditional special-occasion and seasonal varieties—in addition to calendars, stickers, tissue paper, gift bags, holiday decorations, and toys. In 1997 alone, Gibson introduced more than 5,000 new items—over a fifth of the current count. CEO O'Connell asserts that new products will raise 1998 sales by 10 percent.

GLOBAL PRESENCE

In 1996 the company sold off its majority-owned Mexican subsidiary, Gibson de Mexico, S.A. de C.V. Its remaining international operation, Gibson Greetings International Limited, is based in Great Britain. Europe is its primary market outside the United States.

EMPLOYMENT

Eligible employees can receive health and life insurance benefits upon retirement. Gibson sponsors a defined benefit pension plan for employees who meet its criteria. The company contributes tax-deductible amounts. Retirement benefits are calculated according to length of service. In 1998 Gibson closed a plant and let over 400 production employees go when it began to outsource manufacturing as part of a major restructuring move. In an effort to increase efficiency the company made a $35-million investment in information technology and expected to cut its administrative staff by 65. All displaced workers receive a comprehensive severance package, including salary continuation, subsidized medical coverage during a part of the salary-continuation period, professional outplacement assistance, and career counseling.

SOURCES OF INFORMATION

Bibliography

Coleman, Calmetta Y. "Gibson Greetings Makes Headway in Turnaround Bid." *Wall Street Journal,* 18 December 1997.

Davids, Meryl. "Gibson Greets a New Day." *Journal of Business Strategy,* November-December 1997.

De Lombaerde, Geert. "Gibson Cuts R&D Costs with Online Tests." *Business Courier,* 30 January 1998.

"The Front End: Hi There!" *Drug Topics Magazine,* 2 June 1997.

Gibson Greetings Home Page. May 1998. Available at http://www.gibsongreetings.com.

"Gibson Greetings Expands Increasingly Popular Helen Steiner Rice Collection." Gibson Greetings, Inc. News Release, 2 December 1997.

"Gibson Greetings Announces Strategic Online Merchandising Alliances." Gibson Greetings, Inc. News Release, 8 December 1997.

"Gibson Greetings Announces Major Restructuring." Gibson Greetings, Inc. News Release, 31 March 1998.

"Gibson Greetings Brings Fresh Meaning to 'The Recipe Card' with New Chef'n Around Brand." Gibson Greetings, Inc. News Release, 4 May 1998.

"Gibson Greetings Reports Earnings for Fourth Quarter and 1997 Full Year." Gibson Greetings, Inc. News Release, 19 February 1998.

"Gibson Introduces Snaps for Generation X." Gibson Greetings, Inc. News Release, 5 May 1998.

"Gibson: Is Success in the Cards?" *Business Week,* 22 June 1998.

O'Connell, Frank J. "In My View: An Evolution for Card Companies." *Supermarket Business,* September 1997.

Richmond, James "The Next Great Thing." *Newsday,* 21 October 1997.

For an annual report:

write: Corporate Communications, Gibson Greetings, Inc., 2100 Section Rd., Cincinnati, OH 45237

For additional industry research:

Investigate companies by their Standard Industrial Classification Codes, also known as SICs. Gibson's primary SIC is:

2771 Greeting Cards

Gibson Guitar Corporation

FOUNDED: 1894

Contact Information:
HEADQUARTERS: 1818 Elm Hill Pke.
    Nashville, TN 37210 USA
PHONE: (615)871-4500
FAX: (615)889-5509
TOLL FREE: (800)444-2766
EMAIL: relations@gibson.com
URL: http://www.gibson.com

OVERVIEW

Gibson Guitar Corporation is one of the most diversified musical instrument companies in the world, both in terms of product and market reach. In the late 1990s it was a $150-million global company. The top-of-the-line Gibson guitars, featuring Les Paul and other signature models, account for about 50 percent of revenues. The recently energized Epiphone brand of low- and middle-market guitars make up 30 percent, with the remaining 20 percent coming from smaller musical instrument companies that were acquired to broaden the line. Of the guitar models, nearly 50 in all bearing the Gibson name over the past century, one stands out above all the rest: the Les Paul solid-body electric. Similarly, Gibson's, The Explorer, Flying V, and Moderne are also among the most valuable of any Gibson production models today. Gibson celebrated 100 years of musical instrument design and production in 1994.

ANALYSTS' OPINIONS

Gibson's brand name, tarnished under the Norlin Company, has regained respectability. In the late 1990s, according to Paul Majeski, publisher of *Music Trades* magazine in Englewood, New Jersey, "Gibson enjoys universal acceptance with musicians. This has translated into tremendous sales." Gibson launched a web site three years ago on which consumers can order instruments and parts, however, retailers feel the company is attempting to sell around them. Management has been trying to reassure retailers on this issue. There is a dealer referral service on Gibson's Web site.

HISTORY

The earliest documented instrument was made by Orville Gibson, a 10-string guitar, in 1894. In his workshop in Kalamazoo, Michigan, this former shoe clerk combined his love for woodworking and passion for music into new designs for mandolins and guitars. Gibson designed his new mandolins and guitars similar to violins, with carved tops and backs instead of flat ones.

In 1902 the Gibson Mandolin - Guitar Mfg., Ltd. was formed to manufacture instruments with Gibson's designs when it became apparent that he could not keep up with orders for the instruments. Five Kalamazoo businessmen bought rights to his name and patent for $2,500 and hired him as a consultant.

A year after Orville Gibson's death in 1918, Lloyd Loar joined the company and refined many of Gibson's original designs. The Master Model F-5 and L-5 guitars were quickly acclaimed; the F-5 was judged the finest mandolin ever built and the L-5 became the first guitar to take a serious role in the orchestra. The L-5 pioneered the concept of building a specific pitch into the sound box by tuning the f-holes, air chambers, and other structural components. It was during the second decade of the twentieth century that the company relocated many times and opened a factory on Parsons Street in Kalamazoo.

Loar resigned in 1924 when Gibson management did not approve of one of his new radical designs. During the Depression, Gibson entered the toy market, began making violins, and introduced an inexpensive line of "Kalamazoo" acoustic guitars.

During the 1930s and 1940s Gibson introduced the Super 400, an extra large jazz guitar. It also enlarged the size of its L-5 model to compete with the horn section in orchestras. A modified version of the Super 400 became Gibson's first electric model in 1951.

During World War II Gibson suspended production of its musical instruments due to a shortage of materials. In 1944 the company was bought by Chicago Musical Instruments, a music wholesale company. With the end of the war, production resumed in 1946 to fill the pent-up demand for musical instruments. Ted McCarty was hired in 1948 and his tenure as company president lasted from 1950-1966. In 1952 the first Gibson Les Paul made its debut as the first solid body electric guitar. For the first time, two woods—maple for the top and mahogany for the back—were combined on a solid instrument for a musical purpose.

In 1957 Gibson acquired Epiphone and a whole new line was introduced in 1958, expanding Gibson's dealer base. This proved to be an impressive move for Gibson, because in 1965 the company hit record production, shipping over 100,000 Gibson and Epiphone instruments for the only year thus far in Gibson history. The 1960s were a period of incredible growth for the music business in general and Gibson in particular. The explosion of rock

FAST FACTS:
About Gibson Guitar Corporation

Ownership: Gibson is a privately owned company.

Officers: Henry Juszkiewicz, CEO; David Berryman, Pres.; Traci Kaufman, Dir. of Human Resources

Employees: 500

Principal Subsidiary Companies: Gibson's principal divisions are Oberheim, The Epiphone Company, Tobias Musical Instruments, Flatiron Mandolins, Dobro Resonator Guitars, Slingerland Drums, and Steinberger Basses and Guitars.

Chief Competitors: Gibson's competitors are other guitar manufacturing companies. They include: Fender; Ibanez; Washburn; Yamaha; Bigsby; and Jackson.

and roll, jazz, and folk music produced unprecedented demand for guitars of all types. Back orders were as long as two years on many models.

In 1969 Chicago Musical Instruments was purchased by Ecuadorian Co., Ltd. and was renamed the Norlin Music Corporation. The overall quality of Gibson products began to decline and so did the company's profits—at an annual rate of 20 percent each year for three years. Its Nashville factory, opened in 1975, was producing only 75 guitars per day in 1986, and was selling its factory failures at discounts.

Under the leadership of the Norlin Music Corporation and with the recessions of 1980-81, Gibson was on the verge of being dissolved. By the mid-1980s the company was near bankruptcy. Norlin folded all of Gibson's product lines (including its famed acoustic guitars and mandolins), except for a couple of electric guitar brands. With the music market still weak, in 1986 Henry Juszkiewicz and David Berryman purchased the company for $5 million. There has since been a successful corporate turnaround.

A new research and development (R&D) team expanded Gibson's product lines and invented new ones. The Chet Atkins family of guitars were expanded and the SST and SST-12 string guitars were introduced. Gibson revived the Les Paul Classic. Acoustic instruments were also evaluated and new designs created. In 1990 Gibson opened a state of the art facility for acoustic production in Bozeman, Montana, where the dry climate made building conditions ideal.

CHRONOLOGY:

Gibson Guitar Corporation

1894: Orville Gibson makes his earliest known guitar

1902: The Gibson Mandolin-Guitar Mfg. Co., Ltd. is formed

1918: Orville Gibson dies

1921: A Gibson employee invents two of the most important facets of guitar design—the adjustable truss rod and the height-adjustable bridge

1935: The first Gibson electric is introduced

1944: Chicago Musical Instrument Co. purchases Gibson

1952: The Les Paul Model solidbody is introduced

1957: Gibson acquires Epiphone

1965: More than 100,000 Gibson and Epiphone instruments are shipped for the only time in company history

1978: Gibson begins reissuing vintage guitars

1986: Henry Juszkiewicz and David Berryman purchase Gibson

1994: Gibson celebrates its 100th year of continuous operation—the only American guitar maker to do so

STRATEGY

In the music business the best way to win consumers is to get their favorite musicians to play the company's instruments. In order to accomplish this the company recruits celebrities to endorse its products. Among the company's current endorsers are Chet Atkins, Tom Petty, Mathew Sweet, and John Lee Hooker. Gibson has taken an innovative approach to marketing its instruments: targeting consumers, as opposed to the trade (manufacturers and dealers). In order to attract new consumers that Gibson wasn't reaching in *Guitar Player* or other industry magazines, the company began running ads in magazines such as *Esquire, GQ,* and *The New Yorker.* Most importantly these ads include an (800) number that consumers can call for more product information.

As it becomes increasingly apparent that the guitar market will unlikely reach the sales volume of the 1960s'

boom years, Gibson has acquired businesses that make electric basses, amplifiers, mandolins, keyboards, and drums to augment its line of guitars. These include the Flat Iron Mandolin Company in 1987; Tobias, a line of electric bass guitars in the early 1990s; Steinberger Guitars and Basses; Slingerland Drums; Oberheim Keyboards and drum machines; OMI dobros; and Kramer Electric Guitars. In the late 1990s the company had 13 divisions overall. The strategy behind the acquisitions was to get Gibson to compete in multiple markets. Gibson is also "aiming to become more involved in the burgeoning business of computer-based music," according to Joshua Rosenbaum of *The Wall Street Journal.*

Not long after Juszkiewicz took over Gibson he raised prices and reinvested the profits into improving product quality and production. Equally important, Gibson discontinued selling factory seconds—flawed guitars from the factory that had been sold at a discount.

One Gibson strategy that failed miserably in the early years of Juszkiewicz's term was a discount strategy. When the new management took over Gibson in the 1980s, it considered trying to compete with Japanese guitar makers by cutting prices. However, Juszkiewicz discovered that the lower priced guitar didn't sell. In fact, the more the company charged for the guitar, the more the product sold. Gibson management reversed the discount strategy and revenues and earnings grew.

INFLUENCES

In the past there has been some instability in Gibson's 30-person sales force. Henry Juszkiewicz has reorganized it several times since taking over the company, usually with the aim of cutting down on bureaucracy and making sales representatives and managers more responsive to customers. In its most recent reorganization, the company shifted the sales management responsibilities from its headquarters staff to its regional managers.

The company had no product offering in the entry-level and middle market. The Epiphone brand is an example of Gibson's strategy of targeting a specific market segment with a specific brand set aside as a stand-alone company. Gibson's Epiphone division is located in Korea where it employs quality control workers who regularly check production. In the late 1990s Epiphone was boosted to the number two brand.

Sales of musical instruments have always been influenced by trends in the music industry. Matt Umanov, a veteran New York guitar dealer, was quoted in a February 1998 *Wall Street Journal* article as saying, "There have been no guitar heroes, like Eddie Van Halen, for several years now, and that's what spurs sales of guitars." Today's stars are making their music with rap and other songs without guitars. But Gibson Chairman Juszkiewicz says there just might be a "guitar renaissance." He points to music videos and pop music becoming more guitar oriented.

CURRENT TRENDS

Gibson chairman Juszkiewicz would like his company to become a lifestyle company representing the musician lifestyle the way Nike represents the athletic lifestyle. Juszkiewicz recently opened the first Gibson cafe in downtown Nashville and named it Henry's. It is a combination coffeehouse, performance space, and exhibition space for Gibson guitars. It is similar to Planet Hollywood and Hard Rock Cafe. Henry's showcases acts from country bands to gospel singers to mandolin orchestras, and has been attracting tourists, musicians, and record producers. Juszkiewicz's goal is to launch a nationwide chain if it proves successful. The growth of the guitar market has been growing steadily for the past five years and Gibson has clearly benefited.

While focusing on consolidation of its bluegrass division, Gibson acquired a four-story building in Nashville, Tennessee, which will be used specifically for all its bluegrass instruments. The building will include a bluegrass museum, a diner, an outside stage seating 300 to 400 people, and a store in which tourists can purchase bluegrass instruments and other merchandise.

PRODUCTS

Gibson guitars are priced as low as $200, to as high as $100,000 for custom-made models. Gibson's principal instruments and trademarks include Gibson Bluegrass Banjos and Mandolins, Gibson Custom*Art*Historic, Gibson Montana Acoustic Flat Top Guitars, Gibson Strings & Accessories, Gibson USA Electric Guitars and Basses, Gibson Tourwear, Dawn Pro Audio, DOBRO Resonator Guitars and Basses, Epiphone Instruments, Flatiron Mandolins, Obherheim Electronics, RedBear Amplifiers, Slingerland Drums, Steinberger Basses and Guitars, Tobias Basses, and GMI Licensed Products.

Recently the Hallway Entertainment of Nashville, Tennessee, signed a license with Gibson to produce a documentary/video biography on the history of Gibson instruments and the musicians who play them. This documentary will be produced for broadcast as well as for home video release and will feature many legendary musicians. Also, Gibson and Les Paul are in the process of designing a guitar that will incorporate new solid-state electronics. Gibson estimates they have built and sold 500,000 Les Paul guitars over a period of 43 years. The company will continue to revive historic models and design new ones.

CORPORATE CITIZENSHIP

Gibson has been giving increasing attention to the city of Memphis. In the early 1990s it became a sponsor of the Blues Foundation's W.C. Handy and Lifetime Achievement Awards and International Blues Talent Competition. Gibson is also a sponsor of the Foundation's Beale Street Caravan radio program. The goodwill is further reflected in the recent announcement that Blues Foundation president David Less will soon join Gibson in its Gibson Entertainment division. The division, which will have offices in the Memphis facility, is expected to lead the company into new businesses beyond the manufacture of musical instruments. Terry Clements, director of visitor development at the Nashville Convention and Visitors Bureau, stated, "They [Gibson] are outstanding corporate citizens." Gibson sponsors live events such as "Battle of the Bands" with equipment and recording opportunities as prizes. In April 1998 the Epiphone company, partnered with the Red Cross, Nashville's Shiloh music, and local bands for a free concert to benefit the victims of two tornadoes that devastated Nashville's downtown and suburbs.

GLOBAL PRESENCE

Gibson has had a presence in Europe and Asia for 30 to 40 years. Still, global opportunities weren't being effectively exploited until the Juszkiewicz era. In 1986 sales outside the United States were just about $2 million. In the late 1990s, 60 percent of Gibson's products were sold overseas. The number of U.S.-based factories has increased from 1 to 11.

Gibson's global sales have grown 50 percent since 1995. In fact those sales account for half of the company's revenues, up from 20 percent in 1995. The company has begun to devote more resources to finding and managing distributors in markets around the globe. Gibson has incorporated a distribution system and added executives with global experience to operate the international division. This division is currently segmented as western Europe, Pacific Rim, and developing markets including Russia, the Eastern Bloc, South Africa, and Central and South America.

The company also supports its international distributors. Via frequent phone calls, faxes, and e-mail, the company keeps them posted of new products, price increases, and marketing plans. In addition, Gibson holds annual distributor meetings in Nashville, Tennessee, and Europe to discuss sales strategy. Top management also meets with distributors at major music industry trade shows, including the Frankfort Musik Messe, an international music show held annually in Germany.

EMPLOYMENT

Gibson's workforce has grown from 250 in 1986 to approximately 500 in 1998. In fact, part of Gibson's reinvestment of profits went toward increased manpower. The company has six regional teams of five salespersons each, which are headed by a regional manager who works directly with individual division heads for problem solving. Compensation for each team is tied to group accomplishment, with about half of their pay driven by regional performance.

SOURCES OF INFORMATION

Bibliography

Brewer, Geoffrey. "The Front Man." *Industry Week,* March 1997.

Gibson Guitar Corporation Home Page, 21 April 1998. Available at http://www.gibson.com.

McGraw, Jim. "American Classics: The Gibson Guitar." *Popular Mechanics,* 1995.

Rosenbaum, Joshua. "Guitar Maker Looks For a New Key." *Wall Street Journal,* 11 February 1998.

Stevens, Tim. "The Guitar Man." *Industry Week,* 23 June 1997.

For additional industry research:

Investigate companies by their Standard Industrial Classification Codes, also known as SICs. Gibson's primary SIC is:

3931 Musical Instruments

The Gillette Company

OVERVIEW

The Gillette name is synonymous with a wide range of personal care products for men and women. It is the world's leading manufacturer of razor blades, razors (Gillette), alkaline batteries (Duracell), writing instruments (Parker, Paper Mate, and Waterman), and toothbrushes (Oral B). Shaving products account for more than 50 percent of Gillette's profits. Gillette's business also includes toiletries (Right Guard and Soft & Dri), hair removal products and household appliances (Braun).

More than 1.2 million people around the world use one or more of Gillette's products every day. Gillette is the world leader in 13 major consumer product categories. The company has a very extensive global presence and is credited with a strong program of new product development.

COMPANY FINANCES

In a study of the top 50 consumer packaged goods companies reported in *Business Week,* Gillette was 1 of only 17 that managed to achieve above-industry average growth in both sales and profits from 1985 to 1990. Gillette also was numbered among the 7 of these 17 companies that were able to maintain this excellence during the following 5 years.

Although due in part to the acquisition of Duracell, sales have more than doubled since 1991 to $10.1 billion in 1997, a 4-percent increase over 1996. Net income improved at a 16-percent rate to $1.4 billion. Earnings per share were $2.55. Gillette stock's price/earnings ratio was

FOUNDED: 1901

Contact Information:

HEADQUARTERS: Prudential Tower Bldg.
    Boston, MA 02199
PHONE: (617)421-7000
FAX: (617)421-7123
TOLL FREE:
URL: http://www.gillette.com

FINANCES:

Gillette Co.
Sales, 1994-1997
(million dollars)

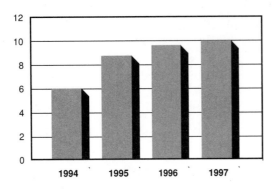

Gillette Co.
1997 Stock Prices
(dollars)

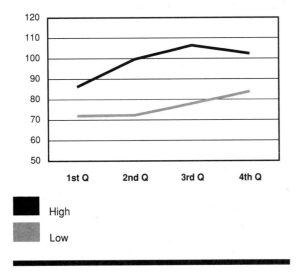

■ High

▨ Low

The January 1998 Value Line Investment Survey reported that the climb in Gillette's profits should continue in 1998, with an almost 18-percent rise in earnings. According to *Business Week,* Wall Street analysts expect this 18-percent rise to continue over the next five years, slightly more than double the rate for the S&P 500. Value Line calls Gillette a good quality stock and ranks it as an average year-ahead selection. However, for the long term Value Line indicates, "Gillette shares offer lackluster appreciation potential through 2000-2002, due, in part, to a solid uptick in the stock's quotation since our October report."

HISTORY

In 1895 King C. Gillette, an ambitious traveling salesman, had two problems. One was his dulled razor and the other was his lack of a "right" product to market. Gillette envisioned an inexpensive, double-edged blade that could be clamped over a handle, used until it was dull, and then discarded. Gillette spent about six years trying to perfect his safety razor, despite pessimistic views of scientists and tool-makers.

In 1901 Gillette joined forces with William Nickerson, a Massachusetts Institute of Technology-educated machinist, who helped Gillette form the American Safety Razor Company. While Gillette raised the $5,000 they needed, Nickerson developed production processes to make Gillette's idea a reality. In 1903, with Gillette as the president of a three-person directorate, the company began production of razors.

In October 1903 the company was renamed the Gillette Safety Razor Company. Product advertising began that year. In 1904 Gillette received a patent on the safety razor and bought a six-story building in Boston. The company paid its first cash dividend in 1906. While earnings increased steadily due to print advertising, Gillette also concentrated on international expansion. In 1905 a London sales branch was established; followed in 1909 by a small manufacturing plant in Paris; and offices in Germany, Austria, Scandinavia, and Russia. Foreign business accounted for 30 percent of Gillette's profits by 1923.

King Gillette fought off challenges for control of the company from John Joyce, a major investor in the company. Gillette bowed out in 1910 after selling a substantial portion of his controlling share to Joyce. Even though Gillette retained the title of president, Joyce took charge of the active management of the company until he died in 1916. Edward Aldred, Joyce's long-time friend and an investment banker, bought Joyce's interest in the company, retained Joyce's management team, and took control.

41 times expected 1997 profits. Fiscal 1997 marked the twentieth consecutive annual increase in dividends per common share paid to Gillette stockholders. It was also the ninety-second consecutive year the company paid cash dividends on its common stock. In calendar year 1997, Gillette stock ranged from a low of $72.00 to a high of $106.38. The annual dividend was $.86. In June 1998 a two-for-one stock split became effective for stockholders.

Financial goals for the company are to increase total spending on research and development, capital spending, and advertising (in combination) at least as fast as sales to assure continued growth.

Gillette supplied 3.5 million razors and 36 million blades to troops during World War I, earning a large number of new loyal customers. Five hundred new employees were hired. In 1921 when Gillette's patent expired, a new and improved safety razor, which sold at the price of the old one, was introduced. Growth and expansion, both domestic and foreign, continued. The company received favorable publicity when it became royal purveyor to the Prince of Wales in 1922 and to King Gustav V of Sweden in 1924, and when the Paris office gave Charles Lindbergh a Gillette Gold Traveler set the day after he completed the first transatlantic flight.

At the end of the 1920s Gillette faced two major problems that led to a loss of confidence in the company and lower stock prices. In 1929 Stock prices fell from a high of $125 to $18. This crisis led to a management reorganization. Gillette made a bold advertising move when it admitted that the blade it had introduced in 1930 was of poor quality. The company then introduced what became its most recognizable product, the Blue Blade. Even though the Blue Blade kept Gillette a leader in the field, profits remained disappointing through the Depression.

In 1939 Gillette restored the company's advertising budget, relying successfully on heavy broadcast sports advertising. During World War II almost all of Gillette's production went to the military. Even though foreign production and sales declined, domestic production more than made up for it. The backlog of civilian demand led to record sales until 1957. During this time Gillette started broadening its product line by introducing brushless shaving cream; ball-point pens and home permanents were added to the product line through acquisitions.

Gillette reorganized in 1964 as a diversified consumer products company. It pursued the strategy of internal development of new product lines and acquisition of other companies to add to its product lines. This strategy brought mixed results. New products, which included Toni hair-color products, Earth Born shampoos, luxury perfumes, and small electronic items (smoke alarms, watches, and calculators) all failed. The acquisition of the West German Braun Company gained the company entry into the European electric-shaver market, but a Justice Department antitrust suit prevented Gillette from introducing the Braun shaver in the U.S. market until 1984. Other companies acquired in this period, including Eve of Roma perfume, Buxton leather goods, Welcome Wagon, and Hydroponic Chemical Company never found the right fit with the company and were later sold.

Colman M. Mockler Jr., who came to Gillette in 1957, took charge of the company in 1975. Mockler sorted through all the new acquisitions, sold off the least successful ones, and retained those that either were successful or had a good line of products that needed to be marketed more efficiently. Mockler also increased Gillette's advertising budget and undertook company-wide cost cutting measures. In 1984 Gillette acquired Oral-B, enabling it to branch into dental-care products.

FAST FACTS:
About The Gillette Company

Ownership: The Gillette company is a publicly held company traded on the New York Stock Exchange, as well as the Boston, Midwest, Pacific, London, Frankfurt, and Zurich Stock Exchanges.

Ticker symbol: G

Officers: Alfred M. Zeien, Chmn. & CEO, 68, $3,416,667; Michael C. Hawley, Pres. & COO, 60, $1,358,333

Employees: 44,000

Principal Subsidiary Companies: Gillette's subsidiaries include: The Gillette Company Andover Manufacturing Center, The Gillette Company Personal Care Division, Oral-B Laboratories, Paper Mate, Braun AG, and Duracell.

Chief Competitors: Due to the diversity of its products, Gillette competes with multinational companies in a variety of industries, including manufacturers of razors, toiletries, stationery products, alkaline batteries, and oral-care products. Chief among the company's competitors are: BIC; Ralston Purina; Bristol-Myers Squibb; Colgate-Palmolive; Johnson & Johnson; Procter & Gamble; Remington Products; Sunbeam; and Warner-Lambert.

The growing fear of fluorocarbons was one of the biggest problems faced by Mockler. He eventually replaced the propellant in Gillette's aerosol cans. This move was followed by new product launches, which recovered a quarter of the deodorant market for Gillette.

Bic was a French competitor that threatened Gillette's pen and Cricket lighter products. Once again Gillette countered by competing with Bic on price while emphasizing the higher quality of its pens and lighters. By 1980 Gillette had improved profitably despite Bic's challenge.

Mockler's policies proved very successful for Gillette, producing a higher profit margin and a surplus of cash. This resulted in a takeover threat from Revlon in 1986. In 1987 two unsolicited requests from Revlon to buy the company were rejected by Gillette's Board of Directors. In response to these takeover threats, Gillette reorganized top management, laid off workers to thin out its workforce, modernized its plants, shifted some pro-

CHRONOLOGY:

Key Dates for The Gillette Company

1901: Traveling salesman King Gillette starts the American Safety Razor Company to manufacture disposable razors

1903: The company is renamed Gillette Safety Razor Company

1904: Gillette receives a patent on the safety razor

1910: King Gillette sells his controlling share

1929: Gillette merges with Auto Strop Safety Razor Company

1936: Gillette Brushless shaving cream, the company's first non-razor product, is introduced

1948: Expands its product line even further by purchasing the Toni Company home permanent maker

1955: Gillette acquires the Paper Mate pen company

1963: Gillette patents a coated, stainless-steel blade

1971: The Trac II, the world's first twin blade system, is introduced

1984: Gillette acquires Oral-B

1990: The Sensor is launched in 16 countries, marking the company's first international launch

1996: Duracell International merges with Gillette

duction to low-cost facilities, and sold many smaller and less profitable operations.

In early 1988 Gillette experienced one of its biggest takeover threats. Coniston Partners sought representation on Gillette's board in an effort to sell or dismantle the company. In 1989, $600 million shares of Gillette convertible preferred stock were purchased by Berkshire Hathaway, of which Warren Buffet owns 9 percent. Buffet agreed to give Gillette the right of first refusal, which lessened the threat of a takeover. With its restructuring completed, Gillette returned to emphasizing its powerful brand names.

In early 1990 Gillette tried to expand its shaving operation by acquiring Wilkinson Sword. However, the Justice Department blocked the sale of Wilkinson's U.S. interests since Wilkinson was number four in the market and Gillette already controlled about half the U.S. mar-

ket. Since 1990 firm's earnings grew an average of 20 percent annually.

Throughout the 1990s Gillette continued acquiring companies with popular brand products. In May 1993 Gillette acquired Parker Pen Holdings Ltd. Thermoscan was acquired in 1995. In 1996 Gillette merged with Duracell International. Duracell is the world's leading producer of alkaline batteries, with nearly 50 percent of the U.S. market. The *Knight Ridder/Tribune Business News* stated, "The consumer giant spawned by the merger will create a marketing powerhouse selling everything from copper-topped batteries to Right Guard deodorant - and play an increasingly dominant role in the world's supermarkets and drugstores."

STRATEGY

Gillette's strategy is a three-pronged focus. Simply put, its mission is to achieve or enhance clear leadership, worldwide, in the core consumer product categories in which it chooses to compete. The company hopes to achieve this through a continuing process of new product introductions. Maintaining a new-product ratio above 40 percent of sales is the objective. A record 49 percent of Gillette sales in 1997 came from products new to the market in the last five years. This is twice the level of innovation at the average consumer-products company.

A vast research and development program is at the core of Gillette's success with its new product introductions. According to *Business Week,* Gillette religiously devotes 2.2 percent of its annual sales, or over $200 million, to research and development (R&D)— roughly twice the average for consumer products. The company aims to prove that consumers can be induced to pay a premium for innovative products that deliver superior performance. The company goal is to increase spending on R&D, capital expenses, and advertising— all combined—at least as fast as sales to assure continued company growth.

INFLUENCES

Several factors influenced Gillette's sales performance in 1997. The strength of the U.S. dollar relative to most foreign currencies reduced sales growth by 4 percentage points. The company faces the challenge of making its other businesses as profitable as its blade business. Shaving had been the business that powered Gillette since early this century. Batteries, toiletries, writing instruments, and toothbrushes, for example, must now account for at least half of Gillette's growth.

CURRENT TRENDS

Gillette's plan for the next five years is continued expansion in global markets including Asia, Russia, and Latin America. It will also continue with increased emphasis on new products.

PRODUCTS

The Gillette Company's brands are organized into six major business segments: blades and razors, toiletries, stationery products, Braun products, Oral-B products, and Duracell products. More than 20 new products were launched in 1997.

Gillette's Sensor brand is its top-of-the-line shaving product. Sensor includes the SensorExcel shaving system for men (introduced in 1993) and for women (introduced three years later). The Atra and Trac II twin-blade shaving systems have been major brands for more than 20 years. Agility, the new women's disposable razor, was introduced in North America in late 1997. Gillette's Good News brand is the best-selling disposable razor in the United States.

In April 1998 Gillette introduced its first triple-blade razor, the Mach3. This razor stars in the company's biggest product launch ever, complete with a multimillion dollar global marketing campaign supported by six years of research and development.

Deodorants/antiperspirants, shave preparations, after-shave products, and skin care products make up Gillette's toiletries line. Gillette Series, Right Guard, Soft & Dri, and Dry Idea are part of the largest toiletries category, deodorants. The Gillette Series and Satin Care for women are two major brands in the shave preparation business. In early 1988 Gillette divested the Jafra line of skin care and color cosmetics. According to the company, Jafra "no longer fit Gillette's business strategy."

Parker, Paper Mate, and Waterman writing instruments and the Liquid Paper line of correction fluids, pens, and DryLine correction film comprise Gillette's stationery products.

The Braun line of hair-removal products is the largest Braun business, led by the Flex Integral shaver and the Silk-epil electric hair epilator for women. Braun's oral care products include the Oral-B plaque removers. Food processors, hand blenders, steam irons, hair dryers, and the Thermoscan infrared ear thermometer are among Braun's household and hair-care appliances.

The Oral-B toothbrush is used by more dentists and consumers than any other brand in the world. Toothpastes, mouth rinses, dental floss, and professional dental products are also manufactured under the Oral-B brand.

Alkaline batteries are Duracell's principle line of business. It also makes specialty and high-power rechargeable batteries. In May 1988 Duracell introduced its new Duracell Ultra high-tech battery. It lasts up to 50 percent longer than ordinary batteries and claims to be the world's longest-lasting alkaline battery for high-technology consumer devices, such as cellular phones and camcorders. In 1997 the company announced that it would discontinue manufacturing rechargeable batteries.

CORPORATE CITIZENSHIP

For Gillette, fulfilling the traditional value of good citizenship has meant "reaching beyond the workplace, through corporate contributions and employee involvement to improve our communities." In the company's headquarters city of Boston, Gillette supports organizations and community programs that help improve education, aid the less fortunate, revitalize inner city neighborhoods, and increase community spirit.

Gillette was a founding corporate sponsor of the YMCA of Greater Boston's Black Achievers program. It also sponsored teams of young men and women as part of City Year Boston, a full-time community service program for youth. A number of internship programs for high school and college students are also offered by Gillette. Also in Boston, Gillette provides financial support for organizations such as the United Way, Dimock Community Health Center, South Boston Neighborhood House, and The Museum of Afro-American History, as well as for mentoring programs at local elementary and middle schools.

In the medical field Gillette contributes significantly to women's cancers research at the Women's Cancer Program of Boston's Dana-Farber/Partners CancerCare. In 1997 Gillette awarded $5 million to this program.

In addition to its strong involvement in community service, Gillette is also committed to its responsibility to the environment. With the company's acquisition of Duracell batteries, the company has placed renewed emphasis on environmental initiatives. Since 1990 Gillette has spent more than $60 million on environmental projects around the globe. In the last eight years, Gillette cut worldwide emissions by 80 percent, reduced packaging by 12 percent, and realized energy efficiency gains of 10 percent.

GLOBAL PRESENCE

Gillette is one of the most globalized companies among Fortune 500 multinational organizations. Foreign operations account for 63 percent of Gillette's total sales and operating profits. Gillette has maintained a vast international market base and is growing its business in emerging markets around the world. Gillette operates 64 manufacturing facilities in 26 countries, and Gillette

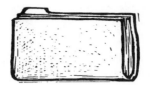

THE SPACE-AGE RAZOR

"One day soon," writes humorist Dave Barry, "the Gillette Co. will announce the development of a razor that, thanks to a computer microchip, can actually travel ahead in time and shave beard hairs that don't exist yet." Gillette hasn't reached this point yet, but it wouldn't be a surprise to find out that the shaving company is feverishly working on such a project in its laboratories. One doesn't usually associate "high-tech" with "shaving," but Gillette works every day to do just that. What do you expect from a company run by a former naval engineer? According to the *Knight Ridder/Tribune Business News*, Gillette CEO Alfred Zeien "talks about 'shaving systems' with the same sort of technical gusto one expects from a Boeing or Hughes engineer." Zeien's attitude permeates Gillette. It's a company that spends huge amounts on R&D and that refuses to release a new product until the next generation is already in development. Gillette has four laboratories devoted just for research, eight for the development of new products, and three engineering centers that work on improving processes and equipment.

This is best exemplified in the story behind the razor that Gillette released in the spring of 1998—the Mach3, the first triple-blade razor. The razor was developed over a seven-year period at a cost of over $750 million. Gillette then spent over $300 million promoting it—meaning over $1 billion was spent on the development and marketing of a *razor*.

To develop this high-tech razor, Gillette put over 500 top-notch engineers on it—some with degrees from universities such as Stanford and M.I.T. The engineers ended up using technology from the semiconductor industry to help build a better blade. They discovered that they could make the blades stronger by dipping them in carbon—the same process used for computer chips. By the time the research and development was complete, Gillette had applied for 35 patents. The stakes involved in the development of the Mach3 were made apparent when it was discovered that one engineer had handed shaver secrets over to the competition. He plead guilty and was sentenced to 27 months in federal prison and ordered to pay $1.2 million in restitution.

Reviews of the new razor were mostly favorable, many commenting on the closer, smoother shave the Mach3 gave. Although some thought it a little pricey, the Mach3 was the top-selling razor during its first full week on the market and, according to Gillette, outsold the closest competition by a two-to-one margin.

Oh, and by the way, the next generation razor was, of course, already in development before the Mach3 was released. It should be out somewhere between 2006 and 2008.

---

products are distributed in more than 200 countries around the world. The most promising new markets for Gillette are in what the company calls its AMEE region—an acronym for Africa, Middle East, and eastern Europe. The company maintains 16 manufacturing facilities and more than 5,500 employees in this region. Gillette attributes its flourishing growth there to its strategy of training local nationals for the highest positions as soon as possible. Among the emerging markets where Gillette is making its presence known are Poland, Russia, the Czech Republic, Turkey, India, Pakistan, and South Africa.

One of the reasons for Gillette's global success is the fact that its product offerings, marketing strategies, and messages are the same for all markets. The global view also extends to the company's hiring and training of managers, as well as to its technology policy—proof of which is Gillette's research and development facilities worldwide. In an article in *Chief Executive*, CEO Alfred Zeien claimed that the organization's

global focus is the glue that holds its disparate businesses together.

EMPLOYMENT

Gillette employs 44,000 people, nearly three-quarters of them outside the United States. Bringing out the finest in each of its employees is the foundation of the company's human resources philosophy, policies, and practices. The company invests about $125 million annually in worldwide training and development programs.

Fortune magazine ranked Gillette number 46 in its 1998 list of the "100 Best Companies to Work for in America." Of the Gillette employees who were randomly chosen to participate in the magazine's survey, 85 percent felt so positively about the company that they indicated their intent to remain with the company until retirement. The company was also cited for its practice of promotion from within.

SOURCES OF INFORMATION

Bibliography

Canedy, Dana. "Gillette, Long a Favorite of Investors, Finds Itself Walking an Edge as Thin as One of Its Razor Blades." *The New York Times,* 28 January 1998.

Donlon, J.P. "An Iconoclast in a Cutthroat World." *Chief Executive (U.S.),* March 1996.

"The Gillette Company." *Hoover's Handbook of American Business 1998.* Austin, TX: Reference Press, 1997.

"The Gillette Company." *Hoover's Online,* 30 July 1998. Available at http://www.hoovers.com.

Hast, Adele. *International Directory of Company Histories,* Vol. III. Detroit, MI: St. James Press, 1997.

Moody's Company Data Report. Moody's Investor Service, 1996.

Symonds, William C. "Gillette's Edge: The Secret of a Great Innovation Machine? Never Relax." *Business Week,* 19 January 1998.

For an annual report:

on the Internet at: http://www.gillette.com **or** telephone: (800)291-7615 **or** write: The Fields Co., 385 Pleasant St., Watertown, MA. 02172

For additional industry research:

Investigate companies by their Standard Industrial Classification Codes, also known as SICs. Gillette's primary SICs are:

2844 Toilet Preparations

3421 Cutlery

3951 Pens and Mechanical Pencils

3991 Brooms & Brushes

Godiva Chocolatier Inc.

FOUNDED: 1929

Contact Information:

HEADQUARTERS: 355 Lexington Ave.
    New York, NY 10017
PHONE: (212)984-5900
FAX: (212)984-5901
TOLL FREE: (800)9GODIVA
URL: http://www.godiva.com

OVERVIEW

Godiva Chocolatier is a manufacturer and retailer of ultra-premium chocolates in the United States and abroad. The company has boutiques in more than 100 locations and more than 1,000 additional outlets in department stores and specialty shops.

COMPANY FINANCES

Since Godiva Chocolatier is a wholly owned subsidiary, financial statements are not published, and Campbell Soup Company does not release financial information for the company. According to the Campbell Soup Company 1997 annual report, "Godiva contributed double-digit sales growth through strong retail sales in the United States and continued expansion in Japan."

ANALYSTS' OPINIONS

According to an analysis of the Campbell Soup Company, published by Deutsche Morgan Grenfell Inc. on February 19, 1997, "Godiva has become a powerful global brand of premium chocolates. Year-to-date sales have increased 20 percent on top of an 11 percent increase in fiscal year 1996 and a 16 percent increase in fiscal year 1995. This growth has stemmed from new products, new stores, and new geographic locations, including Japan and Russia. Management foresees double-digit growth on the top line and in earnings for the foreseeable future."

HISTORY

The Draps family began crafting elegant chocolates in Brussels, Belgium, in 1929. When he opened the first retail shop, Joseph Draps, a son of the founding family, is said to have named the company after the legendary Lady Godiva, who is commonly found depicted in European art.

The Draps worked to create a smooth and rich chocolate. "Through the years," according to company literature, "these standards have been maintained as assiduously as Draps' recipes have been guarded. The finest ingredients in the world have been aggressively sought out, making artificial colors and flavors unnecessary. As a result of this adherence to Draps' heritage, Godiva Chocolates evoke the greatest in confectionery excellence."

Campbell Soup acquired Godiva about 30 years ago, during the 1960s. It started producing chocolates for the American market in 1966 in Pennsylvania. Albert J. Pechenik, formerly head of the subsidiary, is credited with taking Godiva "out of the red into solid profitability." He took the company "from a few boutiques in the East to department stores across the country" in the late 1970s and early 1980s. At that time chocolates sold for about $5 a pound, compared to $16 per pound in the late 1990s. Under Pechenik's direction, Godiva sales reportedly "climbed from $4 million to well over $20 million in less than four years," according to *Forbes* magazine. Godiva was yielding $2,388 per square foot per year in the top 10 department stores, according to Pechenik.

Thomas Fey, who succeeded Pechenik as Godiva president, told *Working Woman* that the company began automating its sales operations in 1987 and equipped its field force with laptop computers "to enhance the existing corporate culture." Fey claimed, "Godiva could have maintained its lead easily for several years without investing in computers," but "wants to keep Godiva on the leading edge."

The company spent approximately $3,000 for each laptop, in addition to software, development, training, and other expenses. "The paramount goal initially," said Fey, "was to reduce paperwork for the sales representatives. If we have cut that load and given them time to do something else—whether it be other work or free time to be with their families—part of our objective has been realized."

In 1994 Godiva undertook a new marketing program under president David Albright. Godiva sales declined in the late 1980s following the recession. In the early 1990s the company sought ways to improve its profits. Its goal was to improve store traffic. The redesign of its stores was the new marketing program's main focus. Godiva changed the decor of its stores from marble floors and black lacquer to creamy white walls, bleached wood floors, and delicate wooden displays. Prior to the redesign, customers had to look through glass showcases

FAST FACTS:
About Godiva Chocolatier Inc.

Ownership: Godiva Chocolatier Inc. is a privately owned company.

Officers: Craig W. Rydin, Pres.

Principal Subsidiary Companies: Godiva Chocolatier Inc. is a wholly owned subsidiary of the Campbell Soup Company.

Chief Competitors: Some chocolate makers competing with Godiva Chocolatier Inc. are: Scharffen Berger Chocolate Maker; Guittard; and Kron Chocolatier.

and rely on the help of a salesperson to make purchases. The purpose of the redesign was to make the chocolates more accessible, with printed price lists and open shelving so that customers could serve themselves. The result was an upturn in worldwide profits and double-digit growth in the new stores.

One of the key elements in Godiva's new marketing program was the inclusion of new, less-expensive products customers could easily purchase on impulse. In 1994 it was estimated at being a $6-million market, which Godiva had "historically ignored," according to author Fara Warner in *Brandweek* magazine. The first new products were coffee, then cocoa and biscotti. Two-piece packages of chocolates for $3.50 were introduced. Then came the Dessert Chocolat in 1996. Godiva's new introductions were an attempt to find a price point and a niche for all its potential customers.

STRATEGY

Very little information is available outside the company about Godiva's business and corporate life. However, the company does disclose that its sales strategy encompasses wholesale, retail (company-owned boutiques), institutional, and direct mail sales. Godiva wholesale accounts include fine department or specialty stores located in major metropolitan areas throughout the country. Examples of wholesale accounts are Bloomingdales, Lord & Taylor, Saks Fifth Avenue, Neiman-Marcus, Jordan Marsh, Hecht's, Macy's, Dayton-Hudson, and Wanamaker's. The company-owned boutiques are located in upscale malls in major metropolitan areas of the United

States. The company's Institutional Sales Program makes Godiva available as an amenity in many luxury hotels as part of their turn-down service, in-room mini bars, or catering service.

A bit more information is available about Godiva's direct mail programs. According to a 1996 article in *Direct* magazine, Craig W. Rydin, president of Godiva Worldwide, said that 6 percent of Godiva's total North American sales and profits came from direct marketing in 1996. "For the 70-year-old company, direct has typically meant the six consumer and two corporate catalogs it mails out each year," according to Rydin. Godiva's six consumer catalogs are mailed in the fall, Christmas, Valentine's Day, spring/Easter, Mother's Day, and summer.

According to the company, Godiva chocolates are positioned to appeal to consumers who buy them for three reasons—for the buyers themselves, for home entertainment, and for "gifting," which accounts for 70 percent of direct marketing sales. Product strategy, catalog design, list management, and customer service make up the four crucial aspects of direct marketing, according to David L. Albright, former president of Godiva Worldwide.

Since the mid-1990s, interactive marketing has taken on greater importance in the company's direct marketing area. In 1994 Godiva was the first Campbell Soup Company to launch a web site. According to Susan M. Dingwall, head of direct marketing for Godiva, the company hoped the web site would bring in 15 percent of its direct mail business in 1996. The Godiva web site includes online ordering, recipes, a list of new Godiva products, a store locator, and an ongoing soap opera entitled, "Murder and Fine Chocolates." Godiva senior marketing manager Adam Rockmore explained in *Direct,* "although women make up only a third of Web surfers, the 8,000 online surveys that customers have completed show that 65 percent to 70 percent are female. Godiva's catalog list is mostly women in the 25 to 65 age bracket with incomes of $50,000 on average."

Godiva has maintained an upscale, golden image for its product. The company has created this image through its advertising, packaging, and distribution. Godiva calls its advertising campaign "silhouettes." This campaign has been designed to "reflect a more approachable, warmer, friendly mood," according to Godiva literature. It is intended to project "a Godiva whose premium image is more generically perceived." Godiva advertises its chocolates in "upper tier" magazines including *Bon Appetit, Forbes, Food & Wine, Travel & Leisure,* and *Gourmet.*

Godiva's chocolates are packaged elegantly and sophisticatedly. Gold boxes, grosgrain ribbon, silk flowers, gilded leaves and berries, collectors' tins, and colorful wrapping paper are offered in a variety of ways on the chocolate assortments. The chocolates are never sold in discount stores or at a reduced price. They are only distributed through upscale department stores and specialty shops.

CURRENT TRENDS

Changing tastes in chocolates is one trend that the Godiva Chocolatier is facing as it plans to modify the way it makes and packages its product. These changes are a result of studies conducted by Godiva and of consumer comments the company received. According to an October 1997 article in *The New York Times,* when Godiva started making chocolates in the United States 30 years ago, the company decided to alter its product slightly from its European chocolates, to reflect a difference in the American palate. "Americans have tended to like their chocolates sweeter, with less intensity, and they have not preferred some favorite European flavors like hazelnut," explained the article. As American tastes are changing, Godiva is adjusting its line of chocolates and including more European-style items, notably four chocolates with hazelnut filling. Godiva is also changing its most popular candy, truffles, by making the hard chocolate coating thinner. New specialized assortments including all-chocolate or caramel and nuts will be made available.

As the American palate has changed, so has the realization that Godiva chocolates sold in the United States and those in Europe are not the same. Americans are becoming more aware of the differences between the chocolates sold here and abroad. These changes will not affect prices.

PRODUCTS

Godiva makes premium chocolates in a myriad of flavors, shapes, and assortments. The Godiva catalog lists approximately 40 different products including chocolates, cocoa, coffee, and biscotti. The Godiva signature assortment is its Gold Ballotin, offered in seven sizes. The Ballotin is a gold box embossed with the Godiva logo and wrapped with a gold tie. The word "ballotin" comes from the French diminutive "ballot," which means small package of wares for sale. There are ballotins to mark every occasion including birthdays, weddings, births, and all holidays. Truffles are another famous Godiva assortment.

Most Godiva products are Kosher and the company's on-line ordering service lists 34 different Kosher items. Coffee, cocoa, and biscotti are recent additions to the Godiva line-up. Dessert Chocolat was introduced by Godiva in 1996 and features three different pieces, which combine two different fillings to make a dessert-like taste—strawberry cheesecake, creme brulee, and machaccino mousse.

GLOBAL PRESENCE

Godiva Chocolatier is expanding globally. In 1998 Godiva had plans to open 30 more retail stores in the United States. Perhaps Godiva's biggest focus is on its expansion efforts in Japan where Godiva has more than 100 distribution points. Additionally, Russia is a new market for Godiva chocolates.

SOURCES OF INFORMATION

Bibliography

Briggs, Jean A. "The Chocolate Soldier." *Forbes,* 17 January 1983.

"Godiva Chocolatier Inc.: History of the Company." New York, NY: Godiva Chocolatier Inc., n.d.

Moreau, Katherine. "Godiva." *Catalog Age,* March 1993.

For additional industry research:

Investigate companies by their Standard Industrial Classification Codes, also known as SICs. Godiva Chocolatier Inc.'s primary SICs are:

2064 Candy & Other Confectionery Products

2066 Chocolate and Cocoa Products

The Goodyear Tire and Rubber Company

FOUNDED: 1898

Contact Information:
HEADQUARTERS: 1144 E. Market St.
   Akron, OH 44316-0001
PHONE: (330)796-2121
FAX: (330)792-2222
URL: http://www.goodyear.com

OVERVIEW

The Goodyear Tire & Rubber Company is the number one U.S. tire maker. Its principal business is the development, manufacture, distribution, and sale of tires throughout the world. Eighty-six percent of the company's 1997 sales have been attributed to car and truck tires. The company also produces and sells a wide variety of other products made from rubber, chemicals, and plastics for the transportation industry including automotive and industrial belts and hoses, molded products, and foam cushioning accessories. In addition, Goodyear provides auto repairs and services through a network of nearly 1000 retail outlets.

Goodyear owns the longest U.S. crude oil pipeline, The All-American Pipeline, which carries oil from California to Texas. The pipeline is operated by Goodyear's Celeron subsidiary.

COMPANY FINANCES

Goodyear achieved strong financial performance in 1997 with income from operations improving for the seventh consecutive year. The company set a record that year for worldwide unit sales, growing twice the industry rate for that year, although revenues were basically flat. Eighty-five percent of Goodyear's revenues were derived from the sale of car and truck tires, while approximately 13 percent of sales came from the company's general products, and 0.9 percent came from oil transportation.

In a 52-week period in 1997, Goodyear stock ranged from a high of $71.30 to a low of $45.00. The company reported earnings per share of $4.71 for 1997. Shareholders received a 7 percent dividend increase, raising the annual dividend rate to $1.20, which was the highest ever. Goodyear's price-earnings ratio was 13.6.

Financial goals for the company are for profitable and sustainable growth and for "cost leadership." The company has set a goal of $20 billion in revenues by 2003.

ANALYSTS' OPINIONS

Analysts have mixed reviews of Goodyear's stock potential in the future. While both *Standard & Poor's* and *Moody's* predict a favorable forecast, the March 1998 *Value Line Investment Survey* ranked Goodyear shares a below-average choice for investing in the year ahead. According to *Moody's,* Goodyear's prospects are positive due to the company's reduction of operating costs and productivity enhancements, and the company's focus on growing its international operations adds to the positive outlook. *Standard & Poor's* rated Goodyear as among the most undervalued of the automotive suppliers. According to its stock reports, Goodyear is "less susceptible to deep cyclical downturns given its primary focus on the replacement market." The shares "make an attractive long-term holding" due to "a steadily strengthening balance sheet, a commitment to a healthy dividend payout, and a $600 million stock buyback program."

HISTORY

Founded in 1898 by Frank and Charles Seiberling, Goodyear was given its name in honor of Charles Goodyear, inventor of the vulcanization process. Goodyear was originally launched as a manufacturer and producer of bicycle and carriage tires. By 1916 the company capitalized on the automotive industry to become the world's largest tire manufacturer.

Looking to expand to foreign countries, the company sought and developed operations in Canada, Australia, Argentina, and the Dutch East Indies by the 1920s. Due to financial entanglements, the two Seiberlings were forced by investment bankers to leave the company. Paul Litchfield took over as the company's CEO in 1926, the year Goodyear was established as the world's largest rubber company.

By the 1930s Goodyear blimps were recognized by people nationwide. With expansion in mind once again, the company purchased Kelly-Springfield (a tire maker) in 1935, increased its number of company stores, and introduced synthetic rubber tires. The company became the U.S. industry leader for tire sales by 1966. Over the next three decades, Goodyear became a master at implement-

FINANCES:

Goodyear
Net Sales, 1994-1997
(billion dollars)

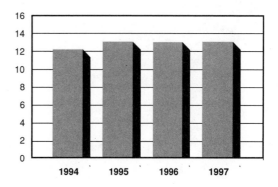

Goodyear
1997 Stock Prices
(dollars)

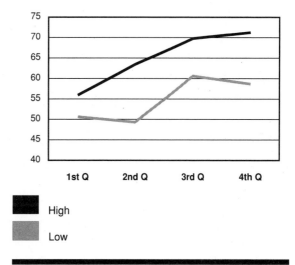

High

Low

ing new technologies, and even supplied the tires used in the Apollo 14 lunar landing in 1971.

The company scrambled to fight a takeover attempt by Sir James Goldsmith in 1986. Goodyear succeeded only after it obtained $1.7 billion by selling all of its businesses unrelated to tires and borrowing $4.7 billion from company stock.

More financial troubles befell the company in 1990 when the tire industry suffered worldwide. Recession, overcapacity, and price cutting added to Goodyear's deep wounds as it struggled through its first financially un-

The Goodyear Blimp flying high in the sky. (Photograph by Joan Slatkin. Archive Photos.)

successful year since the Depression. The company hired Stanley Gault, the retired Rubbermaid CEO known for reviving that company's sales to $1.5 billion.

With Gault in the power seat, marketing procedures changed at Goodyear. Gault cut costs by laying off employees, closing plants, and reducing capital spending. The Goodyear Tire & Rubber Company became profitable once again by 1991, and Gault was chosen as 1992's CEO of the year by *Financial World* magazine.

Several purchases were made by the company in the mid- to late 1990s, increasing the company's global status. In 1994 Goodyear purchased a 60 percent interest in a Chinese automotive hose factory and a 75 percent interest in a Chinese tire factory (Dalian International Nordic Tire Co.). It also purchased 860 Penske Auto centers and more than 300 automotive centers from Montgomery Ward in 1996. That same year the company bought Poland's TC Debica, the country's leading tire manufacturer. Goodyear also introduced Infinitred that year, the only tire available with a lifetime warranty.

In 1997 Sumitomo Rubber Industries formed a strategic alliance with Goodyear, which enabled the companies to manufacture tires for each other in North America and Asia. In January 1997 Goodyear acquired a 60 percent interest in Contred, South Africa's largest manufacturer of tires, power transmissions, and conveyor belts, with 195 retail stores and 41 retreading plants. The remaining 40 percent stake in Contred was purchased by Goodyear for $59 million in March 1998.

STRATEGY

The Goodyear Tire & Rubber Company has faced several strategic shifts over the years. Under the leadership of Samir Gibara, who succeeded chairman Stanley Gault as CEO in 1996, the company has aimed to become number one or number two in each of its markets and to become the lowest-cost manufacturer among the three tire and rubber industry leaders. Some of the company's strategic shifts have included moving production to low-wage countries, incorporating more flexible work rules in the United States, striving to produce innovative products, broadening distribution, and increasing productivity.

Aiming to be ranked as the world's best tire and rubber company by the year 2000, the company has established new development teams to research future trends of the industry. For example, the New Products Development group was established in 1982 to research and predict what consumers would desire in the 1990s. Another group was formed to research and analyze the company's chief competitors. This team studied possible moves competitors would make in the future, such as mergers with other companies, which could affect Goodyear's marketability.

The Goodyear strategy is to improve its profitability by reducing its operating costs and enhancing productivity. Cost containment by the company has included a long-term labor agreement with the United Steel Workers Union and efforts to divest itself of its non-core businesses. The company is also lowering costs through reduction in selling, administrative, and general expenses. Productivity has been improved with the change to seven-day operations at most plants. Goodyear eventually expects to have all its global manufacturing facilities on seven-day work schedules.

Aggressive marketing and distribution strategies also are planned by the company. Goodyear has set a goal of 80 percent as its new product ratio by the year 2000. (The ratio in 1998 was 50 percent.) The introduction of innovative products in an expanded marketplace will help to boost market share.

Goodyear is also utilizing technology to improve quality and cost. In February 1998 the company unveiled a new manufacturing process called IMPACT, an acronym for Integrated Manufacturing Precision Assembled Cellular Technology. Goodyear claims this process is 43 percent more precise than today's production process and allows the company to produce tires 70 percent faster. Changes in tire size and construction can be made in mere minutes with this new process.

INFLUENCES

Goodyear faced highly competitive pricing conditions in the first quarter of 1997. Weak currencies in Asia also negatively influenced the company's financial picture. In April 1997 a strike of nine Goodyear Tire and Rubber Co. factories idled 12,500 workers in seven states for two weeks. The strike cost Goodyear more than $50 million.

CURRENT TRENDS

Goodyear has needed to cut costs due to wavering tire prices. Tire prices had dropped approximately 4.1 percent in 1997, and competitors like Bridgestone increased their global presence. Goodyear's CEO Samir Gibara reduced employment by 5,500 people and sold $90 million worth of assets.

Other profitable growth ingredients have included the company's current focus on innovative products. In North America, Europe, Latin America, and Asia, new products account for nearly 50 percent of tire sales. The company has also implemented new techniques to lessen the time it takes for a new product to get to the market. To do so, the company has expanded its funding in its research and development sectors.

Another focus of Goodyear's profitable growth strategy has been the increase of distribution sites worldwide. In North America, Goodyear's distribution grew by more than 10 percent in 1996. To meet demands, the company

FAST FACTS:
About The Goodyear Tire and Rubber Company

Ownership: The Goodyear Tire and Rubber Company is a publicly owned company traded on the New York Stock Exchange. The stock is also listed on the Chicago Stock Exchange and The Pacific Exchange.

Ticker symbol: GT

Officers: Samir G. Gabira, Chmn., CEO & Pres., 58, 1997 salary $1,571,373; William J. Sharp, Pres., Global Support Operations, 57, 1997 salary $793,260; Robert W. Tieken, Exec. VP & CFO, 59, 1997 salary $682,849; Eugene R. Coller, Jr., Exec. VP, North American Tires, 60, 1997 salary $486,776

Employees: 95,000

Principal Subsidiary Companies: The Goodyear Tire & Rubber Company's chief subsidiaries include All American Pipeline Co.; Brad Ragan, Inc.; Celeron Gathering Co.; and The Kelly-Springfield Tire Co.

Chief Competitors: Goodyear's key competitors are: Bandag; Bridgestone; Continental AG; Cooper Tire & Rubber; Michelin; Pep Boys; Pirelli; and Whitman.

has been searching for new and more profitable retail methods, marketing programs, and telemarketing techniques.

Consistent with the company's focus on profitable growth has been its purchases of other companies and business partnerships. The acquisition of Contred, which was completed in 1998, rounds out the company's re-entry into the South African tire market. An alliance with Sumitomo Rubber Industries Ltd. and its affiliates, Dunlop Tire Corp U.S., and OHTSU Tire and Rubber Co. Ltd. included agreements for marketing and distribution of each other's products and sharing worldwide test facilities. A joint venture with Sava, based in Slovenia in central Europe, will help the company expand its European tire and engineered products market, including hose, power transmission belts, and air springs. In North America, Goodyear purchased the Ultima Rubber Products Co. to extend its retread tire market. Finally, Goodyear made an offer for the shares it doesn't already own in Brad Ragan Inc., a producer and distributor of retread tires.

CHRONOLOGY:

Key Dates for The Goodyear Tire and Rubber Company

1898: Frank and Charles Seiberling found Goodyear in Akron, Ohio

1916: Goodyear becomes the world's largest tire manufacturer

1926: Goodyear becomes the world's largest rubber producer

1937: The crash of the *Hindenburg* ends the dirigible industry for Goodyear

1945: Goodyear begins establishing factories in foreign countries

1951: Annual sales exceed $1 billion for the first time

1961: Annual sales exceed $2 billion for the first time

1969: Annual sales exceed $3 billion for the first time, the first rubber company to top $1, $2, and $3 billion in annual sales

1976: Goodyear is the world's largest radial tire producer

1986: Goodyear has to sell off most of its non-tire interests to survive an attempted takeover

1990: The company suffers a financial loss for the first time since the Depression

1997: Sumitomo Rubber and Goodyear form an alliance to manufacture tires for each other in North America and Asia

Tire customers have expressed a preference for purchasing tire systems, such as balanced tire and wheel assemblies; this preference replaces the desire for individual components like unmounted tires. To answer this trend, Goodyear is positioning tire mounting facilities close to its manufacturing sites in North America, Latin America, and Europe. Goodyear has invested in a new cellular technology plant and a wheel and tire assembly facility in Brazil, near a new General Motors auto plant for which it will be the sole supplier.

PRODUCTS

Goodyear manufactures and markets tires, belts, hoses, and other rubber products for the transportation industry and industrial and consumer markets around the globe. The company produces approximately 150 million tires of all types. Tires and related products include new tires, inner tubes, retreads, repair/maintenance items, and auto repair and service. Goodyear tires include models designed for all types of driving conditions and vehicles including passenger car radials, winter radials, Wrangler light truck radials, and Eagle performance radials.

For passenger cars, Goodyear recently introduced its Extended Mobility Technology (EMT) tires. These tires, called run-flat tires, allow motorists to safely drive at 55 miles-per-hour for up to 50 miles on a damaged tire until they can reach a repair shop. This EMT technology was incorporated on Goodyear's Eagle Aquasteel and Tracker brands in early 1998. Two of Goodyear's more popular passenger car tires are the Infinitred tire, available with a lifetime warranty, and Aquatred tire, for performance under wet driving conditions.

Goodyear's chemical division produces specialty polymer and rubber chemicals for the tire and rubber industry. Coating resins, hydrocarbon resins, and latex are made also. Goodyear rubber and chemicals are used in golf and tennis balls, shoes, automotive and industrial belts and hoses, sealers and paint, bandages and tape adhesives, carpeting, asphalt, housewares, latex gloves, and toys and novelties. Goodyear's chemical division is expanding with a $600 million investment for the production of polyisoprene and synthetic rubber.

Engineered products make up Goodyear's third division. Industrial hose, conveyor belts, air springs, shoe products, molded products, power transmission, and transportation products are produced by this division.

Goodyear's Celeron subsidiaries operate a crude oil pipeline system in the United States that extends 1225 miles from the California coast to central Texas. This system includes an offshore crude oil gathering pipeline in California and crude oil storage facilities.

CORPORATE CITIZENSHIP

Goodyear is a socially responsible corporation and is committed to several environmental and civic projects. The company has a variety of programs that address its focus on environmental accountability. Perhaps Goodyear's biggest challenge is scrap tires. Due to the way tires are manufactured, tire recycling is impossible. Unlike plastics, rubber cannot be returned to its original state for reuse in a new tire. However, scrap tires can be reused or converted to energy. Scrap rubber can be pulverized into powder as a filler in such products as door mats, asphalt, and carpet backing. Goodyear pioneered the use of whole tires as shore barriers, fish habitats, and highway barriers in the early 1970s.

The company faces the seemingly insurmountable problem of huge stockpiles of whole and shredded tires.

According to the company, its priority "is the immediate recycling and recovery of scrap tires through viable, non-subsidized markets." An additional challenge for the company is the annual replacement of 253 million worn out tires by consumers. Technological innovations that have doubled the lifespan of tires, along with improvements in retreading, have reduced the number of discarded tires. Goodyear is a leading advocate for the use of scrap tires as a fuel source to generate energy to run plants and supply electricity to homes.

As a corporate citizen, Goodyear also participates in several programs to help the disadvantaged. For example, more than 100 Goodyear employees partnered with Rockwell Automation to build a house for a needy family as part of the Habitat for Humanity program.

Goodyear contributes to communities in other ways. The Goodyear Highway Hero program honors truck drivers who exemplify heroism and courage by performing heroic acts or outstanding acts of humanitarianism. The University of Akron received a $3 million gift from Goodyear in 1997 to establish the Goodyear Chair of Intellectual Property in the School of Law and the Goodyear Global Scholarship Program in the College of Business Administration. Finally, Goodyear sponsors First Night Akron, one of more than 160 alcohol-free, family-orientated community New Year's Eve celebrations.

GLOBAL PRESENCE

Goodyear is truly a global organization and its brand name is universally recognized. The company markets its products in 185 countries and manufactures them in 80 plants in 27 countries. Approximately 1,000 retail stores are operated in the United States, which accounted for 54 percent of sales in 1996. Europe provided the second biggest market for Goodyear, with Latin America, Asia, and Canada rounding out its foreign operations. With an increased global focus, Goodyear's CEO Samir Gabira has emphasized the importance of acquisition and expansion in every market the company serves.

One fairly new market that appeals to many tire manufacturers is South Africa. Abandoning apartheid (the government policy of racial segregation), South Africa has become democratic. The strict apartheid policies had caused economic tensions and internal conflict in the country, forcing many companies to withdraw their investments in South African businesses. With a democratic government now in place, however, many companies have become eager to re-enter the South African marketplace. South Africa has a wealth of natural resources, an enthusiastic work force, and an increasingly appealing economy.

The Goodyear Tire & Rubber Company abandoned the South African market in 1989 due to apartheid pressures. Purchasing Tycon Pty. Ltd. in the late 1990s, Goodyear had become South Africa's biggest manufacturer of heavyweight conveyor belting and power transmission products. With this purchase, Goodyear also acquired Tredcor, a company with 41 tire retreading locations and 195 distribution facilities.

Another market of recent concern to Goodyear has been North America, where analysts have anticipated an increase in demand for the tire industry. North America has remained Goodyear's primary market, but the anticipated rise was not seen by 1997; research showed that demand in the market fell by 2 percent. Another disappointment for Goodyear has been the pricing struggles in Europe and Latin America, forcing the company to reduce its prices to remain competitive in these regions.

EMPLOYMENT

Goodyear's nearly 95,000 associates are employed in more than 80 plants in the United States and 27 other countries. More than 5,000 employees joined the company through four major acquisitions made in 1996. New hires to Goodyear can find employment at the Akron corporate headquarters or any of the company's worldwide facilities. The company is actively involved in college recruiting and posts current job openings on the Goodyear web site at http://www.goodyear.com/about/employ/jobs.html. In 1998 the company was hiring additional engineers and scientists to support its expanded product and process technology. Goodyear announced that it is adding 160 engineers and scientists at its technical facilities in Akron and Luxembourg and in its North American tire plants, bringing the total of new scientists, engineers, and professionals, including those joining the Training Squadron, to more than 200.

Racial, ethnic, and cultural diversity is actively pursued by the company. Goodyear attributes its establishment of new operations worldwide to its emphasis on diversity. Diversity and sensitivity awareness are part of Goodyear's associate training and education.

Company benefits include a comprehensive array of plans in the FlexChoice program. Some of these benefit plans include medical and prescription drug, dental, vision, long-term disability, and life and accident insurance. Many employees also enjoy a retirement plan, 401K savings plan, paid vacations and holidays, a tire purchase plan, tuition assistance, and a stock purchase plan.

According to *The Value Line Investment Survey,* among Goodyear's attempts at cost-cutting in an effort to improve company finances, was a 30 percent decrease in wages for new employees. Labor agreements reached during the year include continuous seven-day operations in all but one plant. Negotiations also succeeded in reaching an unprecedented six-year labor contract with the United Steelworkers of America.

Goodyear's centennial anniversary was in 1998. Plans for observing the centennial include plant "open houses" and family day activities for employees.

SOURCES OF INFORMATION

Bibliography

Galuska, Peter. "High Pressure at Goodyear." *Business Week,* 5 May 1997.

Goodyear Home Page. 5 May 1998. Available at http://www. goodyear.com.

"Goodyear Sets Tentative Deal with Union." *The New York Times,* 5 May 1997.

"Goodyear Tire & Rubber Co." *Hoover's Handbook of American Business.* Austin, TX: Reference Press, 1998.

Moody's Handbook of Common Stocks, Winter 1997-98, New York: Moody's Investors Service, Inc., 1997.

Narisetti, Raju. "Goodyear Plans Product Improvements to Bolster Sales, and Posts Small Profit." *The Wall Street Journal,* 10 February 1998.

"Remaining Contred Stake Is Bought for $59 Million." *The Wall Street Journal,* 3 March 1998.

Rubber & Plastics News. 4 May 1998. Available at http://www. rubbernews.com.

Standard & Poor's Stock Reports - January 1998, New York: McGraw Hill, 1998.

The Value Line Investment Survey, 13 March 1998. New York: Value Line Publishing, Inc., 1998.

For an annual report:

contact: Investor Relations Dept., 1144 E. Market St., Akron, OH, 44316-0001

For additional industry research:

Investigate companies by their Standard Industrial Classification Codes, also known as SICs. Goodyear's primary SICs are:

2819 Industrial and Inorganic Chemical Manufacturing

3011 Tire and Inner Tube Manufacturing

3021 Rubber and Plastic Footwear Manufacturing

4613 Refined Petroleum Pipelines

Greyhound Lines, Inc.

FOUNDED: 1913 as Hibbing Transportation

OVERVIEW

Greyhound Lines Inc. is the nation's largest intercity bus company, and the only long-haul, nationwide provider of bus service in the United States. The company serves more than 2,600 urban and rural destinations in the 48 contiguous states and Mexico. The company maintains a fleet of 2,400 buses, which cover 60,000 route miles. The focus of Greyhound's business is scheduled passenger transportation, but it also offers limited charter passenger service. In addition, the company operates express package delivery and food service at some locations.

Contact Information:

HEADQUARTERS: 15110 North Dallas Pky.
   Dallas, TX 75248
PHONE: (972)789-7000
FAX: (972)789-7330
TOLL FREE: (800)231-2222
URL: http://www.greyhound.com

COMPANY FINANCES

Greyhound's financial picture has brightened considerably since 1994 when the company lost $116 million due to a poorly devised ticketing policy and declining sales. Greyhound's brightest year in this decade was 1997 when total revenue reached $771 million, up 10 percent from 1996. This figure reflects a 13-percent increase in the number of passengers carried by Greyhound as well as increases in the company's charter service. Ticket sales for the company were up for 11 consecutive quarters. The company reported net income before extraordinary items of $8.4 million for 1997, an improvement of $15 million over the $6.6-million loss reported for 1996.

Greyhound stock ranged from a low of $3.37 to a high of $5.87 over a 52-week period. Greyhound's price-earnings ratio was 46. The company has not paid any dividends on its common stock and does not expect to pay any in the foreseeable future. The company's goal is

FINANCES:

Greyhound Lines Inc.
Operating Revenues, 1994-1997
(million dollars)

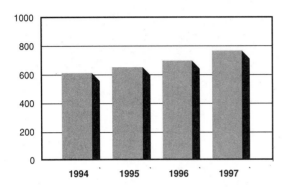

Greyhound Lines Inc.
1997 Stock Prices
(dollars)

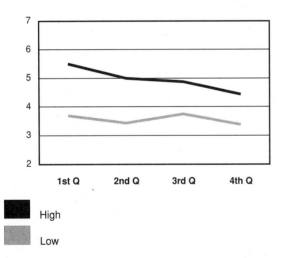

to become a billion-dollar company by the year 2000. Restructuring efforts, begun in 1994, are well underway and the company has more buses, drivers, customer service people, and terminals than it has had since these efforts began.

ANALYSTS' OPINIONS

In May 1995, *Money* magazine recommended 12 stocks that would likely double in value in 12 years. A year later, the magazine reported that all 12—Greyhound among them—were meeting expectations. As *Financial World* reported, by January of 1996 Greyhound's comeback strategy was beginning to win over the most hardened Wall Street skeptics—and CEO Craig Lentzsch deserved the credit. In its January 13, 1997 edition, *Forbes* rated Greyhound stock a good buy, and predicted that it would soon jump in value. At the time of the article, Greyhound stock was trading at nine times 1997 expected earnings. One money manager was quoted as thinking the share price could double within a year.

HISTORY

In 1913 a Swedish immigrant named Carl Wickman created a job for himself by providing transportation for Hibbing, Minnesota, mine workers in his seven-seater Hupmobile. He named his company Hibbing Transportation. (The first real intercity buses were manufactured in 1921 by Safety Coach of Muskegon, Michigan; they were called the "greyhounds" because of their sleek design and grey paint.

Five years later, Wickman and Orville Swan Caesar, who owned several small bus lines, acquired additional lines and united them under the name Motor Transit Corporation. The period following World War I was a boom era for the bus industry, during which the company competed with a number of other lines.

In 1930 the Motor Transit Corporation was renamed the Greyhound Corporation, and the "running dog" became the company's official trademark. Greyhound suffered heavily as a result of the 1929 stock market crash; however, the Depression resulted in increased ridership. By 1946 Greyhound was the leading bus line in the country, carrying one-fourth of all bus passengers. In the mid-1950s the company diversified into industrial leasing, airport auxiliary services, such as baggage handling, and even food service.

After several prosperous decades, which culminated in the buyout of its last remaining rival (Trailways, 1987), Greyhound entered a difficult period. It hit bottom in 1990 when it declared bankruptcy. The company tried to revive profitability by instituting a reservation system. This move proved disastrous for the company because bus passengers did not want to make reservations and when they did make the (unpaid) reservations, they often failed to keep them. In addition, bus customers did not respond well to a new pricing structure, which increased fares for walk-up passengers. These marketing mistakes resulted in a $116-million net loss in 1994, and led to a change in company management. With the ascendancy of Craig Lentzsch, former executive for bus manufacturer Motor Coach Industries, things began to turn around for Greyhound. Lentzch brought back a more convenient ticketing system and more direct routes. Company sales rose 14 percent in two years, and in 1996 the company posted a profit, the first in four years.

Greyhound began to upgrade its fleet of buses and utilize a new phone system for customer ticketing in conjunction with regional bus lines. In 1997 Greyhound acquired Valley Transit, serving south Texas and the Rio Grand Valley, and Carolina Trailways, Inc., serving the mid-Atlantic states. That year the company also acquired a 49-percent stake in the Mexican company Crucero, which operates a bus route between Mexico and Los Angeles. It also reached an agreement to acquire a controlling interest in Golden State, a Hispanic carrier operating in the Southwest. Finally, in 1977 Greyhound purchased the rights to its "running dog" trademark from Viad.

STRATEGY

With the appointment of Greyhound's new management team in late 1994 and early 1995, the company developed a "back-to-basics" operating strategy that remains in place today. This strategy, as stated by the company, focuses on "providing a good customer-oriented product with a capacity-flexible, sound bus operation."

Greyhound contends that as its core demographic customer base expands, company revenues will continue to grow. The company has said that this customer base is growing at a rate that exceeds the U.S. population growth rate as a whole. Greyhound has largely built its business on lower-income clientele. Specifically, the company has identified two groups of customers—the core and the transitional groups. Core passengers come from households with incomes below $15,000 a year. If someone from this group (44 percent of Greyhound's ridership) needs to travel from one city to another, financial circumstances offer few options other than bus transportation.

Transitional riders, on the other hand, are those with household incomes between $15,000 and $50,000—they make up the other 56 percent of Greyhound's ridership. (Persons who make more than $50,000 annually constitute a negligible segment of the passenger bus market.) This group is dubbed transitional precisely because Greyhound cannot count on its continued loyalty. Because of their higher income levels, these customers have other options for travel in addition to buses.

Greyhound has identified key groups among the transitional riders: women with children, grandparents, gamblers traveling to popular gaming spots, college students, members of the military, and workers commuting to jobs. Among the 20 million passengers carried by the company in 1997, primary groups included the elderly and young people; persons in the lower- to middle-income brackets; and minorities, particularly African-Americans and Hispanics. Seniors account for 28 percent

FAST FACTS:
About Greyhound Lines, Inc.

Ownership: Greyhound is a publicly owned company traded on the American Stock Exchange.

Ticker symbol: BUS

Officers: Thomas G. Plaskett, Chmn., 53; Craig R. Lentzch, Pres. & CEO, 48, 1997 base salary $462,241; Jack W. Haugsland, Exec. VP & COO, 57, 1997 base salary $304,037

Employees: 11,700

Principal Subsidiary Companies: Greyhound operates four subsidiary bus lines: Texas, New Mexico, and Oklahoma Coaches, Inc. (TNM&O); Vermont Transit Co. Inc.; Carolina Trailways, Inc.; and Valley Transit Company.

Chief Competitors: The transportation industry is highly competitive. The company's primary sources of competition for passengers are automobile travel, low cost air travel from both regional and national airlines, and, in certain markets, regional bus companies and trains. Some of Greyhound's primary competitors include: AmericaWest; Amtrak; Continental Airlines; Delta; Northwest Airlines; TWA; and U.S. Airways. The company faces intense competition in its package express service from local courier services, the U.S. Postal Service, and overnight, express, and ground carriers. Some of these competitors include: FedEx; UPS; and Yellow Corporation.

of Greyhound's passengers, and another 25 percent are under 25 years old. According to Greyhound, approximately one-third of the U.S. population matches the demographic profiles of its customers. In 1977 the company used a variety of promotional fares to expand its customer base.

Since 1996 Greyhound has provided bus transportation to the nation's most popular casino destinations from nearby metropolitan areas. Frequent departures, competitive fares, direct service to hotels, and a flexible return trip policy make this service especially attractive.

Greyhound is not a company that markets itself on "snob appeal"; rather, its strategy is based on egalitarian principles rooted in moving the maximum number of people the maximum number of miles. Its mission state-

CHRONOLOGY:

Key Dates for Greyhound Lines, Inc.

1913: Carl Wickman started Hibbing Transportation, bussing miners from the city to the mine

1925: Wickman leaves Hibbing and purchases White Bus Line

1926: White Bus merges with several other lines to form Motor Transit Corporation, nicknamed Greyhound

1930: Motor Transit becomes Greyhound Corporation

1946: Wickman retires; Greyhound is the leading bus line

1962: Greyhound purchases Booth Leasing and becomes the largest industrial leasing company in the world

1970: Greyhound acquires Armour Foods, keeping only its meat packing business

1987: Trailways, Greyhound's last remaining rival, is bought out

1997: Greyhound acquires Valley Transit and 49 percent of Crucero, a Mexican busline

ment is: "Provide the opportunity for any person to travel between any two cities in North America with safety, dignity, and convenience . . . "

Pooling agreements with other carriers is one way Greyhound hopes to provide better customer service. These agreements allow the company to coordinate service with other carriers, consolidate terminals, and eliminate redundant schedule offerings. The bottom line is a better choice of departures for its customers and reduced expenses for the company. In 1997, the company received approval to coordinate its service with Adirondack Trailways on all major routes in New York State. Another pooling agreement was made in 1997 with Capital Colonial Trailways.

Intermodal alliances are another opportunity for the company to grow by capitalizing on its ability to serve additional passengers without proportionately increasing expenses. Intermodal alliances are agreements between companies with different modes of transportation. Greyhound entered into such an agreement with Amtrak in 1997—moving many of its terminals to Amtrak train stations to pick up that traffic.

INFLUENCES

Greyhound Lines' business is seasonal in nature and generally follows the pattern of the travel industry as a whole. Peak travel periods are during the summer months and the Thanksgiving and Christmas holiday periods. As a result, the company's cash flows are also seasonal in nature and a disproportionate amount of this cash flow is generated during the peak travel times.

In August 1997 a group of a dozen handicapped persons demonstrated at the Port Authority terminal in New York City. The group was protesting its lack of access to Greyhound's buses. The handicapped demonstrators rolled their wheelchairs in front of a bus, disrupting ticket sales for four hours and backing up bus traffic.

CURRENT TRENDS

In order to implement its "back-to-basics" strategy, Greyhound is focusing on improving customer service. Fares and prices have been changed, and new destinations have been added to its schedules. The company tries to meet the demands of peak holiday travel times by scheduling its buses and drivers accordingly. "Everyday low prices" continues to be the focus of its marketing and advertising campaigns. Advertisements for Greyhound appear on the radio, television, and print media, especially Yellow Pages and magazines. Customers seeking fare and schedule information can call a toll-free phone number around-the-clock.

PRODUCTS

Riders can purchase a 7-, 15-, 30-, or 60-day Ameripass ticket, which allows unlimited travel in the United States during that period. In May 1998 a seven-day pass sold for $199, and a 60-day pass for $599. An international Ameripass for foreign visitors is also available, at comparable fares. Greyhound offers discounts for advance purchase, military personnel, senior citizens, children, and companions of passengers with disabilities. The advance purchase discount is for a 30-day advance purchase for travel anywhere in the United States. Prices are $59 one-way or $118 round trip. Generally, however, Greyhound passengers purchase their tickets on a city-to-city basis.

In addition to its bus service, Greyhound also operates an express package service, Greyhound Package Express. Greyhound offers a new $59 service that offers same-day delivery of packages up to 50 pounds within 500 miles. The company is now focusing on developing door-to-door service in many of its markets.

CORPORATE CITIZENSHIP

Greyhound, in cooperation with the International Association of Chiefs of Police and the National Runaway Switchboard, operates the Home Free program. Teenage runaways who want to return to their family can go to a Greyhound station and receive a free ride on the next bus to their destination.

GLOBAL PRESENCE

Greyhound's major passenger markets are large metropolitan areas, but its business is geographically fragmented. The company's research has shown that its potential riders are concentrated in the northeastern, southern, and industrial midwestern United States, as well as Texas and California. Greyhound believes that the Spanish-speaking markets in the United States and Mexico present an opportunity for growth. In January 1997 Greyhound introduced its first line into the Mexican interior, as opposed to border towns such as Tijuana. Greyhound began service to Ciudad Obregon, halfway down Mexico's west coast. The buses, under the name *Crucero,* feature Spanish videos for riders, and save them the trouble of having to change buses at the border. The fare is $30 for a round-trip ticket from Los Angeles.

EMPLOYMENT

Greyhound has an enormously positive employee environment, symbolized by the "Question and Answer" section in the company's occasional *Conference Call* newsletter for its workers. In the newsletter, employees have an opportunity to address matters of concern, to be answered by top company officers. Particularly remarkable about these newsletters is the fact that they are not simply a place for the company's leadership to pat itself on the back. One issue featured a section entitled "Misses In 1995," including "We failed to meet our on-time performance goal." This attitude of forthright self-appraisal, also evident in the company's annual report, is highly unusual among American corporations. In addition to the irregular *Conference Call,* the company also publishes *The Mirror,* a monthly publication that highlights various issues of importance to employees.

Greyhound employs 11,700 people, including 4,300 drivers, approximately 4,000 terminal employees, 1,200 supervisory personnel, 800 mechanics, 900 telephone information agents, and 500 clerical workers. The 800 maintenance workers belong to a number of unions, including the Amalgamated Transit Union (ATU), International Association of Machinists and Aerospace Workers (IAM), and International Board of Teamsters.

"HOW LONG WILL THIS TRIP TAKE IN DOG YEARS?"

One of Greyhound's more memorable advertising campaigns was launched in 1957 when the ad boys came up with the idea of dressing up a greyhound dog in a jeweled tiara and collar, and then touring the pup around the country. This was at a time when Greyhound sponsored Steve Allen's television program, and the dog was originally called "Steverino" (although this was subsequently changed to the more refined "Lady Greyhound"). Lady Greyhound made innumerable public appearances—both for Greyhound and for charitable causes—before passing on to that great fire hydrant in the sky.

SOURCES OF INFORMATION

Bibliography

Geer, John F., Jr. "Why Greyhound Is No Longer a Dog." *Financial World,* 30 January 1996.

Greyhound Home Page. 21 April 1998. Available at http://www.greyhound.com.

Greyhound Lines, Inc. 1997 Annual Report. Dallas, TX: Greyhound Lines, Inc., 1998.

"Greyhound Lines, Inc.: Some Long-Distance Fares Are Cut to Boost Ridership." *The Wall Street Journal,* 27 August 1996.

"Greyhound Lines, Inc." *Hoover's Handbook of American Business 1998.* Austin, TX: The Reference Press, 1997.

Pierre-Pierre, Garry. "Disrupting Sales at Greyhound, Disabled Protest Bus Access." *The New York Times,* 9 August 1997.

Waxler, Caroline. "Dog Has Its Day." *Forbes,* 13 January 1997.

Zellner, Wendy. "Leave the Driving to Lentzsch." *Business Week,* 18 March 1996.

For an annual report:

write: Inverstor Relations, Greyhound Lines, Inc., PO Box 660606, Dallas, TX 75266-0606

For additional industry research:

Investigate companies by their Standard Industrial Classification Codes, also known as SICs. Greyhound's primary SIC is:

4131 Intercity & Rural Bus Transportation

GT Bicycles Inc.

FOUNDED: 1979

Contact Information:

HEADQUARTERS: 2001 E. Dyer Rd.
   Santa Ana, CA 92705
PHONE: (714)481-7100
FAX: (714)481-7111
URL: http://www.gtbicycles.com

GT Bicycles, Inc. is a leading designer, manufacturer, and marketer of mid- to premium-priced mountain and juvenile BMX bicycles sold under the company's GT Powerlite, Robinson, and Dyno brand names. The company's Riteway Products distribution network is a leading distributor of the company's bicycles, parts, and accessories, as well as parts and accessories of other manufacturers, to 4,000 independent bicycle dealers. GT's juvenile BMX bicycles maintain a dominant market share of the BMX bicycles sold by independent bicycle retailers in the United States. The company offers 37 mountain bicycles (51 percent of revenue), 48 juvenile BMX bicycles (23 percent of revenue), and 14 road/speciality bicycles. GT also distributes one of the broadest lines of private label and branded parts and accessories (26 percent of revenue) in the industry.

GT Bicycles' revenues more than doubled between 1992 and 1997. Net sales in 1997 for GT Bicycles were a record $216.2 million, up from $208.4 million in 1996, $168.9 in 1995, $145.7 in 1994, $123.7 in 1993. Net income for 1997 was $3.2 million, as compared to net income in 1996 of $11.6 million. The company received $1.6 million in life insurance proceeds following the death of its former president and chief executive officer Richard Long in July 1996. Sales of adult bikes were weak, as were sales of domestic parts and accessories. Domestic juvenile bike sales were up from 1996. International sales of juvenile bikes also increased, with sales in Japan topping all the company's foreign divisions in adult and juvenile bikes, parts, and accessories. Overall, however, foreign sales declined as the strong U.S. dollar, especially relative to European currencies, hurt sales in the United Kingdom, France, and Germany. GT Bicycles expected sales in the adult market to continue to be soft in 1998 and beyond, according to a company press release. However, company president Michael Haynes stated, "our superior technology, powerful brand name and broad distribution channels will allow us to gain market share. We plan to continue improving manufacturing efficiencies and to increase the amount of product assembled in our new facility, which should further enhance gross profits."

In October 1995 GT Bicycles issued its common stock in an initial public offering at a price of $14.00 per share. GT Bicycles stock ranged from a low of $5.42 to a high of $10.37 during a 52-week period. The stock's price-earnings ratio is 19.53 and its earnings per share is $.32. The company has never paid a cash dividend and intends to retain its earnings for use in the business.

ANALYSTS' OPINIONS

"Weak earnings earlier this year, a stock price below $10 per share and a market capitalization (share price times shares outstanding) of less than $100 million leave [GT Bicycles Inc.] largely ignored and unloved," according to Robert Frick in a December 1997 article in *Kiplinger's Personal Finance Magazine.* "But those drawbacks camouflage the company's assets, including coveted brand name among kids and a reputation for shrewd marketing and innovation. In short, GT is a perfect buy for investors looking for a small company at a bargain price." Although bike and bike accessory markets are basically flat in the United States, Frick maintained that GT Bicycles has strong ties to its retailers and a good distribution system which extends to Europe and Asia. A strong brand identity among kids and a broad range of products make higher sales a good bet, predicts Frick.

Other analysts are a little more cautious about GT Bicycles. Mark Greenberg, who runs the Invesco Strategic Leisure Fund, said in a November 1997 *New York Times* article, "I don't own any of the bike stocks; that should tell you something. There are such high marketing and development costs that you never seem to make as much money as you'd like." David L. Rose, an analyst at Jefferson Company, in the same article stated, "Cannondale and GT, I think are positioned about as good as you can be in the long term, but it's going to be tough."

Sales of high-end bicycles were sluggish in 1997 and some analysts predicted that the trend would continue intact. According to James Sterngold in *The New York Times,* these sales results are due to large sales of chil-

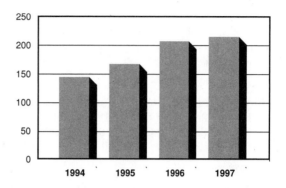

FINANCES:

GT Bicycles
Net Sales, 1994-1997
(million dollars)

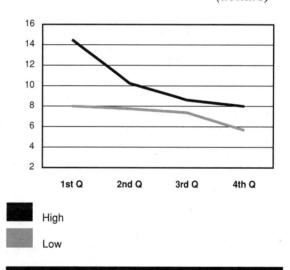

GT Bicycles
1997 Stock Prices
(dollars)

■ High
■ Low

dren's bikes and stores' efforts to reduce inventory to make way for premium bicycles. However, many retailers are behind in responding to the demand for these premium bikes.

HISTORY

Founded in 1979 by Gary Turner and Richard Long, GT Bicycles Inc.'s focus as a company was on product innovation, a focus that still remains. Turner, an engi-

FAST FACTS:

About GT Bicycles Inc.

Ownership: GT Bicycles Inc. is a publicly owned company traded on NASDAQ.

Ticker symbol: GTBX

Officers: Geoffrey S. Rehnert, Chmn., 40; Michael C. Haynes, Pres. & CEO, 45, $312,000; Charles Cimitile, VP Finance & CFO, 43, $175,000; William K. Duehring, COO, 41, $228,000

Employees: 775 (1997)

Chief Competitors: GT Bicycles' primary competitors are: Cannondale; Huffy; Trek; Rockshox; Giant; Mongoose; Raleigh; Schwinn; and Specialized.

neer, built bike frames in his garage for his son to race; Long was a BMX bicycle racetrack operator. Together they founded the company to make dirt track racing bikes for boys. Quickly becoming a hit among the dirt bike fans, sales hit $4 million in two years. Throughout its history, GT focused on design superiority and was credited with countless "firsts" within the bicycle industry. In its early years, GT focused on the application of innovative design and frame composites in the then-rapidly expanding juvenile BMX bicycle market.

In the 1980s GT entered the mountain bike market, a market that was faster growing and pricier than the BMX market. From 1989 through 1994 company revenues increased from $41 to $146 million. In 1998, GT controlled a 40-percent plus share of the independent bicycle retailers' juvenile BMX business. GT completed its initial public offering of stock on October 18, 1995, issuing 3.15 million new shares and receiving net proceeds of approximately $40.2 million, of which approximately $37.1 million was used to repay debt. GT established a rather impressive long term financial record.

In July 1996 Richard Long, GT Bicycles' co-founder, president, and CEO, was killed in a motorcycle traffic accident at the age of 46. The loss was devastating to the company. Long had fought diligently to expand the company's market share. In early 1997 GT consolidated the company's corporate headquarters, manufacturing, assembly, and West Coast distribution facilities into one combined facility in Santa Ana.

STRATEGY

The key to the success of GT Bicycles is its distribution subsidiary, Riteway Products, a leader in the $3-billion parts and accessories market. In order to maximize flexibility and engineering expertise while minimizing capital commitments, the company's manufacturing strategy used a combination of internal manufacturing for its higher end products, and outsourcing for its higher volume, lower cost products.

GT's marketing strategy is targeted at the bicycle retailer, not the end user. GT's research indicated that 50 to 70 percent of a purchase decision is affected by the preferences of the bicycle salesperson, while only 30 percent is affected by the customer's brand preference. High ticket purchases are often affected by a salesperson's input. Other marketing efforts include: annual catalogs, a monthly flyer detailing a variety of products, *Hammerdown* (a newsletter published nine times a year) and *Geardown* (a newsletter published six times a year for all GT dealers). GT also participates with its dealers in direct mail marketing programs three times a year. In March 1998 GT Bicycles began the production of a 30-minute television show, "Crank," for the Fox Sports Network. A nationally syndicated program, "Crank" features BMX and Freestyle cycling and other extreme sports targeted to the after school audience. The company continues to build brand recognition in the market by aggressively targeting the juvenile BMX segment with advertising, sponsorship, and more than 40 juvenile BMX models.

Building brand awareness at an early age and capitalizing on it as each generation matures is GT Bicycles's strategy for continued company growth. Current demographics bode well for the company as teen population growth is expected to outpace the overall population through the year 2010.

INFLUENCES

In March 1998 GT Bicycles initiated a recall of approximately 10,000 bicycles and frame sets manufactured since 1995. The recall affected less than 1 percent of the approximately 2 million bikes GT sold during that period and was the result of 17 reported cracks in the frames of its BMX bicycle models. According to the company, the financial impact of the recall should be minimal, as its warranty and other reserves should cover the recall costs.

The weather also played a role in domestic sales of the company's bicycles in 1998, when the company faced some of the harshest weather conditions in recent history. Its largest winter markets—California, Florida, and Texas—were unseasonably cold and wet, resulting in flat sales of adult and juvenile bikes for the first quarter of 1998.

CURRENT TRENDS

Product development remains a top priority for GT and the company is beginning to realize its goal of developing direct distribution in key international markets. While GT established an important presence in international markets, representing some 30 percent of 1996 revenue, the company perceives an important opportunity to improve the growth and profitability of these markets. Internally, GT is focusing on the implementation of process improvements in manufacturing and distribution functions, which will allow for greater manufacturing efficiencies. In order to quickly fill orders from bicycle dealers, the company's wholly owned distributors maintain significant inventories. The company believes the close relationships with its principle manufacturing sources allow it to introduce innovative product designs and alter production in response to market demand for its product.

The bicycle market has undergone many changes in the recent past. The mountain bike boom of the 1980s has dwindled. In the early 1990s "hybrid" or cross bikes, which combined the ruggedness of a mountain bike with the cruising abilities of a road bike, broke into the market. "Many experts believe the future is in transforming bicycles into high performance status symbols," according to James Sterngold in *The New York Times*. The trend is toward high-technology bikes that appeal to yuppies. They typically have softer suspensions and wider, softer saddles. These bikes are not only comfortable for baby boomers who often complain of wrist, shoulder, and other soreness, but they also come with a hefty price tag, ranging from $600 to $4,000.

PRODUCTS

GT Bicycles designs mountain, street, and juvenile motorcross (BMX) bikes. More than 140 models are available. The company also makes bike helmets and other bike accessories.

GT Bicycles' Superbike 2, a handbuilt, featherlight racing bike, was honored as part of *Popular Science* magazine's annual "Best of What's New" awards. Also, GT formed a partnership with AeroVironment, an internationally renowned developer of energy efficient vehicles, to create Charger Bicycles. Charger Bicycles produces and markets an electric-assist bicycle called the Charger, which features an on-board power control center and a removable battery pack that can be recharged anywhere. Extensive market research has shown substantial worldwide demand for electric bicycles with a growing number of bicycle commuters internationally benefitting from assisted, clean transportation. GT's initial target market will be commuters and recreational riders, and the electric bikes will be sold by GT's Riteway Products distribution network.

Harley-Davidson has licensed GT Bicycles to make Harley-Davidson cruiser bikes. The bikes have a fake gas

CHRONOLOGY:
Key Dates for GT Bicycles Inc.

1979: Gary Turner and Richard Long found GT Bicycles Inc.

1980: GT enters the mountain bike market

1995: GT completes its initial stock offering

1996: Co-founder Richard Long dies

1998: GT holds a 40 percent market share of the independent bicycle retailers juvenile BMX business

tank and the signature Harley-Davidson paint. At the other end of the spectrum, the company's new Jetstream model, with a light aluminum frame and a comfortably soft, wide saddle, is designed to appeal to middle aged baby boomers.

GT has been investing in new materials and manufacturing processes. The most significant new development has been the use of thermoplastics in frame manufacture, which are lighter, stronger, and absorb shock better than steel or aluminum frames. The thermoplastic frame manufacturing process takes less than an hour to complete and costs significantly less than the process for aluminum frames.

CORPORATE CITIZENSHIP

In addition to its sponsorship of independent teams such as the U.S. Cycling Team, U.S. Triathalon Team, Saturn, and Team Shaklee, the company supports and promotes its own Team GT racing and demonstration teams. In 1998 alone, the company supported a GT mountain bicycle racing team, four BMX racing teams, and a number of freestyle demonstration riders who perform at varying venues such as NBA halftime shows, state fairs, school assemblies, trade shows, and corporate events. GT has sponsored more than 1,000 events with its event support program.

GLOBAL PRESENCE

Internationally, GT Bicycles markets its products in 65 countries through 56 independent distributors. The company's wholly owned distributors are Riteway Japan, Riteway France, and Caratti. Distribution facilities are located in the United Kingdom, France, and Japan. The company goal is to expand GT Bicycles into a company with worldwide brand name recognition.

The company is highly dependent on products manufactured by foreign suppliers located primarily in Taiwan and Japan and to a lesser degree the People's Republic of China. The company believes that there are opportunities for expanded sales in foreign markets and intends to increase its sales and marketing efforts in these areas. The company's business is subject to the risks generally associated with doing business abroad, such as delays in shipment, foreign governmental regulation, adverse fluctuations in foreign exchange controls, trade disputes, changes in economic conditions, and political turmoil in the countries in which the company's manufacturing sources are located. The delay or disruption in supply of bicycles or bicycle parts and accessories could have a material adverse effect on the company's business, results of operations, and financial condition. Also, the market for bicycles, parts, and accessories, both in the United States and internationally, is highly competitive. In all its product categories, the company competes with other manufacturers and distributors, some of which have well-organized brand names and substantial financial, technological, distribution, advertising, and marketing resources.

EMPLOYMENT

The company offers profit sharing for all employees who have worked for the company at least 12 months. Also, in 1995 the company's "Stock Purchase Plan" was adopted by the Board of Directors, covering an aggregate of 300,000 shares of common stock. Employees are eligible to participate if they have been employed by the company for at least one year.

SOURCES OF INFORMATION

Bibliography

Beckert, Beverly. "Mission Possible!: First to Market."*Knight-Ridder/Tribune News,* 17 July 1995.

D&B Million Dollar Directory, 1997 Series. Bethlehem, PA: Dunn & Bradstreet, Inc., 1997.

Frick, Robert. "Ready for Takeoff." *Kiplinger's Personal Finance Magazine,* December 1997.

"GT Bicycles, Inc." *Hoover's Online,* 11 May 1998. Available at http://hoovers.com.

"GT Bicycles Inc." *Moody's Investors Service,* 11 May 1998. Available at http://sbweb2.med.iacnet.com.

"GT Bicycles Inc." *News Alert,* 11 May 1998. Availabe at http://www.newsalert.com.

GT Bicycles Inc. Home Page, 11 May 1998. Available at http://www.gtbicycles.com.

La Franco, Robert. "The Battle of the Bikes." *Forbes,* 26 August 1996.

Rowe, Jeff. "Santa Ana, Calif.-Based GT Bicycles to Make Harley Bike." *Knight-Ridder/Tribune News,* 8 August 1996.

Sterngold, James. "Bike Makers Try Comfort and Gizmos to Pump Up Profit." *New York Times,* 30 November 1997.

Teague, Paul E. "Gold Rush! Software, Sensors, Motors, and More Help Athletes Go for the Gold." *Design News,* 24 June 1996.

For an annual report:

telephone: (714)481-7100 **or** write: Investor Relations, GT Bicycles, Inc., 2001 E. Dyer Rd., Santa Ana, CA 92705

For additional industry research:

Investigate companies by their Standard Industrial Classification Codes, also known as SICs. GT Bicycles' primary SIC is:

3751 Motorcycles, Bicycles and Parts

Gucci Group N.V.

OVERVIEW

Capitalizing on its prestigious, long-established name and its brand recognition worldwide, Italian fashion house Gucci has avoided the attention to new trends and fashions that dominates the fashion industry and instead has concentrated on classic, high-profit luxury merchandise such as handbags and perfumes. With 1996 sales rising an incredible 76.1 percent over 1995 and net income growing even faster, the company's famous interlocking-G logo has become more than a symbol of high fashion, it has become a symbol of success. This sales increase is all the more remarkable given that close to 50 percent of Gucci's sales come from Asia, a market that experienced a tremendous economic crisis in 1997 and 1998.

Certainly, a large part of the company's success is due to its refusal to dilute its product offerings with mass market merchandise. The Gucci name remains a symbol of prestige and its accessories are virtually *de rigueur* among the affluent, especially among the many newly wealthy Asians. Although the company's ready-to-wear women's and men's clothing is popular, accessories like handbags, scarves, perfumes, and eyewear drive the company's sales. The company's signature handbags include an A-frame and bamboo bag, as well as hobo and dome bags. Although more expensive than most designer lines, Gucci products are successful in reaching many consumers who want the status of owning a Gucci handbag or watch. That prestige—combined with a major restructuring effort in the early 1990s to streamline production, improve quality, and refurbish stores—sent company revenues skyrocketing in the mid-1990s. Although sales slowed considerably in 1997, largely as a

FOUNDED: 1920

Contact Information:

HEADQUARTERS: Rembrandt Tower, 1
  Amstelplein
  Amsterdam 1096 HA Netherlands
PHONE: +31-20-4621-700
FAX: +31-20-465-3569

FAST FACTS:

About Gucci Group N.V.

Ownership: Gucci Group N.V. is owned by Investcorp S.A., which is a privately owned company.

Ticker symbol: GUC

Officers: Domenico De Sole, CEO; Brian Blake, Exec. VP, Sales; Robert Singer, CFO

Employees: 1,504

Chief Competitors: Some of Gucci's main competitors include: Gianni Versace; Louis Vuitton; and Polo.

result of economic conditions in Asia, the company still posted a healthy 10-percent gain. As of 1998 Gucci operated 154 stores worldwide, about half of them company-owned and half franchised. Gucci products are also sold in department stores, duty-free shops, and by mail order.

COMPANY FINANCES

During fiscal year 1996 Gucci achieved record performances across all distribution channels and product categories, as well as in all geographic regions. Sales for directly operated stores rose 52.6 percent, while wholesaling increased 151.2 percent. Net revenues for fiscal 1996 were up 76.1 percent to $880.7 million, compared to $500.1 million in fiscal 1995. The company showed even stronger growth in 1995, with sales rising from $263 million in 1994 to $500 million in 1995.

Results in 1997 were far less dramatic, but still more than satisfactory. Net revenues for fiscal 1997, including royalties, increased 10.8 percent to $975.4 million, while net income increased 4.2 percent to $175.5 million. Basic earnings per share for 1997 were $2.92, compared to $2.85 in the previous year, while diluted earnings per share were $2.86 in 1997, compared to $2.76 in the previous year. Operating profit as a percentage of revenues was down slightly from 27.2 percent in 1996 to 24.3 percent in 1997. All in all, Gucci was pleased with its performance, with CEO Domenico De Sole attributing the company's success to the company's "disciplined operating philosophy, which is focused on delivering to our customers excellent design, quality products and supe-

rior value, while maintaining strict control over distribution channels and costs."

HISTORY

Guccio Gucci was born to a Florentine craftsman in 1881. He moved to Paris as a young boy and then to London, where he worked his way up to become a Maitre d'Hotel at the Savoy. It was during his time in London that Gucci observed the style and sophistication that enhanced culture. With capital of only 30,000 lira, he returned to Italy in 1920, where he opened the first of many Gucci shops in Florence.

The company's initial success is credited to remarkable leather craftsmanship and accessories for horseback riders. The firm grew slowly and steadily, and Gucci eventually brought in his sons—Aldo, Ugo, Vasco, and Rodolfo—to work for his company. They opened new stores in Milan, Florence, and Rome. Against the elder Gucci's wishes, Aldo and Rodolfo opened the first shops in New York in 1953. Guccio Gucci died that same year. The brothers decided to keep the successful company going, and it flourished. During the ensuing years Gucci's classic products were introduced: the handbag with the bamboo handle; the moccasin with the distinctive snaffle-bit; along with numerous belt clasps, ties, and other accessories. Also during this time, new stores were opened in London, Palm Beach, Paris, Beverly Hills, and Tokyo. By the late 1960s Gucci was among the first Italian brand names to have worldwide recognition.

In 1989 Rodolfo Gucci's son, Maurizio, was named president of the entire group. He brought in Dawn Mello, formerly with Bergdorf Goodman, and it was under her direction that the company made the strategic decision to scale down its product line from 20,000 to 5,000 items. The company concentrated on its most popular items, which included the bag with the bamboo handle, suitcases, shoes, and the "Flora" foulard (lightweight fabric), which had been created by Rodolfo Gucci and the artist Accorenro for Princess Grace of Monaco. With the reduction of its product line, the company also decided to reduce the number of distributors.

In 1993 Maurizio Gucci stepped down and sold his share of the company to Investcorp, an Arabic multinational company that now controls 100 percent of Gucci Group N.V. Even with this change in ownership, Gucci products are still made with the same attention and care that was given to the classic products first introduced by Gucci. Stressing quality, not quantity, has always been the key to Gucci's success and is exemplified in Gucci's motto, "Stay small and remain great." The company's focus on limited lines of high-quality, sophisticated products and a more efficient distribution system paid off handsomely in the 1990s, resulting in record growth and making Gucci one of the most successful product lines in the history of the fashion industry.

STRATEGY

Gucci's strategy is centered around a commitment to the production of limited lines of high-quality, luxury goods distributed primarily through a network of company-owned stores. By holding down the number of different product lines and distribution channels, the company believes it will be better able to present its image consistently and better serve its customers. With this in mind, the company acquired control over subsidiaries in Taiwan and Korea in 1998, calling the acquisitions a key step in the company's "strategy to exercise a high degree of control over our distribution network." According to CEO Domenico De Sole, this would enable the company "to closely oversee every aspect of manufacturing, advertising and distribution in order to present a uniform quality image worldwide." Despite the slump in the Asian economies during the late 1990s, Gucci believed the Asian market still held significant growth potential and regarded the acquisitions as a means of further developing its presence in this market.

To present a more consistent brand image, Gucci has refurbished and expanded many Gucci boutiques, paying particular attention to its growing markets in Japan and western Europe. The company has also updated its merchandising and logistics systems to support the demand for its products.

INFLUENCES

In the 1990s the Gucci Group pulled off one of the most remarkable turnarounds ever seen in the fashion industry. The internal problems that began in the late 1970s and spanned the 1980s led to disputes among the Gucci cousins and eventually to the sale of the company to Investcorp. This resulted in a dramatic restructuring and refocusing effort that saw sales increase by over 60 percent in company-owned stores. Revenues from wholesaling, which includes franchising, duty free stores, and department and specialty stores, rose more than 180 percent.

CURRENT TRENDS

Gucci's record 1996 growth and continued expansion in 1997 and 1998 stabilized the company's leadership role in the market for luxury accessories and clothing. Trends in the fashion industry indicated that the company's decision to focus on accessories rather than clothing had been a wise one. By the mid-1990s, sales of women's apparel—once the driving force of the industry—were not growing nearly fast enough for many companies' bottom lines. Women were spending less time and money on clothes shopping—a development

CHRONOLOGY:
Key Dates for Gucci Group N.V.

1920: Guccio Gucci opens first Gucci shop in Florence, Italy

1953: Guccio's sons, Aldo and Rodolfo, open first shops in New York

1989: Rodolfo's son, Maurizio, is named president

1993: Maurizio Gucci steps down and sells his share of company to Investcorp

1998: Acquires 100 percent of franchisee in Korea, Sung Joo International Limited; Acquires majority share in Taiwanese franchisee, Shiatos Taiwan Co

that benefited those companies offering mid-priced, sporty apparel but seriously damaged "couture" companies. While companies like Givenchy, Oscar de la Renta, Gianni Versace, and other venerated fashion houses struggled to stay afloat, Gucci continued to forge ahead by providing stylish, high-fashion accessories women could use to add a touch of sophistication to otherwise casual wardrobes.

PRODUCTS

Gucci distributes several signature items that are popular around the world. Its finely crafted handbag with the bamboo handle was one of the most significant lines in its wide range of luxury merchandise. The company's ready-to-wear clothing, although accounting for a relatively small portion of its income, has been well received by critics and consumers alike and was showing double-digit growth at a time when many other fashion houses were faced with slumping demand.

In addition to its leather goods, scarves, shoes, ties, watches, gifts, jewelry, eyewear, perfume, and luggage, Gucci has also introduced a collection of table-top accents. Developed under the direction of creative director Tom Ford, this collection includes a set of six glasses made by Murano glassmakers of Venice featuring a modern, striped design and selling for more than $400. The glass set was an instant hit, which encouraged Gucci to continue the collection.

GLOBAL PRESENCE

By 1998 the Gucci Group had 76 company-owned stores and 77 franchises throughout the world, including two stores in China. The initial results of the Chinese stores were well beyond what the company had expected, and CEO De Sole stressed the importance of the company's participation in such markets from a long-term-growth point of view. Gucci's expansion into foreign markets has been made easier since the company's name and reputation precede it wherever it goes.

In 1997, although economic conditions in Asia (which accounts for nearly half the company's revenues) seriously curtailed the company's overall growth, Gucci's retail business in Japan grew at a double-digit rate, with the three men's boutiques opened during 1997 performing well above expectations. The Asian slowdown did not affect Gucci's expansion plans either. The company planned to open six new Gucci stores and another men's boutique in Japan, as well as a flagship location in Tokyo and two stores in the new Hong Kong airport. In 1998 Gucci acquired 100 percent of the Gucci business of Sung Joo International Limited, its franchisee in Korea, as well as a majority share in its Taiwanese franchisee, Shiatos Taiwan Co. Limited.

In the European and American markets, sales through 1998 were growing at a much faster pace than in Asia. Business remained strong in such key markets as Italy, France, and Germany, and the company planned to open new stores in Zurich, Vienna, and Monte Carlo, as well as a 10,000-square-foot flagship store in Milan.

SOURCES OF INFORMATION

Bibliography

"Gucci." *Made in Italy On Line,* 1995.

"Gucci Group N.V." *Hoover's Online,* 4 April 1997. Available at http://www.hoovers.com.

"Gucci Group N.V." *Market Guide Company Snapshot,* 2 February 1997. Available at http://www.marketguide.com.

"Gucci Group N.V. Announces Acquisition of Controlling Interest in Taiwan Franchisee." *Business Wire,* 14 April 1998.

"Gucci Group N.V. Announces Acquisition of the Business Assets of its Korean Franchisee." *Business Wire,* 14 May 1998.

"Gucci Group N.V. Announces Purchase of Five Franchise Stores in Italy; Opens Two Stores in China." *Market Guide News,* 4 February 1997.

"Gucci Group N.V. Announces Record Results for Fiscal 1996." *Business Wire,* 26 March 1997.

"Gucci Group N.V. Announces Results for Fiscal 1997." *Business Wire,* 19 March 1998.

Jones, David. "Focus-Gucci Group N.V. Profits Soar as Growth Continues." *Reuters,* 27 March 1997.

Ward, Timothy Jack. "Currents: Gucci's Latest Can't be Worn." *New York Times,* 1 February 1996.

For additional industry research:

Investigate companies by their Standard Industrial Classification Codes, also known as SICs. Gucci's primary SICs are:

5023 Homefurnishings

5136 Men's/Boys' Clothing;

5137 Women's/Children's Clothing

5139 Footwear

5632 Apparel and Accessory Stores

Guess?, Inc.

FOUNDED: 1981

OVERVIEW

Quality, innovative design, attention to detail, and ingenious marketing campaigns helped brothers Maurice and Paul Marciano build a fashion empire on a foundation of raw denim. Combining an appreciation of the American lifestyle with European flair, the company they founded in 1981, Guess?, Inc., rocketed to the top of the fashion charts in the 1980s with its upscale jeans, casual apparel, sportswear, and accessories. With 1997 sales of about $515 million, Guess was still one of the top U.S. jeans makers. Guess products are sold in more than 100 company-owned stores, as well as through department stores and more than 270 other stores around the world, which are owned by licensees and distributors. The company also brought in substantial revenues by licensing its name for a variety of product lines, including Guess Watches, Baby Guess, Guess Kids, and Guess Eyewear. By the end of the 1990s, however, Guess's reign seemed to be coming to an end. Changing tastes in fashion led to slumping denim sales, and the company's bottom line suffered with 1997 sales dropping more than six percent from 1996.

COMPANY FINANCES

After seeing its 1995 sales plummet to $487 million from $548 million in 1994, Guess appeared to bounce back in 1996 with sales of $551 million. The recovery was short-lived, however. Net 1997 revenues fell 6.5 percent to $515.4 million, and they continued to fall in fiscal 1998, with net revenues for the first quarter at $110.8 million, compared to $135.7 million for the comparable

Contact Information:
HEADQUARTERS: 1444 S. Alameda St.
    Los Angeles, CA 90021
PHONE: (213)765-3100
FAX: (213)744-7840
URL: http://www.guess.com

FINANCES:

Guess?, Inc.
Net Revenues, 1994-1997
(billion dollars)

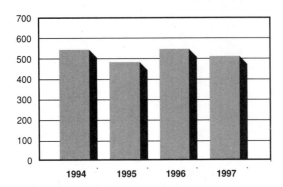

Guess?, Inc.
1997 Stock Prices
(dollars)

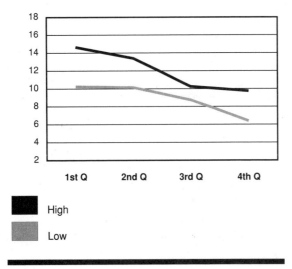

period in fiscal 1997. The story was even worse from an earnings point of view; net earnings for the first quarter of 1998 were $8.0 million, compared to $14.1 million the year before. Between 1993 and 1997 the company's net earnings dropped from $103.5 to $37.5 million. Basic per-share earnings in the first quarter of 1998 were $0.19, versus basic net earnings per share of $0.33 in the prior year.

Also impacting the company's financial results are the general seasonal trends of the apparel and retail industries. Wholesale operations normally do better in the

first and third quarters, while retail performance is usually stronger in the third and fourth quarters.

ANALYSTS' OPINIONS

From a marketing perspective, Guess has been a trendsetter in the fashion industry. Its signature black-and-white print advertisements, as well as color print advertisements, have received numerous prestigious awards from the advertising industry, including Clio, Belding, and Mobius awards for creativity and excellence.

As an investment, however, the company has seemed less solid. Its continued emphasis on jeans has forced it to deal with increased competition in a shrinking market. As Kurt Barnard, president of *Barnard's Retail Trend Report,* said in an analysis of the textile industry, "People are getting tired of jeans." While companies like Levi Strauss and The Gap moved to take advantage of the burgeoning khakis market, Guess responded by introducing higher-quality, more distinctive jeans.

HISTORY

With its origins in the French Riviera, it is perhaps no surprise that the company's eventual success was based on a combination of European chic and supermodel glamour sprinkled with a liberal dose of rugged American individualism. The company began humbly enough in the 1970s with a jeans boutique owned by Georges Marciano in St. Tropez, France. In 1977 Georges, along with brothers Maurice and Armand, moved to Los Angeles where the three founded Guess?, Inc., in 1981. A fourth brother, Paul, joined the firm that same year and it was under his direction that the company launched its famous marketing campaign using supermodels such as Claudia Schiffer and Naomi Campbell. This advertising method was one of the leading factors responsible for making Guess a major brand name.

Guess jeans were met with some skepticism in the early days of the company. One of its premier products was the 3-zip Marilyn jeans, which were aimed at individuals who wanted to make their own fashion statement and express their own sense of style and attitude. According to the company, "After much resistance, Bloomingdale's agreed to sell some two dozen pairs of the Marilyn 3-zip jeans as a favor to the Marciano brothers—within hours, the entire stock sold out."

In 1983 the brothers sold 50 percent of their interest in the company to the Nakash brothers, who owned the Jordache company. A year later the Marcianos tried to buy out the Nakash brothers, arguing that Guess designs had been stolen in order to create a new style for Jordache. The two companies battled in court for five years before finally reaching an out-of-court settlement. The long court battle proved to be a major financial drain; in 1994 the Marciano brothers paid $23.2 million to the law firm that represented them against the Nakashes. The Marciano brothers resumed ownership of Guess, and in 1998 they controlled about 80 percent of the company's shares.

In 1990, the company decided to license its name to other manufacturers, such as Revlon, which marketed perfume using the Guess logo. Within a short time, the company had issued licenses for eyewear, footwear, jewelry, knitwear, and legwear. By 1998 nearly 10 percent of company revenues came from licensing royalties.

Following a disagreement regarding the future of the company, Georges Marciano sold his 40 percent share in the company to his brothers. Georges wanted to take the company mass-market, while the other brothers wanted to remain purveyors of up-market clothing. Soon after the break, Georges launched his own rival company, Yes Clothing.

In 1995 Guess continued with its international expansion and opened its first stores in Spain (in Barcelona and Madrid). In 1997 the company began moving its factories out of the United States to Mexico, blaming the difficulties caused by allegations of unfair and illegal labor practices. The company fought a protracted legal battle with the Union of Needletrades, Industrial & Textile Employees (UNITE), which accused the company's contractors of conducting illegal homework operations. UNITE's confrontation with Guess was carried out through the media as well as in the courts. Consequently, Guess' name was tarnished and the company was forced to defend itself against accusations that its factories were sweatshops. Finally, in April 1998, Guess entered into a settlement agreement; the company admitted no liability and was not found guilty of violating any laws.

STRATEGY

When the Marciano brothers first decided to manufacture denim products, the general consensus was that jeans were outdated and wearing them was no longer considered a fashion statement. But Guess confounded its critics with an ad campaign that portrayed denim as sensual and chic, and this marketing tactic took the public by storm. The company's approach was a radical re-imaging of denim that changed the way a whole new generation looked at jeans. That vision helped spur the trend towards designer jeans that dominated the 1980s and turned Guess into a clothing giant that, for years, set the tone in the denim industry.

Another key element of Guess' merchandising strategy was its "shop-in-shop" merchandising format. This was an exclusive area within a department store that sold only Guess products and used Guess signs and fixtures.

FAST FACTS:
About Guess?, Inc.

Ownership: Guess?, Inc. is a publicly owned company traded on the New York Stock Exchange.

Ticker symbol: GES

Officers: Maurice Marciano, Chmn. & CEO; Paul Marciano, Pres. & COO; Armand Marciano, Sr. Exec. VP, Assistant Secretary & Director; Terence Tsang, VP, Treasurer, & Corporate Controller

Employees: 2,800

Principal Subsidiary Companies: Guess' principal subsidiaries include: Viva Optiques, Pour le Bebe, Sweatshirt Apparel U.S.A., DML Marketing Group, Charles David, and Callanen.

Chief Competitors: Guess' principal competitors include: Levi Strauss; Bugle Boy; Calvin Klein; Chic; Donna Karan; The Gap; J. Crew; Jordache Enterprises; Lands' End; Tommy Hilfiger; VF Corp.; Warnaco Group; and Yes Clothing.

At the end of 1997 there were about 1,270 shop-in-shops, and the company planned to add or remodel approximately 60 shop-in-shops by the end of 1998.

In the 1980s Guess had given new life to denim, making it fashionable and chic. By the mid-1990s, however, jeans were once again losing ground as young people turned away from fashions worn by their elders, and different materials—especially khakis—began to grow more popular in the casual clothing market. While competitors like Levi Strauss and The Gap reduced their emphasis on jeans in favor of the newly-popular khakis, Guess continued to push its jeans. As Maurice Marciano commented in a company press release, "In response, we continue focusing on our core business by expanding our denim and denim-related product offerings."

INFLUENCES

Thanks to the keen business sense and creativity of the Marciano brothers, Guess has managed to keep up with trends and styles as well as devise innovative forms of advertising throughout most of its history. Each brother played a key role in Guess' growth. Maurice was

CHRONOLOGY:

Key Dates for Guess?, Inc.

1981: Georges Marciano, with brothers Maurice and Armand, establish Guess?, Inc.

1983: Brothers sell 50 percent of their interest in company to the Nakash brothers, who owned the Jordache company

1984: Marciano brothers try to buy out Nakash brothers but fail; engage in a five-year court battle before reaching an out-of-court settlement

1990: Markets company name to other manufacturers

1995: Opens first stores in Spain (Barcelona and Madrid)

1997: Begins moving factories out of the United States to Mexico

the chairman and chief executive officer and, at the same time, oversaw the design direction and was the inspiration for the company's spirited and successful expansion since 1982. The company credited Guess' president, Paul Marciano, "with the vision that is the essence of the Guess image—one that has created some of the most innovative and ground breaking images in the history of American advertising." Armand Marciano was responsible for overseeing retail, processing, and customer relations for the entire corporation. Together, the complementary skills and affectionate loyalty of the Marciano brothers helped make Guess a clothing giant.

CURRENT TRENDS

For years its innovative advertising and eye for the latest trends and fabrics helped keep Guess on top of the designer-jeans heap. The company's most famous ads were those that featured black-and-white photos of models and celebrities. The ads were provocative, powerful, eye-catching, and sexy—an irresistible combination that was right on target with Guess' customers.

However, not even the slickest advertising can convince consumers to buy what they no longer want, and by the mid-1990s Guess and its rivals in the fashion industry were forced to confront the fact that consumers seemed to be losing interest in fashion. As a *Hoover's*

industry analysis noted, "Americans' propensity for dressing down is a trend still shaping the apparel industry." However, added *Hoover's,* "too many T-shirts and jeans have translated into threadbare profits." Khakis were the new thing and, according to Kurt Barnard of *Barnard's Retail Trend Report,* khakis were capturing a share of the jeans market. In 1997 sales of men's khakis increased 21 percent over 1995 levels to $2.8 billion, while sales of women's khakis increased 36 percent to $1.5 billion during the same period. Sales of men's jeans, on the other hand, shrank 6.2 percent between 1996 and 1997. Rather than expand into other areas of the apparel market, Guess' response to this competitive trend was to try to capture a larger share of the shrinking jeans market by introducing in 1998 a new line of high-end jeans called Premium Denim. According to Guess, the innovative design and exclusive ring-spun denim will make these jeans "stand alone in the saturated industry of denim jeanswear."

PRODUCTS

Guess has long been known for fashionable products that are not only well made but are also chic and comfortable. The Guess line of clothing includes blue jeans, blouses, dresses, jackets, shirts, skirts, and shorts. Guess also licenses its name for lines of eyewear and children's clothing, as well as various accessories—some of the most popular lines being watches, footwear, and home furnishings. Guess uses several trademarks to distinguish its products, including Guess?, Guess? U.S.A., and Triangle Design.

GLOBAL PRESENCE

While the majority of Guess' business was concentrated in the United States, where the company operated 87 retail and 49 factory outlet stores at the end of 1997, the company also operated on a global level, with 269 retail and outlet stores operated by licensees and distributors. Plans were underway to open about 30 new stores in 1998. Guess also owned and operated a flagship retail store in Florence, Italy. Guess products were sold in over 70 countries, bringing in sales of approximately $34 million in 1996. In May 1997 Guess formed a joint venture in Europe called Maco Apparel, S.p.A. to manufacture and sell Guess jeanswear products throughout Europe.

EMPLOYMENT

Throughout the 1990s Guess was plagued by labor-related problems. Most of these problems involved the company's sub-contractors and were not directly related to Guess itself. Guess regarded its own employees as "one of its most valuable resources." At the end of 1997, 2,800 people were directly employed by the company, with 900 of them working in wholesale and the rest in retail. According to its publicity material, Guess is committed to protecting workers' rights to fair wages and a clean and safe workplace. It has also pledged to be "100% Sweatshop Free" and has initiated a subcontractor compliance program that it calls the most aggressive in the apparel industry.

These measures were initiated after a series of lawsuits were filed against Guess, arising out of the company's relationship with its independent contractors, charging Guess with unfair labor practices, violation of state wage and hour laws, wrongful discharge, and breach of contract. Guess denied all wrongdoing and fought to salvage its image by pointing out that it was the first company to voluntarily sign an agreement with the U.S. Department of Labor to monitor the compliance of its contractors with federal and state labor laws—an agreement Labor Department officials hailed as "truly historic" and "an industry model." The cases were eventually settled, with Guess admitting no liability and being found not guilty of any violations of state or federal law.

Guess offers several programs for its own employees, including various classes, workshops, and training seminars; a Service Awards Program to recognize employees for long-standing service; and a Corporate Recognition Program to honor employees who make an extra effort. None of Guess' employees are represented by labor unions, and the company has never experienced any interruption of its operations due to labor disputes.

SOURCES OF INFORMATION

Bibliography

"Corporate Responsibility." *Guess Home Page,* 27 March 1998. Available at http://www.guess.com.

"Guess History." *Guess Home Page.* 7 May 1998. Available at http://www.guess.com/history/index.html.

"Guess?, Inc." *Hoover's Online.* 7 May 1998. Available at http://www.hoovers.com.

"Guess?, Inc., Reports First Quarter Results." *Guess Home Page,* April 1998. Available at http://www.guess.com.

"Guess? Launches Premium Denim." *Guess Home Page,* 3 June 1998. Available at http://www.guess.com.

For an annual report:

on the Internet at: http://www.sec.gov/Archives/edgar/data

For additional industry research:

Investigate companies by their Standard Industrial Classification Codes, also known as SICs. Guess' primary SICs are:

5023 Homefurnishings

5136 Men's/Boys' Clothing

5137 Women's/Children's Clothing

5139 Footwear

5311 Department Stores

Hallmark Cards, Inc.

FOUNDED: 1910

Contact Information:

HEADQUARTERS: 2501 McGee St.
   Kansas City, MO 64141-6580
PHONE: (816)274-5111
FAX: (816)274-8513
URL: http://www.hallmark.com

OVERVIEW

Hallmark Cards, Inc. wraps up 44 percent the U.S. greeting card market to seal the title of the world's largest maker of greeting cards. Hallmark products—including puzzles, gift wrap, party goods, decorations, and collectibles under a variety of brand names—can be found in drugstores, supermarkets, and discount outlets. The Kansas City-based firm also sells Hallmark products through 4,800 Gold Crown shops, the second largest specialty retail chain in the United States. Wanting to grow but keep its feel-good image, the company bought Revel-Monogram, the world's top maker of plastic model kits, and Binney & Smith, the maker of Crayola crayons and markers. Hallmark racked up net sales of $3.6 billion in 1996, placing thirty-fifth on *Forbes* list of the largest privately held companies in the nation.

Throughout its history, Hallmark has shown innovation in messages, markets, and marketing. The company continues to grow and thrive by offering personal expression products in an increasingly impersonal world. The family-owned business takes great care to make sure that only quality products carry its signature.

ANALYSTS' OPINIONS

"There are a number of things that make Hallmark a top-10 company," said Robert Levering in an interview with *Personnel Journal*. "One of the key things that's very interesting about Hallmark is how it's been evolving in the past 10 years or so. It was very paternalistic in the early 1980s, and it has made a transition from paternalism to a more professionally minded company. It's not all the Hall family anymore running the place. Moving away from paternalism is not something that all companies do successfully.

"While taking the best of (more empowered) companies, they've maintained the good qualities of a paternalistic company—they haven't thrown the baby out with the bath water. They still take care of their people. The people running the place look out for the employees. It's exhibited in the personalized practices and their benefits."

FAST FACTS:
About Hallmark Cards, Inc.

Ownership: Hallmark is a privately held company. The Hall Family retains majority ownership while employees own the remainder.

Officers: Donald J. Hall, Chmn.; Irvine O. Hockaday Jr, CEO & Pres.

Employees: 20,100

Principal Subsidiary Companies: Company subsidiaries include Ambassador Cards, Binney and Smith Inc., Crown Media Inc., EvensonCard Shops Inc., Hallmark Marketing Inc., and Hallmark Metamora Fixture Operations.

Chief Competitors: Hallmark has two main competitors in the greeting card industry and assorted competitors in a variety of other fields. Competitors include: American Greetings; Gibson Greetings; Hasbro; Marvel; Mattel; Time Warner; Turner Broadcasting; Viacom; and Walt Disney.

HISTORY

In 1908 Joyce C. Hall and his two older brothers started the Norfolk Post Card Company in their hometown of Norfolk, Nebraska. Two years later, the 18-year-old quit school, packed up two shoe boxes full of picture post cards, and boarded a train bound for Kansas City. Hall was determined to make his own mark in the boom town, with his own company that would become Hallmark Cards. Drugstores, bookstores, and gift shops quickly snatched up Hall's cards.

The following year Hall asked his brother Rollie to join him in his growing venture. The two opened a specialty shop, named Hall Brothers, that sold gifts, books, post cards, and stationery. In 1915, their business burned down, putting them $17,000 in debt. Joyce Hall recounted the trying times in his autobiography, *When You Care Enough*: "One of the first Hallmark sentiments was made more meaningful by the fire. When you get to the end of your rope, it read, tie a knot in it and hang on. We had to do that a number of times."

Hanging on with the help of a loan, the brothers bought an engraving firm and started manufacturing their own cards with original designs. Brother William joined the company in 1921. By 1922, the brothers had salesmen in all 48 states and added gift wrap to their products.

The continuing history of the company is a litany of firsts in the greeting card business, from the introduction of eye-catching racks full of greeting cards in the 1930s to the development of retail card shops in the 1950s and 1960s.

In 1944, company executive Ed Goodman coined Hallmark's trademark slogan, which it uses to this day: When you care enough to send the very best. The company adopted its crown-and-signature logo in 1949.

The Hallmark Hall of Fame television specials began in 1951. The dramatic series has won consistent praise through the years for quality programming. In 1961, the National Academy of Television Arts and Sciences even awarded an Emmy to Hallmark, the first sponsor ever to receive that honor. The series went on to win more Emmy awards than any other TV show.

The company, with its growth and success after World War II, changed its name in 1954 to Hallmark Cards. Expanding in all directions, the company started selling overseas in 1957. Hallmark then created a low-end line of cards called Ambassador in 1959 to be sold through mass merchandisers, foreseeing the time when card buying trends would shift away from card shops and more toward discount food and drug stores.

Hallmark branched into real estate development in 1967, with the construction of the 85-acre Crown Center complex that envelops the company headquarters near downtown Kansas City. (The center made national headlines in 1981, when two walkways collapsed at its Hyatt Regency hotel and killed more than 100 people.)

Founder Joyce Hall died in 1982. He was preceded in death by brother Rollie, VP and director of sales, in 1968, and brother William, VP and treasurer, in 1971. Donald Hall, Joyce's son, took over as chairman of Hallmark in 1983.

Under Donald Hall, the company continued to try new markets and fields. Hallmark bought Crayon-maker Binney & Smith in 1984. Shoebox Greetings, known for whimsical designs and humorous messages, debuted in 1986. From 1991 to 1994, Hallmark was even in the cable TV business. The company teamed up with National Geographic TV in 1995 to create a series of made-for-television movies.

CHRONOLOGY:

1908: Joyce C. Hall and his two older brothers form the Norfolk Post Card Company in Norfolk, Nebraska

1910: Joyce leaves family business and sets up a mail-order postcard company, Hall Brothers, in Kansas City, Missouri

1912: Hall Brothers adds greeting cards to product line

1915: Fire destroys company's entire inventory, putting it $17,000 in debt

1923: Formally incorporates under the name Hall Brother Company

1938: Advertises in the broadcast medium for first time by sponsoring *Tony Won's Radio Scrapbook* on WMAQ radio in Chicago

1949: Takes out copyright on the company logo

1951: Sponsors first production of the Hallmark Hall of Fame series

1954: Changes name to Hallmark Cards, Inc.

1966: Joyce Hall retires and names son, Donald Hall, president and CEO

1968: Broke ground on the $500 million Crown Center in Kansas City, Missouri

1979: Acquires lithographer, LithoKrome Corporation

1982: Joyce Hall dies; Donald Hall adds chairmanship to his duties

1986: Donald Hall retires as CEO and hands position to President Irvine O. Hockaday Jr.

1994: Posted record-high sales of $3.8 billion

1998: Acquires Irresistible Ink, Inc.; sues S. Schwab Company, Inc. and is awarded $700,000

Between 1990 and 1994 the company's profits remained flat or down, according to *Forbes*. The magazine estimated Hallmark's share of the $5.6 billion (retail sales) domestic card market had dropped to 42 percent, down from 45 percent in five years. Despite the increased competition, which caused the slight decline in market-share, the company posted record-high sales of $3.8 billion in 1994.

Hallmark embarked on a major restructuring in early 1995. In one streamlining effort, the newly-installed management team decided to merge administrative, marketing, and product-development functions. of all the Hallmark card brands. The company reportedly returned to its 45 percent market share.

Still in expansion mode, Expressions from Hallmark arrived in 1996. The new brand fills a gap between the original Hallmark line and the Ambassador line, which first appeared in 1959. The company also created lines to appeal to various ethnic and demographic groups. Hallmark acquired Minneapolis-based Irresistible Ink, Inc. in 1998. The subsidiary provides customized greeting cards for business clients that want direct mail with a handwritten message.

Knowing and guarding the value of a brand that ranks among the top five brands in the nation, Hallmark sued S. Schwab Company, Inc. for using a Hallmark design without the company's permission. The court ordered Schwab to pay $700,000 in damages to Hallmark in 1998.

STRATEGY

Consumers consistently rank the Hallmark brand amongst the top five quality brands nationwide.

In 1996 the company initiated a campaign to capitalize and build on brand loyalty. In one series of advertisements, customers were encouraged to turn over a card to sneak a peek at the brand on the back. Hallmark ran commercials on top TV shows, such as "Seinfeld," "Friends," and "ER." The company also placed print ads on the back covers of more than 100 national magazines. Next Hallmark launched a series of commercials designed to raise the visibility of its Hallmark Gold Crown network of independently owned and operated card and gift shops. Those ads ended with the tagline: "You'll feel better inside."

In 1992 competitor American Greetings introduced computerized card-making kiosks to the marketplace. The following year Hallmark rolled out its Touch-Screen machines that let customers create their own personalized greeting card for about $4. The do-it-yourself business as a whole has yet to catch on with card-buyers. After scaling back on the number of kiosks available in 1996, Hallmark continues to test price points and marketing ploys.

PRODUCTS

Hallmark manufactures some 40,000 products under the brand names of Hallmark, Ambassador, Crayola, Hallmark Connections, Heartline, Keepsake Ornaments,

Liquitex, Magic Marker, Party Express, Revell-Monogram, Shoebox Greetings, Springbok, and Verkerke. Products include mugs, puzzles, bookmarks, calendars, collectibles, gift wrap, greeting cards, and writing papers. Hallmark serves approximately 40,000 retail outlets domestically.

For Easter 1997 Hallmark unveiled a line of Christian greeting cards with an explicit Bible-based theme, sporting lengthy Bible passages and first-hand testimonials on faith. The company hopes to lure the ever-growing market of Christians buyers away from religious bookstores and into Hallmark shops.

CORPORATE CITIZENSHIP

Social responsibility is not a new-fangled concept for Hallmark. The Hallmark Corporate Foundation contributes to various and sundry programs. These include a traveling creative workshop for kids and a group of videos designed to help children develop social skills. In Kansas City, where corporate headquarters are located, the company routinely makes donations to various charitable causes including a $20 million donation from the Hallmark Family and Corporate Foundations for the renovation of the train station and the development of a museum. The company benefits human service, education, health, and arts organizations in the communities in which it operates.

The company has a unique job security plan in which, rather than lose their job to a layoff or euphemistic "work reduction," employees can opt to volunteer in the community while still receiving their usual paychecks. Executives say the sense of goodwill and employee security this program offers employees and the community make this program worthwhile.

GLOBAL PRESENCE

Hallmark products are carried by more than 40,000 retail outlets, including 33,000 mass merchandisers and 7,500 specialty stores throughout the United States. Customers can also shop via computer, buying Hallmark cards and products through America Online. The company distributes its products in more than 100 countries in 20 languages.

EMPLOYMENT

Hallmark Cards Inc. has been repeatedly hailed in the 1990s as "one of the most attractive employers" in the nation for treating employees well. According to *Personnel Journal,* employees are respected in observable ways by the company through its various programs, not the least of which is employment security. The company reportedly supports and assists employees in maintaining a healthy balance between work and family through family care assistance, counseling and education, and job-sharing arrangements. The company encourages open communication through newsletters, computer-monitor signboards, CEO forums, and town hall meetings. Diversity in the halls of Hallmark "includes, but is not limited to: ethnic origin, religion, gender, age, sexual orientation, disability, lifestyle, economic background, regional geography, employment status and thinking style."

In 1995 Hallmark marked its tenth year on *Working Mother* magazine's "100 Best Companies for Working Mothers," and the company has been twice listed in the top 10 in "The 100 Best Companies to Work for in America," by Robert Levering and Milton Moskowitz.

"Hallmark is loaded with literally thousands of Quarter Century Club members—people who have been with Hallmark for 25 years or more," according to *Personnel Journal.* "Around Kansas City, the company enjoys a reputation as a peach of a Bermuda Triangle—folks enter its hallowed halls and never want to leave. A recent union flirtation failed because employees simply didn't demonstrate enough interest in changing anything about the company. And why should they? Thanks to a generous profit-sharing program, employees now own one-third of the company." (Company literature placed employee-ownership at 25 percent in 1998.)

More than 700 people make up Hallmark's creative staff, including artists, designers, stylists, writers, and photographers. Together they crank out roughly 11,000 new and 8,000 re-worked greeting cards a year. Company-paid retreats and foreign trips help keep their muses alive. Creators of the Shoebox line often get inspired through free movie passes and daily screenings of popular television shows, all courtesy of Hallmark.

SOURCES OF INFORMATION

Bibliography

A Centennial Tribute to the Memory of Joyce C. Hall, Kansas City, MO: Hallmark Cards, Inc., 1991.

"Expressions from Hallmark Makes Greeting Card History." *Drug Store News,* 29 April 1996.

Flynn, Gillian. "Hallmark Cares." *Personnel Journal,* March 1996.

Howard, Elizabeth G. "Hallmark's $4 Billion Formula." *The Kansas City Business Journal,* 16 June 1995.

"Robert Levering Tells Why Hallmark Is One of 'The Best.'" *Personnel Journal,* March 1996.

Stern, William M. "Loyal to a Fault." *Forbes,* 14 March 1994.

For additional industry research:

Investigate companies by their Standard Industrial Classification Codes, also known as SICs. Hallmark's primary SICs are:

2678 Stationery, Tablets, and Related Products;

2679 Converted Paper & Paperboard Products

2771 Greeting Cards

Hanes

OVERVIEW

Headquartered in Winston-Salem, North Carolina, Hanes is the world's leading apparel brand and a key part of the $20-billion Sara Lee Corporation. Sara Lee Corporation is a global manufacturer and marketer of brand name products ranging from packaged meats, coffee, and baked goods, to household goods, body care products, and "personal products," which include the various Hanes brands.

Sara Lee Corporation's Personal Products line includes the Intimates, Accessories, Knit Products, and Hosiery business groups, and in 1997 accounted for more than $2 billion of the corporation's nearly $20 billion in sales. The Intimates group primarily markets bras and panties that are manufactured and distributed under several labels including Hanes Her Way. Sara Lee Knit Products manufactures and distributes underwear and active wear for men, women, and children in North America, South and Central America, Europe, and the Asia-Pacific region. Principal brands in this category include Hanes and Hanes Her Way in North America, and Hanes in Europe. The Hosiery group (which also includes the Hanes brand) is the market leader in hosiery markets in North America, western Europe, Australia, New Zealand, and South Africa. Hanes' fiscal 1996 launch of Resilience hosiery was the corporation's most successful.

Hanes Printables is a division of Sara Lee Knit Products, part of the Sara Lee Corporation. Hanes Printables, Hanes Activewear, Hanes Underwear divisions, Hanes Hosiery, and several other Sara Lee divisions/companies are based in Winston-Salem, North Carolina. The division markets high quality blank apparel designed specifically for use in screen printing, embroidery, heat transfers, and so on.

FOUNDED: 1965

Contact Information:

HEADQUARTERS: 3 1st National Plz.
  Chicago, IL 60602-4260
PHONE: (312)726-2600
FAX: (312)558-8653
URL: http://www.onehanesplace.com

FAST FACTS:
About Hanes

Ownership: Sara Lee Corporation, the parent company of Hanes, is a publicly owned company traded on the New York, Chicago, and Pacific Stock Exchanges. The stock also is traded in London and Amsterdam; on the Swiss stock exchanges in Zurich, Geneva, and Basel; and on the Paris Bourse. Options are traded on the American Stock Exchange.

Ticker symbol: SLE

Officers: John H. Bryan, Chmn. & CEO Sara Lee Corporation; C. Steven McMillan, Pres. & COO Sara Lee Corporation; Jonathan Letzler, Pres., Hanes Hosiery; Art Gibel, Pres. & CEO, Hanes Printables

Employees: 141,000 (Sara Lee Corporation)

Principal Subsidiary Companies: Sara Lee Corporation is the parent company of Hanes.

Chief Competitors: Hanes' leading products include underwear, T-shirts, and women's hosiery, putting it in direct competition with Fruit of the Loom and Calvin Klein.

Hanes and other Sara Lee Corporation hosiery products are sold in channels ranging from department and specialty stores to supermarkets, warehouse clubs, discount chains, and convenience stores. Hosiery products are also distributed through catalog sales, the Internet, and Sara Lee stores. In its 1997 Annual Report, the company reported that Hanes, together with the company's other knit products, accounted for 10 percent or more of Sara Lee Corporation's consolidated revenues during each of the previous three fiscal years.

COMPANY FINANCES

In 1997 Sara Lee Corporation's net sales increased 6 percent to $19.7 billion from $18.6 billion in 1996. with growth in the company's Coffee, Knit Products, and Intimate Apparel businesses primarily responsible for the sales growth. For the full year, worldwide Knit Products units increased 9 percent, global Intimate Apparel unit sales rose 1 percent, and worldwide legwear sales fell 2

percent. On the downside, lower margins in the Personal Products segment pushed down the gross profit margin from 38.4 percent in 1996 to 37.8 percent in 1997. Operating income (pretax earnings before interest and corporate expenses) kept pace with sales, however, increasing by 6.2 percent, while net income for 1997 increased 10.1 percent to $1.0 billion and primary earnings per share increased 10.9 percent to $2.03. Similar results were achieved the previous year when net sales increased 5.1 percent to $18.6 billion in 1996 from $17.7 billion in 1995. Over the long term, Sara Lee's focus on consumer fundamentals such as food and undergarments has resulted in steady, if unspectacular, growth.

ANALYSTS' OPINIONS

Sara Lee Corporation is seen by some analysts as a "comfort" stock. Established brand names and a range of products that cover many of life's essentials have made the company a safe, reliable bet for investors. The company's restructuring efforts were also praised. As PaineWebber analyst Roger Spencer told the *Charlotte Observer* in 1994, "This is how you stay good, big and strong, by taking remedial action before you get sick. Good management is supposed to address realities of the marketplace, adjust to them and try to make money. Rather than sit around hoping for a turnaround . . . they're adjusting to what might be a long-term trend."

HISTORY

The history of the Hanes brand is long and complicated. It all began in the 1800s when brothers J. Wesley and Pleasant Hanes formed the P.H. Hanes Tobacco Company, which they later sold to R.J. Reynolds for $175,000. Flush with cash, the brothers immediately launched new ventures with J. Wesley forming Shamrock Mills Co. (men's hosiery) and Pleasant forming P.H. Hanes Knitting Co., which introduced the first set of two-piece men's underwear.

For the next 65 years the two companies operated in parallel while remaining independent. In 1910 Shamrock Mills changed its name to Hanes Hosiery Mill Co. and began to make women's hosiery. A decade later it pulled out of the vanishing men's hosiery business altogether and focused on the fast-growing women's business. Meanwhile, P.H. Hanes expanded into undershirts, briefs, sleepwear, and knitted shorts. In 1965 the two companies merged to form Hanes Corporation, and the new company was listed on the New York Stock Exchange.

In 1972 Hanes "hatched" what was to be the world's most successful hosiery brand ever, L'eggs. The new brand was so successful that it quickly spun off as its own company. Hanes' success and strong brand recognition soon attracted the attention of other corporations and in 1979 the Consolidated Foods Corporation (now Sara Lee Corporation) acquired the Hanes Corporation, including L'eggs. A few years later, in 1986, Hanes introduced yet another brand that was to prove enormously successful—the Hanes Her Way brand of women's apparel—starting with women's panties and quickly expanding to other categories. Hanes Her Way soon rivaled L'eggs for brand recognition and popularity. Hanes scored another coup shortly after, signing up the young basketball star, Michael Jordan, to promote a line of men's underwear.

Through the 1990s Hanes continued to play a key role in Sara Lee's success, generating more than $2 billion in sales in 1997 and helping Sara Lee Corporation maintain its number one position in the intimate apparel markets in the United States, Canada, and Mexico.

STRATEGY

Brands are the key to Sara Lee's success and throughout the 1990s the company's main focus was to build brand equity and improve returns by developing new, value-added products, expanding existing products into new markets, and providing extensive marketing support in order to build leadership brands. As of 1998 Sara Lee had 31 "megabrands," (a brand with sales of more than $100 million) and, in 1997 the company spent almost $2 billion to increase brand recognition with customers.

Sara Lee's strategic focus for the U.S. underwear market was to develop new, value-added products. This included an expanded array of boxer-brief styles, fashion underwear for men, and more upscale panty styles for women. In 1997 the Hanes megabrand was the number one apparel label in the mass channel of distribution for the fourth consecutive year. To counter the effects of the slumping legwear business, Sara Lee planned to increase marketing support for its leading hosiery brands, improve operating efficiencies, and develop high-margin, value-added products that would give consumers more choices in legwear. One of the best-known examples of the company's drive to promote its hosiery products was the Tina Turner Hanes hosiery campaign, which included print, billboard, and television advertising, as well as sponsorship of a North American concert tour.

For all apparel categories, Sara Lee capitalized on its partnership agreement with the 1996 Olympic Games to strengthen the equity of the Hanes and Champion brands.

Hanes and other Sara Lee hosiery continued to respond to changing market forces in the hosiery area during fiscal 1996 through the introduction of shaping and toning products, new colors and textures, increased dura-

CHRONOLOGY:
Key Dates for Hanes

1900: P.H. Hanes Tobacco Company sold to R.J. Reynolds for $175,000

1901: J. Wesley Hanes forms Shamrock Mills Co., specializing in men's hosiery

1910: Shamrock Mills changes name to Hanes Hosiery Mill Co. and makes women's hosiery

1920: Hanes Hosiery pulls out of men's hosiery business to focus on women's hosiery business

1920: P.H. Hanes expands into undershirts, briefs, sleepwear, and knitted shorts

1965: Hanes Corporation is formed when the two Hanes companies merge

1972: Releases the most successful hosiery brand ever, L'eggs,

1979: Hanes Corporation is acquired by the Sara Lee Corporation

1986: Introduces Hanes Her Way women's apparel brand

1989: Signs basketball star Michael Jordan

1992: Introduces new logo and advertising campaign, "Just Can't Wait'll We Get Our Hanes On You."

1997: Generates $19.7 billion in sales, helping Sara Lee maintain number one position in the intimate apparel markets in the United States, Canada, and Mexico

bility, and special occasion hosiery. The global market for sheer hosiery continued to exhibit weakness, and unit volumes fell 9 percent. However, profits for Sara Lee's worldwide sheer hosiery business increased. In the United States, Hanes and other Sara Lee hosiery continued to decrease production capacity and improve inventory flow to maximize returns and profitability. In Europe, Sara Lee continued to reduce manufacturing overhead and excess sheer hosiery capacity.

In late 1997 Sara Lee announced a three-year strategic program designed to increase its competitiveness through a combination of cost-reductions, outsourcing, and elimination of assets "that Sara Lee has determined it does not need to own in order to fulfill its primary mission of building brands on a global basis."

INFLUENCES

In the highly competitive knit products market, success depends on brand recognition, quality, price, and loyalty—all elements that Sara Lee focuses on. Through its combination of superior value, low-cost sourcing, and "megabranding," the company has established itself as a market leader in hosiery and intimate apparel products worldwide. The hosiery business, in particular, is very competitive in both the United States and Europe. In the United States, where Sara Lee's major competitors are other hosiery companies, the company must compete on quality, value, function, service, and distribution. In Europe the primary focus is on quality.

For most of Sara Lee's competitors, the small companies who compete in the unbranded sector of the market, the primary focus is on quality. In a bid to counter slumping sales and increase market share in 1997, Sara Lee launched a new series of hosiery products offering superior fit, durability, and figure control, while continuing its efforts to enhance brand identity and consumer awareness of new products.

CURRENT TRENDS

The T-shirt industry, once a cottage industry populated by tie-dyers, protesters, and small-time rock concert promoters, has become a big-time business for companies such as Hanes. According to a 1996 *U. S. News & World Report* article, 1 billion T-shirts were bought in the United States in 1995 with total sales of $10 billion. "Hanes and Fruit of the Loom are looking to sign a slew of big-name music acts to shirt contracts," the article said. "If they succeed, they will be able to establish huge, vertically integrated T-shirt businesses that control everything from silk-screening to shelf space in stores."

In 1996 Hanes paid $100 million to gain sponsorship and licensing rights for apparel at the Olympic Games in Atlanta. "By the time the sports spectacle is over," said the article, "the company expects to have sold between $400 million and $500 million worth of Olympic T-shirts, about half of all Olympic-licensed merchandise," explains Mike Davis, vice president of Olympic licensing for Hanes. "The Olympics are the equivalent of two Super Bowls a day for 17 days."

By 1998 women's hosiery products had been on a downward slide for several years as trousers and other casual clothes became increasingly popular. To counter this trend, Sara Lee emphasized a wider range of products that offered better fit and control, and increased its marketing activities on behalf of these products.

PRODUCTS

Hanes hosiery products include pantyhose, stockings, combination panty and pantyhose garments, tights, knee-highs, and socks, many of which are available in both sheer and opaque styles.

Hanes Printables products include Hanes T-shirts: Beefy-T, Heavyweight, Standard Weight, and Heavyweight 50/50; Hanes Her Way Essential Accents (includes T-shirts and tank tops for women); fleece products such as Hanes Superheavy Cotton, Ultimate Cotton, Heavyweight, and Activewear.

Hanes also manufactures and distributes men's, women's, and children's underwear and activewear (T-shirts, fleecewear, and other jersey products for casual-wear) in North America, South and Central America, Europe and the Asia-Pacific countries.

In April 1997 Hanes announced a new product line centered on National Basketball Association star Michael Jordan. The Michael Jordan Collection by Hanes, a line of men's underwear, includes ribbed briefs, ribbed boxer briefs, and T-shirts. All the garments are made of cotton and priced from $6 to $13. Jordan helped design the new product. Hanes packaged it in red, white, and black—the colors of Jordan's team, the Chicago Bulls—with a picture of Jordan and the M.J. logo.

CORPORATE CITIZENSHIP

In an unprecedented demonstration of corporate generosity, Sara Lee Corporation announced in June 1998 that it would be giving its renowned art collection to 20 American museums. Calling it a "millennium gift to America," the company promised to donate 35 to 40 paintings and sculptures by the French Impressionists and other popular artists of the modern era. According to Sara Lee CEO John H. Bryant, "Our purpose in making this gift is to demonstrate our strong belief in the importance of good corporate citizenship, and in the positive influence of art on society." President Bill Clinton's wife, Hillary Rodham Clinton, applauded the gift, saying, "In making this gift, Sara Lee Corporation sets an example of involved citizenship that we hope many others will emulate - corporations and individuals alike."

After an internal environmental audit revealed a number of environmentally harmful practices, Sara Lee implemented a program to make sure its production methods and packaging complied with environmental laws and intensified its efforts to reduce its use of natural resources.

GLOBAL PRESENCE

Sara Lee hosiery brands dominate the markets in North America, western Europe, Australia, New Zealand, and South Africa, while its underwear (for men, women, and children) holds the leading market share in the United States. It also holds the leading position in men's and boys' underwear in Mexico. In 1996 the Hanes Her Way brand was a leader in the Mexican bra market and a strong seller in Canada.

Sara Lee's Personal Products business is handled overseas by foreign subsidiaries in dozens of countries around the world. Some of these companies include: Dim S.A.; Grupo Sans, a division of Sara Lee/DE Espana S.A.; Sara Lee Personal Products, S.p.A.; Sara Lee Personal Products (Australia) Pty. Ltd.; Pretty Polly, a division of Sara Lee UK Holdings Ltd.; Vatter GmbH; the Filodoro Group; Sara Lee Hosiery, S.A. de C.V.; Bellia S.p.A. Hanes de Centroamerica S.A.; Hanes de El Salvador, S.A. de C.V; Hanes de Mexico, S.A. de C.V.; Hanes (Deutschland) GmbH; Hanes Dominican Incorporated; Hanes France S.A., France; Hanes Hellas S.A.; Hanes Jamaica Limited; Hanes Panama Incorporated; Hanes Tejidos Costa Rica Limited; and Hanes U.K. Limited.

EMPLOYMENT

During fiscal 1996 Sara Lee Corporation's worldwide restructuring program resulted in 9,422 layoffs. The company announced its restructuring program in 1994, the year it laid off more than 8,000 workers, or about 6 percent of its workforce worldwide. The layoffs came in the wake of slumping U.S. hosiery sales brought on by an increasingly casual lifestyle, and they were heaviest in the company's Winston-Salem, North Carolina-based textile division. At the same time, margins were shrinking as Wal-Mart and other discounters were wrung price concessions from suppliers.

As Sara Lee Corporation is the world's largest company named after a woman, the company believes strongly in promoting the role of women in the modern workforce. Nearly 60 percent of Sara Lee Corporation's employees are women.

SOURCES OF INFORMATION

Bibliography

"About Hanes Printables," 9 May 1997. Available at http://www.HanesPrintables.com/about.htm.

"Corporate Info.," 9 May 1997. Available at http://www.hanes2u.com/corp.html.

"Dressing Down for Dollars/The Booming $10 Billion T-shirt Industry Is Now a Big-Time Business." *U.S. News & World Report,* 13 May 1996.

Edgar Archives, September 1996. Available at http://www.sec.gov.

Hanes Corporate Web Site, 9 May 1997. Available at http://www.hanes.com.

"Hanes Credits Jordan with Assist on Its New Line of Men's Underwear." *Charlotte Observer,* 2 April 1997.

"J. Gordon Hanes, Industrialist, Dies/Hosiery Business Head Also Longtime Arts Supporter." *Charlotte Observer,* 2 September 1995.

Sara Lee Corporation 1997 Annual Report. Chicago, IL: Sara Lee Corporation, September 1997. Available at http://www.sec.gov.

"Sara Lee Corporation Donates Its Renowned Art Collection to 20 American Museums." Sara Lee Corporation Press Release, 3 June 1998.

"Sara Lee Corporation Names Letzler President of Hanes Hosiery." Sara Lee Corporation Press Release, 30 March 1998.

"Sara Lee Corp. to Lay Off 8,000/N.C.-based Textile Division Will Bear the Brunt of the Action; Company Stock Rises." *Charlotte Observer,* 7 June 1994.

For an annual report:

on the Internet at: http://www.sec.gov/Archives/edgar/data/23666/0000912057-97-031412.txt **or** telephone: (800)654-SARA **or** write: Sara Lee Corporation, Investor Relations and Corporate Affairs Department, 3 1st National Plz., Chicago, IL 60602-4260

For additional industry research:

Investigate companies by their Standard Industrial Classification Codes, also known as SICs. Hanes' primary SICs are:

5136 Men's/Boy's Clothing

5137 Women's/Children's

Hard Rock Cafe

FOUNDED: 1971

Contact Information:
HEADQUARTERS: 5401 S. Kirkman Rd.
　　　Orlando, FL 32819
PHONE: (407)351-6000
URL: http://www.hardrock.com

OVERVIEW

Hard Rock Cafe operates and franchises restaurants serving high-quality, moderately priced American-style food and beverages. The Hard Rock Cafe was part of the first wave of popular theme restaurants, focusing on the worldwide fascination with rock 'n roll and its celebrities. The highly charged and informal atmosphere is enhanced by displays of rock memorabilia and a reputation for attracting musicians and other celebrities.

COMPANY FINANCES

Hard Rock Cafes' 1997 sales totalled approximately $400 million. The company is now held by the London-based Rank Organisation, but until 1996 functioned as two distinct corporations—one owned by Rank and one by cofounder Peter Morton. Rank purchased Morton's share for $410 million; however, Morton is still active in the development of new Hard Rock enterprises, including hotels and casinos.

ANALYSTS' OPINIONS

Nation's Restaurant News reported, "The growth of Hard Rock Cafes has slowed, at least in the domestic markets." However, the company's consolidation under Rank management and its expanding interest in hotels and casinos indicate potential for strong growth. *Nation's Restaurant News* calls Hard Rock Cafe "one of the world's best-known, highest-grossing, and most influen-

Rock star Sammy Hager playing at the opening of the Hard Rock Café in Hollywood, California. (*Reuters/Fred Prouser/Archive Photos.*)

tial restaurant creations." The magazine's Theresa Howard noted, "Aligning itself with all things cool under the sun, Hard Rock is ensuring that it regains any ground lost during the heady rise of other entertainment-themed restaurants by positioning itself as the premier international entertainment and leisure company."

HISTORY

The idea for the first Hard Rock Cafe came to a pair of expatriate Americans living in London. Peter Morton, whose family ran Morton's Steakhouse, and Isaac Tigrett, a Memphis native, longed for American hamburgers and ice-cold beer. They wanted a restaurant that would offer food everybody could enjoy in a place in which everyone was treated equally. The pair scraped together $10,000 and acquired a loan to open their first Hard Rock Cafe on June 14, 1971. The venue was a former Rolls Royce showroom in London's Mayfair District. Items on the menu were inspired by Tennessee truck stop fare: burgers, fries, shakes, and apple pies. The restaurant's theme was inspired by a love of American popular music.

FAST FACTS:
About Hard Rock Cafe

Ownership: Hard Rock Cafe is a privately held company.

Officers: James Berk, Pres. & CEO

Employees: 1,500

Principal Subsidiary Companies: Rank Organisation PLC purchased half of Hard Rock Cafe in 1988 and half in 1996.

Chief Competitors: Hard Rock Cafe's competitors include: Planet Hollywood and Official All-Star Cafes.

From its very beginning the Hard Rock Cafe was dedicated to rock 'n roll and everything associated with it. The restaurant name itself was inspired by the art on an album cover: According to corporate mythology, Tigrett was studying the small print on the back sleeve of The Doors' 1970 album *Morrison Hotel* when he noticed the picture of a make-believe cocktail bar called the Hard Rock Cafe.

The restaurants are perhaps most famous for their decor, which is covered with anything and everything related to rock music and the musicians who play it. The chain's first item of memorabilia was a guitar donated by Eric Clapton. Not to be outdone, Pete Townshend sent his guitar along with a note stating, "Mine's as good as his!" The collection grew to more than 35,000 items by 1997. The pieces are circulated periodically from restaurant to restaurant worldwide. The company boasts that it owns some of the most priceless rock 'n roll artifacts on display anywhere in the world.

The first Hard Rock Cafe, in London, has also been a popular spot for the superstars of rock to perform and celebrate. Paul McCartney, Prince, Janet Jackson, Sting, Elton John, George Harrison, and Peter Gabriel are among the stars who have performed there. These events have included informal jam sessions, such as the 1995 performance by Sting and Elton John. Bob Geldof, a British musician known for his Live-Aid efforts and his band the Boomtown Rats, celebrated at the London Hard Rock following his honorary knighthood.

Morton and Tigrett had their differences, however, and by 1979 they went their separate ways. Morton opened his exclusive Morton's restaurant in Hollywood;

three years later he sold his share in the London Hard Rock Cafe for $800,000, and proceeded to open the first Hard Rock Cafe in the United States, which met with opposition from Tigrett.

According to *Nation's Restaurant News,* a legal squabble between the former partners over Morton's disputed rights to Hard Rock ultimately was won by Morton on intellectual-property grounds. The two factions divided up the world for future expansion and split the United States along the Mississippi River. A jointly owned licensing company was set up to control the shared trademark.

Tigrett took his Hard Rock faction (Hard Rock International) public in England in 1983, selling 25 percent of the company for $1 million. He launched the New York Hard Rock a year later. In 1987 his company sold notes representing 23 percent of its equity for $54 million. In 1988, with a total of seven Tigrett-run Hard Rocks operating internationally, he sold the 54 percent he controlled for $108 million, personally pocketing some $30 million. With that money, he opened the first House of Blues in 1992.

Rank Organisation, which purchased Tigrett's interest in the Hard Rock restaurants in 1988, was also able to acquire Morton's share in 1996, shortly before the twenty-fifth anniversary of the cafe chain. The London-based Rank paid $410 million for Morton's Hard Rock Cafes, and with them acquired worldwide control of the Hard Rock brand. The consolidation of the brand under one company would allow expansion and aggressive marketing of the chain. CEO and president James Berk stated in *International Business,* "Unification of the Hard Rock trademark provides an unprecedented opportunity to take an internationally recognized and respected brand and exploit it more fully."

The chain continued to expand under Rank's management. It comprised approximately 80 restaurants in 1998, and planned to open a new restaurant every month until the end of the millenium. The company is also expanding its focus by sponsoring rock tours, co-producing record albums, and forming partnerships with music video cable channel VH1.

STRATEGY

The company's mottoes embody the Hard Rock philosophies: "Love All—Serve All," "Take Time To Be Kind," "All is One," and "Save the Planet." The focus of the original restaurant was on treating all customers equally well, a strategy that has paid off worldwide. The company's anti-elitist—and ostensibly American—stand has made people around the world feel comfortable and welcome in the Hard Rocks, and customers have responded by buying the chain's hamburgers, beers, T-shirts, and pins. Hard Rock Cafe has always placed importance on environmental and humanitarian issues, pursued with a definite sense of "coolness." This emphasis has contributed to the chain's popularity with customers, some of whom could be called "followers," so devoted are they to the restaurants. Hard Rock Cafes around the globe still adhere to the original vision of its founders, which was to provide customers with a complete rock experience.

INFLUENCES

The Hard Rock Cafe and its phenomenal success has inspired many similar ventures, from Dick Clark's American Bandstand Grill to Elvis Presley's Memphis. As the popularity of themed restaurants grows, the competition for customers increases. The toughest competition Hard Rock Cafe faces is from Planet Hollywood, an international movie-memorabilia restaurant chain.

Morton brought a lawsuit against Planet Hollywood in the early 1990s. He explained in a 1994 *Restaurants & Institutions* interview what provoked his action: "Well, to cut through it, we allege that Planet Hollywood misappropriated our trade secrets and know-how and breached fiduciary duties, and this was all while Robert Earl was the CEO of the Rank Hard Rocks and at the same exact time, CEO of Planet Hollywood. He was CEO of both organizations at the same time. I think the right place for the litigation is in the courts, and that's where we are." Morton eventually settled the dispute out of court, but Planet Hollywood remains a strong competitor for the Hard Rock chain.

CURRENT TRENDS

To set Hard Rock Cafe apart from its competitors, management is turning increasingly to the rock 'n roll roots of the organization. In 1977 Hard Rock teamed up with Rhino Records to form Hard Rock Records. The label produces rock 'n roll compilations celebrating the last 25 years of popular music. The company is considering expansion in the area of concert venues, and continues to strengthen a long-time commitment to live music by sponsoring tours of Cafe sites, including a Jonny Lang tour in 1997. Hard Rock Cafe is also sponsoring a weekly show on VH1 that highlights live performances. In addition to the new ventures, Hard Rock Cafe continues to sell its signature T-shirts, pins, and leather jackets.

The link with rock 'n roll is what sets the Hard Rock apart from other "eater-tainment" institutions. Regarding competition with other themed restaurants, founder Morton told *Restaurants & Institutions*, "We've always had competitors out there, and their theming is in a certain way like a Halloween party. They put on a costume. I don't think we put on costumes at the Hard Rock. I think there's a real love for what the Hard Rock has put out there in its association with the rock-music entertainment industry."

CHRONOLOGY:
Key Dates for Hard Rock Cafe

1971: Founded on June 14

1973: Paul McCartney plays at Hard Rock in London

1977: Forms Hard Rock Records

1983: Hard Rock offers stock publicly in England

1985: Participates in Live Aid

1988: Tigrett sells his 54 percent

1990: Launches Signature Series of charity

1991: Veggie burger is introduced

1996: Rank Organization, PLC purchases Hard Rock America

Hard Rock's focus in the past has been on tourists, but the company now aims to be a destination for hometown diners as well. While Hard Rocks continue to be welcome oases for Americans abroad, and wildly popular stops for international (and American) tourists in the United States, a current goal for the chain is to offer such quality food, service, and entertainment that people desire to return to the Hard Rock in their city again and again.

PRODUCTS

In 1998 approximately 80 Hard Rock Cafes operated in more than 30 countries. The company hopes to have more than 100 restaurants in operation by the end of the century. Each location offers logo-emblazoned merchandise, Hard Rock records, and live music events, in addition to food and drink. Peter Morton also operates a Hard Rock hotel and casino in Las Vegas, Nevada. Further development in gaming and lodging may be in the company's future.

CORPORATE CITIZENSHIP

Good global citizenship was one of the cornerstones on which the Hard Rock Cafe was founded, and the company continues to support a wide range of charitable efforts. Environmentalists, AIDS organizations, famine victims, and the homeless are only some of the groups that

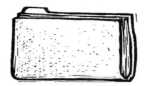

HARD ROCK PLAYS SOFTLY ON THE PLANET

Of all the prescription drugs in the United States, at least one quarter contain active ingredients derived from plants, the majority of which come from tropical rain forests. Although rain forests account for less than 6 percent of the world's land mass, they are unarguably the world's most biologically diverse habitats. The Hard Rock Cafe, in association with Conservation International, strives to protect the valuable rain forests by purchasing sustainable harvested Brazil nuts for dessert toppings. The Hard Rock's slogan "Save the Planet" is a symbol of the Cafe's commitment to saving the environment while simultaneously providing customers with dessert toppings that are easily replenished. By providing an economic incentive for Brazilians to conserve the trees and plants that provide products such as chocolate, coffee, and nuts, the Hard Rock Cafe is actively working against rain forest destruction. Eat at Hard Rock and "Save the Planet."

have benefited from the Hard Rock's social conscience. Specific charities that have enjoyed long relationships with the Hard Rock include Friends of the Earth, PETA (People for the Ethical Treatment of Animals), and the Elton John AIDS Foundation. The company's strong links with the music business fueled its relationship with the Nordoff Robbins Music Therapy Centre, a United Kingdom- and New York-based charity that reaches out to autistic children through the power of music.

Hard Rock Cafe has catered famous charitable rock events by setting up backstage restaurants, and has been a sponsor of such charity rock events as Live Aid, The Wall Concert, The Nelson Mandela Tribute, and tribute events for rock greats Bob Dylan, John Lennon, and Freddie Mercury.

Another humanitarian effort of the Hard Rock is the Signature Series, a special line of T-shirts designed and signed by rock stars and printed in limited editions. Profits from sales of these shirts benefit each artist's charity of choice. More than $4.5 million had been raised by the program by 1996. Participants have included Sting, Elton John, Aerosmith, REM's Michael Stipe, the Grateful Dead, and John Lennon.

In addition to its substantial monetary donations, Hard Rock has increased public awareness of such issues as AIDS, homelessness, environmental abuse, and edu-

cation through music." To continue these social and environmental good works, the company maintains a corporate foundation that oversees contributions and does the administrative work involved in philanthropy.

GLOBAL PRESENCE

Hard Rock Cafes are located throughout North America, Europe, and Asia, as well as in South America, Africa, the Middle East, and Australia. The global thirst for all things American continues to drive the expansion of the chain, offering as it does a glimpse of hip American rock culture. As the planet shrinks through communications and American culture and music permeate world culture, the chain's global possibilities appear limitless.

EMPLOYMENT

Everyone involved in the Hard Rock Cafe has a dedication to the goals expressed in the restaurants' mottoes, and especially to the world of rock 'n roll. Many young members of local waitstaffs are involved in music, whether it be collecting CDs or playing in a garage band. Occasionally, the son, daughter, brother, or niece of a rockstar or popular figure is hired as a waiter, waitress, or even a manager.

SOURCES OF INFORMATION

Bibliography

Bartlett, Michael. "Peter Morton: The Hard Rock Cafe Co-founder Talks About Saving the Planet, the Myth of the All-Wise CEO and Why Gambling Is the Defense Industry of the '90s." *Restaurants & Institutions,* 15 November 1994.

Davis, G. Alisha. "Striking Gold in its Silver Year." *International Business,* July/August 1996.

Howard, Theresa. "Hard Rock Broadens Scope, Keeps Finger on Pulse of Cool." *Nation's Restaurants News,* 30 June 1997.

Kochak, Jacque. "That's Eater-tainment!" *Restaurants Business,* 15 February 1998.

Martin, Richard. "Peter Morton & Isaac Tigrett." *Nation's Restaurant News,* February 1996.

"Morton Sells His Piece of the 'Rock' to Rank." *Nation's Restaurant News,* 17 June 1996.

Soeder, John, "Hard Rock Cafe Reunited." *Restaurants Hospitality,* July 1996.

For additional industry research:
Investigate companies by their Standard Industrial Classification Codes, also known as SICs. Hard Rock Cafe's primary SIC is:

5812 Eating Places

Harley-Davidson, Inc.

OVERVIEW

Harley-Davidson, Inc. was the only major American motorcycle company in the 1990s. It is also considered one of the best-managed companies in the world. Mostly known for its heavyweight motorcycles, the company also produces rocket bikes and touring motorcycles. Harley-Davidson owns nearly 50 percent of the U.S. motorcycle market and 22 percent of the Pacific Rim market.

For several years, the demand for Harleys has far outweighed the supply. Harley enthusiasts have transformed the riding experience into a cultural phenomenon. Dealers have reported a two-year wait for some models and instances of used bikes being sold for more than the list price.

Harley-Davidson prides itself on the quality of its products and the loyalty of its customers. The Harley Owners Group (HOG) is dedicated to building life-long customers and a community of lasting friendships. The group markets the motorcycle experience through apparel, corporate-licensed Harley products, and extensive community involvement.

COMPANY FINANCES

In 1997, worldwide net sales totaled $1.8 billion, a 15 percent jump from the previous year. Of this, 78 percent was from motorcycles, 14 percent from parts and accessories, and 8 percent from merchandise and other sources. The company's operating income in 1997 increased 16 percent from the previous year, reaching $265.5 million. Worldwide motorcycle shipments totaled

FOUNDED: 1903

Contact Information:

HEADQUARTERS: 3700 W. Juneau Ave.
   Milwaukee, WI 53208
PHONE: (414)342-4680
FAX: (414)342-8230
URL: http://www.harley-davidson.com

FINANCES:

Harley-Davidson Net Sales, 1994-1997 (million dollars)

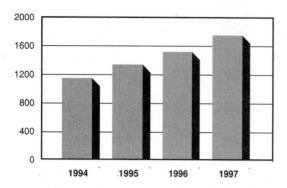

Harley-Davidson 1997 Stock Prices (dollars)

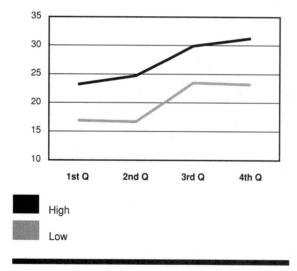

The stock price ranged from $16 3/4 to $31 1/4 per share over the prior 12-month period.

ANALYSTS' OPINIONS

According to *Forbes,* "Doubting Harley-Davidson is almost like spitting on the American flag. Harley's inspiring comeback has been a cheering symbol of the American industrial renaissance. . . . Buying a Harley brings membership into a brotherhood. . . . It's a membership so fiercely loyal to the brand that non-Harley bikers are not welcome at the annual rallies in Sturgis, South Dakota, and Daytona, Florida. . . . It's that loyalty, that intangible asset, that has convinced investors that Harley is a real growth stock. That loyalty may, however, be a wasting asset as hard-core Harley fanatics age."

In 1997, *Industry Week* listed Harley-Davidson among the 100 best-managed companies in the world. *Standard & Poor's February 1998 Stock Report* said to expect consistent above-average growth for the next five years. Projecting 15 percent growth, *Standard and Poor's* highly recommends buying Harley-Davidson stock.

HISTORY

William Harley and William, Walter, and Arthur Davidson produced their first motor-assisted bicycle in 1903. The motorcycle quickly became popular, and most were sold before they went out the factory doors. In 1909, they introduced the V-Twin engine, the feature that quickly became the trademark of the Harley-Davidson motorcycle. This engine enabled motor enthusiasts to travel up to 60 miles per hour—double the maximum speed of its predecessors.

In the early 1900s Harley-Davidson motorcycles were used in U.S.-Mexican border skirmishes with Pancho Villa. Already in use by the nation's police force, World War I placed a high demand on new vehicles. In fact, it had been reported that by the end of the war 20,000 Harleys had been used to support the infantry.

Prior to World War I, an estimated 150 motorcycle companies were competing in the United States. After the Great Depression, however, only Harley-Davidson and Indian remained. Harley-Davidson survived by continuing to support the police and military and by expanding into international markets. World War II again increased demand for motorcycles. The company produced more than 90,000 motorcycles for the American and Allied forces and was awarded by the armed services with honors for excellence in wartime production.

After World War II, motorcycle demand boomed. Consumers acquired increasing amounts of expendable capital and leisure time, and in response the company began producing a variety of recreational motorcycles. Pop-

132,300 units in 1997, 27.3 percent of which was exported throughout the world.

Since going public, Harley-Davidson stock has been a strong performer. In fact, a person who invested $1,000 in the company's stock at the initial public offering (and reinvested all dividends) would have found that the value of their stock had reached $40,670 at year-end 1997. As of March 1997, there were 75,733,097 outstanding shares of common stock. The total market value of common stocks held by nonaffiliates (i.e., people not considered officers of the company) was approximately $2.6 billion.

The 1997 Heritage Springer Softail was designed to resemble the 1948 Harley-Davidson Panhead motorcycle. (Photograph by Mike Poche. AP/Wide World Photos, Inc.)

ular movies of the day such as *The Wild Ones* and *The Great Escape* glamorized the motorcycle lifestyle, and such elements of this culture, including black leather jackets, became increasingly popular. Indian closed down in 1953, leaving Harley-Davidson as the only American motorcycle company in a growing market. The introduction of the Sportster motorcycle in 1957 continued to propel the company's sales.

Although the company's founders died in the 1950s, Harley-Davidson remained family-owned until it went public for the first time in 1965. It merged with American Machine and Foundry (AMF) in 1969, adding considerable resources and financial strength. Also in 1969, Japanese companies began importing motorcycles to the United States. The cheaper imports and Harley's manufacturing problems (due to the company's rapid growth in production) caused sales to drop throughout the 1970s, and the company was put up for sale.

In 1981 more than a dozen members of the Harley-Davidson management team purchased the company in a leveraged buyout. Huge tariffs on Japanese imports saved the company from bankruptcy, giving it enough time to restructure. The company went public again in 1986. Implementing new management techniques and focusing on quality, the team turned the company around. In 1985 Harley-Davidson had only 16 percent of the U.S. heavyweight motorcycle market, but by 1996 had captured nearly 50 percent of the market.

The 1990s brought a continued consumer interest in motorcycles and particularly the Harley-Davidson brand. The company began selling clothing and acquired a finance company and a 49 percent share of the Wisconsin-based motorcycle manufacturer Buell Motorcycle. Buell sold a record 4,415 motorcycles in 1996 and was launched in Europe and Australia in 1997.

STRATEGY

Harley-Davidson's focus on quality has put its products in great demand. But with this demand far exceeding production in 1996, management unveiled a plan to open two new plants and increase production to 200,000 units per year by the company's centennial in 2003. The company has also devoted $40 million to building a new Product Development Center in an attempt to accelerate research and development. To help boost European sales, the company has also introduced Harley-Davidson Legend, a line of cologne, aftershave, and deodorant in this market.

By licensing such products and sponsoring rallies, Harley Davidson has successfully marketed the motorcycle lifestyle. With 380,000 members in more than 100 countries, the Harley Owners Group (HOG) is the largest motorcycle club in the world. HOG focuses on building lifelong friendships and customers. Sponsorship of group chapters has grown 95 percent since 1985, reaching 988 in 1998. More than 70 rallies in 1997 drew in more than 127,000 people around the world.

The company has been protective of its corporate image throughout the years. In 1994, for example, Harley-Davidson banned the use of the Confederate flag from Harley-Davidson T-shirts and other products it licenses. "The decision is by no means a sign of disrespect for the history of the South or the people of the South," said Harley-Davidson spokesman Mark Barbato. "It's more a question of hesitancy to offend people who may consider the flag a symbol of bigotry or racism." To further protect its image, the company sued Lorillard Tobacco to get out of a cigarette licensing deal in 1995.

CURRENT TRENDS

The typical modern Harley rider is a weekend warrior, has a college education, and has a nice chunk of disposable income. "Harley's are hip," claimed one wire service report. "Movie stars, wealthy business leaders, and sports figures ride hogs. So do doctors, lawyers, real-estate executives, and other solid citizens, who shuck their suits and ties for the weekend, deck out in Harley gear and roar off," bringing many a feeling of freedom and adventure.

PRODUCTS

Harley-Davidson makes heavyweight motorcycles, rocket bikes, and touring motorcycles. Models include the

FAST FACTS:
About Harley-Davidson, Inc.

Ownership: Harley-Davidson is a publicly owned company traded on the New York Stock Exchange.

Ticker symbol: HDI

Officers: Richard F. Teerlink, Chmn., 60, 1996 base salary $1,233,751; Jeffrey L. Bleustein, Pres., & CEO, 57, 1996 base salary $732,309; Thomas A. Gelb, VP Continuous Improvement, 1996 base salary $503,116

Employees: 5,200

Chief Competitors: For four decades, beginning in 1953, Harley-Davidson was the only American manufacturer of heavyweight motorcycles. In the 1990s, several startup companies entered the market, including Buell Motorcycle Co., Polaris, and Excelsior-Henderson, but the company's main competitors are still Japanese and European manufacturers including: Honda; BMW; Kawasaki; Suzuki; Yamaha; and Triumph.

CHRONOLOGY:
Key Dates for Harley-Davidson, Inc.

1903: William Harley, along with the Davidson brothers, William, Walter, and Arthur, produce first motor-assisted bicycle; establish Harley-Davidson Motor Company

1909: Introduces the V-Twin engine

1921: Harley-Davidson machine is used by winner of the first race in which motorists reach average speeds of more than 100 miles-per-hour

1941: Company turns entire manufacturing effort toward supplying U.S. and Allied troops in World War I

1953: Becomes the sole American motorcycle manufacturer

1957: Introduces the Sportster model "superbike"

1965: Company goes public

1969: American Machine and Foundry Co. (AMF) buys Harley-Davidson

1975: Vaughn Beals is put at the head of Harley-Davidson; Jeff Bleustein is named chief engineer

1981: Thirteen company executives, with the help of Citicorp, take control of Harley-Davidson from AMF

1984: Establishes SuperRide promotion

1996: Captures nearly 50 percent of the U.S. heavyweight motorcycle market

Electra Glide, Sportster, Fat Boy, Low Rider, and Super Glide. The company also makes motorcycle parts and accessories and offers apparel and corporate-licensed Harley products.

CORPORATE CITIZENSHIP

Behind the rough exterior of the Harley-Davidson image is a company well known for acts of compassion and charity. The company believes that being a leader in the business world means being involved with society at all levels. Among the company's beneficiaries is the Muscular Dystrophy Association, which has received more than $25 million from Harley-Davidson; the Harley-Davidson Foundation Inc., which contributes to such organizations as the United Way, Businesses Against Drunk Drivers, Boy Scouts of America, and the Greater Milwaukee Educational Trust; American Diabetes Association; and many other local organizations throughout the state of Wisconsin. Interestingly, the company also matches employees' volunteer work with monetary contributions.

GLOBAL PRESENCE

In 1997, 27 percent of the company's sales were derived from outside the United States. The company has been selling motorcycles to the Asian market for more than 80 years. Its wholly owned subsidiary in Japan services more than 90 dealers in the Pacific Rim market. In the late 1990s, there were nearly 250 Harley-Davidson dealerships in Europe and 8 European distributorships in Italy, Spain, Scandinavia, South Africa, the Middle East, and central Europe.

Latin America is another area in which heavyweight motorcycles are becoming increasingly popular. Harley-Davidson first introduced its products to this market in the 1920s when it produced motorcycles for the Mexican police force. The company is currently investing a great deal to expand operations in Latin American countries such as Costa Rica, Columbia, Ecuador, Peru, and Venezuela. In July 1998, the company announced the launch of an assembly plant in Brazil. In 1997, Harley-Davidson exported 600 motorcycles to Brazil. Establishing an assembly operation in this country is hoped to greatly increase sales in the country by utilizing its "free-trade zone" rules and eliminating current trade restraints and tariffs.

Harley-Davidson sponsors motorcycle and touring rallies in the United States, Canada, New Zealand, Australia, Japan, and Europe.

EMPLOYMENT

In 1997 employment at Harley-Davidson totaled 5,000. The company provides education and training pro-

HARLEY RIDERS SHARE A COMMON BOND

There is one American product with such loyal support that having the company's symbol tattooed on some body part is akin to wearing a medal: Harley-Davidson motorcycles. Harley riders make up a unique brotherhood, and people from all walks of life often come together to celebrate this common bond. The Harley Owners Group is the largest motorcycle club in the world, with nearly 300,000 members and almost 900 dealer-sponsored chapters worldwide. By creating opportunities for bikers to bond, H.O.G. instills a dedication to Harley-Davidson unmatched by any other motorcycle group. H.O.G. members take part not only in state, regional, and national rallies, but also in international events. In addition to supporting rallies, H.O.G. also sponsors rider safety seminars, motorcycle maintenance classes, and even fundraising events for the Muscular Dystrophy Association. Perhaps more of a lifestyle than a club, the Harley Owners Group epitomizes the entire motorcycle experience.

grams for employees and a gain-sharing program that monetarily rewards employees for helping meet corporate goals. The company's goal of increasing production to more than 200,000 motorcycles per year and their plan to open two new plants by the year 2003 should create many new employment opportunities.

SOURCES OF INFORMATION

Bibliography

Golfen, Bob. "Scalpers Cater to Demand for Harley-Davidson Motorcycles." *Knight-Ridder/Tribune Business News,* 15 November 1994.

"Harley-Davidson, Inc." *Hoover's Company Profiles,* 29 March 1998. Available at http://www.hoovers.com.

"Harley-Davidson, Inc." *Standard & Poor's Stock Report,* 21 February 1998.

Harley-Davidson, Inc. 1997 Annual Report, Harley-Davidson, Inc., Milwaukee, 1998.

Harley-Davidson's Home Page, April 1998. Available at http://www.harley-davidson.com.

Machan, Dyan. "Is the Hog Going Soft?" *Forbes,* 10 March 1997.

Soraghan, Mike. "Confederate Flag Supporters Rev Opposition to Harley-Davidson's Ban." *Knight-Ridder/Tribune Business News,* 29 December 1994.

"That Vroom! You Hear May Not Be a Harley." *Business Week,* 20 October 1997.

For an annual report:
write: Harley-Davidson, Inc., 3700 W. Juneau Ave., PO Box 653, Milwaukee, WI 53201.

For additional industry research:
Investigate companies by their Standard Industrial Classification Codes, also known as SICs. Harley-Davidson's primary SICs are:

3751 Motorcycles, Bicycles and Parts

6719 Holding Companies, NEC

Harpo Entertainment Group

OVERVIEW

Harpo Entertainment is wholly and privately owned by Oprah Winfrey. The company has four divisions: Harpo Productions, Harpo Films, Oprah Winfrey Presents, and Oprah Online. The television talk show *The Oprah Winfrey Show* produces nearly 70 percent of the company's estimated $150 million in revenue. The show is seen in approximately 120 countries and enjoys the highest ratings of any talk show in the world.

Oprah Winfrey is a successful entertainer, known for her ability to connect with people. Although Harpo Entertainment doesn't release strategic plans, the feeling is Oprah wants to bring what she believes is good, wholesome entertainment to her fans. Many of her movies and television specials, for example, deal with strong, courageous women.

COMPANY FINANCES

Harpo is a privately held company; therefore, it doesn't release financial information to the public. Sales estimates for the company ran between $140 and $150 million in 1997, up 7.1 percent from the estimated $140 million the company earned in 1996. In 1986 when Harpo Entertainment gave King World Productions the right to distribute *The Oprah Winfrey Show* through the year 2000, it was said King World received 43 percent of the gross profits for the first two years of the deal. After that, Harpo's take increased from 57 percent to approximately 70 percent. As the show grosses over $180 million per year, Harpo received (after the second year of syndication) over $103 million. *The Oprah Winfrey Show* generates approximately 68 percent of Harpo's income.

FOUNDED: 1986

Contact Information:
HEADQUARTERS: 110 N. Carpenter St.
   Chicago, IL 60607
PHONE: (312)633-1000
FAX: (312)633-1111
URL: http://www.oprahshow.com

FAST FACTS:

About Harpo Entertainment Group

Ownership: Harpo Entertainment Group is a privately held company owned by Oprah Winfrey.

Officers: Oprah Winfrey, Chmn. & CEO; Jeffrey Jacobs, Pres. & COO; Tim Bennett, Pres., Harpo Productions; Doug Pattison, VP & CFO

Employees: 175 (1997)

Principal Subsidiary Companies: The Harpo Entertainment Group consists of Oprah Online, Oprah Winfrey Presents, Harpo Productions, and Harpo Films.

Chief Competitors: Harpo Entertainment Group competes with every film developing firm and production company. Included are: dick clark productions; Dream Works SKG; Sony; and Time Warner.

ANALYSTS' OPINIONS

Oprah Winfrey is one of the most successful entertainers in history. *Forbes* magazine consistently ranks her among the top 10 highest-paid entertainers, ranking her third in 1997. Analysts say her influence is enormous, pointing to the success of her recently launched book club. Some point out that her integrity is practically unquestioned among her viewers; her "every woman" style of relating to her audience and people in general give her credibility. Other fans can relate to Oprah because she tells of personal experiences. In addition, she offers practical advice about how people can improve their lives.

Some critics don't care for what *The Wall Street Journal* called the "Oprahfication" of America. These critics feel talk shows, such as Oprah's, make it too easy for people to feel good about themselves.

HISTORY

Oprah Winfrey began her career as a news anchor in Nashville, Tennessee, at the age of 19. From there she traveled to Baltimore, Maryland, to anchor the evening news on a local station. Soon she switched to co-hosting a local morning talk show called *People Are*

Talking. As the popularity of the show grew, ABC moved her from the affiliate station in Baltimore to the one in Chicago. Oprah began hosting *AM Chicago,* focusing on ordinary people and their concerns. The show soon became number one and was renamed *The Oprah Winfrey Show.*

Oprah wanted to assume more control of her show, so she obtained the syndication rights to it and formed Harpo (Oprah spelled backwards) Entertainment in 1986. After acting in several movies, Oprah decided her production company would also make movies and television specials, and Harpo Films was made a subsidiary. In 1990 Harpo bought a production studio in Chicago. This move made Oprah one of only three women (the others being Mary Pickford and Lucille Ball) in television and film history to own her own production studio.

STRATEGY

Oprah Winfrey's strategy seems to be to control her destiny. *The Oprah Winfrey Show* is extremely successful, with over 20 million viewers. Its success comes from Oprah's feel for so-called ordinary people. She comes across as an ordinary person, with ordinary concerns, and uses these as topics for her show. Her enthusiasm for a topic is evident, as no topic is covered without Oprah's approval.

Prior to the debut of *The Oprah Winfrey Show,* there were few talk shows on the air, but as Oprah's show gained popularity new ones were introduced. Soon there were hundreds to choose from and the hosts fought to distinguish themselves from one another. Some hosts used "tabloid shows" to generate high ratings; such programs focused on negative, the bizarre, and the sensational. Initially Oprah tried to compete with such shows, but eventually she was disgusted by it all. In 1994 Oprah pledged that her show would no longer cover sensational topics, but would focus instead on positive stories that could make a difference in her viewers' lives. Her ratings suffered, falling from the number-one spot. But Oprah fought back, and her show consistently falls in the number-one or number-two spot nationwide.

Through her film division, Oprah seeks to offer movies and programs she believes most people want to see. Keeping control of the company allows her to develop projects others might pass over.

CURRENT TRENDS

Oprah doesn't just follow trends, she creates them. An avid reader, Oprah decided to share some of her favorite books with her audience, and in September 1996 she created Oprah's Book Club. After one year, millions of people who hadn't picked up a book in a long time were avidly reading Oprah's selections. Every book selected, some of them obscure, averaged over a million copies sold, becoming instant best-sellers.

One episode of Oprah's show dealt with "mad cow" disease and the outbreaks occurring in Great Britain. After listening to a guest describe the disease, Oprah commented that she had eaten her last hamburger. That one remark caused beef prices to plunge, creating huge losses for cattle farmers. Texas cattle farmers sued Oprah under a food libel law, but she was found not guilty in a 1998 trial.

PRODUCTS

Harpo Entertainment produces 200 episodes of *The Oprah Winfrey Show* every year. The company also produces movies such as *Beloved;* television specials released under Oprah Winfrey Presents, such as *Before Women Had Wings;* and children's television specials. In the late 1990s Harpo had a five-year movie deal with Disney and a deal with Capital Cities/ABC to produce or star in six made-for-television movies. The company also maintains Oprah Online through the America Online Internet service.

CORPORATE CITIZENSHIP

Because of her background of poverty and abuse, Oprah contributes to charitable organizations that help women and children. In 1997 she attended the President's Summit in Philadelphia, joining the call to volunteerism—something she encourages on her show. Oprah has established educational scholarships at colleges nationwide. In late 1997 she formed the Oprah's Angel Network and encouraged her viewers to get involved. She asks that all share their good fortune with others. One of the features of the Angel Network is the World's Largest Piggy Bank; viewers are asked to contribute their change for college scholarships across the country. Another Angel Network program brings volunteers together to build a Habitat for Humanity home in every market where Oprah's show is carried.

GLOBAL PRESENCE

The Oprah Winfrey Show is seen by more than 20 million people a day on more than 200 televisions in the United States. Estimates indicate the show is seen in anywhere from 64 to 132 foreign countries and is heard and seen over Armed Forces Radio and TV Service.

CHRONOLOGY:

Key Dates for Harpo Entertainment Group

1986: Oprah Winfrey obtains syndication rights to her show and forms Harpo Entertainment

1990: Buys a production studio in Chicago, Illinois

1994: Winfrey pledges her show will no longer cover sensational topics

1996: Creates Oprah's Book Club

1997: Winfrey attends the President's Summit in Philadelphia, Pennsylvania

1998: Winfrey is found not guilty in suit brought upon her by Texas cattle farmers

SHE FEELS YOUR PAIN

It was in 1986, with the syndication of her hour-long talk show, that Oprah Winfrey ushered in the age of television as public confessional. Oprah led the way with her willingness to talk about her own troubled past and has since offered up a steady stream of shows on battered women, alcoholism, and fashion make overs. It is these types of topics that make up the very life-blood of daytime television, and Oprah's most devoted audience can be found among her female viewers. Indeed, Harpo is a predominantly female-run company, and one guest described the show as "a raucous gathering in a ladies' room where women who have just met become instant confidants." It might sound like a strange concept for one of the highest-rated talk shows in television history, but it works.

EMPLOYMENT

Despite her outward openness, Oprah is a private person, and she expects her employees to value and protect her privacy. A demanding perfectionist, Oprah is nonetheless known for her good treatment of employees, who say she is humanistic in her business approach, unlike the typical corporate CEO. Oprah weighs the impact of her decisions on her employees. She is also known to be generous with gifts and even built the Harpo Cafe at the studio.

SOURCES OF INFORMATION

Bibliography

Dickerson, Debra. "A Woman's Woman." *U.S. News and World Report,* 29 September 1997.

"Harpo Entertainment Group." *Hoover's Online,* 25 April 1997. Available at http://www.hoovers.com.

"The Oprah Winfrey Show," 20 April 1998. Available at http://www.oprahshow.com.

Rebello, Stephen. "Brand Oprah." *Success,* May 1998.

Sorkins Directory of Business and Government, Vol. 4, Chicago Edition. St. Louis, MO: Sorkins Directory, Inc., 1998.

"Time 25 - Oprah Winfrey." *Time,* 17 June 1996.

For additional industry research:

Investigate companies by their Standard Industrial Classification Codes, also known as SICs. Harpo Entertainment's primary SIC is:

7812 Motion picture and Video Production

Hasbro, Inc.

OVERVIEW

Hasbro, Inc. is currently the second largest toy maker in the United States, ranked only behind Mattel. The company designs and manufactures a diverse line of toy products and related items throughout the world, including traditional board and card games, electronic and interactive CD-ROM games, puzzles, action toys, plush products, and infant products. Hasbro also licenses a number of trade names and property rights for use in connection with the sale by others of noncompeting toys and nontoy products.

The company is organized into a Toy Group and a Games Group. The Toy Group includes the Playskool, Playskool Baby, Hasbro, Kid Dimension, and Kenner divisions. The Games Group includes the Milton Bradley and Parker Brothers divisions. Milton Bradley produces a line of more than 200 games and puzzles for children and adults. Its most popular products include Scrabble, Battleship, Chutes and Ladders, Operation, and Twister. Parker Brothers' staple products include Trivial Pursuit, Monopoly, Clue, Risk, and Sorry!. Hasbro Interactive develops interactive CD-ROM games based on the company's traditional products such as Monopoly and Battleship. Hasbro's Emerging Business Group has developed the Super Soaker line of water toys, the Koosh soft play items, and a line of interactive candy.

Hasbro continues to market its classic items, such as Tonka Trucks, Nerf products, and its extensive line of Kenner toys. These, and the high-quality infant and toddler products from Playskool and Playskool Kids, are major sources of revenue. The company plans to regain the number-one toy maker position by aggressive marketing, corporate acquisitions, and introducing

FOUNDED: 1923 by Henry and Hilal Hassenfeld as Hassenfeld Brothers Company

Contact Information:

HEADQUARTERS: 1027 Newport Ave.
   Pawtucket, RI 02861
PHONE: (401)431-8697
FAX: (401)431-8535
URL: http://www.hasbro.com

FINANCES:

Hasbro, Inc.
Revenues, 1994-1997
(million dollars)

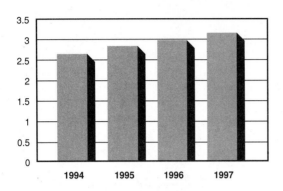

Hasbro, Inc.
1997 Stock Prices
(dollars)

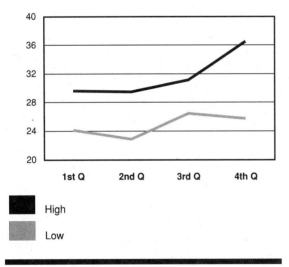

new toys based on popular movies, comic books, and television programs. Hasbro also plans to invest in the further development of CD-ROM games and online gaming.

COMPANY FINANCES

In 1997 worldwide sales totaled $3.12 billion. Of this, 37 percent was derived from two retail outlets: Toys 'R' Us (22 percent) and Wal-Mart (15 percent). Also in 1997 the company spent $386,912 on royalties and product development and approximately $411,574 on marketing programs. Hasbro's current licensing agreements are expected to cost the company up to $500 million in royalties between 1998 and 2005.

As of March 1998, more than 133 million shares of Hasbro's common stock were outstanding. The total market value of the common stocks held by nonaffiliates (i.e., people not considered officers of the company) was approximately $4.49 billion. Hasbro's stock prices ranged from $22 7/8 to $36 3/4 over the prior 12-month period.

ANALYSTS' OPINIONS

Standard & Poor's includes Hasbro in its S&P 500 index, and its February 1998 Stock Report recommends buying Hasbro stock. They expect the company's new products, reduced inventory, and corporate restructuring program will help the stock outperform the market.

Some consumers, however, have been complaining about unfair business practices. A 1998 *Fortune* magazine article notes that many collectors are asking why the toy maker allows its miniature sports collectibles to be sold "out the back door." The article notes that "out the back door" sales are a problem with all toy collectibles, but most seriously with Kenner's Starting Lineup figures. This line of miniature sports action figures initially flopped, but demand for them increased after production was cut and shortages developed—or as the article suggests, were encouraged.

HISTORY

Hasbro traces its origin to an enterprise founded in Providence, Rhode Island, by Henry, Hilal, and Herman Hassenfeld, brothers who had emigrated from Poland. They formed the Hassenfeld Brothers Company in 1923 to distribute fabric remnants. Hilal Hassenfeld became involved in other textiles, and Henry took control of the company. Although he took the role of a father figure at the company, Henry was a tough and shrewd businessman. During the Great Depression, with 200 employees, Hassenfeld Brothers commanded annual sales of $500,000 from sales of pencil boxes and cloth zipper pouches filled with school supplies. At that point, the company's pencil supplier had raised its prices and began to sell its own boxes at prices lower than Hassenfeld's. Henry Hassenfeld responded with a vow to enter the pencil business himself, and in 1935 Hassenfeld Brothers began manufacturing pencils. This product line would provide the company with a steady source of revenue for the next 45 years.

During the late 1930s Hassenfeld Brothers began to manufacture toys. Some of the early products included toy medical kits and modeling clay. During World War II, Henry's younger son Merrill acted on a customer's suggestion to make a junior air-raid warden kit complete with flashlights and toy gas masks.

By 1942, as demand for school supplies declined, the company had mainly focused on toy manufacturing. During this time, Hassenfeld ventured into plastics to better support its toy making. In 1952 Mr. Potato Head became the first toy advertised on television. In the 1960s, the toy division introduced G.I. Joe. An instant success, the doll quickly became their most popular toy.

Although still run by the Hassenfeld family, the company went public in 1968 and changed its name to Hasbro Industries. The pencil and toy divisions were run by different family members in the 1970s, and disagreements regarding finances, leadership, and the company's future direction led to a separation in 1980. The toy division continued to operate under the Hasbro name, and the pencil division became the Empire Pencil Corporation.

Under new CEO Stephen Hassenfeld, Hasbro grew rapidly in the 1980s. He reduced the number of products by one-third in order to concentrate on specific markets. The company also refocused on simpler toys, like Mr. Potato Head-products that were inexpensive to manufacture, could be sold at lower prices, and had longer life cycles. Hasbro introduced a successful line of toys during this time, which included Transformers and a smaller version of G.I. Joe dolls. In 1983, Hasbro purchased much of Knickerbocker's inventory, including Raggedy Ann and Raggedy Andy dolls, from Warner Bros.

In the early 1980s Hasbro was the sixth-best-selling toy maker in the United States, with revenues of $225.4 million and $15.2 million in profit. Hasbro surpassed Mattel as the country's number-one toy maker when it bought Milton Bradley (the nation's fifth-best-selling toy maker at the time) in 1984. The company acquired Cabbage Patch Kids, Scrabble, Parcheesi, and other products from Coleco in 1989. Stephen Hassenfeld died that year, and his brother, Alan, took control of the company.

In 1991 the company purchased Tonka for $486 million and, in that same year, established operations in Greece, Mexico, and Hungary. In 1992 Hasbro purchased Nomura Toys, a Japanese corporation, and acquired a majority interest in the Asian toy distributor Palmyra. In 1994 the company formed a joint venture with Connector Set Limited Partnership to market its K'Nex construction toys outside the United States. It also established operations in Israel, purchased British game maker John Waddington, and the puzzle and board game businesses of Western Publishing. Mattel again became the number-one toy maker in 1994 and attempted a takeover bid for Hasbro. Hasbro blocked the takeover by insisting that antitrust authorities in the United States and Europe would block the sale.

The 1990s were also a time of scandal for the toy maker. The Federal Trade Commission (FTC) accused

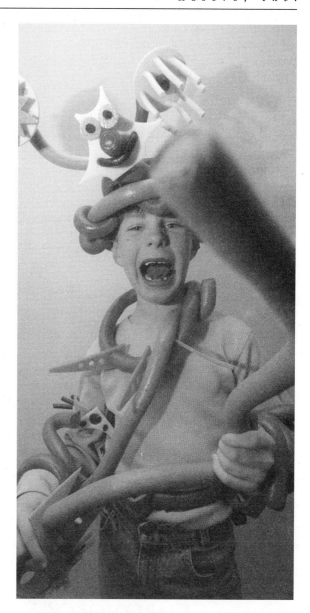

Hasbro's Toobers&Zots are made of colorful soft foam pieces that can be twisted and turned into a multitude of wacky positions. (Photograph by Adam Nadel. AP/Wide World Photos, Inc.)

Hasbro of deceptive advertising and of violating antitrust laws.

STRATEGY

Hasbro plans to surpass Mattel as the number-one toy maker again. Its strategy includes continuously developing and acquiring new products and implementing an aggressive marketing campaign. New products in-

clude computer versions of their popular board games and action figures based on popular television and movie characters.

CURRENT TRENDS

Acquisitions are likely to continue at Hasbro. In 1997 the company announced plans to acquire Tiger Electronics, Russ Berrie's Cap Toys, and OddzOn Products. In 1998 *The Wall Street Journal* speculated that Hasbro might also be eyeing Galoob Toys as a potential acquisition. They also reported that two former Milton Bradley officials had been indicted for tax fraud and money laundering. Although Hasbro settled its deceptive advertising lawsuit with the FTC in 1993, they were still found guilty of violating anti-trust laws in 1997 by entering into vertical agreements with Toys 'R' Us to restrict certain toys to warehouse club retailers.

PRODUCTS

Throughout the years, Hasbro has introduced many nationally recognized products. Toys have ranged from board games to action figures geared toward several age groups. The Kenner division develops Batman, G.I. Joe, and *Star Wars* action figures. These particular products are especially popular toys for children and adult collectors.

FAST FACTS:
About Hasbro, Inc.

Ownership: Hasbro, Inc. is a publicly owned company traded on AMEX.

Ticker symbol: HAS

Officers: Alan G. Hassenfeld, Chmn., Pres. & CEO, 49, 1996 base salary $1,407,900; Harold Gordon, VChmn., 59, 1996 base salary $703,230; Alfred J. Verrecchia, COO, Domestic Toy Operations, 54, 1996 base salary $778,397; George R. Ditomassi Jr., COO, Games & International, 62, 1996 base salary $705,577

Employees: 12,000 (6,500 located in the United States)

Principal Subsidiary Companies: The company's principal subsidiaries are: Kenner, Nerf, Playskool, Milton Bradley, and Parker Brothers.

Chief Competitors: Hasbro's primary competitors are: 3DO; Acclaim Entertainment; Lego; Galoob Toys; Mattel; Nest Entertainment; Nintendo; Ohio Art; Pleasant; Revell; Rubbermaid; SEGA; SLM International; Toy Biz; and Tyco Toys.

CHRONOLOGY:
Key Dates for Hasbro, Inc.

1923: Brothers Henry, Hilal, and Herman Hassenfeld form Hassnefeld Brothers Company

1935: Hassenfeld Brothers begin manufacturing pencils

1942: Company focuses mainly on toy manufacturing

1952: Mr. Potato Head becomes first toy advertised on television

1964: G.I. Joe is introduced

1968: Goes public and changes name to Hasbro Industries

1974: Merrill Hassenfeld becomes CEO and his son, Stephen D. Hassenfeld becomes president

1980: Spins off Empire Pencil; Stephen Hassenfeld becomes CEO and chairman of the board

1984: Becomes country's number-one toy maker with purchase of Milton Bradley

1989: Acquires products from Coleco

1991: Purchases Tonka

1994: Forms joint venture with Connector Set Limited Partnership

1997: Company is found guilty of violating anti-trust laws

THE FORCE IS WITH HASBRO

Not too long ago, in this very galaxy, the most successful film-based merchandising program got its start with the release of the *Star Wars* trilogy, the most successful film series of all time. *Star Wars* spawned a toy and game franchise that was unprecedented. 20 years after their initial release, *Star Wars* toys remained the leading brand among boys.

Kenner produced the original toys in 1976. Hasbro bought Kenner in 1991 and took over the franchise. In 1997, George Lucas, the creator of the *Star Wars* films, released an enhanced version of the trilogy, thus spurring a huge increase in sales for Hasbro. At about the same time, Lucas announced that he was beginning work on the first of three "prequels" to the original trilogy. The first was scheduled to be released in May 1999. The Force proved strong with Hasbro—Lucas awarded the company exclusive rights to make *Star Wars* toys and games related to the prequels. Some estimated that sales of *Star Wars*-related items could surpass $1 billion in 1999—that's a lot of Imperial credits for Hasbro.

Hasbro has capitalized on the *Star Wars* craze by tying it in to some of its other popular games. In 1998, Hasbro released a *Star Wars* edition of Trivial Pursuit. The previous year it had released a *Star Wars* edition of Monopoly that was a complete sellout; later the same year, Hasbro released a CD-ROM version. It included full-motion, 3D versions of *Star Wars* characters and also extensive footage and music from the trilogy. Instead of Boardwalk and Park Place, players vied for galactic properties like Dagobah and Tatooine. Players were also able to play with people from all across the country through Microsoft's Internet Gaming Zone.

Fans can access the center of Hasbro's *Star Wars* Universe through its *Star Wars* home page. There one can view pictures of all Hasbro's *Star Wars* toys and games, many of which can be viewed in 3-D rotating views and video clips. At this web site, kids can access the Death Star Construction Area where they can find instructions on how to create their own *Star Wars* environments. Or you can visit the Mos Eisley Spaceport and see how various Hasbro *Star Wars* figures were developed. Want to discuss *Star Wars* stuff with other fans? Visit the Cantina, the *Star Wars* chat room.

Star Wars has made an indelible mark upon popular American culture—in no small part due to the fact that the last couple of generations of children have grown up playing with *Star Wars* toys such as the Millennium Falcon, X-wing fighters, Darth Vader, and R2D2. With the release of the next trilogy, it's assured that little boys and girls will be pretending to be in the *Star Wars* universe for years to come. And the Imperial leaders at Hasbro's toy Empire couldn't be happier.

The Playskool division is geared toward toddlers and pre-schoolers. Playskool products include Play-Doh, Lincoln Logs, Weebles, and the Easy Bake Oven. The Tonka division manufactures realistic versions of trucks that are well-built and sturdy enough for any playtime adventure.

Milton Bradley and Parker Brothers produces Battleship, Monopoly, Twister, Scrabble, Clue, Risk, and Trivial Pursuit.

CORPORATE CITIZENSHIP

Hasbro donated $6.5 million in 1996 to service programs that help children, their families, and their communities. The company helps disadvantaged children through the Hasbro Children's Foundation and the Hasbro Charitable Trust. The Hasbro Charitable Trust also supports the Hasbro Children's Hospital, which opened in 1994.

GLOBAL PRESENCE

Hasbro manufactures and sells its products throughout the world. The company has subsidiaries on six continents and sells its products through more than 20,000 retail outlets worldwide. International sales accounted for approximately 45 percent of revenues in 1996.

The company relies especially heavily on Chinese manufacturing. Its 1997 annual report expressed concern over the potential impact of the United States or European Union imposing sanctions against China. Such an action could significantly increase the cost of importing toys to the United States and Europe.

SOURCES OF INFORMATION

Bibliography

"Company News' SEC Is Asked to Investigate Trading of Hasbro." *Bloomberg Business News, The New York Times,* 8 May 1996.

"Ex-Officials at Unit of Hasbro Are Indicted on Tax Fraud Charges." *The Wall Street Journal,* 15 April 1998.

Fitzgerald, Kate. "Hasbro, Mattel Play for Keeps in Cyberspace." *Advertising Age,* 15 January 1996. Available at: http://www.conceptone.com/netnews/nn713.htm.

Greenberg, Herb. "Hasbro's Short-Toy Shortage." *Fortune,* 27 April 1998.

"Hasbro, Inc. Company Profile." 19 March 1997. Available at http://www.efund.com/Hasbro_Co_Prof.html.

Hasbro, Inc. Homepage. 20 April 1998. Available at: http://www.hasbro.com/corporate/index.html.

"Hasbro, Inc." *Hoover's Company Profiles,* Hoover's, Inc.: Austin, TX, 1997. Available at: http://www.hoovers.com.

For additional industry research:

Investigate companies by their Standard Industrial Classification Codes, also known as SICs. Hasbro's primary SICs are:

3942 Dolls & Stuffed Toys

3944 Games, Toys, & Children's Vehicles

The Hearst Corporation

OVERVIEW

The Hearst Corporation is a media mega-company that operates newspapers, magazines, book publishing companies, television and radio stations, and many other media outlets, including ventures into new media.

Hearst Magazines is the world's largest publisher of monthly magazines. These include 16 U.S. titles and more than 90 international editions distributed in more than 100 countries. Hearst Newspapers publishes a dozen daily newspapers and seven weekly newspapers, and maintains a Washington news bureau. Hearst Broadcasting operates television and radio stations and a television production company. The formation of Hearst-Argyle Television Inc. in 1997 propelled Hearst into the ranks of leading U.S. television broadcasting groups. Hearst-Argyle, a public corporation reaching more than 10 percent of U.S. television-viewing households, was created when Hearst Broadcasting merged with the former Argyle Television Inc. Hearst is the majority shareholder of Hearst-Argyle Television, which is one of the largest U.S. independent owners of television stations.

Hearst's Entertainment & Syndication Division combines its cable network partnerships, television programming and distribution activities, and various syndication companies. Hearst is a partner or holds interests in several leading cable television networks, including the History Channel, Lifetime, ESPN, ESPN2, A&E, and Classic Sports Network. Another key part of this division is the King Features Syndicate, which is the world's largest distributor of comics and newspaper columns. Among its well read properties are "Hints from Heloise," "Blondie," and "Beetle Bailey."

FOUNDED: 1887

Contact Information:

HEADQUARTERS: 959 8th Ave.
New York, NY 10019
PHONE: (212)649-2000
FAX: (212)765-3528
EMAIL: pphillips@hearst.com
URL: http://www.hearstcorp.com

FAST FACTS:

About The Hearst Corporation

Ownership: The Hearst Corporation is a privately owned company.

Officers: George R. Hearst Jr., Chmn., 69; Frank A. Bannack Jr., Pres. & CEO; Victor F. Ganzi, Exec. VP & COO, 51; Gilbert C. Maurer, Exec. VP, 69

Employees: 15,000

Chief Competitors: A major force in both print and broadcast media, The Hearst Corporation faces competition in all the business in which it operates. Some of its major competitors are: Bertlesmann; CBS; Cox Enterprises; Gannett; K-III; Knight Ridder; McGraw-Hill; New York Times; Reed Elsevier; Time Warner; Times Mirror; Tribune; and Viacom.

Book publishers William Morrow & Co. and Avon Books are the two major imprints of the Hearst Books/Business Publishing division. Morrow is a publisher of hardcover books, while Avon publishes paperbacks. In addition to books published under those two imprints, the division publishes a number of books each year for special audiences, as well as a number of magazines. These range from books on electronic design and automotive engineering to *Floor Covering Weekly* and *Diversion,* a leisure time magazine for doctors.

Hearst's New Media & Technology division is blazing trails on the Internet and elsewhere as technology creates new markets for Hearst products. The division works with all Hearst groups to adapt existing products and resources to formats appropriate for new delivery systems such as the Internet.

Extensive real estate holdings are maintained by the Hearst Real Estate Division. These include timberlands and farming operations in California, along with commercial properties in San Francisco and New York City. The famous Hearst Castle, perhaps the best known piece of Hearst property ever, no longer belongs to Hearst, having been deeded to the state of California after the death of William Randolph Hearst in 1951. Located on the central California coast near San Simeon, the home is today a popular tourist attraction.

COMPANY FINANCES

As a privately held company, Hearst Corp. does not report full details on its financial operations. However,

it is known that 1997 revenue for Hearst reached $2.7 billion, an increase of 5.1 percent over 1996 revenue of $2.57 billion. Revenue in 1995 totaled $2.51 billion, compared with 1994's $2.29 billion.

HISTORY

The history of the Hearst Corporation is overshadowed by the mythos surrounding its founder, William Randolph Hearst. Larger than life is his story and so public that the debate continues as to whether indeed Orson Welles, in his debut film *Citizen Kane,* patterned the life of his Charles Foster Kane after Hearst. There are those who claim Welles originally had another mogul in mind while crafting the movie—possibly Howard Hughes, whose life Welles examined briefly as part of his late-career film *F is for Fake.*

Young Hearst was handed control of the *San Francisco Examiner* in 1887 after his father, George, was elected to the United States Senate; the elder Hearst had reportedly gained ownership of the newspaper as payment for a gambling debt. Hearst's vigor and dramatic revision of the *Examiner* is almost legendary, and indeed is seen as having forever changed the face of American journalism. "He pioneered what might legitimately be called tabloid tactics," according to an article in the British magazine *Campaign,* "introducing cartoon strips and salacious stories to his titles. He was, in fact, the prototype media baron."

Hearst's next purchase was the *New York Journal* in 1895. His acquisitions continued, and in the 1920s Hearst owned newspapers throughout the United States. Company history holds that in that era "one in four Americans read a Hearst newspaper."

It was the *Journal* purchase that put Hearst in a head-to-head battle for circulation with another newspaper magnate, Joseph Pulitzer, owner of the *New York World.* The rivalry during the era of the Spanish-American War gave rise to what is known as "yellow journalism." The newspaper became more than a chronicle of news; it also, under Hearst, became a means by which he communicated his views, both personal and political.

As Hearst continued to acquire newspapers around the country, he also began to look to other emerging media. These included magazines, film, and radio, in all of which the company became involved before 1930. The company, for example, started the Hearst-Selig News Pictorial, a film newsreel production company that dominated film journalism in the 1920s.

For many observers of the Hearst empire, 1935 is seen as the year the company was at its height. Hearst controlled 19 newspapers, King Features Syndicate, international news and photo services (which would become folded into United Press International), 13 magazines, 8 radio stations, and 2 motion picture companies.

Despite his success, in 1937 Hearst had to step down from the business and sell many of his properties, including a portion of his estate in San Simeon, to avert bankruptcy.

Upon Hearst's death in 1951, Richard Berlin, who had overseen the company since 1940, was made chief executive officer. The Hearsts kept a semblance of control over the company through a trust but didn't actually regain control until 1974.

Frank Bennack was appointed head of the company in 1979. Under Berlin the company had been pared down; Bennack, however, went on a spending spree, purchasing television stations, magazines, and other daily and weekly newspapers through the 1980s. Bennack also closed the doors of the legendary *Los Angeles Herald Examiner* in 1989.

New technologies signaled further changes for the Hearst Corporation as the 1990s began. Hearst made a major foray into the so-called new media arena with the establishment of its Hearst New Media & Technology group in 1993. This particular division works to create content in various electronic media based on its existing products.

George Hearst Jr., nephew to the founding family, assumed control of the company as chairman from Randolph A. Hearst in 1996. In March 1997 Hearst and Argyle Television Inc. announced an agreement to merge 6 Hearst television stations with 6 owned by Argyle to form Hearst-Argyle Television Inc. The 12 stations owned by Hearst-Argyle, along with another 3 the company will manage, reach nearly 12 percent of the U.S. television audience. Among the 12 television stations owned by Hearst-Argyle are 9 ABC-affiliated stations, more than any other television station group other than ABC itself.

In January 1998 Hearst announced the acquisition of Medi-Span Inc., an Indianapolis-based supplier of drug product information to the healthcare industry. Medi-Span joins Hearst's First DataBank Inc. of San Bruno, California, to become the corporation's second electronic drug database company. First DataBank, which supplies drug, nutrition, and medical information to healthcare companies and institutions, was acquired by Hearst in 1980.

STRATEGY

The *San Francisco Examiner* and *San Francisco Chronicle* have been in a joint operating agreement since 1965. Under this arrangement, also known as a JOA, two newspapers in the same market maintain separate news and editorial departments but share their business operations and split profits evenly. This San Francisco agreement is to last until 2005. Each paper holds the right of first refusal to buy the other.

CHRONOLOGY:
Key Dates for The Hearst Corporation

1887: William Randolph Hearst gains control of the *San Francisco Examiner*

1903: Starts *Motor* magazine

1895: Purchases the *New York Journal*

1911: Acquires magazine, *Good Housekeeping*

1928: Purchases radio station, WISN in Milwaukee, Wisconsin

1937: Hearst steps down and sells many properties to avoid bankruptcy

1943: All of Hearst's assets are consolidated within The Hearst Corporation

1951: William Randolph Hearst dies of heart attack; Richard Berlin is made CEO

1966: *Journal-American* folds in New York

1974: Hearst family regains control of company

1979: Frank A. Bennack Jr. takes over as CEO

1989: Bennack closes doors to *Los Angeles Herald Examiner*

1993: Hearst New Media & Technology group is established

1996: George Hearst Jr. assumes control as chairman from Randolph A. Hearst

1997: Hearst and Argyle Television Inc. announce agreement to form Hearst-Argyle Television Inc.

1998: Announces acquisition of Medi-Span Inc.

According to a rival news service, "Hearst executives, rebuffed twice on offers to buy the *Chronicle* in recent years, have now proposed closing the *Examiner*. Hearst would hold a minority interest and grant *Chronicle* owners a substantial majority interest, perhaps as much as 60 to 65 percent, in a restructured joint operating agreement." The caveat: Hearst wants control of the combined newspaper. The company acted similarly in its dealings in the San Antonio market in the 1990s. Rumors throughout the 1990s abounded as to the future of the *Examiner.*

"'The *Chronicle* has a capitalization shortage, a lack of a strategic plan, and short-term management', said a [DeYoung] family member [owners of the *Chronicle*].

William Randolph Hearst's San Simeon Estate located in California. (AP/Wide World Photos, Inc.)

THE ENCHANTED HILL

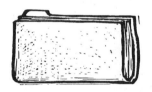

More than 1 million people visit the Hearst Castle each year. William Randolph Hearst built the lavish "La Cuesta Encantada," or Enchanted Hill, during his lifetime, but deeded it to the State of California when he died in 1957. The enormous castle is a result of 28 years of work between Hearst and architect Julia Morgan. The building sits on a hilltop overlooking the Pacific Ocean and rests in the beautiful countryside of San Simeon, California. The architectural masterpiece offers 127 acres of gardens, terraces, and pools; 165 rooms in 4 different houses; and a zoo. Hearst was an avid collector of art and artifacts; and accordingly, his palace is filled with Italian and Spanish treasures. The grounds and castle are open to the public for tours.

'That is a risky environment for the investor. That can be very dangerous. If we get the right deal at the right price, family members will be well-served'."

INFLUENCES

Hearst has had a number of problems in its magazine division; high paper costs, postal price increases, and intensified competition for advertising dollars. In 1995 Hearst announced plans to raise cover prices on some magazines between 18 and 33 percent and to raise ad-vertising rates 5 percent; coupled with this, circulation was cut approximately 10 percent. The annual savings realized was about $20 million per year. "It was an explosive cocktail and advertisers responded with predictable fury," according to *Campaign.* "Kraft Foods pulled all its advertising, worth $30 million, from Hearst magazines, and several other major advertisers, including the fragrance giant, Elizabeth Arden, cut back spending sharply." Bennack also replaced employees within the division, not the least of whom was Helen Gurley Brown, the grande dame of *Cosmopolitan,* who was replaced as editor-in-chief.

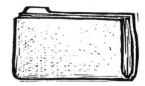

CURRENT TRENDS

Hearst made a major foray into the "new media" arena with the establishment of its Hearst New Media & Technology group in 1993. Designed to guide and manage the company's interests in the media, according to company literature, this particular division works to create content in various electronic medium based on its existing products. Employees are trained at the Hearst New Media Center, which also oversees digital production. In 1995, the company joined with eight other large newspapers to form New Century Network, designed to create a national network for online newspaper services. It also has interests in software applications and products, such as Netscape Communications.

PRODUCTS

Hearst's 12 newspapers include the *Albany Times Union, Beaumont Enterprise, Edwardsville Intelligencer, Houston Chronicle, Huron Daily Tribune, Laredo Morning Times, Midland Dailey News, Midland Reporter-Telegram, Plainview Daily Herald, San Antonio Express-News, San Francisco Examiner,* and *Seattle Post-Intelligencer.* The company publishes weekly newspapers in Texas and Michigan, and has a Washington, D.C. news bureau. It also operates Hearst Entertainment & Syndication, of which King Features Syndicate is a part.

Hearst Broadcasting is one of largest independent broadcasting groups in the nation. The company has television and radio stations in Baltimore, Boston, Milwaukee, and Pittsburgh as well as television stations in Dayton, Tampa, and Kansas City. Hearst has interest in cable networks including Lifetime Television, The History Channel, ESPN and ESPN2, and other stations and production subsidiaries.

Hearst Magazines titles include *Colonial Homes, Cosmopolitan, Country Living, Esquire, Good Housekeeping, Harper's Bazaar, House Beautiful, Marie Claire, Popular Mechanics, Redbook,* and *SmartMoney.* The company also has magazine and newsstand distribution as well as subscription fulfillment services.

The company's business also includes Hearst Books/ Business Publishing (William Morrow & Company, Avon Books), Hearst New Media & Technology (shareholder in New Century Network, Netscape Communications, and Books that Work), and Hearst Real Estate.

CORPORATE CITIZENSHIP

In the spring of 1997 Hearst Corp. announced the formation of a Speakers Bureau program under which senior Hearst executives would visit college campuses to address students on a wide variety of topics relating to the media. The program came as part of an outreach effort by Hearst, following extensive dialogue with pro-

ART IMITATES NATURE

In 1941 Orson Welles directed and starred in the film *Citizen Kane.* It was and still is a cinematic masterpiece. Called the greatest movie of all time by many critics all over the world, *Citizen Kane,* was actually modeled after the life and career of William Randolph Hearst.

Welles played Charles Foster Kane, a newspaper tycoon with a life that paralleled the real life of William Randolph Hearst. The movie portrayed Hearst's wife, mistress, friends, and even his castle, La Cuesta Encantada, in the film called Xanadu. When Hearst found out that the movie portrayed him as uncaring and somewhat mad, he took enormous objection to it. He used his clout to try to block the movie's distribution. When that did not work he tried to buy the negative to destroy it. None of that worked and the movie was released. It is now a classic.

Sadly, *Citizen Kane* was not recognized for what it was at the time of its release. It did not get much theater play, which was partly due to the fact that many theaters would not even show the film because of Mr. Hearst's influence. However, it also lost out for best picture at the Academy Awards in 1941. Critics did not realize the film's greatness until many years later. *Citizen Kane* is now studied by every film major in the world. It is one of the most influential movies of all times. Its style has been copied numerous times and movies have been made about the movie. William Randolph Hearst swore until his death that he had never once viewed the movie, but no matter how adamantly against it he was, it will live on, and so will Mr. Hearst's legend.

fessors, department heads and deans of universities, colleges, and journalism schools, to establish contact with students at graduate and undergraduate levels. In announcing the program, Gloria Ricks, Hearst's deputy director of corporate communications and the overseer of the Speakers Bureau program, said: "We want to build stronger, closer ties with the most recognized and widely acclaimed institutes of higher learning. We know that our future employees and industry leaders are students in America's schools today."

GLOBAL PRESENCE

Hearst distributes more than 90 international editions of its magazines in more than 100 countries worldwide. Hearst Magazines International, which is head-quartered in New York City, oversees the publication of Hearst's leading consumer titles, around the world. These international editions are published through joint ventures, partnerships, and licensing arrangements, using material from the U.S. parent editions and other international editions and creating original content appropriate for each national or regional edition.

In the United Kingdom, the National Magazine Company Ltd., a subsidiary of Hearst since 1910, publishes nine monthly titles, including the British editions of *Good Housekeeping, Country Living, Cosmopolitan, Esquire,* and *House Beautiful,* as well as the popular women's titles *Company, SHE,* and *Zest.*

SOURCES OF INFORMATION

Bibliography

Cook, Richard. "Hearst Buys and Diversifies to Protect its Media Empire." *Campaign,* 21 June 1996.

Ewell, Miranda. "San Francisco Chronicle, Examiner Merger Talks Move Forward." *Knight-Ridder/Tribune Business News,* 22 March 1996.

"The Hearst Corporation." *Hoover's Online,* 17 May 1998. Available at http://www.hoovers.com.

The Hearst Corporation Home Page, 17 May 1998. Available at http://www.hearstcorp.com.

For additional industry research:

Investigate companies by their Standard Industrial Classification Codes, also known as SICs. Hearst's primary SICs are:

2711 Newspapers

2721 Periodicals

2731 Book Publishing

4832 Radio Broadcasting Stations

4833 Television Broadcasting Stations

4841 Cable & Other Pay TV Services

H.J. Heinz Co.

OVERVIEW

H.J. Heinz Company is one of the world's leading producers of processed food products and nutritional services. The company's products include tuna, baby foods, pet foods, beans, ketchup and condiments, dietary foods, frozen foods, and soup. Anchored by Heinz Ketchup, which is used in 4 out of 5 American restaurants and accounts for 47 percent of its market, Heinz brands such as Star-Kist tuna, Ore-Ida frozen potatoes, 9-Lives cat food, and Skippy peanut butter are among the best known in the United States. In 1997, the company produced more than 4,000 varieties of products that were distributed in more than 200 countries and territories around the world. The company's two strongest global brands are Heinz and Weight Watchers.

Heinz's food service division, which sells products to eating establishments and hotels, was the company's leading division as of 1998, producing supplies of ketchup and single-serving packages of condiments, jellies, and syrups. Heinz was also the leading at-home brand of ketchup, accounting for close to 50 percent of the U.S. market in 1997 and close to 19 percent of Heinz's total sales. Heinz also controlled 87 percent of the private label soup market and had leading positions in U.S. markets for frozen potatoes (Ore-Ida brand), tuna (Star-Kist), pet foods (9-Lives and Ken-L Ration); and weight control products (Weight Watchers). Heinz is also a major player in the international baby food market—though less so in North America where it markets infant food under the Heinz and Earth's Best brand names. More than 85 percent of its infant foods are sold outside the United States.

Heinz has a major presence in international markets. Operations outside of North America accounted for more

FOUNDED: 1869

Contact Information:
HEADQUARTERS: 600 Grant St.
Pittsburgh, PA 15219
PHONE: (412)456-5700
FAX: (412)456-6128

FINANCES:

H.J. Heinz
Sales, 1994-1997
(billion dollars)

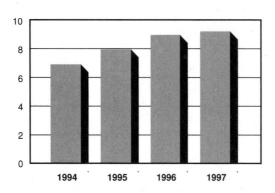

H.J. Heinz
1997 Stock Prices
(dollars)

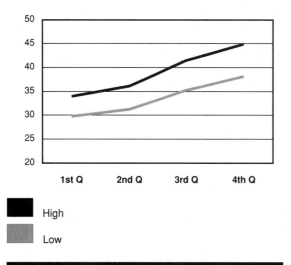

an attempt to boost profits. The replacement of long-time CEO Anthony O'Reilly in 1998 by marketing whiz William R. Johnson was expected to rejuvenate the company and prompted a surge in the value of the company's stock.

COMPANY FINANCES

After posting sales growth of well over 10 percent a year in fiscal 1995 and 1996, Heinz's total revenue for fiscal 1997 rose only 2.7 percent, or $244.7 million, to $9.36 billion from $9.11 billion in fiscal 1996. Sales in fiscal 1998, which ended April 30, 1998, totaled $9.21 billion, down 1.6 percent from fiscal 1997. Sales in fiscal 1994 and 1995 totaled $7.05 billion and $8.09 billion, respectively. Net income in fiscal 1998 totaled $801.6 million, up more than 165 percent from $302.0 million in fiscal 1997. Fiscal 1996 net earnings totaled $659.0 million, compared with $591.0 million in fiscal 1995. For fiscal 1994, Heinz posted net income of $603.0 million.

ANALYSTS' OPINIONS

As of 1996, opinions on H.J. Heinz by some market analysts were mixed. A report by Bear, Stearns & Company in December 1996 stated that Heinz had initiated price increases in several product categories but that the strategy had led to a drop in volume sales. "At this point, we stick to our view that the company's aggressive pricing strategy may continue to cause volume deterioration and market share losses. Furthermore, we believe that the company will likely increase promotional spending during the second half of fiscal 1997 in an attempt to stimulate volume and regain lost share." As a result, Bear Stearns expected Heinz profits to be mediocre and said that its share prices might fall.

While noting that Heinz might have trouble reaching its profit goal in 1997, a report by Dean Witter Reynolds in December 1996 said that the company's six operating segments, with the exception of the Weight Watchers business, were performing "reasonably well" and were continuing to expand their international presence.

One strategy Heinz was pursuing in the mid- to late 1990s was to increase profitability by raising product prices and reducing marketing costs (primarily by reducing advertising support for its brands). This strategy received mixed reviews among industry observers. While increasing short-term profits, some analysts stated that it had led to volume declines for Heinz products in certain categories. Also, in an article in *Advertising Age,* Rance Crain criticized Heinz, saying that it had abandoned the brand advertising that made Star-Kist tuna and 9-Lives

than 40 percent of the company's worldwide sales in 1997. Heinz's best known overseas brands in the mid- to late 1990s were Orlando, Wattie's, Olivine, Farley's, Plasmon, and Guloso.

Although the company's sales continued to climb through the 1990s and Heinz continued to provide a decent return to its investors, its growth was less than spectacular. Intensive competition, a rising U.S. dollar, and decreased advertising were all seen as contributing to Heinz's sluggish growth. In response, the company underwent the most massive restructuring in its history, unloading weaker operations and cutting its work force in

Al Banisch, an executive of the H.J. Heinz Company, presents a bottle of their ketchup with one of the estimated 60,000 entries in their 1997 contest to design a new product label.

(Photograph by Gene J. Puskar. AP/Wide World Photos, Inc.)

FAST FACTS:
About H.J. Heinz Co.

Ownership: H.J. Heinz Company is a publicly owned company traded on the New York Stock Exchange.

Ticker symbol: HNZ

Officers: Anthony J.F. O'Reilly, Chmn., 61, $3,039,015; William R. Johnson, Pres. & CEO, 49, $2,139,820; Paul F. Renne, Exec. VP & CFO, 55; David R. Williams, Exec. VP, 55, $1,101,038

Employees: 40,500 (1998)

Principal Subsidiary Companies: H.J. Heinz Company has a number of operating units focused on six major categories: food service; infant foods; ketchup and condiments; pet food; tuna; and weight control products.

Chief Competitors: Heinz competes with numerous large and small companies around the world. Some of its leading competitors include: Campbell Soup Company; Colgate-Palmolive Company; Del Monte; General Mills; Hormel; Iams; Jenny Craig; Kellogg; RJR Nabisco; Philip Morris Companies; The Quaker Oats Company; Ralcorp; and Sara Lee Corporation.

---

cat food famous. "These brands have been reduced to commodities," said Crain. Companies that advertise well boost the value of their products and services, he stated.

The resignation in April 1998 of the man responsible for these tight-fisted measures, CEO Anthony O'Reilly, was welcomed by Wall Street, which immediately following the announcement in December 1997 pushed the company's stock to a 52-week high. Although analysts such as Nomi Ghez of Goldman Sachs in New York were quick to point out that "Tony O'Reilly has done a great job in building the company," most looked forward to seeing what O'Reilly's replacement, William Johnson, would do.

O'Reilly had also been criticized for his tendency to fill the top positions at Heinz with cronies and yes-men. Here, too, Johnson was expected to make changes. "He'll put people in positions and expect them to perform," said Joseph Jordan, an analyst with PNC Institutional Investment Services, in the *Pittsburgh Business Times*. "Their salaries and incentives will also be at risk if their performance doesn't come through."

HISTORY

In 1856, 12-year-old Henry John Heinz began peddling produce from his family's garden in Sharpsburg, Pennsylvania, to friends and neighbors. In 1869, the 25-year-old entrepreneur formed a partnership with his friend, L.C. Noble, to bottle horseradish in clear glass. Unfortunately, the business went bankrupt in 1875. The next year, however, with the help of his brother John and his cousin Frederick, Heinz created F&J Heinz, a company for which he developed tomato ketchup (1876) and sweet pickles (1880). Henry Heinz gained financial control of the firm in 1888 and changed the name to the H.J. Heinz Company.

Heinz developed a reputation as an advertising and marketing genius. He got the idea for the famous "57 Varieties" slogan in 1896, while riding in a New York streetcar. After seeing a sign for "21 styles of shoes," Heinz conceived the idea for the "57 varieties" trademark, even though his company already had many more products.

Henry Heinz died in 1919, and the business depended on its traditional product lines for the next 50 years, as his son and later his grandson ran the company. In the late 1950s the company began acquiring other food processing firms. In 1958 it purchased a major Dutch food processor, followed by Star-Kist in 1963 (tuna and pet food), Ore-Ida in 1965 (potatoes), and Weight-Watchers in 1978.

In 1979 Anthony J.F. O'Reilly became CEO of Heinz, beginning a period of sustained growth for the company. When Henry Heinz II died in 1987, O'Reilly assumed the additional title of chairman. O'Reilly, with his flamboyant personality, assumed a very public role and became clearly identified with the H.J. Heinz Company. However, in 1997 O'Reilly appeared to clear the way for eventually naming his successor when he said he planned to turn his CEO title over to company president William R. Johnson once the company implemented a restructuring program. By the end of the year, that restructuring program (called "Project Millennia") was well under way and O'Reilly announced his resignation, formally handing over the reins to Johnson in April 1998. Industry-watchers looked forward to the change, expecting Johnson to revive Heinz's marketing operations and institute other beneficial changes.

During the 1990s, Heinz continued to make changes to its core operations. Heinz purchased the pet food division of Quaker Oats Company in 1995 for $725 million. The company also was able to dramatically improve its position in the tuna business, moving from a market share of 30 percent in 1992 to 46 percent in 1997. The growth was produced by an aggressive pricing strategy made possible by extensive cost-cutting on the manufacturing side.

STRATEGY

In the 1990s, H.J. Heinz Company faced challenges such as the changing nature of the retail market and the global economy. Despite these challenges, Heinz's chairman Anthony O'Reilly said in a 1995 article that two guiding principles allowed the company to remain a leader in its product categories: niche leadership and "constant rebirth." By leading in specific product "niches," Heinz was able to maintain its dominant share of the condiments, tuna, weight-loss, and frozen potatoes markets, according to O'Reilly.

"Constant rebirth," according to O'Reilly, involved the continual shifting of management to enable the company to function in a changing environment. Constant rebirth is also made possible through renewal of technology, procurement, pricing, and oversight, he said.

One strategy Heinz was pursuing in the mid- to late 1990s was to increase profitability by raising product prices and reducing marketing costs (primarily by reducing advertising support for its brands)—a strategy that received mixed reviews from industry observers who argued that it had led to volume declines for some Heinz products.

In 1997, Heinz pursued another strategy to improve its profits and make its stock more appealing to investors. In March 1997, Heinz management announced a massive restructuring and reorganization program called "Project Millennia." The plan called for exiting nonstrategic businesses while bolstering core ones, closing or selling 25 of 111 manufacturing plants, cutting 2,500 jobs (from a work force of 43,000), and taking a charge against earnings of $650 million. The plan was expected to generate about $120 million in savings in 1998 and up to $200 million a year once it was fully implemented.

According to the *Wall Street Journal,* Heinz was among the last large food companies to use restructuring to increase earnings. Sales in the food industry were growing at only 1 percent a year in the mid- to late 1990s, and low inflation made price increases on food products hard to implement, the report noted.

Despite the downsizing, Heinz had ambitious financial goals for the late 1990s. Heinz expected sales of about $9.5 billion in fiscal 1997 (and came close with actual sales of $9.3 billion) and planned to increase annual sales to $14 or $15 billion within five years while maintaining earnings growth of 10 to 12 percent per year.

O'Reilly's theme of "constant rebirth" was most forcefully illustrated in 1998 when he handed over stewardship of the company to a dynamic young executive named William Johnson who had built a name for himself in the company's pet food division. Johnson's emphasis on marketing and performance was expected to dramatically change the way Heinz presented itself to the world. Indeed, one of Johnson's first moves was to take the money the company had saved through its restruc-

CHRONOLOGY:
Key Dates for H.J. Heinz Co.

1869: 25-year-old, Henry Heinz forms a partnership with L.C. Noble to bottle horseradish

1875: Horseradish business goes bankrupt

1876: F & J Heinz Company is started with the help of Henry's brother and cousin; tomato ketchup is its first product

1888: Henry Heinz gains financial control of the firm and changes its name to the H.J. Heinz Company

1919: Henry Heinz dies and his son takes over

1958: The company begins acquiring other food processing firms with its purchase of a major Dutch food processor

1979: Anthony J.F. O'Reilly becomes CEO of Heinz

1987: Henry Heinz II dies and O'Reilly assumes title of chairman

1998: O'Reilly resigns and William R. Johnson takes over as chairman

turing efforts and funnel it into advertising and marketing. Though this was exactly what Project Millennia called for when announced in March 1997, industry-watchers saw it as a bold move, indicative of Johnson's new approach.

INFLUENCES

The 1980s and 1990s were the decades of Anthony O'Reilly, a formidable and flamboyant leader whose impact on Heinz was unmistakable. When O'Reilly took over Heinz in 1979, he produced immediate returns of nearly 30 percent and continued to produce an average annual return of 22 percent over the next two decades. But as Heinz floundered in the mid-1990s, stockholders and analysts began to blame O'Reilly and the pressure mounted for him to step down as CEO. He did so in 1998, leaving behind a company valued at nearly $20 billion. It had been worth less than $1 billion when he took control in 1979.

Though long a producer of infant food, it wasn't until 1994, when it acquired U.K. infant food manufacturer

Farley's, that Heinz ran into the infant food marketing controversy. Farley's operations were cited in a 1994 report by the International Baby Food Action Network (IBFAN) for inadequate labeling and improper promotional practices in violation of infant formula marketing guidelines set up by the World Health Organization and UNICEF.

CURRENT TRENDS

One trend in which Heinz was apparently *not* participating in during the mid-1990s was the development of "low-flatulence" beans. Colin Leakey of Girton, England, the son of anthropologist Louis Leakey, succeeded in developing a bean that would not induce flatulence in people who consumed it. However, as of 1997 the bean had not yet caught on, according to press reports.

"While we are interested to understand more about this development," Steve Marinker, a spokesman for the British unit of H.J. Heinz Company, was quoted as saying, "the reality is that beans as a high-fiber product have an effect on the digestive systems that is no greater or no less than any other high-fiber product." As a major producer of baked beans, H.J. Heinz would be a natural candidate for processing and marketing the low-flatulence beans.

PRODUCTS

One new product introduced by Heinz in 1997 wasn't really a new product at all, but rather a creatively repackaged one. In 1996 Heinz sponsored a national contest for children, asking them to create new labels for some of its ketchup bottles.

To publicize the contest, Heinz placed ads in magazines with the headline: "Hey kids, wanna be famous?" and sent posters to school art classes. About 60,000 children sent entries to Heinz. Three labels designed by children were chosen.

The contest started in June 1996 and was accompanied by a $450,000 grant from Heinz to the National Endowment for the Arts for children's art programs. One reason behind the Heinz contest was the importance of children as consumers of the company's products. Children between 4 and 12 spend more than $17 billion per year on their own and directly influence another $172 billion that other people spend, according to one estimate.

CORPORATE CITIZENSHIP

Heinz has contributed to many different charitable and community activities over the years. In 1996, the H.J. Heinz Company Foundation donated $5.6 million to about 900 organizations and announced that it would donate $450,000 to the National Endowment for the Arts (NEA) over a three-year period. The money was to be used specifically to save children's art programs and was the largest single donation the NEA had received since its budget was slashed by the Republican Congress. Meanwhile, Heinz U.S.A. raised money for children's hospitals through its baby food label saving program.

On the environmental front, Heinz has adopted a worldwide policy of refusing to buy tuna caught using gill nets or drift nets or "through the intentional encirclement of dolphin by purse seine nets."

GLOBAL PRESENCE

Heinz was a pioneer in the globalization of its business, exporting products to every continent before 1900. By 1905 Heinz was manufacturing food products in the United Kingdom. In 1996 Heinz generated more than 40 percent of its sales outside the United States. In that same year, Heinz controlled about 90 percent of the jarred baby food business in Australia, Canada, Italy, and New Zealand, and its baked beans were the market leader in the United Kingdom.

Heinz focused more intently on international expansion in the 1980s and 1990s. A key 1980s acquisition was Marie Elisabeth Produtos Alimentares S.A. of Portugal. Heinz also established international subsidiaries, including units in Botswana and Belgium. In 1992 Heinz purchased Wattie's Limited, New Zealand's largest food processing company.

In late 1997 Heinz continued to build its overseas network, acquiring John West Foods Limited in Europe, a majority interest in Pudliszki S.A., one of Poland's top food processors, as well as some other small companies.

SOURCES OF INFORMATION

Bibliography

Crain, Rance. "Heinz Fails to Protect Its Barriers of Entry." *Advertising Age,* 20 February 1995.

"H.J. Heinz Company." *Hoover's Online,* 25 August 1998. Available at http://www.hoovers.com.

"H.J. Heinz Company." *1998 Quarterly Report.* Pittsburgh, PA: H.J. Heinz Company, 1998.

H.J. Heinz Company 1997 Annual Report. Pittsburgh, PA: H.J. Heinz Company, 1997.

Ingrassia, Lawrence. "Dr. Colin Leakey, a Real Bean Counter, Finds Profit Elusive." *The Wall Street Journal,* 1 April 1997.

"Ketchup Sales Improve Flavor of Heinz Profit." *The Financial Post,* 11 March 1998.

Murray, Matt. "Era Is Nearing An End As Heinz's Johnson Assumes More Control." *The Wall Street Journal,* 10 March 1997.

————. "Heinz Unwraps Details of Restructuring; Pretax Charge of $650 Million Planned." *The Wall Street Journal,* 17 March 1997.

O'Reilly, Anthony J.F. "125 Years at the Heinz Table." *Journal of Business Strategy,* May-June 1995.

Richards, Amanda. "Heinz Cans Principles to Protect Brand Role." *Marketing,* 31 August 1995.

Tascarella, Patty. "New Heinz CEO Makes His Presence Felt." *Pittsburgh Business Times,* 23 March 1997.

Tharp, Paul. "Time to Ketchup." *New York Post,* 1997.

For an annual report:

write: Stockholder Relations, H.J. Heinz Company, 600 Grant St., Pittsburgh, PA 15219

For additional industry research:

Investigate companies by their Standard Industrial Classification Codes, also known as SICs. Heinz's primary SICs are:

2033 Canned Fruits, Vegetables, Preserves, Jams and Jellies

2035 Pickled Fruits and Vegetables, Vegetable Sauces and Seasonings, and Salad Dressings

2038 Frozen Specialties, NEC

2091 Canned and Cured Fish and Seafoods

Hershey Foods Corporation

FOUNDED: 1908

Contact Information:
HEADQUARTERS: 100 Crystal A Dr.
   Hershey, PA 17033-0810
PHONE: (717)534-6799
FAX: (717)534-6724
URL: http://www.hersheys.com

OVERVIEW

Hershey Foods Corporation manufactures, distributes, and sells chocolate-related products and candies as well as grocery and pasta products. In 1997 the company controlled one-third of the U.S. candy market, making it the leading manufacturer in North America of chocolate, confectionery, and chocolate-related grocery products. Hershey's nearest competitor, Mars Inc., held just over 20 percent of the market. The company also is the leading producer in North America of brand-name dry pasta products. In addition, Hershey Foods Corporation has international interests and exports its products to more than 90 countries worldwide.

Although once content to rely on its products' quality to generate revenue, the company has gradually revised its policy and has sought to improve its prospects through new product introductions, corporate acquisitions, and specialized marketing campaigns, including thematic merchandising.

COMPANY FINANCES

Hershey Foods Corporation had record sales and earnings in 1997. Sales totaled $4.3 billion in 1997, compared to $3.99 billion in 1996, resulting in profits of $336.3 million and earnings of $2.25 per share. Hershey Foods corporate stock outperformed the S&P 500 during the first three quarters of 1997 by increasing 25.6 percent; its P/E ratio was 115 percent. The stock had a closing price of $62 on December 31, 1997. Hershey Foods' confectionery business is growing at a rate of 6.7 percent.

The corporation has paid a dividend on its common stock every quarter since the first quarter of 1930. The increase paid in September 1997 was the twenty-third consecutive annual increase of the corporation's common stock.

ANALYSTS' OPINIONS

Analysts with Morgan Stanley, Dean Witter expect the company's Hershey Chocolate North America division to provide 87 percent of the company's operating profit in 1998. They project Hershey's gross profit should rise in 1998 primarily due to volume growth.

HISTORY

Milton S. Hershey was born in Pennsylvania and was apprenticed to a candy maker as a teenager. His first candy business was a failure but a later venture with caramels was a success. It wasn't until Hershey visited the 1893 World's Columbian Exposition in Chicago that chocolate became a business interest. He decided then that the future was in chocolates, not caramels: he started the Hershey Chocolate Company the following year. Hershey sold his Lancaster Caramel Company in 1900 and returned to Derry County, his birthplace, to build his chocolate empire. His chocolate factory was completed in 1905. By 1911 the company was posting sales of $5 million and was a pioneer in confectionery mass-production techniques. The name Hershey would become synonymous with chocolate—even though the company did not advertise its products until the 1970s, adhering instead to Milton Hershey's policy of letting the quality of the products vouch for themselves.

In the 1960s Hershey Foods Corporation began expanding beyond its traditional product lines and making acquisitions. Toppings and a liquid baking product were among the line extensions. The company's first acquisition, made in 1963, was the H. B. Reese Candy Company, which had been founded by a former Hershey employee. Hershey Foods further expanded its chocolate and nonchocolate confectionery lines through the 1977 purchase of Y&S Candies, whose products included Twizzlers; the 1988 purchase of Peter Paul/Cadbury, whose products included Almond Joy and York peppermint patties; and the 1995 purchase of Henry Heide, Inc., whose products included Jujyfruits and Wunderbeans jelly beans. In 1996 Hershey purchased Leaf Inc., the leading company in the nonchocolate confections market, from Huhtamaki Oy of Finland. This acquisition, the largest ever by Hershey, added Good & Plenty, Heath, Jolly Rancher, Rain-Blo bubble gum, Whoppers malted milk balls, and other popular candy and chewing gum brands to the Hershey line, and reportedly enhanced the company's position in the chocolate candies market as

FINANCES:

Hershey Foods Corp.
Net Sales, 1994-1997
(billion dollars)

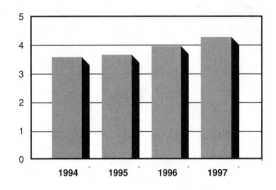

Hershey Foods Corp.
1997 Stock Prices
(dollars)

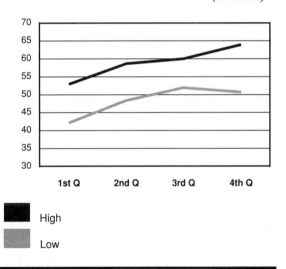

well. Hershey Foods saw an increase in its 1996 net sales of 8 percent over 1995 sales.

Hershey Foods entered the pasta market with the 1966 purchase of San Giorgio Macaroni Company. Since then the company has become the manufacturer of a number of regional pasta brands, the producer of an extensive line of food service pasta products, and the supplier of private-label pasta products to large retail chains and wholesalers. In 1996 Hershey Foods integrated its pasta and grocery operations into a single group. In addition to pasta, the division makes baking products, ice cream toppings, chocolate syrup, peanut butter, and milk products.

These are some of the miniature products manufactured by Hershey Corp. (Photograph by Chris Gardner. AP/Wide World Photos, Inc.)

STRATEGY

After losing a big chunk of its market share to Mars in the 1970s, Hershey Foods began advertising for the first time and diversifying its product lines. In 1997 the company increased summer candy sales by 20 percent through what was called the "largest and most complex [promotion] ever attempted in the candy industry." The promotion, a tie-in with the movie *Lost World,* encompassed several Hershey brands and featured dinosaur-themed candy. A similar campaign tied in with the 1998 movie *Godzilla* featured "Godzilla" packaging and novelty items. The company also has thematic merchandising programs tied to NASCAR, the NFL, and the NCAA Final Four.

INFLUENCES

Late in 1995 Hershey Foods increased wholesale prices on its candy bars and king-sized candy bars by 11 percent to offset higher costs for raw materials and packaging. The increase was the first in more than five years. Also in 1995, the company repurchased stock from the Milton Hershey School Trust. (Hershey Foods repurchased another 9.9 million shares from the trust in 1997.) These and other actions helped boost the company's stock value 40 percent. Hershey Foods' pasta business had a slight decline due to higher durum wheat costs in 1996, and experienced further decline in 1997 due in part to the trend toward away-from-home eating.

In April 1996 Hershey unveiled Sweet Escapes, a reduced fat and calorie candy line, spurred by the consumer demand for such food products. Hershey Foods claims the line is its "most successful new product introduction to date." Also in 1996, Hershey Foods introduced its first hard candies, called TasteTations, and its boxed candies, Hershey's Pot of Gold. In 1997 Hershey Foods introduced Reese's Crunchy Cookie Cups. Reese's is the corporation's largest and most successful brand.

FAST FACTS:
About Hershey Foods Corporation

Ownership: Hershey Foods Corporation is a publicly owned company traded on the New York Stock Exchange since 1927. The Milton Hershey School Trust is the company's majority shareholder.

Ticker symbol: HSY

Officers: Kenneth L. Wolfe, Chmn. & CEO; Joseph P. Viviano, Pres. & COO; William F. Christ, Senior VP, CFO, & Treasurer; Michael F. Pasquale, Pres., Hershey Chocolate North America; Jay F. Carr, Pres., Hershey Pasta & Grocery Group

Employees: 16,200 (1997)

Principal Subsidiary Companies: Hershey Chocolate North America, Hershey Pasta and Grocery Group, and Hershey International are the three operating divisions of Hershey Foods Corporation.

Chief Competitors: The company's primary competitors are: Mars Inc.; Nestle; and Philip Morris.

PRODUCTS

The Hershey Chocolate North America division produces chocolate and nonchocolate candies for consumers in the Americas under the Hershey brand name, as well as other candies, such as Almond Joy, Mounds, Cadbury Creme Eggs, Twizzlers, Reese's peanut butter cups, Sweet Escapes candy bars, Milk Duds, Jolly Rancher, Jujyfruits, and York peppermint patties. One of the company's core brands, Hershey's Kisses chocolates, was introduced in 1907. The candy has been packaged with the trademarked tissue paper plume since a mechanical wrapping machine was put into use in 1921. On July 26, 1971, Hershey's Tropical bar was sent to the moon with Apollo 15 astronauts.

The Hershey Pasta and Grocery group makes a wide range of grocery items, including eight regional pasta brands—American Beauty, Ideal by San Giorgio, Light 'n' Fluffy, P&R, Mrs. Weiss, Ronzoni, San Giorgio, and Skinner—and Hershey's and Reese's baking products and hot cocoa mixes. Hershey's hot chocolate was introduced in 1940, and its instant cocoa mix in 1956. The division holds the leadership position in the chocolate syrup and unsweetened cocoa categories in the United States.

Hershey's product line is diverse, comprising assorted flavors of Luden's throat drops, introduced in 1992; Reese's peanut butter ice cream cups, Hershey's Great American Cafe non-dairy creamers, and Amazin' Fruit drink boxes, all introduced in 1995; two flavors of Hershey's classic caramels, introduced in 1997; and ReeseSticks wafer bars, which appeared in 1998.

CORPORATE CITIZENSHIP

Milton S. Hershey, founder of Hershey Foods Corporation, established a tradition of corporate philanthropy. According to corporate literature, "Mr. Hershey's belief that an individual is morally obligated to share the fruits of success with others resulted in significant contributions to society."

Hershey returned to Pennsylvania's dairy country in 1903 because of the large supply of fresh milk for his products. Once there, he built a plant and developed the community around it. "Some people were suspicious of Mr. Hershey's motives in founding the town and feared that he would take advantage of people who lived there, as had happened in other 'company towns'," writes a Hershey biographer in a corporate history. "But though Mr. Hershey could certainly be autocratic and was criticized for deciding what was important, often without consulting the town's inhabitants, his concern for his workers' welfare was genuine."

Hershey found work for the community even during the Depression, when he built a hotel, a community

CHRONOLOGY:
Key Dates for Hershey Foods Corporation

1894: Milton Hershey starts Hershey Chocolate Company

1900: Hershey sells Lancaster Caramel Co.

1905: Chocolate factory is completed in Derry County, Pennsylvania

1907: Hershey's Kisses are introduced.

1909: Hershey Industrial School is established for orphaned boys

1927: The company incorporates as the Hershey Chocolate Company

1933: Hershey initiates a building campaign to provide jobs during the depression

1945: Milton Hershey dies

1963: Acquires the H.B. Reese Candy Co.

1966: Purchases San Giorgio Macaroni Company

1971: Hershey's Tropical bar goes to the moon on Apollo 15

1988: Acquires Peter Paul/Cadbury

1992: Hershey's introduces Luden's throat drops.

1995: Acquires Henry Heide, Inc.

1996: Purchases Leaf Inc.; introduces Sweet Escapes fat free line and TasteTations hard candies.

1997: Acquires Y&S Candies

building, a sports arena, and new corporate headquarters. No employees were laid off from Hershey during the Depression.

Hershey and his wife, who were childless, established the Hershey Industrial School in 1909. The school for orphaned boys was the primary recipient of Hershey's benevolence, just as it is today. Currently the Milton Hershey School Trust owns 35.5 percent of Hershey Foods common stock and more than three-fourths of the company's voting shares.

Hershey Foods is involved in community philanthropy to this day, primarily through Hershey's Track & Field Youth Program and the Children's Miracle Network.

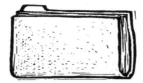

LET THEM EAT CHOCOLATE

Chocolate is a product that is largely derived from cocoa beans, which are imported from warm climate countries such as Brazil, Venezuela, Mexico, Ghana, and Nigeria. Initially, the beans are white when they are harvested, but turn brown when left to dry in the sun. Beans from different countries have different flavors, so they are stored by country of origin when they arrive at the Hershey plant for processing. Hershey has 25 cocoa bean silos, which can hold up to 90 million pounds of cocoa beans. That's the equivalent of 5 1/2 billion chocolate bars or other tasty treats. And remember, as the good folks at Hershey assure us, "Chocolate milk is a good source of many nutrients."

GLOBAL PRESENCE

Hershey International exports Hershey's branded confectionery and grocery products to more than 90 countries. It also markets these products, some of which are designed specifically for their markets. The company has licensing agreements with companies in several Asian nations. Hershey's strongest market outside North America is the Philippines. Products are sold there both at retail and in duty-free shops. The company plans to concentrate its expansion into the Far East, Russia, and China.

EMPLOYMENT

The company attributes much of its success in the mid-1990s to the team concept it promotes. It credits one such team with the development of Sweet Escapes. Other teams have developed means to control quality in Peter Paul Almond Joy candy bars, thereby eliminating missing almonds, and a corporatewide purchasing plan. In 1997 Hershey Foods became one of the few companies with more than 100 employees to extend stock options to every fulltime employee, regardless of position.

Hershey Pasta in Louisville, Kentucky, has employed hearing-impaired people since the 1950s; about 10 percent of all production employees at the Louisville facility are hearing-impaired. Most employees use sign language to circumvent the noisy equipment. Sign language is also taught at the plant.

SOURCES OF INFORMATION

Bibliography

Adding Value: Hershey Foods Corporation Summary Annual Report 1996. Hershey, PA: Hershey Foods Corporation, 1996.

"Hershey Foods Corporation. *Hoover's Online,* 10 March 1998. Available at http://www.hoovers.com.

"Hershey Foods Corporation."*International Directory of Company Histories.* Detroit: St. James Press, 1996.

"Hershey Foods Corporation Announces 1997 Record Sales and Earnings." *PR Newswire,* 28 January 1998.

"Hershey Foods Posts Record Sales, Earnings." *Knight-Ridder/Tribune Business News,* 19 January 1998.

"Hershey Will Make 'Godzilla' Chocolate Bars in Movie Tie-In." *Knight-Ridder/Tribune Business News,* 12 March 1998.

Hershey's Home Page, 16 February 1998. Available at http://www.hersheys.com.

Heuslein, William. "Timid No More." *Forbes,* 13 January 1997.

The Man Behind the Chocolate Bar: An Introduction to Milton S. Hershey 1857-1945. Hershey, PA: Hershey Foods Corporation, ND.

Moody's Investors Service. "Hershey Foods Corporation," 10 February 1998.

Morgan Stanley, Dean, Witter. "Hershey Foods - Company Report," 13 November 1997.

Profile of Hershey Foods Corporation. Hershey, PA: Hershey Foods Corporation, April 1996.

Warner, Mary. "Hershey Foods Offers Stock Options Plan to All Employees." *Knight-Ridder/Tribune Business News,* 26 February 1997.

Warner, Mary. "Hershey Foods Reaches the Non-Chocolate Lead among Candymakers." *Knight-Ridder/Tribune Business News,* 30 April 1997.

For an annual report:
write: Hershey Executive Offices, 100 Crystal A Dr., PO Box 810, Hershey, PA 17033-0810

For additional industry research:
Investigate companies by their Standard Industrial Classification Codes, also known as SICs. Hershey Foods Corporation's primary SICs are:

2064 Candy & Other Confectionery Products

2066 Chocolate And Cocoa Products

2098 Macaroni Spaghetti

Hewlett-Packard Company

OVERVIEW

Hewlett-Packard Company (HP) primarily designs, manufactures, and services electronic products and systems for computation, analysis, and measurement. HP offers more than 25,000 products and maintains manufacturing plants, research-and-development centers, warehouses, and administration facilities in more than 120 countries. Sales of computers and related products and services account for approximately 70 percent of the company's revenue. With 1997 net revenues of $42.9 billion, Hewlett-Packard is the nation's second-largest computer company and one of the fastest growing. The company is number 16 on the Fortune 500 list of the largest U.S. corporations and a leader in most of the markets in which it competes. These markets include servers, workstations, personal computers (including portables), computer peripherals, network equipment, and handheld calculators. Other products include electric test and measurement equipment, analytical instruments, and medical equipment. HP has become one of the largest diversified companies in the world, generating more than 55 percent of its business outside the United States.

ALSO KNOWN AS: HP
FOUNDED: 1939

Contact Information:

HEADQUARTERS: 3000 Hanover St.
   Palo Alto, CA 94304-1185
PHONE: (650)857-1501
FAX: (650)857-7299
EMAIL: students@hp.com
URL: http://www.hp.com

COMPANY FINANCES

Most of Hewlett-Packard's income comes from its broad range of computer products and peripherals, accounting for more than $35 billion of HP's total 1997 revenues. The company is the world's revenue leader for RISC and UNIX-based computers and the second largest supplier of workstations for engineering and business ap-

FINANCES:

Hewlett-Packard Net Revenues, 1994-1997 (billion dollars)

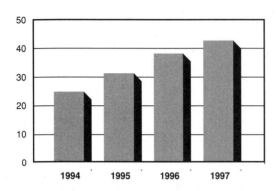

Hewlett-Packard 1997 Stock Prices (dollars)

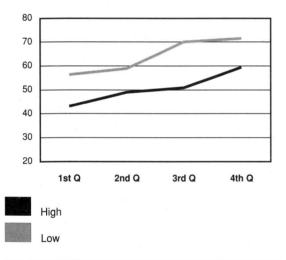

■ High

■ Low

in excellent financial condition enabling it to easily continue investing in future growth.

ANALYSTS' OPINIONS

Second only to IBM among the world's manufacturers of computer equipment and related technologies, Hewlett-Packard's history of consistently strong performance has always appealed to investors and analysts. The company itself remained confident in 1998 that it had the product offerings and resources needed for continuing success, though it warned that future revenue and margin trends could not be safely predicted. Indeed, that unpredictability caused investors to flee HP in the spring of 1998 after the company announced weaker than expected profits in the first quarter. No fewer than six firms and many analysts who had formerly been "bullish" on Hewlett-Packard slashed estimates on HP. HP blamed the drop in earnings on weakness in the Asian market and severe competition in the PC market. Also contributing to the decline was increasing erosion of HP's leading share in the workstation market caused by competitor Dell Computer. Analysts noted that, unlike IBM, Hewlett Packard did not have a major services business to fall back on when times were tough in the hardware market. Nevertheless, though both HP and investors were disappointed by the company's 1998 first quarter results, no one expected the setback to damage the company in the long term. New HP initiatives in the Internet arena also helped boost confidence.

HISTORY

Stanford University electrical engineers William Hewlett and David Packard began their joint venture in 1938 out of a Palo Alto garage with $538.00. They began working on their first product, a resistance-capacity audio oscillator, used for testing sound equipment. Their first order for eight oscillators was from Walt Disney Studios, who used them in the making of the film "Fantasia." Today that same garage is officially designated as a State Historical Landmark and recognized both as HP's birthplace and a Silicon Valley milestone.

Founded as a test-and-measurement company, HP's products quickly gained acceptance from engineers and scientists. When war broke out at the end of 1941, U.S. government orders poured in and the fledgling company expanded rapidly, building the first of its own buildings in 1942. Hewlett and Packard, still a little dazed by their sudden success, had the 10,000-square foot office/laboratory/factory designed so that it could be converted into a grocery store if the electronics business failed. In 1942 HP developed a line of microwave test signal generators and by the end of the war the company was the

plications. Net revenue from the United States rose 12 percent in 1997, while international revenue grew 11 percent and accounted for 56 percent of total revenues. The company boasted a comfortable 1997 operating profit of 10.1 percent and net profit of 7.3 percent, with a return on assets of 9.8 percent. Strong earnings growth contributed to an increase of $1.6 billion in net cash, enabling the Board of Directors to add $1.0 billion to the authorization for repurchase of the company's common stock. During a 52-week period from 1997 to 1998, HP's stock reached a high of $82.00 (and a low of $50.00). Despite losses in early 1998, Hewlett Packard remained acknowledged leader in the field. The company was incorporated in 1947.

The 1950s was a time of growth and maturation for Hewlett-Packard. The company had grown tremendously in the decade since World War II began, from 3 employees in 1941 to 215 in 1951. Revenues had soared from $34,000 in 1941 to $5.5 million in 1951. In 1957 the company made its first public stock offering and in 1958 it made its first acquisition, purchasing the F.L. Moseley company of Pasadena, California. By this time, HP was earning in excess of $30 million and employed nearly 1,800 people.

In 1959 HP ventured overseas for the first time, establishing a sales office in Geneva, Switzerland, and a manufacturing plant in Boeblingen, West Germany. A few years later, the German plant introduced a noninvasive fetal heart monitor and pioneered flexible working hours, an idea soon adopted at HP manufacturing facilities worldwide. The company continued its expansion overseas in 1963 forming a joint venture company, Yokogawa Hewlett-Packard in Tokyo, Japan. By 1965 the company's revenues had quintupled again, climbing to $165 million, and more than 9,000 people around the world worked for Hewlett-Packard.

For most U.S. companies, the 1970s was a time of oil shocks, stagflation, and increasingly agile international competition, but for Hewlett-Packard it was a time of continued innovation and rapid growth. In 1972 HP introduced the world's first scientific hand-held calculator and branched into business computing with the HP 3000 minicomputer. In 1973 the company introduced the industry's first commercial distributed data processing system and, in 1974 it developed the first minicomputer based on dynamic random access semiconductors (DRAMS). This period was also marked by a significant growth in earnings and employment, with revenues cracking the $1-billion mark well before the end of the decade and computer sales accounting for half the company's revenues. The 1970s also saw the long reign of Bill Hewlett and Dave Packard come to an end as they handed over responsibility for management of day-to-day operations to John Young.

As with the economic problems of the 1970s, the bitter recession of the early 1980s left Hewlett-Packard virtually unscathed. Between 1980 and 1985, sales more than doubled from $3.0 to $6.5 billion and employment rose from 57,000 to 85,000. The company launched a dazzling array of new products during this time, including its first personal computer, the HP-85, and its most successful product ever, the HP LaserJet printer. In 1984, HP also pioneered inkjet technology with the introduction of the HP Thinkjet printer. In the late 1990s, the company's inkjet and laser printers remained among the most popular and technologically sophisticated in the world.

The early 1980s also saw HP make its first foray into the world of network computing when its U.K. sub-

FAST FACTS:
About Hewlett-Packard Company

Ownership: Hewlett-Packard is a publicly held company traded on the New York Stock Exchange.

Ticker symbol: HWP

Officers: Lewis E. Platt, Chmn., Pres., & CEO, 57, 1997 earnings $1,811,435; Robert P. Wayman, Exec. VP & CFO, 52, 1997 earnings $1,032,300; Edward W. Barnholt, Exec. VP & General Manager, 53, 1997 earnings $748,592

Employees: 123,500

Principal Subsidiary Companies: Hewlett-Packard has subsidiary companies and facilities in 120 countries and manufacturing operations in 40. Some of these include: Apollo Systems Div.; CSTO Div.; Four Pi Systems Corp.; Hewlett-Packard Co. International Div.; Hewlett-Packard Co. Microwave Technology; Hewlett-Packard Co. Optoelectronics Div.; Hewlett-Packard Co. Personal Computer; Hewlett-Packard Co. Scientific Instruments; and Hewlett-Packard Co. Video Communications Div.

Chief Competitors: Hewlett-Packard's principal rival is IBM, the world's number one computer maker. HP's presence in the high-end workstation market also puts it in direct competition with companies like Sun Microsystems, Inc and Silicon Graphics. Its PC business pits it against leading PC manufacturers such as: Dell Computer; Acer Computer; and Compaq Computer. HP is also a leading player in the printer market where it competes against companies such as Canon; Epson; Lexmark; and Xerox.

sidiary, HP Limited, developed an electronic mail system that was the first of its kind based on minicomputers. At about the same time, HP launched its most massive and expensive R&D effort ever, a five-year program to develop computer systems based on innovative RISC (Reduced Instruction Set Computing) architecture. The new line of computer systems was launched in 1986 and formed the basis for the powerful workstations, which by the end of the decade had transformed the world of computing.

By 1990 HP's revenues had doubled again from 1985's $6.5 to $13.2 billion and the company had moved into the top 50 in the Fortune 500. Though 1992 and 1993

CHRONOLOGY:

Key Dates for Hewlett-Packard Company

1938: Stanford University electrical engineers William Hewlett and David Packard begin work on first product

1939: Hewlett and Packard formalize venture as a partnership

1942: Builds first of its own buildings

1947: Company is incorporated

1957: Makes first public stock offering

1958: Purchases F.L. Moseley company

1959: Establishes offices and plants overseas

1963: Forms joint venture company, Yokogawa Hewlett-Packard in Tokyo, Japan

1972: Introduces first scientific hand-held calculator

1973: Introduces industry's first commercial distributed data processing system

1974: Develops first minicomputer based on dynamic random access semiconductors (DRAMS)

1986: Introduces new family of Spectrum computer systems

1989: Pays $500 million for Apollo Computer

1994: Doubles 1990 earnings, taking in $25 billion

1998: CMP Media study names Hewlett-Packard the most recognized brand in the U.S. technology market

---

saw growth briefly slow down to a less frantic 10 percent or so a year, by 1994 the company had still managed to double its 1990 earnings, taking in $25 billion. During this time HP concentrated on marrying its technologies of measurement, computing, and communication and developed new applications for its computer technology in analytical and medical instrumentation. New products included: the 11-ounce HP 95LX palmtop PC, weighing 11 ounces, which combined Lotus 1-2-3 software with advanced calculation features and data-communication capabilities; the HP SONOS 1500 echocardiograph system for real-time, non-invasive cardiac analysis using ultrasound waves; and a color scanner that allowed computers to read photographs and other visual images.

By the late 1990s Hewlett-Packard ranked as the second largest supplier of information technology in the world. From printers and scanners to desktop PCs and workstations, Hewlett-Packard was a dominant force in the world computing market and, in 1998 a study conducted by New York-based CMP Media named Hewlett-Packard the most recognized brand in the U.S. technology market, even finishing ahead of the ubiquitous Microsoft. Perhaps the company's only weakness was that its main strength lay in hardware, making it slow to take advantage of the many opportunities presented by the explosive growth of the Internet from the mid-1990s on. By 1997 the company was moving to correct this deficiency, however, acquiring VeriFone, the industry leader in electronic-payment systems and beginning development of its "Web Quality of Service" line of technologies, which were designed to prevent system overloads and allow businesses to prioritize transactions during peak usage periods. HP also began developing its own version of Java, a popular and versatile programming system originally developed by Sun Microsystems and widely used on the Internet. HP's plan was to focus on implementing this technology in printers and other devices, allowing them to link into and use a computer's interface to do such things as notify the systems administrator that the toner cartridge was running out, or even query a database and initiate an order for a replacement cartridge.

These moves put Hewlett-Packard in a position to play a more important role in the burgeoning Information Age. As CEO Lew Platt explained in his 1997 Letter to Shareholders, "Software has been one of HP's least visible businesses, but it is vitally important to our future." Thus, a second component of HP's new strategy was to form partnerships with electronic commerce software companies to offer what the company referred to in one press release as a "full-production Internet-commerce environment." Some analysts suggested the moves could give HP a leg up on its major competitor, IBM, in the electronic commerce field, a market expected to grow enormously by the end of the decade. In 1998 it was still too early to tell how things would turn out, but, as HP's consumer marketing campaign put it, the future was clearly one of "Expanding Possibilities."

STRATEGY

Hewlett-Packard's growth has been generated by a strong commitment to research and development in electronics and computer technology combined with a decentralized organization that gives business units considerable decision-making authority. That growth has been accomplished by providing a continuous flow of new products and services to markets they currently serve, and by expanding into new areas. Reflecting the company's continued investments in new technologies, expenditures for research and development accounted for 7.2 percent of total expenditures in 1997, increasing by 14 percent to $3.1 billion, compared with $2.8 billion in 1996. Future increases in research and development expenditures are anticipated in order to maintain the company's competitive position and ensure a steady flow of innovative, high-quality products.

In Hewlett-Packard's 73 divisions worldwide, the company strives to promote industry standards that recognize customer preferences for open systems in which different vendors' products can work together. Collaboration with other companies and technology alliances allow HP to expand into markets it might otherwise be unable to penetrate. For example, HP and Sybase, Inc. teamed up in a joint venture to develop Intel's upcoming 64-bit processor, the IA-64 (Intel Architecture-64-bit). HP and Intel jointly developed the original architecture. The company often bases its product innovations on such standards and seeks to make technology innovations into industry standards through licensing to other companies. For example, during fiscal 1996 the company helped lead the development of the International Cryptography Framework, an industrywide effort to address the issue of security on the Internet.

Like other large companies, HP flexes its financial muscle when necessary to strengthen its dominant position within the market. In acquiring Apollo Computer in 1989, a maker of workstations, HP jumped to the number two position in market sales behind Sun Microsystems, up from number three before the merger. Similarly, in a move aimed at establishing a stronger presence in the growing electronic commerce market, HP partnered with Cisco Systems in 1997 to develop technologies to increase the efficiency and reliability of business on the Internet. This strategy was deemed a shrewd move by analysts who foresaw the possibility of HP capturing a significant share of the electronic commerce market from IBM. As Zona Research senior analyst, Vernon Keenan, told *Wired News,* the move was typical of HP's approach of "going after a competitor that's plowed the market initially." In fact, capitalizing on the innovations of others has always been a key part of HP's strategy. The company built its dominance of the printer market on a printer engine developed by the Japanese company, Canon, and was later sued—first by Apple Computer for copyright infringement and then by Xerox for patent infringement. Similarly, HP's decision to develop its own version of the Java programming system standardized by Sun Microsystems enabled it to gain a foothold in previously inaccessible markets.

produced letter-quality type and could be sold for $3,000 retail. HP's only printer at that time was a $100,000 model sold with the company's minicomputers. HP started developing a new line of printers for consumers, using Canon's new engine. HP was confident that they could develop a cheaper, better product than the Japanese, exploiting HP's brand name and making up on volume whatever profits it had to share with Canon. HP had no experience selling to a broad consumer market. However, Richard Hackborn built up, over 15 years, a printer division that now brings in one-third of HP's revenues and 40 percent of its profits.

Similarly, HP's purchase of Apollo Computer in 1989 leapfrogged it into the number two spot in the market for computer workstations, a field experiencing significant growth in the early 1990s. The company entered the PC field even later, but once again its immense resources allowed it to quickly catch up. In 1992 HP was the sixth leading supplier of personal computers, by 1996 it was the third largest. But while HP was gaining ground in the PC field, it was slow to make its products relevant to the Internet. Competitors like IBM and Sun Microsystems had gotten in on the ground floor and by 1997 had a significant lead in this area. HP responded by forming a partnership with Cisco Systems to develop new Internet business tools and by developing its own variant of the Java programming system originally developed by Sun.

Once HP brings its resources to bear, it is able to compete very effectively, offering customers superior technology, performance, price, quality, reliability, distribution, and service and support. But product life cycles are short and to remain competitive the company will have to continue to develop new products and periodically enhance its existing products. Capitalizing on its early entry into the market, HP has dominated the printer market with its LaserJet and DeskJet brands. The company has worked diligently to create and sustain a competitive advantage through branding, new product development, and aggressive pricing.

Hewlett-Packard has certainly been responsible for its share of innovations over the years, but perhaps its greatest strength lies in its ability to create highly technical products with a user-friendly interface. So strong is HP in this area that in 1997 it was able to lure Donald A. Norman, the former head of Apple's Research Laboratories, to a position at Hewlett-Packard Labs. Said Norman to *Wired,*" I should be able to do tasks without learning a complex technology . . . Today we have to learn tools; I want to make that necessity disappear."

INFLUENCES

In 1981 HP's computer peripherals group manager Richard Hackborn learned that Japan's Canon was working on a prototype of a small, cheap desktop printer that

CURRENT TRENDS

Hewlett-Packard is currently spending millions to develop new products such as printers that can produce photo-quality images from screens, and palm-size sensors that can transmit soil content data from the ground to farmers' PCs. On October 14, 1997, HP and Intel revealed the first details of their jointly defined Explicitly Parallel Instruction Computing (EPIC) technology and IA-64 (Intel Architecture 64-bit). The new technology was expected to offer breakthrough performance for the next-generation of 64-bit high-end workstation and servers. The company also announced a joint strategy with Microsoft to increase the productivity and simplify integration of enterprise computing technology while reducing costs. In another move, HP expanded its share of the computer printer market with new products such as the mopier (makes multiple original prints) and the HP Network ScanJet 5. The company estimated that even a gain as small as 1 percent could significantly increase its printer sales.

But it was in the Internet arena that the company hoped to make its biggest gains. By 1998 the Internet had become the fastest growing segment of the information technology market and all the major companies were scrambling to stake out a piece of the action. The emerging global network and a host of new specialized "information appliances" were revolutionizing the way people gathered and share information. HP believed it had the expertise to help create and manage these data highways, pointing to its expertise in both instrumentation and computing as a key advantage. The company's biggest step in this direction came with its alliance with Cisco Systems, Inc. early in 1997. The two companies agreed to a broad technology-development, Internet solutions, and customer-support alliance that would integrate computing, networking, and network management to supply complete, fully secure Internet-ready networked computing solutions.

Although the company continued to maintain its growth in 1998, earnings for the second quarter of fiscal 1998 were down slightly from the previous year, provoking many investors to sell their shares and pushing down the value of HP's stock. The company blamed the decrease in profitability on lower prices for computers and printers and on economic weakness in Asia.

PRODUCTS

HP's first products were electronic measuring instruments used primarily by engineers and scientists. Later the company extended its range of measurement instruments to serve the areas of medicine and chemical analysis. The eventual move into the computer field was a logical progression based on the need to help its customers collect and manipulate large quantities of measurement data. By the late 1990s, though still a leader in instrumentation, HP was best known for its broad line of computer and computer-based products, including associated software, peripherals, support, and services. In 1998 HP was the world's leading supplier of RISC sys-

tems and UNIX system-based computers and the world's second largest supplier of powerful workstations for engineering and business applications. It was also one of the fastest-growing personal computer companies in the world. HP's PC products include the Pavilion family of PCs for home users, the OmniGo 100 handheld organizer, and the 200LX palmtop PC.

HP is also the world's leading supplier of printers. New products like the HP LaserJet 4000 printers deliver high-resolution 1,200 dots-per-inch print performance at full engine speed and incorporate new technology that allows them to exchange information with printers, scanners, and other devices directly without a PC. The company also introduced a new DeskJet inkjet printer, the 722C that features exclusive new color and photo enhancement technologies that enable it to produce photo-quality images more quickly. Other HP "hardcopy" products include DesignJet large-format printers, ScanJet scanners, OfficeJet all-in-ones, and CopyJet color printer-copiers.

Early in 1997 Hewlett-Packard introduced a new Jet-Direct print server with advanced features designed to save network administrators time and protect a company's network-printing investment. The AdvanceStack Switch 800T that HP started shipping in May 1997 earned a Communications Week Max Award for its 10/100Mbit Ethernet switching. Recently HP teamed up with Intel Corporation and Microsoft to help develop the reference specifications for the NetPC system, the newest class of personal computer. HP also put forth the most affordable scanner ever offered to consumers, the Scan-Jet 5s. HP also introduced the HP-UX system to enable companies to avoid date-related system and application failures in the transition to the year 2000.

CORPORATE CITIZENSHIP

In 1939, the year the company was founded with $538 and no revenues or profits, its ledger showed a $5 gift to the community. Co-founders Bill Hewlett and Dave Packard began a tradition of community involvement with a modest gift to a local charity in Palo Alto, California. Today HP is recognized as a leading giver among corporations in the United States. HP gives a lot of HP equipment, mostly for educational programs. In 1996 the company donated $72 million towards its philanthropy efforts and about 80 percent or $57 million of this amount went to education.

In 1997 the company donated about $61 million in cash and equipment, and was recognized for its philanthropy by the National Society of Fund Raising Executives who awarded it the Outstanding Corporation Award. It also launched the Diversity in Education Initiative, a program aimed at encouraging females and minorities to consider technical careers, and to help improve the teaching of math and science in schools and colleges.

Hewlett-Packard's environmental philanthropy focuses on many areas of concern. Since 1991, HP has donated nearly $4 million in cash and equipment to U.S. conservation and environmental causes. In addition, the company continues to support environmental efforts throughout the world. In Europe HP contributes to a coalition of educational institutions, and government and environmental researchers working to improve the quality of water in several European rivers. This includes the Rhine Basin Program, to which HP Europe has donated more than $5 million. But HP does more than just donate money to environmental programs. It is a leading supplier of measurement and computation systems used for environmental monitoring and strives to develop products that minimize impact on the environment and on human health and safety. Most HP products are designed so that they can be taken apart and recycled. The company also offers customers in several countries a no-cost recycling program for HP LaserJet toner cartridges. Each month, HP recycles or reuses approximately 3 million pounds of material from old products at its product-recovery centers in Grenoble, France, and Roseville, California.

In 1996, HP's commuter transportation department won a U.S. Environmental Protection Agency award for its efforts to improve air quality and reduce traffic congestion by encouraging the use of commute alternatives. Similarly, two HP plants in California were recognized by the Integrated Waste Management Board as among the top-10 waste-conscious businesses for diverting from landfill 92 percent of the solid waste they generated in 1996. Another HP site that uses wastewater from manufacturing to irrigate landscaping won a 1995 award from the California Water Pollution Control Association for its program. Also in 1995, HP Austria won an award cosponsored by the national government and an international environmental organization for the site's environmental efforts. On the energy conservation side, HP's NightDIRECTOR made it possible to switch networked PCs on remotely for off-hours maintenance, instead of leaving them running all night.

GLOBAL PRESENCE

Sales outside the United States make up more than half the company's revenue. HP's total orders originating outside the United States, as a percentage of total company orders, were approximately 56 percent in fiscal 1996, 55 percent in fiscal 1995, and 54 percent in fiscal 1994. Approximately two-thirds of HP's international orders in each of the last three fiscal years were derived from Europe, with most of the balance coming from Japan, other countries in Asia Pacific, Latin America, and Canada. In addition, part of the company's product and components manufacturing, along with key suppliers, are outside the United States. HP is one of the top 10 U.S. exporters.

Hewlett-Packard operates facilities in 10 states, Puerto Rico, and 16 countries, and has 600 sales and support offices and distributorships in more than 120 countries. Sales are made to industrial and commercial customers, educational and scientific institutions, health care providers (including individual doctors, hospitals, clinics, and research laboratories), and in the case of its calculators and other personal information products, computer peripherals and PCs, to individuals for personal use. Foreign sales subsidiaries make up most of the company's sales in international markets. In countries with low sales volume, the company is marketing its products through various representative and distributorship arrangements. Certain sales in international markets, however, are made directly by the company from the United States. The Frankfurt Heart Center, one of Germany's largest cardiac treatment facilities, asked Hewlett-Packard to supply cardiology and patient monitoring equipment and to design a medical information management system that would make all patient data available online.

HP anticipates revenues in China to rise more than 50 percent in 1997 from a total of $550 million in 1996. Furthermore, HP's vice president, Alex Sozonoff, stated, "China has been strategically elevated as the major investment market for Hewlett-Packard." Space TV Systems, Inc. chose HP's MediaStream Broadcast Server as its on-air remedy for the world's first global direct-to-home satellite service that will feature Chinese programming. This joint venture will supply programming to China, Taiwan, Hong Kong, Japan, Korea, Australia, and North America.

HP's heavy dependence on foreign markets hurt the company in early 1998 as the Asian economy struggled in the wake of a region-wide economic collapse. Sales of medical instrumentation and test measurement systems fell and the company found itself posting earnings well short of expectations. The Asian economic problems also put pressure on HP's Asian partners, one of whom, Samsung, was forced to sell its 45-percent share in the company's 13-year-old joint venture, Hewlett-Packard Korea, to HP for $36 million. In addition to bailing out Samsung, HP also announced it would invest $250 to $300 million in South Korea in 1998. Perhaps that is one reason why the company was rated the number 9 most admired company in Asia, compared to its number 10 rating in the United States.

EMPLOYMENT

Hewlett-Packard believes strongly in the principles of equal opportunity and affirmative action for all employees and promotes an informal, non-authoritarian working atmosphere. In fact, HP won the prestigious Catalyst Award, an annual national prize that recognizes organizations for their programs to advance the careers of female professionals. The company also adheres to the belief that it is the employees who make the company's success possible and rewards them for their efforts with regular cash profit sharing and stock-purchase programs. Employees are eligible for profit sharing as soon as they have worked for the company for six months, receiving two bonuses annually. In May 1998, HP distributed $210 million to more than 118,000 employees throughout the world.

SOURCES OF INFORMATION

Bibliography

Fisher, Lawrence M. "Hewlett in $1.15 Billion Deal for Maker of Credit Card Services." *The New York Times,* 24 April 1997.

Glave, James. "Sun's New Headache: H-P's Java." *Wired News,* 20 March 1998. Available at http://www.wried.com/news/.

Hewlett-Packard 1976 Annual Report. Palo Alto, CA: Hewlett Packard Company, January 1977.

Hewlett-Packard 1997 Annual Report. Palo Alto, CA: Hewlett Packard Company, January 1998.

"Hewlett-Packard Company." *Hoover's Handbook of American Business 1997.* Austin, TX: The Reference Press, 1996.

"Hewlett-Packard Company." *Hoover's Online,* 19 July 1998. Available at http://www.hoovers.com.

"Hewlett-Packard 'Copies' Xerox." *Reuters,* 29 May 1998.

The Hewlett Packard Home Page, 29 May 1998. Available at http://www.hp.com.

"Hewlett-Packard Sees China Sales Up 50 Percent." *Market-Guide,* 21 April 1997. Available at http://www.marketguide.com/MGI/INDUSTRY/INDUSTRY.htm.

"HP AdvanceStack Switching Hubs Earn Editor's Choice Award for Performance and Features; Network Computing Ranks HP Above 3Com in Port-switching Comparison." *MarketGuide,* 14 February 1997. Available at http://www.marketguide.com/MGI/INDUSTRY/INDUSTRY.htm.

"HP Announces $4 million Grant Program to Strengthen Educational Opportunities for Women and Minority Engineers; Using Cash Grants, Universities and K-12 Schools Will Partner to Encourage and Prepare Women and Minorities for High-Tech Careers." *MarketGuide,* 27 March 1997. Available at http://www.marketguide.com/MGI/INDUSTRY/INDUSTRY.htm.

"HP Awards $210 Million in Profit Sharing to Employees." *Business Wire,* 28 May 1998.

"HP Breaks the Bad News." *Wired News,* 15 May 1998. Available at http://www.wired.com/news/.

"HP Buys Out Korean Partner." *Wired News,* 27 May 1998. Available at http://www.wired.com/news/.

"HP Jumps Into Java War." *Wired News,* 20 May 1998. Available at http://www.wired.com/news/.

"HP LaserJet 5Si Mopier Wins Best New Product Award at FOSE; HP Also Ranked No. 1 in Federal Government Survey on Competitiveness and Past Performance." *MarketGuide,* 8 April 1997. Available at http://www.marketguide.com/MGI/INDUSTRY/INDUSTRY.htm.

"HP Tackles Year-2000 Issue With Cure 2000 Solution; HP-UX is Year-2000-Ready." *MarketGuide,* 4 March 1997. Available at http://www.marketguide.com/MGI/INDUSTRY/INDUSTRY.htm.

"HP Takes Internet Plunge." *Reuters,* 11 May 1998.

"Industry's Most Powerful 64-Bit Microprocessor Attains Performance Level That Outperforms Competitors By Up To 260 Percent." *MarketGuide,* 4 April 1996. Available at http://www.marketguide.com/MGI/INDUSTRY/INDUSTRY.htm.

"Intel and Microsoft Release NetPC Reference Specification For Broad Industry Review; Product Announcements From PC Manufacturers Expected Within 90 Days; Specification Co-Authored by Compaq, Dell and Hewlett-Packard." *MarketGuide,* 12 March 1997. Available at http://www.marketguide.com/MGI/INDUSTRY/INDUSTRY.htm.

Melville, Richard. "IBM Attracts Investors Fleeing Hewlett-Packard." *MarketGuide,* 14 May 1998. Available at http://www.marketguide.com/MGI/INDUSTRY/INDUSTRY.htm.

"New HP JetDirect 10/100Base-TX Print Server Simplifies Migration to High-Speed Networking; HP Print Server Operates in 10Base-T or 100BaseTX Environments, Making the Transition to Fast Ethernet Easy." *MarketGuide,* 14 April 1997. Available at http://www.marketguide.com/MGI/INDUSTRY/INDUSTRY.htm.

Oakes, Chris. "HP Makes E-Shopper Guarantees." *Wired News,* 11 May 1998. Available at http://www.wired.com/news/.

Pescovitz, David. "Invisible Computing." *Wired News,* 27 May 1998. Available at http://www.wired.com/news/.

"President Clinton Announces Ron Brown Award." *MarketGuide,* 3 April 1997. Available at http://www.marketguide.com/MGI/INDUSTRY/INDUSTRY.htm.

"Space TV Systems Selects HP MediaStream Broadcast Server For Its First Digital Direct-To-Home Satellite TV Service." *MarketGuide,* 7 April 1997. Available at http://www.marketguide.com/MGI/INDUSTRY/INDUSTRY.htm.

"Xerox Sues HP Over Patents." *Reuters,* 14 May 1998.

For an annual report:
on the Internet at: http://www.hp.com **or** write: Hewlett-Packard Company, 3000 Hanover St., Palo Alto, CA 94304

For additional industry research:
Investigate companies by their Standard Industrial Classification Codes, also known as SICs. Hewlett-Packard's primary SICs are:

3571 Electronic Computers

3572 Computer Storage Devices

3575 Computer Terminals

3577 Computer Peripheral Equipment, NEC

3578 Calculating & Accounting Equipment

7378 Computer Maintenance & Repair

Hilton Hotels Corporation

OVERVIEW

The Hilton name has become nearly synonymous with hotel, and rightly so. In 1998 Hilton was the seventh-largest hotel company in the United States, and it has worldwide name recognition through its global hotel and gaming operations. The company develops, owns, manages, and franchises hotels, hotel-casinos, resorts, and vacation-ownership resorts. Through its subsidiaries, Hilton also has interests in designing and furnishing hotels and computer reservation systems for rental cars and hotels.

Hilton's lodgings division includes 231 hotels and resorts across the United States. Of this total, 51 are owned and/or managed by Hilton, while 180 operate under franchise agreements. The company's flagship properties include New York's Waldorf-Astoria, the Hilton Hawaiian Village, and the Chicago Hilton and Towers. Hilton's Grand Vacations subsidiary manages 18 vacation-ownership (time share) resorts in Florida and Nevada. The company continues to expand its hotel operations through the acquisition of full-service properties and through the addition of new mid-price hotels, such as the Hilton Garden Inn properties.

In 1997 Hilton announced a strategic alliance with Britain's Ladbroke Group PLC, owners of the Hilton name outside the United States. The alliance reunites the Hilton name worldwide for the first time in more than 30 years. With more than 400 hotels and resorts in 49 countries, the reunification by both companies adds further luster to Hilton's leadership position in the hospitality industry.

With 16 gaming facilities worldwide, Hilton Hotels Corp. is considered the world's largest casino gambling company. The company's acquisition of Bally Entertainment Corp. in late 1996 helped to vault Hilton into

FOUNDED: 1919

Contact Information:
HEADQUARTERS: 9336 Civic Center Dr.
 Beverly Hills, CA 90210
PHONE: (310)278-4321
FAX: (310)205-4599
URL: http://www.hilton.com

FINANCES:

Hilton Hotels Corp. Revenues, 1994-1997 (billion dollars)

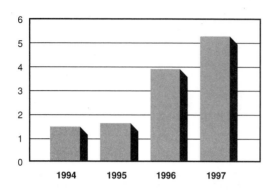

Hilton Hotels Corp. 1997 Stock Prices (dollars)

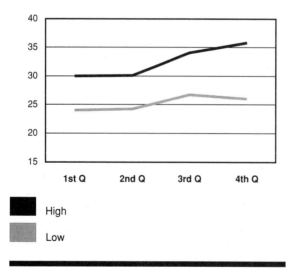

■ High

▨ Low

this leadership position in the world of gaming. Hilton's gaming division owns and operates eight hotel-casinos in New Jersey and Nevada, as well as riverboat casinos in Louisiana, Mississippi, and Missouri. In the Canadian province of Ontario, the company manages the Casino Windsor and the Northern Belle Casino with a partner.

COMPANY FINANCES

In 1997 Hilton Hotels Corporation reported net earnings of $250 million on revenue of $5.30 billion, com-

pared with net income of $82 million on revenue of $3.94 billion in 1996. Per-share earnings of $.94 in 1997 were up sharply from $.41 per share in 1996. In 1995 the company reported a net of $173 million on revenue of $1.65 billion, compared with 1994 net earnings of $122 million on revenue of $1.51 billion. Per-share earnings for 1995 and 1994 were $.89 and $.63, respectively.

In 1997 room rentals accounted for 36 percent of Hilton's total revenue, while its casino operations generated 34 percent of the total. Food and beverage sales brought in another 19 percent of revenue; 1 percent was accounted for by management and franchise fees; and the remaining 10 percent came from other operations.

ANALYSTS' OPINIONS

The appointment of Stephen F. Bollenbach as president and CEO had the pundits opining—overtime—about Hilton's prospects. There is no single consensus, save for general agreement that Bollenbach's appointment was a wise decision.

"[Bollenbach] brings [Hilton] financial acumen—an in-depth knowledge of the hotel business and gaming business [and] he brings leadership skills," said Los Angeles-based hotel consultant Saul Leonard in an article in *Hotel & Motel Management*. "Steve Bollenbach has been a success at every place he's been. I see no reason not to see him continue his success at Hilton."

The investment community also scrutinized the situation. "Bollenbach is also taking steps to market and leverage the respected, if underutilized, Hilton name more aggressively," explains *Financial World*. "[One analyst] explains that Hilton missed the boat on the three-star, limited-service hotel market segment over the past 10 years and is now actively franchising the mid-price Hilton Garden Inn chain. The company expects to have 100 signed franchises by 2000."

Analysts wonder how all of these moves will translate into revenue and earnings gains. While Wall Street is excited about the prospects, its outlook for the company is more modest than Hilton's own. Joyce Minor of Lehman Brothers, for example, expects the stock's price to reach the mid-30s [sic] within a year or so and recommends the stock.

Another analyst, quoted in *Financial World,* insists that "analysts are conservative in their estimates." He also thinks they have "not really given credit for Hilton's hotel acquisitions and what they will mean for earnings growth."

HISTORY

Around the turn of the century Conrad Hilton rented out rooms in his family's home. It was a passion that was to last a lifetime. In 1919 Hilton left New Mexico and headed to Texas, where he planned to buy a bank. Hilton's plans for a career in banking were abandoned when he spotted a small hotel for sale in Cisco, Texas, between Abilene and Fort Worth. With the purchase of this small-town hotel, Hilton launched his career in the lodging business. He soon purchased additional properties, but his plans were stalled by the Depression. Hilton devised a scheme to lease the land on which hotels were located rather than buy the hotels themselves.

Determined to grow his business, Hilton made his way to California, where he began purchasing hotels in 1938. There he met a young starlet by the name of Zsa Zsa Gabor—they were married but later divorced.

Hilton Hotels Corporation was officially formed in 1946 with Conrad Hilton as its president. Trading in the company's stock was begun on the New York Stock Exchange. By 1948 Hilton had amassed enough properties in the United States and Mexico to necessitate the formation of Hilton International to manage his foreign assets. He opened his first European hotel in 1953. The following year he made the biggest transaction in the industry to date when he purchased 10 hotels in the Statler chain for a record $111 million.

Hilton made its first foray into gaming in 1949 when it opened a casino in San Juan, Puerto Rico, at the behest of the governor of Puerto Rico. Barron Hilton tells the story: "My father had been born and raised in the small town of Socorro, New Mexico, and had learned to speak Spanish even before he could speak English. So in responding to the Governor, he wrote back in Spanish. I believe the Governor was touched by this, and that this letter in his native language played a major role in our company securing the agreement to operate what became the Caribe Hilton."

The company continued to acquire properties and began franchising the Hilton name in 1965. Conrad's son, Barron Hilton, was appointed president in 1966 and chairman of the company upon his father's death in 1979; he remains chairman.

Stephen F. Bollenbach gained much attention in the 1990s for putting together Disney's $19-billion acquisition of Capital Cities/ABC while serving as CFO at Disney. He joined Hilton as CEO in 1996. Bollenbach is the first non-family member to head Hilton. Much was made of this transfer of power, and since confidence in Bollenbach was high, the market responded. Hilton's stock rose 21 percent within two days of his hiring.

In 1997 an alliance was hammered out between Hilton and Britain's Ladbroke Group PLC, which owns the rights to the Hilton name outside the United States. The agreement reunites the Hilton name worldwide for the first time in more than 30 years. More than 400 hotels and resorts in 49 countries bear the Hilton name.

FAST FACTS:
About Hilton Hotels Corporation

Ownership: Hilton Hotels Corporation is a publicly owned company traded on the New York Stock Exchange.

Ticker symbol: HLT

Officers: Barron Hilton, Chmn., 70, $600,000; Stephen F. Bollenbach, Pres. & CEO, 55, $945,000; Matthew J. Hart, Exec. VP & CFO, 45, $715,000; Dieter H. Huckestein, Exec. VP & Pres., Hotel Operations, 54, $600,000

Employees: 61,000

Chief Competitors: As a major force in the hospitality industry, Hilton Hotels Corporation faces competition in the hotel and resort industry as well as the gaming business. Major competitors include: Accor; Boyd Gaming; Host Marriott; Hyatt; ITT Corporation; Loews; Marriott International; Mirage Resorts; and Westin.

STRATEGY

In its global strategy to expand its international hotel network, Hilton won some and lost some in the latter half of the 1990s. In 1996 the company acquired Bally Entertainment for $3 billion and announced plans to build 100 Hilton Garden Inns, a mini-chain of mid-price hotels. That same year, Hilton bought out Prudential's interests in six hotels, including Chicago Hilton & Towers, San Francisco Hilton & Towers, and New York Hilton & Towers.

Unsuccessful, however, was Hilton's hostile takeover bid for ITT, the owner of Sheraton hotels and Caesars World. ITT managed to elude Hilton for months through a series of escape maneuvers and eventually accepted a higher offer from Starwood, a real estate investment management company.

INFLUENCES

Among the trends that has shaped the strategy of the lodging industry in recent years, none has been more powerful than the economic boom in the United States

CHRONOLOGY:

Key Dates for Hilton Hotels Corporation

1919: Conrad Hilton purchases a small hotel in Crisco, Texas

1938: Hilton begins purchasing hotels in California

1946: Hilton Hotels Corporation is officially formed with Conrad as president

1953: Hilton opens his first hotel in Europe

1954: The company purchases 10 hotels in the Statler chain for $111 million

1965: The company begins franchising the Hilton name

1966: Barron Hilton, Conrad's son, becomes chairman of the company

1979: Conrad Hilton dies

1997: An alliance between Hilton and the Ladbroke Group PLC (which owns the rights to the Hilton name outside the U.S.) reunites the Hilton name worldwide

and other parts of the world (much of Asia being a notable exception). According to a January 1998 report in *Business Week,* hotel room rates, bolstered by a combination of strong demand and a shortage of hotel rooms, climbed nearly 13 percent during 1996 and 1997.

However, what goes up must eventually come down. *Business Week* reported that U.S. hotel occupancy rates, which slipped slightly from 65.1 to 64.5 percent in 1997, will probably drop more in 1998, according to analyst Bjorn Hanson of Coopers & Lybrand. This slowing in hotel demand puts into question the need for the 140,000 new hotel rooms coming on line in 1998. *Business Week* reported that while the supply of hotel rooms will grow by 3.4 percent in 1998, the demand for rooms will climb by only 2.6 percent. While none of these trends is likely to result in a major industry shakedown, they do indicate that the going may be rougher in the remaining two years of the decade.

A saving grace in all of this for Hilton is the likelihood that demand for space in full-service hotels in gateway cities will continue to be strong. Most of Hilton's holdings fall into this category. Hilton's CEO Stephen F. Bollenbach remarked in *Business Week,* "For our hotels, these are the best of times, and it will continue."

CURRENT TRENDS

In an article assessing the positive aspects of the 1998 outlook for the lodging industry, *Business Week* predicted that room rates will increase by about 5.3 percent and many upscale hotels will continue to experience room shortages. On the downside, however, the article indicated that budget, mid-price, and extended-stay hotels are likely to be hurt by overdevelopment, and that occupancy levels in many parts of the United States are declining.

One trend that Hilton executives have tracked very closely is the growing American love affair with the Internet and electronic business. When marketing executives first campaigned for a sophisticated Internet site that would allow customers to book reservations on-line, those in charge of the bottom line insisted on some guarantees, according to a 1998 report in *InformationWeek.* Dieter Huckestein, president of Hilton's hotel division, said, "We wanted to be leading, not bleeding." According to Bruce Rosenberg, Hilton's vice president of marketing and distribution, every dollar spent on the company's web site generates about $10 in revenue. The company estimates that on-line room reservations produce roughly $2 million of revenue monthly.

PRODUCTS

Hilton Hotels Corporation develops, owns, manages and franchises hotels, hotel-casinos, resorts, and vacation-ownership resorts throughout the United States. The company's major units include Hilton Hotels Divisions, Hilton Gaming Division, Hilton Reservations Worldwide, and Hilton Equipment Corporation. As of early 1998 the company had 231 properties in 7 different product categories, including airport hotels, mid-priced hotels and resorts.

CORPORATE CITIZENSHIP

Hilton Hotels Corporation is involved in numerous charitable activities, particularly in the communities in which their properties are located. Among the corporatewide programs are Kids Voting USA, a national voter-education program, and the Hilton Gaming Scholarship Program, which grants scholarships to the children of employees.

In 1996 Hilton instituted a program for compulsive gamblers at its Australian property. The program provides information on where to seek assistance, as well as crisis intervention training for casino staff.

GLOBAL PRESENCE

For more than 30 years Hilton's domestic and international hotel operations were separated, with Ladbroke Group PLC managing Hilton hotels outside the United States. In 1997 Hilton and Ladbroke negotiated a strategic alliance that linked their operations and reunited the Hilton name worldwide. As part of their agreement, Peter George, Ladbroke's CEO, was given a seat on Hilton's board of directors.

Hilton has gaming operations in a number of foreign countries, including Turkey, Uruguay, and Australia. Conrad International Hotels has luxury properties in numerous international cities, including Jakarta, Brussels, Hong Kong, Dublin, and Barcelona.

EMPLOYMENT

In an effort to optimize the use of its human resources and improve management of team operations through all levels of its business, Hilton has instituted a program of five-day workshops called "Professional Development for Directors of Human Resources." The courses cover such topics as hiring costs, terminations, turnover, training, compensation, internal surveys, and grievances.

Hilton attaches a high level of importance to training at all levels of its operations. According to company literature, "the ongoing training of every Hilton team member is a crucial element of the continued success of the brand. Well-trained team members—from general managers to line workers—provide the consistent service that our customers expect and the quality lodging experience that keeps them coming back to Hilton." Such training begins at the top. New managers attend courses at the Hilton Quality Service Institute. Other training courses, held regionally, cover a variety of job skills as well as customer relations.

SOURCES OF INFORMATION

Bibliography

Gibbs, Melanie F. "Hilton Hotels Corp.: The Sleeping Giant Wakes." *National Real Estate Investor,* February 1997.

Golden, Fran. "Hilton Chief: More Purchases Likely: Hotel Company Looks to Future in Wake of $2 Billion Bally Acquisition." *Travel Weekly,* 13 June 1996.

Golden, Fran. "New Hilton Chief: Chain Will Grow by Investing in Hotels and Gaming." *Travel Weekly,* 27 May 1996.

Goldgaber, Arthur. "Honeymoon Hotelier: Hilton's Stock Quickly Doubled after Stephen Bollenbach Took Over as CEO. Now He Must Deliver." *Financial World,* 21 January 1997.

Henkoff, Ronald, and Andrew Serwer. "It Ought to Be No Contest: Hilton vs. ITT." *Fortune,* 3 March 1997.

Hilton Gaming News. Beverly Hills, CA.: Hilton Hotels Corporation, Winter 1996.

Hilton Hotels Corporation 1995 Annual Report. Beverly Hills, CA.: Hilton Hotels Corp., 1996.

Hilton Hotels Corporation Home Page, 1 June 1998. Available at http://www.hilton.com.

"Hilton Hotels Corporation." *Hoover's Online,* 1 June 1998. Available at http://www.hoovers.com.

Morris, Kathleen. "Industry Outlook: Services: Lodging." *Business Week,* 12 January 1998.

Violino, Bob. "Trends: Hilton Hotels-Reservations Online." *InformationWeek,* 27 April 1998.

For an annual report:

on the Internet at: http://www.hilton.com/corporate/index.html

For additional industry research:

Investigate companies by their Standard Industrial Classification Codes, also known as SICs. Hilton Hotels Corporation's primary SICs are:

5812 Eating Places

6794 Patent Owners and Lessors

7011 Hotels and Motels

Hitachi America, Ltd.

FOUNDED: 1959 as Hitachi New York, Ltd.

Contact Information:

HEADQUARTERS: 50 Prospect Ave.
    Tarrytown, NY 10591
PHONE: (914)332-5800
FAX: (914)332-5555
URL: http://www.hitachi.com

HITACHI

OVERVIEW

Hitachi America, Ltd. is a wholly owned subsidiary of Hitachi, Ltd., a $68.7 billion company with more than 330,000 employees worldwide. Hitachi, Ltd. is the world's largest global electronics and electrical company, manufacturing and marketing a wide range of products including computers, semiconductors, consumer products, and power and industrial equipment. Hitachi America, Ltd. manufactures and markets a broad range of electronics, computer systems and products, and semiconductors, and it provides industrial equipment and services throughout the United States. The company has employees in 7 divisions and 10 subsidiaries around the country. The company's product lines include leading-edge technology in the automotive, computer, power generation, semiconductor, office automation systems, consumer electronics, and telecommunications industries.

COMPANY FINANCES

Hitachi America's annual sales for fiscal 1997, ending March 31, were $3.3 billion, representing 29 percent of Hitachi Ltd.'s overall sales for the year. Per the annual report, Hitachi Ltd. also recorded $80.3 billion in total assets, $47.8 billion in total liabilities, gross profit of $18.3 billion, and $712 million in net income for 1997.

ANALYSTS' OPINIONS

Hitachi Ltd. is ranked by *Fortune* magazine as the world's largest electronics and electrical equipment company. In 1996 sales by the company's Home Electronics Division increased 20 percent, primarily due to sales of projection TVs. In 1997 Hitachi Home Electronics anticipated overall growth of 15 percent, again led by projection TVs. This anticipated growth also reflects the company's expectations for its new product offerings.

According to Victor Nowak, Executive Vice President and General Manager of Hitachi's Automotive Products Division in Detroit, Michigan, Americans benefit from Hitachi's presence in the United States. Mr. Nowak stated, referring to Hitachi's global presence, "Our combined automotive capabilities in Japan, Europe, China, and southeast Asia truly provide our customers in Detroit with the benefits of doing business with a global corporation."

Forbes magazine states that Hitachi is a viable competitor for Intel in the microprocessor market. Hitachi's chip is being installed by five of the seven handheld computer manufacturers. "Hitachi expects its microprocessors to play a leading role in portable devices," said Tsugio Makimoto, executive managing director in charge of Hitachi's semiconductor business.

HISTORY

In 1959 Hitachi, Ltd. established Hitachi New York, Ltd. in Manhattan to sell turbines and power generators. In the 1960s the product line expanded to include industrial equipment and machinery, electron tubes, telecommunications systems, and automotive parts. In 1969 Hitachi New York, Ltd. was renamed Hitachi America, Ltd. to reflect the company's national sales scope. In the 1970s computers and semiconductors became the major focus of Hitachi America's businesses. In 1975 Hitachi America established the International Procurement Group in Tarrytown to buy U.S. goods. By 1979 Hitachi America's primary purpose was marketing and servicing Hitachi, Ltd. products throughout the United States. In 1988, Hitachi America sales surpassed $1 billion.

STRATEGY

The company established the Research and Development (R&D) Division in 1989 with the primary goal of creating new technology for Hitachi's businesses in North America. The division also is linked to the global research and development efforts of Hitachi, Ltd. In another important move, Hitachi America established the Convergent Technologies Group to force its business units to work together. This organization overlays the company's independent divisions and provides a forum for components experts in semiconductors, displays storage, and CD-ROM to exchange ideas and create new

FAST FACTS:
About Hitachi America, Ltd.

Ownership: Hitachi America, Ltd. is a publicly owned company traded on the New York Stock Exchange.

Ticker symbol: HIT

Officers: Tomoharu Shimayama, Pres.; Philip Omsberg, Senior VP & Gen. Counsel; Katsumi Sakurai, VP, Finance; Gerald F. Corbett, Director of Corporate Communications

Employees: 6,329

Principal Subsidiary Companies: Hitachi America, Ltd. is a subsidiary of Hitachi, Ltd., which is headquartered in Tokyo, Japan. Hitachi Ltd.'s principal subsidiaries are Hitachi Automotive Products (USA), Inc.; Hitachi (Canadian), Ltd.; Hitachi Computer Products (America), Inc.; Hitachi Consumer Products de Mexico; Hitachi Electronics (America), Inc.; Hitachi Instruments, Inc.; Hitachi Micro Systems, Inc.; Hitachi PC Corporation (USA); Hitachi Semiconductor (America), Inc.; and Hitachi Telecom (USA), Inc.

Chief Competitors: As a major electronics manufacturer, Hitachi competitors include: Toshiba Corporation; Mitsubishi Electric Corporation; Hewlett-Packard; Sharp Electronics; Sony Corporation; Pioneer Electronics Corporation; Philips Electronics NV; and Matsushita Electric Industrial Co. Ltd..

products. In 1996 Hitachi America merged its computer, office automation, and field engineering divisions. The merger combined divisions with related products or services, which enabled the company to more uniformly and aggressively pursue its business goals.

Hitachi entered into numerous alliances to expand the company's market. For example, the company partnered with Hewlett-Packard to jointly develop a software product, and it partnered with Web TV Networks, Inc. to manufacture boxes. The company formed the International Business Development Group to evaluate and develop strategic alliances for Hitachi in the United States. Hitachi continued its growth in the retail channel by teaming up with Minneapolis-based Best Buy Co., Inc., a Fortune 500 company and one of the strongest merchandisers in the U.S. consumer electronics market, to distribute its Hitachi Visionbook Plus Series of notebook

CHRONOLOGY:

Key Dates for Hitachi America, Ltd.

1959: Hitachi, Ltd. Establishes Hitachi New York, Ltd.

1969: Hitachi New York is renamed Hitachi America, Ltd.

1975: Hitachi America establishes the International Procurement Group

1988: The company's American sales surpass $1 billion

1989: The company establishes the Research and Development (R&D) division

1997: The company announces the development of the world's first DVD-ROM drive

1997: Hitachi America introduces the MP-EGI digital camera

computers to over 280 locations nationwide. In March 1998 Hitachi, Ltd. and Sony Corporation reached a licensing agreement regarding the CPU cores of Hitachi's SuperH mircoprocessors. This move should strengthen the status of the SuperH microprocessors as an industry standard.

INFLUENCES

In 1997 Hitachi America announced the development of the world's first DVD-ROM drive for the notebook, desktop, and workstation markets. Hitachi products must maintain a competitive advantage within the market. Accordingly, the company requires that the parts and materials it purchases come at the most competitive prices. Hitachi is one of the few companies in the world that can develop, manufacture, and market all the essential components of its products.

In the late 1990s Hitachi America debuted a new Hitachi corporate advertising campaign in the United States. This multi-million dollar campaign, sponsored by Hitachi, Ltd., will focus on attracting new consumers through brand recognition, specifically regarding the Ultravision Projection TVs. The television programs selected for the campaign include the "Wonderful World of Disney," "Monday Night Football," and "Home Im-

provement." The print ads will appear in *Entertainment Weekly, Sports Illustrated, Fortune,* and *Forbes* magazines.

CURRENT TRENDS

In 1996 the R&D Division established the Information Technology Group (ITG) at the San Jose Semiconductor Research Lab to focus on leading-edge information technologies for the commercial application of Hitachi's computer products. ITG's first project was to develop data warehouse and data mining application software to operate on commercial parallel computers and servers. The Automotive Products Research Laboratory in Farmington Hills, Michigan, has been experimenting with cleaner burning engines. Its goal is to design a nonpolluting car for the future. The Semiconductor Research Laboratory in Brisbane, California, is creating new technologies in high-speed Digital Signal Processing (DSP). The Digital Media Systems Laboratory in Princeton, New Jersey, is working on the development of digital communications technologies and products. The Information Technology Group in Santa Clara, California, is expanding its activities in the global information infrastructure arena to create a new information system concept. In addition, Hitachi, Ltd. is working to develop high-quality diagnostic instruments for the health care industry. Hitachi America, Ltd. operates three laboratories as well as planning and administration divisions on both coasts. It sponsors research seminars and programs with America's top universities and participates in several residential research programs with U.S. corporations.

PRODUCTS

In response to the advent of the digital era, in July 1997 Hitachi Home Electronics (America) Inc. (HHEA) introduced the MP-EGI digital camera. This camera, the first all-digital device on the market, can capture up to 20 minutes of full-motion video, 3,000 still images, or 4 hours of audio. HHEA also introduced the UltraVision MMV, a multimedia vision 27-inch TV with VGA input—the perfect TV/Monitor for PC gaming and Internet browsing. Additional new products include the HDS-1110S Digital Satellite System, the DVHS Digital VCR, and the GD-2000 double-speed DVD-ROM drive. HHEA has also introduced a new line of fully automatic camcorders, including several 8mm units with a 3-inch LCD display that allows for instant review of videos. Hitachi also plans to introduce a new projection TV line, the FX Series. All in all, the company planned to introduce 45 new products for fiscal year 1997. In the first month of fiscal year 1998, Hitachi, Ltd. released a new PCMCIA I/F card emulator for its most powerful microprocessors, two new models in its series of standard logic integrated circuits (ICs), and a new series of cell-based ICs.

CORPORATE CITIZENSHIP

Hitachi, Ltd. was one of the first Japanese companies to get involved with large-scale philanthropic endeavors and is committed to its responsibility to the community. Since 1976, Hitachi America, Ltd. has created a sophisticated giving program that combines employee volunteerism and direct funding. Hitachi is involved in innovative programs aimed at improving the quality of life in the communities where its employees live and work. The company also invests a portion of its pre-tax profits in charitable and cultural activities. Since 1985, Hitachi's Foundation has made more than 500 grants in American communities.

Hitachi Automotive Products, Inc. operates a Technical Center that provides engineering, design, and development support. To date, it has developed high-quality sensors and control units that are used to reduce car emissions and increase fuel economy while also meeting government diagnostic regulations.

GLOBAL PRESENCE

Hitachi America operates eight manufacturing facilities in the United States and Mexico. The company is organized for the primary purpose of marketing and servicing all Hitachi, Ltd. products, other than consumer goods, throughout the United States. Hitachi products are sold by eight Hitachi America divisions, each serving a specific product line. Principal division offices are located in New York, Atlanta, Houston, Los Angeles, San Francisco, and Chicago. Hitachi's Information Technology Group is expanding its activities in the global information infrastructure arena to create a new information system concept. In 1998 there were 75 Hitachi companies in North America.

Hitachi also reaches more than 200 public broadcasting stations nationwide through its sponsorship of "Real Science!," an educational program aimed at 12 to 16-year olds. The award-winning program is designed to inspire youths to take up careers in science.

EMPLOYMENT

Hitachi America actively seeks individuals in the areas of administration, engineering, sales, finance and accounting, service and support, research and development, and marketing. The company offers its employees pen-

sion plans and severance benefits. It is an equal opportunity employer that exhibits no discrimination.

SOURCES OF INFORMATION

Bibliography

"Career Opportunities at Hitachi PC," 20 April 1998. Available at http://www.hitachi.com/about/jobs.html.

"Health Care Instruments and Systems for the Future." 20 April 1998. Available at http://www.hitachi.co.jp/Sp/TJ-e/1998/revfeb98/rev4701.htm.

"Hitachi America Announces World's First Double Speed DVD-Rom Drive," 4 October 1997. Available at http://www.hitachi.com/New/Docs/970923.html.

"Hitachi America Formed." *Television Digest,* 1 April 1996.

"Hitachi America, Inc.," 4 October 1997. Available at http://www.hitachi.com.

"Hitachi America Ltd.," 22 July 1997. Available at http://sweb3.med.iacnet.com/infotrac/session/245/980/4565067/sig!n163.

"Hitachi and Sony Reach Agreement on Licensing of Super H RISC CPU Cores," 20 April 1998. Available at http://www.hitachi.co.jp/News/cnews/E/980331B.html.

"Hitachi Announces Broad New Line of Consumer Electronics for 1996/97 Season," 6 May 1996. Available at http://www.hitachi.com/New/Socs/960506.html.

"Hitachi Automotive Products (USA), Inc. Names Nowak Executive VP and GM," 2 September 1996. Available at http://www.hitachi.com.

"Hitachi Disc Camcorder Due." *Television Digest,* 18 November 1996.

"Hitachi Foundations," 20 April 1998. Available at http://www.hitachi.co.jp/Int-e/hf.html.

Hitachi, Ltd. 1997 Annual Report. Tokyo, Japan: Hitachi, Ltd., March 1997.

"Hitachi PC Teams With Best Buy Consumer Electronics Stores," 2 September 1997. Available at http://www.hitachipc.com/new/pressreleases/970902.html.

"Hitachi Releases E10A PCMCIA I/F Card Emulator for SH-4 Microprocessor," 20 April 1998. Available at http://www.hitachi.co.jp/New/cnews/E/980413B.html.

"Hitachi Releases the HD74ALVC16835 and the HD74ALVC162385 High-Speed Standard Logic ICs Supporting 100 MHz Memory Bus," 20 April 1998. Available at http://www.hitachi.co.jp/New/cnews/E/980409B.html.

"Hitachi Releases the HG75C Series 0.18-micrometer ASIC High Integration Density Cell-Based ICs," 20 April 1998. Available at http://www.hitachi.co.jp/New/cnews/E/980406B.html.

"Hitachi Sponsors a Third Season of Real Science," 26 September 1996. Available at http://www.hitachi.com/New/Docs/960926.html.

Ryan, Ken. "Hitachi Dishing It Out: To Join DSS Fray by Late Summer." *HFN The Weekly Newspaper for the Home Furnishing Network,* 27 May 1996.

"Web TV's Set-top Boxes." *The Wall Street Journal,* 20 June 1997.

Weinberg, Neil. "A Sleeping Giant Awakes." *Forbes Magazine,* 21 April 1997. Available at http://www.forbes.com/forbes/97/0421/5908045a.htm.

Wirthman, Lisa. "HP and Hitachi Partner on HP-UX to Address Reliability, Availability." *PC Week,* 10 February 1997.

For an annual report:

on the Internet at: http://www.hitachi.com.co.jp **or** telephone: (914)332-5800

For additional industry research:

Investigate companies by their Standard Industrial Classification Codes, also known as SICs. Hitachi America's primary SICs are:

5013 Motor Vehicle Supplies & New Parts

5045 Computers and Computer Peripheral Equipment & Software

5065 Electronic Parts and Equipment

7629 Electrical and Electronic Repair Shops, NEC

Home Box Office Inc.

OVERVIEW

Home Box Office Inc. (HBO) earns applause as the first and by far the most successful pay-television network. The company's core channels, HBO and Cinemax, reach more than 32 million subscribers 24-hours-a-day. Programming includes concerts, hit movies, sporting events, comedy specials, and documentaries. The company also owns a share of Comedy Central. Founded by Time Inc. in 1972, HBO helped pioneer a new field of home entertainment by offering cable television services. HBO reports weekly viewership rose almost 20 percent from 1994 to 1997, however, subscriber growth showed signs of slowing in 1998.

In response to the growing home video market, the network started producing a greater number of original programs and has earned a multitude of awards for its content and programming. HBO produces more than 15 original programs a year, such as the $60-million space exploration series, *From the Earth to the Moon,* and the $14-million Vietnam memoir, *A Bright Shining Lie.* In 1997 HBO won 19 Emmy Awards, beating 3 out of the 4 major broadcast networks.

While the network's schedule of commercially uninterrupted programming features mostly Hollywood motion pictures, HBO refuses to show X-rated films and airs R-rated films only at night. Success stems partly from the company's ability to keep up with entertainment and cable industry trends and technology. In 1997, HBO announced it would begin broadcasting programs in the new high-definition television format beginning in 1998, becoming the first cable service to commit to the new technology that is set to become the standard for broadcast television by 2006.

ALSO KNOWN AS: HBO
FOUNDED: 1972

Contact Information:

HEADQUARTERS: 1100 Avenue of the Americas
New York, NY 10036
PHONE: (212)512-1000
FAX: (212)515-5517
URL: http://www.hbo.com

FAST FACTS:
About Home Box Office Inc.

Ownership: Home Box Office (HBO) is the pay-television programming and marketing division of Time Warner Entertainment Company, L.P. (TWE), which is a subsidiary of Time Warner Inc. TWE is a publicly traded entity on the New York Stock Exchange.

Ticker symbol: TWX

Officers: Jeffrey L. Bewkes, Chmn. & CEO

Employees: 1,500

Principal Subsidiary Companies: Time Warner Inc. is the largest entertainment and information company in the world, with operations in more than 100 countries. Working completely under the Time Warner umbrella, Home Box Office Inc. has two feature film production units, HBO Pictures and HBO NYC Productions. Other HBO business units include: HBO Direct, Inc.; HBO Downtown Productions; HBO Independent Productions; Time Warner Sports; and HBO Home Video.

Chief Competitors: As the most successful pay-TV network in the country, HBO controls some 70 percent of the market. HBO programming also competes against the major broadcast networks for viewers and awards. Its primary competitors include: CBS; DirecTV; GE; Showtime Networks, Inc.; Sony; TCI. and Walt Disney.

COMPANY FINANCES

Throughout the mid-1990s HBO's revenues showed steady growth. In 1994 HBO reported sales of $1.51 billion, compared with 1993's $1.44 billion. In 1996 HBO posted revenues of $1.76 million, up from 1995 sales of $1.60 billion. In 1997 HBO reported operating income of $391 million on sales of $1.92 billion.

ANALYSTS' OPINIONS

Although HBO had a considerable lead in the mid-1990s, industry analysts such as Paul Kagan and Associates contend that HBO's control of the market could continue to erode little by little. The media analysis firm predicted that HBO's share may drop below 70 percent in the late 1990s. Showtime started to run more original movies in the mid-1990s, thereby expanding its popularity and revenues. Observers expect that if Showtime can continue producing quality original movies, it could succeed in stealing large numbers of HBO's subscribers—in 1997 Showtime offered twice as many original movies as HBO.

On the other hand, according to a December 1997 article in *Business Week,* "HBO has become the most efficient profit machine in the Time Warner Inc. empire, with a return on invested capital of about 55 percent. It generates cash flow of well over $400 million a year on revenues of $2 billion and has an asset value of more than $4 billion. 'It just goes from strength to strength,' says Montgomery Securities' John Tinker. 'They cut through the clutter. They create events. They have the best brand. They win'."

HISTORY

Publishing giant Time Inc. started a cable television service called Home Box Office in 1972. The first HBO presentation, a National Hockey League game from Madison Square Garden, went out to 365 cable TV subscribers in Wilkes-Barre, Pennsylvania, on November 8, 1972. HBO's first championship boxing match, featuring George Foreman vs. Joe Frazier, was broadcast live from Kingston, Jamaica. In March 1973 HBO produced the first original pay-television special, the Pennsylvania Polka Festival, from the Allentown (Pennsylvania) Fairgrounds.

HBO's original strategy included purchasing the rights of recently released movies and transmitting them to local cable operators via satellite. The local cable operators would then deliver the programs to their subscribers. In the early to mid-1970s cable subscriptions ran about $6.00 per month with HBO receiving a little over half of this subscription fee, or $3.50. Although stringent federal regulations and the lack of infrastructure—such as cables, satellites, and other equipment needed to provide cable services—plagued the cable industry in the early and mid-1970s, by the end of the decade companies such as HBO had established enough infrastructure to amass sizable customer bases. The number of HBO customers increased from 50,000 in 1974 to 1.5 million in 1978. Aided by more conducive federal policies, HBO posted its first profit in 1977 and started to prosper by the end of the 1970s.

In August 1980 the company launched Cinemax, an all-movie channel that would become the second most watched service after HBO. The company continued to diversify throughout the 1980s. In 1983, with 13.4 million customers, HBO began producing made-for-TV movies and original comedy shows after reaching an agreement with Columbia Motion Pictures and CBS to create a new movie studio, Tri-Star Pictures. The deal also gave HBO the cable-TV rights to all movies produced by the new studio. The following year, HBO also launched another successful division, HBO Home Video, that released its made-for-TV movies as well as movies from Orion Pictures, Miramax Films, and Samuel Goldwyn. In 1987 HBO became the first pay-cable network to win an Academy Award and, in 1989 HBO launched the advertising-supported Comedy Channel.

The 1990s brought even more change, growth, and honors when The *Madonna - Live! Blond Ambition World Tour '90* grabbed the title of highest-rated original entertainment program in HBO history. To pump up the subscriber list, in 1991, HBO started offering customers additional HBO channels at no extra cost. (Researchers would later conclude the move brought greater satisfaction and perceived value for customers and a higher retention rate for HBO.) The company also expanded internationally, adding Hungary and Latin America in 1991 and Asia in 1992. Also that year, HBO worked out an agreement with General Instrument Corporation to begin transmitting digital compressed television in the United States. Original programming on HBO continued to address TV-sensitive subjects, such as AIDS and abortion. The ground-breaking network also continued to win industry accolades, including 17 primetime Emmy Awards in 1993, 34 Cable Ace Awards in 1994, and 4 Golden Globe Awards in 1997. In 1998 the company aired the most expensive original programming venture in HBO history, the $60 million space exploration series *From the Earth to the Moon.*

CHRONOLOGY:
Key Dates for Home Box Office, Inc.

1972: Company is founded by Time, Inc.

1973: Produces first original pay-television special

1977: Posts first profit

1980: Launches Cinemax

1983: Begins producing made-for-TV movies and original comedy specials

1984: Launches HBO Home Video

1987: Becomes first pay-cable network to win an Academy Award

1988: Launches Comedy Channel

1991: Begins offering additional HBO channels at no additional cost

1992: Negotiates agreement to begin transmitting digital compressed television in the United States

1998: Airs most expensive original programming venture in HBO history, the $60 million space exploration series *From the Earth to the Moon*

STRATEGY

HBO continued to dominate the cable television market in the mid-1990s. HBO increased its hold on the market with a simple plan of providing a mix of popular movies, original movies, specialty series, comedy weeklies, and sports shows. In addition, HBO obtained the exclusive television rights from many major movie studios, including a 1995 contract with DreamWorks SKG—the joint venture of Stephen Spielberg, Jeffery Katzenberg, and David Geffen—which extends through 2006. This programming strategy allowed HBO to capture an enormous share of the premium cable channel market. HBO controlled 71.6 percent of the market in 1996, down 0.5 percent from 1995, whereas Showtime held 28.4 percent in 1996, up from 27.9 percent in 1995, according to Jon Schlosser in *Broadcasting & Cable*. Furthermore, HBO's number of subscribers rose to 32.4 million in 1996, while Showtime reported only 9.5 million.

HBO sells no commercials and makes money only by selling its programming services, but the company spends more than $25 million a year to advertise the HBO brand via print, radio, and television.

INFLUENCES

Throughout its history, HBO has faced a number of challenges that have helped to shape the company and make it a stronger player. HBO encountered accelerated competition in the late 1970s and in the 1980s as federal policies made the industry more accessible to other cable service providers. With its offerings and marketing strategy focusing solely on movies, Showtime began to win HBO customers over to its cable channel during this period. In response, HBO stepped up its efforts to secure more movies. HBO started paying higher prices to gain the rights to popular movies and, in 1980, launched its second channel, Cinemax, to compete directly with Showtime. Devoted exclusively to movies, Cinemax was strategically priced lower than Showtime. HBO's strategy paid off, and by 1982 the company's subscribers rose to 9.2 million, or about 50 percent of all cable subscribers. In addition, HBO reported sales of $400 million, and by this time had dwarfed its most significant rival, Showtime, with almost three times as many customers.

HBO's fortunes started to shift again in 1984 because of competition caused by video rentals and the rising cost of cable service. Consequently, HBO watched its share of the market slip from 50.4 percent in 1983 to 48.1 percent in 1984. Nonetheless, by 1985, HBO had 14.6 million subscribers and posted $800 million in revenues. HBO continued to expand its offerings in 1989 by introducing the Comedy Channel. The Comedy Channel faced problems almost immediately because of its somewhat fragmented programming mix and because competitor Viacom, owner of Showtime, had launched a competing comedy channel called HA! Analysts correctly predicted that demand was not strong enough to support two cable comedy stations, so the two channels were merged in 1990, becoming Comedy Central. Also at this time, HBO started to offer multichannel programming to hold on to customers who may have already seen one of the movies the cable service was showing. The company also began to diversify its selections as cable channels became more specialized, targeting smaller segments of the market.

CURRENT TRENDS

HBO intends to increase its focus on original movies and home video sales and rentals. As cable service providers such as Showtime expanded their original movie offerings, HBO responded by following suit in order to maintain its dominance of the industry. HBO's specialty programming remained unparalleled in the mid-1990s and promises to be another key area the company will emphasize in the future to distinguish itself from the competition. Furthermore, HBO anticipates that home video will play an increasingly important role in the company's revenues. HBO experienced heightened growth in its video sales and video rentals in the 1990s. According to research by Warner Home Video, HBO's home video sales may have amounted to as much as $1 billion in 1997.

Moreover, with an array of specialized cable channels, HBO realized it must present a diverse selection of shows, movies, and programs in order to retain its control of the industry. Therefore, HBO introduced sports shows to compete with ESPN, music shows to put pressure on MTV and VH1, women's shows to keep up with Lifetime, and African-American shows to stave off customer losses to BET in addition to its new movie offerings.

PRODUCTS

HBO's core products include numerous hit movies as well as the company's own made-for-cable productions. Moreover, the cable service delivers a variety of shows covering an assortment of sports, including professional football, boxing, and basketball. HBO also recruited veteran comedians such as Dennis Miller, Chris

Rock, and Janeane Garofalo to host weekly comedy shows. For music fans, HBO launched programs such as "Reverb," which features appearances of popular rock artists, and simulcasts of live performances by headliners such as country singer Garth Brooks. The cable service also added shows targeted toward children, including "The Inventors' Specials" and "Happily Ever After." Besides these shows, HBO airs programs dealing with social issues such as drug addiction and AIDS. Since its 1987 airing of *Mandela,* HBO has striven to include programming aimed at African Americans, who as of 1997, constituted 22 percent of HBO's subscribers.

CORPORATE CITIZENSHIP

Home Box Office has earned a well-deserved reputation for responsible programming, devoting a segment of its schedule to programs designed to help make the world a better place. A good example of such programming was HBO's November 1996 family special, *Smoke Alarm: The Unfiltered Truth About Cigarettes,* produced in collaboration with Consumer Reports Television. The documentary, aired in conjunction with 1996's Great American Smokeout, offered a revealing look at the hazards of tobacco, the teenage smoking epidemic, and efforts by the tobacco industry to market their products to children.

HBO's annual all-star Comic Relief benefit has raised millions of dollars for Health Care for the Homeless Projects in a number of American cities. All of the money raised through Comic Relief is allocated to health care and related services that, thus far, provided help to more than a million homeless Americans.

GLOBAL PRESENCE

Not only has HBO led the cable industry in the United States but also throughout the world. In 1997 HBO provided service to more than 40 countries. More than 10 million viewers watch HBO offerings from television sets in Latin America, Asia, and eastern Europe. HBO's Ole, which began in 1991, provides HBO features and Cinemax offerings to South and Central America, Mexico, and the Caribbean. HBO Asia delivers HBO programming, including exclusive Disney releases, to nine countries in Asia, including Singapore, Thailand, Indonesia, and the Philippines. HBO started doing business in eastern Europe in 1991 with HBO Hungary, which offers American, European, and Hungarian films to subscribers. HBO added HBO Poland in 1997 to tap into the developing market for pay-TV services there. The international division of HBO also oversees Time Warner's investment in a regional broadcast station in Hamburg, Germany.

EMPLOYMENT

HBO is looking for bright and committed people to join its team. The company offers opportunities in a variety of fields, including general management, legal, finance, sales and marketing, network programming, and technology and operations. Interested parties are encouraged to check out current job openings at the company's Job Opportunities web site at http://www.homeboxoffice.com/cmp/career.html. Applicants for jobs posted on the web site may send their resume online to HBO.

Resumes and cover letters may also be sent to HBO, Human Resources, 1100 6th Ave., New York, NY 10036; HBO, Human Resources, 2049 Century Park E, Ste. 4100, Los Angeles, CA; or HBO, Human Resources, The Lenox Bldg., Ste. 1600, 3399 Peachtree Rd. NE, Atlanta, GA 30326.

SOURCES OF INFORMATION

Bibliography

HBO Home Page. May 1998. Available at http://www.hbo.com.

Lewis, Scott M. "Home Box Office Inc." *International Directory of Company Histories.* Vol 7. Detroit, MI: St. James Press, 1993.

Schlosser, Jon. "Showtime Fights for Screen Time." *Broadcasting & Cable,* 14 April 1997.

Stevens, Elisabeth Lesly. "Call It Home Buzz Office."*Business Week,* 8 December 1997.

For an annual report:

on the Internet at: http://www.pathfinder.com/@@DqkZow QAsQ59hNn6/corp/hbo/index.html

For additional industry research:

Investigate companies by their Standard Industrial Classification Codes, also known as SICs. HBO's primary SICs are:

4841 Cable and Other Pay Television Services

7812 Motion Picture and Video Production

The Home Depot Inc.

FOUNDED: 1978

Contact Information:

HEADQUARTERS: 2455 Paces Ferry Rd.
    Atlanta, GA 30339-4024
PHONE: (770)433-8211
FAX: (770)431-2685
EMAIL: consumer-affairs@homedepot.com
URL: http://www.homedepot.com

OVERVIEW

Home Depot is the largest home improvement retailer in North America, boasting 690 stores in 43 states and 5 Canadian provinces. These warehouse-type stores, each averaging about 130,000 square feet (including garden center), stock 40,000 to 50,000 home improvement products and are aimed mainly at the do-it-yourself trade. The stores, however, also attract many professional building contractors. Products include lumber, floor and wall coverings, hardware, paint, plumbing supplies, and tools. Home Depot also offers facilities maintenance and repair products through its direct mail subsidiary Maintenance Warehouse, and custom window treatments by direct mail through National Blind & Wallpaper Factory. Much of the company's success has been attributed to its superior customer service, along with low prices and a broad selection of products.

COMPANY FINANCES

In 1997 Home Depot posted net earnings of $1.2 billion on revenue of $24.2 billion. This net earnings figure excludes a pretax, nonrecurring charge of $104 million. This compared with net income of $938 million on revenue of $19.5 billion in fiscal 1996. Per-share earnings of $1.64 in fiscal 1997 represented an increase of 27 percent from the $1.29 per share earned in fiscal 1996. In fiscal 1995 Home Depot's net earnings totaled $732 million on revenue of $15.5 billion, compared with net income of $605 million on revenue of $12.5 billion in fiscal 1994. Per-share earnings in fiscal 1995 were $1.03, compared with $.88 per share in fiscal 1994.

Approximately 34 percent of Home Depot's total revenue in fiscal 1997 was accounted for by sales of building materials, lumber, and floor and wall coverings. Sales of plumbing, heating, lighting, and electrical supplies brought in about 27 percent of the company's total revenue, while seasonal and specialty products accounted for about 15 percent. Sales of hardware and tools brought in about 14 percent of total revenue, and sales of paint and other products accounted for 10 percent.

ANALYSTS' OPINIONS

Home Depot stock, which went up 28,000 percent after the company went public in 1981, slowed almost to a halt in 1993. According to Patricia Sellers in *Fortune* magazine in March 1996, things looked grim and most analysts agreed that the stock and the company had hit a wall. In her in-depth article, Sellers pinpointed the problem as a lack of professionalism. The founders themselves agreed that the company had grown beyond their capacity to manage it in the way they had been doing up to that point. Sellers quoted Donald Keough, one of Home Depot's board members and the retired president of Coca Cola, as saying: "of course there are problems, but they are the problems of success."

In 1997, despite these dire concerns, Home Depot opened more stores in the United States and Canada and announced plans to enter the South American market with a store in Chile. The company unveiled its plan to open a store in Chile in January 1997. A month later, Lisa Goldbaum, writing in *Barron's,* observed that Home Depot stocks remained stalled and predicted that "growth will become increasingly difficult as the company matures and market share gains become harder to achieve."

HISTORY

Home Depot was born in 1978 when Bernard Marcus and Arthur Blank, executives with Handy Dan Home Improvement Centers, found themselves out of work after a corporate takeover at Handy Dan. Joined by Ronald Brill, another Handy Dan employee; and Pat Farrah, former owner of Homeco, the world's first home improvement warehouse, they mapped out a plan for a bigger and better store catering to the needs of do-it-yourselfers. The following year they opened three Home Depot outlets in the metropolitan Atlanta area, adding a fourth outlet in 1980.

Home Depot went public in 1981 and headed south from Atlanta to open four stores in the bustling south Florida market. The following year the company added two more stores in Florida and posted 1982 sales of $100 million.

FINANCES:

Home Depot Revenues, 1994-1997 (billion dollars)

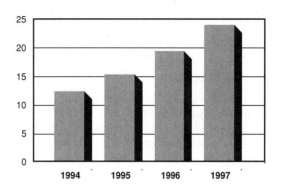

Home Depot 1997 Stock Prices (dollars)

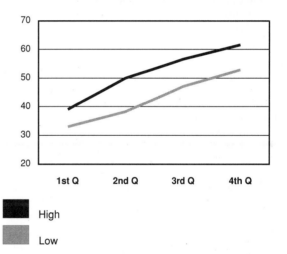

■ High

▨ Low

Throughout the mid-1990s Home Depot was troubled by a series of lawsuits charging gender discrimination. The first of these were filed by female workers on the West Coast who alleged that they were not treated on a equal basis with male employees. In 1997 the company reached a $65 million out-of-court settlement in the class action suit that developed from this initial litigation.

In mid-1997 Blank took Marcus' place as Home Depot's chief executive officer while Marcus retained the chairmanship.

FAST FACTS:

About The Home Depot Inc.

Ownership: The Home Depot Inc. is a publicly owned company traded on the New York Stock Exchange.

Ticker symbol: HD

Officers: Bernard Marcus, Chmn. & Secretary, 68, $2.6 million; Arthur M. Blank, Pres., CEO, & COO, 54, $2.6 million; Ronald M. Brill, Exec. VP & Chief Administrative Officer, 53, $725,000; Larry M. Mercer, Exec. VP, Operations, 50, $530,000

Employees: 125,000

Principal Subsidiary Companies: Home Depot Inc. operates direct mail subsidiaries Maintenance Warehouse and National Blind & Wallpaper Factory.

Chief Competitors: As a large-scale retailer of home improvement products, Home Depot faces competition from other home improvement retailers as well as from major discount retailers that carry large stocks of home improvement products. Major competitors include: Hechinger; Lowe's; Ace Hardware; 84 Lumber; HomeBase; Kmart; Menard; Sherwin-Williams; Payless Cashways; TruServ; Wal-Mart; and Wickes.

In late April 1998 Home Depot announced it had reached agreement with Canada's Molson Companies Ltd. to purchase for C$375 million Molson's 25 percent partnership interest in The Home Depot Canada. This transaction gave Home Depot total control of its Canadian operations. The company's partnership with Molson was formed in 1994 when Home Depot acquired 75 percent of Aikenhead's Home Improvement Warehouse, which then operated 7 home improvement stores in Canada. Since that time The Home Depot Canada has opened another 30 stores in 5 Canadian provinces.

STRATEGY

Home Depot boasts that the key to its strategy is listening to and heeding the wisdom of its associates. Claims of "keeping communications open at all levels, treating our associates with dignity, welcoming creative ideas, and rewarding entrepreneurial thinking by pro-

moting from within" abound throughout Home Depot's promotional literature. By building a loyal workforce and creating good will within the community both through its employees and through its programs, Home Depot has made itself a household name. Offering lower prices, advice, and installation services gives consumers what they're looking for: a partner in home improvement.

Continuing to expand its customer base by opening stores in new locations while encouraging a team attitude among its associates has allowed Home Depot to give all its stores the same down-home feel offering advice, a warm welcome, and superior service. Most warehouse-type stores in the past had concentrated on price and selection but neglected customer service. By putting service first and making associates a part of the big picture, Home Depot quickly stepped to the front ranks of its market segment. Size has not diminished the company's commitment to service and community, making the chain welcomed in most areas.

INFLUENCES

One of the factors that has helped to shape the successful marketing strategy of Home Depot has been the recognition of the amazingly large interest among Americans in home improvement projects, both large and small. To cater to do-it-yourselfers whose goals extend beyond merely making repairs, Home Depot stores boast a design center staffed by professional designers who offer free in-store consultation for home improvement projects ranging from lighting to computer-assisted design for kitchens and bathrooms. The company has also set up EXPO Design Centers in a handful of key markets across the country. Unlike traditional Home Depot stores, the EXPO centers in Atlanta, Dallas, Miami, San Diego, and Westbury, New York, do not sell building materials. The centers focus on interior design and renovation projects, including lighting, floor and wall coverings, and kitchen and bath modernization.

CURRENT TRENDS

One of Home Depot's longtime trends has been that of superior customer service. This trend put Home Depot at the top and will not likely be abandoned. The same can be said of service to the community. Home Depot spotlighted community efforts toward building affordable homes as well as at-risk youth and the environment. The company has designated a $12.5 million philanthropic budget to help meet some of those needs.

Protecting the environment has been another of Home Depot's biggest concerns. Home Depot's environmental program was kicked off after Earth Day 1990. Through the 1990s Home Depot began to use more recycled and recyclable products, made an effort to sell "greener" home improvement products, published EN-VIRONMENTAL PRINCIPALS, which were adopted by the National Retail Hardware Association, and led the industry in a switch to products that were not made from rain forest woods. This trend in environmental protection not only attracts buyers, but protects communities.

PRODUCTS

Home Depot's product line includes all manner of hardware, plumbing supplies, power tools, paint and wall coverings, floor coverings, lumber and building materials, how-to books on home improvement, gardening supplies and plants, and services for information dissemination and installation of products. Home Depot also offers home delivery in many areas.

Home Depot's new products include more of the same with an emphasis on supplying low-cost "green" options for customers. With a trend toward environmental care and awareness, Home Depot's widening selection of environmentally sound, or less destructive, products allows homeowners and contractors alike to build and improve with an environmental conscience.

CORPORATE CITIZENSHIP

With a philanthropic budget of $12.5 million for 1998, much of it directed toward affordable housing, at-risk youth, and environmental causes, Home Depot makes citizenship one of its primary concerns. Most of this budget is put back into the communities where Home Depot stores are located. Home Depot serves the concerns of its employees with a matching gift program and promotes volunteerism among its employees through its Team Depot program, which alerts employees to local volunteer opportunities within the community. Home Depot has also worked with Habitat for Humanity to build housing for those in need.

One of Home Depot's main thrusts in the 1990s toward corporate and world citizenship has been a responsibility toward the environment and toward the promotion of "greener" home repair/improvement products, as well as a reduction in its own wastes, a commitment to recycling, and giving money to environmental groups. In this quest, they have received awards from The national Environmental Development Association (1993), Renew America and the National Awards Council for Environmental Sustainability (1995), and were recognized with the President's Sustainable Development Award (1996).

Home Depot's environmental initiatives have been highly praised and used in the creation of environmental building standards. They publish an Environmental Greenprint to help consumers build and remodel with environmentally safe products and techniques and offer clinics to teach skills locally. Annually, Home Depot

CHRONOLOGY:
Key Dates for The Home Depot Inc.

1978: Founded by Bernard Marcus and Arthur Blank

1980: Opens fourth store

1981: Goes public on the stock exchange

1989: Installs satellite communication network to continually train employees

1994: Acquires 75 percent of Aikenhead's Home Improvement Warehouse

1996: Receives the President's Sustainable Development Award

1997: Begins joint venture with S.A.C.I. Falabella to open first store in Chile; opens 500th store by January

1998: Buys out Molson's 25 percent share of Aikenhead

gives hundreds of thousands of dollars toward environmental safety, cleanup, and education.

GLOBAL PRESENCE

In early 1997 Home Depot announced a joint venture with Chile's S.A.C.I. Falabella to open the chain's first store outside of North America. That outlet was scheduled to open in the Chilean capital of Santiago in August 1998.

SOURCES OF INFORMATION

Bibliography

Berry, Leonard L., Kathleen Seiders, and Larry G. Gresham. "For Love and Money: The Common Traits of Successful Retailers." *Organization Dynamics,* 1 October 1997.

Goldbaum, Lisa. "Home Depot Has Many Fans, But Some Say Growth May Be Harder to Come By." *Barron's,* 27 February 1997. Available at http://kelsey.abcompass.com/abc/art/detail/7508.html.

Home Depot: Greenprint. 5 May 1998. Available at http:/www.homedepot.com.

"The Home Depot, Inc." *Hoover's Online,* 10 May 1998. Available at http://www.hoovers.com.

Home Depot Fact Sheet, the Home Depot: Financial Page, 5 May 1998. Available at http://www.homedepot.com.

"The Home Depot to Open a Store in Chile As Its First South American Location." Chile Press Release, 1997. Available at http://www.homedepot.com/FI/chile/htm.

"Home Depot Eclipses 500 Stores Mark." Opening of Store Press Release, 1997. Available at http://www.homedepot.com.

Krass, Peter. "Home Depot's Bernie Marcus." *Investors Business Daily,* 5 February 1998.

"President's Sustainable Development Award." Home Depot Press Release, 1996. Available at http://www.homedepot.com.

Sellers, Patricia. "Can Home Depot Fix Its Sagging Stock?" *Fortune,* 4 March 1996.

For an annual report:

on the Internet at: http://www.homedepot.com/

For additional industry research:

Investigate companies by their Standard Industrial Classification Codes, also known as SICs. Home Depot's primary SICs are:

5211 Lumber and Other Building Materials

5231 Paint, Glass, and Wallpaper

5251 Hardware

5261 Retail Nursery and Garden

Honda Motor Co., Ltd.

OVERVIEW

Honda Motor Co. ranks among the world's top 10 automakers. The Tokyo-based manufacturer also claims 30 percent of the world's motorcycle market, making Honda the world's top motorcycle maker. Banking on its beginnings as an engine producer, Honda also commands a global presence in power equipment, ranging from snow blowers to lawn mowers to outboard motors.

Honda maintains research and development (R&D) facilities and manufacturing plants around the world. After reading the warning signs of a shaky Asian economy in the late 1990s, Honda accelerated the company's expansion of its manufacturing operations in North America. Long known for its efficient engines, the company continues to work on building low-emission vehicles.

COMPANY FINANCES

In fiscal 1998, which ended March 31, Honda posted net income of $1.96 billion on revenue of $45.06 billion, compared with a net of $1.78 billion on revenue of $42.65 billion in fiscal 1997. In fiscal 1996, Honda reported net earnings of $666 million on revenue of $39.98 billion, compared with net income of $711 million on revenue of $45.82 billion. In fiscal 1998, automobiles accounted for 79 percent of the company's total sales, while motorcycle sales generated 13 percent of total revenue and power products brought in the remaining 8 percent.

The 1998 revenue increase largely can be attributed to the fact that Honda sold more cars in North America and Europe, both regions where the local currencies had

FOUNDED: 1948

Contact Information:
HEADQUARTERS: No. 1-1, 2-chome
    Minami-Aoyama, Minato-ku
    Tokyo 107-8556, Japan
PHONE: 81-3-3423-1111
FAX: 81-3-3423-0511
URL: http://www.honda.com

The 1998 Honda Passport EX sport utility vehicle. (Courtesy of Honda Motor Co., Ltd.)

strengthened considerably against the weakening yen. Increased sales abroad and the favorable currency exchange rate also pumped up profits for the company.

HISTORY

Soichiro Honda, a race car driver and a patent-holding mechanical engineer, founded the Honda Technical Research Institute in Hamamatsu in 1946. Honda started out in business by making motorized bicycles powered by war-surplus engines. The popularity of the motorized bike financed the design and production of Honda's A-type bicycle engine in 1947. The company incorporated as Honda Motor Co. in 1948. Backed by a private investor, the company made its first motorcycle in 1949. Honda quickly followed that introduction with a revolutionary engine that doubled the horsepower of the four-stroke engine.

Riding that engine innovation, the company increased sales and attracted greater financing throughout the 1950s. Honda established offices and factories throughout Japan and moved its head office to Tokyo. By the end of the decade, Honda had won all of the most prestigious motorcycle racing honors in the world.

The company went international with the establishment of American Honda Motor Co. in 1959. The American subsidiary sold its small lightweight motorcycle for just $250, undercutting heavy U.S.-made machines that ran around $1,200. Global expansion continued in the early 1960s with the founding of Honda Deutschland GmbH in Germany, Honda Benelux in Belgium, and Asian Honda Motor Co. in Thailand.

The first Honda automobile was introduced in 1962. In 1965 Honda further expanded its product line with the introduction of the E300 portable generator. The rest of the 1960s and the 1970s were a time of expansion for both automobile and motorcycle models. Plants were also set up around the globe, including Belgium, Malaysia, and Mexico. Honda introduced the Civic compact in 1972, just in time to reap the benefits when gas-guzzling cars lost favor with the American public during the oil crisis of 1973. For the next four years running, the Civic won first place in the now-important U.S. fuel economy tests.

The 1980s continued the trend of new products and racing victories. In 1985 and 1986, the Honda Accord was named Japanese car of the year. Throughout the 1980s Honda's R&D continued creating new products and automobile technologies, like the first in-hub motorcycle anti-lock braking system and the Honda Traction Control System.

During the late 1980s and early 1990s Honda aggressively developed new products and technology. It was also a time of accolades. In 1989, two years before his death, Honda's founder, Soichiro Honda, became the

FAST FACTS:
About Honda Motor Co., Ltd.

Ownership: Honda Motor Co. is a publicly owned company traded on the New York Stock Exchange.

Ticker symbol: HMC

Officers: Yoshihide Munekuni, Chmn. & Representative Director; Hiroyuki Yoshino, Pres. & CEO; Koichi Amemiya, Exec. VP, Representative Director, & Pres., American Honda Motor Company

Employees: 109,400 (1998)

Principal Subsidiary Companies: Honda Motor Co. operates 89 plants in 33 countries. Overseas subsidiaries include: American Honda Motor Co.; Honda Motor Europe Co. Ltd.; Honda France S.A. B.P.; Honda Deutschland GmbH; Honda Belgium NV; AP Honda Motor Co.; Honda Canada Inc.; Honda Australia Pty. Ltd.; and Honda Motor do Brazil Ltda.

Chief Competitors: In addition to other truck, van, and car makers, Honda competes with a variety of manufacturers of other products, including motorcycles, lawn mowers, outboard motors, portable generators, and all-terrain vehicles. The company's primary competitors include: BMW; Catepillar; Daewoo; Fiat; Ford; General Motors; Harley-Davidson; Hyundai; Isuzu; Kawasaki Heavy Industries; Kia Motors; Mazda; Mercedes Benz; Mitsubishi; Outboard Marine; Nissan; Peugeot; Renault; Suzuki; Toyota; Toro; Triumph Motorcycles; Volkswagen; Volvo; and Yamaha.

---

first Asian inducted into the American Automotive Hall of Fame. The Honda Accord became the best-selling car model in the United States in 1989 and once more grabbed top honors in the U.S. Customer Satisfaction Index. The next year, Honda's new president was named *Automotive Industry* magazine's "Man of the Year."

The early 1990s brought continued success. In 1992, Honda announced the first joint venture to manufacture motorcycles in China. Honda overtook Chrysler in 1993 to become the third largest seller of cars in the United States. Then Honda started to lose market share.

Taking heed of the warning signs of a shaky Asian economy in the late 1990s, Honda stepped up the company's plans to expand its manufacturing operations in North America. Honda's motorcycle division started investing heavily in Asia, where a strong demand for motorbikes led to an increase in sales for Honda. The depreciation of the yen boosted the company's overall performance during 1997. In a ground-breaking move that won the envy of other carmakers that year, Honda introduced one frame that can be adapted for numerous models.

The company also made headlines with U.S. court cases in 1997. First, 18 former Honda executives were convicted of engaging in unfair competition, following accusations that the executives took payoffs from a car dealer for more lucrative franchises. Later on, a group of emu ranchers in Texas and Arkansas sued Honda for allegedly disparaging their feathered livestock in a television commercial that mockingly called emu meat the "pork of the future," long after the market for emus had crashed.

BIOGRAPHY:
Consumers are Fonda Honda

If Japan has its version of Henry Ford, that man would be Soichiro Honda. He worked for six years as an apprentice at an auto service station in Tokyo before opening his own branch of the repair shop in 1928. In addition to his mechanical talents, Honda was also a race car driver, and in 1931 he received a patent for his invention of metal spokes, which replaced the wood that had been previously used in wheels. From there, Honda created a company to make piston rings in 1937, and with the advent of World War II, the company found itself making propellers for Japanese bombers. Most of his factory was subsequently destroyed by Allied bombs (as well as an earthquake), and in 1945 he sold it to Toyota. Honda then entered the motorcycle engine-production business, which later expanded to include motorcycle production in its entirety. It wasn't until the 1960s that Honda began producing cars and trucks. He lived to see his corporation expand into one of the most respected companies in the world before dying in 1991.

CHRONOLOGY:

Key Dates for Honda Motor Co., Ltd.

1946: Honda Technical Research Institute is founded by Soichiro Honda in Hamamatsu

1948: The company is incorporated as Honda Motor Co.

1949: Honda makes its first motorcycle

1959: The company goes international with the establishment of the American Honda Motor Co.

1962: A Honda automobile is introduced

1989: Honda's founder, Soichiro Honda, becomes the first Asian to be inducted into the American Automotive Hall of Fame

1993: Honda becomes the third largest seller of cars in the U.S.

1997: Honda introduces one frame that can be adapted for numerous car models

STRATEGY

In May 1996 Honda announced its decision to accelerate its "Automobile Strategy for the Americas," originally established in July 1994. This strategy included expanding U.S. production of automobile engines and automatic transmissions, increasing R&D capabilities in the United States, and boosting local procurement in North America.

By fully utilizing existing resources, Honda was working to improve the competitiveness of its products. This was done by bolstering its R&D from the early stages of the development process and increasing the efficiency of its manufacturing system.

INFLUENCES

The main influences helping to shape Honda's strategy come in two different categories, marketing successes and the opening of overseas subsidiaries and manufacturing plants. In each instance, new technology and new subsidiary locations brought new opportunities to Honda Motor Co.

Honda began its international expansion in 1959 with its move into the United States. The rest of North America and Central and South America slowly followed. Honda then began expanding into Europe and Asia in 1961 and continued to grow around the world throughout the 1980s. According to Honda, this expansion met the goals of "taking manufacturing to our markets." By expanding local economies through R&D centers and manufacturing plants worldwide, Honda lowered costs by cutting the need to transport parts or vehicles and by taking advantage of cheaper labor and a strong yen.

Honda's marketing successes have also influenced the direction of the company. After the introduction of its first car in 1962, Honda became active in the racing arena. Racing successes combined with good sales pushed Honda onward in the automobile industry, acting as an incentive to introduce more models. As each model was well received, proceeds enabled Honda to begin development of newer technologies and models. By the mid-1980s, and again in 1994, the Honda Accord was named Japanese car of the year. By the 1990s the Honda Civic was given the same honor. As Honda's quality became well known, sales grew at an astronomical rate, allowing for more R&D and higher production.

CURRENT TRENDS

Honda's current trend is essentially a continuation of policies and programs set in motion earlier. Honda continues to create new models, open new manufacturing plants and R&D centers, and take advantage of every marketing medium available. These strategies helped to build Honda into the company it is today, and there are no signs that company executives will abandon them any time soon. Honda's reputation for quality has made it a big seller in the United States, and its continued accolades and awards help to bolster that reputation.

The company's move into automobile and motorcycle racing broadened its market to specialty racing cars as well as consumer automobiles. Since the 1960s Honda has been active in formula-1, formula-2, and motorcycle racing.

PRODUCTS

Honda products can be found in 140 countries. Honda's most popular products include the Accord, the Civic, the Prelude, the Acura Integra, and Acura Legend, along with a wide array of motorcycles. The popularity of the Accord and Civic automobiles continues to drive sales in North America. Honda also produces several light trucks, four-wheel drive vehicles, general purpose engines, tillers, outboard motors, generators, water pumps, lawn mowers, and snow blowers. Honda's product line expands nearly every year as they introduce new models.

CORPORATE CITIZENSHIP

According to Honda Motor Co., one of its main objectives is "to conduct all our business activities with the overall objective of serving society." Honda strives to meet this objective by protecting the environment, developing technologies to create a more efficient use of the world's energy, boosting the local economy through job creation, and supporting athletics through scholarships in the United States.

Honda's record with the environment is strong and goes as far back as 1971, when its Civic CVCC was the world's first car to meet the 1970 Clean Air Act's strict emission requirements without the use of a catalytic converter. This trend continued into the 1990s and by the mid-1990s, Honda's Civic lineup used a four-cylinder gasoline engine that received the Low Emissions Vehicle certification from the California Air Resources Board. In 1991, Honda announced a new way to reuse painted car bumpers and became the first car company in Japan to recycle bumpers.

In the United States, Honda shows its corporate spirit through patronage of young people's sports. Since the mid-1990s Honda has been a sponsor for the U.S. Little League Baseball Association of America. Its patronage has helped fund the Little League system, keeping young teams playing. Honda also supports athletics through two different scholarship programs: the Honda Awards Program and the Honda Scholar Athlete Program.

Honda also shows its corporate citizenship by operating manufacturing plants and R&D centers in nearly every country where Hondas are sold, which allows them to boost local economies by offering jobs to the local population. It also allows vehicles to be sold less expensively in each area because there are no costs for importing parts or vehicles. At the same time, with motorcycle plants in China, India, Thailand, and five other Asian countries, Honda actively promotes traffic safety programs as the region becomes more motorized.

GLOBAL PRESENCE

Honda maintains a global network, with 89 plants in 33 countries, supplying Honda products to nearly every country in the world. The company has set up subsidiaries in the United States, the United Kingdom, France, Germany, Belgium, Canada, Australia, Brazil, and Thailand. The company also has manufacturing plants in Belgium, Brazil, Indonesia, Italy, Malaysia, New Zealand, Nigeria, Peru, the Philippines, Taiwan, Thailand, Vietnam, the United States, and the United Kingdom, among others.

Honda's diversified markets include automobile and motorcycle consumers as well as consumers of power products. Because of Honda's early and aggressive international expansion, Honda's markets include the Americas, Europe, Asia, and Australia.

SOURCES OF INFORMATION

Bibliography
American Honda Homepage, 11 May 1998. Available at http://www.honda.com:80.

"American Honda Motor Co. Inc." *Hoover's Online,* 5 May 1998. Available at http://www.hoovers.com.

Derdak, Thomas. "Honda Motor Company Limited (Honda Giken Kogyo Kabushiki Kaisha)." *International Directory of Company Histories.* Detroit: St. James Press, 1995.

"History of Honda Motor Co., Ltd." *Hardin Honda Home Page,* 11 May 1998. Available at http://www.hardin.com/data/m-honda.html.

Honda Japan Homepage, 11 May 1998. Available at http://www.honda.co.jp/home.

"Honda Motor Co., Ltd." *Hoover's Online,* 5 May 1998. Available at http://www.hoovers.com.

For an annual report:
on the Internet at: http://www.honda.co.jp/home/zaimu/a_report/annualreport/ope-hl.html

For additional industry research:
Investigate companies by their Standard Industrial Classification Codes, also known as SICs. Honda's primary SICs are:

3524 Lawn and Garden Equipment

3711 Motor Vehicle and Car Bodies

3714 Motor Vehicle Parts and Accessories

3751 Motorcycles and Parts

Hormel Foods Corp.

FOUNDED: 1891

Contact Information:

HEADQUARTERS: 1 Hormel Pl.
    Austin, MN 55912-3680
PHONE: (507)437-5611
FAX: (507)437-5489
URL: http://www.hormel.com

OVERVIEW

Hormel Foods Corporation has come a long way from its original founding in 1891. George Hormel's original meat packing plant, housed in an abandoned creamery, has grown into one of the leading multinational manufacturers and marketers of food products in the world. Hormel is the producer of consumer-branded meat and food products, many of which are among the best known in the food industry. Among Hormel's most popular products are SPAM, canned luncheon meat, and Dinty Moore stews.

The full range of products produced and marketed by Hormel includes pork products, such as hams, bacon, and sausages; canned luncheon meats, meat spreads, chili, hash, and stews; microwaveable meals; condiments, such as salsas; ethnic foods; and frozen processed foods.

With 110,000 employees worldwide, Hormel is a truly multi-national company. Known until 1991 as George A. Hormel & Co., the company is still headquartered in the town of its birth, Austin, Minnesota, which is also home to Hormel's flagship plant and research and development division. Within the United States, Hormel products are sold everywhere, testifying to the strength of the company's national sales force, which has offices in major cities across the country. Other Hormel manufacturing facilities are located in Stockton, California; Atlanta, Georgia; Aurora, Illinois; Knoxville, and Osceola, Iowa; Wichita, Kansas; Fremont, Nebraska; Oklahoma City, Oklahoma; and Beloit, Wisconsin. Also based in Fremont, Nebraska is a hog slaughtering operation.

Additional raw material for Hormel's pork processing operations comes from the hog slaughtering facility of Rochelle Foods, a wholly owned subsidiary based in Rochelle, Illinois. Jennie-O Foods Inc., another wholly owned subsidiary, is one of the largest U.S. producers of whole and processed turkeys selling to both retail and food service outlets. Jennie-O Foods is headquartered in Willmar, Minnesota. Dan's Prize is a wholly owned Hormel subsidiary, based in Cornelia, Georgia. Dan's Prize's manufacturing facility in Long Prairie, Minnesota produces roast beef, pastrami, corned beef, prime rib, and other cooked meats for delicatessens and other food service operations.

On the international front, Hormel Foods has been particularly active in recent years, though it is no newcomer to exports, having first sold abroad in 1905. Hormel Foods International Corporation (HFIC), also based in Austin, Minnesota, has negotiated international joint venture and license agreements in Australia, China, Colombia, Costa Rica, Denmark, England, Japan, Korea, Mexico, Panama, the Philippines, Poland, Spain, and other countries. HFIC sells to more than 40 nations worldwide.

COMPANY FINANCES

For fiscal 1997, ending October 31, 1997, Hormel reported net earnings of $110 million on revenue of $3.30 billion, up from fiscal 1996 net income of $79 million on revenue of $3.10 billion. Per-share earnings climbed to $1.43 in fiscal 1997 from $1.04 in 1996. In fiscal 1995, net earnings totaled $120 million on revenue of $3.04 billion, compared with fiscal 1994 earnings of $118 million on revenue of $3.07 billion. Per-share earnings in fiscal 1995 were $1.57, compared with $1.54 in fiscal 1994.

In fiscal 1997 meat products accounted for 54 percent of Hormel's total sales, while prepared foods brought in about 27 percent of total revenue. The remaining 19 percent of revenue was accounted for by sales of poultry and other products.

ANALYSTS' OPINIONS

Ralph Acampora, chief technical analyst at Prudential Securities, in an interview in the April 1998 issue of *Money* magazine, said the stock of Hormel Foods, which had hit a new 52-week high only a short time before, was among the handful of small and midcap names he favored. Acampora, who first won Wall Streeters' respect for his accurate prediction in mid-1995 that the Dow-Jones Industrial Average (DJIA) would soon hit the 7000-mark, also predicted the DJIA would top 10,000 in 1999.

FINANCES:

Hormel Foods Net Sales, 1994-1997 (billion dollars)

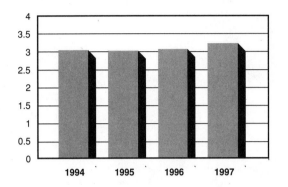

Hormel Foods 1997 Stock Prices (dollars)

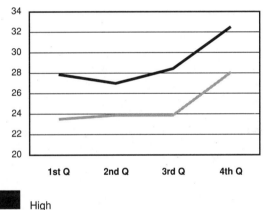

 High

Low

HISTORY

In 1891 George Hormel took an abandoned creamery and turned it into a meat packing plant, including a smokehouse and slaughterhouse. To compete with larger meat processors, Hormel needed to expand. In 1899 he updated facilities to include refrigeration, new pumps and engines, an electric elevator, smokehouses, and a hog kill. Additional land was acquired in 1901 for constructing a casing processing room and a machine shop.

Hormel's Corporate Office building. *(Courtesy of Hormel Foods.)*

Hormel acquired his first patent in 1903 with Dairy Brand and began to open distribution centers. George Hormel established export business in 1905 and by the end of World War I, exports accounted for about 33 percent of the company's yearly sales.

Jay Hormel, George's son, became the company's president in 1929. Jay continued expanding the product line and introduced Dinty Moore beef stew, Hormel chili, and SPAM luncheon meat.

During World War II Hormel sold more than 60 percent of its production to the U.S. Government. In 1941 Hormel was manufacturing 15 million cans of SPAM per week for U.S. servicemen abroad. The brand became so widely known that it became the object of criticism and ridicule that would live on well into the future.

After the war Hormel continued to expand by renovating many of its plants and opening new locations. Canning operations were improved and Hormel began to contract independent canning businesses to produce Hormel items. The company also began producing gelatin from pork skins to make use of its raw material.

New products were also introduced after the war. Mary Kitchen Roast Beef Hash, Corned Beef Hash, and Spaghetti and Beef in Sauce were first offered in 1949. Hormel continued to build new facilities throughout the United States during the 1950s and 1960s. The popular Hormel Cure 81 ham was a major success during the 1960s. The ham was a boneless, skinless, cured ham without the shank.

By the 1980s the meat industry began to shrink. The cost of hogs had increased and Hormel struggled. The company was forced to re-evaluate its place in the market. Hormel left the slaughtering business in 1988. The company moved into the microwaveable foods market and introduced Top Shelf, unrefrigerated meals in a vacuum pack, and its Light & Lean Franks. The company expanded into ethnic foods with its purchase of House of Tsang and Oriental Deli brands. Jennie-O Foods, a turkey-processing business, was also bought by Hormel.

Since the company was expanding to embrace many different types of foods, a decision was made to change its name to Hormel Foods Corporation in 1993. The company had been known as George A. Hormel & Co. for more than 100 years.

In 1996 Hormel set up a joint venture with Patak Spices Ltd., a leading Indian food producer, to market Indian food products in the United States. The company also bought a 21-percent interest in Campofrio Alimentacion SA, a Spanish food company, for $64 million. At home Hormel acquired premium chili producer Stagg Foods.

Rising hog prices sent Hormel's earnings spiraling downward in 1996. The company sold off its subsidiary Farm Fresh Catfish Co. and struck an agreement with El Torito to market El Torito's line of Mexican food products in supermarkets.

STRATEGY

Hormel's strategy has included the acquisition of companies with products that fit into Hormel's product mix. The company purchased Melting Pot Foods in 1995 to further increase its ethnic foods market share.

The company also believes in expanding its operations and enhancing its facilities where it is most cost effective. Hormel constructed a new turkey processing plant in Montevideo, Minnesota, and expanded its gelatin/specialized proteins plant in Davenport, Iowa.

INFLUENCES

Consumer trends have influenced Hormel's business decisions over the years. As consumers became increasingly health-conscious during the 1980s and 1990s, sales of traditional meat products began to decline. To appeal to the consumer for lower fat content, Hormel introduced its Light & Lean 97 brands. The line includes all-beef franks, boneless ham, turkey breasts and smoked dinner links.

Convenience has also been a trend of the 1990s. To meet the customer demand for convenience, Hormel introduced cold cuts packaged in recloseable zippered thermoform.

CURRENT TRENDS

More and more businesses are promoting eating and movie-watching as a desirable combination. In 1994 Hormel teamed up with Ingram Entertainment to cross-promote its food products with Ingram's videos. The agreement allowed Hormel consumers a $3.50 discount on Ingram videos. In 1996 Hormel and New Line Home Video Inc. signed a similar contract to cross-promote the direct-to-sell-through release of "The Adventures of Pinocchio."

Although it has made no commitment to use irradiation in the production of any of its products, Hormel has been dogged since 1996 by Food & Water, a small Vermont-based consumer group unalterably opposed to irradiation of food products. When Hormel sent a couple of observers to a Dallas meeting about the irradiation process, Food & Water contacted the company and demanded a pledge that Hormel would never use irradiation on any of its products. When the company refused, Food & Water placed an ad in Hormel's hometown newspaper implying some sort of link between Hormel and irradiation. As recently as the spring of 1998, Hormel spokesman Allan Krejci said of irradiation: "We haven't yet determined whether we would use it."

FAST FACTS:
About Hormel Foods Corp.

Ownership: Hormel Foods Corp. is a publicly owned company traded on the New York Stock Exchange.

Ticker symbol: HRL

Officers: Joel W. Johnson, CEO, Chmn., & Pres., 54, $970,000; Don J. Hodapp, Exec. VP & CFO, 59, $605,000; Gary J. Ray, Exec. VP, 51, $510,000; Stanley E. Kerber, Group VP, Meat Products, 59, $445,000

Employees: 11,000

Principal Subsidiary Companies: Hormel's principal subsidiaries are Dan's Prize Inc., Hormel Foods International Corp., Jennie-O Foods Inc., and Rochelle Foods.

Chief Competitors: Active in several sectors of the food industry, Hormel Foods Corporation faces competition in all areas of its operations. Some of its major competitors are: Campbell Soup; ConAgra; CPC; General Mills; Goya; Grand Metropolitan; Heinz; IBP; Nabisco Holdings; Nestle; Perdue; Philip Morris; Sara Lee; Smithfield Foods; Thorn Apple Valley; and Tyson Foods.

PRODUCTS

Hormel has three main product lines: meat products, food service, and prepared foods. The meat products group includes such products as Cure 81 ham, Black Label bacon, and Light & Lean meats. The food service sector includes such product lines as Sandwich Maker turkey breast and roast beef and Super Select boneless pork loin and pork chops. Hormel's prepared foods line includes both shelf-stable and frozen foods such as SPAM and Hormel chili.

CORPORATE CITIZENSHIP

During World War I Hormel employed women for the first time. The company and its employees were involved in the war effort, producing meat, buying Liberty bonds, and donating an hour's pay each day to the Red Cross.

CHRONOLOGY:
Key Dates for Hormel Foods Corp.

1891: Founded as George A. Hormel & Co. by George Hormel

1899: George Hormel updates facilities, adding, among other things, refrigeration

1903: Acquires Dairy Brand

1905: Hormel begins selling products internationally

1929: Jay Hormel, George's son, becomes president

1933: Bitter strikers physically remove Jay Hormel from his office and shut off the plant's refrigeration system

1946: Jay Hormel becomes chairman of the board and H.H. Corey becomes president

1949: Introduces Mary Kitchen Roast Beef Hash, Corned Beef Hash, and Spaghetti and Beef in Sauce

1954: Jay Hormel Dies and R.F. Gray becomes Hormel's fourth president

1965: Adds a new 75,000-square-foot sausage manufacturing building to its Austin plant

1986: Acquires Jennie-O foods

1993: Changes name to Hormel Foods Corporation

1995: Purchases Melting Pot Foods

1998: Begins selling products produced at Shanghai Hormel Foods Co. Ltd. in the Chinese market

The Hormel Foundation was instituted to serve religious, charitable, scientific, literary, or educational causes. The foundation financed a research facility at the University of Minnesota called the Hormel Institute. The Institute performed research on fats and other lipids, analyzing their effects on the human body.

Hormel supports education, welfare, and cultural and charitable community service organizations. In education, Hormel has financed scholarships. Hormel has also supported capital building projects. The company has provided funding for cancer, heart disease, arthritis, and diabetes research, and assists hospitals and health clinics. In addition, Hormel has donated financial assistance to organizations for handicapped, elderly, and

homeless people. Hormel also has donated its products to Second Harvest and its food banks. The company has assisted the American Red Cross and Salvation Army with food and donations during emergencies and natural disasters.

GLOBAL PRESENCE

Hormel continues its expansion globally. The company plans to increase its international business through exports, joint ventures, and licensing agreements.

The company sells its products in more than 40 countries. Major markets for Hormel include Australia, Hong Kong, Japan, Korea, Mexico, Panama, Philippines, and the United Kingdom.

In 1994 the company teamed up with Beijing Agriculture Industry and Commerce to establish Beijing Hormel Foods Company Ltd. in China. Under the Hormel brand, western-style meat products were to be marketed to the Chinese but modified to meet local tastes.

In 1995 Hormel formed a joint venture with Grupo Herdez S. A. de C. V. of Mexico called Hormel Alimentos S. A. de C. V. The partnership enabled Hormel to tap into the Mexican market. Also in 1995, Hormel finalized an agreement with Darling Downs Bacon Cooperative Association Ltd. in Australia. The venture, named KR Hormel Foods, replaced a previous licensee agreement. The joint venture greatly increased Hormel's expansion opportunities in Australia.

In January 1998, only weeks before the observance of lunar New Year, products produced at Shanghai Hormel Foods Co. Ltd. first hit the Chinese market. The sausage, hams, hot dogs, and bacon, on sale at Chinese food stores, were produced inside the factories of Shanghai Dachang Meat Processing Complex, Hormel's partner in the joint venture. Plans call for the Shanghai joint venture to process 10,000 tons of meat annually.

EMPLOYMENT

Hormel has had its share of labor disputes. After a bitter labor strike in 1933, Jay Hormel instituted the "Annual Wage Plan" where employees received weekly pay, flexible working hours, and the guarantee of a year's notice before any employee could be terminated. The company also began to offer profit sharing, merit pay, a pension plan, and a joint earnings plan.

The equal opportunity and affirmative action programs instituted by the company provide all persons who apply with the company "due consideration for employment," and protect all persons employed from "discrimination based on race, color, religion, sex, national origin, age, sexual orientation, disability, or being a veteran of the Vietnam era."

Hormel supports the education of its employees. On-the-job training is provided for new employees, and the company sponsors courses and in-house workshops to further educate the workforce.

SOURCES OF INFORMATION

Bibliography

Alaimo, Dan. "'Pinocchio Release Cross-Promoted with Hormel." *Supermarket News,* 9 September 1996.

The Career Guide 1997: Dun's Employment Opportunities Directory. Bethlehem, PA: Dun & Bradstreet, Inc., 1996.

"Corporate Profile." Austin, MN: Hormel Foods Corp., 10 May 1998. Available at http://www.hormel.com/Hormel/company.nsf/lkdocuments/B1?OpenDocument.

"Hormel to Enter Mexican Venture." *Nation's Restaurant News,* 29 July 1996.

"Hormel Enters into New Mexican Venture." *Nation's Restaurant News,* 4 September 1995.

"Hormel Foods Buys Specialty Food Firm." *Nation's Restaurant News,* 2 October 1995.

"Hormel Foods Corporation." *Hoover's Online,* 10 May 1998. Available at http://www.hoovers.com.

"Hormel Meat Products Hit Market." *AsiaInfo Daily News,* 6 January 1998.

Mirabile, Lisa, ed. *International Directory of Company Histories.* Detroit: St. James Press, 1990.

Morrison, Shauna, ed. *Standard & Poor's 500 Guide.* New York: The McGraw-Hill Companies, Inc., 1996.

Nissen, Todd. "Hormel's Light & Lean 97 Hot Dog Takes a Bite out of Wiener Market." *Corporate Report-Minnesota,* March 1994.

Scherreik, Susan. "Dow 10,000? A Top Technical Analyst Explains Why He Sees the Market Soaring." *Money,* 1 April 1998.

"Small Group Targets All Firms That Show Interest in Irradiation." *Denver Post,* 1 April 1998.

"When Grocery Met Video." *Supermarket News,* 18 April 1994.

"Zippered Thermoform Carves Hot Niche for Cold Cuts." *Packaging Digest,* January 1994.

For an annual report:

on the Internet at: http://www.hormel.com/Hormel/COM-PANY.NSF/lkdocuments/B2_5?OpenDocument **or** call Hormel Shareholder Services at: (507)437-5164

For additional industry research:

Investigate companies by their Standard Industrial Classification Codes, also known as SICs. Hormel's primary SICs are:

2011 Meat Packing Plants

2013 Sausages & Other Prepared Meat Product

2032 Canned Specialties

H&R Block, Inc.

FOUNDED: 1955

Contact Information:

HEADQUARTERS: 4410 Main St.
   Kansas City, MO 64111
PHONE: (816)753-6900
FAX: (816)753-5346
URL: http://www.hrblock.com

OVERVIEW

H&R Block is probably best known for H&R Block Tax Services, the largest tax preparation service in the United States, handling approximately 1 in every 7 tax returns filed with the U.S. Internal Revenue Service (IRS). H&R Block operates and franchises about 9,700 tax preparation offices in the United States, Canada, Europe, and Australia. Founder Henry Bloch stated that, "Our biggest competitor is the person who does his own tax return."

H&R Block, Inc. diversified and experimented with products and services in many other areas. The company's subsidiary, Block Financial Corporation, develops and provides home mortgage loans, tax preparation software, temporary employment services, document processing, and sales of mutual funds, insurance, and annuities. In fiscal year 1998, H&R Block served more than 18 million taxpayers in more than 10,000 offices in the United States, Canada, and Australia. The company handled approximately 1 in every 7 regular returns and 51 percent of all electronic returns filed with the IRS that year.

COMPANY FINANCES

Despite losses incurred by the struggling CompuServe Corporation, which H&R Block eventually sold in January 1998, the company reported strong revenue growth in fiscal 1997 with net earnings of $47.8 million, or $.45 per share, and a 16.5-percent increase in revenues to $1.9 billion. H&R Block's previous year's earnings were $177.2 million, or $1.67 a share. The decline in earnings was due entirely to a $186.5-million pretax loss reported by CompuServe Corporation. Excluding the CompuServe results, Block's revenues rose nearly 26 percent from $871.5 million in 1996 to $1.1 billion in 1997. Pretax earnings grew 14 percent to $225.1 million, while earnings per share increased more than 15 percent from $1.18 to $1.36. For the third quarter ended January 31, 1998, the company reported revenues of $208.7 million, a 34.5-percent increase over the previous year. The company also gained $231.9 million on the sale of CompuServe Corporation. The company estimates pegged total earnings for the 1998 fiscal year at $173 million, an increase of 22 percent over 1997.

ANALYSTS' OPINIONS

With efforts to expand into other financial products and services, Joel Friedman, partner in the San Francisco office of Andersen Consulting, was quoted as saying, "They will have to invest heavily in consumer marketing to have customers make the link between what the brand has historically stood for—tax preparation—to other products." In spite of his break with the company, former H&R Block CEO Richard H. Brown said, "I've hung on to my Block stock." Standard and Poor rated the company a "market outperformer" in the spring of 1998.

HISTORY

H&R Block, Inc. was founded in 1955 by Henry and Richard Bloch, who were born and raised in Kansas City, Missouri. They decided to use the incorrectly spelled name in order to prevent people from mispronouncing the name as "Blotch." Henry first decided to start his own business while studying statistics at Harvard Business School, but his plans were put on hold while he served in the U.S. Air Force during World War II.

In 1946 Henry and Richard Bloch opened United Business Company in Kansas City. They offered small businesses bookkeeping, management, and collection, and prepared income tax returns without charge for their business clients. Later they began preparing tax returns separately for a small fee. By 1954 they realized that the time spent on tax preparation interfered with their bookkeeping business and decided they would either have to discontinue the service or make it their primary business. On January 25, 1955 the Blochs sold United Business Company and started H&R Block, Inc., specializing in income tax return preparation. During that tax season, the company grossed more than $20,000, a third of the annual volume of United Business Company.

One reason for the company's success was their unique pricing structure. H&R Block devised a method

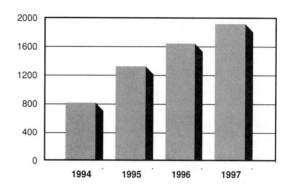

FINANCES:

H & R Block
Revenues, 1994-1997
(million dollars)

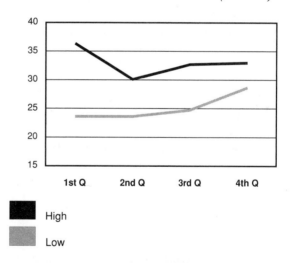

H & R Block
1997 Stock Prices
(dollars)

of charging related solely to the number and complexity of forms and schedules included within the return. The charge did not vary with the size of the tax refund, the client's income, or the time involved. With this same theory still applying to this day, the average charge for completing a return for U.S. customers was only about $70.

When the Blochs realized they could not operate all the offices personally, they began hiring qualified local people. They trained them and let them operate on a franchise or salary contract basis under the H&R Block banner.

FAST FACTS:
About H&R Block, Inc.

Ownership: H&R Block, Inc. is a publicly owned company traded on the New York Stock Exchange, Boston Stock Exchange, Chicago Stock Exchange, Pacific Stock Exchange, and Philadelphia Stock Exchange, Inc.

Ticker symbol: HRB

Officers: Henry W. Block, Chmn., 75; Frank L. Salizzoni, Pres. & CEO, 60 $1,035,608; Ozzie Wenich, Sr. VP & CFO, 55, $394,807; Thomas L. Zimmerman, Pres., H&R Block Tax Services, 48 $424,655

Employees: 1,200 (72,000 during tax season)

Principal Subsidiary Companies: The three major subsidiaries of H & R Block, Inc. are H & R Block Tax Services, H&R Block International, and Block Financial Corporation.

Chief Competitors: While H&R Block faces competition from innumerable small tax preparation services, independent accountants, and larger accounting firms, few pose a significant threat to its core business. The company's most prominent competitors include: Andersen Worldwide; Ernst & Young; and KPMG.

In January 1957 the Blochs opened offices in Columbia, Missouri, and Topeka, Kansas. In 1958 they added Des Moines, Oklahoma City, and Little Rock. H&R Block went public in 1962. By 1969 Block had 3,286 offices throughout the United States, Canada, and Puerto Rico, with volume totaling more than $56 million. By 1978 H&R Block offices prepared more than 1 of every 9 tax returns filed in the United States.

At the saturation point in the tax business, H&R Block began to diversify. In 1978 the company acquired Personnel Pool of America, a temporary personnel agency specializing in health care, for $22.5 million. CompuServe, Inc., purchased by H&R Block in 1980, provided Internet, business network, and Intranet access services. From 1980 to 1987 H&R Block's Block Management Company supplied marketing and administrative services for the nationwide expansion of Hyatt Legal Services, an Ohio chain of storefront legal clinics offering basic legal services at standardized fees. In 1985 H&R Block bought Path Management Industries, a busi-

ness seminar company, which they sold in 1990 at a loss. In 1990 H&R Block acquired Interim Systems for $49.5 million, merged its assets with Personnel Pool of America, and renamed the subsidiary INTERIM Services. In early 1994 H&R Block announced plans to sell INTERIM through an initial public offering. Block Financial Corporation was started in 1993 and Block entered the credit card business with a MasterCard called the H&R Block ValueCard, and later with the CompuServe Visa affinity card and the Websource Visa card.

As the tax preparation business grew, it became apparent that the company needed a reliable source of trained income tax return preparers. It then established its H&R Block Income Tax Schools. H&R Block was one of the first companies to file tax forms electronically with their Rapid Refund service offered in conjunction with the IRS and Sears. In 1986 Block started by filing 22,000 tax returns electronically from two test areas, Cincinnati and Phoenix. In 1997 the company filed more than 8 million returns electronically in the United States and Canada.

On January 31, 1998 the Company finalized the sale of the CompuServe Corporation and received 30.1 million shares of WorldCom, Inc. stock. The transaction was completed with the receipt of $1.03 billion in net proceeds from the monetization of the WorldCom stock in a Block trade on February 2, 1998. The company planned to use the proceeds to grow its core tax and financial services businesses and to fund a stock repurchase plan.

STRATEGY

For years, H&R Block's biggest problem had been what to do with the more than 10,000 empty offices during the eight months of the year when people aren't worrying about taxes. In 1997, the company lost $83 million during the off season. The solution devised by Block CEO Frank Salizzoni, was to market other financial services directly to its tax customers. Though the company's subsidiary, Block Financial Corporation, was already offering a variety of services including mortgages and mutual funds, little had been done to integrate the services with those offered by H&R Block Tax Services. Creating a one-stop financial shopping mall targeted at the company's downscale customer base (a segment largely ignored by other financial service firms) seemed like a sure bet, given Block's international name recognition, extensive network of field offices, and the huge wad of cash it had pocketed following the sale of CompuServe.

In 1998, Salazzoni began testing out the idea. Fourteen Block offices in 4 cities offered an expanded array of services and 14 financial planners were hired to offer investment advice for fees ranging from $10 for a simple plan to $250 for a combination tax preparation and financial plan. Mutual funds, annuities, stocks, and bonds were offered at these 14 offices and Block mortgages were offered in another 30 cities. At the rest of the company's stores, tax customers were asked questions about their non-tax needs. More than half gave the company permission to call them.

INFLUENCES

In 1997 H&R Block paid $250,000 to settle a dispute with the New York City Department of Consumer Affairs over wording in their advertising. Customers did not understand that their instant refunds were actually refund anticipation loans (RALs)—short-term high-interest loans using the future refund as collateral. After settling the disagreement, H&R Block continued to offer RALs in partnership with Beneficial Corporation, one of the leading RAL lenders. "The RAL agreement and the new mortgage business indicate that Block Financial is rapidly evolving into a strategic partner of our Tax Services business," said Block CEO Frank Salizzoni in a 1997 company press release. The success of Block Financial and RALs were soon to prompt the company to consider expanding its array of financial services and delivering them straight to a captive market, the millions of Americans who had their tax returns prepared by H&R Block every year.

CURRENT TRENDS

H&R Block continued to enjoy revenue growth in 1997 and 1998, and the number of clients served worldwide with tax preparation and electronic filing services rose to a record 18.2 million. However, the company's margins were slipping due to bad debt associated with electronic filing, marketing expenses, and costs connected to a new, computerized bookkeeping and management reporting system. Though it seemed unlikely the government would ever fulfill its promises to simplify the tax system, the market for tax preparation services had little room left to expand. To maintain its growth, H&R Block began experimenting an expanded array of services offered right in the tax office. Revenues at offices that offered additional products were more than double those offering only tax services, suggesting that the company was moving in the right direction. Salazzoni, a former airline executive who had already experienced the dangers of expanding too quickly, however, was in no hurry. After all, taxes are one of only two things in life that everyone can count on.

PRODUCTS

Block Premium offices markets financial planning products and services aimed at more upscale clients,

CHRONOLOGY:
Key Dates for H&R Block, Inc.

1946: Henry and Richard Bloch form United Business

1955: Reincorporate under the name H&R Block, deliberately misspelling last name

1956: Opened seven storefront offices in New York City

1962: Company goes public

1964: Initiates legal action against New York franchisees because of unscrupulous practices

1966: Settles out of court with New York franchisees and bought back franchises for more than $1 million

1967: Gain 5,000 new employees who were trained in company's tax school

1972: Opens outlets in 147 Sears department stores

1978: Acquires Personnel Pool of America for $22.5 million

1980: Acquires CompuServe; Bloch brothers enter into joint venture with Ohio attorney and entrepreneur Joel Hyatt

1985: Acquires Path Management Industries

1990: Sells Path Management to American Management Association

1991: Purchases Interim Systems for $49.5 million and merges its assets with those of Personnel Pool of America, renaming subsidiary INTERIM Services

1993: Starts Block Financial Corporation

1994: Announces plans to sell INTERIM through initial public offering

1998: Finalizes sale of CompuServe Corporation and receives 30.1 million shares of WorldCom, Inc. stock

which also allows the company to use some of its offices year-round. To reach other customers who are not coming to them, H&R Block makes tax preparers available for house calls from the 4,300 company-owned offices. They also market a simple kit for writing a will at home, as well as the software programs, Home Legal Adviser, Small Business Attorney, and Kiplinger TaxCut.

Block Financial's new Conductor program offers community banks the means of providing a wide variety of financial services to their customers through CompuServe and the Internet. Using software provided by Jack Henry & Associates, Conductor enables banks to offer such services as bill payment and account access to their customers online.

GLOBAL PRESENCE

With expansion in tax preparation reaching its limits in the United States, growth in Britain allowed H&R Block to increase the number of offices in order to take advantage of changes in their tax laws. These tax laws doubled the number of people who are required to file tax returns. In addition, there are no geographical limits on the financial services that are being marketed through H&R Block's Internet web site.

Aside from the recent expansion of offices in Great Britain, there are more than 1,000 H&R Block offices in Canada, handling over 10 percent of their tax returns, and more than 300 offices in Australia handling 75 percent of the professionally prepared tax returns there. H&R Block, Inc. also owns subsidiaries in Bermuda, Canada, Nova Scotia, Guam, New Zealand, United Kingdom, Germany, Switzerland, France, Sweden, Netherlands, Australia, and Singapore.

EMPLOYMENT

Since April 15 is the deadline each year to file tax returns, the vast majority of H&R Block employees, 79,000 seasonal hired, work only during the first four months of the year. While many of these employees return from year to year, H&R Block's Basic Tax Preparation course supplies new recruits. Every year 60,000 to 100,000 people pay a fee to enroll in the course. The basic course involves 69 hours of classroom instruction and training provided, not only to potential H&R Block employees, but also to employees of other financial institutions, including major banks, mutual fund companies, and brokerage firms. Senior preparers with the company go on to study five different levels of courses.

SOURCES OF INFORMATION

Bibliography

"Compuserve to be Sold to Worldcom." H&R Block Press Release, 8 September 1997. Available at http://www.hrblock.com.

Feder, Barnaby J. "From Storefronts to Supermarkets." *New York Times,* 9 February 1997.

"H&R Block Delivers Tax Tips and Tools on the Internet." H&R Block, Inc. Press Release, 13 February 1997. Available at http://www.hrblock.com/press_releases/taxchecklist.html.

"H&R Block Reports Fiscal Year Earnings." H&R Block, Inc. Press Release, 18 June 1997. Available at http://www.hrblock.com.

"H&R Block Reports Third Quarter Results and Gain On Sale of Compuserve." H&R Block, Inc. Press Release, 23 February 1998. Available at http://www.hrblock.com.

"H&R Block to Spin off CompuServe." *The Daily Reporter,* 21 February 1996.

Hoffer, William. "Bloch the IRS Return." *Nation's Business,* March 1987.

Palmeri, Christopher. " Watch Out, Merrill Lynch." *Forbes Magazine,* 4 May 1998.

For an annual report:
on the Internet at: http://sec.yahoo.com/e/970729/hrb.html

For additional industry research:
Investigate companies by their Standard Industrial Codes, also known as SICs. H&R Block's primary SICs are:

6719 Real Property Lessors Nec.

7291 Tax Return Preparation Services

7363 Help Supply Services

7372 Repackaged Software

7374 Data Processing & Preparation

7375 Information Retrieval Services

8249 Vocational Schools Nec

Huffy Corporation

OVERVIEW

Huffy Corporation is involved in both the manufacturing and marketing of consumer products, ranging from bicycles to lawn and garden tools, and the sales of services to the retail sector. On the consumer products side of its operations, Huffy is divided into five core companies: Huffy Bicycle, Huffy Sports, True Temper Hardware, Washington Inventory Service, and Huffy Service First.

Huffy Bicycle Co., the world's largest seller of bicycles, markets bicycles made in the company's U.S. factories as well as some lower-priced models made for Huffy in Asia. To maintain its position as the world's largest seller of bikes, Huffy has had to take steps to better compete with lower-priced models produced in Asia. Huffy Sports Co. is North America's leading supplier of NBA-licensed basketball backboards, as well as other basketball equipment. True Temper Hardware manufactures and markets a wide range of lawn and garden tools for use at home, on the farm, or by contractors. Washington Inventory Service provides a variety of inventory services to the retail industry through its nationwide workforce equipped with state-of-the-art technology. Huffy Service First is the country's only nationwide supplier of retail services that range from in-home and in-store product assembly and repair services to merchandising services.

COMPANY FINANCES

In 1997 Huffy Corp. posted net earnings of $10.1 million on revenue of $694.5 million, compared with 1996's

Contact Information:
HEADQUARTERS: 225 Byers Rd.
    Miamisburg, OH 45342
PHONE: (937)866-6251
FAX: (937)865-5470
URL: http://www.huffy.com

FINANCES:

Huffy Corp.
Net Sales, 1994-1997
(million dollars)

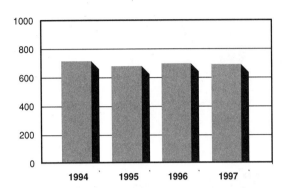

Huffy Corp.
1997 Stock Prices
(dollars)

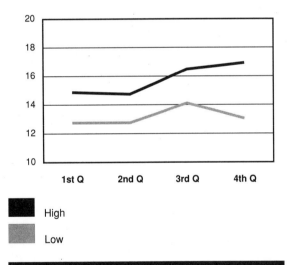

net of $6.5 million on revenue of $701.9 million. For 1995, the company reported a net loss of $10.5 million on revenue of $684.8 million, compared with net income of $17.4 million on revenue of $719.5 million in 1994. Sales of consumer products accounted for 74 percent of the company's total revenue in 1997, while the remaining 24 percent was derived from sales of retail services.

HISTORY

Founded by Horace Huffman in 1924, Huffman Manufacturing Company produced and marketed equip-

ment for service stations, including one of its own inventions, a rigid spout to dispense oil from large drums. During the Great Depression, Horace decided he could make money by providing a more inexpensive means of transportation and, in 1934, Huffman began producing bicycles.

When Horace brought his son into the business a few years later, Horace Jr. was able to double production and increase sales to more than $1 million by 1940. Horace continued to guide the company through World War II and the post-war recession by implementing modern management and manufacturing policies.

The introduction of the company's Huffy convertible bicycle in 1949 proved a big hit with the public. The bike was equipped with training wheels that could be removed once its young users had learned to ride. Huffman's business continued to grow through the 1950s and 1960s. In 1968 the company went public.

The 1970s gave the company's bicycle sales a shot in the arm with the rapid expansion of retail chains opening up a promising new market. In 1977 Huffman Manufacturing changed its name to Huffy Corporation, and the company acquired Frabill Manufacturing, a manufacturer of fishing and basketball equipment. Other acquisitions designed to diversify Huffy's product line followed. In 1982 the company bought YLC Enterprises, a company specializing in product assembly, and Gerico, the producer of Gerry and Snugli baby products. Six years later, Huffy purchased Washington Inventory Service. In 1990, the company bought True Temper, a manufacturer of lawn and garden tools. In 1997 the company acquired Royce Union Bicycle Company, a manufacturer of high-end bicycles.

Mounting competition from foreign bicycle manufacturers, particularly Asian, and a generally sluggish retail market combined to cause a hefty loss for Huffy in 1995. The company answered the competition aggressively with the 1997 introduction of 16 new BMX models.

To tighten the focus of its portfolio, in 1997 Huffy divested Gerry Baby Products Co. Gerry had failed to meet Huffy's criterion of ranking number one or two in its industry, and the company felt that it would need to make a very substantial investment in order to move Gerry into the desired position. Huffy determined the money could better be spent to fund "the internal growth and acquisition strategies to further enhance the number one or number two position held by each of our five core businesses."

STRATEGY

In late May 1998, Huffy Bicycle Co. announced a major restructuring plan to better position itself to compete with Asian manufacturers in the global bicycle marketplace. Under the plan Huffy would reconfigure its manufacturing operations, resulting in a sharp increase in finished goods production at its Farmington, Missouri, plant.

Huffy's goal in restructuring was to maximize operating efficiency by eliminating excess production capacity and reducing annual bicycle operating expenses. An 18-month-long analysis of the international bicycle market by the company revealed a sharp drop in comparable bike prices in the United States in the four years between 1993 and 1997; this decline in prices was blamed on fierce global competition, for which the company said there was no end in sight. This left Huffy with no choice but to fight back aggressively by cutting excess capacity and costs. The long-term goals for its new strategy were to "satisfy consumer demand for value-priced bicycles and to solidify Huffy as a viable U.S. bicycle supplier." Huffy hopes these actions will help it achieve its overall objective of maintaining its leadership in the bicycle industry despite competitors that have successfully driven down retail prices and eroded Huffy's profit margins."

One unfortunate consequence of its restructuring plan, Huffy said, was the need to close the company's 40-year-old bicycle factory in Celina, Ohio, in order to reduce production capacity. Other elements of the plan called for the leasing of a 100,000-square foot U.S. facility to make parts to support its Farmington, Missouri, factory and the continuation of its Asian import program to bring in opening price point bikes.

Huffy said the restructuring reflected some very basic changes in U.S. consumers' buying patterns. It pointed out that in 1997 nearly 60 percent of the bikes sold in the United States were produced by foreign manufacturers. The company said bicycles produced in Asia typically cost 10 to 20 percent less than comparable U.S.-produced models. This leaves companies like Huffy with no alternative but to adopt a competitive mix of domestic and non-domestic products. Huffy said it also planned to develop Mexican sources as alternatives for opening price point bikes currently imported from Asia.

Huffy has outlined five goals to help the company achieve its mission of being "the leading supplier of name brand consumer products and retail services designed to improve consumer lifestyles and enhance the business performance of its retail customers." According to company literature, Huffy "will achieve its vision by attaining prominence in every category of business in which it participates; by directing assets to value-adding activities to become the low-cost supplier of products and services to ensure the highest value to its retail customers and to consumers; by building strong relationships with customers and suppliers to be as efficient as possible; [by having] no single business unit [account] for more than 33 percent of total operating profits; [and by] achieving profitability that ensures consistent returns of at least 15 percent on beginning shareholder equity."

FAST FACTS:
About Huffy Corporation

Ownership: Huffy Corporation is a publicly owned company traded on the New York Stock Exchange.

Ticker symbol: HUF

Officers: Don Graber, Chmn., Pres., & CEO; Paul D'Aloia, Pres., Huffy Sports; Carol A. Gebhart, Pres., Washington Inventory Service; Christopher Snyder, Pres., Huffy Bicycle

Employees: 6,700

Principal Subsidiary Companies: Huffy operates a number of subsidiaries, including Huffy Bicycle Co. and Huffy Service First Inc., both headquartered in Miamisburg, Ohio; Huffy Sports Co., based in Sussex, Wisconsin; Royce Union Bicycle Co.; True Temper Hardware, based in Camp Hill, Pennsylvania; and Washington Inventory Service of San Diego, California.

Chief Competitors: Huffy's competitors include: Bell Sports; Bridgestone; Brunswick; Cannondale; Fremont; GT Bicycles; K2; Lifetime Products; TriStar Aerospace; RGIS Inventory; Specialized Bicycle Components; Trek; and U.S. Industries.

INFLUENCES

One of the forces that has helped shape Huffy's corporate strategy in the 1990s has been the continuing demand from consumers for "new and improved" products. Huffy has tried to answer that call and credits the positive consumer response to many of it product innovations with fueling its turnaround since 1995, when the company suffered a net loss of $10.5 million. During 1997, new products and services—including BMX bikes; the Hercules basketball system, marketed by Huffy Sports in Wisconsin; and expanded in-home assembly services—delivered additional sales in higher margin markets.

CURRENT TRENDS

In early 1998, Huffy expressed optimism that the momentum achieved in 1997, the second consecutive year of increased earnings, would help fuel the continu-

CHRONOLOGY:

Key Dates for Huffy Corporation

1924: Huffman Manufacturing Company is founded by Horace Huffman

1934: Huffman begins producing bicycles

1940: Sales reach over $1 million

1949: Company introduces the Huffy Convertible Bicycle

1968: Company goes public

1977: Huffman Manufacturing changes its name to the Huffy Corporation

1982: Company acquires YLC Enterprises and Gerico

1997: Huffy introduces 16 new BMX model bicycles and sells off Gerico

1998: Company announces a major restructuring plan to better compete with Asian manufacturers

ing financial turnaround that began in 1996. Leaving nothing to chance, in May 1998 the company announced a major restructuring program designed to help the company better compete against Asian bicycle manufacturers. The restructuring plan was designed to eliminate excess manufacturing capacity and trim operating costs.

Introducing the restructuring program, Huffy CEO Don Graber said, "When the restructuring and reconfiguration are complete, Huffy Bicycle Company will be a viable, long-term competitor. We expect performance for 1999 and beyond to be enhanced as a result of this restructuring."

PRODUCTS

Huffy operates in two distinct businesses: consumer products and retail services. Among its consumer product operations, Huffy Bicycle manufactures and markets bicycles and cycling equipment, while Huffy Sports is the leading North American supplier of NBA-licensed basketball backboards, as well as other basketball equipment. True Temper Hardware manufactures lawn and garden tools for use at home or on the farm. Among its retail service companies, Washington Inventory Service, based in San Diego, uses state-of-the-art technology to provide high quality inventory services to retailers. Huffy Service First offers a variety of services, including in-store and in-home product assembly and repair.

GLOBAL PRESENCE

Huffy is engaged in a battle to preserve its leadership in the worldwide bicycle market, challenged by fierce competition from foreign manufacturers, particularly those in Asia. In order to maintain the proper price mix in its bicycle product line, Huffy imports some lower-priced models from Asia, but it hopes to explore the possibility of developing Mexican sources as an alternative supplier of bicycles.

SOURCES OF INFORMATION

Bibliography

"Huffy Corporation." *Hoover's Online,* 18 May 1998. Available at http://www.hoovers.com/premium/profiles/10754.html.

"Huffy Corporation Announces New Bicycle Manufacturing Plan to Confront Fierce Asian Competition." *PR Newswire,* 28 May 1998.

"Huffy Plant to Lay Off Workers." *Associated Press,* 5 June 1998.

"Identity." Huffy Corporation, 1998. Available at http://www.huffy.com/identity/index.html.

For an annual report:

on the Internet at: http://www.huffy.com/balance_sheet.html

For additional industry research:

Investigate companies by their Standard Industrial Classification Codes, also known as SICs. Huffy Corporation's primary SICs are:

3423 Garden Hand Tools

3568 Drive Chains, Bicycle and Motorcycle

3751 Bicycles and Parts

3949 Basketballs and Basketball Equipment and Supplies

5261 Garden Supplies and Tools

IBM

FOUNDED: 1910

ALSO KNOWN AS: International Business Machines
Corporation

OVERVIEW

IBM is the world's largest computer company, with annual sales rapidly approaching 12 figures, about 60 percent of which comes from outside of the United States. In addition to manufacturing hardware and software, IBM has diversified into the areas of Internet service and computer consulting—in 1997 alone, 15,000 new employees joined IBM's services arms. The early 1990s were a time of crisis at IBM, but after a major revamping that began in 1993 and included some downsizing and a reevaluation of the company's strong points and mission, IBM managed to get back into the driver's seat and into the fast lane.

In 1997 the company was awarded the most U.S. patents for the fifth straight year—1,724, 300 more than the second-place applicant and almost 500 more than it received in 1996. Among the most significant was its breakthrough in using copper wiring in place of aluminum in chips, which greatly boosts both the speed and capacity of semiconductors. IBM often licenses its proprietary technology to communications and computer companies, a venture that earns it more than $1 billion per year.

Contact Information:

HEADQUARTERS: New Orchard Rd.
Armonk, NY 10504
PHONE: (914)499-1900
TOLL FREE: (800)426-3333
URL: http://www.ibm.com

COMPANY FINANCES

From a financial standpoint, 1997 was a record year for IBM, and a crucial one for nurturing the company's improving health. Revenues for 1997 reached $78.5 billion, with $19.3 billion representing the company's services businesses. Net earnings were $6.1 billion, up from $5.9 billion in 1996. After the effects of foreign currency

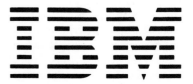

FINANCES:

IBM
Revenues, 1994-1997
(billion dollars)

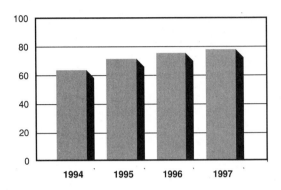

IBM
1997 Stock Prices
(dollars)

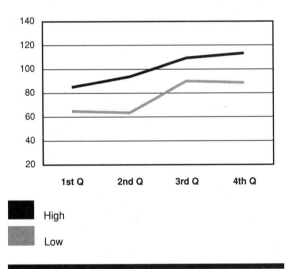

1995 and 1998, the company bought back about $20-billion worth of its common stock. At the close of 1997, there were 623,537 holders of common stock, which split two-for-one in the second quarter. IBM's market valuation, which CEO Louis Gerstner called "the ultimate measure of our performance,"grew by $23 billion. The company ended 1997 with $7.6 billion in cash.

The first quarter of 1998, however, saw IBM's first earnings decline in two years; the trend continued into the second quarter. But on July 30, 1998, IBM stock hit what Reuters described as "a lifetime intraday high" of $133.75, up 6, adding that "virtually all of Wall Street has turned bullish on IBM."

ANALYSTS' OPINIONS

A 1998 report by Salomon analyst John Jones stated, "We believe that IBM's software, PC servers and UNIX RS/6000 servers businesses are doing well." Gerstner would seem to agree. In the 1997 annual report he wrote, "IBM's comeback is on track and doesn't require a major course correction."

HISTORY

In 1910 Charles Ranlett Flint started the earliest ancestor of IBM under the name Calculating-Tabulating-Recording, or CTR, by merging three firms: International Time Recording Co., Computing Scale Co. of America, and Tabulating Machine Co. The last was founded by an engineer, Herman Hollerith, who had invented a tabulating machine—an apparatus that sorted and counted punch cards. This machine was first sold to the U.S. Census Bureau, and later to businesses that needed to organize large amounts of data economically. In 1915 Thomas Watson was hired as CTR's general manager and, by 1920, had built CTR into the leader in tabulating design.

CTR changed its name to International Business Machines—or IBM—in 1924. By focusing on large, custom systems for businesses, the company found that it had fewer competitors than those that made smaller, mass-produced systems. The company leased its products, instead of selling them, and reported profits throughout the 1920s. Initially, IBM held onto its market and customers by making punch cards that only worked with its own machines. By 1932, this policy had led to a U.S. government antitrust suit filed against IBM. At the time, IBM controlled 85 percent of the U.S. market for tabulating, keypunch, and accounting equipment.

The New Deal programs of the Depression years expanded government bureaucracy, which led to a need for large calculators; IBM supplied this equipment. World War II bolstered IBM's sales as well, and increased pub-

fluctuation, earnings improved by 8 percent. During the year, the company invested $5.5 billion in research and development, $300 million more than in 1996, and laid plans for a $700-million microchip development facility that will utilize the newly patented copper technology.

Stockholders' equity in 1997 measured almost $20 billion, and earnings per share were $6.18, up from 1996 earning of $5.53. Since 1996, the quarterly dividend has increased by 76 percent. In April 1997 directors raised the amount by 14 percent and, in April 1998 they increased it by another 10 percent, along with approval to step up the stock-buyback plan by $3.5 billion. Between

An early IBM personal computer and printer, circa 1981. (Courtesy of IBM.)

lic- and private-sector demand for tabulators helping to triple IBM's sales.

In 1956 IBM took the lead in the computer business by introducing its 705 general-purpose business computer. Institutional customers appreciated the way IBM's computers utilized the equipment that they had already leased or bought. The recognizable blue-suited sales force was instrumental in placing IBM's computers into businesses. In 1961 IBM released the Stretch computer system, which used a magnetic memory core and transistors instead of the more primitive vacuum tube technology. With the capability of performing up to three quarters of a million additions per second, the Stretch was the most powerful computer on the market.

In 1970 IBM introduced the first "floppy" (5 1/4 inch) disks, which were made by forming thin wafers of silicon and then cutting them into chips, thus setting the stage for much smaller systems. IBM subsequently released a new system, the 370 family. It was faster and could do more simultaneous tasks than prior systems. In 1973, IBM doubled the storage space on floppy disks with the 3340 disk storage unit, which functioned like main memory but at a much lower cost.

In 1975 IBM attempted to release its first personal computer, the 5100, weighing 50 pounds and costing about $5,000. Sales were disappointing. Realizing that demand for personal computers was minimal at the time, IBM focused on building mainframes. It was not until 1980 that IBM tried again to crack the personal computer

market. By then, many other companies were already making the machines, and IBM was not able to gain immediate control of the market. That same year, it rolled out the IBM 3687 Holographic Scanner, which was used with the IBM 3683 supermarket terminal to read bar codes. Throughout the 1990s, IBM continued to grow by producing many new systems and personal computers, and by providing various consulting services. It expanded its overseas operations and, in the late 1990s, continued to dominate the mainframe and computer-related service markets.

STRATEGY

Bold letters on IBM's rich web site declare, "IBM is about TWO things: 1. Creating the industry's most advanced information technologies; 2. Helping customers apply that technology to improve what they do—and how they do it." Keen insight into the issues facing today's industries allows IBM to design products that deliver maximum impact and long-lasting value. In a December 1997 interview in *U.S. News and World Report,* CEO Gerstner explained IBM's developing view of itself as a provider of solutions to the customer's needs, "Our ability to integrate is a unique advantage of this company. So we said: All right, now let's go build a strategy around integrating the technology into solutions for customers. That was the fundamental decision we made."

FAST FACTS:
About IBM

Ownership: IBM is a publicly held company traded on the New York Stock Exchange.

Ticker symbol: IBM

Officers: Louis V. Gerstner, Chmn. & CEO, 56, 1997 base salary $1,500,000; Douglas L. Maine, Sr. VP & CFO

Employees: 269,465 (1998)

Chief Competitors: Some primary competitors include: Acer Corp; AST Computer; Hewlett-Packard; Gateway 2000; and Microsoft.

CHRONOLOGY:
Key Dates for IBM

1910: Charles Ranlett Flint starts the Calculating-Tabulating-Recording (CTR) firm

1924: CTR changes its name to International Business Machines or IBM

1932: A U.S. Government antitrust suit is filed against IBM

1956: IBM introduces its 705 general-purpose business computer

1961: The company releases the Stretch computer system

1970: The company introduces the first "floppy" disk

1975: IBM releases its first personal computer

1980: The 3687 Holographic scanner is released

1990: IBM researchers move individual atoms

1992: The Think Pad is introduced

1997: Deep Blue, an IBM Supercomputer, defeats the World Chess Champion

1998: IBM announces its "E-business Tools" line

Aside from the company's strategy as a vendor, Gerstner writes in his annual statement that IBM is "committed to maximizing shareholder value and to making productive use of our cash." Since 1995 IBM has made 45 strategic acquisitions. Its acquisition of Lotus Development Corp., the maker of the popular Lotus Notes messaging software, was significant and highly publicized; but each of the other corporate deals has been just as calculated to contribute to IBM's long-term success, as have been the decisions to decline certain takeover opportunities.

INFLUENCES

The hard times of the early 1990s were a great motivator for IBM, which many analysts had written off even before the stock price had fallen into the $40 range. Earnings lagged, and dividends were cut. The departure of CEO John Akers, and the accession of Gerstner (formerly the chairman of RJR Holdings Corp.) marked the start of IBM's slow climb back to viability. The 1997 annual report proudly states, "Our people have worked hard in recent years to reinvent not just the mechanics of their work, but also the soul of their company." However, Gerstner's statement identified one lofty ambition, still unfulfilled: "a return to industry leadership."

CURRENT TRENDS

One current, emerging growth area for IBM is "deep computing," which links high-speed computers and analytical software. A major customer for this technology is the U.S. Department of Energy, for whom IBM is building a supercomputer for use in nuclear-weapons simulation testing. IBM envisions the technology as being useful to the pharmaceutical industry in simulating chemical reactions, and to the business world in providing financial modeling. In the mid-1990s, two celebrated face-offs pitted Russian chess grandmaster Gary Kasparov against "Deep Blue," an IBM RS/6000 SP supercomputer that utilizes deep computing technology. NASA's 1997 *Pathfinder* mission to Mars included an IBM RS/6000 as its onboard flight computer. Also in space that year were several IBM ThinkPad laptop computers missions.

In April of 1998 IBM announced its new "E-business Tools" line, comprised of servers, work stations, PCs, and notebooks for the purpose of facilitating business transactions over the Internet. The products include the Netfinity 3000 and 5500 servers, hard-disk and tape-drive storage devices, the IntelliStation M Pro workstation, the PC 300 PL personal computer, and an enhanced palm-sized computer, all available through IBM's web site. In a *Wired News* interview, IBM's vice president of Internet technologies, John Patrick, said of the development, "This concept that we are on, e-business, is not just e-commerce. It's about making a company into an electronic business where all the transactions become network-centric. When you do this, the transactions go up dramatically. And when the transactions go up, you need more disk space, and processing power, and infrastructure, and systems integration skills, and strategic planning. Well, those happen to be things we are really good at." An extensive marketing campaign in 1997 demonstrated the value of a "networked world."

In May of 1998, IBM announced its plans to support IDT Corp's Net2phone Internet-phone service, which allows long-distance telephone calls to be placed via computer. The software will be included with IBM's Internet access materials.

PRODUCTS

IBM makes leading computer hardware and software, and provides consulting services through its IBM Global Services unit. Hardware products include mainframes, servers, midrange, and desktop machines. Recent introductions include the Thinkpad 560, which weighs only 4.1 pounds and has one of the sharpest and largest screens in its class, and the enlarged Aptiva line of personal computers, which allows the monitor and media drives to be placed on the desktop, with the tower located elsewhere. The IBM Network Station allows businesses to access the Internet on a large scale. IBM's 1996 investment of $4.7 billion in research and development toward embedded microelectronics for digital devices—a method for bringing clear video to desktop computers—yielded the Voice Type Simply Speaking software, which allows the user access to applications by way of voice control. Lotus Notes, dubbed in the 1996 annual report "a human transaction system," allows team members across an organization to integrate their collective work more efficiently. IBM Global Services, a $19-billion business that experienced double-digit growth for more than 20 straight quarters in the mid- and late 1990s, assists customers with installation and implementation of their IBM machinery. In 1998, IBM's Internet service had about 750,000 subscribers.

CORPORATE CITIZENSHIP

IBM is the largest corporate contributor in the world. A $35-million grant program called "Reinventing Education" uses technology to improve education—for adults and children alike—all over the world. In South Africa, the program has provided computers to schools and

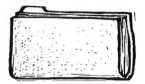

KNIGHT TAKES PAWN

It's a common enough theme in science-fiction—a machine that is more intelligent than the person who created it (think of the supercomputer HAL in *2001: A Space Odyssey*). Human beings have a vested interest in believing that they are smarter than their machines, and that is why chess matches between computers and grandmasters of chess have always elicited considerable comment and media coverage. The best human chess players have always been able to beat the best computer programs, but that all changed in May 1997, when IBM's Deep Blue took on the reigning world champion of chess, Garry Kasparov. Six games later it was official, Deep Blue had defeated Kasparov, and the supremacy of human beings (in chess at least) was at an end. Deep Blue, an IBM RS/6000 SP super-computer, was able to calculate 200,000,000 chess positions per second. And Kasparov? He grumbled that he wanted a rematch.

helped to train teachers to use them. Plans are in place to do the same in Vietnam, Ireland, and India. Annually, IBM donates millions of dollars worth of new technology to more than 1,600 domestic nonprofit health and human services entities via the United Way. During 1997 IBM employees donated $30 million in matching grants to local nonprofit organizations and schools. That same year the Environmental Protection Agency (EPA) recognized the company's efforts to eliminate the use of ozone-depleting chemicals (more than 15 million pounds since 1983). In 1998 President Clinton presented IBM with the Ron Brown Award for Corporate Leadership, which recognizes organizations for excellence in employee and community relations.

GLOBAL PRESENCE

IBM has a presence in more than 160 countries. It works with more than 1,000 businesses in central Europe and Russia alone, and is the leading vendor of personal computers in China. IBM's Global Campus Solution serves universities in the United States, Australia, Latin America, and Europe. Even in its research, IBM expands globally, with labs in Beijing working on Java, a programming language for use on the Internet.

EMPLOYMENT

IBM aims to be an employee-friendly institution. A survey by the National Society of Black Engineers found IBM to be its members' preferred employer. The company and its subsidiaries offer defined benefit and contribution plans to employees and a supplemental retirement plan to certain executives. In 1995, with Gerstner's endorsement, the company sent its long-famous dress code the way of the abacus, no longer requiring suits, hoping to foster comfort at all levels.

SOURCES OF INFORMATION

Bibliography

Behr, Peter, and Brett D. Fromson. "The Monumental Task of Rebuilding Big Blue." *Washington Post,* 26 March 1993.

Berger, Joseph. "Black Jeans Invade Big Blue." *New York Times,* 6 February 1995.

Cook, William J. "Interview with IBM CEO Louis Gerstner." *U.S. News Online,* 19 December 1997.

Faiola, Anthony. "Big Blue—Jeans, That Is." *Washington Post,* 4 February 1995.

"IBM." *Hoover's Online,* June 1998. Available at http://www.hoovers.com.

IBM Home Page. June 1998. Available at http://www.ibm.com.

"IBM Leads in U.S. Patents for Fifth Year in a Row." IBM Press Release, 12 January 1998. Available at http://www.ibm.com.

"IBM Names Chief Financial Officer." IBM Press Release, 14 April 1998. Available at http://www.ibm.com.

"IBM Receives Ron Brown Award for Corporate Leadership." IBM Press Release, 12 February 1998. Available at http://www.ibm.com.

"IBM Stock Hits High as Wall St. Is Solidly Bullish." *Reuters,* 30 July 1998.

"IBM Unveils New Computer Products." *AP,* 15 April 1998.

Jorgensen, Janice, ed. *Encyclopedia of Consumer Brands.* Vol. 3. Detroit: St. James Press, 1994.

Martin, Jonathan. *International Directory of Company Histories.* Vol. 3. Detroit, MI: St. James Press, 1994.

Melville, Richard. "Focus—IBM Says It Earned $1 Billion in First Quarter." *Reuters,* 20 April 1998.

———. "Gerstner: 1997 'A Great Year' For IBM Technology." *Reuters,* 28 April 1998.

Schiesel, Seth. "IBM Teams Up with Internet Phone Service." *New York Times,* 18 May 1998.

For an annual report:

on the Internet at: http://www.ibm.com **or** telephone: (800)426-3333

For additional industry research:

Investigate companies by their Standard Industrial Classification Codes, also known as SICs. IBM's primary SICs are:

3571 Electronic Computers

3572 Computer Storage

3575 Computer Terminals

3577 Computer Peripheral Equipment

7371 Computer Programming Services

7372 Prepackaged Software

7373 Computer Integrated Systems Design

7374 Data Processing and Preparation

7375 Information Retrieval Services

7377 Computer Rental and Leasing

7378 Computer Maintenance and Repair

7379 Computer Related Systems

Intel Corporation

OVERVIEW

Intel Corp. is a manufacturer of microprocessors, chipsets and motherboards, microprocessor peripherals, microcomputers and supercomputers, and semiconductors, including flash memory devices, best known for its "Intel Inside" advertising slogan designed to push its Pentium processors for personal computers. In mid-1997 it was estimated that Intel microprocessors were in more than 80 percent of all personal computers.

COMPANY FINANCES

The first quarter of 1998 showed a 7-percent drop in revenues when compared to the same quarter in 1997, from $6.4 to $6.0 billion. During most of 1997, sales were strong, bringing in a revenue of $25.1 billion, compared to 1996's total of $20.8 billion. At the end of 1997 and beginning of 1998, sales slowed and the company purchased Chips and Technologies, Inc., reducing revenue and Intel's stock value. By mid-1998, stock had risen to the mid-70s, after the company repurchased 22.1 million shares.

Over the years, revenue has consistently risen—from $8.8 billion in 1993, to $11.5 billion in 1994, to $16.2 billion in 1995. In addition, Intel's stock has also risen with earning per share ranging from $1.30 in 1993 to $3.87 in 1997.

ANALYSTS' OPINIONS

In June 1998, shortly after the U.S. Department of Justice accused Microsoft of monopoly, the Federal Trade

FOUNDED: 1968

Contact Information:

HEADQUARTERS: 220 Mission College Blvd.
 Santa Clara, CA 95052-8119
PHONE: (408)765-8080
FAX: (408)765-6284
EMAIL: support@cs.intel.com
URL: http://www.intel.com

FINANCES:

Intel Corp.
Revenues, 1994-1997
(billion dollars)

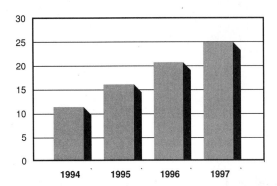

Intel Corp.
1997 Stock Prices
(dollars)

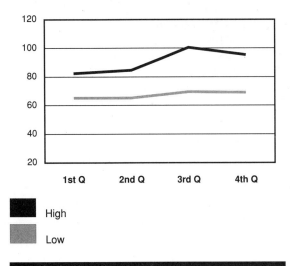

Commission (FTC) filed a complaint against Intel, charging that it had denied three of its customers access to information they needed to design and build systems using Intel's latest technology. The FTC said that Intel had done this because those companies refused to give Intel licenses to their patents. In a story published by *US News Online,* reporters William J. Cook and Warren Cohen said the FTC characterized Intel as "a schoolyard bully who illegally takes the ball away from anyone who won't play by his unilaterally imposed rules." A federal appeals court lifted the injunction on Microsoft, an action that is expected to bode well for its partner Intel, as well.

HISTORY

Intel Corporation was the creation of a couple of engineers who had left Fairchild Semiconductor in 1968 in an entrepreneurial desire to develop large scale integration technology for silicon-based chips. Robert Noyce had been the co-inventor of the integrated circuit while Gordon Moore was primarily responsible for the company's planning, and developed what is known as Moore's Law. He held that chip processing technologies tend to double every year-and-a-half.

"So far," stated a *Fortune* article, "Moore's law has been sustained by a regular cycle: Computer makers and software companies (especially Microsoft) develop new features and programs that require more power. Intel, meanwhile, creates brawny new chips to meet those new demands."

They were aided by a young man who tended to the manufacturing end of the business by the name of Andy Grove. The business was young and no consumer computing devices existed. The calculator was beginning to be introduced in business applications, but computer punch cards were still standard practice.

Marcian "Ted" Hoff, an Intel engineer, invented the microprocessor, and is credited as the man responsible for the personal computer industry. In 1971 he introduced a device known as the 4004—a microprocessor consisting of 2,300 transistors located on a sliver of silicon. It was one-eighth of an inch wide by one-sixth of an inch long. It was seen as an amazing invention, used primarily for calculating.

The 8008 microprocessor, the first chip to be actively marketed, and the one that had been developed with the 4004, first appeared April 1972. This chip moved rudimentary computing from 4- to 8-bit processing. Though this changed the complexion of the industry, it was not until IBM decided in the 1980s to use the Intel 8086 and 8088 microprocessors to create a personal computer. It was about this time that Apple Computer was founded, and began using components from rival Motorola.

"IBM's decision to support the 8086 microprocessor, running an operating system called MS-DOS, resulted in a software company called Microsoft, founded by Bill Gates and Paul Allen." Eventually, these two companies would become the two most powerful firms in a marketplace that is now worth billions of dollars annually," recounted a *Computer Weekly* article commemorating the twenty-fifth anniversary of Hoff's invention.

"Since Intel's launch of the 4004, faster, smaller, and more complex microprocessor devices have been developed. Intel, Texas Instruments, Advanced Micro Devices (AMD), Digital Equipment, Cyrix, and many others have deluged the industry with tiny black microprocessor chips that have altered the courses of our lives," an article in *Computer Weekly* stated. "But Intel has dominated the market for microprocessor chips and looks likely to continue this for quite some time, unless companies such as AMD can break its monopolistic grip.

"The Motorola 68000 microprocessor family has been the single most significant threat to the dominance of Intel in the chip business. Apple's all-out adoption of the 68000 for use in its Macintosh computers forged a market with 12 million-plus loyal customers.

"But Intel saw off this competition, and has beaten off the challenge from firms such as AMD and Cyrix, which introduced Intel-compatible processors in an attempt to hijack Intel's market. During the early 1990s, thanks to a huge investment program in chip manufacturing plants, Intel was able to maintain its position as the only firm able to satisfy the burgeoning demand for PC chips."

Industry estimates are that for each personal computer sold, Intel reaps about $300 in profits. The personal computer, however, is not the only consumer electronic device using Intel technology.

Intel has had its problems even in the midst of its success. The company, in an attempt to protect its technology, was tangled in suits with rival chip makers, particularly AMD. In a 1992 arbitration, Intel was ruled against and AMD's claims regarding a technology exchange upheld. The company took a further hit in 1994 when, shortly after the introduction of the Pentium processor, a problem was found in the chip's calculation abilities. Other concerns surfaced, as well, including the chip's tendency to overheat the circuitry in existing computer systems that had been upgraded.

Intel was integral in the industry celebration of the microprocessor's "birthday" at Comdex, the international computer trade show. This included a museum containing artifacts that showed the microprocessor's history from the Intel 4004 and Busicom calculator to consumer products, such as the TRS-80 and Commodore PET, in addition to modern devices such as smoke detectors—microprocessors are embedded into these.

Grove took over as chief executive officer in January 1987. Since that time Intel's average annual return to investors has been 44 percent. Grove was named chairman May 21, 1997, replacing Moore. The move was seen as being symbolic, since Grove had effectively been running the company since his appointment as chief executive officer.

According to *Fortune,* "Even though he was one of the handful of employees who got the company up and running in 1968, Grove has never been considered a founder—a status reserved for Moore and Noyce. They have been celebrated as legends and visionaries, aided in their success by Andy Grove, the efficient manager. Now he must be considered their equal."

Time Magazine named Grove its "Man of the Year" in the last issue of 1997, featuring his accomplishments

FAST FACTS:
About Intel Corporation

Ownership: Intel is a publicly held company traded on NASDAQ.

Ticker symbol: INTC

Officers: Craig R. Barrett, Pres. & CEO, 58, $2,555,100; Andrew S. Grove, Chmn., 61, $3,255,400; Gordon E. Moore, Chmn. Emeritus, 69

Employees: 64,000 (1997)

Principal Subsidiary Companies: Intel's subsidiaries include: American Communications Exchange Inc.; Intel Corp. Military Special Products Div.; Intel Corp. Personal Computer Enhancement Div.; Intel Corp. Rio Rancho Div.; Intel Corp. Supercomputer Systems Div.; and Intel Products Group.

Chief Competitors: A maker of microprocessors, Intel's primary competitors include: Advanced Micro Devices (AMD); Cyrix; and Motorola.

and vision in a cover story. Shortly afterward, Grove stepped down as president, allowing Craig Barrett to take over the role of CEO.

STRATEGY

Intel has been in the business of introducing cutting-edge technology and getting consumers to pay for the research and development (R&D) of the gee-whiz speeds of its new chips. It is a cyclical process, which also necessitates more R&D of even faster, smaller products. The company does this to constantly renew the need and to keep its margins high. Intel spent $5 billion on capital projects and R&D in 1996, and had record earnings that year—$5.2 billion in earnings on sales of $20.8 billion.

This business model has been compared to the automotive industry's "planned obsolescence." A new model means the old model is not good, or new, anymore, therefore the consumer feels compelled to purchase the newest, latest, greatest product.

According to a 1997 article in *Fortune,* "To ensure Intel's success over the coming five years, he has been maneuvering to make the PC the central appliance in our lives. In Grove's vision, we will use PCs to watch TV,

CHRONOLOGY:

Key Dates for Intel Corporation

1968: Intel is founded

1971: An Intel engineer invents the microprocessor, the 4004 Microchip

1972: The 8008 microprocessor is Intel's first chip to be actively marketed

1981: IBM decides to put an Intel microprocessor into its first PC

1982: Intel creates the 286 chip with 134,000 transistors, the first chip to offer software compatibility with its predecessors

1985: The Intel386 is released with 275,000 transistors and 5 million instructions per second capacity

1993: The Pentium processor debuts with 3.1 million transistors and 90 million instrusctions per second capacity

1994: A problem is found in the Pentium chip's calculation abilities

1997: The Pentium II is released with 7.5 million transistors

1998: Intel and Polaroid announce plans to produce a digital camera using Intel technology

to play complex games on the Internet, to store and edit family photos, to manage the appliances in our homes, and to stay in regular video contact with family, friends, and co-workers. If Grove's vision comes to pass, Intel will thrive. If it doesn't, Intel's strategy falls apart."

"'Intel is on a treadmill of new-product introductions fed by increasing demand for microprocessors," says Scott Randall, a security analyst at SoundView Financial in Stamford, Connecticut. "The day that treadmill slows down is the day their business plan has to be rethought." That's why Grove has boosted the budget for projects that contribute to market development but have nothing directly to do with microprocessors. Such spending has gone from zero in 1990 to more than $500 million in 1996. Intel is the only company in the computer hardware business that can afford that kind of money: Its earnings exceed the aggregate profits of the top ten PC manufacturers combined."

In February 1998, Intel and Polaroid Corporation announced plans to produce an inexpensive digital camera using Intel technology, which would allow a consumer to take still pictures or video images, with use of the Intel 971 PC Camera Kit. This was one of several alliances Intel has made to include its technology in consumer items not normally associated with microprocessors.

CURRENT TRENDS

The trends are pushed by more powerful applications, which in turn necessitate new microprocessors and other new generations of computer products. Intel has been making this an integral part of its business plan. Slowing of computer sales in the United States has made an impact on the market, but again, new technologies and overseas sales keep Intel profits up. Most (71 percent) of Intel's products are sold in North America and Europe, protecting it, to some extent, from exposure to the 1998 Asian financial woes. However, almost one third of its revenues depend on Asian markets, which has entered a turbulent period.

PRODUCTS

Intel makes a wide range of computing products. These include video conferencing products, networking products, and a wide array of embedded devices. The mainstay of Intel's business is its microprocessors or chips. The most current of these is the Pentium line of microprocessors. In 1998 Intel introduced the 333-MHZ Pentium II processor, the first built on Intel's 0.25 micron process technology. Later in that year, it shipped higher MHZ versions designed to support high-volume workstations and servers.

CORPORATE CITIZENSHIP

In 1997, Intel contributed more than $96 million to colleges and universities, K-12 education, and community organizations located where Intel has a major facility. It awarded $2 million in scholarships and prizes at the 1998 Intel International Science and Engineering Fair for high school students held in Fort Worth, Texas. Paleontologist Dr. Richard Leakey presented the Glenn T. Seaborg Notel Trip Awards to two winners, 16-year-old Karen Mendelson of Worcester, Massachusetts and 17-year-old Geoffrey Schmidt of Little Rock, Arkansas which will allow them to attend the 1998 Nobel Prize ceremonies in Sweden.

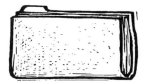

CASHING IN ON THEIR CHIPS

It was in 1947 that Bell Labs invented the transistor and ushered in what might well be termed the Digital Age. Fifty years later, in 1997, Intel introduced its Pentium II processor. How much of an improvement was it on Bell Lab's original transistor? Well, each Pentium II has 7.5 million transistors embedded within it. These microscopic transistors each costs less than a paper clip, and they are etched into wafers of silicon to create their remarkable computing capabilities. How fast are they? They can perform 500 million instructions every second. And just think, in a few years, the Pentium II will be considered a laughably out-of-date antique.

GLOBAL PRESENCE

Intel Corporation owns 102 buildings and leases another 57. Intel has numerous manufacturing plants abroad, including facilities in Ireland, Israel, Malaysia, and the Philippines. In terms of its global sales, the majority come from Europe, with the next largest amount from the Asia/Pacific region.

SOURCES OF INFORMATION

Bibliography

Dailey Paulson, Linda. "Microprocessor Enshrined at Comdex Museum." *Newsbytes,* 19 November 1996.

Fawcett, Neil. "Happy Birthday, Micro!" *Computer Weekly,* 17 October 1996.

Kirpatrick, David. "Intel's Amazing Profit Machine." *Fortune,* 17 February 1997.

For an annual report:

on the Internet at: http://www.intel.com/intel/annual97/s_index. htm **or** telephone: (800)298-0146

For additional industry research:

Investigate companies by their Standard Industrial Classification Codes, also known as SICs. Intel Corporation's primary SICs are:

3571 Electronic Computers

3577 Computer Peripheral Equipment, NEC

3674 Semiconductors and Related Devices

J. C. Penney Company, Inc.

FOUNDED: 1902

Contact Information:

HEADQUARTERS: 6501 Legacy Dr.
    Plano, TX 75024-3698
PHONE: (972)431-1000
FAX: (972)431-1977
URL: http://www.jcpenney.com

OVERVIEW

As the nation's fourth largest retailer, J. C. Penney Company, Inc. earns more than 50 percent of its revenue in department store offerings, which include apparel, accessories, and home furnishings. J. C. Penney also has the largest U.S. catalog operation, which accounts for 13 percent of the company's revenue. Additionally, the company owns the fourth largest U.S. drugstore chain, Eckerd Corporation, which generates roughly one third of J. C. Penney's revenues. Topping off this ensemble, J. C. Penney derives 3 percent of its revenue selling insurance, and the insurance division continues to post record profits.

Under its "new models for profitable growth" philosophy, J. C. Penney wants to capitalize on other proven money makers and cut back on under performers. After closing 75 stores in the United States, the company plans on expanding its international operations, which include stores in Puerto Rico, two stores in Mexico, and one in Chile. J. C. Penney has also upgraded its fashion line and added more private-label clothes to its mix. Like many other retailers, the company offered an early retirement program and thinned out its management ranks, which is expected to save $85 million annually.

COMPANY FINANCES

Total revenue for the J. C. Penney Company jumped from $23.5 billion in 1996 to $30.5 billion in 1997. Even after soft sales in the department store division during the second half of 1997, the company finished with a strong operating performance. The majority of the revenue increase came from the company's drugstore division. Throughout 1996 and 1997, J. C. Penney acquired a series of drugstores, including 1,724 Eckerd drugstores, 272 Fay drugstores, 200 Rite Aid drugstores, and 97 Kerr drugstores. With nearly 2,800 drugstores in total under the Eckerd banner, J. C. Penney formed the nation's fourth largest drugstore chain ranked by sales volume. As a result, total stockholder return for The J. C. Penney Company far outpaced the *Standard & Poor's* 500 retail index for department stores.

ANALYSTS' OPINIONS

According to the 1997 annual report for J. C. Penney, "Our company has increased size, focus, and strength. In the past two and a half years, we have sold some operations that did not fit with our strategic vision while expanding our drugstore business." One retail analyst at Smith Barney Inc. agreed with that assessment. Analyst Gary Giblen commented on J. C. Penney's acquisition of the Eckerd chain of drugstores for the *Austin American-Statesman* in a 1996 article: "The department store arena is pretty crowded. Sears is whipping Penney's butt and gaining customers in the juniors department store category. It's pretty smart for Penney to focus some effort on the drug piece."

HISTORY

The J. C. Penney Company is named for its founder, James Cash Penney. Penney and two former employers opened a dry-goods store, called the Golden Rule, in Wyoming in 1902. According to a Paul Harvey radio broadcast in 1998, Penney and his wife lived above the store and reveled in first-day sales of more than $400. Penney bought out his partners' interest in the store in 1907. The company incorporated in 1913 as The J. C. Penney Company.

A devout Baptist, Penney's moral convictions became the stores' basis for customer service. In fact, the forerunner to J. C. Penney was so named because Penney thought strong morals could form the foundation for solid business practices. In 1914, the store headquarters was moved to New York City from Salt Lake City to facilitate buying and operations. Six years later, the company had about 1,200 stores.

During the Depression, J. C. Penney stores thrived on their reputation for quality and value. The company went public in 1929. After World War II, the company had more than 1,600 stores and sales in excess of $1 billion.

The 1960s brought expansion and diversification. In 1962, the company bought a Milwaukee mail-order firm

FINANCES:

J.C. Penney Revenues, 1994-1997 (billion dollars)

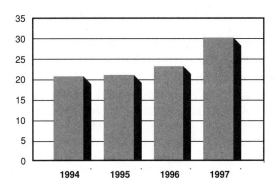

J.C. Penney 1997 Stock Prices (dollars)

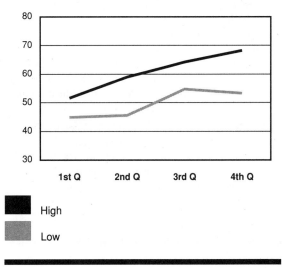

■ High
▨ Low

and started carrying hard goods in 1963. Those two moves meant that J. C. Penney was now able to compete with Sears and Montgomery Ward. J. C. Penney also purchased Treasure Island, a chain of discount stores, and formed an insurance subsidiary from various companies it purchased late in the decade. Thrift Drug was purchased by J. C. Penney in 1969.

The company continued to thrive and, in the 1980s, began fine-tuning its mix of goods. It sold the Treasure Island discount stores in 1981 and ceased selling an array of items in 1983—from paint to tires to fabric. That same year, the company began issuing MasterCard and Visa

FAST FACTS:

About J. C. Penney Company, Inc.

Ownership: J. C. Penney is a publicly held company traded on the New York Stock Exchange.

Ticker symbol: JCP

Officers: James E. Oesterreicher, Chmn. & CEO, 55, 1998 base salary $1,045,621; John T. Cody, Jr., Pres. & COO, J. C. Penney Stores, Merchandising, Marketing, & Catalog, 58, 1998 base salary $614,146; Thomas D. Hutchens, Pres. & COO, International, 57, 1998 base salary $597,786; Francis A. Newman, Pres. & CEO Eckerd Corporation, 48

Employees: 260,000

Principal Subsidiary Companies: J. C. Penney Company, Inc. has three main divisions, including two subsidiaries: J. C. Penney Stores and Catalog, made up of 1,203 domestic and international retail stores carrying family apparel, jewelry, shoes, accessories, and home furnishings; Eckerd Corporation, consisting of 2,778 drugstores selling pharmaceuticals and related products as well as general merchandise; and J. C. Penney Insurance Group, Inc., a direct-marketer of life, health, accident, and credit insurance, as well as non-insurance products.

Chief Competitors: J. C. Penney competes with numerous retail and catalog apparel sellers, as well as with drugstores. Some primary competitors are: American Stores; Avon; Dayton Hudson; Dillard's; Fingerhut; The Gap; Kmart; The Limited; Montgomery Ward; Price/Costco; Sears; Service Merchandise; Spiegel; Walgreen's; and Wal-Mart.

credit cards. J. C. Penney tried to become upscale with the introduction of the famed Halston label to its racks, but the line failed to attract a following. Taking a cue from other retailers, J. C. Penney started to develop its own private label brands, such as Hunt Club and Worthington. The company stopped selling consumer electronics, photography equipment, and sporting goods in 1987.

In 1988, J. C. Penney moved its headquarters out west again, settling in Texas. That same year the company started taking catalog phone orders and offering telemarketing services for other companies.

In the mid-1990s, the company earmarked about $2 billion for store modernization and relocation over a

three-year period. J. C. Penney also realigned its regional operations, grouping its top 10 markets together into a "mega region". The company opened a store in Monterrey, Mexico in 1995. Also that year, free-standing J. C. Penney Home Stores debuted.

Throughout 1996, J. C. Penney embarked on a string of drugstore acquisitions, including 272 Fay drugstores, 200 Rite Aid drugstores, and 97 Kerr drugstores. In 1997, J. C. Penney finalized a $3.3 billion deal to buy 1,724 Eckerd drugstores, but later sold 161 of the stores over antitrust concerns. A sentimental note about the Eckerd acquisition appeared in the 1997 Annual Report for J. C. Penney: "When signs on the Thrift Drug stores in Erie, Pa. changed to Eckerd in 1997, a cornerstone of the American drugstore culture returned to its birthplace—nearly a century after J. Milton Eckerd opened its first pharmacy there in 1898."

Other changes occurred in 1997. William R. Howell, who had served the company as chairman and chief executive officer since 1983, retired from the company in January. Howell had been with the firm 38 years, having started cleaning up the Claremore, Oklahoma, store, managed by his father. Howell was also the last chair of the company to have worked with a known Penney. He was also the longest serving chairman of the board at the company. Additionally, J. C. Penney sold the assets of J. C. Penney National Bank for $740 million, which netted a gain for the company. Streamlining continued as well; the company closed 75 stores in 1997. In early 1998 the company announced plans to cut 5,000 jobs, including 1,700 managerial positions.

STRATEGY

According to an annual report for J. C. Penney, "Our strategy revolves around continuing to fulfill the customer's expectations for value, selection, and convenience: value in terms of the right combination of quality, fashion, and price; selection between recognized national brands and our own exceptional private brands; and the convenience of shopping the store or ordering through the catalog."

J. C. Penney believes its private brands—Jacqueline Ferrar, The Original Arizona Jean Company, The Hunt Club, Stafford, and Worthington—are the most outstanding values in the department store industry today; national brands are still important for their merchandising strategy since they account for about 50 percent of their apparel sales. J. C. Penney's strategy with private brands is to offer products comparable to those in the best known department stores, but at a better price. While insiders applaud retailers for trying the give the customer a better value, insiders also know that retailers realize a much better markup on private-label over nationally branded goods.

On the drugstore front, J. C. Penney has put together a formidable competitor in the industry. The company became the nation's fourth largest drugstore chain in 1997 with the acquisition of the Eckerd Corporation. Building on the strength of the Eckerd name, J. C. Penney decided to put all of its 2,800 drugstores under the Eckerd banner. Sales in the J. C. Penney drugstore division hit $9.7 billion in fiscal 1997, a 13 percent increase over results from the previous year, with comparable store sales rising 7 percent.

Eckerd drugstores pepper the Northeastern, Southeastern, and Sunbelt regions of the United States, home to millions of retirees and aging baby boomers. J. C. Penney already holds the first or second market share in 37 of its 42 major drugstore markets, and it stands ready to benefit from the growing market for pharmaceuticals and health-related products.

CURRENT TRENDS

Online sales at J. C. Penney experienced a six-fold increase in 1997 as more consumers discovered the ease and convenience of shopping via computer. The company improved its World Wide Web store (www.jcpenney.com/shopping) by adding an electronic order form that lets online customers order any item from its print catalogs. The J. C. Penny nationwide gift registry is also available online.

PRODUCTS

The company operates three main divisions. J. C. Penney Stores and Catalog primarily sells family apparel, jewelry, shoes, accessories, and home furnishings. In addition to well-known national brands, the company also sells private-label brands. Private brands include St. John's Bay, The Original Arizona Jean Company, ZONZ, Hunt Club, Stafford, Jacqueline Ferrar, and Worthington. Eckerd Drugstores primarily sells pharmaceuticals, health-related products, and general merchandise. The drugstore division boasts one of the largest in-store photoprocessing operations in the industry as well as one of the largest mail-order prescription services. J. C. Penney Insurance primarily sells life, health, accident, and credit insurance through direct-marketing channels. Membership services include LeisurePlus and MotorPlus discounts on travel. The insurance division counted more than 13 million insurance policies, certificates, and membership accounts in force in 1997.

CORPORATE CITIZENSHIP

J. C. Penney supports various programs in the communities where it operates. Charitable contributions to-

CHRONOLOGY:
Key Dates for J. C. Penney Company, Inc.

1902: James Cast Penney opens a dry-goods store called the Golden Rule in Wyoming

1913: The company incorporates as J. C. Penney Company; the Golden Rule stores are replaced by J. C. Penney stores

1929: The company goes public

1949: J. C. Penney opens its first suburb store

1951: Sales top $1 billion for the first time

1958: J. C. Penney starts taking credit at its stores

1963: The first J. C. Penney catalog is introduced

1987: The company stops selling consumer electronics, photography equipment, sporting goods

1995: Free-standing J. C. Penney Home Stores open

1997: The company buys Eckerd drugstores and sells 161 of the 1,724 stores because of antitrust concerns

taled $27 million in 1997, $24 million of which consisted of cash contributions. The focus for the company is on women's charitable organizations, including programs supporting minority- and women-owned businesses. The company also has supported The United Way; The Susan G. Komen Breast Cancer Foundation Race for the Cure; several women's sporting events, including the LPGA; and other awards for women who are leaders in their field and/or communities.

GLOBAL PRESENCE

J. C. Penney attempted global expansion into Europe in the 1970s. The company had failed ventures in Italy and Belgium until 1982. In the 1990s, the company cautiously ventured into new retailing ventures in Mexico and Chile. Bolstered by a successful venture into Canada, J. C. Penney Insurance plans to launch its first overseas operation in 1998 in the United Kingdom.

SOURCES OF INFORMATION

Bibliography

"J.C. Penney Company, Inc." *Hoover's Handbook of American Business 1998.* Austin, TX: The Reference Press, 1997.

JCPenney Company, Inc. Annual Report. Plano, TX: 1997.

Lasalle, Patricia Ann. "Making Change Work." *SMU Magazine,* Winter-Spring 1997.

"Update on JCPenney." Plano, TX: J. C. Penney Company, Inc., July 1996.

For an annual report:

on the Internet at: http://www.jcpenney.com **or** telephone: (800)953-9421 **or** write: Public Relations Department, J. C. Penney Company, Inc., PO Box 10001, Dallas, TX 75301-4301

For additional industry research:

Investigate companies by their Standard Industrial Classification Codes, also known as SICs. JCPenney's primary SICs are:

5311 Department Stores

5912 Drug Stores & Proprietary Stores

5961 Mail Order Houses

J. Crew Group Inc.

FOUNDED: 1983

OVERVIEW

The J. Crew Group is a clothing company that sells casual style clothing mainly through three mail order catalogs—J. Crew, Popular Club Plan, and Clifford Wills. After making a name in catalog sales, the New York City-based company opened 50 stores to sell its distinctive upscale look to a wider variety of shoppers throughout the United States. J. Crew also operates 60 retail units in Japan in conjunction with ITOCHU Corp., a diverse Japanese concern and the third-largest company in the world. In 1997 J. Crew posted sales totaling $850 million, although rough estimates from industry sources varied greatly for the private company. *Fortune* placed J. Crew among its top 500 privately held companies ranked by sales. With renewed backing by the Texas Pacific Group, J. Crew plans to open even more stores.

Credit for the initial success for the company goes to founder Arthur Cinader. But continued success belongs to his fashion-savvy daughter, Emily Woods, wife of movie producer Cary Woods. Emily Woods assumed the presidency of J. Crew in 1989 at the age of 28. She immediately launched a storefront operation to offset a steep increase in postal rates and ongoing pressures in the cutthroat catalog business. Under Woods, J. Crew broadened its product line, adding career wear and lingerie to weekender classics. To finance her vision of further growth, Woods spearheaded negotiations with the Fort Worth investment partnership.

The clothing company has not entirely folded its mail-order operations. It still prints the three catalogs: J. Crew, offering khakis, corduroys, and clothes to match the up-and-coming, button-down lifestyle of the target

Contact Information:
HEADQUARTERS: 770 Broadway
   New York, NY 10013
PHONE: (212)209-2500
FAX: (212)209-2666
URL: http://www.jcrew.com

FAST FACTS:

About J. Crew Group Inc.

Ownership: The J. Crew Group Inc. is a privately owned company.

Officers: Emily Cinader Woods, Chmn. & Chief Designer, 36; Howard Socol, CEO, 52; Barry Erdos, COO; Michael P. McHugh, VP Finance & CFO

Employees: 6,300

Principal Subsidiary Companies: The Texas Pacific Group, a Fort Worth-based investment partnership, acquired an 88-percent stake in J. Crew Group Inc. in October 1997. The rest of the company belongs to Emily Cinader Woods, daughter of founder Arthur Cinader.

Chief Competitors: J. Crew competes with retail clothiers as well as with mail-order retailers for a share of the men's and women's casual and professional clothing market. The company's competitors include: Ann Taylor; Benetton; Calvin Klein; Dayton Hudson; Eddie Bauer; Land's End; L.L. Bean; Men's Warehouse; Nautica Enterprises; and The Gap.

ative outlook for J. Crew. The forecast came after Standard & Poor lowered the ratings on the company's credit and bank loans. "First quarter revenues and margins should be flat with the prior year; however, the third and fourth quarters will be more critical indicators for any further changes in the credit rating. Should weakness continue, particularly in J. Crew's core catalog segment, the ratings could be downgraded."

Though J. Crew has performed well as a direct marketer of classic apparel items, analysts remained skeptical of J. Crew's bid to convert itself into a fashion retailer fortified by a network of retail stores. Banana Republic towers above J. Crew in its efforts to become a purveyor of vogue clothing. Banana Republic's Gap division operated 226 stores throughout the United States, whereas J. Crew ran only about 50 in 1997.

Nevertheless, observers acknowledge the company's potential to succeed because the director of J. Crew's retail units, David DeMattei, a veteran retailer with more than a decade of experience at Gap Inc. and former chief financial officer of Gap, possesses the experience and know-how needed to help the catalog retailer of traditional apparel capture a new share of the men's and women's urban-professional market. DeMattei, who joined the company in 1995, holds the responsibility of making the company's endeavors bear fruit. Furthermore, analysts responded positively to J. Crew's consideration of selling a share of the company to Texas Pacific, which gave the company extra capital required for its expansions. Unlike direct-marketing retailing, storefront retailing requires considerable investment in sites, employees, and overhead products.

audience of men and women in their 30s; Clifford & Wills, offering moderately priced clothes to career women; and the Popular Club Plan, offering women's apparel, kitchen supplies, and home furnishings. Customers can also browse online through a J. Crew web site.

COMPANY FINANCES

J. Crew showed strong growth in the 1990s. While accounts vary for the privately held company, in 1995 J. Crew reportedly posted sales of $500 million from combined direct-marketing and store sales. Revenue climbed to $750 million the next year. By some accounts, in 1997 sales rose to $850 million, a 70-percent increase in revenues in just two years. *Fortune* placed J. Crew among its top 500 privately held companies ranked by sales.

ANALYSTS' OPINIONS

In May 1998, eight months after Texas Pacific bought the majority of J. Crew, *Credit Wire* issued a neg-

HISTORY

The seeds for J. Crew were planted as far back as 1947, when Mitchell Cinader and Saul Charles founded the Popular Club Plan, a mail-order operation that sold women's apparel and home furnishings. Mitchell's son, Arthur Cinader, inherited the catalog business. Hoping to fill a niche for busy shoppers, Cinader created the J. Crew catalog in 1983. J. Crew sported casual and classic men's and women's clothing such as khakis, chinos, and oxfords. The company posted sales of $3 million in its first year.

J. Crew rolled out the Clifford & Wills catalog for career women in 1984. Also that year, Arthur's daughter, Emily Woods, joined her father. Woods—who personally favors the clean-cut Eastern Seaboard look for her lanky frame—immediately banned polyester. Next, following a widespread industry move to pump up profit margins, she decreed J. Crew would only sell its own private-label brand.

In 1989 Woods became president of J. Crew. That year, the mail-order company faced a 30-percent hike in postal rates. So J. Crew opened its first store, located in New York City, as the first step in its plan to open 50 stores in 5 years. J. Crew was following the lead of fellow mail-order houses, such as Eddie Bauer and Victoria's Secret, that opened storefronts in malls and shopping districts as the number of catalog customers declined. By 1993 J. Crew operated more than 30 stores. That same year, a troubled economy and the resignation of then-president Arnold Cohen forced Cinader to scale back his expansion efforts. Executive shuffles continued throughout the 1990s.

In the mid-1990s the company tried to win new customers by diversifying its product line. In 1995 Vice Chairman and Chief of Design Woods decided to expand the company's offerings to include lingerie. Woods introduced J. Crew's intimates to the company's August catalog, hoping that they would constitute as much as 10 percent of the company's sales by the late 1990s. J. Crew also started marketing home furnishings in 1995.

In 1997 J. Crew found a buyer to finance the company's continued growth. The Texas Pacific Group (TPG) reportedly paid $527 million for an 88-percent stake in the company. (Woods retained a 12-percent stake.) As part of the leveraged buyout Woods got $20 million and her father received $5 million, according to the *Daily News Record*. Further shifting away from the company's mail-order roots, Woods plans to use the cash infusion to open more stores.

J. Crew has restructured under the control of TPG. The company appointed a new CEO, CFO, and COO in 1998. It cut 10 percent of its workforce, eliminating 100 workers in its mail-order division. The company sent out fewer catalogs in the first quarter of 1998, and mail-order sales for J. Crew continued to soften. But during the same period the storefronts pulled in an additional 6 percent in sales, which offset the lost catalog business.

STRATEGY

J. Crew's goal in the mid-1990s was to expand both its retail and direct-marketing divisions. The clothing retailer opened new stores throughout the United States, including one in Los Angeles and one in San Diego. Furthermore, in 1997 J. Crew took its direct-marketing campaign to the Internet, allowing customers to order its product online using its web site catalog. J. Crew planned to update the web site seasonally along with its print catalogs. The company also designed the site to provide customers with assistance and a means for ordering its print catalogs.

J. Crew also concentrates on providing quality merchandise. Known for their meticulousness attention to detail, the father and daughter team of Arthur Cinader and

CHRONOLOGY:
Key Dates for J. Crew Group Inc.

1983: Arthur Cinadar creates the J. Crew catalog

1984: J. Crew creates the Clifford & Willis catalog for working women

1989: The first J. Crew store opens in New York City; Emily Woods, Cinader's daughter, takes over as president

1991: The company expands and starts targeting some catalogs towards Canada

1993: J. Crew signs an agreement with Japanese retailers to open 46 stores in Japan

1995: The company starts marketing home furnishings

1997: The Texas Pacific Group purchases an 88 percent stake in the company

Emily Woods carefully inspect catalogs to assure that they stand out among other companies' catalogs and that they accurately depict J. Crew's products. Former employees report that Woods had photographs re-shot several times in order to capture subtleties of lighting that make the products look more attractive. J. Crew also emphasizes quality merchandise; therefore Emily Woods examines the fabrication and stitching of the garments the company sells.

CURRENT TRENDS

In the mid-1990s J. Crew continued to expand its retail operations. In 1996 it opened a 12,000-square-foot store as its flagship unit in New York's Soho district. A 10,000-square-foot storefront was opened in Japan in cooperation with J. Crew's partner ITOCHU. The flagship store carries many items from the J. Crew catalogs, as well as J. Crew's sophisticated J. Crew Collection line not offered via catalog. Vice chairman Emily Woods announced the company's plans to double the number of retail stores by 2000, adding 15 to 20 stores in 1997 and 1998.

PRODUCTS

J. Crew offers a complete line of men's and women's casual and professional clothing in 50 stores throughout the United States and 60 stores in Japan. On the mail-order side, the company prints three catalogs: J. Crew, offering preppie clothes for men and women in their 30s; Clifford & Wills, offering moderately priced clothes for career women; and the Popular Club Plan, offering women's apparel, kitchen supplies, and home furnishings. A J. Crew web site also lets shoppers buy via computer.

In 1997 J. Crew began to market a new array of clothing that strayed from its trademark wholesome, clean-cut, preppie look and focused more on fashionable styles. As its baby-boomer customer base began to age, J. Crew executives started to consider ways of piquing the interest of a younger group of customers. The new strategy involves some risk, however, as the company tries to reinvent itself and woo new customers, it may alienate its original customer base. These product decisions put the company in face-to-face competition with Banana Republic, a highly successful and well-monied clothing retailer.

CORPORATE CITIZENSHIP

J. Crew and other clothing retailers came under attack for contracting manufacturers in countries with poor human rights records who pay employees low wages and require them to work long hours in "sweatshop" conditions. In response to customers' insistence and a threatened boycott of J. Crew products, in 1997 the company announced it would sever its business connection with Yangon Knit Garment Manufacturing Co. in Burma.

GLOBAL PRESENCE

Through its partnership with ITOCHU J. Crew established a strong presence in Japan in the 1980s and early 1990s. However, by the mid-1990s competitors such as the Gap, Spiegel, and Eddie Bauer had penetrated the Japanese market, offering their products at lower prices than J. Crew. Consequently, J. Crew's merchandise appeared overpriced. Moreover, a recession struck the Japanese economy during that period, making consumers more interested in bargains and discount merchandise. Because of higher labor and rental costs in Japan, J. Crew typically charged more for its products in Japan than in the United States. For example, a Japanese unit would sell a wool sweater for the yen equivalent of $130, while a U.S. unit would charge only $48. Therefore, J. Crew led a campaign to lower prices in Japan and to cut costs in order to hold on to its market share.

SOURCES OF INFORMATION

Bibliography

Bongiorno, Lori. "J. Crew Plays Dress-Up." *Business Week,* 5 May 1997.

Bounds, Wendy. "Fashion: Dressed for Change, J. Crew Reaches Crossroads." *The Wall Street Journal,* 22 August 1997.

———. "J. Crew Catalog Retail Empire Discusses Its Own Sale to Texas Pacific." *The Wall Street Journal,* 21 August 1997.

Edelson, Sharon. "J. Crew Opens Soho Flagship as Prototype." *WWD,* 4 November 1996.

"J. Crew Sets July Debut in L.A." *WWD,* 4 June 1997.

For additional industry research:

Investigate companies by their Standard Industrial Classification Codes, also known as SICs. J.Crew's primary SICs are:

2300 Apparel and other Textile Products

5651 Family Clothing Stores

5961 Catalog & Mail Order Houses

J.M. Smucker Co.

OVERVIEW

J.M. Smucker Company is the leading producer of jams, jellies, and preserves in the United States. The company has branched out in recent years, becoming a leader in such other areas as ice cream toppings and natural peanut butter. In 1997 Smucker's celebrated its one-hundreth year. In addition to fruit products for its own jellies, Smucker's makes the fruit filling for Kellogg's Pop Tarts and Dannon yogurt. The company also owns the juice and concentrate brand R.W. Knudsen.

Smucker's divisions include industrial, food service, beverages, and international. In the mid-1990s the company operated 3 international facilities and 12 plants in the United States. Food processing plants are located in Washington, Oregon, and California, and manufacturing facilities are in Orrville, Ohio; Salinas, California; Memphis, Tennessee; Ripon, Wisconsin; Chico, California; Havre de Grace, Maryland; New Bethlehem, Pennsylvania; Australia; and Canada. The main high-speed jelly and preserve producing plant is in Memphis. That plant also serves as a distribution center for more than 1,500 Smucker products.

The company's founder, Jerome M. Smucker, is remembered by members of the company family for his philosophy of unchanging values. The company still lists its basic values—quality, people, ethics, growth, and independence—on its web page. Employees and managers alike found that holding to these values led the company to be the brand leader in fruit spreads and toppings. While remaining dedicated to its core values, Smucker has also had to grow technologically and remain innovative. A sensitivity to fruit prices has been essential, as has increasing cooperation with other companies in the food industry.

FOUNDED: 1897

Contact Information:

HEADQUARTERS: 1 Strawberry Ln.
   Orrville, OH 44667-0280
PHONE: (330)682-3000
FAX: (330)684-3370
TOLL FREE: (888)550-9555
EMAIL: info@smucker.com
URL: http://www.smucker.com

FINANCES:

J.M. Smucker
Net Sales, 1994-1997
(million dollars)

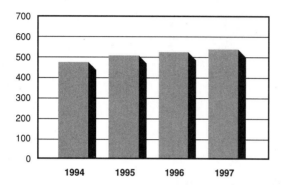

J.M. Smucker
1997 Stock Prices
(dollars)

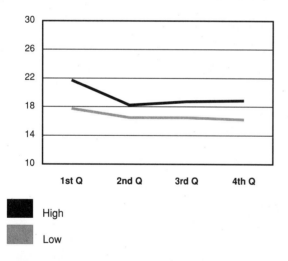

■ High
▨ Low

COMPANY FINANCES

In 1996 J.M. Smucker Co. was ranked number six by *Food Processing* magazine with $528.0 million in sales. Total sales in fiscal 1997 were $542.6 million, while net income was $1.06 per share, or $30.9 million. Sales rose for the nine months ended in January 1998, as did net income. Sales of new and existing products in frozen dairy, yogurt, and bakery, and sales growth in fruit spreads helped results. Contributing to the gain were lower raw materials costs in 1997. Earnings per share that year were $1.23 with the stock price reaching a high of $30 and a low of $16.25.

ANALYSTS' OPINIONS

J.M. Smucker is regarded by many analysts as a high-quality company. Consistent earnings and an eye focused both on the ideals of the company's early history and on current trends have kept the company strong. At the same time, the fact that the company's brands were well recognized meant that Smucker's was in a mature market. It was forced to break out of its mold and expand. In the mid-1990s the company held a market share of close to 40 percent in the retail jam market. As a century-old company, it still focused on quality, independence, and high ethical standards. Some Wall Street analysts would have preferred to see the company make bolder acquisitions to better reach customers at the supermarket. Very few seemed to expect radical changes at this family-run company. Despite its long-standing relationship with Kellogg & Co., which involves reciprocal board seats, analysts doubt the company will sell out.

HISTORY

In 1897 Jerome M. Smucker opened a cider mill in Orrville, Ohio. He also made and sold apple butter in hand-sealed crocks. In 1921 he incorporated his business as the J.M. Smucker Company. In 1955 the company introduced a line of portion-control products.

In 1979 Smucker's began a series of acquisitions that allowed it to enter other markets. It acquired Dickinson's product line that year, and in 1984 it bought R.W. Knudsen Family beverages. Although the latter acquisition was successful, not all of them proved to be so fortuitous. In 1995 Smucker's bought Mrs. Smith's frozen pie business for $80 million. After less than a year, the business was sold to a subsidiary of Flowers Industries Inc.

However, 1995 also saw the acquisitions of After the Fall beverages and Laura Scudder's natural peanut butter, both of which have brought steady growth to the company. Smucker's also was attuned to the health concerns in the United States in the mid-1990s. Smucker's Light rolled out in fiscal 1997, and the late 1990s also saw introductions of low-sugar varieties of many other Smucker products.

J.M. Smucker Co. is still very much a family organization. Paul Smucker, the grandson of founder Jerome, owns about 14 percent of the company and serves as chairman of the executive committee. His sons Timothy and Richard run the company as chairman and president.

STRATEGY

The strategy in the company's early years was to concentrate on a few products, and to manufacture and market them with pride and care. As the next generation grew to run the company, they began to expand their horizons. They made some strategic acquisitions, such as beverage manufacturers, and some alliances, such as that with Kellogg.

In the mid-1990s the company began a strategic planning process that included close to 10 percent of its workforce. Requesting ideas and input from staff members who ordinarily would not be involved in decision making proved to be very effective for Smucker's. Marketing in the 1990s included attention to the increasing health-consciousness of consumers. The slogan "food that is good for you and tastes good" was pegged to the company's new fruit spread, "Bagel Toppers," as well as a fat-free, fruit-based shortening. The company also reformulated its Simply Fruit brand to have longer shelf life and better taste.

Smucker's acquired Kraft's domestic fruit spread business in 1997. That business accounted for a 2-percent share of the market, which was anticipated to be a boon for Smucker's market share. In the 1990s the company also experimented with co-branding, or working with other established brand names to enter a new market. The Smucker's brand name was licensed to Brach and Brock Confections to make Brach's Smucker's jelly beans and fruit chews. Smucker's Dove ice cream toppings came from a similar partnership with M&M/Mars. A 1997 partnership with Naturipe produced two new flavors—vanilla creme and dark chocolate—for Naturipe's Berry Dippers dip for strawberries.

A 1997 marketing campaign featuring Tim and Richard Smucker growing up in Orrville, Ohio, in the 1950s generated nostalgia for Smucker's products in the company's anniversary year. Advertising expenditures in the late 1990s ranged from $9 to $10 million dollars.

FAST FACTS:
About J.M. Smucker Co.

Ownership: J.M. Smucker Co. is a family controlled public company traded on the New York Stock Exchange.

Ticker symbol: SJMA

Officers: Paul H. Smucker, Chmn. of the Exec. Committee, 80, 1997 base salary $356,731; Tim Smucker, Chmn. of the Board, 53, 1997 base salary $366,923; Richard K. Smucker, Pres., 49, 1997 base salary $357,750; Robert R. Morrison, VP, Operations, 63, 1997 base salary $196,000

Employees: 1,950

Principal Subsidiary Companies: J.M. Smucker Co. has several subsidiaries including After the Fall Products Inc.; Dickinson Family Inc.; R.W. Knudsen & Sons; Mary Ellen's Inc.; California Farm Products Div.; JMS Specialty Foods Inc.; and A.F. Murch Co.

Chief Competitors: J.M. Smucker's competitors include: ConAgra; National Grape Co-Op.; and Seagram.

INFLUENCES

The company was influenced by its success in marketing core items to consumers who appreciated freshness, taste, and reliable quality. When it branched out into other areas, the company learned from its mistakes. The 1995 acquisition of Mrs. Smith's frozen baked goods for $80 million proved to be unprofitable, and was sold in 1996. An English subsidiary, Elsenham Quality Foods Ltd., was also less profitable than the company had anticipated; in 1995 Smucker's divested itself of the subsidiary and took a pretax loss of $6 million. However, despite economic uncertainties throughout the century, the J.M. Smucker company built a strong reputation for making high-quality products that sold well.

CURRENT TRENDS

The Smucker family invited analysts to the company headquarters in the mid-1990s for the first time in decades. Despite their company's fairly solid track record, the managers felt compelled to explain their prospects for the future of Smucker's. In 1997 the company invested in new technology, including tailor-made versions of Oracle software developed to improve distribution and help warehouses become more efficient. It consolidated some assembly lines, but hesitated to close plants or impose major layoffs. The company did, however, reduce its number of employees in the late 1990s from more than 2,500 to just under 2,000. It achieved such reductions partly by using outside vendors for transportation, thereby eliminating Smucker's fleet of trucks.

Mass merchandisers and warehouse clubs changed the way many consumers bought shelf goods, and by the late 1980s Smucker was forced to adjust. Distribution lines that had worked before needed to be rethought, and Smucker's fought hard to maintain market share. Private-label competitors took aim at Smucker's, and the company decided to increase advertising expenditures to stay ahead.

CHRONOLOGY:

Key Dates for J.M. Smucker Co.

1897: Founded as a cider mill in Orrville, Ohio by Jerome Smucker

1921: Incorporates as J.M. Smucker Co.

1955: Introduces a line of portion-control products

1979: Acquires Dickinson's produce line

1984: Buys R.W. Knudsen Family

1995: Buys Mrs. Smith's frozen pie business and buys After the Fall beverages

1996: Sells Mrs. Smith's

1997: Celebrates 100 year anniversary; introduces Smuckers Light

PRODUCTS

Jerome Smucker's first product was apple butter. Still, 100 years later, the company is best known for its fruit spreads. But the company that led the way in producing jams, jellies, and preserves also produced dessert toppings such as Magic Shell, syrups and fruit dips, peanut butter brands including Laura Scudder's and Goober's, fruit juices under the R.W. Knudsen and After the Fall brands, pie glaze, and industrial fruit products such as yogurt and bakery fillings.

Smucker's fruit spreads include preserves, jams, jellies, marmalades, fruit butter, and low-sugar and lite varieties of spreads. The increased vigilance about health concerns in the U.S. population led Smucker's to focus on creating the latter varieties. The Simply Fruit brand contains 100 percent spreadable fruit, and the low-sugar varieties have just half the sugar of the regular varieties, with the same amount of fruit per serving. The lite varieties contain fruit and nutra-sweet, creating a fruit spread low in calories and completely sugar-free. Fruit butter is made by cooking fruit pulp and sugar slowly until it develops a thick, butterlike consistency.

Fruit syrups come in 12-ounce jars and in flavors including apricot, blackberry, blueberry, boysenberry, red raspberry, and strawberry. Fruit dips were developed and marketed as a fat-free snack in which to dip fruit. They are sold in 15-ounce tubs in caramel apple or chocolate flavor. A serving of two tablespoons contains no fat and 130 calories.

Smucker's dessert toppings include spoonable toppings, microwaveable toppings, sundae syrup toppings, magic shell topping that hardens on ice cream, and special recipe toppings in hot fudge, butterscotch, and caramel flavors. Peanut butter varieties made by Smucker's include Laura Scudder's Old Fashioned peanut butter in smooth, nutty, and no-salt varieties; Goober, a peanut butter and jelly combination; natural peanut butter in creamy, chunky, and no-salt-added varieties; and reduced-fat peanut butter, which contains 25 percent less fat than the regular natural peanut butter.

Smucker's line of gourmet and specialty foods includs the Dickinson's brand, which is closing in on the top market share in the gourmet/specialty foods segment. The company has expanded efforts at co-marketing and co-branding. The company also saw strong growth in its industrial sector, providing fruit for Dannon yogurt and for Kellogg's Pop Tarts.

Smucker's beverage business centers around the R.W. Knudsen Family line. Simply Nutritious juices were among its successful product introductions of recent years. The juices include vitamins and such herbs as ginseng, echinacea, and wheat grass, and were marketed to health-conscious consumers.

CORPORATE CITIZENSHIP

The community in Orrville, Ohio, respected Smucker's as a good neighbor. Most notable among Smucker's environmental efforts was the introduction in 1995 of a six-pack beverage container made of paperboard. This was to replace the plastic version, which not only threatened wildlife but also was not easily recyclable. The new paperboard container showed the company's commitment to waste reduction, recycling, and animal welfare.

GLOBAL PRESENCE

Smucker's international division includes facilities in Australia, Canada, and Latin America. In 1988 management decided to expand the company's international presence. Growth overall has been steady, although 1997 results were flat due to the divestiture of Smucker's English partner, Elsenham Quality Foods.

The company has manufacturing facilities in Quebec, Canada, and in Victoria, Australia. Smucker's hopes to have a manufacturing presence in Mexico and China during the early twenty-first century. Export sales are strong and growing to the Pacific Rim, and domestic business in Australia also has good margins. The IXL brand has a significant market share in Australia and aims to be that country's most popular brand.

IT MUST BE JELLY, 'CAUSE JAM DON'T SHAKE LIKE THAT

The story goes that in the early nineteenth-century a man by the name of John Chapman strolled about the Ohio countryside, scattering apple seeds wherever he went. He became known as Johnny Appleseed and his legend grew, even as stories about his brothers, Bobby Tomatoseed and Harry Watermelonseed withered on the vine. It was from these apples that J. M. Smucker started up his cider mill business in 1897.

These days, the Smuckers empire is going strong, boosted in part by the 1,500 peanut butter and jelly sand-wiches Americans consume by the time they graduate from high school. That's the equivalent of eating peanut butter and jelly every day for over four years. In fact, it is estimated that the average American consumes 1.7 pounds of jelly annually. Naturally, the company makes many different varieties of jelly, and their motto states, "With a name like Smuckers, it has to be good." Whether or not this claim extends to their quince jelly is a matter of some dispute.

EMPLOYMENT

Top management at Smucker's is said to be quite accessible, and the corporate culture relaxed and informal. Employees call each other by first names, and top managers meet with employees at all major U.S. facilities twice a year. Christmas bonus checks for every employee are calculated at 2 percent of salary, and the bonus also includes a gift and a turkey.

Employees work on task forces and in worker teams and are empowered to make decisions about their day-to-day work. The company earns the respect of its employees by not succumbing to the trend of layoffs and downsizing. Employees are valued and encouraged to meet the highest standards, and the company stresses business ethics that are related to high personal ethics.

SOURCES OF INFORMATION

Bibliography

Byrne, John A. "Strategic Planning." *Business Week,* 26 August 1996.

Hunter, Kris. "Smucker's Plant Manager Emphasizes Quality, Profit." *Memphis Business Journal,* 17 July 1995.

J.M. Smucker Home Page, 16 April 1998. Available at http://www.smucker.com.

Levering, Robert, and Milton Moskowitz. *The 100 Best Companies to Work for in America.* New York: Doubleday, 1993.

Phalon, Richard. "Sticky Times." *Forbes,* 18 November 1996.

Salomon, R.S., Jr. "Wallflowers." *Forbes,* 22 January 1996.

"Smucker's Celebrates 100 Years of Family-Made Goodness." *Frozen Food Digest,* December 1997.

For an annual report:
on the Internet at: http://www.smucker.com/ **or** write: Consumer Services Department, The J.M. Smucker Company, 1 Strawberry Ln., Orrville, OH 44667

For additional industry research:
Investigate companies by their Standard Industrial Classification Codes, also known as SICs. Smucker's primary SICs are:

2033 Canned Fruits & Vegetables

2087 Flavoring Extracts & Syrups, NEC

2099 Food Preparations, NEC

Johnson & Johnson

FOUNDED: 1887

Contact Information:

HEADQUARTERS: 1 Johnson & Johnson Plz.
New Brunswick, NJ 08933
PHONE: (732)524-0400
FAX: (732)524-3300
URL: http://www.jnj.com

OVERVIEW

Johnson & Johnson is the world's leading manufacturer of health-care products for the consumer, pharmaceutical, and professional markets. The New Brunswick, New Jersey-based company produces literally hundreds of products, some well-known to a wide consumer market, such as Band-Aids and Tylenol, and others recognized for their specialty uses, like Ortho-Novum contraceptives and Retin-A dermatological medicine. Still other products, such as wound closure and cardiology products, are known only among medical specialists. The company holds the top spot in many worldwide markets, including disposable contact lenses and blood glucose testing products.

Johnson & Johnson credits a steady stream of new products for fueling its growth. Accordingly, the company ranks among the top 10 companies in the United States for expenditures on research & development (R&D). More than one third of 1997 revenue for Johnson & Johnson came from newly introduced products.

COMPANY FINANCES

Johnson & Johnson reported $22.63 billion in sales for 1997, up 4.7 percent over 1996's $21.62 billion. Net income rose 14.2 percent, from $2.89 billion in 1996 to $3.30 billion in 1997. During a 52-week period from May 1997 to May 1998, Johnson & Johnson's stock reached a high of $77 and a low of $53. The company pays an annual dividend of $1.00 per share.

The company boasts spending more than $8 billion for R&D from 1992 to 1997, including $2 billion for R&D in 1997 alone. The R&D pays off—36 percent of sales came from new products in 1997.

ANALYSTS' OPINIONS

Johnson & Johnson, and its stock, have often received high praise in the national press. In March 1997, *Fortune* magazine rated Johnson & Johnson number six among "America's Most Admired Companies." Michael Sivy, in *Money* magazine's 1997 supplement, predicted the company's stock would enjoy 16 percent or higher growth rates in 1997. *Black Enterprise's* Bruce Hawthorne expressed high faith in the growth potential of Johnson & Johnson stocks, as did a number of other financial commentators in 1996 and 1997.

Less attractive was an ongoing battle between Johnson & Johnson's Tylenol brand and rival American Home Products' Advil brand. Many observers condemned both companies for their negative advertising campaigns. Thomas Petzinger, writing in the *The Wall Street Journal* in October 1996, expressed dismay over Johnson & Johnson's treatment of a small Canadian medical supplies firm, Hart Surgical Inc., whose distribution rights he says the company unfairly appropriated.

HISTORY

In the mid-1800s the concepts of germs and of sterilization against them were novel ones. In 1876 when English surgeon Joseph Lister spoke of germs as "invisible assassins," he still sounded like an alarmist; but one listener who took him seriously was the young American entrepreneur Robert Wood Johnson. Johnson envisioned the use of a practical, sterile surgical dressing, which could be individually wrapped and sealed for use as needed in the operating room. In 1885 he and brothers James Wood and Edward Mead Johnson established a Brunswick, New Jersey, company to produce just that. In 1887 they incorporated their enterprise as Johnson & Johnson.

Johnson & Johnson began mass-producing cotton and gauze dressings for sale throughout the country. The company also published a book in 1888, *Modern Methods of Antiseptic Wound Treatment,* to teach the new practices of maintaining a sterile operating room. In 1897 Edward left and later established the drug company Mead Johnson, which eventually became part of

FINANCES:

Johnson & Johnson Sales, 1994-1997 (billion dollars)

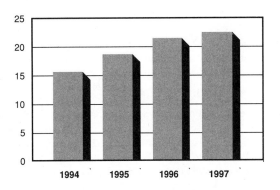

Johnson & Johnson 1997 Stock Prices (dollars)

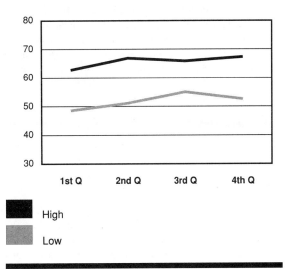

Bristol-Myers Squibb. Robert died in 1910 and James succeeded him as company president. During this era the company introduced its most famous product, Band-Aids, in 1921. The company also established its first foreign affiliate in Canada in 1923, as well as its first one overseas, Johnson & Johnson Ltd. of Great Britain, established in 1924.

Robert Wood Johnson, Jr. took the helm in 1932. Johnson, who would later serve as a general during

FAST FACTS:

About Johnson & Johnson

Ownership: Johnson & Johnson is a publicly owned company traded on the New York Stock Exchange.

Ticker symbol: JNJ

Officers: Ralph S. Larsen, Chmn. & CEO, $2,593,371 1997 base salary; Robert N. Wilson, VC, $1,752,594 1997 base salary; Ronald G. Gelbum, Worldwide Chmn., Pharmaceuticals & Diagnostics Group, $965,014 1997 base salary; James T. Lenehan, Worldwide Chmn., Consumer Pharmaceuticals & Professional Group, $949,380 1997 base salary

Employees: 91,400

Chief Competitors: Because of its diverse product line, Johnson & Johnson competes with multinational companies in a variety of industries including manufacturers, wholesalers, and retailers of pharmaceutical and health care products. Competitors include: American Home Products; Bristol-Myers Squibb; Eli Lilly; Kimberly-Clark; Procter & Gamble; and Smith-Kline Beecham.

World War II, established the strategic principles of decentralization and community service embodied in the company Credo, which continued to prevail into the 1990s. In 1960 Johnson & Johnson introduced perhaps its second most well-known product, the pain-reliever Tylenol.

During the 1980s the company expanded into such product markets as acne medicine, with Retin-A, and contact lenses, with Acuvue. At the end of the decade, it entered into a joint venture with Merck for the marketing of Mylanta antacid medicine. With the fall of Communism, it began selling its products in eastern Europe, and by 1993 it had two facilities in China as well. In 1994 it purchased the Neutrogena line of skin- and hair-care products. The company introduced several revolutionary products in 1996, including Renova wrinkle-reducing cream and the Confide home HIV test. In 1998 Johnson & Johnson strengthened its commitment to women's health with the purchase of two companies:

Biopsys, which makes products for minimally invasive breast biopsies; and Gynecare, which markets minimally invasive medical devices for treating uterine disorders.

STRATEGY

Company president Robert Wood Johnson, Jr. (sometimes referred to as General Johnson) established the company strategy as one of decentralized operations. Instead of growing the central company until it became an unwieldy bureaucracy, he encouraged the establishment of semi-autonomous divisions and affiliates. Thus, the company is said to have as many subsidiaries as it has products. Johnson & Johnson has often acquired other businesses, some of them well known, such as Neutrogena, others involved in specialty product lines for professional use. Whatever the case, Johnson & Johnson strives to maintain the original company's identity and operational framework as much as possible; the company is as likely to enter into a joint venture with another corporate entity as it is to acquire that entity.

This practice of staying loose and flexible has helped it to maintain a competitive edge. When *Fortune* magazine rated Johnson & Johnson sixth out of 431 top U.S. companies in 1997, it cited innovation as the most important secret behind a company's success.

Looking beyond 1998, Johnson & Johnson feels to stay a strong, financially sound company, it must be a leader in the healthcare industry. The company plans to focus on patented advances, driven by technology, which usually have high profit margins. The areas the company sees ripe for growth are skin care, vision care, wound care and healing, diabetes, nutraceuticals, circulatory diseases, minimally invasive therapies, urology, and women's health.

INFLUENCES

General Johnson remained the leading influence on the company many decades after he stepped down from its leadership. In addition to his principle of decentralization that would continue to guide the company's operations, he framed its prevailing values in a succinct statement known as "The Credo," which Johnson & Johnson's corporate literature continues to quote in the late 1990s. The Credo lists four groups to whom the company is responsible—its customers, its employees, the community and environment, and its stockholders.

When a saboteur put cyanide in several bottles of Tylenol in 1983 and eight people died, it could have been the company's downfall. However, Johnson & Johnson handled the crisis in a forthright manner by recalling 31 million bottles and, in the process, spending $240 million, partly on a public relations campaign. The way the company took public responsibility for the product, then introduced a new tamper-resistant cap is now considered a classic business school study on crisis management.

While Johnson & Johnson received praise for its handling of the cyanide crisis, observers question the company's handling of other problems with Tylenol. It seems acetaminophen, the main ingredient in Tylenol, can cause serious problems or even death in doses not much higher than what is recommended. The company has defended over 100 lawsuits against the product, winning some, but losing or settling most. While Johnson & Johnson has been adding more warning labels to the product, some think the company should prominently explain to consumers the extreme consequences of taking too much Tylenol, or Tylenol in combination with certain products. The use of a dosage diary has also been recommended.

CURRENT TRENDS

In the mid-1990s Johnson & Johnson began marketing three revolutionary products. Disposable contact lenses entered the market in 1993, and in 1996 the company won FDA approval for Renova, believed to have a significant wrinkle-reducing effect. Potentially most history making, however, was Confide, the first home HIV test. With home testing becoming a more commonplace event, Johnson & Johnson continually updates its products to make them even more accurate. Hot home testing kits include those for pregnancy, ovulation, blood-sugar, and HIV.

Another leading trend for Johnson & Johnson in the late 1990s was litigation. The most notorious case, in late 1996, involved Confide itself. According to a suit brought by Elliott J. Millenson, the owner of the firm that had invented the breakthrough home HIV test, Johnson & Johnson owed Millenson all returns on sales of the product because the company had fired him without cause, thus violating their contract. Johnson & Johnson was found guilty of firing Millenson without cause and had to return all assets to him. Other complaints included charges in October 1996 that the McNeil Consumer Products division, makers of Tylenol, had misled consumers by marketing its pain relievers with the name of the American Arthritis Foundation on them; and a September 1996 lawsuit by Boehringer Mannheim, which claimed that Johnson & Johnson subsidiary LifeScan had stolen important research documents.

CHRONOLOGY:
Key Dates for Johnson & Johnson

1885: James Wood and Edward Johnson establish Johnson & Johnson

1887: The company incorporates

1888: *Modern Methods of Antiseptic Wound Treatment* is published by the company

1897: Edward Johnson leaves to establish a drug company

1921: Band-Aids are introduced

1949: Johnson & Johnson develops a separate division for the suture business

1959: McNeil Laboratories is acquired

1960: Tylenol is introduced

1981: Frontier Contact Lens is acquired

1989: Johnson & Johnson form a joint venture to manufacture non-prescription products

1994: Purchases the Neutrogena line of skin care products

1996: Confide home HIV test is introduced

1997: Johnson & Johnson is rated sixth out of 431 large U.S. companies by *Fortune* magazine

Litigation, and the high costs brought on by it, may be an almost inevitable by-product of the medical and pharmaceutical business; however, it is extremely unfortunate given the high costs for research and development faced by companies such as Johnson & Johnson. As the professional journal *R&D* reported in October 1996, research and development costs were growing at a faster rate than that of inflation.

PRODUCTS

Johnson & Johnson has more product divisions than most companies have products. These fall generally under the headings of consumer goods, contributing 29 percent of sales; pharmaceuticals, 34 percent of sales; and professional products, 37 percent of sales. The most profitable line is the pharmaceuticals, since the products in that category contributed 56 percent of Johnson & Johnson's net income.

Consumer goods include analgesics, baby care products, contact lenses, feminine hygiene products, first aid products, gastrointestinal products, oral care products, and skin and hair care products. In early 1998 Johnson & Johnson acquired international marketing rights to Benecol, a margarine with an ingredient that reduces cholesterol. In mid-1998 the Food and Drug Administration (FDA) allowed the company to use sucralose, a zero-calorie sweetener, in 15 products. In 1998 Johnson & Johnson planned to introduce disposable contact lenses for those with bifocal and toric prescriptions.

Pharmaceuticals include antibacterials, antifungals, antipsychotics, and family planning products. In 1997 the company introduced Levaquin for treatment of bacterial respiratory illnesses such as community-acquired pneumonia. In 1998 there were plans to introduce Smartstrip, which will allow diabetics to get accurate blood sugar readings without a monitor.

Professional product lines include asepsis/sterilization, biotechnology, diagnostics, endoscopic surgery, interventional cardiology, orthopedics, and wound closure products. In 1998 Johnson & Johnson introduced its second-generation coronary stent, the Palmaz-Schatz Crown Stents. The company is developing crush-resistance stents, stents that will deliver low radiation doses to arteries, and stents that have plaque-fighting medicines already in them.

CORPORATE CITIZENSHIP

Johnson & Johnson, in adherence to its Credo, attempts to "do well by doing good," as one of its brochures states. For instance, the "Focused Giving Program" puts money into biomedical research, which can help find cures for diseases while also opening up profit potential for the company and its shareholders.

The company sponsors a myriad of programs for the community and the environment. Workers in parts of the country participate in "Christmas in April," in which they assist needy local homeowners with repairs, maintenance, and cleaning. The company also supports such charities as the United Way, SAFE KIDS (education for accident prevention), several local arts initiatives, the LIVE FOR LIFE nursing education program, Bridges to Employment (which encourages potential high-school dropouts to explore careers in health care), the Arthritis Foundation, various environmental activities, and global relief for victims of natural disasters.

GLOBAL PRESENCE

Johnson & Johnson has facilities in 50 countries and sells its products in 175 countries worldwide. Of 1997's $22.63 billion in sales, 52 percent were in the United States, 26 percent in Europe, 13 percent in Africa, Asia, and the Pacific, and 9 percent in Canada and Latin America. The Asian market, especially in China, was a ripe area for growth in the latter part of the twentieth and the beginning of the twenty-first century.

EMPLOYMENT

The second item in the four-part Credo that governs Johnson & Johnson's values relates to creating a positive work environment for its employees. Company literature states that Johnson & Johnson strives to provide workers with a situation in which they feel encouraged to make suggestions or even just to complain.

One concrete initiative the company makes on behalf of its employees—and as a corporate citizen—is called the Volunteer Support Program, whereby the company contributes $2 for every $1 contributed by an employee to a qualifying charity. Also, Johnson & Johnson provides extensive child care and even early childhood education facilities for children of its workers.

SOURCES OF INFORMATION

Bibliography

Easton, Thomas, and Stephen Herrera. "J&J's Dirty Little Secret." *Forbes,* 12 January 1998.

Greenwald, John. "Bitter Ads To Swallow." *Time,* 1 April 1996.

Johnson & Johnson. *Discovering Better Health Care Products.* New Brunswick, NJ: Johnson & Johnson, 1997.

The Johnson & Johnson Home Page, 5 May 1998. Available at http://www.jnj.com.

"Johnson & Johnson." *Hoover's Online,* 5 May 1998. Available at http://www.hoovers.com.

"Johnson & Johnson Outlines 'Platforms for Growth' Increases Dividend for 36th Consecutive Year." *Company News On Call,* 11 May 1998. Available at http://www.prnews.com.

"Johnson & Johnson Agrees To Settlement Over Arthritis Drugs." *The Wall Street Journal,* 17 October 1996.

Petzinger, Thomas J. "The Front Lines: Giant J&J Gains a Sales Territory—And a New Enemy." *The Wall Street Journal,* 11 October 1996.

"Pharmaceutical Companies Confront High Cost of Drug Development." *R&D,* October 1996.

Social Responsibility in Action Worldwide. New Brunswick, NJ: Johnson & Johnson, 1995.

For an annual report:

on the Internet at http://www.jnj.com **or** telephone: (800)328-9033

For additional industry research:

Investigate companies by their Standard Industrial Classification Codes, also known as SICs. Johnson & Johnson's primary SICs are:

2834 Pharmaceutical Preparations

2844 Toilet Preparations

3842 Surgical Appliances & Supplies

Keebler Foods Company

FOUNDED: 1853

Contact Information:
HEADQUARTERS: 677 Larch Ave.
Elmhurst, IL 60126
PHONE: (630)833-2900
FAX: (630)530-8773
EMAIL: attpost!klash@elves.attmail.com
URL: http://www.keebler.com

OVERVIEW

By leveraging the strength of its Elfin trademark Keebler Foods has become one of the giants of the snack-food industry. It is the second largest maker of cookies and crackers in the United States after Nabisco. Keebler is a major player in both domestic and institutional snack Markets, and its subsidiary, Bake-Line Products, is the leading manufacturer of private-label cookies and of cookies and crackers for the food service market. Keebler boasts a market share of about 25 percent in an $8-billion industry, in which companies compete fiercely with prices and new products and for valuable shelf space. The ubiquitous Ernie the Elf and "hollow tree" motif help to give Keebler a 98-percent brand-name recognition. It is estimated that 2 out of 3 households in the United States purchase its products.

COMPANY FINANCES

In 1997 total sales exceeded $2.0 billion, up from $1.7 billion in 1996. Gross profit in 1997 was $1.17 billion, up by $259 million from 1996. In addition to marketing initiatives, recent factors in Keebler's financial favor include decreased raw material and packaging costs, as well as streamlined manufacturing processes. Typically, Keebler does not pay dividends on its stock, which has been held publicly since early 1998. Rather, the company prefers to invest its earnings in growth and product development.

Keebler's initial public offering (IPO) in 1998 of approximately 13.5 million shares—with about three quarters sold in the United States—represented ownership of about 16 percent of the company. Upper management holds about 10 percent of the stock, and their annual bonuses are tied to its performance. Keebler is traded on the New York Stock Exchange, and options of Keebler stock are traded on the several option exchanges. The stock began trading at around 26 times expected earnings per share for 1998.

Long-term shareholder value is a central objective at Keebler. In 1998 the board of directors authorized the purchase of up to $30 million in shares of Keebler common stock in order to offset any dilution resulting from the exercise of management stock options. The company bolstered its board to complement the IPO, and Flowers Industries' vice chairman Robert Crozer was elected Keebler's first chairman.

ANALYSTS' OPINIONS

None of the proceeds from the IPO were received by the company, and shares in this mature industry (where 1997's growth was a mere 0.6 percent) are not likely to show the wild upward spurts that are more common in other industries, such as with cutting-edge software producers. Slow and steady growth are more realistic expectations as long as the company continues its trend of introducing viable new products. The company uses financial derivatives in order to hedge against increasing costs of ingredients, but not for speculatory investment purposes. Return on equity in 1997 was 25.7 percent

In 1998 Standard & Poor's raised its rating of Keebler's subordinated debt to double-'B'-plus from double-'B'-minus. The higher rating raised Keebler's corporate credit and bank loan ratings to triple-'B'-minus from double- 'B'-plus. The company's rating outlook is stable, and Standard & Poor's expects Keebler to hold its market position and to maintain a financial profile consistent with its current rating.

HISTORY

Keebler is one of the oldest American food companies. Its long lineage dates ultimately back to a small but popular Philadelphia bakery opened by Godfrey Keebler in 1853, and its larger-scale status dates back to 1927, when the United Biscuit Company of America was formed. By 1944 the United Biscuit Company of America comprised 16 bakeries from Philadelphia to Salt Lake City that made cookies and crackers under a variety of names that sold in all states excluding the West Coast. In 1966 the official company name was changed to Keebler Company. Product distribution was expanded to the West Coast in 1983. In 1974 Keebler was acquired by United Biscuits, one of the largest British food manufacturers. Keebler then operated under its own name as

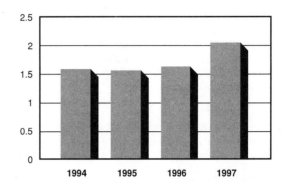

FINANCES:
Keebler Foods Co. Net Sales, 1994-1997 (billion dollars)

a unit of UB Investments U.S., Inc., the American holding company of United Biscuits.

By 1995, when the company was owned by UB Investments Netherlands B.V. (a Dutch subsidiary of Britain's publicly held United Biscuits Holdings PLC), Keebler was put up for sale. In 1996 Flowers Industries (an American baked-goods manufacturer), Artal Luxembourg S.A. (a private investment group), Bermore, Ltd., (another private investment group), and various members of Keebler's current management—all under the name INFLO Holdings Corporation—purchased it for $500 million. In 1997 INFLO was merged into Keebler Corporation, and the company's name was changed to Keebler Foods Company.

In 1996 Keebler bought G.F. Industries Inc.'s subsidiary Sunshine Biscuits, Inc. for approximately $172 million. Sunshine, then the third largest U.S. cookie and cracker maker, had had annual sales of approximately $600 million. At the time of the crucial acquisition, Keebler's president Sam Reed remarked, "A little Sunshine will make our Tree grow," referring to Keebler's trademark cartoon factory and headquarters.

STRATEGY

In 1996, citing increased competition, Keebler integrated the production, distribution, and administrative operations of its Keebler and Sunshine divisions. It shifted production among its plants and closed its facilities in Santa Fe Springs, California, and Atlanta, but did not discontinue any of its brands at that time. It also

FAST FACTS:

About Keebler Foods Company

Ownership: Keebler Foods Company is a publicly held company traded on the New York Stock Exchange. Flowers Industries holds a 55-percent majority interest in the company.

Ticker symbol: KBL

Officers: Sam K. Reed, Pres. & CEO, 51, $1,748,500; Robert P. Crozer, Chmn., 51; E. Nichol McCully, Sr. VP Finance & CFO, 43, $550,810

Employees: 9,500 (1997)

Principal Subsidiary Companies: Keebler Food Company's wholly owned subsidiaries include Bake-Line Products; Elfin Equity Company, L.L.C.; Hollow Tree Company, L.L.C.; Hollow Tree Financial Company, L.L.C.; Johnston's Ready Crust Company; Keebler Company; Keebler Leasing Corp.; and Sunshine Biscuits, Inc.

Chief Competitors: Some of Keebler's competitors include: Campbell Soup; Nabisco Holdings; and Frito-Lay.

closed Sunshine's corporate headquarters in Woodbridge, New Jersey. In 1998 plants were running at about 82-percent capacity.

With the purchase of Sunshine, Keebler started a plan to increase efficiency and to decrease costs. Cost-cutting measures included staff reductions throughout the company, the closing of various production centers, and the consolidation of distribution lines. These initiatives were completed in 1997. The enlarged entity has been able to lower its materials costs by buying in high volume.

INFLUENCES

In 1995 Keebler discontinued its frozen-food lines by selling the assets and stock of those wholly owned subsidiaries (e.g., Bernardi Italian Foods Co. and The Original Chili Bowl, Inc.) to Windsor Food Company. In 1996 it sold off its salty snack division, which had produced a wide variety of pretzels and snack chips. Much of those assets, including a factory in Bluffton, In-

diana, were sold to Kelly Food Products, Inc. Such strategic moves have allowed Keebler to concentrate on competing with Nabisco in the more lucrative cookie and cracker markets. Any additional acquisition of a single competitor would be less significant than the purchase of Sunshine, so product development remains a key factor in expanding the company and increasing its revenues.

CURRENT TRENDS

Since the buyout from United Biscuits and the acquisition of Sunshine Biscuits in 1996, Keebler has focused on its distribution potential. Distribution is a critical step for any manufacturer, particularly at the national level, and Keebler is the only cookie and cracker maker besides Nabisco that has its own national distribution system. Keebler utilizes a "direct store delivery system" (DSD), through which nearly all U.S. supermarkets retail Keebler products. A 1,500-person field sales force visits 30,000 retail stores each week and tracks inventory and sales progress, as well as the appearance of merchandise displays. Keebler is thus able to monitor the products' development all the way down the line to the final point of sale, in addition to their viability as consumer items. DSD sales personnel use handheld computers. The company has incorporated the volume of Sunshine products into its DSD system, which has significantly reduced overhead costs. Keebler sees warehouse-club retailers, drug stores, and convenience stores as essential outlets for further revenue growth. In 1997, its deliveries to warehouse clubs, drug stores, and mass marketers such as Kmart and Wal-Mart increased by more than 30 percent each.

Keebler describes the cookie and cracker business as "impulse driven." Accordingly, it plans to continue its heavy advertising, including an introduction of television commercials for Cheez-It products, to help sustain its market share. Keebler spent close to $70 million in 1997 on advertising and "marketing programs," including a basketball-themed, instant-winner sweepstakes promotion for Cheez-Its. It reports that in-store displays increased by almost 40 percent between 1996-97.

For its Chips Deluxe brand chocolate chip cookies, Keebler has developed advertising aimed at children. Revenues for this brand, for example, increased by 25 percent following a promotional "Create Your Own Cookie Contest." In 1998 the company launched its "Rainbow USA" cookie line—cookies containing red, white, and blue candies—at the strategic time between Memorial Day and the Fourth of July in order to capitalize on patriotic feeling surrounding those holidays. Keebler's sales are seasonally influenced, with cracker sales being heaviest in the fourth quarter as a result of the concentration of food-oriented holidays. It has also used clever marketing to boost sales of Cheez-Its. In 1997 it was able to increase sales of the brand by almost 30 percent (to $213 million) by expanding the popular cracker's theme with new varieties and by improving the appeal of its packaging.

PRODUCTS

In recent years Keebler has narrowed the range of its food products. The company's output currently is limited to diverse ranges of cookies, crackers, ice cream cones, and pie crusts under such familiar names as Hydrox, Ready Crust, Wheatables, Hi-Hos, Zesta, Carr's brands, Town House Crackers, and Cheez-Its. The timeless Cheez-It is the largest-selling snack cracker in the United States. For this perennial favorite, Keebler makes its own cheese. In 1997 Keebler introduced 17 new products, including the successful Cookie Stix.

GLOBAL PRESENCE

International sales are not a significant part of Keebler's business, and historically the company has not pursued such markets very aggressively.

CHRONOLOGY:
Key Dates of Keebler Foods Company

1853: Godfrey Keebler opens a bakery in Philadelphia, Pennsylvania

1927: United Biscuit Company of America is formed, comprised of many bakeries

1966: Keebler becomes the official company name and the brand name for all United Biscuit products

1974: Keebler is acquired by United Biscuit (Holdings) PLC of the United Kingdom

1983: Distribution of all products is expanded to the West Coast

1996: INFLO Holdings Corp. purchases Keebler

1997: INFLO is merged into Keebler and the company name changes to Keebler Foods Company

SOURCES OF INFORMATION

Bibliography

"Amex to Trade Options on Keebler Foods Company." *PR Newswire,* 29 April 1998.

Gottesman, Alan. "Got Cookies?" *Adweek,* Eastern Edition, 9 February 1998.

Husted, Bill, and Matt Kempner. "Keebler Co. to Shut Atlanta Bakery." *Atlanta Journal and Constitution,* 3 March 1996.

"Keebler Agrees to Sell Salty Snacks Brands." *Supermarket News,* 4 December 1995.

"Keebler Foods Company." *Hoover's Online,* 18 August 1998. Available at http://www.hoover's.com.

"Keebler Foods Company Announces Authorization of $30 Million Buyback Program for Common Stock." Keebler Foods Company Press Release, 10 March 1998.

"Keebler Foods Company Announces Initial Public Offering." *Business Wire,* 29 January 1998.

"Keebler Foods Company Announces Initial Public Offering." Keebler Foods Company Press Release, 29 January 1998.

Keebler Foods Company Annual Report 1997. Elmhurst, IL: Keebler Foods Company, 1998.

Keebler Foods Company Home Page, 18 August 1998. Available at http://www.keebler.com.

"Keebler to Merge Two Units." *Supermarket News,* 12 August 1996.

"Keebler's Subordinated Debt Rating Raised to BB+; Outlook Stable." *Business Wire,* 16 April 1998.

King, Sharon R. "Look Who's Leaping from That Hollow Tree." *New York Times,* 25 January 1998.

Molis, Jim. "New Jersey's Sunshine Biscuits Inc. to Merge with Keebler Co." *Columbus Ledger-Enquirer,* 6 June 1996.

Rees, Scott. "Not Such a Sweet Deal." *Barron's,* 26 January 1995.

"Robert P. Crozer Elected Keebler's Chairman of the Board; Five New Directors Elected to Expanded Keebler Board." Keebler Foods Company Press Release, 2 March 1998.

Schlegel, Jeff. "Sunshine Biscuits, Keebler Co. Parent Firms Said to Be Talking Merger." *Asbury Park Press,* 30 May 1996.

For an annual report:
write: Keebler Foods Company Corporate Office, 677 Larch Ave., Elmhurst, IL, 60126

For additional industry research:
Investigate companies by their Standard Industrial Classification Codes, also known as SICs. Keebler's primary SIC is:

2052 Cookies & Crackers

Kellogg Company

FOUNDED: 1906 as Battle Creek Toasted Corn Flake Company

Contact Information:

HEADQUARTERS: 1 Kellogg Sq.
  Battle Creek, MI 49016-3599
PHONE: (616)961-2000
FAX: (616)961-2871
TOLL FREE: (800)962-1413
URL: http://www.kelloggs.com

OVERVIEW

Kellogg Company is the world's largest producer of breakfast cereals and an industry leader in the production of grain-based convenience foods. Despite forays into non-cereal product types, the company has ultimately made its fortune through a commitment to the cereal and grain-based convenience food market. Kellogg's success in this mature and diversified market can be attributed to its aggressive advertising, product innovation, and constant expansion of its consumer base.

COMPANY FINANCES

Growth for the Kellogg Company was slow for the year-ending 1997. Net sales were $6.8 billion, up 2 percent from 1996 sales of $6.67 billion. However, even this modest increase represented improvement over the 1996 year-end loss of 5 percent from 1995 net sales of $7 billion. The company's stock price ranged from $32 to $50 per share through 1997, representing some improvement over its 1996 range of $31 to $40. Net earnings per share for 1997 were $1.32, slightly higher than 1996 earnings per share of $1.25 (however, this modest change also reflects the stock-split that took place on August 22, 1997). The company reported first quarter 1998 earnings per share of $.42, up 11 percent over $.38 reported in the first quarter of 1997.

Operating profits for the company as reported in 1997 were $1 billion, up 5 percent from 1996's total $958.9 million. Of 1997 profits, $706.8 million was earned in the United States (vs. $611.2 million in 1996),

$158.9 in Europe (vs. $204.4 million in 1996), and $143.4 million in all other markets (vs. $143.3 million in 1996).

ANALYSTS' OPINIONS

According to Zacks, current analyst opinion recommends a "hold" on Kellogg stock, meaning for solid investment performance investors should keep what they currently own. A few analysts recommended a "buy" or "strong buy" rating for the company, meaning they would recommend that investors pick up more shares (as of May 1998). Moody's Investors Service, however, was considering a downgrade of Kellogg's long-term debt rating. This was in part due to highly competitive conditions in the United States for the ready-to-eat cereal market, and in part to Kellogg's weaker market share in the United States.

HISTORY

Despite inventing the toasted grain flake in 1894, brothers Will Keith (W.K.) and Dr. John Harvey Kellogg were slow to capitalize on the discovery. W.K. worked for his brother in the Seventh-Day Adventist homeopathic sanitarium at Battle Creek, Michigan. In an effort to produce more digestible bread—one more product in Dr. Kellogg's long line of health foods—the brothers ran boiled wheat dough through rollers. Unfortunately, the mixture was too wet and sticky. One day, after an interruption resulted in dried-out dough, they again ran it through the rollers—this time, it came out in bite-sized flakes, which they then toasted. The grain flake cereal was born.

The brothers' partnership sold the Granose flakes by mail order, until W.K. left to start his own Battle Creek Toasted Corn Flake Company in 1906. At that time, Battle Creek was the undisputed cereal capital of the United States, with close to 40 separate companies. Dr. Kellogg himself continued to sell a similar product until W.K. successfully sued him for rights to the Kellogg name. One of the biggest competitors of the time was C.W. Post, who was once a patient at the Battle Creek Sanitarium.

STRATEGY

If there has been one successful strategy characterizing the history of the Kelloggs company, it is advertising. Upon its founding in 1906, W.K. Kellogg spent more than 30 percent of the company's working capital on an advertisement in *Ladies Home Journal*. The strategy paid off, with demand soon outstripping supply. One racy campaign told consumers to "wink at their grocer and see what you get;" consumers got a free taste test

FINANCES:

Kellogg Co. Net Sales, 1994-1997 (billion dollars)

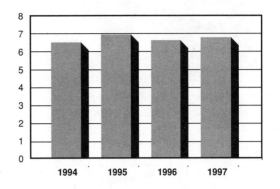

Kellogg Co. 1997 Stock Prices (dollars)

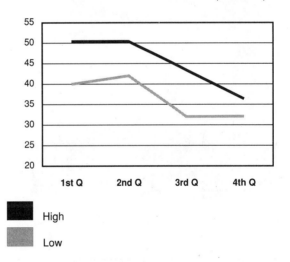

and Kellogg increased its sales. During the Great Depression, despite falling sales, the company followed the retired W.K. Kellogg's advice and added $1 million to its advertising budget. As a result, sales continued to increase throughout the 1930s. In the 1950s, the company capitalized on the postwar baby boom and doubled sales and profits with the introduction of *Tony the Tiger* and other animated hucksters who pitched products on Saturday morning television. Stepped-up advertising was also the solution for sluggish sales in the 1970s. When the company returned to its roots, with renewed emphasis on high-fiber, health-oriented cereals in the 1980s, ad-

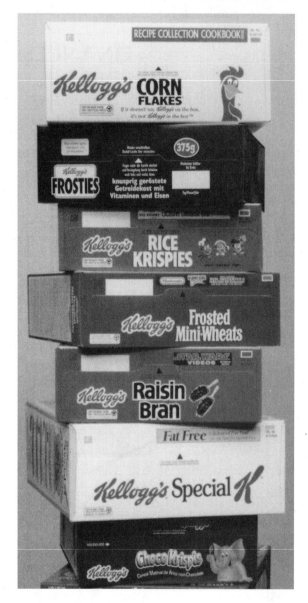

Kellogg's breakfast cereal brands. *(Courtesy of Kellogg Company.)*

vertising was again key in capturing health-conscious consumers.

In addition, the company has put a constant emphasis on market expansion and research and development (R&D). Kellogg's R&D expenditures were approximately $106.1 million in 1997, $84.3 million in 1996, and $72.2 million in 1995. Earnings are typically reinvested to keep the company's facilities and technology up to date.

In 1996, after suffering a substantial decline in sales and earnings, the company placed emphasis on strengthening and repositioning itself for long-term growth. Kel-

logg's strategy featured the company's continued movement towards a goal of improved consumer value combined with pricing restraint and rigorous cost reduction. One major part of the repositioning process was the 1996 purchase of the Asian Ralston Purina Company. Also in 1996, the company repurchased $535.7 million in shares of Kellogg stock, with the Board of Directors authorizing up to $415.1 million in additional purchases for 1997. These purchases, the company asserts, will put long-term upward leverage on earnings per share and provide a "tax-efficient means of transferring cash to our shareholders."

To protect new advanced technology, Kellogg ended their popular plant tours in 1986, Kellogg saw the need for a new public relations resource and the community expressed the need for a new visitor attraction. The not-for-profit Heritage Center Foundation was created to develop, own, and operate the $18-million Cereal City USA complex in Battle Creek. The new complex was scheduled to open in Summer 1998. The 45,000-square-foot complex, a sort of homage to the history and process of cereal production, will include sets, a theater, and other recreational attractions. Backed with contributions from several local foundations, Heritage hired a veteran of the amusement park industry to manage the operation, which it hopes will bring in 400,000 ticket-buying visitors per year. The company lacks a strong merchandise or licensing presence so it will apply for a license to create souvenir merchandise using its cartoon hucksters, like *Tony the Tiger* and *Snap, Crackle, and Pop* for advertising and promotional purposes.

INFLUENCES

In 1996, competitive challenges in the U.S. market, and aggressive store brand competition in the United Kingdom dealt a serious blow to the company's historic performance level. This unprecedented turbulence in Kellogg's two largest cereal markets resulted in a decline in sales and earnings. Though earnings picked up slightly in 1998, the Kellogg Company continues to expand its global markets, partially to compensate for dropping domestic market share.

CURRENT TRENDS

The Kellogg Company's plans for the twenty-first century are to leverage what the company calls its "positive health image." Growing awareness of the benefits of fiber have led Kellogg's to redesign packaging and expand global marketing of bran products such as *Kellogg's All-Bran* and *Kellogg's Complete* wheat and oat bran cereals. The company is heavily promoting these products through its Age+5 campaign, designed to increase children's consumption of fiber.

Kellogg's CEO Arnold Langbo shakes the paw of "Tony the Tiger" after announcing that prices would be cut on their most popular cereals. (Photograph by Mark Cardwell. Reuters/Archive Photos.)

PRODUCTS

Kellogg is, without a doubt, the cereal king—it is the number one seller of cereals. Its principal sales come from ready-to-eat cereals. The company generally markets its products with company-owned trademarks. Products are usually sold directly to the grocery trade for resale to consumers, though broker and distribution arrangements are made in less developed markets. Through its history, the company has acquired several convenience food companies, which account for nearly 20 percent of global sales. In addition to the Kellogg cereals the company also sells *Kellogg's Pop-Tarts* toaster

pastries and *Kellogg's Eggo* frozen waffles. Most recently, Kellogg broadened its global potential with the purchase of the Lender's Bagel Bakery business from Kraft Foods, Inc.

CORPORATE CITIZENSHIP

Kellogg established the W.K. Kellogg Foundation in 1930 and gave it majority interest in his company (the company bought back about 20 percent in 1984). The private grant-making organization was established "to help people help themselves through the practical application of knowledge and resources to improve their quality of life and that of future generations." It provides seed money to organizations and institutions with solution-based programs in the areas of volunteerism, philanthropy, youth, leadership, community-based health services, rural development, and higher education. Grants go mostly to Latin America, the Caribbean, southern Africa, and the United States (particularly Michigan and the Great Lakes region). Early in 1997 the company commenced operations at the new W.K. Kellogg Institute for Food and Nutrition Research in Battle Creek.

Despite the company's charitable activities, its role as the leading cereal maker has not been bereft of criticism. In 1972, the Federal Trade Commission accused Kellogg and other major cereal producers of monopoly business practices, overcharging consumers by more than $1 billion between 1957-72. The American Dental Association blasted the industry for downplaying the sugar content of its presweetened cereals. Kellogg's, to its credit, made no secret of its sugar use, with bold product names like *Sugar Smacks* , *Sugar Corn Pops*, and *Sugar Frosted Flakes*. By the 1990s Kellogg's had changed the names to those lines, calling them *Kellogg's Smacks*, *Kellogg's Corn Pops*, and *Kellogg's Frosted Flakes*. Again, in 1995, U.S. Representative Charles Schumer accused Kellogg and others of price collusion.

FAST FACTS:
About Kellogg Company

Ownership: Kellogg Company is a publicly owned company traded on the New York Stock Exchange.

Ticker symbol: K

Officers: Arnold G. Langbo, 60, Chmn. & CEO, 1997 base salary $980,000; Thomas A. Knowlton, Exec. VP, 1997 base salary $535,000; Donald W. Thomason, Exec. VP Corp. Services. & Technology, 1997 base salary $431,250; Donald G. Fritz, Exec. VP, 1997 base salary $430,000

Employees: 14,339

Chief Competitors: As a leading producer and marketer of grain-based convenience foods, Kellogg's main competitors include: General Mills; Philip Morris; CPC; Malt-O-Meal; Quaker Oats; and Sara Lee.

CHRONOLOGY:
Key Dates for Kellogg Company

1894: Will Keith Kellogg and Dr. John Harvey Kellogg (brothers) invent the toasted grain flake

1906: Kellogg founded as Battle Creek Toasted Corn Flake Co.

1907: Company becomes the Toasted Corn Flake Company

1909: Company becomes the Kellogg Toasted Corn Flake Company

1911: Kellogg has an advertising budget of $1 million

1915: 40% Bran Flakes are introduced

1916: All-Bran is introduced

1921: W.K. Kellogg wins rights to family name

1922: Company becomes the Kellogg Company

1925: W.K. Kellogg begins searching for his replacement as president

1928: Rice Krispies are introduced

1930: W.K. Kellogg Foundation is established

1939: Watson H. Vanderploeg finally fills the role as permanent president

1951: W.K. Kellogg dies

1952: Tony the Tiger is introduced

1969: Kellogg acquires Salada Foods

1976: Purchases Mrs. Smith's Pie Company

1982: The Nutri-Grain line is introduced

1994: Sells Mrs. Smith's frozen pie business

1996: Purchases Ralston Purina Company

GLOBAL PRESENCE

Kellogg is truly a global company, with 29 manufacturing plants in 20 countries and distribution of 120 countries. It currently holds an estimated 39 percent of worldwide volume in the ready-to-eat cereal market. The company's cereal business shows formidable growth both in developing markets of Asia, Latin America, and southern Europe, and in established markets like Canada, Australia, and Mexico. Faced with widespread competition at home, the company aggressively courted European consumers, who in 1995 accounted for 26 percent of total sales. An additional 16 percent of sales came from Asia, Australia, Africa, and Latin America. Kellogg's 1996 decision to reduce prices domestically may increase sales at home, but this may be hampered somewhat by a competitive U.S. market. Overall growth in sales may ultimately depend on success in the global marketplace.

Kellogg is building from a strong global base. Of the top 15 cereal brands in the world, 12 are Kellogg products. In early 1997, the company bought cereal plants in Ecuador and Brazil and finished building a new plant in Thailand. In the eyes of Kellogg's CEO Arnold Langbo, ready-to-eat cereal will be a global growth business for the twenty-first century. In the grain-based food industry, Kellogg Company's global infrastructure goes unmatched. The company's position became even stronger with the 1996 addition of the three Lender's plants, plus the purchase of a Kentucky convenience foods plant. Roll-outs of convenience foods such as its *Kellogg's Nutri-Grain* cereal bars and *Kellogg's Rice Krispie Treats Squares* in the United Kingdom and Austrlia, with plans to move into Latin America during 1998, also helped to accelerate global growth.

EMPLOYMENT

On its web site, the Kellogg's company states, "We are committed to helping Kellogg people reach their full potential and to recognizing their achievements." Toward that end the company provides training and development opportunities, tries to promote from within the company, and works to provide an environment where equal opportunity is awarded and diversity is respected.

SOURCES OF INFORMATION

Bibliography

"Kellogg Company." *International Directory of Company Histories.* Detroit: St. James Press, 1988.

"Kellogg Company Completes Lender's(R) Bagels Purchase." Kellogg Company Press Release, 16 December 1997. Available at http://www.prnewswire.com/K.

BATTLE CREEK ATTRACTION!

On June 1, 1998, Kellogg opened Cereal City USA, a cereal-oriented theme park that they call "the Midwest's newest attraction." After a video tour conducted by a cartoon character with the festive name of "Mr. Grit," tourists can take in the wonders of the "Simulated Cereal Production Line." Warm Corn Flakes are available as you tour the facility, and if that's not enough, you can also top off your visit with a snack of ice-cream and Fruit Loops as you meet Tony the Tiger in person. This "family attraction celebrating cereal" is located in Battle Creek, Michigan. Make your reservations now.

"Kellogg Corporate Headquarters." Available at http://www.kelloggs.com/corp_hq/.

"Kellogg EPS Increases by 11 Percent in First Quarter." *PR Newswire,* 24 April 1998.

Kellogg's 1997 Annual Report. Kellogg Company, 1998. Available at http://www.prnewswire.com/cnoc/AREPORTS/483375.6.

"Letter to Shareholders." *Kellogg's 1997 Annual Report.* Kellogg Company, 1998.

Moody's Industrial Manual. New York: Moody's Investors Service, Inc., 1996.

"Moody's May Cut Kellogg Co Long-Term Debt." Moody's Investors Service Press Release, 28 April 1998.

O'Brien, Tim. "Construction Under Way for Kellogg's $18 million Cereal City USA Center." *Amusement Business,* 13 January 1997.

For an annual report:

on the Internet at: http://www.prnewswire.com/cnoc/AREPORTS/483375.6 **or** telephone: (800)962-1413 **or** write: Kellogg Company, PO Box CAMB, Battle Creek, MI 49016-1986

For additional industry research:

Investigate companies by their Standard Industrial Classification Codes, also known as SICs. Kellogg's primary SICs are:

2041 Flour & Other Grain Mill Products

2043 Cereal Breakfast Foods

2051 Bread, Cake & Related Products

Kelly Services Inc.

FOUNDED: 1946 as Russell Kelly Office Services

Contact Information:

HEADQUARTERS: 999 W. Big Beaver Rd.
   Troy, MI 48084
PHONE: (248)362-4444
FAX: (248)244-4154
TOLL FREE: (888)GO-KELLY
URL: http://www.kellyservices.com

OVERVIEW

In the U.S. temporary personnel business, Kelly Services is one of the Big Three, trailing industry leader Manpower and running almost even with Adecco. It has more than 200,000 clients, mostly companies or government agencies, to whom it contracts out the services of its more than 800,000 temporary workers. On a daily basis, Kelly employs approximately 150,000 temporary employees and 5,000 full-time employees worldwide. The hiring company pays Kelly Services for the labor of its "temporaries," as these employees are often called, and the service in turn pays the employee after receiving its own percentage of the pay. The company has some 1,500 offices worldwide.

The current downsizing trend in corporate America has resulted in an increased demand for the temporary personnel supplied by Kelly Services and its competitors. More and more companies have cut their rosters of full-time employees to the bone, sharply reducing their salary and benefits budgets. When there is a temporary bulge in the workload that can not be met with existing staff, temporary employees are brought in to handle the extra work.

In recent years, Kelly has become increasingly specialized to meet the needs of its customers. The exponential increase in corporate demand for computer-savvy workers prompted Kelly's acquisition in 1994 of ComTrain, a software training business. The same year Kelly acquired Your Staff, a company that leases employees and even entire departments to other companies. To meet the demands of the legal community, in 1995 Kelly purchased Wallace Law Registry, a service that supplies law clerks and paralegals to law firms throughout the country.

COMPANY FINANCES

In 1997 Kelly Services posted net earnings of $81 million on revenue of $3.85 billion, compared with 1996 when net income was $73 billion on revenue of $3.3 billion in 1996. Per-share earnings were $2.12 in 1997, compared with $1.91 in 1996. In 1995 Kelly recorded net earnings of $70 million on revenue of $2.69 billion, compared with a net of $61 million on revenue of $2.36 billion in 1994. Per-share earnings in 1995 and 1994 were $1.83 and $1.61, respectively. Nearly 80 percent of Kelly's total revenue in 1997 was generated by operations in the United States, while the rest came from foreign subsidiaries' business.

ANALYSTS' OPINIONS

Until the mid-1990s financial observers were enthusiastic about stocks in temporary-services companies, but with the slowing of growth on the heels of decreased corporate downsizing, enthusiasm for these stocks began to ebb. *Financial World* suggested that the future did not look as bright for giants such as Kelly as it did for smaller, more adaptable temporary services.

In 1995 *CIO,* a trade magazine for executives in the information industry, named Kelly to its top 100 list of companies with the best business and organizational practices. The company's web site has also won praise as an educational resource for job seekers; *Training & Development* magazine reviewed it as a "Cool Site," and in August 1996 *Human Resource* magazine gave it the "best recruitment advertisement on a web site" award. In bestowing the award, the magazine cited the site's targeting of businesses, its database of Kelly offices, its company profile, and its links to other human resources-related web sites.

HISTORY

In 1946 William Russell Kelly founded Russell Kelly Office Services in Detroit, Michigan, following a stint in the service during World War II. His idea was a novel one for the time: other businesses would bring their clerical work, such as typing or filing, to his company for his employees to perform. Eventually, Kelly saw that his future lay in what people five decades later would have called "outsourcing": providing other businesses with on-site temporary employees.

With his company's strategy set, Kelly incorporated the business in 1952. In 1954 he opened his first branch outside of Michigan, in Louisville, Kentucky. A year later, the company had 35 branches throughout the country. It was renamed Kelly Girl Services Inc. in 1957, and in 1962 the corporation went public. Another—and final—name change came in 1966, when Kelly Girl became Kelly Services Inc.

By the end of 1964 Kelly had 169 offices in 44 states, and opened in Puerto Rico in 1965. Its first international office opened in Toronto in 1968, and in the early 1970s the company established locations in Europe. In 1976 the company acquired the service company Home Care Inc., which it eventually turned into Kelly Health Care.

FINANCES:

*Kelly Services
Sales, 1994-1997
(billion dollars)*

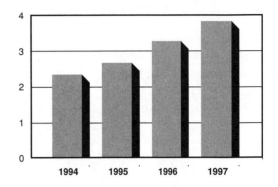

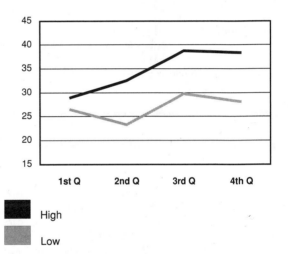

*Kelly Services
1997 Stock Prices (class A shares)
(dollars)*

High

Low

FAST FACTS:

About Kelly Services Inc.

Ownership: Kelly Services is a publicly owned company traded on NASDAQ.

Ticker symbol: KELYA, KELYB

Officers: Terence E. Adderley, Chmn., Pres., & CEO, 64, $1,154,250; Carl T. Camden, Exec. VP, Field Operations, Sales, & Marketing; Robert E. Thompson, Exec. VP, Administration, 54, $615,000; Tommi A. White, Exec. VP, Service, Quality, & Information Technology, 47, $456,250

Employees: 750,000

Principal Subsidiary Companies: Kelly Services is the parent of several foreign subsidiary operations in Australia, Canada, Denmark, France, Ireland, Italy, Mexico, Netherlands, New Zealand, Norway, and the United Kingdom.

Chief Competitors: Kelly's major competitors in the temporary personnel business include: Adecco; Administaff; Interim Services; Manpower; Norrell; Olsten; Staff Builders; Staff Leasing; and Volt Information.

It took Kelly 13 years, from 1973 to 1986, to grow from $100 million in sales to $1 billion; it only took 7 more to grow to $2 billion in 1993. Then, just three years later in 1996, the company surpassed $3 billion in sales. The company introduced PinPoint, an innovative program for teaching software. Also in the mid-1990s, Kelly expanded its services to include highly specialized fields; for example, it could provide scientists to work on a temporary basis.

The late 1980s and the 1990s have seen a sharp increase in Kelly's international activities. Since 1988 Kelly has made nearly 15 acquisitions to expand the company's presence in Europe, Australia, New Zealand, and North America. In 1997 Kelly opened operations in Italy and Russia.

William Russell Kelly, the company's founder and chairman, died in early 1998. Taking over as chairman was Kelly's adopted son, Terence Adderley, who added the chairmanship to his existing responsibilities as president and CEO.

STRATEGY

Kelly Services was the brainchild of the late William Kelly, and even in 1997 (when Kelly was in his 90s), he and adopted son Terry Adderley together controlled 89 percent of the company's stock. From the beginning, Kelly implemented a simple but brilliant strategy: to offer businesses an economical way to meet unexpected workload increases by providing them with temporary staff. These "temporaries" would save the company the cost of hiring and training a new employee, and would eliminate expenses involved in maintaining the employee, such as health care and clerical costs.

Added to this business plan was a growth strategy, which Kelly himself stated thus: "We decided that if we didn't want [a competitor] to knock us off, we'd better go nationwide." Kelly said that at one point the company opened 13 offices in as many days. In this regard, a milestone was achieved in 1979 with the opening of an office in Burlington, Vermont—the fiftieth state with a Kelly facility.

INFLUENCES

In the 1980s and early 1990s the temporary industry was one of the fastest-growing businesses in the United States, due to rampant downsizing that accompanied the many mergers and corporate takeovers of that era. By the mid-1990s, however, downsizing had begun to slow—and so had the temporary business. Therefore, Kelly and other temporary companies had to expand their service lines. As *Financial World* reported in December 1996, high-tech temporaries offered a new area for growth.

CURRENT TRENDS

During the late 1980s and 1990s, Kelly expanded its service line to include a number of specialty areas. Those included temporary services for scientific, home-care, and legal personnel. Also, it introduced a new software program, PinPoint, which helped teach employees how to use other types of software. In 1995 the company began promoting itself on television for the first time in a decade, with ads on the Weather Channel.

Kelly also responded to the trend toward "quality service" in customer relations, a response throughout the marketplace to customer unhappiness with impolite or impersonal treatment by service personnel. The journal, *Purchasing,* reported in August 1994 that Kelly had begun quality training with its personnel through use of an orientation video.

Kelly entered the scientific temporaries field in March 1996. Through this program, the company would provide temporary staff in the areas of research and development, quality assurance/control, product and process development, and a number of other technical areas. At the time of the launch, the company had 7 such offices in operation, with 5 to 10 more scheduled for opening by the end of the year and plans for expansion of the program into Canada and Europe in 1997. The cost to businesses ranged from $9 an hour for laboratory assistants to $35 an hour for physicists, chemists, and other scientists with full doctorates.

PRODUCTS

Kelly offers a wide variety of services in the office clerical, marketing, professional, technical, semi-skilled light industrial, and management lines.

Kelly Business Solutions includes a number of divisions: Kelly Management Services provides office and clerical work ranging from telemarketing to accounting work; Kelly Scientific Resources staffs scientific personnel in such fields as biochemistry and geology; KellySelect is a temporary-to-permanent employee service that allows companies to test out an employee before making the investment in hiring; Partnered Staffing handles chiefly payroll and human resources personnel; and the Wallace Law Registry is a specialty line of legal temporaries, including attorneys. In addition to these services, Kelly Business Solutions offers PinPoint, a software program on CD-ROM. The program teaches employees how to use various other software products such as the word processing, spreadsheet, and database programs produced by Microsoft and Novell.

Kelly Assisted Living Services is a temporary service that provides caregivers for the elderly and disabled.

CORPORATE CITIZENSHIP

In an effort to help men and women leaving the armed services make a successful transition to employment in the private sector, in 1998 Kelly struck an agreement with Hire Quality Inc. Hire Quality developed and maintains the largest career-referral service for veterans and their families. Under the agreement, Hire Quality will supply Kelly with thousands of job applicants each month, each of whom will be prescreened for education, work experience, and skills. This information will be integrated by Kelly into its branch automation system, which will allow its more than 1,200 U.S. offices to match customer job requests with the candidate records provided by Hire Quality.

Announcing the agreement with Hire Quality, Carl Camden, Kelly's executive vice president for field operations, sales, and marketing, said: "In the current tight labor market it's especially exciting for us to have ac-

CHRONOLOGY:
Key Dates for Kelly Services Inc.

1946: William Russell Kelly establishes the Russell Kelly Office Services

1952: The company incorporates

1957: Russell Kelly Office Services is changed to Kelly Girl Services Inc.

1962: Goes public

1966: Company name becomes Kelly Services Inc.

1968: The first international office opens in Canada

1976: Kelly acquires Home care Inc., which becomes Kelly Health Care

1986: Sales top $1 billion for the first time

1995: Introduces PinPoint teaching and testing software

1998: Kelly reaches an agreement with Hire Quality Inc. to attain job applicants

cess to such a highly trained and disciplined group of workers. These men and women have skills and experience in areas such as science, legal, information technology, office, manufacturing, and electronics—all areas where we have many job opportunities."

GLOBAL PRESENCE

Kelly has more than 1,600 offices worldwide. In addition to the United States and Puerto Rico, company facilities are located in Canada, Mexico, the United Kingdom, Ireland, France, Denmark, Norway, Holland, Luxembourg, Switzerland, Spain, Italy, Russia, Australia, and New Zealand. Of its total revenue in 1997, 78 percent was generated in the United States, while the remaining 22 percent came from all the company's foreign operations combined.

EMPLOYMENT

As demand for "temps" has grown worldwide, Kelly has added a number of incentives to encourage temporary employees to sign on with the company. Kelly offers temporaries a week of paid vacation after 1,500 hours worked in a 12-month period. Among the other benefits temporary employees may receive are performance bonuses, health insurance, discounts on stock purchases, and a retirement plan. An employee publication, *The Chronicle,* helps to promote team spirit.

SOURCES OF INFORMATION

Bibliography

Dravo, Ed. "How to Play the Jobs Recovery." *Financial World,* 29 March 1994.

Epatko, Elena. "Temporary Help Firms Put New Emphasis on Training." *Purchasing,* 18 August 1994.

Epstein, Joseph. "Staying Power." *Financial World,* 16 December 1996.

Halliday, Jean. "Kelly Services Forecast: High Visibility on Weather Channel through End of 1996." *Adweek,* 9 October 1995.

"Kelly Services Inc." *Hoover's Online,* 1 June 1998. Available at http://www.hoovers.com.

Kelly Services Inc. 1996 Annual Report. Troy, MI: Kelly Services Inc., 1997.

Kelly Services Inc. Home Page. 1 June 1998. Available at http://www.kellyservices.com/corpinfo/index.html.

Rubis, Leon. "Benefits Boost Appeal of Temporary Work." *HR Magazine,* January 1995.

For an annual report:

on the Internet at: http://www.kellyservices.com/corpinfo/index.html

For additional industry research:

Investigate companies by their Standard Industrial Classification Codes, also known as SICs. Kelly Services' primary SIC is:

7363 Help Supply Services

KFC Corporation

OVERVIEW

KFC Corporation is the largest fast-food chicken franchiser in the world. The company operates more than 5,000 restaurants in the United States and approximately 5,200 more in 79 other countries. KFC is best known for its founder, Colonel Harland Sanders, and his Original Recipe Chicken, with its secret blend of 11 herbs and spices, and the unique package—the red and white bucket of fried chicken.

Colonel Sanders developed his chicken recipe over many years, introducing it at his service station and then at his motel and restaurant in Corbin, Kentucky. He signed his first franchise in 1952 and incorporated in 1955. The company has grown through a succession of owners, including John Y. Brown, Jr.; Jack Massey; Heublein Inc.; R.J. Reynolds Industries; and PepsiCo. In 1997 PepsiCo spun off its restaurant operations, and KFC became a wholly owned subsidiary of Tricon Global Restaurants, which also owns the other former PepsiCo restaurant chains, Taco Bell and Pizza Hut.

ALSO KNOWN AS: Kentucky Fried Chicken
FOUNDED: 1952

Contact Information:

HEADQUARTERS: PO Box 32070
　　Louisville, KY 40232
PHONE: (502)874-8300
FAX: (502)874-2195
URL: http://www.kfc.com

HISTORY

The history of KFC Corporation started long before the first restaurant opened. Harland Sanders (born in 1890) began cooking when he was six years old. His father had died and his mother was working two jobs, so it was up to him to care for his younger brother and sister. He left home at age 15 and held a variety of jobs until he opened a service station in 1929 in Corbin, Kentucky. He continued cooking and occasionally served

A complete KFC classic meal. *(Courtesy of KFC Corporation.)*

customers in his family's dining room in the back of the station. His cooking quickly became popular, so he purchased the motel across the street from his service station, which had a 142-seat restaurant.

In the 1930s the Harland Sanders Court and Cafe became a popular eating place, and Sanders developed his quick method of spicing and pressure-frying chicken. Kentucky's governor made him an honorary Kentucky Colonel, hence the name Colonel Sanders. In 1939 Duncan Hines endorsed the Harland Sanders Court and Cafe in the publication *Adventures in Good Eating.* Gas rationing during World War II cut tourism and forced Colonel Sanders to close temporarily, but after the war

he reopened and remained in business until 1956. Plans for the new I-75 freeway were to entirely bypass Corbin, and this forced the Colonel to sell his motel for $75,000— less than half of its value.

The Colonel began signing franchises in 1952 when he signed with Pete Harman in Salt Lake City, Utah. In 1955 he incorporated and registered the name Kentucky Fried Chicken. When he finally sold the Corbin store in 1956, Sanders, rather than living on his meager savings and Social Security, drove across the country giving samples of his chicken and demonstrations of his cooking methods. A restaurant owner got a franchise by shaking hands with the Colonel and agreeing to pay him a nickel

for each chicken sold. By 1963 Sanders had signed more than 600 franchises in the United States and Canada. By this time he was traveling more than 200,000 miles per year and the business was getting too large for him to run.

In 1964 he sold his interest in the company to a group of investors headed by John Y. Brown, Jr. and Jack Massey. Colonel Sanders agreed to remain the company's spokesman and roving ambassador. In three years the investment group transformed the loosely-knit, one-man operation into a smoothly run corporation. They changed the Colonel's concept of a diner to a fast-food, take-out store; they developed the company's distinctive red-and-white striped buildings; and they opened more than 1,500 take-out stores and restaurants in all 50 states, Canada, Great Britain, Mexico, and Japan. By 1967 Kentucky Fried Chicken was the sixth-largest (by volume) food-service company in the United States.

Kentucky Fried Chicken went public in 1969, but publicity about loose accounting practices caused its stock to plummet. In 1971 Kentucky Fried Chicken merged with Heublein Inc., yet the company remained without a focus throughout the 1970s. Kentucky Fried Chicken found its sales slackening as Heublein introduced many new products, acquired many new stores, and ignored quality control. Poor management also created friction between the parent company and the franchise owners. In 1977 Heublein decided to remake the company. Heublein limited the menu to focus on quality and cut costs, brought back the Colonel's cooking methods, spent $35 million on renovating store fronts, developed better relationships with franchise owners, and developed new marketing strategies. Colonel Sanders continued traveling, averaging 250,000 miles per year, until he was struck with leukemia in May 1980. He died seven months later.

R.J. Reynolds Industries (now RJR Nabisco, Inc.) acquired Heublein in 1982, and PepsiCo, Inc. bought Kentucky Fried Chicken from R.J. Reynolds in 1986. In 1991 Kentucky Fried Chicken changed its name to the KFC Corporation in anticipation of the addition of non-fried menu items. In 1997 PepsiCo spun off all its restaurant subsidiaries to create a new company, Tricon Global Restaurants, Inc. Tricon owns KFC, Taco Bell, and Pizza Hut. With 30,000 restaurants worldwide, Tricon is the world's largest restaurant system.

STRATEGY

In 1996 KFC settled a seven-year contract dispute with its franchisees. In settling the dispute, the company agreed to provide permanent territorial protection to franchisees. In return, KFC would have more direct say in advertising and public relations activities.

Independent of the settlement but in the same spirit of cooperation, KFC established a "Chefs' Council"

FAST FACTS:
About KFC Corporation

Ownership: KFC is a wholly owned subsidiary of Tricon Global Restaurants, Inc.

Ticker symbol: YUM

Officers: Jeff Moody, Pres. & Chief Concept Officer; Terry Davenport, Chief Marketing Officer; Rob Saxton, Chief People Officer; Kathy Corsi, CFO

Employees: 101,680

Chief Competitors: KFC competes with many fast-food, pizza, and restaurant chains. Some of its biggest competitors are: Boston Market; Cracker Barrel; Dairy Queen; Domino's Pizza; Little Caesar's; Long John Silver's; McDonald's; Outback Steakhouse; Ruby Tuesday; and Wendy's.

through which franchisees could have more input into product development. This group, composed of both company employees and franchisees, was responsible for introducing two new products, "Colonel's Crispy Strips" and "Chunky Chicken Pot Pie."

In early 1997 Tricon's CEO, David Novak, announced the "Team 6000" program under which KFC franchisees are urged to open at least one new restaurant each within five years, which would bring the number of KFC sites in the United States to 6,000 company-owned and franchised restaurants.

CURRENT TRENDS

The fast-food industry, always highly competitive, became even more so in the 1990s. In the mid-1990s KFC took several steps to "spice up" its image. It introduced a new logo that featured Colonel Sanders, as well as new packaging that spotlighted the Colonel and his famous fried chicken; brought back the famous bucket of chicken; introduced a number of new products; and focused on home delivery service from 300 of its restaurants.

In numerous cities Tricon restaurants serve both KFC and Taco Bell menus at the same location. This growing trend in the fast-food and gas station industries keeps site costs down and provides two-in-one exposure for the establishments.

CHRONOLOGY:

Key Dates for KFC Corporation

1929: Harland Sanders is selling food out of the back of his service station

1939: Harland Sanders Court and Cafe listed in Duncan Hines' *Adventures in Good Eating*

1945: The restaurant reopens after war-time shutdown due to gas rationing

1952: First Kentucky Fried Chicken franchise opens in Salt Lake City, Utah

1955: Sanders incorporates and registers the name Kentucky Fried Chicken

1956: Sanders sells the cafe

1964: Harland Sanders sells his interest to a group of investors

1971: Kentucky Fried Chicken merges with Heublein, Inc.

1982: R.J. Reynolds acquires Heublein and KFC

1986: PepsiCo purchases KFC

1991: The company name becomes KFC Corporation

1996: PepsiCo spins its restaurants off into Tricon Global Restaurants, Inc.

BIOGRAPHY:

Colonel Sanders

Born in Henryville, Indiana, in 1890, Colonel Harland D. Sanders' lifetime obsession with chicken began at an early age. After years of toil and experimentation, he finally perfected his secret blend of eleven herbs and spices by hand-mixing the spices on a concrete floor on the back porch of his home. He had opened a gas station in Corbin, Kentucky in 1929, and when he began to make some of his customers dinner, word of his "finger-lickin' good" chicken rapidly spread. He began franchising restaurants in 1952, then sold the franchise in 1964, with the provision that he be kept on the payroll for making public appearances. When he died in 1980, he was such a celebrity and revered public figure that his body lay in state in the Kentucky State Capital Rotunda.

PRODUCTS

The Colonel developed his secret blend of 11 herbs and spices while operating the Harland Sanders Court and Cafe. For many years he kept the recipe in his head and personally mixed the spices. The recipe is still a tightly guarded secret. One spice company mixes part of the recipe, and another company mixes the rest; neither company knows the entire recipe.

KFC serves a variety of chicken meals. In addition to their first product, the bucket of fried chicken (available in crispy, barbecued, and roasted styles as well as the Original Recipe version), KFC offers pot pies, roasted chicken, chicken strips, and sandwiches. Some overseas outlets also offer local variations. In Japan, for instance, the KFC menu offers salmon sandwiches in addition to fried chicken.

CORPORATE CITIZENSHIP

KFC sponsors several programs in the company's hometown of Louisville, Kentucky. In 1996 KFC began the "KFCares Neighborhood Partners Program." Each of the 25 KFC restaurants in Louisville received $1,000 to donate to a community project, chosen from proposals submitted by local residents. KFC also supports the "Project Jump Start" early education program in Louisville elementary schools.

GLOBAL PRESENCE

In 1997 KFC of North America (KFCNA) and its franchisees operated 10,200 restaurants in 79 countries worldwide; half of these restaurants were in the United States and Canada. The principal international markets for Tricon's restaurants (including KFC, Taco Bell, and Pizza Hut) are Australia, Japan, China, Korea, Mexico, Spain, New Zealand, Puerto Rico, and the United Kingdom. KFC places emphasis on developing the Asian and eastern European markets. It opened its first restaurant in China in 1987 and its first in Moscow in 1995.

SOURCES OF INFORMATION

Bibliography
"KFC Corporation." *International Directory of Company Histories,* Vol. 7. Detroit, MI: St. James Press, 1993.

KFC Home Page, 26 May 1998. Available at http://www.kfc.com.

"Tricon Global Restaurants." *Hoover's Handbook of American Business 1998.* Austin, TX: The Reference Press, 1997.

"Tricon Global Restaurants." *Standard and Poor's Stock Report,* 21 February 1998.

For additional industry research:
Investigate companies by their Standard Industrial Classification Codes, also known as SICs. KFC's primary SIC is:

5812 Eating Places

Kinko's Incorporated

FOUNDED: 1970

Contact Information:

HEADQUARTERS: 255 W. Stanley Ave.
   Ventura, CA 93002
PHONE: (805)652-4000
FAX: (805)652-4045
TOLL FREE: (800)254-6567
URL: http://www.kinkos.com

OVERVIEW

Kinko's is one of the biggest chains of document copying and business services stores in the world. The company has more than 850 stores equipped with high-speed, digital, and black-and-white copiers; computer rentals; custom printing and finishing services; faxes; mailing services; and overnight drop-off services. Almost all Kinko's stores (company officials prefer to call them "branch offices") are open 24-hours-a-day, 7-days-a-week. The company's goal is to have 2,000 stores by the year 2000.

On January 2, 1997, Kinko's announced the roll-up of the 130 decentralized joint venture, corporate, and partnership entities operating under its name into a single corporate structure. Kinko's founder, Paul J. Orfalea, stated, "Having a more centralized structure offers numerous benefits, including more standardized product, service and pricing structures, more consistent operating principles, . . . and more ownership and career opportunities for our co-workers."

In April 1997 Joseph Hardin, Jr. was named Kinko's Incorporated's president and chief executive officer. Hardin left his post as president and CEO of SAM's Clubs, the wholesale club division of Wal-Mart, to join Kinko's. Orfalea, the company's single-largest shareholder, was named chairperson of the company's 13-member board of directors; seven of its members would be nominated by Clayton, Dubilier & Rice (CD&R) Incorporated, a New York City-based private investment firm. CD&R had invested $214 million in Kinko's stock, representing 30 percent of Kinko's equity; Orfalea and the owners of existing Kinko's entities accounted for most of the remaining equity.

COMPANY FINANCES

Founder Paul Orfalea does not disclose annual sales figures, financial details, or ownership arrangements. However, according to one Los Angeles investment banking firm, the company's annual revenues from its stores exceeded $525 million when it had about 800 locations, based on an estimated $700,000 per store. *Forbes* magazine estimated that the chain posted more than $400 million per year in sales.

ANALYSTS' OPINIONS

Kinko's, once a tiny entity led by a counterculture figure, is now viewed as anything but small. Locally owned copy shops across the country see the California-based firm as a corporate Goliath. In the early 1990s the owners of eight printing, secretarial, and copy services in Sausalito, California, complained to the city council about Kinko's plans to open nearby. They, like the owners of many independent stores nationwide, were certain that Kinko's arrival would hasten their demise and quicken the arrival of a caravan of other national chains ranging from Burger King to Wendy's.

Kinko's has also raised the ire of publishers. A coalition of publishers sued the company for photocopying excerpts from copyrighted books as a service to professors and binding them into anthologies without permission. Kinko's lost the suit and was ordered to pay the plaintiffs $1.9 million in damages and legal fees.

Small business owners and others who use Kinko's 24-hour-a-day services are glad the company exists. One small business owner told the *Greater Lansing Business Monthly,* "Kinko's keeps me looking good with my clients. It's nice to know that if my equipment fails, I can zoom over to Kinko's." Similar opinions are echoed on the company's web site, where users are encouraged to post their own Kinko's stories.

HISTORY

In 1970 Paul Orfalea launched Kinko's with a $5,000 bank loan. The University of California at Santa Barbara graduate opened his first photocopy shop in Isla Vista, California, and christened it Kinko's—the nickname he was given because of his curly reddish hair. The first store, which he leased, shared space in a building that housed a hamburger stand. Orfalea's 100-square-foot establishment contained a rented Xerox copier, an offset press, and some stationery and school supplies. Once the store's clientele grew, the copier was rolled out onto the sidewalk and used as a self-service machine.

To finance new locations, Orfalea took on fellow students, who scouted the West Coast in search of colleges with more than 20,000 students. Once they found the colleges, the scouts set up shops close to the campuses. To save money, the student scouts slept in fraternity houses. Orfalea stuffed flyers in mailboxes and delivered orders, and spent the rest of his days working with fellow hippies he had hired to operate his company's machinery. In 1985 the company opened its first 24-hour store in Chicago.

Kinko's grew rapidly, and by 1990 there were 480 Kinko's locations. Around 1989 the company began moving away from serving college students and began targeting small-business owners. Kinko's operated 635 stores by 1993, 780 in 1995, and more than 850 by 1997.

As Kinko's sought to expand the range of services it offered, it entered into joint ventures and strategic alliances with other companies. For example, it teamed with GTE to link its stores to the World Wide Web through high-speed ISDN connections, and with Netscape Communications' Web browser for its growing fleet of rentable personal computers. When it decided to offer videoconferencing at selected locations, Kinko's teamed up with long-distance carrier Sprint.

In 1997 the company obtained much-needed financing for its expansion strategy when the private investment firm of Clayton, Dubilier & Rice (CD&R) purchased a 30-percent interest in the company for $214 million.

FAST FACTS:
About Kinko's Incorporated

Ownership: Kinko's Incorporated is a privately owned company.

Officers: Paul J. Orfalea, Chmn.; Joseph Hardin, Jr., Pres. & CEO; Karen Sophiea, VP-Marketing

Employees: 23,000

Chief Competitors: Kinko's competes with other companies that offer copying and printing services and access to computers and other business machines, including: Sir Speedy; PIP Printing; American Speedy Printing Centers; Office Depot; and Office-Max.

CHRONOLOGY:

Key Dates for Kinko's Incorporated

1970: Paul Orfalea opens the first Kinko's

1973: Kinko's opens a Los Angeles branch in an old photo booth

1982: Color copies become available at Kinko's

1985: Kinko's opens its first 24-hour shop in Chicago, Illinois

1993: Sprint and Kinko's announce an alliance to offer videoconferencing

1995: Kinkonet, Kinko's electronic document transfer system, is introduced

1997: Clayton, Dublier, & Rice purchase a 30 percent interest in the company

STRATEGY

When competitors such as Sir Speedy and PIP Printing began offering copying services similar to Kinko's, Orfalea shifted gears. His focus centered on a new clientele: small-business owners. A growing number of them were seeking more realistic copies of documents, in larger sizes and in color, as well as sophisticated graphics. So Orfalea began opening 7,000-square-foot stores in suburbs and business districts. In doing so, Kinko's has cashed in on medium and large companies, as well as the small-business market, particularly the growing number of self-employed and home-office workers.

To service all of its new customers, Orfalea provided them access to sophisticated equipment such as laser and color copiers. Instead of buying the machines, he leased them, reducing the need for fresh capital and allowing the company to constantly upgrade its equipment.

Kinko's also introduced new telecommunications and technological services, such as videoconferencing, Internet access, document delivery, e-mail accounts, and other services that would be useful to people conducting business on the road or at remote locations.

In April 1997 Kinko's newly formed alliance with Clayton, Dubilier & Rice was expected to help finance Kinko's international expansion and its ongoing penetration of the U.S. market. Investment proceeds were also expected to be used to finance communication and computing technologies. Prior to forming the alliance, Kinko's launched Kinko's Corporate, an initiative aimed at servicing the needs of larger companies.

INFLUENCES

Over the years, Kinko's has developed a customer base whose loyalty to the company has as much to do with its accessibility and plethora of products and services as it does to the company's focus on customer service.

"Our primary objective is to take care of our customers," the company says in its philosophy statement. "We are proud of our ability to serve them in a timely, helpful manner, and to provide high quality at a reasonable price. We develop long-term relationships that promote mutual growth and prosperity."

CURRENT TRENDS

With the growing number of home-office workers, telecommuters, and self-employed people working at home, Kinko's began promoting itself as "The New Way to Office" in 1997. It began offering a wider range of services, from faxing and Internet access to electronic document distribution and computer rentals. These services also address the needs of mobile professionals who often find themselves away from their offices.

Small businesses continue to be an important target market for Kinko's. By offering access to expensive office equipment and services, Kinko's allows customers to "test drive" high-end technical equipment before making a purchase decision. In many cases, customers can access the equipment at Kinko's without having to make a large capital outlay to own it.

Kinko's recently expanded into new geographic locations to better serve its core customers (small office and home office workers and owners) and closed some of its locations in college towns. In 1997 it announced plans to open more than 30 new Kinko's branches in the metropolitan New York area, especially in suburban Westchester County and Connecticut's Fairfield County, between 1997 and 1999. The fact that Fairfield County is home to more Fortune 500 companies than any other county in the United States also fits in with Kinko's plans to market its services to larger corporations.

In 1997 Kinko's announced plans to open two branches in London, England, in a joint venture with the Virgin Group, a diversified British company that operates music retailing and recording businesses and an airline.

Another recent development took place at the Kinko's Copy Center in Riverside, California, when the Glendale Federal Bank opened a mini-branch there in mid-1997. The bank, believed to be the first to open a branch in a copy center, opened its first branch in a Kinko's in February 1997 in Simi Valley, California. That location attracted $3 million in deposits within the first few months. The bank hopes to reach the small-business owners who use Kinko's services and plans to open in as many as 20 California Kinko's branches over the next year.

PRODUCTS

Kinko's "products" are actually services. One of Kinko's most recent services is Kinkonet (SM), an electronic document delivery service. It electronically sends documents from one Kinko's store to another anywhere in the world. With the aid of free Kinkonet software, a customer can send a document from an office, home, or laptop computer to Kinko's. A Kinkonet worker takes the work request, confirms receipt of it and quotes the customer a price, and then electronically sends it to one or more Kinkonet locations. The company said it built the system with full security devices to ensure that customer information would remain confidential.

On August 1, 1997, Kinko's began offering high-speed Internet access using ISDN lines, which were about 10 times faster than conventional Internet connections. These connections also allowed customers to check their e-mail.

Utilizing new digital printing technology, Kinko's can produce high-quality, full-color copies as fast as 40 copies per minute. Customers can also make use of Kinko's design services to assist in the creation of brochures and other materials.

Some high-tech services, such as compact disk creation and videoconferencing, are only available at selected locations. Videoconferencing is offered at approximatley 140 locations, and up to 15 Kinko's locations can be linked together. If a particular service isn't offered at a location, Kinko's can arrange to set up the services for customers.

In August 1997 Kinko's announced it would begin offering customers free e-mail accounts through a partnership with national e-mail provider Hotmail. Other recently introduced services include KinkoCards (SM), which allows customers to send a free animated greeting card.

CORPORATE CITIZENSHIP

Kinko's uses recycled and chlorine-free paper as well as computer programs that recycle copy paper waste. The company engages in numerous acts of good citizenship. In the early 1990s, for example, the 35 stores of

Kinko's of Ohio Incorporated bought the states of Ohio, Pennsylvania, New York, and New Jersey 70,000 tree seedlings as recompense for paper Kinko's had used.

Kinko's "Environmental Vision Statement" includes the following principles: maximize the use of recycled and environmentally benign raw materials while minimizing the use of virgin natural resources; require waste reduction, product take-back, and sustainable natural resource management programs from our business partners; use energy-efficient technologies and renewable energy sources; continuously strive to eliminate all nonrecyclable waste streams; foster mutually beneficial relationships with businesses that use our by-products as raw materials; and promote the use and sale of environmentally friendly products.

GLOBAL PRESENCE

Only 20 or so of Kinko's 850 branches are located outside the United States. Those are located in Canada, the Netherlands, Japan, South Korea, and Australia. A couple of new locations in London, England, are planned for 1998.

EMPLOYMENT

Kinko's employed about 23,000 people worldwide in 1997 and operated approximately 850 branches, including about 20 in Canada, the Netherlands, Japan, South Korea, and Australia. The staff at a Kinko's location ranges from 20 to 60 people. Although Kinko's is an expanding business in an expanding business world, it tries to make its employees feel like they're members of the Kinko's family.

SOURCES OF INFORMATION

Bibliography

Brooks, Nancy Rivera. "Kinko's to Enter Virgin (Group) Territory." *Los Angeles Times,* 15 July 1997.

Crooks, Michael. "Depend on Kinko's." *Greater Lansing Business Monthly,* November 1997.

Karon, Paul. "The Cutting Edge: Small Office/Home Office." *Los Angeles Times,* 16 June 1997.

"Kinko's Announces New CEO." Kinko's Press Release, 21 April 1997. Available at http://www.kinkos.com/press.press/4964833.

"Kinko's Completes Roll-Up of its 130 Ventures to Become a Unified Corporation: Clayton, Dubilier & Rice Fund Provides $214 Million Equity Investment." Kinko's Press Release, 2 January 1997. Available at http://www.kinkos.com/press/press9176224.

Kinko's Home Page, 19 May 1998. Available at http://www.kinkos.com.

"Kinko's Turns 25 with a Jolt." *Graphic Arts Monthly,* December 1995.

McAuliffe, Don. "Glendale Federal Bets the Bank on Kinko's." *Press Enterprise-Riverside, California,* 14 June 1997.

Monnesh, Sheldon. "Original Copy Cats: Founded with a Loan from a Bank Once Torched by 60s Protesters, Kinko's Now Has Some 800 Copy Shops across the Country. Still, it's Run by Renegade Hippies." 16 May 1997. Available at http://www.wired.com/wired/3.06/departments/electrosphere/kinkos.html.

Moukheiber, Zina. "I'm Just a Peddler." (Kinko's Graphics Corp. Founder Paul Orfalea). *Forbes,* 17 July 1995.

Prenon, Mary T. "Kinko's Unveils Expansion Plan." *Westchester County Business Journal,* 18 August 1997.

Stroh, Michael. "Kinko's Graduates to a Higher Strata." *The Sacramento Bee,* 15 October 1997.

For additional industry research:

Investigate companies by their Standard Industrial Classification Codes, also known as SICs. Kinko's primary SICs are:

7334 Photocopying and Duplicating Services

7377 Computer Rental and Leasing

7389 Business Services, NEC

Kmart Corporation

FOUNDED: 1899

OVERVIEW

Kmart Corporation is the third largest retail chain in the United States behind Wal-Mart and Sears. After reporting staggering losses in 1995 and 1996, Kmart returned to profitability in 1997. Its strategy of returning to its core business as a discount retailer and mass merchandise retailer seemed to be paying off. Since 1993 the company has sold off all its non-core businesses as well as all of its international operations to focus on serving customers in the United States as well as Puerto Rico, Guam, and the U.S. Virgin Islands.

According to the *Kmart Fact Book 1997*, "Kmart's primary target customer group is women between the ages of 25 and 45 years old, with children at home and with household incomes between $20,000 and $50,000 per year." To better serve its core customers, Kmart introduced new product lines such as the Martha Stewart Everyday and Sesame Street lines in 1997, while it implemented hundreds of initiatives aimed at improving customers' shopping experience and the overall performance of the company.

As Kmart refocused itself on its core business, it converted many of its traditional stores into a new prototype called "Big Kmart." Big Kmart stores feature a new layout, an expanded consumable goods section, brighter lighting, wider aisles, and a bigger assortment of goods. By the end of 1997 there were 670 Big Kmart stores operating in several major markets. The company planned to open an additional seven new Big Kmart stores with 520 conversions in 1998. In addition, the company had 99 Super Kmart stores in operation at the end of 1997, with plans to open 3 more in 1998. The Super Kmart centers have about 12.5 million square feet of

Contact Information:

HEADQUARTERS: 3100 W. Big Beaver Rd.
  Troy, MI 48084
PHONE: (248)643-1000
FAX: (248)643-5249
TOLL FREE: (800)635-6278
URL: http://www.kmart.com

FINANCES:

Kmart
Sales, 1994-1997
(billion dollars)

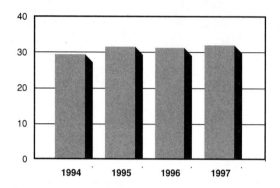

Kmart
1997 Stock Prices
(dollars)

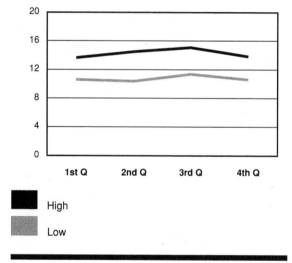

selling space and offer full-service shopping convenience from groceries to general merchandise. They are open 7-days-a-week, 24-hours-a-day.

COMPANY FINANCES

After reporting net losses of $571 million in 1995 and $220 million in 1996 on relatively flat sales of $31.7 and $31.4 billion, Kmart completed its financial turnaround in 1997 with a net income of $249 million on sales of $32.2 billion. Sales per square foot grew from $201 in 1996 to $211 in 1997, due primarily to the successful conversion of an additional 458 traditional Kmart locations to the Big Kmart format. Successful product introductions, such as Martha Stewart Everyday home fashions and Sesame Street children's apparel, also contributed to the company's improved financial performance.

From 1992 to 1996, Kmart's stock lost more than half its market value as share prices plunged from around $24.50 at the end of 1992 (after reaching an all-time high of $28.14 in November 1992) to $10.39 at the end of 1996 (after reaching a low point of $5.89 in early 1996). In 1997 the stock was trading in the $10-$15 range, buoyed by the company's return to profitability. The company's fourth quarter profits in 1997 were the best in five years, prompting analysts to begin recommending Kmart stock.

ANALYSTS' OPINIONS

Analysts and others who followed Kmart appeared convinced the company had been successfully turned around under Floyd Hall's leadership, especially after its strong financial performance in 1997 and the first quarter of 1998. For example, William Armstrong, an analyst with Fahnestock & Co., was quoted in the *Detroit Free Press* after Kmart announced its 1998 first quarter results: "Kmart was really screwed up a few years ago, but they've made comprehensive improvements in management and store-level management, in streamlining national brands and editing their entire merchandise assortment into fewer but better brands."

Kurt Barnard, president of *Barnard's Retail Trend Report* and one of Kmart's harshest critics, said, "Kmart really has managed a turnaround. It's very real, and Kmart has become a formidable competitor in America's retail market place. They've not only plugged the hole in the sinking ship, the engines are going full-speed ahead."

HISTORY

Sebastian S. Kresge founded the S.S. Kresge Company in 1899. It became one of the largest dimestore chains in the United States. The company opened the first Kmart discount department store in 1962 in Garden City, Michigan, a suburb of Detroit. In 1966 company sales topped the $1 billion mark for the first time. There were 162 Kmart stores and 915 total stores in operation. In 1976 S.S. Kresge opened a record 271 Kmart stores in one year. The next year, 15 years after opening the first Kmart store, the company name was changed from S.S. Kresge Co. to Kmart Corporation.

A BIG Kmart storefront. *(Courtesy of Kmart Corporation.)*

In the late 1970s the company bought the Walden Book Company and in the 1980s bought Builders Square, a chain of home improvement stores. In 1981 the two-thousandth Kmart store was opened. By 1985 Kmart owned PayLess Drug Stores Northwest and Bargain Harold's Discount Outlets in Canada. Kmart also ventured into warehouse club retailing, opening PACE Warehouse with a company called Makro. In 1987 it sold most U.S. Kresge and Jupiter stores. Kmart bought The Sports Authority in 1990 and sold PACE Warehouse to Wal-Mart in 1994.

In the early 1990s Wal-Mart leaped ahead of both Kmart and Sears as the leader in the industry. By 1991 Kmart's older and less attractive stores with slimmer merchandise couldn't keep up with Wal-Mart's ultra-modern reputation. Kmart's sales and market share fell behind this mega-merchandiser.

Kmart fought on and bought a large portion of OfficeMax in 1991. In 1992 Kmart purchased 76 percent of Maj, a Czechoslovakian department store. It also announced plans to build 100 stores in Mexico with Grupo Liverpool. Also in that year, the company bought Borders, a chain of book stores. In 1994-95, Kmart spun off OfficeMax and The Sports Authority as public companies through initial public offerings (IPOs) of stock. Proceeds to Kmart were $1 billion for OfficeMax and $405 million for The Sports Authority. It also sold its interest in Coles Meyer in Australia. Facing falling profit margins, Kmart continued to sell its investments. In 1995

Borders Group became a publicly traded company through an IPO; proceeds to Kmart were $566 million.

Searching for a new strategy, Kmart brought in a new CEO, Floyd Hall, and a new management team and board of directors were put in place. More than 200 stores were closed by the mid-1990s, and the company set about to restructure itself and focus on its core business. Rumors of bankruptcy swarmed Wall Street, but Kmart put out a letter in 1996 stating it had no intention of filing such a claim.

In 1996 and 1997 Kmart continued to divest itself of its non-core businesses and its international operations, including its Czech and Slovak stores. Thrifty Payless was spun off as a public company in 1996. In 1997 Kmart sold its interest in Kmart Mexico and all of its Kmart Canada stores. Finally, it divested itself of Builders Square in 1997.

STRATEGY

Kmart was originally a general merchandise discount store. The company got into financial trouble when it tried to diversify into a variety of specialty stores, from book stores to home improvement centers. Since Floyd Hall became head of the company in 1995, Kmart has refocused on its core business. Hall conducted a study to determine a profile for the target Kmart shopper. He

FAST FACTS:

About Kmart Corporation

Ownership: Kmart is a publicly owned company traded on the New York, Chicago, and Pacific Stock Exchanges.

Ticker symbol: KM

Officers: Floyd Hall, Chmn. of the Board, Pres., & CEO, 58, $2,749,500; Donald W. Keeble, Exec. VP Store Operations, 48, $861,200; Laurence L. Anderson, Exec. VP & Pres., Super Kmart, 55; Warren F. Cooper, Exec. VP, Human Resources & Administration, 52

Employees: 265,000

Chief Competitors: Kmart's primary competitors are other discount retailers, especially: Wal-Mart; Target; J.C. Penney; and Sears.

found out that Kmart's primary target customer group was women between the ages of 25 and 45 years old, with children at home and with household incomes between $20,000 and $50,000 per year. Of the 180 million people that shop at Kmart each year, 57 percent are women and 43 percent are men. The core Kmart shopper visited the store an average of 4.3 times a month and made an average purchase of $40 each visit. These core shoppers accounted for 60 percent of total store revenues.

According to Kmart's annual report, the company is focused "on improving our customers' shopping experience through stronger assortments, better stores, convenient service and quality products at great prices." The company's merchandising strategy was focused on three areas: frequently purchased goods, popular national brands, and high-quality private label offerings. Its strategy was to improve its assortment of dominant national brands and be aggressive in pricing them. It wanted to complement that with a strong line of private label products, which included the Martha Stewart Everyday line of home fashions, the Sesame Street collection for children, and Jaclyn Smith and Kathy Ireland apparel, as well as Penske Automotive products and more.

Part of the company's strategy of improving its customers' shopping experience was to convert its older stores into Big Kmart stores, with brighter lighting, wider aisles, bigger assortments, and an expanded consumable goods section. Super Kmart centers have opened, which

feature about 12.5 million square feet of selling space, a broad selection of general merchandise and apparel, and a full assortment of groceries. Super Kmart centers are open 24-hours-a-day, 7-days-a-week. The first Super Kmart center opened in 1991 and numbered nearly 100 by the end of 1997.

Another aspect of Kmart's real estate strategy was to develop a five-year plan for each of the company's top 30 metropolitan markets. Within each of those regions, made up of both urban and suburban areas, Kmart planned to expand its presence.

INFLUENCES

Kmart's poor financial performance of 1995 and 1996 was attributed to overdiversification and a lack of focus. With the company returning to profitability in 1997, Kmart's strategy is driven by the lessons it learned from the past. It is focused on providing its core shoppers with a better shopping experience. It will continue to do what it does best, namely, to provide an assortment of general merchandise at discounted prices.

The company is also influenced by the strong performance of other mass merchandisers, especially Wal-Mart and Sears. It will compete with them in the area of general merchandise, attempting to offer a bigger and better assortment that is more aggressively priced than its competitors. It is unlikely that Kmart will again try to branch out into specialty stores.

CURRENT TRENDS

Now that Kmart has divested its specialty stores and all of its international operations, it is focused on implementing initiatives that will improve customers' experience in the stores and the overall performance of the business. In 1997 the company entered into a strategic alliance with Little Caesars and unveiled a new "KCafe" prototype in about 750 stores.

The company had a more aggressive marketing program in 1997, issuing its first-ever toy catalog. Online shopping and other electronic in-store services were planned for 1998. In 1997 the company introduced an on-line application process for the Kmart credit card. It also introduced an electronic swipe card called the Kmart Cash Card, which replaced Kmart's paper gift certificates and includes a calling card feature provided by AT&T.

PRODUCTS

The company's new products consist of private label brand merchandise and apparel. One of the successes

CHRONOLOGY:

Key Dates for Kmart Corporation

1962: S.S. Kresge opens the first Kmart discount department store in Garden City, Michigan

1966: Sales top $1 billion for the first time

1976: Kresge opens a record 271 stores in one year

1977: The S.S. Kresge Co. becomes Kmart Corporation

1984: Kmart acquires Walden Book Company and Builders Square

1990: Purchases The Sports Authority

1992: The first Super Kmart opens; Purchases Borders Group

1994: The company begins to sell off its non-core business by spinning off Office Max and the Sports Authority

1995: Sells Borders Group

1997: Enters into an agreement with Little Caesars for its KCafe

---

of 1997 was the rollout in March of the Martha Stewart Everyday line of home fashions. In August the Sesame Street line of children's apparel was introduced. It includes clothes for newborns, infants, and toddlers as well as products such as toys, books, and accessories for all ages.

CORPORATE CITIZENSHIP

Kmart has an impressive record of sponsorship, particularly in the March of Dimes WalkAmerica. Kmart has participated faithfully and has consistently been the nation's leading team in this program since 1985. Kmart alone raised $2.5 million for the March of Dimes in 1997.

Kmart also hosts the Kmart Kids Race Against Drugs program. Kids between the ages of 7 and 13 race a converted lawn tractor on a specially designed track at a chosen Kmart location. The racer with the fastest time in each age group receives a 5-foot trophy and a $10,000 scholarship. Stars have been known to make appearances during the event such as Kathy Ireland (model and actress), Michael Andretti (Kmart CART driver), Jeremy Mayfield (Kmart NASCAR driver), Sam Jones (NBA Hall-of-Famer), and Terrell Buckley (Miami Dolphin quarterback). D.A.R.E. (Drug Abuse Resistance Education) representatives have made appearances as well.

Kmart has also been rewarded for its development of the ConSern Loans for Education™ program. This program provides education financing for Kmart associates and their families. The company has assisted over 2,600 individuals in their education and has provided almost $16 million in their efforts.

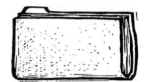

SOMETHING FOR EVERYONE

You're taking care of the last-minute packing for your spring break trip, and suddenly you realize you forgot to pick up suntan lotion. Chances are you're included in the 80 percent of the U.S. population who are within a 15-minute drive of a Kmart store. Over 180 million people shop each year at Kmart, and odds are they're carrying what you need. Each year, Kmart stores stock more than 100,000 items, everything from candy bars to camping gear. Need to do some planting? Kmart sells 83,000 tons of potting soil each year, the equivalent of 342 blue whales. Or perhaps your house is just screaming for a fresh coat of paint. Kmart sells enough paint each year to paint a foot-wide line around the globe 35 times. So when you're looking for that certain something, you just might find it at Kmart.

GLOBAL PRESENCE

As of 1998, Kmart stores were located only in the United States, Puerto Rico, Guam, and the U.S. Virgin Islands. In 1997 Kmart Canada was sold to the Hudson's Bay Company, involving 112 Kmart stores at a price of $54 million. The company's Czech and Slovak operations were sold off in 1996 for $115 million.

EMPLOYMENT

With some 265,000 Kmart associates, Kmart was the sixth largest employer in the United States at the end of 1996. With a renewed emphasis on customer service, Kmart is committed to attracting, retaining, and developing the most talented and highly motivated associates in retailing. Associates may work in a store, distribution center, or at Kmart's headquarters. They are hired and retained on the basis of high standards of performance. Kmart recognizes that its employees are one of its most valuable resources and that success is attained through teamwork. Kmart provides equal employment opportunities regardless of race, religion, color, national origin, sex, or disability.

SOURCES OF INFORMATION

Bibliography

Brauer, Molly. "Kmart Earnings Point to Recovery." *Detroit Free Press,* 14 May 1998.

"For Kmart, Cost-Cutting Pays Off." *The New York Times,* 6 March 1997.

"Kmart Announces Turnaround Strategy." *Gazette Telegraph Online,* 17 February 1996. Available at http://www.gazette.com.

"Kmart Corporation." *Hoover's Online,* 16 March 1997. Available at http://www.hoovers.com.

"Kmart Corporation Announces First Quarter 1998 Earnings; Net Income Increases 236 Percent to $0.10 Per Share." *PR Newswire,* 13 May 1998.

"Kmart Corporation Honored for Its commitment to Providing Education Opportunities for Its Associates and Their Families."

Yahoo! On the Money, 3 December 1996. Available at http://www.yahoo.com.

Kmart Fact Book 1997. Troy, MI: Kmart Corporation, 1997.

Kmart Home Page, 16 March 1997. Available at http://www.kmart.com.

Olijnyk, Zena. "Bay Snaps up Kmart." *Financial Post-Toronto,* 7 February 1998.

Pollock, James. "Kmart Hustles to Get Back in the Game." *Marketing Magazine,* 9 December 1996.

Preddy, Melissa. "Kmart Growth Continues: Emphasis on Revamped Stores, Lower Prices is Paying Off, Hall Says." *Detroit News,* 27 February 1998.

Preddy, Melissa, and David Howes. "Kmart Crafts a Comeback Team." *The Detroit News,* 2 February 1996.

Robinson, Edward A. "America's Most Admired Companies." *Fortune,* 3 March 1997.

"S&P Revises Kmart Corp. (K Mart Corp.) Outlook to Stable." *Yahoo! On the Money,* 14 March 1997.

Sellers, Patricia. "Kmart is Down for the Count." *Fortune,* 15 January 1996.

White, George. "K-Ching!; Kmart Trying to Boost Image, Products." *Los Angeles Times,* 20 February 1998.

For an annual report:

telephone: (248)643-1040 **or** write: Investor Relations, Kmart Corp., 3100 W. Big Beaver Rd., Troy, MI 48084-3163

For additional industry research:

Investigate companies by their Standard Industrial Classification Codes, also known as SICs. Kmart's primary SIC is:

5331 Retail-Variety Stores

Kraft Foods, Inc.

FOUNDED: 1989

OVERVIEW

Kraft Foods, Inc. is a wholly owned subsidiary of Philip Morris Companies, Inc. with more than 70 of the world's best-known brands in almost every category of grocery product, making it the largest manufacturer and distributor of packaged foods in North America. Kraft has 65 manufacturing plants in the United States and Canada, as well as a network of 18 distribution centers. The company posted North American revenues of almost $17 billion in 1997.

Kraft is in the process of selling off nonprofitable, noncore businesses while acquiring others that meet its needs. Four of the Kraft brands have annual sales of more than $1 billion (Kraft, Oscar Mayer, Maxwell House, and Post), and 25 brands post sales of between $100 million and $1 billion annually. Kraft spends heavily in research and development, introducing new products frequently. Kraft brands are backed by some of the industry's largest marketing and advertising campaigns, as well as some of the best tie-ins to other products and charities.

COMPANY FINANCES

In 1997 Kraft had sales of $16.8 billion, up from $16.5 billion in 1996, an increase of almost 2 percent. Higher sales were attributed to increased volume, pricing, and acquisitions. Net earnings rose to $2.9 billion in 1997 from $2.6 billion in 1996. Higher volume, price increases, and lower costs were all credited with fueling the rise in profits. Sales increases in frozen pizzas, ready-to-drink beverages, Taco Bell grocery products, desserts,

Contact Information:
HEADQUARTERS: 3 Lakes Dr.
   Northfield, IL 60093-2753
PHONE: (847)646-2000
FAX: (847)646-2922
URL: http://www.kraftfoods.com

FAST FACTS:

About Kraft Foods, Inc.

Ownership: Kraft Foods, Inc. is a wholly owned subsidiary of Philip Morris Companies Inc., which is a publicly owned company traded on the New York Stock Exchange.

Ticker symbol: MO

Officers: Bob Eckert, Pres. & CEO, 43; Todd C. Brown, Exec. VP & Pres., Kraft Foods Division; Mary Kay Haben, Exec. VP; Betsy D. Holden, Exec. VP & Pres., Kraft Cheese Division

Employees: 39,000 (North America), 73,000 (worldwide)

Principal Subsidiary Companies: Kraft is organized into eight business divisions: beverages and desserts; coffee and cereals; Kraft Canada; Kraft Cheese; Kraft Food Services; The New Meals Division; Oscar Mayer Foods; and pizza.

Chief Competitors: Kraft competes against a variety of businesses, including a number of large manufacturers of food products. There are competitors on both the national and regional levels, as well as those who produce generic and private-label foods. Kraft's major competitors include: General Mills; Kellogg; Nabisco; Pillsbury; Procter & Gamble; and Sara Lee.

and snacks drove Kraft's revenues and profits higher in 1997.

HISTORY

Kraft Foods, Inc. was formed in 1989 and is the result of the combination of three turn-of-the-century companies: Kraft, General Foods, and Oscar Mayer. Each of these companies made significant contributions to the food processing sector.

Kraft was founded in 1903 by J.L. Kraft, who started in Chicago by purchasing and reselling cheese. Kraft's brothers soon became involved in the business, then known as J.L. Kraft & Bros. Co. The company began manufacturing processed cheese in 1914, and the products were soon used by the U.S. armed services during World War I. The company became known for its sponsorship of various radio and television shows, such as the Kraft Music Hall. In 1930, Kraft-Phoenix Cheese Corporation was acquired by National Dairy Products Corporation; the company operated as an independent subsidiary. The parent company changed its name to Kraftco Corporation in 1969, then to Kraft, Inc. in 1976.

In 1895, C.W. Post made his first cereal in Battle Creek, Michigan. Soon he added Grape-Nuts and Elijah's Manna to the original Postum cereal. Post was the first food manufacturer to use advertising, coupons, samples, product demonstrations, and other now-standard techniques to reach consumers. Post died in 1914, but the company continued operations. Postum Cereal Company acquired the Jell-O company in 1925 and began a four-year campaign of acquisitions and heavy product marketing. These acquisitions included the rights to a new process of quick freezing food developed by Clarence Birdseye. The allied companies went through various name changes, with the parent corporation eventually being renamed General Foods Corporation. In addition to Jell-O, the company developed such products as Maxwell House instant coffee, Tang breakfast beverage crystals, and Cool Whip nondairy whipped topping.

Oscar Mayer, a Bavarian immigrant, started his career in the meat business in 1873 as a Detroit meat market "butcher's boy." With the help of his two brothers, he leased a failing Chicago meat market and made it so successful that in 1888 the landlord refused to renew the brothers' lease. The Mayers started from scratch down the street, exacting revenge on the landlord by forcing him out of business. The company specialized in "Old World" meats, sausages, and hams, and had a reputation for quality and customer service. In 1906 it was among the first companies to join the federal meat inspection program. In 1919 the company bought a plant in Madison, Wisconsin, which soon became corporate headquarters. The company, which was a leader in the processed meats industry, continued as an independent meat processor, operated by the Mayer family for about a century. In 1981 Oscar Mayer's stockholders voted to sell the company to General Foods Corporation in order to continue the growth of the business.

In 1985 General Foods Corporation was acquired by Philip Morris Companies Inc. Three years later, Philip Morris purchased Kraft Inc. In 1989 the two companies were combined, forming Kraft General Foods, Inc. The company's name was changed to Kraft Foods, Inc. in January 1995 and reorganized into 11 different divisions, reflecting the company's vast product lines.

STRATEGY

From 1995 to 1997, Kraft and Kraft International sold off several businesses in order to concentrate on key brands and best-selling items. Gone from North American operations in 1997 was a syrup business; in 1996 the company's bagel business was sold; and in 1995 Kraft got rid of its bakery, margarine, specialty oils, marshmallows, caramels, and food service distribution businesses. At the same time, other businesses were acquired to add to Kraft's reputation as a seller of well-known brands. In 1995 Kraft bought Del Monte puddings and in 1996 acquired Taco Bell grocery products.

Through 1996 Kraft made a push to increase brand recognition, particularly for its non-Kraft name brands such as Tombstone and DiGiorno. Prime, a direct-mail program tested by Kraft executives in upstate New York, was just one of the many advertising and consumer incentive programs. The company drew upon a database with data on more than 30 million households to create custom coupon mailings. Another of these programs was "Kraft Simple Answers," a direct-mail and promotion program.

One brand name for which Kraft consistently has attempted to buoy market share is Tang. While the drink doesn't have a large impact on the bottom line, it is a sentimental favorite of the company. Every few years, Kraft tries to get behind Tang, most recently in early 1997 with a campaign targeted at consumers between the ages of 9 and 14. Tang sales were down 13.7 percent in 1995 and 0.9 percent in 1996. The company also did consumer testing designed to reincarnate the powdered space-age beverage as "Extreme Orange."

In another promotion in 1995, Kraft cut prices on its Post and Nabisco lines of cereal by 20 percent. The desired result was to increase long-term business within those brands. Kraft is pushing new cereals and backing the introductions with heavy advertising and marketing, including more than $45 million for the introduction of Oreo O's cereal in 1998.

Kraft is also making a renewed push into the specialty coffee market. Iced coffee and cappuccino sales are expected to reach $2.2 billion, with 41 million people drinking specialty coffee by 2005. Currently, grocery store sales represent only 29 percent of this market, and Kraft wants to push that higher with a new line of iced coffees.

With children having more say in the spending of family budgets, Kraft decided to launch two major promotions each year that tie into children's products. In 1998 the two were the Kraft/Cartoon Network "Get Tooned" promotion, featuring Macaroni and Cheese with superhero shapes; and a tie-in between Nintendo's Yoshi's Story software and Kool-Aid drink mixes and ready-to-drink Bursts.

INFLUENCES

Two of the biggest influences within Kraft Foods Inc. are new product introductions and high international coffee prices. New flavor introductions in the Jell-O line

CHRONOLOGY:
Key Dates for Kraft Foods, Inc.

1895: The Postum Cereal Company, Ltd. is incorporated

1909: James L. Kraft's wholesale cheese distribution business is incorporated as J.L. Kraft & Bros. Company

1915: Kraft develops a cheese that does not spoil and could be packaged in small tins

1924: The company becomes Kraft Cheese Company and goes public

1925: Postum purchases the Jell-O Company

1928: Kraft merges with the Phenix Cheese Corporation to become Kraft-Phenix Cheese Corporation; Postum acquires Maxwell House Coffee

1929: Postum changes the name to General Foods; acquires Birdseye frozen foods

1930: National Dairy Products Corp. purchases Kraft-Phenix

1937: Kraft introduces their famous Macaroni and Cheese dinner

1945: The company becomes Kraft Foods Company

1957: National Dairy reorganizes and turns the subsidiaries into divisions of a single operating company; General Foods purchases the SOS company

1969: National Dairy becomes Kraftco Corporation

1976: Name changes again to Kraft, Inc.

1980: Dart Industries, owner of Tupperware and Duracell, merges with Kraft to become Dart & Kraft

1981: General Foods purchases Oscar Mayer

1985: Philip Morris purchases General Foods

1986: Dart & Kraft is dissolved, Kraft keeps its product line and gains Duracell

1988: Philip Morris purchases Kraft

1989: Philip Morris merges Kraft with General Foods, creating Kraft General Foods, Inc.

1995: Kraft General Foods is realigned into 11 divisions and the name is changed to Kraft, Inc.

have stimulated interest in new and old products, as have the addition of fat-free or reduced-fat products and new items, such as Post Blueberry Morning cereal. The high prices for green coffee beans, particularly the volatility of those prices and their impact on consumers, dramatically changed consumer buying patterns and increased competition within the various lines of coffees, especially in international markets.

Another recent development has been the cereal wars; major companies have been cutting prices and offering larger discounts on coupons. In 1996 and 1997 Kraft developed an aggressive pricing strategy on cereals, offered high-value coupons, and introduced consumer choice coupons. These coupons allow consumers to choose which cereal or cereals to take the discount.

PRODUCTS

The list of Kraft Foods Inc. products includes coffees such as Maxwell House, Sanka, General Foods International coffees, and Maxim; Country Time, Kool-Aid, and Tang drink mixes; Nabisco and Post cereals; Kraft, Miracle Whip, Bull's-Eye, and Sauceworks sauces and condiments; Altoids mints; Tobler and Toblerone chocolates; Jell-O; Shake 'N Bake; Minute Rice; Stove Top; Dream Whip whipped topping mix; Good Seasons salad dressing mixes; Velveeta products, including Velveeta Shells and Cheese; cheeses of all sorts under the brand names Kraft, Velveeta, Old English, Cracker Barrel, Light n' Lively, Athenos, DiGiorno, Polly-O, Philadelphia Brand, Knudson, and others; processed meats under the Louis Rich and Oscar Mayer brands; Cool Whip; Tombstone, Jack's, and DiGiorno pizzas; and Claussen pickles, as well as many other grocery items.

New products are regularly rolled out. In 1998, introductions were planned for Macaroni and Cheese Super Hero Shapes, Cappuccino Coolers, and Oreo O's cereal. Kraft wants to build up both its Minute Rice and Macaroni and Cheese brands, and in 1998-1999 will introduce Cheesy Rice in the famous blue boxes and cheese-flavored Minute Rice in three flavors: white cheddar and herb, four-cheese, and mild Mexican cheddar.

CORPORATE CITIZENSHIP

The majority of charity work undertaken by Kraft Foods involves fighting hunger in the United States. Philip Morris Companies, Inc. reports contributions of more than $100 million between 1990 and 1995. In January 1996, the company donated $1.3 million to Meals-on-Wheels in New York City. This corporate grant was designed to eliminate 1,000 elderly people from a waiting list for meals. Kraft also ran a holiday promotion tie-

in with Meals-on-Wheels in December of 1997 called "Share the Holidays Kraft . . . We're Helping Others Celebrate." Kraft donated $500,000 and helped to increase awareness of the charity. Kraft as a whole and also through specific brands is doing more tie-ins with charities, including Second Harvest, Children's Miracle Network, and Habitat for Humanity. Also through Philip Morris, Kraft Foods has given aid to those involved in disasters, including the Oklahoma City bombing and natural disasters throughout the United States.

GLOBAL PRESENCE

The international business of Kraft Foods, which was reorganized in 1995, includes several regional units: Kraft Foods Asia/Pacific; Kraft Jacobs Suchard Central and Eastern Europe, Middle East and Africa; Kraft Jacobs Suchard Northern Europe; and Kraft Jacobs Suchard Western Europe. Kraft Foods International, which runs these regional divisions, is a separate operating unit from Kraft Foods Inc., but both are wholly owned subsidiaries of Philip Morris Companies, Inc. Kraft Foods International is headquartered in New York.

EMPLOYMENT

A strong believer in promoting from within, Kraft provides training, guidance, and support to make sure that employees who work for the company can advance. It provides a number of organization-wide training programs and also develops its own programs to meet specific needs. However, most of the learning comes on the job.

With a large national and international work force and reflecting the realities of the American work force, Kraft organized nine employee councils in 1994. The councils work within the company and in local communities to promote different cultures, integrate marketing ideas, and recruit and provide support for new employees.

SOURCES OF INFORMATION

Bibliography

"A Brief History of Kraft Foods, Inc." *Kraft Foods, Inc. Archives Department.* Northfield, IL: Kraft Foods, Inc., 1995.

"The Food Chain's Dominant Duo." *Brandweek,* 6 May 1996.

The Kraft Foods Home Page, 8 June 1998. Available at http://www.kraftfoods.com.

Lefton, Terry Thompson. "Playing It Kool." *Brandweek,* 2 March 1998.

"Phillip Morris 10-K Form." 8 June 1998. Available at http://www.sec.gov.

Spethmann, Betsy. "Tang Blastoff." *Brandweek,* 11 March 1996.

Terry-Azios, Diana A. "Kraft Employee Council Unites Hispanics." *Hispanic,* March 1998.

Thompson, Stephanie. "Augmenting Specialty Coffee Push, Kraft Debuts Ice-Cappuccino Mix." *Brandweek,* 2 February 1998.

———. "Kraft Cheesed Off About Rice Biz." *Brandweek,* 6 April 1998.

———. "Kraft, DC Serve Up Heroic Pasta." *Brandweek,* 5 January 1998.

———. "Kraft Drops." *Brandweek,* 26 January 1998.

———. "Kraft Puts Meals On Wheels For Xmas." *Brandweek,* 27 October 1997.

———. "The O's Have It." *Brandweek,* 30 March 1998.

For an annual report:

telephone: (212) 880-5000 **or** write: Investor Relations, Philip Morris Companies, Inc., 120 Park Ave., New York, NY 10017

For additional industry research:

Investigate companies by their Standard Industrial Classification Codes, also known as SICs. Kraft's primary SICs are:

2022 Natural, Processed, and Imitation Cheese

2035 Pickled Fruits and Vegetables, Vegetable Sauces and Seasonings, and Salad Dressings

2043 Cereal Breakfast Foods

2099 Food Preparations, NEC

The Kroger Company

FOUNDED: 1883 as the Great Western Tea Company

Contact Information:

HEADQUARTERS: 1014 Vine St.
    Cincinnati, OH 45202
PHONE: (513)762-4000
FAX: (513)762-1160
URL: http://www.kroger.com

OVERVIEW

The Kroger Company is the largest supermarket chain in the United States, operating almost 1,400 supermarkets and over 800 convenience stores across 24 states. More than 90 percent of its supermarkets are superstores or combination stores (combined supermarkets and drug stores). Most stores also have delis, bakeries, and floral departments. Some supermarkets are like minimalls, including additional services such as coffee shops, fast-food franchises, banks, and barber shops.

Kroger sells grocery and other products under its own name, called a private label brand. The company operates food-processing plants to provide products for the Kroger brand, and generates above-average sales on its private label products.

Kroger has continually sought ways to improve service. It was the first grocery to include a bakery, to sell meat, and to test its food products scientifically. In the 1990s the company streamlined its distribution network, developed a coordinated purchasing program, negotiated nationwide promotions, and instituted a frequent-shopper program.

COMPANY FINANCES

In 1997 sales totaled $26.57 billion, 5.56 percent above 1996 sales of $25.17 billion. More than 90 percent of sales are from supermarkets and approximately 20 percent of those sales are from Kroger's brand products. Kroger's 1997 net income was $411.6 million, up 17.6 percent from net income in 1996 of $349.9 million.

To reduce its large debt, $3.66 billion in 1997, Kroger's aggressively cut costs. Over the two-year period from 1996 to 1997, the company invested $70 million to streamline its distribution network and reduce transportation costs. Despite this, the company's stock prices continued to rise, with a high of $37.31 and a low of $22.69 in 1997. Kroger does not pay dividends on its stock, per agreements with creditors. Despite being heavily leveraged, Standard and Poor's reported that Kroger's "can generate a strong cash flow to pay down debt in a timely fashion."

ANALYSTS' OPINIONS

According to a 1996 Paine Webber report, Kroger is a strong company benefiting from its position as a leader in best practices implementation, its modern store base, and the opportunity to improve its profitability. Kroger "has demonstrated its ability to survive competition with non-traditional competitors, a key strength in modern food retailing," said the report. Paine Webber recommended buying Kroger stock.

In February 1998, Standard & Poor's upgraded Kroger stock from "buy" to "accumulate." S&P cited many factors, including: Kroger's improved buying power, strong cash flow, increased sales of Kroger brand products, a low price/earning ratio, the company's plans for expansion, and an "expected" increase in food prices.

HISTORY

Bernard Kroger founded the Great Western Tea Company in 1883. In 1901 the company became the first grocery to operate its own bakeries. By 1902, Kroger operated 40 stores in the area around Cincinnati, Ohio. That year, the company incorporated and became the Kroger Grocery and Baking Company. In 1904 Kroger bought 14 Nigel meat markets and became the first grocer to sell groceries and meats. In 1928 Bernard Kroger sold his holdings in the company for $28 million. The company operated 5,575 stores (the most in its history). The Kroger Grocery and Baking Company officially became The Kroger Company in 1946.

In the late 1920s, Kroger began acquiring other grocery stores in the midwestern and southern United States. In the 1950s, Kroger purchased companies with stores in Texas, Georgia, and Washington, D.C. In the 1960s, Kroger purchased New Jersey-based Sav-On drug stores and opened its first SuperRx drugstores. In the 1980s, it bought Kansas-based Dillon Food Stores, Kwik Shop convenience stores, M&M Super Markets, and Tom Thumb Food Stores.

In 1988, Kroger fended off two hostile takeover attempts by borrowing large sums of money to "recapitalize." The move left Kroger in serious debt. To pay off this debt, the company had to drastically cut operating

FINANCES:

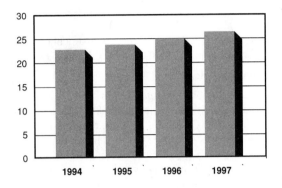

Kroger
Sales, 1994-1997
(billion dollars)

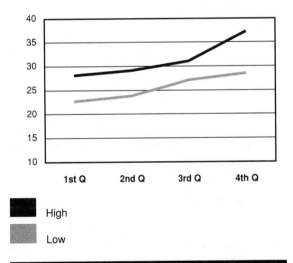

Kroger
1997 Stock Prices
(dollars)

■ High
■ Low

costs and increase the amount of cash produced by its stores. The lower interest rates of the mid-1990s allowed the company to refinance or eliminate a large portion of its debt. The leaner, more efficient Kroger became an even stronger competitor in the supermarket business.

Since its beginning, Kroger has continuously sought ways to improve service. It was the first grocery to operate its own bakery, and the first to offer an in-store butcher shop. In 1930 the company established the Kroger Food Foundation, and became the first grocery to test its food products scientifically. In 1971, Kroger instituted the "open dating" system to assure shoppers of

FAST FACTS:

About The Kroger Company

Ownership: The Kroger Company is a publicly owned company traded on the New York Stock Exchange.

Ticker symbol: KR

Officers: Joseph A. Pichler, Chmn. & CEO, 1997 base salary $471,508, bonus $381,688; David B. Dillon, Pres. & COO, 1997 base salary $351,477, bonus $254,458; Michael S. Heschel, Exec. VP, 1997 base salary $291,292, bonus $207,548; Ronald R. Rice, Sr. VP, 1997 base salary $231,523, bonus $278,006

Employees: 212,000

Principal Subsidiary Companies: The Kroger Company operates more than 1,300 supermarkets under the Kroger name. Its wholly owned subsidiary, Dillon Companies, Inc., operates approximately 250 supermarkets under the names City Market, Dillon Food Stores, Fry's Food Stores, Gerbes Supermarkets, King Scoopers, and Sav-Mor. Dillon also operates approximately 820 convenience stores under the names Kwik Shop, Mini-Mart, Quik Stop Markets, Tom Thumb Food Stores, and Turkey Hill Minit Markets.

Chief Competitors: Kroger supermarket chains have different competitors in different parts of the United States. Some of its biggest competitors are: A&P; Albertson's; Hy-Vee Food Stores; IGA; Meijer; Wal-Mart; SUPERVALU; and Safeway.

---

freshness. In 1972 they added nutritional labeling to the Kroger brand products, and introduced the scanner checkout system. In 1997 and 1998, Kroger began experimenting with self-scanning checkout units.

STRATEGY

As the largest supermarket chain in the United States, Kroger's main business strategy is to be a dominant factor in every market where it operates, "dominant" defined as being the number 1 or 2 chain in each area. In the 1990s, Kroger invested heavily in areas where it held a strong market share and in nearby areas as well, taking advantage of marketing, distribution, and overhead efficiencies. At the same time, the company closed

or sold its stores in areas where it was not a key player. By 1997 Kroger held the number 1 or 2 position in 25 major markets where it operated nine or more stores.

The Kroger Company's growth strategy for 1996 to 1998 had three parts: producing higher profits from existing stores; building increased selling space in its stores; and implementing new technology. According to Kroger, higher profits would come from better customer service and innovative food products, such as ready-to-eat meals. Increased selling space came from a 1996 project that involved spending $520 million on 120 supermarkets. That project increased the company's total selling space (square footage) by 6 to 7 percent. From 1998 to 2000, Kroger plans to invest approximately $800 million on opening or acquiring 100 new stores each year.

The third part of the strategy is new technology. Kroger has been an industry leader in using computer assisted ordering. With this system, employees use portable scanning devices linked to the store's computer via radio frequencies. This allows the stores to make precise decisions on what needs to be reordered. This also reduces the store's inventory needs, and saves money. Kroger has also implemented sophisticated management information systems and distribution systems.

INFLUENCES

In 1930 the Kroger Company played an inadvertent role in creating the modern supermarket. A Kroger manager, Michael Cullen, proposed opening self-service stores, offering groceries at lower prices. Kroger rejected the idea, so Cullen left to start King Kullen, the first supermarket, in Long Island, New York. By 1935, Kroger changed its mind and began operating self-service supermarkets. From the 1940s through the 1970s, the company expanded steadily by acquiring several other supermarket chains.

In the 1980s and 1990s, Kroger faced strong competition from huge "supercenters" operated by discount chains such as Meijer and Wal-Mart. These supercenters combine a discount store and a supermarket in one store. Kroger faced this challenge by opening its own "supercenters," supermarkets including additional services such as coffee shops, fast-food franchises, banks, and barbershops. Kroger has been aggressive in this area, even adding health clubs to some stores. While they take up valuable space and aren't profitable to the company, the health clubs draw in new customers. With profit margins low in the supermarket industry, every idea that brings in new customers also brings in more money to the store.

CURRENT TRENDS

In the 1990s Kroger developed partnerships with food suppliers and local restaurants in the Columbus,

Ohio-area to create in-store food service programs. This allows Kroger to sell prepared food from those restaurants. In some stores, Kroger also offers Mexican, Chinese, and American dishes. In the Georgia area, Kroger installed bagel-baking operations, which are operated under a shared-income contract with the Manhattan Bagel Company. In late 1997, Kroger added a "market within a market"—Vegetarian Markets. These sections within Kroger cater to the growing health consciousness of Americans. Galaxy Foods, a health food manufacturer, already sold products in Kroger and other supermarkets. Galaxy designed the Vegetarian Markets, which are stocked with Galaxy products.

Kroger has traditionally been a leader in adopting new technology. In 1992 the company invested $120 million in a satellite communications system, new front-end scanners and improved in-store computers. This allowed Kroger to develop what it called Efficient Consumer Response (ECR) projects, which helped the chain more efficiently order and restock merchandise. In 1996, Kroger successfully implemented customer self-scanning of grocery purchases at its division in Louisville, Kentucky. New stores in that area are equipped with a self-service checkout system that almost entirely eliminated cashier involvement. Shoppers can scan, bag, and pay for their groceries without a clerk's assistance. Over the next two years Kroger expanded the program, implementing self-service checkouts in Cincinnati and other areas.

Kroger, in partnership with Peapod Delivery System Inc., implemented an online shopping and delivery service in Columbus, Ohio. Shoppers are able to access the Kroger-Peapod service on the Internet, order products on a web site, and have the order delivered to their homes.

PRODUCTS

Kroger has one of the strongest private label (store brand) programs in the United States, selling more than 4,800 products under its label, including grocery, dairy, bakery, and health and beauty aids. The company operates 36 food-processing plants to support the Kroger brand. The private label products account for approximately 20 percent of total sales, several points above the industry average.

CORPORATE CITIZENSHIP

In 1995 the Kroger Company Foundation donated $2.5 million to a variety of community projects. In addition, Kroger's retail divisions and manufacturing plants contributed more than $2.4 million of their operating income and $2.3 million in products to charity and community groups. Thousands of Kroger employees raise funds for charity through bake sales, car washes, and Habitat for Humanity projects. In 1995 Second Harvest,

CHRONOLOGY:
Key Dates for The Kroger Company

1883: B.H. Kroger opens his first store in Cincinnati, Ohio

1901: Kroger is the first grocery store to operate its own bakeries

1902: The Kroger Grocery and Baking Company is incorporated

1904: Meat and groceries are sold under the same roof for the first time

1916: Self-service is tried in the Kroger store

1928: B.H. Kroger sells his stock and retires from active management

1935: 50 Kroger stores take on the new "super market" style

1946: The company becomes The Kroger Company

1952: Sales top $1 billion for the first time

1968: Sales top $3 billion after reaching $2 billion just five years earlier

1972: An experimental scanner checkout system is tested in Kroger

1983: Kroger merges with Dillon Food Stores

1988: Kroger restructures to ward off a hostile takeover attempt, borrowing $5 billion and going into debt

1992: The company invests $120 million in new scanners, satellite communications systems, and better in-store computers

1997: Adds a vegetarian market to its stores; begins testing self-service checkout systems

the national food bank organization, named Kroger its Grocery Distributor of the Year.

SOURCES OF INFORMATION

Bibliography
Amato-McCoy. "Dillon Cos. to Get First of Kroger's 50 Self-Checkouts." *Supermarket News,* 20 April 1998.

———. "Kroger Launches Frequent-Shopper Program in Three Stores." *Supermarket News,* 11 May 1998.

"Galaxy Foods Pioneers Supermarket Health Megatrends; Designs New Vegetarian Markets." *Business Wire,* 24 August 1997.

"The Kroger Co." *Hoover's Handbook of American Business 1998.* Austin, TX: The Reference Press, 1997.

"Kroger Co." *Standard and Poor's Stock Reports,* 1998.

The Kroger Company Home Page, 11 May 1998. Available at http://www.kroger.com.

"The Kroger Company 10-K Form, 23 March 1998." 15 July 1998. Available at http://www.sec.gov.

"The Kroger Company 14A Report, 8 April 1998," 15 July 1998. Available at http://www.sec.gov.

Levs, Joshua, and Bob Edwards. "Supermarket Changes." *Morning Edition, National Public Radio,* 28 November 1997.

For an annual report:

write: The Kroger Company, 1014 Vine St., Cincinnati, OH 45202

For additional industry research:

Investigate companies by their Standard Industrial Classification Codes, also known as SICs. Kroger's primary SIC is:

5411 Grocery Stores

The LEGO Group

OVERVIEW

The LEGO Group, one of the largest toy manufacturers in the world, is owned and managed by the Kirk Kristiansen family in Billund, Denmark. The company operates in 30 countries and has 50 companies worldwide. The company's main business is the manufacturing, development, marketing, and distribution of the LEGO toy system. Its products are sold in more than 130 countries, and an estimated 300 million children have played with LEGO bricks.

LEGO built its leadership position in the construction-toy industry by making children its vital concern. According to a company press release, "Our basic business concept and the foundation for all LEGO products and activities is that we take children and their needs seriously."

The company sees its fundamental task as one of stimulating children's imaginations and creativity, and encouraging them to explore their own world. This corporate mission has allowed LEGO to develop a wide range of products around its basic construction-toy theme. These include products incorporating robotics; media products, such as software, music, video, books, and film for children; educational products for kindergartens and schools; and lifestyle products such as clothes, watches, bed linen, and puzzles.

LEGO also operates two theme parks, one in Billund, Denmark, opened in 1968, and one in Windsor, England, opened near London, in 1996. A third park is scheduled to open in Carlsbad, California, near San Diego, in 1999.

FOUNDED: 1932

Contact Information:

HEADQUARTERS: DK-7190
  Billund 7190 Denmark
PHONE: +45-75-33-11-88
FAX: +45-75-35-33-60
URL: http://www.lego.com

FAST FACTS:
About The LEGO Group

Ownership: The LEGO Group is a privately owned company. It is owned and managed by the Kirk Kristiansen family in Denmark.

Officers: Kjeld Kirk Kristiansen, Pres. & CEO; Mads Ovlisen, Chmn.; Niels Christian Jensen, Exec. VP Marketing & Product Development

Employees: 9,400

Principal Subsidiary Companies: The LEGO Group owns 50 companies in 30 countries, including Lego Systems Inc. in the United States.

Chief Competitors: LEGO competes with other toy manufacturers and specifically with construction-toy manufacturers, including: Tyco Toys Inc.; Rivtik; Tandem Toys; PEDLO; GOMPLA; and K'Nex Industries.

COMPANY FINANCES

Although LEGO is a private company, its annual report is available on the company's web site. For 1997, LEGO reported revenues of 7.6 billion Danish kroner (DKK), or approximately $1.12 billion. Revenues came mainly from sales to retailers and distributors, licensing income, and revenue from LEGOLAND parks, among other sources. That was a 1-percent increase over 1996 revenue of DKK 7.5 billion or $7.28 billion.

Financially, 1997 was not a good year for LEGO. Revenues were up, yet net income for 1997 was only DKK 171 million ($25.3 million), compared with net income of DKK 699 million ($103.4 million) for 1996.

Sales in 1997 stagnated overall compared with a 4-percent increase in 1996. However, the company enjoyed substantial increases, zero growth, and declines in various markets.

ANALYSTS' OPINIONS

Many analysts believe LEGO to be a financially stable company, and the company's expansion in many areas of its business seems to indicate this is true. Also, the company's workforce has increased by more than 50 percent over the past seven years.

With all of its success, LEGO, critics say, still has need for growth. Competition with other toy manufacturers is fierce. The average German family bought six LEGO sets per year per child compared to U.S. figures of 2 or 3 sets per year per child. Many analysts see LEGO's plans to develop new theme parks as a competitive edge. The company plans to open a new theme park every three years starting in 1999. LEGOLAND in Denmark counted 1.3 million visitors in 1996, and LEGOLAND Windsor, near London, had 1.4 million visitors that year after opening in March 1996. Compared to Disneyland's 13.0 million per year, these numbers may seem low, but analysts saw them as promising. LEGO's goal is 1.8 million visitors per year at each of its parks.

HISTORY

In 1932 Ole Kirk Christiansen, a Danish carpenter, went into business with the intent of building houses. Feeling the impact of the depression in the 1930s, most people were not able to afford such luxuries. He looked for other possibilities with his business and began building wooden toys. Combining two Danish words, "Leg Godt" which means "play well," he derived the name LEGO for his company.

By the late 1930s, LEGO produced many different types of wooden toys, including vehicles, animals, and Yo-Yos. In 1947 LEGO began producing plastic toys, which included baby rattles, toy tractors, small dolls, and animals. In 1949 the company introduced Automatic Binding Bricks, which were plastic building bricks. By 1955 the "LEGO System of Play" was introduced. These sets included small molded vehicles and figures along with town maps.

In 1958 Godtred Kirk Christiansen, son of the company founder, invented a new system for coupling the plastic bricks. He developed the tubes placed inside LEGO bricks that made the bricks stick together better. This discovery also increased the nearly endless number of ways bricks could be combined.

The first sales company outside of Denmark was established in Germany in 1956. By 1960, sales companies branched out to include France, Great Britain, Switzerland and Sweden. LEGO entered the U.S. market around 1974 and opened a factory and sales office in Connecticut.

In 1980 the company established its Dacta division to work on educational products for schools. The Dacta line includes complex sets that challenge students to build working machines and solve problems using math and logic.

Continuing to grow over the years, LEGO was ranked as one of the world's top 10 toy manufacturers in

1996, being the single European company on the list. All of the other top 10 toy companies were American or Japanese. In 1997 it introduced a record 103 new products at the annual American International Toy Fair in New York City.

STRATEGY

LEGO's strategy is to provide a wide range of creative experiences, construction toys, educational materials, lifestyle products, family parks, and media products for children all over the world. The development of these products and activities is guided by the company's vision of "Idea, Exuberance, and Values" and the shared belief that children are of vital concern to LEGO.

The company's goal is for the LEGO logo and name to be known among families with children as the strongest brand in the world. While the company's core business area is the development, production, marketing, and distribution of the LEGO toy system, it is also exploring several new product areas. In order to remain competitive, it has increased the rate of new product introductions and lessened the time it takes to develop an idea into a finished product. In 1997 the company introduced more than 180 new products, equal to almost half its entire product line.

INFLUENCES

The Great Depression in the 1930s forced Ole Kirk Christiansen to be flexible with the times. Originally planning to build houses, Christiansen quickly changed his plan to manufacture wooden toys. The invention of plastics allowed LEGO to be the first company to buy a plastics injection-molding machine in 1947. This offered greater selection, capabilities, and strength in the toys LEGO manufactured.

LEGO grew to become one of the top toy manufacturers in the world. With this growth, however, came greater demands. By the 1990s, the company faced fierce competition from companies like K'Nex Industries and Ritvik, maker of Megablocks. Large stores selling toys, such as Wal-Mart and Toys 'R' Us, began to require more selection and faster shipment. LEGO had to shift its strategy to focus on marketing and production.

The company also had to develop new products in a timely fashion. Between 1995 and 1997, the number of products on the market less than one-year-old increased from 48 to 60 percent. In order to get these new products to market faster, LEGO had to reduce total production time significantly, in some cases cutting this time in half. LEGO also had to maintain good relations with big name buyers like Target, Wal-Mart, Toys 'R' Us, and Kmart, which, combined, accounted for nearly two-thirds

CHRONOLOGY:
Key Dates for The LEGO Group

1932: Ole Kirk Christiansen sets up a firm to manufacture stepladders, ironing boards, and wooden toys in Billund, Denmark

1934: The company takes on the name LEGO

1947: LEGO is Denmark's first company to buy a plastic injection-molding machine for toy making

1949: The company introduces plastic Automatic Binding Bricks

1953: Automatic Binding Bricks are renamed LEGO Bricks

1955: The first LEGO System of Play sets are introduced

1958: The current LEGO stud-and-tube coupling system is patented

1967: The DUPLO brick is invented for smaller children

1974: LEGO figures are introduced and are the biggest selling product to date; LEGO enters the U.S. market

1980: Dacta is established to build educational products for schools

1988: The first official LEGO World Cup building championship is held in Denmark

1992: The world record is set for toy rail construction—1,788 feet of LEGO rails and three model locomotives

1996: LEGO is the only European company ranked in the world's top 10 toy manufacturers

1997: Introduces a record 103 new products at the International Toy Fair

of all toy sales. LEGO began giving regular invitations to these companies to tour its Enfield, Connecticut, plant in order to foster good relations.

LEGO's marketing division had to make some adjustments as well. To compete with other toy companies, LEGO began offering coupons with sets purchased at a price of $14 or higher. The company also extended an invitation to consumers to join the LEGO Builders Club, which offers coupons and a LEGO magazine. Part of

LEGO's goal in doing so was to raise membership by 50 percent by the end of 1997.

CURRENT TRENDS

LEGO is accelerating the rate at which it introduces new products. In 1997 it introduced 103 new products at the American International Toy Fair in New York and more than 180 new products during the year. While some of these new products were variations on existing products, many were brand new. Some of the new products incorporate the latest technology, including a "smart" brick with an imbedded computer chip, CD-ROM games, and robotics.

Over the past couple of years, LEGO has made a substantial investment in developing digital products. For many years it has collaborated with the Media Lab at the Massachusetts Institute of Technology (MIT) to lay the foundation for such products as LEGO Mindstorms, a child-friendly programming language, digital LEGO bricks, and CD-ROM titles, among other new products.

LEGO is committed to offering a wider variety of stimulating experiences for children through such diverse offerings as its theme parks and interactive educational exhibits. After opening in March 1998 at The Children's Museum of Indianapolis, the LEGO Ocean Adventure will travel to other children's museums in the United States for one year. It is an interactive, educational exhibit that allows children to immerse themselves in an imaginary ocean environment where they encounter life-size LEGO sharks, dolphins, and other sea creatures. The exhibit provides a wide variety of hands-on activities and unlimited play possibilities for children. Four interactive stations, including a research submarine and a rover building area, are part of the exhibit.

With cutbacks in educational spending in the United States, LEGO closed the U.S. branch of its Dacta division in 1997 and moved its functions to Denmark. The move was part of a global reorganization of Dacta to improve operational efficiency. Overall, Dacta sales in North America, France, and Scandinavia increased during 1997. The company decided to focus on a smaller number of professional institutional suppliers to improve market contact with its educational customers.

In early 1998 LEGO announced an agreement with Lucas Licensing Ltd. under which LEGO will have exclusive rights to manufacture, market, and distribute Star Wars construction toys. With a new Star Wars movie scheduled for release in the United States in May 1999, LEGO planned to introduce its first assortment of LEGO building sets based on the original Star Wars trilogy in early 1999. It was the first such licensing agreement for LEGO.

PRODUCTS

LEGO Media International, a division established in 1996, introduced its first computer game in October 1997 called LEGO Island. Developed in collaboration with Mindscape, one of the world's largest CD-ROM producers, LEGO Island was the biggest-selling computer game in the United States and ranked high on the world's top 10 list of software for children. Three more CD-ROM titles are planned for 1998.

Mindstorms, a new LEGO system that features a building brick with an imbedded microchip, was introduced for 1998. The RCX brick, as it is called, allows children with the help of a personal computer to build and program robots that move and act on their own. Using RCX and traditional LEGO bricks, children build their creature, then use RCX code, a child-friendly programming language, to develop a program. Then they download the program from their computer to the RCX using a special infrared transmitter. Unlike many other LEGO products, Mindstorms is aimed at children, ages 11 and older. However, the company is working on other robotics projects for children as young as 6.

LEGO first presented its Mindstorms technology at the Museum of Science and Industry in Chicago, where the first LEGO Mindstorms Learning Center opened in late 1997. At the Learning Center, children can create their own robots and vehicles using programmable LEGO elements and LEGO's specially developed software.

Other new product introductions in 1997 included many new items in LEGO's PRIMO Baby line. A new Dinosaurs theme surrounded newly released toys in the LEGO DUPLO Preschool line. The LEGO SYSTEM line included additions such as Divers, Fright Knights, U.F.O., Aqua Raiders, and Robo Force. Many new pieces and characteristics accompanied these new products, including domed pieces for constructing futuristic undersea adventures; extra large, curved pieces for making round, space-centered models; heat-activated stickers; and fiber optics capabilities.

LEGO SCALA, a product line designed especially for girls, featured new additions in 1997 to the flexible doll's house system, which allows girls to arrange the various elements however they desire. The dolls—a father, two mothers, three teenage daughters, and a baby—have flexible limbs and are able to hold things in their hands.

CORPORATE CITIZENSHIP

Annually, LEGO gives an international prize (LEGO Prize) of DKK 1 million to people and/or establishments that strive to improve the living conditions of children. This prize is one in which no applications are

The hand of a model engineer places a model car into position under Admiralty Arch at a Legoland theme park. (Reuters/Kieran Doherty/Archive Photos.)

IF THEY COME, THEY WILL BUILD IT?

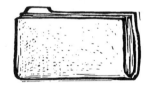

As of spring 1999, America will have a hot new vacation destination for tourists: Legoland, yes, Legoland, will open up in Carlsbad, California. It will feature rides, shows, restaurants, and Lego, Lego, Lego. At the heart of Legoland will be Miniland, where approximately 30 million Lego bricks will be used to create various kinds of displays. This will be the third Legoland theme park worldwide, and the estimated construction cost is in the neighborhood of $130 million. And here you thought Legos were just fiendish toys randomly scattered by small children to cripple barefoot parents in the middle of the night.

taken. Since 1985, 24 individuals, institutions, and establishments in 17 countries have been awarded the LEGO Prize.

LEGO itself has won several awards including the ACITT 1994 Awards, First Prize; Gold Award 1996 Worlddidac Foundation; Best Education Product MacUser 1994 Awards; Presidents Citation International Technology Education Association; Teacher's Choice Learning 91; New Product Awards for The Nursery & Creche '95; 10 Best Children's Educational Products for the Dr. Toy; and Parents' Choice Award 1995.

GLOBAL PRESENCE

Based in Denmark, LEGO products are manufactured and marketed throughout the world. There are LEGO factories in 5 countries: Denmark, Switzerland, the United States, Brazil, and Korea. In 1997 the company's products were sold in more than 130 countries. The company's first computer game, LEGO Island, was marketed in 8 different language versions: English, German, French, Danish, Spanish, Portuguese, Korean, and Japanese.

In declining order, the company's top 10 international markets in 1997 were Germany, the United States, the Benelux countries—Belgium, Netherlands, and Luxembourg—France, Great Britain, Japan, Austria and Hungary, Italy, and Canada.

EMPLOYMENT

In 1997 the number of full-time positions with the company rose to 8,671 from 8,167 in 1996. Of those, 4,260 positions were in Denmark and 4,411 in other countries. Including temporary positions, the company employed 9,867 people worldwide in 1997. The LEGOLAND parks organization accounted for more than 10 percent of LEGO employees worldwide.

SOURCES OF INFORMATION

Bibliography

Broderick, Pat. "Legoland is Ready to Break Ground at Carlsbad Ranch." *San Diego Business Journal;* 31 March 1997.

French, Howard. "Lego Closing out Dacta Division." *Journal Inquirer-Manchester, CT,* 10 January 1997.

French, Howard. "Lego Systems Just Toying with the Competition." *Journal Inquirer-Manchester, CT,* 28 January 1997.

Harrison, David. "Lego, Brady Set to Meet on Huge U.S. Theme Park." *Baltimore Business Journal,* 10 May 1996.

Jackson, Susan. "Putting the Snap Back in LEGO." *Business Week,* 30 December 1996.

Jacobson, Linda. "LEGO Virtual Village: A Collaborative Play Space for Designers." *Silicon Graphics,* December 1996.

"The LEGO Group Acquires Global Star Wars License." LEGO Company Press Release, 12 May 1998. Available at http://www.lego.com.

"The LEGO Group and Mindscape Turn LEGO Bricks into Bytes on CD-ROM." *Coming Soon Magazine,* 25 January 1997.

LEGO Home Page, 12 May 1998. Available at http://www.lego.com.

"LEGO (R) Ocean Adventure Sets Sail." LEGO Company Press Release, 12 May 1998. Available at http://www.lego.com.

McNary, Dave. "Building a Home for Lego Maniacs." *Daily News.* Los Angeles, CA: 21 September 1997.

Oster, Patrick. "From Tiny Plastic Bricks . . . A Mighty Theme Park." *Business Week,* 7 October 1991.

Segel, Dee. "Lego Isn't Just for Building Toys Any More." *The Courant,* 21 August 1995.

Ward, Bruce. "Lego Goes Electronic: New Mindstorms Gives Creative Children Building Blocks of Technology." *Ottawa Citizen,* 30 January 1998.

For an annual report:

on the Internet at: http://www.lego.com **or** write: The LEGO Group, 7190-Billund, Denmark

For additional industry research:

Investigate companies by their Standard Industrial Classification Codes, also known as SICs. LEGO's primary SICs are:

3944 Games, Toys, and Children's Vehicles

7996 Amusement Parks

Levi Strauss & Co.

OVERVIEW

Levi Strauss & Co. is a leading global manufacturer of brand name clothing. In the United States, Levi Strauss is the second largest manufacturer of men's jeans, trailing VF Corp., which makes and markets Wrangler and Lee brand jeans. Along with its signature denim collection, Levi Strauss also manufactures Dockers casual wear. Levi's clothing is sold in various department stores, and the company began opening Original Levi's Stores as well as Dockers Shops. In 1997 Levi Strauss sportswear was sold in more than 30,000 retail outlets.

Levi Strauss relies heavily on advertising. In its efforts to market its products, Levi Strauss uses many different forms of advertising; the company also cooperates with the advertising campaigns of associated retail stores in order to increase the public's awareness of its products.

FOUNDED: 1873

Contact Information:
HEADQUARTERS: 1155 Battery St.
San Francisco, CA 94111-1230
PHONE: (415)544-6000
FAX: (415)501-3939
URL: http://www.levistrauss.com

COMPANY FINANCES

As a privately held company, Levi Strauss does not release complete details of its financial operations. However, it is known that for fiscal 1997, ended November 30, 1997, the company posted worldwide sales of $6.90 billion, down 3.4 percent from sales of $7.14 billion in fiscal 1996. The company's sales in fiscal 1995 totaled $6.71 billion, up more than 10 percent from $6.07 billion in fiscal 1994.

FAST FACTS:
About Levi Strauss & Co.

Ownership: Levi Strauss Associates Inc. is a privately owned corporation.

Officers: Robert D. Haas, Chmn. & CEO; Peter A. Jacobi, Pres. & COO; Gordon D. Shank, Pres., Levi Strauss Americas; Jim Fraser, Pres., Levi Strauss Asia Pacific

Employees: 37,000

Principal Subsidiary Companies: Levi's principal subsidiaries are Levi Strauss International, Levi Strauss North America, Dockers, and Brittania.

Chief Competitors: Levi Strauss's main competition comes from other manufacturers of brand name clothing. These include: Calvin Klein; The Gap; Jordache Enterprises; Liz Claiborne; Tommy Hilfiger; and VF Corp.

HISTORY

In 1847 Levi Strauss arrived in New York from Bavaria to assist his brothers in the opening of a dry goods store. Strauss moved on to San Francisco in 1853 to open his own dry goods business in which his primary product was tent canvas. Strauss' store was frequented mostly by gold rush miners.

Shortly after Strauss arrived, he was informed by a local prospector that the miners were having difficulty finding apparel that was sturdy enough to last through a hard day's work. It was at this time that Strauss developed a pair of pants out of canvas, and it wasn't long before the word spread, and the rugged pants were a hit with the miners.

Strauss went on to make a few more pairs of the canvas pants before he switched to a durable fabric that the French called *serge de Nimes,* and which eventually became known as denim. Strauss later colored the fabric with indigo dye and, adopting a suggestion from Nevada tailor Jacob Davis, reinforced the pants with copper rivets. In 1873 Davis and Strauss produced the first pair of Levi's Patent Riveted 501 waist-high overalls (501 was the lot number). "The pants, which soon became the standard attire of lumberjacks, cowboys, railroad workers, oil drillers, and farmers, were the same (in 1997) as they

were in 1873," according to *Hoover's Online.* Eventually, the copper rivets, found on the pockets and the crotch, were removed.

One of the most recognizable aspects of Levi's jeans was the red label that could be found on the pockets of its famous pants. This was called the "Tab Trademark," and it was introduced to distinguish original Levi's jeans from other brands. Eventually, the decision was made to put a blank red tag on every seventh pair of jeans to protect the company's legal right to the "Tab Trademark." The color of this tag later came to identify the various product lines, including an orange tag to indicate its more quality fabric and styling and the silver tab to indicate its more fashionable line of products.

While the "Tab Trademark" was introduced in 1936, the Levi Strauss company had a recognizable logo many years before. This particular logo was the image of two horses, and it was introduced in 1886.

Strauss continued to manufacture pants and run his wholesaling business until his death in 1902. At that time, the business was turned over to Strauss's four nephews who continued to manufacture blue jeans. The business continued to thrive, and after World War II, Walter Haas Jr. and Peter Haas, who were fourth-generation Strauss family members, took over and eliminated the wholesaling side of the business. Wholesaling was the primary segment of the company's business at the time, but the decision was made to focus on the clothing aspect of the business. By the 1950s Levi's blue jeans became popular with the youth of the day, and by the 1960s the company had introduced women's clothing, as well as expanded overseas.

The decision was made to take the corporation public in 1971, and in that same year there was a licensing agreement made with clothing manufacturer Perry Ellis. The company continued to manufacture its denim line of clothing, but by the mid-1980s profits started to decline. There was also concern about the loss of family tradition within the company. The Haas family returned the business to private ownership in 1985. By 1996 all outstanding stock held by employees was repurchased.

The year 1988 saw the company reorganizing its marketing groups to provide better customer service. Further reorganization took place in 1992 when the U.S., Canadian, and Mexican businesses were merged as one North American entity.

Although Levi's jeans can be found in thousands of retail outlets, the company in 1992 decided to establish and operate its own retail stores called the Original Levi's Store. The women's market also was courted more strongly with the establishment of the Levi's Personal Pair personalized jeans program.

STRATEGY

In order to increase company sales and ensure consumer loyalty, Levi Strauss has continued to develop new products. The company has also employed an intense marketing approach in which it has used several methods of advertising—including the radio, television, and billboards—in an attempt to ensure company recognition while at the same time introducing quality products. Levi Strauss went on to develop Dockers casual wear, and in 1987 the company acquired Brittania, a line of casual clothing. Levi Strauss' focused market strategy and the aggressive expansion of its product line has allowed the company to grow into a clothing giant. Diminishing sales in the 1990s due to increased competition from retailers, big name designers, and private labels forced the company to close 11 plants in 1998. Future plans are to focus on the custom-made jeans and dress slacks market.

To spread the Levi's name far and wide, global marketing media director Sean Dee has an estimated $5-million budget with which to work. Some of this goes into the Levi Strauss web site, which includes product information, store locations, and historical archives. Sponsorship also goes into the mix, with the Levi's name attached to the video-streaming web site Streamland (available at http://www.streamland.com). In addition, to court the young female clothing market, Levi's sponsors the fashion section of the Webzine Kid's Domain (available at http://www.splam.com), targeted at the 6- to 12-year-old crowd.

INFLUENCES

In 1998 the International Trademark Association released the results of a 1991-1995 study on trademark counterfeiting and its impact on worldwide apparel sales. Participating companies estimated a 22 percent loss in sales ($2.1 billion) because of counterfeiting. Levi Strauss is among the companies whose trademark has been infringed upon, with the resulting significant loss of sales.

Increasing overhead costs, along with changing customer tastes, also are causing Levi Strauss to cut back production and revamp products. While other manufacturers have gone abroad, Levi's remains an American-made product. This accounts for higher prices at the store, prices that fewer people are willing to pay. Consumers also want better-fitting, more attractive clothes, and Levi's hopes its custom-designed jeans and dress slacks lines will fill the need.

CURRENT TRENDS

The rise in the demand for casual wear has been a driving force in the development of many different lines of clothing in Levi's history. Along with its world famous line of denim fashions, Levi Strauss introduced Dockers casual pants in 1986. The following year, the company acquired Brittania, which was an addition to their denim and casual line of sportswear. Along with casual wear, Levi Strauss also made the move into apparel that was geared toward individuals interested in a look appropriate for the workplace. This line, introduced in 1995, was called SLATES and featured dress slacks. SLATES was the company's first new brand name since Dockers.

PRODUCTS

Levi Strauss' most recognized form of apparel is its denim line, with articles varying from blue jeans to denim skirts and blouses. The company recognized the need to expand into other areas of the clothing business, and in 1986 introduced the Dockers line, which included casual wear in fabrics other than denim. The Dockers line featured pants and shirts as well as women's apparel. In 1987 Levi Strauss purchased Brittania, which expanded the company's interests in denim and other casual wear, both of which were marketed under the Britannia brand name.

Levi Strauss also looked for ways to sell to individuals interested in clothing appropriate for the workplace. The company wanted to develop a product that was well-made and also would attract consumers who were familiar with the company's existing products. This led in 1995 to the introduction of the SLATES clothing line, dress slacks manufactured with the same quality as the other products produced by Levi Strauss. The division's marketing group spent several months searching for an appropriate name for the new line of pants; it wanted a name that could be spoken in several different languages and had a global appeal. It also wanted a masculine name that ended in "s" like their other products. Nancy Friedman, SLATES marketing director, said, "What we were looking for was an empty vessel, a word that really had no meaning that we could then fill with meaning."

CORPORATE CITIZENSHIP

The company's founder, Levi Strauss, gave much of himself to charities and other philanthropic activities. The company he founded carries on that tradition by encouraging its employees to become involved in the community. Through the Levi Strauss Foundation and Community Involvement Teams, more than $20 million is donated to organizations in nearly 40 countries each year. The company also sponsors AIDS education programs and promotes economic empowerment for the poor.

Providing a good work environment is important to the company. Not only does it practice fair employment practices and keep the work environment healthy, but it

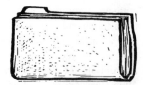

DID YOU KNOW THAT. . .

- The company's headquarters were totally destroyed by the San Francisco earthquake of 1906?

- Belt loops were added to Levi's in 1922 and suspender buttons were retained until 1936?

- Jeans became a part of the collections at the Smithsonian Institution in Washington, D.C.?

- Levi Strauss makes 501 jeans in more than 108 sizes and 20 different fabrics?

- The company uses 1.25 million miles of thread for the production of jeans each year?

- Until 1960, Levi's 501 jeans were called "waist overalls?"

- Levi's began using rivets in their clothing in 1873 because of complaints from miners whose pockets tore due to the weight of ore samples?

also has drawn up Global Sourcing and Operating Guidelines, "a code of conduct to ensure that the company's products are manufactured in a responsible way," for companies that wish to contract with it. Businesses unwilling to follow Levi's guidelines do not get contracts.

GLOBAL PRESENCE

While Levi Strauss' primary sales are in the United States, there are also significant sales in other parts of the world. In 1994 Levi Strauss opened its first company-owned retail outlet on London's fashionable Regent Street. The company also opened affiliates in Argentina, India, and South Africa. Sales in the Americas generated 67 percent of the company's total revenue in fiscal 1997. European sales brought in 26 percent of revenue, while Asia/Pacific sales accounted for the remaining 7 percent.

Levi Strauss has plenty of motivation to expand its reach into international markets. The company's brand name products have been sold in more than 60 countries, and there are further opportunities out there for growth outside the United States. To help guide the company's overseas expansion efforts, Levi Strauss created two new operating divisions: Levi Strauss International and Levi Strauss North America.

In 1998 Levi Strauss decided to try manufacturing and selling its product in China. China's civil rights record had kept the company away in the past. However, now that Hong Kong is once again a part of China, Levi Strauss has felt confident it can find contractors that will adhere to the company's strict labor condition guidelines.

EMPLOYMENT

Levi Strauss offers attractive compensation and benefits packages. It also follows company value statements that guide the employees on their progress, and Levi also stresses the importance of positive employee-management relations. "In 1991 Levi Strauss instituted a team approach to production, and two years later the company's sewing plants adopted Japanese-style production techniques that encourage more worker responsibility," according to *Hoover's Online*.

Levi Strauss also takes great pride in its reputation as a politically correct employer. In accordance with this, the company initiated a rewards program, the Global Success Sharing Plan, which would provide bonuses that are equal to a worker's 1996 base salary if certain goals were met by the year 2002. The company also has agreed to repurchase nearly $4 billion in stock from family and employees. (Family members own approximately 94 percent of Levi's stock.)

Due to shrinking market share, the company closed 11 factories in 1998, laying off more than 6,000 workers. A $200–million employee benefits package was created to help the laid-off employees and the communities affected by the factory closures.

SOURCES OF INFORMATION

Bibliography

Canedy, Dana. "Struggling to Duplicate a Success, Levi Strauss Hopes to Match Performance of Dockers." *The New York Times,* 9 October 1996.

Cuneo, Alice Z. "Levi Strauss Sponsors Splam Site in Effort to Target Girls." *Advertising Age,* 1 September 1997.

Himelstein, Linda. "Levi's Is Hiking Up its Pants (Overcoming Teenage Indifference)." *Business Week,* 1 December 1997.

King, Ralph T. "Its Share Shrinking, Levi Strauss Lays Off 6,395." *Wall Street Journal (Eastern Edition),* 4 November 1997.

Landler, Mark. "Reversing Course, Levi Strauss Will Expand Its Output in China." *New York Times (Late New York Edition),* 9 April 1998.

"Levi Strauss Associates Inc." *Hoover's Online,* 1997. Available at http://www.hoovers.com.

"The Quiet American. (Levi Strauss' R. Haas)." *The Economist,* 8 November 1997.

Rich, Laura. "Insider: Levi's Easy Fit." *Mediaweek,* 16 February 1998.

Rigdon, Joan Indiana. "Levi to Cut 20 of Salaried Staffers, Citing Jeans Demand, Tougher Rivalry." *Wall Street Journal (Eastern Edition),* 20 February 1997.

"Study Shows Global Counterfeiting Activity in the Apparel and Footwear Industries Eating Away at Company Sales." *PR Newswire,* 6 May 1998. Available at http://www.infoseek.com.

"Why Work for Levi Strauss & Co." San Francisco, CA: Levi Strauss & Co., 1997. Available at http://www.occ.com/levi/.

For additional industry research:

Investigate companies by their Standard Industrial Classification Codes, also known as SICs. Levi Strauss' primary SICs are:

5136 Men/Boys' Clothing

5137 Women/Children's Clothing

5699 Misc. Apparel and Accessory Stores

The Limited, Inc.

FOUNDED: 1963

Contact Information:

HEADQUARTERS: 3 Limited Pky.
   Columbus, OH 48230
PHONE: (614)415-7000
FAX: (614)479-7080
URL: http://www.limited.com

OVERVIEW

With 1997 sales of $9.2 billion, The Limited, Inc. is one of the biggest specialty apparel retailers in the United States. With its corporate offices located in Columbus, Ohio, the company operates several chains nationwide, including The Limited, Limited Too, Express, Lane Bryant, Lerner New York, Henri Bendel, Galyan's Trading Company, Victoria's Secret, Structure, and Bath and Body Works. The Limited has acted progressively over the years to keep up with new trends and survive economic challenges and has competitors in many different markets. Due to its efficient operations and willingness to take chances, the company has often had the edge over its competition. The company is known to be aggressive in marketing and began expanding internationally into the United Kingdom.

At the same time, since 1995 it has downsized by closing unprofitable stores, including the 118-store Cacique chain of lingerie stores, and spinning off some of its most profitable chains as public companies. A 1995 public offering of stock in Intimate Brands (parent of Victoria's Secret and Bath and Body Works) left The Limited, Inc. with an 83-percent ownership in Intimate Brands. In 1998 it divested its interest in Brylane Inc., a catalog publisher that grossed $1.3 billion in 1997. Also in 1998, it completed its spin-off of Abercrombie and Fitch, a 156-store upscale casual clothier that had 1997 sales of $521.6 million. Overall, The Limited, Inc. reduced the number of stores it operated from 5,640 in 1997 to about 5,200 in 1998.

COMPANY FINANCES

For 1997 The Limited, Inc. reported net sales of $9.2 billion, up from $8.6 billion in 1996. The increase was due to sales from new stores, as comparable store sales were flat. Women's brands (Express, Lerner New York, Lane Bryant, The Limited, Henri Bendel) accounted for $3.9 billion in sales; Intimate Brands (Victoria's Secret Stores and Catalogue, Bath and Body Works, Cacique, and other) accounted for $3.6 billion in sales; emerging brands (Structure, Limited Too, Galyan's Trading Co., and other) accounted for $1.1 billion in sales; and Abercrombie and Fitch accounted for $522 million in sales.

For 1997, operating income fell to $480 million from $636 million in 1996, due in large part to a one-time charge of $187 million in 1997 for the closure of 5 of the 6 Henri Bendel stores and other charges. As a result, women's brands had an operating loss of $268 million, while the company's strongest performer, Intimate Brands, had an operating income of $505 million. Led by Limited Too, emerging brands reported an operating income of $159 million, and Abercrombie and Fitch was profitable with $84 million in operating income.

The company's stock price improved from trading in the $16-$20 range in early 1996 to a range of $23-$27 at the end of 1997. This change in price reflected Wall Street's approval of the company's restructuring efforts as well as the general strength of the retail sector during that period.

ANALYSTS' OPINIONS

Analysts have recommended The Limited sell some of its divisions and zero in on its target market, 20- to 40-year-olds. Some also believe the women's apparel division, including Limited, Limited Express, Lerner, Lane Bryant, and Henri Bendel should be sold. Others believe the company should drop only its budget apparel line, Lerner, and its plus sizes division, Lane Bryant. According to some critics, Structure stores for young men also have had declining sales and could be sold off.

Industry experts are also concerned because the company has expanded its product line extensively. Its "limited" product line led the company to success and gave it its market advantage in the past. Other critics claim the company has not been run as efficiently as it could have been, and that it has problems with product quality, concepts, and redundancy.

The Limited has also been criticized for lacking identity in a retail marketplace dominated by strong brands. One analyst asked, "Lerner, Limited, what do these stores stand for?"

HISTORY

Leslie Wexner started working at his father's clothing store in 1961. Disagreeing on how to run the business most effectively, Leslie tried to convince his father

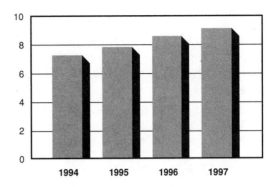

FINANCES:

The Limited, Inc.
Net Sales, 1994-1997
(billion dollars)

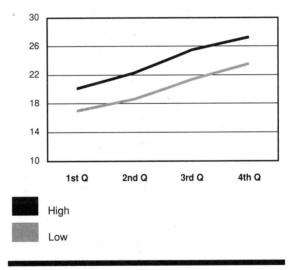

The Limited, Inc.
1997 Stock Prices
(dollars)

■ High

■ Low

to focus on selling sportswear. Wexner's father urged him to open his own store and apply his marketing ideas. Taking his advice, he left his father's clothing business in 1963 and opened the first Limited store in Columbus, Ohio, using $5,000 of borrowed money. Named for its limited selection, The Limited offered mid-priced, fashionable clothing to young women. After the first year the store was such a success that a second store was opened in Columbus. In 1965, Wexner's parents closed their store and joined their son's rapidly growing company.

Sales topped $1 million by 1968 and, in 1969 The Limited's first public stock was issued. However, the

FAST FACTS:

About The Limited, Inc.

Ownership: The Limited Inc. is a publicly owned company traded on the New York Stock Exchange and London Stock Exchange.

Ticker symbol: LTD

Officers: Leslie H. Wexner, Chmn., Pres. & CEO, 60, $2,861,560; Kenneth B. Gilman, VChmn. & Chief Administrative Officer, 51, $2,128,630; V. Ann Hailey, Exec. VP & CFO, 47, $463,152; Andrea Weiss, Exec. VP & Chief Stores Officer

Employees: 131,000 (1998)

Principal Subsidiary Companies: The Limited, Inc. owns and operates the following businesses: Galyan's Trading Co., Henri Bendel, Lane Bryant Inc., Lerner New York Inc., Limited Express, The Limited, Limited Too, Structure, and MAST Industries Inc. In addition, it owns 83 percent of Intimate Brands Inc., which includes Victoria's Secret Stores, Victoria's Secret Catalogue, and Bath and Body Works. It is in the process of divesting its ownership in Abercrombie and Fitch Co. through an exchange of stock.

Chief Competitors: The Limited, Inc. competes with other retailers of women's apparel, including: Banana Republic; Benetton; Body Shop; Charming Shopper; Clothestime; CML Group; Dayton Hudson; Dillard's; Dress Barn; Edison Brothers; Federated; The Gap; J. Crew; Lands' End; Levi Strauss; L.L. Bean; Marks and Spencer; May; Melville; Nieman Marcus; Nordstrom; Spiegel; TJX; and U.S. Shoe.

company's earnings were collapsing due to its rapid growth, so Wexner improved its manufacturing and distribution systems' efficiency. By 1976 the company had 100 stores.

In the early 1980s, The Limited began segmenting the market, or branching off into other specific markets. Over the years the company has marketed many types of apparel and accessories to many types of people. Products sold through its different stores include women's casualwear and sportswear, men's sportswear, children's sportswear, lingerie, toiletries, and perfume.

In 1980 the company began segmenting its market by opening the first Limited Express store (later named

Express). The new store was targeted toward teenagers, selling trendier fashions. By 1982 the Limited Express was so successful that it became a separate business.

In 1982 The Limited became a multidivisional company with the acquisition of Lane Bryant, a clothing store for larger women, and Victoria's Secret, a lingerie store and catalog operation. With the Lane Bryant acquisition, The Limited store discontinued selling its plus sizes and zeroed in on fashionable sportswear for younger women.

Acquisitions in 1985 included Lerner New York, mid-priced stores selling women's casualwear and sportswear, and targeted to a more budget-minded woman, and Henri Bendel, a New York-based company with six stores that specialized in *haute couture*. The Limited made Lerner lucrative within one year and opened the first Lerner Woman in 1986. Company sales for 1985 were $2.4 billion.

Limited Too, a children's fashion store, was opened in 1987 to capture the children's apparel market. Later, the Express store branched off by introducing the first men's line of fashions. The men's store name became Structure in 1987.

In 1988 The Limited acquired Abercrombie and Fitch, an upscale casual clothier, and introduced another lingerie store, Cacique, as sales reached the $4-billion level. Sales continued to grow in the early 1990s as the company introduced Bath and Body Works in 1990. By 1991 sales had reached $6.1 billion.

In 1995 The Limited purchased Galyan's Trading Company, a full-line sporting goods retailer with its own brands. That same year the company began restructuring to become more competitive, hiring away key executives from competitors such as J. Crew and Banana Republic, and downsizing by closing unprofitable stores. It made Intimate Brands (parent of Victoria's Secret and Bath and Body Works) a public company through an initial public offering of stock, but retained an 83-percent ownership. In 1996 Abercrombie and Fitch became a public company, and by 1998, The Limited planned to eliminate its ownership position in the 156-store chain through an exchange of stock.

In 1998 the company divested its interest in Brylane Inc., a catalog publisher, that grossed $1.3 billion in 1997, and closed the 118-store Cacique chain of lingerie stores. Overall, The Limited, Inc. reduced the number of stores it operated from 5,640 in 1997 to about 5,200 in 1998.

STRATEGY

The Limited has taken many steps over the years to reach its goal of becoming the largest and most profitable retailer of women's specialty clothing in the United States. One of the main reasons the company has been so strong in the marketplace is that it was the first store to offer affordable fashions catering to working women.

It produced private-label lines, which were manufactured exclusively for its stores in Third World countries and sold at high profit margins. Higher margins could be maintained due to the desirable image The Limited's private-label lines projected.

Another reason The Limited has been able to keep its market share is its unique sourcing and distribution process. Starting in 1969, the company instituted a system to improve financial controls. Using point-of-purchase terminals, the company was able to monitor inventory from its headquarters. This system enabled The Limited to mark down slow-selling items and restock with a speed that provided an advantage over its competitors. Department stores could not be as flexible. Acquiring MAST Industries, an international apparel purchasing and importing company, was key to this distribution process as well. With The Limited's point-of-purchase terminals and MAST Industries' efficient buying and shipping operations, The Limited was able to restock its shelves with the latest and most popular fashions within a matter of weeks, while competing stores took months to reshelve.

The Limited was willing to be creative and take chances with its marketing ideas. In an effort to win back customer loyalty, The Limited introduced a radio advertising campaign in 1994 targeted at the younger generation, which was the first to be aired in 10 years. The company also started an Italian cafe, Papa Razzi Cucina, in Express stores to attract a larger crowd. Although customers could not shop while eating, the combination store was designed to be casual and convenient.

Since 1995 the company has been refocusing on its women's apparel chains, especially Limited and Express, and downsizing by closing underperforming stores. A new division, Limited Design Services, was formed to upgrade the company's product lines, and the former president of Banana Republic, Maria Holman-Rao, was hired to be in charge.

According to its 1997 annual report, The Limited is mainly interested in brands that are capable of producing $1 billion in annual sales. The company's recent strategy involves building its core brands and eliminating others. According to a "Most Recognized Brands" survey, in only two years the Victoria's Secret brand moved from twenty-sixth to ninth most recognized brand. In 1998 the company sold its Cacique chain of lingerie stores to focus its resources on building the Victoria's Secret brand even more. Overall, the company is seeking to have fewer, but stronger, brands.

INFLUENCES

When the company went public, business expanded astronomically, almost to the point of collapse. The Limited was able to survive by improving the efficiency of

CHRONOLOGY:
Key Dates for The Limited, Inc.

1963: Leslie Wexner opens The Limited in Columbus, Ohio

1968: Sales surpass $1 million for the first time

1969: The Limited goes public

1978: Purchases Mast Industries, a merchandise procurement firm

1980: Launches The Limited Express targeting teenagers

1982: Acquires Lane Bryant and Victoria's Secret

1985: Acquires Lerner New York

1987: Opens Limited Too, a children's clothing store

1988: Acquires Abercrombie and Fitch

1995: Makes Intimate Brands, parent Victoria's Secret, a public company with an initial public stock offering

1996: Abercrombie and Fitch goes public

1998: Announces plans to eliminate its ownership of Abercrombie and Fitch through an exchange of stock

its manufacturing and distribution systems. Improving efficiency became the company's strategy and basis for strength in the market.

Economic challenges and the maturation of the company were obstacles for The Limited. In the early 1980s, the company grew at a phenomenal rate, but in 1984, a marketing mistake challenged The Limited. The company stocked its stores with career clothes, which did not sell very well. With the help of MAST Industries, The Limited quickly developed a new line of clothing and replaced career clothes with this more casual line within a few months, and avoided a possible catastrophe.

All challenges The Limited faced were met with decisive action. In 1988, when stores experienced a slight decrease in business, the company combatted this by expanding its specialty stores with enlarged display windows to attract more customers. In the 1990s, though, impressive storefronts were not enough. Customers wanted fashion and more importantly, value. Comparable store sales declined.

In the move to create more value, The Limited decided to spin off Intimate Brands, which accounted for 17 percent of its best growth business, as a public company in 1995. The Limited kept an 83-percent majority interest in Intimate Brands, which included Victoria's Secret stores and catalog, Bath and Body Works (the personal care product stores), and Cacique (the lingerie stores). Revenue gained from the sale was used to buy back Limited stock and prevent other division stores from closing.

The success of its sourcing and distribution system caused problems for the company. With speedy delivery being the number one priority, quality became questionable and pricing problems developed. Items were being marked down the same day they were put on the shelf, which detracted from the brand's image. The Limited managed to fight these problems while continuing to expand.

CURRENT TRENDS

The Limited began reorganizing its many divisions in 1995 as part of its overall strategy to refocus on women's apparel and create more value for the company's shareholders. It eliminated entire businesses, sold off substantial assets, and strengthened its core brands. The company began closing underperforming stores in 1995 with 79 store closings, followed in 1996 by 135 closings, in 1997 with 186 closings, and in 1998 with a projected 280 closings. The closings affected Limited, Lerner, Express, and Lane Bryant Stores. In 1998 the company closed the 118-store Cacique chain of lingerie stores to focus on strengthening its Victoria's Secret brand.

Two of the company's most profitable divisions, Intimate Brands and Abercrombie and Fitch, were spun off as public companies. While The Limited retained an 83-percent interest in Intimate Brands, it announced in 1998 that it would eliminate its ownership position in Abercrombie and Fitch through an exchange of stock. With the company looking for brands capable of producing $1 billion in annual sales, it was possible other divisions could become publicly owned companies once their performance reached a certain level. Other streamlining measures included cutting back the exclusive Henri Bendel chain from six stores to a single store in New York City.

In order to focus on strengthening its brands, especially its women's apparel stores The Limited and Express, The Limited hired experienced executives away from its competitors and also promoted several executives from within. Rob Bernard, formerly president and chief operating officer at the J. Crew Group, was hired as president of The Limited Stores to reestablish it as a dominant brand. Marie Holman-Rao, former president of Banana Republic, was hired as president of Limited Design Services, a new position responsible for the overall design platform of each business. The position also oversees the quality of each individual business's design organization.

PRODUCTS

The company's products include its many different store chains and the branded merchandise it sells. Its most recent acquisition was Galyan's Trading Company, a retailer for sport and fitness enthusiasts. Other brands on which the company is focusing its resources include Victoria's Secret, which will be supported by a $50-million advertising budget in 1998. Limited Too, a specialty store for girls, is also considered a leader in its segment.

CORPORATE CITIZENSHIP

In 1993, The Limited offered to construct a new vocational center for the Columbus Public School District in Ohio in exchange for 28 acres owned by the Northeast Career Center. The land occupied by the current career center was next to land the company had acquired to build a shopping mall. The company also offered to pay for the building appraisal and travel expenses for school officials to collect ideas by visiting other career centers nationwide. CEO Leslie Wexner is also a major donor to Ohio State University.

GLOBAL PRESENCE

The Limited operates most of its stores within the United States. In 1994 and 1995, in partnership with British apparel retailer Next PLC, The Limited opened five Bath and Body Works stores in suburban London, England, and in Scotland. Next PLC withdrew from the venture in 1996, selling its stake back to The Limited. With those stores doing well, it would be possible for Bath and Body Works to expand into Europe.

Most of the merchandise sold by The Limited is purchased from some 4,000 manufacturers in foreign markets. In 1995, approximately 55 percent of the company's total goods purchased were from foreign outlets.

EMPLOYMENT

The Limited is dedicated to its employees and emphasizes teamwork. It describes its corporate culture as one emphasizing creativity, hard work, and high energy. It is looking for people who are smart, ambitious, outgoing, and interested in making a career with the company. The company promotes from within and has a creative incentive program for its workers.

Benefits vary depending on the level of employment. They include merchandise discounts, participation in a stock purchase plan, a savings and retirement plan, a full dental and medical package, life insurance, and disability income.

SOURCES OF INFORMATION

Bibliography

Coleman-Lochner, Lauren. "Limited to Close 200 Shops." *Record-Bergen County,* 15 January 1997.

Gault, Ylonda. "The Limited Discovers its Limits." *Crains New York Business,* 19 December 1997.

Gebolys, Debbie. "Bath & Body Works Heads Overseas." *Columbus Dispatch,* 25 January 1997.

———. "Limited Agrees to Split with Catalog Operation." *Columbus Dispatch,* 3 March 1998.

———. "Limited Creates Division, Names President." *Columbus Dispatch,* 15 July 1997.

———. "Limited to Shed 2 Chains, Take Charge." *Columbus Dispatch,* 18 February 1998.

———. "The Limited's Executive Suite Sees Changes." *Columbus Dispatch,* 26 June 1997.

———. "New Leader Selected for Limited Stores." *Columbus Dispatch,* 12 August 1997.

Limited Fact Book. Columbus, OH: The Limited, Inc., 1997.

"The Limited, Inc." *Hoover's Handbook of American Business 1996.* Austin, TX: The Reference Press, 1995.

"The Limited, Inc. Announces Successful Completion of Exchange Offer Resulting in the Split-Off of Abercrombie & Fitch Co." *PR Newswire,* 14 May 1998.

The Limited, Inc. Home Page, 6 May 1998. Available at http://www.limited.com.

O'Malley, Christine B. "Limited Pays for Vocational School Study." *Business First-Columbus,* 15 August 1994.

Sahafi, Maya. "The Limited, Inc." *International Directory of Company Histories.* Detroit, MI: St. James Press, 1990.

Sparks, Debra. "Limited Appeal." *Financial World,* 12 August 1996.

Walters, Rebecca. "Limited Stirs Ingredients to Revive Winning Recipe." *Business First-Columbus,* 31 January 1994.

For an annual report:

on the Internet at: http://www.limited.com **or** write: The Limited, Inc., PO Box 16000, Columbus, OH 43216

For additional industry research:

Investigate companies by their Standard Industrial Classification Codes, also known as SICs. The Limited's primary SICs are:

5621 Women's Clothing Stores

5961 Catalog and Mail Order Houses

Little Caesar Enterprises, Inc.

FOUNDED: 1959

Contact Information:
HEADQUARTERS: 2211 Woodward Ave.
   Detroit, MI 48201
PHONE: (313)983-6000
FAX: (313)983-6494

OVERVIEW

Little Caesars Pizza is one of the world's largest pizza chains and a widely recognized brand name. The company is well-known for its "Little Caesar" character, which is used on the company's award-winning, humorous television commercials. It is also used in youth-oriented community programs sponsored by the firm.

As of 1997, Little Caesars was the third-largest pizza chain in the United States, with more than 4,700 retail stores and estimated sales of $2.1 billion. The chain trailed only Pizza Hut (owned by Tricon Global Restaurants) and Domino's Pizza. About two-thirds of all Little Caesars units were franchised to independent operators. In its marketing and advertising, Little Caesars emphasizes the quality of its pizza, which includes Grade A cheese, selected California tomatoes, and high-gluten flour as the main ingredients. As of 1997, Little Caesars was continuing a long-standing promotion of offering two pizzas for the price of one. The slogan for this campaign was "Pizza! Pizza!" In addition to its regular pizzas, Little Caesars offers deep-dish pizzas, individual-sized pizzas, submarine sandwiches, breads, and salads.

Since the beginning, the company was owned by the husband and wife team of Michael and Marian Ilitch, who hold key executive positions in the company. The couple also owns Blue Line Distributing, which distributes food and non-food products to Little Caesars' pizza franchisees on a weekly basis. Outside of their pizza operations, the Ilitches own the Detroit Tigers Baseball Club—American League, purchased in 1992 from Domino's Pizza founder Tom Monaghan for a reported $85 million; the Detroit Red Wings National Hockey League team, purchased in 1982 for a reported $8 million; Olympia Entertainment, a local arena management company; two arenas in Detroit and one in Glen Falls, New York. The Ilitches also own the Fox Theatre in Detroit. In 1996 Little Caesar Enterprises was ranked number 171 in the *Forbes* magazine Private 500 listing.

COMPANY FINANCES

As a private company, Little Caesars does not make public its financial records. Industry estimates put annual sales in 1997 at $2.10 billion, the same as 1996. Sales for 1995 were estimated at $2.05 billion, a slight increase from 1994's $2.00 billion, but down from 1993's $2.15 billion.

ANALYSTS' OPINIONS

Advertising and marketing has been a strong point most commentators agree. The company has gotten exceptional mileage from its two-for-one offerings, dubbed "Pizza! Pizza!" Most of the advertising is light-hearted, using humor to dramatize strong points. The ads do well in "most memorable campaign" surveys and have won several industry awards.

Over the years Little Caesars has been criticized by some of its franchisees as being too strict and having too many rules to follow. For example, franchisees must purchase products from Blue Line Distributing. However, company supporters claim that the rules are necessary to preserve the company's proven method and keep franchisees from cutting corners.

HISTORY

In 1959 Michael and Marian Ilitch, who grew up in Detroit, opened a carryout pizza restaurant west of the city. They called it Little Caesars Pizza Treat. Two years later, they added a second unit. From this small beginning, the Little Caesars chain began to grow. In 1962, the company began to franchise Little Caesars restaurants to independent owner/operators. As it did for other fast food chains, the franchising concept helped Little Caesars grow rapidly. By the late 1990s, Little Caesars had become an international chain with restaurants in all 50 states, Puerto Rico, Guam, Canada, South Korea, Honduras, the Dominican Republic, Turkey, the Philippines, Ecuador, and the Czech and Slovak Republics.

Other milestones in the company's history include opening its first restaurant outside the United States in 1962 in Canada, and introducing the first two-for-one offer in 1974, later called "Pizza! Pizza!" It also introduced flavored crusts in 1990. National delivery was introduced

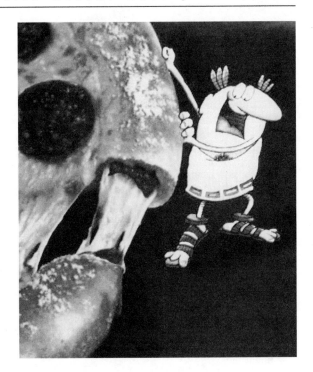

Little Caesar holds a piece of stuffed crust pizza. (Photograph by Richard Sheinwald. AP/Wide World Photos, Inc.)

in 1995, and the first Little Caesars in a hotel was opened in 1995 in Orlando, Florida.

STRATEGY

The growth of Little Caesars was driven by franchising, in which the company licensed the Little Caesars name to local owner/operators for a standard fee. Little Caesars then provided advertising, marketing, services, and products to the owner/operators in exchange for additional fees. In the early 1990s, Little Caesars received 5 percent of its franchisees revenues as royalties and an additional 4 percent for advertising. In 1991 Little Caesars spent $45 million on advertising in the United States. In 1996 it spent $32.7 million on network television advertising and $10.3 million on cable.

When selecting new franchisees, Little Caesars looks for individuals who are able to develop multiple restaurant locations. Before approving a franchisee, the company examines several factors, including overall experience, personal and financial qualifications, and business experience. As of 1997, Little Caesars' franchise fee was $20,000 for the first unit and $15,000 for each additional unit. The company offers third party financing to its franchisees.

FAST FACTS:

About Little Caesar Enterprises, Inc.

Ownership: Little Caesars is a privately owned company controlled by the Ilitch family.

Officers: Michael Ilitch, Chmn. & Pres.; Denise Ilitch Lites, VChmn.; Harsha V. Agadi, COO; Marian Ilitch, Treasurer & Secretary

Employees: 600 (headquarters), 90,000 (total)

Chief Competitors: Little Caesars competes primarily with other pizza chains and to a lesser extent with quick service chains. Its major pizza competitors are: Pizza Hut Inc.; Domino's Pizza Inc.; Hungry Howie's Pizza and Subs; and Papa John's International Inc.

Little Caesars also sponsors regional franchise meetings to review corporate strategies and solicit comments from franchisees. These meetings are used to help franchisees strengthen their operations and marketing programs. Little Caesars also operates a "Franchise Advisory Committee," which is made up of franchise owners and Little Caesars corporate executives who meet on a regular basis to discuss current business issues and review future strategies.

To maintain strong local franchises and ensure consistent products and services across the chain, Little Caesars provides a wide range of services and benefits to its franchisees, including training, business support, and marketing support. The Little Caesars training program covers operations, marketing, and general business information. Services are provided through the Little Caesars franchise services department.

Another key part of Little Caesars business strategy is an ongoing marketing and advertising program. The company launched its first national network television campaign in 1988. After that, the company became known for its humorous, entertaining commercials. The commercials focus on the value and quality of Little Caesars products. From 1992 to 1997, Little Caesars' advertising was ranked by consumers among the top five most memorable campaigns in Video Storyboard Tests Incorporated's annual survey. Little Caesars said that its advertising outranked some other major companies that spent 3 or 4 times more on advertising. The company cut

back its media budget to $51.9 million in 1996, down 22.8 percent from 1994 levels.

In early 1997, the American Association of Advertising Agencies (AAAA) named Little Caesars Enterprises as the winner of its John O'Toole Advertiser Award, which honors outstanding advertising campaigns over a period of time. In a June 1997 interview, Little Caesars Enterprises's new vice president of strategic marketing, Ken Murray said that he was committed to retaining the company's distinctive advertising campaign, which was created by Cliff Freeman & Partners. Little Caesars also maintains ongoing communications and public relations programs in addition to its advertising program. These efforts are coordinated by a corporate communications department.

Unlike its main competitors, Domino's Pizza and Pizza Hut, Little Caesars was exclusively a carryout business until the mid-1990s. The "no-delivery" policy allowed the firm to maintain a significant price advantage over its competitors, according to one press report. However, in July 1995 Little Caesars changed this strategy when it began pizza deliveries at nearly all of its operating units in the United States. Little Caesars said it would hire and train 40,000 new employees to operate the delivery system. It also began a national television campaign to promote Little Caesars pizza and its delivery service.

The firm called its new delivery program a success, even while some observers questioned the move. One observer suggested that Little Caesars should have avoided competing in the delivery segment of the pizza business, citing cases of long waits for both delivery and carryout services at Little Caesars outlets. Instead, it was thought the company should focus on improving efficiency and customer service in the carryout business.

In the 1990s, Little Caesars and other pizza chains were exploring the use of non-traditional retail outlets. For example, in 1991 Little Caesars opened 400 Pizza Stations inside Kmart stores in order to increase customer awareness and market share for both firms. However, some existing Little Caesars franchise owners were upset by the move. They said that the new Kmart units would hurt their sales. Some franchisees banded together to form A.L.C.F. Inc., a group to represent their interests and negotiate with Little Caesars Enterprises.

In 1996, Little Caesars Enterprises and Pizza Hut both entered into strategic alliances with hotel companies. This meant that the pizza firms would provide food service on premises at hotels as well as room service. The alliances were expected to increase sales and improve room service in the hotels and also improve the pizza chains' market share and brand marketing ability. Little Caesars signed an agreement with Holiday Inn Incorporated, while Pizza Hut had agreements with Choice Hotels International Inc. and HFS.

INFLUENCES

Little Caesars has succeeded in differentiating itself from other pizza companies through its humorous advertising and its product offerings. Its 25-year-old "Pizza! Pizza!" campaign was still going strong in he late 1990s. The company also strives to maintain a cohesive franchisee network. The company has stopped bringing in new franchisees during various time periods, while existing franchise owners could open new locations.

CURRENT TRENDS

Many franchise firms, including Little Caesars Enterprises, had to deal with disgruntled franchisees who appeared to be filing increasing lawsuits against franchisors in the mid- to late 1990s. For example, in 1997 some Little Caesars pizza store owners sued the parent company for alleged overcharging for pizza dough and supplies. Earlier, in mid-1995, Little Caesars Enterprises was sued for antitrust violations by a group of Minnesota-based franchisees. The group charged that Little Caesars' requirement that franchisees purchase products from Blue Line Distributing, owned by the Ilitches, constituted an illegal monopoly.

Little Caesars and Kmart Corporation reached an agreement in 1997 whereby Kmart would begin selling Little Caesars pizza in virtually all of its in-store restaurants. Numbering some 1,800 locations, K Cafes ranked among the nation's 10 largest restaurant chains with annual revenues of about $350 million. About 500 Kmart stores have carried Little Caesars pizza since 1991.

PRODUCTS

Little Caesars most recent new product was the "Big! Big!" pizzas introduced in fall 1997. As part of this campaign Little Caesars expanded the size of its pizza by 4 inches. A small pizza would be 14 inches in diameter, for example, rather than 10 inches. In addition, the pizzas would be topped with three-inch pepperoni and extra-large slices of ham.

Little Caesars was actively developing and marketing other new products during the mid- to late 1990s. In October 1996, the firm introduced Pizza by the Foot, designed to be a family meal. The launch was supported by a $10-million advertising campaign created by Cliff Freeman and Partners. The three-foot long pizza came with seasoned Italian bread for a package price of $19.99— with limited-time value pricing of $10.99. During 1997 a new Stromboli Pizza was introduced as part of the Pizza by the Foot offering. The Stromboli Pizza is a fold-over pizza stuffed with tomato, cheese, and pepperoni.

In November 1995 Little Caesars introduced a stuffed crust pizza, following the lead of Pizza Hut, which

CHRONOLOGY:
Key Dates for Little Caesar Enterprises, Inc.

1959: Michael and Marian Ilitch open a carryout pizza restaurant outside of Detroit, Michigan

1962: The company begins to franchise Little Caesars restaurants

1974: Little Caesars stops its delivery service to become carryout only; begins its two-for-one deal

1979: The "Pizza! Pizza!" campaign begins

1982: Becomes the first pizza chain to operate within a sports arena

1987: Little Caesars opens in Alaska, giving the company a franchise in all 50 states

1992: Little Caesars advertising is ranked the number one most recognizable

1995: Reintroduces delivery services

1997: Kmart and Little Caesars reach an agreement in which Kmart would serve Little Caesars pizza in its in-store restaurants

introduced its version of stuffed crust pizza in mid-1995. Little Caesars' Stuffed Crust Pizza had a suggested price of $7.99 for carryout and $9.99 for delivery. The 14-inch pizza pie had string cheese and pepperoni stuffed into the crust.

CORPORATE CITIZENSHIP

In the late 1990s Little Caesar Enterprises was involved in several community activities. It reaches out to the communities in which it operates by working with local school systems and being involved with various community and family/youth groups. The company participates in a number of "adopt-a-school" programs throughout the United States to provide a positive influence on the quality of education.

The company also supports amateur sports programs in the cities where it is located. About 50,000 children participate in Little Caesars sponsored sports annually. The company also helps sponsor youth sports through local amateur athletic organizations and local parks and recreation departments. It participates in programs that support college athletics and professional sports as well.

The company sponsors the Little Caesars Love Kitchen, a mobile pizza operation that works through soup kitchens to provide free pizza to people in need. It also provides relief to victims and relief workers when natural disasters strike.

In the Detroit area, Michael and Marian Ilitch, owners of Little Caesars, have been heavily involved in efforts to revitalize the downtown area. They own two local professional sports teams, have rehabilitated a famous local theater, and built a large office building in downtown Detroit. Individually and with his family, Michael Ilitch has received numerous awards for community service, as well as for contributions to the restaurant industry. These awards have included the "Humanitarian of the Year" award from the March of Dimes and many others.

GLOBAL PRESENCE

Little Caesars has pizza locations in the U.S. territories of Puerto Rico and Guam and in nine other countries: Canada, Czech Republic, Slovakia, South Korea, Honduras, the Dominican Republic, Turkey, the Philippines, and Ecuador.

EMPLOYMENT

Little Caesars employs about 600 people at its corporate headquarters in downtown Detroit and about 90,000 throughout its locations in all 50 states and internationally.

SOURCES OF INFORMATION

Bibliography

Benezra, Karen. "Rattling the Chains." *Brandweek,* 21 April 1997.

Howard, Theresa. "Pizza Hut, Little Caesars Fend off Separate Lawsuits." *Nation's Restaurant News,* 20 November 1995.

CORPORATE KINDHEART

In 1985 Little Caesars introduced a service called the Little Caesars Love Kitchen. The Kitchen consists of a pizza restaurant on wheels that travels to soup kitchens and shelters feeding hungry people in the United States and Canada. The Love Kitchen also travels to help out victims and rescue workers at various disaster sites, including Hurricane Hugo (1989), Hurricane Andrew (1992), the San Fernando Valley earthquake (1994), and the Alfred P. Murrah Federal Building in Oklahoma City (1995).

Kramer, Louise. "Little Caesars Arsenal Grows with Delivery Debut." *Nation's Restaurant News,* 26 June 1995.

Lyons, David. "Hail, Caesars!" *World Traveler,* April 1997.

McDowell, Bill, and Laura Petrecca. "Little Caesars' Big New Idea: Pizza by the Foot." *Advertising Age,* 28 October 1996.

Pittinger, Heather. "Popular and Profitable." *Hotel & Motel Management,* 6 May 1996.

Preddy, Melissa. "Kmart Expands Little Caesars at K Cafes." *Detroit News,* 24 September 1997.

Rinkel, Desiree. "Holy Moly! It's Stromboli; Little Caesars Introduces New Pizza." *PR Newswire.* 10 February 1997.

Stopa, Marsha. "Ilitch: Back in Pizza Biz." *Crain's Detroit Business,* 23 September 1996.

Tannenbaum, Jeffrey A. "Many Franchisers, Ignoring Recession, Rush to Expand." *The Wall Street Journal,* 27 January 1992.

Whalen, Jeanne. "Little Caesars Exec's Goal: Do More with Less." *Advertising Age,* 2 June 1997.

For additional industry research:

Investigate companies by their Standard Industrial Classification Codes, also known as SICs. Little Caesars' primary SICs are:

5812 Eating Places

6794 Patent Owners and Lessors

Liz Claiborne, Inc.

OVERVIEW

Liz Claiborne, Inc. is one of America's leading apparel companies. Its products are sold in department stores and speciality stores worldwide. The company designs and markets fashion apparel and accessories for women; fashion apparel and furnishings for men; and fragrances for men and women. According to the company's annual report, "Each division of the company responds to a different set of lifestyle needs or preferences among the millions of fashion consumers who are our customers." In addition to its divisions, the company's brand name has been licensed to manufacturers and marketers of women's shoes, bed and bath furnishings, optics, sunglasses, and men's suits.

FOUNDED: 1976

Contact Information:

HEADQUARTERS: 1441 Broadway
　New York, NY 10018
PHONE: (212)354-4900
FAX: (212)626-1800
TOLL FREE: (800)578-7070
URL: http://www.lizclaiborne.com

COMPANY FINANCES

After a prolonged slump in the mid-1990s, Liz Claiborne experienced a reversal of fortune. Earnings rose 69 percent in 1996, one of the best gains in the apparel business. Net sales were a record $2.2 billion, with steady gains in women's sportswear, Dana Buchman products, and the outlet stores. In 1997 Liz Claiborne set another record with net sales of $2.4 billion, and earnings per share of $2.65. In the first quarter of 1998, the turnaround continued with net sales of a record $656.0 million, compared with the same period in 1997 when sales were $596.6 million. In addition, strong sales increases were reported in the Casual Sportswear Group, which includes, LizSport, LizWear, and Liz & Co.

FINANCES:

Liz Claiborne Revenues, 1994-1997 (billion dollars)

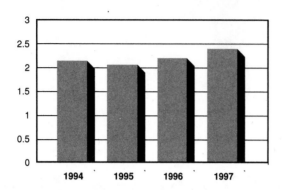

Liz Claiborne 1997 Stock Prices (dollars)

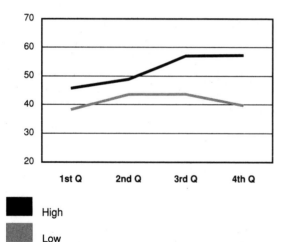

HISTORY

Elisabeth Claiborne had spent 25 years designing women's clothes when Liz Claiborne, Inc. was founded in 1976. Claiborne waited until her son was 21 years old before starting the company so that he would not be adversely affected if the business failed. Her goal was to be a clothing designer, and to build a small, profitable business. Joined by Leonard Boxer, Jerome A. Chazen, and her husband, Art Ortenberg, each of these four original founders invested $50,000 in the company. Loans from family and friends provided an additional $200,000.

In 1981 Liz Claiborne, Inc. became a publicly traded company on the New York Stock Exchange under the symbol LIZ. With revenues of approximately $800 million in 1986, the company appeared on the Fortune 500 list of the top companies in America.

In 1994 Paul Charron became the chief executive officer of Liz Claiborne, Inc. In the same year, sales fell and profits dropped dramatically. Charron, a former navy officer, was quoted by Nancy Rotenier in *Forbes* as saying: "The navy taught me how to operate in a combat zone." Rotenier agreed, saying that "Liz Claiborne, Inc. was practically a combat zone when the naval-officer-turned-marketing executive was brought in from VF Corp. to run it in 1994." Extensive market research indicated that many of Liz Claiborne's fashions had not kept up with current trends, so new styles were introduced, and new products, such as watches and swimwear, were offered. An extensive advertising campaign was launched using supermodel Niki Taylor, which helped the company become one of the largest fashion apparel advertisers. The company used print sources as well as outdoor billboards and bus shelters to advertise its products.

The apparel industry was not growing. The company had to do everything it could to increase its competitiveness in order to gain as large a market share as possible. Charron worked to cut costs using newly introduced information-management technologies. Computer-aided design cut costs and reduced the amount of time it took to go from the design phase to actual products for sale.

ANALYSTS' OPINIONS

Many analysts felt that management strategies at Liz Claiborne, Inc. were sound, and expected company sales and profits to grow. The Special Markets Group, a new moderate line of clothing introduced in Wal-Mart and Sears, Roebuck and Co. was expected to be especially profitable in the late 1990s. According to Raymond S. Cohen in *Value Line Investment Survey,* "Claiborne is committed to the expansion of all its labels in a multilevel strategy that aims to include appeal for all women."

STRATEGY

In the late 1990s growth in the retail industry continued to be sluggish. Liz Claiborne targeted moderate price department store markets through several special labels. Emma James, introduced in 1996, was a new moderate label to be sold in department stores. The label First Issue, which featured relaxed career and everyday wear, was to be relaunched and sold at Sears, Roebuck and Co. stores. The Russ label targeted budget conscious consumers at Wal-Mart stores.

In the company's 1997 annual report, chairman Paul Charron noted that the company was focused intently "on leveraging and extending our core competencies, employing new technologies and devoting ceaseless energy to make us the world's preeminent designer and marketer of fashion apparel and accessories." In practical terms, this included the opening of 461 LizView shops; the launching of the company's consumer web site, which featured an interactive wardrobe planner and a domestic and international store locator; and the Claiborne Changing Room, a mobile showroom in 10 cities that gave apparel tips to men.

INFLUENCES

Liz Claiborne began selling clothing in 1976, a time of growth and customer interest in apparel. Women were joining the work force in record numbers and looking for attractive, reasonably priced clothing to wear to work. The company filled this niche and was very successful through the 1980s. Claiborne clothing and accessories were sold in department stores throughout the country. Sales and profits soared. In the early 1990s this trend changed. Several factors contributed to a decline in fortunes for the company. First, the entire women's fashion business experienced a downturn. Customers were spending less money on clothing and showing more independence about adopting the latest fashion trends. Second, a more relaxed dress code was adopted in the workplace. Third, several competitors joined the market. Styles offered by Liz Claiborne, Inc. were often overshadowed by competitors. Claiborne work was inferior in some cases. According to Teri Agins and Wendy Bounds in the *Wall Street Journal*, "Earnings declined in 1993 and 1994—the year that one of Claiborne's most prestigious retail accounts, Saks Fifth Avenue, dropped the sportswear collection entirely. Saks deemed the clothes not fashionable enough and too widely available elsewhere."

CURRENT TRENDS

When Paul Charron became CEO of Liz Claiborne in 1994, he realized that strong measures would have to be employed to return the company to profitability. Sales had dropped from $2.2 billion in 1993 to less than $2.1 billion in 1995. Profits dropped to $83 million in 1994 from a high of $223 million in 1991. One of his first actions was to conduct market research to determine the changing shopping habits and needs of customers. An innovative approach was used to determine customer preferences by interviewing customers personally at shopping malls and in their homes.

FAST FACTS:
About Liz Claiborne, Inc.

Ownership: Liz Claiborne, Inc. is a publicly owned company traded on the New York Stock Exchange.

Ticker symbol: LIZ

Officers: Paul R. Charron, Chmn. & CEO, 55, $2,239,300; Denise V. Seegal, Pres., 44, $1,331,200; Jorge L. Figueredo, Sr. VP, Human Resources, 37; Samuel M. Miller, Sr. VP Finance & CFO, 60, $574,000

Employees: 7,500

Principal Subsidiary Companies: Liz Claiborne, Inc.'s principal subsidiaries are L.C. Special Markets, Inc.; Claiborne Ltd.; Liz Claiborne Accessories, Inc.; and Liz Claiborne Cosmetics, Inc.

Chief Competitors: As a manufacturer of women's clothing, Liz Claiborne competes with: Jones Apparel Group, Inc.; Rafaella; Tommy Hilfiger Corp.; Nautica Enterprises, Inc.; Ralph Lauren; Banana Republic; Gap Inc.; and Limited Inc.

In addition, Liz Claiborne, Inc. operated its own speciality stores throughout the world to keep in close touch with customers and current trends. After analyzing market research results, the company discovered that women's roles had shifted and that they wanted to simplify the way they dressed. More than anything else, women desired versatility in clothing—clothing that would go from home to work.

Cost-cutting measures were employed to increase profitability. Jobs were cut by 10 percent, and production was consolidated to give the company better control over the quality of it products and to speed up the time it took for products to reach the market. Technology also played a role in Liz Claiborne's success. Computer-aided design technology was used as was LizRIM, a retail inventory management system that allowed items selling very well to be replaced in stores while still in season. Sales rose 25 percent in stores where LizRIM had been installed. Management became much more flexible. Division managers were given greater decision-making authority so they could respond to fashion trends more quickly, and implement new fashion ideas.

Liz Claiborne felt that product presentation and the shopping experience were critical to success and insti-

CHRONOLOGY:

Key Dates for Liz Claiborne, Inc.

1976: Liz Claiborne, Inc. is founded

1981: The company goes public

1985: Expands its line to include men's clothing

1986: Launches its signature scent

1988: Makes the Fortune 500 list—one of the youngest companies to make the list

1989: Elisabeth Claiborne resigns from active management

1992: *Fortune* names Liz Claiborne, Inc. one of the ten most admired corporations in America

1997: Liz Claiborne and Donna Karan International sign a licensing agreement for marketing and distribution

---

tuted two new programs in those areas: LizEdge, a program designed to ensure that products are displayed attractively in stores and LizView, a program that enhances the retail area in which products are sold. Color schemes, fixtures, and signs are designed to attract customers and to suggest coordinated outfits.

Liz Claiborne and Donna Karan International Inc. signed a strategic licensing agreement in 1997 to market and distribute two lines of apparel, DKNY Jeans and DKNY Active throughout the Western Hemisphere. The alliance provided Liz Claiborne with the opportunity to reach new consumer segments. The company noted that megabrands, such as the DKNY line, were central to continued growth and market share gains.

PRODUCTS

Liz & Co., a line of petite clothing, was introduced in 1996, as well as dana b. & karen, the casual career clothing line of the Dana Buchman division. New products included swimwear and watches. Curve for women, and Curve for men were the company's newest fragrances. New designs included fitted jackets with zippers, stretch pants, and five-pocket jeans.

In 1997 the company introduced Liz Claiborne and Elisabeth swimwear and coats, and extended its line of home accessories to include table linens, placemats, napkins, and accessories. Dana Buchman Eyewear, featuring sunglasses with sophisticated styling, were introduced and marketed by Bausch & Lomb.

The company also relaunched the Crazy Horse brand of affordable casual clothing in 1997. The collection was to be available exclusively at J. C. Penney beginning in the Fall of 1998.

CORPORATE CITIZENSHIP

The company's charitable activities are coordinated through the Liz Claiborne Foundation, which works primarily in communities where the company's major facilities are located. They provide assistance to organizations that are involved in helping women and their families. Projects supported by the Foundation include providing educational opportunities for needy children; job training for disadvantaged women; and assisting women who are HIV-positive or have AIDS. The Foundation also provides support to a variety of cultural institutions to enhance the quality of the arts in communities around the country.

Employees of the company are encouraged to volunteer at local nonprofit organizations. An employee-matching-gifts program is used to encourage employees to support a variety of charitable interests.

Liz Claiborne, Inc. is also concerned about domestic and family violence. The program, Women's Work, was established in 1991 to educate and raise public awareness. This program uses billboards and radio announcements to raise awareness, and form partnerships with community groups and local retailers. In 1996 the company used well-known college athletes to deliver public service announcements that discouraged men from engaging in violence in relationships.

GLOBAL PRESENCE

To remain competitive, the company actively worked toward global expansion. By the mid-1990s, products were available in more than 50 countries on 6 continents. In 1995 international sales reached $138.2 million.

Liz Claiborne products were available in Canada, Europe, Asia, and Central and South America by the late 1990s. A substantial portion of the company's products are manufactured by foreign companies. The company has partnerships with yarn mills and textile houses worldwide. Liz Claiborne, Inc. is a member of a Presidential Task Force that had been organized to set up voluntary standards for apparel factories in the United States and in foreign countries. These standards help to insure that apparel companies do not use "sweatshops"—places where employees work long hours for low wages and under poor working conditions—in the manufacturing of their products.

SOURCES OF INFORMATION

Bibliography

Agins, Teri, and Wendy Bounds. "A Flashier Liz Claiborne Fashions a Turnaround." *The Wall Street Journal,* 11 November 1996.

Better, Nancy Marx. "The Secret of Liz Claiborne's Success." *Working Woman,* April 1992.

Cowen, Raymond S. "Liz Claiborne." *Value Line Investment Survey,* 2 February 1997.

D'Innocenzio, Anne. "Charron's Challenge: Sending Liz Claiborne Back to the Stars." *WWD,* 15 March 1995.

———. "The Repackaging of Liz Claiborne." *WWD,* 6 November 1996.

Gault, Ylonda. "A Liz for the '90s." *Crain's New York Business,* 30 September-6 October 1996.

Greenhouse, Steven. "Voluntary Rules on Apparel Labor Proving Elusive." *The New York Times,* 1 February 1997.

Liz Claiborne Annual Report 1995. New York: Liz Claiborne, Inc., 1995.

"Liz Claiborne-Company Report." *Merrill Lynch Capital Markets,* 22 October 1996.

Liz Claiborne Home Page, 29 May 1998. Available at http://www.lizclaiborne.com.

Rotenier, Nancy. "Niki and Me." *Forbes,* 13 January 1997.

Sellers, Patricia. "The Rag Trade's Reluctant Revolutionary." *Fortune,* 5 January 1987.

Sieder, Jill Jordan. "Liz Claiborne Gets Dressed for Success." *U.S. News & World Report,* 26 February 1996.

For an annual report:
on the Internet at: http://www.lizclaiborne.com/highlite **or** write: Liz Claiborne Inc., 1441 Broadway, New York, NY 10018

For additional industry research:
Investigate companies by their Standard Industrial Classification Codes, also known as SICs. Liz Claiborne Inc.'s primary SICs are:

2329 Men/Boys' Clothing, NEC

2335 Women/Juniors/Misses' Dresses

2339 Women/Misses' Outerwear, NEC

2389 Apparel & Accessories, NEC

L.L. Bean, Inc.

FOUNDED: 1912 by Leon Leonwood Bean

Contact Information:

HEADQUARTERS: Casco St.
   Freeport, ME 04033
PHONE: (207)865-4761
FAX: (207)552-2802
URL: http://www.llbean.com

OVERVIEW

L.L. Bean, Inc. is a mail-order company specializing in outdoor products. In 1998 it had 24 different catalogs, representing seasonal items; specialty products for hunting and fly fishing; sporting goods; children's clothing; and household furnishings. In 1996 it distributed more than 115 million catalogs. The company's customer service policies have allowed consumers unlimited returns, as well as replacements of the soles of its Maine Hunting Shoe, the first product carried by the company. Taking advantage of the Internet, the company has considered conducting its mail-order business solely from its web site, allowing L.L. Bean to battle rising shipment costs.

COMPANY FINANCES

In 1998 total revenue for L.L. Bean was $1.07 billion, up from 1997's $1.04 billion. However, both years were slightly lower than 1996's revenue of $1.08, but up from 1995 and 1994, which was $974 and $870 million, respectively.

ANALYSTS' OPINIONS

Many analysts consider retail and mail-order catalogs to be a mature business in the United States. For example, the outdoor-wear market in Japan is approximately $405 million, only one-twentieth the size of the U.S. market. The possibilities for growth in Japan, according to analysts, is partially due to the fast-paced lifestyles, making outdoor activities appealing. For years,

Japanese men worked extremely long hours, thus neglecting their private lives. However, a new trend to explore nature and family-oriented activities developed.

Many analysts have viewed L.L. Bean's outlet stores as a financially rewarding move. These stores, where most merchandise sold has been discounted for various imperfections, have allowed the company to recover approximately $.90 of each dollar's value it would otherwise count as a loss. L.L. Bean says its research has shown that these stores do not take away from mail order sales. In fact, the company claims, catalog sales have been higher where outlet stores exist.

L.L. Bean has been criticized by some for its failures in the European and U.K. markets. Some say the company's poor sense of audience was to blame. One analyst said customers wanting to place an order in these regions faced an ordeal. First, the prices in the catalogs were in dollars and not pounds. Second, the customer had to calculate personal shipping costs, duty fee, and taxes. Also, to place an order required dialing an American number. Some say pricing the merchandise in pounds and making ordering more simple would have attracted more customers there. Consequently, L.L. Bean did not have much success in Europe.

The L.L. Bean classic boot. (*Courtesy of L.L. Bean.*)

HISTORY

L.L. Bean's first product, the Maine Hunting Shoe, launched the company's success. Its first shipment of boots, however, proved faulty in that they all leaked. The rubber-soled, leather upper boots were rapidly fixed at Leon Leonwood Bean's expense, beginning the company's reputation of top quality customer service.

Located in Freeport, Maine, the company sought a mailing list of avid hunters once Maine's hunting licensing system was active in 1917. Leon Bean created a showroom for consumers in the Freeport area. In 1920 he constructed a store located on Main Street in Freeport. By 1937, sales had escalated to $1 million.

During World War II, times would have been tough for the company had the military not allowed Bean to design their boots. Continuing to grow and add products, L.L. Bean began staying open 24-hours-a-day in 1951. The company furthered its growth by adding a women's department store in 1954.

Leon Bean died in 1967 at 94 years of age, and witnessed sales having climbed to $4.8 million. Leon Gorman, Bean's grandson, took over as president. He brought in advanced mailing systems, improved manufacturing systems, and set a goal to attract nonsporting markets. The 1980s proved successful since sales grew steadily, averaging 20 percent each year.

Seeing a potential for growth in Japan, L.L. Bean signed deals with Seiyu and Matsushita. The first catalog and service facility was opened in Japan in 1995.

Also expanding its market, L.L. Bean added a children's clothing line, L.L. Kids, in 1993. Due to overwhelming popularity, the company opened a separate clothing store for kids in 1997.

STRATEGY

L.L. Bean's strategy for success started with a standard Leon Leonwood Bean called "L.L. Bean's Golden Rule." Simply, the rule exemplified his belief: "Sell good merchandise at a reasonable profit, treat your customers like human beings, and they will always come back for more." Customer service remains a large strategic factor in the company's success, backed by a 100-percent satisfaction guaranteed statement found on the company's retail stores and catalogs.

The other ingredients of L.L. Bean's strategy revolve around the way the company functions. For example, its main business has been conducted by mail-order. Factory stores exist, but their purpose has been to sell merchandise returned in a less than flawless state. Some items might have been returned without their original package. Others were items that did not sell well. In other words, the purpose of these factory outlets stores has been to get back the financial loss of those returned or never-sold products.

FAST FACTS:

About L.L. Bean, Inc.

Ownership: L.L. Bean, Inc. is a privately owned company.

Officers: Leon A. Gorman, CEO; Lee Surace, CFO

Employees: 3,600 (1998)

Chief Competitors: L.L. Bean competes with other mail-order companies, as well as store-based retail organizations. Some of its primary competitors include: American Eagle Outfitters; Coleman; Fruit of the Loom; The Gap; Hudson's Bay; J.C. Penney; J. Crew; Lands' End; Levi Strauss; Nautica Enterprises; NIKE; OshKosh B'Gosh; Reebok; Spiegel; Sports Authority; and Timberland.

INFLUENCES

L.L. Bean claims much of its success was a result of its reputation, effective marketing, and enlarged circulation. L.L. Bean's sales dropped in 1989 however, forcing the company to lay off employees in 1991 and 1992. After that setback, the company began prospering rapidly and continued to expand. Increases in the postal rate in 1991 caused the company to charge a shipping and handling fee to its customers for the first time. Also in an effort to offset rising shipment costs, L.L. Bean set its sights on the Internet, creating its own web site as a means of mail-order service. The mail order business, the company's core business, accounted for 87.7 percent of the sales in 1995.

Sales grew by 10 percent—nearly $1 billion in 1995. In spite of these profits, the company offered buyouts and early retirements to eligible employees in 1996. The company claimed sales were $90 million below target range and it had to cut costs for the next three years in order to remain competitive. Considering the fact that from July 1994 to July 1995, 50 percent of American companies did some sort of downsizing, L.L. Bean's cost-cutting efforts seemed ordinary.

Due to market demand, L.L. Bean established L.L. Bean Japan in 1995. L.L. Bean's early efforts to expand throughout Europe and the United Kingdom were not as successful. Some analysts attribute this failure to many factors including a confusing ad campaign and ordering difficulties.

L.L. Bean added L.L. Kids, a children's clothing store, after the popular clothing line demanded its own business in 1996. The fastest portion of L.L. Bean's business in 1996, L.L. Kids grew 29 percent in 1995. The company has claimed it learned a valuable lesson—seize opportunities as they present themselves instead of waiting.

CURRENT TRENDS

The newest trend of L.L. Bean's strategic moves has been to take advantage of technological advances to further its growth. In 1995 the company set up its own web site. Gaining new customers rapidly, the company made plans to put its catalogs on a Net Commerce server. Working with IBM and a consulting firm to develop an interface for users, L.L. Bean hoped to increase its customer volume even further.

Another recent change for the company has been in the area of customer service, long-established as a no-questions-asked, 100-percent satisfaction guaranteed policy. Due to increased dishonesty of many returns, the company has had to develop a more cost-effective return policy. The ability of a customer to return any L.L. Bean item without a receipt at any given point in time prompted some customers to try to return items they had bought at garage sales. One customer even tried to return clothes from a dead relative's closet.

PRODUCTS

Approximately 94 percent of its products carried the L.L. Bean label in 1998. The company manufactures more than 200 different products in six categories: Maine Hunting Shoes, handsewn footwear, sleepwear, dog beds, tote bags, and soft luggage. Bean's manufacturing center in Brunswick, Maine, also functions as a repair and refurbishment shop. In 1996, L.L. Bean reported that it replaced over 25,000 pairs of worn-out rubber bottoms on Maine Hunting Shoes.

CORPORATE CITIZENSHIP

In 1998, L.L. Bean offered its customers an Outdoor Hotline, staffed with employees who could give guidance on outdoor recreation topics, ranging from sea kayaking to backpacking. It offered to help customers plan trips, find the right camp site, or locate areas where particular fish were running.

As a special service to its Internet customers, its web site in 1998 linked to sites containing information on nearly 1,000 parks where they could camp, fish, hike, or swim—presumably using Bean products.

L.L. Bean, a nature-focused company, has committed itself to the environment. In 1996 it was the SCA's EarthWork America corporate sponsor. The efforts consisted of a day-long volunteer program with various conservation projects on the agenda. L.L. Bean also worked with several conservation and recreation groups to maintain the Appalachian Trail and has contributed $20,000 annually to the Grants to Clubs program of the Appalachian Trail conference (ATC). L.L. Bean's contribution has been the largest corporate donation to the organization.

The company also prides itself since, in 1996, it made the Trendsetter List released by the Labor Department in Washington. This list is comprised of retailers and manufacturers who make extra efforts to guarantee their products are not made in sweatshop conditions, including child labor, abusive conditions, and other compromising circumstances. In addition, it tries to support domestic manufacturing, particularly in Maine.

GLOBAL PRESENCE

In 1998, L.L. Bean maintained its Freeport, Maine, retail store and factory outlets in 4 states. It also had 10 retail stores in Japan as well. Because L.L. Bean, Inc. has targeted upper- and middle-class individuals, 50 percent of which are men, Japan became an increasingly profitable market. The Japanese were used to catalogs carrying cheaply made items with no apparent theme, unlike L.L. Bean's appeal to nature. American catalogs, however, offered top quality goods with pictures of top models to help sell them. Hungry for quality merchandise, Japan quickly developed a $20-billion mail order catalog market. L.L. Bean's mail order sales in Japan for 1995 were estimated to be $200 million, equaling 80 percent of international sales for the company.

SOURCES OF INFORMATION

Bibliography

"An Insider's Guide to Catalog Marketing in the UK and Europe." *The Catalog Marketer,* 26 March 1997. Available at http://www.smartbiz.com.

Cooper, Lane F. "Webbing for Dollars: Being a Webmaster Is Taxing, But the Work to Keep an Electronic-Commerce Site Profitable Can Be Herculean." *Web Commerce,* 13 January 1997. Available at http://techweb.cmp.com.

Lee, Louise. "Tired of Shopper Scams, Retailers Are Tightening Policies on Returns." *The News Times,* 18 November 1996.

L.L. Bean Home Page, 17 July 1998. Available at http://www.llbean.com.

"L.L. Bean." *NSM Report Company Profiles,* 14 November 1994. Available at http://dmworld.com.

Morency, R.R. et al. "A Methodology to Implement and Validate

CHRONOLOGY:
Key Dates for L.L. Bean, Inc.

1912: Leon Leonwood Bean invents a boot made out of rubber and leather to keep the feet dry

1917: The company opens its first showroom

1920: The first L.L. Bean store opens

1937: Sales top $1 million for the first time

1951: L.L. Bean stores begin staying open 24-hours-a-day

1954: A women's department store is added

1967: Leon Bean dies

1991: A postal increase causes the company to charge a shipping and handling charge for the first time

1993: L.L. Bean opens a kids line of clothing

1995: The first L.L. Bean catalog and service facility opens in Japan

1997: The kids line proves to be so successful, L.L. Bean opens a separate kids store

Ergonomic Improvements To Computer Workstations at L.L. Bean." *R&D Ergonomics,* 28 March 1997. Available at http://members.aol.com.

"Secretary Reich Releases Labor Department's 1996 Trendsetter List." *News Alert,* 27 November 1996. Available at http://www.newsalert.com.

Semilof, Margie. "Internet World: Hits and Misses." *Interactive Age Digital,* 3 May 1996. Available at http://pubsys.cmp.com.

Smith, Jeff. "L.L. Bean Accepts 340 Offers to Leave, Avoids Layoffs." *Portland Press Herald,* 24 February 1996.

Strosnider, Kim. "L.L. Bean to Build Store in Freeport Just for Kids." *Portland Press Herald,* 29 August 1996.

———. "L.L. Bean to Open on West Coast." *Portland Press Herald,* 16 April 1996.

Yamaguchi, Mari. "Japanese Consumers Embrace American Mail Order Catalogs." *Associated Press,* 10 November 1996. Available at http://www.virtuallynw.com.

Yokoyama, Kiho. "Nature Spawns a Shopping Bonanza." *The Nikkei Weekly,* 14 October 1996.

For additional industry research:

Investigate companies by their Standard Industrial Classification Codes, also known as SICs. L.L. Bean's primary SIC is:

5600 Retail—Apparel and Accessory Stores

Lotus Development Corporation

FOUNDED: 1982

Contact Information:

HEADQUARTERS: 55 Cambridge Pky.
   Cambridge, MA 02142
PHONE: (617)577-8500
FAX: (617)693-1909
TOLL FREE: (800)205-9933
URL: http://www.lotus.com

OVERVIEW

Lotus Development Corporation is a pioneer spreadsheet developer and the world's number six software vendor. The core product line of Lotus Development Corporation is its spreadsheet program, known as Lotus 1-2-3. Spreadsheets assist in analyzing financial data by performing difficult calculations instantly, such as those involving interest rates. This detailed information is presented in a format easy to understand. The company also makes a graphics program, Freelance, as well as e-mail and word processing software, with several products available. In 1995, the most recent year for available independent financial data, Lotus's total revenue was $1.15 billion worldwide.

The company was founded in 1982 when Mitchell D. Kapor, a software programmer, won $500,000 dollars in royalties for a software program that combined charts, statistics, and other challenging calculations. Kapor founded Lotus Development with these royalties. The company's ground-breaking Lotus 1-2-3 spreadsheet program took the still young personal computer market by storm. He quickly earned back the initial investment in its development and promotion. Lotus controlled nearly 18 percent of the business software market four years after it began.

COMPANY FINANCES

As a subsidiary of IBM, Lotus Development does not report independently on its financial operations. In 1995 the company posted total revenue of $1.15 billion, compared with revenue in 1994 of $971 million. Lotus reported 1993 revenue of $981 million, compared with 1992, which was $900 million.

ANALYSTS' OPINIONS

The 1995 merger with IBM generated many views throughout the business world, from negative to positive. A June 3, 1996 article in *PC Week* said that the impact of the merger was still being scrutinized nine months later; but, for the time being, it appeared to be a success. A January 22, 1996 article in *Industry Week,* however, called IBM's decision to merge one of the most "Gutsy Decisions of 1995." Some called it a happy marriage; others, a marriage of convenience. A June 19, 1995 article in *Newsweek* referred to it as a hostile takeover. *PC World* questioned whether Lotus users would feel that they were being "IBMed to death." A July 10, 1995 article in *Fortune* said the move proved IBM could be taken seriously again. *PC Week,* however, on June 19, 1995, asked whether two companies with records of failure could make a successful merger.

HISTORY

Lotus Development Corporation was founded in 1982 by computer programmer Mitchell D. Kapor. As a psychology graduate student in 1978, Kapor had gained experience in the new field of software programming. Kapor designed a program he called Tiny Troll, that combined charts, statistics, and other difficult calculations in a single software package. This creation earned him $500,000 in royalties. It was with this seed capital that Kapor set up Lotus Development.

Kapor launched the Lotus 1-2-3 spreadsheet software in January 1983 with the help of additional investors and a $1-million advertising campaign. The response to the ad campaign was overwhelming. Within a few days Kapor and his investors had made back their money. Eighteen months after its founding, Lotus Development went public. The investors increased their commitment from $5 to $100 million.

By 1986 Lotus held 17.6 percent of the business software market. In July of that same year Kapor left the company, and Jim Manzi took the helm. It was during this time period that a series of failures and unsuccessful product introductions began. The company began to diversify in reaction to industry concerns that Lotus was focusing on a single product, the highly successful 1-2-3. However, Symphony, a database management software program unveiled in 1984, did not sell well. The same was true of Jazz, a database program for Macintosh computers. Competitor Microsoft began to develop a number of innovative competing products, including Excel spreadsheets.

FAST FACTS:
About Lotus Development Corporation

Ownership: Lotus is a subsidiary of IBM, a publicly owned company traded on the New York Stock Exchange.

Ticker symbol: IBM

Officers: Jeff Papows, Pres. & CEO; Michael D. Zisman, Exec. VP, Strategy; J. Philip Dellasega, Sr. VP, Finance, & CFO

Employees: 6,400

Principal Subsidiary Companies: Lotus Development Corporation is a subsidiary of IBM.

Chief Competitors: Lotus Development's major competitors include: Adobe; Computer Associates; Corel; Hyperion Software; Microsoft; Novell; Oracle; Symantec; and Wang.

Lotus experienced a return to better times during the latter part of the 1980s and the early 1990s. First came the adaptation of its spreadsheets and other programs for Windows. Then, in 1990, Lotus introduced AmiPro word-processing software. In 1992, responding to a growing consumer trend, the company introduced its own "office suite," a bundled program of various applications, including spreadsheets and word processing. Also in 1992, it launched Lotus Notes, its e-mail program. IBM chose to use this in its own office plan.

Lotus enjoyed a good relationship with this computer industry giant for several years. Then, in what was widely considered a "hostile takeover," IBM purchased Lotus for $3.3 billion in July of 1995. By February 1997, IBM and Lotus together led the worldwide e-mail market.

Lotus continued as a major competitor on the groupware scene. By the spring of 1998 it boasted more than 22 million users worldwide for its Lotus Notes client software. Notes integrates messaging, calendaring, Web access, and personal task management functions into a single-user interface.

Lotus announced in late spring of 1998 that it had signed definitive purchase agreements with DataBeam Corp. of Kentucky, and Israel's Ubique Ltd., both privately owned companies specializing in real-time communications software. These companies will be acquired by IBM, Lotus's parent, under this agreement. They will

CHRONOLOGY:

Key Dates for Lotus Development Corporation

1982: Mitch Kapor and Jonathan Sachs found Lotus Development; Lotus launches the Lotus 1-2-3 spreadsheet software

1983: Lotus goes public

1985: Purchases Software Arts, the creator of the first spreadsheet software

1986: Kapor resigns and Jim Manzu takes over

1989: Lotus Notes is introduced

1990: Novell backs out of a proposed merger that would have created the largest personal computer software firm

1995: IBM purchases Lotus

1998: IBM announces plans to purchase DataBeam Corp. and Ubique Ltd. to become part of the Lotus Communications Products Division

become part of the Lotus Communications Products Division. Lotus plans to bring a real-time dimension to e-mail, and collaborations in business of all sizes by way of the Internet, as well as the company's individual intranets. Lotus will base this work on its Notes and Domino software, in addition to the gain made from technologies and expertise of DataBeam and Ubique.

STRATEGY

Lotus had a tendency to succeed or fail based on the adaptability of its programs to consumers' needs. This included its compatibility with other software programs, especially operating systems. Lotus started out as an IBM-compatible program. This was a wise move since the 1982 introduction of Lotus followed the 1981 unveiling of the IBM personal computer (PC). The PC became to computers what the Model T had been to automobiles.

Eventually, however, Lotus had to adapt to the Macintosh market as well. This was due to the fact that most software used on IBM machines cannot be accessed on an Apple, or vice-versa. Lotus also had to come to terms with industry giant Microsoft, a major competitor. Mi-

crosoft's Windows program was selling at a rate of 1 million copies a year by 1991. Lotus was forced to adapt to this market also—to stay competitive the company developed a program for Windows that same year.

Lotus hoped that with its acquisition of DataBeam Corp. and Ubique Ltd. in the spring of 1998, the company would achieve its goal of bringing a real-time dimension to its messaging and groupware programs. Both companies, which were privately held, were leaders in the field of real-time communications into the late 1990s.

INFLUENCES

The three biggest milestones in Lotus's development were its initial splashy entrance into the marketplace; its subsequent troubles in the mid-1980s; and its acquisition by IBM. Mitchell Kapor followed two crucial paths with his new company in 1982. First, he tied its product to another successful one, the IBM PC. Then, he launched it with what was considered at the time an almost excessive advertising budget for computer software. The campaign included full-page newspaper and magazine ads, and cost $1 million. However, in only nine months, Lotus sold 110,000 copies of its software at $495 a piece, for a total sales figure of close to $55 million.

Still, in the mid-1980s, as Wall Street observers started to note that 60 percent of the company's profits came from a single product, Lotus was in danger of being viewed as a "one-product company." The decision to diversify followed quickly. First came Symphony, introduced with a large ad campaign at the 1984 Los Angeles Olympics. The program combined word processing with data management and networking. Users found it cumbersome to use. In addition to this complication, the idea of combining software packages that would not take hold until the 1990s, was ahead of its time. Similar problems followed with Jazz for Macintosh. In 1986, however, Lotus began a comeback with a new version of 1-2-3, and a massive expansion into the Japanese market.

IBM's purchase of Lotus in July 1995 signaled a new era for the company. Industry observers in *PC Week* suggested that IBM intended to maintain a hands-off approach, and let Lotus, along with its highly popular Notes program, influence the mother company, rather than the other way around. *Business Week* also held that the success of the merger would be tied closely to the success of Lotus Notes in coming years, and *Black Enterprise* called the merger a sign that IBM was gearing up to enter a "groupware war" with office-suite competitor Microsoft. On the heels of the merger, long-time Lotus chief Jim Manzi stepped down. According to *PC Week,* it appeared that IBM and Lotus's existing managers could not see eye-to-eye. Some "house-cleaning" was necessary.

The growing consumer clamor for real-time communications was the key factor behind the 1998 acquisition of the two companies holding considerable expertise in the field. IBM acquired DataBeam and Ubique Ltd. for integration into Lotus' Communications Products Divsion.

CURRENT TRENDS

Two of the biggest trends in Lotus' business during the late 1990s were "office suites" and "the net"—both the Internet and the intranet. Suites are packages that combine several programs into one bundle. This makes it possible, for instance, for a user to import an object from a graphics program to a slide show; or, to include spreadsheet data alongside word processing. Lotus entered the office suite market with SmartSuite in 1991. The next year, it entered into an agreement with Digital Equipment, to include a copy of SmartSuite for Windows with every computer the company sold.

During this same time period, Lotus established a significant presence in the e-mail and Internet markets with its products Lotus Notes and cc:Mail. A review of computer trade and financial industry publications' articles about Lotus in 1996 and 1997 indicated that many industry analysts believed that Lotus Notes represented the future of the company. The program assists businesses in making the most of the "intranet," the internal network of each business.

Lotus' eSuite was yet another product developed to appeal to businesses increasingly involved in networking. The product represents a new line of business productivity software and technologies designed exclusively for the network computing environment. There are two eSuite product lines: eSuite Workplace and eSuite DevPack.

PRODUCTS

Lotus' product line includes desktop application products, such as SmartSuite; and an integrated applications suite that combines word processing, spreadsheets, and other types of programs. Another key focus for Lotus is communications, with Lotus Notes for workgroup computing, which gave it a foothold in the expanding "intranet" market; cc:Mail, an e-mail program; and, Soft*Switch electronic mail switching. Its most renowned product is its spreadsheet program, 1-2-3, which has versions for DOS, Windows, and Macintosh. In addition, Lotus has the word processing program, AmiPro, and the presentation graphics program, Freelance Graphics.

In late 1996 Lotus announced the introduction of Domino, an Internet (in contrast to intranet) version of Notes. An aggressive marketing campaign followed the announcement. Earlier in 1996, it unveiled ACT! for Notes, which the company developed in cooperation with

Symantec Corporation. The product created user access to Notes databases, and send e-mail. A product designed to appeal to the networking environment is Lotus's eSuite. Two versions are marketed: eSuite Workplace and eSuite DevPack.

In May of 1998, Lotus unveiled plans to offer client-and-server-based products that deliver the advantages of network-based, real-time communication and collaboration to businesses worldwide. This allows the company to utilize the document-based awareness, instant messaging, and real-time conferencing capabilities of Israel-based Ubique Ltd., and Kentucky-based DataBeam Corp., in order to expand the benefits of groupware into a comprehensive *Sametime* collaboration platform, all in conjunction with its own leading-edge collaboration of *Notes* and *Domino*.

CORPORATE CITIZENSHIP

Lotus has placed a high value on its relationships with the worldwide communities where it operates. The company has taken the lead in corporate citizenship through its strong, stated commitment to "socially responsible business practices, including efforts to enhance the quality of life, and level of opportunity afforded individuals within our communities throughout the world."

The company's community-minded initiatives find a focus in the Lotus Philanthropy Program. The program is based on the conviction that its employees should play a key role in identifying and implementing those initiatives. Many Lotus employees are active on policy and grant-making committees, offer technical assistance to nonprofit organizations, and participate in volunteer efforts in the United States and abroad.

GLOBAL PRESENCE

Prior to the merger with IBM, Lotus marketed its products in more than 80 countries worldwide, principally in North America, Europe, and the Pacific Rim. When Lotus became a part of the IBM team, its potential to become a more significant global player was increased. Slightly more than 25 percent of its total revenue is derived from sales outside the United States.

SOURCES OF INFORMATION

Bibliography
Cooper, Charles. "Mega-Deal Is Considered a Short-Term Success." *PC Week*, 3 June 1996.

Cortese, Amy. "Can IBM Keep Lotus Blooming?" *Business Week*, 30 October 1995.

Dellecave, Tom, Jr. "Lotus Makes Play For SPA." *Sales & Marketing Management,* March 1996.

Farber, Dan. "How Will IBM Handle Lotus Marriage?" *PC Week,* 16 October 1995.

Gibson, Stan. "After a Season of Gloom, Can Lotus Blossom Again?" *PC Week,* 1 May 1995.

"IBM: Lotus Development Corp. to Bring Real-time Dimension to Messaging and Groupware." *PressWire,* 20 May 1998.

"Lotus Development Corporation." *Hoover's Online,* 16 August 1998. Available at http://www.hoovers.com.

Lotus Development Corporation Home Page, 2 June 1998. Available at http://www.lotus.com/.

Lundquist, Eric. "IBM Takes Notes Message to Heart." *PC Week,* 15 January 1996.

Sloan, Allan. "Fear of the Future." *Newsweek,* 19 June 1995.

Verespej, Michael A. "Gutsy Decisions of 1995: IBM Goes Shopping." *Industry Week,* 22 January 1996.

Zuckerman, Lawrence. "Lotus Gears Up to Get a Slice of Internet Pie." *The New York Times,* 16 September 1996.

For additional industry research:

Investigate companies by their Standard Industrial Classification Codes, also known as SICs. Lotus' primary SICs are:

4822 Telegraph & Other Communications

7372 Prepackaged Software

7373 Computer Integrated Systems Design

Lucent Technologies Inc.

OVERVIEW

Lucent Technologies manufactures telecommunications equipment and also conducts research and development for new and or improved telecommunications products. The company consists of four main divisions, including: Bell Labs, providing breakthrough research and development support to Lucent Technologies; Systems for Network Operators, with design, manufacturing and support networking systems, and software for communications service providers and wireless operators; Microelectronics Group, which designs, develops, and manufactures integrated circuits, power systems, and optoelectronic components for use in the communications and computing industries; and Business Communications Systems, responsible for designing, manufacturing, selling, and servicing advance voice, data, and multimedia communications solutions for worldwide businesses and the U.S. government.

COMPANY FINANCES

By 1997 Lucent stock prices had grown from the initial value of $27 per share to about $55. The stock rose sharply late in 1997 and on April 1, 1998, it split two-for-one after reaching $140. In May 1998, it was trading in the low 70s.

At the end of the company's second quarter of fiscal 1998 (March 31, 1998), Lucent reported its net income had more than doubled to $180 million over the same quarter of the previous year. According to its 1997 annual report, Lucent's revenues rose steadily in each quarter after its initial public offering, and it achieved

FOUNDED: Lucent was founded in 1995 and made fully independent of AT&T on September 30, 1996

Contact Information:

HEADQUARTERS: 600 Mountain Ave.
   Murray Hill, NJ 07974-0636
PHONE: (908)582-8500
FAX: (908)508-2576
TOLL FREE: (888)458-2368
EMAIL: webmaster@lucent.com
URL: http://www.lucent.com

FINANCES:

Lucent Technologies Revenues, 1994-1997 (billion dollars)

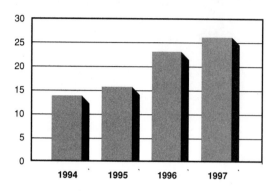

Lucent Technologies 1997 Stock Prices (dollars)

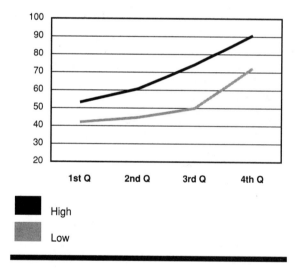

record total revenues in its first fiscal year as an independent company.

In 1997 total sales reached $26.36 billion. Of that total, 59 percent ($15.61 billion) came from systems for network operators, 24 percent ($6.41 billion) from business communications systems, 11 percent ($2.76 billion) from microelectronics, 4 percent ($1.01 billion) from consumer products, and the remaining 2 percent, or $567 million, from other systems and products.

ANALYSTS' OPINIONS

Lucent will be in position by October 1998 to merge with another giant in the technology arena, according to

financial reporter Tiernan Ray of *SmartMoney Interactive* in a May 1998 story. Ray foresees one big purchase or multiple purchases. Ascend Communications, Nokia, Bay Networks, and P-Com would make good strategic choices for a company interested in maintaining dominance in wireless communications and networking technologies, according to Ray.

"Whatever the nature of Lucent's acquisitions, most observers seem to agree that the company's path will bring it more and more into direct competition with Cisco," Ray predicted, citing that Lucent may be the best example of the Silicon Valley business model because "management is running the company more and more as an entrepreneurial shop."

According to another analysis appearing on *Knight-Ridder/Tribune Business News,* "There is a certain unpredictability to the equipment business, where sales ebb and flow." Bear Stearns & Co. expects that Lucent's markets will have grown 10 percent a year from $285 billion in 1995 to $380 billion by the end of 1998.

"The phone market is going to be expanding. There is natural growth and now new competitors," said Alan Sulkin, a former AT&T employee who runs TeqConsult in Hackensack, New Jersey. "The need for new equipment is on the order of $14 billion . . . I think the other Lucent strength is they are not just selling product, they are selling solutions and knowledge of applications, in which all their major competitors . . . are playing catch-up."

HISTORY

Lucent was formed in 1995 in the wake of AT&T's restructuring. AT&T sold 17.6 percent of Lucent in an April 10, 1996 initial public offering. The $3 billion was the largest initial public offering in U.S. history. The company shifted the remaining 82.4 percent of Lucent to AT&T shareholders on September 30, 1996. A share of Lucent was traded for every three AT&T shares owned for a total of 525 million shares of Lucent stock distributed to AT&T shareholders.

The company is the corporate descendant of AT&T's Western Electric manufacturing division that AT&T bought in 1881. Elisha Gray founded the company in 1869, close to the time Alexander Graham Bell patented the first telephone. Also under the Lucent umbrella is Bell Laboratories in Murray Hill, New Jersey, formed in 1925, and credited with the invention of the transistor and the communications satellite, the laser, the cellular phone, and electronic telephone switching. From the time it was founded until the time it was incorporated into Lucent, Bell Laboratories averaged one patent a day. Lucent, however, averaged three patents a day between March and September 1996, and has managed to maintain a high rate of development since its founding.

Lucent designs, builds, and delivers public and private networks, communications systems and software,

consumer and business telephone systems, and micro-electronic components. Under the guidelines of the spin-off/breakup, AT&T kept its services business, including long-distance, wireless, Internet access, satellite television, and a budding local phone service, while Lucent emerged as a new business, positioned to succeed from the start.

In 1996, Lucent Technologies reported a 10-percent increase in revenues between the first quarter of 1995 and the first quarter of 1996, from $4.2 to $4.6 billion. This was attributed to increased sales of systems for network operators and microelectronic products. Those revenues increased in all segments, except consumer products. Further, Lucent reported a $444-million increase in corporate costs of goods sold. In 1997, two years into independent operation, Lucent had revenues of $21.4 billion, a workforce of more than 125,000 employees around the world, and a position as the third-largest private employer in New Jersey.

At the same time, the company experienced losses because of new-company start-up costs and expenses. These included building new information systems and the costs associated with introducing the new company name and logo. In 1997, Lucent faced additional challenges as a result of integrating and consolidating Philips Electronics NV into the company. Ultimately, the company earned more than $1.0 billion in profits in 1996 and $1.1 billion in 1997. At the end of the second quarter of 1998, Lucent reported that revenues were $6.2 million, an increase of 19.6 percent over the same quarter in 1997.

FAST FACTS:
About Lucent Technologies Inc.

Ownership: Lucent is a publicly owned company traded on the New York Stock Exchange.

Ticker symbol: LU

Officers: Roger A. McGinn, Chmn., Pres., & CEO, 51, $2,326,023; Donald K. Peterson, Exec. VP & CFO, 48, $860,971

Employees: 134,000 (1997)

Principal Subsidiary Companies: Lucent's subsidiaries include AG Communication Systems Corp., Lucent Technologies Octel Div., Lucent Technologies Foundation, and Lucent Netcare Messaging SVC.

Chief Competitors: Lucent competes with a variety of companies involved in telecommunications, networking, and information technologies. Some of its competitors include: Ascend Communications; Bay Networks; Nokia; P-Com; and Cisco Systems.

STRATEGY

Lucent is attempting to position itself to take advantage of its various leading positions in subsectors of the telecommunications market. It is tapping into new technologies including the wireless phone market, videoconferencing, and Internet telephony. In 1997, executives predicted the annual growth for Lucent Technologies should range between 10 and 15 percent. The cellular segment, for example, is expected to increase from 100 million subscribers to 1.4 billion by 2010.

Lucent is interested in growth in international, as well as domestic, markets. It has positioned itself as a leader in rapidly changing technologies by offering new products frequently and by responding quickly to evolving industry standards.

CURRENT TRENDS

In the next few years, Lucent is prepared to acquire and invest in new businesses, partner with existing businesses, deliver new technologies, close or consolidate some facilities, reduce its workforce, or withdraw from

markets in order to maintain its competitive edge, according to its 1997 annual report.

In some cases, partnerships may involve competitors. By partnering with a competitor to develop new technology, Lucent has the advantage of sharing the expense, as well as the potential for failure. In June 1998, Lucent announced such an alliance with Motorola in order to develop next-generation digital signal processor (DSP) technology and to cross-license existing DSP architectures. As part of the alliance, Lucent and Motorola will create a joint design center, named StarCore, in the Atlanta area. They hope to have their first products available by mid-1999.

PRODUCTS

Lucent makes equipment for public and business communications systems and is a supplier of systems and software to the world's largest networks, according to the company. It manufactures microelectronic components for communication systems, and computer manufacturers. In conjunction with several strategic partners, Lucent also produces messaging equipment, personal communications products, and switching equipment used in asynchronous transfer mode technology (ATM). One of the company's new areas of research and development is Digital Subscriber Line (DSL) high-speed modem technologies, putting it into direct competition with Cisco Systems.

CORPORATE CITIZENSHIP

Lucent gives back to the community through its Lucent Technologies Foundation, which supports philanthropic initiatives that advance education, addresses the needs of communities where employees live and work, and encourages employee volunteerism and giving. In 1997, the Foundation assisted Australian students living in remote outback areas, coordinated company volunteers working for Atlanta's Habitat for Humanity, and awarded $3 million to education for manufacturing workers. In addition, Lucent employees have established and raised more than $500,000 for the Blind Foundation for India.

GLOBAL PRESENCE

According to one report, Lucent leads the world market for network systems with a customer base that includes AT&T, the regional Bell telephone companies, and countless phone carriers from Saudi Arabia to India and Indonesia. The company has strategic relationships or joint ventures—such as one in Poland with Telekomunikacja Polska S.A.—in more than 12 nations, with a presence in every nation. According to the company's annual report, it has 1.4 million customers in 94 countries. Among them are Brazil, China, Egypt, France, Hong Kong, India, and Indonesia. Lucent has offices or distributors in more than 90 countries, including Bell Laboratories facilities in 17 of those.

EMPLOYMENT

At its start, the company inherited more than 100,000 employees. Soon after the initial public offering, an estimated 22,000 jobs were eliminated, according to a February 1997 article in *Baltimore Business Journal*. There had been expectations the company needed to consolidate even more to survive. By September 30, 1997, Lucent's workforce reflected a reduction of another 18,000 employees, part of a companywide restructuring.

SOURCES OF INFORMATION

Bibliography

Ey, Craig S. "Lucent Enjoys Growth Spurt." *Baltimore Business Journal*, 14 February 1997.

"Lucent and Motorola Join Forces to Develop Advanced DSP Technology." May 1998. Available at http://www.starcore-dsp.com/.

"Lucent 1Q Revs Up 10%, Micro Unit 26%." *Electronic News*, 20 May 1996.

Lucent Technologies: First Annual Report 1996. Murray Hill, NJ: Lucent Technologies, 1996.

1997 Lucent Annual Report. 17 May 1998. Available at http://www.lucent.com/annual97/.

Perone, Joseph R. "New Jersey-Based Lucent Sets Goal of Double-Digit Growth." *Knight-Ridder/Tribune Business News*, 20 February 1997.

Rosenbush, Steven A. "Lucent Prepares to Complete Its Separation from AT&T." *Knight-Ridder/Tribune Business News*, 15 September 1996.

"Who's On Lucent's Shopping List?" *SmartMoney Interactive*, 8 May 1998. Available at http://www.smartmoney.com/smt/story=19980508intro.

For an annual report:

on the Internet at: http://www.lucent.com/annual97 **or** write: Lucent Technologies, c/o The Bank of New York, PO Box 11009, Church St. Sta., New York, NY 10286-1009

For additional industry research:

Investigate companies by their Standard Industrial Classification Codes, also known as SICs. Lucent's primary SICs are:

3613 Switchgear and Switchboard Apparatus

3661 Telephone & Telegraph Apparatus

3669 Communications Equipment, NEC

8731 Commercial Physical Research

Lycos Inc.

FOUNDED: 1995

OVERVIEW

Founded in June 1995, Lycos quickly became one of the leading World Wide Web navigation companies. Through its own web site, it helps Internet users to locate, retrieve, and manage online information, aided by a variety of free services. Lycos uses both searching and indexing technology and has set up 18 WebGuides that cover individual categories of information. It also offers user services such as TOP 5% (a directory of reviews of web sites), PeopleFind, StockFind, CompaniesOnline, and GTE Yellow Pages. As of early 1997, Lycos had cataloged almost 70 million URLs (Uniform Resource Locators) on the World Wide Web.

In April 1996, only 10 months after its founding, Lycos became a publicly traded company, earning the distinction of being the youngest company to go public on the NASDAQ exchange.

Lycos derives its income by selling advertising on its web site and by licensing its technology to other users. In early 1998 Lycos had more than 20 million users, and nearly 500 advertisers were advertising in excess of 800 brands on its web site. Besides its headquarters in Waltham, the company has offices in New York City, San Francisco, and Pittsburgh. Outside the United States, Lycos has offices in Germany, Italy, France, Spain, the Netherlands, and the United Kingdom.

The first half of 1998 saw a flurry of activity to extend Lycos's reach as an online service. On the acquisition front, the company in February acquired Tripod, which firmly established Lycos as one of the World Wide Web's most popular community sites, offering its users tools with which to build home pages. Two months later,

Contact Information:

HEADQUARTERS: 400-2 Totten Pond Rd.
    Waltham, MA 02154
PHONE: (781)370-2700
FAX: (781)370-2800
EMAIL: http://echomail.lycos.com/em_dir/lycos/lycosmail.nsf/email+form?OpenForm
URL: http://www.lycos.com

FINANCES:

Lycos Inc.
Revenues, 1996-1997
(million dollars)

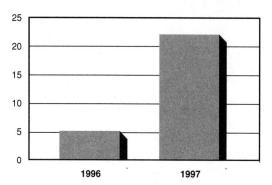

*1995 was the inception period for Lycos Inc.

Lycos Inc.
1997 Stock Prices
(dollars)

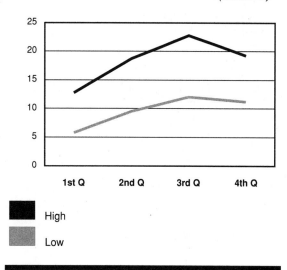

■ High

■ Low

Lycos announced its acquisition of WiseWire Corp. and its technology for Internet directory-building.

The company struck a number of strategic alliances during the first half of 1998. Lycos acquired an interest in PlanetAll, which offers unique contact management technology, as well as a minority stake in GlobeComm Inc., a company that provides Lycos's free e-mail service. Lycos also announced a three-year agreement with AT&T, under which the companies together will develop and market an array of Internet-based communication services for consumers.

COMPANY FINANCES

Founded in mid-1995, Lycos has made significant strides in growing its international revenue during its brief existence. The cost of the expansion deemed necessary to position the company for future growth, however, has been high, resulting in a string of losses. Lycos reported a loss of $6.6 million on revenue of $22.3 million in fiscal 1997 ending July 31, compared with a loss of $5.1 million on revenue of $5.3 million in 1996. The company reported a loss of $2.4 million on revenue of $15.1 million for the third quarter of fiscal 1998 ending April 30, 1998, compared to net earnings of $301,000 on revenue of $12.6 million for the quarter ending January 31, 1998. The value of Lycos stock ranged from a 52-week high of $107 on July 7, 1998 to a low of $11 on June 24, 1997.

HISTORY

In 1994 Dr. Michael L. Mauldin, a research computer scientist at Carnegie Mellon University (CMU) in Pittsburgh, developed the prototype for the Lycos search engine. At the time, most Web users were technologically adept. However, Lycos was designed to offer intuitive assistance to all levels of users. To locate information, Lycos employs automated software robots called spiders, which travel on the Web and download summaries of the most important information that they find. (The name "Lycos" was taken from the Latin term for Wolf Spider, *lycosidae lycosa,* a creature that actively hunts for prey.) The Lycos technology then gives the user a list of the most likely sites on the Web for finding information about a topic, along with summarized information about each site.

Although Lycos became a public company in early 1996, both CMU and Mauldin kept about 8 percent of the company's stock. CMU also retained the Lycos trademark. When Lycos stock was first sold to the public, its value skyrocketed by the hour, and the tiny company suddenly was worth an estimated $177 million. By the end of 1996, Lycos had a host of partners, including Netscape (which agreed to display Lycos prominently on its web site) and AT&T. However, despite the phenomenal rise in revenue during its first two years of existence, from $5.3 million in fiscal 1996 to $22.3 million in fiscal 1997, Lycos still was not operating at a profit by late 1997. Early returns for fiscal 1998 showed sharp increases in revenue but no guarantee the company would finally get into the black.

The company moved aggressively in early 1998 to expand its operation and the quality and scope of its services with the acquisition of Tripod and WiseWire, as well as forming alliances with AT&T, PlanetAll, Japan's Sumitomo Corp., and GlobeComm.

The home page on the Lycos Inc. web site at http://www.lycos.com. (Courtesy of Lycos Inc.)

STRATEGY

Lycos, although it operates in a technologically complex world, has adopted a very simple (although highly ambitious) strategy. As stated in its 1996 annual report, it wants to be "the most widely used place to find information in the world." To achieve this goal, the company uses several means: providing users with a one-stop source of information on a variety of topics, drawing a high volume of traffic to its site by providing free and very accessible online guides, developing innovative advertising possibilities on its site, providing multiple access points to Lycos through its many business partnerships, and developing customized and locally oriented guides. The company also licenses the Lycos name for use in other products, such as books and CD-ROMs, in return for royalty payments. As an example, Lycos Press was established as a joint publishing venture with Simon & Schuster.

In another strategic move to capture repeat business from users, Lycos acquired Tripod, attracted by its strong following among Generation Xers. Lycos is trying to leverage personalized access to a wide variety of content and services, including classified ads, comics, news, sports, yellow pages, maps, travel advice, shopping, and free e-mail.

INFLUENCES

During its extremely short existence, Lycos has had great success. It stands as one of the premier Internet nav-

igational tools in a very crowded field, along with a few others, such as Yahoo!, Infoseek, and Excite. Aside from its well-developed topical WebGuides and customized guides such as PeopleFind, Lycos has been very adept at forming partnerships with major companies (e.g., Netscape, Barnes and Noble, Microsoft) to give itself visibility on frequently visited web sites. It also has attracted hundreds of major advertisers, who have provided a steady source of income and have given visitors to the World Wide Web the message that Lycos is traveling in the most important circles on the Internet.

Lycos also was quick to develop parallel services outside of the United States, with local sites allowing visitors to the Web to search for information in German, French, Spanish, and Italian in addition to English. It also spent its first two years forming partnerships with European companies (e.g., EMAP Internet Sales, a leading online advertising sales firm in the United Kingdom).

Despite all of these innovations and its rapidly rising revenue, Lycos faces enormous competition from other Internet navigational tools. Its chief competitors, and many smaller ones, all are fighting to form partnerships with popular web sites and with major advertisers. The company has yet to report a profit.

Certainly one of the trends helping to shape the company's strategy is the incredible speed with which Americans are abandoning the television set in favor of surfing the Internet. As more and more get bitten by the cyber-bug, the demands facing online services become increasingly more sophisticated. Keeping up with con-

FAST FACTS:

About Lycos Inc.

Ownership: Lycos is a publicly owned company traded on NASDAQ.

Ticker symbol: LCOS

Officers: Robert J. Davis, Pres. & CEO, 41,1997 base salary $298,000; Edward M. Philip, COO, CFO, & Secretary, 32, 1997 base salary $200,000

Employees: 137

Chief Competitors: Lycos's chief competitors include: America Online; CNET; Digital Equipment; Dow Jones; Excite; Infoseek; Microsoft; Netscape; Prodigy; and Yahoo!.

CHRONOLOGY:

Key dates for Lycos Inc.

1994: Dr. Michael L. Mauldin develops the prototype for the Lycos search engine

1995: Lycos is founded

1996: Becomes public company; has host of partners, including Netscape and AT&T

1997: Announces steps to streamline Lycos Pro; Becomes exclusive provider of Microsoft Active Channel Guide

1998: Launches "Personal Guide" for Web users

sumers puts a tremendous burden on Lycos and its competitors.

CURRENT TRENDS

Lycos is operating in a very new and rapidly changing field, surrounded by equally young and eager competitors. As in the Microsoft-Apple and the Microsoft Ex-

plorer-Netscape Navigator rivalries, it is possible that one competitor eventually will become dominant. Lycos is aware of its precarious position and of how its existing partnerships and advertising arrangements could change completely in a short time.

According to company literature, Lycos also is aware of how its "rapid growth has placed, and is expected to continue to place, a significant strain on the company's managerial and operational resources." In the span of two years, Lycos attained over $22 million in revenues, entered into dozens of partnerships, and drew hundreds of advertisers, all with a staff of only 60 employees. Lycos is focusing on how it can manage all of this growth successfully, while still providing its core service: a tool that provides current and easily accessible information to both computer novices and experts.

As the competition among the so-called search engines heats up, the need to streamline the search operation intensifies. In the fall of 1997, Lycos announced it was taking steps to further streamline Lycos Pro, its advanced search engine. Introduced in mid-1997, Lycos Pro proved an immediate success. However, given the competition and the speed with which other companies are introducing advances, Lycos found it necessary to upgrade the service less than six months after roll-out. Among other things, the changes included relevancy controls, allowing users to fine-tune the criteria affecting the ranking of their search results.

PRODUCTS

In mid-1997 Lycos entered into several partnerships that are likely to boost its rank among Internet navigational tools. First it announced a three-year partnership with Barnes and Noble (http://www.barnesandnoble.com), in which the international leader in book sales becomes the exclusive book seller on the Lycos web site. The Discovery Channel Online (http://www.discovery.com) also chose Lycos as its directly linked search engine. Finally, Lycos was selected by Microsoft as the exclusive provider for the Microsoft Active Channel Guide in its new Microsoft Internet Explorer 4.0. Lycos will lead users of Internet Explorer 4.0 into a variety of news, sports, business, entertainment, and lifestyle "channels."

In the first half of 1998 Lycos announced a wide range of product enhancements. In April, the company launched its "Personal Guide," a free service allowing users to personalize Web content, organize their lives, and leverage online communities. Lycos also offers users access to a collection of more than 40,000 pictures and vintage illustrations, including images of contemporary and historical personalities. In early June, Lycos announced it had formed an alliance with Ziff-Davis Inc. to offer the ZDNet software library on the Lycos Internet Web guide.

CORPORATE CITIZENSHIP

In 1997 Lycos joined the call for industry self-regulation of World Wide Web content, by introducing a set of guidelines designed to protect young computer users from inappropriate or misleading banner advertising on web sites. Lycos president, Robert J. Davis, in a company press release said, "Lycos is a gateway to the Internet for millions and millions of people . . . We've always striven for an industry-leading approach to making the Web a safe place for all surfers." Lycos also offers a Kids WebGuide that gives young Web surfers a list of age-appropriate links.

SOURCES OF INFORMATION

Bibliography

Court, Randolph. "Lycos: Cash + Traffic = Good Deal." *Wired News,* 25 March 1998.

"Hot Technology Companies: 287 Firms Qualify in June and July." *Facts Online,* 4 August 1998. Available at http://www.facts-online.com.

"Lycos, Inc." *Dow Jones & Company,* 9 August 1998. Available at http://www.wsj.com.

"Lycos, Inc." *Hoover's Online,* 23 July 1997. Available at http://www.hoovers.com.

"Lycos Reports 158% Growth in Revenues." Lycos Inc. Press Release, 14 May 1998.

"Lycos Supercharges Search with Powerful New Enhancements." *Business Wire,* 14 October 1997.

"Lycos to Feature Envirolink, The Premier Environmental Site on the Internet." Lycos Inc. Press Release, 14 May 1998.

Seminario, Maria. "Lycos Losses Narrow on Sharply Higher Revenues." *Ziff-Davis News Net,* 26 August 1997.

Sippey, Michael. "Eyeballs and Lowballs." *The Netly News,* 10 February 1998.

For an annual report:

on the Internet at: http://www.lycos.com/info/

For additional industry research:

Investigate companies by their Standard Industrial Classification Codes, also known as SICs. Lycos' primary SICs are:

4899 Communications Services

7375 Information Retrieval Services

7379 Computer Related Services